GLOBAL CAPITAL AND NATIONAL INSTITUTIONS

Crisis and Choice in the International Financial Architecture

GLOBAL CAPITAL AND NATIONAL INSTITUTIONS

Crisis and Choice in the International Financial Architecture

Laura Alfaro
Harvard Business School, USA

World Scientific

NEW JERSEY • LONDON • SINGAPORE • BEIJING • SHANGHAI • HONG KONG • TAIPEI • CHENNAI

Published by

World Scientific Publishing Co. Pte. Ltd.
5 Toh Tuck Link, Singapore 596224
USA office: 27 Warren Street, Suite 401-402, Hackensack, NJ 07601
UK office: 57 Shelton Street, Covent Garden, London WC2H 9HE

British Library Cataloguing-in-Publication Data
A catalogue record for this book is available from the British Library.

GLOBAL CAPITAL AND NATIONAL INSTITUTIONS
Crisis and Choice in the International Financial Architecture

ISBN-13 978-981-4280-87-7
ISBN-10 981-4280-87-9

Printed in Singapore by World Scientific Printers

Acknowledgments

This book is composed of cases I have written and taught at Harvard Business School. A number of people have contributed to the creation of this collection of cases. I sincerely thank Rawi Abdelal, Faheen Allibhoy, Namrata Aora, Vincent Marie Dessain, Vinati Dev, Rafael Di Tella, Masako Egawa, Lakshmi Iyer, Ane Damgaard Jensen, Akiko Kanno, Renee Kim, Stephen McIntyre, Camille Tang, Debora Spar, Ingrid Vogel, and Eric Werker. Many colleagues and friends have taught these cases and provided useful comments and suggestions. I am grateful to members of the various teaching groups for taking time to review and comment on many of the cases in this volume. I especially want to thank Rawi Abdelal, Niall Ferguson, Julio Rotemberg, Debora Spar and Dick Vietor for detailed comments. Their suggestions and encouragement have helped to improve them. I am indebted to my students in Business Government and the International Economy (BGIE) and Institutions, Macroeconomics and the Global Economy (IMAGE) for numerous helpful comments and discussions. I also thank my assistant Mary Heanue, who provided valuable help at different stages of each case and volume. I owe special thanks to George Lodge for helping me with my first case and Debora Spar for suggesting this collaboration. I am forever grateful to Fabio Kanczuk for taking time to discuss the cases in this volume and providing emotional support. Many thanks also to Zvi Ruder and Bhupathiraju Shalini at World Scientific for their help in this project.

Acknowledgments

Contents

Introduction

All managers face a business environment in which international and macroeconomic phenomena matter. Understanding these phenomena — the determinants of capital flows, the effects of foreign capital on host countries, the impact of exchange-rate movements, and the genesis of financial and currency crises — is a crucial aspect in making informed managerial decisions. International capital flows can significantly affect countries' development efforts and provide clear investment opportunities for businesses. Adverse macroeconomic phenomena can exert a catastrophic impact on a firm's performance, as evidenced by the many strong companies destroyed by the successive crises in Latin America, the Asian financial crisis, the recent U.S. subprime mortgage crisis and the global financial meltdown of 2008 and 2009. But such episodes can also create business opportunities, and not just for the speculators that profit from them. Managers who have and use a coherent framework for analyzing these phenomena can secure a competitive advantage.

This book presents a series of case studies taught in the Harvard Business School course *Institutions, Macroeconomics, and the Global Economy* (IMaGE). The course addresses the opportunities created by the emergence of a global economy and proposes strategies for managing the risks associated with globalization. The course emphasizes both the economic consequences of policies and the political and institutional context in which they are established and implemented. The material thus bridges a gap between firm- and household-level behavior, which is typically well understood by a managerial audience, and aggregate phenomena, which are often less understood by this audience.

The cases in this book have been designed to give students an appreciation of the critical role of institutions and policies in affecting patterns of international capital flows and the abilities of government to manage them effectively. The case studies in the module are tied together by two broad themes: (1) the determinants and effects of international capital, and (2) policy-makers' management of these flows. The cases approach these themes by exploring institutional detail in deep local context. Students are exposed to key recent events that have shaped the way economists think about these subjects. The events covered have a clear global perspective as the cases are set in Africa, Asia, Europe and Latin America, as well as the U.S. The cases also cover events that occurred during the last three decades as not only do they affect the business environment that managers face today but they also hold important lessons. An important feature the cases reveal is the cyclical nature of international capital flows.

The cases in the book were written to encourage students to consider several fundamental characteristics of the international financial system: Why cycles in international capital flows recur; and how does sovereign debt and domestic debt differ from each other in their contracts, explicit and implicit, and their enforcement. The module also teaches students three key insights from the field of international economics. First, trade in goods is different from trade in financial assets: A financial transaction inherently involves a commitment to pay at a later date. Financial transactions are therefore fundamentally affected by problems of asymmetric information and the risk that the contract will not be enforced, and both problems are exacerbated at the international level. Second, international financial flows are affected by two additional macroeconomic risks that are absent within countries: sovereign risk and the use of different currencies. Third, international capital flows imply additional policy challenges for countries as policy makers face a difficult trade-off among three objectives: monetary policy autonomy, a stable fixed exchange rate, and free capital mobility. Research has demonstrated that local conditions — political objectives, financial markets, firms, and institutions — decisively influence the operation of these basic macroeconomic logics in actual practice. As a whole, the module emphasizes the importance of domestic institutions for effective macroeconomic policy-making, capacious regulations, credible policy commitment, and attracting and using foreign direct investment efficiently.

During the 1990s and early 2000s, the world witnessed an explosion in capital flows at the global level. Gross foreign assets and liabilities stood at two or three times GDP for many countries, as compared to just two decades ago. This explosive growth, especially in emerging markets, has been fueled both by changes in world politics (e.g., the end of the Cold War, collapse of the Soviet Union, shifting political climate in China, and political changes in Latin America and Asia) and advances in technology. Private capital flows — debt finance, equity capital, and foreign direct investment (FDI) — became larger than current and past official capital flows. FDI has become the dominant source of foreign private capital for emerging markets, promising additional productivity gains for recipient countries. Beyond merely adding to the stock of capital, FDI may translate into the promise of better technology, modern management, and greater access to global markets. Portfolio equity liberalization might help in a different way by exposing local companies to the scrutiny of the international capital market (and potentially requiring greater accounting transparency and more effective corporate governance). This new era of foreign capital mobility has also been characterized by low interest rates in industrial countries, growing external imbalances in the U.S. economy, and the rise of China, all of which posed new challenges to policy management.

In 2009, the global economy remained mired in a deep crisis following the subprime meltdown in the U.S. The World Bank, in one of its bleakest assessments yet of the ongoing crisis, estimated that the global economy would contract in 2009 for the first time since World War II. The World Bank's sister organization, the International Monetary Fund (IMF) released a similar outlook. More than US$50 trillion in wealth had been wiped out across borders over the last 18 months. Policy makers across the world found themselves trying to tackle a dizzying array of problems, from rising unemployment to frightened investors to plunging exports. According to one view, shared by many academics and policy makers, the financial sector debacle had its origins in the "global imbalance" — the phenomenon of large current account surpluses in China and a few other countries co-existing with large U.S. deficits. The situation was also a true testimony of how intertwined individual economies had become over the years. With the explosion of international capital flows, financial institutions in various corners of the world had inadvertently participated in the U.S.' debt-financing boom. The effect of policies to deal with the ongoing global crisis and new policy choices remained to be seen.

This book is composed of three intellectual segments: I. *Determinants and Effects of International Capital Flows*; II. *Policies and Strategies for Harnessing the Benefits of Financial Globalization*; III. *Challenges and Policies of Large Economies.* Section I explains the purpose and provides the basic insights of the module. Section II presents a detailed overview of the cases and readings in the module. The last section relates the cases in the module to the main patterns of international capital flows in the last 30 years. It also presents the key insights from the field of international economics covered in the cases as well as the current state of debate among policy makers.

I. PURPOSE AND BASIC INSIGHTS OF THE MODULE

This book focuses on the costs and benefits of international capital and the policies utilized to make it work. It is composed of three intellectual segments.

- The cases in *Determinants and Effects of International Capital Flows* study both potential positive and negative effects in host economies of opening up to international capital flows. In particular the cases analyze the effects of capital flows in the development efforts of countries, with an emphasis on FDI (which has become the main source of private flows to emerging markets) and the policies to attract and maximize FDI's benefits. In addition, the cases in this first segment analyze the effects of international capital flows in the context of financial crisis.
- The second segment of the book, *Policies and Strategies for Harnessing the Benefits of Financial Globalization*, focuses on the strategies to harness the benefits of financial globalization and minimize potential risks. The cases cover policies regarding the management of capital inflows using capital controls, the choice of exchange rate regime, and policies associated with the management of sovereign defaults. The module ends with a discussion of the effects of transfers of capital and debt relief between rich and poor countries.

- The last segment of the book, *Challenges and Policies of Large Economies*, studies the cases of the three largest economies in the world (Japan, China and the U.S.).[1] Because of their economic importance and political power, the policy options available to these countries, and their effects, are in many ways different from the standard "small open economy" cases analyzed previously in the module. The module ends with a discussion of the "global imbalances", the U.S. subpime crisis and the global financial crisis of 2008–2009.

Technical notes on capital controls, foreign direct investment, and sovereign debt and the international financial architecture accompany the cases.

II. OVERVIEW OF CASES AND READINGS

"Botswana: A Diamond in the Rough" (HBS No. 703-027)

Case Synopsis

Since achieving independence in 1966, Botswana has recorded the highest sustained real GDP growth rate in the world. Moreover, Botswana, arguably the most politically stable country in Africa, has enjoyed a democratic regime since independence. The achievements of this small, landlocked country situated in sub-Saharan Africa, appear even more impressive because they have occurred in a region generally associated with economic stagnation and political unrest. The case highlights Botswana's mutually profitable partnership with De Beers as evidence of using FDI as a successful development strategy. Independence leaders such as Sereste Khama and Ketumil Masire gained a broad political base and made far-sighted policy decisions about the country's most important asset, diamonds. The fact that Botswana was able to avoid the natural resource curse that has haunted virtually all natural resource-abundant countries, including Angola, Zaire (Congo), and Nigeria, is largely attributable to the role played by the institutions. But going forward, a weaker diamond market and no strong alternative sector for foreign investment pose major challenges for the nation.

The note "Foreign Direct Investment" (HBS No. 703-018), which provides an overview of the evolution of international business and analysis of cycles of world opinion regarding FDI, is a useful complement to the case.

Teaching Objectives

- Define and differentiate FDI flows from other forms of foreign capital flows.
- Discuss the determinants of and motivations for FDI flows.
- Analyze the benefits of FDI and FDI-led strategies to host countries.

[1]The case book "Institutions Macroeconomics and the Global Economy," by Rafael Di Tella, Huw Pill and Ingrid Vogel (World Scientific, 2005) analyzes in detail the European Union experience.

- Analyze the origins of Botswana's institutions and the role of leadership in the country's development.

Proposed Assignment Questions

1. Is Botswana a success story?
2. What accounts for the country's performance?
3. Is this performance sustainable?

Supplementary Reading List

- Alfaro, L., S. Kalemli-Ozcan and V. Volosovych (2008). "Why doesn't capital flow from rich to poor countries? An empirical investigation," *Review of Economics and Statistics*, 90, 347–368.
- Acemoglu, D., S. Johnson and J. Robinson (2003). "An African Success Story: Botswana." In *In Search of Prosperity: Analytic Narratives on Economic Growth*, D. Rodrik (ed.), Princeton: Princeton University Press.

"Foreign Direct Investment and Ireland's Tiger Economy" (HBS No. 706-007)

Case Synopsis

Ireland's transformation from one of Europe's poorest countries into one of its richest in a short span earned it the nickname "Celtic Tiger." Its spectacular growth is attributed in large part to FDI, particularly from the U.S. Ireland has, through government institutions such as the Irish Development Authority (IDA), focused its energies on attracting foreign investors with a combination of marketing strategies and fiscal and financial incentives. But the remarkable economic record of the 1990s, notwithstanding the efficacy and long-run viability of an FDI-focused growth policy, has come under scrutiny. Can Ireland continue to attract and sustain significant levels of FDI in the face of rising costs and labor shortages at home and increasing competition from eastern European countries, aggressively trying to attract foreign investment and reducing corporate taxes?

The note "Foreign Direct Investment" (HBS No. 703-018), which provides an overview of the evolution of international business and analysis of cycles of world opinion of FDI, is a useful complement to the case.

Teaching Objectives

- Critically assess Ireland's development strategy.
- Discuss and debate the role of FDI, pros and cons as well as benefits and costs, in the context of Ireland's growth.
- Critically assess the merits of government policies for attracting FDI to a host country.

- Discuss the effects of policies for attracting FDI within the context of the European Union.

Proposed Assignment Questions

1. What accounts for Ireland's economic success? What role did FDI play?
2. Should countries subsidize FDI? What are the pros and cons of FDI?
3. Are there lessons for other countries? Can the Irish model be replicated?

Supplemental Reading List

- Alfaro, L., A. Chanda, S. Okalemli-Ozcan and S. Sayek (2004). "FDI and economic growth: The role of local financial markets," *Journal of International Economics*, 64, 113–134.
- Navaretti, G. B. and A. Venables (2004). *Multinational Firms in the World Economy*, Princeton: Princeton University Press.

"Transforming Korea Inc.: Financial Crisis and Institutional Reform" (HBS No. 708-007)

Case Synopsis

In December 1997, Korea, which had prided itself on its remarkable growth over the previous few decades, suffered the humiliation of asking IMF for a record US$58 billion bailout. Korea had emerged from the aftermath of the Korean War (1950–1953) and embarked on an export-led growth strategy that, by the 1980s, had transformed the nation from one of the lowest-income countries in Asia into a major exporter. The country's economy continued to grow at a rapid pace through aggressive state intervention and capital controls, coupled with high savings and relatively low unemployment. By 1996, Korea had become the world's 11th largest economy and joined the Organization for Economic Cooperation and Development (OECD). But just one year later, it was swept up in the Asian financial crisis, which exposed fundamental weaknesses in its economy, ranging from huge bad loans in the banking sector to overcapacity in the manufacturing sector to reckless growth policies pursued by large conglomerates — the engines that had been driving the nation's economic growth. Under the IMF's guidance, Korea launched a sweeping reform plan that overhauled its financial sector, revised its domestic labor laws, and opened up its market to greater foreign investment.

As Korea approached the ten-year anniversary of the financial crisis, reactions were mixed. Some observers praised the country for having made significant improvements in its banking system and overall regulatory environment. But others believed that Korea needed, in addition to regulatory and institutional reforms, to find a new growth model capable of generating sustainable economic growth, especially as neighboring China and Japan seemed to be increasingly threatening its competitiveness in the global export market.

Teaching Objectives

- Explain the role of economic development strategy in the context of a country's political background, recognizing that political constraints, especially if international or domestic political conditions change, might facilitate or hinder growth strategy.
- Understand the benefits of capital mobility versus the potential risks of financial liberalization in the case of Korea, in particular, in relation to the large family conglomerates that dominated the country's economic landscape for decades.
- Grasp the origins of Korea's financial crisis such as vulnerabilities to external shocks and institutional inadequacies, both domestic and global.
- Explore and examine the appropriateness of the policies that the IMF prescribed to a country suffering from financial crisis.

Proposed Assignment Questions

1. How did Korea achieve its economic "miracle"?
2. If Park's strategy up to 1979 was so successful, why did his successors want to change it?
3. Was the financial crisis of 1997 inevitable? What were the main causes of the crisis?
4. Were the IMF's policies appropriate for Korea at that time? Why or why not?
5. How did Korea change through the crisis?

Supplementary Reading List

- Stiglitz, J. (2002). *Globalization and Its Discontents.* New York: W.W. Norton & Company.
- Rogoff, K. (2002). "An open letter to Joseph Stiglitz." Washington DC, http://www.imf.org/external/np/vc/2002/070202.htm, accessed October 2007.
- Joon-Ho, H. and F. Mishkin (2000). "Causes of the Korean financial crisis: Lessons for policy," NBER Working Paper No. W7483, http://ssrn.com/abstract=211229.
- "Gold from the Storm." *The Economist*, June 28, 2007.
- Dornbusch, R., Y. C. Park and S. Claessens (2000). "Contagion: How it spreads and how it can be stopped." World Bank Research Observer, http://siteresources.worldbank.org/INTMACRO/Resources/ClasessensDornbuschPark.pdf, accessed October 2007.

"Capital Controls in Chile in the 1990s (A)" (HBS No. 705-031)

Case Synopsis

In 1991, Chile adopted a framework of capital controls focused on reducing the massive flows of foreign investment coming into the country. Because international interest rates remained low, capital inflows threatened the central bank's ability to manage the exchange rate within a crawling band that aimed to eventually lower the rate of inflation to international levels. Until the Asian financial crisis of 1997 and the Russian debt crisis of August 1998, Chile's economy had performed spectacularly under, or perhaps despite, these controls. But in the aftermath of those crises, the country's economy began to suffer through both trade and financial channels. Its current account deteriorated not only because Chile relied on Asia as a market for one-third of its exports, but also because the price of copper, its largest export product, plummeted as demand from Asia dwindled. Financial flows to Chile, as to emerging markets in general, fell dramatically as investors panicked. By the end of 1999, Chile had experienced Latin America's most severe "sudden stop" of external capital flows. Many private sector observers blamed the controls for unnecessarily adding to the strain and demanded that they be dismantled. But Chile's central bank continued to defend the controls, arguing that they had helped to insulate the country from worse contagion. Chile was thus forced to decide what to do about its system of capital controls in this new economic environment.

A follow-up case, "Capital Controls in Chile in the 1990s (B)" (HBS No. 705-032), discusses the "sudden stop" in external capital flows to Chile in the years after the Asian and Russian crises, and details the changes in Chile's capital controls framework and exchange rate system between mid-September 1998 and June 2003. The case also discusses the impact of the U.S. Free Trade Agreement that went into effect in 2004 on the scope of future capital controls in Chile.

The note "Capital Controls" (HBS No. 702-082), which traces the modern history of capital controls and presents the debate regarding the advantages and disadvantages of international financial market regulation, is a useful complement to the Chile cases.

Teaching Objectives

- Explore the relationships among capital mobility, exchange management, and monetary policy (the "irreconcilable trinity").
- Introduce the mechanics and objectives of capital controls.
- Highlight the academic discussion of, and encourage students to debate, the advantages and disadvantages of capital controls, particularly on inflows.
- Compare Chile's experiences with capital controls in the 1980s and 1990s, and discuss the importance of other policies (such as bank regulation and fiscal policy) to encouraging economic growth and deterring economic crises.

Proposed Assignment Questions

1. Why did Chile institute capital controls in 1991? Did the controls achieve their objectives? What roles did other policies play in Chile's economic success in the 1990s?

2. What were the arguments for and against dismantling the controls in the wake of the Asian and Russian financial crises? What were the alternative policy options? Was Chile in danger of suffering a crisis such as that of 1982?
3. How should the relaxing of controls be sequenced with other policies? What can other countries learn from Chile's experiences?

Supplementary Reading List

- Alfaro, L. and R. Abdelal (2003). "Capital and control: Lessons from Malaysia." *Challenge*, 46, 36–53.
- Edwards, S. (1999). "How effective are capital controls?" *Journal of Economic Perspectives*, 13, 65–84.
- Laurens, B. (2000). "Appendix I: Chile's Experience with Controls on Capital Inflows in the 1990s." In *Capital Controls: Country Experiences with Their Use and Liberalization*, A. Ariyoshi *et al.* (eds.), IMF Occasional Paper 190.
- Cowan, K. and J. D. Gregorio (2007). "International borrowing, capital controls and the exchange rate: Lessons from Chile." In *Capital Controls and Capital Flows in Emerging Economies: Policies, Practices and Consequences*, S. Edwards (ed.), Chicago: University of Chicago Press.

"Malaysia: Capital and Control" (HBS No. 702-040)

Case Synopsis

On September 1, 1998 Malaysia imposed strict currency and capital controls, banning offshore trading of the Malaysian ringgit and restricting outflows of capital. The Malaysian capital controls sparked an enormous controversy in the world of international finance, and they remain at the center of debates among economists and policy makers. These debates include the following questions: Did the Malaysian capital controls successfully insulate the country's economy from the crisis? Did the capital controls promote an economic recovery that outpaced Malaysia's more orthodox neighbors, such as Korea? Does the Malaysian experience hold lessons for other developing countries facing financial crises? The case is designed to encourage students to engage each of these debates. Malaysia: Capital and Control was written for use in Business, Government, and the International Economy (BGIE), a required first-year course at Harvard Business School.

The note "Capital Controls" (HBS No. 702-082) is a useful complement to the case.

Teaching Objectives

- Explore the relationships among capital mobility, exchange management, and monetary policy (the "irreconcilable trinity").

- Deepen understanding of the mechanics and objectives of capital controls as well as the academic discussion of, and encourage students to debate, the advantages and disadvantages of capital controls, particularly on outflows.
- Debates the origins of the Malaysian capital controls.

Assignment Questions

1. What caused the financial crisis in Malaysia?
2. Why did the Malaysian government impose currency and capital controls? Were the controls necessary? Were they effective? What were the benefits and costs? What are the lessons of Malaysia's experiment with currency and capital controls?
3. Why did the international financial community react so negatively to the Malaysian currency and capital controls?
4. What have been the effects of the Malaysian government's attempts to achieve "national unity" between 1971 and 2001?

Supplementary Reading List

- Alfaro, L. and R. Abdelal (2003). "Capital and control: Lessons from Malaysia," *Challenge*, 46, 36–53.
- Jomo, K. S. (2001). "Capital controls." In *Malaysian Eclipse: Economic Crisis and Recovery*, K. S. Jomo (ed.), London: Zed.
- Kaplan, E. and D. Rodrik (1998). "Did the Malaysian Capital Controls Work?" NBER Working Paper No. 8142. Also see Krugman, P. "Saving Asia: It's time to get radical." *Fortune*, September 7, 74–80.
- Krugman, P. (1998). "An Open Letter to Prime Minister Mahathir." reprinted in *Fortune*, September 28, 35–36; Krugman, P. (1999). "Capital control freaks: How Malaysia got away with economic heresy." *Slate*, September 27.

"Brazil 2003: Inflation Targeting and Debt Dynamics" (HBS No. 704-028)

Case Synopsis

In October 2002, Brazilians elected for the first time in the country's history a left-wing president, Luís Inácio "Lula" da Silva. As markets faltered in response, da Silva reaffirmed his commitment to fiscal discipline, a floating exchange rate, and inflation targeting. By August 2003, however, his attempt to change market sentiment was coming under threat, as the country faced a looming recession. Skeptics began to worry that the new PT (Worker's Party) government would be forced to resort to printing money to meet its campaign promises. Moreover, with observers questioning the sustainability of Brazil's large public debt situation in the wake of Argentina's massive default on its public debt at the end of 2001, da Silva was under intense pressure to implement measures that would help spur the economy and deliver immediate results.

Teaching Objectives

- Examine the mechanics of inflation targeting.
- Illustrate the challenges of inflation targeting in emerging market economies, in particular, the conflict with exchange rate management in the context of "fear of floating."
- Develop an understanding of debt dynamics in emerging market economies and the linkages between inflation targeting and other monetary policy approaches,

Proposed Assignment Questions

1. What is inflation targeting? What are the alternatives?
2. Would you buy a Brazilian bond in July 2002? What would be the basis for your decision? What other information would you like to have?
3. How about August 2003? Would you buy a Brazilian bond? What has changed?
4. Is inflation targeting a good strategy for emerging markets such as Brazil?

Supplementary Reading List

- Alfaro, L. and F. Kanczuk (2005). "Debt Maturity: Is Long-Term Debt Optimal?" Harvard Business School Working Paper No. 06-005.
- Guillermo, A. C. and F. S. Mishkin (2003). "The mirage of exchange rate regimes for emerging market countries," *Journal of Economic Perspectives*, 17, 99–118.
- Banco Central do Brasil (2003). "Open Letter to the Ministry of Finance." January 16, http://www.bcb.gov.br, accessed February 2004.
- Fraga, A., I. Goldfajn and A. Minella (2003). "Inflation targeting in emerging market economies," *NBER Macroeconomics Annual*, 18.
- Mishkin, F. S. (2000). "Inflation targeting in emerging-market countries," *American Economic Review*, 90(2), 105–109.

"Rovná Daň: The Flat Tax in Slovakia" (HBS No. 707-043)

Case Synopsis

Robert Fico, the newly elected Prime Minister of the Slovak Republic (Slovakia) in 2006, faced a crucial policy decision — whether to keep the controversial *Rovná Daň*, or 'flat tax' that his predecessor, Mikuláš Dzurinda, had adopted as part of a central piece of economic reform to bring stability and growth to the country. A flat tax was defined as an income tax that applied the same rate to everyone, regardless of one's income level, often excluding deductions or exceptions. During the 1990s, several Eastern European countries such as Estonia had successfully adopted flat taxes; Slovakia followed suit and on January 1, 2004, imposed a flat tax rate of 19% on personal income, corporate income, and Value Added Tax (VAT). According to Slovakia's Ministry of Finance, Ivan Mikloš, the broad objectives of the tax reform were the "creation of a business and investment friendly environment for both individuals and companies; elimination of existing weaknesses and distortionary effects of the tax law; and achievement of a high degree of tax fairness by taxing all types and amounts of income equally." Other goals included luring foreign investors through improved business transparency and simplification of tax laws. Yet despite positive growth, Dzurinda's reform plan had also led to cuts in public spending and high unemployment. Amid growing public discontent over the flat tax, Fico won the election as a critic of the existing tax system and as a proponent of reinforcing the welfare state. His decision whether to keep or overhaul the tax system in a nation suffering from reform fatigue would not only have an impact on the long-term sustainability of reforms, but also on Slovakia's compatibility with the European Union integration.

The note "Foreign Direct Investment," (HBS Note 703–018) serves as a useful complement to the case discussion.

Teaching Objectives

- Understand the general principles of public finance and examine the objectives and purposes of a tax system.
- Understand the role of tax policy within the context of a nation's overall development strategy and its effect on the business environment.
- Explore the principles behind what makes a tax system fair, equitable, and optimal, especially in relation to political economy considerations.
- Review the goals and complexities of adopting a flat tax system and whether it can serve as a fundamental platform for sustainable economic growth and foreign investment.
- Examine the flat tax's compatibility with the European integration initiative, as taxes and welfare systems are at the core of the different capitalist models in Europe.

Proposed Assignment Questions

1. What is a flat tax? Should countries have a flat tax system? What are the best arguments for and against adopting it?
2. Why did Slovakia adopt a flat tax? How does it fit into Slovakia's development strategy?
3. Is the growing interest in flat tax compatible with the European Union's integration initiative in the long run?

Supplementary Reading List

- Rosen, H. S. (2004). *Public Finance*, 7th Ed., Chapter 14, Boston: McGraw Hill.
- Hall, R. E. and A. Rabushka (1995). *The Flat Tax*. Stanford: Hoover Institution Press.
- Krugman, P. (1996). "The Tax Reform Obsession," *The New York Times*, April 4.
- "The Case for Flat Taxes," *The Economist*, April 14, 2005.
- "Flat Taxes," *The Economist Intelligence Unit Views Wire*, January 18, 2007.
- "Slovak Republic," OECD Economic Surveys, Volume 2005/16, September, 2005.
- "The Fundamental Tax Reform, December 2004," Ministry of Finance of the Slovak Republic, http://http://www.finance.gov.sk/en/Default.aspx?CatID=118, accessed September 23, 2007.

"Special Economic Zones in India (A): Public Purpose and Private Property" (HBS No. 709-027)

Case Synopsis

In December 2007, the government of India introduced the Land Acquisition Amendment Bill in the national parliament. The Bill proposed to significantly extend the definition of "public purpose" for which the government could use the power of eminent domain to acquire land from private parties. Under the terms of the proposed bill, if a "public serving" company had acquired 70% of the land for a project, the government could use the power of eminent domain to acquire the remaining 30% on behalf of the company. The bill was introduced as a way to solve the significant problems of land acquisition which were slowing down industrial projects in India. In 2007, farmer protests led to the cancellation of the project to build a Special Economic Zone (SEZ) in West Bengal state. India had enacted the SEZ Act in 2005, to create duty-free areas that were given various regulatory, infrastructural, and taxation benefits, similar to export processing zones in other countries. These zones were designed to attract investment from foreign and domestic sources, and fuel employment in the services and manufacturing sectors. Industrial projects outside SEZs were also facing difficulties in land acquisition. Both the SEZ policy and the proposed bill proved quite controversial, leading to intense debate and widespread protests.

A complementary case, "Tata Motors in Singur: Public Purpose and Private Property (B)" (HBS No. 709-029), details the Tata Motors factory project in Singur, the sequence of events in the subsequent land acquisition dispute, and the final outcome of Tata withdrawing its factory from West Bengal in October 2008 and relocating in Gujarat. This (B) case can also be taught on its own, as a way to analyze business strategy in the face of political risk in emerging markets.

The note "Foreign Direct Investment," (HBS Note 703-018) can complement the case discussion.

Teaching objectives

- Understand that the underpinnings of a private property system include protection against expropriation by the state as well as other individuals, and that violating such protections, even for a "public purpose," can lead to an erosion of perceived security of property.
- Discuss the limits to private property rights, and the circumstances under which governments should be allowed to acquire private property. This is part of the larger question of the appropriate role of the government in facilitating economic development.
- Explore the logic behind setting up SEZs as a development strategy, and the pre-conditions needed for this strategy to succeed. In particular, the students should consider whether the benefits generated by SEZs can justify government intervention in establishing them.
- Analyze the factors driving political risk with regard to land acquisition in emerging markets, and the necessity of involving all stakeholders, not just the current government.

Assignment questions

1. Should the Indian government change the law on eminent domain, so that they can acquire land for SEZs?
2. Is setting up SEZs the right development strategy for India?
3. What could Tata Motors have done in their Singur project to mitigate the protests from farmers?
4. Under what circumstances and to what extent should the government intervene in market transactions?

Supplementary Reading List

- Acemoglu, D., S. Johnson and J. A. Robinson (2001). "The colonial origins of economic development: An empirical investigation," *American Economic Review*, 91(5), 1369–1401.
- Banerjee, A. and L. Iyer (2002). "History, institutions and economic performance: The legacy of colonial land tenure systems in india," *American Economic Review*, 95(4), 1190–1213.

"Creditor Activism in Sovereign Debt: 'Vulture' Tactics or Market Backbone" (HBS No. 706-057)

Case Synopsis

The role of distressed debt funds, also known as "vulture funds," in sovereign debt restructuring was a hotly debated topic, especially after Elliott Associates successfully converted an US$11 million investment in Peruvian bonds into a US$58 million cash payout from the country, representing the full face value of US$21 million plus past-due interest. Many observers derided "vulture" and "rogue creditor" firms such as Elliott that sought to profit from sovereign debt restructurings and maintained that these holdout creditors presented a major obstacle to successful sovereign debt restructurings. But other observers argued that activist investors, in fact, improved the market overall by demonstrating the enforceability of contracts. Elliott and similar firms have changed the "business" of sovereign debt by taking a determined approach to ensure that their contracts are enforced. Contrary to conventional wisdom, holdouts have not tended to derail restructurings. In most incidents, an 80–90% participation level is achieved in restructuring. Argentina's case in 2005, with 76% participation, was an exception. Holding out is risky. Specialized firms like Elliot have been successful, but not every investor can be so. A coordinated international approach might be warranted, however, as it is debatable whether courts in "rich" countries should be making decisions about which defaults are allowable or not due to capacity vs willingness-to-pay problems. It is difficult to keep politics out of the decision, which accounts for the tendency of Europe and the U. S. to take an ambiguous and ambivalent approach to the problem of attachment.

A supplementary note on sovereign debt, "International Capital Markets and Sovereign Debt: Crisis Avoidance and Resolution," (HBS No. 707-018), describes how successive economic crises in the 1990s and early 2000s intensified the focus on reforming the "international financial architecture." Because many of these crises involved defaults on sovereign bonds, an important component of the discussion revolved around the composition of international capital flows and sovereign debt restructuring. With the official sector, private creditors, and sovereign debtors concerned about different issues, proposals surrounding the topic varied widely. The note describes some of the proposals and summarizes their advantages and disadvantages.

Teaching Objectives

- Explore the differences between sovereign debt and corporate debt (ability vs capacity-to-pay problems).
- Highlight the problems of collecting after receiving favorable judgments against countries.
- Debate the benefits and drawbacks of "vulture funds" in sovereign debt restructuring, and analyze their effects on the sovereign debt market more generally.
- Consider whether institutional intervention is required in sovereign debt restructuring.

Proposed Assignment Questions

1. How does one make money in this business? What are the implications of doing business with and buying sovereign debt in the secondary market? How does it differ from corporate debt?

2. Would you like to work for Elliott in this business? What are the implications of "vulture" activities for the sovereign debt market? What are the pros and cons? Do holdouts and "races to the courthouse" threaten to obstruct sovereign debt restructuring?
3. You are an average person in say, Peru, Panama, or Argentina. Do you want Elliott to win or lose its case?
4. Is this the best type of solution to debt problems or is an institutional solution required? Thinking back to the Paris and London Club processes mentioned in the case, what other approaches might possibly address sovereign debt restructuring? What are the complications?
5. Some countries (e.g., Argentina) are thinking about responding by issuing bonds within their jurisdictions. Do you think this makes sense? What are the pros and cons?

Supplementary Reading List

- Alfaro, L. and F. Kanczuk (2005). "Sovereign debt as a contingent claim: A quantitative approach," *Journal of International Economics*, 65(2), 297–314.
- Rogoff, K. S. (1999). "International institutions for reducing global financial instability," *Journal of Economic Perspectives*, 13, 21–42.
- Sturzenegger, F. and J. Zettelmeyer (2006). *Debt Defaults and Lessons from a Decade of Crises.* MIT Press. Earlier draft available as *Defaults in the 90s: Learning to Deal with Crisis*, http://www.utdt.edu/~fsturzen/Defaults%20in %20the%2090s Final.pdf, accessed July 6, 2006.

"Aid, Debt Relief, and Trade: An Agenda for Fighting World Poverty (A)" (HBS No. 707-029)

Case Synopsis

At the 2005 Group of Eight (G8) Summit at Gleneagles, Scotland, world leaders called for full debt relief for the world's poorest countries and agreed to double aid to Africa by 2010. The decision, in the spirit of helping to end world poverty and hunger, was called "real and achievable progress" by British Prime Minister Tony Blair. But critics questioned whether the proposal was a reliable way to fight world poverty and, in particular, whether debt relief or aid could promote investment and economic growth in the world's highly indebted poor countries (HIPCs). The role that bilateral and multilateral institutions such as the World Bank and their conditional aid packages have played in enabling growth and development of the world's poorest countries seemed to be called into question by the G8's announcement. Although observers might be quick to criticize donor policies, there is little consensus regarding the best policy for distributing aid and ensuring that the money is spent efficiently and effectively.

The "Aid, Debt Relief, and Trade: An Agenda for Fighting World Poverty (B)" case (HBS No. 707-040) provides a brief update on the progress made towards debt relief, official development assistance, and trade talks following the 2005 Gleneagles summit.

Teaching Objectives

- Review the challenges to growth and development, the state's role in creating functioning markets, and the interaction between markets and institutions by examining the difficulties and problems facing the world's poorest countries.
- Understand the potential of aid flows and debt relief to promote economic growth by improving efficiency and incentives for investment.
- Differentiate among different kinds of capital flows across sovereign countries — private debt, sovereign-to-sovereign lending, international financial institutions' loans to individual countries, and corporate private debt — and their respective implications.
- Understand the complications involved in aid distribution such as a country's ability (or inability) to accumulate and efficiently spend aid, and the politics of sovereign-to-sovereign lending with respect to whether countries' own political motivations align with the overarching humanitarian issue of trying to resolve world poverty.
- Examine the private sector's role in tackling poverty and health issues around the world, and assess whether and how private funding could be effective by reviewing the non-profit organizations, foundations, and microfinance projects that are emerging in greater numbers.

Proposed Assignment Questions

1. What obligations do rich countries have to assist poor countries?
2. Can debt relief open the doors to growth and investment?
3. Can aid flows help poor nations break out of poverty?
4. What is the role of the private sector in the redistribution of income at the global level?

Supplementary Reading List

- Alfaro, L., S. Kalemli-Ozcan and V. Volosovych (2008). "Why doesn't capital flow from rich to poor countries? An empirical investigation," *The Review of Economics and Statistics*, 90, 347–368.
- World Bank (1998). *Assessing Aid: What Works, What Doesn't and Why?* New York: Oxford University Press.
- Easterly, W. (2003). "Can foreign aid buy growth?" *The Journal of Economic Perspectives*, 17, 23–48.

- Arslanalp, S. and P. B. Henry (2006). "Debt relief," *Journal of Economic Perspectives*, 20, 207–220.
- Burnside, C. and D. Dollar (2000). "Aid, policies, and growth," *American Economic Review*, 90, 867–868.
- Easterly, W., R. Levine and D. Roodman (2004). "Aid, policies, and growth: Comment," *American Economic Review*, 94, 774–780.
- Bulow, J. and K. Rogoff (2005). "Grants versus loans for development banks," *American Economic Review*, 95, 393–397.

"Kinyuseisaku: Monetary Policy in Japan" (HBS No. 708-017)

Case Synopsis

Toshihiko Fukui, the governor of the Bank of Japan (BOJ), faced a complex situation in the fall of 2007. Japan was experiencing the longest business recovery in its post war history. The BOJ had abandoned its zero interest rate policy (ZIRP) in 2006 after five years, and increased rates twice to 0.5%, but was eager to raise them again to more "normal" levels to exert effective monetary policy. However, the timing and approach remained controversial issues. Economic data were mixed and a large public debt burden, approximately 170% of the country's GDP accumulated from past efforts to lift the economy out of its slump through fiscal expansion, could not be ignored. Japan also faced a demographic crisis in the form of an aging population that would increase pension and health-care costs, and thereby place greater pressure on public spending. Moreover, there was growing uncertainty in the global financial markets stemming from the United States' sub-prime mortgage crisis. Although the BOJ had the autonomy to make an independent decision regarding monetary policy, Fukui was placed in a delicate position; numerous factors and different interest groups' concerns would need to be considered in making what would be a critical decision for the future of the Japanese economy.

The case "*Kinyuseisaku*: Monetary Policy in Japan" (B) (HBS No. 709-056) presents the situation faced by authorities as of 2009 and the policy choices open to them amidst the Global Financial Crisis of 2008–2009.

Teaching Objectives

- Analyze the impact of monetary policy on Japan's economic performance over the past few decades.
- Examine the effects and consequences of conducting monetary policy in a deflationary environment.
- Understand the importance of managing expectations to conduct monetary policy effectively and efficiently.
- Evaluate how other policies and factors such as fiscal policy, the banking sector's non-performing loans, and the international financial markets affected Japan's economic recovery and, more specifically, the effectiveness of its monetary policy.

- Explore potential future policy options for improving the nation's current situation.

Proposed Assignment Questions

1. Evaluate Japan's performance over the past two decades. What is wrong with the economy? Is it the lack of supply (structural) or lack of demand problem?
2. Assess the BOJ's actions during the "lost decade" and moving into the early 2000s.
3. How should policy makers address Japan's economic woes? How feasible are the potential solutions? Should the BOJ increase the interest rate? If so, what would be the appropriate timing?

Supplementary Reading List

- Ito, T. and F. S. Mishkin (2006). "Two Decades of Japanese Monetary Policy and the Deflation Problem." In *Monetary Policy with Very Low Inflation in the Pacific Rim*, T. Ito and A. K. Rose (eds.). Chicago: University of Chicago Press, 131–193.
- Bernanke, B. and M. Gertler. "Should Central Banks Respond to Movements in Asset Prices?" http://www.princeton.edu/~bernanke/asset.doc, accessed August 13, 2007.
- Cecchetti, S. G., H. Genberg, J. Lipsky and S. Wadhwani (2000). "Asset prices and central Bank policy." *Geneva Reports on the World Economy 2.* London: Centre for Economic Policy Research.
- Krugman, P. (1998). "It's baaack: Japan's slump and the return of the liquidity trap," *Brookings Papers on Economic Activity*, 2, 137–205.
- Auerbach, A. J. and M. Obstfeld (2003). "The case for open market purchases in a liquidity trap." NBER Working Paper No. 9814. Cambridge: National Bureau of Economic Research.
- King, M. (2004). "The institutions of monetary policy," *American Economic Review*, 94, 1–13.
- Hayashi, F. and E. C. Prescott (2002). "The 1990s in Japan: A lost decade," *Review of Economic Dynamics*, 1, 206–235.

"China: To Float or Not To Float? (A)" (HBS No. 706-021)

Case Synopsis

On July 21, 2005, China revalued its decade-long, quasi-fixed exchange rate of approximately 8.28 yuan per U.S. dollar by 2.1% to 8.11. At the same time, a more market-based exchange rate system was introduced. But many analysts and economists who had been calling for more drastic changes in the dollar-to-yuan exchange rate were disappointed. Modification of China's exchange rate regime had been eagerly anticipated and hotly debated in the preceding months, as China's trade surplus against the United States reached record highs and frictions increased with Europe and Japan. Not only were outside pressures intensifying, but analysts argued that the tightly managed exchange rate was straining China's own economy. They noted that the exchange rate was expensive to sustain and contributed, as well as limited China's flexibility to respond to a potentially overheating economy. It remained to be seen what China would ultimately choose to do with its exchange rate regime.

Additional short cases that can be used to supplement the main case include:

- "China: To Float or Not to Float? (B): Timeline of Changes Relevant to the Chinese Renminbi" (HBS No. 706-022). This case provides updated information on changes to China's exchange rate system and international calls for further flexibility. It starts with the People's Bank of China's July 21, 2005 announcement of the yuan revaluation.
- "China: To Float or Not to Float? (C): Esquel Group and the Chinese Renminbi" (HBS No. 706-023). This case presents a brief overview of China's textile industry and the Esquel Group, and of the reaction of the Hong Kong based manufacturer of cotton shirts with factories in China to the yuan revaluation.
- "China: To Float or Not to Float? (D): Bank of America's Strategic Investment in China Construction Bank," (HBS No. 706-031). Bank of America, the second largest U.S. bank in terms of assets and market capitalization and one of several foreign banks directly participating in China's banking sector reform, had US$3 billion invested in the China Construction Bank, the Chinese state bank. Many analysts considered banking sector reform an important complement to capital account liberalization and further changes to China's exchange rate regime. The case allows discussion about the optimal sequencing of liberalization policies.
- "China: To Float or Not to Float? (E): ABB Investment in China" (HBS No. 706-035). Given its significant presence in China, ABB was among the companies confronted with the challenge of addressing the revaluation of the yuan and the possibility of future appreciation. In 2004, approximately 6% of the company's total worldwide revenues were generated in the local currency. It remained unclear how possible future appreciation might affect ABB's strategy to intensify its use of China as a base for global sourcing. The company was among those exploring opportunities to shift inland, where costs were much lower than in the more popular coastal and capital-city areas.
- "China: To Float or Not to Float? (F): Alcatel and Strong Chinese Competition" (HBS No. 706-036). The Chinese operations of Alcatel, a global communications solution provider based in France, faced strong local competition and a difficult market. Alcatel confronted the question of whether and how it would be able to recover growth in the Chinese market even as initiatives were underway to increase the focus on services over equipment, expand its Chinese research and development presence, and merge with a U.S. competitor, Lucent.

Teaching Objectives

- Link China's exchange rate policy with its development strategy and explore the historical context of, and sustainability of flaws in, China's development strategy.
- Understand the mechanics of China's exchange rate policy, specifically with respect to the role of capital controls and sterilization, and the challenges, risks, and benefits of maintaining a quasi-fixed exchange rate against the U.S. dollar; highlight the importance of sequencing exchange rate reform with banking sector and capital controls reforms.
- Debate what China should do with its exchange rate policy and how different actions will affect businesses located in China and elsewhere.

Proposed Assignment Questions

1. What are the implications of China's exchange rate policy for doing business with and "against" China?
2. How is China's exchange rate policy linked to its development strategy? How would changes in exchange rate policy affect growth in China as well as in the rest of the world?
3. How should changes to China's exchange rate policy be sequenced with banking sector reform and liberalization of capital controls?

Supplementary Reading List

- Prasad, E. and S.-J. Wei (2007). "The Chinese approach to capital inflows: Carrots and sticks, or deeper forces at work?" In *Capital Controls and Capital Flows in Emerging Economies: Policies, Practices and Consequences*, S. Edwards (ed.). Chicago: University of Chicago Press.
- Morrison, W. and M. Labonte (2005). "China's exchange rate peg: Economic issues and options for U.S. trade policy." CRS Report for Congress, RL32165.
- Dooley, M., D. Folkerts-Landau and P. Garber (2004). "The U.S. current account deficit: Collateral for a total return swap." Deutsche Bank Global Markets Research.

"The U.S. Current Account Deficit" (HBS No. 706-002)

Case Synopsis

Investors and policy makers worldwide were confronted with the risk of painful economic consequences arising from the large and growing U.S. current account deficit. The implications of the widening deficit were intensely debated. Among those arguing that the large deficit would eventually resolve itself smoothly, even if it persisted for many years, was Federal Reserve Chairman Alan Greenspan, who anticipated a "benign resolution to the U.S. current account imbalance."[2] Others, such as economists at the World Bank, believed the large deficit risked a sharp and disorderly fall of the dollar, and that necessary macroeconomic adjustment could be painful, for the U.S. as well as for the rest of the world.[3] Despite the ongoing deficit, the gap between foreign holdings of U.S. assets and U.S. holdings of foreign assets was slightly improving. After widening to unprecedented levels, from 4.6% of GDP in 1996 to 23.2% of GDP in 2001, net liabilities fell to 16.3% of GDP in 2006. The improvement was driven by the devaluation of the dollar and the more rapid appreciation of U.S. owned foreign assets (in local currency) than that of U.S. dollar liabilities (in dollars). The *Financial Times asked*: "How long will foreigners be prepared to make such generous 'gifts' to the U.S.?[4] In this environment, Berkshire Hathaway, run by legendary investor Warren Buffett who postulated that current account imbalances would lead to "some chaotic markets in which currency adjustments play a part," announced to shareholders a plan to increase investment in overseas companies to protect against this risk.[5] It remained to be seen what results this currency bet would ultimately yield.

A simulation model (HBS No. 706-701) of the U.S. current account deficit based on Maurice Obstfeld and Kenneth Rogoff's, "Global Current Account Imbalances and Exchange Rate Adjustments," can be used in conjunction with this case.[6]

Teaching Objectives

- Study the drivers of the widening U.S. current account deficit and explore the effects of an adjustment on the world economy and business environment.
- Review the dynamics of the current account including the impact of: domestic savings and investment relative to world savings and investment; trade and international capital flows; international growth and productivity in traded and non-traded goods; prices, interest rates, and exchange rates; and fiscal and monetary policy.
- Emphasize that the current account deficit is the general equilibrium outcome of domestic and international forces.
- Explore the interaction between the current account balance and net liability position including the effect of valuation (e.g., the fact that the net liability position can be brought closer to balance through changes in asset values such as a dollar depreciation that raises the value of foreign assets held by U.S. residents).

[2]Remarks by Chairman Alan Greenspan at the 21st Annual Monetary Conference, co-sponsored by the Cato Institute and *The Economist*, Washington, D.C., November 20, 2003.
[3]World Bank Global Development Finance Report, 2005.
[4]Martin Wolf, "Global Imbalances," Martin Wolf's Economist Forum, *Financial Times*, http://www.ft.com/comment/columnists/ martinwolf, accessed January 30, 2006.
[5]"Buffett skeptical about soft landing for dollar," *Financial Times*, May 6, 2006.
[6]Maurice Obstfeld and Kenneth Rogoff, "Global Current Account Imbalances and Exchange Rate Adjustments." In *Brookings Papers on Economic Activity* 1, edited by George, L. P. and W. C. Brainard (Washington, D.C: Brookings Institution Press, 2005).

- Explore parallels with previous historic periods of U.S. external imbalance.

Proposed Assignment Questions

1. Is Warren Buffett's decision to bet against the dollar a good one? Why or why not?
2. Why has the U.S. developed such large current account deficits?
3. Is the U.S. current account deficit in 2005 sustainable? Is its continual widening a problem? Is the U.S. headed towards crisis? Why or why not?
4. What, if anything, should the U.S. do to reduce its current account deficit?
5. Is global adjustment to external imbalances likely to occur and, if so, how? What could be done to facilitate a smooth adjustment?

Supplementary Reading List

- Dooley, M. P., D. Folkerts-Landau and P. Garber (2004). "The revived Bretton Woods system: The effects of periphery intervention and reserve management on interest rates and exchange rates in center countries." Bureau of Economic Research Working Paper 10332.
- Roubini, N. and B. Setser (2005). "Will the Bretton Woods 2 Regime Unravel Soon? The risk of a hard landing in 2005–2006." Written for the Symposium on the "Revived Bretton Woods System: A New Paradigm for Asian Development?" organized by the Federal Reserve Bank of San Francisco and UC Berkeley, San Francisco.
- Mann, C. L. (2002). "Perspectives on the U.S. current account deficit and sustainability," *Journal of Economic Perspectives*, 16, 131–152.
- Edwards, S. (2005). "Is the U.S. Current Account Deficit Sustainable? And if Not, How Costly Is Adjustment Likely to Be?" Prepared for presentation at the Spring 2005 meeting of the Brookings Panel on Economic Activity.
- Hausmann, R. and F. Sturzenegger (2006). "Global Imbalances or Bad Accounting? The Missing Dark Matter in the Wealth of Nations." Center for International Development, Harvard University, Working Paper No. 124 (Revised September 2006), http://www.cid.harvard.edu/cidwp/124.htm, accessed December 9, 2006.

U.S. Subprime Mortgage Crisis: Policy Reactions (A) (HBS No. 708-036)

Case Synopsis

By early 2008, the U.S. Government and the U.S. Federal Reserve Board had taken various policy measures over the last months to tackle the subprime mortgage crisis that threatened to drag the economy into a recession. The Bush administration approved a fiscal stimulus package exceeding US$150 billion. Interest rates had been repeatedly cut at the fastest pace in decades to 2.25% as of March 2008. In March 2008, the U.S. Federal Reserve Board, in an unprecedented move, played a critical role in orchestrating JPMorgan Chase's purchase of Bear Stearns, the fifth largest U.S. investment bank. This was no ordinary deal between two investment banks on Wall Street. The Fed had consented to cover up to US$29 billion in potential losses from Bear Stearns' risky assets, whose financial woes were linked to the U.S. subprime mortgage crisis. In a separate move, to ease the economy's credit crunch, the central bank also opened a direct credit line for investment banks for the first time in history. The policy broke away from the traditional practice of directly lending to commercial banks only. These moves were all aimed at restoring investors' confidence amid concerns of the widespread impact of the mortgage crisis.

Policy makers, academics, and business leaders were caught in an intense debate over what the best policy response would be, moving forward. Some argued for an aggressive monetary and fiscal expansion to prevent a recession in the U.S. Additional proposals ranged from the Fed and the Treasury to take on a more direct responsibility for financial regulation of investment banks to the provision of aid for the millions of homeowners who now faced foreclosures, unable to meet their housing payments. Many critics, however, viewed the Fed's involvement in the Bear Stearns and some of the proposals advanced to date as a bailout for financial institutions' imprudent lending practices conducted especially in the subprime mortgage sector and homeowners' reckless borrowing.

The case "U.S. Subprime Mortgage Crisis: Policy Reactions (B)" (HBS No. 709-045) complements the discussion and updates events. By March 2009, one year had passed since investment bank Bear Stearns had been bailed out in an effort to stem the subprime mortgage crisis from spiraling out of control. However, the situation had turned from bad to worse. Several big companies that represented the heart of America's financial system, including Lehman Brothers and insurance giant AIG, had faltered. In fact, the U.S. had plunged into the worst financial crisis and recession not seen since the Great Depression. About 2.6 million jobs in 2008 had been axed, coupled with a loss of wealth and depressed consumer confidence. The Bush administration attempted to breathe life back into the economy pushing for a stimulus package, and creating various lending programs for debt-ridden banks. The Fed had dropped interest rates to near zero and pursued quantitative easing policies. Yet as the economy showed few signs of turning around anytime soon, now, the responsibility fell on newly elected President Barack Obama. The new administration pursued a new fiscal stimulus and the new policies to tackle the problems in the financial system. The effectiveness of policies remained to be seen.

The case "Sovereign Wealth Funds: For Profits or Politics?" (HBS No. 708-053) allows for a critical evaluation of the role of sovereign wealth funds.

Teaching Objectives

- Analyze the causes and consequences of the U.S. subprime crisis and in particular their relation to the global imbalances.
- Explore the short-term versus long-term consequences of the policies advanced.

Assignment Questions

1. What explains the U.S. subprime mortgage crisis? Who's to blame?
2. How does the U.S. current account deficit relate to the current subprime mortgage mess? Why is the U.S. current account in such a massive deficit? Is the U.S. current account deficit sustainable? Is its continual widening a problem?
3. What, if anything, should the U.S. do to solve the subprime crisis? What, if anything, should the U.S. do to reduce its current account deficit? Are the solutions compatible?
4. Of all the concerns raised against SWF, which do you find the most persuasive? Should Washington have allowed these government funds to take such large stakes in Wall Street?

Supplementary Reading List

- Cecchetti, S. G. *et al.* (2000). "Asset Prices and Central Bank Policy." Geneva Reports on the World Economy 2. London: Centre for Economic Policy Research.
- Bernanke, B. S. (2002). "Deflation: Making Sure "It" Doesn't Happen Here." Remarks before the National Economists Club, Washington DC. http://www.federalreserve.gov/boardDocs/speeches/2002/20021121/default.htm.
- Bernanke, B. S. and M. Gertler (2007). "Should Central Banks Respond to Movements in Asset Prices?" http://www.princeton.edu/~bernanke/asset.doc, accessed August 13, 2007, p. 1.
- Bernanke, B. S. (2009). "The Crisis and the Policy Response." Speech at the Stamp Lecture, London School of Economics.
- Greenspan, A. (2007). "The roots of the mortgage crisis," *The Wall Street Journal*, December 12.
- Taylor, J. B. "Housing and monetary policy." National Bureau of Economic Research Working Paper 13682.
- Reinhart, C. and K. Rogoff (2008). "Is the 2007 U.S. subprime financial crisis so different? An international historical comparison." NBER Working paper w13761.
- Reinhart, C. and K. Rogoff (2009). "The Aftermath of Financial Crises." NBER Working Paper w14656.

"The First Global Financial Crisis of the 21st Century" (HBS No. N9-709-057)

Case Synopsis

In 2009, the World Bank and the IMF forecasted that the world economy would contract for the first time in the post war period. By then governments around the world had taken various policy measures over the last few months to tackle the subprime mortgage crisis that threatened to drag the economy into a recession. Individual nations tried to stabilize and steer their economies towards recovery through monetary, fiscal, and financial policies. Yet as the global economy faced slower growth stemming from the U.S. mortgage crisis, policy makers were caught in an intense debate over what the "right" solution would be, and the implication of these policies.

Teaching Objectives

- Analyze the global causes and consequences of the U.S. subprime crisis and the relation to the global imbalances.
- Explore the policies available for countries, in particular developing ones, to deal with the consequences of the crisis.
- Analyze the role of coordinated efforts and the role of international institutions in the crisis.

Assignment Questions

1. What explains the global meltdown?
2. Is global adjustment to the crisis and current imbalances likely to occur, and if so, how? What could be done to encourage a smooth adjustment?
3. Are there differences between large and small countries, or developed and developing in terms of the tools available?
4. What should be, if any, the role of the IMF?
5. What can be done to prevent future global crises?

Supplementary Reading List

- World Economic Outlook Update, Global Economic Slump Challenges Policies, International Monetary Fund, January 28, 2009, http://www.imf.org/external/pubs/ft/weo/ 2009/update/01/index.htm

III. INTERNATIONAL CAPITAL FLOWS

A. Patterns of International Capital: 1970s–2000s

Cycles in capital flows, especially in emerging markets, have been observed for nearly two hundred years.[7] The module focuses on events that occurred during the last three decades as they hold important lessons for current policy makers and the business environment that managers face today.

In the late 1970s, banks in the U.S. (and other industrial countries) recycled OPEC surplus to emerging markets, in particular, Latin America. This took place against a background of soaring commodity prices and high inflation in the advanced economies, coupled with low real interest rates and weak loan demand in the U.S. Capital flows through bank lending surged during this period. But in the early 1980s, the situation changed dramatically. Interest rates rose sharply as the U.S. Federal Reserve acted to reduce spiraling double-digit inflation, thus dampening economy activity and lowering commodity prices and demand. As most of the loans had either short maturities or variable interest rates, the prospects for repayment quickly deteriorated. In the summer of 1982, debtor countries, led by Mexico, could not secure the added credit they needed to pay the high interest and offset the shortfall of export earnings. Mexico's debt moratorium in August 1982 sent shock waves around the world, and the highly exposed and leveraged banks retrenched from emerging markets and Latin America in particular.[8] One after another, developing countries experienced currency crises, banking crises, or both. Numerous crises, including some of the worst hyperinflations uncorrelated to wars, occurred in Latin America during the "lost decade" that followed.[9]

The drought in capital flows lasted until 1990. Debt restructuring and negotiation paved the way for a rediscovery of emerging markets.[10] Renewed access to international capital markets in the wake of the resolution of the debt crisis led to a surge in available external capital. Mexico, for example, having implemented a suc-

[7]See Reinhart, C. and K. Rogoff (2004). "Serial default and the 'paradox' of rich to poor capital flows," *American Economic Review*, 94, 53–58; Reinhart, C. and K. Rogoff (2008). "This Time is Different: A Panoramic View of Eight Centuries of Financial Crises," NBER Working Paper w13882; Alfaro, L., S. Kalemli-Ozcan and V. Volosovych (2007). "Capital Flows in a Globalized World: The Role of Policies and Institutions." In *Capital Controls and Capital Flows in Emerging Economics: Policies, Practices, and Consequences*, S. Edwards (ed.). Chicago: University of Chicago Press; and Alfaro, L. and F. Kanczuk (2004). "Capital controls, risk and liberalization cycles," *Review of International Economics*, 12. On longer-term trends, see also Obstfeld, M. and A. Taylor (2004). *Global Capital Markets: Integration, Crisis, and Growth*. Cambridge: Cambridge University Press.

[8]See Alfaro, L. and I. Vogel, "Creditor Activism in Sovereign Debt: Vulture Tactics or Market Backbone," HBS No. 706-057.

[9]See Di Tella, R., H. R. Pill, M. L. de Silanes Gomez, C. F. Violand and I. Vogel. "Bolivia: Globalization, Sovereignty, or Democracy?" HBS No. 702-086; and R. Di Tella, L. Alfaro and E. Reficco, "Bolivia and Evo Morales," HBS No. 707-041.

[10]See Alfaro, L., E. Werker and R. Kim, "Aid, Debt Relief, and Trade: An Agenda for Fighting World Poverty (A)," HBS No. 707-029.

cessful inflation stabilization plan and having signed NAFTA, became the darling of foreign investors.[11]

Notwithstanding the 1994–1995 Mexico crisis, capital flows to East Asian miracle economies such as those to Korea and Malaysia increased no less dramatically, especially after 1995, when short-term interest rates in Japan headed towards unprecedented lows.[12] Other emerging counties such as Chile also experienced a surge of capital inflows.[13] What followed was a period of extreme financial turbulence, starting in Asia and spreading to Latin America and other regions.

After a sharp reduction in capital flows to emerging markets during 1998–2002, spreads narrowed to levels not seen since the early 1990s. This new wave of easy access to cheap international credit found the U.S. current account deficit (the difference between the country's savings and investment) at the core of so-called "global imbalances," with current account surpluses in oil-producing countries, Japan, China, and other Asian countries taking the bulk of the "other side."[14] The nature of the U.S. deficit, however, changed over time. In the late 1990s, the U.S. government increased its savings as firms did the same with their investments, thus accounting for most of the imbalance. But after 2000–2001, although U.S. firms continued to increase their savings, the government and households reduced theirs.

As world savings must equal world investments, changes in the U.S. current account deficit have implications for other countries' current accounts. To sustain the same level of world growth, reductions in the U.S. deficit should be balanced with other countries' deficits or the surplus countries should reduce their surpluses. Authorities in Japan have been struggling with zero (or close to zero) inflation and low growth.[15] In 2005, China adopted a *de jure* floating regime, but *de facto* changes have been limited.[16]

As the world coped with the aftermath of the U.S. subprime crisis, the evolution of global imbalances has had a first-order impact on global growth. In March 2009, the World Bank presented its most dismal outlook for the global economy to date, forecasting negative growth for the full year, a phenomenon not seen since World War II. Individual nations tried to stabilize and steer their economies to-

[11]See Pill, H., "Mexico: The Tequila Crisis 1994–1995," HBS No. 702-093.

[12]See Alfaro, L. and R. Kim. "Transforming Korea Inc.: Financial Crisis and Institutional Reform," HBS No. 708-007; and Alfaro, L., R. Di Tella and R. Kim. "Chronology of the Asian Financial Crisis," HBS No. 708-001. Also see Abdelal R. and L. Alfaro. "Malaysia: Capital and Control," HBS No. 702-040 and Alfaro, L. and A. Kanno. "*Kinyuseisaku*: Monetary Policy in Japan (A)," HBS No. 708-017.

[13]See Alfaro, L., R. Di Tella and I. Vogel. "Capital Controls in Chile in the 1990s (A)," HBS No. 705-031.

[14]See Alfaro, L., R. Di Tella and I. Vogel. "The U.S. Current Account Deficit," HBS No. 706-002; Alfaro, L. and A. Kanno. "*Kinyuseisaku*: Monetary Policy in Japan (A)," HBS No. 708-017; and Alfaro, L., R. Di Tella and I. Vogel. "China: To Float or Not to Float? (A)" HBS No. 706-021.

[15]See Alfaro, L. and A. Kanno. "*Kinyuseisaku*: Monetary Policy in Japan (A)," HBS No. 708-017.

[16]See Alfaro, L., R. Di Tella and I. Vogel. "China: To Float or Not to Float? (A)," HBS No. 706-021.

wards recovery through monetary, fiscal, and financial policies. At the same time, they recognized that the scope and scale of the financial crisis required a greater coordinated effort. Yet at the Group of 20's (G20) summit of top level financial ministers held in the first week of April 2009, there was discord among the nations that accounted for 80% of the world economy on what kind of joint action had to be taken. The U.S. urged other nations to push forward with a greater fiscal stimulus while several European nations, led by France and Germany, stressed the need for greater financial regulation at the global level instead. the global level instead. Although there were underlying differences in domestic constraints that caused the discord among nations on what had to be done, there were also contrasting views on what kind of short and long-term policies would really work.

B. International Capital Flows, Sovereign Risk, and Exchange Rates[17]

The book covers issues that define international economics as a distinct field — the implications of sovereign governments and national currencies, and the determinants and effects of cross-border capital flows. Three basic insights are essential.

First, trade in goods is different from trade in financial assets. Because a financial transaction inherently involves a commitment to pay at a later date, payments are always contingent and hence, fundamentally affected by the problems of asymmetric information (such as moral hazard and adverse selection) and the risk of non-enforcement. Both problems are exacerbated in international financial transactions. Information is generally better shared inside countries than across international boundaries, and it is far easier to use national legal systems to manage contractual disputes than it is to rely on still-weak international legal norms. International capital flows can bring substantial gains by augmenting local savings and improving technology. But under pre-existent distortions, weak institutional settings, and — particularly — under unregulated financial markets, international capital mobility can exacerbate the misallocation of resources, increase the likelihood of financial crises, and impair growth.

Second, international financial flows are affected by two additional macroeconomic risks that are absent within countries. That is, the international financial system is burdened not just by asymmetric information and contract uncertainty. One further consideration is sovereign risk: governments can choose to default on their international obligations. The second complication is that countries generally have their own currencies and the rise and fall of currencies relative to one another

[17]See Obstfeld, M. (2007). "International Finance and Growth in Developing Countries: What Have We Learned?" http://www.growthcommission.org/storage/cgdev/documents/Themes Papers/Paper%20Obstfeld.pdf, accessed January 10, 2008; and Hermalin, B. E. and A. K. Rose (1999). "Risks to Lenders and Borrowers in International Capital Markets," in *International Capital Flows*, M. Feldstein (ed.). Chicago: University of Chicago Press, pp. 363–386.

often can be decisive for investors' returns.[18] Potential net gains from international financial trade are contingent on containing these risks.

The main channel through which international capital mobility exacerbates problems associated with trade in assets is related to sovereignty: the involvement of governments as implicit parties to international contracts.[19] The importance of the recurring phenomenon of countries defaulting on their obligations underscores this problem and has prompted an enormous volume of theoretical and empirical literature.[20] Research has focused on why countries ever choose to pay their debts and why private creditors ever expect repayment, given that repayment incentives for governments are minimal in the relative absence of collateral and that courts have limited ability to extract compliance from sovereign entities in the absence of a supranational legal authority empowered to enforce contracts across borders.

The use of different currencies can generate additional macroeconomic risks.[21] Currency mismatches such as dollar liabilities vs domestic-currency assets, for example, can fuel exchange rate volatility and occasion systemic risk. Developing countries are often characterized by their inability to borrow externally in their own currencies as well as by their extensive domestic liability of dollarization/indexation.[22] This exacerbates problems related to large exchange rate movements. For example, a large depreciation of the domestic currency can lead to an increase in the value of debts relative to assets (in contrast, for example, to the U.S., which can issue debt in local currency). This accounts for the tendency of emerging market floaters to be guided more heavily than industrial countries by exchange-market developments,

---

[18]Even for countries that adopt a foreign currency, sovereignty implies the choice to renege or change. For example, Botswana adopted the pula in 1976 (before the South African Rand was official currency). See Alfaro, L. *et al.* "Botswana: A Diamond in the Rough," HBS No. 703-027.

[19]See Obstfeld, M. and K. Rogoff (1996). *Foundations of International Macroeconomics.* Cambridge: MIT Press; Tirole J. (2002). *Financial Crisis, Liquidity, and the International Monetary System.* Princeton: Princeton University Press; Alfaro, L. and F. Kanczuk (2005). "Sovereign debt as a contingent claim: A quantitative approach," *Journal of International Economics*, 65, 297–314; Alfaro, L. and I. Vogel. "International Capital Markets and Sovereign Debt: Crisis Avoidance and Resolution," HBS No. 707-018; and Alfaro L. and I. Vogel. "Creditor Activism in Sovereign Debt: Vulture Tactics or Market Backbone," HBS No. 706-057.

[20]For surveys of the literature, see Kletzer, M. K. (1994). "Sovereign Immunity and International Lending." In *The Handbook of International Macroeconomics*, F. van der Ploeg (ed.). United Kingdom, London: Blackwell Publishers; Eaton, J. and R. Fernandez (1995). "Sovereign Debt." In *Handbook of International Economics*, Vol. 3, G. Grossman and K. Rogoff (eds.). Amsterdam: Elsevier, North-Holland, pp. 2031–2077; Rogoff, K. and J. Zettelmeyer (2002). "Bankruptcy Procedures for Sovereigns: A History of Ideas, 1976–2001," IMF Working Paper, WP/02/133.

[21]See Alfaro, L. (2005). "Inflation, openness, and exchange rate regimes," *Journal of Development Economics*, 77, 229–249.

[22]See Eichengreen, B., R. Hausmann and U. Panizza (2003). "Currency Mismatches, Debt Intolerance, and Original Sin: Why They Are Not the Same and Why It Matters," NBER Working Paper w10036; Alfaro, L., R. Di Tella and I. Vogel. "Brazil 2003: Inflation Targeting and Debt Dynamics," HBS No. 704-028.

a reduced monetary autonomy phenomenon that Calvo and Reinhart (2002) have labeled "fear of floating."[23]

Third, international capital flows have important macroeconomic consequences, and policy-makers face a difficult trade-off among three objectives: monetary policy autonomy, a stable fixed exchange rate, and free capital mobility. Also known as the "irreconcilable trilogy," the open-economy "trilemma" is that only two of the three goals can be reached simultaneously. When capital outflows surge, as they sometimes do, a central bank that does not want their currency to depreciate must either increase interest rates to attract capital or purchase its own currency using foreign exchange reserves. If the flows of capital are large, a central bank might quickly exhaust its foreign exchange reserves with little influence over the market outcome. Increasing interest rates, on the other hand, can have negative consequences for economic activity and employment. In a country where the financial sector is weak, the consequences can be devastating. Similarly, countries experiencing net capital inflows face appreciating exchange rates and increasing money supply which can lead to undesirable inflation, or fuel bubbles in asset prices. Popping asset bubbles can bankrupt the financial systems of countries with heavily exposed domestic banks, as seen in Japan and many Asian countries in the 1990s. Although central banks can "sterilize" increases in international reserves by selling government bonds and thereby reducing domestic credit, this tends to keep interest rates high. Because the government pays a higher interest rate on its bonds than it receives on its foreign reserve holdings, sterilization represents a non-trivial cost to the government of encouraging continued capital inflows.[24] Sterilization is at best only a temporary policy; the evidence to date suggests some scope for sterilization in the short-run, but gives little indication of its viability as a long-term policy.[25] If capital movements are restricted, however, countries can pursue autonomous monetary policies while maintaining fixed exchange rates.

More generally, international borrowing has to be repaid in the future (ignoring the sovereign risk considerations discussed above), for which some investment in profitable projects is important. As such, adequate domestic incentives to invest foreign capital productively are crucial. However, many times, capital flows abruptly stop with severe negative effects.

The academic literature has identified numerous mechanisms that can lead to currency and financial crises. In the canonical "first-generation" crisis models, a government with persistent money-financed budget deficits is assumed to use a lim-

[23] Calvo, G. A. and C. M. Reinhart (2002). "Fear of floating," *The Quarterly Journal of Economics*, 117, 379–408.

[24] See Alfaro, L., R. Di Tella and I. Vogel. "Capital Controls in Chile in the 1990s (A)," HBS No. 705-031.

[25] Ito, T. and D. Folkerts-Laudau (1996). *International Capital Markets*, Washington: International Monetary Fund; Dominguez K. M. (1999). "The Role of the Yen." In *International Capital Flows*, M. Feldstein (ed.). Chicago: University of Chicago Press, pp. 133–171; Dominguez, K. M. and J. Frankel (1993). "Does foreign-exchange intervention matter? The portfolio effect," *American Economic Review*, 83, 1356–1369.

ited stock of reserves to peg its exchange rate.[26] This policy would ultimately be unsustainable and investors' attempts to anticipate the inevitable floating of the exchange rate would generate a speculative attack on the currency when reserves fall to a critical level. An unsustainable fiscal deficit will lead to reserve losses, current-account deficit, real appreciation, and an inevitable collapse (Southern Cone experiences of the 1970s, Brazil in 1999). In "second generation" models, a government chooses whether or not to defend a pegged exchange rate by trading off short-run macroeconomic flexibility against longer-term credibility.[27] This is potentially a multiple equilibria story. Defending the peg is more expensive (via higher interest rates) if the market believes the defense will ultimately fail. Multiple equilibria are thus occasioned by speculative attacks on the currency originating from a predicted deterioration of fundamentals or via a self-fulfilling prophecy (EMS Crisis in Europe in the 1990s). "Third generation" models were developed to account for the crises of the late 1990s (characterized as currency and financial crises) emphasizing balance sheet effects and implicit government guarantees (Asian financial crisis and Korea in 1997).[28] For emerging markets, in particular, there is a potentially explosive multi-directional interaction among the currency market, government finances, and banking and corporate sectors.

Although crises can sometimes be driven by expectations, their possibility presupposes some weakness in various "fundamentals" of an economy.[29] These might be institutional (for example, quality of bank supervision, quality and transparency of corporate governance, state of domestic financial development, strength of the domestic judicial system) or macro (for example, a competitive real exchange rate, the sustainability of the trajectory of the public debt, the term and currency composition of external debt).

---

[26]See Krugman, P. (1979). "A model of balance of payments crises," *Journal of Money, Credit, and Banking*, 11, 311–25; Flood R. and P. Garber (1984). "Collapsing exchange rate regimes: some linear examples," *Journal of International Economics*, 17, 1–13.

[27]Obstfeld, M. (1994). "The logic of currency crises," *Cahiers Economiques et Monetaires*, 43, 189–213.

[28]See Krugman, P. (1998). "What Happened to Asia?" http://web.mit.edu/krugman/www/DISINTER.html, accessed January 10; Hermalin B. E. and K. Rose, p. 364; Kaminsky G. and C. Reinhart (1999). "The twin crises: The causes of banking and balance-of-payments problems," *American Economic Review*, 89, 473–500; McKinnon, R. and H. Pill (1996). "Credible liberalizations and international capital flows: The overborrowing syndrome," in *Financial Deregulation and Integration in East Asia*, T. Ito and A. O. Krueger (eds.). Chicago: University of Chicago Press; Chang R. and A. Velasco (2001). "A model of financial crises in emerging markets," *Quarterly Journal of Economics*, 116, 489–517.

[29]Of course, inferring causality from empirical associations is always perilous. For example, fiscal rectitude, labor market flexibility, and trade openness typically reflect endogenous government policies, which can be driven by "deeper" political factors that, in themselves, make the economy better able to live productively with an open financial account. It is difficult to believe, however, that a favorable configuration of conventional fundamentals will not make an independent contribution to financial stability. See Obstfeld, M. (2007). "International Finance and Growth in Developing Countries: What Have We Learned?" http://www.econ.berkeley.edu/~obstfeld/280c_sp07/commission.pdf, accessed January 18.

The case of Brazil, for example, shows how fiscal imprudence can generate unstable government debt dynamics in which government borrowing rates rise to reflect higher default probabilities, inducing further borrowing and rate hikes, thus increasing the probability of an eventual crisis.[30] Political economy considerations also play an important role. In South Korea, prior to its 1997–1998 crisis, the fundamental institutional distortions were the political power of *chaebols*, which effectively manipulated the financial system to obtain access to cheap funding, and a pervasive government bailout mentality (moral hazard).[31] The fragility of the financial system became worse with the government's decision, earlier in the 1990s, to open the economy to short-term but not long-term foreign lending.[32]

Troubles associated with early financial liberalization were also a devastating experience for Chile in 1982. Policy makers were forced to dramatically depreciate the local currency and nationalize privately contracted financial-sector external debt. Extensive restructuring of the banking system involved the imposition of strict regulations as the government tried to address currency mismatches on balance sheets. On the currency side, from the mid-1980s, the Chilean peso to U.S. dollar exchange rate was kept within a crawling band and the central parity was adjusted daily to reflect the inflation difference between Chile and its main trading partners. The goal was to maintain competitiveness, although there is a danger in any such system that expectations will feed into inflation, resulting in the accommodation of expectations via the exchange rate. Chile's *encaje*, or unremunerated reserve requirement on foreign capital inflows, although initially maintained, was scrapped in the late 1990s as the regime was tested during the Asian crisis. A noteworthy feature here is that by, for example, adopting a tight fiscal policy and prudent banking regulation, countries can create conditions that minimize risk.

Recent literature suggests that certain structural preconditions for financial inflows can maximize their beneficial effects in an emerging market economy.[33] Even in the case of FDI flows, where research identifies benefits linked to know-how and

[30]See Alfaro, L., R. Di Tella and I. Vogel. "Brazil 2003: Inflation Targeting and Debt Dynamics," HBS No. 704-039.

[31]See Alfaro, L. and R. Kim. "Transforming Korea Inc.: Financial Crisis and Institutional Reform," HBS No. 708-007.

[32]Obstfeld, M. "International Finance and Growth in Developing Countries: What Have We Learned?"

[33]Frederic, S. Mishkin provides an analysis of recent emerging-market crises that places at center stage the way faulty institutional underpinnings have distorted the effects of capital inflows from abroad and led to economic instability. See Mishkin, F. S. (2006). *The Next Great Globalization: How Disadvantaged Nations Can Harness Their Financial Systems to Get Rich*, Princeton: Princeton University Press; Alfaro, L. *et al.* (2004). "FDI and Economic Growth: The Role of Local Financial Markets." find that FDI has a stronger growth-promoting effect when the local financial sector is better developed. Bekaert, G., C. Harvey and C. Lundblad (2005). "Does financial liberalization spur growth?" *Journal of Financial Economics*, 77, 3–55, report the positive effect of liberalization on growth to be greatest when the quality of institutions and level of financial development are high. See also Prasad, E., K. Rogoff, S.-J. Wei and M. A. Kose (2003). "The Effects of Financial Globalization on Developing Countries: Some Empirical Evidence," International Monetary Fund Occasional Paper 220.

managerial skills as well as lower volatility, success stories like those of Ireland and Botswana suggest a key role for domestic policies. During the 1990s and 2000s, an extraordinary consensus emerged among policy makers: nearly all lauded the benefits of FDI.[34] Unlike more liquid capital flows, FDI appeared to be stable and proponents further claimed, quite plausibly, a number of other beneficial effects of FDI for recipient countries, including increased productivity and transfers of technology, managerial skills, and know-how. Governments around the world rushed to reduce taxes and provide special incentives for foreign firms to build plants and, following the example of success stories such as that of Ireland, Eastern Europe embraced the FDI development strategy of lowering taxes.[35] The empirical record indicates that the benefits of FDI are most likely to be realized when capital flows are complemented by a range of domestic policies that enhance stability and growth.[36]

We are living in an era of globalization that is in many ways without historical precedent. Trade and capital flows have been liberalized in many parts of the world. In 2009 the world was coping with the first global slowdown since World War II. Many feared increased protectionism. While the potency of conventional macroeconomic policies may have diminished or been affected as a result of globalization, good policy making and judgment become even more critical. Understanding the implications of these dramatic economic developments is crucial for students in their capacity as managers and leaders in the future.

[34]See Alfaro, L. and Clavell E. "Foreign Direct Investment," HBS No. 703-018.

[35]See Alfaro, L., V. Dev and S. McIntyre. "Foreign Direct Investment and Ireland's Tiger Economy," HBS No. 706-007; Alfaro L. *et al.* "*Rovná Daň*: The Flat Tax in Slovakia," HBS No. 707-043.

[36]Alfaro, L., A. Chanda, S. Kalemli-Ozcan and S. Sayek (2004). "FDI and economic growth: The role of local financial markets," *Journal of International Economics*, 64, 89–112; Alfaro, L. and A. Charlton (2007). "Intra-Industry Foreign Direct Investment." Harvard Business School Working Paper, No. 08-018; Alfaro L. and A. Rodriguez-Clare (2004). "Multinationals and linkages: An empirical investigation," *Economia*, 4, 113–169.

I. Determinants and Effects of International Capital Flows

INSTITUTIONS, POLICIES, AND CAPITAL FLOWS

"Botswana: A Diamond in the Rough," introduces many of the themes in the book. The case examines the use of foreign capital and in particular FDI as a development strategy with an emphasis on the role of domestic institutions in reaping its potential benefits. The motivation for the case is the important but little-known fact that since achieving independence in 1966, Botswana has recorded the highest sustained real GDP growth rate of any country in the world. The mutually profitable partnership between De Beers and the government of Botswana has helped the country to avoid the so-called "resource curse" that has afflicted other African countries with abundant natural resources such as Angola, Congo (former Zaire) and Nigeria. The case highlights the critical behavioral foundations of the resource curse: whether it is manifested depends ultimately on development strategy and effective leadership. Although Botswana might be the exception that proves the rule, that very exceptionality reveals what can be accomplished with effective institutions and policy makers. The case introduces one of the main themes of the course, the role of good policy making and solid institutions in harnessing the benefits of foreign capital. The case also identifies and develops the issues of communication, confidence, coordination, and institutional development and the role of policies that are central to the remainder of the course.

POLICIES AND EFFECTS OF FOREIGN CAPITAL

"Foreign Direct Investment and Ireland's Tiger Economy" provides an opportunity to deepen students' understanding of the topics introduced in the Botswana case, specifically with respect to FDI. The Irish government consciously nurtured an investment-friendly regime and supported institutions like the Irish Development Authority (IDA) that were created to attract and promote investment in Ireland. Foreign firms were lured with generous fiscal and financial incentives. Yet many observers argue that the FDI-centered approach resulted in the marginalization of Ireland's indigenous industry, which has remained on the economic periphery, and contend that overdependence on FDI has made the country's economy more vulnerable to external changes. FDI's potential benefits to a country extend beyond capital inflows and job creation to access foreign technology and markets and increased competition. However, for the benefits of FDI to materialize, host countries must create an overall enabling environment that includes stable macroeconomic conditions, more efficient capital markets, and better human and physical infrastructure. This implies that countries should consider the cost of policies aimed at attracting FDI and those of making investments to improve local conditions. Of course, this is not an either/or choice and the ends are not incompatible; better local conditions not only attract foreign companies, but also enable host economies to maximize the benefits of foreign investment.

The note "Foreign Direct Investment", which provides an overview of the evolution of international business and analysis of world opinion regarding FDI over time, is a useful complement to the Botswana and Ireland cases.

CAPITAL FLOWS: BENEFACTOR OR MENACE?

"Transforming Korea Inc.: Financial Crisis and Institutional Reform" highlights two of the book's main themes. The case underscores the benefits of capital mobility vs potential risks and considers how domestic policies can exacerbate or mitigate those risks. Between 1980 and 2000, output per worker in Korea grew at 5.4% per year. During this period, the country experienced only two years of negative growth: in 1980 in the wake of the second oil shock, the international debt crisis, and the assassination of President Park Chung-Hee; and in 1998 in the midst of the Asian financial crisis that forced Korea to seek from the IMF and World Bank a record US$58 billion emergency rescue package. Prior to the 1997–1998 crisis, the fundamental institutional distortion in Korea was the political power of the *chaebols*, which effectively manipulated the financial system to obtain access to cheap funding. Moral hazard in the form of a government bailout mentality was pervasive. Financial fragility was intensified by the government's decision, earlier in the 1990s, to open the economy to short-term but not long-term foreign lending.

Introduction: Institutions, Policies, and Capital Flows

HARVARD | BUSINESS | SCHOOL

9-703-027
REV: NOVEMBER 29, 2005

LAURA ALFARO
DEBORA SPAR
FAHEEN ALLIBHOY

Botswana: A Diamond in the Rough

Our country is beyond doubt one of the poorest nations in Africa.
—Sir Seretse Khama, President of Botswana, 1966[1]

It has been a remarkable quarter of a century, and every Motswana can take pride in our achievements.
—Ketumil Masire, President of Botswana, 1992[2]

When Botswana gained independence in 1966, its future seemed inestimably bleak. The country was suffering from a four-year drought, had virtually no physical infrastructure, fewer than a dozen university graduates, and depended on British grants to cover its official budget. Externally, the new nation was surrounded by white minority regimes in Namibia, South Africa, and Zimbabwe, all of which were hostile to Botswana's explicitly nonracial approach to government and politics.[3] (See **Exhibit 1a**.) There was little arable land anywhere in Botswana and roughly 800 meters of paved roads; as one long-time resident summarized the situation, "There was nothing worth fighting for."[4]

By the turn of the century, however, Botswana had recorded the highest sustained real output growth rates of any country in the world, averaging over 10% for more than four decades and pushing gross domestic product (GDP) per capita from US$80 to $3,600. Infrastructure, schooling, health care, and the provision of other public services had improved dramatically, and the country remained politically stable, a rare event in its part of the world. Alone among its neighbors, Botswana enjoyed a multiracial and democratic system of government, bolstered by a free press and constitutional protection for freedom of speech, association, and religion.[5]

---

[1] Government of Botswana, *Transitional Plan for Social and Economic Development* (Gaborone: Government of Botswana Printer, September 1966), foreword.

[2] Government of Botswana, *Seventh National Development Plan* (Gaborone: Government of Botswana Printer, 1992), p. i.

[3] For a detailed history, see Thomas Tlou and Alec Campbell, *History of Botswana* (Gaborone: Macmillan, 1984).

[4] Gavin Beevers, director of operations, De Beers, interview by authors, Johannesburg, October 7, 2002.

[5] In addition, all citizens, including the black majority as well as its white and Asian minorities, were represented in senior administrative and political posts without a system of quota representation. Charles Harvey and Stephen R Lewis, Jr., *Policy Choice and Development Performance in Botswana* (London: Macmillan, 1990), p. 1. For comparison with other African nations, see Paul Collier and Jan Willem Gunning, "Why Has Africa Grown Slowly?" *Journal of Economic Perspectives* 13 (Summer 1999): 3–22; Paul Collier and Jan Willem Gunning, "Explaining African Economic Performance," *Journal of Economic Literature* 37 (March 1999): 64–111; William Easterly and Ross Levine, "Africa's Growth Tragedy: Policies and Ethnic Divisions," *The Quarterly Journal of Economics* 112 (November 1997): 1203–1250; David E. Bloom and Jeffrey Sachs, "Geography, Demography,

---

Professors Laura Alfaro and Debora Spar and Faheen Allibhoy (MBA 2003) and Research Associate Vinati Dev prepared this case. HBS cases are developed solely as the basis for class discussion. Cases are not intended to serve as endorsements, sources of primary data, or illustrations of effective or ineffective management.

To a large extent, Botswana's spectacular performance could be traced to its equally spectacular diamond reserves. With roughly 25% of the world's gem-quality diamonds, Botswana had prospered from a diamond mining industry that contributed 30% of the nation's GDP in 2002, 70%–80% of its exports, and 50% of government revenues. All diamond operations were handled by the Debswana Mining Company, a joint venture between the Botswanan government and De Beers, the South African mining giant, which essentially controlled the world diamond market.

To some observers, therefore, Botswana's success was simply anomalous. The country had diamonds and De Beers and had just ridden this quasi-colonial connection toward growth. Once the diamonds ran out, skeptics predicted, so too would Botswana's luck. Others, however, took a broader view. Yes, Botswana had diamonds, but so did far less successful countries such as Angola and Sierra Leone.[6] Yes, it had De Beers, but it also had strong institutions and visionary leaders, plus a government that hewed faithfully to prudent social and macroeconomic policies.[7]

In 2002, these debates were more than academic. For while Botswana maintained sizable diamond reserves, the diamond market was noticeably weaker than it had been in previous decades, and the country had yet to develop strong alternative sectors. Foreign investment outside the diamond industry was weak, and the country was battling the world's highest level of HIV/AIDS infection. As in the past, Botswana sought to address its problems through a careful combination of internal policies and external expertise. But would this combination work in the future as well as it had in the past? Could Botswana remain, in the words of one investor, "an island of virtue in a sea of madness"? And did Botswana's experience hold any lessons for its less successful neighbors?

Background: Laying the Foundations of the Tswana State

Modern-day Botswana is peopled primarily by Tswana, members of related African tribes that migrated to the country from southeast Africa in the middle of the eighteenth century.[8] Linked through language, culture, and intermarriage, the tribes also shared a particular set of customs relating to governance and economic subsistence. A chief, or *kgosi*, governed the tribe and held responsibility for administering the law, performing tribal rituals, and allocating communally owned land. He also owned the tribe's most valuable economic asset—cattle—and earned a tribute for renting out the herd to his tribesmen.[9] While the chief's power was hereditary and absolute, Tswana

and Economic Growth in Africa," *Brookings Papers on Economic Activity* (1998): 207–273; Jeffrey Sachs and Andrew Warner, "Sources of Slow Growth in African Economies," *Journal of African Economies* 3 (October 1997): 335–376; Jeffrey Herbst, *States and Power in Africa: Comparative Lessons in Authority and Control* (Princeton, NJ: Princeton University Press, 2000), pp. 3–7, 11–31, 251–272.

[6] For more on the traditionally poor performance of resource-dependent economies, see Jeffrey Sachs and Andrew Warner, "The Curse of Natural Resources," *European Economic Review* 45 (May 2001): 827–838; Jeffrey Sachs, "Natural Resource Intensity and Economic Growth," in *Development Policies in Natural Resource Economies,* Jorg Mayer and Brian Ayisha, eds. (Cheltenham, U.K.: Elgar, 1999), pp. 13–38; and David Wheeler, "Sources of Stagnation in Sub-Saharan Africa," *World Development* 12 (January 1984): 1–23.

[7] On the role of institutions see Daron Acemoglu, Simon Johnson, and James Robinson, "An African Success Story: Botswana," MIT Working Paper, July 2001; and Daron Acemoglu, Simon Johnson, and James Robinson, "The Colonial Origins of Comparative Development: An Empirical Investigation," *American Economic Review* 91 (December 2001): 1369–1401. On the role of policies see World Bank, *Botswana: A Case Study of Economic Policy Prudence and Growth* (Washington, D.C.: The World Bank, 1999).

[8] There are eight major Tswana tribes, the Bamangwato, Batawana, Bangawaketse, Bakwena, Balete, Bakgatla, Barolong, and Batlokwa, each of which has separate cultural, ethnic, and linguistic identities. A single Tswana person is referred to as a Motswana. The Tswana language and culture is called Setswana.

[9] Acemoglu, Johnson, and Robinson, "An African Success Story," argue that this system of asset management made the Tswana institutionalize private property at a relatively early stage.

tribes also had an institution called the *kgotla*, an assembly of adult males that met periodically to discuss issues of public interest. These tribal meetings were venues in which common people could express their opinions and criticize the chief's policies. While chiefs were not compelled to accept the advice given to them by their tribe, by and large they did, for if individuals or groups were not satisfied with their leader, tradition encouraged them to leave the tribe and form another of their own.[10]

By the turn of the nineteenth century, the Tswana had made contact with various European groups. But because the Tswana land was remote and apparently bereft of resources, few of the Europeans lingered there, preferring more promising territories to the north and south. It was only when Boers from the Cape colony migrated north that the Tswana became involved in the colonial scramble for Africa, and even then their involvement was limited to basic defense, struggling to keep the Dutch-speaking white settlers away from their land and livestock.

In 1884, however, Germany annexed South West Africa (modern day Namibia), and Britain began looking inland to create a buffer zone. Already dominant along the coast of southern Africa, the British were determined to prevent German expansion, particularly since Cecil Rhodes's British South African Company had recently discovered vast reserves of copper, gold, and diamonds in the region. Largely at Rhodes's request, the British government declared the creation of the Bechuanaland Protectorate (Bechuana is an archaic form of Botswana) in 1885. When Rhodes petitioned for direct control of this territory, though, Britain's Queen Victoria yielded to the pleas of the Tswana chiefs and instead placed Bechuanaland under British protection. It would retain that status for the next 80 years.

Throughout this period, Botswana was little more than a colonial backwater. Not even Rhodes thought that the arid land around the Kalahari would yield mineral wealth, and the British were content to administer their protectorate from the relative comfort of Mafeking, located in modern-day South Africa. Approximately 75% of colonial expenditures went to day-to-day administrative matters, and tribal chiefs were allowed, even encouraged, to play their traditional role. The only economic activity of any note was cattle ranching, which predated by far the advent of British rule.

For several decades, the British had planned to roll Bechuanaland eventually into South Africa, consolidating their colonies into a single coherent whole. At the end of World War I, however, the rise of the pro-apartheid National Party in South Africa[11] made union with predominantly black Bechuanaland seem less and less probable. Instead, the British moved slowly to a system of local advisory councils in which tribal chiefs became increasingly involved in debating and approving legislation. The spokesman for all of the chiefs was Tsekedi Khama, head of the Bamangwato, the largest Tswana tribe.

According to tribal custom, the man who would eventually replace Khama was his nephew Seretse, who had left Bechuanaland in 1945 to study law at Oxford. But in 1948 Seretse Khama shocked both Britain and Botswana by marrying a white woman named Ruth Williams. Trying to appease anti-mixed marriage sentiment in South Africa, British authorities banned the younger Khama from returning home. He lived in London with his wife until 1956, when his uncle negotiated his return by promising that both the Khamas would renounce their claims to the Bamangwato chieftaincy. Presumably, the British thought that they had limited Khama's power by reducing him to

[10] For more on traditional Tswana governance, see Thomas Tlou, "The Nature of Batswana States: Towards a Theory of Batswana Traditional Government—the Batswana case," in *Botswana: Politics and Society*, W. A. Edge and M. H. Lekorwe, eds. (Johannesburg: J.L. van Schaik), 1998.

[11] See Rawi Abdelal, Debora Spar, and Katherine E. Cousins, "Remaking the Rainbow Nation: South Africa 2002," HBS Case No. 702-035 (Boston: Harvard Business School Publishing, 2002), pp. 3–4.

an ordinary subject. Instead, exile shaped the man who would become Botswana's most important leader.[12]

Almost immediately upon his return, Khama spearheaded a decade of immense political and constitutional reform. A potent symbol of diversity, he traveled the country from village to village, working to rally the support of each tribe and chief for the creation of an independent nation. In 1958, the advisory councils asked British administrators for permission to launch a legislative council, which in turn led to a consultative process that generated a transitional constitution and development plan. In 1960, the country's first political party, the Bechuanaland People's Party, was formed, taking its inspiration and radical anticolonial stance from the antiapartheid struggle in South Africa. In response, Khama established the Bechuanaland Democratic Party (later the Botswana Democratic Party) with a less confrontational agenda and an appeal to both tribal leaders and an emerging educated elite. With a European education and hereditary claim to the country's largest chieftaincy, Khama was in an unrivalled position.

In 1961, a white paper on self-governance formed the foundation of the new nation. Based, as one analysis described it, on a "marriage between the traditional form of political organization . . . [and] those adapted from the west,"[13] the new government was to comprise a mostly elected national assembly (four of the 36 members would be appointed by the president), a president, and a house of chiefs, whose members would be selected along traditional lines.[14] All citizens were to have an equal vote in the new system, and all votes were blind to both race and tribe. In 1963, these plans were put into place, culminating in the protectorate's first elections in March of 1965. The BDP, led by Khama and his colleague, Ketumil Masire, won handily, and the new government immediately petitioned the British government for full independence. On September 30, 1966, Botswana became a sovereign republic within the British Commonwealth.

Botswana: The Fledgling Nation-State

Botswana at independence was hardly an auspicious place. There were few roads, few graduates, and no resources. Compared to the situation elsewhere on the continent, colonial rule in Botswana had been relatively benign, but it had also left few of the administrative structures found in more actively managed colonies such as South Africa or Rhodesia. The new government thus had no formal institutions to fall back upon, and not even the remnants of a civil service.

Moreover, in 1966 Botswana was suffering through the most severe drought in a century. Famine was widespread, and nearly one-third of the nation's cattle—the major source of both protein and export earnings—had been killed. Over 10% of the new nation's GDP was immediately diverted to importing food, and thousands of Batswanans streamed into South Africa searching for work. On the fiscal side, the government had little in its coffers except menial remittances, and transfers from the British government financed over half of the country's expenditures. Commenting on Botswana's tenuous position, President Khama was characteristically blunt. "There are unique development problems," he wrote, "the lack of independent access to the sea, the presence of powerful neighbors

[12] For a comprehensive history of the first president, Sir Seretse Khama, see Neil Parsons, Willie Henderson, and Thomas Tlou, *Seretse Khama 1921–1980* (Gaborone: Macmillan, 1995).

[13] Ladipo Adamolekin and Philip Morgan, "Pragmatic Institutional Design in Botswana—Salient Features and an Assessment," *The International Journal of Public Sector Management* (1999): 1.

[14] Republic of Botswana, *Constitution of Botswana* (Gaborone: Government of Botswana Printer, 1966), p. 46.

whose racial policies differ greatly from those of Botswana, the lack of a national currency, the inability to impose customs tariffs and so on."[15]

Putting pessimism behind him, though, Khama quickly got down to work. To solve the country's immediate financial needs, he looked to the only available source of funds—development aid, particularly aid that came with technical assistance and from countries (Norway, Denmark, Canada) happy to support an African state that opposed South Africa's apartheid regime.[16] Next, the fledgling government turned to trade, an obvious source of revenue for a country heavily dependent on imports. As a member of the South African Customs Union (SACU), Botswana received a fixed percentage share of the total import taxes generated across the union's members. At Khama's urging, a team of civil servants set out to amend the agreement, securing a larger share of the union's income.[17] The results of this negotiation were twofold: first, Botswana boosted its revenues and spurred cross-border trade; and second, the country was unable to set its own external tariffs or to embrace infant industry policies that prevailed elsewhere in the developing world. In search of revenue, Botswana stumbled onto a remarkably open free-trade regime.[18]

The next target of policy was mining, an area that still evoked relatively little interest in the late 1960s. Both policymakers and foreign mining companies were aware that the lands around Botswana held rich resources: gold and diamonds in South Africa, copper and nickel in Rhodesia (now Zimbabwe) and Zambia. Nothing of any value had been discovered in Botswana itself at this point, but clearly the geological potential was there. Accordingly, in 1967 the Botswanan government passed two laws governing prospecting and mining in the country. They were contentious pieces of legislation and quite remarkable given prevailing sentiment at that time in the developing world. Under the terms of the Mineral Rights in Tribal Territories Act, all mineral resources in Botswana were formally vested with the central government rather than with tribal leaders. The government retained the right to assign all mining concessions, and foreign firms were encouraged to prospect once such concessions had been assigned.

What made this legislation so notable was that tribal chiefs had long retained informal control over their lands. The Mineral Rights Act, by contrast, took these rights and handed them over to a brand new entity, one with only a single year of legitimacy behind it. Moreover, across Africa and the developing world, newly independent states were embracing far more restrictive mining legislation, determined to prevent foreign firms from exploiting their mineral resources. President Khama, however, was firmly committed to an open, centrally governed regime, and he threw the full weight of his position behind it. For several months, as former president Masire recalled, Khama traveled from village to village, convincing tribal chiefs to aspire to the national, rather than tribal, good. Khama's own position as a chief, with traditional control over all Bamangwato lands, helped to bolster his already high credibility. Once the chiefs gave their moral support to Khama, the controversial legislation rapidly became law.[19]

Shortly thereafter, significant reserves of copper-nickel were discovered in Selebi-Phikwe, in the northeastern corner of the country, along with coal deposits farther south at Morupule. In a pattern

---

[15] See foreword in government of Botswana, *Transitional Plan for Social and Economic Development* (1966).

[16] Charles Harvey and Stephen R. Lewis, Jr., *Policy Choice and Development Performance in Botswana* (Basingstoke, U.K.: Macmillan, 1990), p. 51.

[17] The Southern African Customs Union (SACU) included South Africa, Botswana, Lesotho, and Swaziland. The initial fixed share for Botswana was 0.28%, which was amended to 0.31% in 1965.

[18] Several years later, this open-trade policy also helped Botswana gain preferential treatment under the Lôme Convention, allowing Botswana's beef to enter the lucrative European market with a rebate of 90% of the EU import levy. See World Bank, *Botswana: A Case Study of Economic Policy Prudence and Growth*, p. 10.

[19] Ketumil Masire, former president of Botswana, interview by authors, Gaborone, October 8, 2002.

that would be repeated in subsequent mining arrangements, the right to exploit these deposits was given to a publicly quoted company, Botswana RST, whose major shareholders included two multinational mining firms (AMAX and Anglo-American) along with the Botswanan government. Funding for the project came from development institutions such as the World Bank and the Canadian International Development Agency and was backed by guarantees from the foreign mining firms.[20] At a cost of one and a half times the country's GDP, the project was intended to provide government revenues, growth, and employment and to begin a process of diversification away from traditional pastoral activities.

Meanwhile, as Botswana was concentrating on copper and coal, a small team of prospectors from De Beers had begun to look for diamonds. Following the discovery of three small diamonds in the dry bed of the Motloutse River, geologists eventually traced their source to Orapa, a small town some 250 kilometers west of Francistown. (See **Exhibit 1b**.) Because the government had no resources to devote to diamonds at this point, it left development almost entirely to De Beers. Following a brief negotiation, the government formed a joint venture, De Beers Botswana Mining Company, owned 15% by the government of Botswana and 85% by De Beers. De Beers agreed to provide 100% of the capital needed to develop the Orapa Mine and to construct a self-contained township around the mine, including water and power supply, shops, a dairy farm, bakery, housing, health facilities, and a school.[21] Under the prevailing minerals taxation policy, Botswana would receive a combination of profits and royalties from Orapa, as well as an equity stake in the mining operation.

Before long, it became clear that minerals, and diamonds in particular, would indeed be a key element of Botswana's development strategy. In 1966, the Transitional Development Program had stated, "Botswana is a poor country not only in terms of per capita income but also in terms of natural resources."[22] By 1968, once copper-nickel and diamond deposits had been identified, the government modified its position, stating, "Botswana is a poor country but it possesses sufficient natural resources to permit, with outside assistance, rapid development."[23] In effect, the country's growth strategy was based on the belief that mining revenues could quickly be channeled into physical, social, and human capital infrastructure. Because the public sector was cash poor, foreign firms would shoulder the burden of investment in the mining sector, leaving the government to translate mining revenues into basic development objectives: roads and dams, water and electricity, and universal health care. Evaluating the country at this stage, a long-term investor noted, "Because they had nothing, they learned to count the pennies before they spent them."[24]

From De Beers to Debswana: Conflict and Partnership

When Botswana signed on with De Beers, they were not only joining forces with a major multinational firm. They were joining with a hugely idiosyncratic firm, one that engendered suspicion and even hatred in some quarters and that arguably managed the world's most successful international cartel.[25] Based in South Africa, De Beers was both a producer and marketer of gem diamonds. It owned all of the major mines in its home country and had purchasing arrangements with nearly all of the world's other diamond producers. The core of De Beers's strategy, though, and

[20] Harvey and Lewis, pp. 141–143.

[21] Harvey and Lewis, p. 52.

[22] *Transitional Plan for Social and Economic Development* (1966), p. 6.

[23] Republic of Botswana, *National Development Plan 1968–1973* (Gaborone: Government of Botswana Printers, 1968), p. 8.

[24] John Hughes, producer relations, De Beers, interview with authors, Johannesburg, October 7, 2002.

[25] For more on De Beers and the diamond cartel, see Debora L. Spar, *The Cooperative Edge: The Internal Politics of International Cartels* (Ithaca, NY: Cornell University Press, 1994), pp. 39–87.

the secret to its success, is a basic formula first hatched by Cecil Rhodes, who ran the giant Kimberley Mine at the end of the nineteenth century. What Rhodes realized then, and what De Beers has perpetuated ever since, is that diamonds are actually neither rare (geologically speaking) nor precious. Instead, the stones' value is largely derived from the romantic allure that has emerged around them, an allure that De Beers carefully cultivates by limiting the number of diamonds released into the market in any given year. Even today, nearly all diamonds produced in the world pass through a single building in London, the Central Selling Organization (CSO), under the watchful eye of De Beers. There, De Beers's employees carefully sort through each and every stone, grading them by color, size, and other minutely honed factors. The stones are then gathered into small, precise packages and sold at a predetermined price to the "sightholders" who make up De Beers's customer base.

In the early years of the cartel, De Beers could control the diamond market through a fairly straightforward combination of the CSO, which was linked directly to De Beers, and the South African mines, which De Beers owned. There were few other producers of rough gemstones and no other channel for distribution. After World War II, however, new discoveries (in Zaire, Australia, Russia, and Angola) threatened to destroy this lucrative scheme. For if these new diamonds flooded world markets, they would drive prices downward and reduce the monopolistic position that De Beers had long enjoyed. Moreover, if new producers sold their stones to maximize short-term profits, they would undermine the very basis of the diamond market, a market that explicitly linked value with rarity. The romantic appeal of diamonds—the "mystique of scarcity"—would be lost.[26]

Against this background, the prospect of diamonds in Botswana was both alluring and threatening to De Beers. If the company could gain control of any Botswanan fields, it could add substantially to its own stores and thus maintain its prominence in the diamond market. By the same token, if someone else controlled Botswana's mines, then De Beers would face a potential threat right on its own doorstep. The bigger the mines, the bigger the threat—and the opportunity. Accordingly, De Beers's chairman, the legendary Harry Oppenheimer, was keeping close tabs on Botswana's geology. And as the fields around Orapa yielded better and better stones, Oppenheimer slowly upped the ante, letting the Botswanans know that De Beers wanted to double production at Orapa and develop a new mine 40 kilometers southeast of the Orapa township at Lethlakane.

Botswana's response was quite extraordinary, especially given the politics of the time. Rather than nationalizing what now appeared to be a hugely valuable resource, rather than raising taxes and imposing demands, the government simply invoked a clause in the original Orapa agreement that allowed for renegotiation due to changed circumstances. Talks resumed, and the two sides spent months working out what would be unprecedented terms for any diamond-producing nation. Rather than simply continuing to lease land to De Beers, or taking even a small share of the venture's profits, the government of Botswana essentially formed a partnership with De Beers, taking a full 50% share of the De Beers Botswana Mining Company and half the seats on the company's reconstituted board.[27] While full details of the 1975 agreements have never been made public, official press statements described the deal as providing "not less than 65 to 70 per cent" of profits to the government, through a combination of royalties, normal income tax on profits, withholding tax on remitted dividends, and dividends on government's equity holding. Other press reports at the time speculated that the government's share was as high as 75%.

After the deal was signed, *The Financial Times* ran a provocative story entitled "Botswana Joins the Rapacious League." While noting that the deal was undeniably favorable for Botswana, the article also realized how critical it was for De Beers, for even with only 25% of the share of profits, De Beers

[26] Ibid., pp. 52–56.

[27] Details on the agreements between De Beers and the Botswana government are from Harvey and Lewis, pp. 124–138.

would be reaping tremendous rewards from Orapa and Lethlakane.[28] More importantly, it was keeping Botswanan diamonds under its own control and then using this control to exert leverage elsewhere in the diamond industry.[29]

This relationship became even more critical—and profitable—after 1976 when another massive diamond pipe was discovered at Jwaneng in southern Botswana, 120–140 kilometers west of Gaborone. Described by Harry Oppenheimer as "the most significant discovery since the original [South African] Kimberley deposits were found,"[30] Jwaneng was a geological marvel, the richest diamond mine in the world by value. With an urgency hastened by a wave of nationalizations in neighboring African states,[31] De Beers and Botswana hurried back to the bargaining table, creating what Nicky Oppenheimer, Harry's son and successor at De Beers, would later describe as an "incestuous relationship," one that drew De Beers and Botswana into an intimate partnership that neither had incentive to leave.[32]

Under the terms of the Jwaneng agreement, the government of Botswana would receive roughly 72%–80% of the mine's profits. The mine and surrounding township would be built and managed by the De Beers Botswana Mining Company (now regularly called Debswana), and the government would retain 50% ownership in the firm. Explicitly, the government also agreed to play an active role in managing the world's diamond supply, a task that depended almost entirely on withholding stones from the market. In effect, the government agreed not to sell its most valuable source of revenue when De Beers decided that increased sales would have a detrimental effect on prices. Such strategic stockpiling, of course, is the key to any cartel, and the only proven way of maintaining commodity prices over time. It is also, however, extraordinarily difficult to maintain, especially for poor governments that rely overwhelmingly on commodity sales.[33] By tying itself so firmly to De Beers, Botswana was also in effect tying its own hands.

The price of this policy became clear in the early 1980s, when the world diamond market went through a severe depression. CSO sales dropped from $2.7 billion in 1980 to a low of $1.3 billion in 1982, and De Beers enforced quota restrictions on its main suppliers, including Botswana. The resulting loss of revenue caused a sharp deterioration in Botswana's external payments and forced the Bank of Botswana to impose a harsh set of adjustment measures: it devalued the pula, reduced bank lending, raised interest rates, and imposed a freeze on public-sector wage expenditures. Rather than chafing at these measures, however, Botswana stuck by its agreement and continued to stockpile diamonds. By 1984, the diamond market had strengthened dramatically, prices had risen by some 13% and Botswana's economy was back on track.[34]

As a result of its forbearance, however, Botswana had accumulated a massive stockpile of diamonds—an asset that was both essentially useless to the country and a threat, albeit a subtle one, to De Beers. Accordingly, in July of 1987, the partners agreed to a swap. Botswana sold its entire stockpile to De Beers in exchange for an unspecified cash payment and newly issued shares equal to

---

[28] Harvey and Lewis, p. 125.

[29] By the mid-1970s, diamonds from South Africa only constituted 10% of the world's total. If Botswana's diamonds were added to this figure, though, the percent rose to 30%.

[30] Harvey and Lewis, p. 127.

[31] In Zambia, for example, the government had reclaimed the mining fields in 1969–1970, creating a state-owned conglomerate called Zambia Consolidated Copper Mines (ZCCM) and excluding any foreign involvement from the mining industry.

[32] Nicholas Oppenheimer, chairman of De Beers Group and Debswana Diamond Co., interview by authors, Johannesburg, October 10, 2002.

[33] Most commodity cartels have ended in dismal failure. See Jock A. Finlayson and Mark W. Zacher, *Managing International Markets: Developing Countries and the Commodity Trade Regime* (New York: Columbia University Press, 1988).

[34] Bank of Botswana, *1989 Annual Report* (Gaborone: Bank of Botswana, 1989), p. 1.

5.2% of the outstanding shares of De Beers. Once again, the benefits on both sides were clear: De Beers retained control over what concerned the company most, and Botswana expanded its own influence over De Beers. Under the terms of the 1987 agreement, Debswana received the right to nominate two directors of the Diamond Trading Company and the De Beers Board, an unprecedented amount of power for any supplier to De Beers.[35] No other producing country had such direct access to De Beers—not even major producers such as Russia, Canada, or Australia—and no other developing country had negotiated such favorable terms. Botswana had negotiated extraordinarily well. Or, as former President Ketumil Masire recalled, the country was like ". . . a charming young lady who doesn't really have any other suitor in mind but knows that her looks are likely to attract."[36]

An African Miracle: Growth and Structural Change, 1966–1990

For 25 years, this "charming young lady" rode diamonds and prudent governance to growth. Botswana experienced the most rapid growth of output per capita of any country in the world during this period and rose from one of the poorest countries in the world to middle-income status. In real terms, GDP growth averaged 13% per annum over the entire post-independence period, and GDP per capita was about eight times higher in 1989 than it had been in 1966.[37] (See **Exhibits 2, 3,** and **4**.) Measures of overall social welfare such as life expectancy, infant mortality, and schooling had also improved to become among the best in Africa:[38] by 1990, 85% of the rural population was within 15 kilometers of a health facility, and the ratio of nurses to population had improved from roughly 1:17,000 in 1965 to 1:550 in 1989. Ninety percent of children were enrolled in primary school by 1989.[39] (See **Exhibits 9** and **10**.) From a poor rural state dependent upon external aid, Botswana became a financially independent country. By 1976 the government was running persistent surpluses, and Botswana had left monetary union with South Africa to establish its own currency and central bank. Looking back at the strenuous beginning of the country, former President Masire wrote, "The fact that Botswana successfully overcame [these] problems in a relatively short period was an achievement in itself."[40]

Throughout, diamonds played a central role, contributing 40% of GDP, over 80% of national export earnings, and nearly 60% of government revenues in 1990.[41] (See **Exhibits 3** and **7**.) The government openly acknowledged the important role of the private sector in harnessing mining revenues and nurtured investors—both current and potential—with tremendous care. At the same time, however, the government was also equally careful to use the foreigners' money wisely. A series of national development plans, laid out by the Ministry of Finance and Development, provided the organizational framework for future government spending and were strictly followed. As a result, as one observer pointed out, the returns from foreign investment were used "in education, heath, roads, dams, no fancy cars, no palaces."[42] As budget deficits were frowned upon, surpluses became the

[35] For a more theoretical formulation of the relationship between De Beers and Botswana, see Zane A. Spindler and Xavier de Vanssay, "A Public Choice Perspective on Cartels," *Journal of Public Finance and Public Choice* XVIII (2000).

[36] Ketumil Masire, former president of Bostwana, interview with authors, Gaborone, October 8, 2002.

[37] Republic of Botswana, *National Development Plan, 1991–1997*, p. 12.

[38] Harvey and Lewis, p. 1.

[39] Republic of Botswana, *National Development Plan, 1991–1997.*

[40] Bank of Botswana, *1989 Annual Report.*

[41] Most of the government revenue came from royalties, taxes, and dividends from the diamond mines. Republic of Botswana, *National Development Plan, 1991–1997*, p. 177.

[42] Gavin Beevers, director of operations De Beers, interview with authors, Johannesburg, October 7, 2002.

norm and were maintained to offset any sudden revenue reduction caused by a potential downturn in the diamond market.[43]

Meanwhile, to compensate for its small domestic market and less-than-robust financial system, the government had created a host of institutions to fill gaps left by the private sector. On the financial front, for example, two special funds—the Public Debt Service Fund (PDSF) and the Revenue Stabilization Fund (RSF)—were established to channel mineral revenues into long-term loans for local authorities and parastatal bodies.[44] The Botswana Housing Corporation likewise used diamond revenues to finance construction projects, and the Botswana Power Corporation and the Water Utilities Corporation performed the same function for electricity and water. Similar entities, such as the Botswana Development Corporation, the National Development Bank, and the Botswana Enterprise Development Unit were charged with using diamond revenues to diversify the economy away from diamonds, creating new industries and entrepreneurs to replace, or at least augment, the mining sector.

A final piece of Botswana's economic success lay with its ability to manage the "Dutch Disease," a pernicious effect of natural resource discoveries.[45] In many other countries, the rapid development of natural resources (usually oil or gas) has tended to lift the value of the nation's currency, making manufactured goods less competitive and dealing a long-term blow to the development of an industrially based export sector. In Botswana, however, officials at the Central Bank knew from the outset that they would have to manage their currency with care, pursuing an exchange rate policy that maintained the competitiveness of their domestic industry on one hand while mitigating the impact of imported inflation. This was no an easy task, since it essentially meant depreciating the real exchange rate but then letting it appreciate as necessary to moderate the impact of imported inflation.[46] Yet the Botswanans pulled it off, revaluing the pula seven times during the 1980s in order to minimize the internal impact of external shocks. (See **Exhibit 6**.)

They also pulled off what was arguably even more important—a political miracle to match their country's economic success. Elsewhere in Africa, and indeed elsewhere across the developing world, the combination of natural resources and foreign investment had often led to chaos or tragedy. In Nigeria, for example, the discovery of oil in the Niger Delta had done little to pull the country out of economic turmoil or political fragmentation. In Angola, the government and rebels battled for four decades, with both sides using the nation's vast resources—primarily oil and diamonds—to fund their armies.[47] Diamonds also funded horrific wars in Sierra Leone and Congo (formerly Zaire), wars that verged at times on genocide and brought governance to a halt.

But in Botswana, the development of diamonds brought not only prosperity but peace as well. Elections were held every four years, and power passed smoothly from Khama (who died in 1980), to Masire, and thence to Festus Mogae, a former vice president and Oxford-trained economist. "One of the secrets behind the remarkable social and economic progress achieved by this country over the last

[43] Damien Shiels and Debora Spar, "Establishing a Manufacturing Plant in Africa: Owens Corning & Botswana," The Foreign Investment Advisory Service, Occasional Paper Series, 1998.

[44] Harvey and Lewis, pp. 53–54. See also, "Role of Financial Sector in Economic Development," in Bank of Botswana, *2001 Annual Report and Economic Review* (Gaborone: Bank of Botswana, 2001), pp. 65–69.

[45] The name comes from the economic pressures that plagued Holland after the discovery of North Sea gas.

[46] Currently, the pula is pegged to a basket of currencies representing its major trading partners, namely the South African rand and the Special Drawing Right (SDR). The SDR is an artificial "basket" currency used by the International Monetary Fund for internal accounting purposes. For more on the country's exchange rate policy, see Dani Rodrik, "The New Global Economy and Developing Countries: Making Openness Work," Policy Essay No. 24 (Washington, D.C.: Overseas Development Council, 1999), p. 125.

[47] By the time UNITA and the government signed a cease-fire in April 2002, at least half a million people had been killed and one-third of the population had been displaced.

36 years," President Mogae proudly stated, "has been deep respect for democracy and the rule of law."[48] Although the BDP remained the dominant political party, there was no evidence of electoral fraud or political mismanagement in the country and hardly any corruption. (See **Exhibit 12.**) In fact, Transparency International ranked Botswana 24th out of the 102 countries it surveyed, finding the country less corrupt than either France or Portugal.[49] (See **Exhibit 11.**) Jonathan Oppenheimer of De Beers expressed the same sentiment slightly differently. "In Botswana," he noted, "we deal with civil servants as effective principles, whereas in other countries the principles are politicians." [50]

New Challenges

At the turn of the twenty-first century, Botswana was widely regarded as an "African miracle"—a sub-Saharan nation with among the highest growth rates in the world, an enviable social infrastructure, and a politically stable state. Increasingly, analysts were looking to uncover the secrets to Botswana's success: was it private property and legal protection? Foreign investment and economic openness? Institutions that worked, or the luck of benign colonialism? These were more than theoretical questions, of course, or historical curiosity. For in Botswana's success might lie advice to states with more stubborn growth trajectories.

At the same time, however, Botswana itself was beginning to show early signs of trouble. Growth, as one might expect, had slowed in the 1990s, and export earnings were down. Despite the government's best efforts, foreign investment was still just a trickle aside from De Beers, and diversification was limited. The country was also struggling under a devastating outbreak of AIDS, one that threatened, over time, to reverse the social improvements of earlier decades. None of these problems had completely manifested themselves yet, and all seemed amenable to solution. But they were enough to grab the attention of Botswana's top officials and make them start searching for longer-term plans.

The Campaign Against HIV/AIDS

Botswana was hardly alone in dealing with AIDS. Indeed, in 2002, 42 million people in the world suffered from the disease, 30 million in sub-Saharan Africa alone. Millions more were expected to become infected in China, India, and Russia.[51] For the developing world, AIDS was a particularly vicious disease. Treatments that typically cost $10,000 to $15,000 in the United States or Europe were simply out of reach for most people in Africa, and although pharmaceutical companies were slowly reconfiguring their pricing strategies, cheap or generic drugs were still very difficult to find. In most poor countries, the lack of a basic medical infrastructure—of doctors and clinics and a clean water supply—compounded the burgeoning epidemic and compromised any attempt at treatment. By 1990, life expectancy across Africa was starting to decline, an ominous portent of the AIDS epidemic.

---

48 "President Mogae addresses nation, announces seven-point growth plan," *BBC Monitoring Africa,* October 29, 2002. From South African Press Association Web site, http://www.sapa.org.za, accessed October 29, 2002.

49 See Transparency International Web site, http://www.gwdg.de/~uwvw/icr.htm, accessed December 5, 2002. The government was determined to ensure that corruption did not flourish. In 1994 it established the independent Directorate of Corruption and Economic Crime, which had a mandate to investigate corruption cases, implement preventative strategies, and conduct public education. Economist Intelligence Unit, *Botswana: Country Profile* (London: The Economist Intelligence Unit, 2002).

50 Jonathan Oppenheimer, interview with authors, Johannesburg , October 7, 2002.

51 Debora Spar, "Life, Death and Property Rights: The Pharmaceutical Industry Faces AIDS in Africa," HBS Case No. 702-049 (Boston: Harvard Business School Publishing, 2002).

Sadly, the problem was particularly acute in Botswana, where the United Nations estimated that 35.8% of the adult population was infected with HIV/AIDS.[52] In 2001 an estimated 26,000 adults and children died of AIDS, and approximately 69,000 children had been orphaned by the disease. The World Bank further estimated that in the next 10 years AIDS would slice 20% off the government budget, erode development gains, and bring about a 13% reduction in the income of the poorest households.[53]

These overwhelming statistics, however, had not discouraged the government. "We cannot afford to despair," stated the president, "no stone must be left unturned in our struggle against this dreadful disease." [54] The Botswanan government had taken an early and aggressive stance against the disease, highlighting the problem and asking the outside world for help.[55] Unlike many countries that were still entangled in debate about the origins and prevalence of HIV/AIDS, Botswana had been remarkably open about the illness. Led by President Mogae and supported by private foundations and major drug companies, the Botswanan government launched an unprecedented effort to fight the epidemic, focusing on both preventive education and treatment for those already afflicted. Impressed by this attitude, Harvard's renowned AIDS Institute had chosen to base its African operations in Botswana, as did Bill and Melinda Gates's AIDS initiative. When Merck, maker of one of the world's leading AIDS drugs, wanted to experiment with free distribution and treatment, it chose Botswana as its pilot site, confident that the government would both respect Merck's intellectual property and support the medical infrastructure that its program demanded.[56] From the president on down, Batswanans were open about the country's AIDS epidemic, and government offices were plastered with signs urging employees to practice safe sex.[57] The efforts of the Mogae government were evidenced by sharp increases in health expenditure, which rose from 5.2% of total government spending in 1998 to 7.2% in 2001.[58]

Internationally, Botswana's AIDS-fighting policies had won its government great acclaim. Inside the country, however, the disease continued to rage. Life expectancy had plummeted from 60 in 1985 to a terrifying 39 in 2000 and showed no signs of rebounding.

Diamonds and Diversification

During the 1990s, Botswana's economy had moved largely in line with the international diamond market, falling during the recession of 1991–1992 and then rising at the end of the decade. When the

---

[52] See World Bank, *Botswana, Selected Development Impact of HIV/AIDS* (Washington, D.C.: The World Bank, 2001).

[53] For information on the HIV/AIDS epidemic, see the AVERT Web site, www.avert.org/aafrica.htm, accessed December 5, 2002.

[54] "President Mogae addresses nation, announces seven-point growth plan," *BBC Monitoring Africa,* October 29, 2002.

[55] This attitude was in sharp contrast with that of many African states, including South Africa, which denied the disease's prevalence for many years and resisted any plans for treatment or prevention.

[56] See James Austin, Diana Barrett, and James Weber, "Merck Global Health Initiatives (A)," HBS Case No. 301-088 (Boston: Harvard Business School Publishing, 2001).

[57] Debswana was also an early mover in the fight against AIDS, offering in 2001 to cover 90% of the cost of antiretroviral drugs to employees and their spouses. The company had an explicit policy not to discriminate against employees with the disease, and all firms wishing to conduct business with Debswana were required to have their own nondiscrimination policies and programs on AIDS.

[58] The Harvard AIDS Institute estimated that it would cost US$370 per person per year to provide basic treatment to AIDS patients, including testing, counseling, education, and pain relief. Intermediate care, including the provision of antiretroviral drugs to pregnant HIV-infected women, would cost a further US$500, while advanced care for infected adults would cost over US$3,000. Based on these figures, advanced care for all adults currently infected with HIV would cost up to US$1 billion, the equivalent of around 18% of annual GDP. Michael Grunwald, "All-Out Effort Fails to Halt AIDS Spread; Botswana's Program Makes Progress, but Old Attitudes Persist," *The Washington Post,* December 2, 2002, p. A1.

market slumped again in 2001, economic officials in the country readied themselves for another bout of reduced export earnings and the fiscal contraction that this would imply.

As in the past, the government was confident that diamond earnings would bounce back before long. In the meantime, Botswana had a very manageable level of government debt of close to 9% of GDP and reserves of more than six months of imports. Still, government officials were becoming increasingly frustrated with their country's reliance on diamonds and the lack of control this afforded them. President Mogae, for example, publicly expressed his government's "concern" about "the heavy dependence of the country on diamonds,"[59] while Dr. Keith Jefferis and Oduetse A. Motshidishi, deputy governors at the Bank of Botswana, noted that "revenues from diamonds seemed to have reached a plateau." Even if diamond revenues were rapidly to resume, bank officials worried that tax revenues would still grow more slowly than the economy, forcing either an unwanted contraction or an increase in debt.[60]

Outside the country, too, diamonds were suffering. New producers (mostly in Canada) were threatening to exert downward pressure on prices, and activists in Europe and the United States had launched an aggressive campaign against "dirty" or "conflict" diamonds coming from the war-torn states of Congo and Sierra Leone. (See **Exhibit 8**.) Even though Botswana's diamonds were undeniably "clean," the country worried, as the Bank of Botswana's Jefferis put it, that the campaign against conflict diamonds could "threaten the means of existence of this country . . . by painting all diamonds as conflict diamonds."[61]

Clearly, after four decades of diamond-driven growth, Botswana needed to diversify its economy. The country's president stressed this goal, outside advisers reiterated it, and Botswana's 8th National Development Program enshrined it in the aptly entitled plan for *Sustainable Economic Diversification*. But how was diversification to be achieved? One possibility (and a favorite of external advisers) was to proceed with privatization, selling off the various agencies and parastatals that remained tied to the state. Because Botswana did not really need the financial proceeds from privatization, however, pressures to privatize were limited, especially since the public sector provided nearly half of the country's total employment and official unemployment was over 15% in 2000.[62]

Another obvious strategy was to build new industries on the back of diamonds, expanding, for instance, into diamond polishing or cutting. The problem here, though, was that Botswana's relatively strong exchange and wage rates would compromise any polishing or cutting industries from the start, since countries like India (which cut and polished roughly 50% of the world's diamonds) were far more competitive. Likewise, attempts to expand the agricultural sector were limited by recurrent periods of severe drought, and prospects for high-end tourism were vulnerable to political troubles in the region, particularly in neighboring Zimbabwe.

Faced with these limited options, the government chose to focus on the manufacturing sector as its next target. While the sector represented only 5% of GDP, it was responsible for about 10% of all those employed in the formal sector, making manufacturing a viable option for both diversification and job creation. But building this sector was not going to be easy. Botswana was still a very small country stuck between larger countries with uncertain political futures. There were some domestic

---

59 President F.G. Mogae, at the time vice president and minister of Finance and Development Planning, in Barclay's Bank of Botswana, *Barclay's Business Guide to Botswana* (Gaborone: Barclay's Bank of Botswana, Limited, 1997), p. 3.

60 Dr. Keith Jefferis, deputy governor, Bank of Botswana, and Oduetse A. Motshidishi, deputy governor, Bank of Botswana, interview with authors, Gaborone, October 8, 2002.

61 Andrew M. Motsomi, deputy director, Research Department Bank of Botswana, interview with authors, Gaborone, October 8, 2002.

62 Unofficial figures ran as high as 30%.

entrepreneurs, but they were limited in both number and resources, generally bereft of any linkages to outside markets. And thus Botswana reasoned, once again, that investment would need to come largely from foreigners. "If entrepreneurs are to emerge in significant numbers," the Botswana Development Corporation report reasoned, "they must come primarily from abroad."[63]

Attracting Foreign Direct Investment (FDI)

In many respects, foreign investment made perfect sense for Botswana. The country had grown, after all, largely on the back of FDI, and it had an exemplary relationship with its biggest investor. It also received very strong marks from the international investment community, a rare distinction for a developing African state. Moody's and Standard & Poor's had given the country investment-grade status in 2001, and UNCTAD and the African Competitiveness Report had written glowing reports, praising Botswana for its political stability, macroeconomic policy, and transparent legal system.[64] (See **Exhibit 5**.)

Some investors had responded to these attractions. In 1995, for example, Hyundai opened operations in Gaborone, quickly transforming vehicle production into one of Botswana's leading sectors. Lured by a combination of stability, location, and openness, the Korean car manufacturer planned to make Botswana the center of its operations for Africa, shipping cars out of Gaborone under the protected tariff framework of SACU.[65] Production, however, was halted early in 2000 when the South African management group running the plant went into liquidation. According to a report by Barclay's Bank of Botswana, "Hyundai's success in capturing a meaningful share of the South African market from a base in Botswana inevitably aroused opposition from South Africa's established manufacturers. As a result of their lobbying, the South African government altered the tariff regulations under SACU imposing duties on parts imported from South Korea rendering Hyundai's operation in Botswana uncompetitive."[66] A similar fate befell Owens Corning, which opened a fiberglass pipeline in 1992, only to close it in 2001 as the Owens Corning Group withdrew from the global pipe business.

Meanwhile, passage of the Africa Growth and Opportunity Act (AGOA) in 2000 promised to change the landscape of small-scale investment. Using the lure of duty-free access to the U.S. market, AGOA was designed to catalyze the growth of textile investment in Africa and further integrate African states into the global economy. Arguably, Botswana was particularly well positioned to benefit from AGOA, since it offered both relatively low labor rates and the stability that investors customarily sought. As of 2002 five textile companies had already been established, and others were reportedly waiting in the wings.

---

[63] Botswana Development Corporation, *Investment Guide to Botswana* (Gaborone: Botswana Development Corporation, 1997), p. 11.

[64] See UNCTAD, *Botswana: Globalization, Liberalization and Sustainable Human Development* (Geneva: The United Nations, 2000), pp. 7–39; and The World Economic Forum, *African Competitiveness Report* (Geneva: World Economic Forum, 1998), p. 219.

[65] Kenneth Good and Skye Hughes, "Globalization and Diversification: Two Cases in Southern Africa," *Foreign Affairs* 101 (2002): 47; and "The Desert Booms," *The Economist*, November 18, 1999, p. 85.

[66] Botswana is part of the Southern African Customs Union (SACU) and is bound by common external tariffs on imports. SACU, established in 1910, is a customs union among South Africa, Botswana, Lesotho, Namibia, and Swaziland. It has common external tariffs and free trade between member countries. In recent years, the average level of the common external tariff of SACU has been sharply reduced because of South Africa's membership in the WTO. Tariffs range up to 10% on industrial raw materials, up to 30% on industrial plant and equipment, and up to 45% on basic consumer goods. In 1998 the WTO calculated that the weighted external tariff was 15.1% with wide dispersion. For more on the external tariff determination see UNCTAD, *Botswana: Investment Policy Review* (Geneva: The United Nations, 2002), pp. 46–47, and *Barclay's Business Guide to Botswana*, p. 27.

Still, the flow of foreign investment was hardly a flood. Potential investors complained about relatively low labor productivity in Botswana, high transportation costs, and a lack of skilled labor.[67] Tax rates as low as 15% for manufacturing firms still did not attract the kind of firms that Botswana wanted, and a growing range of critics claimed that the low rates, together with a slate of financial incentives, were actually tempting investors to come only for the incentives, leaving Botswana as soon as their tax holidays or capital grants expired.[68] Moreover, outside the mineral sector, Botswana's basic geography—small, landlocked, surrounded by unstable states—remained a powerful disincentive.

The data were not encouraging. Between 1995 and 2001, sub-Saharan Africa received 1.5% of all world FDI inflow. Botswana's FDI inflows in 2001 were $131 million (4.4% of gross fixed capital formation).[69] As Serwalo Tumelo expressed, "We suffer because we are in this region . . . we are on the African continent, and people in Europe and the U.S. don't know Botswana is different."[70]

Vision 2016

In 2002, Botswana found itself at a challenging point. The country had done remarkably well during the four decades since independence, but HIV/AIDS, unemployment, persistent poverty, and slowing growth were all emerging as potential future problems.

In order to attack these issues, a presidential task force produced a statement of the country's long-term goals, a report that quickly became known as "Vision 2016." Initiated by former President Masire, Vision 2016 was a plan for the development of Botswana that highlighted the need for economic diversification through foreign investment and improved productivity. In the vision, national officials pledged that Botswana would be a "prosperous, productive and innovative nation" by the year 2016.[71] Across the political spectrum, Botswanans remained confident of their future. Government officials praised their country's solid foundations—"rule of law, good succession plans, accountability, the right economic incentives"—and even the opposition leader agreed that the country was on the right track.[72] Reflecting back on four decades of growth, former President Masire was customarily modest. "So far," he remarked, "so good."[73]

---

67 See UNCTAD, *Botswana: Globalization, Liberalization and Sustainable Human Development*, pp. 37–39; and The Economist Intelligence Unit, *Botswana: Country Profile*, 2001.

68 For more on Botswana's system of investment incentives, see World Bank, *Opportunities for Industrial Development in Botswana* (Washington, D.C.: The World Bank, April 28, 1993), pp. 169–172. For criticism of these incentives, see Good and Hughes, "Globalization and Diversification," p. 48, and "The Desert Booms," *The Economist*.

69 UNCTAD, *World Investment Report*, 2001. Africa has received a very small part of the large increase in flows of foreign direct investment to developing countries in recent years. However, since Africa's share of global GDP is about 1.1%, Africa receives slightly more than its proportionate share of foreign direct investment (close to 15% of GDP).

70 Serwalo S.G. Tumelo, permanent secretary, Ministry of Finance and Development Planning, Republic of Botswana and director of De Beers Consolidated Mines, interview with author, Gaborone, October 8, 2002.

71 Ibid.

72 Otsweletse Moupo, leader of the Botswana National Front, interview with authors, Gaborone, October 9, 2002.

73 Ketumil Masire, former president of Botswana, interview with authors, Gaborone, October 8, 2002.

Exhibit 1a Sub-Saharan Africa and Botswana

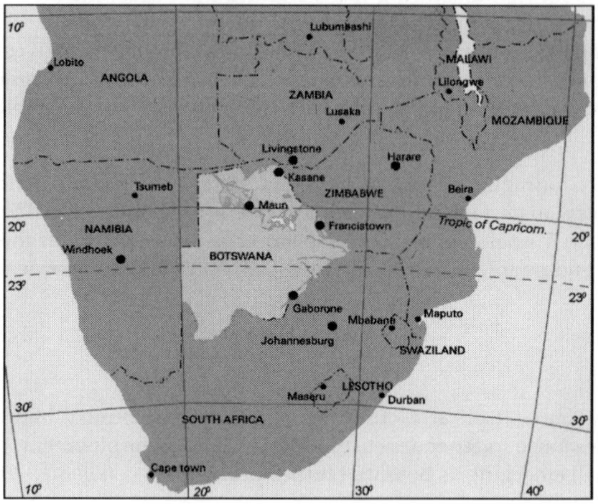

Source: Adapted from Republic of Botwana Tourism Board Web site, http://www.gov.bw/tourism/maps/maps.html.

Exhibit 1b Location of Diamond Mines in Botswana

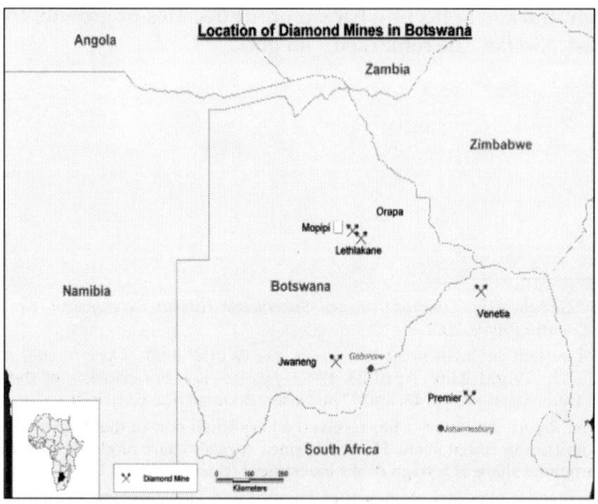

Source: Adapted from Firestone Diamonds Company's Web site, http://www.firestonediamonds.com.

Exhibit 2 National Accounts and Other Economic Data

	1965	1970	1975	1980	1985	1990	1995	2000
Gross Domestic Product (GDP in millions of pula)	32.8	61.3	221.2	771.6	1,828.6	6,539.7	1,2261.7	25,207.8
Real GDP (1995=100)	4.3	6.6	15.3	28.3	46.1	80.7	100.0	135.1
Real GDP Annual Growth (%)	n.a.	8.9	18.4	13.1	10.3	11.8	4.4	6.2
GDP Per Capita (PPP in $US)			839.5	1,985.9	3,434.4	5,341.0	6,035.0	7,651.9
Consumption (in millions of pula)								
Household	29.1	n.a.	131.8	408.9	784.8	2,062.7	4,258.5	7,824.5
Government	7.9	n.a.	41.5	148.7	443.1	1,558.3	3,546.7	7,524.5
Gross Fixed Capital Formation	7.2	n.a.	57.3	248.8	484.0	2,129.9	3,135.2	6,619.4
Changes in Inventories	-5.2	n.a.	44.4	42.1	71.6	384.4	13.7	94.4
Exports of Goods and Services	10.4	n.a.	93.8	410.5	1,074.5	3,658.3	6,071.4	14,108.1
Imports of Goods and Services (-)	16.6	n.a.	147.6	487.4	1,029.4	3,253.9	4,772.5	10,963.1
Expenditure (as a % of GDP)								
Household Expenditure	88.7	n.a.	59.6	53.0	42.9	31.5	34.7	31.0
Government Expenditure	24.1	n.a.	18.8	19.3	24.2	23.8	28.9	29.8
Gross Fixed Capital Formation	22.0	n.a.	25.9	32.2	26.5	32.6	25.6	26.3
Changes in Inventories	-15.9	n.a.	20.1	5.5	3.9	5.9	0.1	0.4
Exports of Goods and Services	31.7	n.a.	42.4	53.2	58.8	55.9	49.5	56.0
Imports of Goods and Services (-)	50.6	n.a.	66.7	63.2	56.3	49.8	38.9	43.5
Other Economic Data								
Inflation Consumer Prices (annual %)	n.a.	n.a.	n.a.	13.6	8.1	11.4	10.5	8.6
Money and Quasi Money—M2 (millions of pula)				236.9	557.4	1,545.9	2,685.6	7,328.5
Money and Quasi Money—M2 as a % of GDP				24.8	20.4	23.9	18.7	27.0
Unemployment as % of Total Labor Force	n.a.	n.a.	n.a.	n.a.	n.a.	n.a.	21.5	n.a.
Population (in millions)	0.5	0.6	0.7	0.9	1.1	1.3	1.5	1.7

Source: Adapted from Bank of Botswana data, IMF, International Financial Statistics, World Bank World Development Indicators.

Exhibit 3 Value Added by Type of Economic Activity as a Percentage of GDP

Economic Sector	1965	1975	1980	1985	1990	1995	1999
Agriculture	42.7	21.1	10.9	5.7	4.9	4.1	2.6
Mining	--	17.1	36.6	48.8	38.2	33.8	33.4
Manufacturing	5.7	7.5	5.0	3.8	4.8	4.6	4.4
Water and Electricity	0.6	2.4	1.6	2.1	1.8	2.2	2.3
Construction	7.8	12.7	8.8	4.5	7.7	6.2	6.1
Trade, Hotels, and Restaurants	9.0	15.7	17.1	12.9	14.0	16.1	10.4
Transport	4.3	1.5	1.5	2.2	3.0	3.4	3.8
Banks, Insurance, and Business Services	20.2	4.8	5.0	6.3	8.6	10.8	11.0
General Government	9.8	15.1	13.0	13.2	15.2	17.1	16.1
Social and Personal Services and Other	--	2.1	0.5	0.5	1.8	1.7	9.9

Source: Adapted from Botswana Central Statistics Office data.

Exhibit 4 Government Finances as Percentage of GDP

	1975	1980	1985	1990	1995	2000
Deficit (-) or Surplus	0.6	-0.2	22.6	12.2	2.2	11.3
Total Revenue and Grants	0.4	39.1	61.3	57.2	44.6	55.7
Total Debt	n.a.	14.7	22.5	12.0	11.7	12.2

Source: Adapted from Bank of Botswana, International Monetary Fund, International Financial Statistics.

Exhibit 5 Sovereign Credit Ratings, 2002 (rating for long-term foreign currency debt, as of February 25)

Country	Moody's[a]	Standard & Poor's[b]
Botswana	A2	A
Brazil	B1	BB-
Egypt	Ba1	BBB-
Mauritius	Baa2	n/a
Slovenia	A2	A
South Africa	Baa2	BBB-

Source: Adapted from Moody's Investor's Service, Standard & Poor's.

[a]Moody's ratings scale runs from Aaa, Aa1, Aa2, Aa3, A1, A2, A3, Baa1, Baa2, Baa3, Ba1, down to C3 and measures risk of government default on long-term foreign currency sovereign debt; ratings of Baa3 and above are investment grade.

[b]Standard & Poor's scale runs from AAA, AA+, AA, AA-, A+, A, A-, BBB+ to D; ratings of BBB- and above are investment grade.

Exhibit 6 Botswana: Balance of Payments and Exchange Rates

Balance of Payments (millions of U.S. dollars)	1975	1980	1985	1990	1995	1999
Current Account	-35.6	-151.1	81.9	-19.3	299.7	516.8
Goods: Exports	142.0	544.5	727.6	1,795.4	2,160.2	2,671.0
Goods: Imports	-181.2	-602.5	-493.8	-1,610.9	-1,605.4	-1,996.5
Trade Balance	-39.2	-58.0	233.8	184.4	554.8	674.5
Balance on Goods and Services	-84.4	-173.1	179.7	18.0	370.9	531.2
Balance on Goods, Services, and Income	-30.4	-206.0	48.2	-87.9	338.5	265.1
Capital Account	n.a.	8.2	5.2	64.7	14.4	20.6
Capital Account: Credit	n.a.	9.1	5.6	65.6	15.4	33.5
Capital Account: Debit	n.a.	-0.9	-0.4	-0.9	-0.9	-12.9
Financial Account	43.5	144.0	123.1	82.6	-33.9	-175.2
Direct Investment Abroad	n.a.	-2.3	-1.5	-7.4	-40.9	-1.5
Direct Investment in Reporting Economy	-38.3	111.6	53.6	95.9	70.4	36.7
Balance of Payments as a % of GDP						
Current Account	-14.0	-14.5	9.4	-0.6	6.9	11.1
Goods: Exports	55.8	52.4	83.6	51.4	49.7	57.5
Goods: Imports	-71.2	-57.9	-56.7	-46.1	-36.9	-43.0
Trade Balance	-15.4	-5.6	26.9	5.3	12.8	14.5
Financial Account as a % of GDP	17.1	13.8	14.1	2.4	-0.8	-3.8
Direct Investment Abroad	n.a.	-0.2	-0.2	-0.2	-0.9	0.0
Direct Investment in Reporting Economy	-15.0	10.7	6.2	2.7	1.6	0.8
Exchange Rates (pula per U.S dollar)						
Official Rate—End of Period	0.87	0.74	2.10	1.87	2.82	4.63
% Annual Change	26.1	-5.9	34.7	-0.1	3.8	3.9

Source: Adapted from Bank of Botswana, International Monetary Fund, International Financial Statistics.

Exhibit 7 Main Exports, Selected Years

	1980	1985	1990	1995	1999
Total Exports (thousands of pula, f.o.b.)	390,437	1,384,284	3,319,091	5,941,470	13,834,682
Principal Exports (percentage of total)					
Meat Products	7.2	7.0	3.2	3.0	1.9
Live Animals	0.0	0.0	0.0	0.0	0.0
Hides and Skins	0.8	0.8	0.6	0.6	0.3
Diamonds	60.4	75.7	78.7	67.0	82.3
Copper-Nickel	20.7	8.7	8.2	5.5	6.0
Textiles	4.0	2.1	3.4	2.5	1.8
Soda Ash	--	--	--	0.4	0.7
Vehicles and Parts	--	--	--	16.1	2.0
Other Goods	6.5	5.6	5.9	4.8	5.1
Direction of Trade (percentage of total)					
Common Customs Area	6.6	5.6	4.7	21.5	6.7
Zimbabwe	3.1	3.0	6.8	3.1	3.9
Other Africa	5.4	1.0	1.6	0.8	0.9
United Kingdom	2.1	3.8	1.2	37.4	69.7
Other Europe	61.3	80.9	85.3	36.1	17.5
United States	21.0	5.3	0.1	0.9	0.6
All Other	0.5	0.4	0.2	0.2	0.7

Source: Adapted from Botswana Central Statistics Office data.

Exhibit 8 World Diamond Mining Production in 2000

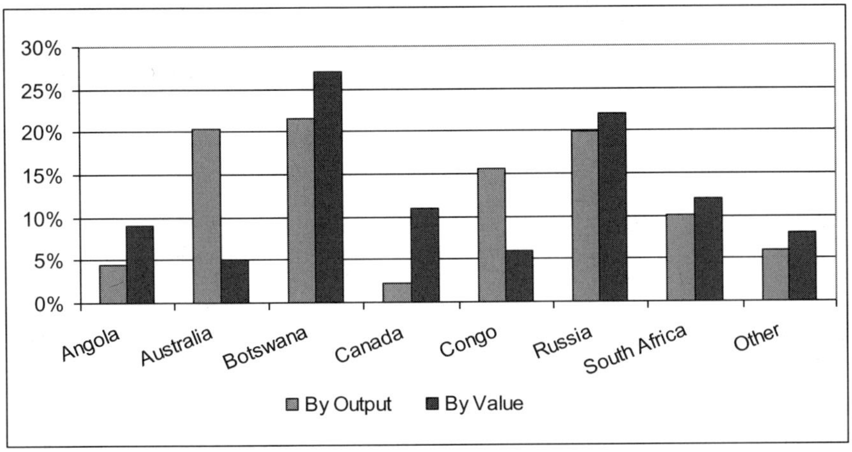

Source: Adapted from World Diamond Registry, New York, 2002 Web site, http://www.diamondregistry.com/News/2002/production.htm; and *Diamond Facts 2000/2001:NWT Diamond Industry Report.*

Exhibit 9 Botswana: Selected Social Indicators

	1970	1980	1990	1999
Population				
Total Population	596,944	941,027	1,326,796	1,611,021
Rural Population	54,416	781,413	720,468	810,599
Urban Population	519,678	159,614	606,328	800,422
Health (per 1,000 people)				
Birth Rate	45.3	47.8	39.4	32.1
Fertility Rate	6.5	6.6	4.2	4.0
Death Rate	13.7	13.0	11.5	10.6
Infant Mortality Rate	97.1	71.0	48.0	38.1
Child Mortality Rate	56.1	35.0	16.0	7.6
Education Enrollment (thousands)				
Primary	83,000	171,900	283,500	323,900
Secondary	3,900	18,300	56,900	148,200
University	100	900	3,700	9,600

Source: Adapted from Botswana Central Statistics Office data.

Exhibit 10 Comparative Statistics

	Birth Rate (per 1,000 people)	Adult Illiteracy Rate	Life Expectancy at Birth	Fertility Rate	GDP Growth (annual %)
1970					
Angola	49.0	--	37.2	6.5	--
Botswana	**49.7**	**53.9**	**51.9**	**6.7**	**17.1**
Brazil	35.0	31.9	58.9	5.0	8.8
China	33.4	48.7	61.7	5.8	14.1
Congo, Rep.	46.0	67.1	45.8	6.3	6.4
India	41.1	66.9	49.4	5.8	3.1
Malaysia	36.2	41.8	61.6	5.5	6.0
Mexico	43.8	25.1	61.7	6.6	6.5
Namibia	42.7	43.0	47.7	6.0	--
Nigeria	50.8	79.9	42.9	6.9	25.0
Sierra Leone	48.7	--	34.4	6.5	8.6
South Africa	39.0	30.2	53.1	5.7	7.3
Zimbabwe	49.3	42.5	50.5	7.3	22.6
1985					
Angola	51.1	--	43.2	7.1	--
Botswana	**41.8**	**36.7**	**60.2**	**5.6**	**7.3**
Brazil	27.2	21.6	64.1	3.2	7.9
China	17.8	28.1	68.3	2.4	12.6
Congo, Rep.	44.1	41.1	51.1	6.3	-1.2
India	32.9	54.8	56.6	4.4	5.5
Malaysia	31.9	23.6	68.9	4.1	-1.1
Mexico	30.3	14.7	69.0	3.9	2.6
Namibia	39.5	29.2	55.1	5.7	0.5
Nigeria	46.6	59.3	47.5	6.5	9.7
Sierra Leone	49.0	--	36.2	6.5	-5.3
South Africa	33.9	21.1	59.4	3.8	-4.0
Zimbabwe	41.4	24.2	56.4	5.8	6.9
2000					
Angola	47.5	--	46.6	6.6	3.0
Botswana	**32.0**	**22.8**	**38.9**	**4.0**	**7.7**
Brazil	19.7	14.8	68.1	2.2	4.5
China	15.1	15.9	70.3	1.9	7.9
Congo, Rep.	42.5	19.3	51.3	6.0	7.9
India	25.3	42.8	62.8	3.1	3.9
Malaysia	24.5	12.5	72.5	3.0	8.3
Mexico	24.8	8.6	73.0	2.6	6.6
Namibia	35.6	18.0	47.2	5.0	3.9
Nigeria	39.6	36.1	46.8	5.3	3.8
Sierra Leone	44.4	--	39.2	5.8	3.8
South Africa	25.8	14.7	47.8	2.9	3.4
Zimbabwe	29.8	11.3	39.9	3.8	-4.9

Source: Adapted from World Bank, World Development Indicators.

Note: In 1999, the Botswanan government reported life expectancy at birth to be 67.6 years.

Exhibit 11 Corruption Perception Index

Country Rank	Country	CPI 2002 Score	Country Rank	Country	CPI 2002 Score	Country Rank	Country	CPI 2002 Score
1	Finland	9.7	36	Belarus	4.8	70	Argentina	2.8
2	Denmark	9.5		Lithuania	4.8	71	Cote d'Ivoire	2.7
	New Zealand	9.5		South Africa	4.8		Honduras	2.7
4	Iceland	9.4		Tunisia	4.8		India	2.7
5	Singapore	9.3	40	Costa Rica	4.5		Russia	2.7
	Sweden	9.3		Jordan	4.5		Tanzania	2.7
7	Canada	9.0		Mauritius	4.5		Zimbabwe	2.7
	Luxembourg	9.0		South Korea	4.5	77	Pakistan	2.6
	Netherlands	9.0	44	Greece	4.2		Philippines	2.6
10	United Kingdom	8.7	45	Brazil	4.0		Romania	2.6
11	Australia	8.6		Bulgaria	4.0		Zambia	2.6
12	Norway	8.5		Jamaica	4.0	81	Albania	2.5
	Switzerland	8.5		Peru	4.0		Guatemala	2.5
14	Hong Kong	8.2		Poland	4.0		Nicaragua	2.5
15	Austria	7.8	50	Ghana	3.9		Venezuela	2.5
16	United States	7.7	51	Croatia	3.8	85	Georgia	2.4
17	Chile	7.5	52	Czech Republic	3.7		Ukraine	2.4
18	Germany	7.3		Latvia	3.7		Vietnam	2.4
	Israel	7.3		Morocco	3.7	88	Kazakhstan	2.3
20	Belgium	7.1		Slovakia	3.7	89	Bolivia	2.2
	Japan	7.1		Sri Lanka	3.7		Cameroon	2.2
	Spain	7.1	57	Colombia	3.6		Ecuador	2.2
23	Ireland	6.9		Mexico	3.6		Haiti	2.2
24	**Botswana**	**6.4**	59	China	3.5	93	Moldova	2.1
25	France	6.3		Dominican Rep.	3.5		Uganda	2.1
	Portugal	6.3		Ethiopia	3.5	95	Azerbaijan	2.0
27	Slovenia	6.0	62	Egypt	3.4	96	Indonesia	1.9
28	Namibia	5.7		El Salvador	3.4		Kenya	1.9
29	Estonia	5.6	64	Thailand	3.2	98	Angola	1.7
	Taiwan	5.6		Turkey	3.2		Madagascar	1.7
31	Italy	5.2	66	Senegal	3.1		Paraguay	1.7
32	Uruguay	5.1	67	Panama	3.0	101	Nigeria	1.6
33	Hungary	4.9	68	Malawi	2.9	102	Bangladesh	1.2
	Malaysia	4.9		Uzbekistan	2.9			
	Trinidad & Tobago	4.9						

Source: Adapted from Transparency International's Web site, http://www.transparency.org/pressreleases_archive/2002/2002.08.28.cpi.en.html.

Exhibit 12 Botswanan National Assembly, 1965–1999

Party	1965	1969	1974	1979	1984	1989	1994	1999
Number of National Assembly Seats Held by Each Party								
Botswana Democratic Party	28	24	27	29	28	31	31	33
Botswana National Front	--	3	2	2	5	3	13	6
Botswana Peoples Party	3	3	2	1	1	0	0	--
BIP/IFP	0	1	1	0	0	0	0	--
Botswana Congress Party	--	--	--	--	--	--	--	1
BAM	--	--	--	--	--	--	0	0
Total Number of Seats	31	31	32	32	34	34	40	40
Percent of Popular Vote								
Botswana Democratic Party	80	68	77	75	68	65	55	54
Botswana National Front	--	14	12	13	20	27	37	25
Botswana Peoples Party	14	12	6	8	7	4	4	--
BIP/IFP	5	6	4	4	3	2	4	--
Botswana Congress Party	--	--	--	--	--	--	--	11
BAM	--	--	--	--	--	--	--	5
Other	1	0	1	0	2	2	0	0
Rejected	--	--	--	--	--	--	--	5
Percent of Seats								
Botswana Democratic Party	90	77	84	91	82	91	67	83
Botswana National Front	--	10	7	6	15	9	33	15
Botswana Peoples Party	10	10	7	3	3	0	0	--
BIP/IFP	0	3	2	0	0	0	0	--
Botswana Congress Party	--	--	--	--	--	--	-	2
BAM	--	--	--	--	--	--	--	0

Source: Adapted from Dr. Mpho G. Molomo and Dr. Gloria Somolekae, "Sustainable Electoral Democracy in Botswana," presented at International IDEA Conference: Towards Sustainable Democratic Institutions in Southern Africa.

Policies and Effects of Foreign Capital

HARVARD | BUSINESS | SCHOOL

9-706-007
REV: MARCH 3, 2009

LAURA ALFARO
VINATI DEV
STEPHEN McINTYRE

Foreign Direct Investment and Ireland's Tiger Economy

—"The World's Best Country," The Economist Intelligence Unit, 2005[1]

In 1987, Ireland was the poorest member of the European Economic Community (EEC, renamed the European Union in 1993) and stood on the verge of default. Debt servicing consumed a third of government revenues, and involvement by the International Monetary Fund (IMF) seemed imminent. Unemployment topped 17%, and gross domestic product (GDP) per capita was 69% of the EEC average.[2] Emigration was a national epidemic, and as university graduates flooded out of the country by the thousands in search of employment, Ireland's prospects seemed to disappear with them.

Over the next decade Ireland underwent a startling economic transformation. Between 1990 and 2000, GDP growth averaged 6.3%, with the highest growth—close to 10%—between 1995 and 2000.[3] By then, Ireland's GDP per capita had surpassed the United Kingdom's, and unemployment had plummeted to 5%.[4] Fiscal surpluses became the norm, the national debt all but disappeared, and emigrants returned in droves. The extent of the revival was unprecedented in the developed world and earned Ireland's economy a nickname: the Celtic Tiger.

The resurgence garnered a great deal of attention worldwide. Scholars, journalists, and politicians sought to identify a "silver bullet"—a single underlying cause of the boom. Some experts attributed the growth to policy initiatives such as collective bargaining and education reforms, or exogenous factors such as EU transfers and favorable exchange rates. But many believed the answer was foreign direct investment (FDI), which swelled throughout the 1990s, averaging over $2.5 billion per year during the latter part of the decade.[5] (See **Exhibits 1a** and **1b** for FDI flows in Ireland.) By 2002, Ireland's per capita stock of FDI was the second highest in the world (after Hong Kong's) and twice the EU average.[6]

In July 2003, the Enterprise Strategy Group (ESG), an independent body of academics and business leaders, was commissioned by the Irish government to report on the future of the economy.[7] The resulting report concluded that FDI did indeed play a major role: "Ireland's performance was driven primarily by a relatively small number of foreign-owned firms who chose Ireland as their base for serving European markets. The effect of these firms on the economy was such that it masked the generally poor performance of the indigenous sector, with the exception of a small number of high-performing firms."[8]

Professor Laura Alfaro, Research Associate Vinati Dev, and Stephen McIntyre (MBA 2005) prepared this case. HBS cases are developed solely as the basis for class discussion. Cases are not intended to serve as endorsements, sources of primary data, or illustrations of effective or ineffective management.

But by then, many experts feared that rising costs, labor shortages, skyrocketing housing prices,[9] and a soaring euro had eroded Ireland's competitiveness and threatened its export-fueled success. There were concerns that as labor market pressures increased, real wages would grow faster than underlying productivity, thereby reducing profits and the incentive for FDI. It also seemed likely that grant incentives, which some argued had been essential in attracting FDI, would be reduced or abolished. Since several regions in Ireland would no longer be categorized as "Objective One" regions, the European Union was poised to significantly curb the level of grant aid that Ireland could offer.[10] In addition, while Ireland had agreed to retain a low corporate tax rate through 2010, there was speculation that it would succumb to EU pressure[11] to increase the tax rate. Others expressed concern about increasing competition from the Eastern European countries, many of which were aggressively pursuing foreign investments and reducing corporate tax rates.[12]

The new realities thus raised questions about whether Ireland could continue to attract significant FDI. If the ESG's contention was correct—that growth was mainly due to FDI—it would radically alter Ireland's policy response and other countries' efforts to emulate the Celtic Tiger. Why was the country so successful in attracting FDI? Was FDI really the driving force behind the boom? What accounted for the economic growth? And, most importantly, could the boom be sustained?

Historical Background

Independence and Civil War

Modern-day Ireland was created in 1921, when, after a two-year War of Independence, Britain and Ireland signed a peace treaty ending nearly eight centuries of British colonial rule. The treaty partitioned the island broadly along religious lines into the Irish Free State, which comprised a predominantly Catholic population, and Protestant-dominated Northern Ireland, which remained a part of the United Kingdom (see **Exhibit 2** for a map of Ireland). Under the treaty, the Irish Free State was required to swear an oath of allegiance to the crown. Irish republicans fiercely opposed the treaty, and a bloody civil war ensued.

In 1923, pro-treaty forces won the war, but Ireland emerged a wounded nation. The new government inherited a severely underdeveloped infrastructure; basic services such as water and electricity were lacking. Unemployment and emigration were high. Furthermore, the country had a virtually nonexistent manufacturing sector. Though undeveloped, the economy was largely agricultural and heavily dependent on trade with the United Kingdom. At first, Ireland pursued a liberal trade policy, but this changed when the leader of the Fianna Fáil political party, Eamon de Valera, became prime minister in 1932.

After winning on a populist platform that emphasized national self-sufficiency, the de Valera government introduced two acts that became symbols of economic, and to some degree political, nationalism. Under the Finance Act of 1932, Ireland's tariffs became twice as high as those in the United States and 50% higher than those in the United Kingdom. The Control of Manufactures Act of 1932 required majority Irish ownership in new manufacturing ventures. The Wall Street crash and Great Depression had provoked a worldwide resurgence in protectionism around this time, and de Valera's policies drew widespread support. In a 1933 lecture at University College Dublin, John Maynard Keynes said, "If I were an Irishman I would find much to attract me in the economic outlook of your present government towards self-sufficiency."[13]

Trade and FDI: The Role of Government

De Valera's government had set Ireland on a path of economic nationalism. But by the 1950s, Ireland's economic stagnation demanded change. A more pro-market agenda began to take hold within the government, which subsequently passed a number of new laws designed to boost the economy. The Finance Act of 1956 introduced export profits tax relief (EPTR). It provided for a 50% tax exemption on profits earned from manufacturing goods, and was set to increase to 100% in 1958.[14] The government also sent the message to the international community that Ireland was open for business; in 1957, Ireland joined the World Bank and the IMF and relaxed restrictions on the Control of Manufactures Act.

In 1958 the finance minister advocated a shift from protectionism to free trade and proposed that the government encourage foreign investment through tax concessions and incentive grants. As a result, between 1962 and 1964 Ireland unilaterally lowered tariffs. In 1965, the Anglo-Irish Free Trade Agreement was concluded. With this agreement, Ireland hoped to achieve free trade of all manufactured goods by 1975. Perhaps most significantly, Ireland joined the General Agreement for Tariffs and Trade (GATT) in 1967.

The new economic programs of the 1960s brought some relief to Ireland. (See **Exhibit 3** for GDP data, **Exhibit 4** for government finances, and **Exhibit 5** for balance-of-payments data.) GDP growth rates surpassed 4% annually, yet high unemployment and poverty continued to plague the nation, and the education system was in a shambles. A 1965 report highlighted the high dropout rate and the dilapidated condition of many schools. In 1968 the minister for education eliminated fees for secondary education, raised the minimum school-leaving age from 14 to 15, and abolished the primary certificate (a form of entrance exam for secondary schools). He also mandated the provision of adequate sanitation and heating. These changes had an immediate impact on the numbers of children entering secondary school.[15]

Industrial Development Authority

The Industrial Development Authority (IDA) was formed in 1949 as a government agency promoting greater investment throughout Ireland.[16] Further, in the 1960s and 1970s, as it became apparent that the government favored an export-focused industrial strategy, the IDA found itself at the center of this new policy environment. With business-friendly legislation as a backdrop, the IDA set out to attract new investments from around the world. Ray Mac Sharry, minister of finance (1982, 1987–1988), and Padraic White, managing director of the IDA (1981–1990), acknowledged, "It (the EPTR) became the IDA's most distinctive investment incentive, and over time its most powerful single weapon in the international industrial promotion battle."[17]

The IDA would have many "wins" in the 1960s. When the pharmaceutical giant Pzifer, in 1969, decided to set up a plant in Cork, it was seen as a major victory for the IDA. However, it was unclear whether it was the promotional efforts *per se* or Irish-American connections that had attracted Pfizer. The IDA officials themselves acknowledged that the company's decision to set up a plant in Ireland was largely due to the efforts of John Mulcahy, a man who had emigrated to America during the Irish Civil War and at the time sat on the Pfizer Board with one-third of the company's shares.

Nonetheless, by the mid-1960s, Ireland was host to a number of foreign firms, including General Electric. Recruiting such reputable firms gave Ireland's efforts instant credibility, and it appeared that a combination of factors, including the government's support for an export-oriented industrial strategy, the IDA's promotional efforts, and American-Irish business ties were working in tandem. Over the next 10 years, 450 foreign companies negotiated new projects or expansions with the IDA.

Yet, over the same period (as competition from Britain, France, and others intensified), the IDA became aware that "Ireland no longer had the investment promotion field all to herself."[18]

Undaunted, the IDA pursued an aggressive plan to position Ireland as the most profitable destination in Europe. Its direct marketing campaign identified promising leads, and the IDA went directly to those companies to make the case for locating in Ireland. The head of the IDA's research and planning section in the early 1970s described the criteria for selecting companies as follows:

1. Pick those that meet basic social and economic criteria such as not too capital intensive, high male-labor content, high use of native raw materials and services, low scale factor.

2. Pick those that offer the best chances of commercial stability and therefore economic stability, by reference to commercial criteria such as high profitability. Pick those with strong growth both in output and international trade.

3. Pick those with high dependence on scarce human resources, such as skilled people, because it implies a greater commitment and tie.

4. Pick those that can take advantage of natural resources and therefore enable us to conserve other resources.[19]

In 1971, the IDA set up task forces and sent executives out on the road to countries such as the United States, Holland, and Sweden to present companies with detailed investment plans.

The IDA also forecasted profits to show companies that there was money to be made by manufacturing in Ireland. In the first year, the IDA executives customized presentations to 105 companies. By 1973, the team had made 2,600 presentations to companies worldwide. By the mid-1970s the IDA's efforts and the promises of the common market brought companies such as Gillette-Braun, Digital, Cross Pens, Baxter Travenol, Syntex, Merck Sharpe, and Warner Lambert to Ireland.

The Turbulent Seventies

With its impending entry into the EEC, Ireland greeted the 1970s with optimism as it anticipated gaining access to the EEC's much larger market. Indeed, with one stroke of legislation, Ireland was able to promise foreign investors a market of upwards of 200 million, as opposed to 3.6 million.

The year of membership, however, also brought the oil crisis of October 1973. Ireland, which imported over 70% of its primary energy requirements, was thrown into turmoil. Moreover, a structural shift in the economy transferred manufacturing growth from traditional indigenous industries to largely foreign-owned and export-oriented modern industries. Foreign firms accounted for less than one-third of total industrial employment in 1973 and simply did not have the capacity to offset the job losses suffered by indigenous industry.[20]

The government was now faced with growing unemployment at home and quadrupling oil prices on the international front. In order to stem the falling living standards, the Fine Gael-Labour coalition launched an ambitious program of public spending, accompanied by major tax cuts. This public-sector expansion was funded through borrowing. Gross expenditure on social welfare grew from 6.5% of gross national product (GNP) to 10.5% from 1973 to 1977. (**See Exhibit 4** for government finances.) In 1977, the government was ousted in the general election, and Fianna Fail returned to power. The new government inherited a large fiscal deficit but continued the trend of deficit spending. In keeping with its election platform, the new government called for increased public spending to lower unemployment and financing of this program by increased borrowing.

By the 1970s, the IDA had secured an unprecedented volume of foreign investment, but persistent unemployment called into question the success of Ireland's industrial policy. To make matters worse, the 1979 oil crisis hit the country, plunging it into a deep recession.

The Question of Industrial Policy—Is FDI Working?

Despite the economic turbulence of the mid and late 1970s, FDI continued to grow. Nevertheless, the IDA endured a steady stream of criticism that the agency-led foreign investment strategy had not done enough to lift the economy. Critics wondered if foreign investors warranted the special treatment they received, noting that despite growth in the pharmaceutical and electronics sectors, the success of the foreign sector was not trickling down to the rest of the economy. They further charged that linkages with foreign subsidiaries and local industry were limited. (See **Exhibit 6** for linkages of foreign firms in manufacturing.) As historian J.J. Lee put it, "The native industry was resolutely refusing to grow."[21] Indeed, when Ireland joined the EEC in 1973, tariff reductions had exposed Irish industry to unprecedented competition, triggering the widespread failure of indigenous firms.

The tide of condemnation eventually led the National Economic and Social Council to commission the Telesis inquiry into Ireland's industrial policy. The resulting 1982 report was not optimistic: "Foreign owned industrial operations in Ireland with a few exceptions do not embody key competitiveness activities in which they participate; do not employ significant numbers of skilled workers; and are not significantly integrated into traded and skilled sub-supply industries in Ireland."[22]

The report stated categorically that the IDA's foreign investment promotion strategy was not as successful as the organization's "propaganda implied."[23] On the contrary, the report alleged that support for foreign firms on the whole, and in the electronics industry in particular, had been excessive. As evidence for its claim, the report noted that only about 30% of the jobs announced by the IDA ever materialized and that jobs created by foreign industries failed to make up for the jobs being lost in traditional Irish industries. The authors went on to argue that no country had succeeded in achieving sustained economic growth without a strong native industry and that for this to happen, the Irish authorities had to insist that foreign companies establish research and development activities in Ireland and favor local sub-suppliers.

The report did not completely blame the multinational corporations (MNCs) for the lack of integration but acknowledged that MNCs had no choice but to source supplies from overseas, since indigenous suppliers lacked essential technical and mechanical expertise.[24] Specifically, the report called for Ireland to work toward "raising the proportion of funds allocated to indigenous export or skilled supply firms from less than 40% . . . to 50% by 1985 and 75% by 1990."[25]

The report suggested that the government select 50 to 75 "winners"—Irish firms whose management had already been deemed top quality—and prop them up to become internationally competitive.[26] The report recommended that weaker companies redeploy their skills toward export-oriented activity with the help of the IDA money.[27] Finally, in what appeared to be a direct assault on the IDA, the Telesis Report stated that the development effort to create a local industry "must be reorganized to emphasize the building of structurally strong Irish companies rather than strong agencies to assist weak companies."[28]

The IDA disputed Telesis's claim that Irish incentives and support for foreign firms were excessive. The IDA pointed to the arrival of big companies such as Apple, Bausch & Lomb, and Fujitsu in 1980[29] as evidence that its strategy was working and blamed the government's mismanagement of the economy, particularly the high inflation rates, for the depressed markets.

Whatever the cause, one historian noted that the efforts to build Irish industry had largely failed:

> Sixty years after independence, fifty years after blanket protection . . . fifteen years after the Anglo-Irish Free Trade Agreement, eight years after entering the EU, a native entrepreneurial cadre of the requisite quality had failed to emerge. Irish-owned industry could not compete internationally. It could not even compete on the home market. Neither carrot nor stick, neither free trade nor protection, had sufficed to create a competitive native industry.[30]

The Eighties: Crisis and Change

Years of excessive government spending and high unemployment took their toll on Ireland's economy. By 1982, the deficit stood at 12% of GDP, and the current account deficit rose to a record of 21% of GDP. In 1983, when Black & Decker and AT&T-owned Telectron announced closures on the same day, it seemed that even the foreign sector, which had thus far appeared resistant to the macroeconomic crisis, had finally succumbed.[31]

By 1987 Ireland was deeply in debt and on the verge of economic collapse. Debt-to-GDP hit 122%, the budget deficit ballooned to 12% of GDP, and unemployment was over 17%.[32] The government introduced widespread reforms, slashing government spending in an attempt to reduce the 22 billion-pound debt (1 Irish pound=1.27 euros). The prime minister explained: "It is imperative that we carry further the progress we have made so far this year in getting public expenditure under control. Unless we achieve further significant cuts in expenditure the growth in public sector debt will continue to be a burden on the economy, inhibiting economic growth and employment and making it impossible for us to get development underway."[33]

Employers, farmers, and unions had all accepted the dismal economic scenario and recognized the need for austere measures in the short term. The government took full advantage of this new environment and forged social partnerships across the political and economic sectors. Aware that these measures would cause considerable pain to the trade unions and their members, the government offered tax reform as a compensating benefit. In 1987, the Program for National Recovery (PNR)—known as social partnership—was created. The *quid pro quo* was pay restraint in return for tax cuts. The net result, it was hoped, would be a real increase in take-home pay for workers and reduced unemployment caused by rising competitiveness. The agreement also promised that welfare would not have to bear a disproportional burden of the fiscal cuts. Before 1987, productivity advances among foreign-owned firms prompted wage increases, which then spread to the indigenous industries. PNR reversed this trend and allowed indigenous firms to lead wage setting according to their slower productivity growth.

The IDA was determined to play a part in the economic recovery. It took advantage of PNR by setting up a program designed to draw labor-intensive service businesses to Ireland. The IDA also used a new advertising campaign to reposition Ireland: it introduced Ireland with the tagline, "We're the Young Europeans," noting that Ireland had the youngest population in Europe.[34] The IDA also shifted its emphasis from tax and financial incentives to an educated workforce and EU membership. As a result of these efforts, the IDA drew a host of new firms to Ireland, including Motorola, Teradata, Stratus, EDS, and Sandoz.

With the fiscal house coming to order and relative macroeconomic stability, the benefits of EU membership began to be felt. The EU's main instrument for supporting social and economic restructuring across the union was the Single European Act (SEA) of 1986. Through this act, the EU made direct transfers to Ireland, providing farming subsidies and disbursing structural funds to be used for infrastructure development. Ireland's annual net receipts from the EU totaled about 6% of GDP from the mid-1980s to the mid-1990s, with roughly two-thirds farm related and one-third structural.[35] Although the absolute figures were high, it was estimated that the transfers contributed less than 3% per year to Ireland's GDP growth rate in the 1990s.[36]

The Nineties: The Emergence of the Celtic Tiger

By 1990, Ireland's GDP growth rate reached 8.5%, and its volume of exports increased by 23.5% from 1985 to 1990. Ireland's competitiveness in the export market had been improved by broadly favorable exchange rates throughout the late 1980s and into the 1990s. A 10% currency devaluation in 1986, coupled with the strength of the dollar and the pound sterling later in the decade, had further boosted competitiveness. In 1996, the government eliminated third-level tuition fees in an effort to further improve the quality of the labor force.

The 1990s were promising times for Ireland. Propelled in part by the American IT boom and the formation of the single European market in 1992, the Irish economy grew rapidly and attracted unprecedented levels of foreign investment. Furthermore, fiscal discipline and reforms, imposed by the Maastricht criteria in 1992, had resulted in lower deficits and debt-to-GDP ratios. Finally, a revaluation of the Irish pound upon Ireland's joining the European Monetary System (EMS) made Ireland's export sector more competitive.

The IDA, aware of EU pressures to increase taxes, had begun lobbying the government to prolong the tax rate. The IDA had conducted studies demonstrating that the low 10% manufacturing tax rate was essential for Ireland to retain its competitiveness relative to other European countries. In 1990 the government extended the 10% rate through 2010.

The combination of low corporate tax and ready access to the European market made Ireland an attractive option.[37] Industries with high operating margins, like pharmaceuticals, were particularly drawn by the low tax environment. Several EU countries were critical of Ireland's corporate tax policy, especially when Ireland began to win sizable portions of FDI from the United States. Some believed that a race to the bottom would develop in Europe, with tax cuts replacing devaluations as a competitive device. But Kieran McGowan, IDA CEO from 1989 to 1999, described the problems other countries would face if they dropped corporate taxes to Irish levels: "They find it hard to replicate our tax policy because they have a large corporate tax revenue stream to begin with. We in Ireland didn't have a corporate sector, so we had nothing to lose."[38]

In the meantime, foreign firms continued to open plants in Ireland, largely due to the IDA's ability to identify and lure target companies (see **Exhibit 7a** for a survey of the economic impact of IDA-supported companies, **Exhibit 7b** for their countries of origin, and **Exhibit 7c** for the IDA's regional offices). International employees spent much of their time making and developing senior contacts in target companies, and the IDA used its on-the-road staff to gather intelligence about market trends. The IDA's annual conference was a key event for consolidating feedback and identifying new trends and patterns. The arrival of computer giant Intel in 1990 was a massive victory for Ireland in general and for the IDA in particular and exemplified the IDA's persistence and imagination. The agency first contacted Intel executives in the late 1970s and nurtured the relationship for more than a decade until conditions were more suitable for investment. The IDA offered Intel a grant package of $157 million, spread over 10 years. But Intel was concerned about the absence of a sufficient supply of experienced engineers. The IDA came up with a plan to address Intel's concern: McGowan compiled a list of Irish engineers working at semiconductor businesses, mainly in the United States, who would be willing to return to Ireland. As McGowan put it, "We presented a booklet to Intel with the names, addresses and phone numbers of 85 people. And I think that impressed them."[39] The hard work paid off, and Intel chose Ireland over Scotland as a location for both its computer system and semiconductor facilities. At the IDA, 1989, the year of the announcement, came to be known as the "year of Intel."[40] By 2004, Intel employed approximately 5,000 people in Ireland.

Over the next few years, almost every major computer company arrived in Ireland: Dell, Gateway, Hewlett-Packard, and IBM all started production. Ireland's share of FDI inflows into the EU tripled between 1991 and 1994, as the country attracted approximately 40% of U.S. electronics investments in Europe.[41] As Michael Dell, founder of Dell Computer, explained in a recent newspaper article:

> What attracted us? [A] well educated work force and good universities close by. [Also,] Ireland has an industrial and tax policy which is consistently very supportive of businesses, independent of which political party is in power. I believe this is because there are enough people who remember the very bad times to de-politicize economic development. [Ireland also has] very good transportation and logistics and a good location—easy to move products to major markets in Europe quickly.[42]

The IDA was also responsible for recognizing Ireland's potential as an offshore call center during an overseas intelligence-gathering mission in the early 1990s. The IDA negotiated a deal with the national telecom company to slash international call rates in return for increased call volumes, and it compiled a list of multilingual workers in order to demonstrate an adequate supply of labor.[43] Ireland built on its first-mover advantage and became the location of choice for pan-European customer contact centers.

The Role of FDI: The Debate

> *The massive inflow of direct investment has been the major positive shock influencing the economy in the 1990s. . . . Ireland's share of OECD total inflows surged in 1990s, reaching a level out of all proportion with its GDP share.*
>
> —Organization for Economic Cooperation and Development (OECD), Economic Survey, 1999

By the early 1990s, the success of the foreign sector was evident, and it became widely accepted that the spectacular rise in Irish exports had come almost entirely from aggressive export-oriented foreign firms. It was also apparent that indigenous exports had stayed flat in real terms and that the domestic economy had generally lagged behind. Critics blamed the FDI-led policy responsible for this change and pointed to several statistics to support their claim. Most notably, there was a high level of unemployment, which ranged between 14% and 16% through the early 1990s.[44] Some claimed that this was a by-product of a "jobless-growth" phenomenon that accompanied the FDI-led policy. They also pointed to the yawning gap between Ireland's GDP and GNP,[45] which they argued demonstrated that foreign companies exported profits. As further evidence of the lack of linkages between domestic and foreign firms, they pointed out that the investment share of Irish national income had shrunk significantly in the early 1990s.

While there was growing evidence that FDI played a crucial role in the Celtic Tiger's growth, it was increasingly acknowledged that the foreign sector had limited ties with local businesses and that an FDI-focused policy had yielded little in terms of creating a vibrant domestic economy. In reaction to this growing criticism, the government split the IDA into two separate entities in 1994. IDA Ireland continued to focus on attracting foreign direct investment, while Enterprise Ireland concentrated its energies on developing indigenous industries. Both organizations reported to Forfás, the national policy and advisory board, an umbrella organization through which powers were delegated to IDA Ireland and Enterprise Ireland.

In 1998 Enterprise Ireland launched the National Linkage Program (NLP).[46] Under the program, NLP representatives would determine a foreign company's sourcing needs and match them with a potential supplier. However, as it became increasingly clear that local suppliers were simply unable to meet foreign standards, the NLP's focus shifted to one of a capacity-building role. Despite the NLP's best efforts, surveys evaluating the program concluded that a ceiling of about 20% of material purchases from within Ireland had been reached. Furthermore, these surveys suggested that it was highly unlikely that this ceiling would be broken, given the inability of local suppliers to produce goods and services for the sophisticated technology sector. The program was scrapped by the end of the decade, vindicating some observers who questioned the long-term benefit of FDI-led growth. As Sean Dorgan, CEO of the IDA, noted, "Perhaps in the past we focused too explicitly on creating linkages. There was an air of protectionism about it." Linkages were hard to measure, but the IDA used as a proxy foreign companies' direct expenditure in the economy.[47] The debate on the question of linkages, which had been at the center of FDI policy in Ireland, was particularly contentious because some believed that linkages alone would spur job growth and the development of a local sub-supplier industry. But some studies concluded that foreign firms tended to have lower linkages than domestic firms and that there were sectoral differences in the extent of linkages created.[48]

Academics who analyzed the interaction of foreign and domestic Irish firms claimed that, in fact, there was little "product-market competition" between the two. The reason behind this, they argued, lay in the different origins and structures of foreign and domestic firms. Foreign firms were largely focused on export markets beyond the U.K., and 80% of their exports came from the chemicals and pharmaceuticals sectors; domestic firms, on the other hand, continued to export primarily to the U.K., and only 10% of their exports came from the chemicals and pharmaceuticals sectors.[49] While the linkages question continued to be debated in Irish policy circles, by the mid-1990s, the falling unemployment rate seemed to vindicate the FDI supporters. In 1998, statistics showed that 47% of the industrial workforce (generating 82% of industrial output) was employed by foreign-owned firms and that some 75% of this FDI came from the United States. Furthermore, data also showed that U.S. foreign affiliates were responsible for 16.5% of Ireland's GDP.[50]

With new employment data as another measure of success, FDI supporters continued to emphasize the positive impact of foreign firms on the Irish economy. Amongst other benefits, supporters pointed out that FDI had brought in substantial corporate tax revenues and additional tax revenues from income tax and indirect taxes.[51] They also pointed out that given the small size of the Irish economy, even the launch of a single new product by an MNC would have a positive effect on economic growth; for example when Pfizer introduced its Irish-produced Viagra, the Irish output of organic chemical products rose by 70%.[52]

Macroeconomic data also supported their claims. Between 1995 and 1999 MNCs directly accounted for 85% of economic growth,[53] though this growth was largely concentrated within three manufacturing sectors—chemicals, computers, and electrical engineering (see **Exhibit 8** for manufacturing ownership and output data). Furthermore, by the late 1990s, Ireland boasted all the big names in the IT industry: Gateway, Dell, AST, Apple, Hewlett-Packard, and Siemens Nixdorf in PCs; Intel, Fujitsu, Xilinx, and Analog Devices in integrated circuits; Seagate and Quantum in disk drives; and Microsoft, Lotus, and Oracle in software (see **Exhibit 9** for software industry statistics). Together these sectors alone accounted for 40% of Irish GDP growth during the 1990s and for 78% of industrial growth in 1998.[54]

While rising FDI had been the theme of the 1990s, the global downturn of 2001 contributed to a large reduction in FDI inflows in Ireland. A 13% job loss at IDA-supported companies accompanied this downward trend and subsequently raised concerns about Ireland's vulnerability to external forces (see **Exhibit 10** for employment in IDA-supported companies and **Exhibit 11** for wages in Ireland). While many saw Ireland's reliance on foreigners as a serious threat, Dorgan claimed it was the inevitable result of globalization. He explained, "Our open economy reduces the distinction between foreign and Irish firms. Global supply is now the reality."[55] Ireland had certainly embraced globalization, topping A.T. Kearney's Globalization Index from 2002 to 2004. Nonetheless, others refuted Dorgan's rationale. Frank Kenny, founder of Delta Partners and a member of the ESG, said:

> The standard line about globalization making global and local firms the same is basically untrue. For example, the senior management of CRH[56] is based in Ireland, so the major decisions are made by people who live and work here. Their kids go to school in Ireland, and they will fight harder to make money here. The fact that CRH is a public company with majority foreign ownership is largely irrelevant.

As FDI dependency and vulnerability entered the narrative of the debate, some commentators worried that the boom was purely a by-product of American growth rather than a self-sustaining, local phenomenon. According to them, Ireland's success at attracting U.S. high-tech companies to its shores in the 1990s coincided with the longest bull market in American history and unparalleled booms in many of the industries targeted by the IDA. Ireland piggybacked on this growth, which led to claims that the Celtic Tiger itself was an illusion—that Ireland's growth was primarily caused by its attachment to the powerhouse U.S. economy.

A journalist lamented Ireland's overdependence: "The fact that we're too reliant on the U.S. is a truism. We're totally plugged into the American economy, and our dependence is made worse by linkages. If Dell pulls out of Ireland, the local haulage company that serves it is in trouble. Many local companies rely on foreign firms for oxygen."[57]

Other attempts to explain the Irish boom focused on the catch-up theory—the inevitable result of prudent economic policies after decades of mismanagement. Worse, some declared the boom to be a chimera born of shady transfer pricing. Low corporate tax rates enticed multinationals to inflate the profits of their Irish subsidiaries. This was often accomplished by booking internal transactions at transfer prices that served to locate a large percentage of the firm's global profits in Ireland.[58] Some observers believed such practices exaggerated Ireland's GDP figures to such an extent that they rendered its economic performance entirely misleading. Others countered that growth rates—as opposed to absolute output levels—remained largely unaffected by transfer-pricing issues. Brian Cogan of Forfás denied the notion that the boom was a fabrication: "Transfer pricing alone would just show up as money flowing in and then out again. It wouldn't explain the decreased unemployment, increased skill level of workers, and higher income levels in the country."[59] Although the impact on Irish GDP was hard to quantify, it was notable that four thriving FDI sectors—cola concentrates, software, pharmaceuticals, and computers—were particularly well placed to benefit from transfer pricing.[60]

The Future of the Irish Economy

The Celtic era, with double-digit growth rates, belongs to the past. Competitiveness has deteriorated.
—OECD Economic Outlook, December 2003

As the new decade dawned, a global slowdown, caused mainly by the American recession, had put the brakes on the Irish economy for the first time in 11 years. The IDA announced record job losses in foreign-owned companies, and the numbers employed in the IT sector fell 11% in 2001 after several high-profile closures, including those of Motorola, Gateway, and General Semiconductors.[61] Ireland faced the threat of new competition from countries in eastern Europe as well as constant pressure from the EU to increase the corporate tax rate, which rose from 10% to 12.5% in 2003 (see **Exhibit 12** for comparative European corporate tax rates and **Exhibits 13a** and **13b** for comparative economic data). While this tax rate was still one of the lowest in Europe, it raised the specter of future tax increases and called into question the sustainability of the low tax rate. Some scholars suggested that as much as 80% of Ireland's FDI inflow was due to its low corporate tax rate,[62] a contention forcefully refuted by an official at Forfás, who noted, "Tax was hugely important, but it wasn't enough on its own."[63]

Ironically, Ireland's economic success of the 1990s had eroded many of its former competitive advantages. Inflation ran well above the EU average, making it the second most expensive country in the Eurozone (after Finland) and prompting widespread use of the term "Rip-off Ireland" by the public and media. Ireland had become an expensive place to do business. Even substantial immigration could not prevent labor shortages, which in turn drove up private-sector wages and put pressure on unions to respond. Fears abounded that social partnership would collapse as unions sought their share of the new wealth. McGowan explained how the backdrop had changed: "In the 1980s, everyone could agree on the need to reduce unemployment. It's not so clear now that people will subordinate their own interests for the national well-being."[64]

The IDA swiftly began to reposition the country, using Ireland's EU membership, educated workforce, and its low wages and tax rate as major selling points. The IDA wanted "to place Ireland at the leading edge of the global economy . . . and [adopt a] broader vision of what constitutes FDI, with less emphasis on job numbers, and a much greater focus on job quality, higher value added activities, and making Ireland a centre for innovation and the strategic management of value chains, rather than just a manufacturing or basic service location."[65] The objective was to reduce Ireland's dependence on manufacturing by targeting underrepresented portions of the value chain such as research and development (R&D), sales, and marketing. The ESG outlined the considerable challenge ahead: "Much of the foreign-owned sector is, by global standards, still positioned at a relatively low point in the value chain. The research and development, marketing and other capabilities that underpin the competitive strength of these enterprises are not for the most part located in their Irish operations."[66]

Prying such activities away from corporate headquarters would not be easy. The IDA believed companies tended to keep R&D close to home, and Ireland did not have an international reputation as a research hub. Furthermore, its peripheral location isolated it from large markets, making sales and marketing more difficult.

Despite the challenges, the IDA was successful in winning approximately 10% of American FDI in Europe in 2003.[67] Once momentum developed in a sector, "reference selling" made it easier to convince the next player to move to Ireland. By 2004, 13 of the world's top 15 pharmaceutical companies had bases in Ireland, 16 of the top 20 medical-device companies, and 7 of the top 10 software designers.[68]

There were some high-profile successes in the technology sector as well. Shortly before going public in 2004, Google established its European headquarters in Dublin. Although the company's celebrated product development function remained in Silicon Valley, the Irish office gained responsibility for online sales and operations in the Europe, Middle East, and Africa markets. A Google manager explained the move:

> There were two determining factors: low tax and a multilingual labor force. Ireland provided a very favorable tax environment, as did Switzerland and the Netherlands, and we were very impressed with the number of different languages available. We could get languages in Switzerland too, but at a much higher labor cost. We didn't feel we could get the same variety of languages in the Netherlands. Furthermore, the IDA was tremendously supportive throughout.[69]

At about the same time, Wyeth, the $16 billion U.S. pharmaceutical company, announced plans to invest 1.5 billion euros in an R&D operation in Ireland, helped in part by a new tax concession for R&D investments introduced by the government in 2004. The development of clusters[70] and stronger links between universities and businesses was seen as crucial to creating a fertile R&D environment, and Science Foundation Ireland (SFI) was established in 2003 to encourage cooperation between education, government, and industry. SFI planned to invest $652 million between 2000 and 2006 in academic researchers and research teams in two fields: biotechnology, and information and communications technology.[71]

The IDA was central to these developments, but some commentators wondered if the agency was overstretching itself. Its *raison d'être* had always been to create jobs, and its success could therefore be easily measured. In an era of full employment, however, the emphasis had shifted from quantity to quality of jobs, and it became harder to assess the IDA's performance. Moreover, the EU was expected to impose limits in 2006 on state aid to firms, thereby removing one tool at the IDA's disposal. More troubling still, the 10 new entrants to the EU threatened Ireland's status as the European export platform of choice. Their low costs and plentiful labor contrasted starkly with the "new" Ireland. Even Ireland's language advantage was neutralized by the prevalence of English throughout eastern Europe. Ireland's tax edge was also under fire, with pressure from Brussels to harmonize corporate taxes throughout the EU, as many Eastern European countries, such as Slovakia, were adopting low tax rates.

Looking Ahead

Ireland's performance since 1987 had been extraordinary, but future growth was expected to be more modest. An IDA economist remarked: "We threw four aces in a row in the 1990s and that won't happen again—but it doesn't have to happen again."[72] Although the Irish had become accustomed to economic success, Dorgan denied that complacency was inevitable: "Perhaps all rich countries get fat and lazy. But I believe we still have the hunger."[73]

Identifying the cause of the boom was crucial to sustaining it, and Ireland's future depended on the lessons learned from the Celtic Tiger years. If growth had been driven by FDI, as the ESG believed, then perhaps the focus should continue to be on attracting better investment from abroad. But what if FDI had not been the primary cause? Was Ireland too dependent on foreigners? Could scarce resources be better spent on reforming education, improving infrastructure, or encouraging indigenous enterprise? Policymakers had many choices going forward.

Exhibit 1a FDI Flows in Ireland, by Type of Investment, 1974–2001 (US$ millions)

Year	1975	1980	1985	1990	1995	2000	2001	2002	2003	2004
Inward Investment										
Equity	n.a.	n.a.	n.a.	n.a.	n.a.	-12728	8879	13771	6240	-8911
Reinvested Earnings	n.a.	n.a.	n.a.	660	2006	9698	9267	13796	19370	11345
Other	158	287	164	-33	-560	28530	-8573	1564	989	8918
Total	158	287	164	628	1447	25501	9573	29131	26599	11352
Outward Investment										
Equity	n.a.	n.a.	n.a.	n.a.	n.a.	3501	1427	9033	714	n.a.
Reinvested Earnings	n.a.	n.a.	n.a.	365	820	1293	2016	2141	2675	n.a.
Other	n.a.	n.a.	n.a.	n.a.	n.a.	-154	660	-2650	139	6565
Total	n.a.	n.a.	n.a.	365	820	4641	4103	8524	3528	6565

Source: Adapted from United Nations Conference on Trade and Development (UNCTAD), Foreign Direct Investment (FDI) database.

Exhibit 1b Ireland: Foreign Direct Inflows (US$ millions)

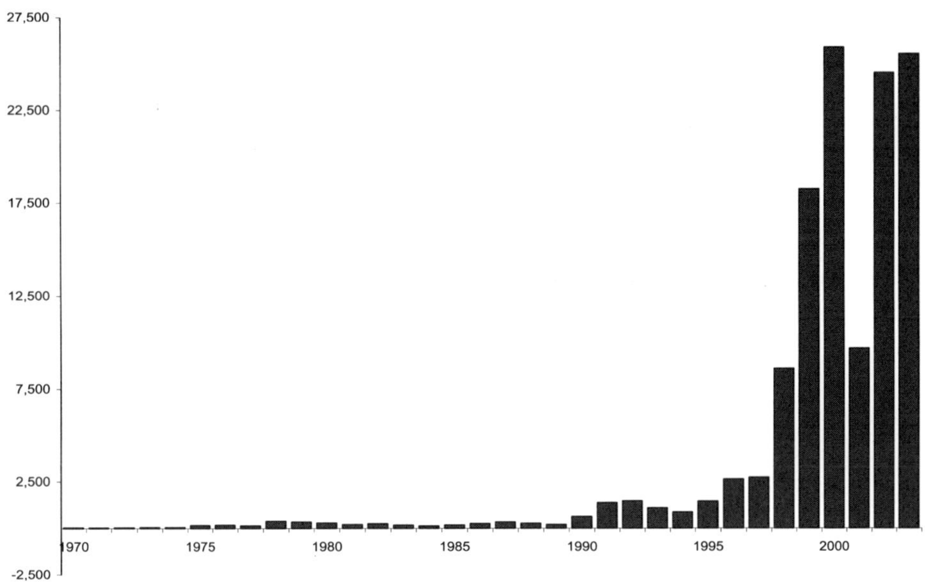

Source: Adapted from UNCTAD, FDI database.

Exhibit 2 Ireland

Source: CIA World Factbook, CIA website, http://www.cia.gov/cia/publications/factbook/geos/ei.html.

Exhibit 3 National Accounts and Other Economic Data

	1960	1970	1980	1985	1990	1995	2000	2001	2002	2003	2004	2005
GDP (constant LCU, millions)	**15,062**	**18,093**	**36,080**	**40,919**	**51,497**	**64,589**	**103,065**	**109,257**	**115,958**	**120,195**	**126,051**	**131,975**
General government final consumption	3,259	5,067	9,352	9,760	9,425	10,786	14,391	16,019	17,359	17,816	18,340	n.a.
Gross capital formation	n.a.	n.a.	9,895	9,120	12,044	13,237	26,140	25,253	25,771	27,092	29,056	n.a.
Change in Inventories	n.a.	n.a.	-2,989	-911	887	856	780	1,091	1,512	1,349	483	n.a.
Household final consumption	11,255	13,159	23,592	23,995	28,547	33,249	48,144	50,665	51,999	53,343	55,053	n.a.
Exports of goods and services	2,179	5,396	10,963	16,191	24,771	45,178	100,720	109,170	115,365	114,468	119,500	n.a.
Imports of goods and services	3,089	7,850	14,734	17,235	24,177	38,717	87,110	92,941	96,047	93,872	96,381	n.a
as a % of GDP												
General government final consumption	21.6	22.3	25.9	23.9	18.3	16.7	14.0	14.7	15.0	14.8	14.5	n.a.
Gross capital formation	n.a.	n.a.	27.4	22.3	23.4	20.5	25.4	23.1	22.2	22.5	23.1	n.a.
Change in Inventories	n.a.	n.a.	-8.3	-2.2	1.7	1.3	0.8	1.0	1.3	1.1	0.4	n.a.
Household final consumption	74.7	69.3	65.4	58.6	55.4	51.5	46.7	46.4	44.8	44.4	43.7	n.a.
Exports of goods and services	14.5	23.8	30.4	39.6	48.1	69.9	97.7	99.9	99.5	95.2	94.8	n.a
Imports of goods and services	20.5	34.6	40.8	42.1	46.9	59.9	84.5	85.1	82.8	78.1	76.5	n.a
GDP (current LCU, millions)	869	2,231	12,891	24,500	36,312	52,530	103,065	115,432	127,992	134,786	146,279	157,915
GDP (current US$, millions)	1,917	4,217	20,863	20,404	47,299	66,326	94,956	103,295	120,452	152,129	181,623	196,388
GDP per capita (constant 2000 US$)	4897	7095	9774	10650	13533	16521	24902	26046	27184	27715	28546	29295
GDP per capita growth (annual % change)		4.1	3.1	1.7	4.9	4.1	8.6	4.6	4.4	2.0	3.0	2.6
GDP per capita, PPP (current international $)	..	..	5605	8519	12720	17816	30532	33348	36264	37171	38827	40942
GNI per capita, PPP (current international $)	..	..	5600	7870	11710	16130	26400	28280	30000	31150	32930	34720
Other Data												
GDP deflator (2000 = 100)	5.8	9.8	35.7	59.9	70.5	81.3	100.0	105.7	110.4	112.1	116.0	119.7
Annual % change		6.1	14.6	10.9	3.3	2.9	4.2	5.7	4.5	1.6	3.5	3.1
Consumer price index (2000 = 100)	6.5	10.3	37.1	66.2	77.9	88.2	100.0	104.9	109.8	113.6	116.1	118.9
Annual % change		5.3	14.1	12.3	3.3	2.5	2.5	4.9	4.7	3.5	2.2	2.4
Productivity Index (1985=100)				100.0	118.0	133.7	163.3	168.1	174.3	177.6	181.9	187.0
Annual % change					3.4	2.5	4.1	2.9	3.7	1.9	2.4	2.8
Population, total (millions)	2.8	3.0	3.4	3.5	3.5	3.6	3.8	3.9	3.9	4.0	4.1	4.2
Unemployment, total (% of total labor force)	n.a.	n.a.	n.a.	16.7	13.0	12.2	4.3	3.7	4.2	4.4	4.4	n.a.

Source: Adapted from World Development Indicators (WDI), World Bank.

Note: All raw data has been taken from the WDI database. Expenditure as a percentage of GDP as well as change in inventories has been manually calculated.

Exhibit 4 Government Finances (billions of Irish pounds)

Year	1980	1985	1990	1995	2000	2001	2002	2003	2004
Budget revenue	4.7	10.4	14.7	20.8	37.5	39.8	43.1	46.5	49.8
Budget expenditure	6.0	12.9	15.7	21.9	33.0	38.7	43.3	46.3	49.6
Budget balance	-1.3	-2.5	-1.0	-1.1	4.6	1.1	-0.2	0.2	0.2
Debt interest payments	0.5	1.6	2.2	2.1	0.9	0.2	0.2	0.3	0.3
Primary balance	-0.8	-0.8	1.2	1.0	5.5	1.3	0.0	0.5	0.5
Public debt	8.3	n.a.	34.6	44.6	43.3	42.2	43.5	43.5	44.3
As a % of GDP									
Budget revenue		43.5	40.4	39.4	36.4	34.5	33.7	34.5	34.1
Budget expenditure		53.8	43.2	41.5	32.0	33.5	33.8	34.3	33.9
Budget balance		-10.3	-2.8	-2.1	4.4	1.0	-0.2	0.2	0.2
Debt interest payments	4.3	6.8	6.2	4.0	0.9	0.2	0.2	0.2	0.2
Primary balance	-6.2	-3.5	3.4	1.9	5.3	1.1	0.0	0.4	0.3
Public debt	66.4	n.a.	95.4	84.7	42.1	36.6	34.0	32.3	30.3
Exchange rate									
Pound:US$ (av)	0.72	1.31	0.79	0.76	1.08	1.12	1.06	0.88	0.80

Source: Adapted from Economist Intelligence Unit.

Exhibit 5 Balance of Payments (US$ billions)

	1975	1980	1985	1990	1995	2000	2001	2002	2003	2004	2005
Goods Exports	3.0	8.2	10.1	23.3	44.4	73.5	77.6	84.2	88.6	100.1	104.1
Goods Imports	-3.5	-10.5	-9.5	-19.4	-30.9	-48.5	-50.4	-50.8	-51.7	-61.1	-67.3
Trade Balance	-0.5	-2.2	0.6	3.9	13.6	25.0	27.3	33.4	36.9	39.0	36.8
Services: Credit	0.6	1.4	1.3	3.4	5.0	18.5	23.5	29.9	42.1	52.7	57.3
Services: Debit	-0.5	-1.6	-1.5	-5.2	-11.3	-31.3	-35.3	-42.8	-54.6	-65.4	-69.8
Balance on Goods and Services	-0.5	-2.4	0.4	2.2	7.3	12.3	15.4	20.5	24.3	26.3	24.3
Income: Credit	0.3	0.8	0.8	3.3	5.1	27.6	28.9	27.2	34.1	43.5	53.9
Income: Debit	-0.4	-1.7	-2.9	-8.2	-12.4	-41.2	-45.2	-49.5	-58.9	-71.4	-84.2
Balance on Goods and Services and Income	-0.5	-3.3	-1.7	-2.7	-0.1	-1.3	-1.0	-1.8	-0.4	-1.6	-6.0
Current Transfers, Net	0.4	1.2	1.0	2.4	1.8	0.8	0.3	0.7	0.5	0.5	0.7
Current Account	-0.1	-2.1	-0.7	-0.4	1.7	-0.5	-0.7	-1.1	0.1	-1.1	-5.3
Capital Account, N.I.E.	0.0	0.0	0.1	0.4	0.8	1.1	0.6	0.5	0.1	0.4	0.3
Direct Investment Abroad	0.0	0.0	0.0	-0.4	-0.8	-4.6	-4.1	-11.1	-5.6	-18.1	-13.8
Direct Investments in Rep. Econ	0.2	0.3	0.2	0.6	1.4	25.5	9.6	29.5	22.4	-11.0	-29.7
Portfolio Investments, Assets	0.0	0.0	-0.1	-0.5	-1.1	-83.1	-111.3	-105.5	-163.8	-168.9	-148.4
Portfolio Investments, Liabilities	0.1	0.2	1.1	0.3	0.8	77.9	89.1	69.4	119.4	186.5	213.5
Other Investments Assets	-0.5	-0.5	0.0	-5.3	-16.6	-37.0	-21.4	-33.2	-65.9	-57.4	-134.1
Other Investments Liabilities	0.7	2.8	-0.1	3.2	16.2	28.9	37.9	49.8	90.5	71.2	117.7
Other, Net	0.0	0.0	0.0	0.0	0.0	0.4	0.4	1.6	-0.5	1.0	-8.2
Financial Account, N.I.E.	0.5	2.7	1.1	-2.0	0.0	7.9	0.0	0.5	-3.5	3.3	-3.0
Net Errors and Omissions	0.0	0.1	-0.4	2.6	-0.2	-8.5	0.4	-0.2	1.4	-4.0	6.2
Reserve Assets	-0.3	-0.7	0.0	-0.6	-2.3	-0.1	-0.4	0.3	1.9	1.4	1.8
Balance of Payments as a % of GDP											
Current Account	-1.4	-10.2	-3.6	-0.8	2.6	-0.5	-0.7	-0.9	0.1	-0.6	-2.7
Goods Exports	33.3	39.4	49.7	49.3	67.0	77.4	75.1	69.9	58.2	55.1	53.0
Goods Imports	-38.7	-50.1	-46.6	-41.0	-46.5	-51.1	-48.8	-42.1	-34.0	-33.6	-34.3
Trade Balance	-5.3	-10.7	3.1	8.3	20.4	26.3	26.4	27.8	24.2	21.5	18.7
GDP (current US$ Billion)	9.1	20.9	20.4	47.3	66.3	95.0	103.3	120.5	152.1	181.6	196.4

Source: Adapted from IMF, International Financial Statistics database, and World Development Indicators (WDI), World Bank.

Exhibit 6 Linkages of Foreign Firms in Manufacturing: Irish Raw Materials as a Percentage of Total Raw Material Purchases

	1986	1989	1992	1995
Nonfood manufacturing	16.2%	16.5%	19.2%	19.8%
(millions)	£353	£546	£734	£1,326

Source: Adapted from Forfás, *Shaping Our Future: A Strategy for Enterprise in Ireland in the 21st Century*, 1996.

Note: Excluding food, drink, and tobacco.

Exhibit 7a Survey of Economic Impact of IDA-Supported Companies (euro billions)

Survey	1999	2000	2001	2002
Sales	42.9	64.02	67.79	69.34
Exports	38.2	58.22	63.14	65.17
Direct expenditure in the economy	11.6	14.26	14.93	14.73
of which:				
Payroll costs	4.0	5.04	5.44	5.34
Irish materials	4.7	4.28	4.51	4.38
Irish services	3.0	4.94	4.98	5.01
Direct expenditure as % of sales	27.1	22.30%	22.00%	21.20%

Source: Adapted from the Annual Business Survey of Economic Impact, coordinated by Forfás and administered by the Survey Unit of the Economic and Social Research Institute (ESRI).

Note: The survey is based on manufacturing and internationally traded services companies with 10 or more employees (excluding IFSC companies). Results can vary from previous estimates due to revisions made by companies and differences in the base of respondents from one survey period to the next.

Exhibit 7b Origins of IDA-Supported Companies, 2003

Origin	No. of Companies	Total Employment
U.S.	489	89,158
Germany	149	11,394
U.K.	118	8,086
Rest of Europe	214	15,602
Asia Pacific	44	2,937
Rest of the World	40	1,816
Total	1,054	12,8993

Source: Adapted from the Annual Business Survey of Economic Impact, coordinated by Forfás and administered by the Survey Unit of the Economic and Social Research Institute (ESRI).

Exhibit 7c IDA Presence: Domestic and International

Source: IDA Ireland website, http://www.idaireland.com/home/index.aspx?id=81, accessed July 17, 2005.

Exhibit 8 Total Manufacturing

Nationality of Ownership	No. of Plants	Total Persons Engaged	Gross Output	Percent of Imported Materials Purchased	Percent of Gross Output Exported
Irish	3,854	111,167	10,379	21.7	35.3
Other EU	318	33,345	3,373	58.4	61.9
of which U.K.	112	12,763	1,575	45.1	39.0
of which Germany	100	10,866	636	79.6	92.3
Non-EU	372	55,491	11,152	68.0	92.8
of which U.S.	267	42,806	8,814	64.3	96.0
Total foreign	690	88,836	14,525	65.6	85.6
Total	4,544	200,003	24,904	42.3	64.7

Source: Census of Industrial Production. Adapted from Frank Barry and John Bradley, "FDI and Trade: the Irish host-country experience," paper presented at the Royal Economics Society Annual Conference, University of Staffordshire, March 24–26, 1993.

Exhibit 9 Software Industry Statistics, 1991–1997

	1991		1993		1995		1997	
	Total	Percent	Total	Percent	Total	Percent	Total	Percent
Total Number of Firms	365	100%	417	100%	483	100%	679	100%
Irish Owned	291	80%	336	81%	390	81%	561	83%
Foreign Owned	74	20%	81	19%	93	19%	118	17%
Total Employment	7,793	100%	8,943	100%	11,784	100%	18,300	100%
Irish Owned	3,801	49%	4,495	50%	5,773	49%	9,200	50%
Foreign Owned	3,992	51%	4,448	50%	6,011	51%	9,100	50%
Total Revenue ($M)	2,699	100%	3,107	100%	4,735	100%	6,245	100%
Irish Owned	234	9%	368	12%	610	13%	739	12%
Foreign Owned	2,465	91%	2,739	88%	4,125	87%	5,506	88%
Total Exports ($M)	2,510	100%	2,872	100%	4,442	100%	5,908	100%
Irish Owned	95	4%	181	6%	357	8%	511	9%
Foreign Owned	2,415	96%	2,691	94%	4,085	92%	5,397	91%

Source: Adapted from Paul. P. Tallon and Kenneth. L. Kraemer, "The Impact of Technology on Ireland's Economic Growth and Development: Lessons for Developing Countries," proceedings of the 32nd Hawaii International Conference on System Sciences, 1999.

Exhibit 10 Employment in IDA-Supported Companies

	1991	1992	1993	1994	1995	1996	1997	1998	1999	2000	2001	2002	2003
New jobs filled	6,904	7,075	8,216	9,961	11,958	13,220	14,685	15,946	17,613	22,994	12,802	11,059	9,182
Number of companies	847	857	876	908	961	1,037	1,099	1,158	1,266	1,250	1,148	1,102	1,054
Full-time employment	75,018	76,218	78,915	85,597	92,424	99,583	108,231	117,864	126,199	141,125	136,277	132,004	128,993
Net change in full-time employment	1,278	1,200	2,697	4,493	6,827	7,159	9,648	8,633	8,335	14,926	-4,848	-4,273	-3,011
% net change	1.70%	1.60%	3.50%	6.30%	8.00%	7.70%	9.70%	7.90%	7.10%	11.80%	-3.40%	-3.10%	-2.30%
Job losses	5,626	-5,875	-5,519	-5,468	-5,131	-6,061	-5,037	-7,313	-9,278	-8,068	-17,650	-15,332	-12,193
Job losses as % of total jobs	7.50%	7.70%	7.00%	-6.40%	-5.60%	-6.10%	-4.60%	-6.20%	-7.40%	-5.70%	-13.00%	-11.60%	-9.50%
Other employment	3,444	4,288	5,334	9,022	11,579	9,488	13,540	15,195	15,665	14,802	12,395	12,362	14,577

Source: Adapted from Forfás Employment Survey, IDA Annual Report 2000, 2003.

Exhibit 11 Wages and Salaries of Affiliates of Foreign TNCs in Ireland, by Industry and Geographic Origin (2000)

Sector/Industry/Region/Economy	Total World	Developed Countries	European Union	Belgium	Denmark	France	Germany	Netherlands	Sweden	United Kingdom	Unspecified EU	North America	Canada	United States	Japan	Unspecified
Total	2712.8	2589	812.4	18.4	73.6	82.2	208.6	50.4	15.7	292.1	71.2	1716	46	1669.7	61.2	123.7
Secondary	2712.8	2589	812.4	18.4	73.6	82.2	208.6	50.4	15.7	292.1	71.2	1716	46	1669.7	61.2	123.7
Food, beverages and tobacco	348.3	10.3	10.3								10.3					338
Textiles and clothing and leather	59.5															59.5
Wood and wood products	44.5															44.5
Publishing and printing	158.4															158.4
Chemicals and chemical products	466.2	401	124				34.7			37.4	51.9	277		277		65.2
Rubber and plastic products	74.5	54.5	39.3				19.7			3.8	15.7	15.3		15.3		
Non-metallic mineral products	36.9	36.9	20.8								20.8	16.1		16.1		20
Metal and metal products	82.7	26	26				13.3			4.8	7.8					56.6
Machinery and equipment	134.8	118.7	53.6				22.5			6.1	25	65.1		65.1		16.1
Electrical and electrical equipment	827.7	1037.4	107.6				43.7			8	55.8	929.9		929.9		-209.7
Precision instruments	287.3															287.3
Motor vehicles and other transport equipment	136	136	111.7								111.7	24.3		24.3		
Other manufacturing	53.1															53.1
Unspecified secondary	2.9	768.2	319.1	18.4	73.6	82.2	74.7	50.4	15.7	232	-227.8	387.9	46	342	61.2	-765.3

Source: Adapted from Forfás Employment Survey, IDA Annual Report 2000, 2003 and United Nations Conference on Trade and Development, UNCTAD, WID.

Exhibit 12 Comparative European Corporate Tax Rates for Substantial Distributed Trading Profits

Country	Tax Rate
Ireland	12.5%
Cyprus	15.0%
Latvia	15.0%
Lithuania	15.0%
Hungary	16.0%
Poland	19.0%
Luxembourg	22.9%
Portugal	25.0%
Slovenia	25.0%
Estonia	26.0%
Germany	26.4%
Czech Republic	28.0%
Sweden	28.0%
Finland	29.0%
Slovakia	29.0%
Denmark	30.0%
U.K.	30.0%
Italy	33.0%
France	33.3%
Belgium	34.0%
Austria	34.0%
Netherlands	34.5%
Greece	35.0%
Malta	35.0%
Spain	35.0%

Source: Adapted from IDA Ireland website, http://www.idaireland.com/home/index.aspx?id=659.

Exhibit 13a Selected EU Countries: Comparative Data

Year	Country	GDP (current US$ Millions)	GDP growth (annual %)	GDP per capita, PPP (current int'l $)	GNI (current US$ Millions)	FDI, net inflows (% of GDP)	FDI, net inflows (% of gross capital formation)	Market Cap. of listed companies (% of GDP)
1985	Cyprus	2,418	4.9	8,158	2,426	2.4	7.9	..
	Czech Republic	..	..	..	..	..	..	..
	Estonia	..	0.5	6,171	..	..	..	..
	France	548,993	2.0	14,182	548,050	0.5	2.4	..
	Greece	41,977	2.5	9,741	42,534	1.1	4.1	..
	Hungary	20,623	-0.3	7,870	19,756	..	..	..
	Ireland	**20,644**	**3.1**	**8,718**	**19,000**	**0.8**	**4.2**	**..**
	Latvia	..	-0.4	6,104	..	..	..	..
	Lithuania	..	..	..	..	..	..	..
	Portugal	25,931	2.8	7,630	24,358	1.1	4.9	..
	UK	455,534	3.6	12,979	451,059	1.2	6.5	..
1995	Cyprus	8,861	6.1	15,648	8,957	2.7	12.5	28.4
	Czech Republic	55,257	6.0	13,144	55,153	4.7	14.3	28.4
	Estonia	4,331	4.5	6,290	4,333	4.7	17.5	..
	France	1,570,256	2.2	22,251	1,573,219	1.5	8.1	33.3
	Greece	120,152	2.1	13,612	123,837	0.9	4.7	14.2
	Hungary	44,656	1.5	9,703	42,967	10.8	47.6	5.4
	Ireland	**67,104**	**9.6**	**17,844**	**60,561**	**2.2**	**11.8**	**38.5**
	Latvia	5,236	-1.0	5,258	5,259	3.4	24.0	0.2
	Lithuania	7,621	3.3	6,302	7,569	1.0	4.3	2.1
	Portugal	112,960	4.3	14,439	112,630	0.6	2.6	16.3
	UK	1,133,633	2.9	21,326	1,129,173	1.9	11.3	124.2
2000	Cyprus	9,147	5.0	19,175	8,603	9.4	..	47.6
	Czech Republic	56,721	3.7	15,450	55,351	8.8	30.0	19.4
	Estonia	5,623	7.9	9,392	5,420	6.9	24.0	32.8
	France	1,327,963	4.0	27,244	1,346,197	3.2	15.6	108.9
	Greece	114,601	4.5	17,057	115,490	1.0	4.0	96.7
	Hungary	47,958	5.2	12,977	45,383	5.8	19.0	25.1
	Ireland	**96,166**	**9.2**	**29,155**	**82,773**	**26.5**	**105.7**	**85.1**
	Latvia	7,833	6.9	7,975	7,814	5.3	22.2	7.2
	Lithuania	11,418	3.9	8,719	10,643	3.3	16.7	13.9
	Portugal	112,650	3.9	18,782	109,813	5.9	21.4	53.9
	UK	1,442,845	4.0	26,476	1,444,479	8.5	48.3	178.6
2005	Cyprus	..	..	..	..	..	..	..
	Czech Republic	123,981	6.1	20,845	117,495	..	..	30.9
	Estonia	13,748	10.5	15,968	13,055	21.8	61.8	25.4
	France	2,126,630	1.2	31,908	2,137,573	3.3	16.5	80.4
	Greece	225,206	3.7	23,377	221,054	0.3	1.2	64.4
	Hungary	110,364	4.3	18,256	103,599	5.8	24.7	29.5
	Ireland	**201,817**	**5.5**	**38,892**	**170,785**	**-14.7**	**..**	**56.6**
	Latvia	16,042	10.6	13,700	15,735	4.6	13.2	15.8
	Lithuania	25,652	7.6	14,584	23,922	4.0	16.1	31.9
	Portugal	183,305	0.4	21,125	180,291	1.8	7.8	36.54
	UK	2,201,591	1.8	33,135	2,249,441	7.2	42.9	138.9

Source: Adapted from World Development Indicators, World Bank

Exhibit 13b Selected EU Countries: Comparative Data

Year	Country	Unemployment Rate	Population, total (thousands)	Employment in agriculture (% of total)	Employment in industry (% of total)	Employment in services (% of total)	Secondary education (% of total)	Tertiary education (% of total)	Life expectancy at birth	Literacy rate, adult
1985	Cyprus	3.3	542	16.4	31.0	50.9	..	..	75.8	92.5
	Czech Rep.	..	10,335	12.1	47.7	40.2	..	..	71.0	..
	Estonia	..	1,529	..	..	..	..	..	70.0	99.8
	France	10.2	55,170	7.6	32.0	60.4	..	..	75.3	..
	Greece	7.8	9,934	28.9	27.4	43.7	..	..	75.0	93.2
	Hungary	..	10,579	..	..	..	..	..	69.0	98.8
	Ireland	**16.7**	**3,540**	**15.6**	**28.4**	**55.6**	**..**	**..**	**73.5**	**..**
	Latvia	..	2,621	..	..	..	..	..	69.3	99.8
	Lithuania	..	3,545	19.7	40.4	39.5	..	..	70.5	99.1
	Portugal	8.6	10,011	23.8	33.8	42.4	..	..	73.4	84.4
	UK	11.3	56,685	2.5	31.2	64.9	..	..	74.6	..
1995	Cyprus	..	651	10.7	25.3	63.0	..	..	77.5	95.8
	Czech Rep.	4.0	10,331	6.6	41.8	51.1	76.9	10.5	73.1	..
	Estonia	9.4	1,437	10.2	34.2	55.6	66.9	17.4	67.8	99.8
	France	11.6	57,844	1.6	27.0	71.4	..	..	77.8	..
	Greece	9.1	10,634	20.4	23.2	56.3	28.0	20.8	77.6	96.2
	Hungary	10.2	10,329	8.0	32.6	59.3	60.5	14.3	69.8	99.2
	Ireland	**12.2**	**3,609**	**11.6**	**28.1**	**59.9**	**31.8**	**24.3**	**75.8**	**..**
	Latvia	18.9	2,515	17.4	28.0	54.0	..	..	66.4	99.8
	Lithuania	17.1	3,632	23.8	28.2	48.0	..	..	69.0	99.5
	Portugal	7.2	10,027	11.5	31.9	56.6	..	..	75.1	89.9
	UK	8.6	58,250	2.0	27.3	70.1	45.0	22.3	76.8	..
2000	Cyprus	4.8	694	5.3	23.3	67.4	40.7	27.0	78.1	97.1
	Czech Rep.	8.8	10,273	5.1	39.5	55.3	78.2	11.3	75.0	..
	Estonia	12.8	1,370	7.2	33.3	59.5	46.4	41.2	70.9	99.8
	France	10.0	58,896	1.6	24.5	73.9	46.0	25.4	78.9	..
	Greece	11.1	10,918	17.4	22.6	60.0	29.9	27.9	78.0	97.2
	Hungary	6.4	10,211	6.5	33.7	59.7	65.2	16.4	71.2	99.3
	Ireland	**4.3**	**3,805**	**7.8**	**28.5**	**62.9**	**..**	**..**	**76.4**	**..**
	Latvia	14.0	2,372	14.5	26.3	59.1	..	..	70.4	99.7
	Lithuania	16.4	3,500	18.7	26.8	54.5	41.4	43.2	72.0	99.6
	Portugal	3.9	10,226	12.6	34.4	52.9	11.9	9.0	76.5	92.2
	UK	5.5	59,743	1.5	25.3	72.8	47.4	26.1	77.7	..
2005	Cyprus	4.7[a]	758	..	..	..	..	..	79.3	..
	Czech Rep.	8.3[a]	10,234	4.0	39.5	56.5	..	..	75.9	..
	Estonia	9.6[a]	1,346	5.3	34.0	60.7	..	..	72.6	..
	France	9.9[a]	60,873	..	..	..	..	..	80.2	..
	Greece	10.2[a]	11,104	12.4	22.4	65.1	..	..	79.0	..
	Hungary	6.1[a]	10,087	5.0	32.4	62.6	..	..	72.6	..
	Ireland	**4.4[a]**	**4,159**	**5.9**	**27.8**	**65.6**	**..**	**..**	**79.4**	**..**
	Latvia	8.7	2,301	12.1	25.8	61.8	..	..	71.4	..
	Lithuania	8.3	3,414	14.0	29.1	56.9	..	..	71.3	..
	Portugal	6.7[a]	10,549	..	..	..	..	..	78.1	..
	UK	4.6[a]	60,227	1.4	22.0	76.3	..	..	78.9	..

Source: Adapted from World Development Indicators, World Bank

[a] Unemployment figures for 2004.

Exhibit 14a Selected Asian Countries: Comparative Economic Data

Year	Country	GDP (current US$ Millions)	GDP growth (annual %)	GDP per capita, PPP (current int'l $)	GNI (current US$ Millions)	FDI, net inflows (% of GDP)	FDI, net inflows (% of gross capital formation)	Market capitalization (% of GDP)
1985	China	304,912	13.5	838	305,753	0.5	1.4	n.a.
	Hong Kong	35,531	0.2	10,125	34,868	..	..	n.a.
	Ireland	**20,644**	**3.1**	**8,718**	**19,000**	**0.8**	**4.2**	**n.a.**
	Korea, Rep.	96,619	6.8	4,533	94,289	0.2	...	n.a.
	Malaysia	31,772	-1.1	3,165	29,535	2.2	8.8	n.a.
	Singapore	17,743	-1.4	7,740	18,302	5.9	13.9	n.a.
1995	China	728,011	10.9	2,515	716,237	4.9	12.5	5.8
	Hong Kong	144,230	3.9	22,026	146,945	..	..	210.6
	Ireland	**67,104**	**9.6**	**17,844**	**60,561**	**2.2**	**11.9**	**38.5**
	Korea, Rep.	517,118	9.2	12,515	515,330	0.3	..	35.2
	Malaysia	88,832	9.8	7,057	84,689	4.7	10.8	250.7
	Singapore	84,291	8.2	18,219	86,424	13.7	40.2	175.6
2000	China	1,198,480	8.4	3,940	1,183,815	3.2	9.8	48.5
	Hong Kong	168,754	10.2	26,214	169,878	36.7	133.4	369.4
	Ireland	**96,166**	**9.2**	**29,155**	**82,773**	**26.5**	**105.7**	**85.1**
	Korea, Rep.	511,658	8.5	16,149	509,443	1.8	..	33.5
	Malaysia	90,320	8.9	8,573	82,712	4.2	15.5	129.5
	Singapore	92,717	10.1	23,594	91,975	17.8	42.2	164.8
2005	China	2,243,853	10.2	6,760	2,254,487	3.5	7.4	34.8
	Hong Kong	177,783	7.5	34,923	177,995	20.2	96.4	566.0
	Ireland	**201,817**	**5.5**	**38,892**	**170,785**	**-14.7**	**24.4**	**56.6**
	Korea, Rep.	791,427	4.2	22,080	790,239	0.5	4.1	90.7
	Malaysia	130,770	5.2	10,887	124,457	3.0	19.1	138.6
	Singapore	116,693	6.6	29,842	112,117	17.2	62.7	178.5

Source: Adapted from World Development Indicators, World Bank.

Exhibit 14b Selected Asian Countries: Comparative Economic Data

Year	Country	Unemployment (% of total)	Population (Millions)	Employment in agriculture (% of total)	Employment in industry (% of total)	Employment in services (% of total)	Tertiary education (% of total)	Life expectancy at birth (years)	Adult Literacy Rate
1985	China	1.8	1,051.0	..	..	..	n.a.	68.3	73.4
	Hong Kong	3.2	5.5	1.6	44.4	54.0	n.a.	76.4	..
	Ireland	**16.7**	**3.5**	**15.6**	**28.4**	**55.6**	**n.a.**	**73.5**	**..**
	Korea, Rep.	4.0	40.8	24.9	30.8	44.3	n.a.	68.5	..
	Malaysia	6.9	15.7	30.4	23.8	45.8	n.a.	68.9	76.3
	Singapore	4.4	2.7	0.7	35.2	63.7	n.a.	72.9	85.6
1995	China	2.9	1,204.9	48.5	21.0	12.2	..	69.4	81.9
	Hong Kong	3.2	6.2	0.6	27.0	72.4	..	78.7	..
	Ireland	**12.2**	**3.6**	**11.6**	**28.1**	**59.9**	**24.3**	**75.8**	**..**
	Korea, Rep.	2.1	45.1	12.4	33.3	54.2	19.2	73.4	..
	Malaysia	3.1	20.3	20.0	32.3	47.7	..	71.5	84.3
	Singapore	2.7	3.5	0.2	31.0	67.9	33.2	76.4	90.7
2000	China	3.1	1,262.6	46.3	17.3	12.7	..	70.3	90.9
	Hong Kong	4.9	6.7	0.3	20.3	79.4	..	80.9	..
	Ireland	**4.3**	**3.8**	**7.8**	**28.5**	**62.9**	**..**	**76.4**	**..**
	Korea, Rep.	4.1	47.0	10.6	28.1	61.2	24.0	75.9	..
	Malaysia	3.0	23.0	18.4	32.2	49.5	..	72.6	88.7
	Singapore	4.4	4.0	0.2	34.2	65.4	36.6	78.1	92.5
2005	China	4.2	1,304.5	..	..	..	n.a.	71.8	n.a.
	Hong Kong	..	6.9	0.3	15.2	84.6	n.a.	81.6	n.a.
	Ireland	**..**	**4.2**	**5.9**	**27.8**	**65.6**	**n.a.**	**79.4**	**n.a.**
	Korea, Rep.	..	48.3	7.9	26.8	65.1	n.a.	77.6	n.a.
	Malaysia	..	25.3	..	..	..	n.a.	73.7	n.a.
	Singapore	..	4.3	..	29.5	69.6	n.a.	79.7	n.a.

Source: Adapted from World Development Indicators, World Bank.

Endnotes

[1] Headline of the article introducing the Economist Intelligence Unit's Quality of Life Survey, *EIU World Report in 2005*, p. 86. The article adds, "Ireland wins because it successfully combines the most desirable elements of the new (the fourth highest GDP per head in the world in 2005, low unemployment, political liberties) with the preservation of certain cozy elements of the old, such as stable family and community life."

[2] "Survey: Tiger, Tiger, Burning Bright," *The Economist*, October 16, 2004, p. 4. Available from Proquest, ABI/Inform, http://www.proquest.com, accessed February 7, 2005.

[3] Calculations based on World Bank data and "Irish Economic Growth: A Brief History of the 1990's," *AIB Quarterly Economic Focus* (Autumn 2000). Allied Irish Banks website, www.fxcentre.com/jb/pdfs/quarterly/q3-2000-15.pdf, accessed February 14, 2005.

[4] "Irish Economic Growth: A Brief History of the 1990's," *AIB Quarterly Economic Focus.*

[5] For more information on the role of FDI in economic growth and the current debate see Laura Alfaro and Esteban Clavell, "Foreign Direct Investment," HBS No. 703-018 (Boston: Harvard Business School Publishing, 2002).

[6] Enterprise Strategy Group, "Ahead of the Curve: Ireland's Place in the Global Economy," July 5, 2004, Forfás website, http://www.forfas.ie/esg/, accessed February 7, 2005.

[7] "Tánaiste Launches Report of Enterprise Strategy Group," Press Release and Summary of Recommendations, July 7, 2004, Forfás website, http://www.forfas.ie/esg, accessed February 14, 2005.

[8] Enterprise Strategy Group, "Ahead of the Curve," p. 5.

[9] Average housing prices had more than doubled since 1995. Martin Wolf, "Ireland's Miracle," *The Financial Times*, July 19, 1999. Available from Factiva, http://www.factiva.com, accessed February 23, 2005.

[10]The European Union classified Ireland's regions into three different categories for structural fund disbursement purposes. "Objective One" regions were those whose development was lagging behind. Specifically, the threshold set for qualification required per capita income, as measured by GDP, to be less than 75% of the EU average. Since Ireland's GDP per head had reached more than 100% in 1998, the government decided to divide the country into two regions. The more affluent eastern and southern counties would experience a gradual phasing out of Objective One status, while 13 border, midland, and western counties retained Objective One status. It was estimated that by 2006, Ireland would be a net contributor to the EU budget and not a net beneficiary.

[11] Germany and Belgium, in particular, with 26% and 34% tax rates, respectively, objected to Ireland's low rate.

[12] For example see Laura Alfaro, Rafael Di Tella and Anne Damgaard Jensen "Rovna Da: The Flat Tax in Slovakia" With Rafael Di Tella and Anne Damgaard Jensen, HBS No. 707-043, 2007.

[13] J.W. O'Hagan, *The Economy of Ireland* (Dublin, Ireland: Gill & Macmillan, 2000), p. 30.

[14] Data and portions of this section were taken from Ray Mac Sharry and Padraic White, *The Making of the Celtic Tiger* (Cork, Ireland: Mercier Press, 2000.

[15] Richard Finnegan and Edward McCarron, *Ireland: Historical Echoes, Contemporary Politics* (Boulder, CO: Westview Press, 2000), p. 109.

[16] IDA had been formed in 1949, after contentious debate within government and civil service quarters (Mac Sharry, p. 187). Some had feared that the new organization would be nothing more than "a gang of crackpot socialist planners" who would hamper private enterprise (Mac Sharry, p. 184. Although IDA was established in 1949 as part of the Department of Industry & Commerce, its authority increased greatly in 1969 when it was incorporated as an autonomous state-sponsored body responsible for all aspects of industrial development.

[17] Mac Sharry and White, *The Making of the Celtic Tiger*, p. 187.

[18] Ibid., p. 190.

[19] Ibid., p. 235.

[20] Ibid., p. 30.

[21] J.J. Lee, *Ireland 1912–1985, Politics and Society* (Cambridge, England: Cambridge University Press, 1989), p. 531.

[22] Paul Tallon and Kenneth L. Kraemer, "Information Technology and Economic Development: Ireland's Coming of Age with Lessons for Developing Countries," Center for Research on Information Technology and Organizations, I.T. in Business, Paper 136, November 1, 1999. Available from http://repositories.cdlib.org/crito/business/136, accessed February 28, 2005.

[23] Lee, *Ireland 1912–1985*, p. 531.

[24] Tallon and Kraemer, "Information Technology and Economic Development."

[25] Lee, *Ireland 1912–1985*, p. 532.

[26] Ibid.

[27] Ibid.

[28] Ibid.

[29] Mac Sharry and White, *The Making of the Celtic Tiger*, p. 203.

[30] Lee, *Ireland 1912–1985*, pp. 535–536.

[31] Mac Sharry and White, *The Making of the Celtic Tiger*, p. 209.

[32] Ray Mac Sharry, "EIB Forum 2004 Speech," European Investment Bank website, http://www.eib.org/forum/docs/ s_macsharry.pdf, accessed February 7, 2005.

[33] Mac Sharry and White, *The Making of the Celtic Tiger*, pp. 68–70.

[34] Some observers cited demographics as a driver of Ireland's success, noting that Ireland's high birth rate in the 1960s and 1970s led to its having the youngest population in Europe by the 1980s. Others noted that young populations often have a destabilizing impact on sluggish economies and saw it as the fuel for growth rather than the trigger.

[35] J.W. O'Hagan, *The Economy of Ireland* (Dublin, Ireland: Gill & Macmillan, 2000), p. 38.

[36] Frank Barry, John Bradley, and Aoife Hannan, "The Single Market, The Structural Funds and Ireland's Recent Economic Growth," May 2001, p. 9.

[37] For more on the impact of corporate taxation on FDI, see M. J. Slaughter, "Host-Country Determinants of US foreign direct investment into Europe," in *Foreign direct investment in the real and financial sectors of industrial countries*, Hermann and Lipsey, eds. (Springer, 2003); and Altshuler, Gubert, and Newlon, "Has US investment abroad become more sensitive to tax rates?" in *International Taxation and Multinational Activity*, J.R. Hines, Jr., ed. (Chicago: University of Chicago Press, 2001). See also Desai, Foley, and Hines, "Chains of Ownership, regional tax competition and foreign direct investment," NBER Working Paper No. 9224, 2002b.

[38] Kieran McGowan, interview by author, Dublin, Ireland, November 5, 2004.

[39] A.V. Vedpuriswar, "Country Scan: Ireland," A.V. Vedpuriswar website, http://www.vedpuriswar.org/articles/ GCEO/Ireland.PDF, accessed February 7, 2005.

[40] Mac Sharry and White, *The Making of the Celtic Tiger*, pp. 219–220.

[41] Colin Coulter and Steve Coleman, eds., *The End of Irish History?: Critical Reflections on the Celtic Tiger* (Manchester, England: Manchester University Press, 2003), p. 38.

[42] Thomas Friedman, "The End of the Rainbow," *The New York Times*, June 29, 2005.

[43] Brian Cogan, interview by author, telephone, October 7, 2004.

[44] World Bank Indicators, WDI database.

[45] Gross national product excludes the profits earned by foreign firms.

[46] Several linkages programs had existed through the early and mid-1980s. The National Linkages Program of the 1980s was launched by IDA. See United Nations Conference on Trade and Development, *World Investment Report 2001:Promoting Linkages* (New York and Geneva: United Nations, 2001), p. 185.

[47] For an overview of the empirical evidence see Laura Alfaro and Andrés Rodriguez-Clare, "Multinationals and Linkages: An Empirical Investigation," *Economia* (Spring 2004); and Holger Gorg and Frances Ruane,

"Multinational Companies and Linkages: Panel-Data Evidence for the Irish Electronics Sector," *International Journal of the Economics and Business* 1 (2001): 1–18.

[48] For more on debate surrounding FDI and linkages in Ireland see Gorg and Strobl, "Multinational companies, technology spillovers and plant survival: evidence from Irish manufacturing," EIJS Working Paper 131, Stockholm School of Economics, 2001.

[49] Giorgio Barba Navaretti and Anthony J. Venables, *Multinational Firms in the World Economy* (Princeton, NJ: Princeton University Press, 2004), p. 209.

[50] F. Desmond McCarthy, "How the Celtic Tiger Did It: Ireland's Rapid Convergence with the Industrial World," World Bank, 2001.

[51] Sean Dorgan, "Is FDI Necessary in Post Celtic Tiger Ireland?" strategy statement by Sean Dorgan, CEO, IDA Ireland, Dublin Economic Workshop Conference, November 11, 2002.

[52] Coulter and Coleman, *The End of Irish History?* p. 39.

[53] Ibid., p. 38.

[54] Ibid., p. 39.

[55] Sean Dorgan, interview by author, Dublin, Ireland, November 3, 2004.

[56] CRH was one of Ireland's largest homegrown multinationals, with revenues of nearly $11 billion.

[57] Frank Fitzgibbon, business editor of the *Sunday Times*. Telephone interview by author, October 26, 2004.

[58] Patrick Honohan and Brendan Walsh, "Catching up with the Leaders: the Irish Hare," Brookings Panel on Economic Activity, Brookings Institute, April 4, 2002, p. 19.

[59] Brian Cogan, interview by author, telephone, October 7, 2004.

[60] Honohan and Walsh, "Catching up with the Leaders: the Irish Hare."

[61] Coulter and Coleman, *The End of Irish History?* p. 39.

[62] Gropp and Kostial (2000)—noted in Barry, p. 18.

[63] Brian Cogan, interview by author, telephone, October 7, 2004.

[64] Kieran McGowan, interview by author, Dublin, Ireland, November 5, 2004.

[65] Dorgan, "Is FDI Necessary in Post Celtic Tiger Ireland?" IDA strategy statement.

[66] Department of Enterprise, Trade, and Employment, "Review of Industrial Performance Policy 2003," September 19, 2003. Available from Department of Enterprise, Trade and Employment, http://www.entemp. ie, accessed February 14, 2005.

[67] U.S. Department of Commerce Bureau of Economic Analysis website, http://www.bea.gov/bea/di/usdcap/cap_03.htm, accessed 2005.

[68] "Ireland Economic Profile," Enterprise Ireland website, http://www.enterpriseireland.com, accessed February 28, 2005; Thomas Friedman, "The End of the Rainbow," *The New York Times*, June 29, 2005.

[69] Sheryl Sandberg, interview by author, Mountain View, California, December 15, 2004.

[70] Clusters are groups of firms all related to the same sector industry.

[71] Science Foundation Ireland, "Introduction to SFI: Helping Ireland Recruit and Retain Research Groups," Science Foundation Ireland website, http://www.sfi.ie/content/content.asp?section_id=207&language_id=1, accessed February 14, 2005.

[72] Raymond Bowe, economist, IDA. Interview by author, Dublin, November 3, 2004.

[73] Sean Dorgan, CEO, IDA. Interview by author, Dublin, November 3, 2004.

9-703-018
REV: MARCH 3, 2009

LAURA ALFARO

Foreign Direct Investment

The export of capital influences and greatly accelerates the development of capitalism in those countries to which it is exported.

Typical of the latest stage of capitalism, where monopolies rule, is the export of capital.

—Vladimir Lenin, 1916[1]

Foreign direct investment (FDI) stirs strong emotions in both home and host (recipient) countries. In home countries these emotions range from fear that firms that invest abroad lower domestic wages, destroy local jobs, and erode technology leadership to the belief that firms must invest abroad in order to remain competitive in an increasingly global environment. In recipient countries, some insist that FDI accelerates economic development by bringing new capital and technologies, while others fear the effects of foreign control of local factors and assets and expect multinational corporations (MNCs) to exploit their size and power to destroy local firms, create economic dependence, and threaten local culture and sovereignty.

In the last two decades, proponents of FDI seem to have gained the upper hand. Worldwide flows of direct investment grew from $57 billion in 1982 to nearly $1,200 billion in 2007. Governments in both developed and developing countries have not only reduced barriers to FDI, but have also offered special incentives to attract foreign firms.

This note briefly reviews motivations and trends of multinational corporations that engage in foreign direct investment as well as the policy debate that surrounds FDI.

Definition and Motivation for Foreign Direct Investment[2]

When a foreign investor purchases a local firm's securities or bonds without exercising control over the firm, that investment is regarded as a *portfolio investment.* When a foreign investor begins a greenfield operation (i.e., constructs new production facilities) or acquires control of an existing local firm, that investment is regarded as a *direct investment.* Since control can be exercised in many ways, the measurement of FDI poses some difficulties. The International Monetary Fund, the United Nations Conference on Trade and Development (UNCTAD), and the U.S. Department of Commerce, among other organizations, classify an investment as direct if a foreign investor holds at least 10% of

[1] Vladimir Lenin, *Imperialism, the Highest Stage of Capitalism* (Indianapolis, IN: Pegasus, [1916] 1968), pp. 127, 129.

[2] The scholarly literature on FDI and multinational corporations is vast and has been surveyed many times. For recent surveys see John H. Dunning, *The Globalization of Business* (London: Routledge, 1993); and Richard Caves, *Multinational Enterprise and Economic Analysis* (Cambridge, U.K.: Cambridge University Press, 1996). See also Debora Spar, "Note on Foreign Direct Investment," HBS Note No. 795-031 (Boston: Harvard Business School Publishing, 1995). For recent trends, see United Nations Conference on Trade and Development (UNCTAD), *Trade and Investment Report* (United Nations, 2001).

Professor Laura Alfaro and Research Associate Esteban Clavell prepared this note as the basis for class discussion.

a local firm's equity.[3] This arbitrary threshold is meant to reflect the notion that large stockholders, even if they do not hold a majority stake, will have a strong say in a company's decisions and participate in and influence its management.

Regardless of measurement difficulties, it is this desire to achieve partial or complete control over the activities of a firm in another country that distinguishes FDI from portfolio investment. An MNC, sometimes referred to as a transnational corporation (TNC), is a firm that owns and controls production facilities or other income-generating assets in at least two countries.

MNCs vary in size, sectors in which they operate, and organizational structures. Firms can invest abroad to serve a market directly; gain access to a supply of inputs, raw materials, or labor; increase operational efficiency; or simply preempt competitors' acquisitions of strategic assets.

However, the fundamental question underlying FDI activities is: Why would an investor be willing to acquire a foreign firm or build a new factory abroad? After all, there are added costs of doing business in another country, including communication and transport costs, higher costs of stationing personnel abroad, and barriers due to language, customs, and exclusion from local business and government networks. In fact, not all firms are multinationals, and while many countries attract and possess many MNCs, other countries neither possess nor attract MNCs.

The answer may seem like the logical extension of a company's pursuing profits in another country: either because it expects larger annual cash flows or a lower cost of capital than the domestic firm. But how can a foreign firm be able to offset successfully the domestic advantage afforded by a local firm's superior knowledge of the market, legal and political system, language, and culture?

One explanation, known as the cost-of-capital theory, is that foreign firms, because of their size or structure, have access to lower-cost funds not available to local firms. This approach, however, has several serious shortcomings. If lower cost of capital were the only advantage, why would a foreign investor endure the troubles and headaches of operating a firm in a different political, legal, and cultural environment instead of simply making a portfolio investment?

Further practices by investors undermine the notion of regarding FDI flows as mainly a way to take advantage of differences in rates of return across countries. Evidence shows that investors often fail to bring all the capital with them when they take control of a foreign company; instead, they tend to finance an important share of their investment in the local market. Moreover, FDI flows, in particular those among developed countries, proceed in both directions and often in the same industry. As MIT economic historian Charles Kindleberger noted, "direct investment may thus be capital movement, but it is more than that."[4]

A more broadly accepted framework derived from the industrial organization literature suggests that firms engage in FDI not because of differences in the cost of capital, but because certain assets are worth more under foreign than local control. An investor's decision, then, to acquire a foreign company or build a plant instead of simply exporting or engaging in other forms of contractual arrangements with foreign firms involves three interrelated aspects: ownership of an asset, location to produce, and whether to keep the asset internal to the firm. First, a firm can possess some *ownership advantage*—a firm-specific asset (such as a patent, technology, process, or managerial or organizational know-how) that enables it to outperform local firms. Second, *locational factors*—such as opportunities to tap into local resources, provide access to low-cost inputs or low-wage labor, or

[3] Note that there is no international consensus on the minimum stake needed to acquire control. In the United Kingdom the percentage is 20%, and in Germany 25%. In addition, countries have changed their definitions over time. Before 1980, for example, Japanese data assumed a 25% minimum stake; after 1980 it decreased to 10%.

[4] Charles P. Kindleberger, *American Business Abroad* (New Haven, CT: Yale University Press, 1969), p. 3.

bypass tariffs that protect a market from imported goods—can also lead to the decision to invest in a country rather than serve the foreign market through exports. Third, the *internalization* of global transactions may be preferable to the use of arm's-length market transactions.[5] In general, the more "imperfect" a market is, the higher the transaction costs and the greater the benefits of internalizing rather than, for example, establishing a partnership or joint venture with a local firm or simply licensing the asset to a domestic firm.

According to this view, the genesis of FDI is the possession of some intangible asset such as technology and know-how that constitutes a potentially important gain for the host country and suggests that FDI can play an important role in modernizing and promoting economic growth in the host country. However, this also means that there might be offsetting costs to the host country. After all, a foreign firm will seek to use this special asset to its advantage and to exploit the monopoly power derived from it. This might result in the transfer of rents away from host-country firms, which may have negative long-term effects on the indigenous base of the economy.

Evolution of International Business and Attitudes toward FDI[6]

The most important driver of FDI flows, in addition to the macroeconomic environment and technological advances, is the attitude of host countries regarding FDI's potential costs and benefits. Policy instruments (trade barriers, direct restrictions against foreign control of local resources or sectors, incentives) have paralleled the prevailing political mood regarding FDI. Over the last century, these attitudes have exhibited remarkable swings.

International investments were already beginning to emerge by the nineteenth century. British firms operated Brazilian gold mines as early as the 1820s; the German conglomerate Siemens made important investments in Russia during the 1850s. However, FDI volumes were still insignificant relative to total economic activity.

International direct investments exploded from the 1880s until the early twentieth century, boosted by economic growth and improvements in transportation and communications and becoming heavily concentrated (55%) in natural resources such as petroleum, coal and iron, and agricultural products. (See **Exhibit 1**.) FDI also became highly concentrated by country of origin and destination. The United Kingdom, the United States, Germany, and France accounted for nearly 85% of outward FDI, while Latin America and Asia, with their abundant natural resources, received almost 55% of inward FDI. Throughout this period, governments did not attempt to control or restrict international private transactions in any systematic way. FDI enjoyed a liberal business environment until the late 1920s.

World War I and the nationalization of foreign property in Russia in 1917 dealt heavy blows to FDI, but it was the onset of the Great Depression in 1929 that marked the end of its golden era. Economic stagnation in the world economy and the breakdown of the international financial system reduced the number of attractive investment opportunities. More importantly, receptivity toward FDI declined during the 1930s, and restrictions increased worldwide as governments became concerned about FDI's potential impact on their economies and national sovereignty. Mexico, for

[5] This approach to the theory of the multinational firm is also known as the OLI framework. See John H. Dunning, *International Production and the Multinational Enterprise* (London: George Allen and Unwin, 1981).

[6] For a historical overview of international business, see Geoffrey Jones, *The Evolution of International Business* (London: Routledge, 1996). On the policy debate, see Edward M. Graham and Paul Krugman, *Foreign Direct Investment in the United States* (Washington, DC: Institute for International Economics, 1995); and Robert Gilpin, *The Challenge of Global Capitalism: The World Economy in the 21st Century* (Princeton, NJ: Princeton University Press, 2000), chap. 6.

example, expropriated the foreign oil industry in 1938. Developing countries, seeking to regain control of their natural resources, denounced the "extractive" nature of FDI, reflecting multinationals' large involvement in the exploitation of natural resources.

Receptivity toward FDI declined even further after World War II following the spread of communism. In this period, attitudes toward FDI were shaped by ideological support for government intervention in the economy in general. Communist countries excluded foreign firms altogether; developing countries began to regulate foreign capital and restrict activities in sectors considered to be in the national interest. Waves of nationalization of key industries followed World War II not only in developing countries but also in European countries such as France and the United Kingdom. Meanwhile, Japan, for example, systematically discouraged inward FDI and managed to restrict it to low levels. FDI activity declined dramatically worldwide.

In the 1960s, a slow resurgence of FDI was largely due to a positive macroeconomic environment. This new wave of FDI, in contrast with that at the turn of the century, was concentrated in manufacturing and in developed countries, with Western Europe, the United States, and Canada accounting for nearly two-thirds of inward FDI. (See **Exhibit 1**.) This shift reflected the declining importance of raw materials in the world economy and the emergence of new market-oriented strategies in the more prosperous developed countries. It was also a consequence of the still-hostile environment that FDI faced in many developing countries. Some manufacturing MNCs, nevertheless, found new opportunities in countries following import-substitution development strategies. With tariff levels kept high to protect domestic industries, some countries allowed MNCs to pursue "tariff jumping" investments and set up factories to cater to the local markets.

Foreign firms' shift from commodities to manufacturing, however, sparked new waves of criticism. Critics argued that foreign firms tended to monopolize rather than diffuse their know-how and that the capital and technology they brought were unlikely to have positive effects on local development. Others argued that MNCs favored imported inputs over locally produced ones, with a consequent negative effect on the trade balance. Critics also maintained that functions with positive externalities such as research and development (R&D) were kept at headquarters, thereby limiting technology transfer and, in the case of international acquisitions, potentially destroying local know-how. Moreover, MNCs were seen to have the undesirable ability to influence local consumption patterns and, protected from local taxation by questionable transfer-pricing practices, exploit their market power to extract huge profits.

Some critics went so far as to assert that MNCs were the main cause of Third World poverty. The dependency theory, which originated in Latin America and swept the world in the 1970s, accused multinationals of being imperialist predators that exploited developing countries. "For every dollar invested by MNCs in the Third World," they argued, "more than one dollar returned to the metropolis in the form of repatriated profits and royalties."[7] Moreover, dependence on MNCs, they claimed, imposed limits on national policies, as governments were restricted by the need to maintain good "investment climates."

Outward FDI was also criticized, as it was construed to be responsible for unemployment and obsolescence of labor in home countries. Others argued that the mobility of FDI reduced labor's bargaining power and led to good jobs with high wages, benefits, and job security being replaced by jobs with low wages and little stability.

---

[7] Ian Roxborough, *Theories of Underdevelopment* (London: Macmillan, 1979), p. 58. See also Fernando H. Cardoso and Enzo Faletto, *Dependency and Development in Latin America* (Berkeley, CA: University of California Press, 1979).

The 1970s and early 1980s were once again difficult times for FDI. Surging oil prices and the debt crisis in developing countries slowed FDI flows. Both developing and developed countries questioned the merits of FDI. The debate in the United States, for example, reached its climax in the middle of the 1980s, as Americans feared the massive flows of Japanese FDI into the country. These concerns even filtered into popular culture: movies such as *Black Rain* and *Rising Sun* portrayed Japanese FDI as sinister. With Japan accounting for 10.5% of global FDI outflows but less than 2.5% of inflows, U.S. businesspeople complained that the United States kept its borders open to Japanese MNCs even as Japan remained largely closed, giving Japanese firms strategic advantages such as economies of scale and scope that could eventually enable them to drive U.S. firms out of the world markets.[8]

But after decades of skepticism, the pendulum swung in favor of FDI in the late 1980s as a broad consensus began to emerge regarding FDI's potential benefits to host economies. FDI began to be portrayed as a means to improve the well-being of the societies in which it operated through the provision of capital, technology, and know-how.

What explains this change in attitude? First, the 1980s debt crisis had severed developing countries' access to credit and portfolio investment. Moreover, the industries in which MNCs were now active—high technology and services—made FDI far more attractive. Finally, the fall of the Soviet bloc reinforced the perception that closed economies and state intervention in economies had failed. As relations improved between MNCs and host countries, governments began to ease restrictions on FDI and increasingly offer incentives in an effort to attract investment and be integrated into the globalized economy. Perhaps one of the most dramatic policy changes occurred in China, as the government gradually opened the domestic market to foreign companies.

During the 1990s, FDI soared, growing more than 20% per year driven by more than 60,000 MNCs with more than 800,000 international affiliates. This recent surge of FDI had its own distinctive characteristics. More than 50% of new investments were in the service sector, and cross-border mergers and acquisitions (M&A) became the main driver of FDI activity. (See **Exhibits 2** and **4**.) Technological developments, especially in telecommunications, and increased competition fostered changes in corporate strategies and forced companies to emphasize business networks and relocate functions. By 2000, intrafirm trade among MNCs accounted for 40% of world trade. Despite a slowdown following a recession in the U.S. economy in 2001, growth of world FDI inflows had resumed by 2004. (See **Exhibit 1**.) UNCTAD forecast strong increases in FDI inflows of around 5% per year for the rest of the decade.[9]

FDI Promotion and Incentives[10]

Although some studies minimize the role government incentives play in foreign investment decisions, both developed and developing countries try to lure foreign investors by granting FDI special treatment.[11] Policies to promote FDI are designed to increase investment revenues and/or reduce costs or risks. Incentives can be fiscal or financial. *Fiscal incentives* are designed to reduce the tax burden of foreign investors. In 1998, 103 countries offered tax concessions to foreign companies

[8] For explanations of the low levels of Japan's inward FDI, see Yasheng Huang, "Note on Foreign Direct Investment in Japan," HBS Note No. 702-029 (Boston: Harvard Business School Publishing, 2002).

[9] See "Boomer Backlash" in *World Investment Prospects to 2010*, by The Economist Intelligence Unit (2006).

[10] For the debate on FDI promotion, see Louis T. Wells, Jr., and Alvin Wint, *Marketing a Country: Promotion as a Tool for Attracting Foreign Investment* (Washington, D.C.: International Finance Corporation, 2000); and Gordon H. Hanson, *Should Countries Promote Foreign Investment?* (New York: United Nations, 2001).

[11] Market characteristics, political factors, economic stability, and strategic considerations appear to be important determinants. See UNCTAD, *Incentives and Foreign Direct Investment* (New York: United Nations, 1996).

that established facilities within their borders. *Financial incentives* include government grants, credit at subsidized rates, government equity participation, and government guarantees. Other incentives include subsidized, dedicated infrastructure, often through duty-free export zones, and foreign exchange privileges. Some host countries require MNCs to establish production facilities in specified industries or regions. Incentives can be granted at the national, state, or municipal level. Direct subsidies are often granted case by case.

A bargaining relationship exists between a firm and host country over the negotiation of incentives. Each seeks to extract maximum concessions from the other following the "obsolescing bargain" pattern.[12] The firm is in the stronger position before an investment, when it can extract maximum concessions. But once the investment is made and knowledge about the techniques spread, the bargaining power shifts to the host country. This is particularly the case for certain projects such as mining, plantation, and infrastructure projects where the benefits of the foreign presence are no longer viewed as essential for the operation of the facility. With the shift in bargaining power, an FDI project can be affected by noncommercial risks such as expropriation, political violence, and breach of contract.

In an effort to minimize these risks, many investors establish relationships (joint ventures, licensing agreements) for the purpose of sharing market knowledge and creating interdependencies with local players. Many investors also purchase political risk insurance from private insurers, who tend to focus on the short to medium term (up to three years); and from export credit agencies (ECAs) and the World Bank's Multilateral Investment Guarantee Agency (MIGA), which cover riskier investments with longer durations.[13]

However, the more conducive environment for FDI has sparked a new debate about the concessions offered to foreign firms. Does FDI warrant special treatment over other forms of investment? If foreign capital is more mobile than local, it could be argued that governments might want to tax income from foreign capital, both FDI and portfolio investment, at lower rates. In general, however, economists argue that for FDI to merit special treatment over other forms of investment, there needs to be some form of market failure such as externalities and spillovers.

Advocates argue that FDI, by its very nature, has important positive effects on host economies beyond the direct capital financing it supplies and the jobs it creates. FDI can help to introduce new processes, managerial skills, and superior know-how into the domestic market while promoting international production networks and access to foreign markets, all of which create valuable productivity spillovers. Increased competition arising from the entry of foreign firms might force local firms to modernize, introduce new technologies, and become more efficient. FDI might also foster linkages with local firms and help jump-start an economy.[14] Finally, countries might want to pursue FDI because of its lower volatility compared with that of portfolio investment flows.

---

[12] For more on the perils of the obsolescing bargain and the risk FDI faces in infrastructure investment, see Louis T. Wells and Eric S. Gleason, "Is Foreign Infrastructure Investment Still Risky?" *Harvard Business Review*, September-October 1995.

[13] MIGA's insurance services, initiated in 1988, are available to investors in all MIGA-member nations (a total of 154 in 2000). In 2001, MIGA insured up to $200 million, 95% of the value of the investment, and up to 40 years. See www.miga.org. In the United States, the Overseas Private Investment Corporation (OPIC) underwrites political risk insurance for U.S. corporations that invest abroad. In 2001 OPIC insured up to $250 million and 20 years, covering 90% of the cost of an investment. See www.opic.gov. In addition to OPIC, there are 18 other ECAs representing 16 industrialized countries.

[14] For an overview of the economics literature on FDI spillovers, see Magnus Blomstrom and Ari Kokko, "Multinational Corporations and Spillovers," *Journal of Economic Surveys*, vol. 12, no. 3 (1998): 247–277. On linkages, see Andres Rodriguez-Clare, "Multinationals, Linkages and Economic Development," *American Economic Review*, vol. 86, no. 4 (1996): 852–873; and Laura Alfaro and Andres Rodriguez-Clare, "Multinationals and Linkages: An Empirical Investigation," *Economia* (Spring, 2004): 113–170.

Others disagree and question whether FDI's potential benefits justify special treatment. In particular, this view has been influenced by empirical studies both at the firm and national levels that show mixed results in terms of growth-enhancing externalities of FDI. A recent survey of empirical work sponsored by UNCTAD finds little evidence that FDI generates positive spillovers in host countries and suggests that a country's capacity to take advantage of these externalities might be limited by local conditions such as infrastructure, education levels, and the policy environment.[15] In sum, generalizations are difficult to make.

Furthermore, some developing countries that have liberalized their policies toward FDI are disillusioned by foreign companies' lack of interest in tapping their markets; FDI remains concentrated in a very few of them. The top 10 developing countries (including China, Hong Kong, Brazil, and Mexico) account for close to 70% of FDI inflows to developing countries, while the 50 least developed countries account for less than 0.5% of global FDI. Sub-Saharan Africa, for example, accounts for less than 1% of total inward FDI. (See **Exhibit 3**.)

Governments continue to believe that FDI warrants special treatment. However, competition for FDI among developing countries has led to increasing concerns that benefits granted by one country—or region within a country—might trigger similar responses by other potential hosts, precipitating a "race to the bottom" that could spiral to the point that incentives granted to foreign firms exceed the social gain of FDI, thus representing a net loss for the "winning" country.

The Future of FDI

Although recent decades have seen unprecedented growth in FDI as governments in both developed and developing countries have liberalized FDI regimes, these policy changes at the national and regional level are not yet reflected at the multilateral level. Despite some bilateral and regional agreements and the partial guidelines related to investment established by the Uruguay Round in 1994, international consensus on FDI practices has yet to be achieved.

The very nature of FDI, the ownership and control of local factors, and the lack of consensus regarding FDI's benefits all limit the possibilities of an international agreement. Such a regime would require rules on right of establishment, national treatment, and nondiscrimination.[16] Moreover, an investment regime would have to deal with rules on sectors that countries tend to restrict (such as finance, culture, and national security), determining which sectors are legitimate and which are not. In the end, governments want to guarantee the best treatment for their firms that invest abroad without relinquishing national sovereignty.

More importantly, the beginning of the twenty-first century has seen a new antiglobalization sentiment and discontent with foreign corporations, which appears to be spreading rapidly. Demonstrations such as those in Seattle in 1999, Genoa in 2001, and Johannesburg in 2002 suggest some questioning of MNCs' activities and FDI. Critics once again warn against the pervasive economic, political, and cultural effects that MNCs can have and voice growing concern that

---

[15] For example, whereas Richard Caves's pioneering work, "Multinational Firms, Competition, and Productivity in Host-Country Markets," *Economica*, vol. 41, no. 149 (1974): 176–193, finds positive FDI spillovers in Australia, Brian J. Aitken and Ann Harrison, "Do Domestic Firms Benefit from Direct Foreign Investment? Evidence from Venezuela," *American Economic Review*, vol. 89, no. 3 (1999): 605–618, find the net effect of FDI on productivity to be small in Venezuela. Macro-level evidence yields little support for the notion that FDI has a positive effect on growth. Hanson's *Should Countries Promote Foreign Investment?* surveys the empirical literature. See also Laura Alfaro, Areendam Chanda, Sebnem Kalemli-Ozcan, and Selin Sayek, "FDI and Economic Growth: The Role of Local Financial Markets," *Journal of International Economics*, vol. 61, no.1 (2004): 113–134.

[16] The right of establishment guarantees that firms of every nationality have the right to invest anywhere in the world; the principle of national treatment requires national governments to treat the subsidiaries of foreign firms as if they were domestic; and the principle of nondiscrimination requires countries not to impose different treatments on firms from different countries.

multinationals have dwarfed the power of governments across the globe.[17] But, as *The Economist* recently noted, "None of this is new."[18]

[17] Noreena Hertz, *The Silent Takeover: Global Capitalism and the Death of Democracy* (New York: Free Press, 2001), p. 109.
[18] "The World's View of Multinationals," *The Economist*, January 27, 2000.

Exhibit 1 FDI Activity, 1917 to 2005

By Origin

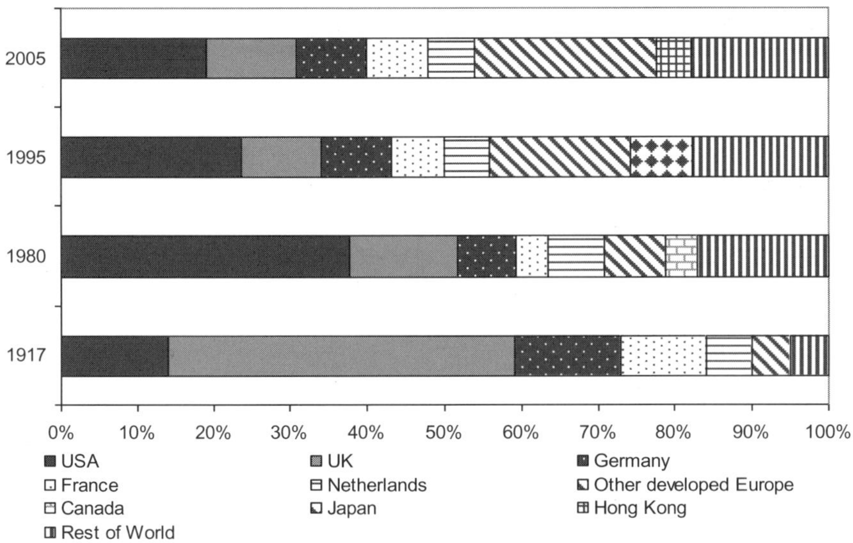

By Destiny

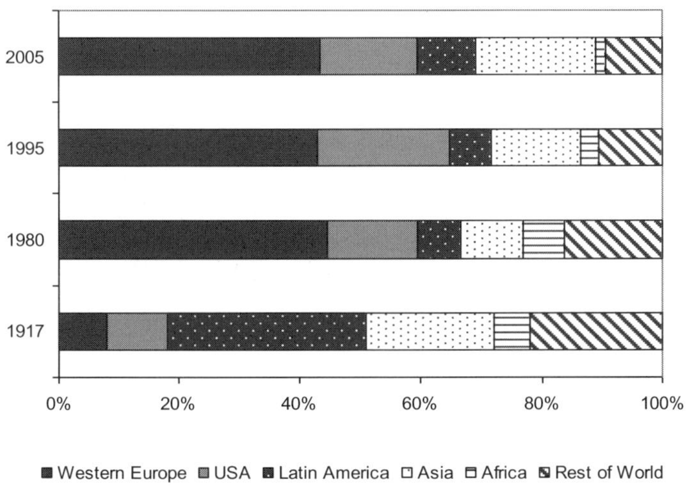

Exhibit 1 (continued)

By Source

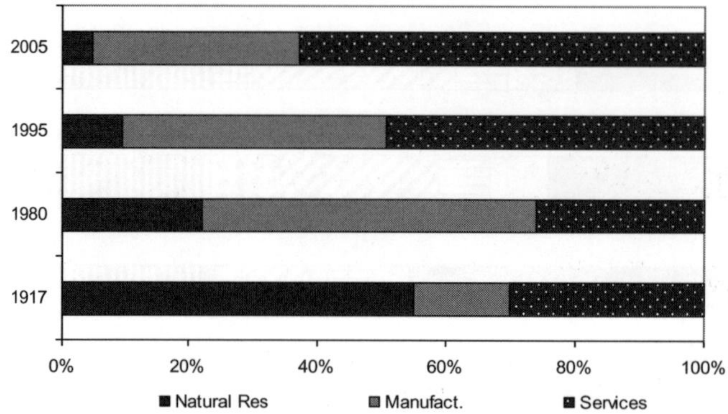

Source: Adapted from Geoffrey Jones, *The Evolution of International Business* (London: Routledge, 1996); and United Nations Conference on Trade and Development, *Trade and Investment Report* (United Nations, 2006).

Notes: Figures expressed as % of total FDI stock.

Exhibit 2 Evolution of FDI and M&As, 1970–2005 (in billions of US$)

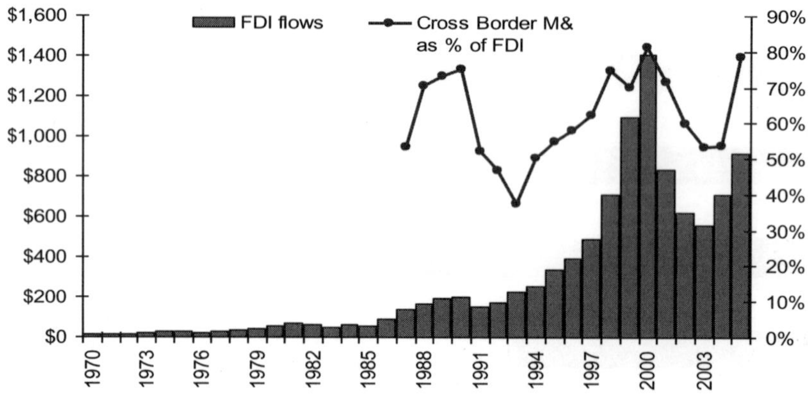

Source: Adapted from United Nations Conference on Trade and Development, *Trade and Investment Report* (United Nations, 2006).

Exhibit 3 Top FDI Recipients among Developing Countries (average 2001–2005)

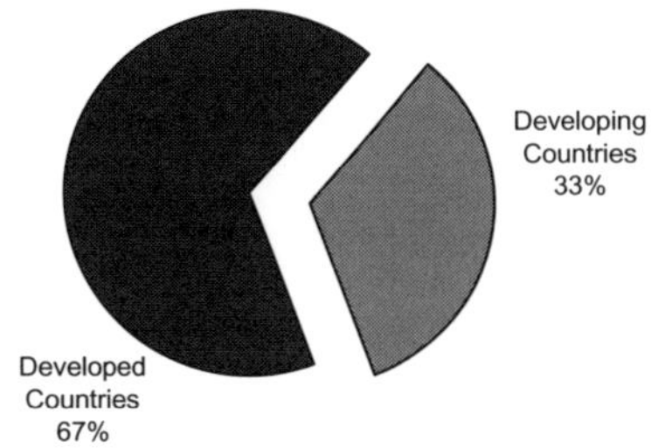

Developed Countries 467,501 million US$
Developing Countries 233,897 million US$

Top 10 Recepients of FDI in Developing Countries
(as a % of FDI to Developing Countries - avg. 2001-2005)

China	24.5%
Hong Kong, China	10.0%
Mexico	8.2%
Brazil	7.0%
Singapore	5.8%
Russian Federation	3.8%
India	2.4%
United Arab Emirates	2.3%
Korea, Republic of	2.2%
Chile	2.1%
Total	**68.4%**

Other Selected Recepients of FDI in Developing Countries
(as a % of FDI to Developing Countries - avg. 2001-2005)

Colombia	1.7%
Turkey	1.6%
Romania	1.5%
South Africa	1.3%
Argentina	1.3%
Malaysia	1.3%
Total	**8.6%**

Source: Adapted from United Nations Conference on Trade and Development, *Trade and Investment Report* (United Nations, 2006).

Exhibit 4 The World's Largest Multinationals (2004—Ranked by Foreign Assets)

				Assets (bn US$)		Sales (bn US)		Employment ('000)	
	Corporation	Country	Sector	Foreign	Total	Foreign	Total	Foreign	Total
1	General Electric	United States	Electrical & electronic equipment	448.9	750.5	56.9	152.9	142.0	307.0
2	Vodafone Group Plc	United Kingdom	Telecommunications	247.9	258.6	53.3	62.5	46.0	57.4
3	Ford Motor	United States	Motor vehicles	179.9	305.3	71.4	171.7	102.7	225.6
4	General Motors	United States	Motor vehicles	173.7	479.6	59.1	193.5	114.6	324.0
5	British Petroleum Company Plc	United Kingdom	Petroleum expl./ref./distr.	154.5	193.2	232.4	285.1	85.5	102.9
6	ExxonMobil	United States	Petroleum expl./ref./distr.	134.9	195.3	202.9	291.3	53.0	105.2
7	Royal Dutch/Shell Group	UK/Netherlands	Petroleum expl./ref./distr.	129.9	192.8	170.3	265.2	96.0	114.0
8	Toyota Motor Corporation	Japan	Motor vehicles	123.0	233.7	103.0	171.5	94.7	265.8
9	Total	France	Petroleum expl./ref./distr.	98.7	114.6	123.3	152.4	62.2	111.4
10	France Télécom	France	Telecommunications	85.7	131.2	24.3	58.6	81.7	206.5
11	Volkswagen AG	Germany	Motor vehicles	84.0	172.9	80.0	110.5	165.2	342.5
12	Sanofi-Aventis	France	Pharmaceuticals	82.6	104.5	15.4	18.7	68.8	96.4
13	Deutsche Telekom AG	Germany	Telecommunications	79.7	146.8	47.1	71.9	73.8	244.6
14	RWE Group	Germany	Electricity, gas and water	78.7	127.2	23.6	52.3	42.4	97.8
15	Suez	France	Electricity, gas and water	74.1	85.8	38.8	50.6	100.5	160.7

The Largest Multinationals from Developing Countries (2004—Ranked by Total Assets)

				Assets (bn US$)		Sales (bn US$)		Employment ('000)	
	Corporation	Country	Sector	Foreign	Total	Foreign	Total	Foreign	Total
1	Hutchison Whampoa Limited	Hong Kong, China	Diversified	67.6	84.2	11.4	23.1	150.7	182.0
2	Petronas - Petroliam Nasional Bhd	Malaysia	Petroleum expl./ref./distr.	22.6	62.9	10.6	36.1	4.0	33.9
3	Singtel Ltd.	Singapore	Telecommunications	18.6	21.6	5.4	7.7	8.7	19.2
4	Samsung Electronics Co., Ltd.	Republic of Korea	Electrical & electronic equip.	14.6	66.7	61.5	79.2	21.3	61.9
5	CITIC Group j	China	Diversified	14.5	84.7	1.7	6.4	15.9	93.3
6	Cemex S.A.	Mexico	Construction	13.3	17.2	5.4	8.1	16.8	26.7

Source: Adapted from United Nations Conference on Trade and Development, *Trade and Investment Report* (United Nations, 2006).

Capital Flows: Benefactor or Menace?

HARVARD | BUSINESS | SCHOOL

9-708-007
REV: MAY 14, 2008

LAURA ALFARO
RENEE KIM

Transforming Korea Inc.: Financial Crisis and Institutional Reform

The crisis will be remembered as a blessing, because it is forcing essential economic changes.
—President Kim Dae Jung, 1999[1]

October 1996 was a triumphant moment for South Korea as the country joined the Organisation for Economic Co-operation and Development (OECD), known as the "rich man's club." Not only had Korea become the second Asian country to join the OECD since Japan's membership in 1964, but it was also the first Asian "tiger" economy to enter the Paris-based club (see **Exhibit 1**).[2] President Kim Young Sam hailed the event as Korea receiving the international community's recognition that its economy was on par with those of other advanced nations. After all, the nation boasted proud achievements: 40 years ago, Korea's future was doubtful, with the country having few natural resources or a significant manufacturing industry as it struggled with the aftermath of the Korean War, which left the country heavily dependent on foreign aid. By 1996, Korea Inc. had transformed itself into the world's 11th-largest economy and a major world-class exporter.

Then, one year later, Korea suffered its worst economic crisis. Swept up in the Asian financial crisis, which rapidly spread from Thailand, Korea was forced to seek a record $58 billion emergency rescue fund from the International Monetary Fund (IMF) and the World Bank, the largest bailout ever put together by the multilateral organizations. This occurred despite positive growth outlooks by the IMF as late as the fall of 1997. Korea plunged into a recession amid crippled investments, high unemployment, and a record number of corporate bankruptcies as the nation pondered—what had gone wrong?

The recession, however, did not last long. Amid sweeping reforms that affected the financial market to the labor market to intellectual property rights, the Korean economy bounced back. Many legal restrictions hindering foreign investment had been lifted, capital markets had been diversified, and companies boasted lower debt-to-equity ratios. The nation had signed a landmark free-trade agreement with the United States, Korea's third-biggest trade partner, which domestic think tanks predicted would add 6% to Korea's annual economic growth over the next 10 years.[3] Other trade pacts were in negotiations in hopes of further boosting Korea's economic growth. Banks' non-performing loans, a key culprit of the crisis, had dramatically contracted. The situation on the macroeconomic front looked encouraging as well, such as Korea holding the world's fifth-largest foreign currency reserves after sinking below $10 billion at one point during the financial crisis.

Professor Laura Alfaro and Research Associate Renee Kim prepared this case. HBS cases are developed solely as the basis for class discussion. Cases are not intended to serve as endorsements, sources of primary data, or illustrations of effective or ineffective management.

Yet as Korea marked its 10-year anniversary of the 1997 financial crisis with positive changes, policymakers were not content. As Jin Nyum, former finance and economy minister, noted, "We have changed a lot over the last decade, but we need to become more innovative, efficient, and transparent to become a true global player."[4] After all, with exports responsible for 40% of the economy's growth, Korea was increasingly feeling pressured, caught between price-competitive goods from China and the more technologically advanced innovative products from Japan in the manufacturing sector (see **Exhibit 2**). There were concerns over how to reform the powerful family-owned conglomerates, known as *chaebol*, which played a major role in the nation's export-led growth strategy through cheap subsidized loans and reckless expansion in the past that crowded out the development of small and medium-sized companies. One ambitious goal was to elevate Korea as the next northeast Asian financial hub and develop its service sector. Thus, what kind of model could usher in the kind of stability and growth that Korea wanted? Could reforms such as the Capital Market Consolidation Act turn Korea into a financial services powerhouse, allowing the nation to grow through a different development platform based on innovation and free-market principles?[5]

Development Strategy

Park Chung Hee (1961–1979): Building Korea Inc.

The foundation of Korea's "economic miracle" began with Park Chung Hee. He was known to be a meticulously organized, pragmatic, and often aloof officer who was educated in the Japanese military academy.[6] The economic situation was dire; there was widespread poverty, no significant manufacturing industry, and per capita income was less than $100. President Park, who rose to power through a military coup in 1961, launched a radical economic reform plan, creating an outward-looking growth strategy through export promotion. This was a clear departure from both the previous administration and other developing nations' policy of focusing on inward-looking growth strategies through import substitution.[7] Park's goal was to establish the nation's basic infrastructure and become self-sufficient, steering the country away from its past dependency on foreign aid. Advocating, "In human life, economics precedes politics or culture," Park nationalized banks, introduced financial subsidies, devalued the currency dramatically, and even set export targets for specific companies.[8] The nation's umbrella labor organization was brought under the government's control, banning all strike activities and imposing repressive labor policies.

Through several five-year economic development plans devised by the powerful Economic Planning Board, the government's economic think tank, the Korean economy geared all efforts toward export promotion (see **Exhibit 3**). Under the slogan "Export Number One," by the end of the first development plan in 1966, exports were increasing at 43% compared with those of Japan and the global export growth rate of 16% and 10%, respectively.[9]

Park's top-down, authoritarian-like leadership, which allowed him to rule the country for two decades, was aided by Korea's strong Confucian culture, which emphasized respect for hierarchy, authority, loyalty, and social harmony, according to Il Sakong, a former chief economic secretary to the president in the 1980s.[10] In addition, there was an emphasis on higher education that generated skilled workers who could quickly learn and improve the foreign technology Korea was importing to manufacture products. For example, Hyundai Motors Co. started to produce cars by 1973, six years after its official establishment. By 1979, it was exporting over 62,000 units of its Pony model, an achievement accomplished through not only hard work but also through foreign loans backed by the government's repayment guarantees and licensed technologies from 26 firms in Italy, Japan, and Britain.[11]

The industrial drive and the *Chaebol* In 1973, Park launched a heavy- and chemical-industry policy (HCI), specifically targeting six industries—steel, shipbuilding, machinery, electronics, nonsteel metal, and petroleum and chemical. Park wanted to shift Korea away from light manufacturing and focus on exporting more higher-value-added products.[12] Part of the president's ambitious foray into such capital-intensive industries included state enterprise Pohang Iron & Steel Co., which the World Bank and other institutions refused to finance, claiming it would not work in a country that had no experience or necessary technology in such industries.

More importantly, the government mobilized big business groups known as *chaebol*, controlled under a single entrepreneur such as Samsung Group founder Lee Byung Chul, to build new industries for exports according to the government's vision. This was achieved after Park arrested prominent entrepreneurs under the Illicit Wealth Accumulation Act. They were forced to parade the streets with placards saying, "I am a corrupt swine."[13] Lee headed the negotiations with Park, securing businessmen's release in exchange for following the government's orders. Daewoo Group Chairman Kim Woo Choong recalled, "The government tells you it's your duty and you have to do it, even if there is no profit."[14] Building on the concept of "bigger is better" to achieve economies of scale, the government allocated policy loans to *chaebol* with special interest rates, which were often negative in real terms. For example, in 1975, the policy loan rate was six percentage points lower than the general bank loan rate of 15.5%, while inflation was close to 25% (see **Exhibit 4**). During this time, policy loans accounted for 60% of total bank loans that flowed to heavy and chemical sectors while import restrictions intensified.[15]

Given that capital markets were underdeveloped, Korean companies primarily relied on debt to finance their investments; thus, the manufacturing sector's debt-to-equity ratio reached about 400% during the 1970s.[16] Favored conglomerates also received foreign capital at rates well below domestic ones through subsidies and repayment guarantees made by the government. Companies aggressively pursued capital to expand their market share and increase exports, which guaranteed cheap credit, investment licenses, and favorable treatment such as tax breaks. "It was a centrally planned economy where the government picked the winners and losers . . . economic theory just didn't work in Korea," according to Tami Overby, president of the American Chamber of Commerce in Korea.[17]

Thus, the triangular relationship among the government, *chaebol*, and banks was born, leading to the country's nickname of "Korea Inc." The top five *chaebol's* valued-added to gross domestic product (GDP) more than doubled to 8.1% in 1978 over five years, while their average growth rate was an impressive 32%.[18] By 1978, their market share of the heavy and chemical industries reached 50%.[19] Meanwhile, import of foreign technology and equipment was encouraged while foreign direct investment (FDI) was not, with Korea's FDI to gross capital formation one of the lowest among east Asian newly industrialized countries amid high entry barriers (see **Exhibit 5**).

The HCI drive, which paved the way for the development and advancement of target industries such as shipbuilding and steel, was done by relying on imported components and technology, such as from Japan, rather than producing them domestically through small and medium-sized companies. The service and light-manufacturing industries were largely ignored, thus creating structural imbalances (see **Exhibit 6**). As a result, Korea's aggressive HCI promotion led to over-investment that coincided with high inflation reaching nearly 30%, rising wages amid growing demand for skilled workers, and the second worldwide oil shock in 1979.[20] To make things worse, Korea fell into political turmoil with the assassination of Park by the chief of the central intelligence agency in October 1979. Korea suffered negative growth for the first time since the 1950s, and the current account balance suffered. An economic crisis seemed inevitable, as foreign debt reached $20.3 billion in 1979 within four years, a growth of 140%, making Korea the fourth-largest debtor in the world.[21]

Chun Doo Hwan (1980–1987): Stability over Growth

A new era was ushered in under the leadership of Chun Doo Hwan, a four-star military general who seized power through a military coup on May 1980.[22] His immediate priority was price stabilization amid staggering inflation and reduction of the nation's foreign debt. Backed by two standby agreements from the IMF, Chun launched a nationwide stabilization program, which involved freezing wages, cutting mass numbers of government employees, and repressing labor unions to control wages. The real exchange rate was depreciated through a 20% nominal devaluation, combined with a sharp reduction in imports.[23] The government's own budget limitations were accompanied by social measures, such as a nationwide campaign that advocated people to save more and spend less.

Despite restrictions on political activities and civil liberties, the Chun administration brought stability by successfully halving the budget deficit and slashing inflation to a single-digit level not seen in two decades, contrary to Latin American countries that were still struggling with similar problems in the early 1980s. In 1986, the economy posted a current account surplus for the first time in modern history,[24] and total foreign debt fell in subsequent years as well (see **Exhibit 7**).

In terms of trade, import liberalization picked up its pace from 1986 amid intense pressure from the United States, Korea's biggest export market, which was running a trade deficit with Korea. As a member of the General Agreement on Tariffs and Trade, Korea introduced preannounced tariff reduction schedules in 1983 and 1988 under the goal of bringing Korea's trade liberalization up to OECD standards by the early 1990s.[25]

However, the pace of financial liberalization was much slower. Four main national banks were privatized between 1981 and 1983. Yet the Finance Ministry continued to appoint bank presidents and dictated even the smaller issues such as when a new bank branch could open. The government also imposed an individual ownership ceiling of 8% on the banks, which was primarily aimed at preventing *chaebol* from entering the banking sector.

Through the Industrial Development Law enacted in 1986, Korea tried to shift away from promoting specific industries and "rationalize" overextended industries, such as shipping, through government-enforced mergers and closures. Seventy-eight companies with a total debt of 7.8 trillion Korean won (KRW) were subject to restructuring over the next two years, which involved a write down or rescheduling of two-thirds of the banks' nonperforming loans.[26] *Chaebol* companies that took over failing firms were given fiscal and financial benefits; as a result, the rationalization only led to the *chaebol*'s continuing expansion and concentration of economic power.

Roh Tae Woo (1988–1993): Economic and Political Transition

The inauguration of Roh Tae Woo, a retired military general and close ally of Chun Doo Hwan, was a historical event as Roh became the first president to be elected through popular vote in more than three decades. It was also the first time presidential power was transferred peacefully in Korea's history. Initially, Roh inherited an economic "golden period," as between 1986 and 1989 external factors known as the "three lows"—low oil prices, low exchange rates, and low global interest rates—favored Korea.[27] As exports surged, the Korean economy started to ease its grip on trade protectionism and financial restraints amid pressure from overseas to open its markets.

However, as the Korean won started to appreciate in the late 1980s, export products started to lose their competitiveness, and Korea's trade surplus contracted more than 60% to $4.3 billion in 1989 from the previous year.[28] Externally, Korean goods were caught between high-quality Japanese goods and low-cost products from southeast Asian countries. Domestically, rising inflation and wages were eroding Korea's competitiveness. The rise of militant labor unions led to thousands of strikes during Roh's presidency demanding better wages and working conditions. Wages increased an average of 20% annually between 1988 and 1991, hindering the government's ability to tame inflation through wage cuts or restraints as it had in the past.[29]

By 1989, Roh faced what he called a "total crisis" as growth slowed to 6.5% after three years of 12% annual average growth.[30] To revive confidence in the economy, the president sacked its more market-oriented, reform-minded economic cabinet in 1990 and replaced it with policymakers who favored old growth policies through export promotion. Initial plans to adopt the "real name" transaction system to create transparency in financial transactions were dropped amid concerns of the economic slowdown. Domestic stimulus packages were introduced, including a massive construction boom to prop up the economy through domestic growth to make up for the falling exports. However, this plan caused the economy to overheat instead.

Roh also tried to tame the *chaebol* by adopting similar measures as his predecessor did, such as imposing credit restrictions and limiting cross-share holdings. In particular, conglomerates were ordered to specialize and select about three core businesses that would be eligible for favorable financial treatment, which sparked bitter complaints among business leaders. The measures did little to reform the *chaebol*; subsidiaries were merely transferred to family members, and conglomerates took advantage of non-banking financial institutions (NBFIs), such as merchant banks, as an alternative source of financing through easier entry restrictions into the nonbanking sector (see **Exhibit 8**). Through ownership of many NBFIs, which enjoyed greater freedom from government control, the *chaebol* secured short-term loans to finance their long-term investment projects. As one economist noted, "The largest *chaebol*, in fact, enjoyed the best of two worlds: they continued to have good access to loans from the banks at controlled interest rates while securing an independent source of capital in newly acquired NBFIs."[31] Overall, Roh's policies pushed the once cooperative business-state relationship into a more confrontational, even hostile one. For instance, the trial of Hyundai Group Chairman Chung Ju Young after he challenged the government's tax probe into his company illustrated *chaebol*'s willingness to voice their complaints with the state, something that was virtually unheard of a decade ago.

In terms of capital controls, Korea had traditionally tightly restricted capital movements: all foreign exchange had to be surrendered to the central bank, and there was a ban on purchasing overseas property. Yet toward the late 1980s, the current account surplus allowed the government to ease restrictions on capital outflows, as the balance-of-payments status guided the government's policies toward transactions related to trade and the capital account.[32] Direct investment inflows were liberalized, including foreign portfolio investment. However, the capital market liberalization, in the absence of bank restructuring or prudent regulation, offset Roh's initiatives such as loan ceilings to restrain the *chaebol*.

The Korean Economy in the 1990s

Kim Young Sam (1993–1997): Era of Globalization

In 1993, Kim Young Sam became the first civilian to be appointed president. Kim's preaching of "globalization" was a far cry from Park Chung Hee's theme of discipline. Coining the term "Korean disease," the absence of authority and endemic corruption that had now appeared at all levels of society, Kim vowed to cure the nation.[33] The first few months in office were dedicated to weeding out corruption from political to business circles. Another continuing ambitious goal from past presidents was to dismantle the *chaebol*, which had become an "octopus with their tentacles stretching throughout the economy" (see **Exhibit 9**).[34]

Despite Kim's initial vow, conglomerates continued to overinvest and expanded their market share and diversification. For instance, the Samsung Group was permitted to enter the auto industry and build a factory in Kim's home province, even though there were three significant domestic automakers in 2004. The top five conglomerates' combined sales alone accounted for 37% of Korea's gross output.[35] Given the size and importance they had in the economy, the collapse of one could threaten the stability of the economy, which reined in the government to keep providing implicit guarantees. Commercial banks continued to carry out their traditional practices of extending loans to conglomerates with little consideration about risk management or default risk, as reflected in their poor profitability (see **Exhibit 10**). In particular, supervision of NBFIs was very weak, with no single agency in charge of monitoring their credit risk or loan policies.

Bid to Join the "Rich Man's Club": The OECD

In addition to the goal of reforming the conglomerates, Kim had another vision—to join the "rich man's club," the OECD. After announcing Korea's intention in 1993, the Kim administration launched a five-year financial liberalization plan to meet the requirements to join the OECD. Key polices included deregulate interest rates to bring domestic rates more in line with overseas rates, abolish "policy loans," make banks more independent, and reduce entry barriers to financial activities, such as raising the foreign ownership ceiling of Korean equities (see **Exhibit 11**).

Most importantly, the capital account was further liberalized. In 1993, firms could borrow abroad either directly or through domestic banks to finance the importation of capital goods through short-term loans, those with a maturity of less than a year. However, stringent long-term foreign borrowing requirements continued to exist, and Korean companies also lacked credibility to borrow at attractive rates for long-term loans, both factors making short-term foreign borrowing more attractive. "In reality, the government should have done a better job in the sequencing of capital market liberalization," recalled an observer.[36] As a result, Korea's foreign debt grew at 33.6% per annum between 1994 and 1996, compared with 17.8% per annum between 1979 and 1985.[37] Merchant banks, which multiplied under Kim, took advantage of lax regulations to engage in offshore borrowings. By the end of 1996, out of their $20 billion total foreign borrowings, 64% were short term, but 85% of their lending activities were long term.[38]

The influx of foreign capital not only into Korea but also to the region in the 1990s stemmed from investors' positive outlook for east Asia. As the "major engine of growth for the global economy," Asian economies were praised for their extraordinary success generated by high savings and investment, a domestic environment that encouraged innovation and modern technology, and outward-looking policies.[39] Their growth, along with financial deregulation, stable exchange rates against the U.S. dollar, low fiscal deficits, and low interest rates in the United States and Japan, attracted almost $100 billion in private flows in 1996, more than double the amount in 1994, the largest inflow of any region with the bulk coming from private creditors.[40]

As 1996 marked Korea's official entry into the OECD, foreign portfolio investment alone surged to $12.4 billion, a 63% increase from that in 1993.[41] The situation on the trade front, however, started to deteriorate. The price of the 64-mega DRAM chip, Korea's leading export product, slumped more than 70%, and the terms of trade fell about 20% in 1996–1997, the biggest drop since the first oil shock in the 1970s.[42] The current account deficit widened, while some critics noted that conglomerates were stretched thin with heavy investments in new facilities. In fact, the top 30 conglomerates' return on assets stood at a mere 0.2% by 2006 compared with 3.2% in 1995.[43] The whole corporate sector's operating income growth rate had slumped to –14% in 1996 compared with 26% the previous year.[44]

Kim failed to pass a new labor law that would have allowed companies the flexibility to lay off workers and control wage hikes amid vehement opposition from labor unions. Meanwhile, short-term debt more than doubled to $98 billion at the end of September 1997 from 1993, consisting of more than half of Korea's external liabilities.[45]

Then Hanbo Steel, one of the top 30 *chaebol*, became the first major conglomerate to go bankrupt in more than a decade under $6 billion of debt in January 1997. Kim's son was also convicted of bribery for helping Hanbo secure new loans to expand, delivering a blow to Kim's already faltering credibility. Two other large conglomerates, Jinro and Sammi, collapsed, marking events unprecedented in Korea's corporate history.

The Asian Financial Crisis

The coming economic crisis will involve bone-carving pain.

—President Kim Young Sam, November 1997[46]

External events around the region started to unfold. In July 1997, Thailand was forced to devalue its currency amid speculative attacks on the baht. Capital fled the region. The Indonesian rupiah and the Malaysian ringgit met similar fates.[47] Yet even as Thailand and Indonesia sought emergency rescue funds from the IMF, Korea initially did not expect to be swept up in the crisis. After all, the IMF had predicted Korea to grow by 6.5% in October 1998.[48] In a confidential report released in the same month, the IMF noted: "The situation in Korea is quite different to that in Southeast Asia, and our assessment is that the weaknesses in the financial sector are manageable if dealt with properly. While there are obvious risks, macroeconomic fundamentals remain strong and the current account deficit is narrowing toward a more comfortable range. External financing is certainly tight but we have confidence in the authorities' ability to prudently manage the situation."[49]

Yet the events in surrounding countries triggered foreign banks to demand repayment on outstanding loans and cancel credit lines. Standard & Poor's, a leading credit-rating agency, downgraded Korea's short- and long-term foreign currency debt. The Korean won came under attack, depreciating more than 20% within November alone (see **Exhibit 12**). The trading band of the currency was expanding up to ±10% from ±2.25% to no avail. Jittery nerves unraveled as the domestic stock market plunged, affecting markets in the United States and Europe as well. Amid efforts to defend the won, the nation's usable foreign currency reserves, which stood at $30.5 billion at October's end, rapidly depleted.[50] Last-minute efforts to avoid seeking help from the IMF were made. "In the late 1970s with the second oil shock, we experience a crisis but survived it. So we thought the same thing would happen; this was a temporary liquidity crisis that we could handle, such as by asking our neighbors like Japan for some help," recalled Byeon Yang Ho, former director general at the Finance Ministry.[51] However, by November 20, as the economic situation continued to worsen and requests for help were turned down, Korea swallowed its pride and announced that it would seek standby loans from the IMF. Within two weeks of negotiations, on December 3, a record $58 billion bailout package was announced.[52]

The announcement, unfortunately, did little to pacify the panic-stricken market or investors. Reports floated that usable foreign currency reserves had sunk to $6 billion and that the nation's short-term foreign debt exceeded $100 billion, more than twice the previous estimate. Bond-rating agencies further slashed Korea's debt to junk-bond status. In addition to the economic turmoil, Korea was facing a presidential election right around the corner. A statement by Kim Dae Jung, a left-wing opposition candidate who later won the election, saying that he would renegotiate the IMF deal created a greater sense of panic among foreign investors.

By mid-December, the unthinkable—national default—was raised as a possibility. Almost all of the $9 billion the IMF had disbursed had been used, and the Korean won had plunged 40% from its level when the deal was announced.[53] Byeon added, "There were people who thought we had no choice but to default, but if we did that, who would trust us again? The effects would have been absolutely devastating for 10, 20 years down the road."[54] The U.S. Federal Reserve and other central banks, recognizing their exposure level to Korea, placed calls to commercial bank executives from the United States to Germany, on vacation for the holidays, to make a choice: reschedule Korea's debt or have the country default. "Frankly, Korea was hours away from declaring national bankruptcy," according to Tami Overby.[55]

It was not until the IMF agreed to the speedier disbursement of $10 billion from the already committed fund with an "IMF-plus" agreement promising broader reforms and major foreign creditors banks' announcement that they would stop calling in the loans and try to roll over the debt that the hemorrhage stopped. A teary-eyed Finance Minister Lim Chang Yuel, known as a nationalistic, tough bargainer, who had been appointed less than a month before in hopes of negotiating a better deal, appeared on national TV to "beg the forgiveness of the Korean people."[56]

Korea's Reaction to the Crisis

We were trapped in a kind of complacent sentiment. So, under those conditions, it was very difficult to change our mind, system, and culture . . . so that kind of financial crisis gave us the momentum to change.

—Jin Nyum, former finance and economy minister, 2007[57]

The election of President Kim Dae Jung initially raised doubts of whether Korea would stick to the conditions of the IMF's loan. Not only was he the first president to be elected from the opposition party, but he was also well-known as a radical populist with strong pro-labor tendencies who had spent his entire life crusading for democracy. Yet Kim vowed to not only implement the IMF program but also to usher in a new fair-market economy that operated according to market principles. In his inauguration speech, Kim said, "All of us are being asked to shed sweat and tears. Let us resolutely march forward hand in hand," as the nation stood on the brink of disaster.[58]

The Korean people, in a remarkable sign of unity, also launched a gold-collection drive, donating symbolic gold rings and bracelets given for birthdays and anniversaries worth more than $2 billion. People braved the cold winter temperatures to line up and donate the gold, which was melted into bars and sold overseas, thus helping to raise much-needed foreign currency for the nation. "I couldn't believe the lines outside the banks . . . where people would give up their own assets for the national good to voluntarily save their country," recalled Overby.[59]

The IMF: Loan and Conditions

The macroeconomic program of the IMF loan focused on a tight monetary and fiscal policy[60] (see **Exhibit 13**). The Korean won, which had traded under a managed float system whereby it was permitted to fluctuate within a given trading band, was required to fully float. To stabilize the exchange rate, the IMF called for high interest rates to restore confidence in the currency. Stanley Fisher, former first deputy managing director at the IMF, explained, "The best approach is to effect a sharp, but temporary, increase in interest rates to stem the outflow of capital" by making it more attractive to hold domestic currency.[61] Foreign currency reserves were required to cover at least two months of imports.

Although high interest rates, which surged beyond 30% at one point, helped to stabilize the exchange rate, they choked the already weak financial institutions and corporations, especially given that inflation was only at around 5%. A severe credit crunch fueled mass bankruptcies as banks refused to not only provide new loans but roll over existing ones. Private consumption froze, and unemployment soared in a country where lifelong employment had been guaranteed, dragging Korea into a recession. Angry jobless workers paraded the streets wearing signs saying the IMF symbolized "I'M Fired."[62] One observer commented, "The IMF was more accustomed to Latin America crises that were caused by high government debt and high inflation, rather than what we experienced, such as the outbreak of our domestic corporate debt problem. Therefore, the IMF probably underestimated how its high interest rate policy would impact Korean companies."[63]

A fiscal austerity program was implemented, which involved the government slashing state spending and raising taxes. The fiscal adjustment was supposed to cover the cost of restructuring the financial sector and restore a sustainable balance of payments, especially the current account deficit.[64] Yet contrary to the initial target of a fiscal surplus of 0.2% of GDP, Korea posted a 5% fiscal deficit in December 1998 (see **Exhibit 14**). Even the former director of the IMF's Asia and Pacific Department admitted, "The depth of the recession was underestimated. In particular, we did not foresee the collapse of investment as a consequence of the problems in the banking system, the virulence of contagion resulting from the working of capital markets."[65]

As similar IMF conditions attached to rescue loans caused recessions in other recipient countries, such as Indonesia, criticisms sparked from various corners of the globe regarding the causes of the crisis, such as the contagion effect. Jeffrey Sachs, professor at Columbia University, noted, "The IMF's seal of approval is a seal of doom."[66] In Korea, the fiscal budget was revised several times throughout 1998. Reversing the initial agreement, the Korean government pushed for an expansionary policy, which included greater social and capital expenditure to create jobs and expand the social safety net. "I basically became a Keynesian," said Jin Nyum.[67] In addition, interest rates on the call rate and the three-year bond were lowered to single-digit levels not seen in decades, which paved the way for companies to lower their debt and encouraged financial institutions to start extending loans again.

Debates regarding the appropriateness of the IMF's austerity approach raged as well. The IMF felt that the U.S. Treasury had ulterior motives in imposing structural changes. "The U.S. saw this as an opportunity, as they did in many countries, to crack open all these things that for years have bothered them," according to a member of the IMF's Asia and Pacific Department.[68] After all, foreign investors had a long list of complaints, ranging from restrictions on stock market investments to automobile imports to inefficient bureaucratic red tape. Martin Feldstein, president of the National Bureau of Economic Research, also argued that the IMF should not use currency crises to force fundamental structural and institutional reforms, unless they were absolutely necessarily to revive access to international funds.[69] On the other hand, some Korean government officials believed that without the crisis, the government would not have been able to push through the necessary financial and corporate reforms that had to be addressed sooner or later. As one observer commented, "Many Korean economists will say that the crisis didn't last long enough, that they would have been able to set up a structure that would make Korea truly competitive if the crisis didn't end so soon."[70]

Wave of Reform

Financial sector Prior to the outbreak of the financial crisis, former President Kim Young Sam had launched a Presidential Commission for Financial Reform in January 1997. The committee proposed several recommendations, which included making the central bank free from the influence of the Finance Ministry, creating a financial supervisory service that would oversee and consolidate the supervision of all financial institutions that was disbursed among different organizations, and deregulating the financial sector. However, due to opposition from various interest groups, the reform proposal was in a deadlock. With the outbreak of the financial crisis "a large portion of what the Financial Reform Committee has been pursuing was included as conditions of the IMF loan," said Hahm Joon Ho, former member of the commission.[71]

Banking-sector reform began with the immediate closure of nonviable banks. More than 700 financial institutions were disposed through closures, mergers, and asset purchase and liabilities assumptions; the number of merchant banks alone shrank from 30 to three by June 2003 (see **Exhibit 15**). Many analysts believed that because the banks had always been under the government's influence and lacked large controlling stakeholders, it was easier for the government to aggressively push through financial-sector reforms. The remaining banks were required to meet international standards of capital adequacy, increase transparency, and improve corporate governance such as by appointing outside directors to their boards.

A total of KRW160 trillion in public funds was used to restructure the financial sector; the bulk of the funds were used to recapitalization and purchase nonperforming loans, which prior to the crisis had been loosely classified as loans in arrears for six months or more (see **Exhibit 16**). Part of the funds were raised by Korea Asset Management Corporation, a state-run agency that primarily focused on disposing the banks' bad debts through domestic and international auctions in the form of asset-based securities.[72] The organization was successful in disposing about a third of the total principal value of the bad loans it had purchased and recovered more than KRW14.3 trillion, 111% of the purchase price of the loans.[73]

Foreign investment Kim was also a big believer in attracting foreign investment, viewing it as a key to restore confidence in the Korean economy and make Korean companies more competitive. The banking sector was one of the first sectors to see this happen with a legal amendment that permitted foreign takeovers and mergers following the crisis. In 1999, U.S.-based Newbridge Capital became the first foreign institution to buy a domestic financial institution, Korea First Bank, one of the first banks nationalized with massive nonperforming loans. Other foreign investments followed, such as Commerzbank of Germany's purchase of a 30% stake in Korea Exchange Bank. With the complete opening of the stock market to foreigners in May 1998, their share of market capitalization of the Korea Stock Exchange surged to 38% in 2001 from 15% in 1997.[74] Various sectors of the economy, including real estate development and investment companies, were liberalized as well.

Tackling the *chaebol* As in the past, trying to reform the *chaebol*, especially given their dominant influence over the economy, posed one of the biggest challenges for the Kim administration. Conglomerates were blamed as causing the nation's worst economic crisis. Thus, they pledged to execute five major reforms: adopt transparent management practices, halt cross-guarantee debt payments among subsidiaries within the same business group, build a healthy financial structure, focus on key businesses, and make majority shareholders and managers accountable.

Conglomerates' debt-equity ratio was ordered to be slashed to 200% within two year from their average of over 500% as of the end of 1997 (see **Exhibit 9b**). The higher interest rate imposed by the IMF was one way to encourage the corporate sector to reduce its traditionally high dependency on debt and focus more on equity.[75] However, conglomerates cut their debt/equity ratios through new stock issues and asset reevaluations rather than through the actual repayment of debts, which did little to improve the companies' profitability.

A "big deal" program took place, whereby top five conglomerates swapped businesses with one another to eliminate overcapacity in certain sectors, sell their smaller unprofitable operations, and focus on their core businesses instead. For example, Hyundai Electronics purchased LG Semiconductors, while Samsung and Daewoo swapped their auto and electronics companies, respectively. The remaining top 30 *chaebol* underwent a "workout" program, led by creditor banks, which primarily focused on rescheduling debt, providing fresh credit, and working through corporate restructuring plans between the creditors and the company. To make companies more accountable for their managerial decisions, corporate governance was introduced, which involved reporting consolidated financial statements, strengthening minority shareholders' rights, and imposing an investment ceiling to a related company of 25% of net assets of a business group.

The collapse of the Daewoo Group, the second-largest conglomerate, in 1999 served as a litmus test of the Kim administration's commitment to corporate reforms. Kim Woo Choong, Daewoo's chairman, recklessly expanded his sprawling empire in 1998 under his belief that he could weather the storm by accumulating more debt. The conglomerate broke up under $80 billion of debt in 1999 as its main creditor, state-run Korea Development Bank, refused to provide or restructure loans, shattering the old belief that the *chaebol* was too big to fail.

Yet the case of Hyundai Engineering and Construction, another *chaebol*-affiliated company, raised doubts as creditor banks, many under the government's control, rolled over loans and worked out debt for equity swaps for the financially nonviable firm. Government officials defended their action, citing that the cost of letting the company go bankrupt outweighed the cost of bailing it out.[76] In addition to the Hyundai Engineering case, transparency of consolidated financial statements for companies still remained weak, and cross-holdings of the top 30 conglomerates actually rose to $32 billion in June 1999, twice the 1997 figure, creating doubts about the effect of corporate reforms.[77]

Economic Recovery

Despite the controversies surrounding the conditions attached to the IMF loan, the economy started to rebound, boosted by exports, especially those of electronic goods, while imports fell dramatically. Korea posted a current account surplus of $40 billion in 1998, reversing its $8 billion deficit suffered in 1997. Labor unions, through a tripartite committee of the government, business, and labor, reluctantly agreed to a landmark decision to legally permit layoffs and allow companies to use contract and temporary workers.

Another boost came from the Kim Dae Jung administration's new paradigm—revive the economy through domestic private consumption, reducing the nation's heavy dependency on exports as the main engine of growth. Credit cards, which had been largely ignored and limited in their capacity, mostly functioning as debit cards, were selected as the new stimulus tool. Merchants were ordered to accept credit cards or face a tax audit. To encourage people to borrow and spend, the government provided various incentives, ranging from large tax breaks for both consumers and merchants to holding monthly lotteries to win up to won 100 million.[78] Companies, eager to attract new customers, signed people up at sidewalk booths with no credit check or address verification. "This was a massive change in a country where people had always been told to save. Now the reversal . . . new promotion was that it was your national, patriotic duty to spend to help revive the economy," commented Chang Yun Sok, country manager of MasterCard Korea.[79]

As a result, the credit card industry played a major role in stimulating consumption and leading the economy out of its recession. The number of credit cards surged to 104 million in 2002 from fewer than 40 million in 1999.[80] Despite a double-digit fall in exports, Korea still grew 3% in 2001, which would have been unthinkable prior to the crisis. Many Koreans chose to use the cash-advance facility as a synthetic revolving card, paying off one credit card loan with another. However, with the lax issuance standards and lack of a positive credit bureau to monitor delinquencies and risk management, the credit card bubble burst in 2003. By the end of September 2003, total credit card debt reached KRW63.4 trillion, about 11% of Korea's GDP[81] (see **Exhibit 17**).

Many observers, including newly elected President Roh Moo Hyun in 2003, criticized Kim Dae Jung for using a short-term stimulus package to pull the economy out of a recession that was not sustainable in the long term. However, with the collapse of LG Credit Card Co., the nation's largest credit card company, Roh provided rescue packages and public funds to avoid another economic crisis on the scale of the 1997 financial crisis.

The Way Forward

By 2007, the 10-year anniversary of the Asian financial crisis, Korea was one of the fastest-growing OECD-member countries. Policymakers, however, deemed additional restructuring of Korea necessary as economic growth had slowed to about 4% in the past few years. Korea's competitiveness in the global economy was caught between the shadow of Japan's advanced technology skills and the threat of China's bustling economic growth and attractiveness for FDI. To boost productivity, the OECD pointed out that Korea needed to further integrate itself into the global economy, such as by attracting more foreign investment and liberalizing trade.[82] Lee Myung-bak, who was elected in 2007 to become the next president, had promoted a "747" vision during his campaign—7% annual growth, per capita income of $40,000, and seventh-largest economy in the world—as a leading theme of his campaign platform. Such growth would have to be accompanied by a new impetus for reform.

Many critics noted that regulatory changes were not enough. The *chaebol* still dominated the economy from President Park's lasting legacy of creating "Frankenstein companies" too big and too difficult to control.[83] Others considered militant labor unions a key weakness in the economy, with frequent strikes not only crippling production and sales at major companies such as Hyundai Motors Co. but also cited as the biggest concern among foreign firms. Foreign investment funds such as Newbridge Capital, which reaped profits from making high-risk investments by buying stakes in distressed Korean financial institutions, were often viewed with hostility in the local press for making what Koreans deemed as excessive profits. As analysts pointed out, "Old habits die hard, and the enactment of legislation more compatible with global trends does not in itself mean that corporate attitudes will change."[84] U.S.-based Lone Star was even accused of stock price manipulation and tax evasion regarding its purchase of a 51% stake in Korea Exchange Bank, depicted as a "demon" by the local press after being hailed as a "savior" for its willingness to invest in troubled financial Korean companies just a few years before.[85]

Observers noted that Koreans had a tendency to emphasize problems more than achievements, despite the optimistic fundamentals, such as sound macroeconomic policy and human capital.[86] After all, the nation had only experienced two years of negative growth in its history since the Korean War—in 1980 with the second global oil shock and debt crisis, and in 1998 with the Asian financial crisis. Did this mean that Korea was simply unable to accept its status in the twenty-first century as a more mature economy, which translated to slower single-digit growth? Could Korea truly become more competitive and stronger if the powerful *chaebol,* which had been the engine of growth, were dismantled? Had the necessary systematic adjustments been made but not accompanied by a national consensus that included a change in workers' and society's mind-set toward globalization?

Exhibit 1 Map of South Korea

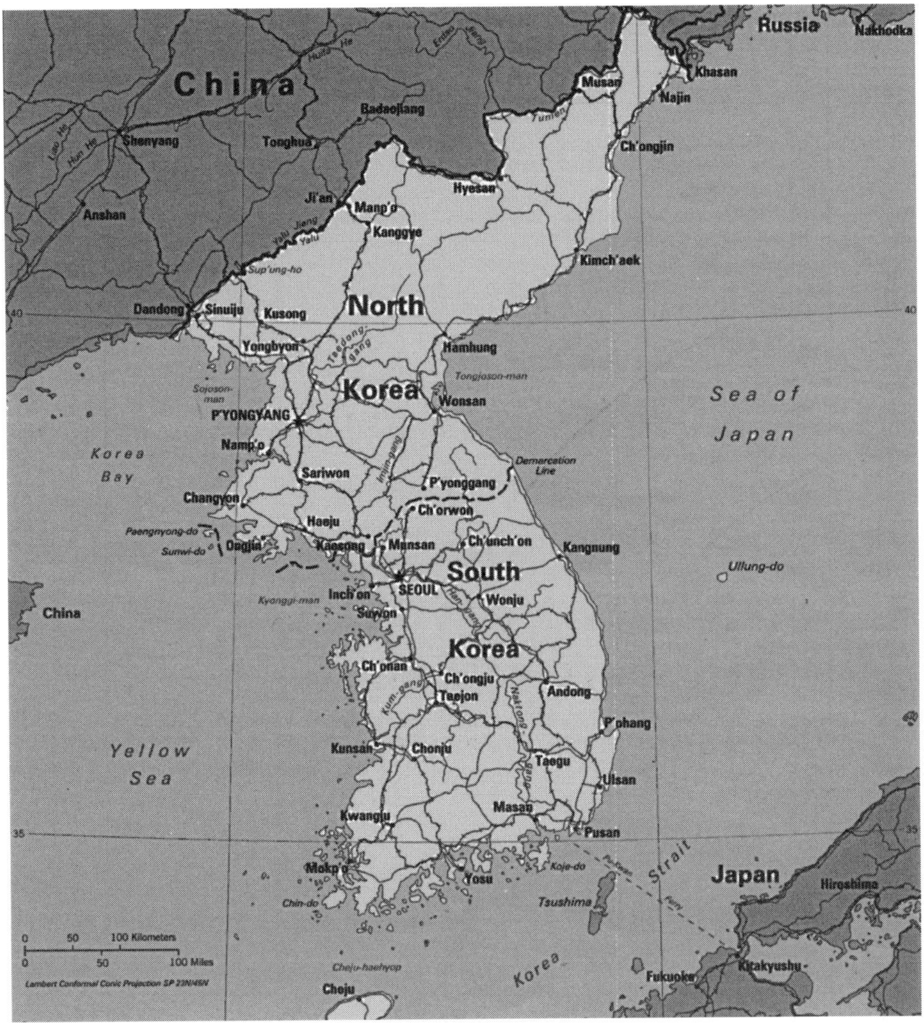

Source: U.S. Central Intelligence Agency.

Exhibit 2a Key Economic Data

	1970	1975	1980	1985	1990	1995	1996	1997	1998	1999	2000	2001	2002	2003	2004	2005	2006
Gross Domestic Product, current prices (Hundreds of Mln US$)	81	215	638	966	2,637	5,173	5,574	5,164	3,461	4,452	5,118	4,820	5,469	6,080	6,809	7,913	8,874
Per Capita GDP, current prices (US$)	-	607	1,673	2,366	6,151	11,471	12,244	11,237	7,477	9,549	10,888	10,177	11,483	12,704	14,173	16,438	18,373
Percentage of GDP:																	
Private	74.5	69.0	62.5	56.6	50.9	52.3	52.7	52.7	49.3	51.9	54.0	55.2	55.7	53.7	51.5	52.6	53.5
Government	9.8	11.2	12.4	11.2	11.8	11.2	11.6	11.6	12.8	12.3	12.1	12.9	12.9	13.3	13.5	14.2	14.8
Gross Fixed Capital Formation	25.6	26.9	32.2	28.8	37.1	37.3	37.5	35.6	30.3	29.7	31.1	29.5	29.1	29.9	29.5	29.3	29.0
Exports of Goods and Services	13.6	26.9	32.1	32.0	28.0	28.8	27.9	32.4	46.2	39.1	40.8	37.8	35.3	37.9	44.0	42.3	43.2
Imports of Goods and Services	23.8	35.4	40.0	31.4	29.0	29.9	31.3	33.0	33.3	32.4	37.7	35.5	33.9	35.6	39.7	39.9	42.1
GDP Growth rate, at 2000 prices (%)	-	5.9	-1.5	6.8	9.2	9.2	7.0	4.7	-6.9	9.5	8.5	3.8	7.0	3.1	4.7	4.2	5.0
GDP Deflator increase rate (%)	-	26.0	24.0	4.8	10.5	7.4	5.1	4.6	5.8	-0.1	0.7	3.5	2.8	2.7	2.7	-0.2	-0.4
Gross Saving Ratio (%)	17.8	19.5	24.7	31.2	37.5	36.3	35.5	35.5	37.5	35.3	33.7	31.7	31.3	32.8	34.9	32.9	31.4
Consumer Price Index (%)	16.0	25.2	28.7	2.5	8.6	4.5	4.9	4.4	7.5	0.8	2.3	4.1	2.7	3.5	3.6	2.8	2.2
M1 (% change)	-	28.7	20.5	16.6	24.2	12.6	13.8	18.2	-3.6	29.6	24.5	18.0	22.5	6.9	8.3	8.5	-0.8
M2 (% change)	-	-	-	-	27.9	19.7	20.9	18.0	23.6	13.5	2.2	6.9	11.5	7.9	4.6	6.9	8.3
Overnight call rates (%)	-	-	-	-	-	12.4	12.4	13.7	14.9	4.9	5.1	4.6	4.2	4.0	3.6	3.3	4.2
Korea Stock Exchange, at year-end[a]	-	-	108.8	138.7	746.0	934.9	833.4	654.5	406.1	806.8	734.2	572.8	757.0	679.8	832.9	1,073.6	1,352.2
Exchange Rate, KRW/US$[b]	316.7	484.0	659.9	890.2	716.4	774.7	844.2	1,695.0	1,200.0	1,135.0	1,263.0	1,313.0	1,185.8	1,192.0	1,035.1	1,007.4	929.5
Foreign Currency Reserves (billion US$)	0.6	1.5	6.5	7.7	14.5	31.9	32.4	19.7	52.0	73.7	95.9	102.5	120.8	154.5	198.2	210.0	238.4
Population (million)	31.9	35.3	38.1	40.8	42.9	45.1	45.5	46.0	46.3	46.6	47.0	47.3	47.6	47.8	48.1	48.3	48.7
Unemployment rate (%)	-	-	-	4.0	2.5	2.1	2.0	2.6	7.0	6.3	4.4	4.0	3.3	3.6	3.7	3.7	3.5
Labor productivity growth (%)	-	-	-	2.9	6.0	6.1	4.7	2.9	-0.9	7.6	4.1	1.8	4.1	3.2	2.8	2.8	3.7

Source: Compiled by casewriter using Bank of Korea, ECOS database, http://ecos.bok.or.kr/EIndex_en.jsp, accessed August 1, 2007; data on population, unemployment rate, and labor productivity growth from Economist Intelligence Unit Country Data, www.eiu.com, accessed August 25, 2007.

[a]Based on January 4, 1980 = 100.

[b]Year-end closing price.

Exhibit 2b Balance of Payments (in million of US$)

	1980	1985	1990	1995	1996	1997	1998	1999	2000	2001	2002	2003	2004	2005	2006
Current Account	**-5,313**	**-795**	**-2,014**	**-8,665**	**-23,120**	**-8,287**	**40,371**	**24,522**	**12,251**	**8,033**	**5,394**	**11,950**	**28,174**	**14,981**	**6,093**
Trade Balance	-4,614	-20	-2,461	-4,365	-15,077	-3,256	41,665	28,463	16,954	13,488	14,777	21,952	37,569	32,683	29,214
Exports	17,245	26,633	63,660	124,934	130,038	138,731	132,251	145,375	176,221	151,478	163,414	197,289	257,710	288,971	331,845
Imports	21,859	26,653	66,121	129,298	145,115	141,986	90,586	116,912	159,267	137,990	148,637	175,337	220,141	256,288	302,631
Services Balance	-723	459	-615	-2,979	-6,179	-3,200	1,024	-651	-2,848	-3,872	-8,198	-7,424	-8,046	-13,658	-18,763
Income Balance	-512	-2,086	-88	-1,303	-1,815	-2,454	-5,638	-5,159	-2,421	-1,198	432	326	1,083	-1,563	-539
Current Transfers Balance	536	852	1,150	-19	-49	623	3,320	1,869	566	-385	-1,618	-2,905	-2,432	-2,482	-3,820
Capital and Financial Account	**6,522**	**1,633**	**2,564**	**16,786**	**23,327**	**1,314**	**-3197**	**2,040**	**12110**	**-3,391**	**6,252**	**13,909**	**7,599**	**4,757**	**18619**
Financial Account:	6,518	1,725	2,896	17,273	23,924	1,922	-3,368	2,430	12,725	-2,660	7,338	15,308	9,352	7,097	21,652
Direct Investment Balance	-20	-358	-263	-1,776	-2,345	-1,605	673	5,136	4,285	1,108	-224	100	4,588	2,010	-3,484
Portfolio Investment Balance	134	1,737	84	11,591	15,185	14,295	-1,878	8,676	11,998	6,583	709	17,907	8,619	-1,728	-22,544
Other Investment Balance	6,405	345	3,075	7,459	11,085	-10,768	-2,162	-11,382	-3,557	-10,351	6,854	-2,699	-3,856	6,815	47,679
Changes in Reserves Assets	-841	41	1,186	-7,045	-1,389	11,922	-30,975	-22,983	-23,771	-7,576	-11,799	-25,849	-38,711	-19,806	-22,112
Errors and Omissions	-369	-878	-1,736	-1,076	1,182	-4,949	-6,200	-3,579	-590	2,934	154	-10	2,938	68	-2,600

Source: Compiled by casewriter using Bank of Korea, ECOS database, http://ecos.bok.or.kr/EIndex_en.jsp, accessed August 1, 2007.

Exhibit 3 Five-Year Development Plans

Plan	Period	Growth Rate	Goals	Policy Initiatives
First	1962–1966	7.1[a] 7.9[b]	• Break away from poverty • Establish a foundation for self-sustainable economic development	1. Develop energy industries such as electricity and coal. 2. Expand social overhead capital. 3. Increase export and develop import substitution industries. 4. Increase agricultural productivity.
Second	1967–1971	7.0[a] 9.7[b]	• Modernize industrial structure • Promote self-sustainability of economic development	1. Improve industrial structure through construction of heavy industries such as steel, machinery, etc. 2. Expand exports and promote import substitutes. 3. Increase farm household incomes. 4. Advance scientific technology.
Third	1972–1976	8.6[a] 10.2[b]	• Harmonize growth, stability, and equity • Realize a self-reliant economy • Develop the national land and balance regional development	1. Develop heavy and chemical industries. 2. Develop self-sufficiency in food staples. 3. Expand exports and improve trade structure. 4. Become more self-sufficient in food supply by developing farming and fishing villages. 5. Improve science, technology, and human resources.
Fourth	1977–1981	9.2[a] 5.7[b]	• Achieve self-sustaining economy • Promote equity through social development • Promote technology and improve efficiency	1. Create self-sufficiency in investment capital. 2. Achieve balance-of-payments equilibrium. 3. Carry out industrial restructuring and enhance international competitiveness. 4. Increase employment and develop manpower.
Fifth	1982–1986	7.5[a] 8.7[b]	• Establish price stability • Improve technology • Restructure government's economic functions	1. Eradicate inflation-oriented economic behavior. 2. Increase competitiveness in heavy industries. 3. Readjust government functions and rationalize fiscal management. 4. Solidify competitive system and promote open-door policy.
Sixth	1987–1991	7.3[a] 9.1[b]	• Establish a socioeconomic system • Pursue industrial restructuring and improvements in technology • Improve national welfare through balanced regional development and income distribution	1. Enhance efficiency and strengthen competitiveness. 2. Expand employment opportunities. 3. Solidify price stability. 4. Realize balance-of-payments surplus and reduce foreign debt. 5. Balance regional and rural development. 6. Promote market economic system and readjust government functions.

Source: Byung-Nak Song, *Rise of the Korean Economy* (Hong Kong: Oxford University Press, 1990), pp. 130–133, Korea Development Institute; *Korea's Economy, Past and Present* (Seoul: Korea Development Institute, 1975), p. 25; and International Monetary Fund Country Statistics.

[a]Forecast.

[b]Actual growth rate.

Exhibit 4 Interest Rate on Bank Loans (%)

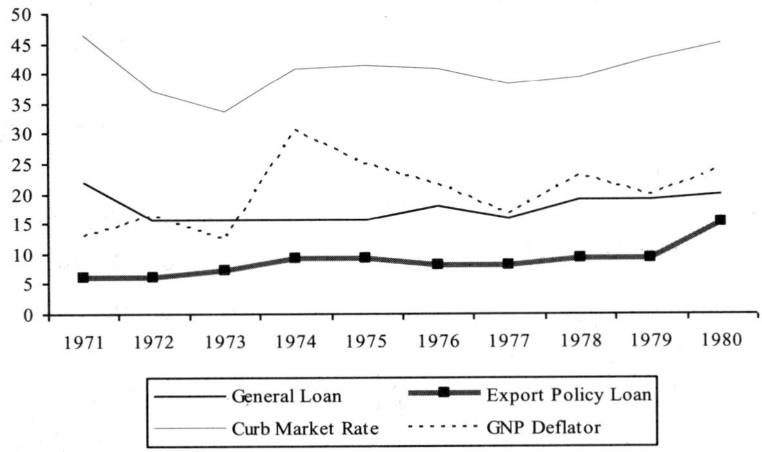

Source: Complied by casewriter based on Il Sakong, *Korea in the World Economy* (Washington, D.C.: Institute for International Economics, 1993), p. 244.

Exhibit 5 Ratio of FDI Inflows to Gross Capital Formation in East Asian Countries (%)

Country	1971–1980	1981–1990	1990–2000	2005
Japan	0.1	0.1	0.2[a]	0.3
Hong Kong	5.1	9.9	32.5	97.0
Korea	1.2	0.9	2.2	3.1
Singapore	15.8	26.2	36.5	78.9
Taiwan	1.3	1.3	2.9	2.3
Indonesia	3.5	1.5	2.2	8.5
Malaysia	13.6	11.3	18.3	15.2
Philippines	1.0	3.8	8.8	7.5
Thailand	2.3	4.8	9.4	7.2
China	0.0	1.5	11.3	9.2

Source: Jang-Sup Shin and Ha-Joon Chang, *Restructuring Korea Inc.* (London: RoutledgeCurzon, 2003), p. 12; and UNCTAD, World Investment Report 2006, http://www.unctad.org/fdistatistics, accessed September 5, 2007.

[a]From 1990 to 1997.

Exhibit 6a Exports and Imports by Major Product

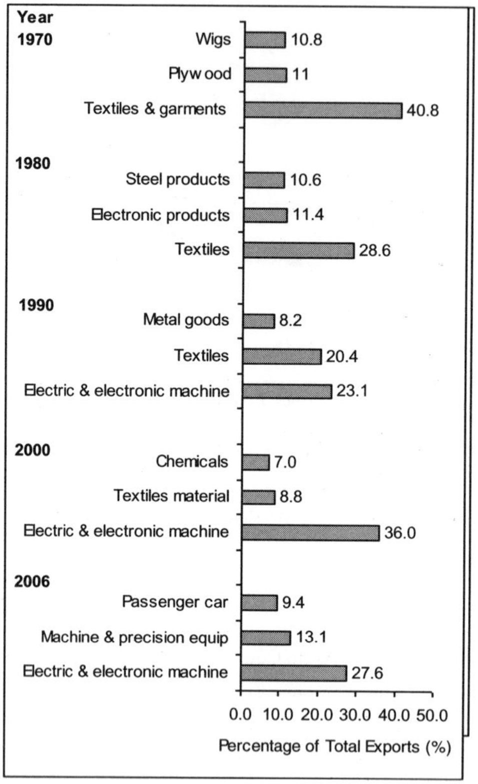

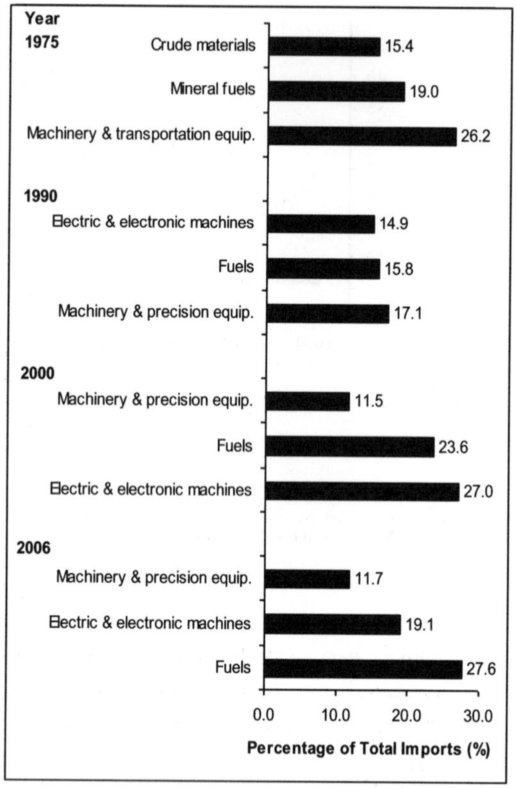

Source: Compiled by casewriter using Bank of Korea, *Economic Statistics Yearbook* (Seoul: Bank of Korea, 2007), pp. 124–125; export data prior to 1990 from Il Sakong, *Korea in the World Economy* (Washington, D.C.: Institute for International Economics, 1993), p. 232; and import data for 1975 from Byung-Nak Song, *The Rise of the Korean Economy* (Oxford: Oxford University Press, 1990), p. 106.

Exhibit 6b Exports and Imports, by Major Trade Partner

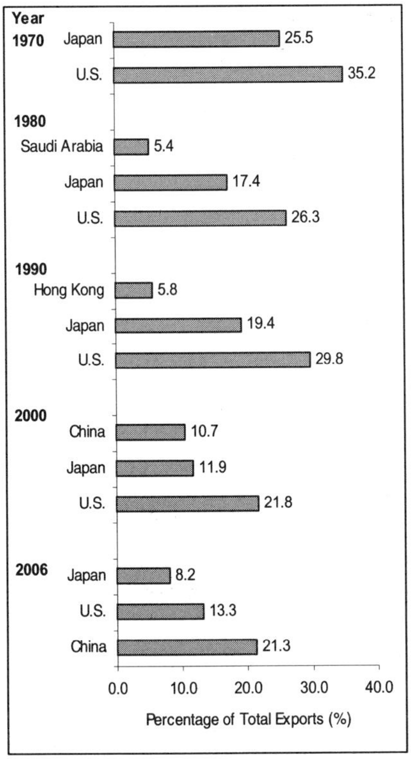

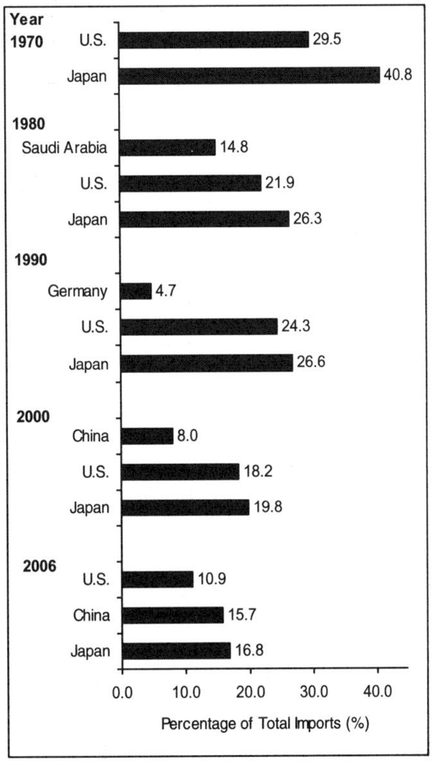

Source: Compiled by casewriter using Bank of Korea, *Economic Statistics Yearbook* (Seoul: Bank of Korea, 2007), pp. 126–129; 1970 data from Il Sakong, *Korea in the World Economy* (Washington, D.C.: Institute for International Economics, 1993), pp. 233–234.

Exhibit 7 Foreign Debt Profile

	Total (in billion of US$)[b]	Short-term Debt (% of total)	Total Debt/GDP (%)	Debt Service Ratio (%)
1960-69[a]	0.5	n.a.	10.6	3.1
1970-79 [a]	8.6	22.3	32.9	15.4
1980	27.2	34.5	44.4	13.3
1985	54.6	33.3	56.5	28.2
1990	47.0	48.5	17.8	12.0
1995	95.0	58.7	18.4	34.5
1996	120.3	59.1	21.6	28.3
1997	145.8	42.8	28.2	14.0
1998	149.1	25.5	43.2	34.9
1999	137.6	30.4	30.9	53.8
2000	130.0	32.4	25.4	74.0
2001	115.3	35.0	23.9	89.2
2002	122.5	38.0	22.4	99.1
2003	133.4	38.1	21.9	116.5
2004	142.6	39.5	20.9	139.6
2005	152.8	43.2	19.3	137.7
2006	176.3	46.7	19.9	135.5

Source: Data from 1960 to 1980 from Jang-Sup Shin and Ha-Joon Chang, *Restructuring Korea Inc.* (London: RoutledgeCurzon, 2003), p. 40; data from 1985 to 2006 from Economist Intelligence Unit Country Data, "Korea," www.eiu.com, accessed August 20, 2007.

[a]Average of annual values.

[b]Total foreign debt after 1980 is defined as total external debt stock, comprising public and publicly guaranteed long-term debt, private nonguaranteed debt, use of IMF credit and short-term debt, at end period.

Exhibit 8a Structure of Corporate Financing (%)

	1980	1985	1990	1995	1997	1998	2000	2005
Direct:	**17.6**	**20.2**	**37.1**	**45.8**	**34.6**	**170.4**	**21.2**	**30.8**
-Commercial paper	4.9	0.3	3.7	16.1	3.7	-41.7	-7.2	3.2
-Corporate bonds	6.0	13.4	21.5	15.3	23.3	163.9	-3.1	7.8
-Stocks	6.7	6.5	11.8	14.4	7.6	48.2	31.6	19.8
Indirect:	**35.2**	**46.7**	**38.3**	**31.8**	**36.7**	**-58.1**	**17.8**	**30.5**
-Bank borrowing	20.2	29.4	15.7	14.9	12.9	0.9	35.4	17.3
-NBFIs borrowing[a]	14.9	17.3	22.6	16.9	23.9	-59.1	-17.6	13.2
Trade Credit	21.5	10.4	6.6	4.9	10.6	-26.9	6.2	3.4
Foreign borrowing	13.0	-2.7	6.1	6.8	2.0	-35.7	23.6	10.1
Govt. borrowing and others	12.8	25.3	11.8	10.7	16.1	50.3	31.2	25.1

Source: Compiled by casewriter using Bank of Korea, "Flow of Funds," Ecos database, http://ecos.bok.or.kr/EIndex_en.jsp, accessed September 5, 2007.

[a]Nonbanking financial institution.

Exhibit 8b Financial Institutions' Market Share (end of period, %)

	1980	1985	1990	1995	1997	1998	2000	2005
Deposits:								
Commercial and specialized banks	70.9	53.6	41.0	27.8	26.4	27.8	42.7	43.0
NBFIs[a]	29.1	46.4	59.0	72.2	73.6	72.2	57.3	57.0
Loans and Discounts:								
Commercial and specialized banks	63.3	58.4	48.3	36.5	34.7	37.9	55.7	70.0
NBFIs	36.7	41.6	51.7	63.5	65.3	62.1	44.3	30.0

Source: Compiled by casewriter using Bank of Korea, *Economic Statistics Yearbook* (Seoul: Bank of Korea, 2007), pp. 38–43; and Joon-Ho Hahm, "Before the Economic Crisis," in *Economic Crisis and Corporate Restructuring in Korea*, eds. Stephen Haggard et al. (Cambridge: Cambridge University Press, 2003), p. 85.

[a]Nonbanking financial institution.

Exhibit 9a Top 15 *Chaebol* in 1997

Unit: billion won

Rank	Name	No. of Affiliates	Assets	Sales	Equity	Debt/ Equity Ratio (%)	Intra-group Trade (%)	Family Ownership (%)	Affiliated Ownership (%)
1.	Hyundai	57	52,821	67,990	9,842	436.7	31.6	13.8	41.6
2.	Samsung	80	50,705	60,113	13,809	267.2	28.2	3.5	42.5
3.	LG	49	37,068	46,674	8,302	346.5	23.7	5.4	34.0
4.	Daewoo[a]	32	34,197	38,243	7,817	337.5	35.6	6.1	31.2
5.	SK	46	22,723	26,640	4,703	383.2	21.4	14.1	30.1
6.	Ssangyong	25	15,804	19,445	3,102	409.5	35.4	3.6	37.5
7.	Hanjin	24	13,907	8,708	2,118	556.6	8.3	18.7	20.3
8.	Kia[a]	28	14,121	12,001	2,289	516.9	33.8	20.8	9.6
9.	Hanwha[a]	31	10,592	9,657	1,244	751.4	20.2	5.9	26.7
10.	Lotte	30	7,753	7,192	2,654	192.1	11.2	3.4	19.4
11.	Kumho	25	7,399	4,443	1,281	477.6	7.1	2.0	37.8
12.	Halla[a]	18	6,627	5,293	306	2,065.7	31.0	18.8	30.5
13.	Dongah[a]	19	6,289	3,885	1,383	354.7	2.6	12.0	42.2
14.	Doosan	25	6,369	4,042	808	688.2	15.8	13.4	35.9
15.	Daelim	20	5,849	4,832	1,118	423.2	26.4	8.8	25.1

Source: Sea-Jin Chang, *Financial Crisis and Transformation of Korean Business Group* (Cambridge: Cambridge University Press, 2003), pp. 12–13.

Exhibit 9b Top 10 Conglomerates, before and after the Crisis

		Assets (in trillion won, year-end)		Debt-Equity Ratio (in %, year-end)	
Rank	Company	1996	1999	1997	1999
1	Hyundai	59.3	88.6	579	152
2	Samsung	54.4	67.4	371	146
3	LG	45.5	47.6	313	148
4	Daewoo	37.5	n/a[a]	472	n/a[a]
5	SK	24.0	40.1	320	133
6	Ssangyong	18.3	9.7	400	634
7	Hanjin	17.6	20.8	908	184
8	Kia	14.5	n/a[a]	524	n/a[a]
9	Hanwha	14.4	11.4	1,215	132
10	Lotte	7.9	15.8	216	76
	Top 30 average			**519**	**164**
	Top 30's average no. of subsidiaries			**27.3**	**19.0**

Source: Michael J. Enright, Jim Newton, and Elyssa Tran, "Daewoo and the Korean Chaebol," University of Hong Kong, Asia Case Research Centre, Case No.01/105C, p. 9, http://www.acrc.org.hk.

[a]Went bankrupt.

Exhibit 10 Overview of Commercial Banks

	1992	1997	1998	2000	2003	2006
Net Income (in trillion won)	n/a	-3.9	-14.2	-2.8	0.7	8.8
Return on Assets (%)	0.6	-0.9	-3.3	-0.6	0.1	1.1
Return on Equity (%)	6.7	-14.2	-52.5	-11.9	2.0	15.6
NPL ratio[a] (%)	7.1	6.1	7.4	8.8	2.7	0.8
BIS ratio[b] (%)	11.1	7.0	8.2	10.5	10.4	12.3
Market share of foreign-owned banks (%)	n/a	8.1	9.3	19.9	28.4	31.1[c]

Source: Financial Supervisory Service, Financial Statistics Information System, http://efisis.fss.or.kr/index.html, accessed September 10, 2007; data prior to 1997 compiled from Joon-Ho Hahm and Frederic Mishkin, "Causes of the Korean Financial Crisis: Lessons for Policy," NBER Working Paper 7483, January 2000, p. 73.

[a]Nonperforming loans are those classified as substandard and below.

[b]Bank of International Settlements ratio of a bank's capital and risk-weighted assets, which is used as an indicator of a bank's capital adequacy.

[c]2005 figure.

Exhibit 11 Financial Reforms during the 1990s, Prior to Joining the OECD

Interest Rate Deregulation

- Took place in four stages (between 1991 and July 1997), liberalizing all lending and borrowing rates, except demand deposit rates

Banks

- Gained freedom to increase capital, establish branches, and determine dividend payments (1994)
- Increased their business scope:
    - Expansion of securities business of deposit money banks (1990, 1993, 1994, 1995)
    - Freedom for banks and life insurance companies to sell government and public bonds over the counter (1995)
    - Permission for securities firms to handle foreign exchange business (1995)

Foreign Exchange Liberalization

- Adopted a Market-Average Foreign Exchange Rate System (1990)
- Set up foreign currency call markets
- Revised Foreign Exchange Management Act to change the basis for regulation from a positive to a negative system (1991)
- Introduced "free KRW" accounts for nonresidents (1993)
- Allowed partial KRW settlements for the export or import of visible items (1993)
- Adopted a Foreign Exchange Reform Plan that provided a detailed schedule for the reform of the foreign exchange market structure (1994)
- Significantly relaxed Foreign Exchange Concentration System (1995)

Capital Market Liberalization

- Foreign investors permitted to:
    - Invest directly in Korean stock markets with ownership ceilings (1992)
    - Purchase government and public bonds issued at international interest rates (1994)
    - Purchase nonguaranteed long-term bonds issued by small and medium-sized firms and non-guaranteed convertible bonds issued by large companies (January 1997)
- Residents permitted to invest in overseas securities via beneficiary certificates (1993)
- Abolished ceiling on domestic institutional investors' overseas portfolio investment (1995)
- Allowed private companies engaged in major infrastructure projects to borrow overseas to pay for construction cost (January 1997)
- Liberalized borrowings related to foreign direct investment (January 1997)

Policy Loans and Credit Control

- Step-wise reduction in policy loans to specific sectors (such as export industries) announced to terminate all policy loans by 1997 (1993)
- Simplified and reduced the controls on the share of a bank's loans to major conglomerates as a portion of banks' total loans

Source: Adopted from Ha-Joon Chang, Hong-Jae Park, and Chul Gyue Yoo, "Interpreting the Korean Crisis: Financial Liberalization, Industrial Policy and Corporate Governance," *Cambridge Journal of Economics* 22 (1998): 737.

Exhibit 12a Foreign Exchange Rate (KRW/US$), June 1997–March 1998

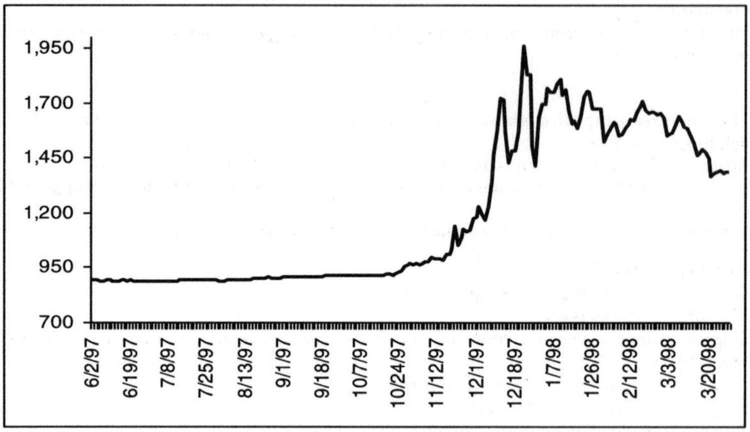

Source: Global Financial Data Database, accessed August 24, 2007.

Exhibit 12b Korea Stock Price Index (KOSPI), June 1997–March 1998

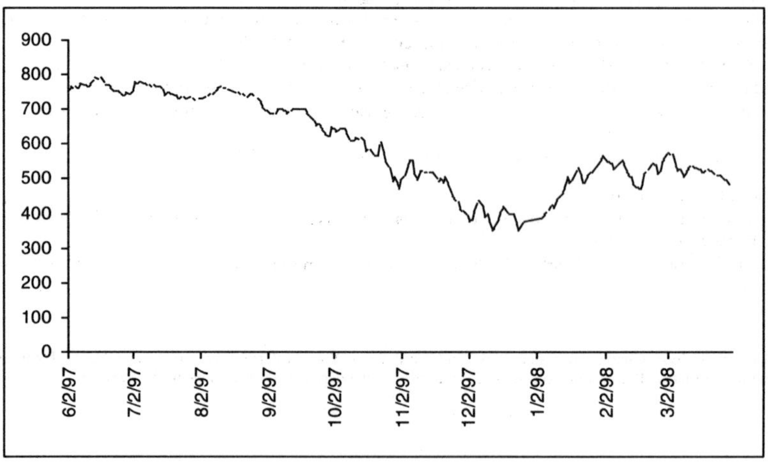

Source: Global Financial Data Database, accessed October 26, 2007.

Exhibit 13 IMF-Led Reforms Implemented by Korea

Measures	Timing
Monetary Policy:	
• Raise call rates to 30%, or above, to stabilize exchange rate	December 1997
• Eliminate interest rate ceiling	December 1997
Capital Account Liberalization:	
• Adopt a free floating foreign exchange rate system	December 1997
• Full liberalization of foreign ownership of listed Korean shares on the Korea Stock Exchange and KOSDAQ	May 1998
• Lift restrictions on M&As by foreigners	February 1998
• Full liberalization of money market instruments	May 1998
• Full liberalization of foreign investment in Korean bonds, beneficiary certificates, and KOSPI futures and options	All completed by July 1998
• Allow foreign banks and brokerages to establish subsidiaries	March 1998
• Permit foreign ownership of land and real estate properties	July 1998
Financial Restructuring:	
• Create Korea Asset Management (KAMCO) to deal with nonperforming loans (NPL)	November 1997
• Identify and suspend 14 insolvent merchant banks and two brokerages	December 1997
• Close five insolvent banks through purchase and assumption	June 1998
• Sell Korea First Bank to Newbridge Capital	December 1998
• Mobilize public funds for recapitalization and NPL purchases	KRW64 trillion in May, 1998; KRW50 trillion in September 2000
• Close, liquidate, and merge more than 600 insolvent nonbanking financial institutions	June 2002
• Financial Supervisory Commission established to plan, coordinate, and oversee banking, insurance, and securities firms restructuring	April 1998
• Strengthen nonperforming loan criteria	July 1998
• Adopt forward-looking asset classification (FLC) system	January 2000
• Strengthen governance, such as introducing outside directors, audit committees, minority shareholders' rights	January 2000
• Bank lending to borrower and its affiliates capped to 25% of bank equity capital; aggregate exposure limit for bank loans in excess of 10% of total capital	January 2000
• Limit bank lending to large shareholders to 25% of equity capital	April 2002
Other measures:	
• Abolish daily exchange rate trading band	December 1997
• Improve labor market flexibility, permit mass layoffs	February 1998
• Cross-subsidiary payment guarantees for businesses tightened to 100% from 200% of net worth	April 1998

Source: Compiled by casewriter from the International Monetary Fund, "Korea Letter of Intent," between December 1997 and July 2000, http://www.imf/org, accessed March 8, 2007; and Wonhyuk Lim and Joon-Ho Hahm, "Turning a Crisis into an Opportunity: The Political Economy of Korea's Financial Sector Reform," in *From Crisis to Opportunity: Financial Globalization and East Asian Capitalism*, eds. Jongryn Mo and Daniel Okimoto (Stanford: The Walter H. Shorenstein Asia-Pacific Research Center, 2006), p. 114–116.

Exhibit 14 IMF's Forecast and Actual Results in 1998

	Real GDP Growth Rate (%)	Inflation (%)	Current Account (billions of US$)	Fiscal Balance (as % of GDP)	Interest Rate	Usable Reserves
Initial Agreement (Dec. 1997)	3.0	5.0	-4.3	0.8% surplus	18–20%	--
Second (Jan. 1998)	1.0–2.0	9.0	3	--	Call rates around 30%	$24 billion by end of March
Third (Feb. 1998)	1.0	Slightly below double digits	8	0.8% surplus	Cautiously and Gradually Down	$30 billion by end of June
Fourth (May 1998)	-1.0	Below double digits by the year's end	21–23	1.2% deficit, but can reach up to 1.75%	Additionally Lower	$32 billion by end of June
Fifth (July 1998)	-4.0	9.0	33–35	Deficit of 4.0%	Flexibly Adjust	$41 billion by end of December
Sixth (Nov. 1998)	Positive Growth in 1999	5.0	20	Deficit of 5.0%	Maintain low interest rates	Rise moderately in 1999 (already reached $45 billion in October)
ACTUAL RESULTS (as of Dec. 1998)	**-6.9%**	**7.5%**	**40.4**	**Deficit of 5.0%**	**-**	**$52 billion**

Source: Compiled by casewriter from Korea, "Letter of Intent and Memorandum of Economic Policies," February 7, 1998 through November 13, 1998, http://www.imf.org/external/country/KOR/index.htm, accessed August 23, 2007; Kim Kyeong-won, "Post-Crisis Transformation of the Korean Economy," Samsung Economic Research Institute, September 2003, p. 316; and Bank of Korea, Ecos database, http://ecos.bok.or.kr/EIndex_en.jsp, accessed August 23, 2007.

Exhibit 15 Financial Industry Restructuring after the Crisis

	Total No. at End of 1997	Type of Resolution: License Revoked	Merger	Other[a]	New Entry	Total No. at June 2003
Banks	33	5	10	-	1	19
Merchant Banks	30	22	6	-	1	3
Securities Companies	36	5	3	2	18	44
Insurance Companies	50	8	6	2	13	47
Investment Trust Companies	31	6	1	-	9	32
Mutual Savings and Finance Companies	231	100	27	1	12	115
Credit Unions	1,666	2	106	463	9	1,104
Leasing Companies	25	9	1	1	4	17
TOTAL	**2,101**	**157**	**161**	**469**	**67**	**1,381**

Source: Adopted from Wonhyuk Lim and Joon-Ho Hahm, "Financial Globalization and Korea's Post-Crisis Reform: A Political Economy Perspective," Korea Development Institute Working Paper 2004-01, p. 21.

[a]Other resolutions included dissolution and asset transfers to bridge institutions.

Exhibit 16 Sources and Uses of Public Funds (November 1997–June 2003)

Unit: trillion won

	KDIC and Others[a]				KAMCO	
	Recapitalization	Capital Contribution	Deposit Payoffs	Purchase of Assets	Purchase of NPLs	TOTAL
Banks	34.0	13.7	0.0	14.0	24.6	86.2
NBFIs:	26.3	3.3	29.8	0.3	14.5	74.2
Merchant Banks	2.7	0.2	17.2	0.0	1.6	21.7
Insurance	15.9	2.9	0.0	0.3	1.8	21.0
Securities & ITCs	7.7	0.0	0.01	0.0	8.5	16.2
Mutual Savings Banks	0.0	0.2	7.9	0.0	0.2	8.2
Credit Cooperatives	0.0	0.0	4.7	0.0	0.0	4.7
Others	0.0	0.0	0.0	0.0	2.4	2.4
TOTAL	**60.3**	**17.0**	**29.8**	**14.3**	**39.1**	**160.4**

Source: Adopted from Wonhyuk Lim and Joon-Ho Hahm, "Financial Globalization and Korea's Post-Crisis Reform: A Political Economy Perspective," Korea Development Institute Working Paper 2004-01, p. 22.

[a]Korea Development Insurance Corporation, state-run agency that handled the resolution of insolvent financial institutions.

Exhibit 17 Outstanding Household Credit (% change)

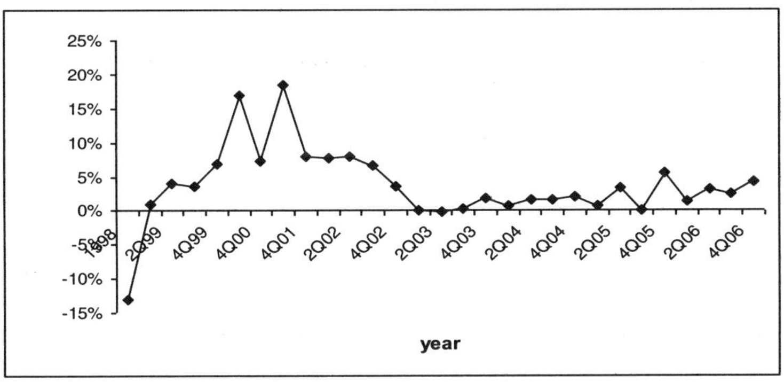

Source: Bank of Korea, "Household Credit Trends," quarterly reports from 1998 to 2006, http://ecos.bok.or.kr/EIndex_en.jsp, accessed September 12, 2007.

Endnotes

[1] Nicholas Kristof, "World Ills are Obvious, the Cures Much Less so," *New York Times*, February 19, 1999.

[2] Hong Kong, Korea, Singapore, and Taiwan are considered the Asian "tiger" economies. A broader definition of east asian "miracle" economies may also include Indonesia, Malaysia, and Thailand.

[3] "South Korea-US FTA to add 6% to GDP in next 10 Years: Think Tanks," *Asia Pulse*, April 30, 2007.

[4] Jin Nyum, casewriter interview, Seoul, June 18, 2007.

[5] Korea's Capital Market Consolidation Act, approved in July 2007, was the nation's version of a "big bang" financial reform that broke down regulatory restrictions for Korea to create domestic investment banks that offer multiple financial services. The goal was to create large-scale investment banks that could compete on the global platform.

[6] Mark Clifford, *Troubled Tiger* (New York: M.E. Sharpe, Inc., 1998), pp. 34–43. For more on Korea's history and economic situation prior to President Park Chung Hee, also see Il Sakong, *Korea in the World Economy* (Washington, D.C.: Institute for International Economics, 1993).

[7] The International Monetary Fund was a strong advocate of import substitution for developing countries at this time. See Forest Reinhardt and Edward Prewitt, "Singapore," HBS No. 793-096 (Boston: Harvard Business School Publishing, 1995), p. 4.

[8] Park Chung Hee, *The Country, the Revolution and I* (Seoul, Hollym Corp., 1970), p. 26.

[9] Kim DoHoon, "Trade Promotion and Economic Development in Korea," available at www.uneca.org/atpc/document/Mainstreaming/trade_promotion_korea.ppt, accessed July 24, 2007.

[10] Il Sakong, p. 9.

[11] Linsu Kim, Imitation to Innovation: The Dynamics of Korea's Technological Learning (Boston: Harvard Business School Press, 1997).

[12] National security concerns were also behind Park's heavy-industries drive in hopes of building a foundation for a defense industry as U.S. troops stationed in Korea were reduced, coupled with the fall of South Vietnam to communism.

[13] Bruce Cumings, *Korea's Place in the Sun: A Modern History* (New York: W.W. Norton & Company, 1997).

[14] Mark Clifford, p. 113.

[15] "The Frankenstein Economy," *The Economist*, June 3, 1995, p. 10.

[16] Il Sakong, p. 37.

[17] Tami Overby, interview by casewriter, Seoul, Korea, June 27, 2007.

[18] The top five *chaebol* were Samsung, Hyundai, Daewoo, Goldstar, and SK. Jang-sup Shin and Ha-joon Chang, *Restructuring Korea Inc.* (London: RoutledgeCurzon, 2003), pp. 28–29.

[19] Shin and Chang, p. 29.

[20] The Middle East construction boom in the 1970s sent hundreds of thousands of Korean workers abroad, thus putting pressure on the domestic economy's labor supply, which needed highly skilled workers to support the HCI drive.

[21] Susan Collins and Won Am Park, "External Debt and Macroeconomic Performance in South Korea," NBER Working Paper Series No. 2596, May 1998, p. 1.

[22] Chun's declaration of power through martial law stirred mass protests and demonstrations, especially in the southern city of Kwangju. To end the protest, Chun sent army tanks and soldiers into the city, killing

hundreds of protestors, branding the incident as the "Kwangju massacre." The brutality of the event haunted Chun throughout his presidency, and in 1996, he was charged for the incident and sentenced to death, only to be pardoned in 1997.

23 Marcus Noland, "South Korea's Experience with International Capital Flows," in *Capital Controls and Capital Flows in Emerging Economies*, ed. Sebastian Edwards (Chicago: University of Chicago Press, 2007), p. 488.

24 Hyung-koo Lee, *The Korean Economy* (Albany: State University of New York Press, 1996), p. 25.

25 Il Sakong, p. 89.

26 Byung-Kook Kim, "The Politics of *Chaebol* Reform," in *Economic Crisis and Corporate Restructuring in Korea*, eds. Stephen Haggard et al. (Cambridge: Cambridge University Press, 2003), p. 59.

27 Hyung-koo Lee, p. 24.

28 Economist Intelligence Unit Country Data, "Korea," www.eiu.com, accessed August 20, 2007.

29 John Burton, "Race to Unchain the Dragon," *Financial Times*, December 7, 1992.

30 Chung In Moon, "Changing Patterns in South Korea," in *Business and Government in Industrialising Asia*, ed. Andrew MacIntyre (New York: Cornell University Press, 1994), p. 155.

31 Byung-Kook Kim, p. 63.

32 R. Barry Johnston, Salim Dabar, and Claudia Echeverria, "Sequencing Capital Account Liberalization: Lessons from the Experiences in Chile, Indonesia, Korea, and Thailand," IMF Working Paper 97/157, November 1997, p. 24.

33 Ed Paisley, "South Korea—Pocketbook Poll: Economic Woes Dominate Voters' Choice," *Far Eastern Economic Review*, Vol. 155, Iss. 49, December 10, 1992, p. 20.

34 "Now it is our turn to Contribute to the World," *BusinessWeek*, July 31, 1995, p. 64.

35 "The Chaebol that ate Korea," *The Economist*, November 14, 1998.

36 Hahm Joon-Ho, interview by casewriter, Seoul, Korea, June 28, 2007.

37 Ha-Joon Chang, Hong-Jae Park, and Chul Gyue Yoo, "Interpreting the Korean Crisis: Financial Liberalization, Industrial Policy, and Corporate Governance," *Cambridge Journal of Economics* 22 (1998): 738.

38 Chang, Park, and Yoo: 739.

39 Michael Camdessus, "The Agenda for Global Financial Cooperation," address to the Association of Japanese Business Studies, Washington, D.C., June 13, 1997, http://www.imf.org/external/np/speeches/1997/mds9708.htm, accessed August 15, 2007.

40 Steven Radelet and Jeffrey Sachs, "What Have We Learned, So Far, From the Asian Financial Crisis?" Harvard Institute for International Development, January 4, 1999, p. 1, http://www.cid.harvard.edu/archive/hiid/papers/aea122.pdf, accessed October 12, 2007.

41 Choi Gongpil, "The Korean Experience with Financial Crisis: A Chronology," Korea Institute of Finance Research Papers 99-06, May 1999.

42 Hahm Joon-Ho and Frederic Mishkin, "Causes of the Korean Financial Crisis: Lessons for Policy," NBER Working Paper 7483, January 2000, p. 29, available at http://www.nber.org/papers/w7483, accessed June 15, 2007.

43 Hahm and Mishkin, p. 76.

44 Ibid.

[45] Marcus Noland, p. 501.

[46] Sang-hun Choe, "South Koreans Accept IMF Bailout—With Humiliation and Anger," *Associated Press*, November 22, 1997.

[47] For a chronology of events of the 1997 Asian financial crisis, see "Asian Financial Crisis: Chronology of Events," HBS No. 708-001 (Boston: Harvard Business School Publishing, 2007). For Malaysia's handling of the financial crisis, see Rawi Abdelal and Laura Alfaro, "Malaysia: Capital and Control," HBS. No. 702-040 (Boston: Harvard Business School Publishing, 2003).

[48] "IMF Mission sees S. Korean 1998 GDP Growth at 6.5%," *Reuters News*, October 15, 1997.

[49] Paul Blustein, *The Chastening* (New York: PublicAffairs, 2003), p. 118.

[50] John Burton, "Seoul Admits Debt Tops $100 billion," *Financial Times*, December 9, 1007.

[51] Byeon Yang Ho, casewriter interview, Seoul, June 21, 2007.

[52] The initial agreement was $55 billion, which consisted of $21 billion from the IMF, $10 billion from the World Bank, and $4 billion from the Asian Development Bank, the remaining $20 billion represented a "second line of defense" pledged by wealthy nations such as the United States, France, and Japan. The World Bank later pledged an additional $3 billion in aid, bringing the total sum of the bailout package to $58 billion.

[53] Blustein, p. 9.

[54] Byeon Yang Ho, interview.

[55] Tami Overby, interview.

[56] Blustein, p. 149.

[57] Jin Nyum, interview.

[58] "Kim Dae-jung Promises Reform Drive—Sworn in as New President in Yoido Ceremony," *The Korea Herald*, February 26, 1998.

[59] Tami Overby, interview.

[60] This section is based on Laura Alfaro and Rafael Di Tella, "Korea: After the 1997 Financial Crisis," HBS No. 707-042 (Boston: Harvard Business School Publishing, 2007).

[61] Stanley Fisher, "The Asian Crisis: A View from the IMF," speech at Midwinter Conference of the Bankers' Association for Foreign Trade, January 22, 1998, http://www.imf.org/external/np/speeches/1998/0122298.htm, accessed August 7, 2007.

[62] "Seattle Comes to Washington," *The Economist*, April 15, 2000.

[63] Hahm Joon-Ho, casewriter interview, Seoul, June 28, 2007.

[64] Timothy Lane, "IMF Supporting Programs in Indonesia, Korea, and Thailand—a Preliminary Assessment," IMF Occasional Paper 178, June 30, 1999, p. 62, http://www.imf.org, accessed March 1, 2007.

[65] Hubert Neiss, "In Defense of the IMF"s Emergency Role in East Asia—a Commentary," *International Herald Tribune*, October 9, 1998.

[66] Peter Passell, "South Korea's Facing Some Difficult Economic Choices," *New York Times*, December 19, 1997.

[67] Jin Nyum, interview.

[68] Blustein, p. 143.

[69] Martin Feldstein, *Foreign Affairs* 77, no. 2 (March/April 1998): 32.

[70] Tami Overby, interview.

[71] Hahm Joon-Ho, interview.

[72] For more about Korea's disposal of bad loans, see George Chacko et al., "KAMCO and the Cross-Border Securitization of Korean Non-Performing Loans," HBS No. 205-037 (Boston: Harvard Business School Publishing, 2005).

[73] KAMCO case, p. 6.

[74] Shin and Chang, p. 108.

[75] Stanley Fisher speech.

[76] Jin Nyum, interview.

[77] Michael J. Enright et al., "Daewoo and the Korean chaebol," University of Hong Kong Case No. HKU143 (University of Hong Kong: August 2001), p. 9, http://harvardbusinessonline.hbsp.harvard.edu/, accessed March 8, 2007.

[78] John Larkin, "Pushing Plastic," *Financial Times*, October 12, 2000.

[79] Chang Yun Sok, casewriter interview, Seoul, June 20, 2007.

[80] Moon Ihlwan, "Koreans' Wallets are Slamming Shut," *BusinessWeek*, July 12, 2004.

[81] Economist Intelligence Unit, *South Korea Country Report*, February 2004, p. 28, http://www.eiu.com, accessed August 9, 2007.

[82] OECD Country Survey, "Korea," June 2007, p. 150, http://www.oecd.org, accessed July 17, 2007.

[83] "Freeing Finance," *The Economist*, June 3, 1995.

[84] "South Korea Country Report," Economist Intelligent Unit, August 2007, p. 21, http://www.eiu.com, accessed August 15, 2007.

[85] Moon Ihlwan, "Public Scorn for Private Equity," *BusinessWeek*, December 4, 2006.

[86] Barry Eichengreen, "The Korean Economy: Higher Cost, Slower Growth, Freer Trade—and the Way Forward," speech delivered to the Ministry of Commerce, Industry and Energy/Korea Trade and Investment Promotion Agency conference on June 20, 2007, Seoul, http://www.econ.berkeley.edu/~eichengr/kotra_paper.pdf, accessed August 10, 2007.

9-708-001
REV: APRIL 23, 2009

LAURA ALFARO
RAFAEL DI TELLA
RENEE KIM

Chronology of the Asian Financial Crisis

In the 1990s, the "Asian miracle" was regarded as the model of successful growth as the newly developing countries in the region, including Korea, Malaysia, and Thailand, attracted investors and capital from around the world. The developing economies of Asia enjoyed an average real GDP growth above 9% during 1992–95, probably unparalleled at any time by any group of economies of comparable size.[1] Thus, in July 1997, when Thailand became the first Asian "tiger" to abandon its fixed exchange rate system in response to speculative attacks on its currency, no one quite expected a domino-like effect to engulf the region. Investors fled Asia, withdrawing their capital at a record pace, not only forcing central banks to spend billions of dollars in failed attempts to defend their currencies, but also to seek the International Monetary Fund's (IMF) assistance for bailouts. As Jeffrey Sachs, Columbia University professor, noted, "In a matter of a few months, the Asian economies went from being the darlings of the investment community to being virtual pariahs."[2]

This case presents a chronology of the major events that took place from the beginning of 1997 to the fall of 1998.

1997

February 5: Somprasong Land Plc, a Thailand-based property developer, misses a $3.1 million interest payment on its foreign debt, the first Thai firm to do so.

March 3: In an effort to boost confidence in its markets, The Bank of Thailand orders financial institutions to raise their provisions for substandard loans and cash-strapped companies to boost their capital standards. Trading of banking and financial shares is suspended on the day of the announcement, but shares tumble in the next day of trading (see **Exhibit 1**).

March 11: Thailand's government proposes a 100 billion baht bailout for troubled financial companies' bad debts incurred through their exposure to the weak property sector. IMF Managing Director Michel Camdessus praises the move and adds that "They are doing exactly what you must do to avoid recurrence of a Mexico-like crisis . . . I don't see any reason for this crisis to develop further."[3]

Professors Laura Alfaro and Rafael Di Tella and Research Associate Renee Kim prepared this case. This case was developed from published sources. HBS cases are developed solely as the basis for class discussion. Cases are not intended to serve as endorsements, sources of primary data, or illustrations of effective or ineffective management.

May 14: The Bank of Thailand adopts selective capital controls to defend the value of the baht by ordering local banks not to sell baht to foreigners in the swap market and by denying short-sellers access to the domestic market.

- "Thais Win Currency Battle, What About the War?" *Reuters News*[4]
- "Thai Currency Tactics Calm SE Asian Markets," *Financial Times*[5]
- "We need more established measures to deal with any future attacks on the baht—something like what they have in Singapore which stops its people from speculating in its own currency. We have a free and open market but we do not open our market to let people bully us." Amnuay Viravan, Thailand's Finance Minister[6]

June 19: Amnuay Viravan, a proponent of defending the currency at all costs, resigns. He is replaced by Thanong Bidaya, head of the Thai Military Bank. A few days later, 16 finance firms are ordered to shut down or consolidate with others, including the prestigious Finance One.

July 2: Thailand allows the baht to float freely for the first time since 1984, after speculative attacks on the currency due to concerns about the health of the economy forced the central bank to spend billions of dollars of its foreign reserves to try and defend the baht. The decision causes the value of the baht to immediately fall by 15%.

- "We felt it was time for them to devalue and face the reality of what their currency was really worth . . . now that they've done it, it helps, I think, to clear the deck." Mark Mobius, President of Templeton Emerging Market Fund Inc.[7]
- "The bank finally did the right thing when it had its back to the wall." *The Herald* [8]
- "The risk is you will see some similar weaknesses of the regional currencies such as the (Indonesian) rupiah and the (Malaysian) ringgit and the peso." *Reuters News*[9]

July 14: Malaysia joins Thailand and abandons its peg to allow the ringgit to float.

July 15: Kia Motors, Korea's third-largest car maker, is placed under bankruptcy protection. It is the fourth among the nation's top 30 conglomerates to go under or narrowly avoid immediate bankruptcy this year, starting with the collapse of Hanbo Steel under $6 billion of debt in January.

July 20: The IMF agrees to provide the Philippines with $1 billion in emergency loans after failing to fend off speculative attacks on the peso.

July 24: Mahathir Mohamad, Malaysia's Prime Minister, accuses George Soros, American billionaire financier, of causing the Malaysian ringgit to depreciate as speculative trading drags the ringgit to a 38-month low against the dollar (see **Exhibit 2**).

August 11: The IMF and other Asian countries approve a $16 billion loan package for Thailand in exchange for a tough economic reform plan, which includes a major restructuring of the financial sector and a tighter fiscal budget.[10]

August 14: Indonesia allows the rupiah to float, abandoning its managed trading band system, after unsuccessfully spending $1 billion to defend the currency and curb speculative attacks (see **Exhibit 3**).

September 20: Mahathir, at the IMF/World Bank annual conference held in Hong Kong, declares that "currency trading is unnecessary, unproductive, and immoral. It should be stopped."[11] George Soros then brands the Malaysian prime minister as "a menace to his own country."[12]

- "Mahathir comments rattle regional markets." *Agence France-Presse*[13]

- "Damage Control, Can Mahathir Get Malaysia Back on Course?" *BusinessWeek*[14]
- "I think Soros's remarks are incorrect because the prime minister's [Mahathir's] criticism against currency speculation and abuse of freedom in the currency trading does not mean that Dr. Mahathir is totally against currency trading." Anwar Ibrahim, Malaysia's Deputy Prime Minister[15]
- "Currency trading is an inherent and very important function in a modern and global economy, and it is integral to global trade." Robert Rubin, U.S. Treasury Secretary [16]

October 8: Indonesia seeks the IMF and the World Bank's help after the local currency falls more than 30% in two months, despite central bank interventions.

October 17: Taiwan floats the new Taiwan dollar.

October 17: Malaysia announces tough fiscal tightening measures, such as reducing the current account deficit and cutting public spending by 2%, in an attempt to prevent the crisis from hurting the economy further.[17]

October 23–28: The Hong Kong stock market loses 25% of its value amid fears over interest rates and pressure on the Hong Kong dollar, sparking other Asian markets and the Dow Jones to tumble. The Korean won begins to tumble.

October 24: Malaysia's Deputy Prime Minister says that Malaysia will not seek help from the IMF, nor does he foresee that it will need help in the near future to weather the regional crisis.[18]

October 31: The IMF announces a loan package for Indonesia of $23 billion, which eventually reaches $40 billion through pledges from other countries. In return, Indonesia closes 16 financially insolvent banks and promises other economic reforms.

- "Reform, Not Aid, Seen Key in Indonesia IMF Package," *Reuters News*[19]
- "Asia Stocks Rally on Indonesia's IMF Package," *Reuters News*[20]
- "The IMF plan may, of course, itself weaken further Mr. Suharto's political position. But if the U.S. administration and the IMF are to avert their worst fears of financial and political instability in Asia, they know that more governments must be prepared to take some painful medicine." *Financial Times*[21]

November 3: Japan's Sanyo Securities, a Top 10 brokerage firm, files for bankruptcy, the first securities company to do so since World War II.

November 19: Korea's Finance Minister, Kang Kyong-shik, is dismissed after being blamed for accelerating the nation's financial problems. Newly appointed Minister Lim Chang-Ryul says, "There is no need for financial help from the IMF"[22] and announces financial measures, such as opening the bond market to foreigners, to stem the rapidly depreciating local currency and weak stock market.

November 21: Korea swallows its pride and announces that it will seek a bailout package from the IMF worth $20 billion as the Korean stock market continues to plunge and the central bank is unable to stem the rapid depreciation of the won (see **Exhibit 4**).

- "Southeast Asia is pretty much a tea party compared to Korea." *Reuters News*[23]
- "Investors are urged to Remain Calm despite Financial Crisis in Asia. Pacific Rim Leaders Say the Turmoil can be Contained. The Issue Tops the Agenda at the APEC Summit." *The Philadelphia Inquirer*[24]
- "If Asia's governments fail to cure their sick banks, their economies' crisis—and its implications for the rest of the world—could grow much worse." *The Economist*[25]

November 24: Yamaichi Securities, another Top 10 brokerage in Japan, collapses.

December 3: Korea, the world's 11th largest economy, announces that it will receive a $55 billion bailout package, led by the IMF, in exchange for a tough restructuring program. Yet concerns over the Korean economy spill over to other regions, such as dragging the Thai baht to a record low. The previous day, the Malaysian ringgit falls to its lowest level since 1973.

December 5: Malaysia's Deputy Prime Minister Anwar Ibrahim announces a severe economic austerity program. The government cuts its 1998 growth rate forecast to 4%–5% from its previous target of 7%. Other measures include: 1) Slashing federal expenditure by at least 18%; 2) Restoring foreign currency reserves by targeting a national reserve worth at least four months of retained imports; 3) Cutting the current account deficit to the equivalent of 3% of GNP from its previous target of 4%; 4) Freezing bailout loans for failing corporations; and 5) Imposing tighter credit policies. The Kuala Lumpur Stock Exchange reacts by surging more than 5%.

December 8: In an unprecedented move, Thailand decides to permanently shut down 56 of its 58 ailing finance companies, a move welcomed by the IMF and the investment community.

December 16: Korea removes the daily foreign exchange rate band of ±10%. As jittery nerves continue to shake Asia, *BusinessWeek*'s editorial section urges, "Dear IMF: Don't Make Asia's Flu Worse," citing that "in a deflationary economic environment . . . typical IMF policy prescriptions can do more harm than good."[26]

December 17: Japan announces a surprise 2 trillion yen tax cut to stimulate its economy; markets react positively to the news.

December 22: Moody's Investors Service downgrades Indonesia, Korea, and Thailand to junk-bond status. Malaysia's rating is cut as well, but remains in the investment-grade ranking. Markets in Korea and Malaysia tumble, yet in Indonesia, the Jakarta exchange rises 1.9% as analysts said a downgrade was expected.[27]

December 23: The World Bank announces $3 billion in emergency loans to Korea, bringing the total of the loan package to $58 billion.

- "We don't know whether we'll default tomorrow or the day after tomorrow . . . . Our warehouse is empty. It's a matter of surviving a day, not a month. I can't believe how the government has been so negligent." Kim Dae Jung, newly elected President of Korea, the first to be elected from the opposition party[28]

December 23: Chinese Premier Zhu Rongji says there will be no devaluation of the yuan, despite the foreign turmoil in Asia.[29]

December 24: The IMF and other world economies agree to the speedier disbursement of $10 billion in loans to Korea, as the initial announcement of the rescue package fails to calm down the market or the depreciation of the won.

December 29: The Indonesian rupiah suffers as reports circulate that the nation's total foreign debt is at around $200 billion, which the government refutes as being closer to $130 billion.

December 30: Major international banks agree to roll over Korea's short-term debt.

1998

January 8: Malaysia's ringgit tumbles to a new all-time low against the U.S. dollar in reaction to a Bank of International Settlements report earlier in the week that Malaysia's short-term debt reached 56% of total borrowings from foreign lenders, higher than previous estimates of 30%; as well as concerns over other regional currencies, despite the central bank's interventions.

January 5: Thai Prime Minister Chuan Leekpai says that Thailand will renegotiate conditions of its rescue package with the IMF, stating that certain conditions set by the multilateral institution, such as a budget surplus of 1% of Thailand's 1998 GDP, cannot be met.

January 12: Peregrine Investments Holdings Ltd., Asia's largest private investment bank based in Hong Kong, files for liquidation, citing exposure to its loans investments in Indonesia. Hong Kong's Hang Seng Index plunges 774 points, or 8.7%.

January 15: Suharto signs a new agreement with the IMF, which includes elimination of Indonesia's monopolies and state subsidies amid concerns of Indonesia's commitment to reforms. The announcement, however, does little to restore investors' confidence.

- "Indonesia Reaches IMF Pact to Speed Reforms—Tougher Accord Expected to Curb Suharto System of 'Crony Capitalism'." *Wall Street Journal*[30]

January 23: Indonesia's rupiah plunges for five consecutive days, losing more than a third of its value. Concerns over Indonesia's financial status and indications that President Suharto could choose B.J. Habibie as vice-president (and Suharto's possible successor) prompt an attack on the local currency. Habibie is known for his unorthodox economic views and large-scale, capital intensive industrial projects, while lacking support from Indonesia's powerful army.

- "Indonesia Faces Debt, Currency Nightmare," *Reuters News*
- "Asian Crisis Worsens as Indonesia Panics," *The Evening Standard*[31]
- "Soaring Ambition: B.J. Habibie, best known for his bold aerospace plans, may be set to take the co-pilot seat as Indonesia's vice-president; Investors are taking flight." Far Eastern Economic Review[32]

January 28: Korea reaches a comprehensive agreement with its global creditors to roll over $24 billion of short-term debt into government guaranteed loans. In hindsight, the *New York Times* says, "Banks were slow to see warning signs in Asia," which stepped up their lending to Asian banks and companies even as signs of trouble emerged.[33]

January 30: Thailand announces the removal of a two-tier currency trading system, in place in since May 1997, which restricted overseas investors' holdings of the local currency, thus making the baht a truly free-floating currency.

February 17: Suharto fires Soedradjad Djiwandono, the independent-minded central bank governor who was a key player in negotiations with the IMF, over a disagreement about plans to create a currency board, and other differences in reforming the Indonesian economy. Most Asian currencies close slightly higher against the U.S. dollar amid speculation that Indonesia may not adopt a currency board in the immediate future.[34]

February 18: Standard & Poor's raises Korea's credit rating (although still in the junk-bond category), removes the nation from CreditWatch, and upgrades its outlook to "stable," citing positive reform efforts.

February 20: Japan's ruling party announces its fourth economic package since October aimed at stimulating the economy, but the yen slips against the U.S. dollar. The package is criticized for failing to include bigger tax cuts or increased public spending. Other G-7 leaders urge Japan to speed up its stimulus efforts (see **Exhibit 5**) amid complaints that the world's second biggest economy, by failing to stimulate its own economy and clean up its reeling banks, is undermining the international effort to restore stability in Asia.

- "U.S. Sees New Villain in Asia Crisis: Japan's Government." *New York Times*[35]
- "The Risks Are Rising: Unless Political Leaders Move Fast, the Current Crisis Will Worsen and Shock World Markets Even Harder. The Key: a Bold Plan to Restore Confidence in the Region's Shaky Banking System." *Fortune* [36]

February 23: Indonesia backs down from plans to adopt a currency board system that would fix the rupiah's exchange rate, coming under pressure from the IMF and other world leaders who argued that it would not be sustainable given the nation's insufficient reserves. The idea of a currency board prompted IMF's (Managing Director) Michael Camdessus to send a letter to the Indonesian president in early February stating that implementation of the plan would prompt the IMF to withdraw funding for the bailout program.

February 24: The IMF agrees to ease key requirements of its bailout package for Thailand—e.g., by allowing a budget deficit of 2% of GDP in 1997 and by reducing interest rates—a "tacit acknowledgement" that the economy is in a worse state that the IMF or the government predicted it was a few months ago.[37] The baht appreciates while the stock market closes down 4.76 points to 517.06, reacting negatively to news that the economy could contract by as much as 3.5% this year.[38]

March 10: Suharto is re-elected to a seventh five-year term as Indonesia's president.

March 19: Chinese premier Zhu Rongji reiterates his commitment to not devalue the yuan, and to defend the Hong Kong currency board at all costs, declaring, ". . . it will have a bearing not only on the development of China but also on the prosperity and stability of Asia."[39]

March 23: The central bank of Indonesia raises key interest rates, one as high as 45%, and abandons a proposed 5% tax on foreign currency purchases. The IMF praised the move as part of the government's strategy to control inflation and strengthen the rupiah.[40]

March 31: Korea signs an agreement with its foreign creditors to roll over 97%, or $22 billion, of its short-term debt, removing a major threat to the solvency of Korean banks.

April 1: Japan unveils its "Big Bang" deregulation of its strictly controlled financial markets; most restraints on foreign exchange trading are lifted and commissions on large equity transactions, previously fixed at set rates, are deregulated.

April 8: Indonesia signs its third letter of intent with the IMF since the beginning of the crisis. It includes a new government-backed plan to restructure $68 billion in foreign corporate debt, and pledges to expedite the pace of banking reform and maintain high interest rates.

May 6: Riots and looting breaks out in Medan, northern Indonesia, as price increases, including a fuel price hike by up to 71%, go into effect as part of the nation's agreement with the IMF.

May 13–14: Riots and violence spreads throughout Jakarta in Indonesia, reportedly causing over a thousand injuries and deaths in two days. Armed troops backed by tanks patrol the streets, and Suharto faces a flood of calls demanding his resignation.

May 21: Suharto steps down after 32 years in power and names B.J. Habibie, the vice-president, as his successor.

May 27: Korea's labor unions launch a two-day nationwide strike in protest of soaring unemployment and mass layoffs; unemployment reaches 6.7% compared to 2.6% last year, with about 8,000 people losing their jobs daily.[41]

May 29: Habibie agrees to hold elections in 1999, following an overhaul of the political system by the national assembly later in the year.

June 13: Japan officially acknowledges that it has fallen into a recession for the first time in 23 years. The economy contracts by 0.7% for the fiscal year ending March 3. Concerns that Japan's woes could hamper Korea's economic recovery send Japan's leading stock index to shed 8.1%, its biggest one-day fall ever. Japan's benchmark Nikkei 225 falls below the 15,000 mark for the first time since January 13, while the dollar soars to an eight-year high, above 145 yen.[42]

- "Wave of Recession in Asia Washes over Japan's Economy, Downturn Steeper than Analysts Feared," *The Washington Times*[43]
- "Japan's Inaction on Yen Indicates It Has Run out of Policy Options," *Dow Jones*[44]

June 17: The U.S. Treasury and the Federal Reserve intervene to prop up the yen, spending about $2 billion to buy the yen after the Japanese currency slumps to an eight-year low amid concerns over the health of the world's second-largest economy including Japanese banks' bad loans. U.S. President Bill Clinton and other world leaders urge Japan to act quickly to resolve its banking problems and find ways to revive the economy.

June 24: Malaysia's Mahathir appoints Dain Zainnuddin, a former finance minister and loyal ally, to the Cabinet with special authority to oversee the nation's economic recovery efforts. Many observers interpret the move as undermining the authority of Finance Minister Anwar Ibrahim; he is a supporter of high interest rates in contrast to Mahathir and Dain, who favor easing monetary policy. Both the ringgit and stock market slip in reaction to the news. The next day, Mahathir criticizes the IMF's prescription of high interest rates, saying "We thought the IMF stance was good, so we adopted that. But we found out it has been very damaging to our economy."[45]

June 25: Indonesia and the IMF announce their fourth agreement, in which the IMF agrees to provide up to $6 billion in extra funding to help Indonesia's fragile economy. The IMF also allows Indonesia to keep fuel and food subsidies in place, after the hike in fuel prices prompted widespread riots in May.

July 23: Malaysia unveils a national economic recovery plan aimed at stabilizing the ringgit, restoring market confidence, and creating financial stability. Measures include temporarily lifting foreign equity ownership in new manufacturing projects until the end of December 1999. Yet the plan fails to stimulate a positive reaction, with the local currency remaining practically unchanged, and the benchmark stock index slipping by 1.5%.

July 28: The IMF agrees to ease monetary and fiscal austerity conditions for Korea as the economy sinks into a deep recession not seen since 1980. The new agreement allows Korea to lower interest rates and expand the budget deficit to 4% of GDP. The IMF also revises its growth forecast, expecting GDP to decline by 4% in 1998, compared to an earlier forecast of 1% made just three months earlier.

August 4: Wall Street's Dow Jones plunges nearly 300 points in its third-biggest point loss, troubled by Asia's economic recovery and weaker corporate earnings.

August 11: Japan's yen slumps to another eight-year low, sending regional stock indexes to take a heavy beating as well. The yen's continuing weakness raises fears and speculations of another round of currency devaluations in Asia.

August 27: Russia's political and economic problems become the latest culprit to hammer stock markets from Tokyo to London to San Paulo, as investors fear that Asia's and now Russia's woes could spread to Europe and Latin America as well.

September 2: Malaysia's Mahathir fires Deputy Prime Minister Anwar Ibrahim, one day after imposing new stricter currency and capital controls, which included freezing Malaysian shares traded on Singapore's over-the-counter market and requiring all ringgits held in offshore accounts to be repatriated within a month. Anwar, who was highly respected outside Malaysia, favored more free-market principles for the economy, contrary to Mahathir's approach.

September 27: Japan's Leasing Corporation, the second biggest leasing company, files for bankruptcy under an estimated $16 billion in debt, the largest bankruptcy filing of a Japanese company since World War II.

September 28: Korea's President Kim Dae Jung announces new measures to try and pull the economy out of its recession, such as lowering interest rates, increasing money supply, and expanding the fiscal budget. Kim also reiterates that there is no possibility of a second currency crisis hitting the nation.[46]

October 9: The U.S. dollar suffers its biggest weekly loss against the Japanese yen since 1971, tumbling more than 10%, as hedge funds dumped dollars to pay back their yen-denominated loans amid concerns of a global financial meltdown. In addition, Japan's Finance Minister Kiichi Miyazawa says he sees no need for a central bank intervention in the foreign exchange markets, further rattling investors' fears.[47]

November 25: IMF Managing Director Camdessus praises Korea and Thailand for their reform efforts and predicts that their economies will start recovering by next year. He also says that although the world should remain cautious, ". . . the worst of the crisis is now over."[48]

Exhibit 1a Thai Baht/U.S. Dollar Exchange Rate

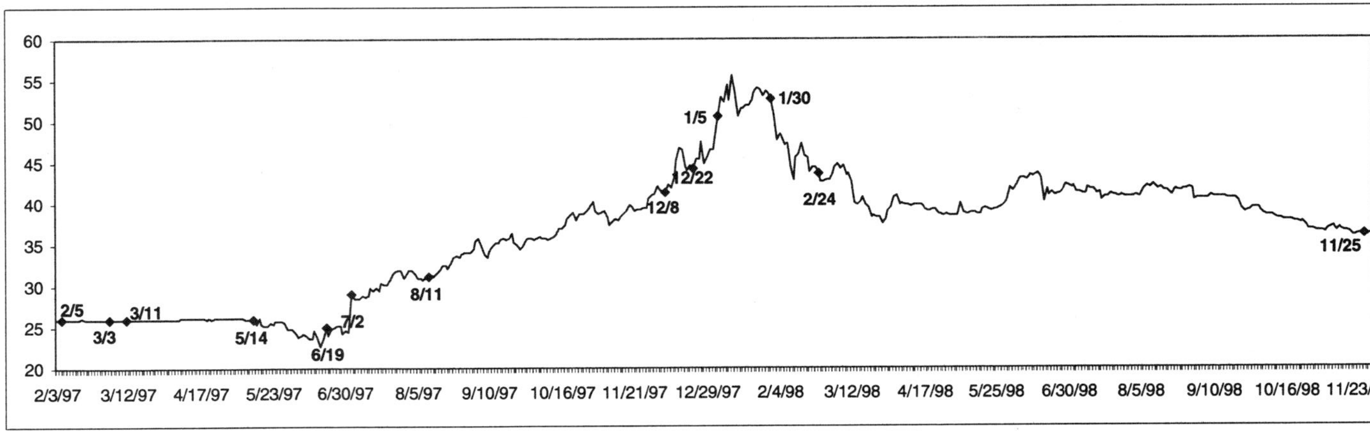

Exhibit 1b Thailand's SET Index

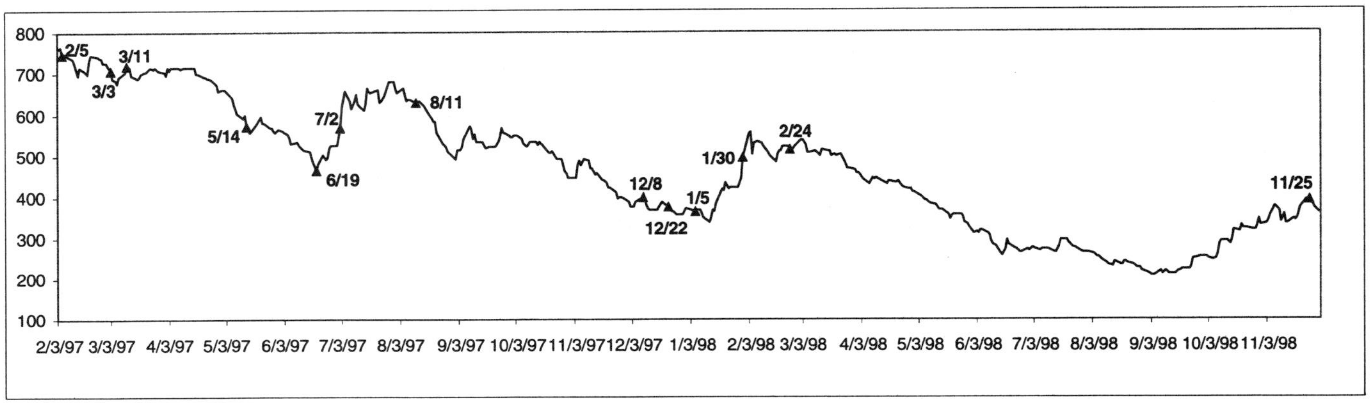

Source: Compiled by casewriter using Global Financial Data, accessed January 28, 2008.

Exhibit 2a Malaysian Ringgit/U.S. Dollar Exchange Rate

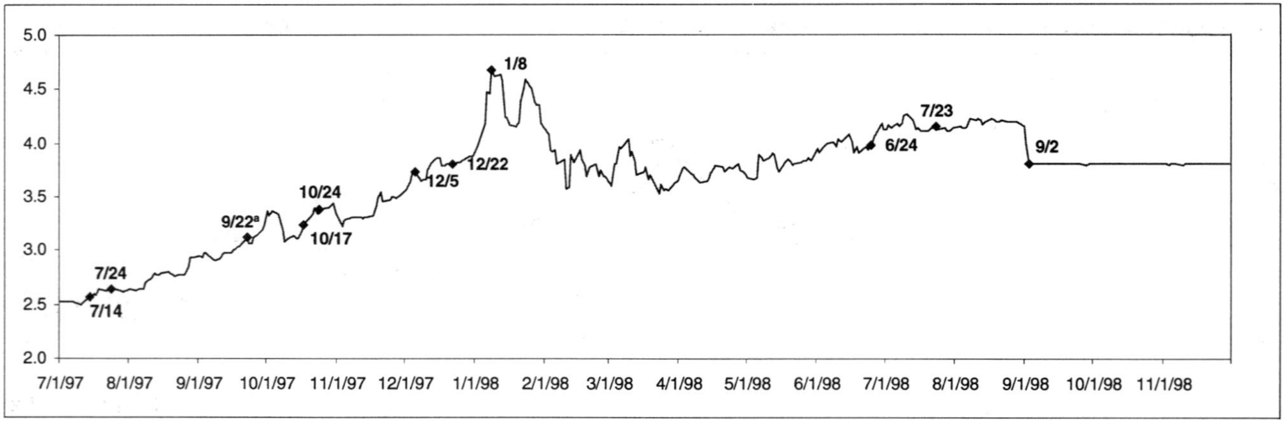

Exhibit 2b Malaysia KLSE Index

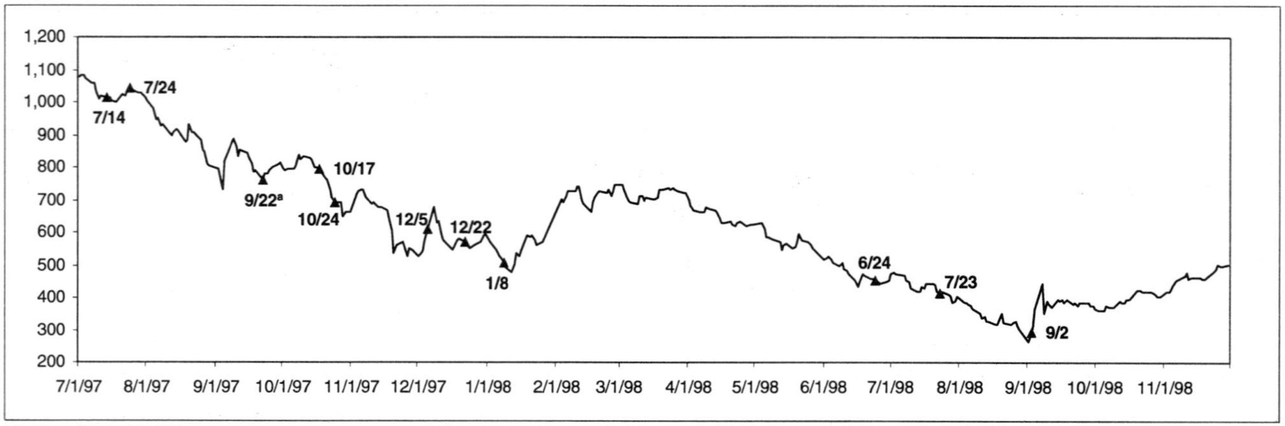

Source: Compiled by casewriter using Global Financial Data, accessed January 28, 2008.

[a] Represents next-day market reaction, since market was closed on the day of the event.

Exhibit 3a Indonesian Rupiah/U.S. Dollar Exchange Rate

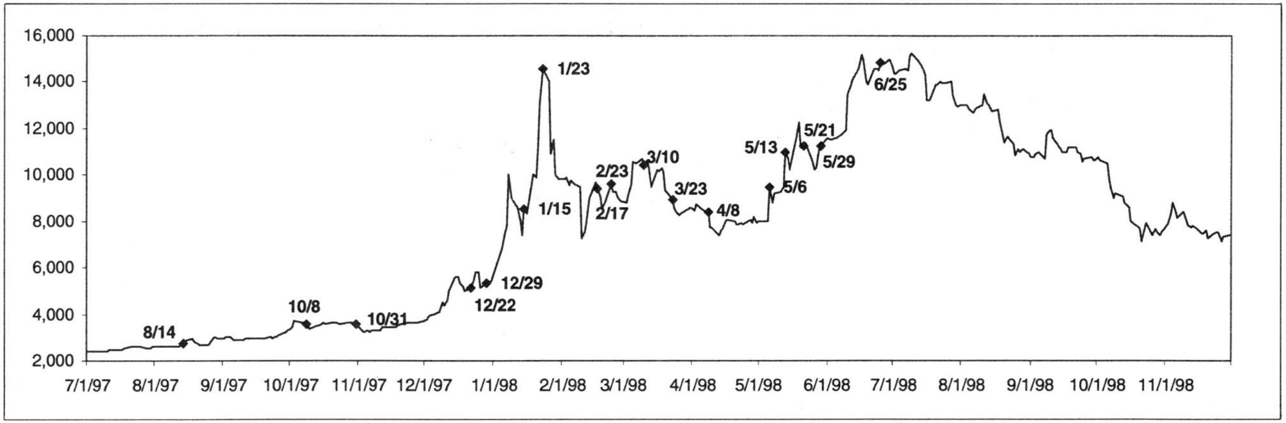

Exhibit 3b Jakarta SE Composite Index

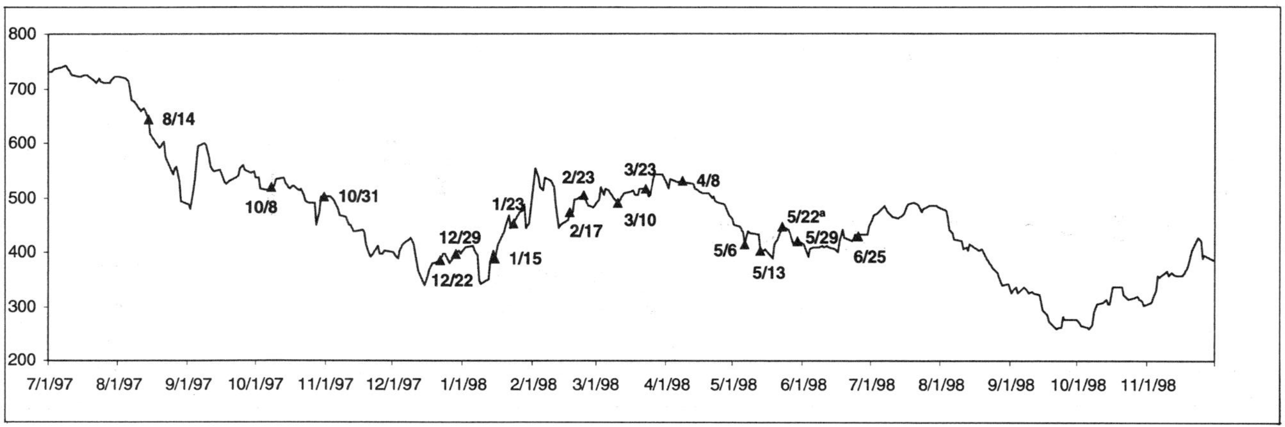

Source: Compiled by casewriter using Global Financial Data, accessed January 28, 2008.

[a] Represents next-day market reaction, since market was closed on the day of the event.

Exhibit 4a Korean Won/U.S. Dollar Exchange Rate

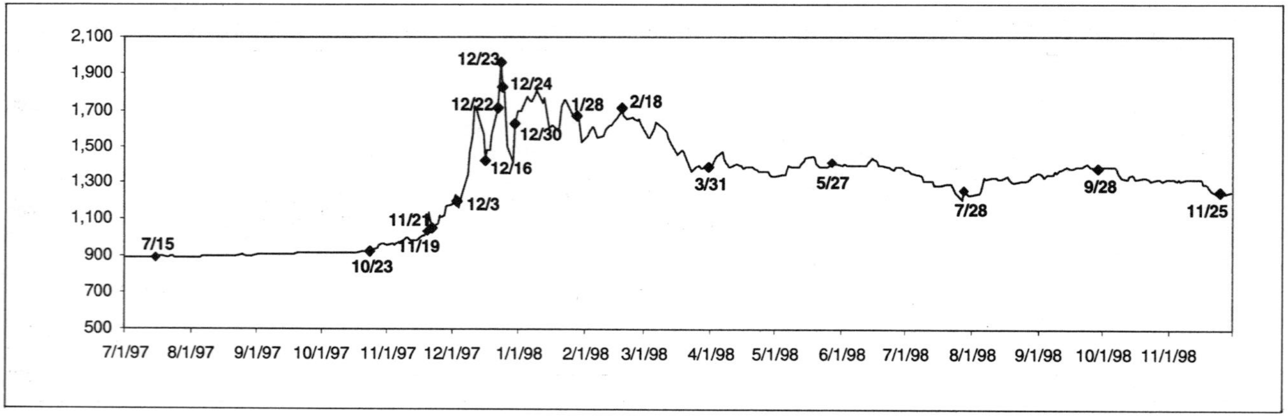

Exhibit 4b Korea Composite Stock Price Index (KOSPI)

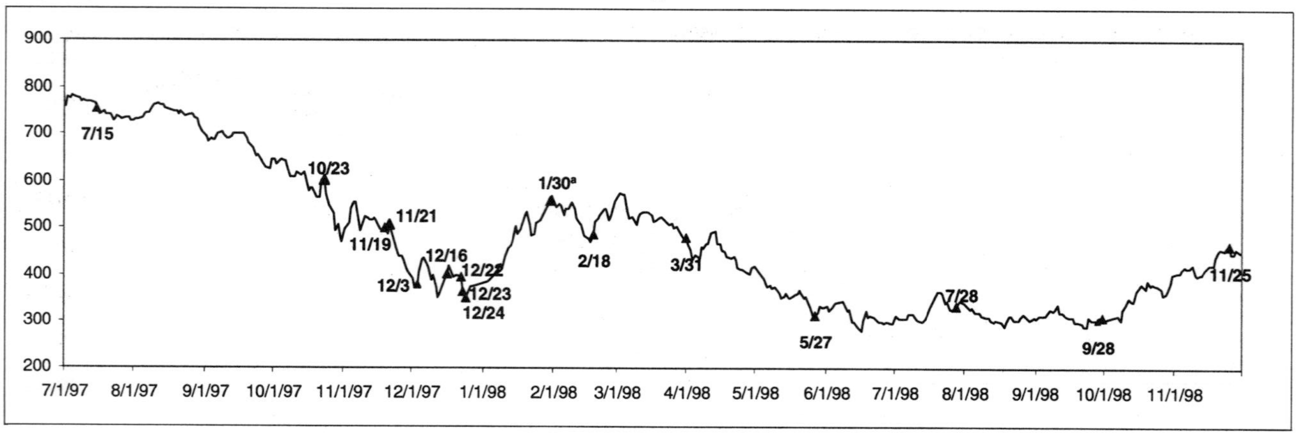

Source: Compiled by casewriter using Global Financial Data, accessed January 28, 2008.

[a] Represents next-day market reaction, since market was closed on the day of the event.

Exhibit 5a Japanese Yen/U.S. Dollar Exchange Rate

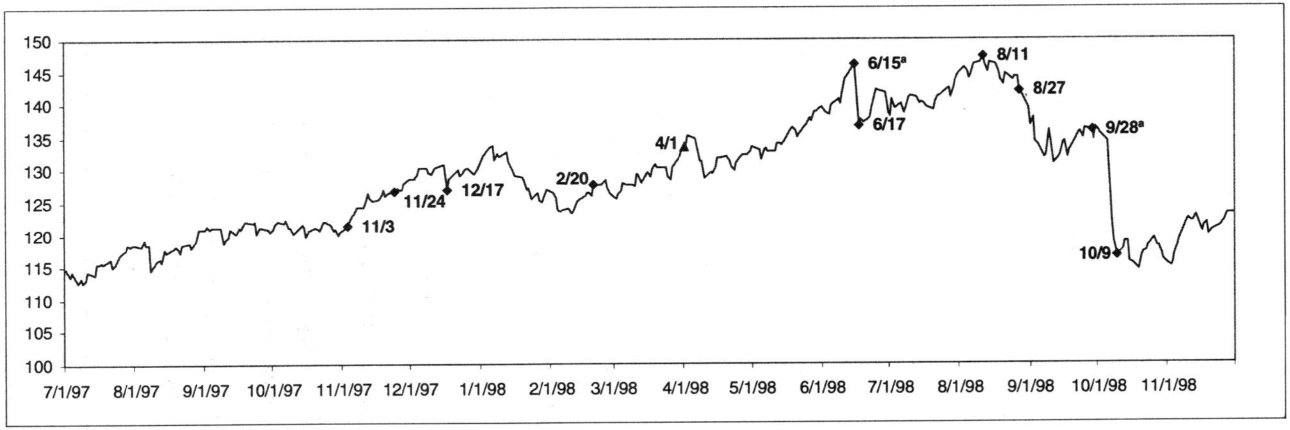

Exhibit 5b Nikkei 225 Index

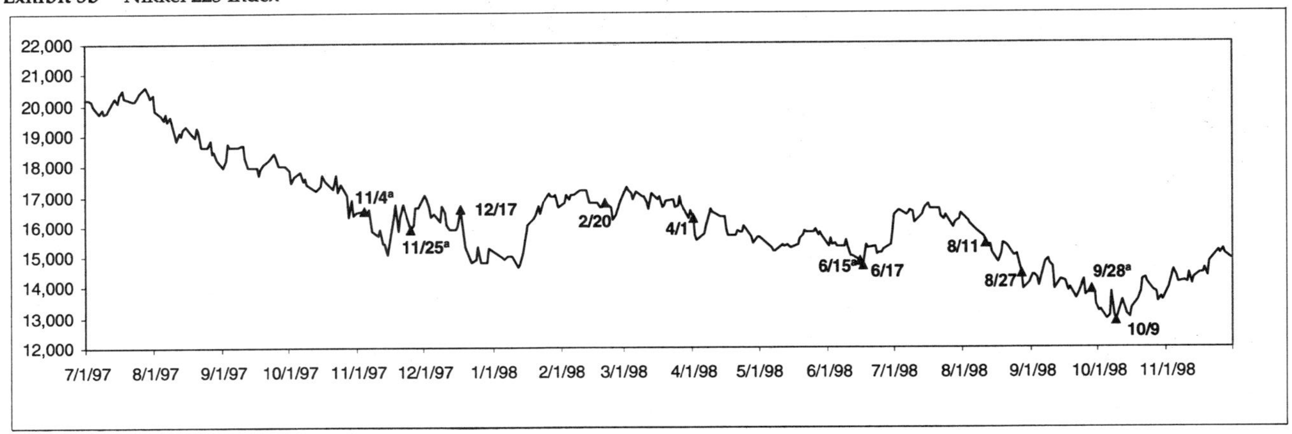

Source: Compiled by casewriter using Global Financial Data, accessed January 28, 2008.

[a] Represents next-day market reaction, since market was closed on the day of the event.

Endnotes

[1] Martin Feldstein, "Refocusing the IMF," *Foreign Affairs* 77, 2 (March/April 1998): 21.

[2] Jeffrey Sachs, "The Wrong Medicine for Asia," *The New York Times*, November 3, 1997.

[3] Ted Bardacke, "Thailand Set to Take on Companies' Bad Debts—IMF Chief Welcomes Move to Impose Discipline," *Financial Times*, March 11, 1997.

[4] Sarah Davison, "Thais Win Currency Battle, What about the War?" *Reuters News*, May 16, 1997.

[5] Ted Bardacke, "Thai Currency Tactics Calm SE Asian Markets," *Financial Times*, May 20, 1997.

[6] "Thailand Seeks Mechanisms to Counter Baht Attacks," *Reuters News*, May 16, 1997.

[7] Thomas Fuller, "Thailand Lets Its Currency Slide, De Facto Devaluation of Baht Is Aimed at Reviving Economy," *International Herald Tribune*, July 3, 1997.

[8] "Tremors as Thailand Floats Baht," *The Herald* (Glasgow), July 3, 1997.

[9] Jonathan Thatcher, "Thailand Neighbours Fear Risk of Currency Infection," *Reuters News*, July 2, 1997.

[10] China, a few days later, pledges $1 billion to help Thailand, bringing the total rescue package to $17 billion.

[11] Alan Friedman, "Soros Calls Mahathir a 'Menace' to Malaysia," *International Herald Tribune*, September 22, 1997.

[12] Ibid.

[13] "Mahathir Comments Rattle Regional Markets," *Agence France-Presse*, September 22, 1997.

[14] Michael Shari, Bruce Einhorn, and Sheri Prasso, "Damage Control, Can Mahathir Get Malaysia Back on Course?" *BusinessWeek*, September 22, 1997.

[15] "Deputy Premier says Financier Soros's Allegations against Premier Mahathir 'Incorrect,'" *BBC Monitoring Service*, September 23, 1997 via Factiva.

[16] Alan Friedman, "Soros Calls Mahathir a 'Menance' to Malaysia," *International Herald Tribune*, September 22, 1997.

[17] For more on Malaysia's handling of the crisis, see Rawi Abdelal and Laura Alfaro, "Malaysia: Capital and Control," HBS No. 702-040 (Boston: Harvard Business School Publishing, 2002).

[18] Sereerema Banoo, "Malaysia Won't Be Seeking IMF Assistance, Says Anwar," *Business Times*, October 24, 1997.

[19] Raju Gopalakrishnan, "Reform, Not Aid, Seen Key in Indonesia IMF Package," *Reuters News*, October 31, 1997.

[20] Marguerite Nugent, "Asia Stocks Rally on Indonesia's IMF Package," *Reuters News*, November 3, 1997.

[21] Gerard Baker and Sander Thoenes, "Needing Tough Treatment—Escalating Crisis in Indonesia," *Financial Times*, November 3, 1997.

[22] "S. Korea Finance Chief says IMF Loan Not Needed," *Reuters News*, November 19, 1997.

[23] Sarah Davison, "S.E. Asia Crisis a '"Tea Party" Compared to Korea," *Reuters News*, November 11, 1997.

[24] "John Whitesides, "Investors Are Urged to Remain Calm Despite Financial Crisis in Asia. Pacific Rim Leaders Say the Turmoil Can Be Contained. The Issue Tops the Agenda at the APEC Summit," *The Philadelphia Inquirer*, November 23, 1997.

[25] "How Far Is Down?" *The Economist*, November 15, 1997.

[26] "Dear IMF: Don't Make Asia's Flu Worse," *BusinessWeek*, December 11, 1997.

[27] "Moody's Blues Spread in Asia," *Associated Press*, December 22, 1997.

[28] Steven Mufson, "South Korea Takes Three More Punches," *Washington Post*, December 23, 1997.

[29] The last major revaluation of the Chinese yuan took place in 1994. "China's Zhu Says No Yuan Devaluation," *Reuters News*, December 24, 1997.

[30] "Indonesia Reaches IMF Pact to Speed Reforms—Tougher Accord Expected to Curb Suharto System of 'Crony Capitalism'," *Wall Street Journal*, January 15, 1998.

[31] Patrick Hosking and Lachlan Colquhoun, "Asian crisis worsens as Indonesia panics," *The Evening Standard (London)*, January 22, 1998

[32] John McBeth, "Soaring Ambition: B.J. Habibie, best known for his bold aerospace plans, may be set to take the co-pilot seat as Indonesia's vice-president; Investors are taking flight." *Far Eastern Economic Review*, January 29, 1998

[33] "Banks Were Slow to See Warning Signs in Asia," *New York Times*, January 28, 1998.

[34] Lara Parpan, "Asian Currencies Stabilize amid Stalemate over Indonesia Plan," *Agence France-Presse*, February 17, 1998.

[35] David Sanger, "U.S. Sees New Villain in Asia Crisis: Japan's Government," *The New York Times*, February 22, 1998.

[36] Jim Rohwer, Tony Paul, and Neel Chowdhury, "Asia's Meltdown," *Fortune*, February 16, 1998.

[37] Sinfah Tunsarawuth and Warangkana Tempati, "Thailand Makes New Promises to IMF; Fund Eases Economic Targets," *Dow Jones Business News*, February 24, 1998.

[38] Anchalee Koetsawang, "Thailand's New Targets Realistic, Analysts Say," *Reuters News*, February 24, 1998.

[39] Andrew Browne, "Zhu Rongji Lays Out Tough Agenda, with a Smile," *Reuters News*, March 19, 1998.

[40] "Indonesia Reserves Decision to Impose 5% Tax on Forex Deals," *Business Times Singapore*, March 24, 1998.

[41] Suh Kyung Yoon, "Huge Strike Hits South Korea," *The Straits Times*, May 28, 1998.

[42] "Japan Stock Prices Fall," *Associated Press*, June 15, 1998.

[43] Willis Witter, "Wave of Recession in Asia Washes over Japan's Economy," *The Washington Times*, June 13, 1998

[44] Willis Witter, "Wave of Recession in Asia Washes over Japan's Economy," *The Washington Times*, June 13, 1998; and Takeshi Takeuchi, "Japan's Inaction on Yen Indicates It Has Run Out of Policy Options," *Dow Jones*, June 15, 1998.

[45] M. Jegathesan, "I'm in Control, Says Malaysia's Mahathir," *Agence France-Presse*, June 25, 1998.

[46] "S. Korea Will Not Suffer Fresh Currency Crisis," *Xinhua News Agency*, September 28, 1998.

[47] "Tokyo Stocks Fall 1% to 13-Year Closing Low as Yen Strengthens," *Dow Jones*, October 9, 1998.

[48] "Worst of the Crisis Seems Over—Camdessus," *Reuters News*, November 25, 1998.

II. Policies and Strategies for Harnessing the Benefits of Financial Globalization

MANAGING CAPITAL INFLOWS

"Capital Controls in Chile in the 1990s (A) and (B)" is a two-case series that explores issues associated with capital mobility, exchange rate management, and policy management (the "irreconcilable trilogy") in the context of a country widely regarded as a "poster child" of reform. Chile had a disastrous early experience with opening its financial markets that culminated, in 1982, in the worst recession experienced by any Latin American country at the time. The country later restructured its domestic financial system and imposed extensive regulation and supervision. In the early 1990s, capital inflows threatened the central bank's ability to both maintain a stable exchange rate (to preserve competitiveness) and lower the inflation rate to international levels. Thus, in 1991, Chile adopted a framework of capital controls. The case presents instructors with an opportunity to analyze the mechanics and objectives of capital controls by focusing on the control of inflows. A comparison is drawn between Chile's experiences with capital controls in the 1980s and 1990s. The case also examines the importance of other policies such as bank regulation and fiscal policy as well as the sequencing of policies with the tightening or loosening of capital controls to encourage economic growth and forestall economic crises. An important teaching point is that the system of capital controls instituted in Chile was complicated and its implementation was neither easy nor trivial: capital controls are complex policy instruments that rely on a central bank with strong enforcement capability.

The note "Capital Controls" summarizes the modern history of international financial market regulation, highlights the advantages and disadvantages of these restrictions, and describes the contemporary debate over controlling short-term capital flows.

MANAGING CAPITAL OUTFLOWS

The case "Malaysia: Capital and Control" (HBS No. 702-040), explores how the Malaysian government managed the financial crisis that swept Asia in 1997–1998, with a focus on Malaysia's imposition of controls on capital outflows. This episode sent shock waves through policy and academic circles around the world, and reopened the debate about the pros and cons of unrestricted capital flows and the effectiveness of controls. The case focuses on the content of Malaysia's internal debate about capital controls, the reasons for the decision to impose them, the reaction of the international financial community, and lessons for other developing countries. Similarly, the case highlights that the implementation of capital controls is neither easy nor trivial. The case is a useful complement to the previous discussion.

CAPITAL FLOWS AND MONETARY POLICY IN EMERGING MARKETS

"Brazil 2003: Inflation Targeting and Debt Dynamics" follows up the discussion by illustrating the challenges of formulating monetary policy in emerging markets, in particular, the conflict with exchange rate management in the context of a "fear of floating." The case also examines the mechanics of inflation targeting, a monetary framework arrangement that countries are increasingly adopting. Inflation targeting implies an explicit institutional commitment to meet a specified and publicly announced numerical inflation rate target or target range within a specified time frame, and emphasizes transparency through communication with the public and the markets about monetary authorities' plans, objectives, and decisions. In addition, the case fosters an understanding of debt dynamics in emerging markets.

CAPITAL MOBILITY AND TAX POLICY

"Rovná Daň: The Flat Tax in Slovakia" explores the impact of increased capital mobility on national tax systems. During the 1990s, several east European countries had adopted flat taxes; Slovakia followed suit and, on January 1, 2004, imposed a flat tax of 19% on personal income, corporate income, and value added tax as part of a central piece of economic reform in hopes of luring foreign investors through improved business transparency and simplification of tax laws. Slovakia's and Ireland's fiscal policies, in an era of increasing European financial integration, thus raised the stakes for European leaders to coordinate and possibly harmonize their tax systems.

INCENTIVES TO INVESTMENTS AND THE ROLE INSTITUTIONS

"Special Economic Zones in India (A): Public Purpose and Private Property," and "Tata Motors in Singur: Public Purpose and Private Property (B)," discuss a popular policy to increase investments and foster development. In 2005, the government of India enacted the Special Economic Zones (SEZ) Act in order to attract foreign investment, generate export revenues and create manufacturing jobs. However, several planned projects faced difficulties in acquiring land for setting up the SEZ. In December 2007, the government of India introduced the Land Acquisition Amendment Bill in the national parliament as a way to solve the significant land acquisition problems which were slowing down industrial projects in India. The Bill proposed to significantly extend the definition of "public purpose" for which the government could use the power of eminent domain to acquire land from private parties. Both the SEZ policy and the proposed Bill proved quite controversial, leading to intense debate and wide-spread protests. Some critics felt that while the SEZ policy might increase manufacturing employment and investment, the resulting land acquisition could threaten the livelihood of millions of farmers and further hamper India's sluggish agricultural sector. Others questioned the necessity of government involvement in land transactions between private landowners and private developers. The case allows for a critical discussion about the appropriate role of the government in fostering economic development.

SOVEREIGN DEBT AND THE INTERNATIONAL FINANCIAL ARCHITECTURE

"Creditor Activism in Sovereign Debt: 'Vulture' Tactics or Market Backbone" highlights the problems associated with coordination at the international level. The case allows students to understand the differences between sovereign debt and corporate debt (ability vs capacity-to-pay problems) through the lens of the fascinating and frequently controversial firm Elliot Associates, which has played an important role in shaping the sovereign debt market. Elliot Associates, a so-called "vulture" fund or "rogue creditor," invested in sovereign debt at discounted prices and sued for full recovery. Many observers deride firms such as Elliott, which seek to profit from sovereign debt restructurings at the expense of countries suffering economic hardship and of the majority of bondholders whose cooperation accommodates the restructurings. Critics believe that these holdout creditors create "collective action problems" and present a major obstacle to successful sovereign debt restructurings. Others argue that activist investors, in fact, improve the market overall by demonstrating the enforceability of contracts. They assert that creditors who receive favorable judgments in support of claims against countries face too many hurdles in collecting.

The session ends with a discussion of the international financial architecture that provides an opportunity for the class to apply and summarize lessons and implications derived from the cases. Successive economic crises in the 1990s and early 2000s — Mexico in 1994, Asia in 1997, Brazil in 1999, and Argentina in 2001 — intensified the focus on reforming the "international financial architecture." As many of these crises involved defaults on sovereign bonds, an important component of the discussion is the composition of international capital flows and sovereign debt restructuring. The note "International Capital Markets and Sovereign Debt: Crisis Avoidance and Resolution," which describes some of the proposals advanced to reform the international financial architecture, is a useful complement to the discussion.

CAPITAL FLOWS BETWEEN RICH AND POOR COUNTRIES

"Aid, Debt Relief, and Trade: An Agenda for Fighting World Poverty (A) and (B)" reviews the challenges of growth and development, the state's role in creating functioning markets, and the potential role of aid and debt relief in promoting economic growth by examining the difficulties and problems that face the world's poorest countries. Amid the debate over aid vs debt relief, the private sector, often backed by wealthy foundations, has emerged as an active donor, but faces scrutiny as to whether it can improve the distribution and function of aid. The case builds on one of the recurring themes of the course: capital, even putatively "free" capital in the form aid, cannot really improve economic performance in a sustained way without being channeled into effective domestic institutions. Although aid can achieve other goals — distributing food and education to those in need, perhaps assuaging the guilt of the world's richest countries and individuals with respect to their sense of obligation to help the poor — unless the much greater challenge of institution-building is taken into account, the current state of affairs is likely to disappoint both donors and recipients.

Managing Capital Inflows

9-705-031
REV: JULY 17, 2007

LAURA ALFARO
RAFAEL DI TELLA

Capital Controls in Chile in the 1990s (A)

In early September 1998, the Central Bank of Chile contemplated whether and how far to loosen the country's capital controls. Fallout from the Asian financial crisis was putting pressure on Chile's economy. Many critics believed Chile's capital controls—in particular the *encaje,* which required foreigners to make a deposit equivalent to a percentage of the value of their investments with the central bank at zero interest for one year—were unnecessarily adding to the strain. As capital inflows, trading on Chile's stock exchange, and exports to Asia dwindled, some Chileans feared a full-blown crisis to rival Chile's painful financial meltdown in 1982.

The external environment had changed dramatically since Chile instituted the *encaje* in 1991. At that time, excessive inflows of capital put a strain on Chile's managed exchange rate regime and on its ability to pursue an independent monetary policy. Supporters argued that Chile's controls had been successful in shifting the composition of inflows to a longer maturity and curbing the flow of speculative funds into the country, thereby helping it avert the type of crises that affected Mexico in 1994 and Asia in 1997.[1] All the while, the country had maintained spectacular economic performance. (See **Exhibits 1–4** for basic macroeconomic data.) Critics of Chile's capital controls, however, attributed Chile's economic success to other policies, such as prudential financial regulation and strong fiscal and monetary policy.[2] They also pointed to the apparent ineffectiveness of the controls in preventing real exchange rate appreciation and in isolating the economy from capital flow reversals.

Despite critiques of Chile's capital controls, they were beginning to attract interest internationally as a way of defending smaller, open economies from volatility in international financial markets.[3] On September 1, 1998, in response to the Asian financial crisis, Malaysia introduced its own series of controls. Declaring that "the free market has failed disastrously,"[4] Malaysian President Mahathir Mohamad prohibited trading of the Malaysian currency outside the country's borders and restricted short-term outflows of capital.[5]

Although Malaysia's framework differed substantially from Chile's by focusing on outflows rather than inflows, Malaysia's move toward and Chile's move away from capital controls prompted heated debate surrounding their use.[6] On the one hand, many stakeholders claimed that controls would hamper the international capital mobility they considered vital for helping emerging economies catch up to the industrial structures and living standards of wealthier countries.[7] On the other hand, other commentators argued that free capital mobility encouraged excessive risk taking and tended to lead to major financial crises.[8] They supported controls as appropriate measures for reducing vulnerability caused by short-term capital flows.[9]

As Central Bank head Carlos Massad contemplated loosening Chile's capital control framework, several questions were particularly relevant: Had the controls been successful in achieving their

---

Professors Laura Alfaro and Rafael Di Tella and Research Associate Ingrid Vogel prepared this case. Research Associate Pamela Arellano provided valuable research assistance. HBS cases are developed solely as the basis for class discussion. Cases are not intended to serve as endorsements, sources of primary data, or illustrations of effective or ineffective management.

objectives? What had been the role of other policies in Chile's economic success in the 1990s? What were the pros and cons of getting rid of controls in the current circumstances? Were there alternatives? Would Chile have to go through another financial meltdown such as that of 1982?

Chile's Socialist Experiment

Between 1932 and 1973, Chile was considered one of the most stable, representative, and reformist democracies in the world. Chile's political system, originally dominated by elite and conservative forces, gradually incorporated most segments of society. Under the 1964–1970 presidential term of Eduardo Frei Montalva, rural workers were granted rights to unionize and strike and achieved increased living standards under small land redistribution programs and better access to education. During his term as president, Frei also intensified the government's state-led development strategy. He took a 51% stake in copper mines controlled by U.S. companies, although under terms critics complained were not favorable enough to Chile. Even though economic growth remained sluggish, the government was able to increase tax revenue through improved collection, allowing it to fund other income redistribution efforts.

Although Frei enjoyed widespread popularity, many elements of Chile's society wanted a more radical nationalist and socialist program. In 1970, after a hotly contested election in which he won 36% of the vote, Salvador Allende—leader of an alliance of socialists, communists, and radicals—became the first elected Marxist head of state in the world. The new government expropriated private enterprises including large estates, banks, the remaining private share in Chile's copper mines, and other industries. Land was redistributed to resident laborers, and factories were turned over to be managed by workers and the state. The government also instituted controls on prices, interest rates, exchange rates, and wages—which were raised dramatically.

In the first year, Allende's programs appeared triumphant as higher real incomes encouraged a "consumer revolution," increasing demand for production and the need for labor. However, the following two years brought economic disaster: price controls created widespread shortages and a thriving black market; deficit spending grew to 25% of GDP; inflation soared above annualized rates of 600%; the economy shrank more than 4% annually; real wages fell 25%; and investment inflows and foreign exchange became scarce.[10]

Political polarization intensified between those who claimed Allende had violated the constitution and destroyed the economy and those who demanded Allende go even further in his redistributive efforts. With Allende lacking the mandate necessary to restore economic or political order, his opponents expected his party to lose power in the March 1973 mid-term elections and, therefore, to be able to force his resignation. When, instead, Allende's party gained seats, his opponents decided more extreme measures were necessary. On September 11, 1973, the military attacked government headquarters. Armed with an assault rifle in an effort to defend his socialist administration, Allende died during the coup under unclear circumstances. The military assumed control over the government and averted civil war through quickly consolidating power.

The Pinochet Years

Army Commander General Augusto Pinochet Ugarte soon emerged as Chile's leader. Pinochet instituted a repressive authoritarian regime and served as president until 1990. Immediately upon seizing power, the military junta declared a state of emergency granting itself draconian powers, dissolved Congress, censored the media, purged universities, outlawed union activity, declared right-wing parties "in recess," and banned left-wing organizations outright.[11] In an effort to stamp out resistance, an estimated 4,000 political opponents were killed by state security, military, and police forces. Thousands of other dissidents were jailed, tortured, or forced to seek asylum abroad.[12]

Having consolidated his power base, Pinochet turned to Chile's economic problems. Beginning in 1975, the dictatorship embarked on a radical transformation of Chile's state-led development strategy. A group of civilian technocrats—known as the "Chicago boys" for their University of Chicago-style economics training—led Chile's conversion to free-market economics. Market-oriented reforms included a dramatic reduction of tariffs, elimination of fiscal deficits, introduction of labor-market flexibility, liberalization of prices, privatization of most of Chile's 400 state-owned companies and banks, and financial liberalization. In 1978, in an effort to fight inflation through relinquishing monetary policy, the process of fixing the exchange rate was begun with the introduction of the "*tablita.*" The "*tablita*" set a pre-announced schedule of devaluations deliberately below the ongoing rate of inflation that converged on a fixed exchange rate in June 1979. By 1981, Chile's economy appeared to have been transformed by what became known as the "Chilean miracle." Inflation dropped to under 10%, the economy was growing at a real rate of 6% annually, fiscal surpluses reached almost 3% of GDP, real salaries grew at 9% per year, and exports tripled.

But Chile's economic boom obscured fundamental problems and proved unsustainable in the face of external constraints such as a rise in U.S. interest rates and brewing debt problems in Mexico. In mid-1982, Chile experienced its severest financial crisis—and the worst in Latin America—since the Great Depression in 1929.[13] Economists sought explanations, focusing on Chile's financial liberalization program, including changes to its capital controls framework and bank reform.

Financial Liberalization up to 1982[14]

Capital controls: During the early years of military rule, the capital account was tightened under increasingly restrictive controls on short-term inflows. Authorities believed large capital inflows hampered anti-inflationary efforts, led to exchange rate appreciation, and created destabilizing pressures on the economy.[15] Non-banks faced restrictions on borrowing from abroad, including a minimum maturity of two years.[16] Bank intermediation of foreign funds was restricted through limits on both the overall level and monthly flow of foreign funds. In April 1978, an additional restriction on short-term foreign debt was introduced. Under Chapter XIV of the Compendium of Foreign Exchange Regulations of Chile's Central Bank requiring foreigners to register their funds with the central bank in order to gain future access to the official foreign exchange market, foreign lenders had to make a non-interest-bearing deposit at the central bank.[17] The unremunerated reserve requirement (URR) ranged from 10% to 25% of the value of loans, depending on maturity (see **Exhibit 5**).[18]

At the same time, incoming foreign direct investment (FDI) was encouraged under Decree Law 600 on Foreign Investment (DL 600), which aimed to regain the trust of long-term international investors after the expropriations during the Allende administration. Under DL 600, which came into effect in 1974, an investor signed a legally binding contract with the Chilean Government that could not be modified unilaterally or by subsequent changes in the law. Under the terms of the contract, investors received a number of specific guarantees, including rules defining repatriation of profits and capital, tax certainty, and guaranteed access to the formal exchange market.[19]

Controls on outflows were less strict. Chileans could purchase $10,000 per month of foreign exchange from the central bank.[20] Foreign direct investment and portfolio investment flows were subject to a minimum stay of two years.

After the exchange rate was fixed in June 1979, authorities expected inflation to fall to international levels. It was thought, therefore, that controls on inflows as a means to manage inflation were less critical. As such, restrictions on bank intermediation of foreign funds were gradually lifted (see **Exhibit 5**). In response, although the two-year minimum term and the URR on foreign loans were still in place, Chile experienced a dramatic increase in total foreign indebtedness, which almost tripled in real terms between 1978 and 1982.[21] (See **Exhibit 6** for external debt data.)

In deciding to lift restrictions on bank intermediation of foreign funds, it appeared that authorities misjudged the speed with which inflation would be reduced. First, institutional inflationary inertia resulting from indexing wages to past inflation proved hard to break.[22] Second, large capital inflows resulting from easing the controls on bank intermediation of foreign funds fueled internal spending, including on nontradable goods such as real estate, which pushed relative prices higher and fueled additional spending. With a fixed exchange rate and inflation rates remaining well above international levels, Chile experienced real appreciation of the peso (see **Exhibit 7**). A vicious cycle was created as the appreciation led to even more inflows; the peso continued to look attractive as investors expected continued inflation-driven appreciation and as the fixed exchange rate was defended through raising domestic interest rates. Once investors perceived an expected devaluation higher than the differential between domestic and international interest rates, it would be expected that inflows would be brought to an abrupt halt,[23] setting the stage for a severe financial crisis.

Banking sector reform: At the time of the military coup, the Chilean banking sector was highly repressed. The government controlled interest rates, rationed and allocated credit, and imposed high reserve requirements. Liberalization of the banking sector—in an effort to reactivate the economy—was therefore given high priority and occurred at a rapid pace. (See **Exhibit 8** for financial liberalization index.) In early 1974, barriers to entry were relaxed. *Financieras* were allowed to operate and to set their own interest rates. In October 1975, commercial banks were also allowed to set interest rates. In 1975, the process of re-privatizing most of Chile's banks was completed. Many of these were bought by private conglomerates—*los grupos*—eager to finance expansion into other areas slated for privatization. In April 1976, credit ceilings were abolished, and an aggressive program for reducing Chile's high reserve requirements on deposits was started.

Chile's banking sector changed dramatically. The number of banks grew from 18 domestic banks and one foreign bank in 1973 to 26 domestic banks, 19 foreign banks, and 15 *financieras* in 1981. The real volume of total credit to the private sector—one measure of the degree of financial intermediation—increased more than 11 times over the same period (see **Exhibit 9**). By 1982, Chile had one of the most highly monetized economies among developing countries.[24]

Chile's banking sector during this period was criticized for lack of effective regulation and supervision. Authorities sought to protect banks from foreign currency risk by requiring that they match foreign currency assets and liabilities (i.e., all foreign currency holdings had to be used to provide foreign currency loans, and, likewise, any foreign currency loans had to be made with foreign currency holdings). Although this regulation succeeded in limiting a bank's direct currency risk, it increased the bank's credit risk, instead, as currency risk was transferred to borrowers. In addition, there was minimal required financial disclosure, improper securing of many loans (many were guaranteed against assets with highly inflated prices), low standards for rules on non-performing loans and loss provisions, and limited oversight of bank activities.[25] As a result, newly privatized banks accumulated large bad loan portfolios. With no limits on lending to related parties, loans were often concentrated in companies either owned or controlled by the same *grupo* that owned the bank.[26] For example, in 1981, 50% of the loans of the largest private bank, *Banco de Chile*, were to other companies owned by the same *grupo*.

In addition, there was an apparent implicit state guarantee on deposits after the government reimbursed 100% of the deposits of several failed financial institutions in 1976 and early 1977. This included the large *Banco de Osorno*, which had a high concentration of bad loans to sister companies within its parent, the Fluxa *grupo*.[27] Although the implicit guarantee averted a substantial run on deposits despite repeated problems with banks and *financieras* in the late 1970s, it led to a situation of moral hazard whereby depositors had no incentive to distinguish between weak and strong banks.[28]

The 1982 Crisis

In mid-1981, a rise in international interest rates led to a tightening of Chilean credit conditions, forcing many firms into bankruptcy. The Chilean government felt it was unnecessary to intervene, citing the advantages of bankruptcies as the "appropriate channel through which an economy gets rid of inefficient investments."[29] International banks continued to pour vast resources into the failing economy until November 1981, when the government was forced to bail out two of Chile's major banks, *Banco de España* and *Banco de Talca.*

The crisis progressed rapidly. In 1982, as international interest rates continued to rise, Chile fell out of favor with international banks amid increased threats of devaluation and financial crisis. In an attempt to improve Chile's standing, the authorities eliminated the minimum stay of two years for capital inflows.[30] Even so, in the first five months of 1982, foreign deposits in commercial banks dropped by 75%.[31] By June 1982, a dramatic drawdown in reserves as pesos were converted to dollars at the fixed exchange rate ultimately forced Chile to intervene by devaluing the peso, despite a 1981 presidential decree guaranteeing that the exchange rate would remain fixed.[32] Many lenders could no longer service their debts at the new exchange rate, worsening the quality of most banks' portfolios and forcing some banks into insolvency. In September, controls on capital outflows were tightened: The limit on the general purpose purchase for foreign exchange was reduced to $1,000 per person per month, and to $3,000 for overseas travel.[33]

The recession was compounded by Mexico's debt default in August 1982 and the international debt crisis. By year-end 1982, real GDP shrank more than 10%, production dropped 25%, and unemployment climbed to almost 20%.[34] Chile eliminated remaining controls on capital inflows.

By the end of 1983, the government had liquidated or nationalized many of Chile's banks and tightly controlled bank operations.[35] Public finances suffered as, despite the lack of a government guarantee, the foreign debt of the liquidated banks was nationalized. In addition, debtors with foreign currency liabilities were subsidized through access to a more favorable exchange rate. Ultimately, bank managers were fired, shareholders bore losses, and fraud was prosecuted,[36] including alleged fraud of a former finance minister who was an official of one of the major *grupos*.[37] The cost of the bailout over the period 1982–1985 was estimated at up to 44% of 1985 GDP.[38]

Recovery and Changes (1983-1989)

With the recession, opposition to Pinochet intensified. Beginning in 1983, demonstrations spread from union members to the middle class to the poor urban population. In addition, Europe and the United States began to demand the restoration of democracy in Chile, one of the last remaining dictatorships in South America. Repressed political parties became emboldened, demanding the lifting of Chile's state of emergency, full amnesty for exiles, and democratic presidential elections. Free elections were finally scheduled for December 1989.

By the time of the elections, Chile was Latin America's best-performing economy, with real growth rates averaging more than 6% since 1984. Much of this growth was based on a rapid expansion of exports, driven both by Chile's trade liberalization strategy and the country's ability to maintain a depreciated exchange rate. Much progress was also made in completing Chile's privatization program as well as in rebuilding the banking sector. In 1986, Chile introduced modern prudential bank regulation and supervision at international standards, and Chile's banking sector became one of the best regulated among emerging markets.[39] (See **Exhibit 10** for data suggesting improvement in Chile's banking system.)

Chile after Pinochet

In December 1989, a new center-left democratic coalition—the *Concertación de Partidos por la Democracia*—was elected to office, led by Patricio Aylwin Azocar. President Aylwin cooperated with the center-right opposition to achieve national reconciliation and the consolidation of democracy. He chose to continue with Pinochet's market-oriented, trade-oriented economic strategy, but with an adjustment aimed to balance "growth with equity."[40] The executive branch of the government began the slow process of changing spending and taxation laws to meet this objective.

After five years of strong growth, Chile's economy began to show some signs of overheating. In the final months of Pinochet's rule, consumer spending had shot up amid uncertainty about what policies the future government might follow. To prevent rising inflation—also prompted by lingering fiscal problems after the mid-1980s bank bailout as well as by the rapidly growing economy—the central bank chose to tighten monetary policy. The rise in the domestic interest rate—combined with a fall in world rates, a general increase in emerging market lending, and an improvement in market sentiment toward the newly democratic country—resulted in a huge surge of capital inflows to Chile. This massive inflow of funds exacerbated the problem of Chile's overheating economy; it was proving difficult for the central bank to keep interest rates high enough to fight an overheating economy without encouraging a flood of inflows that would push up inflation.

Meanwhile, the central bank, which became independent in late 1989, inherited a passive crawling exchange rate band system with a backward-looking central rate defined against the U.S. dollar, with a band width of ±5%.[a] In January 1991, with annual rates of inflation at 27%, the central bank adopted an inflation targeting framework with the goal of quickly reaching international levels of inflation.[b]

Although monetary policy was primarily directed at controlling the rate of inflation, the central bank also tried to influence the real exchange rate. As in the late 1970s, capital inflows raised demand for the peso, putting pressure on the real exchange rate. Exporters complained that the rapid strengthening of the peso—which had appreciated by more than 20% in real terms between 1985 and 1990—was threatening the competitiveness of Chilean goods in international markets.[41] In an attempt to avoid further real appreciation, the central bank intervened in the foreign exchange market, buying foreign currency with pesos. (This increased demand for the dollar, which served to increase its value relative to the peso). In order to help prevent an associated inflationary monetary expansion (as additional pesos were released into the economy), the central bank sterilized its intervention, absorbing the supply of pesos with sales of peso-denominated bonds. This policy was costly at the prevailing interest rate differentials—ultimately pushing the central bank's net worth negative—since the central bank had to forgo higher interest rates on peso assets to hold the U.S.-dollar assets.

On occasion, the central bank accommodated a real appreciation by reducing the central rate, changing the weighting of currencies defining the central rate, or widening the band (see **Exhibit 11**).

---

[a] Under this system, the nominal exchange rate is allowed to fluctuate (somewhat freely) within a specified band. The central parity of the band crawls over time at a rate based on past inflation differentials. In the case of Chile, the center value was adjusted periodically to reflect the difference in inflation between the United States and Chile in the preceding month.

[b] At this time, Chile's inflation targeting framework was less strict than that of Brazil described in "Brazil 2003: Inflation Targeting and Debt Dynamics," HBS case 704-028.

In addition, in November 1995, the central bank introduced a productivity differential in the backward-looking crawl, implying an additional allowable real appreciation of 2% per year. The band was widened from ±5% to ±10% in 1992 and to ±12.5% in early 1997.[42]

Capital Controls in the 1990s (1991-1997)

Chile was finding it impossible to maintain the "irreconcilable trilogy" of autonomy over monetary policy, a managed exchange rate, and free capital mobility.[43] Primarily focused on its ability to maintain the managed exchange rate,[44] the central bank decided to reinstate controls on capital inflows while gradually lifting controls on outflows (see **Exhibits 12a-12c**).[c] At the heart of Chile's capital controls framework was an unremunerated reserve requirement (URR) known as the *encaje*. As in the 1970s, the *encaje* was executed under Chapter XIV of the Compendium of Foreign Exchange Regulations of Chile's Central Bank.

Instituted in June 1991, the *encaje* initially required a 20% interest-free reserve deposit (raised to 30% in 1992) with the central bank for inflows of new loans entering Chile. The holding period was equal to the maturity of the loan, subject to a minimum of three months and a maximum of one year (the holding period was increased to one year regardless of the term of the loan in 1992). As an alternative to making the deposit, investors could pay an up-front fee equivalent to the interest cost of the reserve. Trade credits were excluded from the *encaje* as long as shipment occurred within six months, an exclusion that some observers believed the relatively new central bank authorities included in an effort to obtain the support of exporters—a group that from the beginning had been behind the market-oriented reforms program.[45]

By forcing investors to deposit a proportion of their funds interest-free in the central bank for a specified period, the URR served as an implicit tax on capital inflows that was higher the shorter the term of the funds. The cost of the implicit tax reached up to 10% annually (see **Exhibit 13**) for funds of less than three-month duration.[46] The private sector noted that obtaining central bank approval under the Chapter XIV process was a cumbersome and expensive process. Reams of documents required translation and central bank lawyers reviewed loan covenants in detail, often requesting specific changes to terms. Approval could take weeks, delaying disbursement of funds.

Although some observers noted an overall spirit of compliance with the *encaje*, investors, facing high costs, had a strong incentive to find ways to evade the controls.[d][47] Central Bank President Carlos Massad noted that: "As soon as you impose some form of regulation, the private sector will find a way to evade it. As such, we continually had to revise the system of capital controls to close gaps that kept appearing."[48] This is reflected in the continual valleys and peaks in the power of the *encaje* (see **Exhibit 14**). Through daily compilation and analysis of data related to all transactions seeking approval under Chapter XIV, as well as through *ad hoc* conversations with the private sector, the central bank was able to respond quickly to increase coverage of the *encaje*.

For example, soon after the introduction of the *encaje*, authorities noted a shift in foreign investment from loans to dollar-denominated deposits. In response, the central bank made inflows of foreign currency deposits in commercial banks subject to the URR. In 1995, authorities noticed a marked increase in "secondary ADR" operations, in which an investor takes advantage of the

[c] Decisions relating to capital controls or the exchange rate also required involvement from the Ministry of Finance, which could overrule Central Bank decisions unless all five members of the board of the Central Bank were in agreement.

[d] In contrast, long-term investors were less affected by the implicit tax, which amounted to less than 1% for funds of a three-year duration. As such, since Chile's (explicit) tax rate on dividends was 35% versus a tax rate of 4% on interest, many FDI projects continued to incorporate a large loan component, even though this was subject to the *encaje*.

difference in price of Chilean equities traded on the Santiago stock exchange and the New York Stock Exchange.[49] Soon after, the central bank began to subject secondary ADR operations to the *encaje*. In 1996, after a widely publicized case in which CSFB took a risky position in Chilean short-term securities with long-term funds brought in under the DL 600 mechanism, foreign direct equity investment explicitly became subject to the *encaje* unless it was used to expand productive capacity.[50]

Use of trade credits, which never became subject to the URR (which some observers argued occurred because of heavy lobbying[51]), was popular throughout the period. It became commonplace to structure loans as vendor financing. Many of these loans were straightforward financings of fairly priced goods and equipment. Other loans involved establishing and "trading" with offshore operations, or "sales" at unrealistic prices. Alternatively, an exporter could pay a surplus to collect early on goods, or an importer could pay late in exchange for a higher payment. These "leads and lags" permitted trade credit to substitute for short-term capital.[52] Such misinvoicing of trade was estimated to amount to hidden annual capital inflows reaching nearly 2% of GDP in some years.

Another way in which controls were evaded was through the use of various derivative products. For example, to permit *encaje*-free trading in Chilean equity by foreigners, equity swaps were commonly employed. Under an equity swap, a domestic investor delivered a foreign investor the return on Chilean equities in return for receipt of some interest rate.[53] Alternatively, foreigners could acquire an offshore swap with call features, under which an apparently long-term flow could be converted into a shorter-term loan.[54] For example, an arbitrageur could arrange a long-term credit with a prepayment option in a side contract registered in an offshore center, while keeping the option to roll over the loan if domestic interest rates continue to be attractive.[55] Such structures to evade the *encaje* were thought to be used extensively in Chile.[56]

Economic Performance (1991-1997)

The Chilean economy performed well under the new democracy, and Chile became commonly referred to as Latin America's "poster child" for free-market economic reforms.[57] Between 1991 and 1997, real GDP growth averaged 8% per year while exports recorded annual growth of 11%. Unemployment fell from 8% in 1991 to 6% in 1997. International reserves reached 20% of GDP by the end of 1997. The rate of inflation decreased consistently over the period, falling from an average rate of 22% in 1991 to 6% in 1997. Chile appeared on track to reach its inflation target of 4.5% for 1998 and its longer-term target of 3% annually from 2000. Meanwhile, Chile was forced to maintain domestic interest rates higher than international levels (see **Exhibit 15**). Wages and salaries rose at an average annual real rate of around 4% in 1992–1996 and 2% in 1997.[58]

Furthermore, social conditions were improving. In 1994, the center-left *Concertación*—under the new leadership of Eduardo Frei Ruiz-Tagle (son of former President Eduardo Frei Montalva)—was reelected for another six-year term. President Frei embarked on an ambitious social program. Rates of poverty fell and improvements were recorded in the quality of housing, availability of drinking water, sanitation, transportation infrastructure, public education, and public health services.[59]

There were, however, some looming concerns about the economy as Chile's current account deficit reached 5% of GDP in 1997. The real exchange rate appreciated by an annual average 4% to 5% between 1990 and 1997, threatening the competitiveness of Chilean exports (see **Exhibit 7**). Despite the *encaje*, capital continued to flow into Chile: In 1990–1995, average inflows amounted to 7% of GDP; in 1996–1997 inflows increased to 12% of GDP.[60] Furthermore, according to some data, a large proportion of those inflows appeared to be of a shorter maturity. (See **Exhibits 16a-b**.)

The Asian Financial Crisis (1997-1998)

Chile's economic weaknesses became more relevant amid uncertainty rooted in Asia's financial crisis. A currency crisis hit Thailand in July 1997 and spread throughout East Asia during autumn of that year and into 1998. Initially, President Frei believed the crisis would not impact Chile and embarked on an ambitious spending program, including a 30% increase in salaries over three years along with a bump up in pensions. Many Chileans believed that the *encaje* encouraged the government to be fiscally expansive.[61]

After Russia announced a massive devaluation and unilateral debt restructuring in August 1998, contagion spread to Latin America. Weakened currencies and the beginning of recessionary periods in Asian economies implied a shrunken export market. Chile was particularly affected, as it relied on Asia for one-third of its exports. Prices of copper, Chile's biggest export product, fell almost 40% between June 1997 and June 1998. As a result, Chile's current account deficit was expected to rise to 6% of GDP in 1998—although central bank officials announced commitment to reduce the deficit "at whatever cost."[62]

In addition, several Latin American countries suffered financial setbacks because of investor perception that they shared some of the economic imbalances of Asia and Russia. (See **Exhibit 17** for Latin American and Asian country-level macroeconomic and financial data). By the end of 1998, analysts expected net capital flows to Chile to reach just one-third of their 1997 levels. This reduction reflected both a decline in inflows as well as increased outflows. As in other emerging economies, lower inflows of capital hurt Chile's stockmarket. By mid-September 1998, Chile's main index had declined almost 19% in U.S. dollar terms since the beginning of the year.[63]

In addition, speculators bet against a number of Latin American currencies, fanning fears of devaluations throughout the region. Chile's sizable current account deficit and overvalued currency made the country a particularly attractive target. In 1998, despite capital controls, the Chilean peso suffered three rounds of speculative attacks. The central bank was forced to fight back with large hikes in interest rates and massive interventions in the foreign exchange market.[64] In February 1998, Chile raised the target interbank rate from 6.5% to 8.5%. In June 1998, in a risky effort to enhance credibility, the central bank tightened the exchange rate band from 25% to 5.5% (3% above the center and 2.5% below). Despite these measures, the peso continued to weaken. By the end of August, the exchange rate had fallen to 474 pesos per U.S. dollar, compared with 415 in August the year before. The central bank remained committed to defending the currency. Reserves stood at $15 billion, despite $2 billion of intervention in support of the peso over the prior year. By mid-September, at a cost of real interbank rates of 60%, the peso rose to 469 per dollar (see **Exhibit 11**).[65]

As the peso lost value against the dollar, Chileans with dollar liabilities suffered. Costs for new borrowing were becoming prohibitive; even multinational companies faced peso rates of up to 25% for short-term loans.[66] In response, in mid-1998, in order to offset the increase in the costs of borrowing associated with the deterioration in Chile's sovereign risk premium, the central bank had already partially eased Chile's capital control framework. In June 1998, the authorities reduced the URR from 30% to 10%, but with a warning that it could be increased again at any time.[67] Chile's stockmarket reacted favorably to the decrease. On the day the new rate went into effect, a trader at Chile's largest stockbroker, Larrain Vial S.A., noted: "We're up basically because of the new *encaje* rules. There have been a lot of foreign funds that have ignored Chile due to the *encaje*. Perhaps now, they'll reconsider."[68] In August 1998, the URR was eliminated for capital entering the country to carry out arbitrage of ADRs on the secondary market; the central bank, according to its annual report, "sought to recover the liquidity of Chilean ADRs, along with providing more market stability."[69]

However, complaints about the changes to the *encaje* abounded. On the one hand, economists such as Helmut Reisen, director at the OECD's Development Center, considered the change "a very negative signal to the markets, because it suggests that panic is setting in.... It gives the impression that the *encaje* can be stopped and started at any moment."[70] On the other hand, local critics demanded more. They argued that in this new environment, falling external resources rather than potentially volatile capital inflows were the major concern. Larrain Vial S.A. commented: "The elimination of the secondary ADRs from the *encaje* has revealed itself as insufficient. In Chile, we await new measures to free controls on capital flows."[71] President of Chile's Association of Fresh Fruit Exporters Ronald Bown also argued against the controls: "The best regulator of prices and quantities has been and will continue to be the market, and this is no different in the case of Chile."[72]

Debate

Central bank and government officials supported the capital controls. Massad, head of Chile's central bank argued that by discouraging short-term capital while still attracting longer-terms funds, Chile's controls helped the country achieve a remarkable record of growth and stability.[73] More generally, Massad commented that an "assessment of the Chilean experience has stressed the suitability of capital-account regulation to the circumstances of emerging-market economies."[74] In June 1998, Chile's Finance Minister pointed out that, despite the Asian crisis, Chile's economy was "nowhere near a debacle." Projected economic growth rates were reduced to a still-strong real rate of 5.5%, Chile was proving to be Latin America's leader in productivity for the year, and the economy still benefited from a high savings rate and a large stock of international reserves.

Many in the private sector also appeared to support Chile's capital controls. In a weekly economics report, Goldman Sachs reported that countries, such as Chile, without fully liberalized capital accounts did best in avoiding contagion from the Asian financial crisis.[75] In a July 1998 credit report, after reduction in the URR from 30% to 10%, Duff & Phelps Credit Rating Co. (DCR) wrote, "Chile's firm commitment to sound macroeconomic policies over the last decade underpins DCR's sovereign ratings. In spite of recent volatility in Asian and other markets...macroeconomic management through the crisis has only reaffirmed Chile's high investment grade ratings [AA- for local-currency long-term debt]."[76] In September 1998, credit rating-agency Standard & Poor's commented that it considered Chile to have "the strongest banking system in Latin America;"[77] while Moody's affirmed its confidence in Chile by leaving its sovereign debt rating unchanged while downgrading Brazil and Venezuela and putting Mexico and Argentina on watch.[78]

On the basis of Chile's apparent success with capital controls, many mainstream observers argued that controls were appropriate in helping reduce destabilizing speculation in international financial markets.[79] They argued that free capital mobility encouraged excessive risk taking and tended to lead to major financial crises.[80] Ricardo Ffrench-Davis, an economist at the UN Economic Commission for Latin America in Santiago, argued that controls such as Chile's were justified by the absence of an international regulatory framework designed to "manage bonanzas rather than crises, which are in many ways the inevitable result of badly managed bonanzas."[81] World Bank Chief Economist Joseph Stiglitz commented: "Volatile markets are an inescapable reality. Developing countries need to manage them. They will have to consider policies that help stabilize the economy....These could include sound bankruptcy laws and Chilean-style policies that put some limits on capital flows."[82] International financier George Soros, in testimony to the U.S. Congress, agreed: "To discourage short-term flows, the way for instance Chile has done by imposing a minimum reserve requirement on capital that is there for less than a year, is a good stabilizing move."[83]

Other commentators in the academic, political, and investor communities were less optimistic as emerging-market economies across the world considered introducing their own controls on the movement of capital. Economist Rudiger Dornbusch argued: "The correct answer to the question of capital mobility is that it ought to be unrestricted. Countries must urgently recognize two corollaries: first, the scope for discretionary policies has become extremely limited, and countries stand to gain by enlisting the capital markets in support of good policies, and second, intense capital mobility puts greater burdens on a country to assure that its financial system is well supervised and regulated."[84] Critics of controls focused on the importance of the role of capital inflows in helping emerging economies catch up to the industrial structures and living standards of wealthier countries;[85] the gains from intertemporal trade through a free international market for securities;[86] the problem of capital controls in encouraging corruption;[87] as well as the erosion of the effectiveness of capital controls over time as consumers and firms became better at evading them.[88]

Specifically in the case of Chile, it remained unclear how successful controls had been in meeting their objectives. Former Chief Economist for Latin America at the World Bank, UCLA Professor Sebastian Edwards concluded that the objectives were only partially achieved and only in the short run.[89] Chile's Central Bank Vice-Governor José De Gregorio argued that the success of the *encaje* was overestimated: "Flexibility in exchange rate management and a sound financial system are more important than capital controls in protecting the economy from external shocks and fluctuations in the availability of international capital."[90] Furthermore, small and medium-sized companies complained that the *encaje* made obtaining financing for productive investment substantially more difficult. Between 1996 and 1997, investment costs for smaller firms often exceeded 20% per year, compared with costs for larger firms with access to international markets of only 8%. As one economist pointed out: "This cost could be particularly important for emerging economies in which small firms are valuable engines of job creation and economic growth."[91] Massad concurred that the system discriminated against firms that were unable to evade the controls, but argued that: "The balance between the costs and benefits of the system, in my opinion, clearly pointed to net benefits. It would not have been possible to maintain the exchange rate within the limits of the band without the capital controls."[92]

Furthermore, Massad argued that studies linking controls to corruption were irrelevant in the case of Chile since: "The rules were established, applied, and controlled by the central bank, within which existed extensive permanent monitoring systems as well as a strong tradition of *esprit de corps*."[93] There was agreement that URR-related rent-seeking and corruption costs were small in Chile.[94]

With the debate on capital controls featured in both academic and popular literature, Chile faced a challenging decision. The system of capital controls appeared to have served Chile well in the 1990s—helping the country avert crises such as those in Mexico in 1994 and Asia in 1997. All the while, the country had maintained spectacular economic performance. But what had been the role of other policies? Did it make sense to maintain the controls as a preventative measure? What other policies could Chile pursue to achieve similar goals? How should a further reduction in controls be sequenced with other policies?

Exhibit 1 Chile General Economic Indicators

units as indicated	1974	1976	1978	1980	1982	1984	1986	1988	1990	1992	1994	1996	1998
Per Capita GDP (constant 1995 $)	2,320	2,061	2,336	2,665	2,428	2,445	2,678	2,963	3,283	3,848	4,212	4,858	5,275
Real GDP Growth (% per year)	2.5%	3.4%	7.5%	8.1%	-10.3%	8.0%	5.6%	7.3%	3.7%	12.3%	5.7%	7.4%	3.9%
Unemployment (%)	8.5%	16.0%	13.5%	10.4%	19.6%	13.9%	8.8%	6.3%	5.7%	4.4%	5.9%	5.4%	7.2%
Overall Budget Balance (% GDP)	-5.3%	1.4%	-0.1%	5.4%	-1.0%	-3.0%	-0.9%	1.0%	0.8%	2.3%	1.7%	2.3%	0.4%
M2 (annual % growth)	297%	412%	92%	63%	24%	32%	25%	29%	24%	26%	12%	20%	10%
M3 (% GDP)	14%	21%	21%	28%	38%	38%	40%	39%	41%	40%	39%	44%	45%
Consumer Price Inflation (% per year)	505%	212%	40%	35%	10%	20%	21%	15%	26%	15%	11%	7.4%	5.1%
Stock Market Index (1986=100)	..	..	..	..	..	..	100	175	445	1,043	2,070	1,871	1,372
ICRG Risk Rating1 (0=highest risk to 100=lowest)	..	..	..	..	..	47	48	63	67	74	78	82	75

Sources: Compiled from World Bank Development Indicators (WDI) Online, January 2005; Economist Intelligence Unit (EIU) Country Data, January 2005.

Note: "$" indicates U.S. dollar throughout Exhibits; International Country Risk Guide (ICRG) risk rating is an overall index, ranging from 0 to 100 (highest risk to lowest), based on 22 components of risk. Budget balance data comes from the WDI and differs slightly from data in **Exhibit 3**, which relies on Central Bank of Chile data.

Exhibit 2 Chile National Income Accounts

	1974	1976	1978	1980	1982	1984	1986	1988	1990	1992	1994	1996	1998
GDP (current pesos bns)	**9**	**129**	**488**	**1,075**	**1,239**	**1,893**	**3,419**	**5,918**	**9,246**	**16,123**	**23,715**	**31,237**	**36,535**
Household Consumption	62%	69%	71%	71%	75%	73%	65%	60%	62%	64%	62%	63%	65%
Government Consumption	16%	14%	14%	12%	15%	14%	13%	10%	10%	10%	10%	11%	11%
Gross Fixed Investment	17%	13%	15%	17%	15%	12%	17%	20%	23%	23%	24%	26%	26%
Exports	20%	25%	21%	23%	19%	24%	29%	35%	35%	30%	28%	27%	26%
Imports	20%	21%	24%	27%	21%	25%	26%	28%	31%	28%	26%	29%	30%
Real GDP (constant 1986 pesos bns)	2,746	2,458	2,867	3,309	3,056	3,129	3,419	3,911	4,484	5,436	6,148	7,305	8,039

Sources: Compiled from International Monetary Fund (IMF), International Financial Statistics CD-ROM, December 2003.

Exhibit 3 Chile Central Government Finances (current billions pesos)

	1987	1988	1989	1990	1991	1992	1993	1994	1995	1996	1997	1998
Income	**1,214**	**1,576**	**1,988**	**2,225**	**2,868**	**3,623**	**4,232**	**4,966**	**6,166**	**6,817**	**7,519**	**7,723**
Taxes	821	917	1,112	1,344	2,017	2,631	3,263	3,754	4,405	5,204	5,673	6,007
Copper	116	350	519	451	298	312	163	327	676	402	466	150
Other Income	277	309	358	431	553	680	806	885	1,086	1,211	1,380	1,566
Expenses	**1,206**	**1,456**	**1,675**	**1,991**	**2,641**	**3,280**	**3,954**	**4,615**	**5,285**	**6,130**	**6,806**	**7,565**
Surplus (+) / Deficit (-)	**8**	**120**	**314**	**234**	**227**	**343**	**278**	**351**	**881**	**687**	**713**	**157**
Financing	**8**	**120**	**314**	**234**	**227**	**343**	**278**	**351**	**881**	**687**	**713**	**157**
Net Financial Assets	**-4**	**-62**	**-71**	**23**	**250**	**338**	**5**	**178**	**155**	**84**	**342**	**-332**
Net Loans	-24	22	27	9	-7	4	-26	-14	-36	-15	18	34
Financial Investments	42	41	11	31	58	73	94	141	142	127	153	95
Sale of Financial Assets	-92	-144	-129	-71	-104	-113	-118	-161	-192	-149	-205	-168
Exchange Operations	2	1	0	-84	-4	2	-5	368	-4	-3	-8	-14
Cash	62	5	13	-31	274	317	57	-121	13	13	352	-299
Other	6	14	7	169	33	55	3	-34	232	112	32	19
Net Financial Liabilities	**-12**	**-182**	**-385**	**-211**	**23**	**-5**	**-273**	**-172**	**-727**	**-603**	**-371**	**-490**
Net External Debt	52	91	-20	-62	67	-45	-314	-155	-690	-338	-216	-100
Debt	*106*	*158*	*101*	*148*	*348*	*312*	*95*	*93*	*65*	*52*	*60*	*51*
Amortization	*-54*	*-67*	*-121*	*-211*	*-281*	*-357*	*-409*	*-248*	*-755*	*-389*	*-276*	*-150*
Net Internal Debt	-110	-323	-429	-226	-140	-60	-49	-96	-101	-317	-175	-378
Debt	*3*	*8*	*7*	*7*	*9*	*3*	*0*	*0*	*1*	*0*	*0*	*1*
Amortization	*-113*	*-332*	*-436*	*-232*	*-149*	*-63*	*-49*	*-96*	*-103*	*-317*	*-175*	*-379*
Other	46	51	64	77	96	100	90	79	65	52	20	-12

Source: Compiled from Central Bank of Chile Web site, www.bcentral.cl.

Exhibit 4 Chile Balance of Payments (millions of current U.S. dollars)

	1976	1978	1980	1982	1984	1986	1988	1990	1992	1994	1996	1998
Current Account	**148**	**-1,088**	**-1,971**	**-2,304**	**-2,111**	**-1,191**	**-231**	**-485**	**-957**	**-1,586**	**-3,083**	**-3,918**
Trade Balance	643	-426	-764	63	362	1,092	2,210	1,284	722	732	-1,072	-2,040
Exports	*2,116*	*2,460*	*4,705*	*3,706*	*3,650*	*4,191*	*7,054*	*8,373*	*10,007*	*11,604*	*16,627*	*16,323*
Imports	*-1,473*	*-2,886*	*-5,469*	*-3,643*	*-3,288*	*-3,099*	*-4,844*	*-7,089*	*-9,285*	*-10,872*	*-17,699*	*-18,363*
Net Services	-218	-270	-320	-474	-543	-464	-691	-228	-176	-150	-1	-452
Net Income	-325	-489	-1,000	-2,002	-2,037	-1,904	-1,931	-1,737	-1,881	-2,499	-2,518	-1,889
Net Transfers	48	97	113	109	107	85	181	198	378	331	508	462
Financial Account	**247**	**1,960**	**3,241**	**834**	**-80**	**-2,219**	**-903**	**2,857**	**3,132**	**5,294**	**5,660**	**1,967**
Net Direct Investment	-1	177	213	401	67	313	952	654	537	1,672	3,681	3,144
Outward FDI	*0*	*-4*	*0*	*0*	*-11*	*-3*	*-16*	*-8*	*-398*	*-911*	*-1,298*	*-1,661*
Inward FDI	*-1*	*181*	*213*	*401*	*78*	*316*	*968*	*661*	*935*	*2,583*	*4,979*	*4,806*
Net Portfolio Investment	-6	0	-43	-17	0	-78	-8	361	458	908	1,112	-2,528
Net Monetary Authority Investments	145	304	-36	-58	47	-597	-948	-466	-5	-156	-73	-74
Net General Government Investments	-67	-124	-56	8	142	44	91	243	204	-99	-545	-171
Net Bank Investments	-55	349	1,906	395	-294	-1,537	-1,244	-465	1,568	382	-531	-417
Net Other Investments	231	1,254	1,257	105	-42	-364	253	2,531	370	2,586	2,016	2,012
Net Errors and Omissions	69	-128	51	-69	190	224	-122	-50	372	-557	16	-239
Increase in Official Reserves	464	744	1,321	-1,539	-2,001	-3,187	-1,256	2,323	2,547	3,151	2,594	-2,191
International reserves1 (current $mm, year-end)	461	1,149	4,087	2,471	2,843	3,019	3,840	6,710	9,742	13,740	15,610	16,191
Current-account balance (% GDP)	1.5%	-7.1%	-7.1%	-9.5%	-11.0%	-6.7%	-1.0%	-1.6%	-2.3%	-3.1%	-4.5%	-5.4%
Net FDI (% international reserves)	0%	15%	5%	16%	2%	10%	25%	10%	6%	12%	24%	19%
Net portfolio inv (% international reserves)	-1%	0%	-1%	-1%	0%	-3%	0%	5%	5%	7%	7%	-16%
External debt (% GDP)	57%	48%	44%	71%	103%	119%	81%	63%	46%	44%	34%	41%
Short-term debt (% total external debt)	13.7%	14.9%	21.2%	19.3%	9.7%	8.0%	11.2%	17.6%	16.9%	17.4%	11.4%	5.3%
Nominal exchange rate (pesos/ $; year avg)	13.1	31.7	39.0	50.9	98.5	192.9	245.0	304.9	362.6	420.2	412.3	460.3
Nom exchange rate deprec. (+) (%; pa, year avg)	68.4%	33.0%	4.7%	18.7%	18.9%	17.7%	10.6%	12.6%	3.7%	3.8%	3.9%	8.9%
Real effective exchange rate (1997=100)	...	...	65.0	75.1	102.5	135.7	135.2	126.0	114.5	111.8	99.4	...

Source: Compiled from IMF, International Financial Statistics CD-ROM, December 2003; and WDI Online, January 2005.

Note: "International Reserves" differs from the cumulative increase in "Official Reserves" because of revaluation effects.

Exhibit 5 Controls on Capital Inflows in Chile, 1974–1982

Type of Restriction	Date	Description	
Limitation on maturity of non-bank borrowing	1974	Nonbanks limited to borrowing with maturities > 6 months	
	Apr-76	Nonbanks limited to borrowing with maturities > 2 years	
Unremunerated reserve requirement on foreign borrowing	Apr-78	Average maturity less than 24 months: Forbidden	
		Average maturity between 24 and 35 months: 25%	
		Average maturity between 36 and 47 months: 15%	
		Average maturity between 48 and 65 months: 10%	
		Average maturity of at least 66 months: 0%	
Limit on stock of foreign borrowing by banks	Jan-74	200% of capital and reserves (equity)	
	Jan-75	100%	
	Jun-76	150%	
	Mar-78	160%	
	Apr-78	160%	(+20% extra for fx liabilities with maturities > 36 months)
	Dec-78	180%	(+ 35%)
	Apr-79	180%	(+ 45%)
	Jun-79	free	(limited only by the legal max. debt-to-equity ratio of 20)
Limit on monthly flow of foreign borrowing by banks	Jan-78	5% of capital and reserves (equity)	
	Nov-78	Larger of 5% or US$2 million	
	Jul-79	Larger of 5% or US$1 million	
	Feb-80	Larger of 5% or US$2 million	
	Apr-80	free	(limited only by the legal max. debt-to-equity ratio of 20)

Source: Adapted from Edwards and Edwards, 1986; Cowan and De Gregorio, 2005, p. 12; De la Cuadra and Valdes-Prieto, 1990.

Exhibit 6 Chile's External Debt, 1970–1998

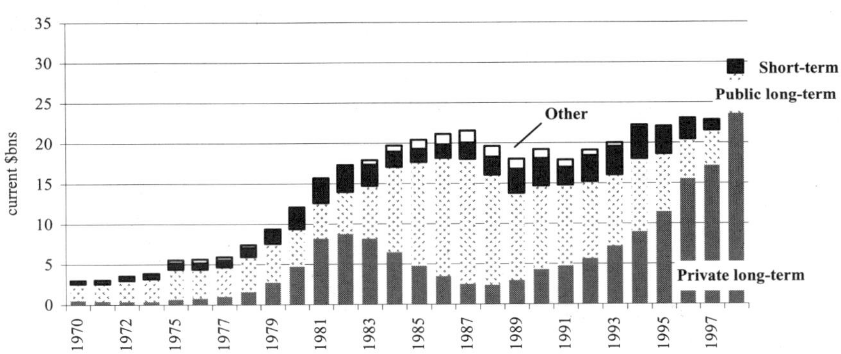

Source: Compiled from WDI Online, January 2005.

Notes: Total external debt is debt owed to nonresidents repayable in foreign currency, goods, or services. Short-term debt includes all debt having an original maturity of one year or less and interest in arrears on long-term debt; public refers to public and publicly guaranteed medium- and long-term debt; private refers to private nonguaranteed medium and long-term debt; other includes use of IMF credit.

Exhibit 7 Chile Real Exchange Rate Index

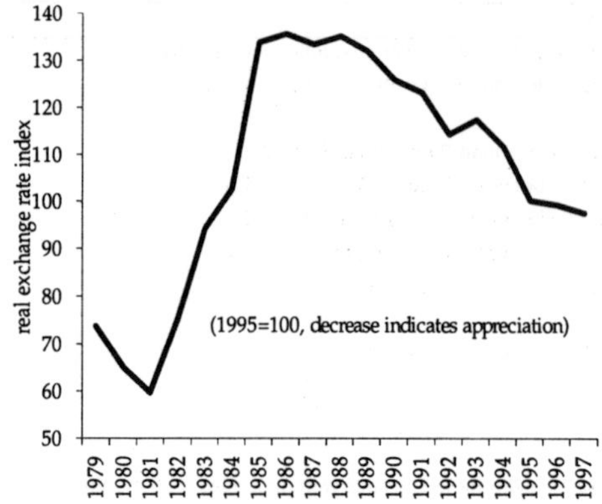

Exhibit 8 Chile Financial Liberalization Index

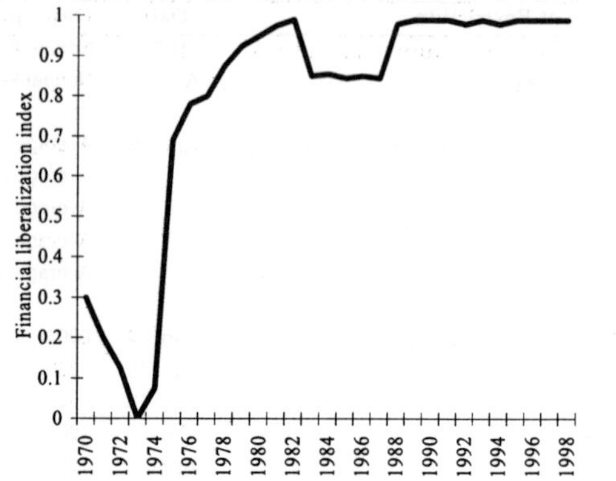

Exhibit 9 Credit to the Private Sector (as % GDP)

Exhibit 10 Measures of Bank Efficiency

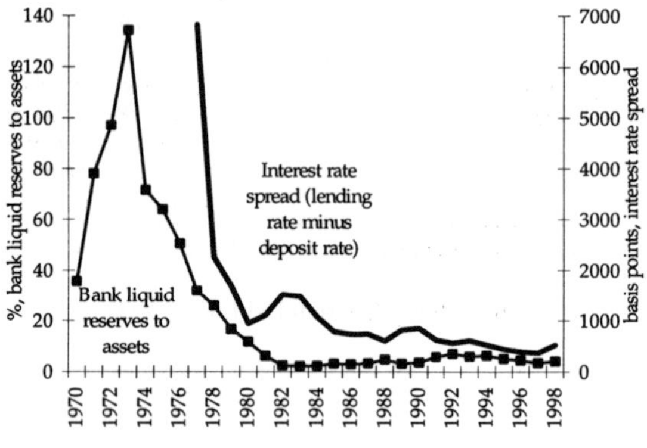

Exhibit 11 Nominal Exchange Rate within Exchange Rate Band (pesos per $)

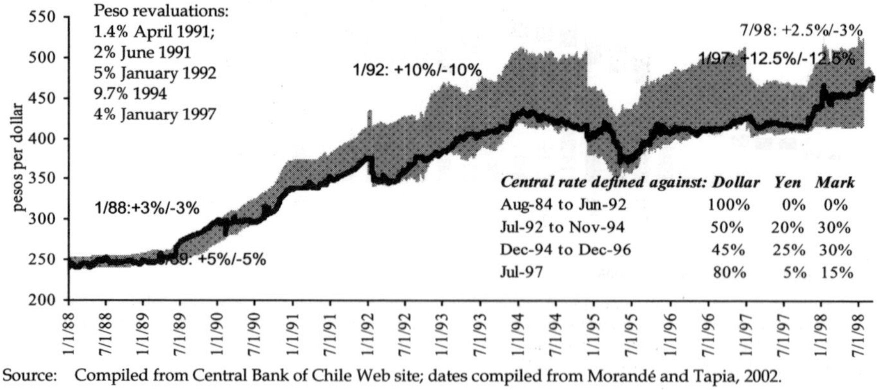

Source: Compiled from Central Bank of Chile Web site; dates compiled from Morandé and Tapia, 2002.

Exhibit 12a Capital Controls in Chile, 1991–1998: *Encaje*

Encaje: *For capital inflows of specified type, deposit of specified amount must be made at central bank for specified time at zero interest. To encourage domestic investors to invest abroad, most investment abroad was guaranteed the possibility to return without having to pay the* encaje.

Date	Rate	Coverage	Deposit /Up-front Fee
1991	(Jun 17) 20%	(Jun 17) All new foreign borrowing. (Jul) + renewed borrowing (close loophole) (Jul) + new credits, excluding trade credit (but including trade credit intermediated by banks) as long as shipment within 6 months (close loophole)	(Jun 17) Deposit must be denominated in currency of credit for term of credit (minimum of 90 days or maximum of one year). (Jun 27) Payment of up-front fee using LIBOR as discount rate also possible (to facilitate enforcement and monitoring).
1992	(May) 30%	(Jan) + foreign currency deposits by locals or foreigners (close loophole) (May) 30% applies to everything but direct borrowing by corporations (which stays at 20%) (Aug) 30% also applies to direct borrowing by corporations (close loophole)	(May) Deposit of 1 year, regardless of term (increase cost) (Aug) LIBOR + 2.5% (increase cost) (Oct) LIBOR + 4.0% (increase cost)
1993		(Oct) trade credit exemption loosened to shipment within 300 days (opens loophole)	
1994			
1995		(Jul) + secondary ADR operations (close loophole) (Dec) - new foreign borrowing to prepay old debt (when new loan of equal or shorter maturity)	(Jan) Up-front fee must be paid in dollars (increase cost) (Sep) Rule introduced that period to purchase foreign exchange after selling ADRs in the domestic market not to exceed five days (close loophole)
1996		(May) + FDI that does not increase productive capacity as decided by FDI committee (close loophole) (Jun) +1 per year limit on credit renewal (close loophole) (Dec) - borrowing < $0.2mm per loan or $0.5mm per year (reduce admin burden)	
1997		(Mar) + all borrowing > $0.1mm per year (Apr) - remittance of funds (principal and profits) from investments by Chileans abroad (Sep) - proceeds from closing positions in derivatives/options in foreign markets	
1998 (to Sep)	(Jun) 10%	(Jun) 10% except for short-term credit lines and foreign-currency denominated deposits, which remained at 30% (adjust to external env.) (Aug) - secondary ADRs (adjust to external env.)	

Sources: Adapted from De Simone and Sorsa, 1999; Laurens, 1999; and Gallego et al., 1999.

Exhibit 12b Capital Controls in Chile, 1991–1998: Non-*Encaje* Inflows

Date	Issuance of Bonds Abroad	Issuance of American Depository Receipts
	Entities wishing to issue bonds or shares abroad were subject to minimum issue amounts and ratings	
	Minimum amount	
1992	$50mm (banks and nonbanks) / 4-yr minimum maturity	$50mm
1993		
Apr-94	$25mm (nonbanks) / $50mm (banks) / 4-yr min. mat.	
Sep-94		$25mm
Jul-95		
Nov-95		$10mm for prior issuers
Sep-96	$10mm (nonbanks) / 4-yr min. mat.	
Apr-98	$5mm (nonbanks) / 4-yr min. mat.	
Apr-98	Minimum amount 0	Minimum amount 0
	Minimum rating	
May-92	Domestic A rating	Domestic A rating
Jun-93	International rating equal to or higher than sovereign risk	
Apr-94	Int'l BBB+ (nonbanks) / BBB (banks)	
Sep-94	Int'l BBB+ (banks subordinated debt)	Int'l BBB+ rating (banks and nonbanks)
Apr-98	Int'l BB (nonbanks) Int'l BBB- (banks subordinate bonds) Int'l A/B (banks nonsub bonds)	Int'l BB (nonbanks) Int'l BBB- (banks)

Sources: Adapted from Gallego et al., 1999; and Annual Report of the Central Bank of Chile, 1998.

Exhibit 12c Capital Controls in Chile, 1991–1998: Outflows

Date	Minimum Stay for Inward FDI	Pension Funds	Commercial Banks	Institutional Investors	Outward Direct Investment
1991	3 years (for DL 600 and Article XIV FDI capita and profits) (from 10 years, as implemented in 1982)		(Feb) 25% of forex deposits can be invested abroad (Apr) 40% forex can be invested abroad		(Feb) Procedures eased (Apr) Financing with forex acquired in informal market allowed (must inform central bank) and period to surrender capital and profits extended from 3 to 4 months (15% of export receipts were exempt)
1992		(Jan) Allowed to invest 1.5% abroad (in investment-grade instruments) (Aug) increased to 3%			(Mar) Export receipts exempt from surrender requirements increased to 50% (from 15%)
1993	(Mar) Conditions for remittance of profits eased				
1994	(Aug) Restrictions on remittance of profits lifted	(Nov) increased to 6%	(Sep) Banks can invest abroad 20% of capital and reserves	(Nov) Mutual funds can invest 30% of portfolio abroad; insurance companies can invest 10% (in investment-grade instruments)	
1995	(Aug) Minimum stay for FDI capital reduced from 3 years to 1 year	(May) increased to 9% (half can be in equity)			(Jul) Export exemption increased to 100%
1996		(Apr) increased to 12%			
1997					(Apr) Repatriation of capital and profits not compulsory
1998 (to Sep)			(Jan) Banks can invest abroad 70% of capital and reserves	(Jun) No limit on mutual fund foreign investment	

Sources: Adapted from Laurens, 1999; De Simone and Sorsa, 1999; and Gallego et al., 1999.

Exhibit 13 Implicit Tax Cost of *Encaje*

	Implicit tax cost of URR (in % per year of total investment value)		
	3-month borrowing	6-month borrowing	1-year borrowing
1991	1.5	1.5	1.5
1992 (January–April)	1.1	1.1	1.1
1992 (May–December)	7.7	3.9	1.9
1993	6.9	3.4	1.7
1994	9.4	4.7	2.4
1995	10.3	5.1	2.6
1996	9.4	4.7	2.4
1997	9.4	4.7	2.4

Source: Adapted from Laurens, 2000, p. 72.

Note: Refer to **Exhibit 12a** for changes impacting the implicit cost.

Calculated as: tax = [r(i*+s) T/(1-r) / D]; r=URR rate; i*=nominal interest rate for currency in which URR is constituted; s=premium applied to investor when borrowing funds to cover the URR (i.e., country risk premium plus specific credit risks); T=the duration of the URR; D=duration of the foreign investment.

Exhibit 14 Effectiveness of the URR

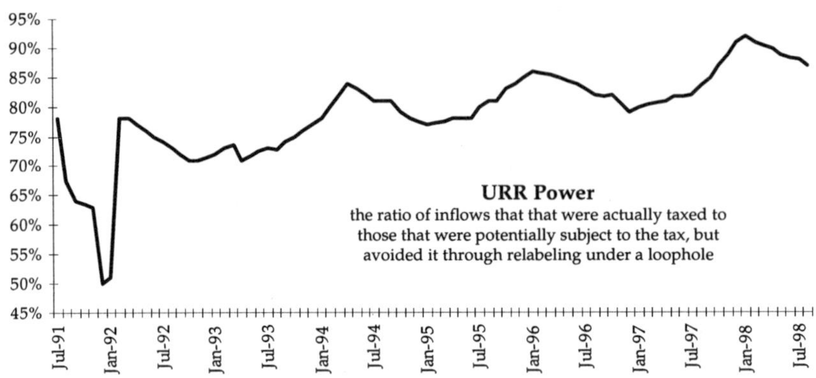

Source: Adapted from (URR power) Gallego et al., 1999, Fig. 3.4.

Exhibit 15 Real Interest Rate Differential, Chile and United States, 1985–1997

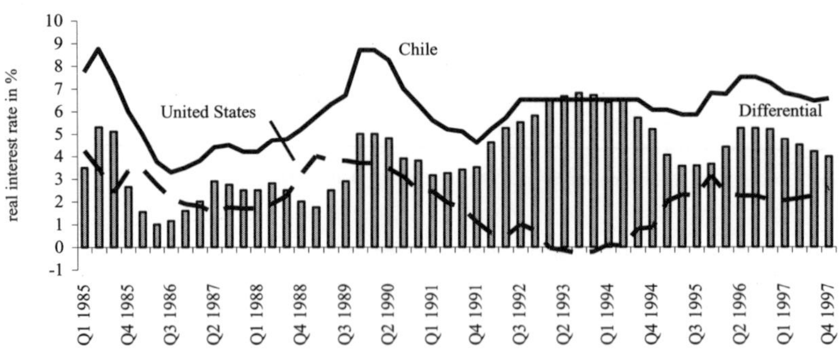

Period Avgs	85-91	92-9
US	2.7	1.3
Chile	5.8	6.5
Differential	3.1	5.2

Source: Adapted from Laurens, 1999.
Note: Chile: from January 1985 to June 1989, average deposit rate for 90-day–1-year bank deposits; from June 1989 to December 1997, 90-day Central Bank of Chile notes rates. U.S.: 3-month Treasury bill rates.

Exhibit 16a Gross Foreign Capital Inflows to Chile

	Inflows of Short-Term Capital (with maturity of one year or less)		Inflows of Long-Term Capital (with maturity of more than one year)		Deposits Subject to URR
	($mm)	(% total inflows)	($mm)	(% total inflows)	($mm)
1988	916,564	96.3	34,838	3.7	-
1989	1,452,595	95.0	77,122	5.0	-
1990	1,683,149	90.3	181,419	9.7	-
1991	521,198	72.7	196,115	27.3	587
1992	225,197	28.9	554,072	71.1	11,424
1993	159,462	23.6	515,147	76.4	41,280
1994	161,575	16.5	819,699	83.5	87,039
1995	69,675	6.2	1,051,829	93.8	38,752
1996	67,254	3.2	2,042,456	96.8	172,320
1997	8,131	2.8	2,805,882	97.2	331,572

Source: Adapted from Edwards 1999, Table 1 (using Chile government data).

Exhibit 16b Composition of Debt in Chile

	Contractual Debt (Central Bank Data)				Residual Debt (BIS Data)			
	Stock of Contractual Short-Term Debt		Stock of Contractual Short-Term Debt Plus Trade Credits		Stock of Residual Short-Term Debt (BIS bank liability due within one year)		Stock of Residual Medium-Term Debt (BIS bank liability due 1-2 years)	
	($mm)	(% total debt)	($mm)	(% total debt)	($mm)	(% total BIS debt)	($mm)	(% total BIS debt)
1991	2,199	11.3	4,346	22.3	3,181	26.8	323	2.7
1992	3,475	16.3	5,841	27.3	4,923	34.4	297	2.1
1993	3,487	15.9	5,769	26.3	5,207	35.6	489	3.3
1994	3,865	15.6	6,859	27.7	6,659	35.1	804	4.2
1995	3,431	13.5	6,891	27.0	7,446	34.7	1,060	4.9
1996	2,635	10.0	7,045	26.8	7,762	29.0	915	3.4
1997	1,287	4.4	5,522	19.0	10,679	31.5	1,230	3.6
1998	1,610	4.9	5,130	15.7	8,935	22.2	1,614	4.0

Source: Compiled from ("Central Bank Data") Cowan and de Gregorio, 2005, pp. 9 and 36; ("BIS Data") EIU Country Data, January 2005.

Exhibit 17 Macroeconomic Indicators around the Asian Financial Crisis

	1996				1997				1998			
	I	II	III	IV	I	II	III	IV	I	II	III	IV
Chile												
Real GDP (% change pa)	6.9	10.7	6.4	5.6	4.3	4.9	8.3	9.0	6.3	5.7	2.8	-1.8
Fiscal Balance (as % GDP; yr-end)		2.3					2.0			0.4		
Nom Exch Rate Depr[1] (+) (% pa)	1.6	9.4	4.1	4.4	0.8	1.7	0.5	3.5	9.5	11.7	12.3	7.7
Current Account Bal (as % GDP; prior tr)		-4.1				-3.7	-3.7	-4.4	-6.0	-6.5	-6.6	-4.9
Stockmarket Index (% change pa $ basis)	-0.5	-17.3	-10.5	-18.2	-1.7	1.0	0.6	-5.5	-16.4	-36.5	-46.9	-30.4
Moody's Bank Financial Strength Rating[2]		C		C		C		C		C		
S&P Sovereign Debt Rating[3]	A-/Stable/A-1											
Argentina												
Real GDP (% change pa)	-0.5	5.3	8.2	9.3	8.3	8.1	8.3	7.8	6.2	6.3	3.5	-0.4
Fiscal Balance (as % GDP; yr-end)		-2.2					-1.5			-1.5		
Nom Exch Rate Depr (+) (% pa)	0.0	0.0	0.0	0.0	0.0	0.0	0.0	0.0	0.0	0.0	0.0	0.0
Current Account Balance (as % GDP; yr-end)		-2.5					-4.2			-4.9		
Stockmarket Index ($ % change pa)	33.3	49.8	29.5	25.2	38.7	33.3	47.2	5.9	0.6	-32.0	-53.8	-37.4
Moody's Bank Financial Strength Rating[2]		D+		D+		D+		D/D+		D/D+		
S&P Sovereign Debt Rating	BB-/Stable/B					BB/Stable/B						
Brazil												
Real GDP (% change pa)	-2.1	1.2	6.5	5.2	4.5	4.5	2.0	2.3	0.7	1.4	0.2	-1.7
Fiscal Balance (as % GDP; yr-end)		0.0					-7.3			-7.8		
Nom Exch Rate Depr (+) (% pa)	10.3	8.9	7.1	6.8	7.2	7.2	7.3	7.4	7.4	7.4	8.1	8.3
Current Account Balance (as % GDP; yr-end)		-3.0					-3.8			-4.2		
Stockmarket Index ($ % change pa)	50.8	54.0	28.9	53.3	70.2	93.9	70.5	34.9	23.0	-28.3	-48.3	-38.6
Moody's Bank Financial Strength Rating[2]		D+		D+		D+		D+		D+		
S&P Sovereign Debt Rating	B+/Positive/—					BB-/Stable/B					BB-/Neg/B	
Mexico												
Real GDP (% change pa)	0.1	6.6	6.9	7.1	6.1	7.1	7.2	6.8	6.3	5.7	4.9	2.9
Fiscal Balance (as % GDP; yr-end)		-0.2					-1.1			-1.4		
Nom Exch Rate Depr (+) (% pa)	10.7	20.6	17.4	2.7	4.5	4.6	3.7	3.0	7.9	13.6	29.2	22.0
Current Account Balance (as % GDP; yr-end)		-0.8					-1.9			-3.8		
Stockmarket Index ($ % change pa)	51.4	21.2	15.2	17.8	16.7	32.8	58.5	51.1	24.0	-15.4	-48.1	-38.0
Moody's Bank Financial Strength Rating[2]		E+		E+		E+		E+		E+		
S&P Sovereign Debt Rating	BB/Neg/—		BB/Stable/B				BB/Positive/B					BB/St/B

Exhibit 17 (continued)

Malaysia	1996-I	1996-II	1996-III	1996-IV	1997-I	1997-II	1997-III	1997-IV	1998-I	1998-II	1998-III	1998-IV
Real GDP (% change pa)	12.3	8.8	9.8	9.4	7.6	8.4	7.2	6.1	-1.5	-5.9	-10.2	-11.2
Fiscal Balance (as % GDP; yr-end)		2.0					2.9			..		
Nom Exch Rate Depr (+) (% pa)	0.0	2.3	0.1	-0.5	-2.3	1.2	27.3	53.9	47.2	65.1	19.0	-2.4
Current Account Balance (as % GDP; yr-end)		-4.4					-5.9			-13.2		
Stockmarket Index ($ % change pa)	16.8	8.2	13.4	25.0	7.1	-6.3	-43.6	-68.8	-59.4	-74.4	-61.5	1.0
Moody's Bank Financial Strength Rating[2]		C+		C/C+		C/C+		D+		D		
S&P Sovereign Debt Rating			A+/Pos/A-1+				A+/N/A-1+	A/Neg/A-1		A-/St/A-2	BBB-/N/A-3	
Thailand												
Real GDP (% change pa)	4.7	6.5	7.8	4.6	1.0	-0.6	-1.6	-4.2	-7.1	-13.9	-13.9	-7.2
Fiscal Balance (as % GDP; yr-end)		2.3					-2.1			-7.7		
Nom Exch Rate Depr (+) (% pa)	2.0	2.8	1.4	1.7	2.9	1.7	43.7	84.5	49.4	64.1	7.6	-22.3
Current Account Balance (as % GDP; yr-end)		-8.1					-2.0			12.7		
Stockmarket Index ($ % change pa)	3.9	-13.1	-16.3	-36.1	-46.9	-58.4	-65.5	-75.7	-56.4	-69.1	-56.7	22.9
Moody's Bank Financial Strength Rating[2]		D+		D+		D/D+		D		E+		
S&P Sovereign Debt Rating			A/Stable/A-1				A-/N/A-1	BBB/N/A-3		BBB-/Negative/A-3		
Korea												
Real GDP (% change pa)	7.3	6.9	6.4	7.0	5.0	5.8	5.0	3.1	-5.4	-8.1	-8.0	-5.4
Fiscal Balance (as % GDP; yr-end)		0.1					-1.2			..		
Nom Exch Rate Depr (+) (% pa)	1.5	6.9	6.9	9.0	14.6	9.6	11.4	100.8	54.2	54.6	52.1	-29.0
Current Account Balance (as % GDP; yr-end)		-4.2					-1.6			11.7		
Stockmarket Index ($ % change pa)	-8.0	-0.8	-19.9	-28.0	-30.0	-29.8	-18.5	-52.3	-59.2	-67.2	-70.2	-20.1
Moody's Bank Financial Strength Rating[2]		D		D		D		D		E+		
S&P Sovereign Debt Rating			AA-/Stable/A-1+				AA-/N/A-1+	B+/CW-N/C		BB+/Stable/B		
Russia												
Real GDP (% change pa)	-2.3	-3.6	-5.7	-3.2	-0.4	-0.7	3.1	3.9	-1.5	-1.0	-8.9	-9.3
Fiscal Balance (as % GDP; yr-end)		0.0					0.0			-5.4		
Nom Exch Rate Depr (+) (% pa)	-0.9	12.6	19.7	19.8	18.0	13.2	8.6	7.2	6.6	7.2	174.1	246.5
Current Account Balance (as % GDP; yr-end)		2.8					0.0			0.1		
Stockmarket Index ($ % change pa)	...	...	...	...	...	...	...	...	...	...	-88.7	-83.4
Moody's Bank Financial Strength Rating[2]	...	...	...	...	...	...	...	...	...	...	...	...
S&P Sovereign Debt Rating						BB-/Stable/B		BB-/Neg/B		B+/St/B	CCC-/N/C	

Sources: EIU Country Data, January 2005; WDI Online January 2005; Standard & Poor's, "Sovereign Ratings History Since 1975," November 2, 2001, http://www.mafhoum.com/press2/72E40.htm, accessed January 2005; and Charles Adams, Donald J. Mathieson, Garry Schinasi, and Bankim Chadha, "Appendix II: The Asian Crisis: Capital Markets Dynamics and Spillover," in "International Capital Markets: Developments, Prospects, and Key Policy Issues," IMF World Economic and Financial Surveys, September 1998.

Notes: 1. Ex rate depr refers to decrease in local currency against $ from same Q-end of previous year. + is depr, - is appr. 2. BFSR is Moody's opinion of a bank's intrinsic strength—the likelihood that the bank will require financial support from shareholders, the government, or other institutions. The ratings range from A (highest) to E (lowest). 3. Standard & Poor's Rating refers to bonds issued in foreign-currency long-term/outlook/short-term (Some countries experienced more than one change in a quarter. The final credit standing only is shown.); CWN refers to on Credit Watch Negative. Order from best to worst is AAA/AA+/AA/AA-/A+/A/A-/BBB+/.... AAA to BBB is investment grade. Below is noninvestment grade.

Endnotes

[1] For mention and criticism of this argument, see Kevin Cowan and José De Gregorio, "International Borrowing, Capital Controls and the Exchange Rate: Lessons from Chile," prepared for the NBER Conference "International Capital Flows," Santa Barbara, CA, February 2005.

[2] For example, the importance of a flexible exchange rate regime and a sound financial system is mentioned in Cowan and De Gregorio 2005, and as discussed in casewriter interview with José De Gregorio, March 9, 2005.

[3] Richard Lapper, "Chilean Capital Controls Come under Local Fire," *The Financial Times*, July 22, 1998.

[4] Darren McDermott and Leslie Lopez, "Malaysia Imposes Sweeping Currency Controls—Such Capital Restrictions Win Credence in Wake of Financial Turmoil," *The Wall Street Journal*, September 2, 1998.

[5] For more on Malaysia's controls, see Rawi Abdela and Laura Alfaro, "Malaysia: Capital and Control," HBS Case No. 702-040.

[6] For further background on capital controls and the debate surrounding their use, see Rawi Abdela and Laura Alfaro, "Capital Controls," HBS Case No. 702-082.

[7] For a brief discussion, see J. Bradford DeLong, "Should We Still Support Untrammeled International Capital Mobility? Or Are Capital Controls Less Evil than We Once Believed?" *The Economists' Voice* (Berkeley Electronic Press) Vol. 1, No. 1, 2004.

[8] See Jagdish Bhagwati, "The Capital Myth: The Difference between Trade in Widgets and Trade in Dollars," *Foreign Affairs*, 77, 1998, pp. 7–12; and Richard N. Cooper, "Should Capital Account Convertibility be a World Objective?" *Essays in International Finance* No. 207, 1998.

[9] For more on this, see essays collected in Sebastian Edwards (ed.) *Capital Controls, Exchange Rates and Monetary Policy in the World Economy* (Cambridge University Press, 1995).

[10] It is unclear how large a role U.S. policy played in Allende's economic failure; at the behest of U.S. President Richard Nixon and U.S. National Security Advisor Henry Kissinger, the U.S. CIA spent $8 million between November 1970 and September 1973 undermining Allende and aiming to "make the economy scream" in an effort to unseat him. For a detailed outline of the involvement of the U.S. CIA in Chile, see Tim Weiner, "All the President Had to Do Was Ask; The C.I.A. Took Aim at Allende," The New York Times, September 13, 1998.

[11] U.S. Library of Congress Chile Country study, available at http://countrystudies.us/chile/3.htm, accessed December 15, 2004; and "Country Profile: Chile," The Economist Intelligence Unit (EIU), 1998.

[12] Larry Rohter, "Chilean Judge Says Pinochet Is Fit for Trial," *The New York Times*, December 14, 2004.

[13] Guillermo A. Calvo and Ernesto Talvi, "Sudden Stop, Financial Factors and Economic Collapse in Latin America: Learning from Argentina and Chile," NBER Working Paper 11153, February 2005 write that it was the worst contraction in Latin America until Argentina 2002.

[14] Sebastian Edwards and Alejandra C. Edwards, "Financial Liberalization, Interest Rates, and the Real Exchange Rate in Chile," UCLA Economics Working Papers 395, UCLA Department of Economics, 1986; Cowan and De Gregorio 2005; and Sergio De la Cuadra and Salvador Valdes-Prieto, "Myths and Facts about Financial Liberalization in Chile: 1974–1982," Pontificia Universidad Catolica de Chile Working Paper No. 128, October 1990.

[15] Edwards and Edwards 1986, p. 3.22.

[16] Cowan and De Gregorio 2005, p. 12.

[17] The Chapter XIV process took approximately one week. For loans, the foreign entity was required to justify to the Central Bank the interest rate being charged, as investors often sought to bring funds in as debt instead of equity and charge an interest rate well above market rates, due to Chile's 35% tax on dividends versus 4% tax on interest. (Discussion of Chapter XIV and DL 600, as well as tax implications, has benefited from casewriter interview with Georges de Bourguignon, Partner Asset Chile, on February 24, 2005.)

[18] De la Cuadra and Valdes-Prieto 1990.

[19] Approval or rejection of investments under DL 600 took 30 to 40 days. For more on FDI in Chile see Karen Poniachik, Executive Vice-President, Chile's Foreign Investment Committee, "Chile's FDI Policy: Past Experience and Future Challenges," OECD Global Forum on International Investment: Attracting Foreign Direct Investment for Development, Shanghai, December 5–6 2002 at <http://www.oecd.org/dataoecd/54/27/2764423.pdf> (accessed February 26, 2005).

[20] $10,000 limit from Patricio Meller, "Un Siglo de Economía Política Chilena (1890-1990)," Editorial Andrés Bello, 1996.

[21] Edwards and Edwards 1986.

[22] Edwards and Edwards 1986.

[23] However, Edwards and Edwards 1986 present evidence showing that investors were not very sensitive to the adjusted exchange rate differential during the period.

[24] Edwards and Edwards 1986, p. 3.3.

[25] Cowan and De Gregorio 2005, p. 19.

[26] Sebastian Edwards, "Capital Inflows into Latin America: A Stop-Go Story?" NBER Working Paper 6441, March 1998, p. 34.

[27] Francisco Gallego and Norman Loayza, "Financial Structure in Chile: Macroeconomic Developments and Microeconomic Effects," Central Bank of Chile Working Paper No. 75, July 2000, p. 7.

[28] For more on moral hazard problems, see Ronald I. McKinnon and Huw Pill, "Credible Liberalizations and International Capital Flows: The Overborrowing Syndrome," *Financial Integration and Deregulation in East Asia*, T. Ito and A. Krueger, eds. (Chicago: The University of Chicago Press, 1996), pp. 1–42; and Graciela L.Kaminsky, and Carmen M. Reinhart, "The Twin Crises: The Causes of Banking and Balance of Payments Problems," *American Economic Review*, 89, 1999, pp. 473–500.

[29] Edwards and Edwards 1986, p. 3.35.

[30] Edwards and Edwards 1986.

[31] Edwards, "Capital Inflows into Latin America: A Stop-Go Story?" 1998, p. 33.

[32] Casewriter interview on January 24, 2005 with Carlos Massad, president of the Central Bank of Chile from 1997 to 2003.

[33] Meller 1996.

[34] Eliot Kalter, Steven Phillips, Marco A. Espinosa-Vega, Rodolfo Luzio, Mauricio Villafuerte, and Manmohan Singh, "Chile: Institutions and Policies Underpinning Stability and Growth," IMF Occasional Paper 231, 2004, <www.imf.org/external/pubs/nft/op/231/op231.pdf> (accessed February 25, 2005).

[35] For details, see Edgardo Barandiarán and Leonardo Hernández, "Origins And Resolution Of A Banking Crisis: Chile 1982-86," Central Bank of Chile Working Paper No. 57, December 1999, pp. 42–46.

[36] Gerard Caprio, Jr., "Safe and Sound Banking in Developing Countries: We're Not in Kansas Anymore," Policy Research Department of the World Bank, January 1997, prepared for the Brookings Conference, "FDICIA: Bank Reform Five Years Later and Five Years Ahead," December 19, 1996.

[37] Edwards and Edwards 1986, p. 3.37.

[38] Bank for International Settlements (BIS), "Bank Restructuring in Practice," BIS Policy Papers No. 6, August 1999, p. 20, Table 6 <http://www.bis.org/publ/plcy06.pdf> (accessed February 25, 2005) sets figure at between 19% and 41%; Bernhard Fischer and Helmut Reisen, "Towards Capital Account Convertibility," OECD Development Center Policy Brief No. 4, 1992, estimate the cost from 1982-1985 at 44% of 1985 GDP; Edwards "Capital Inflows into Latin America: A Stop-Go Story?" 1998, p. 24 estimates value at 20%; Barandiarán and Hernández 1999, p. 54 estimates the cost at 43%of GDP from 1982-1989. It should be noted that a vast majority represented a transfer to nationals rather than to foreigners; Barandiarán and Hernández estimate only 6% of the 43% to represent a transfer to foreigners.

[39] Measures included: a prudential framework establishing high disclosure standards such as requiring the publication of information on banks' asset quality; stringent rules for loan classification and provisioning such that bad loans were recognized early; supervision of credit risk, including borrower foreign exchange exposure; strict limits on connected lending and on bank exposure to foreign exchange risks; the compliance of all banks with international capital adequacy ratios to prevent excessive risk taking; and clear procedures for correction of liquidity or solvency problems. From Francisco Nadal-De Simone and Piritta Sorsa, "A Review of Capital Account Restrictions in Chile in the 1990s," IMF Working Paper WP/99/52, April 1999, p. 14; and Bernard Laurens, "Appendix I: Chile's Experience with Controls on Capital Inflows in the 1990s," in A. Ariyoshi, K. Habermeier, B. Laurens, I. Otker-Robe, J.I. Canales-Kriljenko, A. Kirilenko, "Capital Controls: Country Experiences with Their Use and Liberalization," IMF Occasional Paper 190, May 17, 2000, p. 74.

[40] Daniel Zider, "Key Interviews: Democracy and its Ethical Values," Inter-American Development Bank, (available at <http://www.iadb.org/Etica/Documentos/ayl_democ-i.pdf> as of May 28, 2005).

[41] Sebastian Edwards, "How Effective Are Capital Controls?" *Journal of Economic Perspectives* Vol. 13, No. 4, Fall 1999, p. 76.

[42] For details on the exchange rate regime, see Felipe G. Morandé and Matías Tapia, "Exchange Rate Policy in Chile: From the Band to Floating and Beyond," Central Bank of Chile Working Papers No. 152, April 2002 <http://www.bcentral.cl/esp/estpub/estudios/dtbc/pdf/dtbc152.pdf> (accessed February 25, 2005).

[43] Neely 1999 cites Ronald I. McKinnon and E. Oates Wallace, "The Implications of International Economic Integration for Monetary, Fiscal and Exchange Rate Policies," The International Finance Section, Princeton University, 1966; and Maurice Obstfeld and Alan M. Taylor, "The Great Depression as a Watershed: International Capital Mobility over the Long Run," in *The Defining Moment: The Great Depression and the American Economy in the Twentieth Century*, Michael D. Bordo, Claudia D. Goldin, and Eugene N. White, eds., University of Chicago Press, 1998, pp. 353–402.

[44] Casewriter interview with Carlos Massad on January 24, 2005.

[45] Edwards, "How Effective Are Capital Controls?" 1999, p. 76 cites Raúl Labán and Felipe Larraín. "El Retorno del los Capitales Privados a Chile en los Noventa: Causas, Efectos y Reacciones de Política" *Cuadernos de Economía* No. 103, 1997, pp. 329–362.

[46] Laurens 2000, p. 72.

47 For footnote c: Casewriter interview with Georges de Bourguignon, Partner Asset Chile, on February 24, 2005. See Edwards, "How Effective Are Capital Controls?" 1999 for long-term implied tax rates of the *encaje*.

48 Casewriter interview with Carlos Massad on January 24, 2005.

49 Salvador Valdes-Prieto and Marcelo Soto, "The Effectiveness of Capital Controls: Theory and Evidence from Chile," *Empirica* 25, 1998, pp. 133–164.

50 Many economists have written that there appeared to be a general increase in speculative forms of investment entering the country through the DL 600 mechanism disguised as capital increases in existing FDI projects and direct investments in financial services. They postulated the increase of FDI in financial services in total FDI indicated that inflows were not being directed toward developing or enhancing real assets of enterprises. (For example, De Simone and Sorsa 1999, p. 14, fn 18 cite Guillermo Le Fort and Gonzalo Sanhueza, *"Flujo de Capitales y Encaje en la Experiencia Chilena de los 90,"* Central Bank of Chile unpublished paper, 1997.). Chile's Foreign Investment Committee (responsible for executing DL 600 contracts), however, considered the CSFB transaction an isolated case and did not find evidence of wide-scale abuse of the foreign investment route to investing in Chile. Details surrounding the CSFB transaction are unclear. One explanation was that Credit Suisse First Boston invested $700 million in the equity of a custom-made investment company devoted to holding Chilean short-term debt. (Valdes-Prieto and Soto 1998. Also discussed also in Raúl Labán M. and Felipe Larraín B., "The Return of Private Capital to Chile in the 1990s: Causes, Effects, and Policy Reactions," Development Discussion Paper No. 627, Harvard Institute for International Development, Harvard University, March 1998, p. 25.) Another explanation is that CSFB invested $800 million in long-term securities of 8-year maturity and hedged with short-term securities forwards; This open position lost them $120 million when the Russian crisis hit (Aug 1998) because interest rates rose and the exchange rate was moving the opposite way. See also John Williamson, Stephany Griffith-Jones, Ricardo Gottschalk, "Should Capital Controls Have a Place in the Future International Monetary System," May 2, 2003, prepared for Meeting of the International Monetary Convention held by the Reinventing Bretton Woods Committee in Madrid, May 13–14, 2003.

51 Laurens 2000, p.78 quotes Guillermo Le Fort in paper prepared for the Working Group on Foreign Capital Flows for the Financial Stability Forum, 1999, p. 4.

52 De Simone and Sorsa 1999, p. 14 cites Peter Quirk and Owen Evans, "Capital Account Convertibility: Review of Experience and Implications for IMF Policies," IMF Occasional Paper No. 131, 1995.

53 Peter M. Garber, "Derivatives in International Capital Flow," NBER Working Paper 6623, June 1998.

54 Peter M. Garber, "Buttressing Capital Account Liberalization with Prudential Regulation and Foreign Entry," p. 30, in "Should the IMF Pursue Capital-Account Convertibility?" *Essays in International Finance* No. 207, May 1998.

55 Valdes-Prieto and Soto 1998.

56 Valdes-Prieto and Soto 1998 and Garber "Derivatives in International Capital Flow," 1998.

57 In various press outlets, for example, Rafael Urbina, "Asian Financial Crisis Slows Chilean Growth," *Agence France-Presse*, June 15, 1998.

58 "Country Profile: Chile," The Economist Intelligence Unit (EIU), 1998.

59 Ibid.

60 Laurens 2000, p. 75.

61 Interview with casewriter, April 2005, Alejandro E. Alarcon of Chile's Association of Banks and Financial Institutions.

62 Dow Jones International News, "Chile's Measures—4: Capital Controls End Seen Temporary," September 17, 1998.

63 International Money Marketing, "Investment Market Review—Latin America Hit by Global Slump," September 18, 1998.

64 Cowan and De Gregorio 2005, p. 13.

65 Larrain Vial S.A., Corredora de Bolsa, "Chile: Weekly Report" September 14, 1998.

66 Lapper 1998.

67 Dow Jones International News, "Chile's Measures—4: Capital Controls End Seen Temporary," 1998.

68 Emerging Markets Report, "Chile Midday Stocks Higher On New Reserve Rules; IPSA +0.9%," July 8, 1998.

69 Central Bank of Chile, Annual Report, 1998.

70 Andy Robinson, "El Encaje Chileno Ya es de Quita y Pon," *Cinco Dias*, July 16, 1998.

71 Larrain Vial S.A., Corredora de Bolsa, "Chile: Weekly Report," August 31, 1998.

72 Casewriter interview with Ronald Bown on February 9, 2005.

73 Carlos Massad, "The Liberalization of the Capital Account: Chile in the 1990s," in "Should the IMF Pursue Capital-Account Convertibility?" *Essays in International Finance* No. 207, May 1998.

74 Ibid.

75 David Wessel and Bob Davis, " 'Chinese Solution' begins to hold sway," *The Wall Street Journal*, September 4, 1998, quoting MIT economist Rudiger Dornbusch. See also "Time to Turn off the Tap?" *The Economist*, September 12, 1998, cite weekly Goldman report.

76 Jaime Sanz, "DCR Assigns 'A+' Rating to Chile's PRD Notes Program," Duff & Phelps Credit Rating Co. Press Release, July 16, 1998.

77 Cinco Dias, "Standard & Poor's Rebaja la Perspectiva del BBV y Podria Subir al BCH, con el que esta 'Impresionado,' " September 11, 1998.

78 M. Tallin, "Indigna Clasificacion de Deuda a Latinoamericanos" *El Excelsior*, September 7, 1998.

79 Tobin, James. "A Proposal for International Monetary Reform," *Eastern Economic Journal* 4, 1978, p. 154-159.

80 Edwards "How Effective are Capital Controls," 1999 cites Bhagwati 1998 and Cooper 1998.

81 Lapper 1998.

82 Joseph Stiglitz, "Bleak Growth Prospects for the Developing World," *International Herald Tribune*, April 10-11, 1999, p. 6.

83 Reuters News, "Capital Controls Appropriate in Some Cases—Soros," September 15, 1998.

84 Rudiger Dornbush 1998. "Capital Controls: An Idea Whose Time is Past" in "Should the IMF Pursue Capital-Account Convertibility?" *Essays in International Finance* No. 207, May 1998, p. 20.

85 For a brief discussion, see DeLong 2004.

86 Edwards "How Effective are Capital Controls," 1999, p. 66 cites Maurice Obstfeld and Kenneth Rogoff, *Foundations of International Finance* (The MIT Press, 1996).

87 For a brief discussion, see DeLong 2004.

88 Neely 1999, p. 27 cites Marston 1995 and Barry Eichengreen, *Toward a New International Financial Architecture: A Practical Post-Asia Agenda*, (Institute for International Economics, 1999), who argues that controls do not have to be perfect, but just need to make avoidance costly enough to reduce destabilizing flows.

89 Edwards "How Effective are Capital Controls," 1999, and as confirmed in casewriter interview with Sebastian Edwards, February 14, 2005.

90 Cowan and De Gregorio 2005, and as discussed in casewriter interview with José De Gregorio March 9, 2005.

91 Kristin J. Forbes, "One Cost of the Chilean Capital Controls: Increased Financial Constraints for Smaller Traded Firms," MIT Sloan Working Paper No. 4273-02, December 2002. Edwards "How Effective are Capital Controls," 1999 and Francisco Gallego, Leonardo Hernández, Klaus Schmidt-Hebbel, "Capital Controls in Chile: Effective? Efficient?" Central Bank of Chile Working Paper No. 59, 1999 make a similar point with extensive discussion.

92 Casewriter interview with Carlos Massad on January 24, 2005.

93 Casewriter interview with Carlos Massad on January 24, 2005.

94 Gallego, et al., 1999.

9-705-032
REV: JUNE 23, 2005

LAURA ALFARO
RAFAEL DI TELLA

Capital Controls in Chile in the 1990s (B)

In the fallout of the Asian and Russian financial crises of 1997–1998, Chile reevaluated its system of capital controls. As in the rest of Latin America, the crisis was taking its toll on the Chilean economy.[1]

By September 1998, Chile had experienced an upward surge—from 120 basis points prior to the crisis to over 300—in the premium investors demanded as compensation for the risks associated with investing in the country (compared with an average rise in Latin American sovereign risk premiums from 480 basis points prior to the crisis to over 1,700). Chile also experienced a dramatic fall in net capital inflows, rapid exchange rate depreciation, and a steep reduction in its main stock market index (see **Exhibit 1**).

The central bank responded with increased interest rates, intervention in foreign exchange markets, a tightening of the exchange rate band, and a loosening of controls on capital inflows. In particular, in June 1998, the *encaje*—the requirement that foreigners deposit the equivalent of a percentage of their investments with the central bank for one year on an interest-free basis—was reduced from 30% to 10%. In August, secondary American Depository Receipts operations were exempted from the *encaje*. Finally, on September 16, the unremunerated reserve requirement was reduced to 0% for all capital inflows.

In explaining the loosening of the *encaje* after the Asian financial crisis, central bank President Carlos Massad remarked:

> At this time, we were operating under various circumstances. First, capital inflows had fallen drastically. Second, the exchange rate and Chilean exports weakened, which led the exchange rate to move away from the most appreciated position within the exchange rate band to the most depreciated position within the band. In this scenario, we thought that maintaining the controls on capital inflows was absolutely unnecessary.[2]

At the same time as it loosened the *encaje*, the central bank announced other measures. The target interbank rate was raised from 8.5% to 14%, and the exchange rate band was loosened. The ceiling of the band was increased from 2% to 3.5%, while the floor remained unchanged at 3.5%. By year-end, the band would be allowed to increase gradually to ±5%. The inflation target for 1999 remained at 4.3%.

Professors Laura Alfaro and Rafael Di Tella and Research Associate Ingrid Vogel prepared this case. HBS cases are developed solely as the basis for class discussion. Cases are not intended to serve as endorsements, sources of primary data, or illustrations of effective or ineffective management.

The Wall Street Journal reported: "The measures had little impact on Santiago trading Thursday as Chilean markets paid more attention to events in Brazil and the rest of Latin America, traders said."[3]

Sudden Stop

Despite these measures, the Asian financial crisis brought a degree of economic slowdown to Chile in the following years (see **Exhibit 2**), mirroring the rest of Latin America. Economists Guillermo Calvo and Ernesto Talvi commented:

> Even Chile, a country with very solid economic fundamentals—a track record of sound macroeconomic management, a highly praised and sustained process of structural and institutional reforms that completely transformed and modernized Chile's economy, and an average rate of growth of 7.4% per year between 1985 and 1997, the highest growth rate in LAC-7[4]—and tight controls on the inflows of foreign capital, experienced a sudden and severe interruption in capital inflows.[5]

They noted that between 1989 and their peak in 1998, net capital flows in Chile increased by 2.2% of the gross domestic product (GDP) of the final four quarters leading to the peak—among the smallest booms in Latin America. In contrast, between their peak in 1998 and their minimum in 1999, net capital flows fell by 7.9% of the GDP of the final four quarters leading to the minimum—the largest fall in Latin America. By way of comparison, the average for Latin America was 6.8% of GDP for the boom period and –3.8% of GDP for the bust (see **Exhibit 3**). Calvo and Talvi dub the systemic, large, and largely unexpected interruption in external capital flows to Latin America that followed the Asian and Russian financial crises a "Sudden Stop."

Chile's central bank Vice-Governor José De Gregorio noted that Sudden Stop in the case of Chile was atypical: Unlike in other Latin American countries, the fall in net capital flows was driven by an increase in capital outflows, particularly from pension funds and banks, while capital inflows actually increased. In the case of pension funds—which increased their share of foreign holdings in total portfolios from 1% in 1997 to 10% in 1999, corresponding to outflows of 5% of GDP—it was unclear how much of the increase in outflows could be attributed to macroeconomic events as opposed to a loosening of the capital controls on foreign investment. Banks increased their share of foreign assets in total portfolios from 1% in 1997 to a peak of 6% in 1999, also corresponding to 5% of GDP. The peak occurred after the peso was floated but before country risk had returned to precrisis levels. Bank net dollar asset positions also rose, implying that banks were not simply hedging rising dollar deposits. De Gregorio concluded:

> The rising net asset position and the timing of the foreign asset spike suggest that banks took on a net dollar position to take advantage of arbitrage opportunities that arose prior to the currency being floated in 1999. In effect, Chilean residents were betting against an exchange rate policy that tried to minimize depreciations, while in fact the large negative external shocks pushed the equilibrium real exchange rate upwards.[6]

In addition to Latin America's most extreme capital outflows, Chile also experienced reduced economic growth, a severe drop in asset prices, an abrupt adjustment to its current-account balance, and depreciation of the peso (see **Exhibit 1**). More specifically, average annual GDP growth in Chile fell from 8.3% in the period 1991–1997 to 2.2% in 1999–2002 (compared with an average fall in Latin America from 4.7% to 0.4%; see **Exhibit 4**).[7] The stock market in Chile fell 37% between the second quarter of 1998 and the end of 2002 (compared with 47% for Latin America). Cumulative total external financial flows fell 47% between 1990–Q2 1998 and Q2 1998–2002 (compared with 40% in Latin America overall). The counterpart was an adjustment in Chile's current-account deficit from

6.5% of GDP for the year ending in June 1998 to close to 0% in the following 12-month period (compared with a longer adjustment in Latin America overall). (See **Exhibit 5** for Chilean balance-of-payments data.) From June 1998 to December 2002, the Chilean peso depreciated approximately 50% (compared with 70% in Latin America on average).

Many observers attributed the fact that Chile did not face a financial crisis or severe recession in 1999 to the *encaje,* which they argued successfully reduced Chile's share of short-term debt, shielding the country from financial vulnerability.[8] Other observers disagreed and commented on the limited success of the *encaje* in affecting the level and composition of capital inflows in the 1990s, as well as its failure to prevent massive outflows in the aftermath of the crisis. Furthermore, as De Gregorio noted: "Chile's experience in the early 1980s shows that, even if capital controls are effective in limiting the share of short-term debt, this certainly does not provide a guarantee against currency crises."[9]

Additional Capital Account Liberalization

On September 2, 1999, Chile abandoned its crawling band in favor of a floating exchange rate (see **Exhibit 6**). This occurred for a number of reasons.[10] At the time, the exchange rate was consistently close to the central rate of the band, implying minimal pressures of depreciation or appreciation. In addition, with inflation reaching an annual rate of 3%, the central bank began to focus on maintaining a low rate of inflation rather than setting annual goals for reducing inflation. The crawling peg as a means to reduce inflation therefore became unnecessary. In addition, a freely floating exchange rate would allow Chile to strengthen its inflation-targeting framework by allowing the central bank to focus exclusively on the inflation target. Furthermore, the private sector had become accustomed to hedging currency risk with derivatives and other instruments. By 2005, the value of forward contracts in pesos, often used to hedge currency risk, was equivalent to more than twice the value of Chile's GDNP.[11]

The flotation of the peso allowed the central bank to eliminate Chile's remaining capital restrictions. The minimum stay of one year for inflows of foreign direct investment was eliminated in May 2000. Although the rate of the *encaje* had been set at 0% in September 1998, the central bank had retained the ability to raise it at any time at its own discretion. In April 2001, the *encaje* was eliminated altogether. At the same time, restrictions on issuing American Depository Receipts were lifted, and prior approval from the central bank for the entry of foreign capital into Chilean equity and debt markets as well as for outflows associated with capital returns, dividends, and other investments was no longer required.

In May 2003, bank reserve requirements for foreign currency deposits and local currency deposits were equalized. Prior to this, bank reserve requirements were 19% for foreign currency demand deposits versus 9% for local currency demand deposits, and 13.6% for foreign currency time deposits versus 3.6% for local currency time deposits.[12]

These changes were driven to a large extent by Chile's desire to improve its chances at a free-trade agreement with the United States. Chile's President Ricardo Lagos remarked: "We are going to be opening up capital markets in such a way that it's not going to be an issue on the negotiating table."[13]

U.S. Free-Trade Agreement

In June 2003, after 12 years of bilateral conversation followed by two years of intense negotiation, Chile signed a free-trade agreement with the United States—the first such agreement between the United States and a South American country. The agreement came into force on January 1, 2004.[14]

The United States was strongly against capital controls and demanded language in the agreement to prohibit their future use. The annex to the chapter on investments, however, opened the possibility for exceptions and clarified in detail legal actions investors could take against Chilean authorities in the event of disputes regarding controls on capital movement (see **Annex**). In summary, Chilean authorities would not be liable for the costs associated with restrictive and focused controls on either outflows or inflows during their first year of application—excluding outflows in the form of transfers from foreign direct investment and external debt payments.

In essence, since the effectiveness of controls on capital inflows required a longer-term application, the agreement prevented Chile from reinstituting such controls. (Although the fact that most investment abroad during the period of the *encaje*—equivalent to approximately $27 billion—was guaranteed the right to return any time in the future *encaje* free also played an important role in limiting Chile's ability to reintroduce controls on capital inflows.)[15] Critics such as Consuelo Silva of the Chilean Alliance for Fair and Responsible Trade complained: "Although the free-trade agreement appears to be a trade accord, it is fundamentally a treaty to guarantee the free circulation and protection of U.S. investments and capital." Most observers, however, were optimistic that the free-trade agreement with the United States would benefit Chile's economy through lowering foreign credit costs and stimulating additional trade and foreign investment flows, as well as help to consolidate the country's international image.[16]

Annex

From the Text of Annex 10-C to the U.S.—Chile Free Trade Agreement

Special Dispute Settlement Provisions

Chile

1. Where a claimant submits a claim alleging that Chile has breached an obligation under Section A, other than Article 10.3, that arises from its imposition of restrictive measures with regard to payments and transfers, Section B shall apply except as modified below:

   (a) A claimant may submit any such claim only after one year has elapsed since the events giving rise to the claim;

   (b) If the claim is submitted under Article 10.15(1)(b), the claimant may, on behalf of the enterprise, only seek damages with respect to the shares of the enterprise for which the claimant has a beneficial interest;

   (c) Loss or damages arising from restrictive measures on capital inflows shall be limited to the reduction in value of the transfers and shall exclude loss of profits or business and any similar consequential or incidental damages;

   (d) Paragraph 1(a) shall not apply to claims that arise from restrictions on:

      (i) transfers of proceeds of foreign direct investment by investors of the United States, excluding external debt financing covered in subparagraph (d);

      (ii) and excluding investments designed with the purpose of gaining direct or indirect access to the financial market; or

      (iii) payments pursuant to a loan or bond issued in a foreign market, including inter- and intra-company debt financing between affiliated enterprises made exclusively for the conduct, operation, management, or expansion of such affiliated enterprises, provided that these payments are made in accordance with the maturity date agreed on in the loan or bond agreement;

   (e) Excluding restrictive measures referred to in paragraph 1(d), Chile shall incur no liability, and shall not be subject to claims, for damages arising from its imposition of restrictive measures with regard to payments and transfers that were incurred within one year from the date on which the restrictions were imposed, provided that such restrictive measures do not substantially impede transfers;

   (f) A restrictive measure of Chile with regard to payments and transfers that is consistent with this Annex shall be deemed not to contravene Article 10.2 provided that, as required under existing Chilean law, it does not discriminate among investors that enter into transactions of the same nature; and

   (g) Claims arising from Chile's imposition of restrictive measures with regard to payments and transfers shall not be subject to Article 10.24 unless Chile consents.

2. The United States may not request the establishment of an arbitral panel under Chapter Twenty-Two (Dispute Settlement) relating to Chile's imposition of restrictive measures with regard to payments and transfers until one year has elapsed since the events giving rise to the dispute.

3. Restrictive measures on payments and transfers related to claims under this Annex shall otherwise be subject to applicable domestic law.

Source: Chile-U.S. Free Trade Agreement, available at the U.S. Treasury Web site, http://www.ustr.gov/Trade_Agreements/Bilateral/Chile_FTA/Section_Index.html, accessed February 2, 2005. Refer to the entire text for more details regarding Section A and Section B, as well as Chapter 22, as referred to in the Annex above.

Exhibit 1 Macroeconomic Adjustment in Chile During and After the Asian Financial Crisis

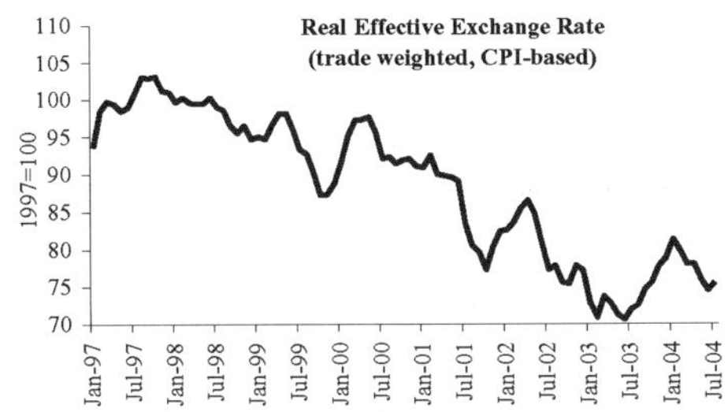

Source: Compiled from EIU Country Data, February 2005.

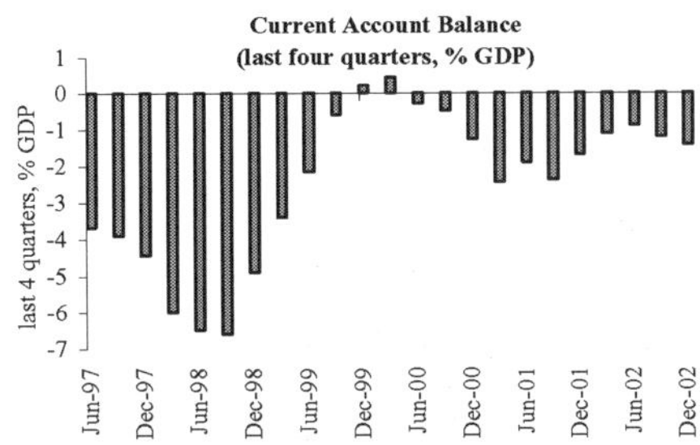

Source: Adapted from Calvo and Talvi, 2005.

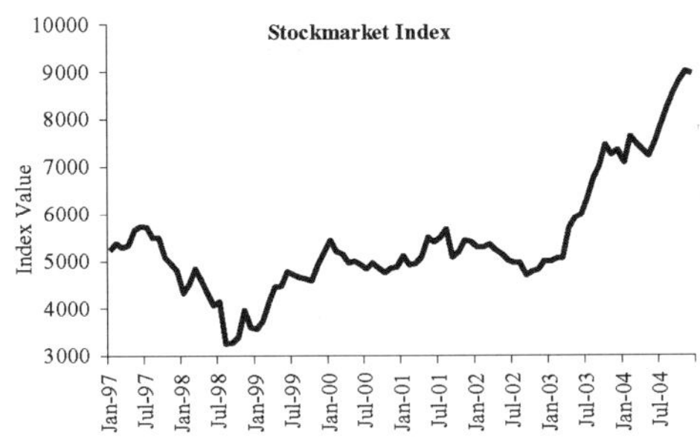

Source: Compiled from EIU Country Data, February 2005.

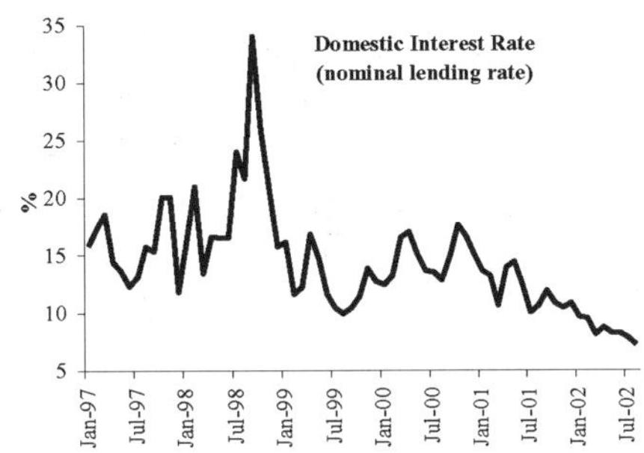

Source: Compiled from EIU Country Data, February 2005.

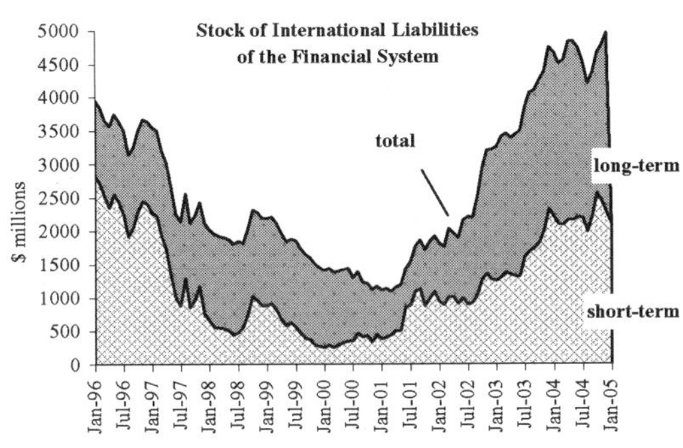

Source: Compiled from Chile Central Bank website.

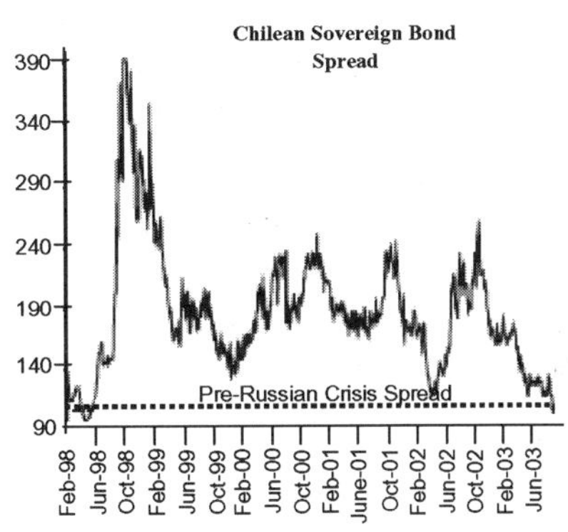

Source: Compiled from Bloomberg, J.P. Morgan EMBI spread.

Exhibit 2 Chile General Economic Indicators

	1997	1998	1999	2000	2001	2002	2003
Real Activity							
Per Capita GDP (constant 1995 $)	5,145	5,275	5,146	5,304	5,385	5,441	5,552
Real GDP Growth (% per year)	7.4%	3.9%	-1.1%	4.4%	2.8%	2.2%	3.3%
Unemployment (%)	5.3%	7.2%	8.9%	8.3%	7.9%	7.8%	...
Money and Prices							
M2 (annual % growth)	9.8%	10.3%	7.8%	6.1%	2.3%	-0.3%	8.1%
M3 (% GDP)	43.6%	45.1%	44.0%	42.9%	42.1%	38.1%	38.2%
Consumer Price Inflation (% per year)	6.1%	5.1%	3.3%	3.8%	3.6%	2.5%	2.8%
Financial Indicators							
Stock market Index (1986=100)	4,794	3,595	5,168	4,869	5,398	4,998	7,337
ICRG Risk Rating1 (0=highest risk to 100=lowest)	80.5	74.8	69.0	74.8	76.3	76.8	77.0
Overall Budget Balance (% GDP)	2.0%	0.4%	-1.4%	0.1%	-0.3%	...	...

Source: Compiled from World Bank Development Indicators (WDI) Online, January 2005; EIU Country Data, January 2005.
Note: $ indicates U.S. dollars throughout Exhibits; International Country Risk Guide (ICRG) risk rating is an overall index, ranging from 0 to 100 (highest risk to lowest), based on 22 components of risk.

Exhibit 3 Growth of Capital Flows in Latin America (% GDP of last four quarters)

	Boom	Bust	
	Q4-1989 vs. max 1998	max 1998 vs. min 1999	max 1998 vs. Q4-2002
Chile	2.4	-7.9	-5.2
Peru[a]	7.4	-7.2	-4.7
Colombia	2.4	-6.6	-3.5
Brazil	8.3	-5.8	-3.8
Venezuela	6.9	-3.5	-17.4
Argentina[a]	8.8	-2.2	-19.5
Mexico	1.2	-1.9	-1.7
Average	6.8	-3.8	-7.5

Source: Adapted from Calvo and Talvi, 2005.
[a]Peru computed from Q3-1990 and Argentina from Q1-1991 to avoid data distortions of hyperinflationary periods.

Exhibit 4 GDP Growth and Investment in Latin America

	GDP (avg annual % change)			Investment (avg annual % change)			Investment Ratio (% GDP)		
	1991–1997	1999–2002	Reversal	1991–1997	1999–2002	Reversal	1997	2002	Reversal
Argentina	6.1	-4.9	-11.0	14.8	-17.9	-32.7	19.4	13.9	-5.5
Chile	8.3	2.2	-6.1	13.7	-5.0	-18.7	27.2	21.1	-6.1
Venezuela	3.4	-2.2	-5.6	18.5	-4.8	-23.3	21.0	14.3	-6.7
Colombia	4.0	0.4	-3.6	9.3	-2.2	-11.5	22.0	15.1	-6.9
Peru	5.3	2.5	-2.8	11.5	-6.5	-18.0	24.0	18.4	-5.6
Brazil	3.1	2.0	-1.1	4.3	0.1	-4.2	21.5	18.1	-3.4
Mexico	2.8	2.7	-0.1	6.9	1.6	-5.3	25.9	24.1	-1.8
Average	4.7	0.4	-4.3	11.3	-5.0	-16.3	23.0	17.9	-5.1

Source: Adapted from Calvo and Talvi, 2005.

Exhibit 5 Chile Balance of Payments (millions of current U.S. dollars)

	1996	1997	1998	1999	2000	2001	2002	2003
Current Account	**-3,083**	**-3,660**	**-3,918**	**99**	**-766**	**-1,192**	**-553**	...
Trade Balance	-1,072	-1,428	-2,040	2,427	2,119	2,054	2,513	...
Exports	*16,627*	*17,870*	*16,323*	*17,162*	*19,210*	*18,466*	*18,340*	...
Imports	*-17,699*	*-19,298*	*-18,363*	*-14,735*	*-17,091*	*-16,411*	*-15,827*	...
Net Services	-1	-136	-452	-737	-648	-918	-957	...
Net Income	-2,518	-2,617	-1,889	-2,233	-2,795	-2,757	-2,536	...
Net Transfers	508	520	462	643	558	428	426	...
Financial Account	**5,660**	**6,742**	**1,967**	**238**	**828**	**1,760**	**999**	...
Net Direct Investment	3,681	3,809	3,144	6,203	-348	3,045	1,140	...
Outward FDI	*-1,133*	*-1,463*	*-1,483*	*-2,558*	*-3,987*	*-1,432*	*-463*	...
Inward FDI	*4,815*	*5,271*	*4,628*	*8,761*	*3,639*	*4,477*	*1,603*	...
Net Portfolio Investment	1,112	1,790	-2,528	-3,223	641	-40	-1,999	...
Outward Equity	*-43*	*-743*	*-2,518*	*-3,474*	*821*	*-2,094*	*-2,922*	...
Outward Debt	*-92*	*-246*	*-792*	*-2,321*	*-55*	*708*	*-281*	...
Inward Equity	*700*	*1,720*	*580*	*524*	*-427*	*-217*	*-317*	...
Inward Debt	*569*	*894*	*262*	*2,054*	*300*	*1,649*	*1,645*	...
Inward Financial Derivatives	*-22*	*165*	*-59*	*-6*	*2*	*-86*	*-124*	...
Net Monetary Authority Investments	-73	-24	-74	-65	36	-47	-2	...
Net General Government Investments	-545	-386	-171	-101	-128	-132	-294	...
Net Bank Investments	-531	-2,045	-417	-2,482	412	602	2,310	...
Net Other Investments	2,016	3,598	2,012	-95	214	-1,667	-156	...
Net Errors and Omissions	16	237	-239	-1,083	255	-1,167	-261	...
Increase in Official Reserves	2,594	3,318	-2,191	-747	317	-599	185	...
Internat. reserves[1] (current $ bns, year-end)	15.6	18.1	16.2	14.9	15.4	14.4	15.3	15.8
Current-account balance (% GDP)	-4.5%	-4.9%	-5.4%	0.1%	-1.2%	-1.7%	-1.3%	-0.8%
External debt (% GDP)	33.5%	30.3%	41.3%	46.9%	49.1%	57.8%	62.3%	...
Short-term debt (% total external debt)	11.4%	5.6%	5.3%	3.4%	6.8%	6.7%	9.0%	...
Direct investment from abroad (% GDP)	7.0%	7.0%	6.3%	12.0%	4.8%	6.7%	2.4%	...
Portfolio investment from abroad (% GDP)	1.8%	3.7%	1.1%	3.5%	-0.2%	2.0%	1.8%	...
Nominal exchange rate (pesos/ $; year avg)	412.27	419.30	460.29	508.78	539.59	634.94	688.94	691.43
Real effective exchange rate (1997=100)	103	100	98	93	94	85	80	73

Source: Compiled from IMF, International Financial Statistics CD-ROM, May 2004 and WDI Online, February 2005.
Note: "International Reserves" differs from the cumulative increase in "Official Reserves" because of revaluation effects.

Exhibit 6 Nominal Exchange Rate within Exchange Rate Band (pesos per $)

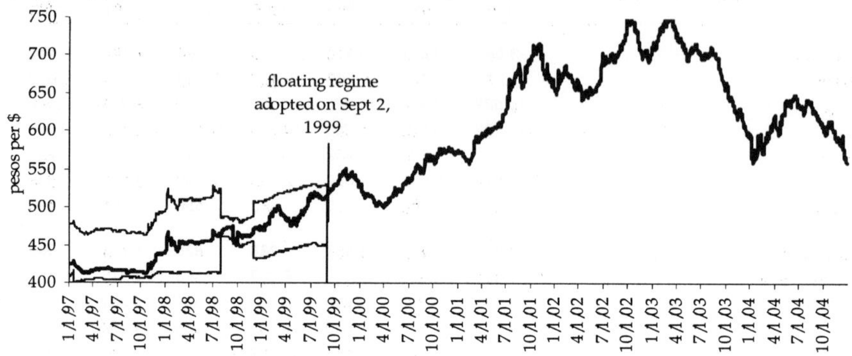

Source: Compiled from Chile Central Bank Web site.

Endnotes

[1] Guillermo A. Calvo and Ernesto Talvi, "Sudden Stop, Financial Factors and Economic Collapse in Latin America: Learning from Argentina and Chile," NBER Working Papers 11153, February 2005: "The anatomy of Chile's macroeconomic adjustment following the Sudden Stop was qualitatively and quantitatively a carbon copy of the average Latin American country."

[2] Casewriter interview with Carlos Massad, January 24, 2005.

[3] "Chile Cuts Capital Controls, Widens Currency's Trading Band," *The Wall Street Journal Interactive Edition,* September 17, 1998.

[4] LAC-7 refers to Argentina, Brazil, Chile, Colombia, Mexico, Peru, and Venezuela. These seven countries represent 93% of Latin America's GDP.

[5] Refer to Calvo and Talvi, 2005 for background for this section.

[6] Kevin Cowan and Jose De Gregorio, "International Borrowing, Capital Controls and the Exchange Rate: Lessons from Chile," prepared for the NBER Conference "International Capital Flows," Santa Barbara, CA, February 2005, and as discussed in casewriter interview with Jose De Gregorio, March 9, 2005.

[7] Calvo and Talvi, 2005.

[8] For criticism of this argument, see Cowan and De Gregorio, 2005, and as discussed in casewriter interview with Jose De Gregorio, March 9, 2005.

[9] Cowan and De Gregorio, 2005, and as discussed in casewriter interview with Jose De Gregorio, March 9, 2005.

[10] For more on Chile's exchange rate history, see Felipe G. Morande, "Exchange Rate Policy in Chile: Recent Experiences," March 2001, available at: http://www.imf.org/external/pubs/ft/seminar/2001/err/eng/morande.pdf, accessed March 9, 2005.

[11] Casewriter interview with Carlos Massad, January 14, 2005.

[12] "Chile finance: Reserve Requirements Cut," Economist Intelligence Unit—*ViewsWire,* January 29, 2003.

[13] Mark Mulligan, "Chile frees capital flows," *The Financial Times,* April 17, 2001.

[14] For more information about the agreement, refer to the U.S. Treasury Web site at http://www.ustr.gov/Trade_Agreements/Bilateral/Chile_FTA/Section_Index.html, accessed February 2, 2005.

[15] Cowan and De Gregorio, 2005, and as discussed in casewriter interview with Jose De Gregorio, March 9, 2005.

[16] "Chile Economy: Details of FTA with US," Economist Intelligence Unit—*ViewsWire,* January 15, 2003.

Endnotes

[illegible]

HARVARD | BUSINESS | SCHOOL

9-702-082
REV: SEPTEMBER 25, 2002

RAWI ABDELAL
LAURA ALFARO

Capital Controls

What used to be a heresy is now endorsed as orthodox.
—John Maynard Keynes, 1944

Only in the waning years of the twentieth century did international financial markets begin to enjoy the freedom from government regulation that they had experienced before the first world war. By 2002, international capital markets had grown to be enormous – 1.2 trillion dollars flowed around the globe per day.[1] The massive size of the market presented policy makers with a serious challenge, as they were forced to grapple with the costs and benefits of such mobile capital.

This note briefly relates the modern history of capital controls and summarizes scholarship on the advantages and disadvantages of international financial market regulation.

Definitions

In a country's balance of payments, international purchases and sales of financial assets are recorded in the capital account.[2] The capital account is usually divided into portfolio investment (purchases and sales of securities such as stocks, bonds, and derivatives) and direct investment (purchases and sales of production facilities and equity investments that lead to managerial control, usually exceeding 10% of a firm).[3] A *capital control* is any policy designed to limit or redirect transactions on a country's capital account.

The International Monetary Fund (IMF) distinguishes between *administrative* and *market-based* capital controls. Administrative (i.e., direct) controls either prohibit or require prior approval for certain capital account transactions. Market-based (i.e., indirect) controls consist of taxes on cross-border capital movements and dual exchange-rate systems.

---

[1] Bank for International Settlements, *Triennial Central Bank Survey* (Basel, 2002). On the types of these capital flows, as well as the reasons for capital flows into developing countries during the 1990s, see Huw Pill, *Portfolio Capital Flows to Emerging Markets*, Harvard Business School Note No. 796-129 (1997).

[2] Standard balance-of-payments terminology changed recently: what was called the capital account is now called the financial account. In this note we use the older terminology, which remains common.

[3] Many balance-of-payments statements also report an "other" category, which includes other transactions in currency and deposits, loans, and trade credits.

Professors Rawi Abdelal and Laura Alfaro prepared this note as the basis for class discussion.

Another way to classify capital controls is according to their function. Controls on inflows, for example, are generally used by policy makers to prevent future crises. The usual justification is an emphasis on the negative macroeconomic implications of large, volatile inflows of capital, including appreciation of the exchange rate. In addition, policy makers generally point to the negative effects of a rapid reversal of short-term capital inflows, particularly for banks' balance sheets and the health of the financial system in general. Chile, for example, regulated capital inflows during the 1990s, as did Malaysia in 1994. Controls on capital outflows, in contrast, are advocated to manage crises as they occur. Generally the objective is to limit the downward pressure on the currency and upward pressure on domestic interest rates by providing authorities with time and autonomy to react. Thailand imposed controls on capital outflows in 1997 as a response to the Asian financial crisis, as did Malaysia in 1998. Of course, it is often difficult for policy makers to separate neatly the effects of controls on inflows and outflows. Restrictions on outflows may deter inflows as well, since investors are generally less willing to put their money in countries that restrict their exit.

A Historical Perspective on Capital Controls

Between the middle of the nineteenth century and the outbreak of World War I many countries adopted the classical gold standard, an international monetary regime that obliged them to maintain the convertibility (i.e., free exchange) of their currencies for all transactions as well as to maintain a fixed price in terms of gold. Controls over the international movement of capital were unusual.[4]

During World War I, however, several countries moved to restrict capital outflows as a means to maintain the tax base for the financing of wartime expenditures. By 1919, most of the countries involved in the war had resorted to capital controls. After the war, following a period of stabilization, many of these controls were relaxed. The onset of the Great Depression, however, led most European countries to impose controls on capital movements again. In the chaotic international financial environment of the 1930s, governments that left the gold standard used controls on capital outflows in their attempts to increase their monetary policy autonomy.[5]

The Bretton Woods era, which followed World War II, produced a rare moment of policy consensus among developed countries. One of the central lessons of the unstable years between the wars was that "volatile," "speculative" flows of capital had been a major cause of monetary and financial instability.[6] The new international financial architecture was designed, therefore, to restrict capital movements as a way to avoid financial instability and ensure governments' policy autonomy. Although the architects of the Bretton Woods agreement envisioned open current accounts, which were exceptional during the 1940s and 1950s, they accepted, and in a few cases even promoted, closed capital accounts. Thus, the Articles of Agreement of the IMF stipulated, "Members may exercise such controls as are necessary to regulate international capital movements...."[7] Compared to the days of the classical gold standard, the Bretton Woods system clearly had overturned the conventional view about international financial markets. As economist John Maynard Keynes, who represented Britain at Bretton Woods, observed, "Not merely as a feature of the transition, but as a

---

[4] See Barry Eichengreen and Marc Flandreau, eds., *The Gold Standard in Theory and History*, 2nd ed. (London: Routledge, 1997). For overviews of these historical periods, see Barry Eichengreen, *Globalizing Capital* (Princeton, N.J.: Princeton University Press, 1996); and Beth A. Simmons, "The Internationalization of Capital," in *Continuity and Change in Contemporary Capitalism*, ed. Herbert Kitschelt, Peter Lange, Gary Marks, and John D. Stephens (Cambridge: Cambridge University Press, 1999).

[5] Barry Eichengreen, *Golden Fetters: The Gold Standard and the Great Depression, 1919-1939* (New York: Oxford University Press, 1992).

[6] See especially Ragnar Nurkse, *International Currency Experience* (Geneva: League of Nations, 1944); and Arthur I. Bloomfield, "Postwar Control of International Capital Movements," *American Economic Review*, vol. 36, no. 2 (1946): 687-709.

[7] Articles of Agreement of the International Monetary Fund, Article VI, Section 3.

permanent arrangement, the plan accords to every member government the explicit right to control all capital movements. What used to be heresy is now endorsed as orthodox."[8]

The Bretton Woods system was not permanent, however. Nor did capital controls remain orthodoxy. In the 1970s, after the collapse of the fixed exchange-rate system, developed countries gradually adopted more liberal policies toward capital flows. There were several reasons for this shift. First, in a world of floating exchange rates capital controls were less necessary, because the exchange rate could in principle adjust to accommodate financial inflows and outflows. Second, the increasing sophistication of financial instruments made it easier to circumvent regulations. Third, the international financial community – including portfolio investors, rating agencies, and international institutions like the Organization for Economic Cooperation and Development (OECD) and IMF – increasingly considered capital controls, particularly on outflows, to be inconsistent with other market-oriented policies.[9] In 1997 Michel Camdessus, then Managing Director of the IMF, argued that the Fund should take upon itself the task of liberalizing capital flows. The IMF's Interim Committee announced that the founding Articles should be amended to "make the liberalization of capital movements one of the purposes of the IMF."[10] Capital controls, once Bretton Woods orthodoxy, were, according to some analysts, becoming heresy again.[11]

Capital account liberalization spread unevenly throughout the world, however. Developed countries embraced liberalization. The United States, Germany, and the Netherlands began the trend in the developed world when they removed their most prominent controls in 1974. The process of European integration resulted in the creation of a common market for goods, labor, and capital, so that by the 1990s all European Union (EU) states had liberalized capital flows.

The policies of developing countries were far more varied. Some countries, such as Singapore and Hong Kong, had always maintained few or no restrictions on capital flows. In East Asia major steps toward liberalization started in the 1970s, accelerating in the 1990s. A number of Latin American countries, which were relatively open during the 1960s, imposed controls during the early 1970s. Then a wave of liberalization was interrupted by increasing restrictions after the debt crisis of the early 1980s. Middle Eastern and east European countries did not systematically liberalize until the 1990s. Most African countries, however, have consistently maintained capital controls for the past 30 years. China and India have also kept many of their capital account restrictions in tact.

The Capital Controls Debate

Policy makers around the world continue to debate the merits of capital account liberalization. For the developed world openness remains the norm, but policy makers and analysts do not always agree on the best policy for developing countries.[12]

[8] Speech to the House of Lords, May 23, 1944.

[9] Benjamin J. Cohen, "Capital Controls: Why Do Governments Hesitate?" in *Debating The Global Financial Architecture*, ed. Leslie Elliott Armijo (Albany: SUNY Press, 2002). Also see Louis W. Pauly, *Who Elected the Bankers? Surveillance and Control in the World Economy* (Ithaca, N.Y.: Cornell University Press, 1997).

[10] Interim Committee Statement on the "Liberalization of Capital Movements Under an Amendment of the IMF's Articles," September 21, 1997.

[11] For example, see Paul R. Krugman, "Saving Asia: It's Time to Get Radical," *Fortune*, vol. 138, no. 5 (1998): 74-80; and Krugman, "Capital Control Freaks: How Malaysia Got Away with Economic Heresy," *Slate*, September 27, 1999.

[12] Robert Wade, "The Fight Over Capital Controls," *Foreign Policy*, no. 113 (1998-99): 41-54.

The Case for Regulation

Columbia University economist Jagdish Bhagwati, famous for his unrelenting support for free trade, argues that markets for capital are inherently different from those for goods. Financial markets are, he argues, more susceptible to crisis because of asymmetric or imperfect information, which can lead to herd behavior. Thus, Bhagwati insists, "[T]he weight of evidence and the force of logic point in the opposite direction, toward restraints on capital flows. It is time to shift the burden of proof from those who oppose to those who favor liberated capital."[13] As MIT economic historian Charles Kindleberger wrote, financial markets have repeatedly experienced manias, panics, and crashes.[14] Underlying these views is the idea that financial markets are subject to wide swings in market sentiment unrelated to market fundamentals, and that crises can therefore be the self-fulfilling prophesies of markets, rather than the result of flawed underlying conditions. John Maynard Keynes offered the classic metaphor:

> [P]rofessional investment may be likened to those newspaper competitions in which the competitors have to pick out the six prettiest faces from a hundred photographs, the prize being awarded to the competitor whose choice most nearly corresponds to the average preferences of the competitors as a whole; so that each competitor has to pick, not those faces which he himself finds the prettiest, but those which he thinks likeliest to catch the fancy of the other competitors, all of whom are looking at the problem from the same point of view. It is not a case of choosing those which, to the best of one's judgment, are really the prettiest, nor even those which average opinion genuinely thinks the prettiest. We have reached the third degree where we devote our intelligences to anticipating what average opinion expects the average opinion to be.[15]

This problem, which is arguably endemic to financial markets, is difficult to solve. While prudential regulation can help to stabilize the domestic market, a government that wants to insulate its economy from additional instability can also limit international capital flows.

Some experts also question the size of the gains and costs from capital account liberalization. "None of the proponents of free capital mobility," Bhagwati notes, "have estimated the size of the gains they expect to materialize, even leaving out the losses from crises that can ensue."[16] But in comparison, the costs of a financial crisis may be staggering, particularly for the banking system.

The relationship between domestic and international financial crises stems in part from the fact that policy makers face a difficult trade-off among three objectives: monetary policy autonomy, a stable exchange rate, and free capital mobility. Also known as the "irreconcilable trilogy," the "incompatible trinity," and, in more radical circles, the "unholy trinity," the trilemma is that only two of the three goals can be reached simultaneously.[17]

---

[13] Jagdish Bhagwati, "The Capital Myth: The Difference Between Trade in Widgets and Dollars," *Foreign Affairs*, vol. 77, no. 3 (1998): 7-12, at p. 12. For a classic argument in favor of an international tax on capital flows, see James Tobin, "A Proposal for International Monetary Reform," *Eastern Economic Journal*, vol. 4, nos. 3-4 (1978): 153-159; and Barry Eichengreen, James Tobin, and Charles Wyplosz, "Two Cases for Sand in the Wheels of International Finance," *Economic Journal*, vol. 105, no. 428 (1995): 162-172.

[14] Charles P. Kindleberger, *Manias, Panics, and Crashes: A History of Financial Crises*, rev. ed. (New York: Basic Books, 1989).

[15] John Maynard Keynes, *The General Theory of Employment, Interest, and Money* (New York: Harcourt Brace Jovanovich, [1936] 1953), pp. 155-156.

[16] Bhagwati, "The Capital Myth," p. 9.

[17] See Paul R. Krugman and Maurice Obstfeld, *International Economics: Theory and Policy*, 5th ed. (New York: Addison-Wesley, 2000), pp. 713-714.

If capital movements are restricted, countries can pursue autonomous monetary policies while maintaining fixed exchange rates. But if countries allow free capital mobility while attempting to maintain fixed exchange rates, they must use monetary policy to defend the currency peg. When capital outflows surge, as they sometimes do, a central bank that does not want the currency to depreciate must either increase interest rates to attract capital or purchase its own currency using foreign exchange reserves. If the flows of capital are large, a central bank might very quickly exhaust its foreign exchange reserves with little influence over the market outcome. Increasing interest rates, on the other hand, can have negative consequences for economic activity and employment. In a country where the financial sector is weak, the consequences can be devastating.

Finally, because capital flows tend to react to economic and political variables that may not be the priorities of governments, some economists and political scientists argue that markets inappropriately limit the autonomy of governments.[18] Dani Rodrik of Harvard's Kennedy School, for example, argues, "A finance minister whose top priority is to keep foreign investors happy will pay less attention to developmental goals."[19] Bhagwati shares this concern with governments' "political independence to run economic policies as they deem fit."[20]

The Case for Liberalization

The most powerful argument in favor of capital mobility is that it facilitates an efficient global allocation of savings by channeling financial resources into their most productive uses, thereby increasing economic growth and welfare around the world.[21] Developing countries with little domestic capital, for example, can borrow to finance investment and thereby attain economic growth without sharp increases in national savings rates. In addition, capital flows increase the opportunities for portfolio diversification and thus provide investors with potentially higher risk-adjusted rates of return. Furthermore, as Stanley Fischer, First Deputy Managing Director of the IMF, argues, capital account liberalization is an "inevitable step on the path of development which cannot be avoided and should be embraced. After all, the most advanced economies all have open capital accounts."[22]

Opponents of capital controls also argue that policy makers cannot actually use regulations to discriminate between short-term and long-term capital flows. Short-term loans, for example, are often rolled over, while long-term assets can be sold in secondary markets. Controls designed to influence flows of portfolio capital may inadvertently deter foreign direct investors.

In addition to favoring the principle of liberalization, some experts point to difficulties in implementation.[23] Many economists argue, for example, that capital controls have become ineffective in the face of the ever-increasing sophistication of financial markets. Markets have evaded regulations by over-invoicing and under-invoicing imports and exports, for example, as well as by innovating in financial derivatives. Improvements in information technology have made it easier to buy and sell

---

[18] See Susan Strange, *Mad Money: When Markets Outgrow Governments* (Ann Arbor: University of Michigan Press, 1998).

[19] Dani Rodrik, "Who Needs Capital-Account Convertibility?" in *Should the IMF Pursue Capital-Account Convertibility?*, No. 207, Princeton Essays in International Finance, May 1998, p. 65.

[20] Bhagwati, "The Capital Myth," p. 9.

[21] See Maurice Obstfeld, "The Global Capital Market: Benefactor or Menace?" *Journal of Economic Perspectives*, vol. 12, no. 4 (1998): 9-30.

[22] Stanley Fischer, "Capital-Account Liberalization and the Role of the IMF," in *Should the IMF Pursue Capital Account Convertibility?*, p.2.

[23] For two recent reviews, see Sebastian Edwards, "How Effective are Capital Controls?" *Journal of Economic Perspectives*, vol. 13, no. 4 (1999): 65-84; and Akira Ariyoshi, Karl Habermeier, Bernard Laurens, Inci Otker-Robe, Jorge Ivan Canales-Kriljenko, and Andrei Kirilenko, *Capital Controls: Country Experiences with Their Use and Liberalization*, IMF Occasional Paper No. 190 (2000).

assets across national borders, thereby making regulators less effective. Additionally, capital controls create incentives for circumvention. Harvard economist Richard Cooper criticizes "the discretion given to officials to approve exceptions to general prohibitions on international capital movements, giving rise to possibilities of favoritism and corruption."[24] Even when controls are effectively implemented, they impose administrative costs.

Although the inherent fragility of financial intermediaries – based on the mismatch between their liquid liabilities and illiquid assets – suggests the need for some government protection from panicked capital outflows, many economists argue that prudential domestic regulation and effective monetary and fiscal policies can fulfill this role better than direct controls. Stanford's Ronald McKinnon and Harvard's Huw Pill argue, "Often indirect methods will suffice. Reserve requirements (implicit taxes on intermediation) imposed on the banks' foreign borrowing, plus very tight rules governing the net foreign exchange exposure of banks and other financial institutions, can reduce risk taking directly while having the incidental effect of restricting capital inflows."[25]

Some analysts argue that capital markets provide a useful discipline on policy makers. As MIT economist Rudiger Dornbusch notes, "The capital market fulfills an important supervisory function over economic policy. Governments may be disinclined to have the bond market look over their shoulders, but savers and investors should welcome it."[26] In this way of thinking governments that pursue macroeconomic policies of which markets disapproved would be punished by capital outflows and rising domestic interest rates. The IMF's Stanley Fischer acknowledges that policy makers may not wish to "admit that the capital markets are only the messenger, delivering a verdict on their performance. Rather, they may be tempted to shoot the messenger."[27]

Finally, granting, as Fischer does, that "markets are not always right," liberalization may be worth its risks. "Sometimes inflows are excessive, and sometimes they are sustained for too long. Markets tend to react late, but then, to react fast and sometimes excessively," he notes. Still, Fischer concludes, "the potential benefits of liberalizing capital flows outweigh the costs."[28]

---

[24] Richard N. Cooper, "Should Capital-Account Convertibility be a World Objective?" in *Should the IMF Pursue Capital Account Convertibility?*; and Cooper, "Should Capital Controls Be Banished?" *Brookings Papers on Economic Activity*, no. 1 (1999): 89-125.

[25] Ronald McKinnon and Huw Pill, "The Overborrowing Syndrome: Are East Asian Economies Different?" in *Managing Capital Flows and Exchange Rates: Perspectives from the Pacific Basin*, ed. Reuven Glick (Cambridge: Cambridge University Press, 1998), p. 353. Also see Ronald McKinnon and Huw Pill, "Credible Liberalizations and International Capital Flows: The Overborrowing Syndrome," in *Financial Deregulation and Integration in East Asia*, ed. Takatoshi Ito and Anne Krueger (Chicago: University of Chicago Press, 1996).

[26] Rudiger Dornbusch, "Capital Controls: An Idea Whose Time Has Past," in *Should the IMF Pursue Capital-Account Convertibility?*, p. 20.

[27] Fischer, "Capital-Account Liberalization and the Role of the IMF," p. 3.

[28] Fischer, "Capital-Account Liberalization and the Role of the IMF," p. 3.

Managing Capital Outflows

HARVARD | BUSINESS | SCHOOL

9-702-040
REV: APRIL 23, 2003

RAWI ABDELAL
LAURA ALFARO

Malaysia: Capital and Control

Malaysia Boleh (Malaysia Can)
—Malaysian national motto

Dr. Mahathir Mohamad, Malaysia's prime minister since 1981, faced one of the biggest challenges of his political career when the Asian financial crisis of 1997-98 spread from Thailand to his own country. By 2001, Prime Minister Mahathir was satisfied that his government's unorthodox approach to the crisis had been the correct one. He explained, "I have been trained as a doctor. And unless you get your diagnosis right, you're not going to cure the patient." Rejecting the view that corruption and "cronyism" had caused the crisis, Mahathir offered an alternate interpretation: currency speculators had undermined the economies of Southeast Asia by "treating the currencies as commodities." Mahathir continued: "We were able to overcome our economic problems by preventing currency traders from fiddling around with our currency."[1]

Mahathir had been unwilling to turn to the International Monetary Fund (IMF) for financial assistance during the crisis. According to the prime minister, he and his advisors "decided that under no circumstances must we surrender ourselves to the IMF." Mahathir complained that the "IMF thinks that all countries are the same."[2] The Malaysian government insisted on maintaining its autonomy.

"More than any other country," the prime minister argued, "Malaysia needed to have control over its economy. Malaysia's economic focus was not only on GDP growth, but also the distributive aspects of growth."[3] The distribution of which he spoke was that among the country's diverse ethnic and racial communities. A basic distinction between the *Bumiputeras* (literally, "sons of the soil"), including Malays and other groups of indigenous Malaysians that together constituted 63% of the population, and the non-*Bumiputeras*, referring to the Chinese and Indian communities, had informed economic policy-making for decades. Thus, Mahathir insisted, "Recovery must be accompanied by the equitable distribution of the economic pie between the *Bumiputeras* and non-*Bumiputeras*. Failure to do so could result in the kind of race riots which broke out in May 1969."[4] These riots, the defining political event of Malaysia's independent statehood, continued to cast a long shadow over the country. "Foreign control over the economy would not take into consideration the need for us to establish parity among the different races of the country," the prime minister explained, "which is absolutely necessary for political stability."[5]

Professors Rawi Abdelal and Laura Alfaro prepared this case with the assistance of Research Associate Moya Connelly, Diaan-Yi Lin (MBA 2002), and Monisha Saldanha (MBA 2001). HBS cases are developed solely as the basis for class discussion. Cases are not intended to serve as endorsements, sources of primary data, or illustrations of effective or ineffective management.

Malaysia's controversial solution to the crisis, introduced on September 1, 1998, was to eliminate offshore trading of the Malaysian ringgit and to restrict outflows of short-term capital, first administratively and later with an exit tax. The introduction of the currency and capital controls seemed to coincide with economic recovery. The Malaysian government, as well as some analysts, argued that the new regulations had helped to insulate the economy from the international financial crisis and promote growth. "As it has been shown," Mahathir explained in 2001, "we were right."[6]

Other observers, however, disagreed. "The Malaysian flirtation with capital controls," according to Nobel laureate Merton Miller, "must be written off as a failure, and one whose costs will be borne by the Malaysian people for many years to come."[7] And emerging markets guru Mark Mobius, emphasizing the longer run reputation effects of the measures, insisted: "Consider the attitudes of investors. If you talk to people off the record – most foreign investors don't want to talk except if they're off the record – they'll tell you the controls were a disaster."[8] Scholars failed to reach a consensus about the necessity, effectiveness, and underlying goals of the controls.[9]

The stakes in the debate over Malaysia's response to the Asian financial crisis were large. Three questions were particularly important: Did the currency and capital controls work? Were the controls appropriate behavior by a government committed to openness to world markets? Would the Malaysian experience hold lessons for other developing countries facing financial crises? Indeed, the Malaysian currency and capital controls also sparked debate about the future of the international financial architecture – the balance between financial market freedom and a government's ability to manage its own economy.

Background: Colonial Malaya

British influence on the Malay peninsula originated with the arrival of the East India Company on the island of Penang in 1786. The colonial administration expanded across the peninsula through a series of treaties of protection signed with local rulers. The colony came to be known as Malaya.[10]

The British encouraged immigrants from India and China to work in Malaya's tin mines and rubber plantations, particularly after 1850. The immigrants from China joined an already established Chinese community, which had lived and worked in Malaya for centuries. Many of these mining areas grew eventually into the colony's urban and commercial centers, which the Chinese communities came to dominate. Although some of the immigrants appear to have planned to return to China, many eventually came to see themselves as a permanent part of the economic and social fabric of the colony. Still, the idea that these people were "Chinese" and "Indian" became institutionalized in the practice of the colonial administration.[11]

Malays were considered by the British, as well as by themselves, to be the rightful owners of Malaya. The colonial administration sought to ensure for Malays a significant role in the politics and economics of the territory by favoring Malay interests in education, public affairs, and the economy, and to maintain "balance" among the various races[12] that composed the society of Malaya.

These racial communities came to be distinguished primarily by their languages and religions. One observer has noted, "To be a Malay is to be, by definition, a Muslim," and to speak Malay.[13] The Chinese and Indian communities both were more diverse with regard to language and religion. Despite the fact that these categories – Malay, Chinese, and Indian – described groups of people with heterogeneous, often divergent interests, they served as shorthand to describe a central political reality of Malaysia: the management of racial and ethnic diversity.

The Governance of Independent Malaysia

After having fallen under the control of the Japanese empire during the Second World War, Malaya acquired political independence in August 1957. In the years leading up to independence representatives of Malaya's ethnic and racial communities joined together to negotiate a set of compromises about how the new state would be governed. According to the 1957 census, approximately half of the new country's population was Malay, a little more than a third Chinese, and most of the remaining Indian. (See **Exhibit 2**.) In exchange for their acknowledgment of Malay predominance, the Chinese and Indian communities were assured of citizenship and protection of their languages and cultures. In politics the bargain was to be maintained by an Alliance, formed officially in 1954, among a few key parties: the United Malays National Organization (UMNO), the Malayan Chinese Association (MCA), and the Malayan Indian Congress (MIC). More generally, ethnically based political parties reinforced the common conceptualization of Malays, Chinese, and Indians as discrete groups with potentially inconsistent interests. The *Barisan Nasional* (National Front), which consisted of UMNO, MCA, and MIC, as well as several opposition parties, ruled Malaysia from 1974 through the end of the century.

In September 1963 Singapore, whose society was overwhelmingly of Chinese descent, and the territories of Sabah and Sarawak, located on northern Borneo, joined Malaya to form the Federation of Malaysia. Lee Kuan Yew, the leader of Singapore's ruling party, questioned the Malaysian government's privileging of ethnic Malay interests. The resulting tensions between the leaders of Malaya and Singapore over the political priorities of their government led, in part, to Singapore's expulsion from the Federation in August 1965.[14]

Malaysia's delicate political balance was seriously threatened in May 1969 by a series of riots that followed the Alliance's poor showing in an election. (See **Exhibit 15**.) The Alliance had anticipated another uneventful electoral victory. In the elections of May 10 it won less than half of the votes, however, and its majority in parliament, composed of 104 seats, declined from 89 to 66. The primary cause of the Alliance's fall from grace was an apparent polarization of the electorate: within the Malay, Chinese, and Indian communities political rivals of UMNO, MCA, and MIC who advocated more aggressive assertion of each community's interests vis-à-vis the others had taken votes from the *Barisan* parties.

Many Malays believed that the election posed a threat to their political dominance. Some members of Chinese opposition parties proclaimed their opportunity to eliminate the government's favoritism of Malays. On May 13, 1969, these tensions erupted into riots in Kuala Lumpur. The riots bitterly and violently divided Malaysia's racial communities. Hundreds were killed; stores and houses were burned.[15] The next day the government declared a state of emergency, suspending the constitution and parliament until February 1971.

The riots led to a period of soul-searching for Malaysian political leaders. Mahathir, a founding member of UMNO who had been expelled from the party in 1969 after criticizing its leadership, offered an analysis from what he considered the Malay perspective in a book entitled *The Malay Dilemma*. The book, which was banned in Malaysia, began by asking, "What went wrong?"

> This is the question that anyone sympathetic to or interested in Malaysia must be asking since 13 May 1969. What went wrong in a multiracial, multilingual, and multireligious country which for twelve years had enjoyed racial harmony and cooperation, that tolerance and understanding could be so abruptly terminated and the various races should sullenly glare at each other and reject a way of life that apparently began long before independence?[16]

Mahathir's answer emphasized the disappointment and resentment of Malays at the wealth of Chinese communities in Malaysia, and his analysis was shared by a number of important Malaysian political leaders. (See **Exhibit 3a**.) The government therefore sought to address the issue of inter-ethnic and inter-racial wealth distribution by implementing what it called a New Economic Policy (NEP) in July 1971.

The primary goal of the NEP was to promote "national unity," which was understood to be "unattainable without greater equity and balance among Malaysia's social and ethnic groups."[17] The NEP was based on a "two-pronged" approach to Malaysian development. The first part of the plan emphasized the reduction and eradication of poverty in general. The second goal was to "accelerate the process of restructuring Malaysian society to correct economic imbalance, so as to reduce and eventually eliminate the identification of race with economic function." The government set an ambitious target for redistribution: within a generation – by 1990 – *Bumiputeras* would "own and operate" at least 30% of the total "economically productive" assets in the country. In 1970 the figure stood at 2.4%.[18] (See **Exhibit 3c**.)

The government sought to "restructure" Malaysia's economy through a variety of regulations and agencies charged with overseeing aspects of the transformation. Although the specific laws, agencies, and institutions changed over the course of the NEP period, several mechanisms remained central to the government's efforts. Explicit quotas were used to alter employment and ownership patterns. In addition, the government established the *Bumiputera* trust agencies to purchase and hold shares on behalf of Malays and other *Bumiputeras*. A number of government agencies sought to cultivate a *Bumiputera* commercial and industrial community with financial and technical assistance for entrepreneurs. The Industrial Coordination Act of 1975 stipulated that all industrial enterprises with 25 or more employees required an operating license, which would be granted primarily to firms that conformed to the NEP's guideline of 30% *Bumiputera* equity participation. The government also required commercial banks to lend at subsidized rates to *Bumiputera*-owned firms.[19]

Malaysia's leaders were quite concerned, however, that the other racial communities of Malaysia would resent the government's distributional priorities, a fact that would undermine, rather than promote, "national unity." They were, in particular, worried that Malaysia's Chinese community would feel as though authorities were expropriating their hard-earned wealth.[20] The NEP, therefore, was to be "based upon a rapidly expanding economy" as a means to "ensure that no particular group will experience any loss or feel any sense of deprivation."

Development Strategy

During the 1970s the Malaysian government sought to promote the export of manufactured goods as the focus of its development strategy, rather than the export of raw materials and commodities, rubber, timber, and tin, in which Malaysia was abundantly endowed.[21] The government intended to lure high-technology foreign direct investment with a variety of tax incentives. These policies appeared to work: a number of Western manufacturing firms, including Intel, National Semiconductor, and 3M, invested heavily in Malaysia.[22]

In 1980, frustrated by the insufficient pace of economic development and a lingering worldwide economic slowdown, the government implemented a new policy to improve the country's infrastructure and upgrade its industrial base, including the production of steel and cement. The Heavy Industries Corporation of Malaysia (HICOM), a state-owned enterprise, was set up to pursue this ambitious agenda. Particularly celebrated was the promotion of an automobile industry and a "national car," the Proton Saga, the product of a joint venture between HICOM and Mitsubishi Motors.

The Malaysian government's increasingly ambitious development plans required a rapid expansion of public expenditures during the early 1980s. At the same time, commodity prices declined during the international recession of 1980-82, and Malaysia's current account balance deteriorated as a result. Malaysia thus found it necessary to borrow heavily from abroad, and its external debt tripled at the very moment that international bank lending was drying up after the debt crisis of 1982. The government reversed its earlier promotion of public enterprises. Malaysia found that its privatization policy, announced in 1982 by the new prime minister, Mahathir, could be designed to further the goals of the NEP by placing newly private firms in the hands of *Bumiputeras*.[23]

The Malaysian economy suffered another crisis during the second half of 1985. Commodity prices had continued to plummet. The government was forced to cut public spending drastically and allow the ringgit to depreciate. As the economic situation worsened, investors became particularly concerned about the health of the banking system, which had financed a real estate and asset market boom.[24] A number of financial institutions experienced runs, which had not been seen in Malaysia for nearly 20 years, and the entire financial system appeared increasingly fragile. Malaysian authorities intervened by taking over troubled institutions. The central bank, Bank Negara Malaysia (BNM), also sought to avert future financial crises by imposing prudential regulations, including conservative provisions against loan losses and restrictions on foreign borrowing. Domestic firms complained about the restrictions on foreign borrowing, citing lower borrowing costs abroad, but Bank Negara held firm.[25] The government favored foreign equity and domestic debt over external borrowing, and continued to keep public spending under control. (See **Exhibit 4-6.**)

Following the crisis of 1985-86, the Malaysian economy began to grow rapidly, and the foreign investors whom the government had sought to lure arrived in droves. The country received unparalleled levels of capital inflows, both short- and long-term, attracted by strong economic fundamentals, high interest rates, and market expectations of ringgit appreciation. In addition, the government promoted foreign direct investment specifically designed for export by relaxing NEP regulations and licensing requirements.[26]

Satisfied that it had reduced its external vulnerability to financial crises, the government began to promote the domestic capital market. Malaysia therefore further liberalized capital inflows and, in 1990, effected the separation of the Kuala Lumpur Stock Exchange (KLSE) from the Stock Exchange of Singapore (SES), on which Malaysian firms had been listed since Singapore and Malaysia had been part of a single state. Interestingly, however, one institutional link between the two exchanges continued to exist throughout the 1990s: the Central Limit Order Book (CLOB), an over-the-counter market that allowed investors in Singapore to trade Malaysian stocks without actually selling or buying on the KLSE. Instead, a Singaporean institution known as the "Central Depository" held the Malaysian stocks on behalf of all CLOB investors. CLOB remained a source of tension between Malaysian authorities, who objected to the practice, and their Singaporean counterparts.

The Malaysian Economy in the 1990s

In 1990 the government assessed the record of the 20-year-old NEP.[27] Much had been achieved. Economic growth had been rapid: an annual average of close to 7% for two decades, below the government's 8% target but still faster than that of most developing countries.[28] Yet some observers suggested that the distributional priorities of the NEP – and the resulting "cronyism" of Mahathir's self-described "Malaysia Incorporated" – had slowed Malaysia's growth.[29] Poverty rates had fallen dramatically, from nearly 50% in 1971 to approximately 15% in 1990. (See **Exhibit 3b**.) Employment patterns had changed a great deal. *Bumiputeras* exceeded the 50% target in professional and technical occupations. But *Bumiputeras* fell far short of the 50% target for administrative and managerial positions, comprising by 1990 only 22% of those employed in positions of authority.

The government's distributional goals with regard to equity presented a mixed picture. (See **Exhibit 3c**.) *Bumiputera* ownership of the shares of relevant firms had risen from 2.4% to 20.3%, a significant increase but less than the 30% target of 1971. Some observers noted, however, that this *Bumiputera* ownership was concentrated among relatively few wealthy Malays. Reliable data on intra-ethnic distribution were scarce.[30]

Then, in February 1991, Prime Minister Mahathir announced Malaysia's most ambitious development agenda to date: Vision 2020. Like the NEP, Vision 2020 was meant to serve as the organizing set of principles for Malaysian political and economic development.[31] The main goal was to become a "fully developed country" within 30 years.[32] Malaysian authorities also decided in 1990 to inaugurate the Federal Territory of Labuan, geographically part of Malaysia but designated an "offshore" financial center.[33] An active offshore market for the ringgit had already developed – primarily in Singapore.

By the end of 1993, Malaysian authorities had become concerned with the ringgit's strength in international currency markets. They also feared that foreign capital inflows, which resulted in a sharp increase in external liabilities in the banking system, could quickly reverse themselves.[34] In February 1994, therefore, Bank Negara imposed a number of direct and market-based temporary controls on capital inflows. Initially, capital markets reacted somewhat negatively to the controls, though little controversy arose. As the capital account surplus decreased, Bank Negara eased the controls, dismantling them completely in August 1994.

With the passing of this episode Malaysia resumed its liberalization policies. By 1997, banks could borrow abroad and lend foreign exchange to residents and non-residents, although foreign currency borrowing by residents required approval. Portfolio inflows were unrestricted and portfolio outflows were subject to ceilings only for corporations that had borrowed domestically; and foreign direct investment, both inward and outward, was completely free except for a few sectoral restrictions.

The economy boomed during the mid-1990s. Massive amounts of capital were channeled into electronics and other export-oriented sectors, as well as real estate, including, most famously, Kuala Lumpur's Petronas Twin Towers, the tallest buildings in the world. As a percentage of total output, Malaysia's market capitalization was the highest in the Asia-Pacific Economic Cooperation (APEC) region. The government budget deficits of the late 1980s and early 1990s had turned into surpluses. The ringgit, though not pegged, remained stable at around 2.5 per U.S. dollar. Inflation was low and stable. Unemployment was low, and the high growth rates were accompanied with significant improvements in living standards. (See **Exhibit 4-6, 14.**)

The Asian Financial Crisis

In early 1997 there were few signs of trouble, none of which appeared to concern foreign investors, who continued to flock to Malaysia and the other rapidly growing countries of east and southeast Asia. Indeed, the countries of the Association of Southeast Asian Nations (ASEAN) seemed very much the places to be. They earned nearly universal acclaim for their economic success: decades of rapid growth fueled by high savings and investment rates, set against a backdrop of low inflation, government budgets that were either in surplus or modest deficit, and the accumulation of foreign exchange reserves. (See **Exhibit 13**.) Their growth, along with financial deregulation, stable exchange rates against the U.S. dollar, and low interest rates in the U.S. and Japan, attracted huge capital flows to the region. In November 1996 the headline of the *IMF Survey* pronounced that "ASEAN's Sound Fundamentals Bode Well for Sustained Growth."[35]

Some observers pointed to signs of vulnerability, including exchange-rate policies designed to reduce volatility relative to the U.S. dollar, which then encouraged domestic financial institutions to accumulate large amounts of short-term foreign currency denominated loans. Others worried that these policies had also led to overvalued exchange rates and, therefore, slowing export growth and current account deficits. But few analysts predicted serious turmoil in foreign exchange markets; fewer still foresaw the full-fledged financial meltdown that would follow in its wake.[36]

As analysts look back on the crisis, they found the first warning signs in Korea and Thailand. In January 1997 a leading South Korean chaebol, Hanbo Steel, collapsed under the weight of its US$6 billion debt, becoming the first bankrupt chaebol in a decade. Two others, Sammi Steel and Kia Motors, followed suit.[37] In February Somprasong, a Thai finance company, missed payments on its foreign debt, leading many to worry that similar Thai firms were over-indebted and over-exposed to the real estate sector. Almost overnight, foreign lending ceased and property prices began to fall. Over the next six months the Bank of Thailand lent over US$8 billion to distressed financial institutions. Capital fled Thailand as concerns spread that the combination of financial problems and slow export growth would ultimately require devaluation of the Thai baht. In response, the Bank of Thailand committed US$28 billion of its US$30 billion in liquid foreign exchange reserves to forward contracts in defense of the baht. In May the government imposed controls on capital outflows, but the controls were systematically circumvented. Thailand was finally forced to allow the baht to float on July 2, 1997.

The devaluation of the Thai baht triggered capital outflows from Indonesia, Korea, Malaysia, and the Philippines. Initially, these governments defended their currencies by intervening in foreign exchange markets – using the reserves of their central banks to purchase their own currencies. Ultimately, however, markets overwhelmed the governments, as massive amounts of capital fled the region. One by one, Asian governments allowed their currencies to float freely and depreciate.

Even in late autumn 1997 informed observers viewed the crisis as a temporary setback. In October the IMF predicted that the Korean economy would grow 6% in 1998, above a regional average of 5.4%.[38] But capital continued to flee Asia. Several more rounds of capital flight, currency depreciation, and widespread corporate failures turned the currency crisis into a financial disaster. The entire region fell into recession, and the years of the "Asian Miracle" seemed to have come to an abrupt end.

Four of these five countries – Indonesia, Korea, the Philippines, and Thailand – turned to the IMF for financial assistance and agreed to implement IMF-designed economic programs, which were geared toward "restoring confidence and preparing the ground for a solid rebound from the current difficulties."[39] The IMF offered standby arrangements of approximately three years to Thailand for US$17.2 billion, Indonesia for US$40 billion, Korea for US$57 billion, and the Philippines for US$1 billion.[40] The Fund imposed conditions, which included tight fiscal and monetary policies, extensive bank closures and restructuring, and improvement in banking regulation and supervision, as well as structural reforms, such as the liberalization of foreign trade and the dismantling of monopolies.[41] Yet capital flight, currency depreciations, and plummeting stock prices continued throughout the end of 1997 and the first half of 1998, with little indication that confidence would return to the region. Indeed, violent riots, which turned against the ethnic Chinese minority, wreaked havoc in Indonesia, eventually forcing the resignation in May 1998 of President Suharto, who had ruled for thirty years.

Some observers worried that these IMF-imposed reforms had actually worsened the crisis. IMF-imposed tight fiscal and monetary policies, according to this view, exaggerated the economic slowdown, while the Fund's insistence on closing insolvent banks led to runs on otherwise sound financial institutions.[42] In any case, Malaysia, unlike the others, did not turn to the IMF for help.

Malaysia's Response to the Crisis

On July 14, 1997, less than two weeks after the devaluation of the Thai baht, Bank Negara, under pressure from international currency markets, stopped defending the currency. The resulting depreciation of the ringgit triggered a vicious cycle of capital outflows and asset price deflation, which, in turn, put increasing pressure on the banking system. Non-performing loans increased, accelerating as the economy contracted. The situation hit hardest those financial institutions that had expanded most aggressively into real estate and share purchase lending. Rumors about the weakness of MBf Finance, Malaysia's largest finance company, triggered runs on deposits.[43] During the first half of 1998 the economy contracted by 5%.

In August and September 1997 Malaysian authorities sought to stem the tide of capital outflows. Bank Negara, for example, imposed limits on domestic banks' offering forward currency transactions to non-residents.[44] Also, Mahathir established a fund to support plunging share prices on the KLSE: shares sold by selected Malaysians would be bought by the fund at a premium, while those sold by foreigners would fetch market prices. Some observers interpreted the fund as a mechanism for protecting political allies of the government.[45]

The prime minister appeared to be frustrated by the behavior of foreign investors. In September, after a meeting with foreign fund managers, Mahathir "described them as 'serious investors' rather than manipulators of the local stock market," which he had labeled them earlier.[46] At the annual meetings of the World Bank and International Monetary Fund in Hong Kong on September 20, 1997, Prime Minister Mahathir attacked "speculators" and called for a ban on "unnecessary, unproductive and immoral" currency trading.[47] Two days later, Mahathir blamed the likes of George Soros for Malaysia's troubles, calling him a "moron." Soros replied that Mahathir "is a menace to his own country."[48]

Meanwhile, Anwar Ibrahim, deputy prime minister and finance minister, confirmed the postponement of several infrastructure projects, vowed to reduce Malaysia's current account deficit, and announced that Malaysia would cut public spending by 2%. The *Wall Street Journal* observed, "Anwar Ibrahim is winning credit as the calm voice of economic reason, particularly among the foreign traders and investors who may matter most to Malaysia's economic stability."[49]

On December 3, 1997, Anwar announced a major austerity package. Government spending was cut by 18%. Bank Negara ended its effort to restrain interest rates. The ringgit recovered some of the value it had lost, as did the KLSE. These policies seemed to mark a shift toward orthodoxy, of the sort the IMF had proposed to Malaysia's Asian neighbors. Mahathir wrote: "What the Minister of Finance, together with the central bank, had done was to implement a virtual IMF without the IMF loans; namely, a combination of tight monetary and fiscal policies, raising the interest rate to defend the exchange rate, attempting to strengthen the banking system through more stringent prudential standards, and cutting down public expenditure to improve the current account balance."[50]

In January 1998, Mahathir announced the formation of a National Economic Action Council (NEAC) to deal with the financial crisis. The PM worked closely with the NEAC to formulate an effective response. Unsatisfied with Finance Minister Anwar's approach, Mahathir summoned Nor

Mohamed Yakcop, former head of foreign exchange trading at Bank Negara.[51] Together, behind the scenes, they began to formulate a policy to control capital outflows and currency speculation. All the while, Anwar continued to implement the "virtual IMF" policies.

Nor Mohamed explained his and the Prime Minister's approach to the problem:

> The reason why we thought that what was happening was not fair was: the guys who were selling ringgit were not the guys who were owning ringgit; or, to put it the other way, they were not the ones who were investing in Malaysia. These are the guys who had never spent a single cent in Malaysia, sitting in the offices of some bank – and borrowing the ringgit and short-selling the ringgit. ... So how do you stop the guys from borrowing? Actually it's easier to stop the guy who has the ringgit from lending to currency speculators. So that's basically what we did. We passed a rule that said that those guys with ringgit cannot lend to speculators, cannot lend to another non-resident. You can do whatever you want with the money ... but you cannot lend to another non-resident because the non-resident who borrows will most likely be a speculator.[52]

As Mahathir recalls, few members of the NEAC responded favorably to his proposal to control capital outflows and currency speculation: "There was objection, especially from people who were familiar with conventional banking, who were very familiar with the world's opinion about things, and they said that the whole world will just descend on us and just crush us flat."[53] The NEAC's members insisted that "Malaysia would be a pariah, shunned by the world's banks," he later wrote.[54]

In June 1998, Mahathir recalled former finance minister Daim Zainuddin to the Cabinet and gave him considerable authority within the NEAC, a fact that led some observers to question the status of the current minister, Anwar. That same month, at UMNO's general assembly, UMNO Youth leader Ahmad Zahid Hamidi criticized the "nepotism" and "cronyism" of the party's leaders with prominent businesspeople. It was widely believed that the criticisms had been encouraged by Anwar, who reportedly hoped to gain even greater power within the party.

The government also, meanwhile, moved to shore up the financial system. In the late spring of 1998 Malaysian authorities created an asset management company, *Danaharta,* to acquire non-performing loans from banks and begin to manage them centrally. And in the summer *Danamodal* was set up by the government to recapitalize selected banks, while the Corporate Debt Reconstructing Committee, a joint public-private initiative, was created to facilitate debt restructuring. The government encountered difficulty, however, raising funds for these organizations, and was unable to provide enough liquidity to stabilize the banking sector.

The NEAC launched its National Economic Recovery Plan in July 1998, seeking to stabilize the ringgit, restore market confidence, and maintain financial market stability.[55] The economic situation continued to worsen, however. Malaysian authorities became increasingly frustrated, even baffled by the collapse of the exchange rate: "For what reason did we deserve to have our currency depreciated by 30 to 40%, especially given our fundamentals?"[56] Interest rates in the offshore ringgit market were more than 40%, compared to only 11% rates in Malaysian banks. The second quarter of 1998, during which the economy contracted by 6.8%, was the country's worst performance since World War II.

On September 1, 1998 Bank Negara imposed new regulations, which included: a requirement that all ringgit held offshore be repatriated within a month; a prohibition of ringgit lending to non-residents; a 12-month waiting period for non-residents to convert ringgit proceeds from the sale of Malaysian securities held in external accounts; and restrictions on residents' investment abroad without prior approval from Bank Negara.[57] (For details, see **Appendix**.) Accompanying the currency and capital controls was a new fixed exchange rate regime, which set the value of the ringgit at 3.8

per U.S. dollar, the market rate on September 2. According to Nor Mohamed, "We knew this was not really the value of the ringgit, but this is what the market feels. We cannot say we know better than the market."[58]

Bank Negara explained the move to the markets in a press release:

> The over-riding objective of the new measures is to regain monetary independence and insulate the Malaysian economy from the prospects of further deterioration in the world economic and financial environment. ... The new measures are based on the following considerations: i. To limit the contagion effects of external developments on the Malaysian economy; ii. To preserve the recent gains made in terms of the policy measures to stabilize the domestic economy; and, iii. To ensure stability in domestic prices and the ringgit exchange rate and create an environment that is conducive to a revival in investor and consumer confidence and facilitate economic recovery. These measures will be removed should normalization in the global financial environment take place. ... These changes, however, will not affect the business operations of traders and investors or the normal conduct of economic activity.[59]

In a related move, the KLSE had, the day before, announced that it no longer recognized transactions on CLOB, Singapore's over-the-counter market for Malaysian shares. According to the *Asian Wall Street Journal*, "Malaysian authorities froze the shares in the CLOB accounts on the Kuala Lumpur exchange, making it impossible for account holders to take their money out. So some 172,000 mostly Singaporean small investors have had their investments locked up in Malaysia."[60]

Bank Negara then aggressively reduced interest rates, which fell from 8.9% to 5.5% by the end of the week. The government passed a fiscal stimulus program. And the KLSE rallied from a low of 262 on September 1 to 445 on September 7. (See **Exhibits 11, 12a-b**.) Malaysia also pursued reforms in the financial and corporate sectors, including measures to consolidate the banking system. Although *Danaharta* and *Danamodal* had achieved only limited success in the summer of 1998, after the imposition of the currency and capital controls the government was finally able to raise enough funds for these institutions primarily through the sale of government bonds in the domestic market. By the end of 1999, *Danaharta* had assumed responsibility for non-performing loans worth RM45.5 billion (US$12 billion).

Relying on well-institutionalized links with the banking system, as well as its traditional prudential supervision, Bank Negara successfully administered the controls through the banks.[61] IMF economists remarked:

> [T]he authorities closely monitored the activities of the commercial banks and at times exercised moral suasion to ensure enforcement of the regulations. ... [The effectiveness of the controls reflected] strict implementation and enforcement of the measures by Bank Negara Malaysia and a disciplined banking system, which strictly interpreted the measures and has not sought out potential loopholes.[62]

Moreover, the bane of capital controls in Latin America – black markets – apparently did not complicate the imposition of Malaysia's new regulations, the Fund's economists noted. The controls thus were "effective in achieving the objective of eliminating the offshore ringgit market."[63]

Mahathir and his advisor, Nor Mohamed, were circumspect, however, about the implications of their policies for the international financial system. "Other developing countries are very different. They cannot implement what we implemented," Mahathir argued. "The reason why Malaysia could is because we don't borrow."[64] Nor Mohamed added, "To do this you must have foreign exchange – external reserves."[65]

The Political and Economic Fallout

The Malaysian government was concerned about the reaction to the controls of two important communities: domestic and international. The local banking community and foreign and local firms within Malaysia would have to deal with the regulations on a daily basis. Additionally, the international financial community shared firmly held beliefs about the balance between public authority and international markets in a globalizing world, beliefs of which Malaysian authorities had been notably critical.

Anwar and Mahathir

The reactions of these two communities was colored by Prime Minister Mahathir's second surprise policy change, which followed quickly on the heels of the first: on September 2, 1998, the day after the imposition of currency and capital controls, Mahathir fired his Deputy Prime Minister and Minister of Finance, Anwar Ibrahim. Anwar's dismissal came as quite a shock. He had been highly respected outside of Malaysia. Even more important, Anwar had, since his accession to the offices of Deputy President of UMNO and Deputy Prime Minister in 1993, been groomed as Mahathir's successor. According to the *Wall Street Journal*, "The sacking Wednesday night of Malaysian deputy prime minister Anwar Ibrahim signaled the end of a battle for the soul of an important nation."[66] Anwar had been "Malaysia's main link to the International Monetary Fund," and under him Malaysia "had pursued an IMF-sanctioned, free-market approach to the crisis."[67] After a few days Prime Minister Mahathir named himself Finance Minister.[68]

The relationship between Anwar and Mahathir had not always been comfortable. When Mahathir had recruited Anwar into UMNO in 1982, an accomplishment Mahathir described as a "major coup," he had sought to placate his conservative Islamic critics. Anwar had been head of ABIM, the Malaysian Muslim Youth Movement, an Islamic organization that became, under Anwar's leadership, increasingly critical of the government. Amid speculation that he would join a rival party, Anwar's membership in UMNO helped to secure the *Barisan*'s convincing 1982 electoral victory. Upon becoming deputy president of UMNO and deputy prime minister in 1993, Anwar began to assert his own policy priorities, which were not always shared by Mahathir. Mahathir and Anwar frequently pledged support to one another, however, and rarely disagreed publicly.[69]

Still, most observers had believed Anwar was on track to become PM. In May 1997, Mahathir had appointed Anwar acting prime minister and acting president of UMNO during a two-month leave of absence. But Anwar's role in the government had been increasingly precarious since the recall of Daim to the cabinet in June 1998.

Subsequent to his dismissal from office on September 2, and expulsion from UMNO on September 3, Anwar's situation turned from bad to worse.[70] Shortly thereafter Malaysia's High Court released detailed affidavits alleging sodomy by Anwar, though they were later retracted amidst allegations of police coercion.[71] Mahathir told reporters that Anwar's sacking and expulsion were necessary because of the former Finance Minister's "low morality."[72] Anwar was then arrested on September 20. When Anwar appeared in court on September 29 with a swollen eye and bruises he complained of having been beaten "severely" while in police custody.[73] In April 1999, following a five-month trial, Anwar was convicted of obstruction of justice and sentenced to six years in jail. In August 2000 Anwar was convicted of sodomy charges as well.[74] Throughout this, Anwar called for reform (*reformasi*), even Mahathir's resignation; a considerable number of Malaysians rallied in his support, going so far as to demonstrate in the streets at the risk of government reprisals.

Reactions within Malaysia

Initially, the complexity of the controls created a great deal of confusion in the local banking community, among foreign investors, and the public in general. According to a knowledgeable source at Citibank in Kuala Lumpur, there was "general misperception, questions from clients – 'How do we get our money out?' 'Would they do it again?'"[75] Another prominent member of the local banking community noted that there was, "initially, a lot of confusion and uncertainty. And a lot of clarifications."[76] Foreign direct investors in Malaysia also expressed their concerns that the new regulations, which relied on a firm distinction between long- and short-term investors, would interfere with their operations. However, both bankers and businesspeople within Malaysia felt that Bank Negara, and Malaysian authorities in general, were very responsive to their questions and concerns.

Indeed, Bank Negara conducted an extensive education campaign, placing detailed descriptions of the control measures, updates, and clarifications on its web site, as well as setting up a 24-hour telephone "hotline" to answer specific questions. Bank Negara noted in its press release, "As we are embarking into uncharted territory, the measures announced today will be implemented flexibly to deal promptly with any problem that might emerge."[77]

The Bank was particularly keen to address the concerns of foreign direct investors, with which Malaysian authorities were eager to maintain a "constant dialogue," according to Daim Zainuddin, former head of the NEAC.[78] For example, after foreign investors expressed concerns about limitations on profit repatriation, Bank Negara significantly revised the policy.[79] Foreign investors welcomed the support of the authorities. "Feedback is the breakfast of champions," opined Nicholas S. Zeffreys, President of American Malaysian Chamber of Commerce.[80] Many foreign investors welcomed the stability brought by the fixing of the exchange rate. "When it was first introduced," Philip Yates of 3M observed of the radical policy change, "I think most of us here were fairly pessimistic about it, not believing that what they were doing was going to help. But I must say in retrospect, it offered a fair amount of stability in a period during which stability was pretty important."[81] Still, concerns arose about the long-run competitiveness of Malaysian exports if other currencies in the region depreciated.

Reactions outside Malaysia

The reaction of the Western media to Malaysia's handling of the crisis was in general quite negative.[82] Partly this reflected the fact that the currency and capital controls appeared to buck the trend toward the globalization of financial markets. "The world was moving until recently in the opposite direction. The International Monetary Fund last year moved to make unrestricted capital flows a condition of membership in the global economy," wrote two reporters for the *Wall Street Journal*.[83] And *Business Week* observed, "Malaysia's controls have deeply frightened global investors because they amount to a financial Roach Motel: Money can get in, but it can't get out. Investors are more sympathetic to limits on the inflow of capital."[84]

Rating agencies, such as Fitch IBCA, Moody's, and Standard and Poor's, downgraded Malaysia's sovereign risk rating. Fitch IBCA insisted that the "arbitrary" imposition of capital controls would damage Malaysia's creditworthiness and downgraded the government's debt to "junk bond" status.[85] According to a spokesperson for Fitch, "We are in no doubt about Malaysia's ability to service its debt. It is a question of willingness to do so. If Malaysia can change rules in an arbitrary fashion once, it can do so again."[86] In addition, on September 4, 1998, days after the capital controls were imposed, Morgan Stanley Capital International (MSCI) removed Malaysia from its developed market series, and then dropped Malaysia from the MSCI emerging market index.[87] (See **Exhibit 8**.)

Similarly, the reaction of U.S. government officials was not favorable. According to U.S. Deputy Treasury Secretary Lawrence Summers, "It would be a catastrophe if countries were to develop the idea that somehow withdrawing from the global system was right and that building the foundation for a market economy was wrong."[88] Summers also argued that capital controls "make unsustainable policy errors more tempting. They repel new capital inflows."[89]

Portfolio investors were, of course, the least pleased. Investors in the KLSE were frustrated by the restrictions on taking their money out of Malaysia. Templeton's Mark Mobius, who had touted Malaysia during the mid-1990s, was incensed: "If we congratulate Malaysia on its policy of locking up US$2 billion of Singaporean investors in the CLOB system indefinitely and locking up US$8 billion to US$10 billion of institutional investors' money up for one year and then imposing a tax on that money, then the future of emerging markets around the world will be threatened."[90] The governor of Bank Negara was accused in a press conference of having "stolen people's money" with the new regulations.[91]

Furthermore, the status of investors in Singapore's CLOB remained unclear, and the process of sorting out their ownership claims in the end took several years.[92] The acrimony between Malaysians and Singaporeans over CLOB, and the fact that the most active offshore ringgit market was located in Singapore before the currency controls eliminated it, led some Singaporeans to claim that Mahathir's policies were oriented primarily against them.

Not all developed countries reacted as negatively. Japan, for example, appeared tacitly to support Malaysia's experimentation with the regulation of international capital. Japan also became a major source of external finance to Malaysia during the period 1998-2000.[93]

Officials within the Malaysian government were not surprised that the international financial community had reacted so negatively to their new regulations. Nor Mohamed observed that the "market, the world was not in the mood to listen."[94] Mahathir insisted, "I'm not surprised at all, because I speak the truth and the press doesn't like the truth."[95] Dr. Zeti of Bank Negara recalls, "The World Bank closed us off. It was supposed to disburse a loan to us for US$1 billion, for education, and it stopped the disbursement because of the controls, and because of the other policies that we were implementing."[96] The Minister of International Trade and Industry, Rafidah Aziz, held a series of seminars in the U.S. in mid-September and in Europe in mid-October "to explain the new currency measures" to potential foreign direct investors.[97]

The Debate

The Malaysian experience with capital and currency controls raised two crucial questions. First, had they provided the Malaysian government with greater policy autonomy from international financial markets? Second, if so, did the Malaysian government use its autonomy prudently?

The government defended the controls, insisting that they obviously increased its autonomy from domestic and international markets. With its enhanced autonomy the government could maintain the distributional priorities of its economic policies as well as reflate the economy by lowering interest rates and increasing government spending and bring stability to the exchange rate. Malaysian authorities also argued that the controls had allowed them the autonomy to stabilize the financial system and avoid the widespread closure of weakened financial institutions, which was often a condition of the IMF stabilization programs.[98] For example, in May 1998 Bank Bumiputera and Sime Bank had declared enormous losses. In September the government announced that *Danaharta* would acquire 65% of Bank Bumiputera's and 95% of Sime Bank's non-performing loans.[99]

But the same policies were interpreted differently outside of the Malaysian government. A prominent critic asserted, "The window of opportunity offered by the capital controls regime has been abused by certain powerfully-connected business interests, not only to secure publicly funded bailouts, but even to consolidate and extend their corporate domination, especially in the crucial financial sector. Capital controls have been part of a package focused on saving friends of the regime, usually at the public expense."[100] From this perspective the capital controls had allowed the government to recapitalize an inefficient and corrupt financial system and reschedule the debts of an uncompetitive corporate sector. Many banks had been saved from certain disaster. Bank Bumiputera, created in 1966, had been bailed out three times – in 1985, 1989, and in 1997, before the financial crisis.[101] There were other examples. Renong, a large *Bumiputera*-owned conglomerate, was bailed out twice over the course of 1997 and 1998.[102] And Petronas, the state-owned oil company, bailed out the Proton automobile manufacturer.[103]

Others suggested that by the time Malaysia had imposed its currency and capital controls the crisis had already ended, a great deal of financial capital had already exited the country, and the rest of the region was already recovering as well.[104] Malaysia's recovery had been aided, in part, by the U.S. decision to lower interest rates in October 1998. (See **Exhibits 12a-b**.)

Another issue was whether there would be longer-term costs to Malaysia's reputation as a result of its regulation of international capital. At least one analyst was unconcerned, noting that "bankers have very little memory. They just want to make money."[105] On the other hand, perhaps Malaysia would have more difficulty attracting the long-term investors on which it had based so much of its development plans. Other analysts thus were concerned that with the currency and capital controls Malaysia "broke the faith of long-term investors."[106] The editors of a prominent business daily observed, "the thousands of foreign investors who had the rules changed on them overnight do have cause to complain. The way Kuala Lumpur treated them will shape foreign perceptions of Malaysia as a place to do business for years to come."[107] Malaysian authorities had sought to control outflows of short-term capital even as they encouraged inflows of long-term capital, but it was not clear that such a rigid separation was possible.[108]

Finally, representatives of the Malaysian government and the financial market disagreed, perhaps predictably, about whether governments should have autonomy from international markets. The prevailing view in the market was that it exerted "good discipline on the management of the country."[109] To these arguments, Mahathir replied, "The idea that the market will discipline government is sheer nonsense."[110]

Challenges for the Future

In February 1999, the government replaced the regulation preventing portfolio capital from leaving the country with a sliding scale of exit taxes on capital gains, ranging from 10 to 30%. In September 1999, Bank Negara replaced the two-tier tax with a flat 10% exit tax, which it subsequently abolished in February 2001. Meanwhile, both the IFC and Dow Jones reinstated Malaysia in their global indices by the end of 1999, and Malaysia returned to MSCI's emerging market index in May 2000.

The country's experience with currency and capital controls at an end, the Malaysian government set about the tasks of managing its economy. Malaysia's leaders continued to lobby for reform of the international financial architecture. Mahathir insisted, "I think countries should be allowed to regulate inflows and outflows of capital to some extent – not absolutely. People who invest in other countries want to feel certain that they can take out their money. That's fine. But when you have a whole lot of them pulling out suddenly, obviously you're going to end up very poor." Although Malaysia had, in his assessment, successfully implemented its currency and capital controls, he worried that "most developing countries, I'm afraid, will not be able to do it. That is why a change in the international system must be done in order to protect the weak countries."[111]

In terms of its long-term development plans, some Malaysian authorities worried about managing the country's transition up the value chains of manufactured goods. With ever greater flows of FDI headed to China than to Malaysia, one of the country's major sources of growth and technological learning appeared less secure than it once was. Still, Mahathir argued, "We are convinced that we will find a niche for ourselves."[112]

Politically, the country faced a number of serious challenges. Although Mahathir and UMNO had survived the crisis surrounding Anwar's dismissal, arrest, and imprisonment, the *Barisan Nasional*'s performance in the November 1999 election was one of its weakest to date. The *Barisan*'s share of the vote fell from 66% (in 1995) to 56%, a result of a split in the Malay vote. Some observers suggested that Anwar's allegations of corruption and calls for reform had encouraged many Malays to defect from the *Barisan*. After the late 1970s the government also had to deal with what some have called Malaysia's "Islamic resurgence," which consisted primarily of the rise of politically active Malays who sought a greater role for their stricter interpretation of religious principles in the governance of the country.[113] Anwar's popularity among socially conservative Malays created the possibility that the two trends could soon be linked.

Finally, after three decades, the government still had to contend with the Malay dilemma – balancing growth with inter-ethnic equity. "National unity" remained as important a social goal as ever. Malaysia's Vision 2020 plan foresaw a country that was developed, egalitarian, and harmonious. Prime Minister Mahathir, having already helped to transform Malaysia once, believed his country would achieve its goals: "I think the idea that you cannot change things is unacceptable. You can change anything."[114]

Appendix: Press Release: Measures to Regain Monetary Independence
Bank Negara Malaysia, September 1, 1998

Existing	New
ECM 2: Dealings in gold and foreign currency No restriction on foreign exchange contracts between authorized dealers and non-residents.	ECM 2: Dealings in gold and foreign currency No change, except for External Account holders.
ECM 3: External Accounts Transfer between External Account holders freely allowed. No restrictions on credits and debits to an External Account.	ECM 3: External Accounts Transfers between External Accounts would require prior approval for any amount. Transfers to resident accounts in Malaysian banks are permitted until 30 September 1998. Thereafter, such transfers require approval. Sources of funding the External Account are limited to: Proceeds from sale of ringgit instruments, securities registered in Malaysia or other assets in Malaysia; Salaries, wages, commissions, interest or dividend; Sale of foreign currency. Use of funds in the account is limited to purchase of ringgit assets in Malaysia.
ECM 4: General payments Generally residents were freely allowed to make payments to non-residents for any purpose, provided, for an amount of RM100,000 and above: a Form P is completed; and the resident does not have any domestic borrowing (if the payment is for investments abroad in any form); or the payment is made in foreign currency if in relation or consequential to a guarantee (for non-trade purposes).	ECM 4: General payments Generally residents are freely allowed to make payments to non-residents for any purpose up to **RM10,000** in ringgit or its equivalent in foreign currency (reduction in amount), except for all payment for imports of goods and services. Residents are freely allowed to make payments to non-residents in foreign currency only, for amounts exceeding RM10,000 equivalent. However, investments abroad in any form and payments under a guarantee for non-trade purposes require approval. Form P is completed for amounts exceeding RM10,000 equivalent.
ECM 5: Export of goods Prescribed manner of payment for exports is in foreign currency or ringgit from an External Account.	ECM 5: Export of goods Prescribed manner of payment for exports is in foreign currency only, other than currencies of Israel, Serbia and Montenegro.
ECM 6: Credit facilities to non-residents Non-resident correspondent banks and non-resident stockbroking companies were permitted to obtain credit facilities in aggregate up to RM5 million from banking institutions to fund mismatch of receipts and payments through their External Accounts.	ECM 6: Credit facilities to non-residents Domestic credit facilities to non-resident correspondent banks and non-resident stockbroking companies **are no longer allowed**.
ECM 9: Investments abroad Residents with no domestic borrowing were allowed to make payment to non-residents for purposes of investing abroad. Corporate residents with domestic borrowing were allowed to invest abroad up to the equivalent of RM10 million per calendar on a corporate group basis.	ECM 9: Investments abroad Residents with no domestic borrowing are allowed to make payment to non-residents for purposes of investing abroad, up to an amount of **RM10,000** or its equivalent in foreign currency per transaction. **All residents require prior approval** to make payments to non-residents for purposes of **investing abroad**, for an amount exceeding RM10,000 equivalent in foreign currency.

Existing	New
ECM 10: Foreign currency credit facilities and ringgit credit facilities from non-residents Residents were allowed to obtain ringgit credit facilities of below RM100,000 in the aggregate from any non-resident individuals.	ECM 10: Foreign currency credit facilities and ringgit credit facilities from non-residents Residents are not allowed to obtain ringgit credit facilities from any non-resident individuals.
ECM 12: Securities There was no restriction on the secondary trading of securities registered in Malaysia, between residents and non-residents, and between non-residents and non-residents. For transfer of securities registered outside Malaysia from non-resident to a resident, the resident was subject to the rules on investments abroad.	ECM 12: Securities Ringgit securities are required to be deposited with authorized depositaries. Ringgit securities held by non-residents must be transacted through an authorized depositary for good delivery. All payments by non-residents for any security registered in Malaysia must be made in foreign currency or in ringgit from an External Account. All proceeds in ringgit received by a non-resident from the sale of any resident security must be retained in an External Account (subject to the conditions on such accounts). However, should the ringgit security be held for more than one year, proceeds from the sale of such securities can be: - Immediately converted to foreign currency; or - Credited to the External Account. All payments to residents for any security registered outside Malaysia from non-residents, must be made in foreign currency.
ECM 13: Import and export of currency notes, bills of exchange, assurance policies, etc. A traveler (resident and non-resident) was freely allowed to import or export any amount of ringgit notes or foreign currency notes, which are on his person or in his baggage. Export of foreign currencies required approval. Authorized dealers were allowed to import any amount of ringgit notes, subject to reporting on a monthly basis to Bank Negara Malaysia.	ECM 13: Import and export of currency notes, bills of exchange, assurance policies, etc. A resident traveler is permitted to import: - Ringgit notes up to RM1,000 only; and - Any amount of foreign currencies. A resident traveler is permitted to export: - Ringgit notes up to RM1,000 only; and - Any amount of foreign currencies up to the equivalent of RM 10,000. A non-resident traveler is permitted to import: - Ringgit notes up to RM1,000 only; and - Any amount of foreign currencies. A non-resident traveler is permitted to export: - Ringgit notes up to RM1,000 only; and - Foreign currencies up to the amount of foreign currencies brought into Malaysia. Prior approval is required for the import and export of ringgit notes and the export of foreign currency notes, ***other than*** as permitted above. **Transitional provision** Up to 30 September 1998, permission is given to a traveler (resident and non-resident) to import any amount of ringgit on his person or in his baggage.
ECM 15: Labuan International Offshore Financial Center Licensed Offshore Banks were allowed to trade in ringgit investments up to permitted limits.	ECM 15: Labuan International Offshore Financial Center Licensed Offshore Banks are no longer allowed to trade in ringgit instruments.

Exhibit 1 Map of Malaysia

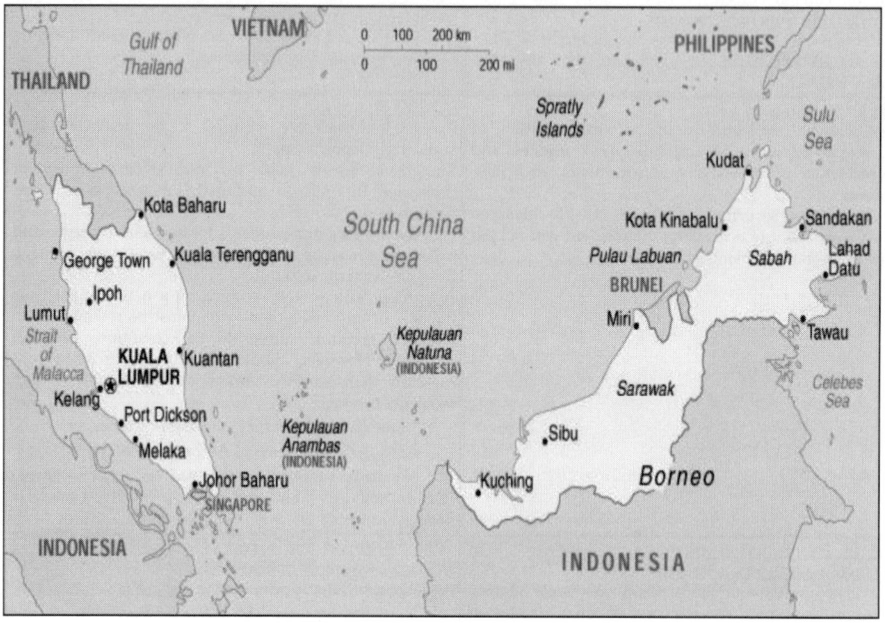

Source: Central Intelligence Agency.

Exhibit 2 Population by Ethnic Group

Year	Malay (%)	Chinese (%)	Indian (%)	Other (%)	Total (in millions)
1947	49.3	38.3	10.9	1.5	4.9
1957	49.8	37.2	11.1	2.0	6.3
1970	53.1	35.4	10.6	0.8	8.8
1980	55.3	33.8	10.2	0.7	11.4
1999	62.5	26.6	7.5	3.5	21.1

Sources: Adapted from Donald Snodgrass, *Inequality and Economic Development in Malaysia* (Kuala Lumpur: Oxford University Press, 1980); K.S. Jomo, *A Question of Class* (New York: Monthly Review Press, 1988); Economist Intelligence Unit (EIU), *EIU Country Profile Malaysia Brunei* (2000); Institute of Strategic and International Studies (Malaysia), www.jaring.my/isis/merc/populati.htm.

Note: May not add up to 100% due to rounding.

Exhibit 3a Income Distribution by Ethnicity (1970)
(as a percentage of total households, in Malaysian ringgit)

Income range (per month)	Malay	Chinese	Indian	Other
RM 1-100	22.9	2.6	1.3	0.2
RM 100-199	19.1	7.8	4.4	0.1
RM 200-399	10.4	11.9	3.5	0.1
RM 400-699	3.0	5.3	1.2	0.1
RM 700 and above	1.3	3.7	0.8	0.3
Total	56.7	31.3	11.2	0.8

Source: Government of Malaysia, *Mid-Term Review of Second Malaysia Plan* (Kuala Lumpur, 1973).

Note: Data are for Peninsular Malaysia only.

Exhibit 3b Incidence of Poverty in Peninsular Malaysia

(In percentages)	1970	1980	1990	1995	2000[a]
Households below poverty line	49.4	33.8	15.0	9.1	5.5

Sources: Adapted from Government of Malaysia, *Third Malaysia Plan* (Kuala Lumpur, 1976); Government of Malaysia, *Sixth Malaysia Plan* (Kuala Lumpur, 1991); Government of Malaysia, *Seventh Malaysia Plan* (Kuala Lumpur, 1996); Government of Malaysia, *Eighth Malaysia Plan* (Kuala Lumpur, 2001).

[a]Figures for 2000 refer to all of Malaysia, which comprises Peninsula Malaysia, Sabah, and Sarawak.

Note: The poverty line income is, according to the official definition, the monthly income necessary to cover minimum nutritional requirements and essential nonfood expenses.

Exhibit 3c Ownership Distribution by Ethnicity (share capital[a] of Limited Companies)

(In percentages)	1970	1975	1980	1985	1990	1995	2000
Bumiputera	2.4	9.2	12.5	19.1	19.3	20.6	19.1
Individuals & Institutions	1.6	3.6	5.8	11.7	14.2	18.6	17.4
Trust Agencies	0.8	5.6	6.7	7.4	5.1	2.0	1.7
Non-Bumiputeras[b]	28.3	37.5	44.5	47.7	46.8	43.4	40.3
Chinese	27.2	n.a.	n.a.	45.3	45.5	40.9	37.9
Indians	1.0	n.a.	n.a.	1.2	1.0	1.5	1.5
Others	n.a.	n.a.	n.a.	1.3	0.3	1.0	0.9
Nominee Companies	6.0	n.a.	n.a.	7.2	8.5	8.3	7.9
Foreigners	63.4	53.3	43.0	26.0	25.4	27.7	32.7
Total (RM million)[c]	5,329	15,084	32,420	77,964	108,377	179,792	310,076

Sources: Adapted from Government of Malaysia, *Second Malaysia Plan* (Kuala Lumpur, 1971); Government of Malaysia, *Third Malaysia Plan* (Kuala Lumpur, 1976); Government of Malaysia, *Mid-term Review of Fourth Malaysia Plan* (Kuala Lumpur, 1983); Government of Malaysia, *Seventh Malaysia Plan* (Kuala Lumpur, 1996); Government of Malaysia, *Eighth Malaysia Plan* (Kuala Lumpur, 2001)

[a]At par value.

[b]Data for 1975 and 1980 includes shares held by nominee companies.

[c]Excludes shares held by federal, state and local governments.

Exhibit 4 National Accounts and Other Economic Data

	1960	1970	1975	1980	1985	1990	1995	1996	1997	1998	1999	2000
Gross domestic product (GDP)												
(Millions of current ringgit)	6,837	12,155	22,332	53,308	77,547	119,081	222,472	253,732	281,889	284,474	299,662	339,420
Percentage of total												
Private consumption	62.0	61.6	58.6	50.5	52.0	51.8	47.9	46.0	45.3	41.5	41.6	42.5
Government consumption	12.9	16.4	17.6	16.5	15.3	13.8	12.4	11.1	10.9	10.0	11.2	10.7
Gross fixed capital formation	12.0	17.7	25.1	31.1	29.8	33.0	43.6	42.5	43.1	26.8	22.2	25.7
Exports of goods & services	56.2	46.1	45.5	57.5	54.9	74.5	94.1	91.6	93.2	114.4	121.3	125.7
Imports of goods & services	-43.7	-44.4	-47.2	-55.0	-49.7	-72.4	-98.0	-90.2	-92.3	-92.6	-96.6	-105.8
Real GDP (1995=100)	n.a.	16.1	23.6	35.6	45.7	63.6	100.0	110.0	118.1	109.4	115.7	125.6
Annual growth rate of real GDP	n.a.	n.a.	8.0	8.5	5.1	6.9	9.5	10.0	7.3	-7.4	5.8	8.5
(on previous value shown)												
Annual growth rate of price deflator	n.a.	n.a.	4.6	9.6	2.5	2.0	3.5	3.7	3.5	8.9	-0.4	4.4
Population (in millions)	8.1	10.4	11.9	13.7	15.7	18.1	20.7	21.2	21.7	22.2	22.7	23.3
Unemployment rate	n.a.	n.a.	n.a.	5.6	6.9	5.1	2.8	2.5	2.5	3.3	3.4	n.a.
Federal Budget Surplus as a percentage of GDP	n.a.	-3.7	-8.2	-6.9	-5.7	-3.0	0.9	0.7	2.4	-1.8	-3.2	-5.8
Public Debt as a percentage of GDP	n.a.	n.a.	n.a.	44.0	82.4	81.4	47.8	35.9	32.5	36.3	37.7	n.a.

Sources: Adapted from Bank Negara Malaysia, *Monthly Statistical Bulletin* (www.bnm.gov.my); International Monetary Fund, *International Financial Statistics* (CD-ROM, 2000); World Bank, *World Bank Indicators* (CD-ROM, 2001)

Exhibit 5 Selected Financial Economic Indicators, 1996-1999, 1997Q1-2000Q1[a]

	1996	1997	1998	1999	97Q1	97Q2	97Q3	97Q4	98Q1	98Q2	98Q3	98Q4	99Q1	99Q2	99Q3	99Q4	00Q1
Average bank lending rate (%)	10.1	10.6	12.3	8.5	10.1	10.5	10.7	11.2	12.5	13.5	12.6	10.0	9.6	8.7	8.1	7.8	7.8
Loans extended by banking system (% growth)																	
Manufacturing	14.8	18.5	2.0	1.3	n.a.	n.a.	n.a.	18.5	10.5	12.3	10.2	2.9	-2.9	1.5	2.6	1.3	3.5
Property	26.8	34.0	6.9	-6.6	n.a.	n.a.	n.a.	34.0	27.9	20.1	11.6	6.9	5.7	-5.8	-5.3	-6.6	-7.2
Share Market Performance																	
KLSE Composite Index[b]	1,238	594	586	812	1,203	1,077	815	594	720	456	374	586	503	870	736	763	922
Market capitalization (MYR billions)	807	376	375	553	845	745	585	376	453	286	249	375	318	503	490	561	632

Sources: Adapted from Bank Negara Malaysia, *Monthly Statistical Bulletin* (www.bnm.gov.my); International Monetary Fund, *International Financial Statistics* (CD-ROM, 2000).

[a]All growth rates on a year on year basis.

[b]KLSE Composite Index is the Kuala Lumpur Stock Exchange Composite Index.

Exhibit 6 Balance of Payments (US$ millions)

	1980	1985	1990	1991	1992	1993	1994	1995	1996	1997	1998	1999	2000
Goods exports	12,963	15,251	28,806	33,712	39,823	46,238	56,897	71,767	76,985	77,538	71,883	84,052	98,429
Goods imports	-10,569	-11,677	-26,280	-33,321	-36,673	-43,201	-55,320	-71,871	-73,137	-74,029	-54,378	-61,404	-77,576
Trade balance	2,393	3,574	2,526	391	3,150	3,037	1,577	-104	3,848	3,509	17,505	22,648	20,853
Service balance	-1,821	-1,992	-1,626	-2,190	-2,347	-3,104	-2,732	-3,379	-2,437	-2,570	-1,610	-2,816	-2,951
Income balance	-836	-2,188	-1,872	-2,473	-3,143	-3,211	-3,595	-4,144	-4,690	-5,366	-3,904	-5,497	-7,514
Transfers balance	-2	7	102	89	172	288	229	-1,017	-1,182	-1,509	-2,462	-1,728	-1,979
Current account	-266	-600	-870	-4,183	-2,168	-2,990	-4,521	-8,644	-4,461	-5,936	9,529	12,607	8,409
Direct investment net	934	695	2,332	3,998	5,183	5,006	4,342	4,178	5,078	5,137	2,163	1,553	1,761
Portfolio and other investment net	497	1,234	-549	1,623	3,563	5,798	-3,054	3,464	4,399	-2,940	-4,714	-8,172	-8,037
Financial account	1,431	1,929	1,783	5,621	8,746	10,804	1,288	7,642	9,477	2,197	-2,551	-6,619	-6,276
Net errors and omissions	-701	-181	1,038	-202	40	3,536	73	-761	-2,503	-136	3,040	-1,276	-3,142
Change in reserve assets	-464	-1,148	-1,951	-1,236	-6,618	-11,350	3,160	1,763	-2,513	3,875	-10,018	-4,712	1,009
Current account balance (% of GDP)	-1.1	-1.8	-2.0	-8.5	-3.7	-4.5	-6.1	-9.7	-4.4	-5.9	13.1	16.0	9.4
Total external debt (% of GDP)	28.8	54.8	39.7	38.5	37.9	41.9	38.7	41.3	42.0	50.5	65.3	62.5	n.a.
Short-term debt (% of total)	n.a.	n.a.	9.6	14.1	23.5	25.0	19.3	19.1	25.7	25.3	19.9	14.3	11.2
Foreign reserves, end of year ($bn)[a]	4.4	4.9	9.8	10.9	17.2	27.2	25.4	23.8	27.0	20.8	25.6	30.5	29.5
Nominal exchange rate (Malaysian ringgit per US$)	2.2	2.3	2.7	2.8	2.5	2.6	2.6	2.5	2.5	2.8	3.9	3.8	3.8
Real effective exchange rate (base year = 1977)[b]	137.6	150.9	102.1	99.5	105.7	104.7	101.7	101.3	105.1	100.0	79.0	81.6	n.a.

Sources: Adapted from International Monetary Fund, *International Financial Statistics* (CD-ROM, 2000); Bank Negara Malaysia, *Monthly Statistical Bulletin* (www.bnm.gov.my).

[a]Includes adjustments to the total value of assets to reflect currency and other gains and losses incurred, real and unrealized, in the period.

[b]An increase in the real effective exchange rate index represents a real appreciation.

Exhibit 7 Net Portfolio Investment into Malaysia by Country (in millions of ringgit)

	1993	1994	1995	1996	1997	1998	1999	2000
United States	2,699	3,452	6,295	3,038	-342	142	-900	412
Australia	13	-102	145	-54	-46	-15	-275	71
China	23	-2	-47	7	-398	158	2	-17
Japan	1,473	593	-304	-441	-531	662	1,591	-133
Hong Kong	6,759	-7,132	-2,598	313	-21,825	-1,444	-376	-1,967
United Kingdom	-432	4,959	1,571	1,642	88	1,191	-417	-2,100
Singapore	14,310	12,209	75	2,607	-4,936	-2,146	-286	-4,402
Other Countries	806	52	223	1,654	-365	197	1,728	581
Total	25,651	14,029	5,360	8,766	-28,355	-1,255	1,067	-8,717

Source: Adapted from Bank Negara Malaysia, *Monthly Statistical Bulletin* (www.bnm.gov.my).

Exhibit 8 Sovereign Debt Ratings History[a]

Standard & Poor's[b]

	Foreign Currency Debt		Local Currency Debt	
Date	Long Term	Short Term	Long Term	Short Term
11/10/99	BBB	n.a.	A	A-1
9/15/98	BBB-	A-3	A-	A-2
7/24/98	BBB+	n.a.	A+	A-1
4/17/98	A-	A-2	AA-	n.a.
12/23/97	A	A-1	AA	n.a.
8/18/97	n.a.	n.a.	n.a.	A-1 (+)
12/29/94	A+	A-1 (+)	n.a.	n.a.
6/28/93	n.a.	n.a.	AA+	n.a.
12/7/92	n.a.	A-1	n.a.	n.a.
9/13/90	A-	n.a.	n.a.	n.a.

Fitch[c]

	Foreign Currency Debt		Local Currency De
Date	Long Term	Short Term	Long Term
12/7/99	BBB	F2	A-
9/9/99	BBB- (+)	F3 (+)	n.a.
7/26/99	n.a.	F3	n.a.
4/26/99	BBB-	n.a.	n.a.
9/9/98	BB	B	BBB
8/13/98	BBB-	F3	A-

Moody's[d]

	Foreign Currency Debt	
Date	Long Term	Short Term
10/17/00	Baa2	P-3
7/12/00	Baa3 (+)	NP (+)
9/14/98	Baa3	NP (+)
7/23/98	Baa2	P-3
6/4/98	A2 (-)	n.a.
12/21/97	A2	P-2
10/2/95	n.a.	P-1
3/15/95	A1	n.a.
1/20/95	A2 (+)	n.a.
3/11/93	A2	n.a.
3/12/90	A3	n.a.
11/18/86	Baa1	n.a.

[a] Changes in future expectations are in parenthesis.

[b] Long-term debt is categorized from highest grade to lowest grade as AAA, AA+, AA, AA- A+, A, A-, BBB+, BBB, BBB-, BB+, BB, BB-, B+, B, B-, CCC+, CCC, CCC-, CC, C, and D. Investments categorized as BBB- and above are investment grade. Short-term debt is characterized as A-1+, A-1, A-2, A-3, B, C and D. Investments characterized as A-3 and above are investment grade.

[c] Long-term debt is categorized from highest grade to lowest grade as AAA, AA+, AA, AA- A+, A, A-, BBB+, BBB, BBB-, BB+, BB, BB-, B+, B, B-, CCC+, CCC, CCC-, CC, C, DDD, DD, and D. Investments categorized as BBB- and above are investment grade. Short-term debt is characterized as F1+, F1, F2, F3, B, C and D. Investments characterized as F3 and above are investment grade.

[d] Long-term debt is categorized from highest grade to lowest grade as Aaa, Aa1 ,Aa2, Aa3, A1, A2, A3, Baa1, Baa2, Baa3, Ba1, Ba2, Ba3, B1, B2, B3, Caa1, Caa2, Caa3, Ca, and C. Investments categorized as Baa3 and above are investment grade. Short-term debt is characterized as P-1, P-2, P-3, and NP. Investments characterized as P-3 and above are investment grade.

Source: Adapted from Bloomberg.

Exhibit 9a Exchange Rate per U.S. Dollar (1997-1999)

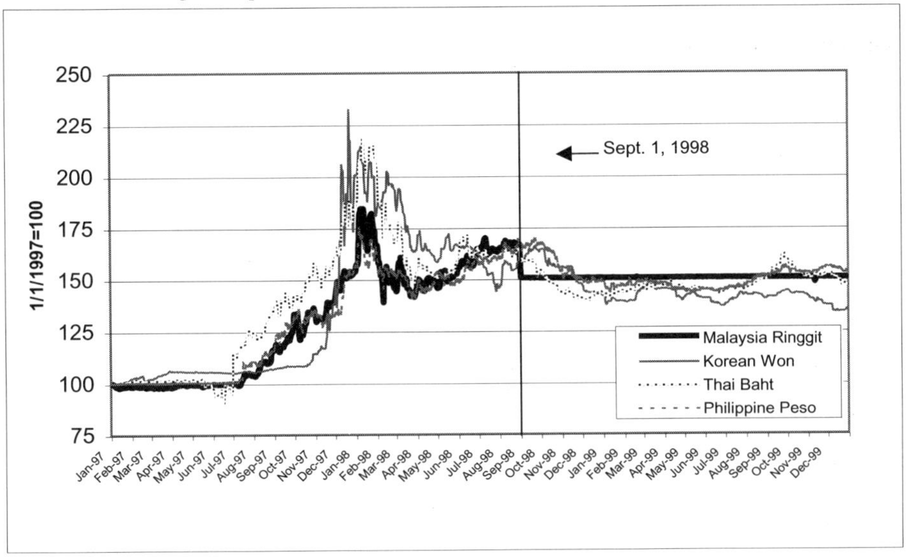

Source: Bank Negara Malaysia (www.bnm.gov.my).

Exhibit 9b Malaysian Ringgit per U.S. Dollar (July - September 1998)

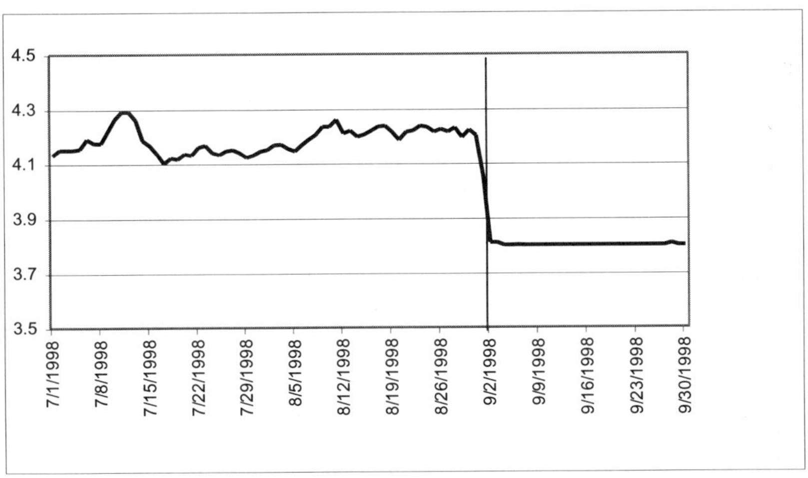

Source: Bank Negara Malaysia (www.bnm.gov.my).

Exhibit 10 Kuala Lumpur Stock Exchange (1997-2000)

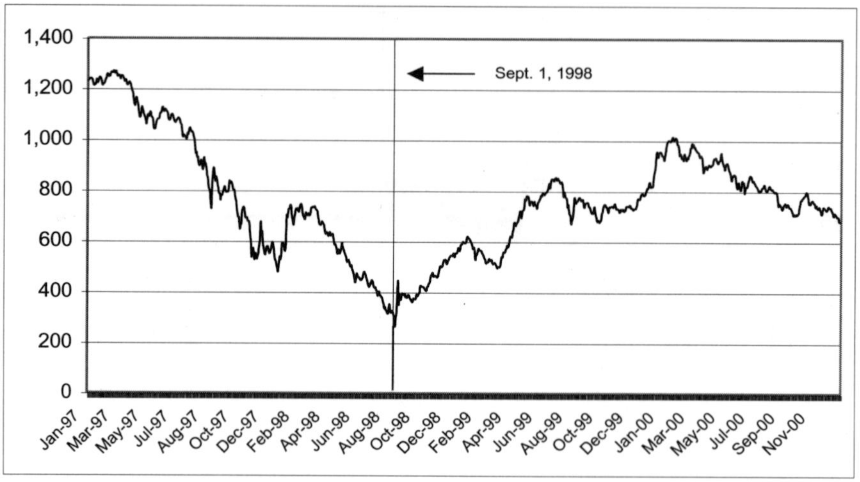

Source: Bank Negara Malaysia (www.bnm.gov.my).

Exhibit 11 Comparative Stock Exchange Indices

Dates	Malaysia	Korea	Philippines	Indonesia	Thailand
8/24/1998	317.20	305.15	1,323.11	370.55	233.15
8/25/1998	324.17	310.23	1,310.19	367.14	230.22
8/26/1998	324.49	317.56	1,287.02	360.93	227.50
8/27/1998	313.51	313.92	1,266.99	354.95	226.85
8/28/1998	302.91	309.32	1,194.71	339.02	218.85
8/29/1998		304.79			
8/30/1998					
8/31/1998		310.16	1,192.25	342.44	214.53
9/1/1998	**262.70**	**309.71**	**1,191.76**	**325.85**	**211.09**
9/2/1998	294.59	314.40	1,197.77	329.63	207.59
9/3/1998	313.07	314.78	1,192.95	334.79	207.40
9/4/1998	363.44	314.22	1,159.38	325.56	207.31
9/5/1998		315.83			
9/6/1998					
9/7/1998	445.06	328.22	1,186.93	335.81	220.56
9/8/1998	349.56	326.35	1,192.08	330.41	212.85
9/9/1998	389.65	329.22	1,157.43	325.76	213.98

Source: Adapted from Bloomberg.

Exhibit 12a Comparative Interest Rates

Dates	Malaysia[a]	Korea[b]	Philippines[c]	Indonesia[c]	Thailand[b]
8/24/1998	9.48	9.30	16.00	62.00	10.00
8/25/1998	9.54	8.91	16.00	59.75	9.00
8/26/1998	9.47	8.58	16.00	59.21	7.00
8/27/1998	9.50	8.23	16.00	61.73	7.00
8/28/1998	9.37	8.59	16.00	58.80	6.25
8/29/1998	8.86				
8/30/1998					
8/31/1998		8.52	16.00	58.50	9.00
9/1/1998	**8.47**	**8.64**	**16.00**	**58.40**	**8.00**
9/2/1998	7.83	8.51	16.00	58.84	14.25
9/3/1998	6.95		16.00	59.40	7.00
9/4/1998	6.21	8.50	16.00	58.72	6.50
9/5/1998	5.52				
9/6/1998					
9/7/1998	5.58		16.00	57.55	5.00
9/8/1998	6.12	8.40	16.00	57.15	6.00
9/9/1998	5.86	9.45	16.00	57.25	5.50

Sources: Adapted from Bloomberg; Bank Negara Malaysia (www.bnm.gov.my).

[a]Daily average interbank money market rates
[b]Call rate
[c]Overnight rate

Exhibit 12b Interest Rates - Selected Countries

	Malaysia	Korea	Philippines	Indonesia	Thailand	United States
1996	6.98	12.44	12.34	13.96	9.23	5.30
1997	7.61	13.24	12.89	27.82	14.59	5.46
I - 98	9.60	23.93	17.83	57.92	20.64	5.52
II - 98	9.97	18.64	14.53	66.31	18.03	5.50
III - 98	8.35	10.21	14.19	74.18	9.57	5.53
IV - 98	5.92	7.16	13.47	52.76	3.84	4.86
I - 99	5.25	5.68	12.70	39.96	2.69	4.73
II - 99	3.14	4.81	10.02	28.95	1.48	4.75
III - 99	2.56	4.78	8.48	13.21	1.51	5.09
IV - 99	2.57	4.76	8.78	12.22	1.41	5.31
2000	2.66	5.16	9.91	10.32	1.95	6.24

Source: International Monetary Fund, *International Financial Statistics* (CD-ROM, 2000).

Note: Interest rates refer to money market rates, except that for the United States, which is the federal funds rate.

Exhibit 13 Comparative Economic Indicators

	1994	1995	1996	1997	1998	1999
Korea						
GDP growth (%)	8.3	8.9	6.8	5.0	-5.8	10.9
Investment rate (% of GDP)	36.5	37.2	37.9	34.2	20.9	n.a.
Government fiscal balance (% of GDP)	0.3	0.3	0.1	-1.3	-3.8	-4.6
Current account (% of GDP)	-1.0	-1.7	-4.4	-1.7	12.6	6.0
Foreign reserves (in months of imports)	2.6	2.5	2.3	1.4	5.1	5.8
Nominal exchange rate (to the US dollar)	803.4	771.3	804.5	951.3	1,401.4	1,188.8
Real exchange rate (100=1997)	90.0	90.6	91.1	81.8	56.2	60.6
Stock market index	1,027.4	882.9	651.2	376.3	562.5	1,028.1
External debt (% of GDP)	18.0	17.5	22.3	28.7	43.4	31.9
Short term debt (% of total)	43.7	54.3	57.5	39.3	20.2	26.8
Bank lending to private sector (growth rate, %)	20.1	15.4	20.0	22.0	n.a.	n.a.
Inflation rate (CPI, %)	7.7	7.1	3.9	3.1	5.3	-2.0
Singapore						
GDP growth (%)	11.2	8.4	7.5	8.0	1.5	5.4
Investment rate (% of GDP)	33.5	34.5	37.0	38.7	33.5	n.a.
Government fiscal balance (% of GDP)	16.3	14.6	10.6	11.7	n.a.	n.a.
Current account (% of GDP)	16.4	17.3	15.9	15.8	20.9	25.0
Foreign reserves (in months of imports)	5.9	5.7	6.0	5.5	7.3	7.0
Nominal exchange rate (to the US dollar)	1.5	1.4	1.4	1.5	1.7	1.7
Real exchange rate (100=1997)	98.4	100.0	103.5	105.7	101.8	95.4
Stock market index	533.6	555.4	536.1	425.9	382.5	668.8
External debt (% of GDP)	10.8	9.8	10.7	n.a.	n.a.	n.a.
Short term debt (% of total)	13.3	14.6	19.8	n.a.	n.a.	n.a.
Bank lending to private sector (growth rate, %)	15.3	20.3	15.8	12.7	n.a.	n.a.
Inflation rate (CPI, %)	3.1	2.6	1.2	1.4	-1.5	-1.3
Indonesia						
GDP growth (%)	7.5	8.2	7.8	4.7	-13.2	0.8
Investment rate (% of GDP)	30.1	31.9	30.7	31.8	14.0	n.a.
Government fiscal balance (% of GDP)	0.9	2.2	1.2	-0.7	-2.4	n.a.
Current account (% of GDP)	-1.6	-3.2	-3.4	-2.3	4.2	4.1
Foreign reserves (in months of imports)	3.2	2.9	3.5	3.0	5.3	6.1
Nominal exchange rate (to the US dollar)	2,160.8	2,248.6	2,342.3	2,909.4	10,013.6	7,855.2
Real exchange rate (100=1997)	111.3	107.6	111.4	100.0	48.7	72.4
Stock market index	469.6	513.8	637.4	401.7	398.0	676.9
External debt (% of GDP)	61.0	61.5	56.7	63.1	152.7	105.3
Short term debt (% of total)	18.0	20.9	25.0	24.1	13.3	13.3
Bank lending to private sector (growth rate, %)	23.0	22.6	21.5	46.4	n.a.	n.a.
Inflation rate (CPI, %)	7.8	9.9	8.7	12.6	73.1	15.2
Thailand						
GDP growth (%)	8.9	8.8	5.5	-1.3	-9.4	4.2
Investment rate (% of GDP)	40.3	41.6	41.7	30.1	25.3	n.a.
Government fiscal balance (% of GDP)	1.9	2.9	2.4	-0.9	-3.5	-2.7
Current account (% of GDP)	-5.6	-8.1	-8.1	-2.0	12.8	10.0
Foreign reserves (in months of imports)	5.4	5.0	5.1	4.1	6.4	6.7
Nominal exchange rate (to the US dollar)	25.1	24.9	25.3	31.4	41.4	37.8
Real exchange rate (100=1997)	109.8	108.0	113.5	100.0	86.3	91.5
Stock market index	1,360.1	1,280.8	831.6	372.7	355.8	481.9
External debt (% of GDP)	45.4	49.4	50.0	62.9	77.4	77.5
Short term debt (% of total)	44.5	49.5	41.4	37.2	27.3	24.3
Bank lending to private sector (growth rate, %)	30.3	23.8	14.6	19.8	n.a.	n.a.
Inflation rate (CPI, %)	5.1	6.0	4.0	3.0	8.7	-4.3

Sources: Adapted from World Bank, *World Development Indicators* (CD-ROM, 2000 and 2001); EIU data, www.eiu.com; Bloomberg, *World Equity Indices;* International Monetary Fund, *International Financial Statistics* (CD-ROM, 2000).

Exhibit 14 Socio-economic Development, Various Countries

	Malaysia	Thailand	Singapore	Indonesia	China	Korea	United States	Japan
GDP per capita (PPP)								
1980	2,621	1,421	5,471	795	422	2,711	12,674	9,029
1990	5,328	3,821	13,768	1,858	1,338	8,596	22,537	19,062
1998	8,137	5,456	24,210	2,651	3,105	13,478	29,605	23,257
Life expectancy at birth (years)	72.0	72.3	77.2	65.4	69.9	72.6	76.5	80.5
Adult literacy rate (age 15 above)	86	95	92	86	83	98	100	100
Population with access (%):								
to safe water	78	80	100	76	75	92	100	100
to sanitation	67	96	100	66	38	63	100	100
Doctors/1,000 people	0.5	0.4	1.4	0.2	2.0	1.3	2.7	1.9
TVs/1,000 people	174	289	348	136	292	346	844	719
PCs/100,000 people	59	22	458	8	9	157	459	237
Main phone lines/1,000 people	198	84	562	27	70	433	661	503
Mobile phones/1,000 people	99	32	346	5	19	302	256	374
Internet hosts/1,000 people	18	4	188	1	0	38	975	107

Sources: Adapted from World Bank, *World Development Indicators* (CD-ROM, 2001); World Resources Institute (www.wri.org).

Exhibit 15 Federal Election Results (number of seats)

Parties	1959	1964	1969	1974	1978	1982	1986	1990	1995	1999
Barisan Nasional (BN, National Front)[a]										
United Malays National Organization (UMNO)	48	52	50	61	70	70	83	71	88	72
Malaysian Chinese Association (MCA)	19	27	13	19	17	24	17	18	30	28
BN Sarawak				15	23	19	21			
Malaysian Indian Congress (MIC)	7	10	3	4	3	4	6	6	6	7
BN Sabah				16	13	10	15			
Gerakan Pakyat Malaysia[b]				5	4	5	5	5	7	7
Parti Pesaka Bumiputera Bersatu (PPBB)								10	13	10
Partai Islam sa Malaysia (PAS)[c]				14						
Other	0	0	0	1	0	0	1	17	18	24
Total Barisan Nasional	74	89	66	135	130	132	148	127	162	148
Barisan Alternatif (BA, Alternative Front)										
Partai Islam sa Malaysia (PAS)[c]	13	9	12		5	5	1	7	7	27
Democratic Action Party (DAP)		1	13	9	16	9	24	20	9	10
Gerakan Pakyat Malaysia[b]			8							
Parti Bersatu Sabah (PBS)								14	8	3
Parti Melayu Semangat '46 (S46)								8	6	0
Others & Independents	17	5	4	10	3	8	4	0	0	5
Total Barisan Alternatif	30	15	37	19	24	22	29	49	30	45
Total Parliamentary Seats[d]	104	104	103	154	154	154	177	176	192	193

Source: Adapted from James Jeduason, *Ethnicity and the Economy* (Singapore: Oxford University Press, 1989); Gordon Means, *Malaysian Politics* (Singapore: Oxford University Press, 1991); Economist Intelligence Unit (EIU), *EIU Country Profile Malaysia Brunei (2000).*

[a]Prior to 1974 the ruling coalition, called the Alliance, was comprised of UMNO, MCA and MIC. In 1974, the Alliance invited more parties into its coalition and was officially renamed the *Barisan Nasional.*

[b]Gerakan joined the BN in 1974, after a strong showing in 1969.

[c]PAS joined the BN for the 1974 elections, but in all other elections before and after has been an opposition party.

[d]Parliamentary districts are determined by the Malaysian Election Commission and are periodically reviewed and adjusted based on population increases and shifts.

Endnotes

[1] Authors' interview with Dr. Mahathir Mohamad, Prime Minister of Malaysia, Kuala Lumpur, October 8, 2001.

[2] Authors' interview with Dr. Mahathir Mohamad, Prime Minister of Malaysia, Kuala Lumpur, October 8, 2001.

[3] Mahathir Mohamad, *The Malaysian Currency Crisis: How and Why It Happened* (Petaling Jaya: Pelanduk, 2000), pp. 19-20.

[4] Mahathir, *The Malaysian Currency Crisis*, p. 20.

[5] Authors' interview with Dr. Mahathir Mohamad, Prime Minister of Malaysia, Kuala Lumpur, October 8, 2001.

[6] Authors' interview with Dr. Mahathir Mohamad, Prime Minister of Malaysia, Kuala Lumpur, October 8, 2001.

[7] Merton Miller, "Currency Controls Inevitably Fail," *Business Times*, July 9, 1999.

[8] "The Controls were 'Crazy': The Critic Expects Investors to Punish Malaysia," *Asiaweek*, September 17, 1999.

[9] For an introduction to the scholarly debate, see K. S. Jomo, "Capital Controls," in *Malaysian Eclipse: Economic Crisis and Recovery*, ed. K. S. Jomo (London: Zed, 2001). Also see Mark Beeson, "Mahathir and the Markets: Globalization and the Pursuit of Economic Autonomy in Malaysia," *Pacific Affairs*, vol. 73, no. 3 (2000): 335-352; Rudiger Dornbusch, "Malaysia: Was It Different?" NBER Working Paper No. 8325, October 2001; Stephan Haggard, *The Political Economy of the Asian Financial Crisis* (Washington, D.C.: Institute for International Economics, 2000); Ethan Kaplan and Dani Rodrik, "Did the Malaysian Capital Controls Work?" NBER Working Paper No. 8142, February 2001; Dwight Perkins and Wing Thye Woo, "Malaysia: Adjusting to Deep Integration," in *The Asian Financial Crisis: Lessons for a Resilient Asia*, ed. Wing Thye Woo, Jeffrey D. Sachs, and Klaus Schwab (Cambridge, Mass.: MIT Press, 2000); Steven Radelet and Jeffrey Sachs, "The Onset of the East Asian Financial Crisis," in *Currency Crises*, ed. Paul R. Krugman (Chicago: University of Chicago Press, 2000); and Maria Toyoda, "Malaysia's Ethnic Cleavages and Controlled Liberalization," in *The Political Economy of International Financial Crises*, ed. Shale Horowitz and Uk Heo (Lanham, Md.: Rowman and Littlefield, 2001). Paul Krugman's views in the popular press received a great deal of attention as well. See Paul Krugman, "Saving Asia: It's Time to Get Radical," *Fortune*, vol. 138, no. 5 (1998): 74-80; Krugman, "An Open Letter to Prime Minister Mahathir," September 1, 1998, reprinted in *Fortune*, vol. 138, no. 6 (1998): 35-36; Krugman, "Malaysia's Opportunity?" *Far Eastern Economic Review*, vol. 161, no. 38 (1998): 32-33; Krugman, "Capital Control Freaks: How Malaysia Got Away with Economic Heresy," *Slate*, September 27, 1999.

[10] For a historical overview, see Grenelle Bauer-Scott and Bruce R. Scott, *Malaysia (A)*, Harvard Business School Case 792-101 (1992), pp. 3-8. Also see Barbara Andaya and Leonard Andaya, *A History of Malaysia* (London: Macmillan, 1982); and Ian Buruma, *God's Dust* (New York: Noonday, 1990), ch. 3.

[11] On the issue of these "Chinese" communities throughout Southeast Asia, see Benedict Anderson, "Introduction," *The Spectre of Comparisons: Nationalism, Southeast Asia, and the World* (London: Verso, 1998), pp. 12-16. Also see Charles Hirschman, "The Meaning and Measurement of Ethnicity in Malaysia," *Journal of Asian Studies*, vol. 46, no. 3 (1987): 555-582.

[12] In this case we occasionally use the word "race" to refer to the Malay, Chinese, and Indian groups in Malaysia because it is common practice, officially and unofficially, among Malaysians. In some other countries these groups might also be referred to as "ethnicities" or "ethnic groups." We do not attempt to distinguish between "race" and "ethnicity" as categories to designate differences among these communities.

[13] Ziauddin Sardar, *The Consumption of Kuala Lumpur* (London: Reaktion, 2000), p. 132.

[14] See Mohamed Noordin Sopiee, *From Malayan Union to Singapore Separation: Political Unification in the Malaysia Region, 1945-65* (Kuala Lumpur: University of Malaya Press, 1976).

[15] The official death toll is 196, the majority of whom were non-Malay. See *The May 13 Tragedy: A Report of the National Operations Council* (Kuala Lumpur, 1969). On the politics of the period, see especially Karl von Vorys, *Democracy without Consensus: Communalism and Political Stability in Malaysia* (Princeton, N.J.: Princeton University Press, 1975).

[16] Mahathir Mohamad, *The Malay Dilemma* (Singapore: Times Books International, 1970), p. 4.

[17] This quote, as well as those that follow, is from *The Second Malaysia Plan Document* (Kuala Lumpur, 1971), pp. 1-5. See also Bauer-Scott and Scott, *Malaysia (A)*, pp. 23-29; R. S. Milne, "The Politics of Malaysia's New Economic Policy," *Pacific Affairs*, vol. 49, no. 2 (1976): 235-262; and Edmund Terence Gomez and K. S. Jomo, *Malaysia's Political Economy: Politics, Patronage, and Profits*, 2nd ed. (Cambridge: Cambridge University Press, 1999), ch. 2.

[18] The plan initially targeted Malay ownership specifically. The government then broadened its restructuring goal to include the other indigenous groups of Malaysia, who, together with Malays, composed the *Bumiputera*. Diaan-Yi Lin, "Distribution and Development: Malaysia's New Economic Policy and After, 1971-2001," Individual Student Research Report, Harvard Business School, autumn 2001, p. 15.

[19] See Lin, "Distribution and Development," pp. 16-22. The ICA threshold was later raised to 75 employees. Also, as early as 1967 export-oriented companies were allowed 100% foreign equity ownership.

[20] On the ways in which Chinese businesspeople dealt with the constraints of the NEP, see James Jesudason, *Ethnicity and the Economy: The State, Chinese Business, and Multinationals in Malaysia* (Singapore: Oxford University Press, 1989).

[21] See Forest Reinhardt, *Malaysia in the 1990s (A)*, Harvard Business School Case 797-074 (1997), pp. 2-4.

[22] Gomez and Jomo, *Malaysia's Political Economy*, pp. 16-18. Also see David Lim, *Economic Growth and Development in West Malaysia* (Kuala Lumpur: Oxford University Press, 1973).

[23] R. S. Milne and Diane K. Mauzy, *Malaysian Politics Under Mahathir* (London: Routledge, 1999), pp. 56-59. Also see Gomez and Jomo, *Malaysia's Political Economy*, ch. 4.

[24] After the early 1970s, the banking system went through rapid expansion with major lending towards real estate and equities as the country enjoyed high growth rates. The Kuala Lumpur Stock Exchange Composite Index rose from 100 in 1977 to a peak of 427 in 1984. Between 1975 to 1983, rental prices of good quality residential and commercial property roughly

tripled. See Andrew Sheng, "Bank Restructuring in Malaysia, 1985-88," World Development Report Working Paper, September 1989, p. 8.

[25] Authors' interview with Dr. Zeti Akthar Aziz, Governor of Bank Negara Malaysia, Kuala Lumpur, October 8, 2001.

[26] Lin, "Distribution and Development," pp. 30-31.

[27] K. S. Jomo, "Whither Malaysia's New Economic Policy?" *Pacific Affairs*, vol. 63, no. 4 (1990-91): 469-499, at pp. 472-479.

[28] Government of Malaysia, *A Review of the First Outline Perspective Plan, 1971-1990* (Kuala Lumpur, 1990).

[29] Christopher Adam and William Cavendish, "Background," in *Privatizing Malaysia*, ed. K. S. Jomo (Boulder, Colo.: Westview, 1995).

[30] See Gomez and Jomo, *Malaysia's Political Economy*, ch. 5.

[31] Government of Malaysia, *Vision 2020* (Kuala Lumpur, 1991).

[32] A number of other government plans made the means to Mahathir's goals more specific. These included the 1991 National Development Policy, as well as the 10-year Second Outline Perspective Plan for 1991-2000 and the Sixth Malaysia Plan for 1991-95.

[33] See Prema-Chandra Athukorala, *Crisis and Recovery in Malaysia* (U.K.: Edward Elgar, 2001), p. 25.

[34] Initially, the government attempted to sterilize the inflows in order to prevent further appreciation of the exchange rate. However, sterilization operations proved to be both expensive – given the shortage of government paper and the need to issue Bank Negara Malaysia bills to conduct open market operations – and ineffective since they kept interest rates high. See Alora Ariyoshi Akira, Karl Habermeier, Bernard Laurens, Inci Otker-Robe, Jorge Ivan Canales-Kriljenko, and Andre Kirilenko, *Capital Controls: Country Experiences with Their Use and Liberalization*, IMF Occasional Paper No. 190, 2000, p. 95.

[35] IMF, *IMF Survey*, November 25, 1996.

[36] See Richard H. K. Vietor, *Asia's Financial Crisis*, Harvard Business School Case 798-081 (1999); Huw R. Pill and Donald H. Mathis, *Bahtulism, Collapse, or Resurrection? Financial Crisis in Asia, 1997-98*, Harvard Business School Case 798-089 (1998); and Joseph P. Gownder and Louis T. Wells, *Chronology of the Asian Financial Crisis*, Harvard Business School Case 799-145 (1999). Also see Morris Goldstein, *The Asian Financial Crisis: Causes, Cures, and Systemic Implications* (Washington, D.C.: Institute for International Economics, 1998); Gregory W. Noble and John Ravenhill, eds., *The Asian Financial Crisis and the Architecture of Global Finance* (Cambridge: Cambridge University Press, 2000); T. J. Pempel, ed., *The Politics of the Asian Economic Crisis* (Ithaca, N.Y.: Cornell University Press, 1999).

[37] See Yasheng Huang, *Korea: On the Back of the Tiger*, Harvard Business School Case 700-097 (2001).

[38] IMF, *World Economic Outlook* (Washington, D.C.: IMF, October 1997).

[39] IMF, *Annual Report of the Executive Board* (Washington, D.C.: IMF, 1998), p. 25.

[40] The Philippines' existing IMF-support program was extended and augmented in 1997.

[41] Stanley Fischer, "The Asian Crisis: A View from the IMF," Address to the Midwinter Conference of the Bankers' Association for Foreign Trade, Washington, D.C., January 22, 1998. See also "Fischer Presents IMF Perspective on Origins, Implications of Asian Crisis," *IMF Survey*, January 26, 1998.

[42] Radelet and Sachs, "The Onset of the East Asian Financial Crisis," p. 107. Also see Jeffrey Sachs, "The Wrong Medicine for Asia," *New York Times*, November 3, 1997.

[43] Athukorala, *Crisis and Recovery in Malaysia*, p. 118.

[44] Jomo, "Introduction," in *Malaysian Eclipse*, ed. Jomo, p. xxvii.

[45] James Kynge, "Malaysian PM sets up GBP 12bn fund to support market," *Financial Times*, September 4, 1997.

[46] "Mahathir tries to reassure foreigners," *Financial Times*, September 8, 1997.

[47] Quoted in John Riding and James Kynge, "Complacency Gives Way to Contagion," *Financial Times*, January 13, 1998.

[48] David Wessel and Darren McDermott, "Soros and Malaysia's Mahathir Cross Swords," *Wall Street Journal*, September 22, 1997.

[49] Raphael Pura, "Malaysia's Finance Chief Gains in Stature: Anwar Emerges from Economic Crisis as Voice of Reason," *Wall Street Journal*, September 22, 1997.

[50] Mahathir, *The Malaysian Currency Crisis*, p. 26.

[51] "The former Adviser of the central bank was summoned by the Prime Minister for a briefing." Mahathir, *The Malaysian Currency Crisis*, p. 32.

[52] Authors' interview with Nor Mohamed Yakcop, Special Advisor to the Prime Minister, Kuala Lumpur, October 11, 2001. The controls banned offshore trading in ringgit instruments among offshore banks operating in Malaysia and prevented Malaysian banks from offering domestic credit to non-residents. To prevent further offshore ringgit activities, conducted primarily in Singapore, the use of ringgit in foreign trade was banned and, effective September 30, all offshore ringgit deposits were no longer legal tender. A one-year ban on the repatriation of proceeds from foreign portfolio investment was designed to restrict currency outflows.

[53] Authors' interview with Dr. Mahathir Mohamad, Prime Minister of Malaysia, Kuala Lumpur, October 8, 2001.

[54] Mahathir, *The Malaysian Currency Crisis*, p. 36.

[55] See NEAC, *National Economic Recovery Plan: Agenda for Action* (Kuala Lumpur: Economic Planning Unit, Prime Minister's Department, August 1998).

[56] Authors' interview with Dr. Zeti Akhtar Aziz, Governor of Bank Negara Malaysia, Kuala Lumpur, October 8, 2001.

[57] See Akira et al., *Capital Controls*, p. 98.

[58] Authors' interview with Nor Mohamed Yakcop, Special Advisor to the Prime Minister, Kuala Lumpur, October 11, 2001.

[59] Bank Negara Malaysia, "Press Release: Measures to Regain Monetary Independence," September 1, 1998.

[60] "CLOBbered Investors," *Asian Wall Street Journal*, July 1, 1999.

[61] Authors' interview with Dr. Zeti Akhtar Aziz, Governor of Bank Negara Malaysia, Kuala Lumpur, October 8, 2001.

[62] Akira et al., *Capital Controls*, pp. 99-100.

[63] Akira et al., *Capital Controls*, p. 99.

[64] Authors' interview with Dr. Mahathir Mohamad, Prime Minister of Malaysia, Kuala Lumpur, October 8, 2001.

[65] Authors' interview with Nor Mohamed Yakcop, Special Advisor to the Prime Minister, Kuala Lumpur, October 11, 2001.

[66] "Malaysia's Self-Isolation," *Wall Street Journal*, September 3, 1998.

[67] Darren McDermott, Raphael Pura, and David Wessel, "Malaysian Currency Controls Roil Asia Markets – Billions of Dollars at Risk in Financial Contracts; Finance Minister Fired," *Wall Street Journal*, September 3, 1998.

[68] Sheila McNulty, "Finance Role Taken Over by Mahathir," *Financial Times*, September 8, 1998.

[69] For more on the relationship between Anwar and Mahathir, see Milne and Mauzy, *Malaysian Politics Under Mahathir*, ch. 7.

[70] "Anwar Dipecat Dari UMNO" (Anwar is Expelled from UMNO), *Utusan Malaysia*, September 4, 1998; "Konspirasi Pihak Atasan Jatuhkan Saya, Anwar" (Anwar: 'There is a Conspiracy at the Highest Level to End My Career'), *Utusan Malaysia*, September 4, 1998.

[71] Sheila McNulty, "The Doctor Orders Complete Rest," *Financial Times*, September 5, 1998; and "No Room for Rivals in Mahathir's Malaysia," *Economist*, September 26, 1998. See "Mengaku Diliwat Anwar – Sukma" (Two Men Admit Being Sodomized by Anwar), *Utusan Malaysia*, September 20, 1998. Both men were sentenced to six months in jail.

[72] "Punca Anwar Dipecat Bakti Perangai Tidak Bermoral Terlalu Kukah, PM" (PM: Anwar's Removal Due to His Low Morality), *Utusan Malaysia*, September 9, 1998.

[73] On the retracted affidavits and Anwar's allegations of abuse, see Amnesty International, "Malaysia: The Arrest of Anwar Ibrahim and His Political Associates," October 3, 1998.

[74] "The Verdict on Anwar," *Wall Street Journal*, August 9, 2000.

[75] Authors' interview with Hsiu-Yi Lin, V.P., e-Business Head, Cash Mgmt and Trade, Citibank Berhad, Kuala Lumpur, October 9, 2001.

[76] Authors' interview with Windsor Newton Hall, CEO, J. P. Morgan, Kuala Lumpur, October 10, 2001.

[77] Bank Negara Malaysia, "Press Release: Measures to Regain Monetary Independence," September 1, 1998.

[78] Authors' interview with Daim Zainuddin, Kuala Lumpur, October 10, 2001.

[79] The one-year stay period was replaced with an exit tax on February 1999. The policy was further revised on September 1999.

[80] Authors' interview with Nicholas S. Zeffreys, President of American Malaysian Chamber of Commerce, Kuala Lumpur, October 8, 2001.

[81] Authors' interview with Phillip Yates, Managing Director, 3M, Kuala Lumpur, October 10, 2001.

[82] For example, see "Dr. Mahathir's Noxious Remedies," *Economist*, September 26, 1998. See also Mark Clifford and Pete Engardio, "Renegade Economy," *Business Week*, September 21, 1998; Mark Landler, "Goodbye World! – Two Asian Economies Seek to Keep Global Markets at Bay," *New York Times*, September 12, 1998; Darren McDermott, Raphael Pura, and David Wessel, "Malaysian Currency Controls Roil Asia Markets – Billions of Dollars at Risk in Financial Contracts; Finance Minister Fired," *Wall Street Journal*, September 3, 1998.

[83] Darren McDermott and Leslie Lopez, "Malaysia Imposes Sweeping Currency Controls," *Wall Street Journal*, September 2, 1998.

[84] Peter Coy, Manjeet Kripalani, and Mark Clifford, "Capital Controls: Lifeline or Noose?" *Business Week*, September 28, 1998.

[85] Sheila McNulty and Edward Luce, "Kuala Lumpur Orders Increase in Lending," *Financial Times*, September 10, 1998.

[86] Quoted in Sheila McNulty and Edward Luce, "Kuala Lumpur Orders Increase in Lending," *Financial Times*, September 10, 1998. See also "Malaysia Rating," *The Independent*, September 10, 1998.

[87] Morgan Stanley Capital International, "Malaysia to be Removed from MSCI EAFE," Press Release, Geneva, September 4, 1998.

[88] Quoted in Nancy Dunne, "Summers in Financial Crisis Plea," *Financial Times*, September 10, 1998.

[89] Quoted in Nance Dunne, "Summers Sees IMF Policies Dealing with Global Crisis," *Financial Times*, October 23, 1998.

[90] Templeton Franklin Investment Services (Asia) Limited, Press Release, September 6, 1998.

[91] Authors' interview with Dr. Zeti Akhtar Aziz, Governor of Bank Negara Malaysia, Kuala Lumpur, October 8, 2001.

[92] Sheila McNulty, "Financial Crisis Reignited Old Tensions with Singapore: KL's Curbs on the Markets Hit at the Heart of the City-State," *Financial Times*, September 10, 1998. See also "Daylight Clobbery," *Economist*, July 10, 1999; "Still CLOBbered," *Asian Wall Street Journal*, December 16, 1999; and "Malaysia's Millennium Bug," *Wall Street Journal*, December 20, 1999. A comprehensive solution was announced in February 2000.

[93] See "Japan Sokong Kawalan Tukar Asing Malaysia" (Japan Defends Malaysia Capital Control Policy), *Utusan Malaysia*, October 6, 1998.

[94] Authors' interview with Nor Mohamed Yakcop, Special Advisor to the Prime Minister, Kuala Lumpur, October 11, 2001.

[95] Authors' interview with Nor Mohamed Yakcop, Special Advisor to the Prime Minister, Kuala Lumpur, October 11, 2001.

[96] Authors' interview with Dr. Zeti Akhtar Aziz, Governor of Bank Negara Malaysia, Kuala Lumpur, October 8, 2001. On the World Bank's delayed disbursement of the US$1 billion loan package, see "Ramai Kurang Jelas Kawalan Pertukaran" (Many Still Not Clear on Malaysia's Exchange Controls), *Utusan Malaysia*, October 24, 1998.

[97] "Kawalan Mata Wang Tidak Jejaskan Pelabur" (Currency Controls will not Impact Foreign Investors), *Utusan Malaysia*, September 16, 1998; and "Rafidah to Explain Malaysia's Latest Economic Measures," *Utusan Express*, September 28, 1998.

[98] Authors' interview with Daim Zainuddin, Kuala Lumpur, October 10, 2001. See also Athukorala, *Crisis and Recovery*, p. 100.

[99] When *Danaharta* acquired banks' non-performing loans, they were removed from banks' balance sheets.

[100] Jomo, "Capital Controls," p. 215. Also see Simon Johnson and Todd Mitton, "Cronyism and Capital Controls: Evidence from Malaysia," NBER Working Paper No. 8521, October 2001.

[101] Gomez and Jomo, *Malaysia's Political Economy*, pp. 193-194.

[102] Perkins and Woo, "Malaysia," pp. 238-239.

[103] Johnson and Mitton, "Cronyism and Capital Controls," p. 20.

[104] See, for example, Stanley Fischer, "Exchange Rate Regimes: Is the Bipolar View Correct?" *Journal of Economic Perspectives*, vol. 15, no. 2 (2001): 3-24, at p. 11.

[105] Authors' interview with Daniel Lian, Vice President, Morgan Stanley, Singapore, October 12, 2001.

[106] Authors' interview with Bernard Eschweiler, Managing Director, J.P. Morgan, Singapore, October 12, 2001.

[107] "CLOBbered Investors," *Asian Wall Street Journal*, July 1, 1999.

[108] Authors' interview with Jeanette Wong, Managing Director and Senior Country Officer, J.P. Morgan, Singapore, October 12, 2001.

[109] Authors' interview with Victor C. S. Liew, Executive Vice President, Treasury, Overseas Union Bank, Singapore, October 12, 2001.

[110] Authors' interview with Dr. Mahathir Mohamad, Prime Minister of Malaysia, Kuala Lumpur, October 8, 2001.

[111] Authors' interview with Dr. Mahathir Mohamad, Prime Minister of Malaysia, Kuala Lumpur, October 8, 2001.

[112] Authors' interview with Dr. Mahathir Mohamad, Prime Minister of Malaysia, Kuala Lumpur, October 8, 2001.

[113] Milne and Mauzy, *Malaysian Politics under Mahathir*, pp. 80-89.

[114] Authors' interview with Dr. Mahathir Mohamad, Prime Minister of Malaysia, Kuala Lumpur, October 8, 2001.

Capital Flows and Monetary Policy in Emerging Markets

HARVARD | BUSINESS | SCHOOL

9-704-028
REV: MAY 18, 2004

LAURA ALFARO
RAFAEL DI TELLA

Brazil 2003: Inflation Targeting and Debt Dynamics

The PT [Workers' Party] follows socialist ideology, and socialism is the final objective of the party.[1]

—Lula, 1989

I am going to call up the bankers and say: "Look, I recognize our debt, but, between paying interest to you guys and filling the bellies of the people, I am going to stick with the Brazilian people. As long as there are children dying of hunger in Brazil, I will not have the means to pay down the debt."[2]

—Lula, 1998

Brazil has changed. The union movement has changed. I have changed.[3]

—Lula, 2002

In October 2002, Brazilians elected a left-wing president, Luís Inácio "Lula" da Silva, for the first time in that country's history. Lula, who had emerged from humble origins to become a leader in the trade union movement and founder of the PT (*Partido dos Trabalhadores*, Workers' Party), was expected to herald a new era in Brazilian politics. In his 2002 presidential campaign, he promised to improve opportunities for the poor in one of the world's most unequal societies. Despite his radical past, during which he argued for socialism and the repudiation of Brazil's public debt, he promised to pursue social reform under the orthodox economic policy framework inherited from the administration of his centrist predecessor, President Fernando Henrique Cardoso.

But markets remained skeptical and worried that Lula had committed to Cardoso's framework of fiscal discipline, a floating exchange rate, and inflation targeting only to win the election. Amid growing uncertainty surrounding what radical changes the PT might in fact implement once in office, the stock market fell, the country risk premium increased, prices crept higher, and the currency weakened dramatically in the last months of 2002. Brazil's central bank was forced to respond by raising interest rates to their highest levels in more than three years.

Upon taking office in January 2003, Lula attempted to change market sentiment, embarking on an aggressive plan to generate a large primary fiscal surplus that would help ensure debt repayment and promote macroeconomic stability. He also implemented a popular "Zero Hunger" program and began work toward important pension, tax, and bankruptcy reforms.

By mid-2003, however, his attempt to change market sentiment was coming under threat as the country faced a looming recession. Skeptics began to worry that the new PT government would be forced to steer away from orthodox policies to meet its campaign promises. Furthermore, after Argentina's massive default on its public debt at the end of 2001, observers were questioning the

---

Professors Laura Alfaro and Rafael Di Tella and Research Associate Ingrid Vogel prepared this case. Andrea Fernandez (MBA '04) provided some helpful assistance. This case was developed from published sources. HBS cases are developed solely as the basis for class discussion. Cases are not intended to serve as endorsements, sources of primary data, or illustrations of effective or ineffective management.

sustainability of Brazil's debt situation. Lula was under intense pressure to deliver results immediately and implement measures that would help spur the economy.

Lula's vice president, José Alencar, pointed to the interest rate as one such measure. He argued that the high rates imposed by the Central Bank of Brazil under the inflation-targeting framework placed the country at a competitive disadvantage and stymied growth:

> Interest rates should be reduced in a more consistent way since we are now starting to experience deflation. When the government first took office, yes, there was a risk of inflation rekindling, but now the situation has changed. The country needs to return to a path of growth so that the current economic environment isn't further aggravated. We already have lost two decades, and this should not be allowed to happen again.[4]

Despite Lula's emphasizing his commitment to the autonomy of Brazil's central bank in setting the interest rate, critics were demanding a rate reduction at the bank's monthly meeting, which was due to take place on August 20. But the central bank had stated it would loosen monetary policy only gradually, as it feared that abrupt moves could bring back inflationary pressures in the short term and compromise sustainable growth in the medium term. It also needed to maintain its credibility as focused on fighting inflation.

In mid-August 2003, all eyes were on Brazil: Would the central bank reduce its benchmark interest rate (the Selic)[a] amid signs that inflation had been contained around 15% and the exchange rate stabilized? And by enough to ease Brazil's growing debt burden? Or would it remain cautious and seek to reaffirm its independence by choosing to maintain the rate at a high 24.5%?

Brazil Before Inflation Targeting[5]

As the world's eighth-largest economy in terms of purchasing-power parity and fifth-largest country in terms of both population and land area, Brazil was considered to have enormous potential for becoming an important world economic power. But the country seemed to have problems in fulfilling that potential. For almost 40 years, Brazil had followed an import-substitution strategy characterized by massive government investment targeting key industries and protection against international competition through high tariff and nontariff barriers. For decades, the strategy appeared to be successful: Brazil grew by 7% per year between 1950 and 1980 (from 1964 under repressive military rule) and created a large and diversified industrial sector. It also, however, left the country with the largest external debt in the developing world and a tendency for high inflation. When oil prices shot up in 1979 and interest rates rose in response, the Brazilian economy crumbled. In 1981, gross domestic product (GDP) fell by more than 4% while fiscal deficits increased, inflation skyrocketed, and public and private investment fell. Along with most of Latin America, Brazil defaulted on its debt in 1982.[b] In 1985, the military regime finally lost its hold.

With the return of democracy, hopes for Brazil rose anew. But a series of stabilization programs that aimed to solve the problem of triple-digit inflation all failed, and the 1980s became known as the "lost decade." Finally, in 1993, Finance Minister Fernando Henrique Cardoso announced the Real Plan. This new stabilization plan introduced the *real* as Brazil's currency, which was tied to the dollar through a crawling peg. Inflation dropped dramatically, from 50% per month in mid-1994 to

[a] The Selic interest rate is the interest rate for overnight interbank loans collateralized by government bonds registered with and traded on the *Sistema Especial de Liquidação e Custódia.*

[b] Although Brazil did not repudiate its debt, it stopped paying interest.

approximately 2% per month by the end of 1994. On the basis of this success, Cardoso easily won the presidential elections in 1994.

Upon taking office, Cardoso introduced a development model based on opening Brazil's closed economy through privatization, deregulation, trade liberalization, and encouragement of foreign direct investment (FDI). A period of price stability and economic growth followed but was accompanied by underlying problems. The appreciation of the real led to increasing current account deficits. Furthermore, nonfinancial primary fiscal deficits persisted from 1995–1999 after failed attempts by the government to reform the tax system and introduce public spending reductions, particularly on wages and pensions. The external imbalance and fiscal deficits were partly financed by FDI, medium- and long-term debt in the international bond market, and substantial inflows of short-term portfolio capital attracted by high interest rates. As a result, Brazil's net-public-debt-to-GDP ratio increased from 30% at the start of 1995 to 42% at the start of 1999. (See **Exhibits 1–4** for basic macroeconomic data.)

Brazil had again become vulnerable to volatility in global capital markets. The Asian crisis in mid-1997 led to a first wave of speculative attacks against the real. In response, the central bank sharply increased interest rates. The Russian crisis in mid-1998 put further pressure on Brazil's crawling peg and led to a halt in capital flows to the country. The central bank was forced to raise rates even higher. In October 1998, Cardoso was reelected for a second term on the basis of promises to continue to defend the currency. Toward this end, he secured a $42 billion assistance package from the International Monetary Fund (IMF). In December 1998, however, the government failed to gain sufficient congressional support for IMF austerity measures, and investors began to lose confidence in the country. In early January 1999, full-scale capital flight ensued—with speculative capital fleeing the country at a rate of $200 million per day—after the state of Minais Gerais defaulted on debt payments. After a second state declared it would also default, capital flight peaked at $1 billion in one day, and Brazil could no longer defend its currency. On January 12, the central bank, hoping to implement a managed float, devalued the real by 8%. Three days later, the central bank was forced to float the currency fully.

In early March 1999, the real plummeted to 2.16 to the dollar, from 1.21 in early January (see **Exhibit 5**). Financial analysts were predicting deterioration of all macroeconomic fundamentals, including inflation's escalating to annual rates of 30% to 80% and negative GDP growth of –3% to –6%.[6] In response, in March 1999, Brazil's central bank announced that its goal was to bring inflation down to a single-digit annualized rate by the last quarter of 1999 (see **Exhibit 6**). To this end, it raised the basic short-term interest rate (the Selic) from 39% to 45% (see **Exhibit 7**). On July 1, the central bank formally adopted a new strategy: a full-fledged inflation-targeting framework behind a floating currency.

Inflation Targeting Worldwide

Inflation targeting was introduced in the 1990s—initially in industrial countries and later in emerging-market economies—with the objective of keeping inflation close to a long-run low level. During this period, there was a strengthening belief among economists and central bankers that low inflation helped to promote economic efficiency and growth in the long run.[7] New Zealand was first, in 1990, to formally introduce a clear and credible commitment to a specific inflation target. The country had a poor economic track record relative to other Organization for Economic Cooperation and Development (OECD) members, with a decade of inflation rates at the upper end of the OECD range (in excess of 10%) combined with growth rates at the bottom of the range. After a foreign exchange crisis forced New Zealand to break its peg to the U.S. dollar in 1985, the government asked the central bank to focus strictly on maintaining low inflation rather than a mix of objectives including low inflation, high employment, and growth. After five years, a formalized inflation-targeting framework was officially introduced.[8] Other countries followed with their own systems: Canada in 1991, the United Kingdom in 1992, Sweden in 1993, and Australia later in 1993. By 2003, 20 countries in total were classified as having adopted full-fledged inflation-targeting frameworks (see **Exhibit 11**),[9] while the central banks of more than 40 countries had the explicit aim of achieving low and stable inflation.

Alternatives to Inflation Targeting

Inflation targeting was only one of a number of monetary regimes on which central banks could base their policy decisions. Some economists argued that central banks should target the growth rate of nominal GDP. It was argued, though, that this approach suffered from weaknesses when compared to inflation targeting: price information was more frequently published, more timely, and more accurately reported than output information; inflation targeting was more capable of delivering short-term stability; the concept of inflation was more easily understood by the public than nominal GDP (which could be confused with real GDP); and a nominal GDP target would be subject to more political contention.[10]

Alternatively, some economists were in favor of a "just do it" approach of monetary policy without explicit targets. The United States appeared to have experienced success under a strategy of responding to signs of future inflation with "preemptive strikes," without any strict or announced inflation target.[11] U.S. monetary policy makers would officially deny that they targeted indicators other than inflation. However, critics cited the Federal Reserve Bank's announcement after the 1987 stock market crash that it would increase liquidity as evidence that it was using the stock market as a target.

More common than GDP targeting or a "just do it" approach were strategies aiming to control the evolution of the price level. Economists described that in doing so, central banks essentially had three options: the adoption of an exchange rate anchor, a monetary anchor, or an inflation-targeting framework.[12] With an exchange rate target, countries relied on a peg to a stable currency to control inflation. The target had the advantage of being simple to implement and monitor, and something over which the central bank had direct control. At the most extreme, countries could implement a currency board[a] or directly adopt the stable currency as its own, such as through dollarization. As such, monetary policy would be relinquished completely. Maintaining a fixed exchange rate constrained the central bank's ability to respond to shocks and (not relevant in the case of dollarization) was difficult under the growing and unstable cross-border movement of capital.[13]

Targeting a monetary aggregate became popular in the 1970s after most industrial countries adopted flexible exchange rate regimes. Under this approach, the central bank sought to control inflation by aiming for particular rates of monetary growth that could be expected to deliver desired rates of inflation. In contrast to exchange rate targeting, monetary targeting allowed central bankers to adjust monetary policy to domestic conditions. After continued failure to meet targets and persistent instability in the relationship between monetary growth and inflation, however, monetary targets began to be replaced by inflation targeting.[14]

[a] Under a currency board, a central bank had to convert currency on demand at a fixed exchange rate, and money supply was restricted to the level of hard-currency reserves. For more details, see "Argentina's Convertibility Plan," HBS Case No. 702-002.

Inflation Targeting Defined

Full-fledged inflation-targeting frameworks included a number of important components. First, countries made an explicit institutional commitment to meet a specified numerical inflation rate target or target range within a specified time frame. This became the primary goal of monetary policy, to which other goals were subordinated. Second, monetary-policy strategy was made transparent through communication with the public and the markets about the plans, objectives, and decisions of the monetary authorities. Third, countries publicly announced their targets on a regular basis. As such, the targets provided an anchor for private market expectations as well as for monetary authorities. Fourth, countries had institutional arrangements in place to ensure that the central bank would be held accountable for reaching specified targets. In New Zealand, for example, the finance minister retained the right to dismiss the central bank governor in the case of missed targets.[15]

Since inflation targeting required credibility in pursuit of inflation objectives, most countries granted operational independence to their central banks. Although in many cases the government was responsible for setting the target, the central bank was free to pursue the target independently.

Central banks had to develop models to predict the effects of given actions (e.g., changes to interest rates) on inflation. Inflation forecasts were assumed to have a *predictable* relationship with inflation; were *controllable* in that monetary authority instruments were capable of affecting projected inflation outcomes; and were a *lead indicator* of future inflation since they were explicitly forward looking.[16] An important feature of inflation targeting was that monetary authorities were required to consider inflation in subsequent periods in addition to in the immediate period. Monetary authorities could conceivably affect inflation in the immediate period through measures, such as appreciating the exchange rate, that were unsustainable. Given longer-term inflation targets, however, monetary authorities would be deterred from implementing them. This was particularly relevant given the long lags (up to two years in some cases) in the effect of monetary policy on the price level.[17]

For the most part, reviews of inflation targeting were positive. Many economists argued that countries adopting inflation targeting experienced low and stable inflation rates without inordinately sacrificing economic growth or destabilizing their economies.[18] Ben Bernanke, a governor of the U.S. Federal Reserve Board, stated: "Central banks that have switched to inflation targeting have generally been pleased with the results they have obtained. The strongest evidence on that score is that, thus far at least, none of the several dozen adopters of inflation targeting has abandoned the approach."[19] Other economists pointed out that the positive performance of countries adopting inflation targeting could be explained by external factors, such as an overall low inflationary international environment over the period.[20] These economists conceded, however, that inflation targeting appeared to do no harm and even possibly had other benefits, such as promoting more open and transparent policymaking. As Bernanke stated, inflation targeting made "the role of the Central Bank more consistent with the principles of a democratic society."[21]

Challenges in Emerging-Market Economies

Many economists noted that emerging-market economies faced special challenges in implementing inflation-targeting frameworks. Fundamental issues included a tendency toward fiscal indiscipline, high rates of dollarization, credibility problems, and vulnerability to external shocks.

Inflation targeting required fiscal discipline—a feature considered lacking in general in many emerging-market economies. If fiscal deficits were to become too large, countries might be forced to borrow heavily and erode existing debt through price increases.[22] Even just the possibility that such a scenario could occur in the future served to increase expected inflation in the present. Hence, in order to keep inflation at a long-run low level, it was a prerequisite that governments incorporated fiscal discipline into their primary objectives.[23]

A high degree of liability dollarization (with obligations of banks, corporations, and governments denominated in dollars while revenues were largely denominated in local currency) was also pointed out as a problem.[24] The exchange rate flexibility required by inflation targeting could cause financial instability by allowing large and sudden currency depreciations to increase the burden of dollar-denominated debt dramatically. Emerging-market economies could not, therefore, afford to ignore the exchange rate completely when conducting monetary policy. As such, however, those countries operating under an inflation-targeting framework ran the risk of transforming the exchange rate into the nominal anchor for monetary policy, even if only in the eyes of the public. This was especially true since in countries with poor histories of monetary stability, the exchange rate tended to be a focal point for inflationary expectations.[25]

Emerging-market economies were also seen to suffer from weak institutions and low credibility—in their financial systems as well as both fiscal and monetary policymaking. As elaborated by Brazil's former central bank governor, Arminio Fraga:

> Institutions in emerging economies tend to be weaker than in developed economies. Central banks are no exception. In this context, the adoption of inflation targeting represents an effort to enhance the credibility of the monetary authority as committed to price stability. . . . Given the history of low credibility, private agents assign some positive probability that the central bank will renege on its commitment to the targets. As a result, the expected inflation and consequently the actual inflation tend to be higher than with a perfectly credible monetary authority.[26]

Because of credibility problems, emerging-market economies tended to adopt more formal frameworks for inflation targeting, and their central banks were reluctant to miss inflation targets even temporarily for fear of undermining anti-inflationary credibility. One economist pointed out that inflation targeting was designed to introduce some flexibility into monetary policymaking (e.g., in comparison to fixed exchange rates) but that "credibility problems will force precisely those emerging markets where a flexible approach to inflation targeting is most valuable to adopt a relatively rigid version."[27]

The vulnerability of emerging-market economies to large external shocks led to high volatility of the exchange rate and contributed to the problems associated with high degrees of dollarization. It also made inflation forecasting more difficult, thereby compounding credibility problems.[28] First, commodity items comprised a large proportion of the consumer price inflation basket of lower-income countries. With very high price volatility and reliance on the external environment, commodity items could, in the words of one economist, "wreak havoc with the forecastability of consumer price inflation."[29] Second, domestic financial conditions of emerging-market economies were highly sensitive to international capital flows. So-called sudden stops in capital flows to emerging-market economies could easily destabilize these economies, resulting in high inflation.[30]

Many economists argued that higher volatility of inflation results in emerging-market economies, combined with the intrinsic limits of forecasting models, justified the use of bands around inflation targets and a clear process to adjust targets. Fraga outlined the credibility trade-off: "The target is adjusted in order to take into account primary effects of change in relative prices and of past inertia that will be accommodated. The new target is publicly announced. Although there is a credibility loss stemming from the target change itself, the gains in terms of transparency and communication are more significant."[31]

Brazil's Inflation-Targeting Framework

Unlike the gradualist approaches of its inflation-targeting Latin American neighbors, Brazil developed the technical and institutional infrastructure required for its full-fledged inflation-targeting regime in just four months. Under this "big bang" approach, targets were set immediately at single-digit levels.[32] Specifically, on July 1, 1999, Brazil formally adopted the new monetary policy framework and set year-end inflation targets (based on the IPCA Broad Consumer Price Index) for the current and following two years at 8% for 1999, 6% for 2000, and 4% for 2001, with a tolerance interval of ± 2%.

Transparency and accountability were important parts of the framework. The central bank's Monetary Policy Committee (Copom) met at regular monthly intervals to set interest rates and announced decisions immediately. It published the minutes of its monthly meetings and a quarterly inflation report that provided detailed information on economic conditions. In the case of breached targets, the central bank governor was required to issue an open letter addressed to the minister of finance explaining the underlying causes and planned corrective measures.[33]

The central bank built models of the transmission mechanism of monetary policy to prices. Given the problems associated with exchange rate volatility, the central bank intervened in exchange rate markets when necessary. It did so as transparently as possible in order to avoid losses in credibility of the central bank's commitment to inflation targeting. Accordingly, the central bank defined the most important transmission channels to inflation as working through aggregate demand (total spending in the economy) and the exchange rate. Permanent changes in the Selic were estimated to take between one and two quarters to impact aggregate demand, which, in turn, took an additional quarter to be perceived in consumer price inflation. The exchange rate channel was estimated to have a shorter transmission lag lasting just one quarter. The pass-through to the overall inflation index of currency depreciation was estimated to be smaller than the pass-through of aggregate demand.[34] (See **Exhibit 15** for a diagram of the transmission mechanism.)

Brazil's Initial Performance under the Framework

Brazil's economy, for the most part, performed well under the inflation-targeting framework in its initial years. The central bank met its inflation targets of 8% in 1999 and 6% in 2000, with actual inflation registering 8.9% and 6.0%, respectively. At the same time, the economy grew by 0.8% in 1999 (an improvement over analyst expectations of negative growth) and by 4.3% in 2000. Growth was prompted by numerous factors: the Selic had fallen from a peak of 45% in March 1999 to 19% by the end of 1999 and to 15.75% by the end of 2000; confidence in Brazil improved, reflected by a fall in the country risk premium from 15% in January 1999 to around 7.5% at the end of 1999 and in 2000 (see **Exhibit 8**); and the currency stayed relatively steady, fluctuating between 1.7 and 2.0 reais to the dollar throughout both years. In support of the inflation-targeting framework, the country succeeded in generating a primary fiscal surplus of 3.1% in 1999. On the negative side, real wages fell by 5% in 1999 and by 1% in 2000, and unemployment officially stood at a relatively high 14% (unofficial estimates were much higher). In addition, Brazilian companies with large dollar debts became worried that under the new framework the central bank would no longer target the exchange rate, in particular since at its weakest it had depreciated more than 80% against the dollar.

Brazil's economic success faltered in 2001. That year, the country experienced economic growth of only 1.4% and missed its inflation target of 4%, with inflation registering 7.7%. In its formal open letter of explanation to the finance minister, the central bank cited contagion from Argentina's economic crisis. The central bank argued that the loss of confidence that Argentina's impending default brought to the Latin American region as a whole, combined with a deceleration in the world economy and the 9/11 terrorist attack on the United States, led to a significant depreciation of the real,[35] which peaked at 2.78 to the dollar (representing an accumulated depreciation over the year of 43%) in mid-October before falling back to 2.32 by the end of the year. The central bank continued to anticipate a downward trend in inflation, however, concluding that "shocks are not expected to reoccur with the same magnitude."[36]

Electoral Uncertainty

The central bank was wrong: An even bigger shock hit the Brazilian economy in 2002. After a relatively mild first half of the year, uncertainties regarding the presidential elections of October 2002 brought turmoil to the economy in the second half. As PT (Workers' Party) candidate Luís Inácio "Lula" da Silva began to lead against his center-right government-backed opponent in the electoral polls, markets reacted with skepticism. Brazilian bonds were downgraded, and the country risk premium climbed to above 20%. Meanwhile, the currency was approaching 4 reais to the dollar—representing a loss in value exceeding two-thirds since the beginning of the year. As the private sector holding dollar debt was collapsing, the government was forced to impose emergency economic measures, including lowering reserve requirements, tapping into a line of credit with the IMF, and buying back $3 billion of foreign debt.

Multibillionaire investor George Soros, who was heavily invested in Brazil, warned that a victory by Lula would "unleash chaos," including market expectations of default on Brazil's $260 billion in public debt.[37] He argued that because of this, Lula was sure to lose the presidential race. In Brazil's leading financial newspaper, *Folha de São Paulo,* Soros commented: "In ancient Rome, only the Romans voted. In modern global capitalism, only U.S. financial agents vote, not Brazilians." As Wall Street appeared to band together in support of the government-backed candidate, Lula accused international speculators of committing "economic terrorism" against his campaign.[38]

Luís Inácio "Lula" da Silva

Lula spent most of his adult life labeled as a revolutionary and radical militant committed to reversing Brazil's enormously unequal society, in which the poorest 50% of the population accounted for only 10% of national income, through anticapitalist methods. He appeared to have a personal rather than simply an ideological commitment to reducing inequality in the country. (See **Exhibit 12** for comparative data on social indicators.)

Unlike other Brazilian politicians, most of whom were a part of the Brazilian "elite," Lula grew up in extreme poverty. He was the seventh of eight children, born in 1945 to farm workers in the arid and impoverished northeastern Brazilian state of Pernambuco. When Lula was seven years old, his family migrated to the state of São Paulo, where Lula worked as a street vendor, shoeshine, and delivery boy. After finishing elementary school at the age of 12, Lula embarked on a two-year technical degree as a machine operator. Upon graduation, he obtained a permanent job at a metalworks where, four years later, he lost a finger in a workplace accident.[39]

While the factory was Lula's opening to politics, an older brother was the impetus. Lula refused to follow his brother's lead in becoming a member of the then-banned Communist Party but eventually agreed to his suggestions to become active in the metalworkers union in the automaking hub of São Bernardo do Campo, outside São Paulo. In 1972, he was elected first secretary of the syndicate. In 1975, after demonstrating superior negotiating and leadership skills and a pragmatic approach to obtaining jobs and benefits, he was elected its president with 98% of the vote. Under his direction, the union held a huge wave of strikes that, with participation in excess of 100,000 workers, solidified the labor movement and challenged Brazil's military dictatorship. In 1980, the military regime imprisoned him for 31 days. Later that year, with the government's easing of political restrictions, Lula founded the leftist *Partido dos Trabalhadores* (PT, Workers' Party). These struggles for democracy endeared him to the liberal and intellectual elite.[40]

Previous Elections

In 1982, in the first elections allowed by the military dictatorship, Lula finished fourth in the race for governor of São Paulo. In 1986, he was elected to the legislature, where he was argued to be ineffectual because of his insistence on pursuing extremist positions.[41] In 1989, Lula ran for president for the first time. He surprised the world when he came close to winning—garnering 47% of the vote in the runoff election—despite his persona as an extremist revolutionary and rumors generating a "red scare" with the specter of government confiscation and reallocation of private property.

In 1994 and 1998, Lula ran for president again, both times against Fernando Henrique Cardoso. In 1994, he mistakenly campaigned on anticipated failure of the Real Plan and won only 27% of the vote. In 1998, he did only marginally better, with 31% of the vote. It was argued that the threat of intensified economic crisis had deterred voters from the leftist candidate promising to default on the public debt and undo free-market reform.

Most analysts believed his third failed challenge for the presidency in October 1998 would be his last, but Lula was selected as the PT's candidate once more in 2002. Although he struggled to appeal to centrist voters, the economic crisis and political scandals involving the ruling party boosted the PT's appeal as a protest vote for those disillusioned with the austerity measures of the Cardoso government. Perhaps most importantly, Lula gave up his radical rhetoric for a campaign message of "peace and love" in an attempt to appeal to the center ground and the international community.[42]

Lula Wins the Election

Lula's change of tack proved successful. In the October 6, 2002 election, he won 47% of the vote, more than any other candidate but just shy of the 50% plus one vote required for an outright win. The runoff, against government-backed candidate José Serra, was scheduled for October 27. Markets remained unconvinced by his apparent transformation to capitalism and reacted poorly to the continued uncertainty surrounding the election. Specifically, investors feared that Lula cared little about corporate profits and could lead the country to default on its foreign debt. In mid-October, the real climbed to 3.96, just shy of the psychological barrier of 4 reais per dollar, prompting the Central Bank of Brazil to call an extraordinary meeting of the Copom. In an effort to halt a further plunge of the currency and rein in inflation, the Copom raised the Selic overnight rate from 18% to 21%—its highest rate and steepest increase in more than three years. Brazilian stocks fell 4.6% in response. In addition, the country risk premium climbed to almost 23% and foreign investment slowed.

Serra made a televised statement attacking Lula for what he said were contradictory pledges of change to common people and continuity to businesses: "If Lula is elected, we will be facing two possibilities. If he fulfills the recently assumed commitments to businessmen, it will be the biggest election fraud. And, if he tries to fulfill his 'magical' promises to the population, it will be the ruin of Brazil."[43]

Despite such dire warnings, Lula received a decisive 61% of the vote in the runoff election and was set to assume the presidency on January 1, 2003. Lula reaffirmed his willingness to stand by market-friendly policies: He voiced commitment to fiscal discipline, pledged that Brazil would honor its obligations to international lenders, and appointed a credible economic team. Lula chose highly regarded Antonio Palocci Filho, a former physician and moderate PT mayor known for his caution and pragmatism, to become finance minister. Henrique Meirelles, an experienced commercial banker, was selected to replace popular central bank president Arminio Fraga. Despite Lula's previous promise that he would not appoint a "mini-Fraga," Meirelles was expected to retain many of the advisers of his predecessor. Markets calmed somewhat, and the real gained strength against the dollar in response.

But skepticism persisted in the last few months of 2002 amid continued mixed signals from the future president. Some observers were uneasy about Lula's close relationships with Cuba's Fidel Castro and Venezuela's President Hugo Chavez.[44] They also questioned how Lula would fulfill his campaign promises to double the minimum wage, create jobs, improve health care, and carry out land reform. Some worried that he would be forced to resort to unorthodox economic policies, such as defaulting on the external debt or printing money and thereby rekindling runaway inflation. As a result, the central bank raised the Selic twice more at its regularly scheduled meetings in 2002, to 22% in November and to 25% in December.

Debt Dynamics

Lula inherited a weakly performing economy. As in 2001, Brazil missed its 2002 inflation target, this time with an actual rate of 12.5% versus its target of 3.5%. (See **Exhibit 13** for an inflation components breakdown and **Exhibit 10** for data on money growth.) As a result, the 2003 inflation target was raised to 8.5% (from 4%) and the 2004 target to 5.5% (from 3.75%).[45] GDP growth was only 1.5%. Official unemployment remained high at 12% in 2002 (unofficial numbers were much higher). Furthermore, the net-public-debt-to-GDP ratio had increased from 42% at the beginning of 1999 to 57% at the end of 2002.

In the aftermath of Argentina's massive default in early 2002, many observers were questioning the sustainability of Brazil's growing public debt. In order for the debt-to-GDP ratio to remain stable or decrease, the primary surplus plus increases in GDP needed to be large enough to cover interest payments on the debt and any hidden liabilities. Depending on assumptions about inflation, interest rates, the exchange rate, the primary surplus, GDP growth, hidden liabilities, and how much should be netted from gross debt, some economists predicted Brazil would be forced into a massive debt restructuring while others predicted a healthy, consistently declining net-public-debt-to-GDP ratio.[46]

Since approximately 48% (425 billion reais) of Brazil's net debt of 881 billion reais was linked to the Selic at the end of 2002, central bank decisions surrounding the interest rate had a significant impact on Brazil's debt burden. With another 42% (373 billion reais) of the net debt linked to foreign currencies, a fall in the real also served to increase the debt-to-GDP ratio dramatically. The Central Bank of Brazil estimated that the exchange rate depreciation of 52.3% against the dollar in 2002 led to a 148 billion real increase in the debt.[47] (See **Exhibit 14** for more details about and data on debt dynamics.)

Lula Initiates Change

In an effort to improve Brazil's economic situation, Lula's government implemented a number of measures. Palocci raised Brazil's primary fiscal surplus target from 3.75% of GDP, as agreed on with the IMF, to 4.25%. At the same time, the government was working toward congressional approval of four important and sensitive reform packages.

The government's first- and highest-priority reform package involved the public pension system, thought to be among the most generous in the world, which was estimated to be running a deficit of more than 4% of GDP while benefiting only 2.5 million people. Previous governments had attempted such reform in the past, but to no avail—largely because of resistance from the PT itself. The second priority was a planned tax reform. The reform would aim to make Brazil's tax system easier to administer and would promote social justice through making some taxes progressive. Third, the government wanted to rewrite bankruptcy laws in favor of creditors—such as through making collateral easier and quicker to recover—in order to enable banks to lend at lower rates and expand credit. Banks would benefit from provisions clarifying bankruptcy proceedings, while distressed companies would find it easier to emerge intact from bankruptcy under the proposed laws.

The government's fourth legislative priority centered on granting the nominally autonomous central bank full independence to set short-term interest rates and pursue its inflation-targeting objectives. Proponents argued that granting the central bank formal independence would strengthen Brazil's institutional framework and boost market confidence. Under proposed legislation, the central bank president and directors would have fixed terms that did not coincide with changes in government. In addition, the central bank would no longer report to the finance ministry.[48]

Confronting an Incipient Recession

Lula's approval ratings soared with his early success in establishing credibility and working toward major reform. Between January 2003 and July 2003, polls showed that between 74% and 84% of Brazilians approved of his "personal performance."[49] In July 2003, the country risk premium fell to an average 775 basis points from a high of 2,300 during the election period. Despite dour predictions prior to the election, Brazil avoided large-scale capital flight. By mid-August 2003, with the exchange rate having appreciated significantly over the year while inflation remained high, it appeared that Brazil's debt situation would show improvement in the short term. In addition, the government hoped to raise 1.7 billion reais in 2004 from the proposed changes to public pensions, enough to cover the cost of Lula's Zero Hunger antipoverty program. Recognizing that nearly a quarter of the population lived on less than half the minimum wage of $80 a month and 15% lacked enough money for proper nutrition, Lula also began work on other antipoverty and redistributional initiatives. He planned to coordinate several dozen programs that transferred money to the poor in an effort to improve their reach and efficiency. Under the reorganization, local groups were to be given a more significant role in identifying beneficiaries and monitoring the programs.

Many critics, however, complained that Lula failed to do enough for the poor. Specifically, they claimed that the Zero Hunger program was ineffectual and simply a public relations tool. Furthermore, the latest GDP growth numbers threatened to halt the momentum behind Lula's reform campaign; the economy was anticipated to retract for a second consecutive quarter. (See **Exhibit 9** for industrial production data.) With recession looming, observers worried that Lula's popularity would erode and with it the political strength required to sustain austerity and push reforms through a reluctant Congress. It was feared that representatives of various vested interests might seize the opportunity to challenge free-market reforms introduced by former President Cardoso. Some state governors (who often had significant influence in the capital) were already starting to press for a relaxation of the fiscal-responsibility law, which had put an end to the spending excesses of local government.

The Decision

The central bank was under increasing pressure to respond to Brazil's slowed growth at its regularly scheduled August meeting by lowering the Selic overnight rate. The central bank had been forced to increase the rate to 25.5% in January 2003 and 26.5% in February 2003 in the face of mounting inflation. Although the rate was then reduced to 26% in June and 24.5% in July, many critics, including PL Vice President José Alencar, complained that the rate was too high and put Brazil at a competitive disadvantage vis-à-vis its neighbors. Consistent with Alencar's position, some observers praised Brazil for responding to shocks in the past by increasing its inflation targets. Referring to a past episode, one economist wrote:

> The procedure followed by the Banco Central do Brasil has several very important advantages and is a textbook case for central bank response to shocks. First, the procedure has tremendous transparency. . . . Second, the central bank recognized that not adjusting the inflation target was just not credible because the market and the public clearly recognized that inflation would overshoot the initial target. Thus adjusting the target was absolutely necessary to retain credibility for the central bank, because to do otherwise would have just signaled to the markets that the central bank was unwilling to be transparent. Third, by discussing alternative paths for the inflation rate and why the particular path using the adjusted target was chosen, the central bank is able to demonstrate that it is not . . . an "inflation nutter" who only cares about controlling inflation and not about output fluctuations. By its procedure of outlining that lower inflation paths would lead to large output losses, the Banco Central do Brasil demonstrated that it is not out of touch with the concerns of the public because it indeed does care about output losses, just as the public and the politicians do.[50]

Some market participants, aware that Lula retained the power to withdraw support for the central bank president or even fire him, were demanding that the government intervene to assure lower rates. Lula, however, stood firm in his conviction that the central bank should remain independent. He continued to defend central bank president Meirelles, as he had when Vice President Alencar attacked him for failing to reduce rates in May.

In fact, inflation targeting itself was being lambasted. Critics complained that it did not work in an economy vulnerable to buffeting from the outside world. Others thought that the targets were too ambitious and the central bank too rigid in trying to meet them. They also pointed out that a long time lag existed between monetary policy and its effect on prices. Still other critics of inflation targeting contended that since inflation was not directly under the control of the central bank, it was not a sensible target. Furthermore, they argued that in emerging-market economies, there was always going to be a tendency to look at and respond to changes in the exchange rate, regardless of any inflation-targeting commitment.

The central bank faced a challenging decision. Most indications showed that inflation had been contained and the exchange rate stabilized. Furthermore, Brazil required lower rates to be able to continue to pay down its debt. But the Copom had an aggressive inflation target to meet, and a third consecutive year of missed targets could seriously threaten the credibility of the institution. It also needed to make its independence in decision making clear, particularly as high-ranking government officials were so publicly critical.

Exhibit 1 Brazil General Economic Indicators

% change pa	1990	1991	1992	1993	1994	1995	1996	1997	1998	1999	2000	2001	2002
Real GDP Growth	n.a.	1.1	-0.6	4.9	5.8	4.2	2.7	3.3	0.2		4.3	1.4	1.5
Real Per Capita GDP Growth	n.a.	-0.5	-2.1	3.3	4.3	2.8	1.3	2.0	-1.0	-0.3	3.3	0.4	0.6
Consumer Price Inflation	1,621.0	433.3	1,112.5	2,477.3	916.5	22.4	9.6	5.2	1.7	8.9	6.0	7.7	12.5
Stock Market Index ($ value)	n.a.	n.a.	n.a.	n.a.	-83.7	-14.1	53.3	34.9	-38.6	70.2	-18.3	-25.0	-45.5
Average Real Wage Increase	n.a.	n.a.	n.a.	n.a.	5.8	10.3	7.4	2.1	-0.4	-5.4	-0.5	-8.2	-2.2
M1 Growth	n.a.	400.0	960.0	2,000.0	2,194.7	25.7	29.9	22.4	7.5	13.6	18.9	12.8	28.3
units as shown													
Nominal Exchange Rate (reais per dollar, end-period)	n.a.	n.a.	n.a.	n.a.	0.8	1.0	1.0	1.1	1.2	1.8	2.0	2.3	3.5
Real Ex. Rate (increase = appreciation, 1997=100)	109.5	89.2	78.7	80.6	85.8	93.5	98.7	100.0	96.8	63.9	69.4	58.2	52.9
Unemployment (%)	8.0	9.0	10.6	9.9	9.5	8.7	10.1	10.6	14.2	14.1	13.3	11.3	11.7
Primary Public Sector Surplus (+) or Deficit (-) (% GDP)	-5.8	-0.4	-3.8	-9.3	-6.1	n.a.	n.a.	-0.9	-0.1	3.2	3.4	3.6	3.9
International Reserves (current $ bns, year-end)	9.2	8.8	23.3	31.7	38.5	51.5	59.7	51.7	43.9	35.7	33.0	35.9	37.8
Net-Debt-to-GDP ratio (year-end)	n.a.	n.a.	n.a.	n.a.	29.2	30.5	33.3	34.3	41.7	48.7	48.8	52.6	56.5
Foreign Debt (current $ bns, year-end)	120.0	121.0	129.1	144.1	152.4	160.5	181.3	198.0	241.0	243.7	238.8	226.4	227.1

Source: Created by casewriter based on data from Economist Intelligence Unit (EIU) Country Data, August 2003; Ministerio Da Fazenda, *Boletim de Acompanhamento Fiscal*, September 2003; and *Banco Central do Brasil Annual Report*, 2002 and 1997.

Exhibit 2 Brazil National Income Accounts (billions of constant 1996 U.S. dollars)

	1990	1991	1992	1993	1994	1995	1996	1997	1998	1999	2000	2001	2002
Gross Domestic Product	**100%**	**100%**	**100%**	**100%**	**100%**	**100%**	**100%**	**100%**	**100%**	**100%**	**100%**	**100%**	**100%**
Household Consumption	59%	59%	59%	58%	59%	62%	63%	62%	62%	61%	61%	61%	59%
Government Consumption	20%	20%	21%	20%	19%	19%	18%	18%	19%	19%	18%	18%	18%
Gross Fixed Investment	19%	20%	18%	19%	20%	21%	21%	22%	22%	20%	21%	20%	19%
Exports	7%	6%	7%	8%	8%	7%	7%	7%	8%	8%	9%	10%	10%
Imports	4%	5%	5%	6%	7%	9%	9%	10%	10%	9%	9%	9%	8%
Real GDP (constant 1996 US$ bns)	648.9	655.7	652.0	684.1	724.0	754.7	775.0	800.7	801.9	808.1	843.1	854.7	867.6
Nominal GDP (current US$ bns)	465.0	407.7	390.9	438.4	546.2	704.2	775.0	807.7	787.7	536.6	601.7	510.6	452.4

Source: Created by casewriter based on data from EIU Country Data, November 2003.

Note: GDP does not equal sum of components because of rebasing to 1996, which alters the relative importance of individual components.

Exhibit 3 Brazil Balance of Payments (millions of current U.S. dollars)

	1990	1991	1992	1993	1994	1995	1996	1997	1998	1999	2000	2001	2002
Current Account	-3,823	-1,450	6,089	20	-1,153	-18,136	-23,248	-30,491	-33,829	-25,400	-24,225	-23,215	-7,696
Trade Balance	10,747	10,578	15,239	14,329	10,861	-3,157	-5,453	-6,652	-6,603	-1,261	-698	2,650	13,143
Exports	*31,408*	*31,619*	*35,793*	*39,630*	*44,102*	*46,506*	*47,851*	*53,189*	*51,136*	*48,011*	*55,086*	*58,223*	*60,362*
Imports	*-20,661*	*-21,041*	*-20,554*	*-25,301*	*-33,241*	*-49,663*	*-53,304*	*-59,841*	*-57,739*	*-49,272*	*-55,783*	*-55,572*	*-47,219*
Net Services	-3,761	-3,891	-3,342	-5,590	-5,346	-7,495	-8,059	-9,309	-9,045	-6,983	-7,162	-7,759	-5,038
Net Income	-11,608	-9,651	-7,997	-10,322	-9,091	-11,105	-12,177	-16,344	-19,617	-18,844	-17,886	-19,743	-18,191
Net Transfers	799	1,514	2,189	1,603	2,423	3,621	2,441	1,814	1,436	1,688	1,521	1,638	2,390
Capital Account	35	42	54	81	173	352	494	482	375	339	273	-36	433
Financial Account	-5,441	-4,868	5,889	7,604	8,020	29,306	33,428	24,918	20,063	8,056	29,376	20,331	-3,102
Net Direct Investment	324	89	1,924	801	2,035	3,475	11,667	18,608	29,192	26,886	30,498	24,715	14,084
Net Portfolio Investment	512	3,808	7,366	12,322	44,732	9,235	20,832	10,058	18,419	3,800	6,955	77	-5,119
Net Government	-3,438	-3,897	-2,289	-2,767	-36,154	-1,652	-3,817	381	-1,728	-4,949	1,514	1,149	-1,626
Net Other	-2,839	-4,868	-1,112	-2,752	-2,593	18,248	4,746	-4,129	-25,820	-17,681	-9,590	-5,609	-10,441
Net Errors and Omissions	-296	852	-1,393	-815	-442	1,447	-1,992	-3,160	-2,911	240	2,557	-498	-901
Balance/Change in Official Reserves	-9,525	-5,424	10,639	6,890	6,598	12,969	8,682	-8,251	-16,302	-16,765	7,981	-3,418	-11,266
Nominal GDP (current US$ bns)	465.0	407.7	390.9	438.4	546.2	704.2	775.0	807.7	787.7	536.6	601.7	510.6	452.4

Source: Created by casewriter based on data from IMF, *International Financial Statistics CD-ROM,* November 2003.

Exhibit 4 Brazil Government Finance

as % current GDP							2003		
	1997	1998	1999	2000	2001	2002	June	July	August
Primary Revenue of the Central Government	15.7	17.3	18.5	18.1	19.1	20.5	20.1	20.0	19.9
Primary Expenses of the Central Government	15.5	16.5	16.5	16.3	17.3	18.1	17.3	17.1	17.0
Social Security	*-0.3*	*-0.8*	*-1.0*	*-0.9*	*-1.1*	*-1.3*	*-1.4*	*-1.4*	*-1.5*
Errors and Omissions	-0.5	-0.3	0.3	0.0	0.0	0.0	0.0	0.0	0.0
Primary Result of the Central Government	-0.3	0.5	2.3	1.8	1.8	2.4	2.8	2.9	2.9
Primary Result of the State Governments	-0.7	-0.4	0.2	0.4	0.6	0.6	0.8	0.7	0.7
Primary Result of the Municipal Governments	n.a.	0.2	0.1	0.1	0.3	0.2	0.1	0.1	0.1
Primary Result of the State Enterprises	0.1	-0.4	0.6	1.1	0.9	0.7	0.7	0.7	0.6
Primary Result of the Public Sector	**-0.9**	**-0.1**	**3.2**	**3.4**	**3.6**	**3.9**	**4.4**	**4.4**	**4.3**
Interest Payments	5.2	7.8	12.4	7.9	8.8	14.4	11.0	9.3	11.0
Nominal Result of the Public Sector	-6.1	-7.9	-9.2	-4.5	-5.2	-10.5	-6.6	-4.9	-6.7
Central Government	*-2.6*	*-5.2*	*-6.1*	*-3.1*	*-3.7*	*-6.6*	*-2.8*	*-1.8*	*-3.3*
State Governments	*-3.0*	*-1.8*	*-2.7*	*-1.8*	*-1.9*	*-3.3*	*-3.4*	*-2.9*	*-2.9*
Municipal Governments	*n.a.*	*-0.2*	*-0.5*	*-0.3*	*-0.1*	*-0.6*	*-0.6*	*-0.6*	*-0.6*
State Enterprises	*-0.5*	*-0.5*	*0.1*	*0.7*	*0.6*	*0.0*	*0.3*	*0.5*	*0.2*
Harmonized Nominal Result of the Public Sector[a]	n.a.	-7.5	-5.8	-3.6	-3.6	-4.7	-5.5	-6.0	-6.2
Central Government	n.a.	-4.9	-2.7	-2.3	-2.1	-0.8	-1.7	-2.9	-2.9
Privatizations	2.1	2.9	0.6	1.8	0.2	0.3	n.a.	n.a.	n.a.

Source: Compiled from Ministry of Finance of Brazil, *Boletim de Acompanhamento Fiscal*, September 2003.

[a]Excludes effect of exchange rate on the stock of internal, real-denominated debt indexed to the exchange rate.

Exhibit 5 Real/Dollar Exchange Rate

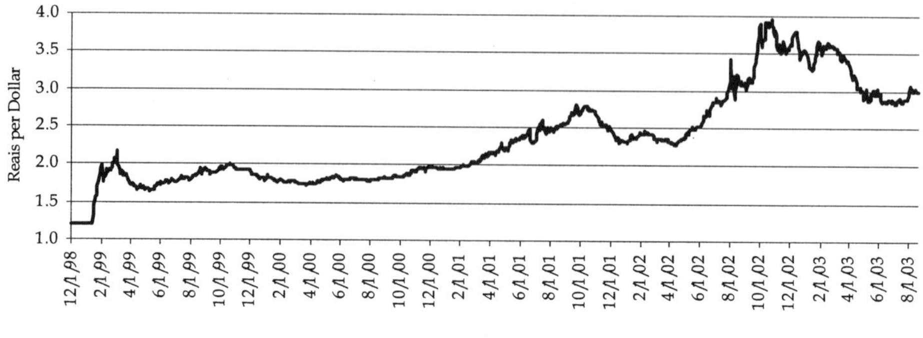

Source: Compiled from Banco Central do Brasil data.

Exhibit 6 Brazil Monthly CPI (% change over previous year, period average)

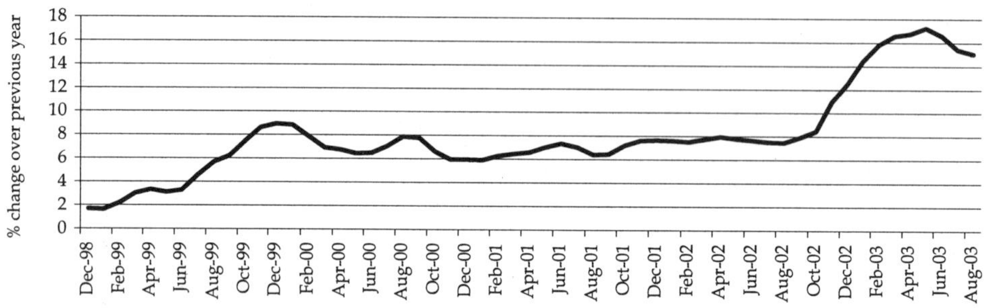

Source: Compiled from EIU Country Data, November 2003.

Exhibit 7 Selic Rate, as Set by Copom

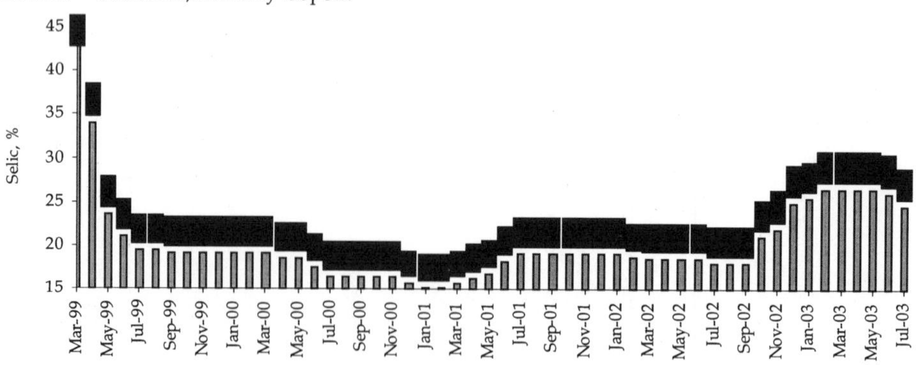

Source: Compiled from Banco do Brasil Web site.

Exhibit 8 J.P. Morgan Emerging Market Bond Index, Brazil

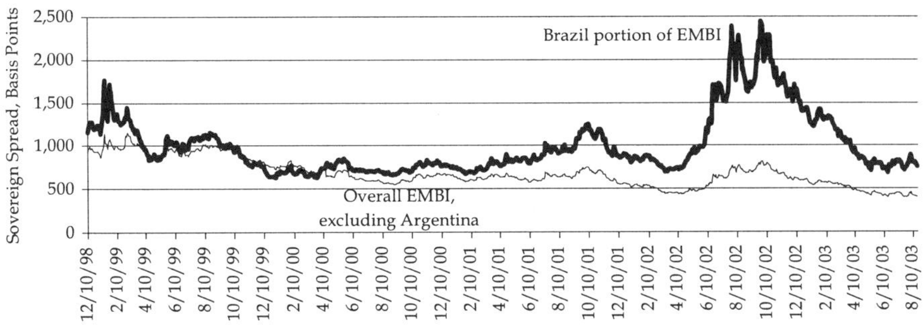

Source: Compiled from JP Morgan data.

Exhibit 9 Monthly Industrial Production Index (1996=100, seasonally adjusted)

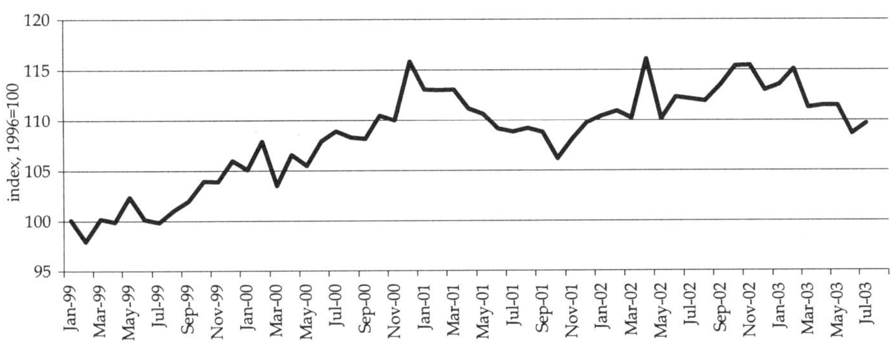

Source: Created by casewriter based on data from EIU Country Data, November 2003.

Exhibit 10 Money Growth in Brazil (% change over previous year)

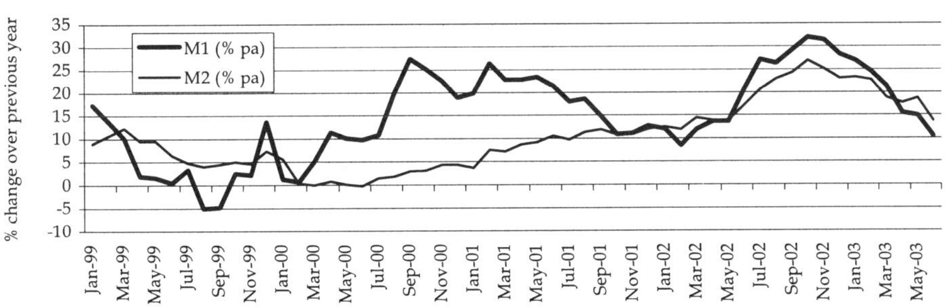

Source: Created by casewriter based on data from EIU Country Data, November 2003.

Exhibit 11 List of Countries Adopting Inflation Targeting (as of June 2003)

	Date of Adoption Inflation Targeting	Initial Target	Inflation Right Before IT Adoption	Inflation 12 Months After IT Adoption
Developed Economies				
New Zealand	Mar-90	3%–5%	7.03	4.52
Canada	Feb-91	3%–5%	6.83	1.68
United Kingdom	Oct-92	1%–4%	3.57	1.35
Sweden	Jan-93	2% (± 1%)	1.76	1.7
Australia	Apr-93	2%–3%	1.22	1.74
Switzerland	Jan-00	<= 2%	1.63	0.9
Norway	Mar-01	2.5	3.64	1.1
Iceland	Mar-01	2.5% (–1.5%+3.5%)	4.05	8.72
Average		*2.8*	*3.72*	*2.71*
Median		*2.5*	*3.61*	*1.69*
Emerging-Market Economies				
Chile	Jan-91	15%–20%	27.31	19.47
Israel	Jan-92	14%–15%	18.03	10.74
Peru	Jan-94	15%–20%	39.49	13.71
Czech Republic	Jan-98	5.5%–6.5%	9.98	3.5
South Korea	Jan-98	9%(± 1%)	6.57	1.46
Poland	Oct-98	<=9.5	10.44	8.82
Mexico	Jan-99	<=13%	18.61	11.03
Brazil[a]	Jun-99	8% (± 2%)	3.15	6.51
Colombia	Sep-99	15%	9.22	9.35
South Africa[b]	Feb-00	3%–6%	2.65	7.77
Thailand	Apr-00	0%–3.5%	1.04	2.47
Hungary	Jun-01	7% (± 1%)	10.78	4.87
Average		*10.3*	*13.11*	*8.31*
Median		*9.3*	*10.21*	*8.3*

Source: Adapted from Fraga, 2003, p. 6.

[a]In Brazil, the inflation of the period previous to the adoption of inflation targeting was in part a result of the over-appreciation of the domestic currency.

[b]First target established for 2002.

Exhibit 12 Social Indicators (most recent between 1997 and 2002)

	Gini Index[a]	Infant Mortality (deaths per 1,000 live births)	Life Expectancy at Birth (in years)	Secondary School Enrollment (% gross)	Tertiary School Enrollment (% gross)	Adult Illiteracy (% people over 15)	Sanitation Facilities (% population with access)	Fixed-Line and Mobile Phone Subscribers (per 1,000 people)
Brazil	60.7	31	68.6	n.a	17%	12%	76%	385
U.S.	40.8	7	78.0	95%	73%	n.a.	100%	1,121
Argentina	n.a.	16	74.3	97%	48%	3%	n.a.	416
Chile	57.5	10	75.9	75%	38%	4%	96%	575
Ecuador	43.7	24	70.4	57%	na	8%	86%	170
Mexico	51.9	24	73.6	75%	21%	8%	74%	354
Venezuela	49.5	19	73.7	59%	29%	7%	68%	373

Source: Compiled from World Bank, *World Development Indicators Database Online,* December 2003.

[a]The Gini Index measures the degree of income inequality. A higher number represents more inequality.

Exhibit 13 Contributors to Inflation

	2001		2002	
	As % Contribution	Percentage Point Contribution to Total Inflation	As % Contribution	Percentage Point Contribution to Total Inflation
Exchange Rate Pass-through	38%	2.9	46.4%	5.82
Market-Price Inflation (Excluding Exchange Rate Pass-through, Inertia, and Expectations)	28%	2.4	18.2%	2.28
Contract-Price Inflation (Excluding Exchange Rate Pass-through, Inertia, and Expectations)	24%	1.7	14.8%	1.85
Expectations	n.a.	n.a.	13.2%	1.65
Inflation Inertia	10%	0.7	7.4%	0.93
Total	**100%**	**7.7**	**100%**	**12.53**

Source: Adapted from Banco Central do Brasil Web site.

Exhibit 14 Debt Dynamics in Brazil

	all values in billions reais, unless noted	2001	2002	2003 est.
a	Total net debt	660.9	881.1	1,093
b	**Foreign currency-linked debt** as % total net debt		42.4%	42%
c=a*b	Value		373.4	463
d	Interest rate (avg LIBOR + avg sovereign spread)		15.4%	10%
e	Depreciation (avg monthly year-to-date against dollar)		26.1%	-12%
f=d+e	Total interest rate		42%	-2%
g=c*f	*Interest cost*		*155.2*	*-9*
h	**Selic-linked debt** as % total net debt		48.3%	48%
i=a*h	Value		425.9	528
j	Interest rate (avg Selic rate)		17.9%	25%
k=i*j	*Interest cost*		*76.3*	*130*
l	**Inflation-linked debt** as % total net debt		9.3%	9%
m=a*l	Value		81.8	101
n	Interest rate (avg TIPS + avg sovereign spread)		15.6%	11%
o	Inflation		12.5%	15%
p=n+o	Total interest rate		28.1%	26%
q=m*p	*Interest cost*		*23.0*	*26*
r=g+k+q	Total interest cost		254.4	148
s	Minus primary surplus		52.9	65
t	Plus hidden liabilities		9.9	12
u=r-s+t	Equals increase in debt		211.5	94
v	Nominal GDP	1,200	1,322	1,536
w	Nominal GDP used by BCB for debt calculations	1,257	1,559	1,812
x	Real economic growth	1.4%	1.5%	1.25%
y=a/w	Total net debt as % GDP	52.6%	56.5%	
$z=(a_{prior\ year}+u)/w - y_{prior\ year}$	Change in debt/GDP ratio		3.4%	-2.7%
$aa=y_{prior\ year}+z$	Calculated total net debt as % GDP		56.0%	53.8%

Source: Casewriter calculations, based on debt model presented in Williamson (2002).

a. From BCB Annual Report; 2003e = a2002+u2002.

b. Calculated from BCB Annual Report as 100% external debt + % of FX-linked debt in domestic debt; 2003 proportions assumed consistent - although not equivalent to c+g.

e. Not a cash cost, but a revaluation effect; this is just an approximation, since some foreign debt is not dollar-linked.

h. Calculated from BCB Annual Report as % of Selic-linked debt (plus most "other" debt) in domestic debt.

l. Calculated from BCB Annual Report as % of IGP- and IPCA-linked debt in domestic debt.

n. TIPS are U.S. inflation-protected securities.

o. Yearly inflation; not a cash cost but a revaluation effect.

s. 4% of GDP in 2002; 4.25% of GDP in 2003.

t. 0.75% GDP (as in Williamson and Goldfajn).

v. From BCB Annual Report: Annual nominal GDP at December prices deflated by the centered IGP-DI based on a series published by the IBGE (therefore recognizing the significance of inflation over the year); 2003 estimated as GDP 2002 * (1+ inflation 2003 + GDP growth 2003).

w. From BCB Annual Report; 2003 estimated as GDP 2002 * (1+ inflation 2003 + GDP growth 2003).

Exhibit 15 Transmission Mechanism, as Defined by Banco Central do Brasil

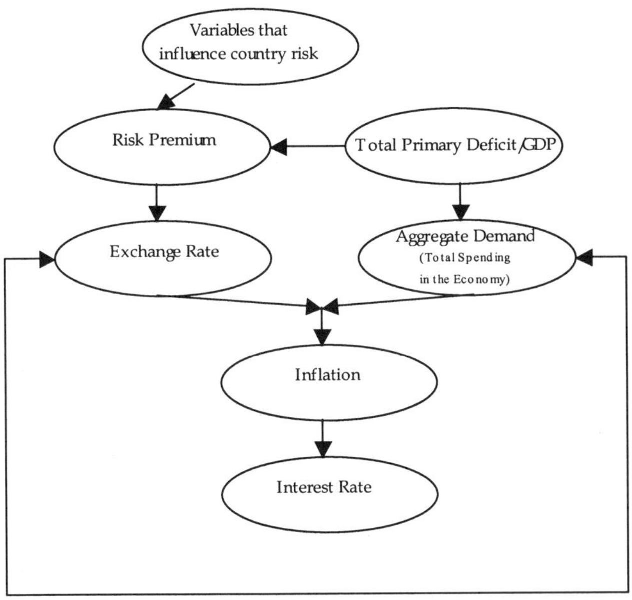

Source: Adapted from Joel Bogdanski, Alexandre Antonio Tombini, and Sergio Ribeiro da Costa Werlang, "Implementing Inflation Targeting in Brazil," paper presented at the IMF Seminar on Implementing Inflation Targets, March 20, 2000, available at <http://www.imf.org/external/pubs/ft/seminar/2000/targets/werlang.pdf> (May 13, 2004). For quantitative model behind diagram, see source.

Endnotes

1 As quoted in "Eleições 2002: La Muda a História, Vinte Anos na Oposição," *Veja,* October 30, 2002, pp. 39–41 (translated by casewriter).

2 As quoted in "Eleições 2002: La Muda a História, Vinte Anos na Oposição," *Veja,* October 30, 2002, pp. 39–41 (translated by casewriter).

3 As quoted in "Os Quatro Presidenciáveis: Um Flagrante de Lula, Serra, Ciro, e Garotinho no Calor da Campanha," *Veja,* September 25, 2002, p. 88 (translated by casewriter).

4 Heliana Frazão, "Vice-Presidente Critica Juros Altos e Diz Que 2003 É um 'Ano Perdido,'" *O Globo,* August 18, 2003.

5 This discussion draws largely on Laura Alfaro, "Brazil: Embracing Globalization?" HBS Case No. 701-014 (Boston: Harvard Business School Publishing, 2001). It also uses information from the Embassy of Brazil in the United States, available at <www.brasilemb.org> (November 2003).

6 Arminio Fraga, "Monetary Policy During the Transition to a Floating Exchange Rate: Brazil's Recent Experience," *Finance & Development,* Vol. 27, No. 1, March 2000.

7 For more on this, see Ben S. Bernanke, Thomas Laubach, Frederic S. Mishkin, and Adam S. Posen, *Inflation Targeting: Lessons from the International Experience* (Princeton, NJ: Princeton University Press, 1999), p. 16.

8 Between 1985 and 1990, New Zealand targeted inflation under a looser framework. For more on New Zealand's experience, see Reserve Bank of New Zealand Web site, particularly <http://www.rbnz.govt.nz/speeches/0076721.html> (accessed December 2003).

9 Arminio Fraga, Ilan Goldfajn, and André Minella, "Inflation Targeting in Emerging Market Economies," *NBER Macroeconomics Annual 2003,* Vol. 18, June 2003, p. 6.

10 Bernanke, et al., *Inflation Targeting,* pp. 301–308.

11 Bernanke, et al., *Inflation Targeting,* pp. 301–308.

12 "The Move to Inflation Targeting," *Finance & Development: Back to Basics,* June 2003.

13 Bernanke, et al., *Inflation Targeting,* p. 303.

14 For more on monetary growth targets, see Michael G. Rukstad, "Paul Volcker and the Federal Reserve: 1979–1982," HBS Case No. 386-055; and Huw Pill, "Fighting the Last War (A): Controlling British Inflation, 1973–1992," HBS Case No. 797-048.

15 Frederic S. Mishkin, "Inflation Targeting in Emerging-Market Countries," *AEA Papers and Proceedings,* Vol. 90, No. 2, May 2000, pp. 105–109; and Barry Eichengreen, "Can Emerging Markets Float? Should They Inflation Target?" Banco Central do Brasil Working Paper Series, No. 36, February 2002.

16 As in the introduction to Andrew G. Haldane, *Targeting Inflation: A Conference of Central Banks on the Use of Inflation Targets Organized by the Bank of England* (London: Bank of England, 1995), p. 5.

17 This is discussed in more detail in Alex Bowen, "British Experience with Inflation Targetry," in Leonardo Leiderman and Lars E. O. Svensson, eds., *Inflation Targets* (London: Centre for Economic Policy Research, 1995), pp. 53–68.

18 Vittorio Corbo and Klaus Schmidt-Hebbel, "Inflation Targeting in Latin America," Central Bank of Chile Working Papers, No. 105, September 2001; and "The Move to Inflation Targeting," June 2003.

19 Ben S. Bernanke, "A Perspective on Inflation Targeting," *Business Economics,* Vol. 38, Iss. 3, July 1, 2003.

20 For example, Laurence Ball and Niamh Sheridan, "Does Inflation Targeting Matter?" NBER Working Paper No. 9577, March 2003, which argues it can be explained by regression to the mean.

21 Bernanke, et al., *Inflation Targeting.*

22 Frederic S. Mishkin, "Inflation Targeting in Emerging-Market Countries," *AEA Papers and Proceedings,* Vol. 90, No. 2, May 2000, p. 107.

23 Fraga, et al., "Inflation Targeting in Emerging Market Economies," p. 24.

24 Mishkin, "Inflation Targeting in Emerging-Market Countries," May 2000, p. 107; discussed more fully and technically in Fraga, et al., "Inflation Targeting in Emerging Market Economies," and Eichengreen, "Can Emerging Markets Float? Should They Inflation Target?" pp. 27–34.

25 Fraga, et al., "Inflation Targeting in Emerging Market Economies," p. 29.

26 Fraga, et al., "Inflation Targeting in Emerging Market Economies," pp. 14–15.

27 Eichengreen, "Can Emerging Markets Float? Should They Inflation Target?" p. 41.

28 Eichengreen, "Can Emerging Markets Float? Should They Inflation Target?" pp. 23–27.

29 Eichengreen, "Can Emerging Markets Float? Should They Inflation Target?" p. 25.

30 Guillermo Calvo, Leonardo Leiderman, and Carmen Reinhart, "Inflows of Capital to Developing Countries in the 1990s," *The Journal of Economic Perspectives,* 10 (1996): 123–139; and Guillermo Calvo and Carmen Reinhart, "When Capital Flows Come to a Sudden Stop: Consequences and Policy," in Peter B. Kenen and Alexander K. Swoboda (eds.), *Reforming the International Monetary and Financial System* (Washington, DC: International Monetary Fund, 2000).

31 Fraga, et al., "Inflation Targeting in Emerging Market Economies"; Eichengreen, "Can Emerging Markets Float? Should They Inflation Target?" p. 23, also discusses this.

32 Klaus Schmidt-Hebbel and Alejandro Werner, "Inflation Targeting in Brazil, Chile, and Mexico: Performance, Credibility, and the Exchange Rate," Working Papers, Central Bank of Chile, 2002.

33 Open letters are available on Brazil's central bank Web site, <www.bcb.gov.br>.

34 Joel Bogdanski, Paulo Springer de Freitas, Ilan Goldfajn, and Alexandre Antonio Tombini, "Inflation Targeting in Brazil: Shocks, Backward-looking Prices, and IMF Conditionality," BIS Paper No. 12, November 2001, pp. 356–384. This is actually more complicated—requires that expectations remain consistent with the model and that the policy change is a sufficiently small departure from the initial position.

35 Open letter available on BCB Web site, "Open Letter, January 16, 2002, From Arminio Fraga Neto to Finance Minister," <www.bcb.gov.br> (accessed December 2003).

36 Ibid., p. 11.

37 Mario Osava, "Politics–Brazil: Potential Lula Victory Shakes up Investors," *Inter Press Service,* June 21, 2002.

38 "Front-Runner's Edge in Brazil Worries Foreign Investors," *The Boston Globe,* September 22, 2002.

39 This section draws on a number of popular sources, including Mario Osava, "Elections–Brazil: Lula, From Revolutionary to Social Democrat," *Inter Press Service,* October 4, 2002; Ray Collitt and Richard Lapper, "Victory in Sight for Brazil's Lula," *The Financial Times,* September 27, 2002; Gabriella Gamini, "Poor Boy from the Factory Floor – The Favourite – Brazil Election," *The Times,* October 3, 2002; and Jonathan Karp, "A da Silva Landslide is Expected in Brazil: Exit Polls Show Him with 63% of the Ballot in Runoff Against Serra," *The Wall Street Journal,* October 28, 2002.

40 Ibid.

41 Francisco Figueroa, "Lula: Proletarian in Armani Suit," EFE News Service, October 4, 2002.

[42] "Brazil Risk: Political Stability Risk," Economist Intelligence Unit Riskwire, August 29, 2003.

[43] As quoted in Andrei Khalip, "Brazil Lula Set for Runoff Win, Rival on Warpath," *Reuters News*, October 20, 2002.

[44] The two were front row guests at his inauguration, as discussed in Clinton Porteous, "Lula's Revolution: Tackling the Social Time Bomb of Brazil," *Australian Financial Review*, January 24, 2003.

[45] The change is outlined in the Open Letter from the Governor of the Central Bank of Brazil to the Finance Minister, January 21, 2003, available at <www.bcb.gov.br> (accessed December 2003).

[46] John Williamson, "Is Brazil Next," International Economics Policy Briefs, No. PB 02–7, August 2002; Ilan Goldfjan, "Are There Reasons to Doubt Fiscal Sustainability in Brazil?" Banco Central do Brasil Technical Note No. 25, July 2002; Carlo A. Favero and Francesco Giavazzi, "Why Are Brazil's Interest Rates So High?" Working Papers from IGIER (Innocenzo Gasparini Institute for Economic Research), No. 224, Bocconi University, July 2002; and Morris Goldstein, "Debt Sustainability, Brazil, and the IMF," Institute for International Economics, Working Paper No. WP 03–1, February 2003. Williamson uses a net-debt-to-GDP ratio of 66% and presents a mixed message; under multiple equilibria, could go either way. Goldfjan uses the BCB's net-debt-to-GDP ratio of 58% and presents a more optimistic picture. Favero and Giavazzi are much less optimistic. They use a much higher debt figure, do not augment the primary surplus to allow for the income that the government receives on the assets that they have netted out, and project a continuing real depreciation of the real. Goldstein is less optimistic as well.

[47] As presented in the 2002 Annual Report of the Banco Central do Brasil, p. 98. Not all foreign-currency-linked debt was dollar denominated, explaining the difference between the central bank's estimate of 148 billion reais and 197 billion reais, which would result from 373 billion reais x 0.523.

[48] "Lula 'twixt Inflation and Recession," *The Economist*, June 21, 2003.

[49] As polled by Sensus Opinion Research Institute.

[50] Frederic S. Mishkin, "Comments on Fraga, Goldfajn and Minella, 'Inflation Targeting in Emerging Market Economies,'" NBER, August 14, 2003.

Capital Flows and Tax Policy

HARVARD | BUSINESS | SCHOOL

9-707-043
REV: APRIL 9, 2009

LAURA ALFARO
RAFAEL M. DI TELLA
VINCENT DESSAIN
ANE DAMGAARD JENSEN

Rovná Daň: The Flat Tax in Slovakia

It will be of little avail to the people, that the laws are made by men of their own choice, if the laws be so voluminous that they cannot be read, or so incoherent that they cannot be understood; if they be repealed or revised before they are promulgated, or undergo such incessant changes that no man, who knows what the law is to-day, can guess what it will be to-morrow.

—James Madison, 1788[1]

Public Finance is nothing else than a sophisticated discussion of the relationship between the individual and the state.

— Former Czech Prime Minister Václav Klaus[2]

With the joy of the election victory in June 2006 quickly fading, Robert Fico of the party Direction-Social Democracy (SMER-SD) had a heavy weight on his shoulders. He had taken over as the new prime minister of the Slovak Republic (Slovakia) from Mikuláš Dzurinda, who had been in office since 1998. During his eight years in office, Dzurinda implemented a comprehensive reform program. It included the reorientation of foreign policy, as well as the reform of the social, pension, healthcare, and the legal systems. But the central piece of the reform was the *rovná daň*, or "equal tax," a drastic simplification of the tax system implemented on January 1, 2004.[3] Its main feature was a flat tax rate of 19% on personal income, corporate income, and value-added tax (VAT).

Dzurinda had hoped that the reforms would bring stability and growth to the country. "The tax reform benefited all income groups and had very positive fiscal results," then Deputy Prime Minister and Minister of Finance Ivan Mikloš agreed. But despite significant economic growth and major investment projects in Slovakia, resistance to the reforms was growing. Indeed, the World Bank and the Organization for Economic Co-operation and Development (OECD) had lent indirect support to Slovak trade unions following their arguments that the disposable incomes of the poorest households had been negatively affected by the reforms, at a time when unemployment was still at 13.5% (in the second quarter of 2006).[4] Fico himself had been labeled a populist as he rode the 2006 election on the public's discontent with market reforms. The disconnect was threatening to become a regional phenomenon in Eastern Europe.[5] "He's a marketing man with a good nose for what is attractive for people and what is not," commented one SMER-SD insider.[6] Fico had also proclaimed that he aspired to reinforce the welfare state[7] and had also ruled out some of the previously announced privatization, announcing a desire to keep strategic companies under state control.[8]

Professors Laura Alfaro and Rafael M. Di Tella, Executive Director of the HBS Europe Research Center Vincent Dessain, and Research Assistant Ane Damgaard Jensen prepared this case. HBS cases are developed solely as the basis for class discussion. Cases are not intended to serve as endorsements, sources of primary data, or illustrations of effective or ineffective management.

Reform fatigue also included the flat tax: the public was rejecting large parts of the reform program. Fico had been swift to react, choosing to split up the 19% VAT rate to a standard rate of 19% and a reduced rate of 10% for drugs and some medical goods starting January 2007; he also made some changes to the unpopular healthcare reforms.[9] In December 2006, Fico introduced a so-called "millionaires' tax," which gradually cut the non-taxable portion of income for Slovaks earning more than SKK 46,700 per month (EUR 1,353 or USD 1,803), around 2.6 times the average Slovak wage.[10] Fico even appeared to consider the possibility of reneging on the previous government's commitment to adopt the euro.

While these changes were a step back in the eyes of the reformers, Mikloš described them as small: "These two or three changes are just cosmetic; they were made for propaganda reasons to be able to say that they made changes to the flat tax." As Fico was deciding whether to ride public discontent with cosmetic changes or a major overhaul of the flat tax, observers noted that this decision also impacted his objective of reinforcing the welfare state and the scheduled adoption of the euro, which required strict financial discipline. Indeed, it was becoming harder to sell the flat tax reforms as *rovná daň*, or even as compatible with the popular European project. Unaffected by populist labels, Fico was prepared to examine further the economic reforms of the technocrats. Not many were prepared to bet on the survival of such reforms.

A Historical Perspective on Slovakia[11]

In 1993, Czechoslovakia broke into two independent countries, officially establishing the Czech Republic and the Slovak Republic (see **Exhibit 1**). Under Communist rule since the end of World War II, the Slovaks were ruled from Prague effectively following a Czech agenda, while the industrial gap between the two, which was already large, kept widening. During the late 1960s, the leader of the Communist Party of Czechoslovakia, Alexander Dubcek, wanted to create "socialism with a human face," and initiated several reforms, including liberalization and federalization efforts. However, Soviet military forces, helped by other Warsaw Pact countries,[12] invaded and reversed the reforms. Other attempts at reform were suppressed until the fall of the Berlin Wall in 1989. Czechoslovakia's non-violent rejection of its Communist regime became known as the Velvet Revolution. Along with the fall of the Soviet Union, this revolution brought democracy to the region and allowed playwright Vaclav Havel, formerly imprisoned as a dissident, to become the new Czechoslovak president.

Post-1989 The first free elections in Czechoslovakia were held in 1990, with reform of the Communist constitution and the introduction of a market economy as high priorities. However, two years of political turmoil eventually led to the creation of two independent states. On January 1, 1993, the Velvet Divorce marked the peaceful split of Czechoslovakia into the Czech and Slovak Republics (see Exhibit 2). As a new country, Slovakia had to adjust to its newfound independence, build up state and government bodies from the ground, and establish a new currency. In 1994, Josef Moravcik took over as prime minister with an agenda of economic reform. Almost 250 companies, with total market value of SKK 130 billion (USD 4.1 billion), were privatized.

A 1994 election gave Vladimir Mečiar a mandate to form a government. Respected for his role in pushing for Slovakia's independence, Mečiar attempted to shield the new country from unemployment and declining living standards. He refocused on domestic rather than foreign investments while strengthening economic relations with Russia. He also slowed down privatization, put an end to liberalization, and nationalized some already privatized entities, including radio and television. A World Bank study noted that only some groups benefited from the remaining privatization efforts: *The New York Times* noted that Mečiar gave a privatized steel mill in Kosice to a close associate, who subsequently wasted significant funds. This was not uncommon, as the president of the Kosice region explained: "The idea of owning something here is that I should get money out of it, build a big house, buy a Mercedes, take my vacation in Tahiti or my winters in Thailand. They didn't realize that to own a company means you have to take care of it, develop it, invest in it."[13]

Mečiar also struggled with the social agenda. Despite the existence of several minority groups, Mečiar required that only Slovak should be spoken by public employees and during public ceremonies, worrying international observers. In addition, it was noted that the Roma population was subject to widespread neglect in the political system.[a] Slovakia applied for membership in the European Union (EU) in 1995, but by 1997, the European Commission decided that the country was still not ready to start membership negotiations. *The Economist* noted that Mečiar was the reason why the EU would not consider membership negotiations with Slovakia.[14] Nevertheless, Mečiar was still supported by some parts of the population.

The Dzurinda Government[15]

In the 1998 election, Mečiar received the largest percentage of votes cast but was unable to form a government. Slovakia began a new era as Mikuláš Dzurinda of the Slovak Democratic and Christian Union (SDKU) became prime minister. An engineer by training, in 1990 he cofounded the conservative Christian Democratic Movement (KDH) and held various government posts, including transportation, budget, and finance. In 1997, several parties in the opposition created the Slovak Democratic Union, with Dzurinda as the spokesman.[16]

Dzurinda formed a coalition government with three other parties with the objective of reinforcing democracy. While Mečiar had an ongoing conflict with the president, Dzurinda redefined presidential power, strengthened his political independence, and introduced direct elections.[17] He also gave independence to the state-owned Slovak Television and Slovak Radio, which had been strictly controlled under Mečiar.[18] Further, Dzurinda made fighting corruption a key priority.[19] Observers maintained that corruption had lost its "systematic character that set apart Slovakia during the Mečiar years."[20]

Dzurinda also reoriented Slovakia's foreign policy, obtaining candidate status in the EU in 1999 and starting membership negotiations one year later. The EU required a long accession process for the 10 candidate countries;[21] as part of the process Slovakia demonstrated compliance with the political and economic conditions that were required.[b] The country also pursued and obtained membership in the North Atlantic Treaty Organization (NATO) and the OECD. In the 2002 election, Dzurinda again obtained a slim majority in parliament despite Mečiar's party again receiving the largest percentage of votes.

Slovakia on the Path to Reform

Slovakia's fiscal position deteriorated, with high unemployment and low levels of foreign direct investment (FDI) compared with its neighbors (see **Exhibits 3, 4,** and **5**).[22] Throughout the 1990s,

[a] The Roma constituted about 10% of the population and lived mainly in the eastern part of the country, the majority in poor and isolated settlements with 80%–100% unemployment.

[b] Before the EU enlargement in 2004, the EU consisted of Belgium, France, Italy, Luxembourg, the Netherlands, Germany, Denmark, Ireland, the United Kingdom, Greece, Portugal, Spain, Austria, Finland, and Sweden; also known as the EU-15.

Slovakia had been a laggard in reform among the Visegrád Group.[c] Dzurinda therefore aimed to rebuild investors' trust and to offer significant incentives for choosing Slovakia over other countries.

Dzurinda's second government was more effective.[23] Mikloš explained, "We were actually quite fortunate, because the Slovak National Party, which was against reform, was split into two just before the election. They didn't make the threshold, which created a political opportunity for us." Popular support was going to be a challenge. In 2003 the prime minister outlined, "We are about to enter into a tough and challenging era, when we will have to put these reforms through not only in terms of legislation but we will have to gain the broadest possible public support for them."[24]

Labor reform In 2003, the government introduced a New Labor Code, which included several measures to make the labor market more flexible. The working week was increased from 40 hours to 48 hours, In addition, workers could work and rest during flexible hours, part-time agreements could be arranged, and companies could grant workers an indefinite number of fixed-term contracts. Also, severance payments were reduced and it was made easier for companies to dismiss workers.[25]

Social reform As unemployment rates had increased during Dzurinda's first term, one of the top objectives was to give unemployed people greater incentives to work by cutting social benefits. The reform made social assistance dependent on participation in volunteer work or retraining programs.[26] Dzurinda noted that "only profound and systemic changes to the labour market, in the social charges and the social system, can result in reduced unemployment and increased efficiency."[27] In turn, unemployment benefits were reduced from one year to six months (see Exhibit 6).

Healthcare reform The government aimed to limit expenditures to basic needs and lower the Slovaks' expectations of the healthcare system.[28] "We are facing very difficult and politically risky measures in the area of healthcare," Dzurinda highlighted in early 2003.[29] The reform was set in motion in June 2003 and consisted of a redefinition of healthcare, excluding elements that did not directly relate to healthcare or healthcare services. User fees were introduced, while hospitals were restructured, facilitated by decentralization and partial privatization.[30]

Pension reform The reform made it mandatory for Slovaks to invest 9% of gross pay in private pension companies, in an attempt to replace the state-funded pay-as-you-go system. Further, the retirement age was increased to 62 for men and women (from 60 and 55–57, respectively). From 2007 the joint contribution element of the pension scheme would be suspended and benefit levels would depend only on contributions paid to social insurance providers.[31]

Privatization A major element of the reform program included privatization of state-owned enterprises. The state sold its 62% stake in the national airline Slovenske Aerolinie in 2004, as well as its 66% stake in the monopoly electricity provider Slovenske Elektrarne in 2005, both to foreign interests.[32] The OECD regarded the privatization efforts positively, but encouraged a more rapid privatization of Slovak Telecom as well as further privatization of the Slovak Railways, the gas monopoly Slovensky Plynarensky Priemysel, and the oil pipeline operator Transpetrol.[33]

Tax reform In 2004, the personal income tax (CIT), the corporate income tax (CIT), and the value-added tax were all set to 19%. The flat tax replaced 21 different tax rates, including two separate VAT rates and a five-band rate structure on wage income (see Exhibit 7). With the tax reform, the government also abolished the dividend tax, the real estate transfer tax, and the inheritance and gift taxes, while it abandoned a majority of income tax exemptions, in particular tax holidays for newly established companies.[34] Dzurinda stated that "these reforms will only be

---

[c] The Visegrád Group was an alliance of the Czech Republic, Hungary, Poland, and Slovakia.

successful if they are interrelated and implemented as a joint project."[35] According to the Ministry of Finance, the broad objectives of the tax reform were the "creation of a business and investment friendly environment for both individuals and companies; elimination of existing weaknesses and distortionary effects of the tax law; and achievement of a high degree of tax fairness by taxing all types and amounts of income equally."[36]

The Flat Tax

A flat tax was usually defined as an income tax that applied "the same rate of tax to everyone and to each component of income" and that allowed "computation of the tax base with no deductions from total income except personal exemptions and strictly defined business expenses."[37] (See **Appendix** for more on public finance.)

Historically, most European countries operated with flat tax rates for all incomes during the nineteenth century. Most countries, however, abandoned them after World War I when progressive taxes were implemented to fund increased government spending.[38] Nevertheless, Hong Kong adopted a 16% flat tax in 1947, while in the U.K., Jersey and Guernsey adopted flat taxes of 20% (in 1940 and 1960).[39]

Indeed, variations of the flat tax had been pursued at different times in the U.K. in attempts to simplify and increase the fairness of the tax system. For example, in April 1990, after years of struggle, Prime Minister Margaret Thatcher implemented the Community Charge as the "best and fairest way of paying for local government." The Community Charge replaced property taxes and became widely known as the poll tax because it applied the same amount to every individual resident in a given area, with exceptions for students and those on income support.[40] Local authorities established their own poll tax depending on the size of their populations and the services provided, but while Thatcher maintained that each citizen should pay about GBP 600 (USD 969), actual figures varied substantially and were often much higher. Millions of citizens refused to pay and protesters took to the streets as anger escalated into violence. Protesters argued that the tax was unfair and did not take a person's ability to pay into consideration.[41] A wealthy person in a rural area with few local services might pay a low poll tax, while a poorer individual in a large city with a high local budget might pay a higher poll tax.[42] The protests constituted the most serious revolt since Thatcher was inaugurated in 1979 and even members of her own Conservative party rebelled.[43] Thatcher resigned in November 1990, taking the poll tax with her. Thatcher's successor, John Major, replaced the unpopular tax with the Council Tax, which in some ways resembled the poll tax.

In the U.S., repeated proposals to move toward a flat tax system had been made. In recent times, for example, an enthusiastic proposal for the flat tax came from Steve Forbes, with one simple rate of 17% on personal income and 17% on corporate profits. Forbes argued—with historic evidence from the Harding-Coolidge tax cuts in the 1920s, the Kennedy cuts in the 1960s, and the Reagan cuts in the in 1980s—that "lower tax rates lead to more economic activity, which leads to more government revenue." According to Forbes, the federal income tax code had been amended 14,000 times in history, and the tax system was 60% larger in 2005 than it was after Reagan.[44]

Pat Buchanan, a fellow Republican and presidential candidate in 2000, was also in favor of a flat tax, although in a different format. While Buchanan maintained that Forbes's proposal would benefit "the boys down at the yacht basin," his own suggestion was based on a single-rate tax plan that would keep deductions from mortgage interest and charitable contributions and tax investment income.[45] Buchanan spoke in favor of a 15% personal income tax, while corporate rates would be flat and significantly reduced for small businesses.[46] Most recently, Bush established a panel to look into the possibilities of an American flat tax. Bush eventually managed to cut income tax rates, but no official flat tax proposal had been made.[47]

The idea of flat taxes had impeccable academic credentials. In 1962, Milton Friedman had advanced the idea of a flat tax in his book *Capitalism and Freedom*. The 1976 Nobel laureate in economics remained an ardent advocator of the flat tax. In a 1996 commentary he noted:

> The purpose of taxes should be to raise revenue to finance government expenses. A major purpose of taxes today is to enable legislators (and presidents) to raise campaign funds by inserting or removing loopholes in our present, obscenely complicated tax code. A single tax rate on all income (or consumption) above an exemption would restore the tax system to its proper purpose. It would make it difficult, if not impossible, to manipulate the tax code to favor, or punish, special interests. Finally, the same rate on all would render it difficult to raise the tax rate. Today Congress can raise taxes because it can persuade a sizable fraction of the populace that somebody else will pay. With a flat tax, no more, "Don't tax me, don't tax thee, tax the man behind the tree!"[48]

Stanford economist Robert E. Hall and political scientist Alvin Rabushka also supported a flat tax in the U.S. In a 1985 book, they advocated implementing a 19% flat tax. While economists generally argued that optimal taxation depended on the tradeoff between efficiency and fairness, Hall and Rabushka claimed that this equity should be embodied in horizontal equity, in the fact that "every tax payer pays taxes in direct proportion to his income." They maintained that lower tax rates would encourage economic activity, while higher tax rates would foster tax avoidance and evasion. The base of the business tax would be the difference between receipts from sales, including exports, and payments for purchases of inputs and capital goods and payments to employees. The tax on workers' income would be assessed on any kind of compensation to labor (including the value of fringe benefits) and on pension benefits.[49] With a flat tax rate of 19%, Hall and Rabushka predicted an increase in output from a larger work effort of 3% for the U.S. economy. Other benefits included potential reductions in interest rates, since the absence of deductions would make it less attractive to borrow and hence reduce the demand for credit.[50] (See **Exhibit 8** for average hours worked in selected OECD countries.)

A key argument was the claim that simplicity would lower the administrative burden; however, this was disputed by opponents who claimed that the range of conceptual and administrative problems involved in defining income would not disappear merely because a flat tax was introduced.[51] This argument was also put forth by economist Paul Krugman who noted that the gains from overhauling the U.S. tax system would be small—less than a 1% increase in the nation's income—and could even be negative. He maintained that while some people might gain from a flat tax, many in the middle class would lose, partly due to elimination of the tax deduction on home mortgages, which would be an inevitable way of assuring some income for the Treasury, Nevertheless, the economy as a whole would suffer: tax analysts asserted that flat taxes were usually promoted with the assurance of "unrealistically" low tax rates, which would create a vast budget deficit, harming the economy instead of accomplishing the opposite.[52]

Flat Tax Experiences in Post-Communist Countries

During the 1990s, several Eastern European countries adopted flat taxes, with the Baltic state of Estonia as the pioneer (see **Exhibit 9**). After regaining its independence from the Soviet Union in 1991, the country launched a bold reform program, including macroeconomic stabilization, fast liberalization, and privatization. In 1994, Estonian Prime Minister Mart Laar implemented a 26% flat tax.[53] An economic advisor to the Estonian government outlined, "While countries which have opted for a 'soft' transition still suffer from a long decline, which seems endless, Estonia has survived the hardships and its future outlook is much brighter."[54] Nevertheless, Estonia's path toward the flat tax had been a coincidence, as the prime minister noted:

> I was so ignorant at the time that I thought that what Friedman wrote about the benefits of privatization, the flat tax and the abolition of all customs rights, was the result of economic reforms that had been put into practice in the West. It seemed common sense to me and, as I thought it had already been done everywhere, I simply introduced it in Estonia, despite warnings from Estonian economists that it could not be done. They said it was as impossible as walking on water. We did it: we just walked on water because we did not know that it was impossible.[55]

Laar's advice to other countries was to keep reforms simple: "Do reforms in a way that you can administrate."[56] The Baltic neighbors Latvia and Lithuania followed Estonia's example, and since then a large number of post-Communist states implemented various versions of the flat tax. Laar outlined that a flat tax "could be applied in any country, and in most countries where it has been applied, it has shown satisfactory results. . . . In Estonia, which has a large population of farmers, it has reduced inequality, created more income for the government and lowered the poverty rate."[57]

Some argued that the flat tax was popular in Eastern Europe due to the region's unique history. Under the Communist regime the population worked for the state and paid no taxes per se. Following the collapse of the Soviet Union, governments across the region created tax systems with Western European models in mind, often resulting in relatively high marginal rates. But tax collection in the chaotic transition period proved difficult. "From the public's point of view the tax system seemed unfair," an economist at the Brookings Institution explained. The effects on tax collection were particularly large in Russia, a country with an enormous underground economy. After the implementation of the flat tax in Russia in 2001, personal income tax revenue rose from USD 8.3 billion that year to USD 20.5 billion in 2004.[58] The waves from Russia were felt in the U.S., as *The Wall Street Journal* put it: "We never thought we'd live to say this, but a Russian-style flat tax reform would be in America's interest too."[59]

The Implementation of the Flat Tax in Slovakia

In Slovakia, the idea of the flat tax originated within the Christian Democratic Party and the Alliance of the New Citizen in their 2002 election programs. "These two junior parties made no professional studies or estimates; they simply put a flat tax of 14% and 16% on the agenda as an idea," Minister of Finance Mikloš remembered.

Mikloš had studied economics at the London School of Economics and the University of Economics in Bratislava. He moved into politics in the beginning of the 1990s as Minister for Administration and Privatization of National Property. During the Mečiar years, Mikloš headed an economic think tank and held numerous international trusteeships. Under Dzurinda, Mikloš held several important posts, including Deputy Prime Minister and Minister of Finance.[60] "My party supported the idea of a flat tax, but we wanted some experts to estimate its economic feasibility. After the election, we put it in our government program that we would analyze the possibility of a flat tax. The details were not clear, but we knew that we wanted to simplify the system."

Minister of Finance Mikloš established a small working group with the purpose of analyzing the introduction of a flat tax. According to Martin Bruncko, Mikloš' financial advisor, it had the advantage of being small. "There are too many experts in developed economies to make things work.

I would say that there were about six, maybe seven, serious economists in this country when we were doing the tax reform." He explained: "One of the main problems in Slovakia was that we had this very typically European overburdened and overregulated business environment. One of the top three concerns of business was the complexity and the frequent changes of the tax system."

The working group was effective and quickly came up with a conclusion; after two weeks of reflections and calculations, the flat tax was on the agenda. According to Bruncko, "the debate was rather simplified and there was hardly any resistance to the idea. When we were attacked in the media it was usually for the fact that the reform allegedly did not go far enough—and that the flat tax rate should be at most 15% and not 19%."

Some people felt like they were not included in the debate, however. The Confederation of Trade Unions of the Slovak Republic (KOZ), which represented 450,000 union members, was against the flat tax, which was perceived as regressive. Also, KOZ believed that the introduction of indirect taxes through a higher VAT would primarily hit low income groups. Vladimír Mojš, KOZ vice president for Economic Policy and Social Partnership, claimed that KOZ was not consulted when the Dzurinda government proposed the reforms. "A text was circulated to us and we were given 10 days to react. This was of course not enough. In any case our objections were not at all taken into account."

Mikloš knew that a higher and unified VAT was unpopular with the trade unions. Nevertheless, he stressed the importance of fiscal consolidation, which inevitably included a higher level of unified VAT. The experts in the working group agreed on the economic feasibility of the flat tax, but from a political point of view they did not support it. Mikloš recalled, "Many of them thought that it would be impossible to pass this unified VAT in Parliament. But I really wanted to give it a try."

Estimates of the effect came in from various parties: the Ministry of Finance, the IMF, and independent think tanks. Each had different results. Ľudovít Ódor, director of the Research Department at the National Bank of Slovakia, was one of the key people behind the calculations. He explained: "It's much easier to estimate the outcome of a change in VAT, but since we don't have good data on personal income tax in Slovakia, it is almost impossible to predict exactly what will happen." He continued, "So we had to construct a model of the distribution of income with the little data we had. I used a combination of the log-normal distribution model in the low end and the Pareto distribution model in the high end."

Initially, Mikloš wanted a 20% flat tax with the promise of a fiscal deficit of 3.5% of GDP. "Dzurinda had confidence in me, but others in the coalition thought that a 19% or 20% VAT was too high. 'It will destroy us politically,' they said to me." Nevertheless, an agreement was reached; a 19% flat tax with the promise of a fiscal deficit of 3.9% of GDP. But the proposal had to pass Parliament as well, as Mikloš remembered: "When we tried to pass the tax reform in 2003 the atmosphere was not good. The opposition, the trade unions, and the media had created widespread public fear about the earlier reforms. They maintained that the reforms would have adverse consequences for low-income groups and only benefit the rich. It was a very difficult time for us to pursue further reforms."

A strategy was therefore needed to convince Parliament, coalition members, and Slovaks that a flat tax could benefit the country. "We wanted to give the reforms a good image," Bruncko remembered. "Because of the poor relations with the Slovak media, Mikloš found that the only way to convince them to report favorably on the reforms was if they read it in Western newspapers. In that way they wouldn't claim that it was government propaganda. Our friends in the German media, for instance the *Frankfurter Allgemeine Zeitung*, ran big stories that created a lot of attention."

The Ministry of Finance drafted the Tax Reform Concept for 2004 to 2006, which was approved by the Slovak Cabinet on June 5, 2003.[61] On January 1, 2004, the 19% flat tax went into effect. It replaced five tax rates on personal income, ranging from 10 to 38 percent, while the personal and spouse allowances were increased significantly. The single VAT rate of 19% was introduced as of May 1, 2004.[62] Under the previous system (with multiple rates), it was possible to claim refunds on inputs at the higher VAT rate and sell output taxed at the lower rate, which had resulted in refunds exceeding domestic VAT collections.[63]

The Ministry of Finance noted:

> The tax reform was designed with a view to introducing in Slovakia a modern tax system which gives the people an incentive to work more, or vigorously look for a job, and gives the entrepreneurs an incentive to invest and thus create new jobs. In this manner, the reform should facilitate dynamic and sustainable economic growth which is the main prerequisite for raising the standard of living of the population.[64]
>
> The simplification of the tax law dramatically improves its transparency and business-friendliness. It eliminates one of the main business barriers identified in Slovakia by business surveys—i.e., the excessive complexity and frequent changes in the tax laws. Thus, the implementation of the tax reform should positively affect the business environment in the medium-term and long-term and should serve as a major stimulus for further FDI.[65]

Slovakia's Performance

From 2000, the Slovak economy grew rapidly, consumer price inflation fell, and unemployment decreased (see **Exhibit 10**).[66] FDI increased, which according to the OECD was due to the macroeconomic stabilization and the assertive structural reforms. While some investments focused on privatized companies, many were greenfield investments, particularly in manufacturing and service activities.[67] The Business Alliance of Slovakia argued that the number of companies in Slovakia had increased significantly from 2001 to 2005 (see **Exhibit 11**). The Slovak Investment and Trade Development Agency (SARIO) also had an important role to play in facilitating the initial moves for foreign companies interested in investing in Slovakia, such as finding a partner or a production site, getting information about trade fairs, assistance with legal issues, and so forth.

The car industry was one of the major industries that had a newfound interest in Slovakia. Following a 10-year tax exemption, Volkswagen started production and assembly in Bratislava in 2001, while PSA Peugeot-Citroën and Hyundai Motors in 2003 and 2004 announced their plans for manufacturing sites to become operational in 2006 and 2007. Slovakia was expected to become the top per capita car manufacturer in the world in 2007.[68] The presence of car producers was expected to promote further clustering: Eight subcontractors had their eyes on Slovakia, worth a total of USD 300 million.[69]

Slovakia won widespread international acclaim for its reforms. "The country stands out among its regional peers. It went for across-the-board reforms that have significantly improved the business climate," a senior economist at the World Bank noted.[70] "One sign that the Slovak reforms are indeed attractive to foreign investors is the reaction of neighboring countries," an IMF economist stated, referring to Austria's and Hungary's tax-cut efforts.[71]

In 2004, tax revenues fell as a share of GDP compared with 2003, which was in line with IMF expectations (see **Exhibit 12**). According to the IMF, the flat tax reduced distortions in the economy and was simpler to administer, while the collection of the personal and corporate income taxes was stronger than predicted. Welfare reforms improved the control of spending and benefit abuse was restrained,[72] while the New Labor Code made the labor market more flexible.[73] However, the IMF noted that labor taxes were only modestly reduced for many. Welfare reform reduced the marginal tax rate.[74] Still, in 2004, employment stagnated despite economic growth.[75]

According to Mikloš, the implementation of the flat tax had benefited all income groups and had not increased the inequality in the country. Richard Sulík, advisor to the current and former finance ministers, also argued that the flat tax left all income groups better off. "A flat tax is the most equal tax system you can imagine. Everyone pays the same share of their income. That is why we call it *rovná daň*, equal tax, here in Slovakia. I prefer this model to a Western European model."

Nevertheless, the reforms did not keep Slovakia from providing subsidy schemes to attract FDI. Hyundai Motors' greenfield investment was encouraged by investment incentives, including state aid worth SKK 1.6 billion (USD 47 million). The Minister of Economy promised that aid would not exceed 15% of the total value of the investment, as required by EU regulation, but observers were suspicious, in particular given the intense competition Slovakia had with Poland over winning the investment.[76]

Some problems emerged, however. One of the most visible was the unequal transformation of the country. Observers noted that investors generally preferred to locate near Bratislava in the west. "We don't have the resources to pay a site for Peugeot-Citroën like they did in Trnava," the President of the Kosice region Rudolf Bauer stated.[77] In September 2005, Markus Huber of the *Stuttgarter Zeitung* maintained that because of the flat tax, the regions in the East had spent less money on schools, hospitals, and much-needed infrastructure.[78] Others charged that the young and qualified benefited the most, with "growing differences between regions and social classes."[79] (See **Exhibit 13**.)

Observers argued that the tax collection had remained stable simply because FDI had increased, even questioning whether the flat tax was in fact the reason for the investment boom. One newspaper asserted that "the low salaries and the almost nonexistence of unions play an even larger role."[80] Only 21% of the work force was unionized, while the minimum wage was EUR 183 (USD 232), the third-lowest in the EU.[81]

To many, job creation measures had been insufficient. "The reform has not contributed to the creation of jobs and the budget is so restricted that the state is no longer taking care of transportation, culture, and education," the president of KOZ outlined.[82] Others emphasized the lack of initiatives for small and medium-sized firms. "as if the arrival of multinationals could solve the unemployment problem all by itself." One newspaper agreed: "The majority of citizens have seen nothing yet, except for an increase in the cost of living, which has restrained consumption."[83] Indeed, an IMF economist noted that the subsistence minimum (the national poverty line) had increased since the tax reform.

The Roma population Slovakia's Roma population had been particularly hit by the reforms due to the reductions in social benefits to large families.[84] The Roma reacted with violent riots in February 2004, which constituted the worst episode of civil disorder since the collapse of the Communist regime.[85] More than 20,000 police and military personnel were deployed, mainly in the eastern part of the country.[86] Michal Vasecka of the Institute of Public Affairs was not surprised by the violence. "This reform, which is necessary for the financial health of Slovakia, was envisaged for 90% of the population, but not for the remaining 10%, of which the majority are Roma."[87] The government brought the looting and rioting under control but had to restore confidence throughout the national and international environment by committing itself to improving the conditions in Roma settlements, which often lacked running water, electricity, and sanitation. Nevertheless, critical issues such as poor education, discrimination in employment, and poverty traps remained unaddressed.[88]

Pensions and healthcare The deregulation of energy prices and the unification of the VAT rates had increased costs of essentials such as heating, food, and transportation, which affected retired people significantly. To counterbalance the inequality, the Minister of Labor and Social Affairs had been forced to grant a one-off bonus worth SKK 1,000 to pensioners during the summer of 2004.[89] The user fees had reduced the number of consultations but had not led to improvements in hospitals. Working conditions appeared unattractive for doctors and hospital workers, with some choosing to work in Vienna, only 60 kilometers from Bratislava.[90] Slovakia was hit by weeks of strikes during the spring of 2006. "Only four countries in Europe spend less than Slovakia on healthcare. It's less than 6% of GDP," the strikers noted. The strikes were well received by the population.

Reactions in the EU

On November 28, 2005, Slovakia joined the EU's exchange rate mechanism (ERM)[d] two years ahead of schedule, making the country a candidate to adopt the euro in January 2009. As such, Slovakia followed the Baltic countries along the path toward adopting the common currency, well before Poland, Hungary, and the Czech Republic.[91] In 2005, Slovakia was close to adhering to the budget deficit of 3% of GDP, the ceiling defined by EU's Stability and Growth Pact.[e]

The European Commission and some member states supported Slovakia. "In Europe, our reforms were supported mainly by Ireland [and] the U.K., as well as other new member states," Ódor explained. "But there was no unique consensus on this issue, as politicians in some countries, in particular Germany and France, heavily criticize our ideas." Indeed, Germany and France criticized what they deemed excessively low taxes for their effect in keeping investments and jobs out of Western Europe (see **Exhibits 14, 15** and **16** for comparative data).[92] Bruncko explained: "Chancellor Schröder said that he considered the flat tax in Slovakia to be tax dumping. The fact that he said that was actually the best kind of marketing we could have hoped for. 'Where is this country with a 19% tax rate?' companies suddenly started asking."

Ódor noted that the Slovak flat tax also sparked a discussion in Germany during the 2005 election. During the election, a flat tax plan with a 25% rate was proposed by a professor named Paul Kirchhoff, Chancellor Merkel's shadow finance minister. However, Kirchhoff's ideas caused a stir within the middle class.[93] Angela Merkel saw her lead shrink by 15 points until Professor Kirchhoff distanced himself in order to stop causing harm to her campaign.[94]

The flat tax debate in Germany continued: In October 2005, major newspaper *Die Welt* ran a story on the Estonian flat tax. The author wondered whether the flat tax reform was viable in the long term, as the weak healthcare and education systems would eventually cause problems for company growth. The article argued for the importance of developing a welfare system that could in fact support a well-qualified working population. Finland, for example, had a social benefits package five times larger than Estonia's.[95] In an article at the time, Mikloš explained his position:

> The European economy is weakened. If the slow economic growth persists, this leads not only to a declining standard of living of its citizens but inevitably also to a declining role of the European Union as political force in the world. To avoid this, Europe has to finally bring itself to undergo deep structural reforms. . . . However, these neoliberal reforms will inevitably undermine the European social model and result in the loss of a large part of the social benefits

[d] The European Exchange Rate Mechanism (ERM) was introduced in 1979 and later modified. It was seen as a means to reduce exchange rate variability and achieve monetary stability in preparation for the introduction of the euro.

[e] The Stability and Growth Pact was adopted in 1997 and stated that members of the European Monetary Union should have an annual budget deficit no higher than 3% of GDP, and that public debt should be lower than 60% of GDP.

that we have built up over the past 50 years. So much for the simple story of the allegedly fundamental economic and social dilemma that everybody knows by heart nowadays.[96]

The flat tax also irritated some EU-15 members who questioned whether it was appropriate to maintain present EU funding levels to Eastern Europe through the Structural Funds[97] given that the countries did not collect much in taxes.[98] Meanwhile, the strength of the Slovak koruna[f] worried analysts in early 2007, as the overwhelming majority of countries entering the Eurozone had exchanged their currency at a rate that was at the center of their fluctuation band. Given the lack of precedent in terms of large revaluations of the central parity before the adoption of the euro, critics believed that Slovakia could still miss the 2009 euro adoption date (see **Exhibit 17**).[99]

The 2006 Elections in Slovakia

According to *The Economist*, Robert Fico's SMER-SD won the election due to the short-term effects of the Dzurinda reforms.[100] "The negative parts of the reforms, especially the VAT increase, were immediately very visible," Mikloš pointed out. "The positive effects of the reforms, such as the reduced income tax, were not that visible because they were not directly reflected in prices."

A former Communist and a deputy since 1991, the 42-year old lawyer Fico had founded SMER-SD in 1999 and gradually absorbed all non-Communist left-wing parties.[101] Fico reoriented the ideological profile of the party along modern social democratic lines.[102] He earned the populist label by heavily criticizing the flat tax and the healthcare reform and by calling for increased government intervention in the economy. "Fast economic growth will no longer be for the benefit of a narrow group of people," Fico said.[103] Sulík commented, "Before the election, Fico promised to abolish the flat tax and reintroduce a progressive tax. After the election, the new minister of finance offered me a key position as his advisor. I accepted this offer, which made me able to defend the flat tax. As a result, we'll keep the flat tax at least through 2007."

Fico's coalition partners were the LS-HZDS, still led by former Prime Minister Mečiar, and the extreme-right SNS, led by Jan Slota. Slota was a notorious figure who expressed severe antagonism toward the Hungarian minority and had publicly stated that the country's Roma population was a problem that could be solved with a "big whip and a small yard."[104] This caused concern in the international community. Some argued that voters had simply had enough of reforms. "The common phenomenon in all these countries is transition fatigue," maintained a political analyst at the DZ Bank in Budapest. Other observers agreed that the rise of populism and nationalism was due to frustrations that had been suppressed during the reform years and the process of admittance to the EU.[105]

Local players requested change, as Slovakia remained complex to operate in. "The Bratislava Stock Exchange is dead, mainly due to the lack of private property rights enforcement," Vice President of The Business Alliance of Slovakia Ladislav Mikuš asserted. "There are no local investors and no entrepreneurial spirit." Fico's proposal for a "millionaires' tax" and the creation of two rates for the VAT drew political fire. Mikloš, for example, was not impressed. "I consider this a political marketing move and a punishment of the higher middle class."[106]

An initial reaction was to continue unfolding the reforms: in 2006 Fico also abolished some of the healthcare fees introduced by Dzurinda and suspended privatization initiatives,[107] including the rail transport company ZSSK Cargo[108] and the Bratislava Airport.[109] In a clear change from the Dzurinda

[f] Slovakia's currency since 1993.

government, he distanced himself from the Bush administration by visiting the once-shunned Cuban embassy and withdrawing Slovak's contingent from Iraq.[110] Many of his supporters were expecting Fico to deliver on his promises to reinforce the welfare state. "I really respect the role of the state," Fico said in a 2007 interview. "The first task of the government is to guarantee that if someone is in a bad social situation, not because of his behavior, but objectively, he should be looked after by the state in a way that enables him to live in normal, humane conditions."[111]

Appendix: Tax and Public Finance Terms[112]

It's time for a complete overhaul of our income tax system. I still tell you, it's a disgrace to the human race.
—U.S. presidential candidate Jimmy Carter, 1976[113]

Calculating an individual's tax liability The first step is to calculate adjusted gross income, which is the total income from all taxable sources (including but not restricted to wages, interest, rents, dividends, profits, royalties, prizes, and unemployment compensation) minus expenses incurred in earning the income. The next step is to subtract exemptions and deductions (such as charitable contributions, medical expenses, state income taxes) in order to arrive at taxable income, which is the amount of income subject to taxation. The final step is to calculate the amount of tax to be paid. This is done via a rate schedule, which indicates the tax liability connected to each level of taxable income.

Defining income One has to be able to define income in order to calculate tax liability. This has proven to be tricky, but public finance economists generally refer to the Haig-Simons[a] definition: "Income is the money value of the net increase in an individual's power to consume during a period," which means the amount consumed plus net additions to wealth. Even though this traditional standard will not make the administration of income tax straightforward, some economists argue that this definition is ideal as it is as broad as possible as well as being attractive for fairness and efficiency reasons. According to Harvey S. Rosen, if "people in equal positions should pay equal taxes," as is indicated by horizontal equity, all sources of income should be taxed. Nevertheless, if people's ability to earn that income varies, then the H-S definition could generate unfair outcomes. However, economists note that neutrality "in the sense of equal tax rates on all types of income may not be efficient."[114]

The following table lists some terms that pertain to tax and public finance.

Term	Definition
Income tax	Tax on an individual's income.
Corporate tax	A tax on the net income of the entity of a corporation; the individuals who own a corporation.
Consumption tax	A tax on spending. Individuals are taxed on what they spend instead of what they produce.
Poll tax	A tax that levies a set amount per individual.
Value added tax (VAT)	A tax that applies the equivalent of a sales tax to every operation that creates value.
Average/effective tax rate	Ratio of taxes paid to income.
Marginal tax rate	The change in taxes paid with respect to a change in income.
Flat Income Tax	A tax schedule such that the marginal tax rate is constant throughout the range of income.
Progressive tax system	When the average tax rate increases with income.
Regressive tax system	When the average tax rate decreases with income.
Distribution of the tax burden	Share of taxes paid by different income groups; relates to fairness (incidence of taxation).
Horizontal equity	People in equal positions should pay equal taxes.
Vertical equity	Tax burden should be distributed fairly across people with different abilities to pay.
Exemptions	Forgone taxes that would normally be collected from an individual or an organization.
Deductions	Special provisions in the law for mortgage interest, charitable contributions, etc.
Exclusions	Moving expenses, retirement, contributions, etc.
Credits	Sums that can be credited against tax liabilities.
Tax avoidance	Altering behavior in such a way as to reduce one's legal tax liability; legal.
Tax evasion	Not paying taxes legally due; illegal.
Laffer curve (developed by economist Arthur B. Laffer in 1979)	Government revenue does not necessarily increase when the tax rate increases. (At high rates, either people decrease hours worked or compliance decreases.) Governments can maximize their tax revenue by setting the tax rate at an optimum point: a tax rate above this point could be lowered without any loss of revenue for the government.

Source: Compiled from Harvey S. Rosen, *Public Finance*, 7th ed. (McGraw-Hill, 2005); and Robert E. Hall and Alvin Rabushka, *The Flat Tax*, 2nd ed. (Hoover Institution Press, 1995).

[a]Economists Robert M. Haig and Henry C. Simons developed this definition in the 1920s and 1930s.

Exhibit 1 Maps

1a) Map of Slovakia

Source: http://www.lib.utexas.edu/maps/cia07/slovakia_sm_2007.gif, accessed April 2007, Courtesy of the University of Texas Libraries, The University of Texas at Austin.

1b) Map of Europe

Source: http://www.lib.utexas.edu/maps/europe/europe_ref_2006.pdf, accessed April 2007, Courtesy of the University of Texas Libraries, The University of Texas at Austin.

Exhibit 2 Timeline after Slovakia's Independence

Year	Event
1993 January	The Velvet Divorce. Czechoslovakia splits and Slovakia is born.
1993 January	Slovakia is admitted to the UN and the OSCE.
1993 February	The Slovak Parliament elects Michal Kováč (Movement for a Democratic Slovakia) as President. Vladimír Mečiar of the same party becomes Prime Minister (after election in 1992) in a coalition government.
1993 June	Slovakia is admitted to the Council of Europe.
1994 March	End of first Mečiar government following no-confidence vote from Parliament. New coalition led by Jozef Moravčik of the Democratic Union of Slovakia.
1994 September	Mečiar wins election and starts second term with another coalition in December.
1995 January	Slovakia is admitted to the World Trade Organisation (WTO).
1995 March	Slovakia signs Treaty of Friendship and Cooperation with Hungary, guaranteeing the existing border and ethnic minority rights.
1995 June	Slovakia officially asks for European Union membership.
1995 November	A new law restricting official use of any language other than Slovak gives rise to international condemnation.
1997 May	Slovak referendum on admittance to NATO. Referendum cancelled due to less than 10% voter turnout.
1997 December	Slovakia is ruled out of the first group candidate countries for the negotiations of EU and NATO enlargement.
1998 March	President Kováč ends his term. Constitutional stalemate as Parliament fails to agree on successor. Prime Minister Mečiar assumes Presidential powers, prompting protest demonstrations and EU condemnation. Dismisses nearly half the country's ambassadors and overturns several Kováč decisions.
1998 September	Mečiar loses election to opposition. Mikuláš Dzurinda heads new coalition government.
1999 January	The Slovak government announces planned measures of economic stabilization.
1999 January	Parliament ends months of constitutional crisis by passing new law allowing for the President to be directly elected by the people.
1999 May	Rudolf Schuster of the Civic Reconciliation Party wins Slovakia's first direct Presidential election.
1999 July	The Parliament approves law to improve the status of minority languages.
1999 December	The EU decides to initiate membership negotiations with Slovakia.
2000 December	Slovakia joins the OECD.
2001 February	Parliament approves changes to Slovakia's constitution, a step towards EU and NATO membership. The new constitution decentralizes power in Slovakia, increases the authority of the state audit office, strengthens the independence of the judiciary and gives greater recognition to minority rights.
2001 December	Regional elections in Slovakia with voter turnout of 26% and 22% during the two rounds.
2002 January	Eight new regional parliaments created under amended constitution, one of the key requirements for EU entry.
2002 September	Dzurinda wins second term as Prime Minister during election and forms centre-right coalition government.
2003 May	92.46% of Slovaks vote in favor of EU membership in referendum.
2004 March	Slovakia is admitted to NATO.
2004 April	Ivan Gašparovič is elected President, defeating former Prime Minister Mečiar in the second round.
2004 May	Slovakia joins the EU as one of 10 new member states.
2005 November	Slovakia joins ERM II as preparation to membership of the eurozone.
2006 June	SMER leader Robert Fico wins election and becomes Prime Minister in coalition government.

Source: Adapted from Antoine Marès, *Histoire des Tchèques et des Slovaques* (Éditions Perrin, 2005); Stanislav J. Kirschbaum, *A History of Slovakia—The Struggle for Survival*, 2nd Edition (Palgrave Macmillan, May 2005); and BBC Slovakia Country Profile, http://news.bbc.co.uk/1/hi/world/europe/country_profiles/1870906.stm, accessed October 2006.

Exhibit 3 National Income Accounts, 1993–2006

SKK Million	1993	1994	1995	1996	1997	1998	1999	2000	2001	2002	2003	2004	2005	2006
Household consumption	227835	260998	305988	350145	392261	436292	484821	532853	592057	643471	687560	768857	844180	941779
Government	99877	102846	124899	153834	155195	174162	169257	187763	209199	225347	249136	270730	272234	297442
Gross fixed capital formation	123374	131819	144248	205846	243539	281774	249792	242277	291027	303481	302782	327087	394618	432084
Changes in inventories	-21970	-27884	-1953	15088	2961	-17215	-14406	1757	10814	19001	-4275	25481	34770	42740
Exports	233214	296372	336172	345778	405045	466487	517940	661682	741313	788589	927747	1018830	1136850	1402200
Imports	250964	268502	323570	415451	474106	551453	555235	685018	823815	868405	950285	1055730	1211520	1478200
GDP	411366	495649	585784	655240	724895	790047	852169	941314	1020590	1111480	1212670	1355260	1471130	1635500
GDP (current US$ millions)	13369	15467	19402	20828	21201	22179	20381	20218	20887	24234	32665	41094	46412	-
GDP vol. 1995 prices	512849	544674	585784	632817	669113	693786	695988	701013	723628	753418	784756	827258	877197	926484
Growth rate GDP vol. 1995 prices, %		5.8	7.0	7.4	5.4	3.6	0.3	0.7	3.1	4.0	4.0	5.1	5.7	5.3
GDP deflator (2000=100)	59.7	67.8	74.5	77.1	80.7	84.8	91.2	100.0	105.0	109.9	115.1	122.0	124.9	130.1
Growth rate GDP deflator, %		11.9	9.0	3.4	4.4	4.9	7.0	8.8	4.8	4.4	4.5	5.7	2.3	4.0
GDP per capita (constant 2000 US$)	2819	2982	3146	3333	3481	3622	3673	3752	3901	4081	4263	4495	4761	-
GDP per capita, PPP (constant 2000 int. $)	8370	8895	9320	9888	10363	10800	11035	11304	11723	12312	12665	13439	14722	-
Population (million)	5.3	5.3	5.4	5.4	5.4	5.4	5.4	5.4	5.4	5.4	5.4	5.4	5.4	-

Source: International Financial Statistics database, the International Monetary Fund, accessed January and April 2007. For GDP (current US$ millions), GDP per capita (constant 2000 US$), and GDP per capita, PPP (constant 2000 international $): World Development Indicators database, The World Bank, accessed January 2007. Growth rate of GDP vol. 1995 prices and Growth rate GDP deflator: Calculated by case authors.

Exhibit 4 Foreign Direct Investment, Net Inflows (% of GDP), Selected Countries, 1993–2005

	1993	1994	1995	1996	1997	1998	1999	2000	2001	2002	2003	2004	2005
Brazil	0.29	0.56	0.69	1.45	2.43	4.05	5.33	5.45	4.42	3.60	2.01	3.01	1.91
China	6.25	6.04	4.92	4.69	4.64	4.29	3.58	3.20	3.34	3.39	2.87	2.84	3.54
Hungary	6.09	2.76	10.76	7.28	9.09	7.11	6.88	5.89	7.54	4.59	2.62	4.63	5.89
Czech Republic	1.90	2.14	4.65	2.31	2.25	5.98	10.50	8.79	9.12	11.29	2.21	4.12	n/a
India	0.20	0.30	0.60	0.63	0.87	0.64	0.48	0.78	1.14	1.11	0.76	0.79	0.82
Ireland	2.20	1.51	2.16	3.53	3.38	12.51	18.98	26.52	9.13	24.00	14.27	-5.96	-14.73
Mexico	1.09	2.60	3.32	2.76	3.20	2.95	2.85	3.06	4.36	2.93	2.39	2.77	2.44
Poland	2.00	1.90	2.63	2.87	3.12	3.70	4.33	5.45	3.00	2.09	2.12	5.10	3.17
Russia	0.28	0.17	0.52	0.66	1.20	1.02	1.69	1.05	0.90	1.00	1.84	2.62	1.98
Slovak Republic	1.49	1.74	1.22	1.68	0.82	2.53	1.74	10.15	7.58	16.94	1.71	3.07	4.11
Turkey	0.35	0.47	0.52	0.40	0.43	0.47	0.43	0.49	2.31	0.62	0.73	0.95	2.70

Source: Adapted from World Development Indicators database, The World Bank, accessed April 2007.

Exhibit 5 Unemployment

5a) Unemployment Rates, Total, 1994–2005

	1994	1995	1996	1997	1998	1999	2000	2001	2002	2003	2004	2005
Czech Republic	4.3	4.1	3.9	4.8	6.4	8.6	8.7	8.0	7.3	7.8	8.3	7.9
France	11.7	11.1	11.6	11.5	11.1	10.5	9.1	8.4	8.9	9.5	9.6	9.9
Germany	8.3	8.0	8.5	9.2	8.8	7.9	7.2	7.4	8.2	9.1	9.5	9.4
Hungary	11.0	10.4	9.6	9.0	8.4	6.9	6.3	5.6	5.6	5.8	6.0	7.2
Ireland	14.3	12.3	11.7	9.9	7.5	5.7	4.3	3.8	4.3	4.6	4.5	4.4
Italy	10.6	11.2	11.2	11.2	11.3	11.0	10.1	9.1	8.6	8.4	8.0	7.7
Japan	2.9	3.1	3.4	3.4	4.1	4.7	4.7	5.0	5.4	5.3	4.7	4.4
Poland	14.4	13.3	12.3	10.9	10.2	13.4	16.4	18.5	19.8	19.2	18.8	17.7
Slovak Republic	13.7	13.1	11.3	11.9	12.6	16.8	18.7	19.4	18.7	17.5	18.2	16.3
United Kingdom	9.3	8.5	7.9	6.8	6.1	5.9	5.4	5.0	5.1	4.9	4.7	4.8
United States	6.1	5.6	5.4	4.9	4.5	4.2	4.0	4.7	5.8	6.0	5.5	5.1
EU15	10.4	10.0	10.1	9.8	9.3	8.5	7.6	7.2	7.6	7.9	8.1	7.9
OECD total	7.6	7.3	7.2	6.9	6.8	6.6	6.2	6.4	6.9	7.1	6.9	6.6

Source: Compiled from OECD Factbook 2007, http://oberon.sourceoecd.org/vl=3799538/cl=23/nw=1/rpsv/factbook/06-02-01.htm, and World Development Indicators database, The World Bank, accessed April 2007.

Note: As a percentage of civilian labor force.

5b) Unemployment in Slovakia by Quarter, 2001–2006

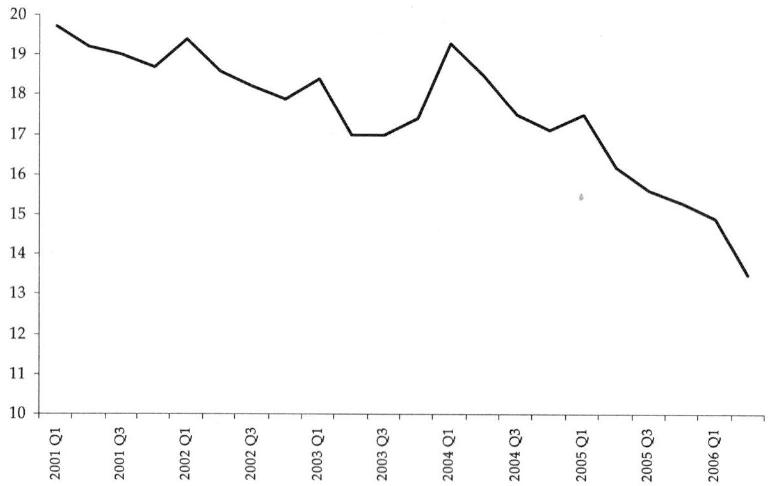

Source: Adapted from Labour Force Sample Survey, the Statistical Office of the Slovak Republic, http://www.statistics.sk/webdata/english/index2_a.htm, accessed October 2006.

Exhibit 6 Social Reform: Monthly Social Assistance Benefits, SKK

Previous System, until December 2003	
Income top-off, material need for "subjective reasons"[a]	
Individual	1,450
Income top-off, material need for "objective reasons"[a]	
Individual	2,900
Dependent minor child	1,000
Non-dependent child	1,600
Maximum per family	10,500

New System, from September 2004[b]	
Basic benefit	
Single person	1,530
Individual parent with up to four children	2,450
Individual parent with more than four children	3,640
Couple without children	2,660
Parents with up to four children	3,630
Parents with more than four children	4,850
Pregnancy allowance[c]	350
Allocation allowance / protection allowance	1,500
Housing bonus: one-person household	780
Housing bonus: multiple-person household	1,330
Healthcare allowance, per person	50

Source: David Moore, "Slovakia's 2004 Tax and Welfare Reforms," IMF Working Paper 05/133, July 2005, p. 35.

[a]The previous system distinguished between material need for "objective" and "subjective" reasons. "Objective" reasons included involuntary unemployment—an inability to find work despite search efforts. "Subjective" reasons included an individual voluntarily leaving a job or refusing a job offer. Material need was usually deemed to be for "subjective" reasons for households in the system for more than 24 months.

[b]The activation allowance was increased in April 2004. Basic benefits were indexed in September 2004.

[c]Paid only to a single person or couple without children.

Exhibit 7 Tax Reform

7a) Corporate Income Tax in Slovakia, 2004 and 2003

	2004	2003
Tax rate	19%	15%
		18%
		25%
Dividend tax	0%	15%
Composite taxation of capital income	**19%**	**36.3%**

Source: Zdenko Krajčír and Ľudovít Ódor, "First Year of the Tax Reform, or 19 Percent at Work," Financial Policy Institute, Ministry of Finance of the Slovak Republic, September 2005, p. 14.

Note: According to The National Bank of Slovakia, the 15% rate was applicable to companies in the agricultural sector (more than 50% of turnover from agriculture), while the 18% rate was applicable to companies that employed people with disabilities (at least 50% of employees).

7b) Personal Income Tax in Slovakia, 2004 and 2002

	2004	2002	
		Income range, rate on the rate + fixed amount	
Tax rate	19%	SKK–SKK 90,000	10% + SKK 0
		SKK 90–SKK 180,000	20% + SKK 9,000
		SKK 180,000–SKK 396,000	28% + SKK 27,000
		SKK 396,000–SKK 564,000	35% + SKK 87,480
		SKK 564,000 and more	38% + SKK 146,280
Deductible items			
Taxpayer	SKK 80,832[a]	SKK 38,760 (SKK 48,000 if handicapped)	
Spouse	MAX (SKK 80,832 minus spouse's income, 0)	SKK 12,000 if had no income	
Old-age pensioners	SKK 0	SKK 0 (SKK 8,400 if partially disabled; SKK 16,800 if disabled)	
Dependent child	SKK 0	SKK 16,800 (SKK 22,800 if handicapped)	
Tax credit			
Dependent child	SKK 4,800 only if parent's annual gross income exceed 6 x minimum wage, i.e., SKK 36,480	SKK 0	

Source: "Slovak Republic: The Quest for Equitable Growth in the Slovak Republic," a World Bank Living Standards Assessment, Report No. 32433-SK, Poverty Reduction and Economic Management Unit, Europe and Central Asia Region, September 22, 2005, p. 52.

[a]The amount is set to 19.2 times the minimum subsistence level as of January every year.

7c) Corporate Income Tax Rates, Percent, 1995–2004

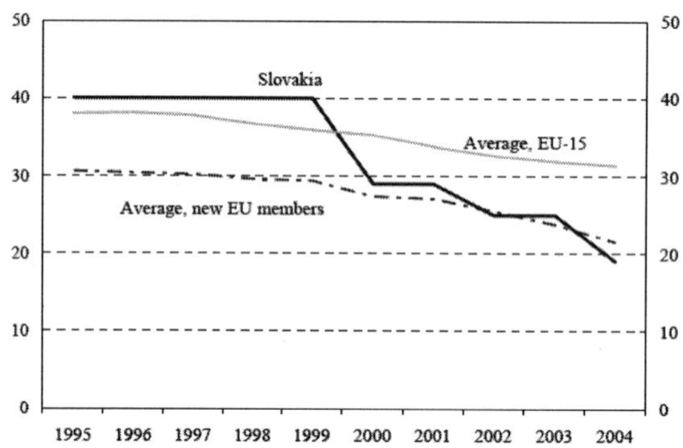

Source: David Moore, "Slovakia's 2004 Tax and Welfare Reforms," IMF Working Paper 05/133, July 2005, p. 21.

7d) Average Personal Income Tax Rate, Percent of Gross Income

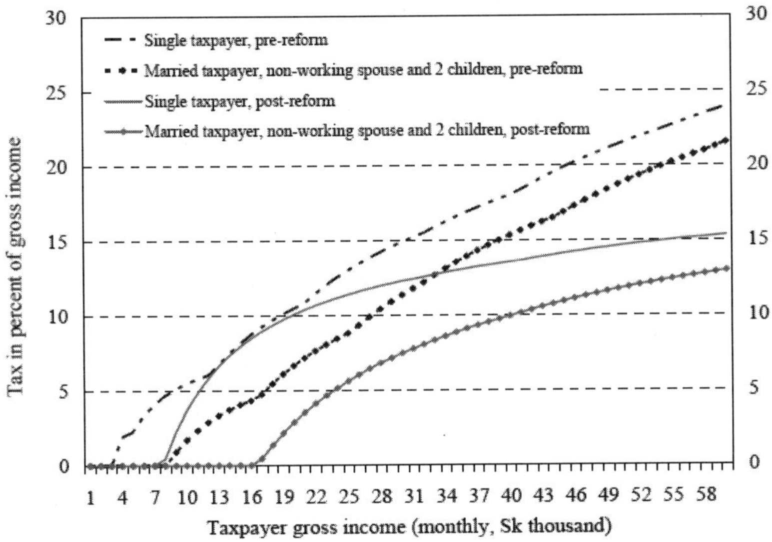

Source: David Moore, "Slovakia's 2004 Tax and Welfare Reforms," July 2005, p. 22.

7e) Marginal Effective Tax Rates, Personal Income

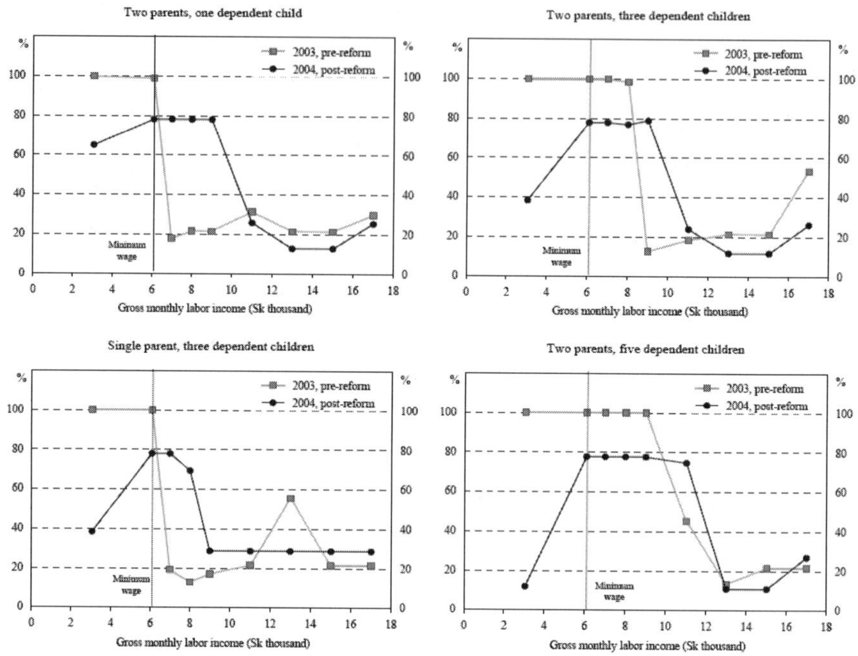

Source: David Moore, "Slovakia's 2004 Tax and Welfare Reforms," July 2005, p. 18.

7f) Tax Structure, Including Social Contributions (in Percent of GDP)

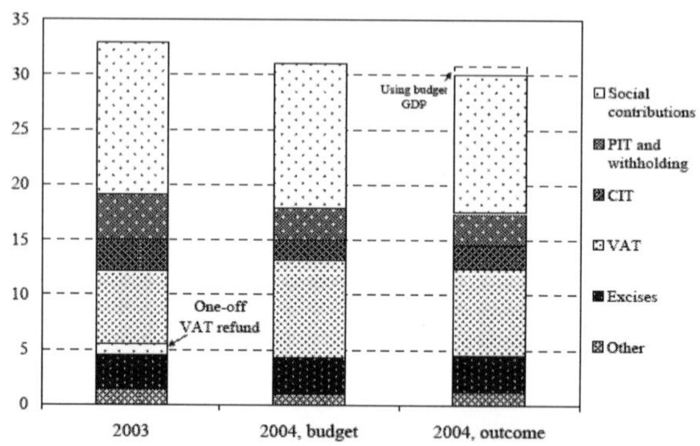

Source: David Moore, "Slovakia's 2004 Tax and Welfare Reforms," July 2005, p. 10.

Exhibit 8 Average Hours Worked, Selected OECD Countries, 1970–2005

	1980	1985	1990	1995	2000	2001	2002	2003	2004	2005
Czech Republic	-	-	-	2,064	2,092	2,000	1,980	1,972	1,986	2,002
Finland	1,850	1,814	1,771	1,776	1,750	1,734	1,727	1,720	1,724	1,714
France	1,844	1,732	1,702	1,651	1,592	1,579	1,537	1,532	1,555	1,546
Germany	1,746	1,665	1,572	1,534	1,473	1,458	1,445	1,439	1,441	1,437
Hungary	2,228	2,012	1,975	2,039	2,061	2,019	2,026	1,997	1,996	1,994
Ireland	1,947	1,897	1,911	1,823	1,688	1,679	1,666	1,646	1,642	1,638
Italy	1,983	1,924	1,934	1,889	1,871	1,866	1,844	1,820	1,813	1,801
Netherlands	1,613	1,517	1,456	1,344	1,368	1,368	1,338	1,354	1,357	1,367
Poland	-	-	-	-	1,988	1,974	1,979	1,984	1,983	1,994
Slovak Republic	-	-	-	1,879	1,811	1,799	1,746	1,673	1,737	1,739
Spain	2,003	1,855	1,824	1,815	1,815	1,817	1,798	1,800	1,799	1,769
Sweden	1,517	1,538	1,561	1,626	1,625	1,603	1,580	1,563	1,585	1,587
United Kingdom	1,769	1,762	1,767	1,739	1,708	1,711	1,692	1,683	1,669	1,672
United States	1,819	1,841	1,836	1,849	1,841	1,819	1,814	1,806	1,808	1,804
Slovenia	-	-	-	2,086	1,866	1,847	1,916	1,920	1,858	1,868

Source: OECD Factbook 2007, http://titania.sourceoecd.org/vl=3144083/cl=39/nw=1/rpsv/factbook/06-01-05.htm, accessed April 2007.

Exhibit 9 Flat Tax Implementation, after 1994

9a) The Eastern European Wave

Country	Year	Rate after Reform	Rate before Reform	CIT Rate, after Reform	Change in Basic Allowance
Estonia	1994	26	16–33	26	Modest increase
Lithuania	1994	33	18–33	29	Substantial increase
Latvia	1995	25	25 and 10	25	Slight reduction
Russia	2001	13	12–30	37	Modest increase
Serbia	2003	14			
Ukraine	2004	13	10–40	25	Increase
Slovakia	2004	19	10–38	19	Substantial increase
Georgia	2005	12	12–20	20	Eliminated
Romania	2005	16	18–40	16	Increase
Kyrgyz Republic	2006	10	10–20	20	
Republic of Macedonia	2007	12	15–24	15	

9b) Countries Considering Adopting Flat Taxes

Possible adopters	
Costa Rica	Mongolia
The Czech Republic	Poland
Mauritius	Slovenia

Sources: "The case for flat taxes," *The Economist*, April 14, 2005; "Slovak Republic: The Quest for Equitable Growth in the Slovak Republic," a World Bank Living Standards Assessment, Report No. 32433-SK, Poverty Reduction and Economic Management Unit, Europe, Central Asia Region, September 22, 2005; Michael Keen, Yitae Kim, and Ricardo Varsano, "The 'Flat Taxes': Principles and Evidence," IMF Working Paper 06-218, September 2006; and Alvin Rabushka, "The Flat Tax Spreads to Central Asia and the Indian Ocean," Hoover Institution, OP-EDS & COMMENTARY, August 8, 2006, http://www.hoover.org/pubaffairs/dailyreport/archive/3556692.html, accessed April 2007.

Exhibit 10 Economic Indicators for Slovakia

10a) Prices, Production and Labor, 1993–2006

SKK Million	1993	1994	1995	1996	1997	1998	1999	2000	2001	2002	2003	2004	2005	2006
Money	116,615	123,820	149,657	173,350	165,658	146,833	153,058	185,964	225,566	244,771	353,971	404,722	468,041	524,322
Quasi-money	137,353	174,452	203,388	236,763	280,113	320,977	369,164	415,478	447,580	456,035	414,497	415,854	381,814	448,920
Discount rate (end of period)	12.0	12.0	9.8	8.8	8.8	8.8	8.8	8.8	7.8	6.5	6.0	4.0	3.0	-
Producer price index	65.1	71.6	78.1	81.3	85.0	87.7	91.1	100.0	106.6	108.8	117.9	121.9	127.7	138.3
Consumer price index	54.1	61.3	67.4	71.3	75.7	80.7	89.3	100.0	107.3	110.9	120.4	129.5	133.0	138.9
Av. monthly wages index	47.1	55.1	62.9	71.3	80.7	87.5	93.9	100.0	108.2	118.2	125.7	138.5	151.1	164.1
Industrial output index	74.3	78.0	86.1	88.3	89.4	94.2	92.2	100.0	106.9	113.7	119.5	124.2	129.0	141.7
Unemployment rate (%)	n/a	13.7	13.1	11.3	13.0	13.7	17.3	18.2	18.3	17.8	15.2	14.3	11.7	10.4
Exchange rate (USD/SKK, yearly av.)	30.8	32.0	29.5	30.7	33.7	35.3	41.5	46.4	48.4	45.3	36.8	32.3	31.1	29.7

10b) Government Finance, 1996–2003

SKK Million	1996	1997	1998	1999	2000	2001	2002	2003
Deficit (-) or surplus	-8,540	-28,430	-28,663	-26,637	-27,464	-32,012	110,172	-33,537
Deficit as % of GDP	-1.30%	-3.92%	-3.6,3%	-3.1,3%	-2.92%	-3.14%	9.91%	-2.77%
Total revenue and grants	254,769	265,402	274,888	315,683	325,614	331,821	366,636	387,288
Revenue	254,510	265,146	274,677	315,436	325,402	331,649	366,552	387,242
Grants	259	256	211	247	212	172	84	46
Exp. & lending minus repayments	263,309	293,832	303,551	342,320	353,078	363,833	256,464	420,825
Expenditure	266,814	290,026	303,952	317,447	368,407	366,901	434,127	438,960
Lending minus repayments	-3,505	3,806	-401	24,873	-15,329	-3,068	-177,663	-18,135
Total financing	8,540	28,430	28,663	26,637	27,464	32,012	-110,172	33,537
Domestic	12,761	21,518	-6,057	-2,112	-681	24,080	-104,078	36,489
Foreign	-4,221	6912	34,720	28,749	28,145	7,932	n/a	-2,952
Total debt by residence	153,910	194,125	215,605	238,061	274,870	417,450	399,947	439,097
Domestic	120,741	144,581	141,813	133,625	137,849	293,003	289,132	335,130
Foreign	33,169	49,544	73,792	104,436	137,021	124,447	110,815	103,967

Source: International Financial Statistics database, the International Monetary Fund, accessed January and April 2007.
For exchange rate data, years 1993 and 1994: Slovakia Country Report, The Economist Intelligence Unit, accessed April 2007.
For exchange rate data, years 1995–2006: http://www.oanda.com/convert/fxhistory, accessed April 2007.

10c) Balance of Payments, 1993–2003

USD Million	1993	1994	1995	1996	1997	1998	1999	2000	2001	2002	2003	2004	2005	2006
Current account	-579.7	670.6	390.0	-2090.4	-1,961.3	-2,126.5	-1,155.1	-694.3	n/a	-1,955.0	-281.9	-1507.0	-4,091.0	-4,442.0
Goods exports, F.O.B.	5,452.5	6,706.1	8,590.8	8,823.8	9,640.7	107,20.2	10,201.3	11,896.1	n/a	14,460.1	21,944.0	27,752.0	32,030.0	41,747.0
Goods imports, F.O.B	-6,364.6	-6,645.4	-8,820.1	-11,106.5	-11,725.2	-13,070.9	-11,310.3	-12,790.6	n/a	-16,625.7	-22,592.7	-29,208.0	-34,480.0	-44,617.0
Trade balance	-912.1	60.7	-229.2	-2,282.7	-2,084.5	-2,350.7	-1,109.0	-894.5	n/a	-2,165.6	-648.7	n/a	n/a	n/a
Services, credit	1,938.6	2,261.4	2,378.5	2,065.6	2,167.4	2,292.0	1,899.3	2,240.9	n/a	2,811.8	3,297.0	n/a	n/a	n/a
Services, debit	-1,666.3	-1,599.7	-1,838.0	-2,027.5	-2,094.3	-2,275.5	-1,844.0	-1,805.4	n/a	-2,350.9	-3,056.1	n/a	n/a	n/a
Balance on goods and services	-639.8	722.4	311.2	-2,244.6	-2,011.4	-2,334.2	-1,053.7	-459.0	n/a	-1,704.8	-407.8	n/a	n/a	n/a
Income, credit	185.2	155.4	249.7	223.5	315.2	437.4	268.4	268.0	n/a	341.8	907.3	n/a	n/a	n/a
Income, debit	-223.5	-275.4	-263.5	-270.3	-438.4	-595.3	-567.8	-623.1	n/a	-790.5	-1026.2	n/a	n/a	n/a
Balance on goods, serv. & inc.	-678.2	602.4	297.5	-2,291.4	-2,134.6	-2,492.2	-1,353.1	-814.1	n/a	-2,153.5	-526.7	n/a	n/a	n/a
Current transfers, N.I.E., credit	216.3	165.8	242.5	482.9	540.4	645.0	466.0	343.8	n/a	480.5	536.5	n/a	n/a	n/a
Current transfers, debit	-117.8	-97.6	-149.9	-282.0	-367.1	-279.3	-268.1	-224.0	n/a	-281.9	-291.8	n/a	n/a	n/a
Capital account, N.I.E.	563.9	84.0	45.6	30.3	0.0	70.4	157.6	90.8	n/a	110.2	102.1	n/a	n/a	n/a
Financial account, N.I.E.	-153.3	70.8	1,211.2	2,267.9	1,780.1	1911.5	1,788.8	1,472.4	n/a	5,230.1	1,661.1	n/a	n/a	n/a
Direct investment abroad	-60.6	-13.9	-10.1	-47.7	-95.3	-144.9	376.1	-21.5	n/a	-3.3	-23.6	n/a	n/a	n/a
Dir. invest. in rep. econ., N.I.E.	198.8	269.9	236.1	350.8	173.7	562.1	354.3	2,052.5	n/a	4,104.2	559.3	n/a	n/a	n/a
Portfolio investment assets	-773.6	-26.1	156.8	-12.2	-81.2	-57.4	247.4	-194.7	n/a	264.5	-742.2	n/a	n/a	n/a
Portfolio investment liabilities, N.I.E.	464.6	304.5	53.5	28.9	92.7	841.4	405.0	1,015.9	n/a	288.5	168.3	n/a	n/a	n/a
Financial derivatives, assets	n/a	0.0	0.0	0.0	0.0	0.0	n/a	n/a	n/a	-0.1	-43.3	n/a	n/a	n/a
Financial derivatives, liabilities	n/a	0.0	0.0	0.0	0.0	0.0	n/a	0.6	n/a	3.1	59.9	n/a	n/a	n/a
Other investment assets	-412.2	-547.6	-115.6	-334.3	-1,028.2	190.3	1,713.3	-973.1	n/a	737.8	-20.0	n/a	n/a	n/a
Other investment liabilities, N.I.E.	429.7	84.0	890.6	2,282.3	2,718.4	519.9	-1,307.3	-407.2	n/a	-164.7	1,702.5	n/a	n/a	n/a
Net errors and omissions	183.2	379.7	144.4	162.2	280.1	-333.1	-14.3	50.7	n/a	298.3	26.8	n/a	n/a	n/a
Reserve assets	-103.6	-1,256.3	-1,590.1	-245.4	-46.9	544.8	-724.8	-794.2	n/a	-3,683.6	-1,508.0	n/a	n/a	n/a
Use of fund credit and loans	89.5	51.2	-201.2	-124.6	-52.1	-67.2	-52.2	-125.5	n/a	0.0	0.0	n/a	n/a	n/a
Total external debt (USD billion)	n/a	n/a	5.7	7.7	10.0	11.8	12.5	12.1	11.1	13.1	18.2	22.1	25.8	30.4
Debt-service ratio, paid (%)	n/a	n/a	11.3	11.9	11.3	15.3	15.3	19.2	16.9	19.4	13.7	15.4	13.7	11.2
Current account balance (% of GDP)	-4.0	4.0	2.0	-10.0	-9.0	-10.0	-6.0	-3.0	n/a	-8.0	-1.0	n/a	n/a	n/a

Source: International Financial Statistics database, the International Monetary Fund, accessed t January 2007.
For total external debt (USD billion) and debt-service ratio: Slovakia Country Report, The Economist Intelligence Unit, accessed January and April 2007.
For current account balance (% of GDP): World Development Indicators database, The World Bank, accessed January 2007.
Current account, goods exports, and goods imports for 2004, 2005, and 2006, Slovakia Country Report, The Economist Intelligence Unit, accessed April 2007.

Notes: Data for 2001 not available through the International Financial Statistics Database.
2005 and 2006 data for total external debt (USD billion) and debt-service ratio: Economist Intelligence Unit estimates.
Current account, goods exports, and goods imports for 2005 and 2006: Economist Intelligence Unit estimates.

Exhibit 11 Foreign Activities in Slovakia

11a) Flow of FDI by Sector in Slovakia (New Equity plus Reinvested Earnings), 1997–2004

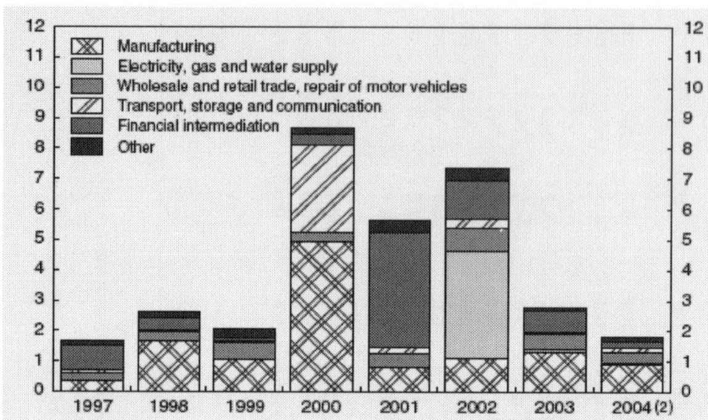

Source: "Slovak Republic," OECD Economic Surveys, Volume 2005/16, September, 2005, p. 29.

Note (2): First three quarters.

11b) Foreign Companies with Substantial Investments in Slovakia by 2006

U.S. companies	Non-U.S. companies
U.S. Steel	Volkswagen
Whirlpool	Hyundai Kia
Kimberly-Clark	Peugeot-Citroën
Emerson Electric	Getrag Ford
Tower Automotive	Deutsche Telecom
Delphi	Ruhrgas
Johnson Controls	Intesa BCI
ON Semiconductor	UniCredito
Citibank	Raiffeisen Group
IBM	Enel
Molex	Siemens
Visteon	
Dell	

Source: 2006 Investment Climate Statement: Slovakia, U.S. Department of State, http://www.state.gov/e/eb/ifd/2006/62032.htm, accessed September 2006.

Exhibit 12 Tax Revenues in 2004 and 2003

	2004 (after reform)				2003 (before reform)	
In SKK billion	Plan	Share on Total	Reality	Share on Total	Reality	Share on Total
Tax revenues	232.0	100.0%	233.5	100.0%	217.6	100.0%
Direct taxes (PIT, CIT, WIT)	62.2	26.8%	68.9	29.5%	82.7	38.0%
Personal income tax (PIT)	27.1	11.7%	34.1	14.6%	39.9	18.3%
Corporate income tax (CIT)	23.7	10.2%	29.1	12.5v	33.6	15.4%
Withholding income tax (WIT)	11.4	4.9%	5.7	2.4%	9.1	4.2%
Indirect taxes (VAT & excise)	157.0	67.7%	149.5	64.0%	118.3	60.9%
VAT	113.8	49.1%	104.9	44.9%	80.7	41.9%
Excise duties	43.2	18.6%	44.6	19.1%	37.6	19.0%

Source: "Slovak tax reform: one year after," Peter Goliaš (Institute for Economic and Social Reforms, INEKO) and Robert Kičina (Business Alliance of Slovakia, PAS), April 2005, http://www.ineko.sk/reformy2003/menu_dane_paper_golias.pdf, accessed November 2006.

Exhibit 13 Impact of Benefits on Income Inequality, 2002 and 2004 (percent)

Type	Net Income + Child Allowance		Net Income + Parental Allowance		Net Income + Social Assistance Benefit and Scholarship	
	2002	2004	2002	2004	2002	2004
Gini index	36.6	37.4	37.4	37.8	33.1	33.9

Source: "Slovak Republic: The Quest for Equitable Growth in the Slovak Republic," a World Bank Living Standards Assessment, Report No. 32433-SK, Poverty Reduction and Economic Management Unit, September 22, 2005, p. 68.

Exhibit 14 Cost of Labor, Social Indicators, Exchange Rates, Selected European Countries

14a) Social Contribution Rates, Selected European Countries, Percent of Gross Labor Income, 2003

	Employee	Employer	Total
Slovakia (2003)	**12.8**	**38.2**	**51.0**
Slovakia (2004)	**13.4**	**35.2**	**48.6**
Czech Republic	12.5	35.0	47.5
Hungary	12.5	32.0	44.5
Poland	25.0	20.4	45.4
EU-15 average[a]	12.5	24.1	36.6

Source: David Moore, "Slovakia's 2004 Tax and Welfare Reforms," IMF Working Paper 05/133, July 2005, p. 16.

Note: Unless otherwise indicated, data refer to 2003 and are based on the average production wage.

[a]Unweighted, excludes Denmark.

14b) Nominal Effective Exchange Rates, Visegrád Countries and Euro Area, 1993–2005

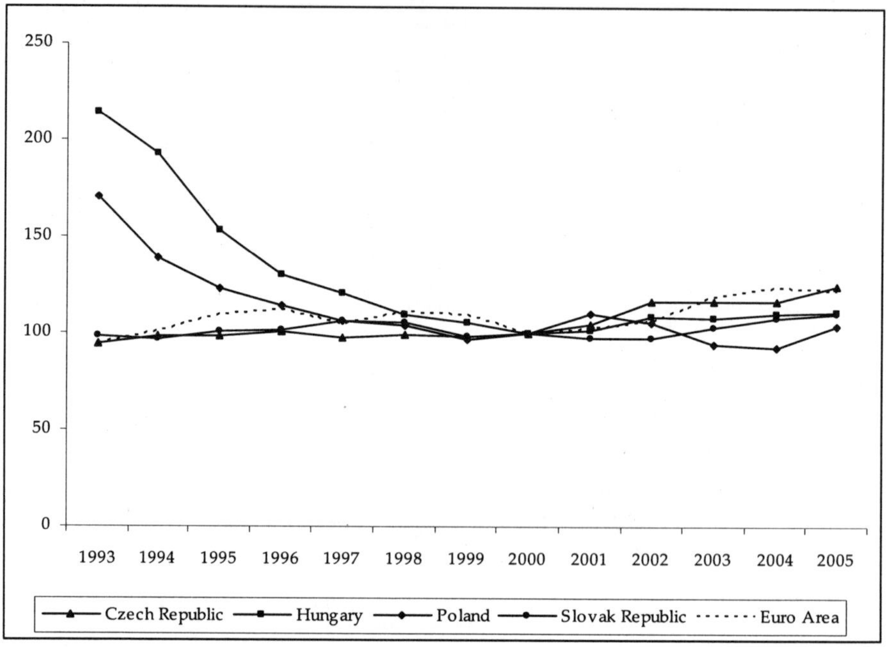

Source: Adapted from OECD Factbook 2007, http://titania.sourceoecd.org/vl=3546018/cl=11/nw=1/rpsv/factbook/04-02-02.htm, accessed April 2007.

Note: Year 2000 = index 100.

Exhibit 15 Statutory Corporate Income Tax Rates on Retained Profits versus Effective Average Tax Burden of Companies in Europe

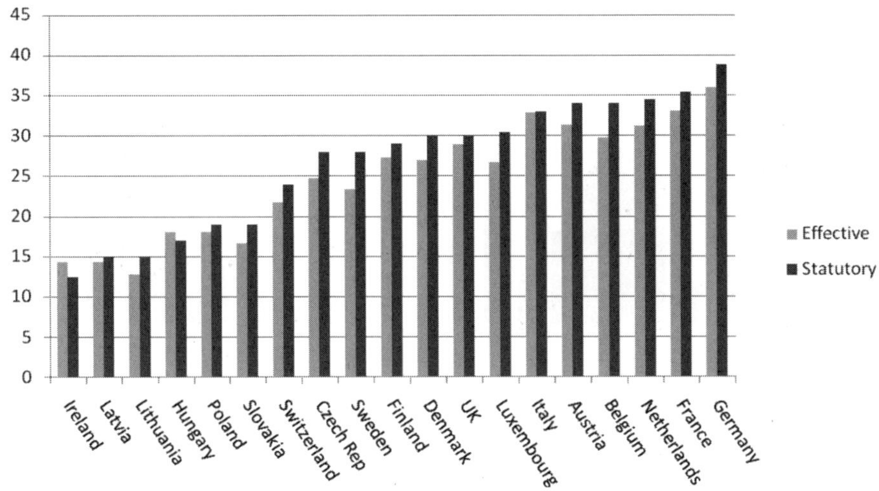

Source: Adapted from Anne-Marie Brook and Willi Leibfritz, "Slovakia's introduction of a flat tax as part of wider economic reforms," OECD Economics Department Working Papers No. 448, October 3, 2005, pp. 21–22.

Note: 2004 data for Slovakia, Germany, Czech Republic, Hungary, Poland, Latvia and Lithuania; 2003 data for other countries.

Exhibit 16 GDP per Capita, Constant 2000 US$, Selected European Countries, 2005

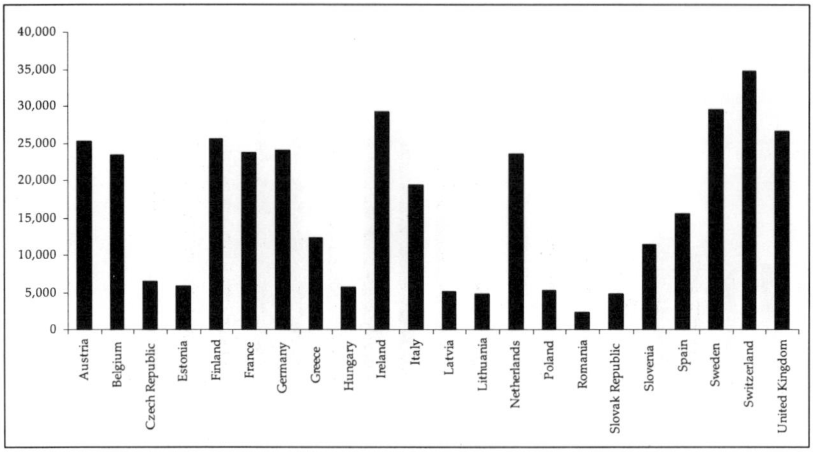

Source: World Development Indicators database, The World Bank, accessed January 2007.

Exhibit 17 The Slovak Koruna within Its ERM II Band, from November 2005 to February 2006

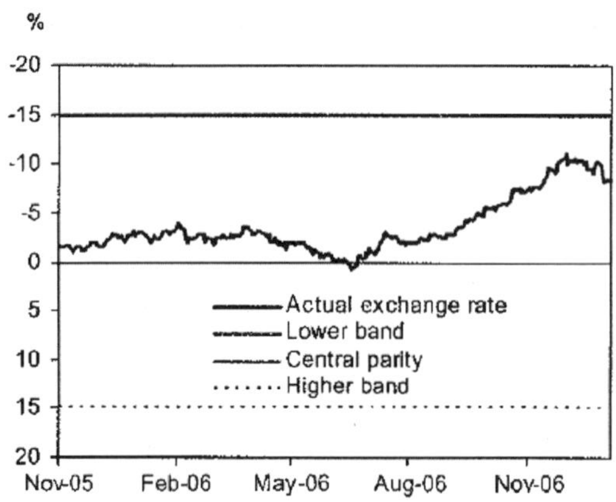

Source: New European Markets Analyst, Issue 07/03, February 2, 2007, GS Global Economic website, https://portal.gs.com, accessed March 2007.

Note: Up = appreciation.

Endnotes

[1] James Madison, The Federalist No. 62, "The Senate," *Independent Journal*, February 27, 1788, http://www.constitution.org/fed/federa62.htm, accessed October 2006.

[2] Harvey S. Rosen, *Public Finance*, 7th ed. (McGraw-Hill, 2005), p. 3.

[3] Stanislav J. Kirschbaum, *A History of Slovakia—The Struggle for Survival*, 2nd ed. (Palgrave Macmillan, May 2005), p. 303; and "Slovak Prime Minister Mikuláš Dzurinda's Speech at the Charles University," Prague, July 24, 1999, http://www.government.gov.sk/dzurinda_en/agenda/aktuality_start.php3?id_ele=1109, accessed October 2006.

[4] "Slovak Republic: The Quest for Equitable Growth in the Slovak Republic," a World Bank Living Standards Assessment, Report No. 32433-SK, Poverty Reduction and Economic Management Unit, Europe and Central Asia Region, p. xvii, September 22, 2005.

[5] "The populist choice," *The Economist*, June 19, 2006.

[6] Robert Anderson, "Leading from the front but striving for consensus," Special Report Slovakia, *Financial Times*, February 20, 2007, p. 4.

[7] Slovakia Country Report, The Economist Intelligence Unit, August 2006, accessed January 2007.

[8] "The Manifesto of the Government of the Slovak Republic," August 2006, p. 10, http://www-8.vlada.gov.sk/data/files/1902.pdf, accessed November 2006.

[9] Ibid.

[10] Peter Laca, "Slovak MPs change tax laws to set ground for budget," *Reuters News*, December 6, 2006.

[11] When no other source is indicated in these notes, information was compiled from Stanislav J. Kirschbaum, *A History of Slovakia—The Struggle for Survival*, 2nd ed. (Palgrave Macmillan, May 2005).

[12] The Warsaw Pact was established in 1955 to counterbalance NATO and included the Soviet Union, Albania, Bulgaria, Czechoslovakia, German Democratic Republic, Hungary, Poland, and Romania. The organization was dissolved in 1990.

[13] Edmund L. Andrews, "An American Giant Places a Bet in Eastern Europe," *The New York Times*, November 30, 2000.

[14] "Mikuláš Dzurinda, Slovakia's turn for the better," *The Economist*, December 9, 1999.

[15] When no other source is indicated in these notes, information was compiled from Stanislav J. Kirschbaum, *A History of Slovakia—The Struggle for Survival*, 2nd ed. (Palgrave Macmillan, May 2005); or from interviews.

[16] Biography of Mikuláš Dzurinda on Wikipedia, http://en.wikipedia.org/wiki/Mikul%C3%A1s_Dzurinda, accessed February 2007.

[17] "Slovak Prime Minister Mikuláš Dzurinda's Speech at the Charles University," Prague, July 24, 1999, http://www.government.gov.sk/dzurinda_en/agenda/aktuality_start.php3?id_ele=1109, accessed October 13, 2006.

[18] Slovakia Country Report, The Economist Intelligence Unit, 4th Quarter, November 199, accessed October 2006.

[19] Speech of H. E. Mikuláš Dzurinda, prime minister of Slovakia, during The Economist Conference, held in Bratislava, February 10, 2003, World Investment News, http://www.winne.com/topinterviews/dzurindaspeech.htm, accessed October 2006.

[20] Comments by Grigorij Mesenznikov of the Institute of Public Affairs in Bratislava in Pasquier Sylvaine, "Slovaquie Opération mains propres," *L'Express*, November 7, 2002.

[21] The 10 countries were Cyprus, Czech Republic, Estonia, Hungary, Latvia, Lithuania, Malta, Poland, Slovakia, and Slovenia.

[22] Slovakia Country Report, The Economist Intelligence Unit, 3rd Quarter, September 1998.

[23] Slovakia Country Report, The Economist Intelligence Unit, January 2004.

[24] Speech of H. E. Mikuláš Dzurinda, prime minister of Slovakia, during The Economist Conference, held in Bratislava, February 10, 2003, World Investment News, http://www.winne.com/topinterviews/dzurindaspeech.htm, accessed October 2006.

[25] Anne-Marie Brook and Willi Leibfritz, "Slovakia's introduction of a flat tax as part of wider economic reforms," OECD Economics Department Working Papers No. 448, October 3, 2005, p. 10.

[26] David Moore, "Slovakia's 2004 Tax and Welfare Reforms," IMF Working Paper 05/133, July 2005, pp. 4–6.

[27] Speech of H. E. Mikuláš Dzurinda, prime minister of Slovakia, during The Economist Conference, held in Bratislava, February 10, 2003, World Investment News, http://www.winne.com/topinterviews/dzurindaspeech.htm, accessed October 2006.

[28] Peter Pažitný, Rudolf Zajac and Anton Marcinčin, "Reform Agenda: Health Reform in Slovakia," Ministry of Health of the Slovak Republic, 2005.

[29] Speech of H. E. Mikuláš Dzurinda, prime minister of Slovakia, during The Economist Conference, held in Bratislava, February 10, 2003, World Investment News, http://www.winne.com/topinterviews/dzurindaspeech.htm, accessed October 2006.

[30] Peter Pažitný, Rudolf Zajac and Anton Marcinčin, "Reform Agenda: Health Reform in Slovakia," Ministry of Health of the Slovak Republic, 2005.

[31] Slovak Ministry of Labor, Social Affairs and Family, "Reform of the Pension System in the Slovak Republic," Bratislava, January 2003; and Slovakia Country Report, The Economist Intelligence Unit, November 2003, pp. 22–23.

[32] "Slovak Republic," OECD Economic Surveys, Volume 2005/16, September, 2005, p. 110.

[33] Ibid.

[34] David Moore, "Slovakia's 2004 Tax and Welfare Reforms," IMF Working Paper 05/133, July 2005, p. 4.

[35] Speech of H. E. Mikuláš Dzurinda, prime minister of Slovakia, during The Economist Conference, held in Bratislava, February 10, 2003, World Investment News, http://www.winne.com/topinterviews/dzurindaspeech.htm, accessed October 2006.

[36] Ministry of Finance of the Slovak Republic, "The Fundamental Tax Reform, December 2004," http://www.finance.gov.sk/EN/Default.aspx?CatID=118, accessed April 2007.

[37] Harvey S. Rosen, *Public Finance*, 7th ed. (McGraw-Hill, 2005), p. 384.

[38] Bernard Mofokeng, "Pros and cons for a flat tax versus progressive tax," *Business Day*, February 13, 2006.

[39] Ibid.

[40] *Poll* means "head" in Old English.

[41] Margaret Harris, "Pool tax revolt may topple Thatcher," *Sun Herald*, March 11, 1990.

[42] "Mrs. Thatcher's Pool Tax," editorial, *The Washington Post*, March 12, 1990.

[43] Philip Webster, "Thatcher will push ahead on poll tax Bill," *The Times*, April 20, 1988.

[44] Steve Forbes, "One Simple Rate," *The Wall Street Journal*, August 15, 2005.

[45] Dan Goodgame, "Is this tax flat unfair?" *TIME*, January 29, 1996, http://www.time.com/time/magazine/article/0,9171,984012-1,00.html, accessed February 2007.

[46] Margo Thorning, "Fundamental Tax Reform: A Comparison of the Major Proposals," American Council for Capital Formation, February 1996, http://www.accf.org/publications/reports/sr-fundtaxreform96.html, accessed February 2007.

[47] Pete du Pont, "The 25 Fat Years—Ronald Reagan's election marked America's economic turning point," WSJ.com OpinionJournal from *The Wall Street Journal* editorial page, February 28, 2006.

[48] "The Flat Tax: 'Nutty' It's Not," *The Wall Street Journal*, February 22, 1996.

[49] "In effect, the HR flat tax is a consumption-type, origin-based value-added tax (VAT) collected by the subtraction method, supplemented by a (nonrefundable) tax credit against labor income." Michael Keen, Yitae Kim, and Ricardo Varsano, "The 'Flat Taxes': Principles and Evidence," IMF Working Paper 06-218, September 2006.

[50] Robert E. Hall and Alvin Rabushka, *The Flat Tax*, 2nd ed. (Hoover Institution Press, 1995).

[51] Harvey S. Rosen, *Public Finance*, 7th ed. (McGraw-Hill, 2005), p. 384.

[52] Paul Krugman, "The Tax-Reform Obsession," originally published in *The New York Times*, April 4, 1996. Found on http://www.pkarchive.org/economy/TaxReformObsession.html, accessed February 2007.

[53] "The case for flat taxes," *The Economist*, April 14, 2005.

[54] "Estonia emerges from recession, forecasts growth," *Reuters News*, January 7, 1994.

[55] "Former Estonian Prime Minister Mart Laar Wins Friedman Prize for Liberty," Cato Institute, http://www.cato.org/special/friedman/index.html, accessed October 2006.

[56] James Morrison, "Watching the Russians...," *The Washington Times*, June 2, 1997.

[57] "To Grow or Not to Grow," editorial, *The Wall Street Journal*, October 11, 2006.

[58] Brian Whitmore, "Eastern Europe embraces flat tax; former communist nations see revenue rise, cheating decline," *The Boston Globe*, February 22, 2005.

[59] "Flat Tax Fever," editorial, *The Wall Street Journal*, July 11, 2003.

[60] CV of Ivan Mikloš from the OECD, http://www.oecd.org/dataoecd/36/63/31721650.pdf, accessed February 2007.

[61] Dušan Zachar, "Reforms in Slovakia 2003–2004," INEKO, July 2004.

[62] "National Report on Economic Reform of the Product and Capital Markets," Bratislava, November, 2003, http://ec.europa.eu/economy-finance/epc/documents/2004/nationalreportsobservers/Slovakia-en.pdf, accessed October 2006.

[63] David Moore, "Slovakia's 2004 Tax and Welfare Reforms," IMF Working Paper 05/133, p. 12, July 2005.

[64] Zdenko Krajčír and Ľudovít Ódor, "First Year of the Tax Reform, or 19 Percent at Work," Financial Policy Institute, Ministry of Finance of the Slovak Republic, p. 8, September 2005.

[65] "National Report on Economic Reform of the Product and Capital Markets," Bratislava, November, 2003, http://ec.europa.eu/economy-finance/epc/documents/2004/nationalreportsobservers/Slovakia-en.pdf, accessed October 2006.

[66] Statistical Office of the Slovak Republic, http://www.statistics.sk/webdata/english/index2_a.htm, accessed October 2006, and Slovakia Country Report, The Economist Intelligence Unit, August 2006.

[67] "Slovak Republic," OECD Economic Surveys, Volume 2005/16, September, 2005, p. 26.

[68] Ibid., p. 29.

[69] Slovakia Country Report, The Economist Intelligence Unit, p. 29, May 2004.

[70] Nick Spiro, "Central & Eastern Europe: EBRD—CEE Success Accentuates Halted Reforms in EU—The New Central and Eastern European Members of the EU Are Setting the Pace on Economic Reform, Stimulating A Liberalising Shake-up That the Rest of the Union Has Been Trying," *The Banker*, May 1, 2005.

[71] David Moore, "Slovakia's 2004 Tax and Welfare Reforms," IMF Working Paper 05/133, July 2005, p. 20.

[72] David Moore, "Slovakia's 2004 Tax and Welfare Reforms," IMF Working Paper 05/133, July 2005.

[73] Anne-Marie Brook and Willi Leibfritz, "Slovakia's introduction of a flat tax as part of wider economic reforms," OECD Economics Department Working Papers No. 448, October 3, 2005, p. 10.

[74] The rate at which an individual loses net income, whether through higher income taxes or withdrawal of benefits.

[75] David Moore, "Slovakia's 2004 Tax and Welfare Reforms," IMF Working Paper 05/133, July 2005.

[76] Slovakia Country Report, The Economist Intelligence Unit, May 2004, p. 21.

[77] "La Slovaquie prépare l'Europe au forceps," *Ouest France*, October 14, 2003.

[78] Markus Huber, "Unüberschaubares Chaos im Flat-Tax-Land; Der Regierung in der Slowakei droht nach zahlreichen internen Querelen die Ablösung," *Stuttgarter Zeitung*, September 24, 2005.

[79] See political scientist Radovan Geist in "La Slovaquie a amélioré ses finances mais pas l'emploi," *Le Monde*, March 24, 2004.

[80] "La Slovaquie a amélioré ses finances mais pas l'emploi," *Le Monde*, March 24, 2004.

[81] "Slovakia's Minimum Wage the Third Lowest in EU Jan 2006–Eurostat," *Slovakian News Digest*, July 14, 2006.

[82] "La Slovaquie a amélioré ses finances mais pas l'emploi," *Le Monde*, March 24, 2004.

[83] "La Slovaquie suspend ses réformes libérales," *La Tribune*, March 15, 2006.

[84] The government argued that relying too much on benefits had added to the marginalization of the poorest groups, in particular Roma communities: Roma accounted for one-fifth of overall unemployment in Slovakia, while 80% were dependent on social assistance benefits. The Roma constituted about 10% in settlements which often lacked electricity and running water, while the Roma lacked basic education and were subject to discrimination, despite having lived in Slovakia since the 14th century. The Roma population was particularly affected by the reforms, which had different consequences for families of different sizes; benefits remained roughly the same for smaller families, while families with four or more children had their benefits reduced.[84] If a family with five children received between SKK 10,900 and 13,800 in 2003 (between USD 280 and 355), the family could only count on receiving between SKK 7,060 and 10,390 (between USD 215 and 315) after the reforms. Also, evidence showed that it took longer than estimated to initiate the activation programs. "La révolte monte dans les ghettos roms de Slovaquie," *Le Monde*, February 27, 2004, David Moore, "Slovakia's 2004 Tax and Welfare Reforms," IMF Working Paper 05/133, July 2005.

[85] Slovakia Country Report, The Economist Intelligence Unit, May 2004, pp. 13–14.

[86] "Slovaquie—Vaste déploiement policier face aux Tsiganes," *Reuters*, February 24, 2004.

[87] "La révolte monte dans les ghettos roms de Slovaquie," *Le Monde*, February 27, 2004.

[88] Slovakia Country Report, The Economist Intelligence Unit, May 2004, pp. 13–14.

[89] Ibid., p. 21.

[90] "La Slovaquie se met au minimum social," *La Tribune*, October 6, 2004.

[91] Rainer Schäfer, "Slovak Republic: Full steam ahead to the euro," Regional Focus Economy & Markets, Dresdner Bank, December 2005.

[92] The EU Structural Funds are allocated by the EU for support for poorer regions in Europe. The current programs run from January 1, 2000, to December 31, 2006, with a €195 billion budget. Together with the Common Agricultural Policy and the Cohesion Funds, the Structural Funds constitute the bulk of EU funding, as well as the majority of total EU spending.

[93] Stephane Dupont, "Le Grand Soir fiscal ne fait plus reçette en Europe," *Les Echos*, October 12, 2005.

[94] James Mackenzie, "German experts unveil corporate tax reform plan," *Reuters News*, January 30, 2006; Daniel Schwammenthal, "The Weekend Interview with Paul Kirchhof: 'This Professor from Heidelberg'," *The Wall Street Journal*, October 29, 2005.

[95] Max Reval, "Der Charme des schlanken Staates; Estnische Debatten über die Flat Tax," *Die Welt*, October 12, 2005.

[96] Paragraph freely translated by case author. Ivan Mikloš, "Das beste Steuersystem der EU; Wie eine 'Flat Tax' mit Effiziens, Trasparenz und Allokationsneutralität für eine gedeihliche wirtschaftliche Entwicklung sorgt," *Frankfurter Allgemeine Zeitung*, September 3, 2005.

[97] The EU Structural Funds were allocated by the EU for support of poorer regions in Europe. The latest programs ran from January 1, 2000 to December 31, 2006, with a €195 billion budget. Together with the Common

Agricultural Policy and the Cohesion Funds, the Structural Funds constituted the great bulk of EU funding, as well as the majority of total EU spending.

[98] "Reaping the European Union Harvest," *The Economist*, January 6, 2005.

[99] New European Markets Analyst, Issue 07/03, February 2, 2007, GS Global Economic website, https://portal.gs.com.

[100] Slovakia Country Report, The Economist Intelligence Unit, May 2006.

[101] Robert Anderson, "Leading from the front but striving for consensus," Special Report Slovakia, *Financial Times*, p. 4, February 20, 2007.

[102] Michael Shafir, "Slovakia's Robert Fico: A Man to Be Trusted or Feared?" *RFE RL Reports*, May 29 2002, http://www.rferl.org/reports/eepreport/2002/05/11-290502.asp, accessed February 2007; and biography of Robert Fico on Wikipedia, http://en.wikipedia.org/wiki/Robert_Fico, accessed February 2007.

[103] "Slovakia's Flat Tax Challenged," http://nospeedbumps.com/?p=932, accessed February 2007.

[104] "The populist choice," *The Economist*, June 19, 2006.

[105] Estimation by Jiri Pehe, political analyst and director of New York University in Prague, as quoted in Associated Press Newswires, Vanessa Gera, "Eastern Europe in political disarray amid fatigue over economic sacrifice," October 22, 2006.

[106] "Slovak Parliament okays higher income tax for rich," *CTK Business News*, December 6, 2006.

[107] Slovakia Country Report, The Economist Intelligence Unit, August 2006, p. 8.

[108] Ibid.

[109] "Review of major steps taken by Slovak governments in 2006," *CTK Daily News*, December 7, 2006.

[110] Robert Anderson, "Industry shrugs off political shock," Special Report Slovakia, *Financial Times*, February 20, 2007, p. 1.

[111] Robert Anderson, "Leading from the front but striving for consensus," Special Report Slovakia, *Financial Times*, February 20, 2007, p. 4.

[112] The following paragraphs draw heavily from Harry S. Rosen, *Public Finance*, 7th ed. (McGraw-Hill, 2005).

[113] Robert E. Hall and Alvin Rabushka, *The Flat Tax*, 2nd ed. (Hoover Institution Press, 1995), p. 5; Jimmy Carter, "1976 Democratic National Convention Acceptance Address," http://www.americanrhetoric.com/speeches/jimmycarter1976dnc.htm, accessed November 10, 2006.

[114] Harvey S. Rosen, *Public Finance*, 7th ed. (McGraw-Hill, 2005), pp. 359–364.

Incentives to Investments and
the Role of Institutions

9-709-027
REV: MARCH 26, 2009

LAURA ALFARO
LAKSHMI IYER

Special Economic Zones in India: Public Purpose and Private Property (A)

Government has no other end, but the preservation of property.

—John Locke, Second Treatise of Government, 1690

The State shall, in particular, direct its policy towards securing that the ownership and control of the material resources of the community are so distributed as best to subserve the common good.

—Constitution of India, Article 39 (b)

On March 14, 2007, police opened fire on villagers protesting against a Special Economic Zone (SEZ) being built in Nandigram, a quiet farming community in India's eastern state of West Bengal. Following the enactment of the SEZ Act in 2005, many private sector investors and state governments in India had been acquiring land to set up these duty-free enclaves that were deemed foreign territory for the purposes of trade operations.[1] Firms were given many regulatory, infrastructure and tax benefits for locating in these zones. The Nandigram SEZ project was a joint venture between the state-owned West Bengal Industrial Development Corporation and Indonesia's Salim Group, which planned to build a major chemical hub. The SEZ required acquiring more than 14,000 acres of land, mostly under agricultural use. The project, though approved by the government in 2005, encountered significant resistance from local villagers and opposition political parties, who argued that the land had been forcibly acquired by the government at below-market rates. They contended that the SEZ's ambitious plans could displace thousands of farmers.

The tension in the region climaxed in March 2007, when fourteen villagers were killed in clashes with the local police. The incident resulted in widespread negative views of the West Bengal government. Gopal Krishna Gandhi, the governor of the state, said that the news of the incident filled him with "cold horror."[2] Ashok Mitra, the state's finance minister, criticized his own party for this action. A newspaper editorial condemned the party machinery for becoming the "sword arm of an industrialization policy that involves settling complicated property rights issues."[3] Many public figures, including social activists, writers and actors, joined the protests against the project. Responding to the public outrage, the state's Chief Minister Buddhadeb Bhattacharjee apologized for the police action and scrapped the Nandigram SEZ project.[4] Furthermore, the central government in New Delhi announced a national freeze on land acquisitions by the government for SEZ development. In November 2007, the West Bengal High Court characterized the police action in Nandigram as "totally unconstitutional" and directed the government to pay compensation to people affected by the action.[5]

Professors Laura Alfaro and Lakshmi Iyer prepared this case with the assistance of Namrata Arora, Researcher at the India Research Center. HBS cases are developed solely as the basis for class discussion. Cases are not intended to serve as endorsements, sources of primary data, or illustrations of effective or ineffective management.

India's SEZ policy aimed to provide manufacturing and services-sector employment to India's growing labor force of over 515 million people. The policy was also aimed at attracting foreign direct investment (FDI) to the country. Kamal Nath, India's minister of commerce and industry and one of the biggest proponents of SEZs, viewed the creation of SEZs as a "golden milestone in the process of broadening and deepening India's export base."[6] Business leaders such as Sunil Munjal of the $3.2 billion Hero Group, the world's largest manufacturer of bicycles and motorbikes, called the SEZ policy an "absolutely brilliant idea."[7]

Many of these new industrial ventures faced difficulties in acquiring the necessary land for their projects, in the face of large-scale land fragmentation and farmers' reluctance to sell their land to industrial enterprises. Even if private developers were able to assemble the majority of the land parcels needed for an economic development project, a relatively small minority of landowners often refused to sell or, recognizing that they were in a position to exert leverage, held out for exorbitant prices. By one estimate, more than 200 SEZ projects were involved in land acquisition disputes as of August 2008.[8] In Gujarat state, the Essar Group proposed to reduce the size of its planned Jamnagar SEZ by 80% in the face of land acquisition problems.[9] In Maharashtra, the state government conducted a referendum in September 2008 on the proposed Reliance SEZ in Raigad; more than 6000 farmers voted, the results of which had yet to be made public.[10] In September 2008, Tata Motors' proposed car manufacturing plant at Singur in West Bengal state was opposed by local farmers amidst allegations that the land had been acquired illegally, leaving thousands homeless.[a]

In an attempt to resolve these land acquisition issues, the United Progressive Alliance (UPA) government, headed by the Congress Party, introduced the Land Acquisition Amendment bill in Parliament in December 2007, which proposed to significantly extend the ability of the government to acquire land. The bill specified that if a "public serving" company had acquired 70% of the land needed for a project, the government could use its power of "eminent domain" to acquire the remainder. But politicians remained divided on the issue of land acquisition for SEZs. Even though her own party had introduced the bill, Sonia Gandhi, president of the Congress Party, opined that "prime agricultural lands should not be compromised for industry and SEZs in particular."[11]

The proposed bill, as well as the SEZ policy, generated widely differing views within civil society regarding the appropriate role of government in facilitating economic development. Should the government be involved directly in solving land transaction issues between two private parties, as the proposed bill would allow? Was the SEZ policy the best way to accelerate India's economic growth?

India's Economic Reforms since 1991

After attaining independence from the British in 1947, the Indian economy functioned under the *License Raj*, a system where complex licenses and regulations were required in order to set up a business. The Indian government, led by Prime Minister Jawaharlal Nehru, believed that businesses needed to be heavily regulated in a planned economy with significant government ownership in several sectors. Laws such as the Foreign Exchange Regulation Act (FERA), which limited foreign investors' equity to 40%, forced established foreign companies such as Mobil Oil, Coca-Cola and IBM out of the Indian economy. Indian businesses too were heavily taxed and had to obtain permission from the government for activities ranging from laying off employees to increasing production capacity. The resultant business environment proved to be highly bureaucratic and corrupt. Between the 1950s and 1980s, India's growth rate remained at a low 3.5% per annum.

---

[a] See "Tata Motors in Singur: Public Purpose and Private Property (B)" HBS 709-029, for more details on this project.

In 1991, India faced a severe balance of payments crisis precipitated by large government budget deficits and high inflation.[12] This proved to be the stimulus for a major economic liberalization program, spearheaded by Finance Minister Manmohan Singh, who was elected Prime Minister in 2004. Industrial licensing was eliminated and significant sectors of the economy were opened up for private participation. India gradually integrated into the world economy: import licensing was abolished, import duties were sharply reduced, and many restrictions on FDI were lifted.[13]

These reforms led to a number of successes. Investment increased from 24% of gross domestic product (GDP) in 1990 to 37% in 2007; growth rates accelerated to more than 9% per annum by 2005; and the proportion of the population living below the poverty line declined from 36% in 1993 to 27.5% in 2005 (see **Exhibit 1** for macroeconomic indicators).[14] India attracted $65 billion in FDI between April 2000 and May 2008, the bulk of which was concentrated in the services, computer software and hardware, construction, and telecommunications sectors (see **Exhibit 3** for the distribution of FDI by sector). The economy transitioned from being mainly dependent on agriculture to being service-oriented. The software industry, backed by the high quality of Indian engineers and IT professionals, witnessed growth rates of more than 50% per annum between 1992 and 2001. Indian firms became increasingly global. After the acquisition of the Anglo-Dutch steel firm Corus in 2007, Tata Steel was one of the top five steel companies in the world. In 2008, Tata Motors unveiled the world's cheapest car, the Nano, and also purchased the Jaguar and Land Rover brands from Ford.

Despite these successes, a number of concerns about the reform and growth process cast doubts on its sustainability. One criticism was that India had focused too much on trade and industrial reform and, as a result, had largely undermined agriculture, a sector which employed about 60% of the nation's workforce. Laws such as the Essential Commodities Act of 1955, which initially protected the farmer by regulating and controlling the production, distribution and pricing of essential commodities, had become archaic and hindered agricultural growth.[15] The Congress Party's surprising victory in the 2004 national elections over the ruling proponents of liberalization, the Bharatiya Janata Party (BJP), reflected farmers' disappointment with liberalization. The national budget of 2006 announced a more agro-friendly policy, and initiatives were introduced to raise efficiency in the agrarian sector. However, stagnant farming yields and reduced capital investment continued to plague the sector. Farming contributed a modest 18% to the country's 2008 GDP of over $1 trillion (**Exhibit 1**).

Manufacturing as a share of GDP had increased only marginally over the past three decades, from 22% in 1980 to 27% in 2006 (**Exhibit 1**). The sector was hampered by restrictive labor laws, tough competition from China, and moderate corporate investment. India was ranked 134 out of 175 countries in a 2005 World Bank survey on the ease of starting a business,[b] compared with China at 93 and Malaysia at 20 (see **Exhibit 4** for international comparisons of the business environment). Unskilled laborers who wanted to move out of the agricultural sector found it hard to find employment in the tepid manufacturing sector. Skill shortages were an addition source of concern. For example, in Maharashtra, one of India's largest and most prosperous states, a sizeable 17% of the workforce was minimally skilled and unlikely to find jobs in the manufacturing sector, as the state faced a projected shortage of 2.1 million skilled laborers by 2012.[16]

On the macroeconomic front, potential weaknesses remained. The combined fiscal deficit of the federal and state governments remained high at 6.4% of GDP in 2006-07.[17] The balance on goods and services had consistently been in deficit for the past three decades, despite the growth of the export sector (**Exhibit 2**). FDI inflows of $23 billion in 2007 lagged far behind those of countries like China, which attracted nearly $84 billion, or Brazil, at $35 billion (**Exhibit 4**). Portfolio investment inflows in

[b] This ranking is the average of the country's percentile rankings on procedures, time, cost, and minimum capital requirements to register a business.

most years were much higher than FDI inflows. For many, this was a particular source of concern, since such flows of capital could be quickly reversed. Further, despite reductions in commodity prices during second half of 2008, inflation remained high. The increasing cost of living bore heavily on low-income families, who had seen large price increases in basic commodities. The cost of rice had risen 20% and the cost of edible oils had risen 40% just in 2008.

A widely prevalent view was that India's growth was taking place despite government policies, not because of them. Fareed Zakaria, editor of *Newsweek International*, remarked, "India's growth is messy, chaotic and largely unplanned. . . . [I]t is not top-down but bottom-up. . . . India does not have a government that rolls out the red carpet for foreign investment. But it has vast and growing numbers of entrepreneurs who want to make money. And somehow they find a way to do it, overcoming the obstacles, bypassing the bureaucracy."[18]

In light of these issues, Indian policy makers envisioned that creating Special Economic Zones made sense as a strategy to attract stable long-term investment and create jobs. SEZs had been established in many countries across the world, with a mixed record of success.

Special Economic Zones around the World

Special Economic Zones (SEZs) were defined as specifically delineated duty free enclaves that were deemed foreign territory for the purposes of trade operations, duties and tariffs.[19] The term Special Economic Zones covered a broad range of more specific zone types, including Free Trade Zones (FTZ), Export Processing Zones (EPZ), Free Zones (FZ), Industrial Estates (IE), Free Ports and Urban Enterprise Zones.[20] SEZs were set up in Argentina and Uruguay in the 1920s, but the rapid development of free trade zones across the world dates from the late 1960s and the early 1970s (see **Exhibits 5** and **6** for details on the worldwide development of SEZs).

Although purposes and objectives varied, many SEZs were created to provide an internationally competitive environment for exports relatively free of regulatory encumbrances.[21] Others were seen as a way to develop the manufacturing sector and create jobs.[22] Taiwan established SEZs in 1965, for example, as part of its larger strategy to free agricultural land for industrial uses. In 1980, the three SEZs in Taiwan (Kaohsiung City, Nanze and Taizhong) contributed a sizeable 7% towards the nation's overall export volume.[23] However, as the infrastructure and duty-free incentives available throughout Taiwan improved throughout the 1980s, the importance of SEZs waned. In the United States, Urban Enterprise Zones (UEZs) were created in the 1980s in states like New Jersey to jumpstart economic activity and alleviate poverty in urban areas. The state's 32 zones created over 150,000 jobs that resulted in $24 billion of private investment.[24] In a significant step veering away from isolationism, North Korea announced in 2002 that it was creating an SEZ on its northwest border with China. However, this venture fell flat when its key promoter was arrested in China later that year on charges of fraud.

Overall, the effectiveness of SEZs had been fiercely debated over the last forty years. Some were perceived as successful while others were seen as creating few benefits for the country and as draining government resources.[25] Proponents of SEZs identified those established in Hong Kong, South Korea, Singapore and Taiwan as one of the factors helping these developing countries increase non-traditional exports. However, other SEZs tended to be enclaves largely cut off from the rest of the economy, dedicated to extractive industries or serving as isolated export platforms with few, if any, net benefits to the country. Critics pointed to failed experiences in the Dominican Republic, Egypt, Ghana, Guatemala, Senegal and Tunisia. In the words of one expert, "EPZs and Free Trade zones have a very problematic record."[26]

China was often considered the greatest SEZ success story. After the Communist revolution in the 1940s, all land was owned by the government, but a special ordinance enacted in the 1980s allowed land within the Shenzhen SEZ, in southeastern China, to be leased to private owners for periods of fifty to a hundred years.[27] Such special ordinances were credited with being the first steps towards market competition for Chinese land. Beginning in 1980 (even before the leasing of land was officially permitted), China established SEZs in Zhuhai, Shantou, and Xiamen, as well as in Shenzhen, all in southeastern regions where large areas of arid land were available for development.

SEZs in China were seen as an experimental setting for capitalism where private entrepreneurs were granted overall minimal government intervention in an otherwise managed economy. They were offered select tax benefits, including customs duty exemptions, reductions in corporate taxes, and a five-year tax holiday for energy and transportation projects (see **Exhibit 7** for a comparison of SEZs in India, China and other countries).[28] Progressive labor practices such as collective bargaining were introduced in some SEZs.[29] Their strategic proximity to the coast facilitated trade, and their size offered employment opportunities to millions of migrant workers.

In part as a result of its successful SEZs, China's GDP and exports grew at annual rates of 10% and 11% respectively, during the 1980s.[30] By 2004, the 54 national-level SEZs accounted for an impressive 22% of all foreign direct investment. Though Chinese SEZs witnessed unprecedented economic success, harsh working conditions, dangerously high pollution levels and soaring crime rates were all raising concerns, making some question the merits of this strategy to achieve accelerated growth.[31]

The World Trade Organization (WTO) rules on subsidies formally prohibited granting export subsidies after January 1, 2003. However, SEZs were deemed to be compliant with WTO rules as long as the incentives offered were not contingent on export performance, and there were no restrictions on sales to the domestic market.[32]

Special Economic Zones in India

India set up Asia's first export processing zone (EPZ) in 1965 in Kandla, followed by one in Mumbai in 1972. Though SEZs evolved from EPZs, there were major structural differences between the two policies. While the EPZ Policy and SEZ Act both aimed to create industrial zones to attract FDI, develop infrastructure, and offer financial incentives, the SEZ Act catered to a larger industrial base and had more relaxed rules and regulations (see **Exhibit 8** for differences).

The government's objectives in setting up SEZs in India were multifold. Aside from generating additional economic activity across rural and urban sectors, the government aimed to promote exports of goods and services, increase investment from domestic and foreign sources, create additional jobs, and develop India's infrastructure.[33] With 45.5% of India's land area uncultivable, the government viewed the SEZ scheme as a way to use such land optimally. SEZs were permitted either to house multiple industries or to specialize in a particular industry. Specialized SEZs catered to sectors such as information technology, gems and jewelry, and biotechnology (see **Exhibit 9** for the sectoral distribution of approved SEZs).

Salient Features of the SEZ Act of 2005

The SEZ Act of 2005 was widely supported by all political parties. Under this Act, SEZs in India were granted the power by the central government to operate as islands of economic activity within the nation, with firms being offered a number of tax, regulatory and infrastructure incentives to locate in these zones. Firms within SEZs did not have to pay import duties on raw material and other inputs to production. They were completely exempt from income tax on all export income for the first five years and were allowed a 50% exemption for the next ten years. They did not have to pay service taxes or central and state sales taxes. Many states chose to provide additional incentives to attract investment. For instance, SEZ developers in many states did not have to pay "stamp duty," a percentage owed to the government for any land transaction. They also received an exemption from duties on goods used in the construction of the SEZ.

Companies wanting to locate in an SEZ were provided "single-window clearance," where they could get all necessary approvals, including environmental, construction, and employment clearances, at a single point. Activities conducted within the SEZ were not closely supervised by customs authorities, with the company's self-declaration serving as the basis for most customs regulation. There were no export targets on companies, as long as net foreign exchange earnings were positive. Indian banks were allowed to set up offshore units in SEZs, which were exempt from domestic banking regulations and could access international financial markets at international rates.[34]

Consistent with the definition of SEZs as foreign territory for trade purposes, goods going into the SEZ from non-SEZ parts of India were treated as exports, and goods coming from the SEZ into the rest of India had to pay the usual import duties. Since firms in SEZs were exempt from import duties and generally enjoyed the benefits of operating within tax havens, some were concerned that there might be "large scale smuggling from SEZ India to non-SEZ India."[35]

Most Indian labor laws applied within SEZs. These laws were extremely restrictive: among other things, any company employing more than 100 workers could not fire people without government permission and had to notify the labor commissioner about every single person working on a night shift. In addition, no worker could work more than 75 hours of overtime in a quarter.[36] However, laborers within SEZs were required to give a thirty-day notice before going on strike. This was in contrast to the situation in the rest of India where they could go on strike without notice except for workers in public utility services such as water or electricity.

Setting up an SEZ

Under the SEZ Act of 2005, SEZs could be set up by the central or state government, the private sector, or a joint collaboration between the government and the private sector. If the SEZ was privately developed, either a foreign company or an Indian company could spearhead the project. Developers were given a great deal of flexibility in the provision of infrastructure to SEZs. They could choose to build all forms of social and economic infrastructure themselves, outsource projects such as roads and power plants to co-developers, or build and share infrastructure for common use with another nearby SEZ.

There was a multi-stage process for setting up an SEZ. In the first stage, an organization identified an area and applied for an in-principle clearance from the central government's Board of Approval. The organization also had to obtain consent of the state government in the form of a "No Objection Certificate."[c] At this point, the project was said to be "In Principle Approved." In the second stage, once the central and state governments had granted clearance to proceed, developers applied for formal approval along with a self-declaration that a certain quantity of land had been obtained to set up the SEZ; at this point the project was said to be "Formally Approved." In the third stage, once the state conducted physical inspection of the land and all necessary paperwork was done, the Ministry of Commerce approved setting up the SEZ, and the project was said to be "Notified."

The Commerce Ministry set up the SEZ Export Promotion Council to facilitate the establishment of SEZs by providing an interface between the private sector and central and state governments. One

[c] The Salim SEZ in Nandigram, West Bengal, had completed this first phase of approval.

of the most significant roles of the Council was to hold SEZ "Open Houses" as a meeting point for government officials and corporations. Open Houses were held six to eight times per year throughout the country. Anita Arjundas, director of the Mahindra World City SEZ in Chennai, was very positive about these initiatives. "The Open Houses have been helpful, and their agendas have fallen into a smooth rhythm. They are a great place to discuss smaller problems that have obvious and quick solutions. Naturally, larger problems take much longer to resolve, but we are glad that such a forum exists not only in name but in practice."[37]

As of March 2008, there were 136 In-Principle Approved SEZs, 453 Formally Approved SEZs, and 207 Notified SEZs (see **Exhibit 10** for SEZ locations).[38] The total land requirement for the Formally Approved SEZs was approximately 642 square km, while for the Notified SEZs it was 284 square km.[39] Southern, western and northern India, with their history of capital rich industry and foothold in information technology, experienced the most aggressive SEZ development while the eastern states lagged behind. Nationally, SEZs employed 336,235 people directly and an additional 220,506 indirectly as construction workers and casual laborers. Total private investment in SEZs was approximately $17 billion and exports generated from SEZs experienced a 381% increase between 2003 and 2008 (see **Exhibit 11** for SEZs' performance).

The Mahindra World City Experience

Mahindra World City, located in the southern Indian state of Tamil Nadu, 45 kilometers from Chennai, was India's first operational SEZ (see **Exhibit 12** for Mahindra World City's performance). It was a multi-sector SEZ that catered to the IT, auto component, and apparel sectors. The SEZ was located on 1,400 acres of land, and was developed by Mahindra & Mahindra Limited, one of India's largest conglomerates with a presence in the automotive, financial services, farming equipment and IT industries. Mahindra planned to retain 30% of the land and lease the rest to other firms. This was lower than the norm in some other countries. For instance, in Singapore, most developers retained 90% of the land for themselves. Anita Arjundas of Mahindra World City recounted, "We were originally looking at creating an industrial park outside Chennai for ancillary motor parts production. The industry at the time was going through a slump. But we figured that auto-industry requirements—solid infrastructure, minimal bureaucratic hassles, availability of a skilled workforce—would apply for any other industry too, so why not build a multi-purpose SEZ?"[40]

The Mahindra World City SEZ successfully reduced the regulatory and infrastructure burdens on industry. Sriram Sivaram of Madras Engineering Industries Private Limited (MEIL) said by way of illustration: "Before the SEZ Act, establishing a 100% subsidiary in India took almost nine months and dozens of trips to New Delhi. However at World City, given MEIL's export track record and the support of the Mahindra team, approval was granted in two months. Further, getting a new power connection is often the biggest problem faced by many new facilities, as there is insufficient overall supply and insufficient distribution capacity. In the case of World City, the Tamil Nadu Electricity Board made necessary arrangements to meet the demand of the entire SEZ."[41]

The tax incentives proved to be another big advantage. P. N. Mathur of Nestronics Private Limited, a Singapore-based electronics company, explained, "After Singapore experienced the risk of SARS, we decided to look for an alternative manufacturing facility in Asia.[42] We visited Thailand and Vietnam in addition to India, and if the SEZ policy had not been enacted, there would have been stiff competition with other Asian countries. But with the SEZ, the tax and infrastructural advantages made our decision to come to India a no-brainer." Nestronics began commercial production at World City in 2006, where the firm found the system of self-declaration for customs very useful. "You could say that since firms located inside SEZs were highly visible, they were granted a greater level of trust by the government," said P. N. Mathur.[43]

Despite being in an SEZ, firms located in Mahindra World City still faced some challenges. These included difficulties in hiring the best talent due to the 90-minute commute from Chennai city, complying with the detailed paperwork requirements of Indian labor law, and managing the congestion and customs delays at Chennai airport. Mathur voiced his concerns at an Open House held in January 2007. As a result, the secretary of the Commerce Ministry came to Chennai to meet with Nestronics and the airport authorities. Mathur remarked, "The ministry took personal interest in sorting out our problems. After seeing that level of commitment, I was sold on the SEZ promise."[44]

Two factors contributed to Mahindra's success in acquiring land. First, the company had already acquired most of the land for an auto ancillary parts plant before the SEZ Act came into place. In fact, the process of land acquisition took more than four years. The second factor was the long-term view taken by the company towards developing SEZs. "The basic difference is we did not look at it as a real estate business but as an infrastructure business. The profits can wait. . . . You have to look at this business with a 10-to-12 year timeframe, unlike in real estate, where you have a 2-to-3 year timeframe," said Arun Nanda, vice-chairman of Mahindra Lifespaces. Mahindra World City broke even in 2008, eight years after the project began. In 2008, Mahindra successfully set up another 2500-acre multi-purpose SEZ near Jaipur in Rajasthan state. Land acquisition for this project was also successful, thanks to the cooperation of the state government, and the acquisition of an extra 1,000 acres for relocating displaced people.[45]

The Debate over Land Acquisition

Private Property in India

The Indian Constitution made an explicit commitment to protecting private property, stating that no person "shall be deprived of his property save by authority of law."[46] In practice, this meant that an active private market existed for land transactions in India. Land transactions were under the purview of state governments, which imposed varying levels of "stamp duty" on them, as well as different local zoning rules.

Many SEZ developers faced hurdles in acquiring land through the private market. The generally small sizes of plots and high degree of land fragmentation required companies to negotiate with large numbers of small landowners. A Delhi-based SEZ expert pointed out that many developers of zones were unable to assemble contiguous land parcels because some landowners refused to sell. [47] Anita Arjundas of Mahindra World City agreed that theoretically the idea that companies could acquire their own land at market prices appeared reasonable. However, in reality, she said, companies were unable to do so because some land owners were unwilling to sell at any price, and as word leaked out of a corporation's interest in the land, other land owners held out for unreasonable pay-outs. For example, Tata Metaliks, a subsidiary of Tata Steel, had planned a 500,000 ton steel plant next to its existing unit in the state of West Bengal. However, it had to put this project on hold for three years when it could not acquire 100 out of the 350 needed acres. The delay pushed up the cost of the project by 150%.[48] Companies also faced public relations risks if land brokers or aggregators hired by them used coercion to meet their targets.

Many companies felt that the government needed to intervene to resolve these land acquisition problems. "Land owners do not want to sell their plots to developers, even at market prices. Even if the state governments are given permission to acquire up to 25 per cent of the land for a zone to serve contiguity purposes, it will be of great help," said Navin M. Raheja, chief managing director of Raheja Developers, which had a Notified 255-acre zone in Haryana state but was having trouble acquiring the land to expand it to a 5,000-acre SEZ.[49]

A major concern about SEZs was that developers were using the SEZ policy to increase their own real estate portfolios. India's central bank, in fact, had notified banks to treat the financing of SEZ developers as real estate loans.[50] Rahul Bajaj (MBA 1964), chairman of Bajaj Auto, India's second-largest motorcycle company, expressed concern that SEZs were turning into "land scams."[51] "This is how people feel: the process is corrupt and politically motivated," said Vilol Khaladkar, a property rights lawyer. "Middlemen will first purchase huge chunks of land at throwaway prices in anticipation of government. Then they will get the land included in a SEZ, and sell the land to the developer at a much higher price. Therefore, the lion's share of the profit is made by the middlemen."[52] The erosion of popular support was encapsulated by Jena Bai, an activist who led a fishing community in Gujarat to initiate a legal battle to block the development of an SEZ that would prevent their boats from reaching the sea. "As far as we understand, the government and company are one. We have no faith that anyone will protect our rights."[53]

Land Acquisition by Government: The Power of Eminent Domain

The Indian government had a legal means to acquire land from private citizens. The Land Acquisition Act of 1894 specified that land could be acquired by the government for "public purpose" on payment of "just compensation." A similar provision existed in the "takings clause" of the Fifth Amendment to the United States Constitution, granting the state the power of "eminent domain." The U.S. Supreme Court's 2005 decision in Kelo v. City of New London, concerning the purposes for which the city could acquire land through eminent domain, illustrated the difficulties of interpreting such legal provisions.

In the United States, federal, state and local governments had traditionally used the power of eminent domain to acquire private property for public uses such as building highways and railroads. The legal system had changed considerably over time in its support for unilateral "takings." In the nineteenth century, courts had often supported actions which damaged private property but nevertheless promoted development. One such ruling was the verdict in the case of *Wolcott v. Upham* (1827), when the Supreme Judicial Court of Massachusetts ruled in favor of a manufacturing company which flooded a neighbor's land in the process of building a mill.[54]

The dispute that led to the *Kelo* decision went back to 1998, when Pfizer Pharmaceuticals began constructing a research facility in New London, Connecticut. To capitalize on the new Pfizer facility and help spur further economic growth, the city created the New London Development Corporation, which planned to purchase nearby properties and convert them into retail and office space, a hotel, and residences. The corporation was able to purchase most properties, but ten owners refused to sell. At this point, the city invoked the principle of eminent domain to obtain their land.

The property owners sued the city government, arguing that the corporation's proposed economic development activity did not constitute "public use" as allowed by the Fifth Amendment. In 2005, a divided Supreme Court ruled in a 5-4 decision that economic development could justify the transfer of property from one private party to another under the principle of eminent domain. In his majority opinion Justice Stevens stated, "Promoting economic development is a traditional and long accepted function of government..."[55] Justice Sandra Day O'Connor, in a dissenting opinion, stated, "[N]early any lawful use of real private property can be said to generate some incidental benefit to the public. Thus, if predicted (or even guaranteed) positive side-effects are enough to render transfer from one private party to another constitutional, then the words 'for public use' do not realistically exclude any takings, and thus do not exert any constraint on the eminent domain power."[56]

There was a significant negative reaction to this ruling in the U.S. Several states changed their laws in order to limit the reach of eminent domain. In 2006, President Bush issued an executive order stating that the federal government could only use eminent domain "for the purpose of benefiting the general public and not merely for the purpose of advancing the economic interest of private parties to be given ownership or use of the property taken."[57]

Implementing Eminent Domain in India

The interpretation of both "public purpose" and "just compensation" was the subject of controversy in India as well. In the original Land Acquisition Act of 1894, "public purpose" applied only to town or rural planning, establishing government owned enterprises, or providing for poor people displaced by government actions. The act specifically stated that public purpose "does not include acquisition of land for companies."[58] However, an amendment in 1984 broadened the term "public purpose" and gave the government greater flexibility in deeming projects, for example those related to export, investment, and infrastructure, as being useful to the public. This view of public purpose was disputed on a variety of projects prior to the SEZ Act of 2005. For example, the Narmada Bachao Aandolan (Save the Narmada Movement), initiated in 1985, involved widespread agitation against building a series of large hydroelectric dams on the Narmada River in Gujarat. The government had proposed these dams for irrigating drought prone areas, but the displaced landowners felt that they were not being fairly compensated for their land, and that the dams were neither beneficial to the public nor environmentally sound.[59]

The definition of "just compensation" also remained "wide open for interpretation," said property rights lawyer Vilol Khaladkar. "Compensation was not necessarily the market rate, it was just the attempt on the part of the government to suitably reimburse the landlord."[60] Yogendra Garg, director of the Ministry of Commerce's SEZ division, explained, "In India, historically, when land was bought, the actual transaction price was not revealed to the government, primarily to save on stamp duty and capital gains tax. Sizeable amounts were paid in cash and thus not declared to the government. The documents registered with state or local governments reflected only the amounts transacted through the banking channels. When the government determined value at the time of acquisition, it was largely guided by the prices declared in the official documentation. The average rate so determined was often lower than the actual market value. Though we were aware of this reality, and corrective actions such as fixing a locality-wise minimum value have been taken in a number of states, compensation was largely determined by the prices declared at the time of registration."[61]

Farmers faced additional problems in trying to obtain the full value of their land. In India's agrarian society, land was usually inherited from one generation to another without a proper will or land title, and there were often disputes over rightful ownership.[62] The usual process of implementing eminent domain left farmers with very little time to protest. "The process is that the district collector posts a notification with the price which the government will pay. Farmers have 48 hours to respond—most of them may not even see the notice in this period—after which the land acquisition agent goes around with eviction orders to make sure the land is acquired," explained Jayant Sinha (MBA 1992), advisor to the opposition Bharatiya Janata Party (BJP) on policy issues.[63]

It was not clear whether market price paid for the value of the land was enough to persuade farmers to sell. Subir Gokarn, chief economist of Standard & Poor in India explained, "If the price is right, people will sacrifice the emotional attachment they have to their land, but if you no longer have the guarantee of living off the land, then what do you do?" Though SEZs were expected to generate substantial employment, farmers were often not qualified to hold these semi-skilled or highly skilled positions. Tayab Ali Mandar, a farmer in West Bengal's Joymalla village remarked, "We know only farm work, we don't know any paper-pencil work."[64]

Reforming Land Acquisition

In order to quell the rising controversy about land acquisition, the Indian government proposed the Land Acquisition Amendment bill of 2007 in which the term "public purpose" was broadened to include strategic, naval, military or air force purposes, public infrastructure projects, or any purpose useful to the general public. In a bid to resolve the problems of land acquisition, the amendment also specified that the government could acquire 30% of the land provided that 70% of the required land had already been acquired by private parties.

The amendment proposed other significant changes. First, it made provisions to compensate not just the land owners but also all those dependent on the land for a livelihood, such as tribal people, landless laborers, or those with tenancy rights. Second, it specified that payment must be made within one year from the date of declaration of intent to acquire the land. Third, it required social impact assessments where large scale displacement was involved. Fourth, for speedy redress, civil courts were replaced by a judicial body at the state and national levels which could be staffed by members without judicial qualifications or experience, such as government officials.

The initial reactions to the proposed amendment were mixed. Proponents believed that companies would welcome the clarity of the amendment in planning their projects. They envisaged that by infusing transparency and a degree of fairness into the land acquisition process, the protests against corporate India, such as those witnessed in Nandigram and Singur, would be mitigated. However, Jayant Sinha, an advisor to the opposition Bharatiya Janata Party (BJP) on policy issues, characterized the bill as "deeply flawed" because of the lack of a comprehensive land use planning process, the difficulty of establishing property rights, and the lack of any provision to arrive at a "just compensation" for the owners of the land.[65]

After being introduced in Parliament in December 2007, the bill was referred to the Standing Committee on Rural Development for review. The committee published its report in October 2008. In general, the views of the committee were against extending the power of eminent domain as proposed because the definition of public purpose in the proposed bill was "too vague and can be misused." Further, the provision allowing the government to step in to acquire the final 30% of the land was likely to result in higher costs for the government because land values would have appreciated after the company had acquired the initial 70%, and because the government would be bound to provide relief and rehabilitation expenses to the holders of the land it acquired. In fact, government assistance with relocation and other relief could pose a question of equality: those who had sold earlier to the company would not be eligible for it, while those whose land was acquired by the government for the same project would be.[66] The reservations expressed by the Committee were likely to cause problems in the passage of the bill in Parliament.

As industry in India awaited legal reforms, lessons could be learnt from successful projects such as the construction of the Cochin International Airport in the southern state of Kerala, where the state acquired 1,300 acres of land from 2300 farmers through a negotiated settlement between the state, local representatives, developers and landowners. As part of the rehabilitation package, the state provided alternative land, financial compensation, shares in the new airport project, a free air ticket and a job to one member of each displaced family, while denying contract work and jobs to leaders of protests. [67] The airport, which began operations in 1999, was the fourth largest international airport in India, and one of the most efficient in the world.[68]

The Aftermath of Nandigram: Tata Motors in Singur

After the High Court ruling of November 2007 directing the government to pay compensation to the victims in Nandigram, the residents who had been evicted from their land returned to their homes. However, fresh violence broke out in May 2008 between residents and representatives of the Communist Party of India-Marxist (CPM), the ruling party in West Bengal. In local elections held in May 2008, the residents of Nandigram voted decisively against the CPM.

The cancellation of the Nandigram SEZ did not end controversies over land acquisition for other industrial projects. On October 3, 2008, Ratan Tata (HBS AMP, 1971) formally announced that Tata Motors was halting its project in Singur, West Bengal. Tata Motors had begun constructing a plant in 2006 to manufacture the Nano, slated to be the world's cheapest car, and had invested nearly $300 million in the project. The state of West Bengal had allocated 997 acres of land for the plant. However, after the project was underway, the main opposition party claimed that it would displace thousands of farmers and that their land had been acquired under questionable circumstances. Massive farmer protests, demanding that 400 acres of the land be returned to local farmers, forced the company to suspend work on the plant in September 2008.[69]

In an open letter to the citizens of West Bengal, Ratan Tata asked whether "they would like to support the present government of Mr Buddhadeb Bhattacharjee to build a prosperous state with the rule of law, modern infrastructure and industrial growth," or whether they would prefer to see West Bengal "consumed by a destructive political environment of confrontation, agitation, violence and lawlessness?"[70] This question was relevant to the entire industrialization policy of the Indian government. How would Tata's decision affect the prospects of attracting investment in Indian manufacturing? Would passing the Land Acquisition Amendment Act resolve the disputes over property rights? How would India's economic growth and reform process evolve in view of these challenges?

Exhibit 1 Composition of Gross Domestic Product in India

	1980	1990	1995	2000	2001	2002	2003	2004	2005	2006	2007
Gross Domestic Product (billion Rs)	1,360	5,687	11,918	21,023	22,790	24,546	27,546	31,494	35,803	41,458	47,132
Real GDP at 1999-2000 prices (billion Rs)			13,970	18,643	19,726	20,483	22,228	23,884	26,129	28,643	31,229
Real GDP growth rate				5.9%	5.8%	3.8%	8.5%	7.5%	9.4%	9.6%	9.0%
Components of GDP (%)											
Consumption	73%	67%	63%	65%	65%	64%	63%	60%	58%	57%	56%
Investment	21%	24%	27%	24%	24%	25%	26%	31%	34%	35%	37%
Government expenditure	10%	11%	11%	13%	12%	12%	12%	11%	11%	10%	10%
Exports	7%	7%	11%	13%	13%	15%	15%	18%	21%	23%	22%
Imports	10%	8%	12%	14%	14%	16%	16%	20%	24%	26%	25%
GDP by Sector (%)											
Agriculture, forestry & fishing, mining & quarrying	40%	34%	30%	26%	26%	24%	24%	22%	22%	21%	n.a.
Manufacturing, construction, electricity, gas & water supply	22%	23%	24%	24%	23%	24%	23%	24%	24%	25%	n.a.
Trade, hotels, transport & communication	17%	18%	20%	22%	23%	24%	25%	26%	26%	27%	n.a.
Financing, insurance, real estate & business services	7%	11%	12%	13%	13%	14%	13%	14%	14%	14%	n.a.
Public administration, defense and other services	13%	14%	13%	15%	15%	15%	14%	14%	14%	14%	n.a.

Source: Compiled by casewriter from <http://indiabudget.nic.in/es2007-08/chapt2008/tab13a.pdf>, accessed November 2008, and International Monetary Fund, International Financial Statistics Database.

Exhibit 2 India's Balance of Payments (million USD except as noted)

	1980	1990	1995	2000	2001	2002	2003	2004	2005	2006
Current Account Balance	(1,785)	(7,037)	(5,563)	(4,601)	1,410	7,060	8,773	780	(7,835)	(9,415)
Export of Goods	8,303	18,286	31,239	43,247	44,793	51,141	60,893	77,939	102,176	123,617
Import of Goods	(13,947)	(23,437)	(37,957)	(53,887)	(51,212)	(54,702)	(68,081)	(95,539)	(134,702)	(166,695)
Trade Balance	(5,644)	(5,151)	(6,719)	(10,640)	(6,419)	(3,561)	(7,188)	(17,600)	(32,526)	(43,078)
Services-credit	2,971	4,625	6,775	16,684	17,337	19,478	23,902	38,281	55,831	75,354
Services-debit	(2,981)	(6,090)	(10,268)	(19,187)	(20,099)	(21,039)	(24,878)	(35,641)	(47,989)	(63,537)
Net Services	(10)	(1,465)	(3,493)	(2,503)	(2,762)	(1,561)	(976)	2,640	7,842	11,817
Income - credit	1,058	436	1,486	2,521	3,524	3,188	3,491	4,690	5,082	7,795
Income - debit	(523)	(3,693)	(5,219)	(7,414)	(7,666)	(7,097)	(8,386)	(8,742)	(11,475)	(12,059)
Net Income	535	(3,257)	(3,734)	(4,893)	(4,142)	(3,909)	(4,895)	(4,052)	(6,393)	(4,264)
Transfers - credit	3,347	2,853	8,410	13,548	15,140	16,789	22,401	20,615	24,120	27,449
Transfers - debit	(14)	(17)	(27)	(114)	(407)	(698)	(570)	(822)	(877)	(1,340)
Net Transfers	3,334	2,836	8,382	13,434	14,733	16,091	21,831	19,793	23,242	26,109
Capital Account	(0)	0	(0)	716	0	0	(0)	(0)	(0)	0
Financial Account	483	5,528	3,861	9,623	7,995	11,985	16,421	22,229	21,622	37,776
Direct Investment Outflow	-	-	(117)	(510)	(1,398)	(1,678)	(1,879)	(2,179)	(2,495)	(9,670)
Direct Investment Inflow	-	-	2,144	3,584	5,472	5,626	4,323	5,771	6,677	17,453
Portfolio Investment Liabilities	-	-	1,590	2,345	2,853	1,022	8,216	9,037	12,144	9,549
Other Investment Assets	(318)	(611)	(1,179)	1,712	(381)	4,850	4,018	2,899	(5,580)	(44)
Other Investment Liabilities	802	6,139	1,423	2,492	1,449	2,164	1,742	6,701	10,876	20,488
Errors & Omissions	(361)	(432)	970	331	(715)	(190)	471	637	769	(4,623)
Change in Reserves	1,663	1,941	733	(6,069)	(8,690)	(18,854)	(25,665)	(23,646)	(14,555)	(23,737)
Exchange Rates (Rupees per USD)	8.10	16.65	33.60	43.51	46.00	47.98	48.16	45.31	44.80	44.29

Source: Compiled by casewriter from International Monetary Fund, International Financial Statistics Database.

Exhibit 3 Foreign Direct Investment by Sector (Apr 2000-May 2008)

Sector	FDI (million USD)	% FDI Inflows
Services	14,255.78	21.85
Computer Software and Hardware	7,476.50	11.88
Construction	4,324.50	6.57
Telecommunications	4,073.78	6.37
Housing and Real Estate	3,745.32	5.56
Power	2,642.89	4.11
Automobiles	2,582.47	4.05
Metallurgical Industries	2,377.38	3.57
Petroleum and Natural Gas	2,006.80	3.01
Chemicals (other than Fertilizers)	1,518.57	2.41
Ports	1,474.45	2.16
Drugs and Pharmaceuticals	1,289.55	2.04
Electrical Equipments	1,186.90	1.84
Trading	1,150.96	1.72
Cement and Gypsum Products	986.88	1.57
Hotel and Tourism	963.49	1.48
Consultancy Services	931.67	1.46
Information and Broadcasting (Including Print Media)	889.47	1.35
Electronics	715.53	1.16
Food Processing Industries	699.10	1.14
Textiles (Including Dyed, Printed)	538.99	0.84
Other	8,974.33	13.86
Total	64,805.31	100.00

Source: Fact sheet on Foreign Direct Investment, Department of Industrial Policy and Promotion, Ministry of Commerce and Industry. http://dipp.nic.in/fdi_statistics/india_fdi_May2008.pdf, accessed November 2008.

Exhibit 4 International Comparisons of Business Environment and FDI Inflows

	India	China	Brazil	Russia	Malaysia	South Korea	Indonesia
GDP (2007), billion USD	1,171	3,280	1,314	1,291	181	970	433
FDI (2007), billion USD	23	84	35	52	8	3	7
FDI/GDP (%)	1.96	2.55	2.63	4.06	4.65	0.27	1.60
Ease of doing business ranking (1=best in the world)	134	93	121	96	20	23	129
Days to start a business	35	35	152	28	13	17	76
Cost of hiring a new worker (% of salary)	17	44	37	31	NA	NA	NA
Firing costs (weeks of wages)	56	91	37	17	75	91	108
Protecting investors rank	33	83	60	60	4	70	53
Ease of tax system rank	158	168	151	98	21	43	116
Total tax rate (% profit)	81	77	72	54	35	34	37
Days to enforce a simple credit contract	1420	292	616	178	600	230	570
Years to close a business (bankruptcy)	10	2	4	4	2	2	6
Bankruptcy recovery rate (cents on the dollar)	13	32	12	29	39	81	14

Source: Compiled by casewriter from World Investment Report, 2008. www.unctad.org/wir, accessed October 2008 and World Bank, World Development Indicators (revised September 2008).

Exhibit 5 Worldwide Development of Export Processing Zones

Years	1975	1986	1997	2002	2006
Number of countries with EPZs	25	47	93	116	130
Number of EPZs or similar types of zones	79	176	845	3000	3500
Employment (millions)	n.a.	n.a.	22.5	43	66
-- of which China	n.a.	n.a.	18	30	40
-- of which other countries with figures available	0.8	1.9	4.5	13	26

Source: http://www.ilo.org/public/english/dialogue/sector/themes/epz/epz-db.pdfwww.ilo, accessed Nov. 2008.

Exhibit 6 Employment Generation in Special Economic Zones by Region

Geographical area	Number of Zones	Employment
Asia	900+	55 741 147
-- of which China		40 000 000
-- of which bonded factories in Bangladesh		3 250 000
Central America and Mexico	155	5 252 216
Middle East	50	1 043 597
North Africa	65	643 152
Sub-Saharan Africa	90+	860 474
United States	713	340 000
South America	43	459 825
Transition economies	400	1 400 379
Caribbean	250	546 513
Indian Ocean	1	182 712
Europe	50	364 818
Pacific	14	145 930
Total (estimated)	3 500+	65 980 763

Source: http://www.ilo.org/public/english/dialogue/sector/themes/epz/epz-db.pdfwww.ilo, accessed November 2008.

Exhibit 7 Comparison of Special Economic Zones across countries

	China	India	Brazil	Bangladesh	Sri Lanka
Number of SEZs	15	207 notified; 453 formally approved	1	8	12
Average size	300 sq km	1.4 sq km	10,000 sq km	1.5 sq km	1.5 sq km
Tax incentives	1/2 normal tax rate in the third and fourth year after profits begin. Full taxes after 5 years.	Exemption from income, sales, service and central taxes.	Exemption from import and municipal taxes; 88% tax reduction for import of raw materials.	Ten-year exemption from income taxes and customs duties; no import duties; allowed to sell 20% of good to domestic market.	Ten-year tax holiday for developers; income tax exemption of 10% for 2 years; exemption from customs duties.
Investment	17.03 billion USD	7.96 billion USD	N.A.	1.04 billion USD	0.29 billion USD
Zone Exports	145.06 billion USD	4.9 billion USD	1.97 billion USD	11.7 billion USD	4.27 billion USD
Definition of Public Purpose for government acquisition	Land Administration Law, Article 21 (1988): Economic, cultural, national defense construction projects, public works projects.	Land Acquisition (Amendment) Bill (2007): Redefines 'public purpose' as land acquired for defense purposes, infrastructure projects, or for any project useful to the general public where 70 percent of the land has already been purchased.	The Constitution, Article 5, 182 & 184 (1988): Public use, social interest, or for purposes of agrarian reform of rural property which is not performing its social function.	Ordinance 11 of 1982 provides for the acquisition of land for public purpose by paying a compensation of 150% of market price. The use of the acquired property for any purpose other than the purpose for which it was acquired is generally forbidden.	

Source: http://www.ilo.org/public/english/dialogue/sector/themes/epz/epz-db.pdf, accessed November 2008.

Exhibit 8 Major Differences between the EPZ Policy and the SEZ Act in India

	Economic Processing Zone Policy (1965)	Special Economic Zones Act(2005)	Implication for Companies
FDI Approval	Government board is required to approve FDI	100% FDI investment	Simplified and speedier FDI inflows into SEZ
Tax Exemption	Income tax exempt for the first 5 years, to be phased out by 2009	100% income tax exempt for the 5 years, 50% for 2 more years thereafter, 50% of the ploughed back export profit for the next 3 years	Companies with SEZ have greater income tax incentives
Retention of Foreign Exchange Earnings	Retain 70% foreign exchange earnings in EEFC (Exchange Earner Foreign Currency Account)	Retention of 100% export earnings by SEZ units in EEFC account	Companies within SEZs have a better control over foreign exchange earnings
Sectors	Focused mainly on manufacturing	Manufacturing, trading activities, and services	SEZ sector focus is more expansive
Export Performance (EP) & Net Foreign Exchange Earnings as % of exports (NFEP)	Minimum EP & NFEP required (varies by state and industry)	No minimum EP required. Positive NFEP required (varies by state and industry)	Companies within SEZ have more freedom in meeting export performance requirements
Domestic Tariff Area(DTA)* Sales	50% of exports qualify for DTA Sales	Units within SEZs can sell unlimited products to DTAs, however sales would be subject to applicable import duties	SEZs have greater access to the national market, but would be required to pay import duties
Duty on Imported Raw Materials	Duty free- raw materials have to be used within 1 year	Duty free- raw materials have to be used within 5 years	SEZ units have a longer period within which to use imported raw materials.
Certification of Imports	Imports need attestation of government authority	Imports on self-certification basis	SEZs have a simpler customs procedure making the import of goods easier

Source: Government of India, Special Economic Zones Act, 2005. http://www.sezindia.nic.in/SEZ%20Act,%202005.pdf, accessed April 2008.

*Domestic Tariff Area is the area within India which is outside the Special Economic Zone.

Exhibit 9 Sectoral Distribution of Approved Special Economic Zones, May 2008

Sectors	In-Principle Approvals	Formal Approvals	Notified SEZs
Aviation/Aerospace	1	1	-
IT/Electronic hardware/Semiconductors	12	282	135
Textiles	14	17	8
Pharma/Chemicals	3	20	13
Petrochemicals & petrol	1	1	1
Multi-product	51	20	9
Building products & materials	1	1	-
Beach & Mineral	1	1	-
Bio-tech	1	21	4
Ceramic & glasses	-	1	-
Engineering	11	17	9
Multi-services	8	14	4
Metallurgic engineering	-	1	-
Electronic products	4	3	3
Auto and related	4	3	1
Energy related	-	-	-
Footwear/leather	2	7	4
Gems & Jewelry	4	9	2
Power/alternate energy	1	4	1
Free Trade Warehousing Zones (FTWZ)	6	4	1
Metal/stainless steel/foundry	5	6	3
Food processing	2	4	3
Non-conventional energy	-	1	1
Plastic processing	1	-	-
Handicrafts	1	4	1
Agro	2	3	1
Port-based multi-product	-	6	2
Airport based multi-product	-	1	-
Writing & printing paper mills	-	1	1
Total	136	453	207

Source: Ministry of Commerce, Government of India, "Special Economic Zones in India- Introduction." http://sezindia.nic.in/HTMLS/about.htm, accessed May 2008.

Exhibit 10 SEZ Locations in India

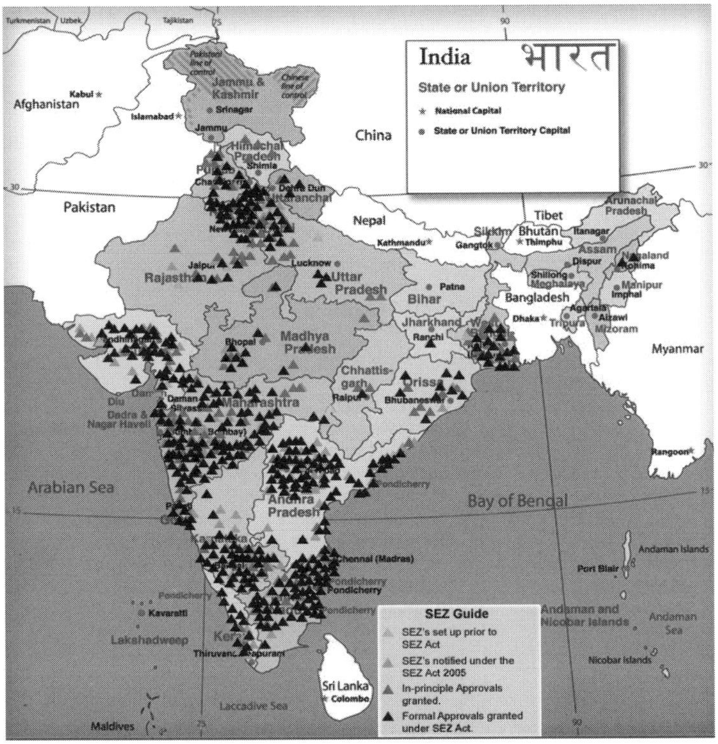

Source: Seminar Magazine (February 2008). Permission to use map granted by Seminar.

Exhibit 11 Performance of EPZs and SEZs in India

	EPZs Established under the EPZ Policy of 1965	SEZs notified after SEZ Act 2005
# of firms	1,525	294
Direct employment	238,242	97,993
Total private investment (billion Rs)	78.6	693.5
Exports 2006-2007 (billion USD)	9.1	0.1
Exports 2007-2008 (billion USD)	17.6	2.1

Source: http://sezindia.nic.in/HTMLS/visiblegains-sez.html, accessed October 2008.

Exhibit 12 Overview of Mahindra World City, Chennai

Total area	1500 Acres
Area under social/residential infrastructure	325 Acres
Area under product specific zones	841 Acres
IT (Services & Manufacturing)	10 companies including Cap Gemini, Helios & Matheson, Infosys, Mastek, Nestronics, Renault Nissan & Co.
Auto Ancillaries	8 companies including Brakes India, Madras Engineering Industries Limited (MEIL), Sundaram Group
Apparel & Fashion Accessories	9 companies including Capella Fashions, Hangers Plus, Leather Crafts India, Tuk Tuk Exports
Direct employment (June 2008)	8500
Projected direct employment by 2016	100,000
Exports (2008)	0.21 billion USD
Projected exports by 2016	1.7 billion USD
Total investment	0.45 billion USD
Projected investment by 2012	1 billion USD
Distance from Chennai International Airport	35 km
Distance from Chennai Seaport	55 km

Source: Mahindra World City.

Endnotes

[1] Government of India, Ministry of Commerce & Industry, Special Economic Zones, http://www.sezindia.nic.in/sez.asp, accessed March 2007.

[2] http://www1.timesofindia.indiatimes.com/articleshow/1800463.cms, accessed November 2008.

[3] http://www.indianexpress.com/news/India-Nirman/25736/, accessed November 2008.

[4] "Buddha Scraps Nandigram SEZ Project," *Indian Express* Online Edition. http://www.expressindia.com/fullstory.php?newsid=83866, accessed April 3, 2007.

[5] http://www.hinduonnet.com/fline/fl2423/stories/20071207508512100.htm, accessed November 2008.

[6] http://commerce.nic.in/May05_release.htm

[7] Response to author's question, Annual Bank Conference in Development Economics keynote address, Cape Town, June 2008.

[8] "Land Acquisition: Whirlwind of Chaos," *Business World*, August 30, 2008. http://www.businessworld.in/index.php/Corporate/Land-Acquisitions.html, accessed November 2008.

[9] http://sify.com/finance/fullstory.php?id=14775423, accessed November 2008.

[10] http://www.rediff.com/money/2008/sep/24sez.htm, accessed November 2008.

[11] *Manmohan Singh's next big move*. Asia Times. October 2006. http://www.atimes.com/atimes/South_Asia/HJ11Df01.html, accessed August 6, 2008.

[12] Johri, Devika & Miller, Mark, "Devaluation of the Rupee: Tale of Two Years, 1966 and 1991." Center for Civil Society. http://www.ccsindia.org/ccsindia/policy/money/studies/wp0028.pdf

[13] See "India on the Move," HBS Case 703-050 for a detailed description of India's reform process.

[14] http://planningcommission.nic.in/news/prmar07.pdf, accessed November 2008.

[15] Government of India, Ministry of Consumer Affairs, Food & Public Distribution, http://fcamin.nic.in/Events/EventDetails.asp?EventId=1216&Section=Annual%20Report&ParentID=0&child_continue=1&child_check=0, accessed March 2007.

[16] Confederation of Indian Industry (CII), "Study on Mapping of Manpower Skills in Maharashtra-2012." Mumbai, 2008.

[17] Economic Survey 2007-08, Ministry of Finance, government of India. http://indiabudget.nic.in/es2007-08/chapt2008/chap35.pdf, accessed November 2008.

[18] http://www.fareedzakaria.com/articles/newsweek/030606.html, accessed October 2008.

[19] Government of India, Ministry of Commerce & Industry, Special Economic Zones, http://www.sezindia.nic.in/sez.asp, accessed March 2007.

[20] Unlike most SEZs, urban enterprise zones are not treated as foreign territory, although like other SEZs they provide favorable tax treatments and other advantages.

[21] Government of India, Ministry of Commerce & Industry, Special Economic Zones, http://www.sezindia.nic.in/sez.asp, accessed March 2007.

[22] See Karima Omar and William A. Stoever, *Transnational Corporations*, Vol. 12, No.1 (April 2008).

[23] "Export Processing Zones in Asia: A Comparative Study." *Asian Survey*, Vol. 32, No. 11, (November 1992), p. 1032. University of California Press.

[24] http://www.state.nj.us/njbusiness/locationdata/uez/about.shtml

[25] See Theodore Moran (2002) *Beyond Sweatshops: Foreign Direct Investment and Globalization in Developing Countries,* Washington D.C.: Brookings Trade Forum; Y.W. Rhee and T. Belot (1990), "Export Catalysts in Low-Income Countries: A Review of Eleven Success Stories," World Bank Discussion Paper, 72, Washington D.C.: World Bank and discussion in Omar and Stoever (2008).

[26] Theodore Moran (2002) Beyond Sweatshops: Foreign Direct Investment and Globalization in Developing Countries, Washington D.C.: Brookings Trade Forum, p. 17.

[27] Zhu, Jieming. "Changing land policy and its impact on local growth: The experience of the Shenzhen special Economic Zone, China, in the 1980s." *Urban Studies*, Dec 94, Vol. 31 Issue 10, p. 1611.

[28] Firoz, Nadeem. "Foreign Investment Opportunities and Customs Law in China's Special Economic Zones." *International Journal of Management*, Vol. 20 No. 1, March 2003.

[29] Tsui, Anna. "Collective Contracts in the Shenzhen Special Economic Zone in China." *The International Journal of Comparative Labour Law and Industrial Relations*, Winter 2006.

[30] Vijaya Ramachandran and Rachel Cleetus. "Export Processing Zones: The Chinese Experience and its Lessons for Tamil Nadu" http://www.cid.harvard.edu/archive/india/pdfs/china_epz0899.pdf

[31] http://www.nytimes.com/2006/12/19/world/asia/19shenzhen.html?pagewanted=1&_r=1

[32] "Export Processing Zones at risk? The WTO rules on subsidies: what options for the future?" UNCTAD Press Release, January 23, 2003. http://www.unctad.org/Templates/webflyer.asp?docid=3154&intItemID=2261&lang=1, accessed November 2008.

[33] Chapter 6- External Sector. Economic Survey 2006-2007. Ministry of Finance, Government of India. www.indiabudget.nic.in, accessed March 2007

[34] http://economictimes.indiatimes.com/articleshow/1975792.cms, accessed November 2008.

[35] http://www.sezindore.com/policy_india.htm, accessed November 2008; *"JD(U) asks PM to scrap SEZ Act."* Financial Express. October 3, 2006. http://www.financialexpress.com/news/JD(U)-asks-PM-to-scrap-SEZ-Act/179532/, accessed July 2008.

[36] "Labor rigidity in India keeps firms on edge," *International Herald Tribune*, February 29, 2006. http://www.iht.com/articles/2006/02/09/business/toyota.php, accessed November 2008.

[37] Interviews with Anita Arjundas, March 2, 2007 and September 29, 2007.

[38] Ministry of Commerce, Government of India. Special Economic Zones in India- Introduction. http://sezindia.nic.in/HTMLS/about.htm, accessed June 2008

[39] Ministry of Commerce, Government of India. Special Economic Zones in India- Introduction. http://sezindia.nic.in/HTMLS/about.htm, accessed April 2008

[40] Interviews with Anita Arjundas, March 2, 2007 and September 29, 2007.

[41] Interview with Sriram Sivaram, July 28, 2007.

[42] SARS is a serious respiratory disease that authorities feared might reach epidemic proportions in 2003.

[43] Interview with P.N.Mathur, July 18, 2007.

[44] Interview with P.N.Mathur, July 18, 2007.

[45] "Mahindras cash in on early SEZ appeal," *Business Standard*, July 29, 2008. http://www.businessstandard.com/india/storypage.php?autono=329919, accessed November 2008.

[46] Constitution of India, Article 300A. http://lawmin.nic.in/coi/coiason29july08.pdf, accessed November 2008.

[47] "Land acquisitions for SEZs get stuck." Rediff.com. July 21, 2008 . *http://www.rediff.com/money/2008/jul/21sez.htm*, accessed July 2008.

[48] "Tata Flight Fear brings government Back to land Acquisition." May 13, 2008. http://www.telegraphindia.com/1080513/jsp/bengal/story_9263777.jsp, accessed July 2008.

[49] http://www.rediff.com/money/2008/jul/21sez.htm, accessed November 2008.

[50] "Treat SEZs like real estate, says RBI Governor," *The Indian Express*, page 2, September 22, 2006.

[51] *"Fields of gold: Dionne Bunsha detects the makings of another Indian mutiny."* New Internationalist http://findarticles.com/p/articles/mi_m0JQP/is_404/ai_n21026854, accessed July 2008.

[52] Interview with Vilol Khaladkar, June 30, 2008.

[53] "Se(i)zing the coast and the countryside" SEMINAR 582, February 2008; "Fishermen move Gujarat HC against Adani SEZ," The Economic Times, 15 Jul, 2008. http://economictimes.indiatimes.com/Infrastructure/Fishermen_move_Gujarat_HC_against_Adani_SEZ/articleshow/3238186.cms, accessed July 2008.

[54] See David A. Moss, Tiffany Morris and Sarah Brennan, "The American System," HBS Case 704-036 for details on the evolution of the U.S. legal system.

[55] http://straylight.law.cornell.edu/supct/html/04-108.ZO.html.

[56] http://straylight.law.cornell.edu/supct/html/04-108.ZD.html.

[57] Executive order of June 23, 2006. http://www.worldnetdaily.com/news/article.asp?ARTICLE_ID=50779, accessed December 2008.

[58] The Land Acquisition Act 1894, Section 3(f)(viii). http://dolr.nic.in/hyperlink/acq.htm.

[59] http://www.narmada.org/, accessed July 2008.

[60] Interview with Vilol Khaladkar, June 30, 2008.

[61] Interview with Yogendra Garg, July 16, 2007.

[62] Indian Trust Management: Land Fractionation, January 10, 2007 http://www.peoplelandandwater.gov/ost/v2-2006-11-18-plw61.cfm, accessed August 1, 2008.

[63] Interview with Jayant Sinha, May 16, 2008.

[64] http://www.nytimes.com/2008/09/17/world/asia/17india.html.

[65] Jayant Sinha, "A Case of Public Acts and Private Ambitions," *Outlook Business*, September 20, 2008. http://business.outlookindia.com/inner.aspx?articleid=2037&subcatgid=938&editionid=55&catgid=12, accessed December 2008.

[66] "Thirty-ninth Report on 'The Land Acquisition (Amendment) bill, 2007'," Standing Committee on Rural Development, October 21, 2008, p 35. http://164.100.47.132/committeereports/Rural%20Development/REP-RURAL-39E-F.pdf, accessed November 2008.

[67] "How Cochin avoided a Singur," *Times of India*, September 7, 2008, page 23.

[68] "Interview with S. Bharath, Managing Director of CIAL," *Outlook Business*, April 19, 2008. http://business.outlookindia.com/inner.aspx?articleid=1293&editionid=36&catgid=11&subcatgid=11.

[69] See "Special Economic Zones in India (B): Tata Motors in Singur" (HBS Case 709029) for further details on the Singur project, and the negotiations among the stakeholders.

[70] http://www.thehindubusinessline.com/2008/10/20/stories/2008102050880800.htm, accessed November 2008.

HARVARD | BUSINESS | SCHOOL

9-709-029
FEBRUARY 11, 2009

LAURA ALFARO
LAKSHMI IYER
NAMRATA ARORA

Tata Motors in Singur: Public Purpose and Private Property (B)

On October 3, 2008, Tata Motors announced the cancellation of their car manufacturing plant at Singur, in the state of West Bengal in India. The decision came in the face of widespread protests from local farmers, who claimed that their land had been acquired by the state government under questionable circumstances. Similar problems over land acquisition issues affected many other industrial projects in India, posing a significant threat to the government's initiatives to spur employment in the manufacturing and services sectors.[a]

Tata Motors, India's largest passenger and commercial vehicle manufacturer, was part of the Tata Group of companies, which comprised 96 operating companies in seven business sectors: information systems and communications, engineering, materials, services, energy, consumer products and chemicals. The Tata Group collectively employed 202,000 people across six continents and reported revenues in 2006 of $21.9 billion, equivalent to 2.8% of India's total gross domestic product.[1] Since 2000, Ratan Tata (HBS AMP 1971), the chairman of the Tata Group, had actively internationalized the group's operations and Tata Motor's 2008 acquisition of the British Jaguar and Land Rover brands from Ford Motors was part of the Group's international expansion strategy.[2] On the domestic front, Tata Motors was the market leader in the light commercial vehicle segment, and was also increasing its presence in the passenger car segment with the introduction of the Tata Indica and Tata Indigo.

In 2003, Ratan Tata embarked on his vision to build a "people's car" that would be the lowest priced car in the world. The Tata Nano, priced at $2,500 (100,000 Indian Rupees) was unveiled in January 2008 amidst enthusiasm and skepticism. The two-cylinder engine, four-door compact car was slated to meet safety requirements as well as emission norms. The Nano had 20% more seating capacity and was almost half the price of its nearest competitor in India. Experts commented that "the little car from India could lead to an overhaul in the global auto industry, which was always geared to earn big profits from big cars."[3] However, others worried that the Nano could lead to "more traffic congestion, more global warming, more highway fatalities and more demand for oil." For Tata Motors itself, the Nano presented major challenges. With an estimated cost of $380 million to $435 million for developing the new model, industry analysts expected that it would take Tata Motors five years to break even on the Nano.[4]

---

[a] See Laura Alfaro and Lakshmi Iyer, "Special Economic Zones in India: Public Purpose and Private Property (A)," HBS Case 709-027.

Professors Laura Alfaro and Lakshmi Iyer and Research Associate Namrata Arora of the India Research Center prepared this case. This case was developed from published sources. HBS cases are developed solely as the basis for class discussion. Cases are not intended to serve as endorsements, sources of primary data, or illustrations of effective or ineffective management.

States across India aiming to boost their industrial growth invited Tata Motors to set up their first Nano plant. Along with the northern states of Uttarakhand and Himachal Pradesh, which received special tax concessions from the central government, the eastern state of West Bengal was also shortlisted by the company. After a series of negotiations, Tata Motors announced its first Nano factory in Singur, West Bengal, on May 18, 2006. Ratan Tata remarked, "We have come to believe that West Bengal is the most investor-friendly state in the country...The investment is a reflection that the Tata Group has faith in the investment climate and the government of Bengal."[5] This was a significant endorsement of Chief Minister Buddhadeb Bhattacharya's strategy of actively inviting private investment to the state, a radical departure from the historical stance of the Communist Party of India-Marxist (CPM).

West Bengal offered Tata Motors a host of incentives. In addition to reduced electricity charges, and a loan of $40 million at a discounted interest rate, the state allocated 997 acres of fertile multi-crop agricultural land for the Tata project. The state government acquired this land by using the eminent domain provisions of the Land Acquisition Act of 1894, citing that the land would be used for public purpose.[6] West Bengal provided 645.67 acres of land to Tata Motors for their mother plant on a ninety-year lease; 290 acres were allocated for a vendor park which would host various ancillary units for the Nano and 60 acres were reserved for the state-run West Bengal Industrial Development Corporation for setting up required infrastructure for the Tata factory. Tata Motors was to pay rent for their land at a gradually increasing rate: $250,000 annually for the first five years, with a 25% increase every five years until the thirtieth year; $1.25 million thereafter with a 30% increase every 10 years until the sixtieth year; and a fixed fee of $5.25 million after the sixtieth year.[7]

Soon after the announcement of the Nano project, protests began in Singur over what some viewed as "forcible" acquisition of land. The protests were led by opposition leader Mamata Banerjee of the Trinamool Congress, who contended that close to 400 acres, owned by more than 2000 farmers, had been acquired illegally and without adequate compensation and should therefore be returned to the farmers. She even undertook a 25-day hunger strike in December 2006 as a mark of protest against the government. The state government, supported by a High Court ruling in January 2008, stated that land had been legally acquired for public interest through the Land Acquisition Act, and urged all farmers to accept the compensation package offered by the state.[8] The state had offered compensation to 13,000 farmers in 2007 at the market rate of $17,000 and $24,000 per acre for single-crop and double-crop land, respectively, amounting to a total payment of approximately $28 million. However, once the Tata project began, the price of industrial land in Singur soared, with some plots valued at $80,000 per acre, leaving many farmers resentful over the payment they had received.

The demand for returning 400 acres was problematic for both Tata Motors and the farmers. Even if Tata Motors could retain enough land for its own plant, its suppliers, who had invested $110 million towards construction and procurement of their equipment and machinery, would be forced to relocate, increasing the cost of production and jeopardizing the Nano's 100,000 rupee price tag.[9] For the farmers, the disputed holdings were scattered across the plant site, making land repatriation even more challenging. Ratan Tata, expressing his frustration over the increasing unrest in Singur remarked, "If anybody is under the impression that because we have made this large investment of about Rs 15,000 crore [$300 million], we will not move, then they are wrong..."[10]

In September 2008, the State government offered additional compensation to the farmers, amounting to 50% of the price originally offered for the land and agreed to return 70 acres of land within the Tata plant. The opposition rejected the offer, citing that there was "no guarantee that they [West Bengal] will keep their promise on the package."[11] Anticipating a gridlock in Singur between the government and the farmers, other states in India began inviting Tata Motors to relocate within their borders. On October 3, 2008, Tata Motors officially announced that the Nano factory was closing its operations in Singur, stating that "an environment of confrontation, agitation and violence" had compelled the company to withdraw from the state.[12]

On October 8, 2008, Tata Motors announced the relocation of their Nano factory to the western state of Gujarat, one of India's most developed states which generated 20% of the nation's industrial output. Gujarat provided similar incentives as the West Bengal government had, along with 1100 acres of acquired land in the Sanand municipality at a rate of $7,000 per acre. Ratan Tata remarked, "We chose Gujarat because of the conducive and industry-friendly environment as well as infrastructure. Also, the location of the land that was being offered was very attractive."[13] Narendra Modi, Gujarat's Chief Minister, announced that the project would generate close to 300,000 cars per year, making the state a "force to reckon with in the automobile sector."[14]

Though Tata Motors celebrated their entry in Gujarat, the events that transpired in Singur continued to weigh on the company's mind. Farmers in Sanand had filed a case in December 2008 stating that their land had been forcibly acquired without adequate compensation, leaving Tata Motors to wonder if they could face a similar fate of opposition in Gujarat, crippling their ambitious Nano project.[15]

Tata's experiences epitomized the challenges of land acquisition in India. The Land Acquisition Amendment Bill, introduced in Parliament in December 2007, aimed to extend the ability of the government to acquire land for "public serving" companies, but it remained uncertain if the Bill would be passed.

Endnotes

[1] "Tata Motors: The Tata Ace" HBS Case 108-011.

[2] "House of Tata: Acquiring a Global Footprint" HBS Case 708-446.

[3] http://www.newsweek.com/id/123068.

[4] http://online.wsj.com/article/SB119993102461279857.html.

[5] http://www.telegraphindia.com/1060519/asp/bengal/story_6243151.asp.

[6]http://www.wbidc.com/images/pdf/Agreement%20between%20TML,%20WBIDC%20and%20Government%20of%20West%20Bengal.pdf. See "Special Economic Zones in India: Public Purpose and Private Property (A)," HBS Case 709-027 for details of the Land Acquisition Act of 1894.

[7]http://www.wbidc.com/images/pdf/Agreement%20between%20TML,%20WBIDC%20and%20Government%20of%20West%20Bengal.pdf.

[8] http://www.livemint.com/2008/01/19001146/Singur-land-acquisition-is-leg.html.

[9] http://knowledge.wharton.upenn.edu/india/article.cfm?articleid=4318.

[10]http://economictimes.indiatimes.com/The_Week_That_Was/Review_of_Corporate_for_the_week/articleshow/3397580.cms.

[11] http://sify.com/news/crime/fullstory.php?id=14758449&cid=14182467.

[12] http://www.telegraphindia.com/1081017/jsp/frontpage/story_9980686.jsp.

[13] http://www.business-standard.com/india/storypage.php?autono=336735.

[14] http://www.business-standard.com/india/storypage.php?autono=336735.

[15] "Sanand farmers file petition on Nano land compensation," *Times of India*, December 4, 2008. http://timesofindia.indiatimes.com/Ahmedabad/Sanand_farmers_file_petition_on_Nano_land_compensation_/articleshow/3789628.cms, accessed December 30, 2008.

Capital Mobility and the International Financial Architecture

HARVARD | BUSINESS | SCHOOL

9-706-057
REV: DECEMBER 6, 2007

LAURA ALFARO

Creditor Activism in Sovereign Debt: "Vulture" Tactics or Market Backbone

A loan to a foreign government is an act of faith.
—Herbert Feis, 1930

On June 10, 2005, Argentina announced what it considered the successful conclusion of its global exchange offer aiming to restructure $82 billion in defaulted government debt.[a,1] A total of $62 billion—implying a 76% participation rate, under the usual rate of above 90% in other restructurings worldwide[2]—was tendered in the exchange between January 10, 2005 and February 25, 2005, making it the largest bond exchange in history. It was also one of the most complex, covering 152 bonds in eight different jurisdictions.[3] (See **Exhibit 1** for selected details on 66 bonds.) Under the terms of the exchange, bondholders tendering their bonds were compensated with new discounted bonds. Investors accepted an average "haircut"—realized investor losses calculated as the percentage difference between the present values of old and new instruments discounted at the yield prevailing immediately after the exchange—of around 73%.[4]

Argentina's debt restructuring process, however, was far from over. It remained to be seen what would happen with the remaining bondholders representing $20 billion in claims who chose not to participate in the exchange. Argentina made it clear that it intended to repudiate the debt of holdout creditors.[5] However, with untendered bonds trading at 30% of the face value of the original bonds[6]—just five percentage points below where the new bonds were trading—it was clear that the market foresaw the possibility of some degree of compensation. Indeed, before the exchange, activist holdouts had "raced to the courthouse" in New York, Germany, and Italy seeking to acknowledge their right to payment and then to collect against Argentine assets located outside of Argentina.[7] Two funds, EM Ltd. (owned by Styrofoam cup billionaire Kenneth Dart) and NML Capital Ltd. (controlled by hedge fund Elliott Associates), were particularly aggressive in their strategy. The funds, which had purchased Argentine bonds at a discount and sought to recover the full face value, delayed settlement of Argentina's exchange offer by two months through legal interventions that aimed to force Argentina to use bonds tendered in the exchange by other creditors to pay EM's and NML's claims. After this effort ultimately failed in spring 2005, the two funds explored other possibilities for attachment, including Argentine Central Bank reserves held in New York.

---

[a] For more on the background of Argentina's economic problems and default, refer to "The 2001 Crisis in Argentina: An IMF-Sponsored Default?" HBS No. 704-004. The following is a brief overview: Between 1998 and 2001, Argentina had endured an increasingly severe recession and multiple failed attempts to restore growth and control government spending. Interest rates soared and foreign investment had dried up. On December 5, 2001, the IMF declared that Argentina had not done enough to control its public deficit and stopped disbursing funds to the country. The stage was set for Argentina to default on its $141 billion in foreign debt outstanding, in what would become the largest sovereign default in history. On January 3, 2002, Argentina formally went into default as expected on a portion of its foreign debt, missing a payment of $28 million on an Italian lira bond; this became the largest government default in history.

Professor Laura Alfaro and Research Associate Ingrid Vogel prepared this case. HBS cases are developed solely as the basis for class discussion. Cases are not intended to serve as endorsements, sources of primary data, or illustrations of effective or ineffective management.

This was not Elliott Associates' first foray into litigation in sovereign debt markets. After several other successful attempts at litigation in sovereign debt markets over the years, in 2000 the hedge fund managed to convert an $11 million investment in Peruvian bonds with a face value of $21 million into a $58 million cash payout from the country, representing the full face value of the bonds plus past-due interest. The case brought attention to Elliott and highlighted the problems associated with debt restructuring. On the one hand, many observers derided firms such as Elliott and Dart as "vultures" or "rogue creditors" who sought to profit on sovereign debt restructurings at the expense of countries suffering economic hardship and of the majority of bondholders whose cooperation allowed the restructurings to take place.[8] Critics believed that these holdout creditors created "collective action problems" and presented a major obstacle to successful sovereign debt restructurings. On the other hand, it was argued that activist investors actually improved the market overall. For example, a BCP Securities broker noted: "Thank God for Elliott Associates. Thank God for the NML lawsuit. Because that is the thing that keeps sovereign lending alive—those lawsuits, and the glimmer of hope . . . they give to creditors that they can reclaim part of their investment. Showing that this recourse exists is the thing that is going to allow future lending to occur."[9]

Debt Restructuring

Background

Until the mid-1970s—following the shutting down of the international markets after widespread defaults in the 1930s—debt flows to most developing countries were generally restricted to international organizations and government-to-government loans. During the late 1970s, banks replaced governments of industrial countries as lenders to developing countries.[10] Commercial bank credit extended by private international banks was usually in the form of syndicated loans.

Enforcing terms of sovereign debt contracts had complications relative to enforcing corporate debt. In particular, sovereign immunity prevented sovereigns from being sued in foreign courts without their consent. Immunity extended to commercial transactions between private individuals and foreign states as well, although as early as the 1930s bondholders had the U.S. State Department or Foreign Office apply diplomatic pressure on defaulting countries.[11] In order to distance the executive from direct responsibility for the fate of private-sector lenders to sovereign debtors,[12] governments introduced more restricted views of sovereign immunity, such as the U.S. Foreign Sovereign Immunities Act of 1976 (FSIA) and the United Kingdom State Immunity Act of 1978. By clarifying the rights of sovereign creditors in the event of default and allowing private individuals to sue a foreign government in U.S. courts for activities related to commerce, including sovereign bonds, these laws were argued to have helped the sovereign lending market develop.[13] Suing sovereigns also became more commonplace as a result of a covenant waiving sovereign immunity, which became part of many debt contracts.[14]

Although sovereign immunity laws played a diminished role in protecting sovereign debtors from creditor suits, they did limit the ability of creditors to collect against governments in the event of a favorable court judgment. Since few sovereign assets were located outside of national borders, collection by creditors in the event of default was difficult. Many countries were generally careful to organize their commercial activities in separate corporations to keep their assets untouchable.[15] In addition, under the FSIA and similar laws in other countries, central bank assets, including international reserves, were usually protected against attachment.[16] This was true even in cases where the central bank was the issuer of the debt. Because the Bank for International Settlements

(BIS) in Switzerland was also protected against attachment proceedings,[17] governments and central banks in some cases placed assets with the BIS.

Bank Advisory Committees

The Paris and London Clubs, acting as the primary avenues of negotiation between developing-country governments and their creditors, attempted to fill the vacuum caused by difficulties enforcing sovereign debt contracts in the event of default. Established in 1956, the Paris Club structured negotiations in which official creditors rescheduled payments and resolved debt problems associated with intergovernmental loans. Members usually included the G-7 countries and several other principal OECD members. World Bank and International Monetary Fund (IMF) representatives were also invited. Relying on agreement by consensus, negotiation among the debtor and its creditors continued until unanimity of all parties was achieved.[18]

The London Club used a similar framework for rescheduling debt payments and servicing, but was geared toward commercial bank creditors rather than official creditors. Banks with the largest exposure would generally form a committee, referred to as the Bank Advisory Committee (BAC), to cater to the interests of all affected commercial banks—usually around 10 to 15. The process encouraged collective action in resolving debt disputes and discouraged litigation. For example, syndicated loan contracts typically contained "sharing clauses" that forced any member of the syndicate to share any payments extracted through litigation or settlement with the remaining members. The BAC derived power relative to debtors by blocking new lending from members before a debt restructuring agreement.[19]

During debt restructurings in the 1980s, banks often provided refinancing to distressed debtor countries rather than forcing them into default. Banks adopted this tactic because, first, they perceived the debt crisis that began in the late 1970s as related to problems of liquidity rather than solvency.[20] Second, banks had a regulatory incentive against declaring a creditor in default—a prerequisite for litigation—since they would be required to write down the value of the loans on their books. A legal academic noted that the "effect of these pressures was a de facto replication of the U.S. Bankruptcy Code's automatic stay of collection actions against a debtor. The banks were effectively unable to pursue their collection rights even though those rights were fully enforceable."[21] There were also additional reasons that banks chose not to force default. They generally desired profitable local operations in the countries being restructured; banks playing legal hardball could face retaliation against local operations whereas a debtor friendly deal might be rewarded, for example with lucrative local banking licenses. Furthermore, any bank that took legal action against one debtor would likely be avoided by other debtors, closing off more new business than the value of a single recovery could offset.

The Debt Crisis

The onset of the emerging market debt crisis in 1982, precipitated by Mexico's announcement that it was no longer able to service its external debt, put these institutions to the test. Unfortunately, they proved inadequate to deal with the extreme problems posed by the crisis, prompting the emergence of other programs intended to resolve debt problems. In retrospect, academics argued that economic impacts on debtor countries were prolonged due to the failure of effected commercial banks and their own governments to reach agreement on who should bear the costs of debtor defaults.[22]

In 1985, U.S. Treasury Secretary James Baker proposed the Baker Plan. He argued that economic growth in heavily indebted nations was a prerequisite for solving debt problems. Multilateral institutions such as the IMF and World Bank were called upon to increase their lending to developing countries by up to 50%. Commercial banks were asked to contribute an additional $20 billion to finance indebted countries' market-oriented reforms, designed and sponsored by the World Bank. The U.S. agreed to an expansion of World Bank funds to support such programs. By encouraging reform and promoting growth, the Baker Plan aimed to restore private capital inflows. Despite these initiatives, between 1982 and 1987, the 15 most heavily indebted countries demonstrated little or no growth under the Baker Plan, and debt problems remained an important constraint on economic performance.[23]

The Brady Plan

The failure of the Baker Plan forced the international financial community to consider debt forgiveness in addition to debt rescheduling. The most prominent proposal was the Brady Plan, suggested by U.S. Treasury Secretary Nicholas Brady in 1989, which encouraged banks to restructure past loans to developing country governments with the ultimate objective of cultivating a climate of sustained economic growth. In March 1989, Brady outlined his agenda to the financial community at a debt conference: "We renew our efforts to create and foster world growth. . . . These past seven years we have faced a major challenge in the international debt problem. . . . Ultimately, resolution depends on a great cooperative effort by the international community."[24]

Mexico's 1990 Brady restructuring provides an example of how the plan worked.[25] Banks could exchange their outstanding loans in arrears to Mexico for newly issued 30-year discount dollar-denominated Brady bonds, with principal and 12–18 months of interest secured by U.S. Treasury bonds. The bonds adopted New York covenants—which required the consent of each bondholder to any proposal to modify payment terms—instead of English covenants, which allowed a super-majority holding 75% of the value of the bonds to make modifications. Banks chose between several options on the terms of the bonds. In the end, they elected to convert 49% of total indebtedness into "par bonds" that provided the same face value as the loans but at a rate of interest well below the market rate and 41% into "discounted bonds" with substantially discounted principal but with a market rate of interest. In the case of the remaining 10% of total indebtedness, banks opted to abstain from the swap options and instead lend new funds equivalent to 25% of their outstanding medium and long-term exposures. Of the three options, providing new money proved the most lucrative over time.

In total, around $202.8 billion of debt was restructured under Brady deals in around 18 countries, resulting in $63.7 billion of debt relief. Average interest rate spreads on the debt fell from 17/16 to 13/16 over LIBOR, while the average maturity of the debt increased from 15 to 30 years. Furthermore, the average price of a country's debt traded in the secondary market increased from 32 cents on the dollar in the year prior to restructuring to 42 cents in the month of the Brady deal.[26] Brady-type operations were credited with enabling debtors and Bank Advisory Committees to reach agreements that allowed debtor countries new access to financial markets.[27]

Post-Brady Restructurings

Although the Brady deals instilled investor confidence in participating countries, problems quickly reemerged as real interest rates increased during the early 1990s. For example, despite its successful debt restructuring, by late 1994 Mexico experienced severe economic problems and was again headed toward default. A large bailout package organized by the U.S. in early 1995 helped the country ultimately avoid default, and the economy recovered rapidly.[28] Another financial crisis erupted in Asia in 1997, when Thailand floated its currency in response to repeated speculative attacks. Economic crisis quickly spread to the Philippines, Malaysia, South Korea, and Indonesia. Currency devaluations across the region sharply increased the servicing costs on foreign-denominated debt, forcing many countries to the brink of default. South Korea ended up reaching a comprehensive agreement with global creditors to exchange $24 billion in short-term debt for government-guaranteed bonds. Other countries followed suit.[29]

Most debt restructurings between 1998 and 2005 focused on sovereign bonds—usually governed under New York or English law—held by a widely dispersed group of creditors, mostly non-banks. Many of these bonds represented converted bank debt, such as under the Brady restructurings. Although bondholder representation was harder to coordinate than bank representation during the 1980s,[30] the restructurings were generally completed relatively quickly.[b] In large part, this was due to take-it-or-leave-it offers, which aimed to be attractive enough to achieve wide participation and therefore result in a sustainable debt burden and corresponding improvement in debt-service capacity for the debtor. Investment banks often served as financial advisors on the offers, which were usually preceded by informal discussions with creditors rather than formal negotiations. Coordination was encouraged by making the offers contingent on acceptance by a given supermajority of creditors (often 80%–90%). Creditors who chose not to participate in the exchanges of original bonds for bonds with a payment stream of lower present value were faced with the alternatives of holding an illiquid instrument, selling at depressed prices, or engaging in uncertain litigation.[31] (See **Exhibits 2**, **3**, and **4** for historical information on sovereign debt defaults.)

As in the 1980s, the IMF was involved in these sovereign debt workouts. Lee Buchheit, partner at New York law firm Cleary Gottlieb Steen & Hamilton LLP, who had served as counsel to multiple governments seeking debt renegotiations, explained: "The integration of the world's financial and trading markets has forced the official sector to view a sovereign debt problem in one country as a potential source of disruption elsewhere. The financial and geopolitical consequences of an unmanageable debt crisis can no longer be neatly contained in a single country, or even a single region."[32]

Legal Issues in Sovereign Debt Restructuring

In the late 1980s, creditor banks began provisioning against loan losses and writing off their loans, and a secondary market in loans was created. This allowed specialized investors—which became known as distressed debt funds or "vulture funds"—to buy discounted debt and sue for full recovery. By 2005, there were many incidences of such creditors bringing suits. On the one hand, some analysts considered litigation as playing an important part in maintaining the viability of sovereign debt markets. On the other hand, litigation risked disrupting or delaying sovereign debt restructurings. Two "collective action problems" were often discussed in this context. First, free riders or holdouts highlighted the problem that creditors as a whole would be better off agreeing to a restructuring that left debtors with a sustainable debt burden, whereas each creditor individually would be better off if it were repaid in full while all other creditors agreed to a restructuring. Facing few holdouts, a sovereign might choose to go forward with its restructuring and to accept the risk of litigation. However, too many holdouts would leave the sovereign unable to restructure. "Runs to the courthouse" involved creditors attempting to preempt other creditors by suing for full recovery before a restructuring.[33] In some cases investors were able to secure better terms than the rest of the creditors. (See **Exhibit 5** for various details on selected litigation.)

[b] Argentina's restructuring discussed in this case is an exception, in that it took more than four years to complete.

Anne O. Krueger, first deputy managing director of the IMF, described the collective action problem in sovereign debt restructuring:

> Developments in the composition of international sovereign borrowing over the past decade—notably the shift away from syndicated bank loans toward traded securities as the principal vehicle for the extension of financial credits to sovereigns—have improved the efficiency of international capital markets. In particular, they have broadened the investor base for financing to emerging market sovereigns and have facilitated the diversification of risk. But the increasingly diverse and diffuse creditor community poses coordination and collective action problems in cases in which a sovereign's scheduled debt service exceeds its payments capacity. This leads to considerable uncertainty among all participants as to how the restructuring process will unfold, and contributes to reluctance by the sovereign, its creditors, and the official sector to pursue a restructuring, other than in the most extreme circumstances. This, in turn, increases the likely magnitude of the loss of asset values, which is harmful to the interests of both debtors and creditors.[34]

An early example of holdout litigation was Allied Bank attempting to recover from Costa Rica after the country suspended debt payments to a 39-member bank syndicate in 1981. Allied was the only bank not to participate in the restructuring, choosing instead to sue. Allied was ultimately successful in getting a favorable judgment in U.S. courts, which concluded that "while parties may agree to renegotiate conditions of payment, the underlying obligations to pay nevertheless remain valid and enforceable."[35] In an *amicus curiae* brief,[c] the U.S. Justice Department referred to the fact that Costa Rica's unilateral imposition of exchange controls was inconsistent with U.S. policy.[36] Ultimately, the U.S. government encouraged Allied to accept the same package offered to the syndicate. Although Allied did no better than the other creditors, the case was important in that it demonstrated that sovereigns could not expect protection in the event of default.[37]

An early case in which a holdout strategy succeeded in yielding a better result than a negotiated offer involved the Dart family in Brazil. In the early 1990s, the Dart family acquired $1.4 billion worth of restructured Brazilian public sector debt from the 1980s at a steep discount. In 1992, Brazil again needed to restructure its debt and made an offer that all creditors, including Dart, accepted.[38] Subsequently, Brazil modified the terms of the exchange. Dart declined the new terms. All debt other than that of Dart and, at the request of the Brazilian government,[39] $1.6 billion held by state-owned Banco do Brasil was converted. When Dart tried to accelerate payment of the debt's principal—which required consent of holders of at least half of the outstanding amount—Banco do Brasil blocked the acceleration. Dart sued in a New York court, arguing that Banco do Brasil had colluded with the Brazilian government and that its vote should therefore not count.[40] In May 1995, the court rejected Dart's appeal.[41] The lawsuit was eventually settled, with Brazil paying Dart $77 million in past-due interest and agreeing to remain current on the debt. In October 1996, Dart securitized the cashflow on its position in the amount of $1.1 billion,[42] implying that Dart came out much better than creditors that accepted the Brady exchange.[43] The Dart case set many precedents that proved useful in subsequent holdout litigation, such as confirming a holdout's right to litigate on the basis of a claim acquired in the secondary market.[44]

[c] "*Amicus curiae*" is Latin for "friend of the court." An *amicus curiae* brief is filed with the court by a party not directly involved in a case, but who may believe its interests will be affected by the outcome of the case.

Pravin Banker Associates in Peru

Peru, with unpaid interest payments dating back to 1984, was one of the 18 debtors restructuring under the Brady Plan. In October 1995, Peru reached an agreement with its creditors, represented by a Bank Advisory Committee, outlining a Brady initiative aiming to cover around $8 billion of defaulted sovereign debt.[d]

In 1990, New York investment and trading boutique Pravin Banker Associates bought $9 million of Peruvian debt on the secondary market at a 73% discount. Shortly after, Pravin sold the majority of its claim, but retained debt with a face value of $1.4 million. Pravin received regular interest payments from the state bank *Banco Popular de Peru* on its debt until the bank faced temporary liquidity problems in February 1992. Pravin notified *Banco Popular* that this represented a breach of contract triggering acceleration, such that payment of all principal and accrued interest was immediately due and payable.

In December 1992, the government of Peru decided to liquidate the troubled state bank. Instead of participating with other creditors in the debt restructuring process, Pravin sued *Banco Popular* in a New York court to attempt to recover the full face value of the debt Pravin held.

On the one hand, the court acknowledged the argument made by the debtor that Pravin's suit could initiate a "race to the courthouse" and therefore disrupt Peru's ongoing debt negotiations under the Brady plan. On the other hand, it was the court's role to enforce valid contracts. Although lawyers for Peru tried to argue that Pravin should not be allowed to recover the full face value of the debt since the firm acquired the debt at a deep discount, Pravin maintained that the terms of the contract it held associated with the debt remained unchanged, irrespective of the conditions under which the debt had been purchased on the secondary market.

Initially, the New York court accepted Peru's argument that the case could interfere with Peru's Brady negotiations and granted two stays of litigation. Subsequently, in October 1995, Peru announced its Brady deal. On January 19, 1996, with Brady negotiations complete, the court judged against Peru and granted Pravin a $2.16 million ruling plus future interest payments. With its small claim, Pravin was considered by a legal academic to be "irksome to both the country and its other creditors, but not about to bankrupt the Peruvian treasury or scuttle the country's contemplated Brady deal."[45] Indeed, Pravin's litigation ultimately brought the firm little benefit; Pravin was only able to recover from Peru an amount close to what it would have received under the Brady terms.[46]

Elliott Associates

Shortly after Pravin's victory against Peru in court, hedge fund Elliott Associates, L.P. began to acquire non-performing debt guaranteed by the Peruvian government at a large discount. Elliott, an investment firm established in 1977, had more than $5.2 billion of capital under management as of July 1, 2005.[47] A 2004 *Euromoney* article described the company as a highly conservative hedge fund—with compound annual returns over 27 years of 14.1% and volatility just one-third that of the S&P 500 index—that had its roots in convertible arbitrage strategies.[e48] After the stock market bust of 1987,

[d] For more on Peru's economic background through the mid-1980s, refer to "Fresh Start? Peru's Legacy of Debt and Default," HBS No. 703-001.

[e] Convertible arbitrage involves buying convertible securities (i.e., bonds, preferred stock, or debentures with an option for the holder to exchange the security for common stock of the issuing corporation) and shorting the corresponding stock (e.g.,

Elliott shifted gradually away from trading and arbitrage strategies and into what Elliott founder Paul Singer, whose background was as a lawyer, described as "value-added investing." He stated: "We like to create value rather than merely identify it. If we just identify value, we can't make money unless the market moves the security in the predicted direction."[49] This involved opportunities around the world to make money through pursuing legal strategies.[50] Columbia Professor Charles Calomiris described Elliott's business strategy as "taking the creditor rights principles of the United States, as well as the strong tradition of rule of law, and applying them—with optimism and endurance—to the 'realpolitik' world of sovereign debt; and occasionally winning."[51]

For example, as a large hedge fund, Elliott could take a significant stake in the debt of distressed companies and get actively involved in the workout process,[52] such as in the case of WorldCom's bankruptcy in which the firm served on the creditor committee.[53] Singer described his thinking on distressed debt: "[for most distressed debt investors] active involvement is considered a cost of doing business. To us, it doesn't go that way. Active involvement is a primary driver for Elliott. We start by asking whether we can get involved and create value."[54] Elliott also got involved in legal strategies on the shareholder side. For example, Elliott led a group of investors in preferred shares[f] in German hair-care company Wella to challenge Proctor & Gamble (P&G) in its takeover of the company. Consistent with how the shares were trading in the market, P&G offered 30% less for preferred shares than for common shares. Elliott argued that, under the German Takeover Act of 2002,[55] P&G was required to offer the same price for all shares—even though preferred shares were trading at a lower price than common shares at the time of the takeover—whereas P&G lawyers argued that the act allowed companies to pay different prices for different classes of shares.[56] After more than six attempts in the U.S. and Germany to challenge the legality of prices offered in P&G's takeover of Wella, Elliott was ultimately successful in getting P&G to raise its offer price.[57]

In 1995, the company began to allocate a small portion of its capital—never exceeding 2%[58]—to both performing and non-performing sovereign debt.[59] In a *LatinFinance* editorial, Singer described Elliott's approach to sovereign debt:

> Sovereign debt—both current and distressed—has many characteristics similar to corporate debt, and there are many routes to the creation of value. Elliott has traded sovereign debt without ever contacting the issuer, has participated in restructurings, and has negotiated directly with sovereigns both individually and as part of groups. When faced with an intractable debtor, Elliott occasionally has brought suit to enforce its rights, as we might in a non-sovereign context. Litigation is always a last resort: it is expensive, time-consuming and often protracted.[60]

Elliott had resorted to this "last resort" previously. In Panama, for example, the hedge fund had acquired $17.5 million of sovereign debt worth $70 million from original creditors in October 1995.[61] Subsequently, Elliott refused to participate in the 1995 Brady restructuring and sued the Republic of Panama in a New York court for the full value of the debt. The court—and later a federal court—ruled in favor of Elliott. In late 1997, Elliott was able to get full repayment by obtaining attachment orders. One order was directed against U.S. assets of the national telecommunications company which Panama was about to privatize. The second order would have interfered with a large new bond issue in New York. Both the value of the privatization deal and the proceeds received from the bond issue were an order of magnitude larger than Panama's payment to Elliott. Elliott was reported to have made about $46 million in profits from the transaction.[62]

---

through borrowing shares from a broker and selling them before buying them back to return to the broker—ideally at a lower price). The strategy can be profitable if the convertible security is priced incorrectly relative to the stock.

[f] Preferred shares take precedence over ordinary shares in the order of payment but do not have voting rights.

Elliott Holds Out in Peru

Elliott engaged another litigation strategy related to the sovereign debt of Peru. Between January and March 1996, Elliott spent $11.4 million on 1983 Letter Agreements of *Banco de la Nacion* and *Banco Popular de Peru* with a face value of $20.7 million. (See **Exhibit 6** for a timeline of Elliott in Peru.) Immediately after completing its acquisition, and while Peru was still negotiating with the Bank Advisory Committee on the exact terms of the Brady deal, Elliott started to make demands for full payment. It was later revealed that Peru secretly repurchased about $1.7 billion in debt at deeply discounted prices on the secondary market as original debt renegotiations were under way. The *Financial Times* wrote: "Essentially, that means the government misled creditors about its ability to repay them in order to win better terms."[63]

It came as no surprise when Elliott chose not to participate in the Brady Exchange Agreement initiated by Peru in October 1996. Instead, on October 8, Elliott filed suits in New York against Peru and *Banco de la Nacion* seeking a judgment for the full face value of the debt plus interest. Elliott also sought a prejudgment attachment order against assets of Peru used for commercial purposes in the U.S. that were intended as collateral for the Brady closing. On the grounds that a favorable judgment would jeopardize the ability of Peru to close the Brady deal, the court initially denied Elliott's motions. The court described the strong differences between the sides, writing: "In the well-turned phrase of highly skilled counsel for Elliott, the prospect of a recalcitrant debtor 'makes Wall Street tremble'"; Whereas, in the judge's words, Peru considered Elliott "a blackmailer seeking to disrupt the national policies of Peru and the United States as expressed in the Brady Plan."[64]

In March 1997, Peru's Brady Exchange Agreement closed, with collateral held in trust protected from Elliott and a verbal promise from Peru not to provide extra benefits to holdout creditors. One year later, a trial was finally held in New York on the case. Before the beginning of the trial, and unnoticed by Peru's lawyers, Elliott acted through wholly owned affiliate Manchester Securities Corp. to amend a New York law retroactively in order to be able to collect interest on interest.[65]

On August 6, 1998, the court found for Peru based on the New York champerty doctrine dating back to the 1840s that made buying debt "with the intent and for the purpose of bringing an action or proceeding thereon" unlawful.[66] Peru's lawyers noted that Elliott began buying discounted Peruvian debt after Pravin Banker Associates' favorable judgment and that the firm had in the past targeted other "struggling nations" with litigation.[67] Elliott took a two-pronged approach in addressing this setback. The fund appealed the case in September, claiming that the champerty doctrine did not apply since intent to sue was only secondary to Elliott's intent to have its obligation paid in full. Elliott, again through Manchester Securities Corp., also convinced two New York state legislators to introduce a bill to amend the champerty doctrine. The bill cleared the state senate, but failed to pass the assembly before legislators went into recess.[68] Peru's lawyers got involved in the process, arguing that "Latin American countries have made the case that New York would be hurting its international credibility if it passed this special bill for Elliott."[69] Elliott was also aided by *amicus curaie* briefs filed on its behalf. For example, in December 1998, The Bond Market Association in New York wrote to the appeals court to request a ruling in favor of Elliott:

> As stated by the district court, restricting the rights of lenders or investors to assign debt contrary to the terms of a contract is at odds with the strong public policy—incorporated in federal and state law—in favor of the free alienability of property. . . . Similarly, the well-established rule that debts that are valid and due are legally enforceable should not be lightly set aside. It is important for this Court to interpret [the champerty doctrine] in a way that does not create a dangerous degree of uncertainty for market participants as to the collectibility of debts acquired in the secondary market. The Association therefore respectfully requests the

> Court to apply the statute in a manner that does not allow a purchaser's "champertous intent" to be readily raised as a defense to summary enforcement whenever a debt has been purchased at a discount or when the debtor is financially distressed. Such a result would be profoundly unsettling to a trillion dollar marketplace.[70]

In October 1999, the appeals court ruled in favor of Elliott. The appellate court argued that "the acquisition of a debt with intent to bring a suit against the debtor is not a violation of the statute where, as here, the primary purpose of the suit is the collection of the debt acquired."[71] In other words, the court decided that the rule was not violated since Elliott had decided to litigate only after Peru informed debt holders that it did not intend to repay the full value of the debt, implying that Elliott's primary goal was not necessarily to litigate but to satisfy a valid debt. As such, the case was sent back to the trial court to calculate damages. Peru tried to get a rehearing, but did not succeed. Peru's lawyers affirmed: "Peru will continue to play tough. They (Elliott) may have advanced (their case) but they're still a long way from getting anything more than a Brady (restructuring debt deal) out of Peru."[72]

Given the favorable decision at the appeals court, the trial court in November 1999 accepted Elliott's request for attachment on any commercial property of Peru and *Banco de la Nacion* located in New York. Given that there was almost no such property, Elliott requested that the restraining order also be applicable to all foreign branches of New York banks. This request was denied.

In June 2000, the trial court entered judgment for Elliott in the amount of $55.7 million, representing both principal and past-due interest, as well as to recover post-judgment interest. However, collecting from Peru was continuing to prove difficult. In response to the attachment order, Peru was careful to channel funds through financial centers other than New York to meet international financial obligations and to receive proceeds from international loan agreements and other commercial transactions. Otherwise, Elliott would be able to seize Peru's funds to pay down the $56 million obligation. Peru's efforts were complicated by Elliott's motions to attach property abroad, in particular in Germany, the Netherlands, Belgium, England, Luxembourg, and Canada. However, for the time being, Peru managed to stave off Elliott's attachment efforts.

Collecting on the Judgment

With its efforts to collect frustrated, Elliott adopted a new strategy focused on barring Peru from meeting its Brady bond interest payment due on September 7, 2000. The terms of the Brady deal required Peru to deliver $80 million to Chase Manhattan Bank in New York on September 6. Elliott obtained a restraining order on Chase to prevent the bank from transferring funds received from Peru to the Brady bondholders. Elliott also obtained restraining orders against the clearinghouses that Chase would use to transfer the interest payment to investors. These included U.S. clearinghouse Depository Trust Company (DTC) and European clearinghouse Euroclear through motions against Morgan Guaranty Trust Company of New York as operator of Euroclear, and Bank of New York as cash custodian of Euroclear.

Peru was forced to find an alternative route to meet its interest obligation. The terms of the Brady Exchange granted a 30-day grace period, after which a legal default would be incurred, triggering the right for bondholders to call for repayment on the full $3.8 billion in outstanding Brady bonds. A rumored agreement to transfer the funds with the Bank of International Settlements, which was immune from lawsuits and attachments, ultimately failed.[73] Other banks and clearinghouses were reluctant to cooperate with Peru because of fears of future lawsuits by Elliott. For example, European clearinghouse Clearstream agreed to cooperate, but only in return for indemnity from Peru. This did not prove possible.

On September 21 and 22, Elliott won a judgment from a New York court for the right to serve additional restraining orders against Chase, DTC, Morgan, and Bank of New York if a deposit or transfer occurred. Chase, Morgan, and Peru all challenged the orders as in violation of the June 2000 decision, but to no avail.

As part of its strategy to attach Brady interest payments, Elliott filed a motion on September 22, 2000, before the Commercial Court of Brussels to prevent clearinghouse Euroclear from accepting or paying out cash related to interest payments on the Brady bonds. Initially, the court rejected the petition. Elliott appealed on September 25 and received a favorable judgment the next day from the appeals court. The court ruled that financial institutions clearing their operations via Euroclear could be fined the equivalent of $2.5 million if they accepted money from Peru in payment for the overdue coupon via that clearing institution.[74] The court argued that it agreed with Elliott's efforts to prevent Peru from "using the possibilities offered by the Euroclear System in order to make discriminatory payments in a legal environment that avoids the effect of the American judgments."[75] In its decision to issue the injunction, the court considered Elliott's interpretation of the *pari passu* clause in debt contracts. (The term comes from the Latin noun *"passus,"* meaning "step, pace, or stride," and the adjective *"par,"* meaning equal or like.) The use of the term in debt clauses was as follows: "The Guarantor [i.e., the Republic of Peru] represents and warrants as follows: (...) (c) The obligations of the Guarantor hereunder do rank and will rank at least *pari passu* in priority of payment with all other External Indebtedness of the Guarantor, and interest thereon." The court noted that "it appears from the basic agreement that governs the repayment of the foreign debt of Peru that the various creditors benefit from a *pari passu* clause that in effect provides that the debt must be repaid pro rata among all creditors. This seems to lead to the conclusion that, upon an interest payment, no creditor can be deprived of its proportionate share."[76] In other words, obligations of other bondholders could not legally be met if Peru was in default to Elliott.

On September 29, 2000, faced with the prospect of being forced to default by missing its interest payment, Peru decided to settle with Elliott. Peru paid $58.45 million to the firm and was able to meet its interest obligations to Brady bondholders within the grace period.

Reactions to Elliott in Peru

The conclusion of the case led to consternation from many perspectives. Legal commentators questioned the validity of Elliott's broad interpretation of the *pari passu* clause, which assumed that payment to all holders of debt have the right to a proportional share of any payments on the debt.[77] A more conventional interpretation simply stated that a claim in question would not have lower priority than other unsecured claims.[78] Although commentators agreed that the *pari passu* clause interpretation would not necessarily hold in future situations, it was often argued that lack of clarity surrounding the interpretation of the clause introduced uncertainty to the debt restructuring process.[g]

[g] Indeed, in March 2004, a Brussels court ruled on a similar claim by distressed debt fund LNC. LNC sought to apply a broad interpretation of the *pari passu* clause to justify blocking Nicaragua's payments to bondholders until it used a portion of such funds to help settle arrears with other creditors. The court avoided ruling on *pari passu*, but struck down an injunction that required the Euroclear payments system to pay all creditors whenever the government serviced its performing debt. (Felix Salmon, "Pari passu clause is a threat to the markets," *Euromoney*, May 1, 2004.) In 2005, analysts noted that efforts were underway in the Belgian legislature to prevent creditors from obtaining injunctions interfering with distributions by Euroclear, or by any other banking institution. (Charles D. Schmerler, "Defaulted Sovereign Debt, Litigate It! Creditors no longer hesitate to go to court, and the debate now centers on enforcement. Developments in Litigation; Class Actions; Pari Passu Clauses; Reforms Are Proposed; Conclusion," *New York Law Journal*, February 22, 2005.) Furthermore, legislation was introduced at the EU level that would avert further court orders preventing Euroclear from receiving and channeling payments on behalf of

The perspective from the financial community was mixed. On the one hand, the *Financial Times* wrote: "It also irked a number of Wall Street banks, which felt that Elliott violated the principle of restructuring. This holds that if each creditor forgives some debt, the ailing borrower will ultimately be better able to repay them all. For this, they characterized Elliott as a 'free rider' who has profited from their generosity."[79] The IMF's Anne Krueger also denounced Elliott directly:

> But the more recent success of an aggressive legal strategy employed against Peru by a vulture company called Elliott Associates underlines the power that holdout creditors retain. The threat of disruption remains likely to deter countries from seeking a necessary restructuring for longer than is desirable either for the country itself or for the international community. . . . It is not clear if Elliott's strategy would survive legal challenge in future cases. But this case—and the possibility that rogue creditors will open other legal avenues—shines a spotlight on what is a missing element in the international community's current approach to the roles of the public and private sectors in debt restructuring.[80]

More generally, it was also argued that supporting creditor rights as in the case of Elliott in Peru was undesirable. For example, Harvard Economist Kenneth Rogoff noted:

> There is also a case for having rich countries make it more difficult, not less, to enforce sovereign debt contracts in rich-country courts. . . . Though this would almost certainly reduce debt flows to many countries in the short run, it would lead to a strengthening of the international financial system in the long run, reducing reliance on debt and helping support the evolution of greater flows in equity and direct foreign investment.[81]

Other critics of the case focused on humanitarian issues. Liana Cisneros, head of the Latin American Campaign of Jubilee 2000—an activist organization that sought to convince leaders of G-7 countries to forgive the debt of the world's poorest countries—argued: "These people are trading in human misery. Elliott Associates, L.P. are picking over the bones of the Peruvian economy like a pack of vultures. It may be just business to them, but to the Peruvians it represents schoolbooks, medicine, and clean water. The U.S. Treasury must investigate this case as a matter of urgency and take immediate steps to stop these scandalous practices." A press release from Jubilee 2000 explained that the organization "condemns these practices and is calling for tough controls to ensure that when a country faces economic bankruptcy private investors cannot see their own payments met at the expense of other creditors or of the government itself."[82]

While the U.S. government refrained from involvement in this specific debate, the U.K. government was more outspoken. U.K. Chancellor of the Exchequer[h] Gordon Brown in a 2002 speech at the UN noted:

> We particularly condemn the perversity where Vulture Funds purchase debt at a reduced price and make a profit from suing the debtor country to recover the full amount owed—a morally outrageous outcome. . . . Whenever a country has to defend a legal case it has to divert considerable time, attention and resources away from focusing on poverty reduction, health and education and we must do everything we can to stop this shameful practice.[83]

On the other hand, many investors lauded "vulture funds" like Elliott for providing essential liquidity in difficult markets as well as for supporting creditor rights. For example, Hans Hume of

---

bondholders. (See International Monetary Fund, "Progress Report to the International Monetary and Financial Committee on Crisis Resolution," April 12, 2005, p. 26.)

[h] A role similar to the Treasury Secretary in the United States.

Van Eck Global, which managed a $160 million distressed debt fund, noted: "The reality is that countries have been very cavalier about their debt restructurings, and the banks have allowed them to do so." Along these lines, many investors questioned the government's willingness versus its capacity to pay down its debt.

Argentina's Restructuring

Bondholders repeatedly sought to negotiate and nearly always formed creditor committees, only to be stiff-armed by debtors, who did not want to have to negotiate. They preferred instead to make unilateral offers. There were no collective action problems, but, rather, a concerted refusal to deal on the part of the sovereign debtors.[84]

— Jay Newman, Elliott Associates

By late 2004, almost 140 lawsuits (including 15 class action suits, the first time such suits were used in the context of sovereign debt) had been filed both by distressed debt funds and retail investors against Argentina in courts in New York, Italy, and Germany. Many suits resulted in favorable judgments, including a $725 million judgment in favor of EM Ltd.—associated with Dart Capital, and a $172 million judgment in favor of NML Capital Ltd.—an offshore fund controlled by Elliott.[85] The concern that this "race to the courthouse" could block or seriously impair the exchange, however, did not materialize. Although two class action litigants did attempt to prevent the exchange offer, a New York court ruled against them in November 2004, allowing the offer to go ahead in January 2005 and reach completion in February.

EM and NML, who had bought Argentine bonds at a discount and sought to recover the full face value, came close to attaching assets. In March 2005, they managed to obtain a freeze on $7 billion in existing defaulted Argentine bonds that had been tendered to the Bank of New York in January and February as part of the exchange.[86] Their lawyers argued that during the instant in which the old bonds were exchanged for the new ones, they would be the property of Argentina, not other bondholders, and therefore open for attachment. The appeals court ultimately ruled against EM and NML and lifted the freeze in late May 2005, but supported the decision of the lower court, which it held "acted within its discretionary authority to vacate the remedies in order to avoid a substantial risk to the successful conclusion of the debt restructuring. That restructuring is obviously of critical importance to the economic health of a nation."[87] This judgment was in line with previous U.S. support of Argentina. In January 2004, the U.S. government and the Federal Reserve Bank of New York filed *amicus curiae* briefs in support of the Argentine government's pursuit of a declaratory judgment from a New York court that would forbid creditors in pending cases from adopting a broad interpretation—as in the case of Elliott in Peru—of the *pari passu* clause to enforce their judgments.[88] Jay Newman of Elliott Associates expressed consternation over the fact that

> Some U.S. courts appear to believe that their job is to defer to foreign sovereigns, even when it means ignoring the plain language of contracts entered into under New York law. The compact between borrowers and lenders is that debt contracts are enforceable. If a sovereign is held to a different standard of enforceability, it vitiates the contract and erodes both the rule of law and confidence in the U.S. judicial system. In the long run, what is more important to the U.S. economy: enforcing contracts in accordance with their terms or permitting a small, self-interested group of defaulting regimes to redefine our system of contract and law?[89]

Although EM and NML were unsuccessful in initial efforts to attach assets, the firms ended up delaying settlement of the exchange—which had been planned for April 1—until early June. In response to the U.S. court's support of Argentina, Harvard Law School Professor Hal Scott noted:

> Developed country governments persist in weakening and not strengthening creditor rights. By intervening in support of Argentina, the United States is endorsing the view that an expansion of creditor rights would impede progress between creditors and Argentina. This is a dangerous view that is also prevalent in Europe—for example with the 2005 amendment of European law explicitly providing that no funds to be credited to a Euroclear account can be attached. Such signals from the United States and Europe that creditors should not interfere with restructuring indicate that the international system is moving in the wrong direction. Given that there is no clear bankruptcy procedure for sovereign defaults, foreign policy ought to be heading in the other direction.[90]

Critics of Elliott gloated about the firm's failure in this particular attachment effort. For example, *LatinFinance* magazine wrote: "The ruling apparently . . . leaves Dart, Elliott, and other vultures holding worthless bonds. They risked losing everything by refusing to participate in the February debt exchange. . . . The vultures took a risk and lost. They should pay the price." Elliott responded with a reply editorial:

> The statement that vultures took a risk, lost and should pay the price is breathtaking. What "price" should creditors pay when a debtor decides—either opportunistically or for reasons of political expediency—that it will not honor contractual obligations? . . .
>
> If debt could not be freely traded in a secondary market by firms such as ours, economic growth would be far lower because lenders, knowing they were locked into the credit, would be far more risk-averse about lending money. The ability to sell their loans in a liquid and legally mature market enables lenders to reduce their exposures to particular types of credits, and is an essential driver of lending to less-than-triple-A borrowers. However, nobody would purchase debt without the assurance that the debt could be enforced in accordance with its original terms. Thus, far from being "vultures," secondary-market purchasers of debt provide essential support to the corporations and sovereigns that need to borrow. . . .
>
> We believe that capital goes where it is welcome. Sometimes capital has a short memory, but countries ignore the rule of law and contract at their peril. Countries where laws and contracts are consistent, predictable and fair attract capital and entrepreneurs. Countries that use power arbitrarily will never attract lending and investment on a grand scale. These principles transcend the easy and seductive benefits of not paying one's debts, or railing against creditors, instead of pursuing the people who actually lost, mismanaged, stole, or wasted the borrowed money in the first place.[91]

In early 2006, EM and NML were back in court again, claiming that $105 million in reserves held by the Argentine Central Bank in New York should be used to pay down their claims. Although a New York court ruled in favor of Argentina, appeals were still ongoing in January 2006.

The results of litigation in Argentina were being closely watched. It remained to be seen whether Elliott would succeed in ultimately getting a full repayment or favorable settlement in Argentina as it had in Panama and Peru. Some observers feared that Elliott's success in Peru would encourage other investors to use litigation or the threat of litigation to seek better restructuring terms and worried that this would threaten globally negotiated debt deals. Other observers believed that the situation in Argentina showed that creditors had too little power. Professor Scott, for example, noted: "Although holdouts have many legal rights, in the end they face huge obstacles in collecting. As such, their legal rights ultimately make little difference. Despite this, investors continue to buy foreign bonds, which is a puzzle. Creditors seem to disregard the outcomes of previous histories of default in evaluating the future. Can this go on forever?"[92]

Exhibit 1 Argentina's 2005 Bond Exchange (January–February); Selected Instruments[1]

Name	Amount Outstanding (US$ mm)	PV[2] (US$)	New Value[3] (US$)	Haircut	Name	Amount Outstanding (US$ mm)	PV[2] (US$)	New Value[3] (US$)	Haircut
Bonte 02	1,513.4	108.1	37.9	64.9%	Hidro	18.2	96.3	34.1	64.6%
Bonte 03	732.9	120.5	38.0	68.5%	Bonex 92	150.0	13.3	4.7	64.3%
Bonte 03F	143.1	114.0	38.5	66.2%	Radar 1	349.5	112.3	38.6	65.6%
Bonte 04	508.7	129.8	37.9	70.8%	Radar 2	351.7	115.9	38.0	67.2%
Bonte 05	759.5	142.0	38.1	73.2%	Radar 3	361.9	117.5	38.5	67.2%
Bonte 06	225.2	144.9	38.1	73.7%	Radar 4	232.0	115.5	38.6	66.6%
Bonte 27	3.4	150.0	38.6	74.3%	Celtic 2	279.1	112.9	38.6	65.8%
FRAN	383.5	311.4	39.5	87.3%	Span 02	130.1	117.7	38.0	67.7%
FRN 04	225.9	120.0	38.3	68.1%	Letras T90	448.5	103.8	37.5	63.9%
Global 03	1,794.4	118.8	37.7	68.3%	Letras T10a	119.7	103.9	37.5	63.9%
Global 05	821.6	139.1	37.8	72.8%	Letras T10b	116.8	103.8	37.5	63.9%
Global 06	1,185.4	143.8	38.4	73.3%	Letras T10c	25.0	103.9	37.5	63.9%
Global 08	5,024.7	147.8	37.7	74.5%	Letras T10d	30.8	103.8	37.5	63.9%
Global 09	1,197.0	155.9	38.5	75.3%	RML	561.8	108.4	38.3	64.7%
Global 10	775.0	156.7	38.9	75.2%	Pagare III	4.0	107.6	38.6	64.1%
Global 12	465.3	174.5	39.3	77.5%	Pagare IV	11.3	110.3	38.7	64.9%
Global 15	718.2	166.7	37.7	77.4%	Pagare V	1.4	112.4	38.1	66.1%
Global 17	1,903.7	169.3	39.3	76.8%	Pagare VI	20.7	126.8	37.8	70.2%
Global 18	104.6	216.8	39.9	81.6%	Pagare A	197.8	111.9	37.9	66.1%
Global 19	146.8	178.8	39.2	78.1%	Pagare B	130.0	107.6	38.0	64.7%
Global 20	121.7	178.0	39.3	77.9%	Pagare C	75.0	106.1	38.1	64.1%
Global 27	809.5	147.4	38.6	73.8%	Pagare 200x	15.0	144.7	38.9	73.1%
Global 29	125.0	138.0	38.6	72.0%	Global F	181.6	100.5	27.8	72.3%
Global 30	166.0	154.0	39.3	74.5%	FRB	1,637.2	59.5	21.2	64.4%
Global 31	13.2	178.7	39.3	78.0%	Discount	800.5	99.6	62.0	37.8%
Global31M	8,595.2	214.5	39.9	81.4%	RA $02	20.3	40.8	13.7	66.4%
PRE 4	259.9	26.4	6.4	75.9%	RA $07	5.8	48.1	13.8	71.4%
PRE 6	73.5	107.4	41.7	61.2%	RA $08	248.6	44.3	13.5	69.5%
PRO2	332.6	73.3	25.2	65.6%	PRE 3	9.9	9.1	2.1	76.9%
PRO4	452.3	126.9	46.7	63.2%	PRO1	39.2	20.7	9.2	55.5%
PRO6	527.6	91.5	31.7	65.4%	PRO3	1.0	33.6	14.1	58.0%
PRO8	14.7	101.2	41.7	58.8%	PRO5	96.9	32.8	11.1	66.1%
PRO10	51.5	103.6	37.7	63.6%	PRO9	30.3	36.7	13.2	63.9%
Total weighted average haircut									**72.9%**

Source: Compiled from Sturzenegger and Zettelmeyer 2005.

[1] Excludes a number of U.S. and Argentina issues.

[2] Represents present value per bond, including past-due interest and principal.

[3] This is actually a weighted average of five different options: 35-year bond in US$ with step-up coupon and no face value reduction; 35-year bond in AR$ with step-up coupon and no face-value reduction; 30-year bond in US$ with step-up coupon and face-value reduction of 66.3%; 30-year bond in AR$ with step-up coupon and face-value reduction of 66.3%; 42-year capitalizing bond in AR$ with face-value reduction of 30.1%.

Exhibit 2 Foreign Currency Sovereign Debt in Default of Selected Countries, 1824–2004[1]

	1824–1834	1867–1882	1890–1900	1911–1921	1931–1940	1976–1989	1998–2004
Europe							
Austria		1868		1914	1932,38,40		
Greece	1824		1893		1932		
Germany					1932, 39		
Hungary					1931, 41		
Italy					1940		
Poland					1936, 40	1981	
Portugal	1834, 50		1892				
Russia	1839			1917		1991	1998
Spain	1820, 31, 51	1867, 82					
Turkey		1876		1915	1931, 40	1978	
Ukraine							1998, 2000
Latin America and Caribbean							
Argentina	1830		1890	1915[1]	1930s[1]	1982	2001
Bolivia		1874			1931	1980, 86, 89	
Brazil	1826		1898, 1902	1914	1931, 37	1983	
Chile	1826	1880			1931	1983	
Colombia	1826, 50	73, 79, 80	1900		1932, 35		
Costa Rica	1827	1874	1895		1937	1983	
Ecuador	1826, 32	1868	1894	1906,09,11,14	1929, 31	1982	1999
Guatemala	1828	1876	1894, 99		1933	1989	
Mexico	1827,33,44,54	1867		1914	1928	1982	
Nicaragua	1828		1894	1911, 15	1932	1979	
Panama					1932	1983, 87	
Paraguay	1827	1874	1892	1920	1932	1986	2003
Peru	1826	1876			1931	1976, 78,80,84	
Uruguay		1876	1891	1915	1933	1983	2003
Venezuela	1826, 48, 60	1864, 78	1892.1898			1982	
Africa							
Angola (and Cameroon)						1985	
Congo (and Niger and Zambia)						1983	
Cote d' Ivoire						1983	2000
Egypt		1876					
Gabon						1986	1999, 2002
Gambia						1986	
Morocco			1903			1983, 86	
Mozambique						1980, 83	
Nigeria						1982, 86, 92	2002
Sierra Leone						1983, 86	
South Africa						1985, 89, 93	
Sudan						1979	
Uganda						1980	
Asia and Middle East							
Indonesia							1998,2000, 02
China				1921	1939		
Philippines						1983	
Pakistan							1998, 99
Vietnam						1985	

Source: Compiled and adapted from David T. Beers and John Chambers, "Sovereign Defaults Set to Fall Again in 2005," Standard & Poor's RatingsDirect, September 28, 2004; and Sturzenegger and Zettelmeyer 2005, Table 1.1.

[1]Refers to federal or central government obligations, except Argentina in 1915 and 1930s. Some dates fall outside of debt clusters identified, but are included anyway.

Exhibit 3 Rate of Sovereign Defaults on Foreign Currency Bonds and Loans (1975–2002)

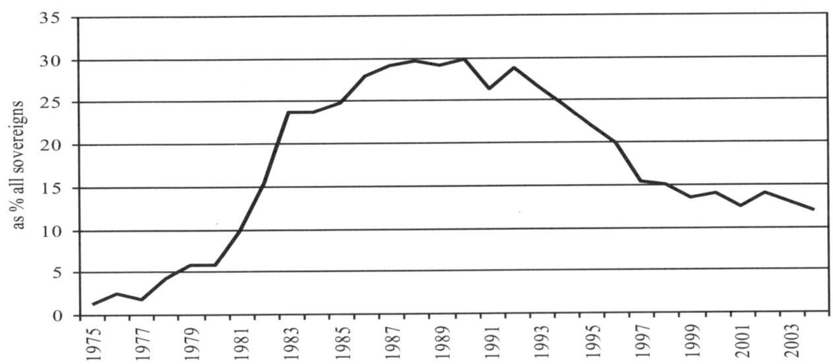

Source: Compiled from "Sovereign Defaults Set to Fall Again in 2005," Standard & Poor's RatingsDirect, September 28, 2004.

Exhibit 4 Amount of Foreign Currency Sovereign Bonds and Loans in Default (1980–2002)

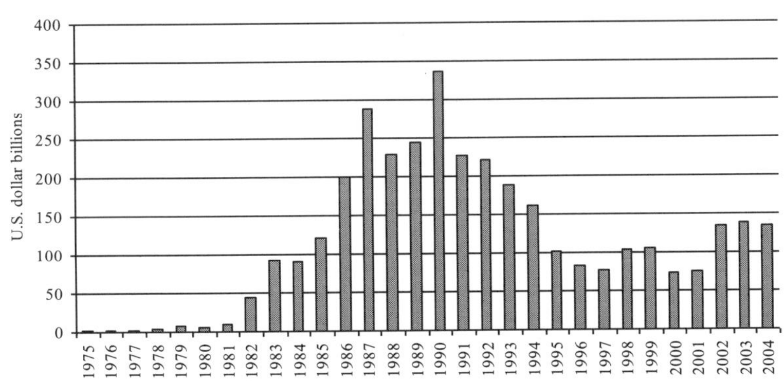

Source: Compiled from "Sovereign Defaults Set to Fall Again in 2005," Standard & Poor's RatingsDirect, September 28, 2004.

Exhibit 5 Selected Cases of Sovereign Litigation

Debtor	n/y[1]	Face Value of Claim	Litigation	Outcome
Yemen	n	$8.2 million	1999; attached central bank assets in Germany	Settled at 1/3 face value (July 2001)
Uganda	y	$5.5 million	Sued Bank of Uganda in U.K.	Court orders payment of $20.6 mm
Uganda	y	$1.3 million	Sued government and Bank of Uganda	Court orders payment of $2.7 mm
Uganda	y	$10.5 million	Ugandan court rules in favor of banks	
Ethiopia	y	$100 million	Yugo did not participate in the IDA buyback; wants full payment	Ethiopia has approached the International Chamber of Commerce for arbitration
Guyana	y	$6 million	Commenced mid-July 2001	In arbitration with ICSID
Nicaragua	n	$87 million	1999; LNC awarded judgment in NY. Could not attach assets. Won judgment in U.K.	LNC, van Eck, and GP Hemisphere trying to attach assets in Switzerland where Nicaragua keeps reserves.
Nicaragua	n	$50 million		
Nicaragua	n	$13 million		
Cameroon	n	$8 million	1997; Favorable judgment in U.K. Attaches Embassy assets	Govt appealed unsuccessfully
Honduras	y	$1.5 million ($17 million with interest from 1975)	First initiated in 1989	No (IDA buyback proposal refused)
Cameroon	n	Ecu 3.8 million	1998; Favorable judgment in U.K.	Attached 150,000 sterling in U.K.; Cameroon attempts retrial in Paris
Congo	n	$27 million, with accrued interest and legal fees	Won in U.K.; attachment order in U.K./Europe. Recognition of U.K. judgment and enforcement in California.	U.S. judge has ordered injunction against paying any creditor prior to Red Mountain. Settled in June 2002 for $8.2 million.
Ivory Coast	n	$8-10 million	Default in 1981; settled in 1994	Settled
Congo	y		Sought and won injunction in France to intercept wire transfers	Money is transferred by French Development bank via wire
Congo	n	$6–$7 million	Default in 1981; settled in 1994	Settled
Zambia	n	$40–$45 million	Won attachment with Bank of England on Zambian currency notes (from the printing press)	Settled in full for $100 million (with interest arrears)
Poland	n	Swiss Francs 5 million	1995	Settled
Ecuador	n	$6 million	1995	Paid in full
Peru	n	$64 million with interest & legal fees	Initiated 1996	$58 million settlement
Panama	n	$48 million	Initiated 1996	$71 million settlement, with interest arrears
Brazil	n	$1.4 bn princ. + $80 mn int.	1994; no attachment or accelerated payment	Received past-due interest, will get payment in full on original schedule
Turkmenistan	n	$3.8 million	Sued	Paid in full

Source: Compiled from Manmohan Singh, "Recovery Rates from Distressed Debt," IMF Working Paper 03161, August 2003; and Sturzenegger and Zettelmeyer 2006.

[1] y indicates that claim holder is original holder; n indicates that claim holder bought debt in secondary market.

Exhibit 6 Timeline of Elliott in Peru

October 1995	Peru government announces Brady deal (after Bank Advisory Committee agrees to restructure Peru's defaulted commercial bank loans).
January 1996	Pravin Banker Associates gets favorable judgment—ultimately, Pravin only collects something close to Brady terms.
January-March 1996	2 weeks after Pravin decision, Elliott begins acquisition of $20.7 million (face value) of commercial bank loans that were intended to be part of the Brady deal for $11.4 million.
March/April 1996	Immediately after completing its acquisition, and while Peru was still negotiating with the BAC on the terms of the Brady deal, Elliott starts to demand full payment.
October 1996	Peru executes Brady Exchange Agreement. Elliott refrains from participation.
October 8, 1996	Elliott files suit against Peru and *Banco de la Nacion* (BN) and ex-parte motion for prejudgment attachment (of collateral for the Brady closing).
October 1996	Court denies motion for attachment, plus a summary judgment motion filed later. Court says it does not want to jeopardize Peru's ability to close the Brady deal.
1997	Elliott, through wholly owned affiliate Manchester Securities Corp., is successful in amending a law to allow collection of interest on interest retroactively. The change goes unnoticed by Peru.
March 7, 1997	Brady Exchange Agreement closes (with collateral held in trust for Brady bond holders to be protected from Elliott). It is later revealed that Peru bought $1.7 billion face value in its own bonds at a deep discount during negotiations.
March 1998	Elliott trial held.
August 1998	New York Court finds for Peru based on "champerty" defense.
September 1998	Elliott files appeal, and, through Manchester Securities Corp., tries to introduce legislation overturning champerty law. Peru and other Latin American countries argue against the change, which ultimately does not go through.
December 1998	The Bond Market Association in New York writes brief on behalf of Elliott.
October 20, 1999	U.S. Court of Appeals agrees with Elliott and sends case back to trial court to calculate damages. Peru tries to get a rehearing, but fails.
November 2, 1999	Trial court grants Elliot attachment and restraining order on commercial property of Peru and BN located in NY (but there was almost no property held by Peru and BN in NY). Elliott requests that the order also apply to foreign affiliates of NY banks. Motion fails.
January 18, 2000	Court rejects Elliott's petition to apply restraining order to foreign branches of New York banks served by the orders.
June 22, 2000	NY Court judges in favor of Elliott and enters judgment for Elliott in the amount of $55.7 million (principal plus past-due interest) plus recovery of post-judgment interest; also authorizes execution of decision against any property of Peru and BN used for commercial activity in U.S.
September 2000	Elliott goes after interest payment to Brady bondholders as attachable assets. Gets restraining orders against the New York Fiscal Agent for the Peruvian's Brady Bonds

	Chase Manhattan Bank, European clearinghouse Euroclear, U.S. cash custodian Depository Trust Company, and Euroclear U.S. operator Morgan Trust Guaranty Trust Company of New York. Chase is ordered to retain any money received from Peru to be used for the interest payment of Brady bondholders. Peru has a hard time avoiding NY to make payments to bondholders. Elliott attempts to close payments through other countries as well, with attachment motions on Brady interest payments in England, Belgium, and Luxembourg; international banks and clearinghouses were reluctant to cooperate with Peru because of fears of new lawsuits by Elliott. Peru explored paying through BIS, which is immune from lawsuits and attachments, but this did not work out, for unknown reasons.
September 7, 2000	First Peru Brady coupon is due—need to transfer $80 million to Chase in U.S. on September 6, 2000. The bonds' credit rating is reduced. 30-day grace period is utilized; by October 7, 2000, non-payment on bonds would trigger $3.837 billion due. Political instability is intense and there are threats of a military coup after Peru's President Alberto Fujimori is caught in bribery scandal.
Sept 21, 22, 2000	NY Courts grant Elliot right to serve additional restraining orders on Chase, DTC, Morgan, and the Bank of New York if a deposit or transfer occurred from Peru. Peru, Morgan, and Chase challenge the orders.
September 22, 2000	Elliott files motion before Commercial Court of Brussels to prevent Euroclear from accepting or paying out cash from Peru intended to pay interest on Brady bonds. The Brussels court rules that Elliott cannot prevent Euroclear from paying the interest to other bondholders.
Sept 25, 2000	Elliott appeals Brussels decision.
Sept 26, 2000	Brussels' Appeals Court reverses decision because payment of interest to others violates principle of *pari passu,* as described by Elliott witness NYU Professor Andreas F. Lowenfeld before the Southern District Court of New York.
Sept 29, 2000	Peru settles with Elliott so it will be able to make payments on Brady bonds (did not wait for result of challenge of Peru and Morgan and Chase against the order). Peru paid $58.45 million to Elliott and had all restraining orders lifted.
October 5, 2000	Peru pays its Brady interest.

Source: Compiled from Sandoval 2002; Gulati and Klee 2001; IMF 2001.

Endnotes

1 See, for example, press release at http://www.clearstream.com/swing/dispatch/en/binary/swing_content_pool/downloads/pdf_attachments/Arg_Ann_100605.pdf, accessed March 2006.

2 Hal S. Scott, International Finance: Transactions, Policy, and Regulation (Foundation Press, 12th Edition, 2005.

3 *Euromoney*, "Argentina: Sovereign finally closes debt restructuring," July 1, 2005.

4 Federico Sturzenegger and Jeromin Zettelmeyer, "Haircuts: Estimating Investor Losses in Sovereign Debt Restructurings, 1998–2005," IMF Working Paper 05137, July 2005, available at http://www.imf.org/external/pubs/ft/wp/2005/wp05137.pdf, accessed April 2006.

5 Michael Casey, "Argentina Battles Bond Holdouts in New Asset Freeze Case," Dow Jones Newswires, January 26, 2006.

6 *Euromoney* 2005.

7 Federico Sturzenegger and Jeromin Zettelmeyer, *Defaults in the 90s: Learning to Deal with Crisis*, available at http://www.utdt.edu/~fsturzen/Defaults%20in%20the%2090sFinal.pdf, accessed July 6, 2006. Forthcoming December 2006 as *Debt Defaults and Lessons from a Decade of Crises* (MIT Press).

8 The case later introduces these critics, including IMF First Deputy Managing Director Anne Krueger, UK Chancellor of the Exchequer Gordon Brown, Jubilee 2000, and *LatinFinance* magazine.

9 Sophie Roell quoting Walter Molano in "Americas: Argentina—Legal Drama Unravels Debt Exchange Scheme—Argentina's Debt Exchange Plan Is in Limbo After a Court Froze Argentine Assets on US Soil, Including $7bn Worth of Bonds," *The Banker*, June 1, 2005.

10 See, for example, Michael Dooley, "A Retrospective on the Debt Crisis," in *Understanding Interdependence: The Economics of Open Economy*, edited by Peter Kenen (Princeton University Press, 1994).

11 For a more extensive discussion, see Lee C. Buchheit, "The collective representation clause," *International Financial Law Review* vol. 17, iss. 9, September 1998, pp. 9–11.

12 For a historical discussion of this topic, see Lee C. Buchheit, "The Role of the Official Sector in Sovereign Debt Workouts," *Chicago Journal of International Law*, vol. 6, no. 1, Summer 2005.

13 Jeremy Bulow and Kenneth Rogoff, "Cleaning Up Third World Debt Without Getting Taken to the Cleaners," *Journal of Economic Perspectives*, Winter 1990, pp. 31, 40–42. For further discussion on issues related to the FSIA, see Working Group of the American Bar Association, "Reforming the Foreign Sovereign Immunities Act," 40 *Columbia Journal Transnational Law* 489, 2002, pp. 517–518, available at http://www.lfip.org/lawe506/documents/reforming_the_foreign_sovereign.htm, accessed July 6, 2006.

14 Scott 2005, p. 738.

15 Carol S. Remond, "U.S. Court Rules in Favor of Creditor Suing Peru," *Dow Jones International News*, October 21, 1999.

16 Scott 2005, p. 739. This, however, was not the case in Germany, where under German law, reserves were open for attachment (see Sturzenegger and Zettelmeyer 2006 for more information).

17 See Article 55, Bank for International Settlements, *Basic Texts*, February 2006, available at www.bis.org, accessed July 6, 2006.

18 For more information on the Paris and London Clubs, consult *Crisis? What Crisis? Orderly Workouts for Sovereign Debtors* (London: Centre for Economic Policy Research, 1995), pp. 20–27; and Scott 2005.

19 Nouriel Roubini and Brad Setser, "Bailouts or Bail-ins? Responding to Financial Crises in Emerging Economies," Institute for International Economics, August 2004, p. 331 available at http://www.iie.com/publications/chapters_preview/378/8iie3713.pdf, accessed June 9, 2006.

20 Michael P. Dooley, "A Retrospective on the Debt Crisis," NBER Working Paper No. 4963, December 1994.

21 Philip J. Power, 1996, "Sovereign Debt: The Rise of the Secondary Market and Its Implications for Future Restructurings," *Fordham Law Review,* Vol. 64, No. 6, May 1996, pp. 2701–2772, as quoted in Sturzenegger and Zettelmeyer 2006, p. 43.

22 Dooley 1994.

23 World Debt Tables External Finance for Developing Countries, 1994–1995 Volume 1: Analysis and Summary Tables (Washington DC: World Bank, 1994), Chapter 2, pp. 25–27.

24 U.S. Department of the Treasury, Office of International Debt Policy.

25 See Scott 2005, pp. 703–706, for further details on the example provided.

26 See Serkan Arslanalp and Peter Blair Henry, "Is Debt Relief Efficient?" *The Journal of Finance* Vol. IX, No. 2, April 2005.

27 World Debt Tables External Finance for Developing Countries, 1994–1995 Volume 1: Analysis and Summary Tables (Washington DC: World Bank, 1994), chapter 2, pp. 25–27.

28 Huw Pill, "Mexico: The Tequila Crisis 1994–1995," HBS No. 702-093.

29 Huw Pill, "Bahtulism, Collapse, Resurrection? Financial Crisis in Asia: 1997–1998," HBS No. 798-089.

30 See Buchheit 1998 for more about this.

31 Sturzenegger and Zettelmeyer 2006, p. 11.

32 Buchheit 2005, and interview with casewriter July 24, 2007.

33 Nouriel Roubini and Brad Setser, "Improving the Sovereign Debt Restructuring Process: Problems in Restructuring, Proposed Solutions, and a Roadmap for Reform," Institute for International Economics paper, May 25, 2005, available at www.iie.com/publications/papers/roubini-setser0303.pdf, accessed July 3, 2006.

34 Anne O. Krueger, *A New Approach to Sovereign Debt Restructuring* (Washington, DC: IMF, 2002) available at http://www.imf.org/external/pubs/ft/exrp/sdrm/eng/sdrm.pdf, accessed April 2006.

35 Statement of Interest of the United States of America in Opposition to the First Amended Complaint, CIBC Bank and Trust Co., Ltd. v. Banco Central Do Brasil, S.A. and Citibank, N.A, 94 Civ. 4733 at 11 (S.D.N.Y. 1994), citing Allied, 757 F.2d at 519–520.

36 Arturo C. Porzecanski, "From Rogue Creditors to Rogue Debtors: Implications of Argentina's Default," available at http://www.american.edu/cas/econ/Brown%20Bag%20Papers/FromRogueCreditorsToRogueDebtors. pdf, accessed June 9, 2006.

37 Sturzenegger and Zettelmeyer 2006, p. 43.

38 Dart was the fourth-largest creditor in the debt.

39 Lee C. Buchheit and G. Mitu Gulati, "Sovereign Bonds and the Collective Will," *Emory Law Journal* 51, fall 2002, pp. 1340–1341 (except amount of $1.6 billion, which comes from Sturzenegger and Zettelmeyer 2006).

40 Buchheit and Gulati 2002.

41 The legal title of Dart's position was transferred to CIBC Bank and Trust Co. (Cayman) Ltd. before the lawsuit. Regarding this case, Sturzenegger and Zettelmeyer 2006 wrote: "as in the *Allied Bank* case, the U.S.

government filed a brief, but with the opposite thrust, urging the court to reject the Darts' claim for acceleration of principal on the grounds that holdouts that had purchased debt in the secondary market should not be allowed to take a free ride on debt workouts agreed by a majority of creditors." Sturzenegger and Zettelmeyer 2006 quoted Power 1996: "The United States observed that its concern in CIBC was a 'mirror image' of its concern in *Allied* ten years earlier. In *Allied*, the United States had been concerned that a judgment for Costa Rica would encourage sovereign debtors to use the courts to extract better terms from creditors than they could obtain through negotiation. In CIBC, conversely, the United States was concerned that a judgment in favor of the Darts would encourage creditors to use the courts to gain unfair concessions from sovereign debtors." Other legal commentators disagreed with this interpretation, noting that the brief ended on a mild note, simply stating that a U.S. court should apply New York law to a New York law-governed agreement.

42 Securitized through the sale by a Cayman trust of Trust Certificates.

43 Sturzenegger and Zettelmeyer 2006, p. 43.

44 Sturzenegger and Zettelmeyer 2006.

45 Power 1996, as quoted in Sturzenegger and Zettelmeyer 2006, p. 48.

46 Carol S. Remond "Despite Ruling Reversal, Peru Stands Firm to Creditor," Dow Jones, November 1, 1999.

47 Represents combined funds of Elliott Associates, L.P. and its sister fund Elliott International, L.P. according to Toronto Stock Exchange Press Release, "Elliott Associates, L.P. and its Sister Fund, Elliott International, L.P., File Schedule 13D Disclosing Enterasys Ownership" August 15, 2005, available at: http://tsedb.theglobeandmail.com/servlet/WireFeedRedirect?cf=GlobeInvestor/tsx/config&date=20050815&archive=prnews&slug=2005_08_15_13_3336_1425087, accessed April 2006.

48 Felix Salmon, "Elliott Associate's aggression captures low-risk returns," *Euromoney*, February 1, 2004. For background on the company, see also Phil Davis, "Elliott's activist chief has no time for cheats but denounces aggressive tactics," *Financial Times*, April 10, 2006.

49 *Euromoney* 2004.

50 *Euromoney* 2004.

51 Interview with casewriter, June 27, 2006.

52 *Euromoney* 2004.

53 Stephen Taub, "Hedge Fund Bankruptcy Role Seen Probed," CFO.com, November 30, 2005, available at: http://www.cfo.com/article.cfm/5244187/c_5244601?f=archives&origin=archive, accessed April 2006.

54 *Euromoney* 2004.

55 For more on takeover laws within Europe, see Huw Pill, "The EU'S 13th Directive on Takeover Bids: Unlucky for Some?" HBS No. 703-014.

56 *International Financial Law Review*, "Shareholders to challenge Wella takeover as unconstitutional," August 2003, available at http://www.iflr.com/includes/magazine/PRINT.asp?SID=511943&ISS=12022&PUBID=33, accessed April 2006.

57 Data on six attempts is from Paul Hoskins and Nicola Leske, "RPT-Wella rebels undeterred as defeat by P&G looms," Reuters, February 3, 2004, available at http://www.forbes.com/work/newswire/2004/02/03/rtr1238923.html, accessed April 2006. Raised offer price (12%) data is from Arindam Nag, "The Skeptic: Adecco's DIS Bid Exposes German Loopholes," Dow Jones International News, March 20, 2006.

58 *Euromoney* 2004.

59 Paul Singer and Jay Newman, "Myths and Realities," *LatinFinance* editorial, September 2005.

[60] Singer and Newman 2005.

[61] Mark Cymrot, "Why lenders should back sovereign bankruptcy rules," *International Financial Law Review*, October 1, 2002.

[62] *Euromoney* 2004.

[63] Joshua Chaffin, "Craft of investing in distressed debt comes under scrutiny," *Financial Times*, October 25, 2000

[64] *International Financial Law Review* 2002.

[65] Carol S. Remond, "Deadbeat Countries May Soon Face More Lawsuits," Dow Jones International News, May 16, 2000; applies to section 5-527 of the New York State's General Obligation Law.

[66] As quoted in Eduardo Luis Lopez Sandoval, "Sovereign Debt Restructuring: Should We Be Worried About Elliott?" Harvard Law School Program on International Financial Systems, May 2002, p. 10, available at http://www.law.harvard.edu/programs/pifs/pdfs/eduardo_sandoval.pdf, accessed April 2006.

[67] Joshua Chaffin, "Craft of investing in distressed debt comes under scrutiny," *Financial Times*, October 25, 2000.

[68] Carol S. Remond, "U.S. Court Rules in Favor of Creditor Suing Peru," Dow Jones International News, October 21, 1999.

[69] Carol S. Remond, "Despite Outcry, U.S. Resists Being Drawn into Debt Fight," Dow Jones International News, August 5, 1999.

[70] Amicus brief is available at http://www.bondmarkets.com/story.asp?id=1242, accessed April 2006.

[71] Remond, "Deadbeat Countries May Soon Face More Lawsuits," 2000.

[72] Remond, "Despite Outcry, U.S. Resists Being Drawn into Debt Fight," 1999.

[73] Carol S. Remond, "Peru Settles Creditor Dispute with Elliott for $58 Million," Dow Jones Newswires, September 29, 2000.

[74] Remond, "Peru Settles Creditor Dispute With Elliott For $58 Million," 2000.

[75] Sandoval 2002, p. 18, footnote 40.

[76] Sandoval 2002, p. 19, footnote 44. See also Charles G. Berry, "'Pari Passu' Means What Now?" *New York Law Journal; Corporate Restructuring and Bankruptcy*, March 6, 2006; Charles D. Schmerler, "Defaulted Sovereign Debt? Litigate It! Creditors no longer hesitate to go to court, and the debate now centers on enforcement," *New York Law Journal*, February 22, 2005; Mitu Gulati and Kenneth N. Klee, "Sovereign piracy," *Business Lawyer*, February 2001; and International Monetary Fund, "Involving the Private Sector in the Resolution of Financial Crises Restructuring International Sovereign Bonds," January 2001.

[77] For a detailed background on the clause, see Lee C. Buchheit and Jeremiah S. Pam, "The *Pari Passu* Clause in Sovereign Debt Instruments," 53 *Emory Law Journal* 869, 2004. Buchheit and Pam were with the firm that acted as counsel to the governments of Peru and Argentina in their restructurings.

[78] Gulati and Klee 2001. See also Sandoval 2002 for an extensive discussion.

[79] Joshua Chaffin, "Craft of investing in distressed debt comes under scrutiny," *Financial Times*, October 25, 2000.

[80] Anne Krueger "International Financial Architecture for 2002: A New Approach to Sovereign Debt Restructuring." Address by Anne Krueger, First Deputy Managing Director, International Monetary Fund, given at the National Economists Club Annual Members' Dinner, American Enterprise Institute, Washington, DC, November 26, 2001, http://www.imf.org/external/np/speeches/2001/112601.htm, accessed April 2006.

81 See Kenneth S. Rogoff, "International Institutions for Reducing Global Financial Instability," *Journal of Economic Perspectives* 13, Fall 1999, pp. 21-42; and Carmen M. Reinhart and Kenneth S. Rogoff, "Serial Default and the 'Paradox' of Rich to Poor Capital Flows," *American Economic Review*, vol. 94, May 2, 2004, pp. 53–58.

82 Jubilee 2000 Coalition, "'Vulture fund' investors make millions out of third world debt crisis," available at http://www.jubileeresearch.org/jubilee2000/news/vulture141000.html, accessed April 2006.

83 HM Treasury, "Financing a World Fit for Children," speech given by the Chancellor of the Exchequer, Gordon Brown, at the United Nations General Assembly Special Session on children, New York, May 10, 2002, available at http://www.hm-treasury.gov.uk/newsroom_and_speeches/press/2002/press_46_ 02.cfm, accessed April 2006.

84 Interview with casewriter, June 27, 2006.

85 Interview with casewriter, June 27, 2006; and *El Cronista Comercial*, "Economia: Blackman reveló que Elliott es acreedor del país," February 15, 2005.

86 Casey, "Argentina Battles Bond Holdouts in New Asset Freeze Case," 2006.

87 International Monetary Fund, "IMF Progress Report on Crisis Resolution," September 21, 2005, p. 5, available at http://www.imf.org/external/np/pp/eng/2005/092105.pdf, accessed July 6, 2006.

88 For more details, including citations for briefs, see Arturo C. Porzecanski, "From Rogue Creditors to Rogue Debtors: Implications of Argentina's Default," available at http://www.american.edu/cas/econ/Brown%20Bag%20Papers/FromRogueCreditorsToRogueDebtors.pdf, accessed June 9, 2006; and Nouriel Roubini and Brad Setser, "Bailouts or Bail-ins? Responding to Financial Crises in Emerging Economies," Institute for International Economics, August 2004, available at http://www.iie.com/publications/chapters_preview/378/8iie3713.pdf, accessed June 9, 2006.

89 Interview with casewriter, June 27, 2006.

90 Interview with casewriter, May 26, 2006. Also addressed in Hal S. Scott, *International Finance: Transactions, Policy, and Regulation* (Foundation Press, 12th Edition), 2005.

91 Singer and Newman, *LatinFinance*, 2005.

92 Interview with casewriter, May 26, 2006.

HARVARD | BUSINESS | SCHOOL

9-707-018

REV: MAY 23, 2007

LAURA ALFARO

International Capital Markets and Sovereign Debt: Crisis Avoidance and Resolution

Successive economic crises of the 1990s and early 2000s—including Mexico in 1994, Asia in 1997, Brazil in 1999, and Argentina in 2001[1]—intensified focus on reform of the "international financial architecture." Because many of these crises involved defaults on sovereign bonds, an important component of the reform discussion revolved around the composition of international capital flows and sovereign debt restructuring. Proposals surrounding the topic varied widely, with the official sector, private creditors, and sovereign debtors all focused on different issues.[2]

One set of proposals focused on avoiding crises altogether. These included specific unilateral measures, such as encouraging countries to protect themselves against excessive short-term capital flows or to avoid borrowing more capital than they could efficiently use.[3] Proposals also included various market-based solutions, such as adopting debt instruments that would require payments to investors only during periods of economic growth.

Another set of proposals focused on managing and resolving debt crises more effectively. In this regard, suggestions included clarifying the process for sovereign debt restructuring through setting up new international institutions and introducing changes in legal frameworks at the national and international level. Another suggestion included introducing changes to clauses in sovereign debt contracts in order to minimize problems of collective action in restructuring.[a]

Each proposal had its pros and cons and obstacles to adoption. Which among them would be politically palatable and capable of achieving the desired outcome—particularly with regard to encouraging countries to repay their debts when they could—remained to be seen. This note briefly describes some of the proposals and summarizes recent scholarship on their advantages and disadvantages.

Government versus Corporate Bankruptcy

The importance of the reoccurring phenomenon of countries defaulting on their obligations prompted an enormous volume of theoretical and empirical literature about sovereign debt.[4] Initially, most of this research focused on why countries chose to pay their debts at all (or why private creditors ever expected repayment). The problem originated from the fact that repayment incentives for sovereign debts were minimal, since little could be used as collateral and the ability of a

[a] For a detailed discussion of the case of distressed debt investor Elliott Associates in Peru's sovereign debt restructuring, see Laura Alfaro, "Creditor Activism in Sovereign Debt: 'Vulture' Tactics or Market Backbone," HBS No. 706-057, June 9, 2006.

Professor Laura Alfaro and Research Associate Ingrid Vogel prepared this case. This case was developed from published sources. HBS cases are developed solely as the basis for class discussion. Cases are not intended to serve as endorsements, sources of primary data, or illustrations of effective or ineffective management.

court to force a sovereign entity to comply was extremely limited, especially given the lack of a supranational legal authority capable of enforcing contracts across borders.[5]

Harvard economist and former Director of the IMF Research Department Kenneth Rogoff highlighted the issue by asking: "Why, exactly, are debtor countries willing to make repayments of any kind, partial or full? . . . Whereas the debate over why countries repay may seem rather philosophical, it is quite dangerous to think about grand plans to restructure the world financial system without having a concrete view on it."[6]

In a now-famous paper from 1981, economists Jonathan Eaton and Mark Gersovitz developed a model that aimed to answer this question. They described as a paradox the existence of a market for private loans to governments, since there was no explicit mechanism deterring a government from repudiating its external debts.[7] They described that countries chose to borrow from international markets in bad periods—for example, when export production was poor—and repay in good periods—such as times of ample production. Countries wishing to engage in international borrowing to smooth income in this way were encouraged to repay their debts in order to avoid retaliation by private creditors in the form of exclusion from future borrowing. In addition to identifying this reputational cost, academics identified other incentives and punishment mechanisms that encouraged countries to repay debt.[8] These included the ability of creditor countries to interfere in trade credits[9] and the risk of substantial temporary losses in economic output following financial crises.[10] Another mechanism often mentioned was potentially high legal costs in the context of collective action problems such as holdout creditors and rushes to the courthouse.[11]

IMF Deputy Managing Director Anne Krueger described the problem of collective action in debt restructuring:

> A sovereign borrower with an unsustainable debt burden and a diffuse group of creditors may find it very difficult to get them to agree collectively to a restructuring that reduces the net present value of its obligations to a manageable level. Even if the restructuring would be in the interests of creditors as a group, some may consider that their interests would best be served by trying to "free-ride" in the hope that ultimately they can secure repayment in line with their original contracts.[12]

In this context, many scholars and policymakers lamented that bankruptcy provisions designed for firms did not apply to sovereigns.[13] In contrast to sovereigns, businesses could protect themselves from "free-riding" creditors by filing under Chapter 11 of the U.S. Bankruptcy Code. Chapter 11 offered a clear timeline of 120 days in which the debtor had the exclusive right to propose a reorganization plan. Approval of the reorganization plan required that within each creditor class, a simple majority of all creditors and representation of at least two-thirds of the value of the debt in the class voted in favor of the plan. This implied that a plan could not be upset by just a few holdout creditors. If a plan were rejected, new plans could be proposed by the debtor or creditors. Chapter 11 also allowed suspension of interest payments and offered protection by forbidding debt collection actions. Another important element was making new financing available, with new debt senior to existing debt.

In some cases, municipalities unable to meet debt payments were offered similar protections under Chapter 9 of the U.S. Bankruptcy Code. As Secretary of the Treasury in 2000, Lawrence Summers noted that municipalities were able to borrow at much lower interest rates and had far fewer incidences of default than sovereign borrowers.[14] It was argued that elements from Chapter 9 could be borrowed in defining a process for sovereign debt restructuring to help arbitrate between the needs of creditors and debtors in restructuring negotiations. For example, Chapter 9 limited court interference with the political or government powers of the municipality and gave certain groups that might be affected by the reorganization a right to be heard, which was intended to better balance the interests of creditors against the welfare of citizens.[15]

Institutional Reform

Sovereign Bankruptcy Mechanism

Like a patient with toothache avoiding a trip to the dentist, a debtor country will all too often delay a necessary restructuring until the last possible moment, draining its reserves and increasing the eventual cost of restoring sustainability.[16]

—IMF Deputy Managing Director Anne Krueger, 2002

Between 2001 and 2003, IMF staff and management advocated adoption of a Sovereign Debt Restructuring Mechanism (SDRM) to define a clear and predictable process for sovereign debt restructuring. They believed the lack of coordination in the existing process raised the costs of restructuring to the debtor. As such, countries waited too long before engaging in a restructuring, thereby risking turning a temporary liquidity problem—such as inability to meet an interest payment due to a cyclical economic downturn—into a longer-term solvency problem. A solvency problem could turn into a full-blown economic crisis that could trigger further crises within a region or beyond. Furthermore, Krueger believed that the existing process exacerbated creditor coordination difficulties and exposed the sovereign to litigation from "vulture" creditors who opted out of a proposed settlement and sued for a higher payout. Such litigation was thought both to drive up the costs of restructuring and increase the risk of delay or even failure in coming to an agreement.[17]

In this context, Krueger believed that the sovereign debt restructuring process would benefit from borrowing some elements of domestic bankruptcy proceedings as defined under Chapter 11. Many provisions—particularly those most attractive to debtors—were included in the proposed SDRM. First, the SDRM had a *cramdown* feature that would allow a qualified majority of creditors to bind the minority in a restructuring agreement. Second, an *automatic stay* feature would shield the debtor from legal action by individual creditors after the suspension of payments and while negotiations were taking place. Third, a *debtor-in-possession* feature would facilitate the sovereign's ability to attract new financing from the private sector during the workout period and thus help stimulate economic growth[18] as well as reduce reliance on loans provided by the IMF.[19] A further provision focused on *creditor protection* by preventing the sovereign debtor from making payments to nonpriority creditors and from adopting poor economic policies.

The SDRM would involve the IMF establishing a separate independent judicial body—within the IMF but not subject to IMF review—that would oversee the restructuring process to ensure that SDRM provisions were applied appropriately. Krueger explained:

> Use of the mechanism would be for the debtor to request, not for the Fund to impose. If a debtor can reach agreement with creditors of its own accord, then it would be under no pressure to resort to the mechanism. Indeed, the existence of a predictable framework should in itself help catalyze agreement without the need for formal activation. This is what happens in well-designed domestic bankruptcy regimes. Most restructurings take place "in the shadow of the law" rather than in court.[20]

Ultimately, the SDRM failed to gain sufficient support for acceptance, which would have required amending the IMF Articles of Agreement. Critics were numerous, including the administration of U.S. President George W. Bush. They argued that the statutory modifications required at the international and national levels were too significant, and that it would be politically impossible to grant such comprehensive powers to a new international institution.[21]

In addition, the likely effectiveness of the SDRM was questioned. On the one hand, some observers believed that the SDRM's focus on collective action problems was insufficient to stimulate smoother debt workouts. For example, economists and investors argued that the creditor litigation problem had not posed a significant risk to successful debt restructurings, even after creditors became more diffuse and uncoordinated in the 1990s.[22]

On the other hand, private creditors tended to argue that making debt restructurings smoother would negatively affect a sovereign's incentives to repay its debts and could lead to higher premiums on sovereign debt investments or even the exclusion of some countries from the sovereign debt market altogether.[23] They believed that the current approach already put creditors at a disadvantage. Unlike a creditor of a bankrupt firm, private creditors were unable to impose policy conditionality, had no prospect of being able to change the sovereign's "management," and could not force a sovereign to present a restructuring proposal within a defined period of time.[24] In addition, even if a creditor successfully sued a sovereign for failing to meet its obligations, the creditor's ability to collect against such a judgment was limited, since most sovereign assets were located within the sovereign's territory and therefore inaccessible.[25]

In this context, many private creditors argued that improving sovereign debt markets required that creditor rights be strengthened.[26] For example, Harvard Law School Professor Hal Scott suggested allowing creditors to attach debtor assets that were currently protected, such as central bank foreign currency holdings at the Bank for International Settlements in Basel.

International Crisis Insurance Funds

Another proposal involved initiating an insurance fund that would bail out countries when they faced debt problems. Countries would finance the fund through premium payments and would have to prequalify for assistance in that transfers would be conditional on the country having adopted good macroeconomic policies before the crisis. The program would be different from the IMF's existing lender-of-last-resort function[27] in debt crises by facilitating transfers rather than just loans and by addressing problems of unsustainable debts rather than just liquidity shortages. The benefit of such a program was that, in theory, good macroeconomic policies could be defined that would ordinarily prevent a crisis, thus reducing the chances of a crisis. Furthermore, debtor moral hazard problems associated with IMF lending—which were argued to encourage countries to borrow more than they otherwise would or delay engaging in or agreeing to debt restructuring negotiations in hopes of a bailout[28]—would in theory be mitigated. Unlike in IMF practice, assistance would be dependent on good policies having been adopted before the crisis.

A similar program involved establishing an insurance fund to protect investors.[29] Again, borrowing countries would finance the fund through premium payments. The official sector would refuse to bail out uninsured debt, forcing investors to choose between lower returns on insured debt versus higher returns on uninsured debt. It would mitigate creditor moral hazard problems by making private investors less inclined to make bad loans or to stall agreeing to a sovereign debt restructuring in hopes of a bailout. Rogoff explained: "If private agents are engaged in risky activities that generate negative externalities—which include not only the costs of bailouts but the costs of greater vulnerability to financial crises—then, in an ideal theoretical world, the activities of such agents should be taxed."[30]

There were numerous criticisms of such proposals.[31] First, it was argued that official sector promises not to bail out countries would not be credible and that moral hazard problems would therefore remain unsolved. Not only would the official sector still need to focus on ensuring global financial stability, but it would also likely continue to be concerned about the welfare of countries requiring assistance. Second, it would be difficult to define actuarially fair insurance premia from participating countries. Not only might countries be reluctant to pay for insurance to cover unlikely events, but the diversity of circumstances surrounding past crises would complicate the process of determining how to price the insurance. Third, as in criticisms of the SDRM, it would be difficult from a political perspective to invest the insurer with the necessary regulatory power. Fourth, in the case of the debtor insurance fund, defining "good" macroeconomic policies would be challenging. Sound policies could differ both among countries and over time, since what was "good" in one area might depend on policies adopted in other areas, on the state of the economic cycle, and on various characteristics of the economy. Furthermore, determining whether countries had adhered to good policies might be impossible, such that in some cases deserving countries might be turned away or undeserving countries might be bailed out. Fifth, it could be difficult to limit the role of politics in deciding which countries got access.

Emerging Market Debt Stabilization Fund

Another proposal involved mitigating "sudden stops" in capital flows to emerging economies that led to debt crises more directly. For example, Chief Economist of the Inter-American Development Bank Guillermo Calvo recommended intervening to stabilize emerging market debt indices such as the JPMorgan Emerging Market Bond Indices EMBI+ or EMBI Global.[32] Calvo noted that IMF-led crisis lending "operates more like a fire department than like a central bank. Liquidity is sprayed where fire is found, not on the system as a whole in the manner of a central bank faced with a liquidity crisis."[33] In response, he suggested the creation of an emerging market fund that would buy emerging market debt if prices fell substantially, such as during the Mexican crisis of 1994 and the Russian crisis of 1998. The fund would intervene on a case-by-case basis without a mechanical intervention rule, depending on whether a downturn appeared to be driven by fundamental factors. Supporting the EMBI would reduce a key source of contagion and reduce the need for IMF crisis lending.

Calvo had responses to many of the possible criticisms of such an emerging market fund. First, he argued that the fund could outperform the market and that any possible losses the fund might face would theoretically wash out over the long term. Second, possible moral hazard problems that the largest individual countries comprising the EMBI+ might face would be prevented through requiring countries that benefit from the fund to follow good economic policies—particularly related to public debt—that would help ensure solvency.

Although Calvo noted that only 1% of the debt instruments of the United States, Japan, and Germany (the G-3) would capitalize the fund in the amount of one-third of EMBI+ debt, it was unclear how the fund would be financed and who would bear the risk associated with the fund's performance. Furthermore, some economists questioned how a fundamental spread increase could be differentiated from a global liquidity problem.[34]

Contract Modifications

Other proposals suggested modifications to bond clauses in sovereign debt contracts. The major focus was on introducing collective action clauses (CACs) that would facilitate restructuring through addressing difficulties of creditor coordination. After the failure of the SDRM, the IMF was a strong proponent of CACs. Undersecretary of Treasury for International Affairs John B. Taylor also supported CACs as a measure to clarify the sovereign debt restructuring process. He believed that the clarity they provided would reduce the likelihood of crises occurring and mitigate crises that did occur. In a 2002 speech, he noted:

> In our view, the most practical and broadly acceptable reform would be to have sovereign borrowers and their creditors put a package of new clauses into their debt contracts. The clauses would describe as precisely as possible what happens when a country decides it has to restructure its debt. In this way the contracts would create a more orderly and predictable workout process. Such clauses represent a decentralized, market-oriented approach to reform because both the contracts and the workout process described by the contracts are determined by the borrowers and lenders on their own terms.[35]

Majority Action Clauses

The most popular proposal was to introduce majority action clauses that would allow a supermajority of creditors to bind all creditors to changes in financial and other terms of sovereign bonds in a restructuring. This was intended to ensure that debt restructuring negotiations would not be blocked by a dissenting minority holding out for better terms.

Specifically, this would require making terms in U.S. contracts more similar to terms in English contracts. Although many terms of sovereign bonds issued under U.S. law—accounting for approximately 69% of the total of $154 billion sovereign bonds outstanding in 2002—could be amended with representation of bondholders holding 50% or 66⅔% of the value of the bonds, changes to contractual terms such as payment dates and amounts required unanimous consent of all creditors.[36] (See **Exhibits 1a** and **1b** for sample text.) This constraint had its roots in the Trust Indenture Act of 1939 restricting the use of majority action clauses in corporate issues, which aimed to prevent a majority of creditors from abusing a minority. In contrast, changes to all terms of debt issued under English law, including those related to payment, were permitted with the consent of bondholders holding 75% of the value of the bonds represented at a meeting with certain quorum requirements. In effect, requiring that bondholders be present at the meeting implied that a lower percentage was actually required to make changes. (See **Exhibit 2** for sample text.) Many English law bonds also had provisions making it difficult for individual bondholders to initiate litigation.

Various groups submitted proposals for new draft majority action clauses. The Group of Ten recommended following the English law standard of allowing changes to payment terms with agreement of bondholders representing 75% of the value of the bonds (although not requiring that bondholders be present at a meeting). (See **Exhibit 3** for sample text.) Private creditor groups pushed for a higher majority action threshold of 90%, which would provide them with more leverage to obtain better terms in a restructuring. They argued that a lower percentage would give sovereigns too much negotiating power, particularly since a large proportion of bondholders might be citizens of the country engaging in the restructuring and therefore subject to pressure from the government to abuse foreign creditors.[37]

Initially, countries resisted including majority action clauses in their sovereign bonds. Although debtor countries were largely in favor of the clauses to improve their leverage in the sovereign debt restructuring process, they worried that such changes would come at the price of higher costs of borrowing.[38] Lee Buchheit, a lawyer who had supported many governments in sovereign debt restructurings, explained: "Bond issuers and underwriters are in the business of selling bonds, not preparing for future restructurings. Majority action clauses are thus viewed in the same light as prenuptial agreements: extraordinarily useful at the end, but distinctly unromantic at the beginning."[39]

Other Collective Action Clauses

In addition to majority action clauses, other types of collective action clauses were also recommended. Taylor suggested introducing a clause that would delegate negotiation of restructuring with the debtor to a *creditor representative*. A process for specifying how the representative would be chosen and how it would function would be defined in the contract. As part of its powers, the representative would have the exclusive right, acting on behalf of a set percentage of bondholders, to initiate litigation.[40] Such a clause would pose a major obstacle to holdout creditors and could have the effect of imposing a standstill on litigation at the outset of negotiations.[41]

A further contract modification often recommended was to introduce *sharing clauses* into sovereign debt contracts. Sharing clauses were standard in syndicated commercial bank loans but were not common in publicly issued bonds.[42] They required that creditors share proceeds *pro rata* with other creditors in the event of payment following litigation. As such, sharing clauses sought to reduce litigation from individual creditors. Critics of sharing clauses questioned whether the clauses would deter litigation, given that there might be only a few residual holdouts. Furthermore, they noted that majority action clauses would solve the problem of holdout creditors disrupting the sovereign debt restructuring process, making sharing clauses unnecessary.[43]

Modification of *acceleration clauses*—defining in what circumstances creditors were entitled to demand full payment of interest and principal—was also recommended. Most sovereign bonds issued under either U.S. or English law required the vote of creditors representing 25% of the value of the debt to accelerate payments. The Group of Ten recommended that the 25% threshold be adopted in all debt contracts. The threat of acceleration was thought to serve a disciplining function on debtors by increasing the potential cost of default. In cases where the majority of creditors agreed to a restructuring and tendered their bonds in an exchange offer, achieving 25% of the value of the remaining old bonds would be relatively easy.[44]

Terms to address the problem of aggregation were also suggested. Economists Barry Eichengreen and Ashoka Mody explained the significance of the aggregation problem as follows:

> Collective action clauses, which are specific to the individual debt contract, might not suffice to deal with the broader problems of information sharing and creditor coordination that arise when the government in default has multiple debt obligations, as is typically the case. Collective action clauses provide for a bondholder assembly and qualified majority voting, debt instrument by debt instrument, on whether to accept a restructuring offer, but they do not specify a way of aggregating the preferences of creditors holding different issues. If the holders of some issues refuse the government's offer, they may have to be paid in full or bought out at par. The government will have fewer resources to share with other issue holders, who may then reject its restructuring offer. This may create a first-mover problem.[45]

By 2005, despite a number of criticisms of CACs, their use became widespread (see **Exhibit 4**). In a progress report, the IMF explained how it encouraged adoption: "Staff continues to maintain an active dialogue with private market participants and debt managers from a number of emerging market countries . . . and to encourage the use of CACs both in the context of the use of Fund resources and the Fund's surveillance activities."[46] Between September 2004 and September 2005, more than 90% of all sovereign bonds issued by value as U.S.-law-governed sovereign bonds had adopted CACs. For example, CACs were included in all of the U.S.-law-governed bonds issued under the 2005 Argentine debt exchange (but not in the Argentine-law government bonds).[47] The share of issues with CACs in the total value of the stock of outstanding sovereign bond issues from emerging market countries increased from 31% at the end of 2002 to 53% by mid-2005.

In most cases, CACs related to acceleration and majority action, including adopting a 75% threshold, were included. CACs that would block litigation by individual bondholders or enable aggregation of different sovereign bonds were included in only a few cases. (See **Exhibit 5** for a list of recommended contract provisions, as well as their adoption in 2004 and 2005.)

Financial Innovation

GDP-Linked Bonds

Distinct from the IMF's objective of protecting against self-fulfilling runs and liquidity problems, the objective of introducing bonds indexed to real variables was to protect against output shocks. Ideally, a real variable would be selected that influenced a country's ability to pay down its debts. For example, this could include oil prices for an oil exporter or GDP of trading partners for a highly export-dependent economy. Alternatively, factors affecting the economies of some countries might be too diffuse to capture in a single measure, in which case a broad economic variable such as domestic GDP might be appropriate.[48] In the case of GDP-linked bonds, bonds would promise to pay an interest coupon based on the issuing country's growth rate. As such, required interest payments would be higher when economic performance was stronger and lower when economic performance was weaker.

GDP-linked bonds were seen to have many advantages for both borrowers and investors. First, the bonds facilitated counter-cyclical fiscal policy by allowing governments to service more debt when they could afford to and service less debt in difficult times.[49] With traditional bonds, emerging market economies were often forced to undertake fiscal retrenchment during periods of slow growth in order to maintain access to international capital markets.[50] Second, by restricting the range of variation of the ratio of debt to GDP, GDP-linked bonds would reduce the likelihood of a crisis.[51] Third, investors would benefit in that the instruments could be used to offer equity-like exposure to a country[52] and to provide a diversification outlet for low-growth countries wanting to take a stake in high-growth countries.[53]

Despite the benefits of the instrument, adoption was not widespread. This was attributed to a number of factors, three of which were considered of primary importance.[54] First, critics worried about the moral hazard implications of GDP-linked bonds, noting that they could induce governments to be less careful about avoiding recessions. A related and more plausible problem was that governments might be motivated to misreport GDP data by underreporting growth. Other critics noted that even if governments did not misrepresent data, accurate growth data was difficult to capture. It was suggested that problems associated with economic data could be overcome through delegating growth measurement to an independent agency or subjecting the process to international audits.

A second major challenge involved establishing sufficient liquidity such that the instruments could be actively traded without investors requiring large premiums. It was recommended that international institutions create incentives for adoption through moral suasion or even through adopting GDP-linked debt in some of their own lending. Third, there were concerns related to the difficulty of pricing the bonds,[55] although it was noted that pricing problems applied in general to new complex financial products and, as was the case with other products, would be overcome as the instruments became more popular.

The possibility of a market being created for GDP-linked bonds of emerging economies was enhanced by the introduction of a GDP-linked security in Argentina's debt restructuring package.[56] Each new bond issued under the restructuring had a GDP-linked warrant attached that would be eligible to trade independently after November 29, 2005.[57] (See **Exhibit 6** for details on the instrument.) Some observers argued that some creditors may have been more inclined to participate in the exchange because of the offer of the securities.[58]

VIX-Based Hedge to Manage Reserve Holdings

To smooth against the impact of sudden reversals in capital flows, many emerging market countries chose to hold large international reserves. The pros and cons of this were debated,[59] with many economists concluding that the policy was expensive and exposed countries to risks associated with exchange rate and interest rate fluctuations of reserve currencies. Various strategies could be adopted to help overcome these downsides by providing reserves only when needed.[60]

For example, MIT economist Ricardo Caballero suggested a central bank reserve management strategy that incorporated assets correlated with sudden stops. Specifically, he evaluated conditioning reserve-building payouts on movements of the VIX volatility index. The VIX was a measure of market expectations of near-term volatility conveyed by option prices on the S&P 500, which was considered to provide a barometer of investor sentiment and market volatility.[61] Jumps in the VIX were highly correlated with sudden stops in emerging economies (see **Exhibit 7**). According to calculations based on data between January 1990 and December 2003, when the VIX spiked, an emerging market economy had a 41% chance of experiencing a sudden stop compared with an 11% chance when the VIX was stable.[62] Caballero concluded that by adopting a reserve strategy that involved a central bank buying options that would pay out in the case of a VIX spike, an average country could experience a 40% rise in its reserves on entering a sudden stop, compared with losing 13% of its reserves if there was no sudden stop.[63] Caballero noted:

> Institutional investors seldom immobilize large amounts of cash to insure against jumps in volatility and risk-aversion—except in the case of extremely frequent events, which sudden stops are not. The use of derivatives and the creation of the VIX are designed precisely to satisfy hedging needs. Why should central banks, which are the quintessential public risk management institutions, not adopt best practices for risk management?[64]

On the one hand, the VIX was considered a useful variable to which to tie payments. It was highly correlated with sudden stops, so it would provide reserves when they were needed. In addition, it would avoid problems of moral hazard by being exogenous to country actions. Furthermore, it would attract investors who did not usually invest in emerging markets, which would avoid the crowding out of demand for other emerging market assets.[65]

On the other hand, there were some weaknesses with the VIX-based hedging strategy. First, it was unclear how reliable the relationship between the VIX and sudden stops would remain. Second, the VIX captured problems specific to the United States, whereas an ideal index would weigh U.S. events that were likely to have worldwide systemic effects differently from those that were likely to have effects in the United States only. However, Caballero noted that if such hedging practices were adopted, better-suited indices would likely be developed to meet the needs of emerging economies.[66] Third, it could be considered imprudent for a central bank to engage in aggressive hedging strategies, since during periods of extraordinarily high market volatility, counterparties might be unable to deliver on their contracts.

Local Currency Bonds

Mismatches in the currency denomination of government assets and liabilities in countries with large foreign currency debt burdens implied that currency crises fed directly into debt crises through reducing debt service capacity. By issuing more local currency debt, countries would avoid problems of currency mismatches.

On the one hand, emerging market countries faced difficulties when attempting to borrow abroad in their own currencies.[67] Explanations for this so-called "original sin" problem included the lack of liquidity in local currency instruments as well as the fact that international investors preferred the protection offered by foreign currency instruments from emerging market inflation and exchange rate fluctuations. Furthermore, investors questioned the credibility of countries committing to policies to maintain stable currencies. The World Bank attempted to stimulate the market by issuing debt in emerging market currencies.[68]

On the other hand, countries could reduce currency mismatches through issuing local currency debt domestically. Even countries with histories of financial instability were able to do so after a sufficient period of currency stability and credible monetary and fiscal policy. For example, as part of the $35.2 billion in new bonds issued under its 2005 restructuring, Argentina issued $15.5 billion worth of peso-denominated bonds under Argentine law.

Unilateral Measures

There were also unilateral steps that countries could undertake to help protect themselves against debt crises.[69] Following the financial crises of the late 1990s, policy groups and academics argued that developing countries could reduce contagion and other problems arising from financial crises through better financial regulation and supervision, improving fiscal accounts, increasing debt maturities, and adopting floating exchange rate regimes.[70] They also recommended reducing debt levels, for example by encouraging foreign direct investment, which was thought to be more stable and bring more benefits. Increasing transparency of information that would support the formulation of sound economic policies and effective functioning of financial markets,[71] such as basing monetary policy on inflation targeting, was also considered important.[72] Other measures mentioned were controls on capital flows, such as those adopted in Malaysia in 1998 to manage outflows and those adopted in Chile in 1991 to manage inflows.[73]

Exhibit 1a U.S. Amendment Clauses (example 1)

The following bond clause comes from the Republic of Guatemala, 8½% Notes due 2007, U.S. $150,000,000. In most sovereign bonds issued under the law of a U.S. jurisdiction, amendments or modifications to the instrument are permitted with the consent of holders of 51% (or sometimes 66⅔%) of the bonds. However, the consent of each affected bondholder is required to defer a payment date, reduce any amount of principal or interest due under the bond, change the currency of payments or take certain other enumerated actions.

Modifications, Amendments and Waivers

With (i) the affirmative vote, in person or by proxy thereunto duly authorized in writing, of the holders of not less than 66% in aggregate principal amount of the Notes then Outstanding represented at a meeting duly called and held as specified above, or (ii) the written consent of the owners of 66% in aggregate principal amount of the Outstanding Notes, the Republic and the Fiscal Agent may, upon agreement between themselves, modify, amend or supplement the terms of the Notes or, insofar as affects the Notes, the Fiscal Agency Agreement, in any way, and such holders may make, take or give any request, demand, authorization, direction, notice, consent, waiver or other action provided by the Fiscal Agency Agreement or the Notes to be made, given or taken by holders of Notes: provided, however, that no such action may, without the consent or affirmative vote of the holder of each Note affected thereby: (A) change the due date for the payment of the principal of, or any installment of interest on, any Note, (B) reduce the principal amount of any Note, or the portion of such principal amount which is payable upon acceleration of the maturity of such Note, or the interest rate thereon, (C) change the currency in which any payment in respect of any Note is payable, (D) reduce the proportion of the principal amount of the Notes the vote or consent of the holders of which is necessary to modify, amend or supplement the Fiscal Agency Agreement or the terms and conditions of the Notes or to make, take or give any request, demand, authorization, direction, notice, consent, waiver or other action provided thereby to be made, taken or given, or (E) change the obligation of the Republic to pay Additional Amounts (as defined below). Any such modification, amendment or supplement shall be binding on the holders of Notes.

Exhibit 1b U.S. Amendment Clauses (example 2)

The following bond clause comes from Republic of Indonesia, 7¾% Bonds due 2006, U.S. $400,000,000. A minority of emerging market sovereign bonds issued under the law of a U.S. jurisdiction employ a more abbreviated amendment clause that requires the unanimous consent of affected creditors to change the terms of payment of the bonds.

Modification

The Republic may modify any of the terms or provisions contained in the Bonds in any way with the written consent of the holders of not less than 51% in principal amount of the Bonds at the time outstanding, provided that (i) if any such modification would change the terms or currency of payment of the principal amount of or interest on any Bond or the amounts thereof or affect the rights of holders of less than all the Bonds at the time outstanding, the consent of the holders of all the Bonds affected thereby is required and (ii) if any such modification would reduce the aforesaid percentage needed for authorization of such modification, the consent of the holders of all outstanding Bonds is required.

Source: Excerpts from Republic of Guatemala and Republic of Indonesia government documents, quoted in Buchheit and Gulati, "Sovereign Bonds and the Collective Will," Georgetown-Sloan Project on Business Institutions Working Paper No. 34, March 2002.

Exhibit 2 English Majority Action Clause

The following contract clause comes from the Republic of Moldova, 9.875% Notes due 2002, U.S. $75,000,000. It permits changes to the payment terms of a bond with the consent of bondholders representing 75% (by amount) of the bonds voting at a bondholders meeting that meets certain quorum requirements.

12. Meetings of Noteholders, Modification and Waiver

(a) Meetings of Noteholders

The Agency Agreement contains provisions for convening meetings of Noteholders to consider matters relating to the Notes, including the modification of any provision of these Conditions or the Deed of Covenant. Any such modification may be made if sanctioned by an Extraordinary Resolution (as defined below).

The quorum at any such meeting for passing an Extraordinary Resolution shall be two or more persons holding or representing a clear majority of the principal amount of the Notes for the time being outstanding, or at any adjourned meeting two or more persons being or representing Noteholders whatever the principal amount of the Notes for the time being outstanding so held or represented, except that at any meeting the business of which includes consideration of proposals, *inter alia,* (i) to modify the maturity of the Notes or the dates on which interest is payable in respect of the Notes, (ii) to reduce or cancel the principal amount of, or interest on, the Notes, (iii) to change the currency of payment of the Notes, or (iv) to modify the provisions concerning the quorum required at any meeting of Noteholders or the majority required to pass an Extraordinary Resolution, the necessary quorum for passing an Extraordinary Resolution shall be two or more persons holding or representing not less than 75 per cent, or at any adjourned such meeting not less than 25 per cent, of the principal amount of the Notes for the time being outstanding.

As used in this Condition 12, "Extraordinary Resolution" means a resolution passed at a meeting of the Noteholders duly convened and held in accordance with the provisions contained in these Conditions and the Agency Agreement by a majority consisting of not less than 75 per cent of the persons voting thereat upon a show of hands or if a poll shall be duly demanded then by a majority consisting of not less than 75 per cent of the votes given on the poll. An Extraordinary Resolution passed at any meeting of Noteholders will be binding on all Noteholders, whether or not they are present at the meeting.

Source: Excerpts from Republic of Moldova government documents, quoted in Buchheit and Gulati, "Sovereign Bonds and the Collective Will," Georgetown-Sloan Project on Business Institutions Working Paper No. 34, March 2002.

Exhibit 3 Example of a Collective Action Clause

The following excerpt is from Bolivarian Republic of Venezuela, Prospectus describing offer of up to $4.8 billion in debt securities, September 21, 2004.

Approval

The following description does not apply to any series of Debt Securities that has been designated Collective Action Securities. See "Approval (Collective Action Securities)" below for a description of the corresponding terms and conditions applicable to Debt Securities that have been designated Collective Action Securities.

Venezuela and the fiscal agent may modify, amend or supplement the terms of Debt Securities of any series and the Fiscal Agency Agreement as it relates to those securities, or the holders may take any action provided by the Fiscal Agency Agreement or the terms of their Debt Securities with:

- the approval of the holders of either a majority in aggregate Outstanding principal amount of the Debt Securities of that series or not less than 66⅔% in aggregate Outstanding principal amount of the Debt Securities of that series that are represented at a meeting of holders, whichever is less; or
- the written consent of the holders of not less than a majority in aggregate Outstanding principal amount of the Debt Securities of the relevant series.

However, each holder of a Debt Security of a particular series must consent to any amendment, modification or change that would:

- change the due date for the payment of principal, any premium, or any interest on the Debt Securities;
- reduce the principal amount of the Debt Securities;
- reduce the portion of the principal amount of the Debt Securities that is payable upon acceleration of the maturity date;
- reduce the interest rate on the Debt Securities or any premium payable upon redemption of the Debt Securities;
- change the currency or place of payment of principal of or any premium or interest on the Debt Securities;
- permit early redemption of the Debt Securities or, if early redemption is already permitted, set a redemption date earlier than the date previously specified;
- reduce the percentage of principal amount of the holders of the Debt Securities whose vote or consent is needed to modify, amend or supplement the Fiscal Agency Agreement or the terms and conditions of the debt securities or to take any other action; or
- change Venezuela's obligation to pay additional amounts.

Approval (Collective Action Securities)

The following description applies only to series of Debt Securities that have been designated Collective Action Securities.

Venezuela and the fiscal agent may modify, amend or supplement the terms of Debt Securities of any series and the Fiscal Agency Agreement as it relates to those securities, or the holders may take any action provided by the Fiscal Agency Agreement or the terms of their Debt Securities with:

- the affirmative vote, in person or by proxy, of the holders of not less than 66⅔% in aggregate Outstanding principal amount of the Debt Securities of that series that are represented at a meeting of holders; or
- the written consent of the holders of not less than 66⅔% in aggregate Outstanding principal amount of the Debt Securities of the relevant series.

However, without the consent or affirmative vote, in person or by proxy, of holders of at least 85% in aggregate Outstanding principal amount of the Debt Securities of a particular series, no amendment, modification or change may be made that would:

- change the due date for the payment of principal, any premium, or any interest on the Debt Securities;
- reduce the principal amount of the Debt Securities;
- reduce the portion of the principal amount of the Debt Securities that is payable upon acceleration of the maturity date;
- reduce the interest rate on the Debt Securities or any premium payable upon redemption of the Debt Securities;
- change the currency or place of payment of principal of or any premium or interest on the Debt Securities;
- permit early redemption of the Debt Securities or, if early redemption is already permitted, set a redemption date earlier than the date previously specified;
- reduce the proportion of principal amount of the holders of the Debt Securities whose vote or consent is needed to modify, amend or supplement the Fiscal Agency Agreement or the terms and conditions of the debt securities or to take any other action;
- change Venezuela's obligation to pay additional amounts;
- change the definition of "Outstanding" with respect to the Debt Securities;
- change the governing law provision of the Debt Securities;
- change the Republic's appointment of an agent for service of process or its agreement not to claim and to waive irrevocably any immunity in respect of any actions or proceedings based on the Debt Securities;
- change the ranking of the Debt Securities as described under the heading "—Nature of Obligation"; or
- in connection with any offer to acquire Debt Securities in exchange for cash or new securities of the Republic or any of its political subdivisions or instrumentalities, change any event of default under the Debt Securities.

...

Certain Amendments Not Requiring Holder Consent

Venezuela and the fiscal agent may, without the vote or consent of any holder of Debt Securities of a series, amend the Fiscal Agency Agreement or the Debt Securities of that series for the purpose of:

- adding to Venezuela's covenants for the benefit of the holders;
- surrendering any of Venezuela's rights or powers;
- providing collateral for the Debt Securities;

- curing any ambiguity or correcting or supplementing any defective provision contained in the Fiscal Agency Agreement or the Debt Securities; or
- changing the terms and conditions of the Fiscal Agency Agreement or the Debt Securities in any manner which Venezuela and the fiscal agent may determine and which is not inconsistent with the Debt Securities and will not materially adversely affect the interests of the holders of the Debt Securities.

Collective Action Securities

The Republic may designate a particular series of Debt Securities to be "Collective Action Securities," the specific terms of which will be described in the prospectus supplement relating to such securities. Collective Action Securities will have the same terms and conditions as the securities described under the heading "Description of the Debt Securities" in this document, except that such Collective Action Securities will contain the provisions regarding amendments, modifications, changes and waivers described under the heading "Meetings and Amendments—Approval (Collective Action Securities)" above instead of the provisions described under the heading "Meetings and Amendments—Approval."

Source: Excerpt from Bolivarian Republic of Venezuela government documents, Prospectus describing offer of up to $4.8 billion in debt securities, September 21, 2004, available at http://www.mf.gov.ve/archivos/20011013/Euro%202015.pdf, accessed November 2, 2006.

Exhibit 4 Emerging Markets Sovereign Bond Outstanding, Issuance by Region and Governing Law

	2002		2005	
	U.S. dollar bns	%	*U.S. dollar bns*	%
Africa				
Total outstanding issuances	10	100%	12.4	100%
Total with CACs	4.2	42%	7.6	61%
New York	4.3	43%	6.8	55%
Of which: with CACs	...	...	2.4	19%
English	2	20%	3.6	29%
German	0.3	3%	...	...
Japanese	2.2	22%	1.6	13%
Asia				
Total outstanding issuances	29.8	100%	43.9	100%
Total with CACs	8.9	30%	18.4	42%
New York	19	64%	30.6	70%
Of which: with CACs	...	...	8	18%
English	6.4	21%	8.2	19%
German	0.7	2%	0.7	2%
Japanese	2.6	9%	2.2	5%
Eastern Europe				
Total outstanding issuances	74.8	100%	107.7	100%
Total with CACs	45	60%	86	80%
New York	14.5	19%	26	24%
Of which: with CACs	...	...	10.9	10%
English	39.7	53%	70.2	65%
German	14.8	20%	6.3	6%
Japanese	5.3	7%	4.9	5%
Latin America				
Total outstanding issuances	146.9	100%	172	100%
Total with CACs	30.6	21%	68.2	40%
New York	90.7	62%	133.4	78%
Of which: with CACs	...	...	49.5	29%
English	22.3	15%	15.7	9%
German	19.9	14%	12.2	7%
Japanese	8.3	6%	3	2%
Middle East				
Total outstanding issuances	16.2	100%	20.7	100%
Total with CACs	8.8	54%	13.2	64%
New York	12.5	77%	16	77%
Of which: with CACs	5.2	32%	8.6	42%
English	3.5	22%	4.3	21%
German	...	...	...	...
Japanese	0.2	1%	0.2	1%
Total				
Total outstanding issuances	277.7	100%	356.7	100%
Total with CACs	97.5	35%	193.4	54%

Source: Adapted from International Monetary Fund, "Progress Report on Crisis Resolution," September 21, 2005, p. 18.

Exhibit 5 Collective Action Clauses: Comparison of Recommendation and Adoption by New York Law-Governed Bonds between September 2004 and September 2005

Provisions	G-10 Recommendations	Argentina, Brazil, Colombia, Dominican, Republic, El Salvador, Guatemala, Hungary, Indonesia, Italy, Lebanon, Mexico, Panama, Peru, Philippines, Turkey, Uruguay, and Venezuela
Amendment of Key Terms	75% threshold based on either outstanding principal or principal held by those present at a duly convened meeting.	75% based on outstanding principal (except the Lebanon bond, where the threshold is based on duly convened meeting).
Aggregate Voting	None.	Argentina, DR, and Uruguay: 85% of the aggregate outstanding principal of all affected series (taken in aggregate) and 66⅔% of outstanding principal of each affected series (taken individually).
Disenfranchisement	Bonds owned or controlled directly or indirectly by the issuer or its public sector instrumentalities.	Generally bonds owned directly or indirectly by the issuer or its public sector instrumentalities.
Acceleration	25% of outstanding principal.	25% of outstanding principal (except the Lebanon bond, where each bondholder has the right to accelerate upon default).
De-acceleration	Between 50% and 66⅔% of outstanding principal.	• Argentina, Colombia, DR, Hungary, Indonesia, Mexico, Peru, Philippines and Venezuela: 50% of outstanding principal. • Uruguay: 66% of the outstanding principal. • Brazil, El Salvador, Guatemala, Italy, Panama and Turkey: 66⅔% of outstanding principal • Lebanon: none.
Initiation of Proceedings	• Mandate the use of a trust or an equivalent legal structure where the trustee can be instructed by 25% to initiate lawsuits. • Pro rata distribution of recovered proceeds under trust structure	Individual bondholder, except the Argentina, DR, Indonesia and Uruguay bonds where the trustee has a limited monopoly over initiation of proceedings whose recovery would be distributed pro rata.
Engagement Provision	• Appoint a bondholder representative for the life of the bond. • 66⅔% to appoint at anytime any person to represent all holders in negotiation with the issuer or other creditors.	None, except the Hungary bond that allows 50% of outstanding principal to "appoint any persons as a committee to represent the interests" of holders in the event of a default or acceleration or following any public announcement by the issuer of a restructuring
Information Provision	A covenant requiring the issuer to provide certain types of information over the life of the bond and following a default.	None.
Documentation	Trust or an equivalent legal structure.	Fiscal agency agreement, except Argentina, DR, Indonesia, and Uruguay which utilized a trust structure.

Source: Adapted from International Monetary Fund, "Progress Report to the International Monetary and Financial Committee on Crisis Resolution," September 21, 2005, p. 19; and April 12, 2005, p. 9.

Exhibit 6 Description of Argentine GDP-Linked Instruments

The text below is from "Prospectus Supplement (to Prospectus Dated December 27, 2004), the Republic of Argentina Offers to Owners of Each Series of Bonds Listed in Annex A to this Prospectus Supplement," January 10, 2005.

The GDP-linked Securities

Securities Offered ...... GDP-linked Securities that expire no later than December 15, 2035.

Each GDP-linked Security will be originally issued as a single unit with the underlying Par, Discount or Quasi-par. During the period of 180 days following the first day of the Settlement Date, each GDP-linked Security will remain attached to and trade as a single unit with the underlying Par, Discount or Quasi-par. Upon expiration of this 180-day period, the GDP-linked Securities and the underlying Pars, Discounts or Quasi-pars will automatically detach and will no longer constitute a single unit. Thereafter, the GDP-linked Securities will trade independently from the underlying Pars, Discounts or Quasi-pars.

Notional Amount ...... Each GDP-linked Security will have a notional amount equal to the corresponding Eligible Amount of Eligible Securities tendered and accepted. If the Eligible Securities tendered and accepted are not in the same currency as the GDP-linked Securities you are entitled to receive, the corresponding notional amount of the GDP-linked Securities will be determined using exchange rates in effect on December 31, 2003.

There are no principal payments in respect of the GDP-linked Securities. Holders will not receive any payments during the life or upon the expiration of their GDP-linked Securities other than as described below.

Payments ...... Any payments on the GDP-linked Securities are contingent upon the performance of Argentina's GDP (as described below) and subject to the conditions described below. Payments made on the GDP-linked Securities will be based on the notional amount of GDP-linked Securities.

Payment Currency ...... The payment currency of the GDP-linked Securities will be the currency of the New Security to which the GDP-linked Securities are initially attached, which may be U.S. dollars, euro or pesos.

Calculation Date ...... The calculation date for the GDP-linked Securities will be on November 1 of each year following the relevant reference year (as defined below), commencing on November 1, 2006.

Payment Date...... Subject to the conditions specified below, Argentina will make payments on the GDP-linked Securities on December 15 of each year following the relevant reference year. The first payment, if any, will occur on December 15, 2006.

Reference Year ...... The reference year for the GDP-linked Securities will be a calendar year, commencing in 2005 and ending in 2034.

Base Case GDP ...... The base case gross domestic product ("Base Case GDP") for each reference year is set forth in the following chart:

Reference Year	Base Case GDP (1993 pesos in millions)	Reference Year	Base Case GDP (1993 pesos in millions)
2005	287,012.52	2020	458,555.87
2006	297,211.54	2021	472,312.54
2007	307,369.47	2022	486,481.92
2008	317,520.47	2023	501,076.38
2009	327,968.83	2024	516,108.67
2010	338,675.94	2025	531,591.93
2011	349,720.39	2026	547,539.69
2012	361,124.97	2027	563,965.88
2013	372,753.73	2028	580,884.85
2014	384,033.32	2029	598,311.40
2015	395,554.32	2030	616,260.74
2016	407,420.95	2031	634,748.56
2017	419,643.58	2032	653,791.02
2018	432,232.88	2033	673,404.75
2019	445,199.87	2034	693,606.89

The Base Case GDP will be adjusted in accordance with any changes to the year of base prices (currently 1993).

Actual Real GDP ...... The actual real gross domestic product ("Actual Real GDP") is the gross domestic product of Argentina in constant pesos for each calendar year as published by the *Instituto Nacional de Estadistica y Censos* ("INDEC").

Actual Real GDP is currently calculated by INDEC using the year 1993 as the year of base prices. If in any year, the year of base prices for calculating Actual Real GDP is changed by INDEC, the Base Case GDP will be adjusted accordingly. For example, if Actual Real GDP for 2006 with 1993 prices is X, and with 2000 prices is Y, then the Base Case GDP = Base Case GDP as per chart above multiplied by a fraction, the numerator of which is Y and the denominator of which is X.

Actual Nominal GDP... The actual nominal gross domestic product (""Actual Nominal GDP") is the gross domestic product of Argentina in current pesos for each calendar year as published by the *Instituto Nacional de Estadistica y Censos* ("INDEC").

Payment Conditions... Argentina will make a payment on GDP-linked Securities in respect of any given reference year only if the following three conditions are met:

- for the reference year, Actual Real GDP exceeds Base Case GDP;
- for the reference year, annual growth in Actual Real GDP exceeds the Growth rate in Base Case GDP for such year (for your reference, the Base Case GDP for 2004 is Ps.275,276.01 million, measured in 1993 pesos); and
- total payments made on a GDP-linked Security do not exceed the payment cap for that GDP-linked Security.

Annual growth of "Actual Real GDP" for any reference year will be calculated by dividing actual Real GDP for that reference year by the Actual Real GDP for the year preceding that reference year, minus one. For purposes of this calculation, the Actual Real GDP for the relevant reference year and the preceding year will each be measured using the same year of base prices, with Actual Real GDP for the year preceding the reference year adjusted, if necessary, to reflect any changes in the year of base prices implemented during such reference year (for an example of how this adjustment is effected see ""Ì Actual Real GDP" above).

Excess GDP ...... The excess gross domestic product for any reference year ("Excess GDP") is the amount, if any, by which Actual Real GDP (converted to nominal pesos, as described below) exceeds the Base Case GDP (converted to nominal pesos, as described below). Excess GDP will be expressed in billions.

For purposes of determining Excess GDP for any reference year, each of the Actual Real GDP and Base Case GDP for that reference year will be converted into nominal pesos by multiplying it by a fraction, the numerator of which is the GDP Deflator (as defined below) for that reference year and the denominator of which is the GDP Deflator for the year of base prices used to calculate Actual Real GDP and Base Case GDP for that reference year. As noted above, 1993 is currently the year of base prices, and the GDP Deflator for that year is one.

GDP Deflator ...... The GDP deflator for any given year ("GDP Deflator") is the quotient that results from dividing the Actual Nominal GDP for such year, by the Actual Real GDP for the same year, in each case as published by INDEC.

Payment Amount ...... On each payment date, holders of GDP-linked Securities will be entitled to receive payments in an amount equal to the Available Excess GDP (as defined below) for the corresponding reference year, multiplied by the aggregate notional amount of GDP-linked securities they hold. ""Available Excess GDP" is an amount per unit of currency of notional amount of GDP-linked Securities, determined in accordance with the following formula:

Available Excess GDP = (0.05 X Excess GDP) X unit of currency coefficient

where:

- "Excess GDP"' is expressed in billions of nominal pesos, and
- the "unit of currency coefficient" is as set forth in the following table:

Currency	Unit of Currency Coefficient
U.S. dollars	1/81.8 = 0.012225
Euro	1/81.8 X (1/.7945) = 0.15387
Pesos	1/81.8 £ (1/2.91750) = 0.004190

The unit of currency coefficient represents the proportion that one GDP-linked security with a notional amount of one unit of currency bears to the aggregate Eligible Amount of all Eligible Securities outstanding as of the date of this prospectus supplement (approximately U.S.$81.8 billion), calculated using exchange rates in effect on December 31, 2003.

For purposes of effecting payments on GDP-linked Securities, Available Excess GDP will be converted to the relevant payment currency using the average free market exchange rate of pesos to the applicable payment currency during the 15 calendar days preceding December 31 of the relevant reference year.

All calculations for payments on the GDP-linked Securities will be performed by the Ministry of Economy and Production of Argentina.

Annex F to this prospectus supplement contains sample calculations related to payments on GDP-linked Securities.

Payment Cap..... The total amount to be paid during the life of the GDP-linked Securities, per unit of GDP-linked Security, will not exceed 0.48, measured per unit of currency. We refer to this amount as the "payment cap for GDP-linked Securities." For example, if you receive GDP-linked Securities in a notional amount equal to U.S.$1 million, the payment cap for your GDP-linked Securities would equal U.S.$480,000.

If the payment cap for a GDP-linked Security is reached in a payment year prior to the scheduled expiration of the GDP-linked Securities, the GDP-linked Securities will be deemed to have expired in such year.

If, for any given year the aggregate payment due under a GDP-linked Security is greater than the amount remaining under the payment cap for that Security, then the remaining amount available under the payment cap for that GDP-linked Security will be distributed to the holder of that security.

Governing Law..... The governing law of each GDP-linked Security will be the same as the governing law of the New Security to which the GDP-linked Security is initially attached.

Source: Excerpt from Argentine government documents, "Prospectus Supplement (to Prospectus Dated December 27, 2004), the Republic of Argentina Offers to Owners of Each Series of Bonds Listed in Annex A to this Prospectus Supplement," January 10, 2005, available at http://www.mecon.gov.ar/finanzas/downloadus_prospectus_and_prospectus_supplement.pdf, accessed November 2, 2006.

Exhibit 7 Daily VIX Series with Crisis Periods Highlighted, January 1990 through December 2003

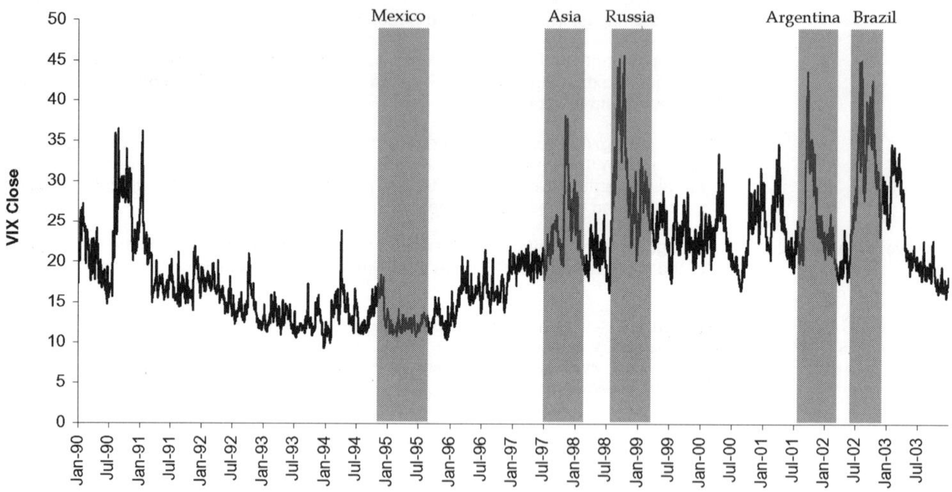

Source: Adapted from Figure 2 in Caballero and Panageas, "Contingent Reserves Management," 2006, using data compiled from Chicago Board Options Exchange (CBOE) website, "New Methodology: VIX data for 1990-2003," available at http://www.cboe.com/micro/vix/historical.aspx, accessed October 31, 2006.

Note: On its website, CBOE defines VIX as "a key measure of market expectations of near-term volatility conveyed by S&P 500 stock index option prices."

Endnotes

[1] For more on this episodes, see Huw Pill, "Mexico: The Tequila Crisis—1994–95," HBS No. 702-093, June 12, 2002; Huw Pill, "Bahtulism, Collapse, Resurrection? Financial Crisis in Asia: 1997–1998," HBS No. 798-089, 1998; Laura Alfaro and Rafael Di Tella, "Brazil 2003: Inflation Targeting and Debt Dynamics," HBS No. 704-028, February 3, 2004; Rafael Di Tella, "The 2001 Crisis in Argentina: An IMF-Sponsored Default?" HBS No. 704-004, October 27, 2003.

[2] See Carmen M. Reinhart, Kenneth S. Rogoff, and Miguel A. Savastano, "Debt Intolerance," Brookings Papers on Economic Activity, 2003, v2003(1), pp. 1–74; Nouriel Roubini and Brad Setser, "Improving the Sovereign Debt Restructuring Process: Problems in Restructuring, Proposed Solutions, and a Roadmap for Reform," prepared for conference "Improving the Sovereign Debt Restructuring Process" co-hosted by the Institute for International Economics and the *Institute Francais des Relations Internationales,* Paris, March 9, 2003; Kenneth S. Rogoff, "International Institutions for Reducing Global Financial Instability," *Journal of Economic Perspectives* 13, Fall 1999, pp. 21–42; Martin Feldstein, "Refocusing the IMF," *Foreign Affairs*, March/April 1998, pp. 20–33; Barry Eichengreen, *Financial Crises and What to Do About Them* (Oxford: Oxford University Press, 2002); and Laura Alfaro, Sebnem Kalemli-Ozcan, and Vadym Volosovych, "Capital Flows in a Globalized World: The Role of Policies and Institutions," in Sebastian Edwards, editor, *Capital Controls and Capital Flows in Emerging Economies: Policies, Practices and Consequences* (National Bureau of Economic Research, forthcoming).

[3] See, for example, discussion in Hal S. Scott, "Sovereign Debt Defaults: Cry for the United States, Not Argentina," Washington Legal Foundation, Critical Legal Issues, Working Paper Series No. 140, September 2006.

[4] For surveys of the literature see M. Kenneth Kletzer, "Sovereign Immunity and International Lending," in *The Handbook of International Macroeconomics*, edited by Frederick van der Ploeg, (United Kingdom: Basil Blackwell Publisher, 1994); and Jonathan Eaton and Raquel Fernandez, "Sovereign Debt," in *Handbook of International Economics* Vol. 3 (Amsterdam, New York and Oxford: Elsevier, North-Holland, 1995) edited by Gene Grossman and Kenneth Rogoff, pp. 2031–2077; and Kenneth Rogoff and Jeromin Zettelmeyer, "Bankruptcy Procedures for Sovereigns: A History of Ideas, 1976–2001," IMF Working Paper, WP/02/133, August 2002.

[5] Maurice Obstfeld and Kenneth Rogoff, *Foundations of International Macroeconomics* (Cambridge, Massachusetts: MIT Press, 1996).

[6] Rogoff, "International Institutions for Reducing Global Financial Instability," 1999.

[7] Jonathan Eaton and Mark Gersovitz, "Debt with Potential Repudiation: Theoretical and Empirical Analysis," *Review of Economic Studies* Vol. 48, April 1981, pp. 284–309.

[8] Jeremy Bulow and Kenneth Rogoff, "Sovereign Debt: Is to Forgive to Forget?" *American Economic Review* 79, 1989, pp. 43–50 show, on theoretical grounds, that reputational effects are not enough to induce countries to repay debt. Instead, foreign creditors must be able to impose direct sanctions in order to induce sovereign debtors to repay. Subsequently, Harold L. Cole and Patrick J. Kehoe, "Models of Sovereign Debt: Partial versus General Reputations," *International Economic Review* 39, 1998, pp. 55–70, show that the ability of reputation to support debt depends on the alternatives open to the country, its relationships in the international arena, and assumptions made about institutions.

[9] Eaton and Gersovitz, "Debt with Potential Repudiation," 1981.

[10] Michael P. Dooley, "Can Output Losses Following International Financial Crises Be Avoided?" NBER Working Paper 7531, February 2000.

[11] Discussed, for example, in Rogoff and Zettelmeyer, "Bankruptcy Procedures for Sovereigns," 2002. Overall, the evidence on why countries repay debt remained inconclusive. See, for example, Laura Alfaro and Fabio Kanczuk, "Sovereign Debt as a Contingent Claim: A Quantitative Approach," *Journal of International Economics* 65, No. 2, 2005, pp. 297–314; Andrew Rose, "One Reason Countries Pay Their Debts: Renegotiation and International Trade," *Journal of Development Economics* 77(1), 2005, pp. 189–206; Sule Ozler, "Have Commercial Banks Ignored History?" *American Economic Review* 83, 1993, pp. 608–620; Barry Eichengreen and Richard Portes, "Debt and Default in the 1930s: Causes and Consequences," *European Economic Review* 30, 1986,

pp. 599–640; and Federico Sturzenegger and Jeromin Zettelmeyer, *Defaults in the 90s: Learning to Deal with Crisis*, available at http://www.utdt.edu/~fsturzen/Defaults%20in%20the%2090sFinal.pdf, accessed July 6, 2006, forthcoming December 2006 as *Debt Defaults and Lessons from a Decade of Crises* (MIT Press).

[12] Anne Krueger, "New Approaches to Sovereign Debt Restructuring: An Update on Our Thinking," speech delivered at International Monetary Fund Conference on "Sovereign Debt Workouts: Hopes and Hazards," Institute for International Economics, Washington, D.C., April 1, 2002, available at http://www.imf.org/external/np/speeches/2002/040102.htm, accessed October 24, 2006.

[13] For discussion about Chapter 11 bankruptcy in relation to sovereign debt restructuring, see Christopher G. Oechsli, "Procedural Guidelines for Renegotiating LDC Debts: An Analogy to Chapter 11 of the U.S. Bankruptcy Reform Act, Virginia Journal of International Law Vol. 21, No. 2, pp. 305–341, as referenced in Rogoff and Zettelmeyer, "Bankruptcy Procedures for Sovereigns," 2002; Patrick Bolton, "Toward a Statutory Approach to Sovereign Debt Restructuring: Lessons from Corporate Bankruptcy Practice Around the World," IMF Staff Papers, Vol. 50, Special Issue, 2003; Andrei Shleifer, "Will The Sovereign Debt Market Survive?" *American Economic Review* Vol. 93, May 2003, pp. 85–90; and Rogoff and Zettelmeyer, "Bankruptcy Procedures for Sovereigns," 2002.

[14] Quoted in Shleifer, "Will The Sovereign Debt Market Survive?" 2003.

[15] Kunibert Raffer, "International Debts: A Crisis for Whom?" Economic Development and World Debt, edited by H.W. Singer and Soumitra Sharma (London: Macmillan Press, 1989), pp. 51–62, as cited in Rogoff and Zettelmeyer, "Bankruptcy Procedures for Sovereigns," 2002.

[16] Krueger, "New Approaches to Sovereign Debt Restructuring," 2002.

[17] The literature is discussed in Rogoff and Zettelmeyer, "Bankruptcy Procedures for Sovereigns," 2002, including Jeffrey Sachs, "Managing the LDC Debt Crisis," *Brookings Papers on Economic Activity* Vol. 2, pp. 397–431, and Benjamin J. Cohen, "Developing Country Debt: A Middle Way," *Princeton Essays in International Finance* 173 (Princeton: Princeton University Press, 1989).

[18] See Krueger, "New Approaches to Sovereign Debt Restructuring," 2002, summarized in Lee C. Buchheit and G. Mitu Gulati, "Sovereign Bonds and the Collective Will," *Emory Law Journal* 51, Fall 2002, pp. 1340–1341; and in Mihir Desai, "Redesigning Sovereign Debt Restructuring Mechanisms," HBS No. 204-110, March 2004.

[19] Discussed, for example, in Steven L. Schwarcz, "Sovereign Debt Restructuring: A Bankruptcy Reorganization Approach," Cornell Law Review Vol. 85, 2000, pp. 101–187, as cited in Rogoff and Zettelemeyer, "Bankruptcy Procedures for Sovereigns," 2002.

[20] Krueger, "New Approaches to Sovereign Debt Restructuring," 2002.

[21] Rogoff, "International Institutions for Reducing Global Financial Instability," 1999.

[22] This view is expressed in Andy Haldane and Mark Kruger, "The Resolution of International Financial Crises: Private Finance and Public Funds," Bank of Canada Working Paper 2001-20, November 2001; Roubini and Setser, "Improving the Sovereign Debt Restructuring Process," 2003; and Sturzenegger and Zettelmeyer, *Defaults in the 1990s*, 2006.

[23] Sturzenegger and Zettelmeyer, *Defaults in the 1990s*, 2006.

[24] Jeremy Bulow and Kenneth Rogoff, "Sovereign Debt: Is to Forgive to Forget?" *American Economic Review* 79, 1989; and Shleifer, "Will the Sovereign Debt Market Survive?" 2003.

[25] For a more detailed discussion, see Laura Alfaro, "Creditor Activism in Sovereign Debt: 'Vulture' Tactics or Market Backbone," HBS No. 706-057, June 9, 2006.

[26] See, for example, Scott, "Sovereign Debt Defaults: Cry for the United States, Not Argentina," 2006, and Shleifer, "Will the Sovereign Debt Market Survive?" 2003.

[27] In addition to its role providing advice and technical assistance on policy reform to correct structural imbalances, the IMF served a lender-of-last-resort function. The fifth of its six objectives defined in its Articles of Agreement states: "To give confidence to members by making the general resources of the Fund temporarily available to them under adequate safeguards, thus providing them with opportunity to correct maladjustments in their balance of payments without resorting to measures destructive of national or international prosperity." In order to address such problems, the IMF could choose to grant a loan package at market rates of interest contingent on the sovereign accepting a policy conditionality plan—requiring, for example, reduced government spending or exchange rate devaluation. (See IMF website at http://www.imf.org/external/pubs/ft/aa/index.htm.)

[28] See, for example, Hal S. Scott, *International Finance: Transactions, Policy, and Regulation* (Foundation Press, 12th Edition, 2005), p. 736; and Adam Lerrick and Allan H. Meltzer, "Sovereign Default: The Private Sector Can Resolve Without a Formal Court," *Quarterly International Economics Report*, Gaillot Center for Public Policy (Pittsburgh: Carnegie Mellon University), April 2002, as cited in Rogoff and Zettelmeyer, "Bankruptcy Procedures for Sovereigns," 2002.

[29] Idea of financier George Soros, as discussed in Rogoff, "International Institutions for Reducing Global Financial Instability," 1999, p. 20.

[30] Rogoff, "International Institutions for Reducing Global Financial Instability," 1999, p. 21.

[31] For criticisms, see Sturzenegger and Zettelmeyer, *Defaults in the 1990s*, 2006, pp. 191–192; and Rogoff, "International Institutions for Reducing Global Financial Instability," 1999, p. 21.

[32] Guillermo A. Calvo, "Crises in Emerging Market Economies: A Global Perspective," NBER Working Paper No. 11305, April 2005, available at http://www.bis.org/events/conf060619calvo.pdf, accessed October 28, 2006.

[33] Ibid.

[34] Takatoshi Ito, "Comments on Guillermo A. Calvo, "Crises in Emerging Market Economies: Global Perspective," Bank of International Settlements, Fifth BIS Annual Conference 2006, Brunnen, June 19–20, 2006, available at http://www.bis.org/events/conf060619/ito.pdf, accessed October 28, 2006.

[35] "Sovereign Debt Restructuring: A U.S. Perspective," Remarks By John B. Taylor, Under Secretary Of Treasury for International Affairs at the Conference "Sovereign Debt Workouts: Hopes and Hazards?" Institute For International Economics Washington, D.C., April 2, 2002, available at http://www.ustreas.gov/press/releases/po2056.htm, accessed October 28, 2006.

[36] Scott, *International Finance: Transactions, Policy, and Regulation*, 2005, p. 746.

[37] Ibid.

[38] Ibid., p. 748.

[39] Lee C. Buchheit and G. Mitu Gulati, "Sovereign Bonds and the Collective Will," *Emory Law Journal* 51, fall 2002.

[40] Taylor, "Sovereign Debt Restructuring: A U.S. Perspective," 2002.

[41] Scott, International Finance: Transactions, Policy, and Regulation, 2005, p. 748.

[42] Lee C. Buchheit, "Changing Bond Documentation: The Sharing Clause," *International Financial Law Review*, July 1998, p. 17.

[43] Lee C. Buchheit, "Sovereign Debtors and Their Bondholders," Unitar Training Programmes on Foreign Economic Relations, p. 23.

[44] Scott, *International Finance: Transactions, Policy,* and Regulation, 2005, p. 747.

[45] Barry Eichengreen and Ashoka Mody, "Is Aggregation a Problem for Sovereign Debt Restructuring?" January 2003, available at http://www.econ.berkeley.edu/~eichengr/research/aeapapers&proceedings5jan15-03.pdf, October 28, 2006.

[46] International Monetary Fund, "Progress Report on Crisis Resolution," September 21, 2005, available at http://www.imf.org/external/np/pp/eng/2005/092105.pdf, accessed October 28, 2006.

[47] According to IMF, "Progress Report," 2005, total issue was 35.2 billion. Half was issued under Argentine law and did not include CACs. Half was issued under other laws and did include CACs.

[48] Sturzenegger and Zettelmeyer, *Defaults in the 1990s*, 2006, p. 198.

[49] Eduardo Borensztein and Paolo Mauro, "The Case for GDP-indexed Bonds," *Economic Policy* Vol. 19, No. 38, 2004, pp. 166–216.

[50] Stephany Griffith-Jones and Krishnan Sharma, "GDP Indexed Bonds: Making it Happen," DESA Working Paper No. 21, April 2006, available at http://www.un.org/esa/ffd/BackgroundPaper.doc, accessed October 28, 2006.

[51] Eduardo Borensztein and Paolo Mauro, "Reviving the Case for GDP-Indexed Bonds," IMF Policy Discussion Paper, PDP/02/10 available at http://www.internationalmonetaryfund.org/external/pubs/ft/pdp/2002/pdp10.pdf, accessed October 28, 2006.

[52] Eduardo Borensztein, Marcos Chamon, Olivier Jeanne, Paolo Mauro, and Jeromin Zettelmeyer, "Sovereign Debt Structure for Crisis Prevention," IMF Occasional Paper 237, 2004, available at http://www.internationalmonetaryfund.org/external/pubs/nft/op/237/op237.pdf, accessed October 28, 2006.

[53] United Nations, "Report on the brainstorming meeting on 'GDP-Indexed Bonds: Making It Happen," 2005.

[54] Borenzstein et al., "Sovereign Debt Structure for Crisis Prevention," 2004; summarized in Sturzenegger and Zettelmeyer, *Defaults in the 1990s*, 2006.

[55] Ibid.

[56] Prospectus Supplement (to Prospectus Dated December 27, 2004), The Republic of Argentina Offers to Owners of Each Series of Bonds Listed in Annex A to This Prospectus Supplement, January 10, 2005, available at http://www.mecon.gov.ar/finanzas/download/us_prospectus_and_prospectus_supplement.pdf, accessed October 28, 2006.

[57] IMF, "Progress Report," 2005.

[58] Griffith-Jones and Sharma, "GDP Indexed Bonds," 2006.

[59] See, for example, Laura Alfaro and Rafael Di Tella, "China: To Float or Not to Float? (A)," HBS No. 706-021, March 2, 2006; and Laura Alfaro and Fabio Kanczuk, "Optimal Reserve Management and Sovereign Debt," Harvard Business School Working Paper No. 07-010, July 2006.

[60] Sturzenegger and Zettelmeyer, *Defaults in the 1990s*, 2006.

[61] See description available on Chicago Board Options Exchange website at http://www.cboe.com/micro/vix/introduction.aspx, accessed October 28, 2006.

[62] The study authors define a sudden stop in this case as falling reserves combined with a decline in capital flows equivalent to 5% of GDP relative to flows in the previous two years. The term was coined by Guillermo Calvo in "Capital Flows and Capital Market Crises: The Simple Economics of Sudden Stops," *Journal of Applied Economics* 1, 1998, to describe the crises of the 1990s characterized by external shocks and abrupt reversals of capital flows.

[63] Ricardo J. Caballero and Stavros Panageas, "Contingent Reserves Management: An Applied Framework," in *External Vulnerability and Preventive Policies*, edited by Ricardo Caballero, César Calderón, and Luis Felipe

Cespedes, Santiago, Chile, Central Bank of Chile, 2006, available at http://www.bcentral.cl/eng/stdpub/studies/centralbanking/pdf/v10/399_420caballero_panageas.pdf, accessed October 28, 2006.

64 Caballero and Panageas, "Contingent Reserves Management," 2006.

65 Sturzenegger and Zettelmeyer, *Defaults in the 1990s*, 2006.

66 Caballero and Panageas, "Contingent Reserves Management," 2006, p. 419.

67 Barry Eichengreen, Ricardo Hausmann, and Ugo Panizza, "Currency Mismatches, Debt Intolerance and Original Sin: Why They Are Not the Same and Why It Matters," NBER Working Paper No. 10036, October 2003.

68 Eichengreen, Hausmann, and Panizza, "Currency Mismatches, Debt Intolerance and Original Sin," 2005.

69 Rogoff, "International Institutions for Reducing Global Financial Instability," 1999, p. 23.

70 For a discussion of debt maturity, see Laura Alfaro and Fabio Kanczuk, "Debt Maturity: Is Long-Term Debt Optimal?" Harvard Business School Working Paper No. 06-005, October 2005.

71 For example, see Basel Committee On Banking Supervision, "Supervisory Lessons To Be Drawn From The Asian Crisis," BIS Working Papers No. 2, June 1999, available at http://www.bis.org/publ/bcbs_wp02.pdf, accessed October 28, 2006, pp. 41–42.

72 For more on inflation targeting, see Laura Alfaro and Rafael Di Tella, "Brazil 2003: Inflation Targeting and Debt Dynamics," HBS No. 704-028, February 3, 2004.

73 For more on capital controls, see Laura Alfaro and Rafael Di Tella, "Capital Controls in Chile in the 1990s (A)," HBS No. 705-031, March 8, 2005; Rawi Abdelal and Laura Alfaro, "Malaysia: Capital and Control," HBS No. 702-040, April 15, 2002; and Rawi Abdelal and Laura Alfaro, "Capital Controls," HBS No. 702-082, April 3, 2002.

Capital Flows Between Rich and Poor Countries

HARVARD | BUSINESS | SCHOOL

9-707-029
REV: JULY 17, 2007

LAURA ALFARO
ERIC WERKER
RENEE KIM

Aid, Debt Relief, and Trade: An Agenda for Fighting World Poverty (A)

You may say I'm a dreamer. But I am not the only one.

—John Lennon, 1971

At the 2005 Group of Eight (G8) summit in Gleneagles, Scotland, leaders of Canada, France, Germany, Italy, Japan, Russia, the United Kingdom, and the United States called on the International Monetary Fund (IMF) and the World Bank to forgive 100% of their debt claims on 18 of the world's poorest countries. In the biggest African aid deal in history, the G8 also agreed to double aid to Africa by 2010. The announcement followed the heels of a pledge by the EU-15[1] to increase aid to the developing world to 0.7% of their collective gross domestic product (GDP) by 2015. In the spirit of helping to end world poverty, G8 leaders also promised to open their markets to freer trade for products from heavily indebted poor countries (HIPCs, see **Exhibit 1** for the list of countries). As British Prime Minister Tony Blair said of the Gleneagles declaration: "It isn't the end of poverty . . . but it is the hope that it can be ended. It isn't all everyone wanted, but it is progress—real and achievable progress."[2]

HIPC members, it was believed, owed more money to their creditors than they could ever repay (see **Exhibit 2**). Many believed debt forgiveness was the only way to promote investment and growth in highly indebted countries. Others questioned whether debt relief could help eradicate poverty. According to a report by the National Bureau of Economic Research, a U.S.-based nonprofit economic research institution, "Debt relief is unlikely to help the world's poorest countries, because . . . their main difficulty is not debt overhang but an absence of functional economic institutions that provide the foundation for profitable investment and growth."[3]

To Kenneth Rogoff, former IMF chief economist and Harvard professor, the main beneficiaries of the Gleneagles debt-relief proposal were the rich countries that garnered good political press at a trivial cost.[4] "At first glance, it seems incredibly generous and statesman-like for G8 leaders to endorse debt relief for the world's poorest nations. But no one really expects the debts to be paid anyway," noted Rogoff. "If the G8 are serious about helping the poor countries, they should start with finding a reliable way to support grant aid and promote accountability for donors and recipients, not debt relief."[5]

Professors Laura Alfaro and Eric Werker and Research Associate Renee Kim prepared this case. HBS cases are developed solely as the basis for class discussion. Cases are not intended to serve as endorsements, sources of primary data, or illustrations of effective or ineffective management.

Jeffrey Sachs, director of the Earth Institute at Columbia University, concurred, asserting that aid was the only way to extract many of the poorest countries from their plight: "When they [people] are utterly destitute, they need their entire income, or more, just to survive. This is the main reason why the poorest are most prone to becoming trapped with low or negative economic growth rates. They are too poor to save for the future and thereby accumulate the capital that could pull them out of their current misery."[6] In the 1990s, Mozambique's total debt service, for example, was 34.5% of exports, while gross savings were a mere 4.8% of GDP.[7] Nicaragua's total debt service was even higher at 38.7% of GDP, while gross savings were –0.9% of GDP.[8] Without sufficient savings, countries could not overcome their shortage of capital.

Others questioned whether more aid would really help the poor. Critics argued that HIPCs had the resources to meet their obligation but had squandered aid funds through poor project design and administration, corrupt politics, and unscrupulous officials. William Easterly, former World Bank official, pointed to the case of Tanzania, where foreign donors spent $2 billion over 20 years to build roads, achieving no improvement in the road network, just growth in bureaucracy.[9] Others noted the example of countries such as China and India, which were growing rapidly without substantial aid and were likely to meet the United Nations' Millennium Development Goals to combat poverty and hunger (see **Appendix A**).

Thus, the G8's announcement at Gleneagles led to several questions: Could aid flows help poor nations break out of poverty? Could debt relief open the door to growth and investment? What obligations did rich countries have to assist the poor?

Postwar International Aid

New Institutions, New Visions

The end of World War II brought world leaders together to restore international financial stability and peace. The IMF and the World Bank were conceived at the 1944 Bretton Woods Conference on the premise that postwar peace would fail if the world economy was not rebuilt. The World Bank would lend internationally to facilitate postwar economic development, while the IMF would stabilize and regulate international monetary exchange (see **Appendix B** for more on the main international financial institutions, or IFIs). In 1947, the General Agreement on Tariffs and Trade (GATT), a set of international laws designed to liberalize trade by reducing tariffs, was established on the premise that free trade would help economic revival.

Launched in 1945, the UN gave the world a forum whereby international grievances—and ultimately the case for development—could be made on a peaceful, ongoing basis. Through the subsequent establishment of subsidiary agencies such as the United Nations International Children's Emergency Fund (UNICEF) in 1946, the World Health Organization (WHO) in 1948, and the UN Development Program in 1965, the UN came to play a direct and substantial role in poverty alleviation, public health, and economic growth.

Yet the newly created financial institutions faced challenges early on. After two years of lending to Europe, including the World Bank's first loan to Credit National of France (worth $250 million), one of the largest loans in real terms made by the bank in its first 50 years,[10] the United States, frustrated with the bank's limitations, launched the Marshall Plan in 1947. Over the next four years, the Marshall Plan dispensed $13 billion in aid, about 1.1% of U.S. annual GDP at the time, to western Europe.[11] When defending the boldness of the Marshall Plan, former U.S. Senator Arthur

Vandenberg observed, "It does little good to extend a 15-foot rope to a man drowning 20 feet away."[12] The plan was widely hailed as a key factor behind Europe's rapid return to economic security and came to symbolize the potential benefits of bold foreign assistance.

As European recovery took hold in the 1950s, attention shifted toward developing countries. Intellectual support for development aid came from Evsey Domar's 1946 article "Capital Expansion, Rate of Growth, and Employment."[13] A Russian-born, Manchurian-raised MIT economist, Domar assumed that production capacity was proportional to the stock of capital (machinery) and called the difference between the required investment for targeted growth and the country's savings "the financing gap." Private financing was assumed to be unavailable to fill the gap, so donor agencies like the World Bank could meet the shortfall with foreign aid. Although Domar later explained that his theory was not applicable for long-term growth, the idea had already taken root in many circles.[14]

At the same time, the Soviet model of state economic planning, including administrative control of investment, became an important alternative model of economic development throughout the developing world. Apart from the complementarity of this approach with the communist and socialist political programs that many followers (voluntary or otherwise) of Soviet Russia adopted, state economic planning and state control over investment had an appeal to modernizing leaders faced with weak political and economic institutions.[15]

The deepening of the Cold War politicized both aid and trade, as the antagonists distributed significant volumes of funds and weaponry to help win and maintain the political support of developing nations. The United States was the biggest foreign-aid donor in the 1950s. Its foreign aid increased 25% in real terms during the Kennedy administration (1960–1963) and then reached a historical maximum of 0.6% of GDP under President Lyndon Johnson (1963–1968).[16] Loan volumes rose from the 1950s, with an increasing share going to low-income countries (see **Exhibits 3, 4,** and **5**).

In 1960, the World Bank formed the International Development Association (IDA) to specifically provide loans with generous terms to the poorest countries. The IDA's creation represented emerging acknowledgement that the focus of aid should be on poverty alleviation, with an emphasis on those most in need.[17]

Many governments in poor countries welcomed foreign aid and borrowed heavily, trying to industrialize quickly though import substitution. They typically invested in infrastructure and capital-intensive industries, protecting domestic markets from international competition with high tariff and nontariff barriers.

Oil Shocks, Debt Buildup

The quadrupling of oil prices in the early 1970s hurt countries around the world. Many developing countries borrowed heavily to stay afloat. The decade also marked the end of continuous growth in the West and the generous aid flows seen in previous years.

During this period, the IMF and the World Bank extended their mandate. The IMF offered short-term loans to help countries cope with increased oil costs. Embracing the IDA's agenda, the World Bank in 1973 announced a new "basic needs" approach to development that targeted poverty reduction rather than economic growth. Then-World Bank President Robert McNamara called on nations to "give greater priority to establishing growth targets in terms of essential human needs; in terms of nutrition, housing, health, literacy and employment."[18] World Bank loans to support basic needs programs rose from 5% of total loans in 1968 to 30% by 1980.[19]

While the second oil price hike in 1979 further drove up the cost of developing countries' imports, commodity prices slumped in the early 1980s, lowering the value of their exports. To fill the gap, governments borrowed even more, increasing their existing debt to sometimes crushing levels. In Latin America, debt was accumulated at an increase of more than 20% a year.[20] Meanwhile, the U.S. Federal Reserve raised interest rates dramatically to curb inflation at home. Because many countries had borrowed at a variable interest rate, higher international interest rates automatically increased the cost of both new loans and payments on outstanding debt. The results in the developing world: recession, inflation, devaluation, rising interest rates, and real-wage reductions. In Latin America, the 1980s came to be called the "lost decade."

The 1980s: Debt Crises and Debt Relief

Unsolved debt problems, not debt per se, are an obstacle to investment. It is hard for a man to establish a relationship with a lender if the estranged wife keeps barging in claiming alimony. [21]

—Rudiger Dornbusch, Ford Professor of International Economics, MIT, 1993

The onset of the emerging market debt crisis was triggered by Mexico's announcement in August 1982 that it was no longer able to service its external debt. By October 1983, 27 nations, including 16 from Latin America, owed $239 billion and had either rescheduled their debts or were in negotiations to do so.[22] Mexico, Brazil, Venezuela, and Argentina together owed commercial banks $176 billion, about 74% of the total developing countries' debt at that time.[23]

However, even as late as the spring of 1982, there were few predictions that a full-blown debt crisis would erupt. The IMF's 1982 World Economic Outlook noted that despite a few payment problems, most Latin American economies would recover during that year and continue to borrow strongly from the international financial community.[24] The situation deteriorated, yet an official debt-relief plan backed by major creditor countries did not emerge. Rather, according to a former assistant director at the IMF, the strategy was to "coordinate" continued bank lending until IMF programs could put the debtor countries back on track.[25] In addition, by restructuring loans or postponing repayment, major Western banks did not actually have to write off loans or sacrifice earnings. However, by the mid-1980s, as the heavily indebted countries saw their purchasing power collapse, inflation soar, and unemployment surge, bankers and creditor countries were forced to recognize that the crisis was more serious than they had initially perceived.

The debt crisis gave the IMF a new role: lending to countries on the brink of default. The organization moved into the development field, establishing the Structural Adjustment Facility and the Enhanced Structural Adjustment Facility to extend medium-term loans with disbursement contingent upon macroeconomic adjustments such as currency devaluation, reduced state spending, and higher domestic interest rates. The World Bank initiated similar programs of its own, setting economic-austerity conditions on loans it disbursed to troubled countries. By the mid-1980s, however, some observers concluded that the austerity policies implemented by many borrowers in order to qualify for such loans only prolonged and deepened their debt problems.[26] Sebastian Edwards, former chief economist at the World Bank, pointed out, "The policy packages were designed for effectiveness in the short run, not for efficiency, income distribution, or welfare considerations."[27] The lack of progress in resolving the debt crisis sent policymakers back to the drawing board.

The Baker Plan In 1985, James Baker, U.S. Treasury secretary during the second Reagan administration, argued that economic growth in heavily indebted nations was a prerequisite for solving debt problems. Baker called upon IFIs to increase their lending to developing countries by up to 50%. Commercial banks were asked to contribute an additional $20 billion to finance market-oriented reforms for indebted countries sponsored by the World Bank. In return, the United States agreed to increase World Bank funds to support such programs. By encouraging reform and promoting growth, the Baker Plan aimed to restore private-capital inflows. Yet between 1982 and 1987, the 15 most heavily indebted countries demonstrated little or no growth under the Baker Plan, and their debt remained an important constraint on their economic performance.[28]

The Brady Plan The more prominent proposal came from Nicholas Brady, U.S. Treasury secretary under George H. W. Bush, who sought to annul debt through collaboration with private-sector lenders. In March 1989, Brady outlined his agenda to the financial community at a debt conference: "We renew our efforts to create and foster world growth. . . . These past seven years we have faced a major challenge in the international debt problem. . . . Ultimately, resolution depends on a great cooperative effort by the international community."[29] That is, resolution would result only if governments coordinated private-sector debt-relief efforts, forcing creditors to accept some losses.

Brady's proposal reflected academic arguments that debtor countries' economic hardships were prolonged due to the affected commercial banks' and governments' failure to agree on who should bear the costs of debtors' defaults. Brady's plan was also echoed by Princeton economist Paul Krugman, who argued that the developing countries' debt problem was a problem of *debt overhang*, "the presence of an existing 'inherited' debt sufficiently large that creditors do not expect with confidence to be fully repaid."[30] Excessive debt could force a government to use inflationary finance, raise taxes to meet debt payments, or possibly default in the future. This threat could hinder private investment and then undermine growth. Krugman argued that in such cases, both borrowers and lenders could gain from debt relief. If the implicit tax on investment fell, corporations and individuals in the borrowing country could make efficient investments that would promote growth.

Under the Brady Plan, 16 debtors—Argentina, Bolivia, Brazil, Bulgaria, Costa Rica, the Dominican Republic, Ecuador, Jordan, Mexico, Nigeria, Panama, Peru, the Philippines, Poland, Uruguay, and Venezuela—reached debt-relief agreements with their private creditors between 1989 and 1995.[31] The commercial banks wrote off a fraction of the debt owed to them, and the countries agreed to implement major economic reforms, such as reducing inflation and liberalizing trade. Countries issued "Brady bonds" with maturities up to 30 years, with repayment usually backed or collateralized by U.S. Treasury zero-coupon bonds. In total, over $60 billion of debt, about 5% of the Brady countries' GDP, was forgiven.[32] In the month of the Brady deal, the average country's debt jumped to 42 cents on the dollar in the secondary market, compared with 32 cents the year before the new debt plan.[33] In the five years after the agreements were signed, Brady countries received $210 billion in net capital inflows, GDP per capita grew from an average zero to 1.6% per year, and stock market indices rose 60%, increasing market value by $42 billion.[34] The Brady Plan also helped to revive the Third World debt market; the secondary market turnover for Brady bonds alone amounted to $1.58 trillion in 1995, while a total of $190 billion of debt was restructured into $37 billion worth of bond issues.[35] After the plan, the composition of capital flows in the Brady countries shifted away from the public sector to the private sector in the form of foreign direct investment (FDI) and equity (see **Exhibit 5**).

The 1990s: New Conditions, New Proposals

As Cold War superpower competition waned in the 1990s, attention to and support of developing-country allies also faded. Foreign aid declined largely due to three events: the end of the Cold War, fiscal problems of the Organization for Economic Co-operation and Development (OECD) countries, and growth in private-capital flows to developing countries. Financial assistance as a means to promote security and political interests lost its purpose after the Cold War. Furthermore, when countries such as the United States and Great Britain struggled with fiscal deficits, aid (although a small portion of OECD countries' spending) was cut. Foreign aid from OECD countries fell to 0.22% of their GNP in 1997, the smallest share of their GNP since comparable statistics were compiled in the 1950s.[36]

As the world's poorest countries suffered from low, sometimes negative growth rates, major anti-poverty movements took place around the world, such as the Jubilee 2000 Campaign. Started by British Christian aid groups, the campaign demanded that creditors cancel all HIPC debts and that debtors use the resulting savings to fight poverty. Many advocators believed that by forcing creditors to accept losses, debt relief would remove the uncertainty associated with debt issues to pave the way for new capital inflows and improve the living standards in poor countries. The movement gained support from over 24 million petitioners and was endorsed by celebrities including Irish rock singer Bono and spiritual leaders such as Pope John Paul II and the Dalai Lama.[37]

Donors that continued to distribute foreign aid into the 1990s increasingly emphasized good governance, human rights, democratization, participatory development, transparency and accountability, and environmental issues. Among the IFIs, stabilization and adjustment remained priorities in the first half of the 1990s, despite their internal debates over the appropriate development roles of state and market. The question of the effectiveness of aid gained greater prominence as most of sub-Saharan Africa showed poor economic growth, coupled with reports that indicated aid did little to help promote growth in the absence of sound economic and government policies (see **Exhibits 6** and **7**).[38] Amid criticisms, the World Bank tried to improve the effectiveness of aid and encourage development in recipient countries by launching the HIPC Initiative.

The HIPC Initiative

While many countries under the Brady Plan regained stability and growth and initiated partially successful economic reforms, other heavily indebted countries failed to grow. By 1992, the present value of the debt from the 33 most indebted low-income countries had more than doubled in 10 years to over six times their annual exports.[39]

In 1996, the World Bank and the IMF launched the HIPC Initiative. The plan called on all creditors, including multilateral ones, to provide a new start to the poorest and most heavily indebted countries by cutting down their excessive debt burdens to a more manageable level. To qualify for debt relief, a country had to meet two conditions: GNP per capita below $695, and a debt burden deemed "unsustainable" after full use of Paris Club debt-relief mechanisms. (The Paris Club was an informal voluntary group of 19 countries that sought coordinated solutions when a debtor nation faced payment difficulties).[40] In 1998, the 41 countries that met these criteria owed $221 billion, of which about a fifth was owed to international financial institutions.[41]

Under the original framework of the HIPC Initiative, only six countries reached their "completion points" to receive irrevocable debt relief for implementing IFI-dictated economic reforms. Because the results were so limited, an enhanced HIPC initiative was launched in 1999 to "provide deeper and faster debt relief to a larger group of countries," such as reducing the threshold that qualified a country's debt burden as "unsustainable."[42]

However, the 22 countries that received debt relief by the year 2000 experienced almost the same growth rates as the 16 countries that had not.[43] There was little change in the post-implementation period between 2001 and 2003 as well. Most HIPC countries lagged behind the rest of the world in many development indicators (see **Exhibit 8**); they also performed dismally in global surveys of corruption and competitiveness (see **Exhibits 9** and **10**). Researchers argued that HIPCs lacked the economic institutions for growth and investment to be successful compared to the more developed Brady countries.[44] "Debt reduction alone is not a sufficient instrument to affect the multiple drivers of debt sustainability," the World Bank concluded. "Sustained improvements in export diversification, fiscal management, the terms of new financing, and public debt management are also needed, measures that are outside the ambit of the HIPC Initiative."[45]

The Gleneagles Summit

The crises of poverty and indebtedness were particularly acute in Africa. As the challenges Africa faced started to gather greater support at the yearly G8 summits, OECD aid to sub-Saharan Africa rose to $23.7 billion in 2003 from $13.8 billion two years prior.[46] Describing the situation in Africa as a "scar on the conscience of the world," in February 2004 British Prime Minister Blair set up a Commission for Africa consisting of G8 members and African governments to attract foreign aid, liberalize trade, and provide debt relief.[47] The commission's recommendations, which framed Britain's agenda at Gleneagles, were subsequently endorsed by Germany and France at the January 2005 World Economic Forum. Envisioning a "Marshall Plan" for Africa, Blair believed that Africa was a problem "beyond the power of any single country . . . a solution requires coordinated international action and, above all, leadership, which the G8 is uniquely placed to give."[48]

Through the Multilateral Debt Relief Initiative (MDRI), the July 2005 G8 summit at Gleneagles promoted the forgiveness of as much as $55 billion in debt owed to three multilateral lending agencies—the IMF, the World Bank, and the African Development Fund. The eligible countries were those that had reached, or would reach, the "completion point" under the HIPC Initiative.[49] Debt relief would begin after compliance with the most recent economic programs prescribed by the World Bank and the IMF. The World Bank expected the MDRI to effectively double the volume of debt relief already under way from the enhanced HIPC initiative.[50] In addition, to ensure that the debt forgiveness would not compromise the organizations' financing capacity, the G8 agreed to provide additional funds to the institutions.

The OECD stated that increased aid commitments made at the summit would add about $50 billion annually by 2010 to the $79 billion the biggest donor countries spent on aid in 2004.[51] Of the $50 billion, Africa would get about half, roughly doubling aid receipts.

The G8 communiqué also promised a substantial reduction in trade-distorting agricultural subsidies, open markets for HIPC products, significant aid for trade, and policy space for HIPC nations to develop and direct their own trade and development strategies. In addition, they committed to providing "nearly universal" access to life-saving treatment to fight HIV/AIDS and to work toward an "AIDS-free generation in Africa."

Concluded Gordon Brown, U.K. Chancellor of the Exchequer: "We are talking about a new deal between the rich countries and poor countries of the world. We will ask other countries to follow and we will continue the campaign until we succeed so that there is debt relief for all the poor countries of the world. Our cause requires more than a week's work at Gleneagles; it requires a lifetime's work crusading for social justice."[52]

Reactions and Debate

We don't have capital . . . we need assistance because we have a poor level of infrastructure. Foreign aid is one way for us to get businesses that can employ some workers and bring down unemployment. Foreign aid gives us capital that can be used for development.[53]

—Julio Cabral Maboula, a taxi driver in Mozambique, 2006

Nicaragua's officials don't repay the debt because they know they can get away with it.[54]

—Dona Berta, domestic worker, Nicaragua, 2006

The commitments made by the G8 pleased many campaigners; the celebrities and nongovernmental organizations (NGOs) that had pushed for such steps considered it a big victory. Nigeria's President Olusegun Obasanjo, head of the African Union in 2005, called the deal a "breakthrough" with African issues being tackled "realistically,"[55] while South African President Thabo Mbeki said, "The most important thing about the decisions of the G8 is that they have put specific sums of money and specific time frames to a programme that, in reality, we had agreed to some time back."[56]

On the other hand, the Catholic Agency for Overseas Development stated that the commitments did not justify the "hope and hype" regarding the summit, and ActionAid noted the "yawning gulf between expectations raised and policy promises delivered."[57] Jubilee USA pointed out that the amount of promised debt cancellation was "wholly insufficient" for countries to meet the UN's Millennium Development Goals.[58] Furthermore, skeptics pointed out failures in aid administration and the harmful influence of both international and domestic political considerations on aid disbursal and poverty alleviation. In Rogoff's opinion, the debt relief proposal of Gleneagles was a farce, or "empty gesture," in that it did not include "a better framework for future aid flows."[59]

No debt overhang Some critics argued that debt relief would do little to address the real problem behind HIPCs' poor economic status—the lack of roads, schools, hospitals, and clean water as well as basic institutions that could stimulate investment and growth.[60] Private-capital flows had never been a significant fraction of total net resources for HIPCs, nor did the debt relief provided under previous initiatives lead to greater flows of FDI; in fact, official flows, such as grants, became more important (see **Exhibit 5**). Another concern was that debt relief could crowd out aid, as the flow of aid had decreased significantly with the previous HIPC initiative.[61]

Effectiveness of aid Empirical studies of the effects of aid on growth in poor countries reached mixed conclusions. Some studies found aid to have a limited effect on growth, but the magnitude of the influence depended on the initial country conditions in terms of business environment and other factors.[62] In an influential paper, World Bank economists found that aid to poor countries could be effective in promoting growth if a country's fiscal, monetary, and trade policies were sound.[63] (Further extension of the data set, however, demonstrated the effects of that study to be less than robust.)[64]

Research by former chief economist at the IMF Raghuram Rajan and his IMF colleague Arvind Subramanian suggested that aid inflows had systematically adverse effects on a country's competitiveness, as reflected in a decline in the share of labor-intensive and tradable industries in the manufacturing sector.[65] They found evidence suggesting that these effects stemmed from overvaluation of the real exchange rate caused by aid inflows. In an example of so-called Dutch disease, aid flows could harm the noncommodity sectors of the economy.

Others argued that donor agencies had favored development projects that were overly expensive and not sustainable, such as massive dams that had been environmentally dubious and expensive for recipient nations to maintain.

Failures in administration A crescendo of voices had begun to lay blame at the foot of the donors. In the mid-1990s, "50 years is enough" became a rallying cry by academics, NGOs, and IFI skeptics arguing that the World Bank and the IMF should be dismantled. In November 1998, the U.S. Congress established a commission to evaluate Washington's future policy toward IFIs. The commission's results, known as the "Meltzer Report," revealed that the World Bank had a 73% project failure rate in Africa by the bank's own criteria.[66] Despite its claims of helping the poorest countries, more than two-thirds of the World Bank's nonaid resources went to 11 countries with easy access to capital markets.[67]

The Meltzer Report argued that donors suffered from large bureaucracies and undermined the effectiveness of their own programs through a failure to coordinate with other donors or ineffective monitoring and evaluation systems.[68] Former World Bank President James Wolfensohn conceded, "There is a large pick-up to be had in just coordinating and better implementing what the development community is doing already."[69]

Other critics highlighted the fact that more money needed to flow to the actual recipient because a significant amount never reached its intended objectives. Of every dollar given to Africa, an estimated 16% went to consultants from donor countries, 26% went into emergency aid and relief operations, and 14% went into debt servicing.[70] How much of the remaining 40% escaped patronage channels to benefit the intended recipients was not known.

Beyond coordination, other problems were cited. According to Easterly, foreign aid was dominated by "planners" who faced complex information problems in administering grand projects in the absence of local institutions and organizations: "Planners at the global top simply don't know what, when, and where to give to poor people at the global bottom."[71] Multiple agencies performed multiple tasks; no one was accountable for their performance or output. Instead, Easterly advocated that donors rely on social/policy entrepreneurs he called "searchers" to find grassroots solutions to poverty in a piecemeal fashion. Others agreed that donor agencies and countries did not necessarily know what was best and that aid would be more effective if there were greater "country ownership" or broader participation among government and community groups in recipient countries in setting priorities and designing programs.[72]

Primacy of politics Politics was another factor influencing aid types, amounts, recipients, and—indirectly—the success or failure of aid efforts. Up to half of U.S. bilateral aid was given as security-supporting assistance, for example, and was allocated on the basis of U.S. strategic goals, not recipient needs. In 2004, the United States spent 90% of its $1 billion in food aid on U.S. produce.[73] The amount of U.S. aid a country received also rose when that country joined the UN Security Council as a rotating member.[74] France and Britain favored their former colonies. As a result, some aid money ended up in the hands of dictators and regimes that did not prioritize development or the public interest (see **Exhibits 11** and **12**).[75]

In the new millennium, the United States and Europe became concerned that a rising China was again politicizing aid, particularly in Africa. China's President Hu Jintao announced in 2005 that his government would provide $10 billion in preferential loans and export credits over three years to help poor nations that imported Chinese products to improve their infrastructure. This triggered worries that such investments would be made without regard to the abuses perpetrated by recipient governments.[76] For example, China invested in the Sudan, which was accused of war crimes against its own people, and provided loans to Angola, whose government was criticized for rejecting greater scrutiny of its finances.[77] But the strongest response World Bank President Paul Wolfowitz could muster was a plea: "We hope that new development partners will work together with the old to satisfy the real needs of the population, so money is used for development and not for pursuing political needs."[78]

Not enough funding? Other critics suggested that the $2.3 trillion in aid given to developing countries by the West needed to be put in context. Spread over 50 years, this amount averaged $46 billion annually. Excluding the aid going to middle-income countries such as Israel, Egypt, and Jordan, annual HIPC aid averaged $26 billion, or $14 per person per year in low-income countries.[79]

According to economist Jeffrey Sachs, several developing countries were too poor to grow and needed substantial additional assistance: "The poorest countries are stuck in a 'poverty trap' from which they cannot escape without an aid-financed big push."[80] Noble Prize winner and MIT economist Paul Samuelson had made a similar argument: "[The backward nations] cannot get their heads above the water because their production is so low that they can spare nothing for the capital formation by which their standard of living could be raised."[81] Benjamin Mkapa, president of Tanzania, advocated for total debt cancellation for poor countries because it was "a scandal that we are forced to choose between basic health and education for our people and repaying historical debt."[82]

Successful cases of aid Despite the criticisms over aid, several programs designed by IFIs had been hailed as successes by the World Bank, such as those in Botswana in the 1960s, Bolivia in the 1980s, and Uganda in the 1990s.[83] In 1986, when President Museveni took over leadership of Uganda after a civil war, the nation was overwhelmed with economic problems ranging from inflation to budget deficits. With guidance from the IMF and the World Bank, Uganda adopted a macroeconomic stabilization and growth program that involved liberalization of its markets and a restrictive fiscal policy.[84] Uganda then curbed inflation and achieved an annual per capita growth rate of 3.3%, consistently ranking among the top economic performers in Africa.[85] In the case of Bolivia, amid hyperinflation in the 1980s, the country pursued structural reform programs as recommended by the "Washington consensus," which the World Bank believed directly helped to curb inflation, liberalize trade, and reform taxes.

Specific programs designated to fight poverty had thrived on a global scale as well. Sachs cited Asia's "green revolution" (whereby scientifically improved wheat and rice yields helped to end hunger in the region); the eradication of small pox; campaigns against malaria, polio, and African river blindness; the spread of family planning; and the mobile phone revolution in Bangladesh as examples of small programs that were eventually scaled up and benefited the poor around the globe.[86] Others noted that past conditions and incentives tied to aid brought proper trade policies, legal reforms, good governance, private entrepreneurship, and investment in health and education.[87]

The Search for New Approaches

Greater Liberalization of Trade

The World Bank estimated that full global trade liberalization would increase the income of sub-Saharan African countries by 1.1% of their GDP, greater than the benefit for high-income countries and higher than the average for developing countries. Another study suggested full trade liberalization would lift 127 million people, over 10% of the world's very poor, out of extreme poverty.[88]

While the United States and Europe offered large cuts in farm aid and export subsidies at the World Trade Organization talks in Hong Kong in 2005, by 2006 the Doha Round was on the brink of collapse. Many believed that a Doha deal could bring enhanced trade with the potential to lift millions of HIPC citizens out of poverty, and a vast chorus of world leaders warned that the failure of the Doha talks would lead to a lost opportunity to alleviate poverty in developing countries.[89]

An Oxfam report complained, "The US and EU promised they would open their markets to agriculture and industrial goods from developing countries, but have created so many loopholes they are actually offering very little."[90] Indeed, according to Nobel prize-winning economist Joseph Stiglitz, the last round of trade negotiations (the Uruguay Round) had actually left the poorest countries worse off. He noted:

> While the developing countries were forced to open their markets and eliminate subsidies, the advanced developed countries continued to subsidize agriculture and kept trade barriers against those products which are central to the economies of the developing world. Rich countries collect tariffs four times higher on their imports from poor countries than on imports from other rich countries.[91]

Specific trade agreements to help HIPCs had been passed, such as the 2000 U.S. African Growth and Opportunity Act (AGOA). Extended until 2015, AGOA eliminated tariffs on more than 6,000 products for 37 African countries.[92] Yet sub-Saharan Africa accounted for a little over 1% of U.S. exports and slightly more than 2% of U.S. imports.[93] Of total AGOA imports by the United States, 92% were petroleum products. Non-oil exports actually fell by 16% in 2005. As African countries still exported only a fraction of the products eligible for entry duty free, data indicated that AGOA was far from a panacea.

Sachs argued that free trade in agriculture was not a solution for poor countries. He believed that many developing countries were net food importers and if Europe and America cut off subsidies to their own producers, higher food prices could harm them more than help them. Africa, for example, would unambiguously benefit from trade liberalization in tropical products (cotton, sugar, bananas), but subsidies for these products were only a small part of the reported $300 billion in agricultural support for farmers in rich countries. Large food exporters such as the United States, Canada, Argentina, Brazil, and Australia would benefit the most from freer agricultural trade, not the HIPCs.[94] Stiglitz also questioned the benefits of simply lowering barriers: "Market access is not enough. Without assistance to overcome gaps in infrastructure, boost product quality and connect to international supply chains, tariff cuts have little effect on trade for the poorest nations."[95]

Aid Based on Selective Criteria

The idea that only good governments with strong institutions could use aid effectively harked back to an idea pushed by the World Bank since the early 1990s.[96] On the basis of this concept, the United States launched the Millennium Challenge Account (MCA) in 2004. Run by the Millennium Challenge Corporation, the MCA provided aid to countries that ruled justly, invested in their citizens, and encouraged economic freedom. Countries' "scorecards" were made public, unlike the decisions made by other aid agencies. According to the *Economist*, the MCA may have encouraged countries to reform to qualify for aid in the future; it was also to be judged not by the amount of dollars it handed out but by the changes aid initiated in the recipient countries.[97]

Grants, not Loans

Others simply advocated for more grants, arguing that development-debt-financed projects did not generate high returns, loans were unlikely to be repaid, and funds were not well allocated by development banks in the first place.[98] For some experts, a shift to grants would increase transparency (making subsidies explicit) and minimize loan "pushing" that simply expanded already troubled countries' debt loads.[99] Another goal was to break the cycle of lending and debt forgiveness that had overshadowed the poorest countries' balance sheets for the previous few decades. Increasingly, donors had tried to improve the composition of aid by favoring more grants over loans. Bilateral aid grants more than doubled, to about $53 billion in 2005 from $25 billion in 1997.[100]

Increasing Role of Private Funding

Private funding started to play a significant role in global development efforts, such as in scientific breakthroughs. Established in 1913, the Rockefeller Foundation had sponsored research leading to the discovery of a yellow-fever vaccine in 1928 and improved crop yields in the developing world. The Bill and Melinda Gates Foundation, created in 2000, financed extensive research into AIDS, tuberculosis, malaria, and other diseases that afflicted the poor. U.S. private international aid, including remittances, was estimated to be around $62 billion, more than three and a half times the official development assistance given by the U.S. government in 2003.[101]

Despite their large endowments, U.S. foundations donated only 5.5% of their assets to charity annually, a number barely above the legal minimum of 5%, according to research by Harvard professors Michael Porter and Mark Kramer. The rest was invested "to create financial, not social, returns."[102] It remained to be seen whether the privately funded sources of development aid were better managed and more effective at eliminating poverty and disease than official donor agencies.

Migration of Workers

Yet another alternative was to allow a greater mobility of workers. Migration—particularly temporary schemes to allow workers from developing countries to work on short-term projects in rich countries—could enable workers from poor countries to fill labor shortages in rich countries and send part of their pay back to their families. Indeed, the flow of remittances from migrant workers in rich countries already exceeded aid flows from rich countries.[103] However, the issue was a politically sensitive one in developed countries.

The Next Step

With inequality between nations at an all-time high, the plight of poor countries had become impossible to ignore. According to the World Bank, more than 1 billion people lived in extreme poverty, defined as living on less than $1 a day (see **Exhibits 13** and **14**).[104] There were 2.6 billion people who lived on less than $2 a day.[105] Ten million children died annually from easily prevented diseases; 3 million died of AIDS each year.[106] One billion people lacked access to clean water, and 2 billion lacked access to sanitation.[107] Meanwhile, the gap between rich and poor countries grew ever wider (see **Exhibit 15**).

Foreign aid and debt relief were global redistribution on a potentially massive scale. The mixed track record of both donors and of HIPC borrowers over the previous six decades, however, had left many questioning their ability to lift poor countries out of poverty. Had aid failed to achieve its purposes? Should the rich countries keep trying to help the poor through traditional aid and debt-relief measures? If so, what was the best way to improve the effectiveness of aid?

Exhibit 1 Low-Income and Brady Countries, as of October 2006

Low-Income Countries[a]			Brady Countries[b]
HIPCs [c,d] *Receiving debt relief*	Other HIPCs	Non-HIPCs	
Benin	Burundi	Bangladesh	Argentina
Bolivia	Central African Republic	Bhutan	Bolivia
Burkina Faso	Chad	Cambodia	Brazil
Cameroon	Comoros	India	Bulgaria
Ethiopia	Côte d'Ivoire	Kenya	Costa Rica
Ghana	Democratic Republic of Congo	Lao PDR	Dominican Republic
Guyana	Eritrea	Lesotho	Ecuador
Honduras	Guinea	Moldova	Jordan
Madagascar	Guinea-Bissau	Mongolia	Mexico
Malawi	Haiti	Myanmar	Nigeria
Mali	Kyrgyz Republic	Niger	Panama
Mauritania	Liberia	Nigeria	Peru
Mozambique	Nepal	Pakistan	Philippines
Nicaragua	Republic of Congo	Papua New Guinea	Poland
Níger	São Tomé Príncipe	Solomon Islands	Uruguay
Rwanda	Sierra Leone	Tajikistan	Venezuela
Senegal	Somalia	Uzbekistan	
Tanzania	Sudan	Vietnam	
Uganda	The Gambia	Yemen, Rep.	
Zambia	Togo	Zimbabwe	

Source: World Bank, "Heavily Indebted Poor Countries," as of October 2006, http://go.worldbank.org/4IMVXTQ090, accessed December 1, 2006, and compiled by casewriter using World Development Indicators database, accessed December 1, 2006; and Serkan Arslanalp and Peter Blair Henry, "Is Debt Relief Efficient?" *The Journal of Finance* 60 (April 2005): 1022.

[a]Low-income countries are those with 2004 GNI per capita of US$825 or less.

[b]Brady countries are those which suffered from excessive debt during the 1980s that was alleviated by the relief plan engineered by former U.S. Treasury Secretary Nicholas Brady, under which international commercial banks agreed to write down a substantial fraction of the countries' debt.

[c]Heavily indebted poor countries. By 1999, the following countries were not part of HIPC: The Gambia, Comoros, Eritrea, Haiti, Kyrgyz Rep., and Nepal. Another six countries (Angola, Kenya, Myanmar, Yemen, Vietnam, and Equatorial Guinea) did not participate but exited the program afterwards.

[d]By 2002, the following countries were not part of HIPC: Eritrea, Haiti, Kyrgyz Rep., and Nepal, whereas Myanmar and Lao PDF participated in the 2002 initiative, then exited afterwards.

Exhibit 2 External Debt and Foreign Direct Investment by Region

	Sub-Saharan Africa	East Asia and Pacific	Middle East and North Africa	Latin America and Caribbean
Total External Debt (billion US$)				
1970	6.92	8.58	4.82	32.56
1980	60.67	60.73	64.48	242.82
1990	176.80	234.08	139.54	444.63
2000	211.00	498.03	145.23	758.67
2004	235.06	588.89	163.93	778.97
Total External Debt (as % GDP)				
1970	10.65	6.91	13.40	19.80
1980	21.98	16.55	29.17	33.00
1990	57.73	35.67	50.35	40.39
2000	62.65	29.64	32.45	38.23
2004	44.43	22.38	29.81	38.35
Total External Debt (as % Exports)				
1970	53.60	...	39.53	176.43
1980	74.20	...	93.23	230.03
1990	221.57	139.74	159.57	258.23
2000	188.01	81.37	99.43	180.15
2004	131.16	54.21	73.03	145.90
Owed to private creditors (billion US$)				
1970	1.57	1.00	1.11	7.65
1980	16.39	18.23	26.42	99.46
1990	35.69	68.27	45.57	206.24
2000	26.17	99.96	26.54	259.78
2004	26.32	84.37	39.60	289.28
Foreign Direct Investment Net Flows (% of GDP)				
1970	0.17	0.17	0.40	0.73
1980	0.05	0.38	0.69	0.87
1990	0.41	1.58	0.26	0.76
2000	1.96	2.60	1.08	4.04
2004	2.17	2.46	1.06	3.02
Total Debt Service (% of exports of goods, services, and income)				
1970	...	...	...	...
1980	7.46	...	14.77	36.35
1990	13.54	17.47	21.36	23.82
2000	11.57	11.35	13.19	38.62
2004	7.92	6.83	10.60	26.39

Source: Compiled by casewriter using World Development Indicators database, accessed January 2007, and Global Development Finance database, accessed January 2007.

Exhibit 3 Total U.S. Foreign Aid

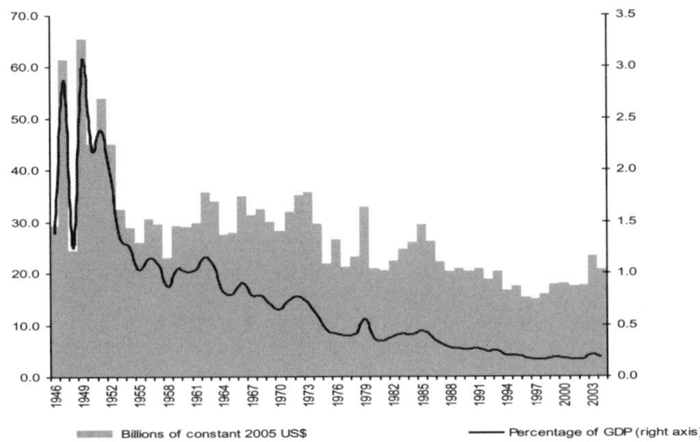

Source: Adapted from "Foreign Aid: An Introductory Overview of US Programs and Policy," CRS Report for Congress, January 19, 2005, p. 16, http://shelby.senate,gov/legislation/ForeignAid.pdf, accessed April 12, 2007.

Exhibit 4 Net Official Development Assistance

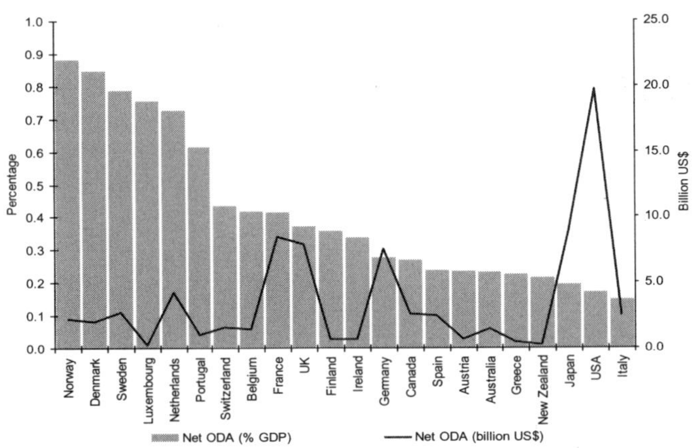

Source: Organization for Economic Co-operation and Development, http://www.oecd.org/dac/stats/dac/dcrannex, accessed April 5, 2007.

Exhibit 5 Annual Capital Flows by Group of Countries[a]

	1970–1979		1980–1989		1990–1999		2000–2005	
	Billions of U.S. Dollars	Percentage of GDP	Billions of U.S. Dollars	Percentage of GDP	Billions of U.S. Dollars	Percentage of GDP	Billions of U.S. Dollars	Percentage of GDP
HIPCs (all)[b]								
Net resource transfers[c]	**3.29**	**6.32**	**7.44**	**7.01**	**11.34**	**8.91**	**17.87**	**10.36**
New lending	3.66	7.07	7.86	7.55	7.84	6.12	9.54	5.76
Net Debt	3.56	6.82	8.06	7.73	6.47	5.07	6.30	3.79
Net FDI	0.11	0.25	-0.20	-0.18	1.36	1.03	3.22	1.96
Portfolio Equity	0.00	0.00	0.00	0.00	0.02	0.01	0.02	0.01
Grants	1.03	1.90	3.95	3.62	8.48	6.68	13.00	7.46
Total debt service (-)	1.37	2.61	4.33	4.12	4.94	3.87	4.51	2.73
HIPCs (receiving debt relief)[b]								
Net resource transfers	**1.63**	**6.75**	**4.84**	**8.24**	**8.16**	**10.88**	**12.26**	**12.08**
New lending	1.88	6.44	4.84	8.43	5.52	7.32	6.74	6.87
Net Debt	1.88	6.32	4.94	8.59	4.39	5.86	4.77	4.78
Net FDI	0.00	0.12	-0.10	-0.16	1.12	1.46	1.97	2.08
Portfolio Equity	0.00	0.00	0.00	0.00	0.01	0.01	0.00	0.00
Grants	0.60	2.32	2.32	3.81	5.77	7.72	8.47	8.23
Total debt service (-)	0.82	3.40	2.29	3.91	3.12	4.15	2.86	2.91
Brady Countries[b]								
Net resource transfers	**8.51**	**2.31**	**-9.85**	**-1.23**	**31.97**	**1.78**	**7.67**	**0.36**
New lending	21.05	5.58	31.05	3.94	105.11	6.06	158.94	7.64
Net Debt	20.08	5.25	30.46	3.88	72.43	4.18	120.01	5.75
Net FDI	0.96	0.33	0.47	0.05	24.47	1.35	35.36	1.74
Portfolio Equity	0.00	0.00	0.12	0.01	8.21	0.53	3.57	0.15
Grants	0.44	0.12	1.24	0.16	2.79	0.18	3.76	0.17
Total debt service (-)	12.97	3.39	42.13	5.33	75.92	4.46	155.02	7.46

Source: Compiled by casewriter using data on net resource flows and grants from the Global Development Finance 2006; data on GDP, aid, and total debt service from the World Development Indicators database, accessed January 2007.

[a]Aid includes both official development assistance (ODA) and official aid. Some net resource transfers may not add up precisely as some countries' complete disaggregated data was unavailable.

[b]See **Exhibit 1** for list of countries.

[c]Net resource transfers = new lending (debt + portfolio equity + foreign direct investment) + grants - debt service, where debt = net resource flows on long-term debt (excluding IMF), including the payments on profit remittances. Portfolio equity = sum of country funds, depository receipts (American or global), and direct purchases of shares by foreign investors. Foreign direct investment = sum of equity capital, reinvestment of earnings, other long- and short-term capital as shown in the balance of payments. Grants (exclude technical cooperation) = legally binding commitments that obligate a specific disbursement for which there is no repayment requirement. Debt service = sum of principal repayments and interest payments in the year specified.

Exhibit 6 Total Foreign Aid to Sub-Saharan Africa, 1965–2004[a]

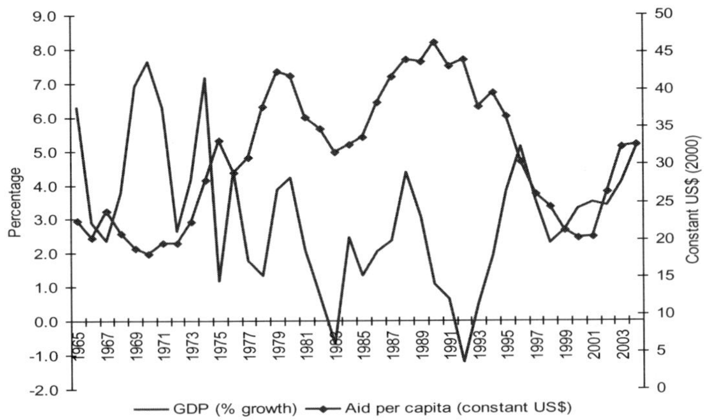

Source: Compiled by casewriter using World Development Indicators database, accessed January 2007.

[a]Sub-Saharan African countries are South Africa, Mauritius, Namibia, Botswana, Swaziland, Kenya, Seychelles, Ghana, Ethiopia, Zambia, Uganda, Nigeria, Malawi, Gambia, Lesotho, Cape Verde, Gabon, Benin, Mozambique, Cote d'Ivoire, Tanzania, Comoros, Senegal, Mauritania, Madagascar, Equatorial Guinea, Togo, Cameroon, Zimbabwe, Sudan, Mali, Angola, Guinea, Rwanda, Niger, Burkina Faso, Burundi, Central African Republic, Sierra Leone, Sao Tome and Principe, Eritrea, Congo Republic, Chad, Guinea-Bissau, Congo Dem. Republic.

Exhibit 7 GDP Growth and Poverty: Sub-Saharan Africa

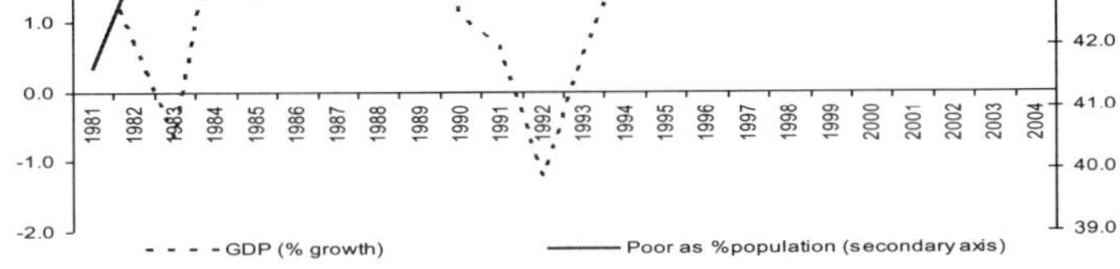

Source: Compiled by casewriter using World Development Indicators database, accessed January 2007.

Exhibit 8 Development Indicators by Country Group

	Year	HIPCs[a]	Sub-Saharan Africa	East Asia & Pacific	Europe & Central Asia	Latin America
Economic Indicators						
GDP per capita (constant 2000 US$)	2005	307.1	559.7	1,351.8	2,603.6	4,036.8
Population, total (million)	2005	554.2	741.4	1,869.5	1,885.3	551.4
Average GDP growth rate	2000–5	2.6	4.1	8.2	5.1	2.6
Average GDP growth rate	1990s	3.0	2.0	8.5	-1.7	3.0
Average GDP growth rate	1980s	1.7	2.2	7.8	..	1.7
Average GDP growth rate	1970s	5.6	4.0	6.5	..	5.6
Gross capital formation (% of GDP)	2004	19.8	19.0	34.4	23.3	21.0
Trade (% of GDP)	2004	59.1	62.7	82.4	82.7	45.5
Gross domestic savings (% of GDP)	2004	11.4	20.0	37.8	23.5	24.0
Inflation, consumer prices (annual %)	2005	8.9	8.7	..	..	7.2
Development Indicators						
School enrollment, secondary (% gross)	2004	22.3	29.8	70.9	90.5	84.7
Fertility rate, total (births per woman)	2004	5.3	5.3	2.0	1.6	2.5
Health expenditure, total (% of GDP)	2003	5.0	5.0	..	..	6.5
Households with television (%)	2002	12.8	14.8	79.6	91.8	88.2
Immunization, DPT (% of children ages 12–23 months)	2004	72.7	63.9	86.6	93.4	90.8
Improved sanitation facilities (% of population with access)	2004	33.0	37.0	50.6	85.4	77.2
Improved water source (% of population with access)	2004	57.2	56.2	78.5	91.9	91.0
Life expectancy at birth, total (years)	2004	49.1	46.2	70.3	68.8	72.2
Personal computers (per 1,000 people)	2004	8.2	15.1	38.2	109.7	92.7
Prevalence of HIV, total (% of population ages 15–49)	2005	4.2	6.2	0.2	0.7	0.6
Telephone mainlines (per 1,000 people)	2004	19.3	10.3	187.9	..	179.5

Source: Compiled by casewriter using World Development Indicators database, accessed January 2007, and based on casewriter's calculations.

[a]Heavily indebted poor countries.

Exhibit 9 2006 Corruption Perceptions Index (rank out of 159 countries; first to least corrupt)

Country Rank	Country	Country Rank	Country	Country Rank	Country
1	Finland	57	El Salvador	111	Nicaragua
	Iceland	59	Colombia		Paraguay
	New Zealand	60	Turkey		Timor-Leste
4	Denmark	61	Jamaica		Vietnam
5	Singapore		Poland		Yemen
6	Sweden	63	Lebanon		Zambia
7	Switzerland		Seychelles	121	Benin
8	Norway		Thailand		Gambia
9	Australia	66	Belize		Guyana
	Netherlands		Cuba		Honduras
11	Austria		Grenada		Nepal
	Luxembourg	69	Croatia		Philippines
	United Kingdom	70	Brazil		Russia
14	Canada		China		Rwanda
15	Hong Kong		Egypt		Swaziland
16	Germany		Ghana	130	Azerbaijan
17	Japan		India		Burundi
18	France		Mexico		Central African Republic
	Ireland		Peru		Ethiopia
20	Belgium		Saudi Arabia		Indonesia
	Chile		Senegal		Papua New Guinea
	USA	79	Burkina Faso		Togo
23	Spain		Lesotho		Zimbabwe
24	Barbados		Moldova	138	Cameroon
	Estonia		Morocco		Ecuador
26	Macao		Trinidad and Tobago		Niger
	Portugal	84	Algeria		Venezuela
28	Malta		Madagascar	142	Angola
	Slovenia		Mauritania		Congo, Republic
	Uruguay		Panama		Kenya
31	United Arab Emirates		Romania		Kyrgyzstan
32	Bhutan		Sri Lanka		Nigeria
	Qatar	90	Gabon		Pakistan
34	Israel		Serbia		Sierra Leone
	Taiwan		Suriname		Tajikistan
36	Bahrain	93	Argentina		Turkmenistan
37	Botswana		Armenia	151	Belarus
	Cyprus		Bosnia and Herzegovina		Cambodia
39	Oman		Eritrea		Cote d'Ivoire
40	Jordan		Syria		Equatorial Guinea
41	Hungary		Tanzania		Uzbekistan
42	Mauritius		Dominican Republic	156	Bangladesh
	South Korea	99	Georgia		Chad
44	Malaysia		Mali		Congo, Democratic Republic
45	Italy		Mongolia		Sudan
46	Czech Republic		Mozambique	160	Guinea
	Kuwait		Ukraine		Iraq
	Lithuania	105	Bolivia		Myanmar
49	Latvia		Iran	163	Haiti
	Slovakia		Libya		
51	South Africa		Macedonia		
	Tunisia		Malawi		
53	Dominica		Uganda		
54	Greece	111	Albania		
55	Costa Rica		Guatemala		
	Namibia		Kazakhstan		
57	Bulgaria		Laos		

Source: Transparency International, http://www.transparency.org/policy_research/surveys_indices/global/cpi, accessed March 27, 2007.

Exhibit 10 Global Competitiveness (ranking out of 117 countries)

Country	Ranking	Country	Ranking
Finland	1	Colombia	57
United States	2	Bulgaria	58
Sweden	3	Ghana	59
Denmark	4	Kazakhstan	61
Taiwan	5	Croatia	62
Singapore	6	Namibia	63
Iceland	7	Costa Rica	64
Switzerland	8	Brazil	65
Norway	9	Turkey	66
Australia	10	Romania	67
Netherlands	11	Azerbaijan	69
Japan	12	Tanzania	71
United Kingdom	13	Argentina	72
Canada	14	Panama	73
Germany	15	Indonesia	74
New Zealand	16	Russia	75
South Korea	17	Morocco	76
UAE	18	Philippines	77
Qatar	19	Algeria	78
Estonia	20	Armenia	79
Austria	21	Serbia-Montenegro	80
Chile	23	Vietnam	81
Malaysia	24	Pakistan	83
Israel	27	Ukraine	84
Hong Kong	28	Macedonia	85
Spain	29	Uganda	87
France	30	Nigeria	88
Belgium	31	Venezuela	89
Slovenia	32	Mali	90
Kuwait	33	Mozambique	91
Thailand	36	Kenya	92
Czech Republic	38	Gambia	94
Hungary	39	Bosnia and Herzegovina	95
Tunisia	40	Albania	100
Slovakia	41	Dominican Republic	102
South Africa	42	Tajikistan	104
Lithuania	43	Malawi	105
Latvia	44	Ethiopia	106
Greece	46	Madagascar	107
Italy	47	East Timor	108
Botswana	48	Zimbabwe	109
China	49	Bangladesh	110
India	50	Cameroon	111
Poland	51	Cambodia	112
Mauritius	52	Benin	114
Uruguay	54	Kyrgyzstan	116
Mexico	55	Chad	117
El Salvador	56		

Source: World Economic Forum, "Global Competitiveness Report," September 28, 2005, http://www.weforum.org/en/initiatives/gcp/Global%20Competitiveness%20Report/index.htm, accessed January 10, 2007.

Exhibit 11 Debt That Can Be Attributed to Dictators, in Billions of U.S. Dollars

Country	Leader	Debt Attributed to Dictators	External Debt 1999	Total GDP 1999
Indonesia	Suharto	126	151.22	140.00
Brazil	Military	100	245.21	536.63
Argentina	Military	65	145.66	283.52
Philippines	Marcos	40	58.32	76.16
Syria	Assad	22	22.37	15.87
South Africa	Apartheid	22	23.91	133.18
Pakistan	Military	19	33.89	62.97
Sudan	Nimeiry/al-Mahdi	17	16.13	10.68
Thailand	Military	14	96.77	122.34
Nigeria	Buhari/Abacha	14	29.13	34.78
Chile	Pinochet	13	34.81	73.00
Zaire/Congo	Mobutu	13	12.05	4.71
Algeria	Military	5	28.00	47.59
Iran	Shah	5	9.91	105.52
Kenya	Moi	4	6.47	12.90
Ethiopia	Mariam	4	5.54	7.62
Bolivia	Military	3	5.55	8.28
Somalia	Siad Barre	2	2.61	NA
Paraguay	Stroessner	2	3.38	7.74
Malawi	Banda	2	2.74	1.78
El Salvador	Military	1	3.79	12.46
Liberia	Doe	1	2.08	0.44
Haiti	Duvalier	1	1.19	4.20

Source: Compiled by casewriter using Joseph Hanlon, "Defining "Illegitimate Debt," in *Sovereign Debt at the Crossroads*, eds. Chris Jochnick et al. (New York: Oxford University Press, 2006), p. 122. Data on external debt and GDP from World Development Indicators database, accessed January 2007.

Exhibit 12 Net Official Development Assistance Disbursements to the 10 Largest Recipients (in billions of dollars, average over period)

1990–1999		2000–2002		2003–2004	
Egypt	2.23	Indonesia	1.35	Iraq	3.24
China	1.82	China	1.18	Dem. Rep. of Congo	3.09
Indonesia	1.47	Egypt	1.12	Afghanistan	1.45
Poland	1.33	Serbia & Montenegro	1.05	China	1.36
India	1.07	Mozambique	1.00	Vietnam	1.07
Philippines	0.90	Vietnam	0.94	Ethiopia	1.03
Bangladesh	0.75	Tanzania	0.88	Tanzania	1.00
Mozambique	0.72	India	0.78	Egypt	0.98
Thailand	0.70	Pakistan	0.76	Indonesia	0.85
Tanzania	0.68	Bangladesh	0.57	Jordan	0.76

Source: World Bank, "Global Development Finance 2006," p. 83, http://www.econ.worldbank.org, accessed March 29, 2007.

Exhibit 13 People Living on Less than $1 a Day (million)

	1981	1987	1993	1999	2002
East Asia & Pacific	796	426	415	282	214
China	634	308	334	223	180
Europe & Central Asia	3	2	17	30	10
Latin America & Caribbean	36	45	52	54	47
Middle East & North Africa	9	7	4	8	5
South Asia	475	473	476	429	437
Sub-Saharan Africa	164	219	242	294	303
Total	**1,482**	**1,171**	**1,208**	**1,096**	**1,016**
Excluding China	848	863	873	873	835

Source: Compiled by casewriter using World Development Indicators database, accessed January 2007.

Exhibit 14 Share of People Living on Less than $1 a Day (percentage)

	1981	1987	1993	1999	2002
East Asia & Pacific	57.7	28.0	24.9	15.7	11.6
China	63.8	28.5	28.4	17.8	14.0
Europe & Central Asia	0.7	0.4	3.7	6.3	2.1
Latin America & Caribbean	9.7	10.9	11.3	10.5	8.9
Middle East & North Africa	5.1	3.2	1.6	2.6	1.6
South Asia	51.5	45.0	40.1	32.2	31.2
Sub-Saharan Africa	41.6	46.8	44.0	45.7	44.0
Total	**40.4**	**28.4**	**26.3**	**21.8**	**19.4**
Excluding China	31.7	28.4	25.6	23.1	21.1

Source: Compiled by casewriter using World Development Indicators database, accessed January 2007.

Exhibit 15 Income Gap (gap between first and fifth quintiles of GDP per capita)

Year	Ratio
1820	3:1
1870	7:1
1913	11:1
1960	48:1
1970	65:1
1980	66:1
1990	72:1
2000	87:1

Source: Compiled by casewriter using World Development Indicators database, accessed January 2007; United Nations Human Development Report (1999); and Andrew Simms, "Ecological Debt," in *Sovereign Debt at the Crossroads*, eds. Chris Jochnick et al. (New York: Oxford University Press, 2006), p. 90.

Appendix A

UN Millennium Development Goals, To Be Achieved by 2015 (adopted September 2000)

Eradicate extreme hunger and poverty:

- Reduce by half the proportion of people living on less than a dollar a day with a base year of 1990
- Reduce by half the proportion of people who suffer from hunger

Achieve universal primary education:

- Ensure that all boys and girls complete a full course of primary schooling

Promote gender equality and empower women:

- Eliminate gender disparity in primary and secondary education preferably by 2005, and at all levels by 2015

Reduce child mortality:

- Reduce by two thirds the mortality rate among children under five

Improve maternal health:

- Reduce by three quarters the maternal mortality ratio

Combat HIV/AIDS, malaria, and other diseases:

- Halt and begin to reverse the spread of HIV/AIDS
- Halt and begin to reverse the incidence of malaria and other major diseases

Ensure environmental sustainability:

- Integrate the principles of sustainable development into country policies and programmes; reverse loss of environmental resources
- Reduce by half the proportion of people without sustainable access to safe drinking water
- Achieve significant improvement in lives of at least 100 million slum dwellers by 2020

Develop a global partnership for development:

- Develop further an open trading and financial system that is rule-based, predictable and non-discriminatory, includes a commitment to good governance, development and poverty reduction—nationally and internationally
- Address the least developed countries' special needs. This includes tariff- and quota-free access for their exports; enhanced debt relief for heavily indebted poor countries; cancellation of official bilateral debt; and more generous official development assistance for countries committed to poverty reduction.
- Address the special needs of landlocked and small island developing states
- Deal comprehensively with developing countries' debt problems through national and international measures to make debt sustainable in the long term
- In cooperation with the developing countries, develop decent and productive work for youth
- In cooperation with pharmaceutical companies, provide access to affordable essential drugs in developing countries
- In cooperation with the private sector, make available the benefits of new technologies—especially information and communications technologies

Source: http://www.un.org/millenniumgoals/#, accessed December 1, 2006.

Appendix B

International Financial Institutions

The World Bank Established in 1945 as the International Bank for Reconstruction and Development (IBRD), the World Bank grew into a group of five international organizations responsible for providing finance and advice to countries for economic development and poverty reduction, and for encouraging and safeguarding international investment. The World Bank made loans at preferential rates to member countries and grants to the poorest countries. Loans or grants for specific projects were often linked to wider policy changes in the sector or the economy. Its five agencies were the IBRD, which focused on financial and technical assistance for middle-income and creditworthy poor countries; the International Development Association, which provided the same assistance to the world's poorest countries; the International Finance Corporation, which provided loans, equity, structured finance, and risk management products and advisory services to build the private sector in developing countries; the Multilateral Investment Guarantee Agency, which promoted foreign direct investment into developing countries; and the International Centre for Settlement of Investment Disputes, which facilitated the settlement of investment disputes between governments and foreign investors. (http://www.worldbank.org)

The International Monetary Fund The IMF was established in 1945 to maintain the international monetary system of payments and exchange rates to facilitate business flows between member countries. While emphasizing sound economic policies among member countries, the IMF also allowed its resources to be used temporarily by countries experiencing financial difficulties due to balance-of-payment problems. IMF lending expanded over time to attach conditional economic strategies such as Structural Adjustment Loans on countries accepting its loans. (http://www.imf.org)

Regional Development Banks

The **African Development Bank** (AfDB) was established in 1964 to promote economic and social development in Africa. It was a conglomeration of the AfDB, the African Development Fund, and the Nigeria Trust Fund. Over 40 years, the AfDB Group financed 2,885 operations totaling $47.5 billion. Over the years, it placed increasing emphasis on the role of women, education, and structural reforms and lent its support to key initiatives such as debt alleviation for HIPCs and the New Partnership for Africa's Development (NEPAD). (http://www.afdb.org/)

The **Asian Development Bank** (ADB) was established in 1966 to promote economic and social development in Asian and Pacific countries through loans and technical assistance. It was a multilateral development financial institution owned by 66 members, 47 from the region and 19 from other parts of the globe. ADB's mission was to help its developing member countries reduce poverty and improve the quality of life of their citizens. (http://www.adb.org/)

The **Inter-American Development Bank** (IDB, or IADB) was established in 1959 to support Latin American and Caribbean economic/social development and regional integration by lending mainly to public institutions. The bank was owned by 47 member countries, 21 of which were lenders. The IADB was the main source of multilateral financing for economic, social, and institutional development projects as well as trade and regional integration programs in Latin America and the Caribbean. (http://www.iadb.org/)

The **Islamic Development Bank** (IDB) was established in 1973 as a multilateral development financing institution. It was founded by the first conference of finance ministers of the Organization of the Islamic Conference (OIC). The bank officially began its activities on 20 October 1975. On the basis of paid-up capital, the main shareholders of the bank were Saudi Arabia, Kuwait, Libya, Turkey, UAE, Iran, and Egypt. IDB's goal was to foster the economic development and social progress of member countries and Muslim communities in nonmember countries individually as well as jointly in accordance with the principles of shari'ah (Islamic jurisprudence). (http://www.isdb.org/)

Source: Compiled by casewriter.

Endnotes

[1] The EU-15 included European Union member countries prior to May 2004: Austria, Belgium, Denmark, Finland, France, Germany, Greece, Ireland, Italy, Luxembourg, the Netherlands, Portugal, Spain, Sweden, and the United Kingdom.

[2] "G-8 Aid Offer Falls Short of Expectations," *All Africa*, July 11, 2005.

[3] "G8 Debt Relief Plan Unlikely to Help Poor—Study," *Reuters News*, May 8, 2006.

[4] Kenneth Rogoff, "Debt Relief an Empty, Backward Gesture," *Business Day* (South Africa), June 21, 2005.

[5] Kenneth Rogoff, "The False Promise of Debt Relief," *Project Syndicate*, June 2005.

[6] Jeffrey Sachs, *The End of Poverty: Economic Possibilities for Our Time* (New York: Penguin Books, 2005), pp. 56–57.

[7] World Development Indicators database, accessed March 29, 2007.

[8] Ibid.

[9] William Easterly, *The White Man's Burden* (New York: Penguin Press, 2006), p. 165.

[10] For more about early World Bank history, see http://web.worldbank.org/WBSITE/EXTERNAL/EXTABOUTUS/EXTARCHIVES/0,,contentMDK:20080726~pagePK:36726~menuPK:214047~piPK:36092~theSitePK:29506,00.html, accessed December 12, 2006.

[11] "G8 and African Leadership in the War on AIDS and Extreme Poverty," DATA, June 2004, available at http://www.data.org/archives/G82004report.pdf , accessed January 25, 2007.

[12] Taken from U.S. Secretary of State Madeleine Albright's Harvard University commencement address, June 5, 1997, transcript available at http://gos.sbc.edu/a/albright3.html, accessed December 17, 2006.

[13] Evsey Domar, "Capital Expansion, Rate of Growth, and Employment," *Econometrica* 14 (April, 1946):137–147.

[14] William Easterly, *The Elusive Quest for Growth* (Cambridge, MA: MIT Press, Inc., 2001), p. 28.

[15] For an influential formulation of this argument, see Samuel P. Huntington, *Political Order in Changing Societies* (New Haven, CT: Yale University Press, 1968).

[16] Easterly, *The Elusive Quest for Growth*, p. 33.

[17] David Lumsdaine, *Moral Vision in International Politics: The Foreign Aid Regime, 1949–1989* (Princeton, NJ: Princeton University Press, 1993), p. 240.

[18] William Clark, "Robert McNamara at the World Bank," *Foreign Affairs* 60, Issue 1 (Fall 1987): 173.

[19] Lumsdaine, p. 248.

[20] Sebastian Edwards, *Crises and Reform in Latin America* (Oxford: Oxford University Press, 1995), p. 17.

[21] Rudiger Dornbusch as quoted in Serkan Arslanalp and Peter Blair Henry, "Research Paper No. 1931," Research Paper Series, Stanford Graduate School of Business, April 2006, p. 6.

[22] Federal Deposit Insurance Corporation, "History of the Eighties—Lessons for the Future, Volume 1: An Examination of the Banking Crises of the 1980s and Early 1990s," p. 191, http://www.fdic.gov/bank/hisotrial/history/191_210.pdf, accessed February 7, 2007.

[23] Ibid.

[24] Edwards, p. 19.

[25] Michael Dooley, "Retrospective on the Debt Crises," in Peter B. Kenen, ed., *Understanding Interdependence* (Princeton, NJ: Princeton University Press, 1995), p. 270.

[26] William Savitt and Paul Bottorf, *Global Development: A Reference Handbook* (Santa Barbara, CA: ABC-CLIO, 1995), pp. 50–96.

[27] Edwards, p. 26.

[28] Laura Alfaro, "Creditor Activism in Sovereign Debt: 'Vulture' Tactics or Market Backbone?" HBS No. 706-057 (Boston: Harvard Business School Publishing, 2006).

[29] U.S. Department of the Treasury, Office of International Debt Policy.

[30] Paul Krugman, "Financing vs. Forgiving a Debt Overhang," *Journal of Development Economics* 29 (November 1988): 254. See also Jeffrey Sachs, "The Debt Overhang of Developing Countries," in G.A. Calvo et al., eds., *Debt, Stabilization and Development* (Oxford: Basil Blackwell, 1989).

[31] The Brady deal announcements were made on the following dates: Argentina—April 1992, Bolivia—March 1993, Brazil—August 1992, Bulgaria—November 1993, Costa Rica—November 1989, Dominican Republic—May 1993, Ecuador—May 1994, Jordan—June 1993, Mexico—September 1989, Nigeria—March 1991, Peru—October 1995, Philippines—August 1989, Poland—March 1994, Uruguay—November 1990, and Venezuela—June 1990.

[32] Serkan Arslanalp and Peter Blair Henry, "Helping the Poor to Help Themselves: Debt Relief or Aid?" in Chris Jochnick and Fraser A. Preston, eds., *Sovereign Debt at the Crossroads* (New York: Oxford University Press, 2006), p. 178.

[33] Serkan Arslanalp and Peter Blair Henry, "Is Debt Relief Efficient?" *The Journal of Finance* 60 (April 2005): 1023. In addition, the average spread of the loans fell to 13/16 over LIBOR on the discount bounds after the restructuring from 17/16 over LIBOR before the Brady Plan. The average maturity of debt increased to 30 years from 15 years.

[34] Serkan Arslanalp and Peter Blair Henry, "Policy Watch, Debt Relief," *Journal of Economic Perspectives* 20 (Winter 2006): 4.

[35] Carol Palombo, "Brady Bonds: Past, Present and Future," *LatinFinance*, July 17, 1996, via Factiva, accessed May 25, 2007.

[36] World Bank, "Assessing Aid: What Works, What Doesn't, and Why," World Bank Policy Research Paper, 1998, p. 7, http://www.worldbank.org, accessed January 25, 2007. © The World Bank Group.

[37] For a supporter's account of the campaign's development, see www.jubileedebtcampaign.org.uk/?lid=282, accessed December 17, 2006.

[38] For more information, see World Bank, "Assessing Aid," Policy Research Report, 1998.

[39] World Bank, "Debt Relief," http://web.worldbank.org, accessed March 29, 2007. © The World Bank Group.

[40] http://www.clubdeparis.org; also see Lex Rieffel, *Restructuring Sovereign Debt: The Case for Ad Hoc Machinery* (Washington, D.C.: Brooking Institution Press, 2003).

[41] Ralf Hepp, "Consequences of Debt Relief Initiatives in the 1990s" (2005), p. 7, available at SSRN, http://ssrn.com/abstract=819645, accessed December 18, 2006.

[42] World Bank, "Global Development Finance 2006," p. 88, http://econ.worldbank.org, accessed March 27, 2007. © The World Bank Group.

[43] Hepp.

[44] Arslanalp and Henry, "Helping the Poor Help Themselves: Debt Relief or Aid?"

45 World Bank Independent Evaluation Group, "Debt Relief for the Poorest: An Evaluation Update of the HIPC Initiative," April 11, 2006, http://siteresources.worldbank.org/INTDEBTDEPT/Resources/ieghipcupdatereview2006.pdf, accessed March 29, 2007. © The World Bank Group.

46 "Africa, the G8, and the Blair Initiative," CRS Report for Congress, available at http://www.fas.org/sgp/crs/row/RL32796.pdf, accessed February 19, 2007.

47 Christopher Adams, "Blair to Launch New Drive Against Poverty in Africa," *Financial Times*, February 25, 2004.

48 "A Year of Huge Challenges—Tony Blair," *The Economist*, January 1, 2005.

49 Under the HIPC Initiative, a "completion point" is reached when countries maintain macroeconomic stability under a World Bank or IMF-directed program, implement important structural and social reforms, and carry out a poverty reduction strategy satisfactorily for a year. Then, creditors will provide irrevocable debt relief. For more information about HIPC programs and their implementation, see World Bank, "Steps of the HIPC Initiative," http://web.worldbank.org/WBSITE/EXTERNAL/TOPICS/EXTDEBTDEPT.

50 World Bank, "Debt Relief."

51 Richard Manning, *OECD Observer*, No. 251, September 2005.

52 "Britain's Finance Minister Calls for 'New Deal' to Wipe Out World Poverty," *Agence France Presse*, March 23, 2006.

53 Casewriter interview.

54 Ibid.

55 "Nigeria: Obasanjo Defends G8 Agreement," *Africa News*, July 10, 2005, via LexisNexis, accessed February 9, 2007.

56 "South African President Hails Decisions Reached at G8 Summit," *BBC Monitoring International Reports*, July 10, 2005, via LexisNexis, accessed February 9, 2007.

57 "Between Hype and Hope," *The Economist*, July 16, 2005.

58 "G8 Debt Agreement a Step Forward, but Analysis Finds Deals Fall Short of What is Needed to Address Global Crises," Jubilee USA Press Release (Washington, D.C., July 8, 2005).

59 Kenneth Rogoff, "The False Promise of Debt Relief," *Project Syndicate*, June 2005.

60 Serkan Arslanalp and Peter Blair Henry, "Helping the Poor to Help Themselves: Debt Relief or Aid?" in *Sovereign Debt at the Crossroads*, Chris Jochnick and Fraser A. Preston, eds. (New York: Oxford University Press, 2006), p. 176.

61 Ibid., p. 187.

62 Carl-Johan Dalgaard, Henrik Hansen, and Finn Tarp, "On the Empirics of Foreign Aid and Growth," *The Economic Journal*, 114 (June 2004): F191–F216.

63 Craig Burnside and David Dollar, "Aid, Policies, and Growth," *American Economic Review* 90:4 (September 2000): 847.

64 William Easterly, Ross Levine, and David Roodman, "Aid, Policies, and Growth: Comment," *American Economic Review* 94:3 (June 2004): 774.

65 Raghuram G. Rajan and Arvind Subramanian, "What Undermines Aid's Impact on Growth?" IMF Working Paper WP/05/126, June 2005.

66 Available at http://www.house/gov/jec/imf/meltzer/htm, p. 13, accessed January 22, 2007.

[67] Ibid., p. 40.

[68] The World Bank and other donor agencies operated a "monitoring and evaluation" system (M&E) whereby certain programs were immediately reviewed to see which activities were efficient and effective and therefore should be expanded or terminated. However, the M&E function had yet to amend the administrative problems of aid due to various issues, from appraisal methods to poor coordination. For more information, see "Monitoring and Evaluation Operations Manual," UNAIDS, http://www1.worldbank.org/hiv_aids/docs/M&EManual.pdf, accessed May 22, 2007.

[69] Sachs, *The End of Poverty*, p. 277.

[70] Ibid., p. 310.

[71] William Easterly, "The Utopian Nightmare," *Foreign Policy* Issue 150 (Sept/Oct 2005).

[72] Radelet, Clemens, Bhavnani, "Aid and Growth: The Current Debate and Some New Evidence," Center for Global Development, February 2004, p. 6.

[73] "Aid Is Not the Answer," *The Wall Street Journal*, August 31, 2005.

[74] Ilyana Kuziemko and Eric Werker, "How Much Is a Seat on the Security Council Worth? Foreign Aid and Bribery at the United Nations," *Journal of Political Economy* 114:5 (2006); see also Alberto Alesina and Beatrice Weder, "Do Corrupt Governments Receive Less Foreign Aid?" *American Economic Review* 92: 4 (September 2002): 1126.

[75] David Lumsdaine, *Moral Vision in International Politics: The Foreign Aid Regime, 1949–1989* (Princeton, NJ: Princeton University Press, 1993), pp. 50–51.

[76] Michael Phillips, "G-8 Warns Loans by Rising Nations May Swamp Poor," *The Wall Street Journal*, June 12, 2006.

[77] "G8 Warns Loans by Rising Nations May Swamp Poor," *Reuters News*, April 25, 2006.

[78] Sachs, *The End of Poverty*, p. 277.

[79] Steve Radelet, "Reply to Easterly: Evidence Beats Rhetoric, Every Time," *CATO Unbound*, April 9, 2006, http://www.cato-unbound.org/2006/04/09/steve-radelet/evidence-beats-rhetoric/, accessed January 10, 2007.

[80] Sachs, pp. 244–259.

[81] Paul Samuelson, *Economics: An Introductory Analysis* (New York: McGraw Hill, 1961), p. 49.

[82] Speech to the Jubilee Debt Campaign, http://www.jubileedebtcampaign.org.uk/, accessed January 10, 2007.

[83] World Bank, "Assessing Aid," p. 1.

[84] For more information about Uganda and its reform policies, see Huw Pill, "Uganda and the Washington Consensus," HBS No. 798-047 (Boston: Harvard Business School Publishing, 1998).

[85] Jayati Datta-Mirta, "Uganda: Policy, Participation, People," Country Assistance Evaluation, World Bank, 2001, p. xv.

[86] Sachs, pp. 259–265.

[87] Steve Radelet, "Reply to Easterly: Evidence Beats Rhetoric, Every Time."

[88] Thomas W. Hertel and L. Alan Winters, "Estimating the Poverty Impact of a Prospective Doha Development Agenda," *The World Economy* 28:8 (August 2005): 1057.

[89] Joseph Stiglitz and Andrew Charlton, "The Doha Round Is Missing the Point," *Financial Times*, December 13, 2005.

[90] "Gleneagles 'Has Not Reduced Infant Mortality,'" *The Independent*, June 9, 2006.

[91] Stiglitz and Charlton.

[92] For more information, see Office of the United States Trade Representative, "2006 Comprehensive Report on U.S. Trade and Investment Policy Toward Sub-Saharan Africa and Implementation of the African Growth and Opportunity Act," p. 9, http://www.ustr.gov/assets/Document_library/Reports_Publications/2006, accessed April 2, 2007.

[93] Ibid., p. 17.

[94] Sachs, p. 282.

[95] Stiglitz and Charlton.

[96] See John Page, Nancy Birdsall, Ed Campos, W. Max Corden, Chang-Shik Kim, Howard Pack, Richard Sabot, Joseph Stiglitz, and Marilou Uy, *The East Asian Miracle: Economic Growth and Public Policy* (New York: Oxford University Press, 1993).

[97] "A Choosier Approach to Aid," *The Economist*, April 23, 2005.

[98] "Grants or Loans?" World Bank Public Policy for the Private Sector Note No. 287, March 2005, http://rru.worldbank.org/Documents/PublicPolicyJournal/287Harford_Klein.pdf, accessed April 2, 2007.

[99] Jeremy Bulow and Kenneth Rogoff, "Grants versus Loans for Development Banks," *American Economic Review* 95(2) (May 2005): 396.

[100] World Bank, "Global Development Finance 2006," p. 3.

[101] Carol C. Adelman, "America's Total Economic Engagement with the Developing World: Rethinking the Uses and Nature of Foreign Aid," available at http://www.hudson.org/files/publications/Rethinking_Foreign_Aid.pdf, accessed January 25, 2007.

[102] Michael E. Porter and Mark R. Kramer, "Philanthropy's New Agenda: Creating Value," *Harvard Business Review* (November–December 1999): 122.

[103] Stiglitz and Charlton.

[104] "World Development Indicators," World Bank, 2006, Table 2.7.

[105] Ibid.

[106] UNICEF and USAID data, cited in William Easterly, *The White Man's Burden* (New York: Penguin Books, 2006), p. 8.

[107] UNICEF, United Nations, and World Bank data, cited in William Easterly, *The White Man's Burden*, p. 8.

HARVARD | BUSINESS | SCHOOL

9-707-040
REV: JULY 16, 2007

LAURA ALFARO
ERIC WERKER
RENEE KIM

Aid, Debt Relief, and Trade: An Agenda for Fighting World Poverty (B)

At the 2006 Group of Eight (G8) Summit held in St. Petersburg, Russian President Vladimir Putin presented energy security, education, and the fight against infectious diseases as central themes. Although aid and trade remained on the agenda, the pressure to keep the momentum of the G8's commitment to aid from 2005 fell largely on British Prime Minister Tony Blair.

A progress report presented at the summit by "Debt, AIDS, Trade, Africa" (DATA), a lobby group cofounded by rock star activist Bono, criticized the efforts the G8 had made over the previous year. While the wealthy countries had largely followed through with the promise to forgive eligible heavily indebted poor countries (HIPC) debt and had made some progress in providing medication and treatment for those with AIDS in Africa and other poor regions, they had made little progress in freeing their markets to HIPC trade. According to Bono, "Overall, there is one cheer on debt, half a cheer on AIDS, and boos and wolf-whistles for what is happening on trade."[1]

As of mid-2006, 29 HIPCs had qualified for debt cancellation and agreed to a new set of international financial institution (IFI)-approved economic policies. These policies included "sound" macroeconomic frameworks and balanced development strategies. Of these 29 countries, 19 had received some debt relief (see **Exhibit 1**). Over the course of the year leading up to the 2006 G8 summit, the multilateral lending agencies had forgiven $55 billion.

Paul Vallely, coauthor of the report published by the Commission for Africa, an organization established by Blair, pointed out that the countries that obtained debt relief in 2006 had an extra $1 billion to spend on worthwhile programs. Debt relief had enabled free health care in Zambia, construction of rural feeder roads for poor farmers in Ghana, food for 3.7 million people hit by drought in Tanzania, and the hire of 50,000 teachers to enroll 3.5 million more children into school in Nigeria as examples of progress.[2]

---

[1] Lesley Wroughton, "Bono Accuses Rich Nations of Faltering on Africa," *Reuters News*, June 29, 2006.

[2] Paul Vallely, "G8 Africa: Gleneagles Did Succeed," *New Statesman*, July 3, 2006.

Professors Laura Alfaro and Eric Werker and Research Associate Renee Kim prepared this case. HBS cases are developed solely as the basis for class discussion. Cases are not intended to serve as endorsements, sources of primary data, or illustrations of effective or ineffective management.

Official development assistance had to continue to steadily increase if it were to reach the additional $25 billion committed by 2010 (see **Exhibit 2**). Yet aid extended by G8 nations in 2005 averaged 0.27% of their gross national income (GNI), or $90 per person, well below the United Nations' target of 0.7%.[3] Even with the Gleneagles 2010 target achieved, G8 aid would only be 0.36% of GNI.[4] While the United States dominated aid giving in total amounts in previous decades, aid as a percentage of GNI was the lowest for the United States among the G8 (see **Exhibit 3**).[5] Although the total amount of aid from G8 members increased 37% from its 2004 level, Oxfam International argued that these numbers were overstated: a full 80% of the rise comprised debt cancellations for Iraq and Nigeria.[6] If those items were removed, overall G8 aid had increased only 9% in 2005.

The situation did not improve in 2006, as overall assistance, excluding for Iraq and Nigeria, actually fell 1.8%.[7] Total official development assistance in real terms declined for the first time since 1997.[8] Jeffrey Sachs, special advisor to the UN Secretary General, said, "By design, to avoid accountability, the G8 refused to put forward clear and predictable year-by-year commitments towards 2010," making it difficult for African countries to plan investments based on expected aid receipts.[9]

World leaders agreed that greater strides needed to be made to conclude the World Trade Organization's Doha Round of trade talks and acknowledged the importance of aid for trade to help developing countries. The G8 expected spending on aid for trade to increase to $4 billion but did not specify how or when.[10] Meanwhile, mutual recriminations and lack of progress in removing trade barriers nearly caused the collapse of the Doha Round of talks in mid-2006 as the United States, the EU, and other countries failed to cut their subsidies, support, and tariffs on domestic agricultural goods.

[3] "The View from the Summit—Gleneagles G8 One Year On," Oxfam Briefing Note, June 2006, http://www.oxfam.org.uk/what_we_do/issues/debt_aid/downloads/g8_gleneagles_oneyear.pdf, accessed March 12, 2007.

[4] "G8 Aid Promises Don't Add Up: Oxfam," *Agence France Presse*, June 9, 2006.

[5] "Gleneagles Promises Forgotten with Africa off the Agenda," *The Daily Telegraph*, July 18, 2006.

[6] Oxfam Briefing Note.

[7] "Development Aid from OECD Countries Fell 5.1% in 2006," OECD, April 3, 2007, http://www.oecd.org/document/17/0,2340,en_2649_201185_38341265_1_1_1_1,00.html, accessed April 9, 2007.

[8] Ibid.

[9] Alan Beatie, "Africa Aid Stalls Despite G8 Pledge," *Financial Times*, April 3, 2007.

[10] G8 Summit Documents, "Trade," http://en.g8russia.ru/docs/16-print.html, accessed February 7, 2007.

Exhibit 1 Estimated Debt Relief Provided by International Development Association (IDA) under HIPC and Multilateral Debt Relief Initiative (MDRI) (in millions of dollars)[a]

		Of which:	
Country	Total Debt Relief by IDA	HIPC Relief	Estimated MDRI Relief
Benin	814	124	690
Bolivia	1,804	287	1,517
Burkina Faso	1,154	420	734
Cameroon	1,133	266	867
Ethiopia	3,616	1,278	2,337
Ghana	4,429	1,446	2,983
Guyana	322	133	189
Honduras	1,293	108	1,185
Madagascar	2,213	444	1,768
Mali	1,553	292	1,262
Mauritania	721	173	548
Mozambique	2,361	1,055	1,306
Nicaragua	1,148	383	765
Niger	1,156	409	748
Rwanda	1,056	709	347
Senegal	2,018	164	1,854
Tanzania	3,961	1,157	2,804
Uganda	3,764	984	2,780
Zambia	2,760	885	1,875
Total	**37,276**	**10,715**	**26,560**

Source: World Bank, "Multilateral Debt Relief Initiative MDRI Fact Sheet," http://siteresources.worldbank.org/INTDEBTDEPT/Resources/mdri_eng.pdf, accessed March 27, 2007.

[a]Data applies to the 19 HIPC completion-point countries as of July 1, 2006.

Exhibit 2 Total Official Development Assistance (ODA) Aid Needed to Reach Additional US$25 Billion by 2010 (in billions of US$)[a]

	2004	2005	2006	2007	2008	2009	2010
Canada	0.9	0.8	1.0	1.1	**1.3**[b]	1.3	1.3
France	4.1	5.0	5.2	**5.5**	6.2	7.0	**7.7**
Germany	2.5	2.5	3.1	3.8	4.4	5.1	**5.8**
Italy	1.2	1.2	2.1	2.9	3.8	4.6	**5.5**
Japan	1.8	1.8	2.3	**2.7**	3.1	3.4	3.4
United Kingdom	3.3	3.5	4.2	5.0	**5.8**	6.4	**7.1**
United States	4.7	5.2	5.9	6.6	7.4	8.1	**8.8**
G8 Total	18.3	20.0	23.8	27.7	31.9	35.9	39.6
OTHER DAC[c] Donors Targets	7.8	6.7	7.6	8.7	9.8	11.0	12.1
Total All DAC	26.2	26.6	31.4	36.4	41.8	46.9	**51.6**

Source: Adpted from "DATA Report 2006," Debt AIDS Trade Africa, p. 29, http://www.thedatareport.org/pdf/DATAreport.pdf, accessed March 12, 2007.

[a]Most figures are based on a simple linear trajectory.

[b]The bolded figures represent the years when G8 donors have set targets.

[c]OECD's Development Assistance Committee (DAC), including all OECD members.

Exhibit 3 Donor Share in Total Official Development Assistance (ODA) (in percent)

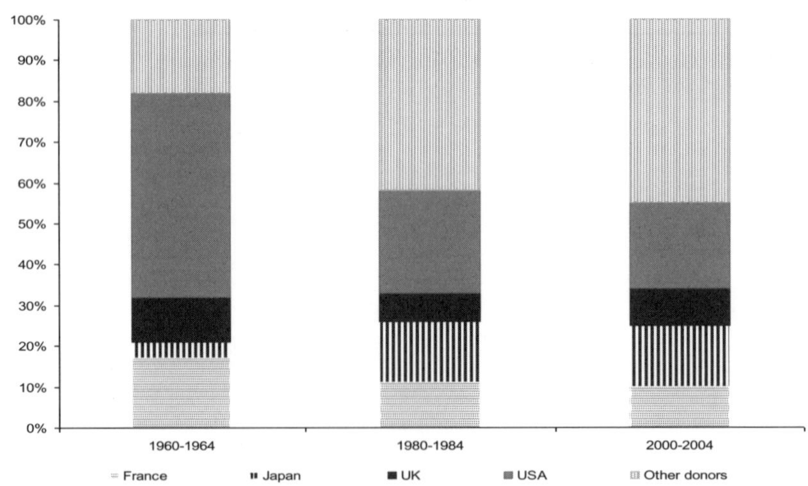

Source: Adapted from OECD, 2005, as published in Sanjeev Gupta et al., "Are Donor Countries Giving More or Less Aid," IMF Working Paper, January 2006, p. 5, http://www.imf.org/external/pubs/ft/wp/2006/wp0601.pdf, accessed April 12, 2007.

III. Challenges and Policies of Large Economies

The cases of the three largest economies of the world — Japan, China, and the U.S. — are examined next. Due to these countries' economic and political importance, the issues and policy options open to them are in many ways different from those studied in the standard "small open economy" cases. The module ends with discussion of current financial crisis.

MONETARY POLICY IN JAPAN

"*Kinyuseisaku*: Monetary Policy in Japan (A)" reviews Japanese monetary policy over the last two decades with an emphasis on the experience of deflation. After what seemed like a miracle performance, the Japanese economy fell stagnant for more than a decade. The "lost decade" has been attributed to many problems: burst of the bubble, bank problems and non-performing loans, failed fiscal policy, and slow structural reforms. But many critics point to failed monetary policy, as deflation is a monetary phenomenon. The case accommodates a critical analysis of the policies that the country implemented and an in-depth discussion of monetary policy, tools, and mechanisms and their effectiveness. "*Kinyuseisaku*: Monetary Policy in Japan (B)" updates the case to the current dilemma faced by authorities as they deal with the Global Financial Crisis of 2008–2009 with a history of high debt levels and low interest rates.

EXCHANGE RATE POLICY IN CHINA

"China: To Float or Not to Float? (A)" links China's exchange rate policy with its development strategy.[1] On July 21, 2005, China revalued its decade-long, quasi-fixed exchange rate of approximately 8.28 yuan per U.S. dollar by 2.1% to 8.11, and introduced a more market-based exchange rate system. Yet the move fell short of many analysts' and economists' expectations. Extensive controls on capital movements into the country that had helped counter some inflationary pressure were increasingly becoming a target of debate as China continued to integrate itself into the world economy. An important objective of the case is to impart an understanding of the mechanics of China's exchange rate policy, specifically, the role of capital controls and policy sterilization, as well as the challenges, risks, and benefits associated with maintaining a quasi-fixed exchange rate against the U.S. dollar. Comparisons with the Chile case encourage students to recognize that the policy motivations and institutional capacity of the government are essential to informed understanding of both the purpose of the regime and the conclusions that governments and market participants should draw from those countries' experiences. The case also emphasizes the importance of sequencing exchange rate reform with changes to the banking sector and capital controls. To foster a debate about what

[1] "China: To Float or Not to Float (B): Timeline of Changes Relevant to the Chinese Renminbi" (HBS No. 706-022) provides updated information on further changes to China's exchange rate system and international calls for greater flexibility.

China should do with its exchange rate policy and assess the impacts of different choices on businesses located in China and elsewhere, any of the following complementary short cases can be assigned: "China: To Float or Not to Float? (C): Esquel Group and the Chinese Renminbi" (HBS No. 706-023); "China: To Float or Not to Float? (D): Bank of America's Strategic Investment in China Construction Bank" (HBS No. 706-031); "China: To Float or Not to Float? (E): ABB Investment in China" (HBS No. 706-035); and "China: To Float or Not to Float? (F): Alcatel and Strong Chinese Competition" (HBS No. 706-036).

THE U.S. CURRENT ACCOUNT DEFICIT AND GLOBAL IMBALANCES

The U.S. current account deficit of close to US$800 billion in the mid 2000s had been referred to as a paradox, a conundrum, and a threat. Considered at the core of so-called "global imbalances," the deficit caused consternation among policy makers around the world. Current account surpluses in poor and emerging economies took the bulk of the "other side" — China, East Asia, oil (non-OECD) exporting countries, and other emerging economies account for close to 75% of the foreign lending to the U.S. The goal of the case is not only to analyze the implications of the U.S. deficit on the world economy and business environment, but also to make sense of the deficit in the context of traditional macro and international economic tools. As world savings finances world investments (that is, the sum of the world's current account deficit has to add to zero), changes in the U.S. current account deficit have implications for other countries' current accounts. As such, the evolution of the global imbalances has a first-order impact on world exchange rates, world patterns of exports and imports, international capital flows, and global growth. Building on the discussion in the *China* case, in addition to historical comparisons to U.S. current accounts deficits in the 1970s and 1980s, the case emphasizes that "politics" — the political pressures for potentially chaotic adjustments — are the main threat to what seems to be an "equilibrium" with economic incentives of the main parties aligned to sustain "global imbalances." A model of exchange determination as outlined in "The U.S. Current Account Deficit Spreadsheet" (HBS No. 706-701) complements the discussion. The model, which incorporates three areas — the United States, Europe, and Asia — can be used to calibrate bilateral real exchange rate changes in response to various scenarios under which global current account imbalances might adjust.

THE U.S. SUBPRIME CRISIS

The cases "U.S. Subprime Mortgage Crisis: Policy Reactions (A) and (B)" focus on the difficulties faced by the U.S. economy in 2008 and 2009 and the policy responses of the U.S. fiscal and monetary authorities highlighting events such as the Fed's role in orchestrating JPMorgan Chase's purchase of Bear Stearns, quantitative easing, the fiscal stimulus and the various plans to address the problems in the financial system. The cases also advance different policies that have been proposed to deal with consequences but also the causes behind the crisis. The case "Sovereign Wealth Funds: For Profits or Politics?" complements the discussion. Sovereign Wealth Funds, (SWFs), broadly defined as an investment fund owned by a national or a government, were gaining prominence across the globe, especially with their recent investments in troubled U.S. financial firms that had suffered significant losses from the subprime mortgage crisis.

GLOBAL FINANCIAL CRISIS

The case "The First Global Crisis of the 21st Century" discusses the world implications of the U.S. meltdown. Many analysts believed the large U.S. deficits raised the risk of a sharp and disorderly macroeconomic adjustment that could be painful, for the U.S. as well as for the rest of the world. By 2009, governments had taken various policy measures over the last few months to tackle the subprime mortgage crisis that threatened to drag the economy into a recession. Yet as the global economy faced slower growth stemming from the U.S. mortgage crisis, policy makers were caught in an intense debate over what the 'right' solution would be and the implication of these policies on global imbalances.

Monetary Policy in Japan

HARVARD | BUSINESS | SCHOOL

9-708-017
REV: APRIL 9, 2009

LAURA ALFARO
AKIKO KANNO

Kinyuseisaku: Monetary Policy in Japan (A)

By the fall of 2007, over a year had passed since the Bank of Japan (BOJ) had abandoned the zero interest rate policy (ZIRP). Japan was experiencing a gradual business recovery that had lasted more than 65 months, the longest in its postwar history. Confident that the worst was over, the BOJ had increased interest rates twice during the past year. Toshihiko Fukui, the governor of the BOJ, commented at a press conference held after the BOJ raised rates in early 2007 that "the benchmark rate of 0.5% is extremely low for an economy with a 2% real growth rate."[1]

Many analysts believed that Fukui did not want to repeat the bank's mistake of the 1980s when its lax monetary policy fueled a bubble economy; the collapse of the bubble condemned Japan to years of deflation and low growth.[2] Real estate prices in some of the metropolitan areas had started to rise and Fukui was concerned about the possibility of a new burst of inflation. "To prevent anything like that happening again, Mr. Fukui has insisted the bank adopt a more forward looking approach," reported *The Economist*.[3] Japan's ZIRP was originally designed to help firms and banks burdened by debt; but with much healthier balance sheets, the subsidy was no longer needed. Normalization of interest rates would also promote further restructuring of "zombie companies." Economists noted further adverse effects of the prolonged low interest-rate policy. Cheap money could promote inefficient investments; and low rates might discourage consumers from spending, since Japanese households enjoyed high levels of savings.

Others, however, were quick to criticize a possible rate hike, fearing a rerun of August 2000 when the BOJ raised rates prematurely, killing off a nascent recovery and aggravating Japan's deflation. Although the economy had enjoyed five years of growth, it was still haunted by falling prices. The core measure of consumer prices (CPI, excluding fresh food but including energy) fell by 0.1% in the 12 months to September 2007. The BOJ had slashed its inflation forecast for the year to only 0.1%.[4] It was difficult, however, to accurately assess the trend of the CPI because prices of many items such as food and daily commodities were on the rise, while prices of some high-priced goods such as digital consumer electronics and computers were falling, which brought down the overall statistical figure[5] (see **Exhibits 1** and **2**).

John Lipsky, first deputy managing director of the International Monetary Fund (IMF), who visited Japan in May 2007 for the fund's regular policy dialogue with Japanese officials, commented that "Japan's expansion continues to be firmly established."[6] However, his report recommended that monetary policy should remain focused on securing price stability and durable growth and that "a rate hike should be delayed until inflation expectations have recovered and the prospective CPI trend is firmly rising."[7] It also stressed the importance of reducing the government's debt which "remained uncomfortably high as pressures from an aging society were building."[8]

Professor Laura Alfaro and Research Associate Akiko Kanno prepared this case with the assistance of Masako Egawa, Executive Director of the HBS Japan Reseach Center. HBS cases are developed solely as the basis for class discussion. Cases are not intended to serve as endorsements, sources of primary data, or illustrations of effective or ineffective management.

While the BOJ had the autonomy to make decisions on monetary policy, there were various factors that Fukui had to take into account. Fukui was aware that the government did not welcome a rate hike that might dampen the economy. Moreover, Japan's public debt amounted to approximately 170% of GDP, and the government wanted the interest rate of Japanese government bonds to be low so that interest payments on the public debt would not increase (see **Exhibits 3**, **4** and **5**). There were also growing uncertainties about the global financial markets stemming from the United States' subprime mortgage crisis.[9] Other factors, however, hinted that an interest rate hike was necessary: rates in Japan were the lowest among developed nations (see **Exhibit 6**).

Although it was clear that the very low interest rates had to be raised at some point, Fukui needed to seek the appropriate timing and approach. The past experience of "too little, too late" actions that sparked the bubble economy urged Fukui to raise rates as soon as possible, while the August 2000 experience of raising rates prematurely made him cautious.

Monetary Policy History of Japan

Postwar Period

The making of Japan's economic miracle When World War II ended, the Japanese economy was devastated. Although the country had few natural resources and had to rely on imports for much of its energy and raw materials, the Japanese people were determined to rebuild the nation. Under the slogan "catch up with and overtake Western countries," people worked hard, saved, and invested in infrastructure and capital assets. In 1961, the Ikeda administration set out a plan to double the country's national income by 1970 ("income-doubling plan"), which required an average economic growth of 7.2% per year for 10 years.[10] The result far exceeded the plan, with economic growth during the decade averaging more than 10%. In 1968, Japan overcame Germany and became the country with the world's second-largest GDP. The country shifted to a heavy-industry-oriented economy, with machinery, petroleum products, and iron and steel industries growing at high rates.[11]

Political system Japan's postwar political system was based on parliamentary democracy. In 1955, the Liberal Party and the Democratic Party merged to form the Liberal Democratic Party (LDP) ushering in a stable one-party rule system. The Ministry of Finance (MOF) and Ministry of International Trade and Industry (MITI)[12] had especially strong powers and authority. MITI determined industrial policy through control of imports and foreign direct investment. In addition to managing the country's fiscal policy, the MOF held strong power in the country's monetary and financial matters. The MOF also had a supervisory function over the policies of the BOJ, the central bank.[13] The BOJ had implemented Japan's monetary policy since its establishment in 1882. The Bank of Japan Law of 1942 reorganized the bank along nationalistic lines, strongly reflecting the wartime period.[14] The bank's objective was stated as "the regulation of the currency, control, facilitation of credit and finance, and maintenance and fostering of the credit system, pursuant to national policy, in order that the general economic activities of the nation might adequately be enhanced."[15]

During this period, the BOJ undertook a stop-go policy[16] as the economy went through business cycles closely linked to the balance of trade. However, its decisions were often influenced by government policy. For example, in 1961, the BOJ decided to raise interest rates in May after the trade balance turned to a deficit. However, the measure was not implemented until July, because the Ikeda cabinet was pursing the "income-doubling plan."[17] Nevertheless, between 1955 and 1972, wholesale prices remained stable with only a 1% annual increase throughout the period.[18] Consumer prices remained stable at first (about 1% growth between 1955 and 1960), but started to rise in the latter half of the period (about 5% annual growth).[19]

The 1970s: Oil Shocks and Dollar Shocks

Dollar shocks On August 15, 1971, U.S. President Nixon announced the end of the gold standard and pressed Japan and other Western countries to revalue their currencies against the dollar. In December 1971, the Smithsonian Agreement revalued the yen to ¥308 per dollar from ¥360 per dollar. However, market pressure for further devaluation of the dollar remained strong as the U.S. trade deficit jumped in 1972 and the Japanese trade surplus soared. In February 1973, after numerous attempts to prevent the dollar's devaluation, Japan and other major countries decided to shift to the floating exchange rate system. As a result, the yen appreciated to ¥254 per dollar.

Oil shocks With the "oil crisis" of 1973, Japan suffered from soaring energy prices since almost 90% of its energy was supplied from overseas. Eventually Japan was able to ensure its oil supply, but the rise in the price of energy and petrochemical products created sharp inflation. Wholesale prices increased by 37.2% and consumer prices by 24.9% in 1974.[20] In an attempt to stop inflation, the BOJ raised its lending rate five times from 4.25% in October 1972 to 9% in December 1973. This monetary tightening was effective in slowing down economic activities. For the first time since the end of WWII, Japan experienced negative growth (-0.4%) in 1974. On the other hand, the CPI inflation rate, which had jumped to 25% in 1974 from 11.7% in 1973, returned to 11.7% in 1975.[21]

In December 1979, oil prices tripled following the Iranian Revolution. Inflation rose from 4% in 1979 to 7.8% in 1980. This time the BOJ acted quickly by raising the bank's lending rate from 6.25% to 9%, which was effective in containing inflation which decreased to 4.9% by 1981.[22] In August 1980, as wholesale prices peaked, the BOJ cut its lending rate to 8.25%.[23]

The Bubble Era

Despite these shocks, the Japanese economy continued to grow. The strong economy was led by the export of manufactured goods. The depreciation of the yen caused by the 1979 oil shock reopened the gap between the ¥/$ exchange rate and the ¥ cost of manufacturing, allowing extensive export growth. As a result, Japanese exports in a few industries, especially cars, auto parts, steel, consumer electronics, and machine tools, began to swamp American production. Japan was slow to open its markets, and the United States, having become uncomfortable with the impact of Japanese imports on its economy, threatened Japan with "reciprocity" legislation that could close U.S. markets to asymmetrical trade. A series of U.S. trade complaints brought temporary and "voluntary" limitations to Japan's onslaught of exports, while the United States tried to adjust.[24] In the meantime, U.S. President Ronald Reagan implemented large-scale tax cuts and high interest rates ("Reaganomics") in an attempt to end stagflation, resulting in trade and fiscal deficits and a strong dollar. The value of the dollar eventually climbed 63%. The weakened yen only reasserted Japan's competitiveness to export.

Plaza Accord In order to cope with the too-strong dollar, on September 22, 1985, the finance ministers of France, West Germany, the United States, the United Kingdom, and Japan (the Group of Five [G-5]), met at the Plaza Hotel in New York and announced their agreement to intervene to depreciate the U.S. dollar. Within a few weeks, the dollar began to fall and by the latter half of 1986, the exchange rate was around 150~160 ¥/$, marking the beginning of *Endaka* (high yen) (see **Exhibit 7**). Countries also undertook cooperative measures to lower interest rates and decrease interest rates differentials. In 1986, both the United States and Japan lowered their official discount rate four times, narrowing the interest-rate differences from about 5% before the Plaza Accord to nearly 2%[25] (see **Exhibit 8**).

Louvre Accord In February 1987, the G-5 gathered in Paris and agreed to end the continuing decline of the dollar and to cooperate to stabilize the international currency market. After the Louvre Accord, countries continued to lower interest rates in order to avoid weakening the dollar, while the United States, in turn, raised interest rates. As a result, Japan lowered its official discount rate to a historical low of 2.5%, and the U.S./Japan interest-rate differential widened to 5% by May 1987.[26]

By 1988, the United States, Japan, and Germany all marked high economic growth rates. As economic growth accelerated, countries raised interest rates to avoid overheating. However, the BOJ maintained the 2.5% discount rate throughout 1987 and did not raise it until May 1989; by then, the Bundesbank had already raised its rate four times.[27] Since the 1950s, the BOJ had been using wholesale prices as the indicator for assessing monetary policies, and it was believed that despite rising asset prices, the BOJ did not tighten its monetary policy because of relatively stable wholesale prices.[28]

With low interest rates, the Japanese economy prospered. Despite the high yen, net exports soared, and Japan's current account surplus became the world's largest. Backed by the huge surplus, the Japanese invested in land, stock, and other assets, which resulted in price hikes for all assets and ultimately triggered what came to be called the "bubble economy." The Nikkei Stock Average went from 18,701 yen at the end of 1986 to its peak at 38,957 yen in late 1989, triple its level in 1985. Land prices also soared, with the urban land price index of six major cities increasing by 500% between 1980 and 1992.[29] The strong yen enabled Japanese companies to buy U.S. equities and real estate, including the landmark Rockefeller Center in New York (see **Exhibits 9, 10,** and **11**).

Burst of the "bubble economy" The official discount rate of 2.5% was maintained for over two years until the newly appointed BOJ governor Yasushi Mieno raised it three times in 1989 (to a high of 4.25%) to cool down the economy and prevent inflation. The tightening was delayed because both the BOJ and the MOF were afraid that higher interest rates would strengthen the yen further. When a rumor of a fourth interest-rate rise spread in early 1990, the market reacted, anticipating higher interest rates. The yield on Japanese government bonds jumped from 5% to 7% and bond prices fell sharply. Stock prices plunged, with the Nikkei Stock Average falling from 38,000 yen in January to 29,000 yen in just one month. By August 1990, the BOJ had raised the interest rate to 6% in order to prevent inflation, which was anticipated following the break out of the Gulf War in 1991 and the subsequent rise in the price of energy and imported goods.[30] At that point, the economy abruptly stopped growing and land prices started to fall. The bubble had burst, and the period of Japan's overconfidence, excessive consumption, and overseas expansion came to an end. By 1992, the Japanese economy had plunged into a recession. Stock prices continued to tumble, with the Nikkei Stock Average reaching 15,000 in the summer of that year. "The asset price bubble occurred under very benign conditions, with low inflation and good financial conditions," noted Masayoshi Amamiya, director-general of the BOJ's monetary affairs department. "It's like a balloon: you can control the pace of growth, but once it bursts, you cannot control the pace of explosion."[31]

The Lost Decade

Japanese corporations, especially the financial institutions, were hard hit by the fall in asset prices. During the bubble era, many companies had made large investments in the stock market, and the fall in stock prices meant huge losses in capital assets. Weaker land prices also had serious consequences, striking not only the real estate sector, but also the banks that had extended loans to real estate companies; in many cases, land assets were used as collateral[32] (see **Exhibit 12**).

In December 1991, the official discount rate of 6% was lowered to 4.5%. However, the economy remained stagnant and land prices continued to fall. The official interest rate was lowered repeatedly until the rate finally reached 0.5% in September 1995,[33] a historic low since the introduction of official discount rates (see **Exhibit 8**).

In the meantime, non-performing loans (NPLs[34]) soared as land prices continued to decline. By FY 1992, there was 12.8 trillion yen worth of NPLs held by the Japanese banks[35] (see **Exhibit 13**). These loans had traditionally dominated the country's financial markets, while development of the capital market lagged behind. Companies relied on bank loans, and because banks played such a vital role in funding businesses, the relationship between companies and their banks became increasingly mutually dependent. This close relationship led to the problem of "ever-greening," where banks continued to extend new loans to failing companies, both to try to recover losses before they became apparent and under the false belief that real estate market would soon rebound.[36] In addition, banks themselves did not have the capacity to realize large losses by writing off bad loans.[37]

Although the MOF had always been reluctant to activate fiscal stimuli in order to try to maintain a balanced budget, in 1992 the MOF adopted a stimulus package of 10.7 trillion yen, followed by a series of similar packages, was adopted in order to overcome the deflationary state.[38] Fiscal measures were focused on spending increases rather than tax reductions, on the grounds that such an approach had a more immediate effect. However, partly because the measures were adopted later, this approach did not see immediate results. Although the fiscal stimuli may have contributed to offsetting a further decline of the economy, the introduction of the packages resulted in a drastic increase in public debt.

By 1995, the economic slowdown hit the small financial institutions such as housing loan companies and credit unions, and second-tier regional banks failed. Housing loan companies, which had expanded their business during the bubble economy by providing not only housing loans to individuals but also real estate loans to businesses, were deeply hit by the downturn. The housing loan companies had been funded by financial institutions such as agricultural banks. In 1996, after great controversy, 680 billion yen of public funds were injected in to an institution set up specifically to collect bad debt held by the housing loan companies (the institution later became part of The Resolution and Collection Corporation) on the basis that failure of the agricultural banks could trigger a crash of the entire financial system. There was strong criticism of the use of taxpayers' money to bail out the housing loan companies. There was also criticism of the responsibility of supervisory authorities such as the MOF and the Ministry of Agriculture, Forestry, and Fisheries, as well as the financial institutions that had been lax in providing funds to the housing loan companies. The bailout measure left ambiguity over the government's principles for the use of public funds.[39]

Financial crisis Despite these events, in the second half of 1995, the economy started to recover. The economy improved further when the government pre-announced a consumption tax rate increase, as people tried to buy more before the tax was implemented in April 1997. However, when the tax was actually raised from 3% to 5% and the temporary special income-tax cut expired in April (as planned), the growth of the economy stopped. This trend was exacerbated by the Asian currency crisis and the financial crisis that struck the Japanese banking industry later that year. Although the MOF had assured the public back in 1995 that no major bank would fail, three major banks—Hokkaido-Takushoku, Long-term Credit Bank, Nippon Credit Bank—failed in 1997 and 1998.[40] In 1998, the government decided to allow banks to apply either book value or the "lower of cost or market" (LCM) accounting method in assessing the value of stocks held by banks. If a bank chose to apply the book value method, then the bank would not have to write down a valuation loss unless the share price plunged to less than 50% of the book value. Because banks' capital would not be influenced by the fluctuation of stock prices, this measure was expected to ease the credit crunch.[41] Further, the government injected capital into the financial system in March 1998, but this turned out to be insufficient. In March 1999, the government made a second capital injection amounting to 7.5 trillion yen, which finally was effective in ending the financial crisis[42] (see Exhibit 14).

The accumulated disposal cost of NPLs held by all banks between April 1992 and March 1999 had amounted to 65.7 trillion yen (85.9 trillion yen after including government's capital injection and other assistance). Most Japanese banks had insufficient provisioning.[43] In 1999, the NPLs of Japanese banks consisted 7.8% of GDP, far exceeding the scope of the U.S. Savings & Loan Association crisis (see **Exhibits 15, 16,** and **17**). "In retrospect, I think we probably underestimated the magnitude of the potential size of the NPLs," recalled Hiroshi Nakaso, director-general, financial markets department of the BOJ. "In early 1990s, bad debt was considered a problem of smaller financial institutions and only few expected that it could develop into a major crisis involving major banks."[44]

Monetary Policy under the New Bank of Japan

In 1997, the Bank of Japan Law was revised for the first time in 55 years and went into effect in April 1998. The main objective of the revision was to give the BOJ greater independence from the government.[45] In addition to other changes, under the new BOJ law, executives could not be dismissed during their office term;[46] the number of Policy Board members was increased from seven to nine members—a governor and two deputy governors of the BOJ, and six Deliberative members appointed by the Cabinet from among those with academic expertise or experts in economy or finance. Government representatives (such as the minister of finance and the minister in charge of economic and fiscal policy, or a designated delegate) were able to attend meetings and express views or submit proposals, or make a request to postpone a Policy Board decision; but they had no voting rights.[47] Despite granting considerably more independence to the BOJ, the new law also specified that the BOJ should maintain close contact with the government so that currency and monetary control and the basic stance of the government's economic policy should be mutually harmonious (Article 4).[48] The BOJ was also required to provide the public with greater transparency on the content of its decisions, as well as its decision-making process for controlling its currency and monetary policies.[49]

Hayami Era

In March 1998, Masaru Hayami was appointed as the 28th governor of the BOJ. Hayami was a former BOJ executive director, who had left the bank 17 years ago and had held important posts such as the chairman of the Japan Association of Corporate Executives. His appointment coincided with the implementation of the new BOJ law.[50] Hayami expressed his aspirations in his first press conference:

> I would like to raise three issues as my goal. First, carry the new law into effect by enforcing the two principles "independence" and "transparency" as prescribed in the law. Second, carry out the financial market reform and realize the "Free," "Fair," and "Global" capital market announced by the Hashimoto government in November 1996 (Big Bang). Third, regain accountability of the BOJ. In terms of interest rate policy, the key issue is finding the appropriate timing to raise the rate which has been maintained at an extremely low level, and such timing will come when we have confirmed that self-sustaining recovery of the economy is underway.[51]

Zero interest rate policy Since 1995, the BOJ had applied the uncollateralized call rate, or the policy interest rate, instead of the official discount rate[52] as the bank's operating target for money market operations (see **Exhibit 25** for glossary). The failure of several major financial institutions in 1997 and 1998 increased overall economic instability. In September 1998, the uncollateralized call rate was lowered from just below the level of the official discount rate of 0.5% to 0.25%. However, economic conditions continued to worsen, with asset prices falling further and bad debt plaguing the books of the nation's banks. In order to prevent the economy from falling into a deflationary spiral and to ease the severe conditions for corporate financing, in February 1999 the BOJ decided to pursue further monetary easing by encouraging the uncollateralized overnight call rate to "move as low as possible"—thus the ZIRP.[53] At an April 1999 press conference, the governor revealed his intention to maintain the ZIRP "until deflationary concerns were dispelled."[54] A few months later, Hayami noted that "[m]onetary policy alone cannot solve all problems. We should recognize that the zero interest rate policy is an unusual and emergency measure. To truly revitalize the Japanese economy we must forcefully promote structural reform."[55]

The economy started to recover in 1999 after the ZIRP was introduced. A second capital injection to banks was implemented the following month, which stabilized the Japanese financial system and put an end to the Japan premium. The economy also benefited from the worldwide IT stock-price increases. By the spring of 2000, Governor Hayami started to suggest the possibility of terminating the ZIRP:

> We are drawing closer to seeing evidence of deflationary concerns disappearing. Companies' capital investment is gradually increasing, [and] although recovery of personal consumption is still weak, we can see signs that employment and wages are bottoming out.[56]
>
> Once we are able to see evidence that deflationary concerns are disappearing, we would like to terminate the zero interest rate, which was an emergency measure, and would like to regain a greater degree of freedom in terms of monetary policy.[57]
>
> [The] Japanese economy has the capacity to absorb a higher interest rate.[58]

On the other hand, government officials, business leaders, and many economists were more skeptical about the basis for implementing a tightening policy. Haruhiko Kuroda, vice minister of the MOF, commented, "The economy is improving gradually, and is not yet at a point where we should make any policy changes."[59] Hiroshi Okuda, chairman of the Japan Economic Federation and Toyota Motor Corporation, said, "We should wait and see the result of the April to June economic growth rate coming out in September before making decisions on ZIRP."[60] Prime Minister Mori also expressed his view that the "Japanese economy is not yet on a full-fledged recovery track, and we expect the BOJ to adopt appropriate policy measures."[61]

However, in August 2000, the BOJ decided by majority vote (7–2) to lift the ZIRP and encourage the uncollateralized overnight call rate to move to 0.25%. The central bank stated, "At present, Japan's economy is showing clearer signs of recovery, and this gradual upturn, led mainly by business fixed investment, is likely to continue. Under such circumstances, the downward pressure on prices stemming from weak demand has markedly receded."[62] Government officials attending the Monetary Policy Meeting (MPM) with no voting rights, however, submitted a motion to delay the voting for one month. This motion was rejected (8–1). Hayami asserted that the change in rates only represented a shift from a "super-super easy" credit policy to "super easy credit," emphasizing that this policy would be maintained until the economy was on a firm recovery track.[63]

Views on the change were divided. A national newspaper expressed support for the decision: "We have always said that since the policy was supposed to be an emergency refuge, it should be lifted as soon as possible."[64] Another national newspaper commented, "We can hardly expect that just raising the interest rate from zero to 0.25% will have the effect of promoting structural reform or stimulating consumption. On balance, impatiently lifting the ZIRP at this delicate stage was unnecessary."[65] A business paper pointed out that "[t]he government's exercise of its right to demand postponement of voting, especially when it was obvious that the motion would be rejected, had left a bitter aftertaste. It highlighted the fact that they did not respect the decisions of the BOJ which was supposed to have been granted independence, and it also led BOJ to lose market confidence over its ability to implement monetary policy."[66]

Only two months after the BOJ lifted the ZIRP, the Japanese economy took a downturn due to the strong yen and the worldwide economic slowdown triggered by the burst of the IT bubble (see **Exhibit 18**). The CPI inflation rate turned sharply negative and economic conditions deteriorated toward the end of 2000. The BOJ had to seek ways to stimulate the economy. In the MPM held on February, 2001, the BOJ decided to reduce the uncollateralized overnight call rate (policy interest rate) from 0.25% to 0.15% and the official discount rate from 0.5% to 0.25% (see **Exhibit 19**). The measures, however, were not effective in stimulating the economy.

Quantitative easing On March 19, 2001, the BOJ decided to make a significant change and implement a policy known as quantitative easing. "It was the first time any central bank adopted this approach,"[67] recalled Kazuo Ueda, professor at the University of Tokyo and former member of the MPM.[68] Instead of using the interest rate as a monetary policy instrument, the new policy applied the balance of BOJ's current account—the sum of financial institutions' reserves held at BOJ—as the main target for monetary operations.[69] The central bank set a higher target (five trillion yen) than the average required reserve held at the time (approximately four trillion yen). This meant that enough liquidity had to be provided into the market to enable financial institutions to place excess funds at the BOJ. The central bank injected liquidity by buying government bonds, bills, and equity shares held by banks. (Later in 2003, the BOJ decided to purchase asset-backed securities (ABS) that passed certain criteria and screening by the BOJ.[70])

Although the policy instrument differed, quantitative easing was considered to be, in effect, a return to ZIRP. This policy reversal, only seven months after the ZIRP was originally lifted, prompted criticism. The BOJ was accused of neglecting to make a thorough diagnosis of the economy and misjudging economic conditions. There was also the belief that the BOJ's desire to assert its independence led to the premature decision to lift the ZIRP.[71] In fact, the governor of the Bank of England, Mervyn King, commented in an article that "the BOJ was granted independence at a time when it was necessary for the monetary policy to be coordinated between the MOF and the BOJ."[72]

The new policy was controversial. Proponents believed that lowering interest rates to zero would flood the economy with enough cash to raise prices, while critics argued that quantitative easing could lead to a disastrous wave of hyperinflation. After announcing the rate cut, Hayami urged the government to introduce much-needed structural change: "The Bank of Japan strongly hopes that comprehensive steps will proceed rapidly on all fronts toward structural reform under the government's decisive leadership."[73]

That year, the target balance of the BOJ current account was increased from six trillion yen in August to 10–15 trillion yen in December. "Many tools were invented to inject liquidity into the banking system. Even if the banks had enough liquidity, we had to keep on injecting money to meet the target," reflected Nakaso of the BOJ.[74] However, as the financial sector still struggled with bad debt, the monetary easing measure was not effective in turning the economy around. Hayami, in the press conference after the announcement, commented, "as the long and short term interest rates have been kept at extremely low levels, the effect of raising the target amount cannot be assured."[75] Nobuyuki Nakahara, one of the MPM members, later criticized Hayami for expressing such a skeptical view toward the new policy.[76] In October 2002, the Nikkei Stock Average fell to below the 9,000 yen level, and the current account target was further raised to between 15 and 20 trillion yen.

Fukui Era

Upon expiration of Hayami's five-year term, Toshihiko Fukui was appointed as the new governor of the BOJ in March 2003. Fukui had been deputy governor of the BOJ before resigning to work in the private sector in 1998. When Fukui took the helm of the BOJ, Japan had been experiencing prolonged deflation. The world economy was also facing uncertainty as a result of the war in Iraq (which had just begun) and the SARS epidemic in East Asia.

Upon his appointment, Fukui stated in his inaugural press conference that "a central bank conducting monetary policy with very little room left for interest rate reductions was like a boxer fighting with his hands tied behind his back."[77] However, he made statements expressing his strong intention to put a stop to deflation by working more closely with the government. There was also a change in rhetoric from the Hayami era. Fukui made clear on numerous occasions that the BOJ intended to maintain the quantitative easing policy until the year-on-year increase in the CPI became stable at zero or above. This commitment strengthened the effect of the easing policy, since the market participants could anticipate monetary easing as long as the year-on-year increase of CPI remained negative[78] (see **Exhibit 20**). Nakaso commented, "An important new element was the 'time horizon' concept to create the market expectation that interest rates would remain flat until the CPI showed positive growth."[79] The details of conditions needed to terminate the policy were clarified in the MPM held in October 2003:

> (1) Not only the most recently published CPI should register zero percent or above, but also that such tendency should be confirmed over a few months; 2) The BOJ needed to be convinced that prospective CPI was not expected to register below zero percent; 3) The above two conditions being the necessary condition for termination, there might be cases [where] the BOJ would judge it appropriate to continue with quantitative easing even if they were fulfilled.[80]

Aware of criticism that the BOJ's implementation of monetary policy had not been timely enough, Fukui took a more aggressive approach. As soon as he assumed office, Fukui decided to raise the current account target several times to reach between 30 to 35 trillion yen in January 2004. Chikahisa Sumi, director of policy and legislative issues division of the Financial Services Agency, looked back and commented: "Many people criticized the quantitative easing policy when it was being implemented, as unorthodox, or a *foie gras* method where you were simply pumping in money into the system. However, I believe it was effective as a signal to the public about availability of money so people could take risks."[81]

Economic recovery By 2004, stock prices started to pick up and the Nikkei Stock Average reached the 11,000 level. In 2005, signs of economic recovery became clearer. The BOJ Outlook Report for April projected a relatively long period of growth, albeit at a moderate pace in 2005 and 2006.[82] There had been progress in adjustments of companies' excessive production capacity, labor, and debts, and corporate profits had recovered, exceeding the level at the end of the bubble (see Exhibit 21). On the finance side, progress had been made in reducing NPLs and restoring the soundness of the financial system. This was pursued as part of the Koizumi administration's overall effort to implement structural reforms, which also included the restructuring and consolidation of major industries such as steel, paper, and energy. Despite such improvements, companies remained skeptical of the recovery and were using profits to reduce interest-bearing liabilities; they were also continuing to restrain labor costs, which contributed to the stalled CPI.

In the second half of 2005, growing confidence in Japan's economic recovery and solid corporate earnings led to a rise in the equity market. The year-on-year change in the CPI reached zero from small negative figures.[83] Fukui and other BOJ members on various occasions made comments suggesting that quantitative easing would end once the conditions (i.e., continued positive growth in the CPI) were met. "With the year-on–year change in the CPI becoming zero percent in October, it is clear to everybody that quantitative policy is nearing an end," Fukui said in a speech to local business leaders in December of that year. He further stated that "quantitative easing was a very unusual policy and the framework restricted the bank's free hand in monetary policy as the BOJ had committed to maintain the easing policy until CPI posted a sustainable rise. And we expect the year-on-year change in the CPI to turn positive in November and December and to stay in positive territory with a wider margin in the January–March period."[84]

On the other hand, the government and ruling coalition (LDP and New Komeito) argued that the time was not ripe. Prime Minister Junichiro Koizumi had told reporters just a few days earlier that "it was too early to end the quantitative easing policy, and that the BOJ should be careful not to rush to change its present policy."[85] The government feared that the economy would backslide into deflation if the BOJ ended the policy prematurely. If deflation returned, the government would not be able to pursue its current structural reforms. The government was also concerned that termination of the policy might trigger a rise in the long-term interest rate. Because the government had an enormous fiscal deficit, any interest rate hike would significantly increase the interest payments on government bonds.

Termination of quantitative easing policy On March 9, 2006 the BOJ (by a 7–1 vote) finally lifted the quantitative easing policy, citing that the three conditions for termination were satisfied. The monetary policy instrument was switched from the BOJ current account balance to the uncollateralized overnight call rate. Just a few days earlier, the cabinet had openly warned that "if BOJ is going to go ahead with the termination of the quantitative easing policy, it must be ready to take responsibilities in case the policy shift does not work out."[86] The decision by Fukui was backed by the strength of the domestic economy, which posted a 5.5% real growth rate in the October–December 2005 period. The European central banks raised interest rates as well, while the U.S. Federal Reserve Board had also suggested to Congress a possible interest rate rise in March and May.

While announcing the shift in policy, the BOJ also pledged that the uncollateralized overnight call rate would remain effectively at zero percent in order to ease fears that termination of the easing policy might trigger an interest rate hike and dampen the economy. The bank also announced guidelines to prevent the market from falling into turmoil: gradual reduction of the outstanding balance of current accounts at the BOJ;[87] continued purchases of long-term interest-bearing Japanese government bonds for some time;[88] the inflation rate that Policy Board members understood as price stability from a medium- to long-term viewpoint in the conduct of monetary policy was agreed to lie within an approximate range between zero and two percent.[89]

The government said that it would respect the BOJ's decision, since the bank had promised to continue to support the economy with a zero interest rate policy. The chief cabinet secretary commented at a news conference, "We understand that the so-called zero-interest rate will continue and the easy money situation will be maintained. We want the BOJ to continue in a responsible manner [and] not to reverse the situation, in line with the significant policy goal of overcoming deflation in concert with the government."[90] The stock market reacted favorably to the announcement of the policy shift, since investors saw the change as putting an end to weeks of uncertainty.

Lifting of zero interest rate policy As the economy continued to recover steadily after the lifting of the quantitative easing policy, the focus shifted to when the BOJ would also exit from the zero interest rate policy. In the Outlook Report of April 2006, the BOJ had projected that the country's economy would experience a sustained period of expansion. Exports and corporate profits (which had marked four consecutive years of growth) remained strong. CPI annual inflation turned positive toward the end of 2005, followed by higher inflation in the beginning of 2006.[91]

In July 2006, the BOJ decided, by a unanimous vote, to abandon the ZIRP and encourage the uncollateralized overnight call rate to remain at around 0.25%.[92] The bank's decision to raise interest rates for the first time in more than five years was backed by solid growth of the economy. The year-to-year change in the May CPI (excluding fresh food) was positive. For seven consecutive months, the annual change in the CPI had been positive.[93] Fukui showed confidence in the state of the economy, commenting that the economy was stronger and more resilient to outer shocks compared with 2000, and therefore was unlikely to fall back to deflation as it did after the policy shift in 2000. Fukui also noted that "the BOJ will step carefully in adjusting interest rate levels, after gauging economic and price conditions," stressing that the termination of ZIRP did not mean the BOJ was planning repeated rate hikes.[94] The government and the ruling party, which had been opposed to lifting the quantitative easing policy, were more receptive to the policy change. A leading newspaper commented that "[t]he BOJ has managed to take an important step to proceed with normalizing its monetary policy in line with the economic growth."[95]

The market had already factored in the potential for a rate hike and did not overreact to the policy change because the May CPI and other economic figures had already revealed the solid state of the economy. Most companies had also already expected the interest rate hike, and were not largely affected by the termination of ZIRP. Moreover, major companies had already gone through financial restructuring, and about 30% of them were said to have no debt on their portfolios, since financing methods had become more diverse due to the development of the capital market. What was a concern to companies, however, was future interest rate hikes. From the tone of Fukui's press conference on the termination of ZIRP, most analysts and market participants did not expect another hike during the year 2006.[96]

Additional interest rate hike In January 2007, many market watchers anticipated an interest rate hike with the release of strong numbers in December. However, to their surprise, the BOJ decided to maintain the policy interest rate at 0.25% by a split vote of 6–3. In particular, Fukui and the two deputy governors agreed that the BOJ should wait for additional information to analyze and confirm the positive trend of consumer prices. Some market analysts agreed with the BOJ's decision given the remaining uncertainties. However, the decision left the impression that the BOJ had yielded to political pressure. Hidenao Nakagawa, the secretary general of the ruling LDP, had openly expressed opposition to a rise in rates, suggesting that the government exercise its right to postpone the BOJ's decision. Finance minister Koji Omi denied putting pressure on the BOJ, and Fukui stressed that the decision was based on careful analysis by the board members.[97]

Then in February 2007, the BOJ decided to raise the policy interest rate by 0.25% (vote of 8–1). The dissenting vote cited concerns over the future trend of consumer prices.[98] However, the majority agreed that the "Japanese economy was likely to continue its moderate expansion with a virtuous circle of production, income, and spending in place. Consumer prices, from a long-term perspective, are likely to increase as a trend, since the utilization of resources has been increasing and the economic expansion is expected to continue."[99] Although economic conditions were similar to the previous month, the announcement of strong economic figures (an October–December economic growth rate of near 5%) and the fact that Federal Reserve Board Chairman Ben S. Bernanke had recently showed confidence in a soft landing of the U.S. economy, worked in the favor of the policy change. Japanese government officials expressed their opinion that the BOJ should not rush to raise interest rates, but did not demand postponement of the decision. The BOJ confirmed in the announcement that "the Bank would adjust the level of interest rates gradually while maintaining the accommodative financial conditions ensuing from the very low interest rates for some time."[100]

The Interest Rate Debate

In an October 2007 BOJ report, the bank assessed that "the economy was expanding moderately; however, the pace of improvement in the household sector had remained slow relative to the strength in the corporate sector. The economy is likely to continue its sustained expansion, although there are uncertainties regarding overseas economies and global financial markets. The rate of real GDP growth in fiscal 2007 and 2008 is likely to register around 2 percent on average."[101]

Some critics argued that the ultra-loose monetary policy with near-zero interest rates had proved to be effective in turning around the unusually long and deep economic stagnation. Others, however, noted that persistently low interest rates had created some problems. First, low interest rates distorted the allocation of financial resources. Many borrowers could raise funds with more or less similar costs, regardless of differences in their credit ratings. Thus, poorly managed companies could easily survive without going through necessary restructuring or going bankrupt. Second, a large portion of incomes had shifted from the household sector to the corporate sector due to the low interest income of households and the low funding costs of corporations. Companies in the course of restructuring concentrated on improving profits while keeping the distribution of profits to labor low. This had helped the recovery of corporate activities, while allowing personal consumption to improve only moderately (see **Exhibit 22**). Such a situation, however, had also led to the enlargement of income disparities. Third, the wide interest-rate differential with other countries had induced large capital outflows, often called the "carry trade" (transactions featuring borrowing in yen and investing in higher-yielding currencies).[102] Although the effects of the subprime crisis and the weakening dollar remained to be seen, the carry trade came with a potential risk of financial instability in the event of a quick reversal of such capital flows.

For the BOJ, normalization of interest rates was a high priority because the BOJ could not effectively exercise its monetary policy as long as the interest rates were close to zero. The question was not whether the low interest rates needed to be corrected, but the appropriate timing and approach. "The key is the fact that the forward rate curve still maintains a positive slope. The market still believes in the growth story—that there will be a series of rate hikes," commented Nakaso of the BOJ.[103] However, the bank was cautious about enforcing premature rate hikes, since it did not want to repeat what happened in 2000 when the economy quickly reversed into deflation after the lift of ZIRP. According to a survey conducted by the *Nikkei Shimbun*, 60% of major corporations considered that the timing of the benchmark interest-rate hike in February was appropriate, while many executives expressed concern over further rate hikes. For example:[104]

> My understanding is that the interest rate raise enforced in February was not aimed at controlling prices but was more of an adjustment of the interest rate levels based on the past monetary policy of BOJ. Business recovery has not extended to local regions and medium- and small-sized companies, and personal consumption has not recovered either. [Nobuo Yamaguchi, chairman of the Japan Chamber of Commerce and Industry][105]

> We are beginning to see some bright signs in the market, such as a good sales record of premium beer products. However, personal consumption is not strong yet and we still do not have a strong sense of business recovery. It is important to maintain sustainable economic expansion that is led by private-sector demand. The BOJ should keep watch over the financial market and control sharp hikes in the interest rates. [Nobutada Saji, CEO of Suntory, Ltd.][106]

Although the economy had been on an uninterrupted recovery track for several quarters, to some critics, the current price performance did not justify a higher rate. The core consumer prices had been either very stable or even slightly moving downward, partly due to an increase in imports of low-priced products from countries that had recently joined the world economy, and because of continued technological innovation. "If you consider the risks additional rate hikes may have on the economy, perhaps the best way is to just wait and see at the present interest rate level," commented Hiromichi Shirakawa, chief economist of Credit Suisse Securities Japan, "but that argument does not seem to work easily for the BOJ."[107]

Separately, there had been debates among scholars and policy makers on whether "inflation targeting" should be introduced to enhance the transparency of monetary policy direction. Takatoshi Ito, professor at the University of Tokyo and member of the government's Council on Economic and Fiscal Policy, supported the application of inflation targeting. "By doing so, the BOJ can secure a reasonable distance between the government, as the Bank would be given authority to make any decision as long as it agrees with the inflation targeting framework."[108] However, critics such as Teizo Taya, special counselor at the Daiwa Institute of Research, questioned the effectiveness of the policy: "I understand the positive elements of the inflation targeting policy, however, I have doubts over whether the policy can be implemented effectively in the world of near zero interest rates."[109]

Many critics believed that if the BOJ had had an inflation target of two percent inflation in the 1990s, not only might it have introduced the ZIRP earlier than March 1999, but the BOJ would not have lifted ZIRP in August 2000, since deflation was still going on at the time. However, others argued that deflation could not have been avoided even if inflation targeting had been applied, although the degree of deflation might have been reduced. The BOJ had so far been opposed to such numerical targeting since the bank wanted to retain some room for its own discretionary judgment.[110] In October 2000, the board agreed (8–1) that it was not appropriate to define price stability by numerical values. There were criticisms that the BOJ was afraid to take any unprecedented actions that might be judged a failure later because of its recently gained independence and the need to establish credibility.

On the other hand, most political leaders wanted the BOJ to maintain the current monetary policy as long as possible. "The government will continue to pursue economic growth. I expect BOJ to fully understand our goal and make appropriate decisions," commented then-Prime Minister Shinzo Abe.[111] "Interest rate hikes could trigger a vicious cycle which could cause setbacks in political reform and contraction of the economy," criticized Hidenao Nakagawa, LDP secretary-general.[112] The cabinet and the mainstream of the ruling coalition parties were anxious to promote economic growth to increase overall tax revenue without raising tax rates. The MOF and many political leaders, backed by the OECD and the IMF, believed that fiscal consolidation was more urgent than monetary neutralization. Japan had public debt of approximately 170% of GDP, the largest among the developed countries. The MOF was anxious to normalize fiscal conditions since a rise in long-term interest rates meant increased interest payments on the huge government debt.[113]

In terms of the exchange rate, the wide interest-rate differentials had weakened the yen. Although the weak yen had benefited Japanese exports, it had also encouraged trading partners to demand a stronger yen. Under the new BOJ law, the BOJ had secured the autonomy of a monetary policy aiming at domestic price stability, but it was made clear that the BOJ would not have authority over the exchange rate policy. The exchange rate authority, MOF, was seemingly complacent about the continued export-led growth supported by the weak yen. Because exchange rates and domestic prices influenced each other, the BOJ could not ignore the value of the currency.

Others wondered whether it was sufficient for the BOJ to monitor mainly price performance to realize price stability. There were views that "a central bank concerned in stabilizing inflation about a specific target level is likely to achieve superior performance by adjusting its policy instruments not only in response to its forecast of future inflation and the output gap, but to asset prices as well."[114] Others emphasized the role of bank supervision, rather than monetary policy, for preventing and managing bubbles.[115] The BOJ was also required to coordinate with the Financial Supervisory Agency

(FSA), established in 1998 as the primary regulator of financial institutions and financial markets, and the MOF, in charge of fiscal and exchange policies.

Structural issues Japan had several structural issues that were closely related to the state of the economy. One of the most serious concerns was the demographic crisis. According to the 2005 population census, the population had declined from the previous year for the first time in the postwar period. The total population was expected to continue decreasing, due to the fact that more than 20% of the population was over 65 and the total fertility rate was low at around 1.3 per woman.[116] The so-called baby-boom generation was reaching retirement age in 2007. If participation of women and the elderly in the workforce remained at the same level, the labor participation rate was expected to decline to 54% in 2030 from 60% in 2007.[117] The demographic trends were directly linked to the increasing concerns over pension and health-care costs. Japan ran a pay-as-you-go pension system and needed periodic adjustments in payment and/or premiums to accommodate changes in demographics and other circumstances[118] (see **Exhibit 23**).

In terms of labor, the unemployment rate had slowly declined from the 5.5% peak in 2002 to 4.0% in September 2007 (see **Exhibit 24**). But the improvement in the employment rate had not led to improvements in the wage level because the ratio of part-time and temporary employment had increased. Wages of part-time employees were lower than those of regular employees—64% lower for men and 70% lower for women.[119] There was also a change in the lifestyles of the younger generation, with more people choosing not to find a permanent occupation and remaining as part-timers even after graduating from high school or college, with critics noting the loss of benefits associated with skill development through on-the-job training. There were also disparities among regions and industries and sectors. Retail and services were hiring more people, while construction and wholesale were hiring fewer; regions that had relied on public works were suffering high unemployment, while regions that had strong industries geared toward exports such as cars and auto-parts manufacturing had better employment opportunities.

Others noted the changes in the market structure. The business grouping and the so-called "keiretsu" relations continued to exist; however, the close relationship between banks and their borrowers (the "main bank" relationship) had been eroding since the banking crisis of the 1990s, due to the stricter lending policies of banks and the increased access to capital markets in Japan as well as abroad on the part of borrowers. Similarly, cross-shareholding between corporations and business partners or main banks had decreased as well.

The Decision

The BOJ faced a challenging decision. Recently disclosed October economic figures showed mixed results. Corporate results were improving and business investments were generally on the increase, while private consumption remained flat. There was a sharp decline in housing and construction starts due to a change in the regulation of construction standards. "Developments in the global financial market and the global economy continue to warrant attention," noted Fukui in the BOJ semiannual report to the House of Representatives.[120]

Exhibit 1 GDP and Components

Year	Nominal GDP (trillions of yen)	Private Consumption (% of GDP)	Government Consumption (% of GDP)	Gross Fixed Investment (% of GDP)	Exports (% of GDP)	Imports (% of GDP)	Real GDP (2000 prices) (trillions of yen)	GDP growth rate(%)	Real GDP per capita ($US at PPP)
1980	240	54.8	13.5	32.0	13.6	14.6	301.3		8,968
1981	259	54.2	13.6	31.0	14.6	13.9	310.3	3.0	10,036
1982	272	55.3	13.8	29.8	14.4	13.7	319.0	2.8	10,873
1983	283	56.0	14.1	28.2	13.8	12.1	324.2	1.6	11,408
1984	301	55.4	13.9	27.7	14.9	12.3	334.1	3.1	12,117
1985	323	54.6	13.5	27.9	14.3	10.9	351.1	5.1	13,045
1986	339	54.3	13.5	27.8	11.3	7.3	361.7	3.0	13,665
1987	352	54.6	13.6	28.6	10.3	7.3	375.1	3.7	14,495
1988	379	53.6	13.2	30.3	9.9	7.7	400.7	6.8	15,949
1989	408	53.4	13.0	31.4	10.4	8.8	421.9	5.3	17,357
1990	440	53.2	12.9	32.4	10.4	9.5	444.1	5.3	18,913
1991	468	52.9	13.0	31.8	10.0	8.4	458.9	3.3	20,163
1992	481	53.7	13.4	30.6	9.8	7.7	463.3	1.0	20,762
1993	484	54.6	13.8	29.3	9.1	6.9	464.2	0.2	21,229
1994	487	54.9	14.7	28.5	9.1	7.1	470.4	1.3	21,703
1995	493	55.1	15.1	28.0	9.2	7.8	479.6	1.9	22,514
1996	504	55.2	15.3	28.4	9.8	9.3	493.1	2.8	23,556
1997	516	55.2	15.3	27.8	10.9	9.8	500.8	1.6	24,288
1998	505	56.0	15.9	25.8	10.9	9.0	490.1	-2.1	23,997
1999	498	57.0	16.5	25.5	10.3	8.7	490.0	-0.02	24,303
2000	503	56.2	16.9	25.2	11.0	9.5	503.9	2.8	25,640
2001	498	57.1	17.5	24.7	10.6	9.9	504.7	0.2	26,258
2002	491	57.7	18.0	23.3	11.4	10.0	506.0	0.3	26,920
2003	491	57.5	18.0	22.8	12.0	10.4	513.4	1.5	27,849
2004	498	57.1	17.9	22.7	13.3	11.4	527.3	2.7	29,411
2005	501	57.1	18.1	23.1	14.3	12.9	537.2	1.9	30,850
2006	508	56.8	17.9	23.8	16.1	14.9	548.9	2.2	31,992

Source: Adapted from The Economist Intelligence Unit; Country Data—Annual Time Series, 2007.

Exhibit 2 Money Supply and Prices

Year	Stock of Money M1[a] (trillions of yen)	Stock of Quasi Money[b] (trillions of yen)	Stock of Money M2[c] (trillions of yen)	M2 Growth Rate (% pa)	Corporate Goods Price Index[d] (2000=100)	Consumer Price Index (1996=100)	Inflation Rate (% change of consumer prices pa)	GDP Deflator Inflation (% change of GDP deflator 1996=100)
1981	86.79	304.89	391.68	11.8	115.0	80.0	4.91	4.49
1982	91.93	336.15	428.08	9.3	115.5	82.2	2.74	2.19
1983	91.99	372.42	464.41	8.5	114.8	83.7	1.89	2.36
1984	98.13	402.82	500.95	7.9	114.9	85.6	2.25	3.16
1985	101.01	443.75	544.76	8.7	114.0	87.3	2.05	2.35
1986	111.22	483.56	594.78	9.2	108.6	87.9	0.62	1.68
1987	116.63	534.22	650.85	9.4	105.2	88.0	0.12	0.29
1988	126.21	583.75	709.96	9.1	104.7	88.6	0.65	0.75
1989	129.91	658.10	788.01	11.0	106.7	90.6	2.29	2.30
1991	142.88	745.84	888.72	5.5	109.4	96.4	3.27	2.96
1992	147.79	770.17	917.96	3.3	108.4	98.1	1.71	1.64
1993	157.58	800.95	958.53	4.4	106.7	99.3	1.27	0.55
1994	164.14	834.53	998.67	4.2	104.9	100.0	0.69	-0.84
1995	190.77	848.58	1,039.35	4.1	104.1	99.9	-0.12	-0.51
1996	208.78	870.10	1,078.88	3.8	102.4	100.0	0.13	-0.56
1997	249.81	891.75	1,141.56	5.8	103.0	101.8	1.77	0.62
1998	261.65	915.72	1,177.37	3.1	101.5	102.4	0.67	0.03
1999	290.37	919.98	1,210.35	2.8	100.0	102.1	-0.33	-1.27
2000	300.18	926.34	1,226.52	1.3	100.0	101.4	-0.71	-1.74
2001	312.63	705.17	1,017.80	-17.0	97.7	100.6	-0.76	-1.25
2002	381.43	645.81	1,027.24	0.9	95.7	99.7	-0.90	-1.55
2003	397.90	642.50	1,040.40	1.3	94.9	99.5	-0.25	-1.61
2004	414.08	629.16	1,043.24	0.3	96.1	99.5	-0.01	-1.08
2005	438.77	607.22	1,045.99	0.3	97.7	99.2	-0.27	-1.25
2006	439.72	599.07	1,038.79	-0.7	100.7	99.4	0.24	-0.91

Source: Compiled from the Economist Intelligence Unit; Country Data—Annual Time Series, 2007; The Bank of Japan, http://www.boj.or.jp/type/stst/dlong/price/cgpi/index.htm. Pre 2003 data estimated from discontinued M2 definition (exclude cash and deposits held by securities companies and Tanshi companies none resident deposites held by Japan Post Bank).

[a]Money M1 = total supply of notes and coins + demand deposits.

[b]Quasi Money = assets with properties resembling those of M1.

[c]Money M2 = M1 + quasi money.

[d]The Wholesale Price Index was changed to The Corporate Goods Price Index in 2001.

Exhibit 3a Fiscal Accounts

(billions of yen)	1995[a]	1997	1999	2000	2002	2004	2006[b]
Government Revenue	59,310	61,713	56,863	60,357	48,706	49,407	55,988
Government Expenditure	75,939	78,470	89,037	89,321	83,674	84,897	83,458
Paying Interest Expense	10,708	10,600	10,494	9,987	8,634	7,331	7,880
Interest Expense / Expenditure (%)	14.1%	13.5%	11.8%	11.2%	10.3%	8.6%	9.4%
Long-term Government Debt (balance)	296,991	357,471	448,777	490,748	535,710	563,922	594,498

Source: Adapted from Ministry of Finance, www.mof.go.jp/jouhou/syukei/sy030m.pdf.

[a]April to March fiscal year.

[b]2006 figures are for the revised budget.

Exhibit 3b General Government Debt (% of GDP)

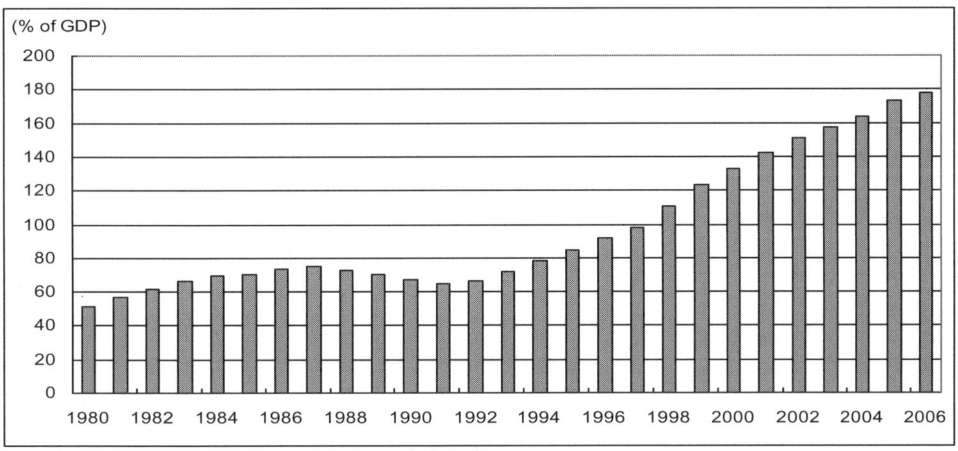

Source: Adapted from The Economist Intelligence Unit; Country Data—Annual Time Series, 2007.

Exhibit 4 Unit Labor Costs

Source: Yardeni.com.

Exhibit 5 Bond Yield and Other Interest Rates

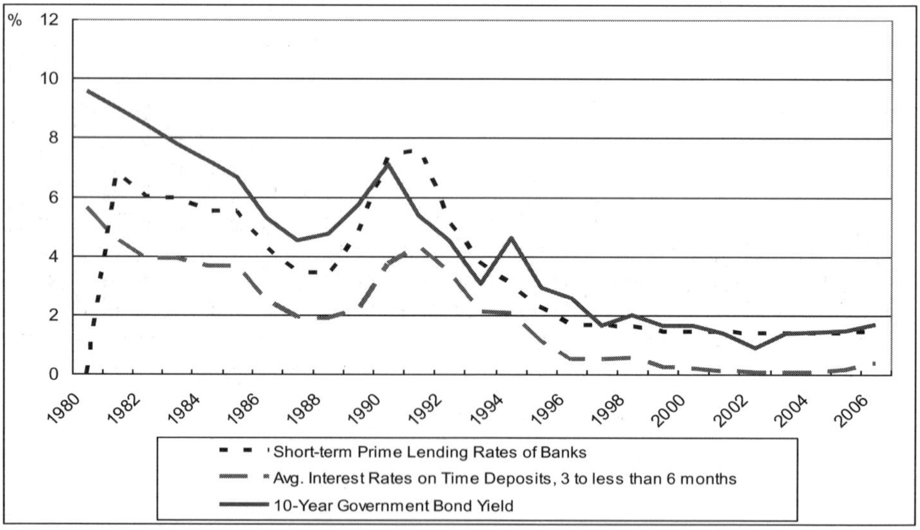

Source: Adapted from The Economist Intelligence Unit; Country Data—Annual Time Series, 2007.

Exhibit 6a Major Countries' Short-Term Interest Rates[a]

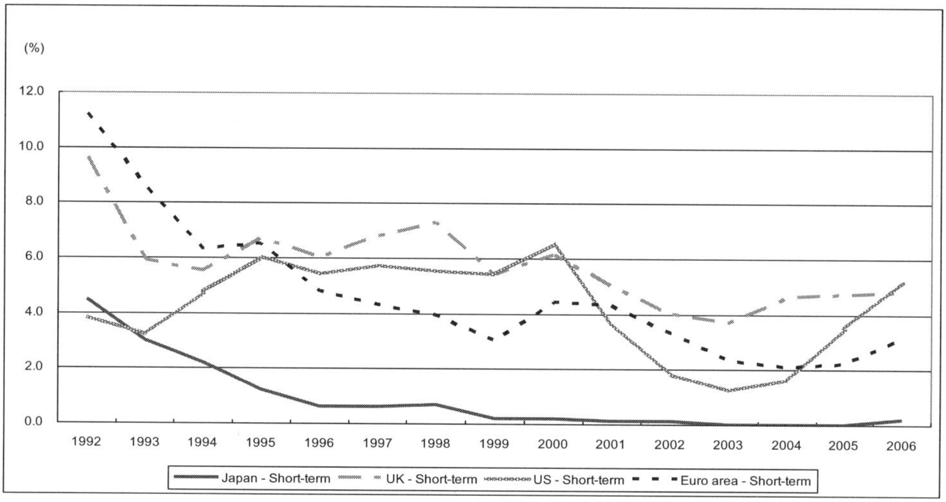

Exhibit 6b Major Countries' Long-Term Interest Rates[b]

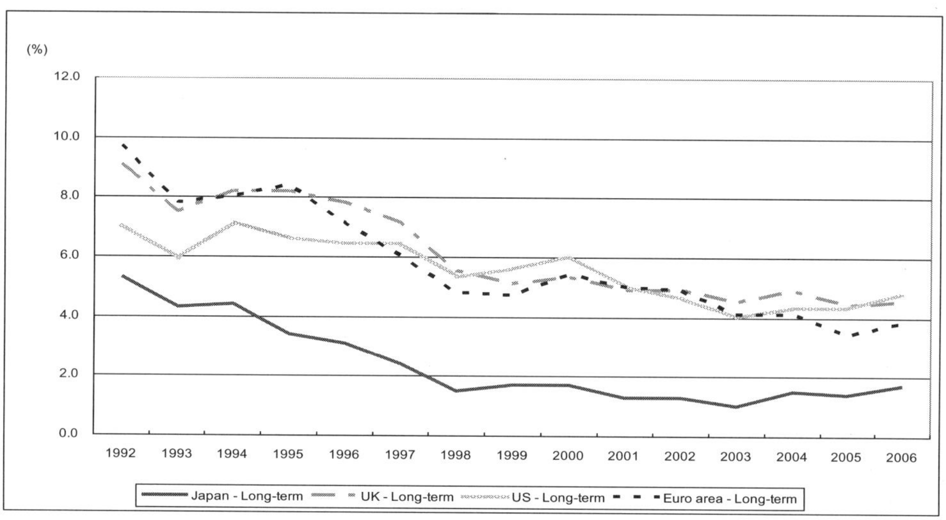

Source: Adapted from OECD Economic Outlook No. 81 database, May 2007.

[a]Three-month money market rates or rates on approximately similar financial instruments.

[b]10-year benchmark government bond yields or yields on approximately similar financial instruments.

Exhibit 7 Japanese Yen/US Dollar Exchange Rate (end-of-period)

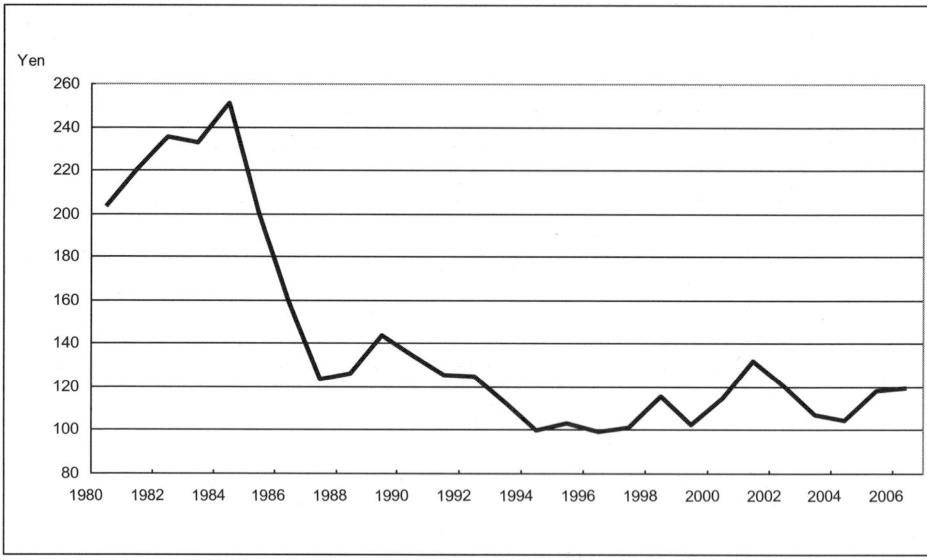

Source: Adapted from The Economist Intelligence Unit; Country Data—Annual Time Series, 2007.

Exhibit 8 Bank of Japan's Official Discount Rate[a]

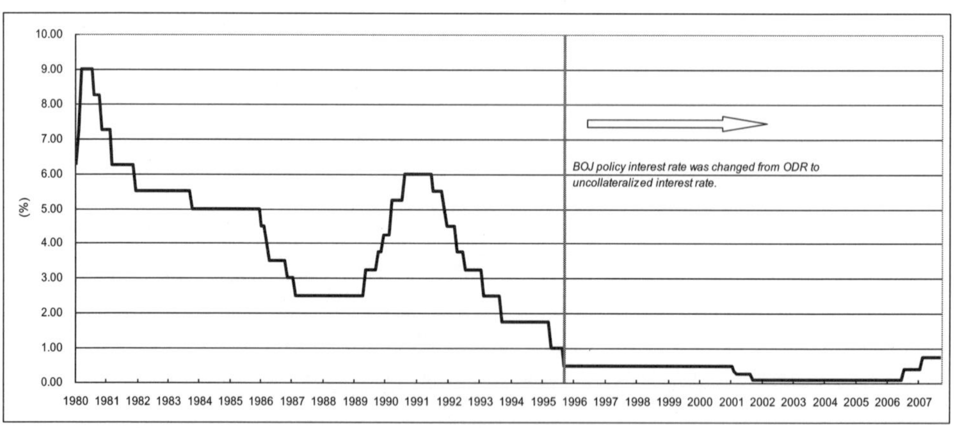

Source: Adapted from Bank of Japan, http://www.boj.or.jp/en/type/stat/boj_stat/discount.htm.
[a]In 2006, the "official discount rate" was changed to the "basic loan rate."

Exhibit 9 Balance of Payments (1980–2006)

(US$ billions)

	1980	1985	1990	1995	2000	2001	2002	2003	2004	2005	2006
Current Account	-10.8	49.2	35.9	111.0	119.6	87.8	112.5	136.2	172.1	165.8	170.5
Exports	126.7	174.0	280.4	428.7	459.5	383.6	395.6	449.1	539.0	567.6	615.8
Imports	-124.6	-118.0	-216.8	-296.9	-342.8	-313.4	-301.8	-342.7	-406.9	-473.6	-534.5
Trade Balance	2.1	56.0	63.6	131.8	116.7	70.2	93.8	106.4	132.1	94.0	81.3
Net Services	-12.1	-11.9	-44.7	-57.4	-47.6	-43.7	-42.2	-33.9	-37.9	-24.1	-18.3
Net Income	0.8	6.7	22.5	44.3	57.6	69.2	65.8	71.2	85.7	103.4	118.2
Net Transfers	-1.5	-1.7	-5.5	-7.7	-9.8	-7.9	-4.9	-7.5	-7.9	-7.6	-10.7
Financial Account	18.9	-53.5	-21.5	-64.0	-75.5	-48.2	-63.4	71.9	22.5	-122.7	-102.3
Direct Investment	-2.1	-5.8	-46.3	-22.5	-23.3	-32.3	-22.9	-22.5	-23.2	-42.2	-57.0
Portfolio Investment	-6.3	-0.3	7.0	-50.5	-36.0	-46.3	-105.9	-95.1	23.0	-13.3	127.5
Other Capital (net)	27.3	-47.4	17.8	9.0	-16.2	30.4	65.5	189.6	22.7	-67.2	-172.9
Errors & Omissions	-3.1	3.8	-20.9	13.8	16.9	3.7	0.38	-16.9	-28.9	-15.9	-31.4
Reserve assets				-60.8	-58.3	-40.1	-46.1	-187.1	-160.9	-22.3	-32.0

Source: Adapted from International Financial Statistics, August 2007, July 2001, 1997, and 1994, International Monetary Fund; Balance of Payments 1997, Japan Ministry of Finance.

Exhibit 10 Nikkei Stock Price Index (1980–2006)

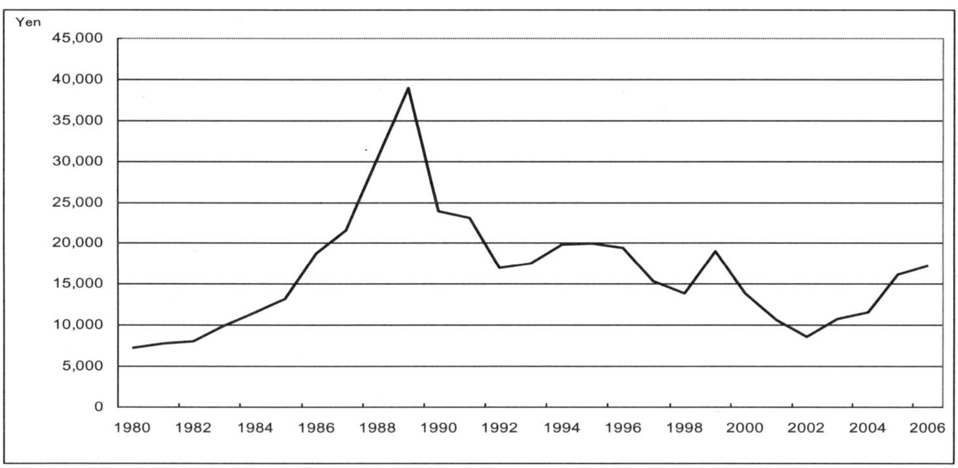

Source: Adapted from The Economist Intelligence Unit; Country Data—Annual Time Series, 2007.

Exhibit 11 Foreign Direct Investment

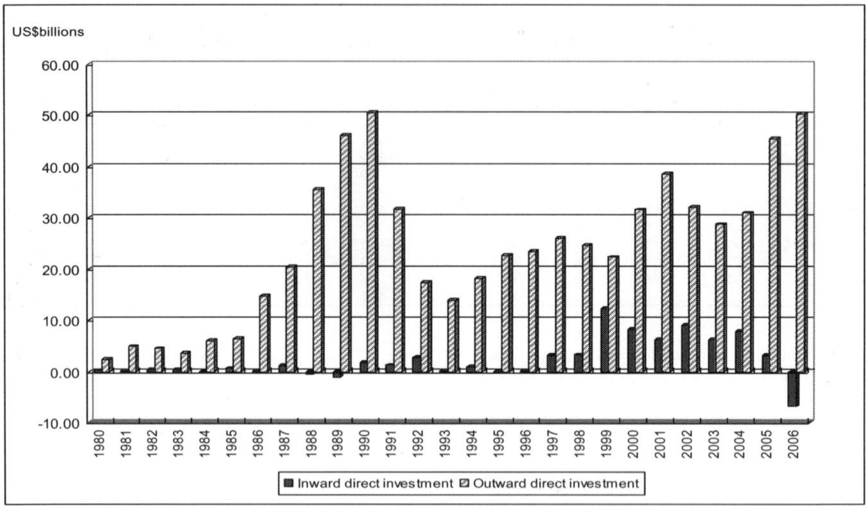

Source: Adapted from The Economist Intelligence Unit; Country Data—Annual Time Series, 2007.

Exhibit 12 Land Prices (year-on-year growth rate of official land prices for commercial land)

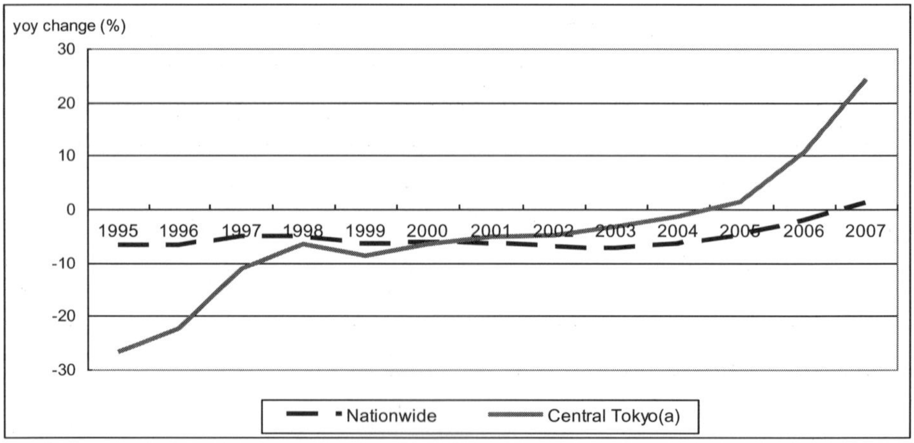

Source: Adapted from Hitomichi Shirakawa, Satoru Ogasawara, and Tomoko Shirotori, "Japan Economics Quarterly," October 2007, Credit Suisse Securities (Japan) Ltd., p. 35.

[a]Central Tokyo contains the Chiyoda, Chuo, Minato, Shinjuku, Bunkyo, Taito, Shibuya, and Toshima wards.

Exhibit 13 Amount of Loans (all domestic banks)

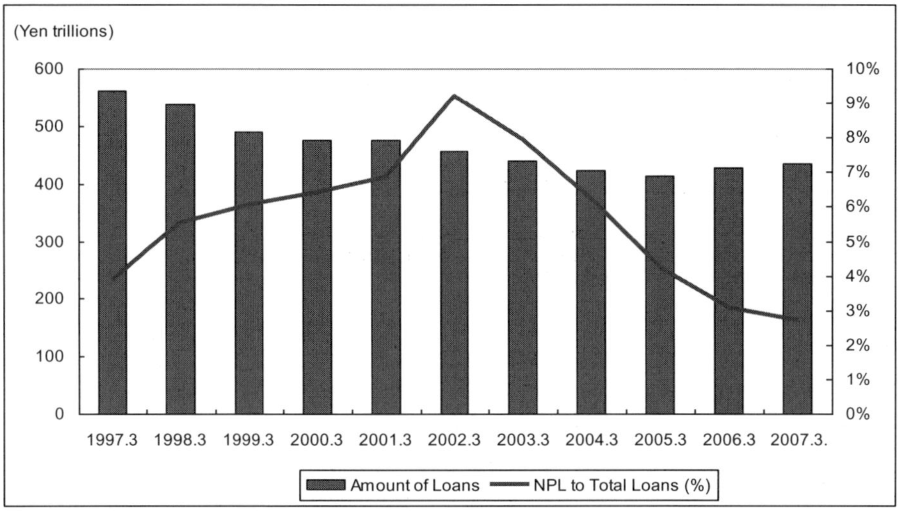

Source: Adapted from FSA data available at http://www.fsa.go.jp/status/npl/20070809/data05.pdf; Japanese Bankers Association data at http://www.zenginkyo.or.jp/stats/year2_01/index.html.

Exhibit 14 Profits and Loan Loss Charges of All Domestic Banks

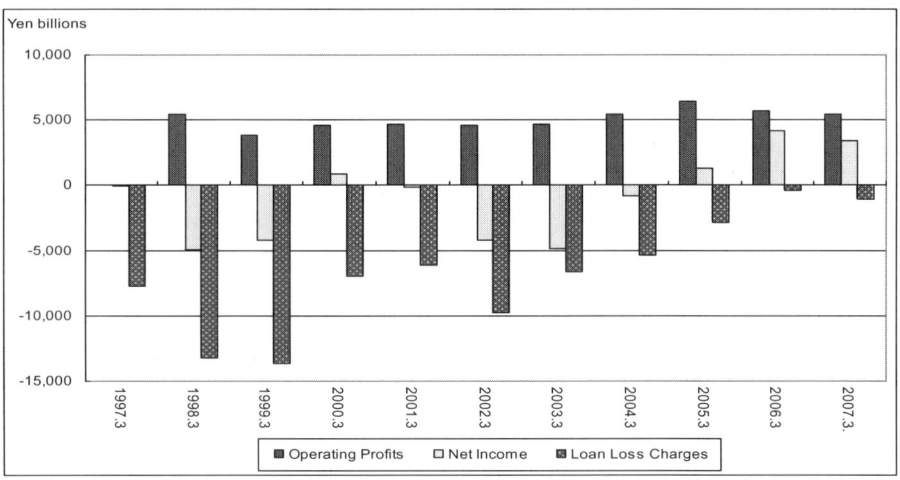

Source: Adapted from Japanese Bankers Association data, http://www.zenginkyo.or.jp/stats/year2_01/index.html.

Exhibit 15 NPL Ratios Comparison of U.S., Sweden, and Japan

		NPLs / GDP[a]	Assets / GDP	NPLs / Assets
Japan	(1999)	7.8%	217.4%	3.6%
United States	(1991)	2.9%	63.3%	4.5%
Sweden	(1992)	13.2%	130.1%	10.1%

Source: Adapted from Hiroshi Nakaso, "The financial crisis in Japan during the 1990s: how the Bank of Japan responded and the lessons learnt," BIS Papers No. 6 (Basel, Switzerland, October 2001), p. 59.

[a]NPLs/GDP = assets/GDP x NPLs/assets

Exhibit 16 Loan Losses and Bank Profits of Swedish and Japanese Banks in the 1990s

	Accumulated Loan Losses (A)	Average Annual Profit before Loan Losses (B)	A / B
Japan (all banks) (Yen trillion)	65.7 (FY1992 - 99)	4.97 (Avg. operating profit)	13.2
Sweden (major banks) (SEK billion)	204 (1991-97)	31.7 (Avg. annual profit)	6.4

Source: Adapted from Hiroshi Nakaso, "The financial crisis in Japan during the 1990s: how the Bank of Japan responded and the lessons learnt," BIS Papers No. 6 (Basel, Switzerland, October 2001), p. 59.

Exhibit 17 Use of Public Funds for Financial Restructuring (U.S., Sweden, Norway, Finland, and Japan)

	Public Funds Used	Ratio to Nominal GDP	
Japan	70 trillion yen	14%	
United States	U$ 200.8 billion	3%	Expenditure on Resolution Trust Corporation, Federal Savings and Loan Insurance Corporation, and interest payment for bonds issued by the Resolution Funding Corporation
Sweden	SEK 65.9 billion	4%	Total expenditure until July 1994
Norway	NOK 24.9 billion	3%	Total expenditure until July 1993
Finland	FIM 33.5 billion	7%	Total expenditure until July 1995

Source: Adapted from Hiroshi Nakaso, "The financial crisis in Japan during the 1990s: how the Bank of Japan responded and the lessons learnt," BIS Papers No. 6 (Basel, Switzerland, October 2001), p. 60.

Exhibit 18 GDP Growth of Japan and Other Major Countries

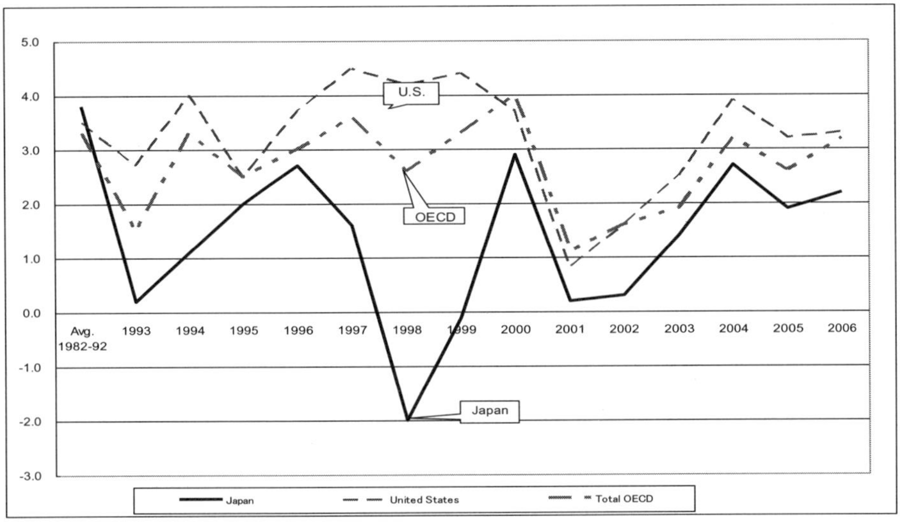

Source: Adapted from OECD Economic Outlook No. 81 database, May 2007.

Exhibit 19 Bank of Japan's Current Account Target, Outstanding Balance, Overnight Call Rate

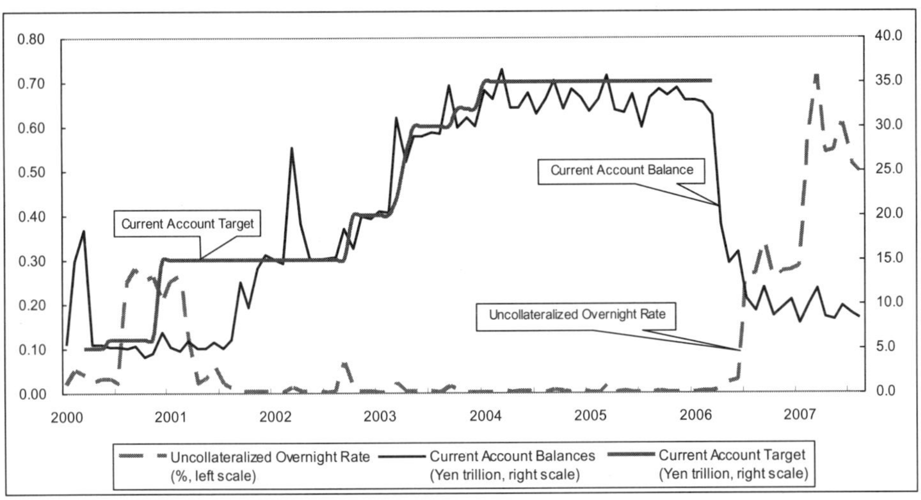

Source: Adapted from Bank of Japan, "The Basic Discount Rate and Basic Loan Rate" tables, Monetary Base table, and Bank of Japan's Transactions Stock table.

Exhibit 20 Consumer Price Index (% change per year)

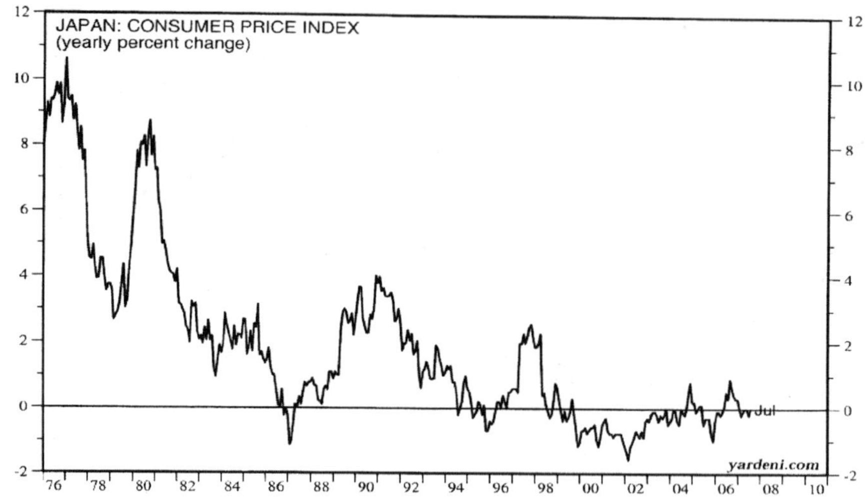

Source: Yardeni.com

Exhibit 21 Return on Equity (Listed Japanese Companies)[a]

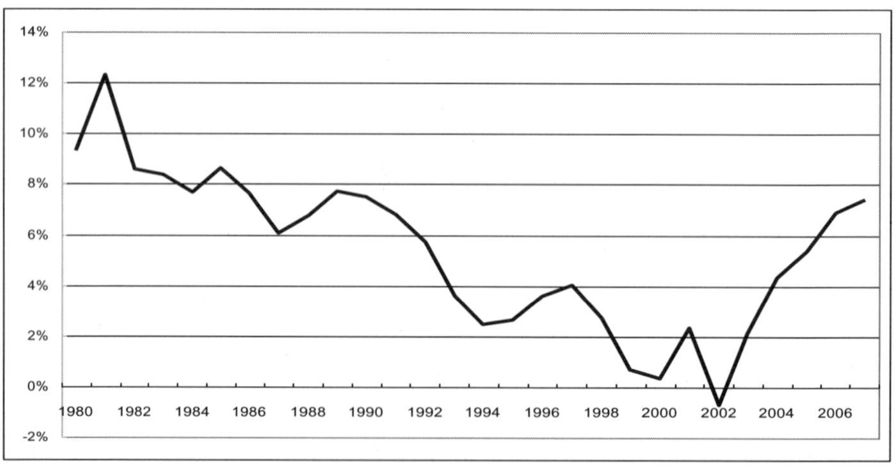

Source: Adapted from Summary of Earnings Digest (April–March business term, listed companies) 2007, Tokyo Stock Exchange, Inc.

[a]Listed companies are companies in 29 industries, and include all manufacturing and non-manufacturing companies except the financial industry. (April–March business term)

Exhibit 22 Savings per Household (thousands of yen)

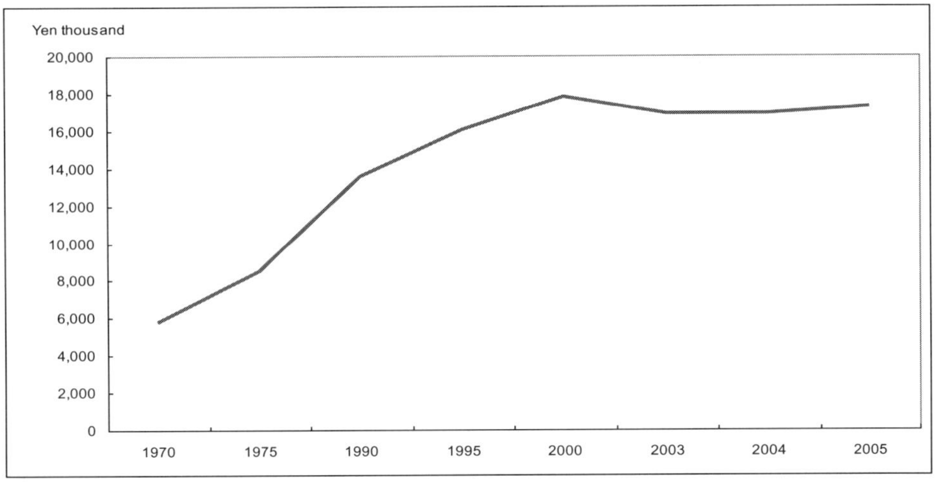

Source: Adapted from Statistics Bureau & Statistical Research and Training Institute data, http:// www.stat.go.jp/data/nihon/zuhyou/n/900800.xls.

Exhibit 23 Trends in Ratio of Public Expenditure by Function

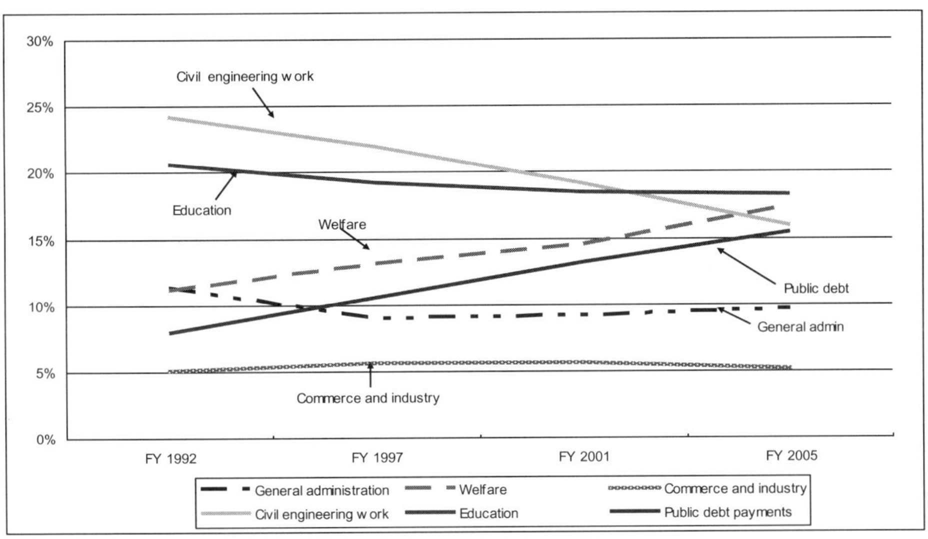

Source: Adapted from White Paper on Local Public Finance 2007, p. 15, Ministry of Internal Affairs and Communications.

Exhibit 24 Unemployment Rate

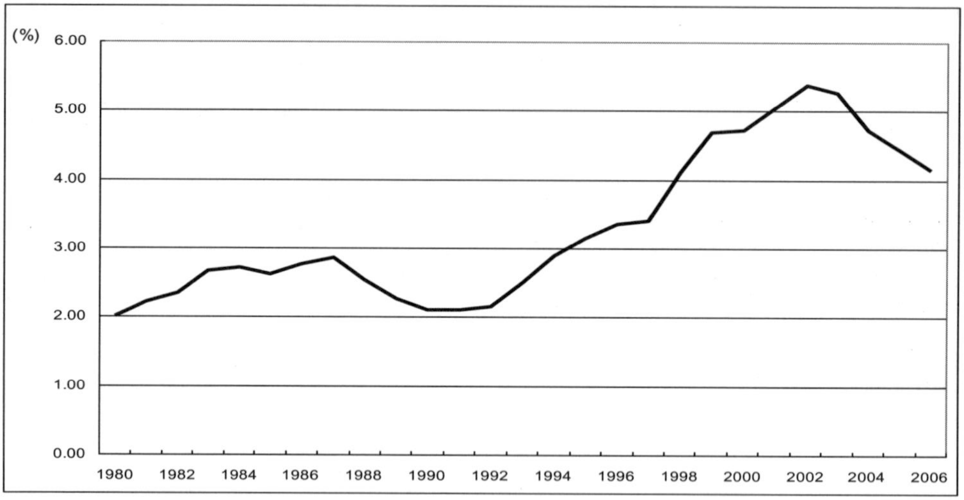

Source: Adapted from The Economist Intelligence Unit; Country Data—Annual Time Series, 2007.

Exhibit 25 Glossary of Financial Terms

Bank of Japan Current Account: The account that private financial institutions held at the Bank of Japan. Financial institutions were required to hold a certain percentage of customer deposits as reserves (required reserves) in this account. Transactions of funds between the BOJ and the financial institutions were made through this account. In the quantitative easing policy, the BOJ used the current account as a means for monetary operations by setting a target balance that exceeded the amount of the required reserve, which in effect lowered the overnight call rate to close to 0%.

Capital Adequacy Ratio: The ratio of a bank's capital to its credit exposure. The Bank for International Settlement (BIS) required banks engaged in international operations to maintain a capital adequacy ratio of 8%.

Carry trade: Transactions that involved borrowing in yen at a low interest rate and investing in higher-yielding currencies.

Inflation targeting: To first set and make public a certain target inflation rate (level of prices), and to conduct monetary policy through the use of interest rates, by steering actual inflation toward the target.

Japan premium: The additional premium that overseas banks charged when lending funds to Japanese banks with low credit ratings.

Official Discount Rate: The interest rate applied when the Bank of Japan lent funds to private financial institutions.

Overnight uncollateralized interest rate: The rate akin to the federal funds rate in the U.S. It was the interest rate that private financial institutions paid for borrowing overnight funds in the inter-bank market. The level of this rate would influence other interest rates such as the banks' lending rate to companies and individuals, which thereby controlled the prices of commodities. When the Bank of Japan reverted to the zero interest rate policy in March 2001, the BOJ abandoned the call rate as the target and started targeting the amount of deposits held at the central bank.

Policy interest rate: The rate the BOJ directly controlled to stabilize the prices of commodities. The BOJ set a target for the uncollateralized call rate, which was the interest rate that private financial institutions paid for borrowing overnight funds in the inter-bank market. The level of this rate would influence other interest rates such as the banks' lending rate to companies and individuals, which thereby controlled the prices of commodities.

Source: Adapted by casewriter from Bank of Japan, http://www.boj.or.jp, accessed December 5, 2007; Nomura Securities, http://www.nomura.co.jp/terms/, accessed December 5, 2007; and Takeo Hoshi and Anil K. Kashyap, "Japan Economic and Financial Crisis: An Overview," *Journal of Economic Perspectives* (Winter 2004).

Endnotes

[1] "BOJ Governor Press Conference on 0.25% Interest Rate Raise," *The Nikkei Shimbun*, February 22, 2007, p. 1.

[2] "A hikers' guide to Japan," *The Economist*, February 22, 2007.

[3] Ibid.

[4] "Saving Grace," *The Economist*, May 3, 2007.

[5] "Why doesn't the CPI increase?—Evolution of PCs Is Pulling Down the Figures," *The Nikkei Shimbun*, August 12, 2007, p. 27.

[6] Michiyo Nakamoto, "Japan Warned Against Further Rate Rise," FT.com, May 24, 2007.

[7] "2007 Article IV Consultation with Japan—Concluding Statement of the IMF Mission," IMF, http://www.imf.org/external/np/ms/2007/052407.htm, accessed July 5, 2007.

[8] Ibid.

[9] Statement by Toshihiko Fukui, governor of the BOJ, concerning the bank's *Semiannual Report on Currency and Monetary Control* before the Committee on Financial Affairs, House of Representatives, on November 2, 2007.

[10] Takenori Inoki, *Nihon no Kindai 7: Keizai seicho no Kajitsu 1955–1972* ["A History of Modern Japan 1955–1972: Fruits of Economic Development"] (Tokyo: Chuokoron Shinsha, Inc., 2000), p. 135.

[11] Richard H. K. Vietor, *How Countries Compete—Strategy, Structure, and Government in the Global Economy* (Boston: Harvard Business School Press, 2007), p. 36.

[12] The ministry was changed to Ministry of Economy, Trade and Industry (METI) in 2001.

[13] In 1998, the Financial Supervisory Agency was established as an administrative organ of the prime minister's office, responsible for inspection and supervision of private sector financial institutions and securities transactions. FSA website, http://www.fsa.go.jp/en/about/pamphlet.pdf, accessed July 12, 2007.

[14] In 1949, after WWII, an amendment was made to the Law, and the Policy Board was established as the bank's highest decision-making body. The Policy Board members consisted of the governor, two government representatives (one from MOF and another from Economic Planning Agency), and four industry representatives who were appointed from private institutions. However, actual decisions were made at board meetings which the governor, deputy governors, and executive directors of BOJ attended, and the Policy Board simply confirmed the decisions reached at the board meetings.

[15] Bank of Japan website, http://www.boj.or.jp/en/type/exp/about/expboj.htm.

[16] For example, whenever the economy overheated, it led to a current account deficit, which would call for monetary tightening measures (raising of interest rates), which would lead to a current account surplus, which would then lead to monetary easing (lowering of interest rates).

[17] Tetsuji Okazaki, "Japan Monetary Policy and Macro Economy: Reassessment from the Historical Perspective," *Financial Review*, June 1999 (Tokyo: Ministry of Finance, Policy Research Institute), pp. 3–9.

[18] Yoshio Suzuki, *Nihon no Kinyuu Seisaku*, ["Monetary Policy of Japan"] (Tokyo: Iwanami Shoten, 1993), p. 22.

[19] Suzuki, p. 23.

[20] Ibid., pp. 36–37.

[21] The inflation rate is the annual percentage change of yearly averages of consumer price indices, not end-of-period data. International Monetary Fund, http://www.imf.org/external/pubs/ft/weo/2002/02/data/pcpi_b.csv, accessed July 9, 2007.

[22] Ibid.

[23] Suzuki, p. 45.

[24] Richard H. K. Vietor, "Japan: Deficits, Demography, and Deflation," HBS No. 706-004 (Boston: Harvard Business School Publishing, 2006), p. 2.

[25] Suzuki, p. 88.

[26] Ibid., p. 90.

[27] Ibid., p. 94.

[28] Tetsuji Okazaki, "Japanese Monetary Policy and Macro Economy: Reassessment from an Historical Perspective," *Financial Review,* June 1999 (Tokyo: Ministry of Finance, Policy Research Institute), pp. 17–18.

[29] Kazuo Ueda, *Zero Kinri to no Tatakai* ["A Battle against Zero Interest Rate"] (Tokyo: Nikkei Shimbun Sha, 2005) p. 146.

[30] Suzuki, pp. 129–130.

[31] Casewriter's interview with Masayoshi Amamiya, November 2007.

[32] Suzuki, p. 132.

[33] Bank of Japan website, http://www.boj.or.jp/type/stat/boj_stat/discount.htm, accessed June 4, 2007.

[34] Non-performing loans were also referred to as Risk Management Loans, which included the total amount of loans to legally bankrupt companies and loans past due for six months or more. In 1995, risk management loans were reclassified, and NPLs included loans for which interest rates were reduced. From 1997, risk management loans included loans past due for three months or more, and restructured loans.

[35] FY1992 ended in March 1993.

[36] Takatoshi Ito and Frederic S. Mishkin, "Two Decades of Japanese Monetary Policy and the Deflation Problem," in *Monetary Policy with Very Low Inflation in the Pacific Rim,* eds. Takatoshi Ito and Andrew K. Rose (Chicago: The University of Chicago Press, 2006) p. 138.

[37] The Bank for International Settlement (BIS) required banks engaged in international operations to maintain a capital adequacy ratio of 8%. When calculating it, banks were allowed to count in 45% of unrealized gain of stockholdings as capital. However, after the bubble burst, stock prices plunged and banks' unrealized profits on stocks disappeared. As a result, banks' capital adequacy ratio became considerably lower, and they could not afford to lower the ratio any further. Ueda, pp. 163–164.

[38] During 1990s, eight economic stimulus packages totaling approximately 120 trillion yen, including 60 trillion yen of public investment and 16.4 trillion yen of tax reductions, were adopted. As a result, general government debt as a percentage of GDP reached 130% in 2000, which was the worst among OECD countries.

[39] "View on risk management, Kosai Yutaka of Japan Center for Economic Research," *The Nikkei Kinyu Shimbun,* June 20, 1996, p. 1.

[40] Ito and Mishkin, pp. 138–139.

[41] Before 1998, stocks held by banks were assessed by the "lower of cost or market" method, whereby losses were recorded in case the market price of a stock was lower than the acquisition (book) value. From April 2001, the market value was applied. ("How should banks accommodate the new financial stability law—worries on application of book value to stocks held by banks—banks could have different views," *The Nikkei Shimbun,* February 18, 1998, p. 7.)

[42] Ito and Mishkin, p. 139.

[43] Hiroshi Nakaso, "The financial crisis in Japan during the 1990s: how the Bank of Japan responded and the lessons learnt," BIS Papers No. 6 (Basel, Switzerland, October 2001), p. 18.

[44] Casewriter's interview with Hiroshi Nakaso, November 2007.

[45] In the original BOJ Law, the MOF was given the authority to instruct the BOJ regarding policy making. Also, the MOF was involved in the selection process of the BOJ governor, although the cabinet officially made the appointment and there was a convention to appoint an ex-MOF high official as the governor of BOJ every other term. Under the former law, Policy Board members were the governor, two government representatives—one from MOF and the other from the Economic Planning Agency—and four industry representatives.

[46] Except for limited circumstances such as health conditions. Bank of Japan website, http://www.boj.or.jp/en/type/law/bojlaws/bojlaw1.htm, accessed June 8, 2007.

[47] Bank of Japan website, http://www.boj.or.jp/en/type/law/bojlaws/bojlaw1.htm, accessed June 8, 2007.

[48] Ibid.

[49] "In addition to monetary policy, the BOJ was responsible for prudential (financial stability) policy. BOJ had the power to step in and look at a financial institution's balance sheets. The primary regulator of financial institutions was the Financial Supervisory Agency, but the BOJ had the power to conduct on-site and off-site examination." Casewriter's interview with Hiroshi Nakaso, November 2007.

[50] The new Policy Board now had four new members; two from the business community (Toshio Miki, chairman of Nittetsu Shoji Co., Ltd. and Nobuyuki Nakahara, honorary chairman of Tonen Corporation) and two from academia (Kazuo Ueda, University of Tokyo and Eiko Shinotsuka, Ochanomizu University), in addition to the two other members (Yasuo Gotoh and Susumu Taketomi) who had been appointed before the revision of the law. The six deliberative members, and governor and two deputy governors of BOJ held regular (two times a month, in principle) Policy Board meetings called Monetary Policy Meetings (MPMs) to discuss and make decisions regarding monetary policy exclusively. The new members were expected to revitalize the board which used to be criticized as a "Sleeping Board," where the board just rubber-stamped the decision made at BOJ's internal executive meetings. After the meetings, the governor held press conferences to announce any decisions taken, and minutes were released one month after the meetings.

[51] "BOJ Governor Press Conference—Interest Rate Raise Depends on Economic Recovery," *The Nikkei Shimbun*, "Instability of Financial System Has Hit the Bottom," March 23, 1998, p. 16.

[52] When deregulation of interest rates was completed in 1994, the strong linkage between the official discount rate and deposit rates ceased to exist, and interest rates were determined by arbitrage in the market. Thus, the uncollateralized overnight call rate became the policy interest rate, and the official discount rate served as the upper limit of the overnight call rate. The term "official discount rate" was changed to "the basic discount rate and basic loan rate" in 2006. "Change in the Term for the So-called 'Official Discount Rate' in Statistics," August 11, 2006, Bank of Japan website, http://www.boj.or.jp/en/type/release/zuiji_new/nt_cr_new/ntdis01.htm, accessed January 15, 2008.

[53] "BOJ Annual Review 1999," p. 5, Bank of Japan website, http://www.boj.or.jp/en/type/law/bojlaws/bojlaw1.htm, accessed June 11, 2007.

[54] "BOJ Governor, Continue ZIRP until Deflationary Concerns Are Dispelled," *The Nikkei Shimbun*, April 14, 1999, p. 5.

[55] Speech given by Masaru Hayami at the Japan National Press Club in Tokyo on June 22, 1999. Bank of Japan website, http://www.boj.or.jp/en/type/press/koen/kako/ko9907b.htm, accessed November 8, 2007.

[56] May 19, 2000, scheduled briefing. "Gradually Nearing the End of Deflationary Concerns—Also Keeping a Watch on US Economy," *The Nikkei Shimbun*, May 20, 2000, p. 5.

[57] June 14, 2000, press conference, "Remarks on Termination of ZIRP," *The Nikkei Shimbun*, June 30, 2000, p. 5.

[58] July 10, 2000 briefing at the International Settlement Bank held in Basel Switzerland. "Recent Remarks regarding Termination of ZIRP," *The Nikkei Shimbun*, July 18, 2000, p. 3.

59 "Minister of Finance and Others Comment against Possible Lift of ZIRP," *The Nikkei Shimbun*, June 7, 2000, p. 2.

60 Ibid.

61 Ibid.

62 "Change of the Guideline for Money Market Operations," August 11, 2000, Bank of Japan website, http://www.boj.or.jp/en/type/release/zuiji/kako02/k000811.htm, accessed June 14, 2007.

63 "Bank of Japan Votes to Lift Zero Interest Rate Policy," Media Resources—*Japan Brief*, Foreign Correspondence Center of Japan, August 28, 2000.

64 Ibid.

65 Ibid.

66 "Bitter After Taste Left after Lift of ZIRP," *The Nikkei Shimbun*, August 12, 2000, p. 2.

67 From 1979 to 1982, the Federal Reserve Bank adopted a similar approach, but in the opposite direction, by targeting non-borrowed reserves in an attempt to contain inflationary pressure in the economy.

68 Casewriter's interview with Kazuo Ueda, November 2007.

69 The monetary base includes the amount of current account at the BOJ. In normal times, excess reserves would be unlikely to stimulate the economy. However, an expansion of the monetary base might be beneficial even if it did not produce a significant increase in the money supply when the interest rate was zero (when conventional monetary tools were no longer effective because lenders would not accept a negative interest rate, since hoarding cash provided a higher return). Liquidity might help avoid a potential financial crisis; it might encourage financial institutions to take more risks in portfolio management (taking positions in long-term bonds, equities, and foreign bonds) which might contribute to stimulating the economy indirectly; it might provide a signal that the monetary base would be higher than it would be once the deflation was over. For more, see Takatoshi Ito and Frederic S. Mishkin, p. 177. On potential signal effects, see Alan, J. Auerbach and Maurice Obstfeld, "The Case for Open Market Purchases in a Liquidity Trap," NBER Working Paper No. 9814 (Cambridge: National Bureau of Economic Research, July 2003).

70 ABS were based on banks' loans as well as account receivables held by small and medium-sized companies. "BOJ to purchase ABS—to support financing of small and mid-sized companies to bring about reform in corporate financing," *The Nikkei Shimbun*, July 25, 2003, p. 5.

71 "Lift of ZIRP—Leaving an Unpleasant Aftertaste," *The Nikkei Shimbun*, August 15, 2000, p. 3.

72 Mervyn King, "The Institutions of Monetary Policy," *American Economic Review* (May 2004): 11.

73 P. Landers and P. Dvorak, "Deflation Fighter: Japan's Central Bank Issues Wakeup Call on Flagging Economy," *The Wall Street Journal*, March 20, 2001.

74 Casewriter's interview with Hiroshi Nakaso, November 2007.

75 Nobuyuki Nakahara, *Nichigin Ha Darenomonoka* ["Who Controls the BOJ?"] (Tokyo: Chuokouron Shinsha, 2006), p. 192.

76 Ibid, pp. 191–193.

77 Speech by Toshihiko Fukui, *Challenges for Monetary Policy in Japan*, at the Spring Meeting of the Japan Society of Monetary Economics, June 1, 2003, Bank of Japan website, http://www.boj.or.jp/en/type/press/koen/k0306a.htm, p. 2, accessed June 20, 2007.

78 Summary of speech by Toshihiko Fukui at a meeting with business people in Nagoya, September 3, 2003, Bank of Japan website, http://www.boj.or.jp/en/type/press/koen/k0309a.htm, p.4, accessed June 20, 2007.

[79] Casewriter's interview Hiroshi Nakaso, November 2007.

[80] Minutes of the Monetary Policy Meeting, October 9 and 10, 2003, Bank of Japan website, http://www.boj.or.jp/en/type/release/teiki/giji/g031010.htm, pp. 15-16, accessed June 20, 2007.

[81] Casewriter's interview with Chikahisa Sumi, November 2007.

[82] "Outlook for Economic Activity and Prices," April 2005, Bank of Japan website, http://www.boj.or.jp/en/type/release/teiki/tenbo/gor0504.htm, accessed June 20, 2007.

[83] "Financial Markets Report—Developments during the Second Half of 2005," January 2006, Bank of Japan website, http://www.boj.or.jp/en/type/ronbun/mkr/mkr0602.htm, accessed June 21, 2007.

[84] "Easy Monetary Policy Near End: Fukui," *The Japan Times*, December 9, 2006.

[85] Ibid.

[86] "Distance between BOJ and Government Widens as the Government Pressure BOJ by Asking for Absolute Liability," *The Nikkei Shimbun*, March 10, 2006, p. 2.

[87] "Change in the Guideline for Money Market Operations," March 9, 2006, Bank of Japan website, http://www.boj.or.jp/en/type/release/zuiji_new/k060309.htm, accessed June 21, 2007.

[88] Ibid.

[89] "The Introduction of a New Framework for the Conduct of Monetary Policy," March 9, 2006, Bank of Japan website, http://www.boj.or.jp/en/type/release/zuiji_new/k060309b.htm, accessed June 21, 2007.

[90] "BOJ lifts ultra loose policy," *The Japan Times*, March 10, 2006.

[91] "Outlook for Economic Activity and Prices," April 2006, Bank of Japan website, http://www.boj.or.jp/en/type/release/teiki/tenbo/gor0604.htm, accessed June 23, 2007.

[92] "Change in the Guideline for Money Market Operations," July 14, 2006, Bank of Japan, http://www.boj.or.jp/en/type/release/zuiji_new/k060714.pdf, accessed June 23, 2007.

[93] "BOJ Decision to Lift ZIRP—Government Acceptance Implies Silent Pressure," *The Nikkei Shimbun*, July 16, 2006, p. 3.

[94] Ibid.

[95] "BOJ terminates zero-rate policy," *The Japan Times*, July 15, 2006.

[96] "Special Feature: Impact of Termination of ZIRP," *Weekly Diamond*, July 29, 2006, pp. 14–18.

[97] "Widely awaited BOJ rate hike a no-show," *The Japan Times*, January 19, 2007.

[98] Deputy Governor Kazumasa Iwata, a former University of Tokyo Professor who had worked for the cabinet office's director-general, cast the dissenting vote.

[99] "Change in the Guideline for Money Market Operations," February 21 2007, Bank of Japan website, http://www.boj.or.jp/en/type/release/zuiji07 /k070221.pdf, accessed June 25, 2007.

[100] Ibid.

[101] "Outlook for Economic Activity and Prices," October 2007, Bank of Japan, p. 1.

[102] It was difficult to estimate the total transaction amount as definitions varied, but it was said to have amounted to $80 billion or even $500 billion at one time in 2007. "Skeptical View on the Myth Concerning Reversal of Yen Carry Trade," *Weekly Economist* (Mainichi Shimbunsha), August 21, 2007, p. 34.

[103] Casewriter's interview with Hiroshi Nakaso, November 2007.

[104] "Quick Corporate Executives Survey on Additional Interest Raise—60% of Major Corporations Consider the Timing as Appropriate," *The Nikkei Shimbun*, February 22, 2007, p. 9.

[105] Ibid.

[106] Ibid.

[107] Casewriter's interview with Hiromichi Shirakawa, November 2007.

[108] "Special Report—Behind the Scenes of BOJ Shelving Rate Raise, and the Consequences," *Weekly Toyo Keizai*, February 3, 2007, pp. 30–32.

[109] "A Debate on Whether the BOJ Should Implement Inflation Targeting," *Weekly Toyo Keizai*, May 13, 2006, p. 103.

[110] Ito and Mishkin, p. 167, and the author's interview with the casewriter.

[111] "Government and the Ruling Party Cautious against Additional Rate Raise," *The Nikkei Shimbun*, January 13, 2007, p. 5.

[112] Ibid.

[113] "A Defeated General Speaks of the Lost Battle," *Nikkei Business*, October 2006, pp. 185–188.

[114] Stephen G. Cecchetti, Hans Genberg, John Lipsky, and Sushil Wadhwani, "Asset Prices and Central Bank Policy," *Geneva Report on the World Economy No. 2*, http://people.brandeis.edu/~cecchett/Genive_Report.htm, accessed August 13, 2007. Ben Bernanke of the FRB had a different view that price stability was the most important indicator, and that "changes in asset prices should affect monetary policy only to the extent that they affect the central bank's forecast of inflation." See Ben S. Bernanke and Mark Gertler, "Should Central Banks Respond to Movements in Asset Prices?" http://www.princeton.edu/~bernanke/asset.doc, accessed August 13, 2007.

[115] Ito and Mishkin, p. 141. See also Takatoshi Ito, "Looking forward on monetary policy and supervision policies to protect against bubbles," in *Asset Price Bubbles: The Implications for Monetary, Regulatory, and International Policies*, eds. W.C. Hunter et al. (Chicago: MIT Press, 2003), pp. 547–552.

[116] The average number of children that a woman would give birth to over her lifetime.

[117] "Working Population Expected to Decrease to Two-Thirds by 2050, Based on Government Estimation, Key is Participation of Women and the Elderly," *The Nikkei Shimbun*, February 22, 2007, p. 3.

[118] In 2004, the Koizumi government implemented a reform to prevent the system from going bankrupt from the rapid increase of retired people. Premium rates were increased; benefit levels were dropped. The eligibility age for retirement had already been lifted from 60 to 65 in 2000. However, the government subsidies for the basic pension still had to rise to keep the revised benefit rate on schedule. Richard Vietor, "Japan: Deficits, Demography, and Deflation," pp. 5–7.

[119] "What's the Difference between Regular and Part-time Employees?" *The Nikkei Shimbun*, October 16, 2007, p. 19.

[120] Statement by Toshihiko Fukui, governor of the BOJ, concerning the Bank's *Semiannual Report on Currency and Monetary Control* before the Committee on Financial Affairs, House of Representatives, on November 2, 2007.

9-709-056
MARCH 27, 2009

LAURA ALFARO
AKIKO KANNO

Kinyuseisaku: Monetary Policy in Japan (B)

At the start of the year 2009, the Bank of Japan (BOJ) governor, Masaaki Shirakawa faced a dire situation. The prospect of the Japanese economy looked grim, as the global recession triggered by the U.S. subprime mortgage meltdown had brought about serious negative impact to the country.

End of Fukui Era

In March 2008, Toshihiko Fukui, the governor of BOJ was expected to end his term later that month. When he assumed office in 2003, the stock market was at historical low since the burst of the bubble economy with Nikkei 225 Stock Average moving near the 7,000 yen level. During his five years as Governor, the economy recovered. As the end of his term neared in March 2008, the stock prices had reached the 12,000 level and the policy interest rate was increased to 0.5% following the end of quantitative easing and the zero interest rate policy (ZIRP).

As the Japanese economy started to feel the impact of the worldwide recession, the BOJ was shook by the confusion of finding a successor to Fukui. The BOJ governor was appointed by the Cabinet and required approval by both houses of the Diet. However, as a result of July 2007 Upper House election, the two houses were ruled by different parties; the Upper House by the opposition party (Democratic Party of Japan), and the Lower House by the governing coalition party (Liberal Democratic Party). The twist in the Diet caused turmoil in the appointment of the new BOJ governor.

On March 12th, the Upper House voted down the government's initial choice: BOJ deputy governor Toshiro Muto based on the reason that his background as a former vice finance minister could weaken the BOJ's independence from the government. The next candidate, Koji Tanami, governor of the Japan Bank for International Cooperation and also a former vice minister was also rejected by the Upper House. The rejection on March 19th came on the same day that Fukui's term expired. As the two parties blamed each other for the delay in appointment of successor, BOJ found itself without a governor for the first time in its postwar history.[1]

Masaaki Shirakawa, serving as the acting chief to take care of the BOJ's day-to-day operations expressed his determination in the press conference held on the day of his appointment, "We are in an unusual situation in that the BOJ governor's seat is vacant, but the economy and financial markets move every day without a pause, and any halt in BOJ operations cannot be accepted."

Professor Laura Alfaro and Research Associate Akiko Kanno prepared this case. This case was developed from published sources. HBS cases are developed solely as the basis for class discussion. Cases are not intended to serve as endorsements, sources of primary data, or illustrations of effective or ineffective management.

Appointment of Masaaki Shirakawa as the Governor of BOJ

On April 9th, 2008 Shirakawa was appointed as the governor of BOJ, three weeks after Fukui's term had expired. Shirakawa, who had joined BOJ in 1972, was versed in not only monetary policy but also regulatory matters. In July 2006, he had retired from the BOJ to become a professor at Kyoto University School of Government. Upon departure of Fukui, he had been called back to become the deputy governor, and just a few weeks later, found himself to be the governor of BOJ. The media and market received him as a specialist of monetary policy, and a well fit person for the post. The new governor faced a difficult situation. The U.S. crisis had caused grave damage to the global economy. Central banks in major economies implemented various measures including reduction in policy interest rates. In the meantime, the political row resulted in giving rise to doubts about independency of BOJ and further "accelerated a negative image of Japan as a country with no sense of crisis."[2]

BOJ's Outlook report issued at end of April 2008 viewed that although "there were downside risks to the economy stemming from uncertainties regarding future developments in overseas economies, the economy is likely to continue its moderate growth from fiscal 2008 through fiscal 2009."[3] In the monetary policy meeting held the following month, the policy board decided unanimously to maintain the policy interest rate at the 0.5% level. Shirakawa stated that bank losses related to subprime related loans were still at a level which could be absorbed by the financial institutions' periodical income and did not pose serious risk to the financial system.[4] The direct impact of the U.S. financial crisis on Japanese banks appeared to be limited because the Japanese banks had significantly reduced international exposure during the stagnation period of the 1990s.

Lehman Shock

The financial crisis intensified when Lehman Brothers Holdings filed for bankruptcy on September 15th, 2008. The bankruptcy was followed by failure or near failure that led to acquisitions by competitors of other large financial institutions. As Japan was primarily an export-led economy, the deepening financial crisis in the U.S. and the slowdown in international trade had direct negative impact on Japanese companies. The weakening of the U.S. economy triggered a sharp increase in the value of the yen, which also affected the country's exports.

On October 8th, the Federal Reserve Board (FRB), European Central Bank (ECB) and four other central banks announced that they would take a concerted step to cut policy interest rates by 0.5%.[5] On the same day BOJ issued a statement welcoming the policy decision by the six central banks, and that BOJ would cooperate by providing liquidity to the market, however not by cutting rates on the basis that that the Japanese policy interest rates were already at a very low level and that moderate domestic economic conditions were being maintained.[6]

The coordinated efforts were not enough to bring the financial turmoil under control. Concerns over deepening worldwide recession led to sharp appreciation of the yen from around 105 to the dollar in mid September to 95 to the dollar in late October. The Nikkei 225 stock average plunged to near the 7,000 yen level. Sense of serious crisis and worsening of domestic economy began to daunt. At the Monetary Policy Meeting held on October 30th, the BOJ decided to cut interest rate by 0.2% and to encourage the uncollateralized overnight call rate to be at around 0.3%. The FRB had implemented an additional rate cut a day earlier, and the ECB was expected to follow.

In November, major auto manufacturer Toyota announced that consolidated sales for the financial year ending March 2009 would decrease by two trillion yen (down by 62.5%), and net profit would be decrease by 700 billion yen (down by 56%) respectively from the original May earnings estimates.

Additional Rate Cut

By the end of 2008 global markets continued to fall as the U.S., the euro area continued to deteriorate and economic growth in emerging markets fell.[7] The yen continued to appreciate against the dollar reaching 89 to 90 to the dollar, reflecting concerns over a harsher U.S. recession. In Japan, one after another, companies announced downward revisions of their earnings forecasts. Major manufacturers curtailed production, and few announced lay-off of non-regular workers. As manufacturing plants tended to be located in the suburbs, many contract plant workers had been provided with company housing. As a result of the layoffs, those workers ended up not only jobless, but also without places to live. The number of non-regular workers had surged since the deregulation of 2004 which allowed contract workers in manufacturing industries. Without adequate safety net, the unemployment had emerged as one of the most urgent economic, social and political problems.

Fiscal measures were being awaited under such economic conditions however the political confusion was preventing the government to act promptly. Moreover, the large public debt disabled the government to implement large scale economic stimulus measures.

At the Monetary Policy Meeting held on December 19th, just three days after the US FRB cut its interest rate almost to zero, the BOJ decided to reduce the policy interest rate to 0.1% from 0.3%. The BOJ also announced that it would introduce unconventional measures such as outright purchasing of commercial papers, and increase outright purchases of Japanese government bonds (JGBs),[8]based on the judgment that additional measures utilizing money market operation tools were necessary for the effects of extremely low policy interest rates to prevail in financial markets and corporations.[9] Although extensive bond purchasing by the BOJ was a key part of the quantitative easing policy, Shirakawa insisted that he had not returned to quantitative easing.[10] A few days after the BOJ announcement, Toyota revised its earning forecast: expected net profit would be 50 billion yen, a decrease by 500 billion (90%) from the revised forecast announced just over a month ago.

Policy Decisions

At the start of 2009 the Japanese economy looked gloomy. The rapid deterioration of exporting companies had led to worsening of unemployment, further accelerating the slowdown of the economy. In early March, the government vowed to implement additional fiscal action. The government indicated possible measures to support the stock market and announced the use of part of its foreign reserves (nearly $1 trillion) to provide loans to Japanese companies operating abroad. "A contingent and extraordinary step," announced Kaoru Yosano, finance minister, "to help the many Japanese companies facing difficulty raising foreign currency funds from the market".[11] Toyota said its US financing arm aimed to seek dollar funds through the new program. Later that month, the BOJ increased its purchases of JGBs by nearly a third, the latest in a series of ever more assertive measures to respond to the global financial crisis and a fierce domestic recession.[12]

Exhibit 1 GDP and Components

Year	Nominal GDP (trillions of yen)	Private Consumption (% of GDP)	Government Consumption (% of GDP)	Gross Fixed Investment (% of GDP)	Exports (% of GDP)	Imports (% of GDP)	Real GDP (2005 prices) (billions of yen)	GDP growth rate(%)
2000	503	56.2	16.9	25.2	11.0	9.5	4,268.8	2.8
2001	498	57.1	17.5	24.7	10.6	9.9	4,275.6	0.2
2002	491	57.7	18.0	23.3	11.4	10.0	4,287.1	0.3
2003	491	57.5	18.0	22.8	12.0	10.4	4,349.7	1.5
2004	498	57.1	17.9	22.7	13.3	11.4	4,468.0	2.7
2005	502	57.0	18.1	23.3	14.3	12.9	4,553.9	1.9
2006	508	57.1	17.9	23.4	16.1	14.9	4,647.3	2.1
2007	515.8	56.3	17.9	23.4	17.6	15.9	4,656.9	2.4
2008	507.4	57.8	18.5	23.0	17.5	17.3	4,721.5	-0.7
2009	*484.9*	*59.1*	*19.7*	*20.9*	*12.5*	*12.1*	*4,441.4*	*-5.9*
2010	*483.2*	*59.2*	*20.1*	*20.8*	*12.4*	*12.6*	*4,449.3*	*0.2*

(2009 and 2010 figures are forecasts derived from Cabinet Office Japan, except for Read GDP figures calculated by EIU)

Source: Compiled from the Economist Intelligence Unit; Country Data- Annual Time Series, March 2009.

Exhibit 2 Bond Yield and Other Interest Rates (2003 ~ 2008)

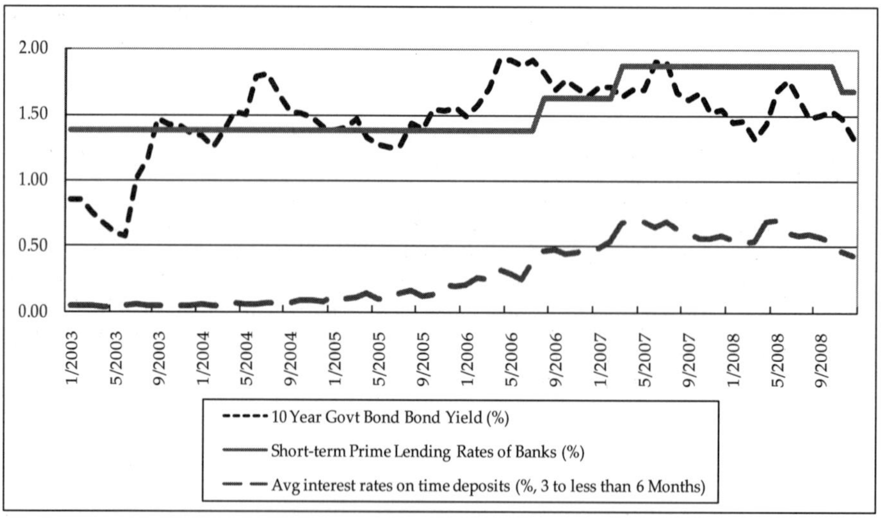

Source: Compiled from the Economist Intelligence Unit; country Data- Monthly Indicators, March 2009.

Exhibit 3 Fiscal Accounts (2003 - 2008)

(billions of yen)	2003[a]	2004	2005	2006	2007[b]	2008[c]
Government Revenue	47,071	49,407	54,251	53,976	58,372	57,713
Government Expenditure	82,416	84,897	85,520	81,446	83,804	83,061
Paying Interest Expense	7,780	7,331	7,029	7,044	8,555	9,341
Interest Expense / Expenditure (%)	9.4%	8.6%	8.2%	8.6%	10.2%	11.2%
Long-term Government Debt (balance)	525,173	563,922	590,500	594,498	607,065	614,677

a April to March Fiscal Year
b 2007 figures are the revised budget
c 2008 figures are budget

Source: Adapted from Ministry of Finance data available at www.mof.go.jp/jouhou/syukei/siryou/sy-new.htm, accessed March 2009.

Exhibit 4 Balance of Payments (2003 - 2008)

(US$ billions)	2003	2004	2005	2006	2007	2008
Current Account	136.2	172.1	165.8	170.5	210.5	157.3
Exports	449.1	539.0	567.6	615.8	678.1	749.5
Imports	-342.7	-406.9	-473.6	-534.5	-573.3	-710.5
Trade Balance	106.4	132.1	94.0	81.3	104.8	39.0
Net Services	-33.9	-37.9	-24.1	-18.3	-21.3	-21.7
Net Income	71.2	85.7	103.4	118.2	138.5	153.0
Net Transfers	-7.5	-7.9	-7.6	-10.7	-11.5	-13.0
Financial Account	71.9	22.5	-122.7	-102.3	-187.2	-
Direct Investment	-22.5	-23.2	-42.2	-57.0	-51.3	-
Portfolio Investment	-95.1	23.0	-13.3	127.5	73.1	-
Other Capital (net)	189.6	22.7	-67.2	-172.9	-209.1	-
Errors & Omissions	-16.9	-28.9	-15.9	-31.4	17.3	-
Reserve assets	-187.1	-160.9	-22.3	-32.0	-36.5	-

Source: Adapted from Economist Intelligence Unit; Country Data- Annual Time Series, March 2009; International Financial Statistics, March 2009, August 2007, July 2001, International Monetary Fund.

Exhibit 5 Nikkei 225 Stock Average Price Index (2003 - 2009)

Source: Compiled from the Economist Intelligence Unit; Country Data- Monthly Indicators, March 2009.

Exhibit 6 Japanese Yen/US Dollar Exchange Rate (end-period, 2003 - 2009)

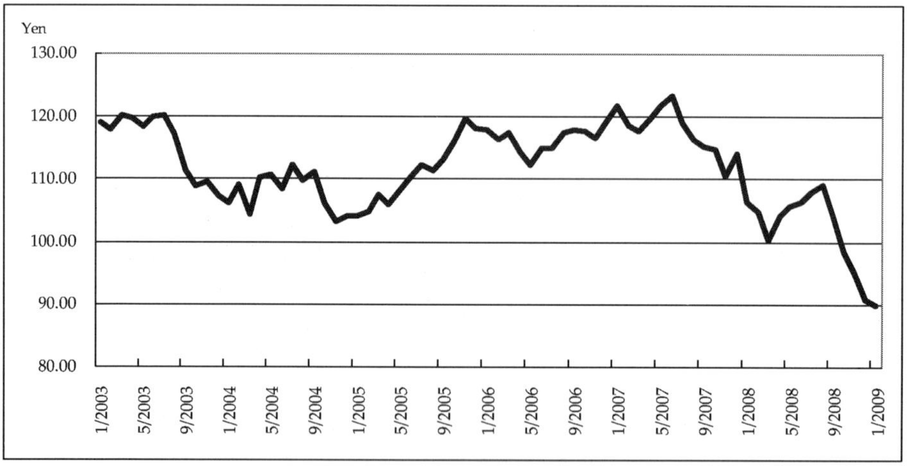

Source: Compiled from the Economist Intelligence Unit; Country Data- Monthly Indicators, March 2009.

Endnotes

[1] On March 20th, only the two new deputy governors, Masaaki Shirakawa – former executive director of BOJ, and Kiyohiko Nishimura - a member of the BOJ's Policy Board since 2005, were appointed. The two deputy governors also required approval by both houses of the Diet.

[2] Critics by Yasuihide Yajima, a senior economist at NLI Research institute. "Shirakawa takes acting charge of BOJ helm," The Japan Times, March 22nd, 2008

[3] "Outlook for Economic Activity and Prices (April 2008)," Bank of Japan

[4] "BOJ Governor - slowdown in the economy for evident, maintain policy interest rates and closely watch inflation risks," *Nikkei Newspaper*, May 21, 2008, p3

[5] Coordinated cut in policy interest rates was enforced by FRB (2.0% to 1.5%), ECB (4.25% to 3.75%), U.K. (5.0% to 4.5%), Canada (3.0% to 2.5%), Sweden (4.75% to 4.25%), and Switzerland (3.0% to 2.5%). 4 other countries also announced to cut rates at the same timing.

[6] "10 Central Banks to cut rates by 0.5%, BOJ to provide liquidity – concerted effort to mitigate the effect of market disruption," *Nikkei Newspaper*, October 9th, 2008, p1.

[7] "Minutes of the Monetary Policy Meeting on December 19th, 2008," The Bank of Japan, page 3

[8] The BOJ announced that it would increase the amount of outright purchases of JGBs from 1.2 trillion yen per month to 1.4 trillion yen per month (16.8 trillion yen per year). It would also expand the range of JGBs accepted in outright purchases by adding 30 year bonds, floating-rate bonds, and inflation-indexed bonds as eligible JGBs to be accepted.

[9] "Minutes of the Monetary Policy Meeting on December 19th, 2008," The Bank of Japan, page 26.

[10] "Bank of Japan slashes rates to 0.1%," *Financial Times*, December 19th, 2008.

[11] "Japan taps forex reserves to ease crunch," *The Financial Times*, March 3 2009.

[12] "Bank of Japan to step up its bond purchases," *Financial Times*, March 19, 2009.

Exchange Rate Policy in China

HARVARD | BUSINESS | SCHOOL

9-706-021
REV: DECEMBER 1, 2008

LAURA ALFARO
RAFAEL DI TELLA

China: To Float or Not To Float? (A)

Step-by-step reform is a better way of reform. The experience of the past 26 years bears testimony to the success of China's incremental way of reform, which is suitable for Chinese economic development and national condition. In making reform in the future, we will continue to adhere to the principle of taking one step at a time. [1]

—China's Central Bank Governor Zhou Xiaochuan, September 2005

On July 21, 2005, China revalued its decade-long quasi-fixed exchange rate of approximately 8.28 yuan[a] per U.S. dollar by 2.1% to 8.11. Simultaneously, China's central bank, the People's Bank of China, announced that an undisclosed basket of currencies would serve as the yuan exchange rate reference and that the daily trading band of 0.3% against the dollar would be maintained (see **Appendix** for full text of announcement).[b] Many analysts and economists had been calling for a much more dramatic change to China's exchange rate regime. They believed the real trade-weighted value of the renminbi was undervalued by up to 30% to 35% and were expecting an immediate revaluation of at least 5% to 10% against the U.S. dollar followed by the introduction of a wider trading band to allow increased flexibility of the exchange rate.[2]

A change to China's exchange rate regime had been eagerly anticipated and much debated in the preceding months as China's trade surplus—particularly against the United States—reached record highs. As U.S. imports from China soared and U.S. manufacturing jobs declined, protectionist pressures in the United States intensified. Members of the U.S. Congress accused China of illegally manipulating its exchange rate by keeping the yuan fixed against the U.S. dollar as the dollar lost value between 2002 and mid-2005, in particular against European currencies. They argued that the quasi-fixed exchange rate gave China an unfair competitive advantage in trade and threatened to impose tariffs against China if it did not revalue its currency. The European Union and Japan reinforced pressure on China to revalue as a necessary step to unwind global financial imbalances.[3]

On the one hand, many economists—focusing on the strain the tightly managed exchange rate imposed on China's economy—agreed that China needed to institute more flexibility. They noted that not only was the exchange rate expensive to sustain, but it contributed—as well as limited China's flexibility in responding—to a potentially overheating economy. Although China's extensive

---

[a] China's currency is generally known as renminbi, but the unit of measurement is the yuan (similar to the terms "sterling" and "pound" in the United Kingdom).

[b] On August 10, the composition of the basket (but not the weightings) was announced. The main currencies were revealed to be the U.S. dollar, euro, Japanese yen, and South Korean won. See "China: To Float or Not To Float (B)," HBS 706-022, for a timeline of further updates to China's currency regime.

Professors Laura Alfaro and Rafael Di Tella and Research Associate Ingrid Vogel prepared this case. HBS cases are developed solely as the basis for class discussion. Cases are not intended to serve as endorsements, sources of primary data, or illustrations of effective or ineffective management.

controls on the movement of capital into the country helped to counteract some inflationary pressure, controls were becoming more porous as China increasingly integrated with the world economy.

On the other hand, a smaller group of economists believed that China should resist demands for exchange rate flexibility to avoid a scenario of falling foreign direct investment (FDI), deflation, and economic decline.[4] It was feared that political and social stability could be threatened if a sharp appreciation reduced exports and forced multinational companies with factories in China to shift production to other low-cost regions such as India or Southeast Asia.[5]

Initially, observers interpreted the 2.1% revaluation and shift to peg the yuan against a basket of currencies as indications that the country was embarking on a sustained gradual shift toward increased flexibility in the medium term, ultimately allowing the yuan to appreciate much further against the U.S. dollar.[6] However, observers soon began to complain that the change was too small to make an impact on resolving domestic or international economic imbalances and feared that little additional flexibility in the exchange rate would be forthcoming.[7] Former International Monetary Fund (IMF) Chief Economist Kenneth Rogoff commented: "No one knows whether China's baby step is the start of something much bigger, as China's authorities hint one day and deny the next. By relenting just a little to intense global pressure to revalue its exchange rate, the Chinese leadership has masterfully stifled the growing chorus of demands to rein in its growing trade surplus."[8]

It remained to be seen what China would ultimately choose to do with its exchange rate regime. Was the small change merely symbolic, or was it a significant first step toward greater exchange rate flexibility and the authorities' stated goal of eventual capital account convertibility? What was the impact of China's exchange rate policy on doing business with and "against" China? Was this part of a broader reform agenda? More generally, what were the implications for China's development strategy and growth in the Chinese as well as the world economies?

China's Gradual Transition to a "Socialist Market Economy"[9]

China, with a population of 1.3 billion, has a land mass slightly smaller than the United States. After China's unification in 221 BC, a series of imperial dynasties controlled the country. In 1911, nationalist forces overthrew China's last dynasty and established the Republic of China. Years of violent conflict ensued, internally between nationalist and communist forces and externally against the Japanese, who aggressively encroached into Chinese territory. In 1949, four years after Japanese occupation was ended, the Communist Party, under the leadership of Mao Zedong, emerged victorious over nationalist forces and established the People's Republic of China. Mao embarked on major reforms, such as the "Great Leap Forward" (1957–1960) and the "Cultural Revolution" (1966–1976), which eventually abolished private property and established a centrally planned economy. Over time, these reforms were blamed for causing major economic and social upheaval. A more moderate governing body, led by former Secretary General Deng Xiaoping, eventually took control of the Communist Party after Mao's death in 1976.[10]

Deng inherited an economy lagging well behind its newly industrializing neighbors such as Japan, Singapore, Taiwan, Hong Kong, and the Republic of Korea. Concluding that the Maoist vision of a centrally planned economy had failed to encourage efficient economic growth, the new Communist Party leadership decided to introduce fundamental reforms in the agricultural sector, state-owned enterprises, the banking sector, international trade, and foreign investment. Change was introduced incrementally, with programs tested in a few localities before being introduced nationally. In general, reforms expanded the role for markets under what Deng labeled transition to a "socialist market economy." At the same time, maintenance of the Communist Party and its political system was always emphasized. With the death of Deng in 1997, reform continued under Jiang Zemin (1998–2003) and Hu Jintao (2003–present).

Between 1978 and 2004, gross domestic product (GDP) grew at an average 9.5% annual rate, real per capita incomes multiplied by more than seven, FDI increased from zero to $64 billion annually, and trade increased from 10% of GDP to 79% of GDP. (See **Exhibits 1–4** for basic background macroeconomic data.) Although per capita GDP remained low at 15% of the U.S. level, on a purchasing power parity basis China stood as the world's second-largest economy. (See **Exhibit 5** for comparative economic indicators.)

Agricultural Reform

The first wave of reforms under Deng took place in the agricultural sector, which employed 71% of China's labor force in 1978. After initial measures increasing procurement prices for farm products and enhancing state investment in the sector, reforms focused on introducing market-based incentives into agricultural production. For example, households that had previously been required to produce strictly to a plan defined at the community level were permitted to plan for and sell excess produce on the open market for profit after delivering a contracted amount to the community at a fixed procurement price.[11]

In the first decade under the reforms, agricultural production and rural incomes grew rapidly. Rural workers channeled savings into local industrial enterprises, known as town and village enterprises (TVEs), which focused predominately on production of agricultural equipment and simple manufactured products. Increased farming productivity released labor to support TVEs.[12] By 1986, rural enterprises employed 21% of the rural labor force and produced over half the value of rural output.[13]

Between the late 1970s and the mid-1980s, more than 100 million workers shifted away from farming. By 2005, the share of China's labor force employed in agriculture, including both farming and TVEs, declined to about 50%.[14] Decline resulted from both increased farming productivity as well as attractive opportunities—exemplified by soaring nonrural industrial incomes—in other sectors. With an estimated 150 million–200 million surplus agricultural workers,[15] farm incomes stagnated and income inequality in China widened. Prohibitions on farmers owning land—which could be used as collateral to fund further investment—and a lack of infrastructure, such as cold warehouses, were thought to be posing impediments to further development of the sector.[16]

State-Owned Enterprise Reform

In 1978, state-owned enterprises (SOEs) accounted for 78% of industrial output and provided 19% of total employment. SOEs operated in a range of sectors—such as financial services, telecommunications, energy, chemicals, automobiles, construction, textiles, food, retail, consumer electronics, and white goods, among many others—and provided housing, education, health care, and lifetime employment for their workers. Attempts to introduce market-based incentives into SOEs—such as allowing them to sell goods beyond planned quotas at market prices and to retain profits to reinvest or distribute to workers as bonuses, permitting managers to hire and fire employees, and shifting the source of capital from government budget allocations to interest-bearing loans that had to be repaid—had mixed results. Productivity improved, but less than for private enterprises and TVEs, which enjoyed much more freedom than the SOEs.

By 1990, although the share of SOE production in industrial output had fallen to 55%, its share of total employment was still 18%.[17] In 1998, more than two-thirds of SOEs generated a loss,[18] and the government estimated that 30% were effectively bankrupt. Studies suggested that approximately one-third of the 100 million SOE workers could be laid off with no effect on output.[19] In an effort to improve performance, the government embarked on a program of privatizing SOEs and reducing subsidies.[20]

By 2005, a large proportion of small and medium-sized SOEs had changed ownership structure or had been shut down, while large SOEs still dominated vital, heavily protected sectors including financial services, power, and telecommunications.[21] Between 1998 and 2001, SOEs shed 26 million workers. Laid-off workers had to compete with an additional 15 million new workers coming into the labor market each year for an estimated 11 million–12 million additional jobs being generated annually in China.[22] Although some observers considered SOEs to be a drag on China's economy,[23] continued major reform had to be considered alongside the social and political stability SOEs provided.

Banking Sector Reform

The poor financial performance of SOEs directly impacted China's banking sector. China's banking system was charged with carrying out policy lending in line with central government planning, including financing SOEs despite their poor performance in repaying loans. Commercial considerations, such as evaluating the risks of projects and counterparties, were disregarded since enterprise viability was dictated by the government.[24] In 1994, in an attempt to allow China's four state banks to become commercially oriented, the government created three new policy banks to focus on government-directed lending. However, until 1998, the government still issued binding credit targets across sectors.

By the mid-1990s, loans to SOEs accounted for more than 70% of the total loans of China's four state banks.[25] A large proportion of SOE loans eventually became nonperforming (NPLs).[c] At year-end 2001, official estimates of the share of NPLs in total loans of the four state banks stood at more than 30%. By mid-2005, after an ongoing government program to reduce NPLs to improve the balance sheets of the state banks and bring their capital adequacy ratios in line with international standards,[26] NPLs at the four state banks fell to $122 billion, representing 10% of their total loans.[27] Combining the NPLs at the state banks with $32 billion in NPLs in the rest of China's banking system and an estimated $150 billion in NPLs transferred to and remaining at four asset management companies yielded $304 billion in total NPLs, representing 18% of GDP. Unofficial estimates of NPLs were much higher, at up to $650 billion.[28]

China engaged in an aggressive program to improve bank balance sheets and reduce the stock of NPLs through transfers and bailouts. In 1998, the government injected $33 billion into the four state-owned banks after a special government bond offer. In 1999, the four state banks (plus one policy bank) transferred $170 billion in NPLs to four asset management companies (AMCs) in exchange for bonds paying 2%.[29] In 2003, $45 billion of China's extensive stock of foreign exchange reserves were transferred to two state banks. The banks were prohibited from converting these dollar assets into renminbi.[30] In 2004, the same two banks transferred $34 billion in NPLs to AMCs, and another bank (not state owned) transferred $5 billion.[31] By mid-2005, a third state bank received a $15 billion injection and transferred $30 billion of NPLs to AMCs.[32] The AMCs were achieving average cash recovery rates of 20%,[33] an amount thought to be insufficient to cover the interest on the bonds issued

[c] A loan was nonperforming when its interest and principal remained unpaid.

and the loans obtained from the Chinese central bank to fund the initial NPL transfer.[34] Many analysts expected the AMCs to generate large losses that would eventually have to be covered by the state.[35] There was also concern that expectations that banks would continue to receive capital injections and opportunities to transfer further NPLs to AMCs at par was creating an environment of moral hazard and poor decision making.[36]

Despite progress in reducing the stock of existing NPLs, analysts believed that flows of new NPLs would become a growing problem. Between 2003 and 2005, banks added $1 trillion in new loans to their books. Low interest rates convinced firms to invest in what many analysts worried was excess capacity, potentially contributing to an unsustainable investment boom.[37] In fact, with nominal interest rates lower than increases in producer prices, some firms faced negative real interest rates and were substituting capital for labor.[38] Goldman Sachs Hong Kong Managing Director Fred Hu commented: "Considering that banks' capacity for risk management remains weak, the current credit boom, if unabated, could increase the risk of new NPLs. . . . The authorities are therefore well justified in flagging their concerns now and beginning to take preemptive measures to prevent a new wave of NPLs."[39] As new NPLs threatened to continue to accumulate, NPLs as a share of GDP were forecast to rise, even in the face of growing GDP.

Analysts believed improvements since 2003 in regulations concerning China's banking system could help state banks to address NPL flow problems and, more generally, become more commercially oriented.[40] In April 2003, the formation of the China Banking Regulatory Commission with the mandate to improve the supervision and regulation of the banking system initiated a wave of important banking reforms.[41] Over the following 18 months, China's central bank introduced measures liberalizing lending interest rates, such as increasing and later removing lending interest rate ceilings for commercial banks.[42] Banks had previously been unable to require significantly higher interest rates to compensate appropriately for risks associated with lending to new or smaller firms in the private sector. The central bank also initiated differentiated reserve ratios based on asset quality and capital adequacy; weaker banks faced higher reserve ratios and, therefore, limits on business expansion.[43] Furthermore, in 2003, limits on foreign ownership of Chinese banks were increased from 15% to 20%.[44] In anticipation of the full opening of China's banking sector to foreign competition in 2006, foreign strategic investors began increasing stakes in China's large banks.[d] Analysts expected foreign investors to share technical expertise and improve corporate governance practices, leading to overall improvement of China's banking sector.[45]

Trade Reform

Another pillar of Deng's reform program was opening China's relatively closed economy to trade. China had kept itself isolated during the Cultural Revolution while its newly industrializing neighbors followed a strategy of export promotion to drive rapid economic growth. Deng believed China's economy would benefit from following a similar strategy and instituted a number of policies to liberalize trade. The government slowly dismantled its system of centralized planning of trade by allowing more market-based decision making and reduced tariffs. Trade liberalization policies were further strengthened with China's 2001 membership in the World Trade Organization (WTO).[46]

Prior to the reforms, the combined value of China's exports and imports rarely exceeded 10% of GDP. By 2004, this value rose to 67%, making China the world's third-largest trading nation, behind the United States and Germany. Between 1977 and 2004, China's share of world trade increased from

---

[d] See "China: To Float or Not To Float (D)," concerning Bank of America's strategic investment in China Construction Bank, HBS No. 706-031, for more details on foreign bank strategic investment in China.

0.6% to 6.0%. Strong trade growth continued. Between 2001 and 2004, exports and imports of goods both increased by an annual average 30%. In the first seven months of 2005, exports grew 32% over the same period in 2004, compared with 14% for imports.[47]

The composition of China's exports changed over time (see **Exhibit 6**). In the earliest years of the reform, exports consisted predominately of agricultural and petroleum products. In the 1990s, exports shifted into labor-intensive manufacturing, particularly textiles, toys, and shoes. In the early 2000s, assembly of imported components in consumer electronics, computers, and information technology products became increasingly important.[48] By the mid-2000s, Chinese production had entered new sectors, such as furniture and auto parts, and was expanding shares in automobiles and aerospace.[49] In addition, China began to grow its exports of products, such as steel, that it had previously imported.[50]

China's spectacular trade growth and apparent move of its exports up the value-added chain[e][51] were creating tensions with its trade partners, particularly the United States. In 2004, China's trade surplus in goods with the United States reached $80 billion, a 37% increase over 2003 (see **Exhibit 7**). A strong protectionist movement emerged, with U.S. manufacturers arguing that China's maintenance of a fixed exchange rate against the U.S. dollar allowed Chinese goods an unfair advantage in the U.S. market and hurt U.S. employment (see **Exhibit 8**). For example, the U.S. textile industry directly attributed the closure of 18 plants and the loss of 16,000 jobs during the first half of 2005 to imports from China.[52] In June 2005, U.S. Congressional Representatives Mark Green of Wisconsin, Chris Chocola of Indiana, and Robin Hayes of North Carolina introduced draft legislation they titled the CHINA Act (Currency Harmonization Initiative through Neutralizing Action), which called for levies on Chinese imports to compensate for currency manipulation. They argued:

> American businesses can compete with anyone in the world when there's a level playing field, but not when the deck is stacked against us. Good people are losing their jobs and our economy is taking a big hit because of China's unfair trade practices, and it's time we send them a strong message. ... For years, China has flooded our markets with illegal transshipments and manipulated its currency to place unfair tariffs on American goods sold in China. It is time for these policies to stop.[53]

Other countries also became uncomfortable with China's growing dominance in exports. For example, in mid-2005, the EU negotiated an agreement with China that limited the growth in EU imports of some categories of Chinese textiles to no more than 8%–12.5% per year until the end of 2008.[54] Although it had an $11 billion trade surplus with China in 2004, Brazil also became concerned by its unequal partnership with China; China continued to import basic commodities from Brazil while exporting growing quantities of value-added goods. Brazilian manufacturing firms were frustrated by China's unwillingness to import Brazilian value-added goods and argued that Brazil's trade surplus with China would eventually turn into a deficit.[55]

In the United States, discount retailers that imported from China also came under attack. In 2003, the U.S. trade union AFL-CIO testified before the U.S. Congress:

> Rifts within the business community have contributed to the U.S. government's passivity and failure to act to date. Companies that produce in China for the U.S. market, retailers, and importers clearly benefit from an undervalued Chinese currency, as well as from the abuse of workers' rights. Wal-Mart, for example—alone responsible for almost $10 billion of the U.S. trade deficit with China [Wal-Mart imports from China reached $18 billion in 2004]—has

[e] For example, for a discussion of strong Chinese competition in the telecommunications sector, see "China: To Float or Not To Float (F)," concerning Alcatel and strong Chinese competition, HBS No. 706-036.

openly supported current Chinese government policies with respect to the yuan. On the other hand, companies actually producing in the United States—whether for the domestic market or for export—face debilitating and unsustainable disadvantages from both currency manipulation and violation of workers' rights in China.

American policymakers have a choice to make in trade relations with China. They can side with the importers and outsourcers, and stand by passively as China takes advantage of its WTO membership and access to the U.S. market, abusing its own workers and artificially undervaluing its currency in order to undercut American workers and domestic manufacturers. Or they can take a stand for American jobs and act now to ensure that China plays fair in the global economy.[56]

However, many observers disagreed with the conclusion that Chinese imports were unquestionably hurting the U.S. economy. For example, it was estimated that over 50% of Chinese export operations relied on the final assembly of products using imported inputs and that the domestic value-added on Chinese exports to the United States was only about 20%.[57] Council of Economic Advisers Chairman Greg Mankiw argued that U.S. "job losses are . . . more closely related to declines in domestic investment and weak exports than to import competition."[58] Furthermore, many observers, including U.S. Federal Reserve Chairman Alan Greenspan, warned of the negative impact U.S. protectionism could have on the U.S. and world economies. Noting benefits of Chinese imports to U.S. consumers, in 2003, Greenspan remarked:

I do not doubt that the vast majority of us would prefer to work in a less stressful, less competitive environment. Yet, in our roles as consumers, we seem to relentlessly seek the low product prices and high quality that are prominent features of our current frenetic economic structure. In particular, America's discount retailers have responded by learning to profit as intermediaries between consumers and low-cost producers, whether located in Guangdong province in China or Peoria, Illinois. Retailers who do not choose their suppliers with price and quality uppermost in mind risk finding themselves in liquidation. . . .

If the renminbi were to rise, presumably U.S. imports from China would fall as China loses competitive position to other low-wage economies. But would, for example, reduced imports of textiles from China induce increased output in American factories? Far more likely is that our imports from other low-wage countries would replace Chinese textiles.[59]

Foreign Investment Reform

An important factor in China's phenomenal export growth was the country's pursuit of policies encouraging the establishment of foreign-invested factories; in 2004, foreign-invested firms produced about half of China's exports (see **Exhibit 9**).[60] However, initial reform of international investment, particularly FDI, proved controversial. Over time, Chinese concerns that FDI implied relinquishing control of Chinese assets to foreigners and threatened the socialist character of the economy were balanced against the recognition that FDI could transfer useful technical and managerial skills.

In 1980, four coastal special economic zones were established that exempted foreign-invested firms from central government trade plans, released them from Chinese labor regulations, and introduced preferential tax treatment over domestically funded firms.[f] At the same time, regulations limited foreign investors to export-oriented operations and required them to form joint-venture

[f] For more on China's incentives to foreign investors, refer to "China: To Float or Not To Float (E)," concerning ABB investment in China, HBS No. 706-035.

partnerships with Chinese firms in order to transfer technology or use local content. FDI growth was modest, and external loans dominated China's capital inflows.[61]

In the 1990s, the government introduced rules allowing foreign investors to establish wholly foreign-owned enterprises with no knowledge-transfer requirements, to receive favorable treatment in additional geographical areas, and to manufacture and sell a wide range of goods in China's increasingly attractive domestic market. With regulations hindering foreign portfolio flows and external borrowing, such as the segregation of China's stock market between residents and nonresidents and strict international loan ceilings,[62] foreign investors interested in China leaned toward FDI as opposed to securities and loans as a way to invest in the country. As a result, FDI increased rapidly and came to account for more than 70% of China's total capital inflows.[63]

By 2004, China was the world's largest recipient of FDI with an annual inflow of $64 billion and a cumulative total balance of $564 billion. The majority of inflows was from Japan and other emerging market economies of Asia (see **Exhibit 10**) and was utilized in manufacturing, particularly electronics. Wholly owned foreign enterprises accounted for approximately 65% of new FDI in China and dominated high-tech exports.[64] However, FDI remained small as a percentage of total investment in China and small compared with domestic savings levels in China approaching $500 billion per year.[65]

Despite its impressive growth, FDI lost its dominance in China's capital inflow composition starting in 2001. This trend was accelerated in 2003 and 2004 (see **Exhibit 4a**). Both domestic and foreign investors came to expect an imminent renminbi revaluation and increased their shorter-term renminbi-denominated assets and foreign currency-denominated liabilities, despite controls restricting non-FDI and non-current account capital.[66] This shift was apparent in both the current account and the financial account. In addition, it was widely conjectured that the large shift in the "errors and omissions" category of the balance of payments from a net outflow to a large net inflow position represented "hot money" entering the country while evading capital controls.[67] Errors and omissions typically included unrecorded flows in the financial account.[68]

On the current account, anecdotal evidence pointed to early collection of export receipts and increased use of trade credit for imports.[69] In addition, there was a surge in private remittance inflows, a category designed to capture, for example, tourist expenditures and cash transfers from workers and family members living overseas. The Chinese government, which had traditionally encouraged such dollar inflows, moved in late 2004 to require banks to report unusually large remittance inflows if they were accompanied by related dollar sales in excess of $10,000 daily.[70]

On the financial account, Chinese households and firms were taking out dollar-denominated loans through Chinese banks.[71] Relaxed official restrictions on cross-border bank flows allowed a degree of capital mobility between China and the rest of the world.[72] Unrecorded flows within errors and omissions were thought to include the conversion of foreign currency deposits held offshore into renminbi deposits held at Chinese banks, which occurred despite the relatively poor condition of these banks and despite controls on capital inflows. This shift occurred as Chinese households and corporations returned funds that they had moved out of the country in the 1990s to avoid taxes and to avoid the consequences of possible depreciation (which did not transpire) of the renminbi during and after the Asian financial crisis of 1997 and 1998.[73] Despite the existence of controls on outflows of capital, Chinese capital flight was estimated to have reached $100 billion a year from 1997 to 2000.[74] (See **Exhibit 11** for data on China's bank deposits.)

Worried about the role of "hot money" in contributing to economic crises, China put on hold its official mid-1990s goal to move to full convertibility on the financial account by the early 2000s.[75] Economist Paul Krugman lauded China's caution: "Controls are often evaded, and they are a source of lots of corruption, but they still give China a degree of policy leeway that the rest of Asia desperately wishes it had."[76] In 2004, new controls were introduced aimed at closing loopholes that allowed money to flow into China through the financial account. For example, domestic foreign-funded banks were forbidden from converting debt contracted abroad into renminbi and became subject to the same quota on offshore borrowing as Chinese banks. In addition, capital brought into the country as FDI could only be converted into renminbi upon proof of a domestic payment order.[77] However, as former head of the IMF's China Division Eswar Prasad noted: "Continued rapid trade expansion creates a growing scope for getting around capital account restrictions. As China becomes increasingly integrated into the global economy in the context of its WTO accession, with commitments to further liberalization of trade and the opening-up of the financial sector, its capital controls are likely to become even more porous."[78] Observers feared that speculators would find ways to place bigger bets on currency movements and, therefore, could pose risks to China's financial system.[79]

While tightening controls on inflows, the Chinese authorities loosened controls on outflows of capital. For example, in 2004, state and private domestic insurance firms were allowed to invest a portion of their portfolios offshore, and Chinese citizens emigrating abroad were allowed to transfer personal assets with them.[80] Chinese officials hoped stimulating outflows would ease some appreciating pressure on the renminbi. (See **Exhibit 12** for a timeline of capital and exchange controls in China.)

The Yuan Controversy

Yuan Background

In the pre-reform period, the yuan was fixed at a deliberately overvalued rate to subsidize imports of capital goods that could not be produced internally. Maintaining the overvalued yuan led to excess demand for foreign currency relative to supply and required strict exchange controls.[81] Starting in 1980, the government aimed to correct the overvalued yuan by steadily lowering its inflation-adjusted value. In 1986, exchange controls were loosened slightly with the introduction of a dual exchange rate system. Under the system, China's central bank fixed the official exchange rate while allowing limited free exchange on a parallel market. Domestic export firms were required to surrender most of their foreign receipts to the central bank for exchange into yuan at the official rate, while foreign firms were allowed to trade all of their export receipts at the market rate. Because the official rate was generally much higher than the market rate, this policy put domestic exporters at a disadvantage.

In 1994, in the face of inflation rising above 20% and a credit boom, the government decided to implement an economic stabilization plan. The core of the plan was a new exchange rate regime that abolished the dual exchange rate and fixed a new rate at the market rate of 8.28 yuan per dollar.[82] In 1996, the currency became fully convertible for current account transactions, such that importers could purchase foreign exchange without restriction and exporters could retain all export earnings.[83] By 1998, inflation was reduced to negligible levels.

During the Asian financial crisis of 1997 and 1998, China's exchange rate came under threat. Many of China's neighbors were forced to devalue their currencies in the face of speculative pressures. China maintained its peg to the U.S. dollar and was lauded for preventing a round of competitive devaluations.

After the Asian crisis, growing capital flows into China put pressure on the exchange rate. In order to keep the value of the yuan from rising against the U.S. dollar in the face of these inflows, China's central bank intervened by exchanging incoming dollars for renminbi at the fixed yuan exchange rate and using the dollars to buy dollar assets such as U.S. Treasuries. By 2004, China had become second only to Japan in holdings of U.S. Treasury bonds. The accompanying release of renminbi into the Chinese economy threatened to fuel domestic inflation and to overheat the economy.[84] Given its capital controls, China had some scope to offset inflationary pressure through increasing interest rates. Officials also counteracted inflationary pressure through sterilization, under which loans to commercial banks were reduced, reserve requirements were increased, and yuan-denominated bonds were issued to absorb liquidity and keep the monetary base from expanding.[85] For example, China's central bank issued sterilization paper amounting to $87 billion in 2003, $182 billion in 2004, and $89 billion in the first quarter of 2005. As such, sterilization bonds offset only half of the increase in reserves between 2003 and mid-2005, implying that the remainder of the increase in reserves contributed to money growth (see **Exhibit 1**).[86] With state banks required to purchase the bonds at high prices (low interest rates), economists expressed concern that the government's sterilization costs were kept down at the expense of the banks' balance sheets and worried that China's financial stability was being threatened.[87]

Furthermore, excess reserves appeared to create an imbalance on China's external balance sheet. MIT Professor Yasheng Huang noted: "When FDI inflows are financing the growth of China's foreign exchange reserves, that amount of FDI is not used productively to develop the Chinese economy. . . . This is surely a strange outcome. The Chinese are striving to give up the ownership of their economy only to use the capital surpluses to invest in low-yielding government bonds in America."[88] However, economists Michael Dooley, Peter Garber, and David Folkerts-Landau argued that the imbalance was necessary to support China's development strategy, with reserves and current account surpluses serving as collateral for FDI inflows.[89]

Pressure to Revalue

Beginning in 2003, in the face of China's complicated and, by some measures, costly exchange rate management regime, the future of the yuan policy became a popular topic. On the one hand, most observers took it for granted that the yuan was undervalued. They pointed to the loss in the value of the dollar against other major currencies between 2001 and mid-2005 and to China's rapid foreign exchange reserves accumulation. In addition, they noted that faster labor productivity growth in China relative to its trade partners was a fundamental force putting upward pressure on the renminbi (see **Exhibit 13**).[90] They also pointed to China's excess exports and associated inflow of dollars as evidence of an undervalued exchange rate. More specifically, another study estimated yuan undervaluation against the U.S. dollar of at least 35% based on the price level of goods and services in China compared with those of its trade partners.[91]

As a result, China came under significant pressure to revalue its currency. While politicians and manufacturing representatives outside of China were predominately concerned with protecting their own countries' and firms' trade interests, many economists believed the Chinese policy of pegging the yuan to the U.S. dollar was straining China's own economy.[92] With a fixed exchange rate and leaky capital controls, China was limited in its ability to correct its apparently overheating economy through increasing interest rates, since higher interest rates would attract further capital inflows and put additional inflationary pressure on the economy and appreciating pressure on the currency. Furthermore, the central bank's ability to continue to sterilize monetary base growth associated with capital inflows was becoming limited.[93] Observers worried that excess liquidity would result, exacerbating the problem of the overheating economy. As former head of the IMF's China Division Prasad remarked:

> While exchange rate flexibility by itself is hardly going to be a panacea, attaining monetary policy independence through greater flexibility will eventually remove an important shackle that has hindered financial sector reforms and restrained other key aspects of the move toward a more market-oriented economy. This will also provide a useful tool to deal with external shocks that China will increasingly become exposed to as it continues its integration with the world economy.[94]

There were also calls for additional yuan flexibility from Europe, Japan, and Latin America. For example, European Central Bank President Jean-Claude Trichet, speaking on behalf of the G-7, called for more flexibility to address global economic imbalances: "Our main message collectively is to call for a smooth, orderly appreciation of the currencies of some emerging Asian countries."[95]

Timing of the move to more flexibility was also debated. In a *Korea Herald* editorial, former IMF Chief Economist Rogoff concluded that China should proceed with a liberalized exchange rate immediately:

> Indeed, over the longer term, the biggest concern for China is that some day money will be trying to get out. Even China's vast reserves will not be enough to stave off a painful devaluation. It is a lot easier to exit from a fixed exchange rate regime when the pressures on the currency are upwards. While it may seem hard to imagine that the speculative tide might ever turn against China, exchange-rate pressures can turn in an instant. Today's darling currency can be tomorrow's dog. Considering China's huge and growing income inequalities, and its massive disguised rural unemployment, it is easy to imagine a period of political instability that sends investors heading for the exits. Mix in China's shaky financial system and the prospect of trade sanctions after an altercation over, say, Taiwan, and it is clear that the yuan might not always be a one-way bet.
>
> Last but not least, the Chinese authorities desperately need to maintain the country's breakneck economic growth in order to preserve the Communist Party's legitimacy. But, as the economy becomes richer and more complex, there will be no escaping the market imperative in internal credit allocation. . . . Indeed, the need to pursue financial liberalization to maintain growth is a central reason why middle-income countries are so prone to financial crises. That's why Chinese authorities should move to greater flexibility now, and not wait until it is too late.[96]

Questioning the Push to Devalue

On the other hand, several analysts and economists argued that the yuan was not undervalued. They noted that the dramatic increase in the yuan's value between 1994 and 2001 was only slightly offset by inflation differentials against China's trade partners since 2001. They also pointed out that large increases in exports, which some observers attributed to the undervalued currency, were matched by large increases in imports.[97] In addition, they explained the increase in China's foreign exchange reserves with short-term speculative flows, which tended to feed on themselves and bore little relation to true macroeconomic fundamentals.[98] Furthermore, they noted that shortly after the July 2005 revaluation, the value of renminbi nondeliverable forward (NDF) contracts—instruments that allowed foreign investors with local currency exposure to hedge against (or currency speculators to bet on) future renminbi movements without needing to exchange renminbi—implied expected further revaluation of only about 5% over 12 months.[99]

Furthermore, other economists argued that China maintained a substantial degree of autonomy over monetary policy despite the fixed exchange rate. Bank for International Settlements (BIS) economists Guonan Ma and Robert N. McCauley estimated that the average spread between the three-month money-market yield on renminbi held onshore and the offshore counterpart ranged from negative 400–1,000 basis points in 1999–2001 to positive 400–1,000 basis points by late 2003 and early 2004. The yield gap indicated that capital controls effectively segmented onshore and offshore markets, while onshore interest rates higher than the offshore counterpart indicated underlying appreciation pressure on the yuan but effective capital controls limiting capital inflows into the yuan. They concluded:

> Despite considerable sanctioned or unsanctioned leaks on China's capital account, official capital and foreign exchange restrictions have so far remained a binding and substantial barrier to cross-border flows. In the short term, this barrier could provide the Chinese authorities some scope to use domestic interest rate adjustments to achieve their desired mix of external and internal policy objectives.[100]

Furthermore, some economists, although agreeing that the yuan was undervalued, questioned the need for China to further change its foreign exchange management. For example, soon after the currency regime change was announced in July 2005, Morgan Stanley economist Andy Xie commented:

> The prolonged battle with China over its currency should serve as a lesson to those who staked their names or political capital on changing China, in my view. China is too big to be pushed around easily. In the globalization game, Chinese are the minimum wage workers while Americans have the most high-paying jobs. It is just difficult to "punish" minimum wage earners in today's world. This is why, I believe, the people who have been very vocal about pushing China towards revaluation may be more cautious in future. . . . China's priority is stability. Currency flexibility should not be allowed to conflict with this goal, in my view. Given that China is in transition, as an industrializing, and urbanizing economy with 300 million surplus workers, it faces immense challenges beyond the experience of many in the west. It is extremely unlikely that China could tolerate substantial currency volatility.[101]

Commenting on the July 2005 appreciation, Stanford economist Ronald McKinnon warned against downward pressure on interest rates that could lead China into a zero-interest liquidity trap much like the one Japan had suffered since the mid-1990s. He also remarked on the importance of maintaining stability of the exchange rate and not "squandering" the credibility invested in the 10-year-old peg.[102] In November 2005, Columbia University economics professor Robert Mundell, who won the Nobel Prize in Economics in 1999, remarked: "A common figure cited for another move, 20 to 25 percent, would be devastating to China, which would cause deflation, cut economic growth, cut off foreign direct investment and would destabilize Asia."[103]

To Float or Not To Float . . .

In late August 2005, the People's Bank of China Governor Zhou Xiaochuan commented on the challenges facing businesses, as well as on the responsibility of other countries in resolving global economic imbalances:

> I think it's very clear that China is introducing a new exchange rate mechanism. It is not a one-time adjustment. . . . The important thing is that it has started to float and over time market forces will play a more and more important role. . . . It is a gradual way to expand the role of market forces, because we need time for Chinese companies and the public to adapt to

> the new system. They need to learn how to live with the new exchange rate mechanism and familiarize themselves with financial instruments like foreign exchange forwards, and others, to hedge their exchange rate risk. . . . Our investment demand has been very strong for several years, so we are now trying, to some extent, to slow down investment and enhance the household consumption demand to improve the economic structure. . . . I think exchange rate policy does work to some extent to achieve a more balanced economic structure, but domestic demand policy is more important than the exchange rate. . . . On the other side we would like to see what kind of policy actions and adjustments happen in the United States, the eurozone and Japan.[104]

Among those companies affected was Hong Kong-based textiles manufacturer Esquel Group, with major factories in China. Esquel had a degree of natural protection against yuan appreciation, including some dollar-denominated costs as well as the ability to shift production to other locations such as Malaysia, Vietnam, Mauritius, and Sri Lanka. However, the company intended to proactively address the possible changes in exchange rate regime through improving its cost structure as well as growing its sales in China. Esquel Executive Director K.L. Lee explained: "It is important for us to make changes as we can in preparation. It will have a significant impact on our business strategy."[g]

As other firms in China and elsewhere contemplated the impact of the changing exchange rate regime on their business models, economists and analysts continued to explore the impact on China's overall development strategy and prospects for future growth. Changes in the exchange rate regime were complicated by China's extensive controls on the movement of capital into and out of the country and by its problematic banking sector.

It remained to be seen when—and even whether—additional flexibility to the exchange rate would be introduced and what the results would be.

---

[g] Interview with casewriter. See "China: To Float or Not to Float (C)," concerning the Esquel Group and the Chinese Renminbi, HBS 706-023, for more on Esquel Group and its response to the exchange rate regime changes.

Exhibit 1a China General Economic Indicators

units as indicated	1978	1982	1986	1990	1994	1998	2000	2001	2002	2003	2004
GDP (current $ billions)	147	202	296	355	543	946	1,081	1,176	1,271	1,417	1,649
Per Capita GDP (constant 2000 $)	153	193	288	364	552	752	856	913	983	1,067	1,162
PPP Per Capita GDP (constant 2000 $)	674	850	1,269	1,597	2,435	3,372	3,821	4,089	4,379	4,727	5,085
Real GDP Growth (% over prior year)	...	9.0%	8.9%	3.8%	12.6%	7.8%	8.0%	7.5%	8.0%	9.3%	9.5%
Population (billions)	0.96	1.01	1.07	1.14	1.19	1.24	1.26	1.27	1.28	1.29	1.30
Unemployment (%)	...	...	...	...	...	6.4%	8.2%	9.3%	9.7%	10.3%	9.9%
M2 Growth (% over prior year)	4%	15%	30%	29%	32%	15%	.12%	15%	19%	20%	15%
M2 (% GDP)	24%	40%	55%	70%	88%	126%	144%	150%	163%	175%	176%
Domestic Credit to Private Sector (% of GDP)	51%	58%	77%	88%	89%	114%	125%	125%	136%	147%	141%
Consumer Price Inflation (% up over prior year)	...	...	...	18.8%	24.1%	-0.8%	0.3%	0.7%	-0.8%	1.2%	3.9%
Producer Price Inflation (% up over prior year)	...	...	...	...	19.5%	-4.1%	2.8%	-1.3%	-2.2%	2.3%	6.1%
Short-term external liabilities (current $ billions)	...	2.3	6.1	9.3	17.5	17.3	13.1	56.3	65.9	88.3	117.6
Short-term external liabilities (% up over prior year)		-6%	-5%	35%	14%	-45%	-14%	331%	17%	34%	33%
Short-term external liabilities (% total external liabilities)		28%	26%	17%	17%	12%	9%	30%	35%	42%	47%
Market Capitalization of Listed Companies (% GDP)		...	...	...	8%	24%	54%	45%	36%	48%	39%

Source: Compiled from World Bank WDI Database, September 2005, and Economist Intelligence Unit (EIU) Country Data, September 2005.

Note: Unemployment is based on EIU Country Data, which cites National Bureau of Statistics, China Statistical Yearbook as the source. It refers to recorded official unemployment as a percentage of total labor force and is, according to the EIU, widely considered to be a gross underestimate.

Exhibit 1b Bilateral Nominal Exchange Rate (yuan per dollar) and Index of Yuan Dollar Real Exchange Rate (decrease in real exchange rate index implies real appreciation of yuan)

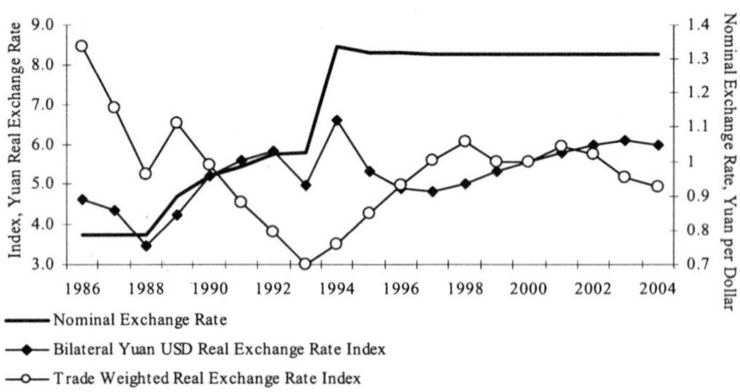

Source: Casewriter calculation based on data from International Monetary Fund, International Financial Statistics Online, accessed May 2006.

Note: Real exchange rate indices based on consumer prices.

Exhibit 2 China National Income Accounts

current yuan billions or % GDP	1978	1982	1986	1990	1994	1998	2000	2001	2002	2003	2004
Nominal GDP	362	529	1,020	1,855	4,676	7,835	8,947	9,731	10,517	11,725	13,652
Household Expenditure	49%	50%	52%	50%	44%	46%	48%	46%	44%	41%	42%
Government Expenditure	13%	15%	13%	12%	13%	12%	13%	13%	13%	13%	12%
Gross fixed capital formation	30%	28%	30%	26%	36%	35%	36%	38%	40%	44%	45%
Exports of goods and services	5%	9%	12%	18%	25%	22%	26%	25%	29%	34%	40%
Imports of goods and services	5%	7%	15%	14%	23%	17%	23%	23%	26%	32%	39%
Real GDP (PPP U.S. billion dollars at 1996 prices)	...	*878*	*1,385*	*1,857*	*2,960*	*4,205*	*4,863*	*5,228*	*5,647*	*6,173*	*6,762*

Source: Compiled from World Bank WDI Database, September 2005, and EIU Country Data, September 2005.

Exhibit 3 China Government Accounts from the National Bureau of Statistics of China

current yuan billions	1978	1980	1985	1990	1994	1998	2000	2001	2002	2003	2004
Total Government Revenue	**113**	**116**	**200**	**294**	**522**	**988**	**1,340**	**1,639**	**1,890**	**2,172**	**2,640**
Taxes	52	57	204	282	513	926	1,258	1,530	1,764	2,002	2,417
From Enterprises	57	44	4	8	...	...	...	...	...	...	...
Subs. to Loss-making Enterprises	...	...	-51	-58	-37	-33	-28	-30	-26	-23	-22
From Construction Funds	...	...	15	19	5	...	...	...	...	...	...
Budget Adjustment Fund	...	...	...	13	6	...	...	...	...	...	...
Extra Charges for Education	...	...	...	...	6	11	15	17	20	23	30
Other Revenue	4	15	28	30	28	83	94	122	133	169	215
Total Government Expenditure	**112**	**123**	**200**	**308**	**579**	**1,080**	**1,589**	**1,890**	**2,205**	**2,465**	**2,849**
Economic Construction	72	72	113	137	239	418	575	647	667	691	793
Social, Cultural, & Educ. Dev.	15	20	41	74	150	293	438	521	592	647	749
National Defense	17	19	19	29	55	93	121	144	171	191	220
Administrative Expenses	5	8	17	41	85	160	277	351	410	469	552
Other Expenditure	4	4	11	27	50	115	178	226	365	467	534
Balance	**1**	**-7**	**0**	**-15**	**-57**	**-92**	**-249**	**-252**	**-315**	**-293**	**-209**
Balance as % GDP	*0.3%*	*-1.5%*	*0.0%*	*-0.8%*	*-1.2%*	*-1.2%*	*-2.8%*	*-2.6%*	*-3.0%*	*-2.5%*	*-1.5%*

Source: Compiled from National Bureau of Statistics of China, "China Statistical Yearbook 2005," September 2005, and author calculations.

Notes: Government expenditures include interest payments on domestic and foreign debts from 2000.

Exhibit 4 China Balance of Payments

current U.S. dollar billions	1982	1986	1990	1994	1998	2000	2001	2002	2003	2004
Current Account	**5.7**	**-7.0**	**12.0**	**7.7**	**29.3**	**20.5**	**17.4**	**35.4**	**45.9**	**70.0**
Current Account as % GDP	***2.8%***	***-2.4%***	***3.4%***	***1.3%***	***3.3%***	***1.9%***	***1.5%***	***2.8%***	***3.2%***	***4.2%***
Goods trade balance	4.2	-9.1	9.2	7.3	46.6	34.5	34.0	44.2	44.7	59.0
Goods exports	*21.1*	*25.8*	*51.5*	*102.6*	*183.5*	*249.1*	*266.1*	*325.7*	*438.3*	*593.4*
Goods imports	*16.9*	*34.9*	*42.4*	*95.3*	*136.9*	*214.7*	*232.1*	*281.5*	*393.6*	*534.4*
Services trade balance	0.5	1.6	1.5	0.1	-4.9	-5.6	-5.9	-6.8	-8.6	-9.7
Services exports	*2.5*	*3.8*	*5.9*	*16.6*	*23.9*	*30.4*	*33.3*	*39.7*	*46.7*	*62.4*
Services imports	*2.0*	*2.3*	*4.4*	*16.3*	*26.7*	*36.0*	*39.3*	*46.5*	*55.3*	*72.1*
Net income balance[3]	0.5	0.2	1.1	-1.0	-16.6	-14.7	-19.2	-14.9	-7.8	-3.5
Income credit	*1.1*	*1.1*	*3.0*	*5.7*	*5.6*	*12.5*	*9.4*	*8.3*	*16.1*	*20.5*
Income debit	*-0.6*	*-0.9*	*-2.0*	*-6.8*	*-22.2*	*-27.2*	*-28.6*	*-23.3*	*-23.9*	*-24.1*
Net transfers	0.5	0.4	0.3	1.3	4.3	6.3	8.5	13.0	17.6	22.9
Capital Account	**0.0**	**0.0**	**0.0**	**0.0**	**0.0**	**0.0**	**-0.1**	**0.0**	**0.0**	**-0.1**
Financial Account	**0.3**	**5.9**	**3.3**	**32.6**	**-6.3**	**2.0**	**34.8**	**32.3**	**52.8**	**110.7**
FDI, net	0.4	1.4	2.7	31.8	41.1	37.5	37.4	46.8	47.2	53.1
FDI inflows	*0.4*	*1.9*	*3.5*	*33.8*	*43.8*	*38.4*	*44.2*	*49.3*	*47.1*	*54.9*
FDI ouflows	*0.0*	*-0.5*	*-0.8*	*-2.0*	*-2.6*	*-0.9*	*-6.9*	*-2.5*	*0.2*	*-1.8*
Portfolio investment assets	0.0	0.0	-0.2	-0.4	-3.8	-11.3	-20.7	-12.1	3.0	6.5
Equity	*0*	*0*	*0*	*0*	...	...	*0*	*0*	*0*	*0*
Debt	*0.0*	*0.0*	*-0.2*	*-0.4*	*-3.8*	*-11.3*	*-20.7*	*-12.1*	*3.0*	*6.5*
Portfolio investment liabilities	0.0	1.6	...	3.9	0.1	7.3	1.2	1.8	8.4	13.2
Equity	*0.0*	*0.0*	*0.0*	...	*0.8*	*6.9*	*0.8*	*2.2*	*7.7*	*10.9*
Debt	*0.0*	*1.6*	*0.0*	*3.9*	*-0.7*	*0.4*	*0.4*	*-0.5*	*0.7*	*2.3*
Other investment assets	-0.8	-0.3	-0.2	-1.2	-35.0	-43.9	20.8	-3.1	-17.9	2.0
Monetary Authorities	...	...	...	...	*-2.4*	*-7.3*	*-5.4*	*0*	*0*	*0*
General Government	*-0.5*	*0.1*	*-0.1*	*-1.1*	...	...	...	*0.0*	*0.0*	*0.0*
Banks	*0.0*	*0.0*	*0.0*	...	*2.8*	*-21.4*	*16.8*	*-10.3*	*-15.7*	*3.0*
Other Sectors	*-0.3*	*-0.5*	*-0.1*	*-0.1*	*-35.5*	*-15.2*	*9.4*	*7.2*	*-2.2*	*-1.0*
Other investment liabilities	*0.7*	*3.3*	*1.1*	*-1.5*	*-8.6*	*12.3*	*-3.9*	*-1.0*	*12.0*	*35.9*
Monetary Authorities	*0.0*	*0.5*	*-0.1*	*1.0*	*-5.4*	*0.0*	*0.0*	*0.0*	*0.0*	*0.0*
General Government	*0.5*	*3.9*	*3.1*	*5.2*	*0.0*	*3.2*	*1.1*	*0.0*	*-2.8*	*1.0*
Banks	*-0.5*	*-1.7*	*-2.3*	*-5.2*	*-3.2*	*-8.3*	*-1.3*	*-1.7*	*10.3*	*13.4*
Other Sectors	*0.7*	*0.5*	*0.4*	*-2.5*	*0.0*	*17.5*	*-3.8*	*0.7*	*4.5*	*21.6*
Net Errors and Omissions	**0.3**	**-1.0**	**-3.1**	**-9.8**	**-16.6**	**-11.9**	**-4.9**	**7.8**	**18.4**	**24.3**
Increase in Official Reserves	**6.3**	**-2.0**	**12.0** [2]	**30.5**	**6.4**	**10.6**	**47.3**	**75.5**	**117.1**	**205.0**
Total Reserves (including gold)[1]	**17**	**16**	**34**	**58**	**153**	**172**	**220**	**298**	**416**	**623**
Total reserves in months of imports	10.5	5.2	8.5	5.9	9.9	7.4	8.8	10.2	10.6	11.8
Total Foreign Exchange Reserves	11	11	30	53	149	168	216	291	408	615
% change in fx reserves	124%	-10%	65%	136%	5%	7%	28%	35%	40%	51%

Source: Compiled from World Bank WDI Database, September 2005; Prasad and Wei 2005, p. 46; and author calculations.

Notes: 1. "Total Reserves" differs from the cumulative "Increase in Official Reserves" because of revaluation effects. 2. Increase in Official Reserves in 1990 is not equivalent to the sum of Current Account, Financial Account, and Net Errors and Omissions because of a data discrepancy. 3. Explanation of steep decrease in net income balance, as described in OECD document available at http://stats.oecd.org/mei/default.asp?lang=e&subject= 13&country=CHN. Prior to 1995, data on reinvested earnings were included indistinguishably in direct investment equity but were not accounted for in investment income in the current account. As a result, reinvested earnings were implicitly included in net errors and omissions in those years. Beginning in 1995, the State Administration of Foreign Exchange (SAFE) has collected such data separately and included them in investment income. It collects the data for other investment income from banks and other SAFE sources. Since 1996, it has also drawn such information from the ITRS and from data compiled by the Ministry of Foreign Trade and Cooperation (MOFTEC).

Exhibit 5 Comparative General Economic and Institutional Indicators (2004, except where indicated)

	Nom. GDP (US$ billions at PPP)	Popula-tion (mns)	GDP per Head ($ at PPP)	Internat'l Reserves, Import cover (months)	Current Account Balance as % GDP	Inward FDI as % GDP	Trade in Goods as % GDP (2003)	Life Expect. at Birth (2003)	Control of Corruption[a] (rank out of 204 countries)	Measure of Capital and Exchange Controls[b]
Argentina	505	39	13,070	8.5	2.0%	2.8%	33.3%	74.5%	117	10
Brazil	1,544	179	8,620	7.9	1.9%	3.0%	25.1%	68.7	95	9
Chile	182	15	11,810	6.5	1.5%	8.1%	55.9%	76.4	24	6
China	7,613	1,300	5,860	12.2	4.1%	3.3%	66.0%	70.8	121	15
Germany	2,343	83	28,370	1.3	3.8%	-1.4%	56.2%	78.3	15	1
Hong Kong	213	7	31,130	5.0	9.9%	20.5%	294.8%	80.1	20	2
Indonesia	835	238	3,500	5.6	1.1%	0.4%	44.9%	66.9	168	11
Japan	3,834	127	30,111	...	3.7%	0.2%	19.9%	81.7	29	2
Malaysia	272	26	10,690	6.7	12.5%	2.5%	174.8%	73.0	71	14
Mexico	1,027	105	9,790	3.6	-1.1%	2.5%	54.9%	73.6	105	11
Netherlands	532	16	32,700	0.7	2.9%	-0.1%	108.9%	78.5	11	1
Singapore	132	4	31,200	6.4	28.4%	12.7%	297.8%	...	2	5
South Korea	1,011	48	20,970	8.9	4.1%	1.2%	...	62.8	78	12
Taiwan	604	23	26,820	15.8	6.1%	0.6%	...	...	54	...
Thailand	518	65	8,020	5.5	4.3%	0.9%	109.4%	69.3	103	13
U.K.	1,884	60	31,520	1.0	-2.2%	3.7%	38.7%	77.6	12	2
U.S.	11,734	293	40,050	0.6	-5.7%	0.9%	18.5%	77.4	16	4

Source: Compiled from World Bank WDI Database, October 2005; IMF, Annual Report on Exchange Arrangements and Exchange Restrictions, 2004; and EIU Country Data, October 2005.

[a]From World Bank Governance Indicators, http://www.worldbank.org/wbi/governance/govdata/index.html, accessed October 2005, a measure of the extent of corruption, conventionally defined as the exercise of public power for private gain. It is based on polls of experts and surveys.

[b]Based on IMF, Annual Report on Exchange Arrangements and Exchange Restrictions, 2004. This measure simply sums the number of controls present of 16 possible controls. See **Exhibit 12** for list of controls.

Exhibit 6 Chinese Exports and Imports by Major Commodity

	2001		2002		2003		2004		2005 (Jan-Jul)			
U.S. dollar billions	Ex-ports	Im-ports	Ex-ports	Im-ports	Ex-ports	Im-ports	Ex-ports	Im-ports	Ex-ports	Change (2004 Jan-Jul)	Im-ports	Change (2004 Jan-Jul)
Live animals, food products, & tobacco	15.3	8.9	17.3	8.7	20.6	12.6	22.3	17.5	14.6	23%	39.7	2%
Mineral products	9.9	22.5	9.8	24.5	12.7	37.7	16.6	67.1	12.1	36%	50.3	38%
Oil	*8.4*	*17.5*	*8.4*	*19.3*	*11.1*	*29.2*	*14.5*	*48.0*	*10.2*	*30%*	*34.4*	*35%*
Chemicals	12.8	19.1	14.6	24.3	18.5	31.8	24.6	42.9	18.3	48%	29.2	25%
Plastics	8.3	17.3	10.0	19.8	12.5	24.7	16.9	32.8	12.6	39%	21.5	20%
Leather goods	8.4	3.4	9.3	3.5	11.6	4.1	13.7	5.1	7.7	13%	3.1	5%
Wood & related goods & wood pulp	4.9	10.3	5.9	11.6	7.4	13.3	9.9	15.5	6.9	32%	9.7	5%
Textiles	49.9	16.3	57.9	17.0	73.3	19.3	88.8	23.0	58.3	22%	13.0	-8%
Footwear	12.2	0.4	13.4	0.4	15.6	0.5	18.4	0.6	12.7	23%	0.4	11%
Stone, glass, ceramics	4.2	1.9	5.5	2.1	6.9	2.6	9.3	3.2	6.7	35%	1.8	-5%
Base metals	16.1	21.9	18.9	26.3	25.1	39.4	43.7	48.6	33.9	61%	32.9	14%
Machinery & electrical appliances	84.8	96.4	115.9	125.4	172.4	175.4	247.8	233.7	167.4	30%	143.1	12%
Vehicles	9.3	10.0	10.4	11.5	15.6	17.5	21.0	19.5	15.7	43%	9.9	-17%
Optical equipment	8.4	10.6	9.5	14.4	13.1	26.2	19.1	41.3	12.6	48%	25.1	10%
Total incl. others	**266**	**244**	**326**	**295**	**438**	**413**	**593**	**561**	**408**	**32%**	**358**	**14%**

Exhibit 7 Chinese Exports and Imports by Trade Partner

	2001		2002		2003		2004		2005 (Jan-Jul)			
U.S. dollar billions	Ex-ports	Im-ports	Ex-ports	Im-ports	Ex-ports	Im-ports	Ex-ports	Im-ports	Ex-ports	Change (2004 Jan-Jul)	Im-ports	Change (2004 Jan-Jul)
U.S.	54.3	26.2	70.0	27.2	92.5	33.9	124.9	44.7	86.9	33%	27.6	4%
EU												
Germany	*9.8*	*13.8*	*11.4*	*16.4*	*17.5*	*24.3*	*23.8*	*30.4*	*17.3*	*42%*	*16.7*	*-6%*
Netherlands	*7.3*	*1.5*	*9.1*	*1.6*	*13.5*	*1.9*	*18.5*	*3.0*	*13.6*	*47%*	*1.7*	*-2%*
U.K.	*6.8*	*3.5*	*8.1*	*3.3*	*10.8*	*3.6*	*15.0*	*4.8*	*10.2*	*34%*	*3.0*	*12%*
Italy	*4.0*	*3.8*	*4.8*	*4.3*	*6.7*	*5.1*	*9.2*	*6.5*	*6.8*	*33%*	*4.0*	*12%*
France	*3.7*	*4.1*	*4.1*	*4.3*	*7.3*	*6.1*	*9.9*	*7.7*	*6.5*	*19%*	*5.0*	*23%*
Hong Kong	46.5	9.4	58.5	10.7	76.3	11.1	100.9	11.8	63.2	22%	7.0	10%
Japan	45.0	42.8	48.4	53.5	59.4	74.2	73.5	94.4	26.7	21%	30.8	3%
ASEAN												
Singapore	*5.8*	*5.1*	*7.0*	*7.1*	*8.9*	*10.5*	*12.7*	*14.0*	*8.8*	*34%*	*9.1*	*18%*
Malaysia	*3.2*	*6.2*	*5.0*	*9.3*	*6.1*	*14.0*	*8.1*	*18.2*	*5.6*	*31%*	*10.7*	*6%*
Indonesia	*2.8*	*3.9*	*3.4*	*4.5*	*4.5*	*5.7*	*6.3*	*7.2*	*5.1*	*58%*	*4.5*	*11%*
South Korea	12.5	23.4	15.5	28.6	20.1	43.1	27.8	62.3	10.9	43%	23.1	21%
Latin America	8.2	6.7	9.5	8.3	11.9	14.9	18.2	21.8	12.4	33%	14.1	17%
Africa	6.0	4.8	7.0	5.4	10.2	8.4	13.8	15.6	10.2	44%	11.5	38%
Taiwan	5.0	27.3	6.6	38.1	9.0	49.4	13.5	64.8	9.2	29%	39.3	9%
Canada	3.3	4.0	4.3	3.6	5.6	4.4	8.2	7.4	6.2	44%	4.4	3%
Australia	3.6	5.4	4.6	5.9	6.3	7.3	8.8	11.6	5.7	27%	8.9	42%
Russia	2.7	8.0	3.5	8.4	6.0	9.7	9.1	12.1	6.1	50%	8.9	25%
Total incl. others	**266**	**244**	**326**	**295**	**438**	**413**	**593**	**561**	**408**	**32%**	**358**	**14%**

Source (6&7): Compiled from EIU China Country Reports, various issues.

Exhibit 8 United States: Change in Number of Employees by Sector (yearly percentage change)

	2000	2001	2002	2003	2004
Total nonfarm	2.2	0.0	-1.1	-0.3	1.1
Total private	2.1	-0.3	-1.7	-0.4	1.3
Natural Resources & Mining	0.2	1.2	-3.8	-1.9	3.3
Construction	3.7	0.6	-1.6	0.3	3.4
Manufacturing	-0.3	-4.8	-7.2	-4.9	-1.2
Wood products	*-1.2*	*-6.3*	*-3.3*	*-3.1*	*2.0*
Nonmetallic mineral prods	*2.5*	*-1.8*	*-5.2*	*-4.2*	*2.1*
Primary metals	*-0.5*	*-8.2*	*-10.8*	*-6.3*	*-2.4*
Fabricated metal products	*1.4*	*-4.3*	*-7.6*	*-4.5*	*1.3*
Machinery	*-0.8*	*-5.9*	*-10.1*	*-6.5*	*-0.7*
Computer & electr. prods	*2.2*	*-3.9*	*-13.8*	*-10.1*	*-2.1*
Elect. equip. & appliances	*0.5*	*-5.8*	*-10.8*	*-7.4*	*-2.8*
Transportation equipment	*-1.5*	*-5.7*	*-5.6*	*-3.0*	*-0.6*
Furniture & related prods	*2.2*	*-5.5*	*-6.0*	*-5.2*	*0.0*
Miscellaneous manufac'ing	*0.5*	*-2.5*	*-3.7*	*-3.6*	*-1.2*
Food manufacturing	*0.2*	*-0.1*	*-1.6*	*-0.5*	*-1.3*
Beverage & tobacco prods	*-0.6*	*1.0*	*-0.8*	*-3.8*	*-2.7*
Textile mills	*-4.8*	*-12.0*	*-12.6*	*-10.2*	*-8.7*
Textile product mills	*-0.5*	*-4.9*	*-5.4*	*-7.9*	*-0.9*
Apparel	*-10.6*	*-14.2*	*-15.7*	*-13.2*	*-8.8*
Leather and allied prods	*-8.1*	*-15.7*	*-13.4*	*-11.4*	*-3.6*
Paper and paper products	*-1.8*	*-4.5*	*-5.4*	*-5.6*	*-3.3*
Printing & related activ.	*-1.0*	*-4.8*	*-8.0*	*-3.7*	*-2.3*
Petroleum and coal prods	*-3.6*	*-1.7*	*-2.5*	*-3.2*	*-1.3*
Chemicals	*-0.2*	*-2.2*	*-3.3*	*-2.3*	*-2.1*
Plastics and rubber prods	*0.4*	*-5.8*	*-5.5*	*-3.8*	*-1.1*
Service-providing	2.5	0.8	-0.2	0.4	1.3
Private service-providing	2.5	0.6	-0.6	0.4	1.6
Government	2.4	1.6	1.9	0.3	0.2

Source: Compiled from Bureau of Labor Statistics, "Employment, Hours, and Earnings from the Current Employment Statistics survey (National)," 2004.

Exhibit 9 Chinese Trade by Type of Enterprise

	2001		2002		2003		2004		2005 (Jan-Jul)			
U.S. dollar billions	Ex-ports	Im-ports	Ex-ports	Im-ports	Ex-ports	Im-ports	Ex-ports	Im-ports	Ex-ports	Change (2004 Jan-Jul)	Im-ports	Change (2004 Jan-Jul)
State owned	113.2	103.5	122.9	114.5	138.0	142.5	153.6	176.5	96.2	17%	110.9	9%
Foreign invested	133.2	125.9	169.9	160.3	240.3	231.9	338.6	324.6	232.9	33%	205.7	15%
Collective	14.2	8.0	18.9	9.5	25.1	13.2	31.8	17.7	20.9	21%	7.9	15%
Other (mostly private Chinese firms)	5.5	6.2	13.9	11.0	34.9	25.2	69.4	42.7	58.0	73%	29.2	22%
Total	**266**	**244**	**326**	**295**	**438**	**413**	**593**	**562**	**408**	32%	**358**	14%

Source: Compiled from EIU China Country Reports, various issues.

Exhibit 10 Sources of FDI in China

Country	Cumulative FDI: 1979–2004		Annual FDI by Country (as % total)					Annual FDI by Country (in US$ billion)
	Amount ($ U.S. bn)	% of Total	2000	2001	2002	2003	2004	2004
Hong Kong	242	43%	38%	36%	34%	33%	30%	19.0
United States	48	9%	11%	10%	10%	8%	6%	3.9
Japan	47	8%	7%	9%	8%	9%	9%	5.5
Taiwan	40	7%	6%	6%	8%	6%	5%	3.1
Virgin Islands	37	7%	9%	11%	12%	11%	11%	6.7
South Korea	26	5%	4%	5%	5%	8%	10%	6.2
EU	...	...	11%	9%	7%	7%	7%	4.7
Total	**564**	**100%**	**100%**	**100%**	**100%**	**100%**	**100%**	**64**

Source: Compiled from Prasad and Wei, 2005, p. 41, and Wayne M. Morrison, "China's Economic Conditions," CRS Issue Brief for Congress, April 25, 2005, available at http://fpc.state.gov/documents/organization/45465.pdf, accessed September 28, 2005.

Notes: Some FDI from Hong Kong is thought to represent roundtripping of funds to take advantage of the favorable tax treatment of foreign investment over domestic investment in China. While shares from Hong Kong have fallen over recent years, shares of small economies such as the Virgin Islands and Western Samoa have risen. It is thought that these smaller economies could now be accounting for some of the roundtripping flows.

China collects data on contracted and utilized FDI. Utilized FDI is contracted FDI that actually occurs. Data in the table refer to utilized FDI.

Exhibit 11 Deposits Held by Domestic Residents at Chinese Banks

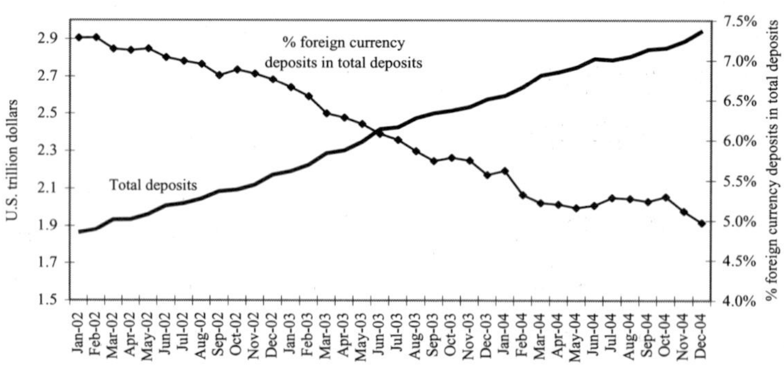

Source: Compiled from People's Bank of China website, http://www.pbc.gov.cn/english/diaochatongji/tongjishuju/, accessed November 2005, and author calculations (2005 data not available at time of writing).

Exhibit 12a Timeline of Capital Controls in China

"y" indicates controls present	1997	1998	1999	2000	2001	2002	2003	2004
Controls on payments for invisible transactions and current transfers	y	y	y	y	y	y	y	y
Proceeds from exports and/or invisible transactions								
Repatriation requirements	y	y	y	y	y	y	y	y
Surrender requirements	y	y	y	y	y	y	y	y
Capital Transactions								
Controls on:								
Capital market securities	y	y	y	y	y	y	y	y
Money market instruments	y	y	y	y	y	y	y	y
Collective investment securities	y	y	y	y	y	y	y	y
Derivatives and the other instruments	y	y	y	y	y	y	y	y
Commercial credits	y	y	y	y	y	y	y	y
Financial credits	y	y	y	y	y	y	y	y
Guarantees, sureties, and financial backup facilities	y	y	y	y	y	y	y	y
Direct investment	y	y	y	y	y	y	y	y
Liquidation of direct investment					y	y	y	y
Real estate transactions	y	y	y	y	y	y	y	y
Personal capital movements		y	y	y	y	y	y	y
Provisions specific to: *Commercial banks and other credit institutions*	y	y	y	y	y	y	y	y
Institutional investors			y					

Source: Compiled from IMF, Annual Report on Exchange Arrangements and Exchange Restrictions, 1997–2004.

Exhibit 12b Summary of China's Capital Controls, 1997–2005

On Capital and Money Market Instruments	
Nonresident purchases	Nonresidents may purchase only RMB-denominated B shares; purchases of money market instruments were not allowed. Beginning in 2004, domestic purchase of A shares was allowed for "Qualified Foreign Institutional Investors," the largest and longest established banks, insurance, and securities firms. QFIIs must set up RMB accounts with domestic banks and use domestic securities companies. No single QFII could own more than 10% of any firm listed in Shanghai or Shenzhen, total QFII ownership of any firm could not exceed 20%. QFII (closed end QFII) capital remittance was permitted after 1(3) year(s) in increments of 20% at 3(1) month intervals.
Nonresident sale or issuance	Not allowed
Resident purchase abroad	Not allowed, except for financial institutions approved by SAFE and authorized enterprises
Resident sale abroad	Sale or issue abroad of securities other than stocks requires PBC and SAFE approval
On Derivatives and Other Instruments	
Nonresident purchases	Not allowed
Nonresident sale or issuance	Not allowed
Resident purchase abroad	Activity by financial institutions subject to review of qualifications and limits on open forex positions (no more than 20% of forex working capital)
On Commercial and Financial Credits	
By residents to nonresidents	Not allowed for industrial and commercial enterprises; Lending by financial institutions subject to SAFE review and a forex asset-liability ratio
To residents from nonresidents	Except for foreign-funded enterprises, external borrowing of commercial credit may only occur through SAFE-approved financial institutions. All transaction amounts must be registered with SAFE and are subject to forex balance requirements except for maturities less than 90 days.
On Direct Investment	
Inward direct investment	All MOFTEC approved nonresidents are free to invest in China, with no foreign exchange restrictions on inward remittances. Some sectors are off limits, however. Beginning in 2004, the ceiling on foreign bank ownership of a Chinese bank was raised from 20% to 25%, and the ceiling for any one bank was raised from 15% to 20%.
Outward direct investment	MOFTEC approval, SAFE registration and review of investment risks and the source of foreign exchange assets required
Nonresident Deposit Accounts/Foreign Currency Deposit Accounts	
Reserve requirements	13% for RMB deposits, 5% for foreign currency deposits in domestic banks, and 3% (5%) for foreign currency deposits in foreign funded enterprises for over (under) 3 months. As of January 2005, reserve requirements on accounts domestic- and foreign-currency denominated domestic were unified at 3%.
Liquid asset requirements	Bank (nonbank) forex liquid assets must be 60% or more of liquid liabilities and 30% (25%) of total foreign exchange assets. Total deposits with 90-day maturity, deposits in both domestic and foreign banks, funds used for purchasing foreign currency denominated securities, deposits with the central bank, and cash holdings should be 15% (10%) or more of total foreign exchange assets.

Source: From Rawi Abdelal and David Lane, "Chrysanthemum and Dragon: JAFCO Asia in China," HBS No. 706-012, which is adapted from Qing Wang, "Appendix II. Evolution of Capital Controls in China," in Eswar Prasad and Shang-Jin Wei, "The Chinese Approach to Capital Inflows: Patterns and Possible Explanations," NBER Working Paper 11306, April 2005, pp. 34–40 (which is based on IMF, "Exchange Arrangements and Exchange Restrictions Annual Report," various years).

Notes: PBC: People's Bank of China, the central bank.
SAFE: State Administration for Foreign Exchange.
MOFTEC: Ministry of Foreign Trade and Economic Construction.

Exhibit 13 Labor Productivity Growth (%) in Selected Countries

	2000	2001	2002	2003	2004	2005 (est.)
China	7.0	6.1	7.0	8.3	8.4	8.2
United States	1.1	0.7	1.9	1.8	3.1	1.9
Hong Kong	9.1	-0.8	2.5	3.5	6.0	3.6
Japan	2.6	0.7	1.0	1.6	2.4	1.4
South Korea	4.0	1.8	4.1	3.3	2.7	2.5
Germany	1.3	0.8	0.6	0.8	1.3	0.2
Netherlands	6.4	-0.1	-0.1	0.3	2.9	0.9
United Kingdom	2.2	1.4	1.2	1.5	2.3	1.2

Source: Compiled from EIU Country Data, September 2005.

Note: "Labor Productivity" measured as real GDP per person employed.

Appendix

July 21, 2005 Text of "Public Announcement of the People's Bank of China on Reforming the Renminbi (RMB) Exchange Rate Regime":

With a view to establish and improve the socialist market economic system in China, enable the market to fully play its role in resource allocation as well as to put in place and further strengthen the managed floating exchange rate regime based on market supply and demand, the People's Bank of China, with authorization of the State Council, is hereby making the following announcements regarding reforming the RMB exchange rate regime:

1. Starting from July 21, 2005, China will reform the exchange rate regime by moving into a managed floating exchange rate regime based on market supply and demand with reference to a basket of currencies. RMB will no longer be pegged to the U.S. dollar and the RMB exchange rate regime will be improved with greater flexibility.

2. The People's Bank of China will announce the closing price of a foreign currency such as the U.S. dollar traded against the RMB in the inter-bank foreign exchange market after the closing of the market on each working day, and will make it the central parity for the trading against the RMB on the following working day.

3. The exchange rate of the U.S. dollar against the RMB will be adjusted to 8.11 yuan per U.S. dollar at the time of 19:00 hours on July 21, 2005. The foreign exchange designated banks may since adjust quotations of foreign currencies to their customers.

4. The daily trading price of the U.S. dollar against the RMB in the inter-bank foreign exchange market will continue to be allowed to float within a band of +/- >0.3% around the central parity published by the People's Bank of China, while the trading prices of the non-U.S. dollar currencies against the RMB will be allowed to move within a certain band announced by the People's Bank of China.

The People's Bank of China will make adjustment of the RMB exchange rate band when necessary according to market development as well as the economic and financial situation. The RMB exchange rate will be more flexible based on market condition with reference to a basket of currencies. The People's Bank of China is responsible for maintaining the RMB exchange rate basically stable at an adaptive and equilibrium level, so as to promote the basic equilibrium of the balance of payments and safeguard macroeconomic and financial stability.[105]

Endnotes

1 Colleen Ryan, "Revaluing Yuan a Gradual Affair," Australian Financial Review, September 12, 2005.

2 For example, see Morris Goldstein and Nicholas R. Lardy, "China's Revaluation Shows Size Really Matters," op-ed in *The Financial Times,* July 22, 2005, where they estimate 10%. Other commentators were less optimistic, estimating 5%. Value of 35% is from Frankel.

3 See, for example, Nerys Avery, "China's Trade Surplus Widened to $10.3 Bln in July (Update2)," *Bloomberg,* August 11, 2005, at http://quote.bloomberg.com/apps/news?pid=10000006&sid=aI6ubprxXtFM&refer=home, accessed November 2005.

4 See, for example, "Mundell Rules Out Further Yuan Appreciation," *Industry Updates,* November 18, 2005; and Ronald McKinnon, "China's Exchange Rate," available at http://www.stanford.edu/~mckinnon/briefs/WSJopedrev.pdf, accessed January 6, 2006. A version of this paper was published in *The Asian Wall Street Journal,* June 27, 2003.

5 See, for example, discussion in David Barboza and Joseph Kahn, "Chinese To Stop Tying Currency Only To Dollar," *The New York Times,* July 22, 2005; and David Barboza, "For Foreign Companies in China, a Rising Yuan Is Hard to Swallow," *The New York Times,* October 15, 2005. See also discussion in "China: To Float or Not To Float (C): Esquel Group and the Chinese Renminbi," HBS No. 706-023.

6 See, for example, Nouriel Roubini, "Whither the Yuan?" The Wall Street Journal Online, July 21, 2005.

7 See, for example, Eswar S. Prasad, "Next Steps for China: Why Financial Sector Reform is a Crucial Element of a Long-term Growth Strategy," *Finance & Development,* September 2005, p. 1.

8 Kenneth Rogoff, "China's Baby Step," *Project Syndicate,* August 2005.

9 Terminology used by Deng to define the economy. For discussion of term, see, for example, Carlos Wing-Hung Lo, "Socialist Legal Theory in Deng Xiao-Ping's China," *The Journal of Asian Law,* Volume 11, Number 2, Spring 1998, at http://www.columbia.edu/cu/asiaweb/v11n2Carlos.htm, accessed November 2005.

10 For more on this topic, see Robert E. Kennedy, "China: Facing the 21st Century," HBS No. 798-066, January 14, 2002. See also U.S. government-developed documents including U.S. Department of State Bureau of East Asian and Pacific Affairs, "Background Note: China," March 2005, available at http://www.state.gov/r/pa/ei/bgn/18902.htm, accessed November 2005; and Federal Research Division of the Library of Congress Country Studies/Area Handbook Series sponsored by the U.S. Department of the Army, available at http://countrystudies.us/china/, accessed November 2005.

11 See Kennedy, 2002, and Library of Congress Country Studies.

12 See Kennedy, 2002.

13 See Library of Congress Country Studies.

14 See U.S. Department of State, 2005.

15 See, for example, Eswar Prasad, Thomas Rumbaugh, and Qing Wang, "Putting the Cart Before the Horse? Capital Account Liberalization and Exchange Rate Flexibility in China," IMF Policy Discussion Paper, January 2005, p. 7, which mentions 150 million according to Chinese authority estimates.

16 See, for example, EIU China Country Report, June 2005.

17 See Kennedy, 2002.

18 See Financial Yearbook of China, 2002.

19 See Kennedy, 2002, and Georges Desvaux, Michael Wang, and David Xu, "Spurring Performance in China's State-owned Enterprises: The Government Must Give a Performance-based System Space to Take Hold," *The McKinsey Quarterly*, 2004 Special Edition.

20 For a detailed discussion of the process, see "Marketization of State-Owned Enterprises," China.org.cn, November 7, 2003, available at http://www.china.org.cn/english/2003chinamarket/79517.htm, accessed November 2005.

21 See *The McKinsey Quarterly*, 2004 Special Edition.

22 Drew Brick, Ray Heung, and Jun Yuan, "Chinese Banks: Trip Report on Bank Reform," Morgan Stanley Fixed Income Research, July 21, 2005; and Ramon Moreno, "Reforming China's Banking System," Federal Reserve Bank of San Francisco Economic Letter, May 31, 2002, available at http://www.frbsf.org/publications/economics/letter/2002/el2002-17.html, accessed November 2005.

23 U.S. Department of State, 2005.

24 Morgan Stanley, 2005, p. 4; and Prasad, 2005.

25 Kennedy, 2002, pp. 11–12.

26 Prasad, 2005.

27 Based on data from China Banking Regulatory Commission.

28 See, for example, discussion in Franklin Allen, Jun Qian, and Meijun Qian, "China's Financial System: Past, Present, and Future," Working Paper 05-17, Wharton Financial Institutions Center, University of Pennsylvania, July 21, 2005. See citation in Xu.

29 Xu (differs from 157) from Morgan Stanley, 2005, p. 5.

30 However, one of these banks, China Construction Bank (CCB), mitigated this risk by purchasing an option to sell the $22.5 billion in dollars back to Huijin (an AMC) at 8.27 renminbi per dollar. The option was exercisable in 2007, and CCB was to pay 5.6 billion renminbi to Huijin in 2007 as an option premium. Deutsche Bank analysts noted that, in effect, the option was a handout from the government to CCB. The option payment was equivalent to 3% of the value of the total amount of $22.5 billion. At the point when the put option was bought, the 12-month nondeliverable forwards (NDFs) for renminbi would have cost double the amount but for a one-year hedge versus the three-year hedge obtained by CCB. (Source: Alan Chua, Tom Quarby, and Sandy Hu, "China Construction Bank: Built for a Positive Future; Initiate with a Buy," Deutsche Bank Company Focus Company Research, November 1, 2005.)

31 PricewaterhouseCoopers, "China NPL Investor Survey 2004: A Survey of the strategies, preferences and expectations of the China non-performing loan foreign investment community," November 2004, available at http://www.pwc.com/extweb/service.nsf/docid/EEDAB19B628FBDE685256F8D007BC771/$file/ChinaNPLSurvey.pdf, accessed November 2005.

32 Morgan Stanley, 2005.

33 Based on data from China Banking Regulatory Commission website, www.cbrc.gov.cn.

34 For more on this, see Min Xu, "Resolution of Non-Performing Loans in China," New York University Leonard N. Stern School of Business, Glucksman Institute for Research in Securities Markets Research Paper, April 1, 2005, available at http://w4.stern.nyu.edu/glucksman/docs/Xu_2005.pdf, accessed November 2005.

35 See data from China Banking Regulatory Commission as well as Pieter Bottelier, "China's Emerging Domestic Debt Markets: Facts and Issues," discussion paper for a conference on Chinese economic policy reform organized by The Center for Research on Economic Development and Policy Reform, Stanford University,

September 18–20, 2003, available at http://scid.stanford.edu/events/ChinaMirror2004/PBottelier2004.pdf, accessed November 2005.

36 See, for example, Nouriel Roubini and Brad Setser, "China Trip Report," April 2005, available at http://pages.stern.nyu.edu/~nroubini/ChinaTripReport-Roubini-Setser.pdf, accessed November 2005.

37 Prasad, 2005; and Goldstein and Lardy, 2005.

38 Roubini and Setser, April 2005.

39 Fred Hu, "China's Credit Boom: Causes and Implications," discussion paper for a conference on Chinese economic policy reform organized by The Center for Research on Economic Development and Policy Reform, Stanford University, September 18–20, 2003, available at http://scid.stanford.edu/events/China2003/Hu%209-18-03.pdf, accessed November 2005.

40 See Morgan Stanley, 2005 for discussion.

41 Morgan Stanley, 2005.

42 Ibid.

43 Ibid.

44 Thomas E. Quarmby, Alan Chua, and Sandy Hu, "Bank of Communications: Nice at half the price; Initiate coverage with Sell," Deutsche Bank Company Research, June 23, 2005.

45 Prasad, 2005; and Morgan Stanley, 2005.

46 For more on this topic, see Nicholas R. Lardy, "Trade Liberalization and Its Role in Chinese Economic Growth," prepared for an International Monetary Fund and National Council of Applied Economic Research conference, "A Tale of Two Giants: India's and China's Experience with Reform and Growth," New Delhi, November 14–16, 2003.

47 See EIU China Country Report 2005.

48 Lardy, 2003.

49 U.S.–China Economic and Security Review Commission, "U.S.-China Trade, 1989–2003: Impact on Jobs and Industries, Nationally and State-by-State," prepared by Robert Scott of the Economic Policy Institute, available at http://www.uscc.gov/pressreleases/2005/05_01_11pr.htm, accessed November 2005.

50 As discussed in Roubini Setser, April 2005; and EIU China Country Report 2005, p. 36.

51 Nouriel Roubini and Brad Setser, "Will the Bretton Woods 2 Regime Unravel Soon? The Risk of a Hard Landing in 2005-2006," prepared for the symposium on the "Revived Bretton Woods System: A New Paradigm for Asian Development?" organized by the Federal Reserve Bank of San Francisco and UC Berkeley, San Francisco, February 4, 2005, p. 14.

52 EIU China Country Report.

53 See press release issued from the office of U.S. Congressional Representative Phil English of Pennsylvania on behalf of Phil English, Mark Green of Wisconsin, Chris Chocola of Indiana, and Robin Hayes of North Carolina, "CHINA Act to Raise Stakes on U.S.-China Negotiations," June 21, 2005, available at http://usinfo.state.gov/eap/Archive/2005/Jun/21-320938.html, accessed November 2005.

54 Memo of the European Union, "The EU-China textile agreement," Brussels, June 12, 2005, available at http://europa.eu.int/comm/trade/issues/sectoral/industry/textile/memo100605_en.htm, accessed November 2005.

55 Grace Fan, "The Asia Factor," *Latin Trade*, March 2005.

56 Excerpt from testimony of Thea M. Lee, assistant director of public policy, AFL-CIO, before the Commission on U.S.-China Economic and Security Review: "China's Industrial, Investment, and Exchange Rate Policies: Impact on the U.S.," September 25, 2003, available at http://www.aflcio.org/mediacenter/prsptm/tm09252003.cfm, accessed November 2005.

57 Prasad, Rumbaugh, and Wang, 2005, pp. 6–7.

58 "U.S.-China Economic Relations—N. Gregory Mankiw, Ph.D.," congressional testimony by Federal Document Clearing House, October 30, 2003, statement of N. Gregory Mankiw, Ph.D., chairman, Council of Economic Advisers, Committee on House Ways and Means, October 30, 2003.

59 Excerpt from remarks by U.S. Federal Reserve Board Chairman Alan Greenspan before the World Affairs Council of Greater Dallas, Dallas, Texas, December 11, 2003, available at http://www.federalreserve.gov/boarddocs/speeches/2003/20031211/default.htm, accessed November 2005.

60 See EIU China Country Report 2005.

61 OECD Directorate for Financial, Fiscal and Enterprise Affairs, "Main Determinants and Impacts of Foreign Direct Investment on China's Economy," Working Papers on International Investment, Number 2000/4, December 2000, available at http://www.oecd.org/dataoecd/57/23/1922648.pdf, accessed November 2005.

62 Prasad, Rumbaugh, and Wang, 2005, p. 26.

63 OECD, 2000.

64 George J. Gilboy, "The Myth Behind China's Miracle," *Foreign Affairs*, July/August 2004.

65 Prasad and Wei, 2005.

66 See various sources, including Prasad and Wei, 2005; Prasad, Rumbaugh, and Wang, 2005; and Guonan Ma and Robert N. McCauley, "Are China's capital controls still binding?" prepared for joint RIETI/BIS/BOC conference, "Globalization of Financial Services in China: Implications for Capital Flows, Supervision and Monetary Policy," Beijing, March 19, 2005, available at http://www.rieti.go.jp/en/events/05031901/pdf/5-1_ma_2.pdf, accessed November 2005.

67 Mentioned in academic papers such as Prasad, Rumbaugh, and Wang, 2005, p. 11, and Ma and McCauley, 2005, as well as nonacademic publications such as EIU China Country Report 2005.

68 See Prasad, 2005, for more on this discussion.

69 Prasad, Rumbaugh, and Wang, 2005, p. 16.

70 Ma and McCauley, 2005, p. 3.

71 Prasad, Rumbaugh, and Wang, 2005; Roubini and Setser, April 2005, p. 16; and Ma and McCauley, 2005, p. 6.

72 Ma and McCauley, 2005, p. 6.

73 Prasad and Wei, 2005, p. 11.

74 Prasad, Rumbaugh, and Wang, 2005, p. 16.

75 Prasad and Wei, 2005, p. 19.

76 Paul Krugman, "Saving Asia: It's Time to Get Radical," *Fortune*, September 7, 1998. Corruption in China is discussed in Wei Li, "Corruption During the Economic Transition in China," December 2001, available at

http://faculty.darden.virginia.edu/liw/papers/zif-c3.pdf, accessed November 2005. Referring to Wei-ding Huang, *The Hidden Economy in China* (Beijing: Commercial Publishing House, 1996), Li describes in footnote 12: "One particular corruption scheme involves diverting bank loans given to a state-owned organization into private investment accounts on the stock market or into private real estate investments. Corrupt officials keep the upsides of these investments, but leave the banks to pick up the downside risks. Although no reliable statistics are available, it is believed that a good portion of China's non-performing bank assets is linked to official corruption."

77 IMF, Annual Report on Exchange Arrangements and Exchange Restrictions, 2004; Ma and McCauley, 2005, p. 6 for foreign-bank quota information.

78 Prasad, Rumbaugh, and Wang, 2005, p. 16; and as discussed with Prasad in casewriter interview.

79 See, for example, Dow Jones Chinese Financial Wire, "China PBOC Yi: No Official Yuan Revaluation Expected," September 15, 2005, which mentions speculators increasing bets.

80 IMF, 2004.

81 See Lardy, 2003, for more on the history of China's exchange rate regime.

82 For more on the history of China's exchange rate regime, see also Barry Eichengreen, "Chinese Currency Controversies," prepared for the Asian Economic Panel, Hong Kong, April 2004.

83 Lardy, 2003.

84 Testimony of Chairman Alan Greenspan, "China," Committee on Finance, U.S. Senate, June 23, 2005, available at http://www.federalreserve.gov/boarddocs/testimony/2005/20050623/default.htm, accessed November 2005.

85 For more discussion, see Alan Greenspan, "Current Account," remarks before the Economic Club of New York, New York, March 2, 2004, available at http://www.federalreserve.gov/boarddocs/speeches/2004/20040302/default.htm, accessed November 2005.

86 For further discussion on Chinese sterilization, see Morris Goldstein, "No Official Yuan Revaluation Expected," chapter in C. Fred Bergsten and John Williamson, *Dollar Adjustment: How Far? Against What?* (Washington, DC: Institute for International Economics, November 2004).

87 Greenspan testimony, June 2005.

88 Yasheng Huang, "Internal and External Reforms: Experiences and Lessons from China," *Cato Journal* 21, Spring/Summer 2001, p. 62, available at http://www.cato.org/pubs/journal/cj21n1/cj21n1.html, accessed August 2005. Article is based on book, Yasheng Huang, *Selling China: The Institutional Foundations of Foreign Direct Investment during the Reform Era* (New York: Cambridge University Press, 2002). Roubini and Setser, April 2005, make the same point.

89 Michael Dooley, David Folkerts-Landau, and Peter Garber, "The US Current Account Deficit: Collateral for a Total Return Swap," Deutsche Bank Global Markets Research, August 2004.

90 Prasad, 2005.

91 Jeffrey Frankel, "On the Renminbi: The Choice between Adjustment under a Fixed Exchange Rate and Adjustment under a Flexible Rate," NBER Working Paper 11274, April 2005.

92 See, for example, Greenspan testimony 2005.

93 See, for example, "Overview and Policy Messages: Mobilizing Finance and Managing Vulnerability," *Global Development Finance*, 2005, p. 5, available at http://siteresources.worldbank.org/INTGDF2005/Resources/gdf05_overview.pdf, accessed November 2005; see also Greenspan testimony, 2005.

[94] Prasad, 2005, p. 4.

[95] "Trichet Says G7 Wants Further Appreciation of Emerging Asia Currencies," *AFX Asia*, September 14, 2005.

[96] Rogoff, 2005.

[97] See "Yuan Step at a Time: The Case for a Big Revaluation of the Chinese Currency is Weaker than Commonly Claimed," *The Economist*, January 20, 2005; and Neil C. Hughes, "A Trade War with China?" *Foreign Affairs*, July/August 2005, available at http://www.foreignaffairs.org/20050701faessay84407/neil-c-hughes/a-trade-war-with-china.html, accessed November 2005.

[98] Discussed in Prasad, 2005; and "Yuan Step at a Time," 2005.

[99] "The Renminbi: The Possibility of Change, and its Likely Effects," New Zealand Treasury Report, July 12, 2005, available at http://www.treasury.govt.nz/release/renminbi/tr2005-1406.pdf, accessed November 2005.

[100] Ma and McCauley, 2005, p. 8.

[101] Andy Xie, "China: What Can 2% Do?" Morgan Stanley Global Economic Forum, July 26, 2005, available at http://www.morganstanley.com/GEFdata/digests/20050726-tue.html, accessed November 2005.

[102] Ronald I. McKinnon, "China's New Exchange Rate Policy: Will China Follow Japan into a Liquidity Trap?" *The Economists' Voice*, Vol. 3: No. 5, Article 2, 2006. Also available at http://www.bepress.com/ev/vol3/iss5/art2.

[103] "Mundell rules out further yuan appreciation," *Industry Updates*, November 18, 2005.

[104] Comments from Zhou published in Andrew Balls, "China's Bank Chief Seeks to Allay Renminbi Fears," *The Financial Times*, August 29, 2005. See also "Yuan Shift Appears Unlikely Soon," *The Wall Street Journal*, August 29, 2005.

[105] The People's Bank of China, "Public Announcement of the People's Bank of China on Reforming the RMB Exchange Rate Regime," July 21, 2005, available at http://www.pbc.gov.cn/english//detail.asp?col=6400&ID=542, accessed November 2005.

HARVARD | BUSINESS | SCHOOL

9-706-022
REV: MARCH 13, 2009

LAURA ALFARO
RAFAEL DI TELLA

China: To Float or Not To Float? (B)

Timeline of Changes Relevant to the Chinese Renminbi

July 21, 2005 China's central bank revalued its exchange rate 2.1%, from approximately 8.28 yuan per U.S. dollar to 8.11. Simultaneously, it announced that a basket of currencies will serve as the yuan exchange rate reference and that the daily trading band of 0.3% against the dollar will be maintained.

July 26, 2005 After speculation in the media and by academics that China will revalue its exchange rate in further discreet steps, China's central bank clarified in a "Solemn Statement of the Spokesman of the People's Bank of China" that no further revaluations should be expected and that further changes in China's exchange rate regime will be made following the principle of "gradualism."

August 2, 2005 China's central bank announced that domestic banks in China, including commercial banks and policy banks, as well as foreign banks and their branches in mainland China can apply for approval to engage in currency forwards and swaps (not involving interest rate swaps). Previously, only China's four state banks and three of China's joint-stock commercial banks were licensed for such transactions. Banks would be responsible for verifying that the domestic entity was engaging in forward purchase and sale of (or swaps involving) foreign exchange for transactions under the current account or for specific allowed transactions under the capital account.[1]

August 8, 2005 China's central bank announced that qualifying nonbanks will be able to participate directly in the foreign exchange spot market based on true currency demands, as well as in currency forwards and swaps.

August 10, 2005 China's central bank revealed the individual currencies making up the yuan reference currency basket. Currencies with prime importance included the U.S. dollar, the euro, the yen, and the South Korean won. Currencies with secondary importance included the pound sterling, Singapore dollar, Malaysian ringgit, Australian dollar, Canadian dollar, Russian rouble, and Thai baht. Specific weightings of the currencies were not revealed.

Professors Laura Alfaro and Rafael Di Tella and Research Associates Ingrid Vogel and Renee Kim prepared this case. This case was developed from published sources. HBS cases are developed solely as the basis for class discussion. Cases are not intended to serve as endorsements, sources of primary data, or illustrations of effective or ineffective management.

September 14, 2005 Chinese President Hu Jintao met with U.S. President George Bush. Among other topics, they discussed China's exchange rate regime. Bush urged China to adopt a fully flexible exchange rate.

September 23, 2005 China's central bank announced that the yuan will be allowed to fluctuate against the reference basket of currencies (excluding the U.S. dollar) by ±3% per day, as compared with ±1.5% previously. The daily band of the yuan against the dollar was maintained at ±0.3%. China's central bank also announced changes liberalizing bank foreign exchange dealings. For example, the spread between the selling and buying prices of foreign currencies quoted by banks to their customers was widened.

October 11, 2005 U.S. Treasury Secretary John Snow started his one-week tour of China. In a meeting on October 18 including U.S. Federal Reserve Chairman Alan Greenspan, Securities and Exchange Commission head Christopher Cox, Chinese Finance Minister Jin Renqing, and People's Bank of China Governor Zhou Xiaochuan, China's exchange rate regime was discussed. China committed in a formal statement at the conclusion of the meeting "to strengthen the role of market forces in their managed floating exchange rate regime." Snow also encouraged China to encourage more consumer spending and financial reform.[2]

October 24, 2005 China's State Administration of Foreign Exchange (SAFE) published new rules effective December 1 aimed at closing loopholes used in yuan hedging. The new rules widened SAFE's definition of short-term overseas debt to include specific trade-related receivables and payment obligations.

November 8, 2005 The United States and China signed a trade deal limiting the growth of Chinese exports to the United States in 34 categories of textiles. For most categories, growth was limited to 8%–10% in 2006, 12.5% in 2007, and 15%–16% in 2008. (The EU-China trade agreement lasted only until 2007.) The United States had been imposing a 7.5% growth limit under World Trade Organization (WTO) safeguard procedures.

November 16, 2005 With President Bush heading to China in a few days to discuss the value of the yuan and other issues with Chinese leaders, Senators Charles Schumer (Democrat, New York) and Lindsey Graham (Republican, South Carolina) said they will delay a vote on a bill to impose a 27.5% tariff on imports from China until March 31.[3]

November 19, 2005 In a joint news conference with Hu Jintao, Bush said: "We'll continue to work with China to help implement its July commitment to a flexible, market-based currency." Most analysts agreed that there were no breakthroughs on currency issues or trade deficits.[4]

November 28, 2005 The U.S. Treasury Department announced that China's steps in reforming the fixed exchange rate between the yuan and the dollar were sufficient to the degree that China will avoid being categorized a currency "manipulator," which could have led to WTO export sanctions.

December 3, 2005 At the Group of Seven (G-7) meeting of finance ministers and central bank governors, China was put under pressure for further exchange rate flexibility. In a communiqué issued at the conclusion of the meetings, the G-7 announced: "We expect that further flexible implementation of China's currency system would improve the functioning and stability of the global economy and the international monetary system."[5]

January 4, 2006 China introduced an over-the-counter (OTC) operations and a market-maker system for the interbank foreign exchange market and authorized the China Foreign Exchange

Trading System to announce the central parity of China's yuan against the dollar, euro, yen, and Hong Kong dollar at 9:15 a.m. each day (instead of taking the closing price as the midpoint for trading in the following session). These measures made trading the yuan easier and were thought to provide the technical basis for an eventual more market-based system. At the same time, China's central bank announced: "The People's Bank of China is responsible for maintaining the RMB exchange rate basically stable at an adaptive and equilibrium level, so as to promote the basic equilibrium of the balance of payments and safeguard macroeconomic and financial stability."[6]

January 16, 2006 China's reserves reached $818.9 billion at the end of 2005, just below Japan's $846.9 billion (China used $60 billion in 2005 to recapitalize state banks). China's trade surplus more than tripled to $102 billion in 2005.[7]

January 26, 2006 At the World Economic Forum in Davos, Switzerland, People's Bank of China (PBOC) Governor Zhou Xiaochuan defended China's exchange rate policy while committing to slow the rate of foreign exchange accumulation by increasing domestic demand, rebalancing the economy gradually away from net exports, and promoting consumption—particularly in rural areas. He also noted that the U.S. dollar accounted for less than 50% of the basket of currencies defining the reference rate.

April 21, 2006 During his visit to the United States, Chinese President Hu Jintao reiterated China's commitment to introduce more flexibility into its exchange rate regime and to "take positive steps in such areas as expanding market access."[8]

April 21, 2006 Finance ministers and central bankers at the G-7 meeting issued a statement calling on China and other emerging markets with trade surpluses to increase exchange rate flexibility "for necessary adjustments."[9]

April 28, 2006 The PBOC raised the benchmark one-year interest rates by 0.27% to 5.85%.

May 10, 2006 The U.S. Treasury announced that it will not formally brand China a currency manipulator, while promising that it will "actively and frankly" push China towards greater flexibility of the renminbi.[10]

August 19, 2006 The benchmark one-year lending interest rate increased for the second time this year, rising 0.27% to 6.12%.

August 27, 2006 The Chicago Mercantile Exchange began trading of futures and options contracts of the yuan.

September 15, 2006 Zhou Xiaochuan, PBOC governor, said China will "sooner or later" expand the trading band for the yuan, but declined to mention a specific timetable while attending the International Monetary Fund and World Bank annual meetings in Singapore.[11]

September 22, 2006 U.S. Treasury Secretary Henry Paulson, in his first trip to China since his appointment to the position, warned that China still hasn't gone far enough to let the yuan rise; "I just know that I'd like even more flexibility" in the yuan's value.[12]

September 22, 2006 China's State Administration of Foreign Exchange approved the trial of foreign exchange reforms in Binhai, a new development area in Tianjin. The new regulations allowed banks to develop offshore finance, imposed no limit on the amount of foreign exchange that could be transformed between headquarters and branches, and lowered the threshold for individuals to hold shares in foreign listed companies.

January 15, 2007 China announced that its foreign currency reserves passed $1 trillion at the end of December, an increase of more than 30% from a year ago. The world's largest reserves were equivalent to about 40% of China's annual economic output.[13]

February 1, 2007 The central bank liberalized its individual foreign exchange regime, raising the annual quota for individual foreign exchange transactions to $50,000 from $20,000 for individual settlement and individual purchases of foreign exchange.

March 9, 2007 China announced its decision to create a new fund to invest the country's massive foreign currency reserves into more diverse and aggressive investments from current investments, which were mostly in U.S. Treasury bonds and other government securities.

March 17, 2007 China's central bank raised interest rates for the third time since April, 2006. The key benchmark one-year interest rate rose to 6.39%, another 0.27% increase.

March 13, 2007 The Chicago Mercantile Exchange said it will list E-mini futures on the FTSE/Xinhua (R) china 25 Index, scheduled to begin trading on May 20, becoming the first U.S. exchange to list futures on the Chinese equity market.

March 31, 2007 The United States imposed tariffs ranging from 10.9% to 20.4% on Chinese high-quality glossy paper, on grounds of fighting alleged Chinese government subsidies. For more than 20 years, U.S. trade policy had been to refrain from imposing duties on non-market economies.[14] The United States posted a record $232.5 billion trade deficit with China last year.

May 18, 2007 In an effort to cool down the economy, the PBOC 1) raised the key benchmark one-year lending interest rate 0.18% to 6.57%, 2) increased banks' reserve requirement ratio by 0.5% to 11.5%, and 3) agreed to widen the trading band of the yuan from 0.3% to 0.5%. The move came a few days before Washington and Beijing's second Strategic Economic Dialogue meeting, aimed at discussing the two countries' trade imbalances.

June 14, 2007 The U.S. Treasury Department, in its semiannual review of foreign currencies, came short of labeling China a currency manipulator amid harsh criticisms and demands for trade action against China.

September 21, 2007 China's central bank governor Zhou said there was no timetable for full convertibility of the yuan, but the government was "quite concerned" about asset prices as inflation reached an 11-year high in August (see **Exhibit 1 and 2**).[15] The previous week, the central bank raised the benchmark interest rates by 0.27% to 7.29%, the fifth increase this year (see **Exhibit 3**).

November 9, 2007 The yuan appreciated 0.6% for the week, its biggest weekly gain since the revaluation (see **Exhibit 4**). Two days earlier, the Chinese central bank's third quarter monetary policy report revealed that the government would "strengthen the coordinated use of interest rates and the exchange rate to help stabilize expectations of inflation," a change in stance from the past of emphasizing the use of other monetary tools, such as bank reserves, to fight inflation.[16]

December 5, 2007 China's state media agency reported that the government decided to shift to a "tight" monetary policy from a "prudent" one in 2008, following a three-day closed-door Community Party leaders' economic conference.[17] Some economists indicated that the move could lead to a faster appreciation of the yuan, which would help fight rising inflation.

December 11, 2007 U.S. Treasury Secretary Paulson warned Beijing that it needs a more flexible exchange rate policy given the country's rising inflation and growing asset bubbles; last month, China's annual consumer price inflation jumped to 6.9%, an 11-year high.

January 11, 2008 China's foreign currency reserves, the world's largest, reached $1.5 trillion as of the end of 2007, a 43% increase from the same period in the previous year. The government also announced that China's trade surplus hit a record $262.2 billion last year.

January 16, 2008 China increased banks' reserve requirement ratio to 15%, just after the last rate hike to 14.5% in the previous month, as part of the central bank's 'tight' monetary policy.

February 14, 2008 IMF Managing Director Dominique Strauss-Kahn said, "...we encourage a faster pace of appreciation that would be helpful for addressing China's key economic challenges and would also contribute to preserving global economic stability," although the yuan was moving "in the right direction."[18]

March 7, 2008 Zhou Xiaochuan, China's central bank governor, said the government will rely more on domestic policies to fight inflation, rather than exchange rate reforms, despite many analysts' belief that a greater appreciation of the yuan may be unavoidable to help fight China's rising inflation.[19] China's goal was to rein in inflation at 4.8% in 2008.

March 18, 2008 China's central bank raised banks' reserve ratio requirement for the second time this year by 0.5% to 15.5%. The decision followed the previous week's announcement that inflation rose 8.7% in February, an 11-year high.

March 23, 2008 Japanese Finance Minister Fukushiro Nukaga indicated that greater efforts to increase the yuan's flexibility would be beneficial for the Chinese economy. His counterpart, Minister Xie Xuren, said China will continue to maintain a "moderate monetary fiscal policy and continue its monetary tightening."[20]

April 2, 2008 U.S. Treasury Secretary Paulson noted that China had made "very material progress" and that the yuan's strength will help to combat rising inflation.[21] Year-to-date, the yuan had already appreciated more than 4% against the dollar.

April 10 2008 The yuan strengthened to close past 7.00 against the dollar for the first time in more than a decade, driven by the overall weakness of the U.S. dollar and growing indications that the PBOC may be willing to let the yuan appreciate with domestic inflation rising at a fast pace.

May 7, 2008 IMF Managing Director Strauss-Kahn said the Chinese yuan still needed to appreciate more quickly, especially as, "too much of the dollar adjustment has been forced on free-floating currencies like the euro and the Canadian dollar"[22] (see **Exhibit 4**).

May 14, 2008 China's central bank released its quarterly monetary policy report and for the first time, directly linked its exchange rate policy to battle inflation, citing that the yuan's flexibility would "allow for the optimum allocation of resources and curb rising prices."[23]

May 15, 2008 The U.S. Treasury's semiannual report to Congress on major trade partners' exchange rate policies concluded that although the Chinese currency remained undervalued, China was not a currency manipulator.

July 1, 2008 Taiwan started to let its local banks legally trade the Chinese yuan for the first time in five decades. The new measure allowed each individual to exchange up to 20,000 yuan as part of Taiwan's cross-strait economic liberalization policy.

August 1, 2008 Amid speculations that China may try to slow the pace of the yuan's appreciation to support economic growth, the yuan weakened 0.35% against the dollar, its biggest weekly depreciation since the 2005 revaluation. President Hu Jintao commented that the country's priority was to maintain steady growth in contrast to his stance earlier this year that China would focus to try and tame inflation.

August 6, 2008 China announced revised foreign exchange regulations aimed at reducing the pressure on the yuan to appreciate. As more investors flocked to the yuan this year, China's reserves continued to increase to reach $1.8 trillion by the end of June, despite a weaker trade surplus and domestic stock markets. The new measures included allowing China's domestic companies to keep their foreign exchange income offshore and lifting the need to seek approval for outward foreign direct investments.

September 15, 2008 For the first time in six years, China's central bank cut the one-year benchmark lending rate, lowering it by 0.27% to 7.20% (see **Exhibit 3**). Smaller domestic banks' reserve requirement ratio was reduced by 1.0% to 16.5%, effective September 25. However, global financial turmoil prompted by the collapse of U.S. investment bank Lehman Brothers outweighed the rate cut; the benchmark Shanghai Composite Index tumbled 4.5% the following day.

October 8, 2008 The PBOC joined other central banks around the world in a coordinated rate cut to help address the jittery global financial markets; China's one-year lending rate was lowered for the second time by 0.27% to 6.93%.

November 10, 2008 China revealed a four trillion yuan stimulus package, about 6% of the country's GDP to combat slowing growth. The government also announced that it was shifting to "moderately easy monetary policies," especially as concerns of rising inflation diminished.[24]

November 26, 2008 China's central bank cut the benchmark one-year interest rate for the third consecutive time, reducing it by 1.08%. It was the PBOC's biggest rate cut in about a decade amid growing concerns about the nation's economic growth. The yuan barely moved against the dollar to close at 6.83.

December 1, 2008 The yuan tumbled to the bottom of its daily trading band limit for the first time. The currency fell 0.7% to close at 6.885 against the dollar, a record one-day loss since the 2005 revaluation, amid rising speculation that the PBOC would adjust its exchange rate policy and allow the yuan to depreciate to help stimulate the economy.

December 3, 2008 After falling to the bottom of its daily trading band for two consecutive days, China's central bank stepped in to sell U.S. dollars and help unfreeze the foreign exchange market. The next day, Commerce Minister Chen Deming said the yuan's depreciation was completely normal and the recent movement was a reflection of a stronger dollar, not a weaker yen.

January 22, 2009 U.S. Treasury Secretary nominee Timothy Geithner told Congress that the newly elected Obama administration "believes that China is manipulating its currency," and noted that a strong greenback was in the United States' national interest.[25]

January 25, 2009 China's state-owned media agency reported that PBOC Vice Governor claimed that Geithner's remarks were inconsistent with facts and that "the Chinese government has never used so-called currency manipulation to gain benefits in its international trade."[26]

January 28, 2009 At the World Economic Forum held in Davos, Switzerland, Wen Jiabao said China was targeting an 8% growth rate for 2009, compared to the 9% growth experienced in 2008. Although the global financial crisis had "a rather big impact" on China's economy, Wen said the nation would focus on expanding domestic consumer demand to drive growth.[27]

January 29, 2009 Premier Wen Jiabao, during a trip to Germany, defended the yuan exchange rate policy, citing that it adhered to a market-oriented principle and it was not to be blamed for fluctuations in world exchange rates.

February 16, 2009 The G-7's top economic officials, including U.S. Treasury Secretary Geithner, praised China for its efforts to stabilize the global economic crisis and "continued commitment to move to a more flexible exchange rate."[28] In their meeting last April, ministers had encouraged the further appreciation of China's exchange rate.

March 4, 2009 Wen Jiabao, in his annual address to the National People's Congress, emphasized that China would keep the yuan stable at an appropriate and balanced level, rather than flexible, as he noted in last year's speech.

March 10, 2009 Commerce Minister Chen Deming announced a gradually reduction in export taxes to zero. He said the government would also provide financial support to struggling exporters. According to economic data released the following day, China's exports tumbled for the fourth consecutive month in February, falling by a worse-than-expected 25.7% from the previous year. February's trade balance recorded a $4.8 billion surplus, the smallest in three years.

Exhibit 1 China's Consumer Price Index (% Change)

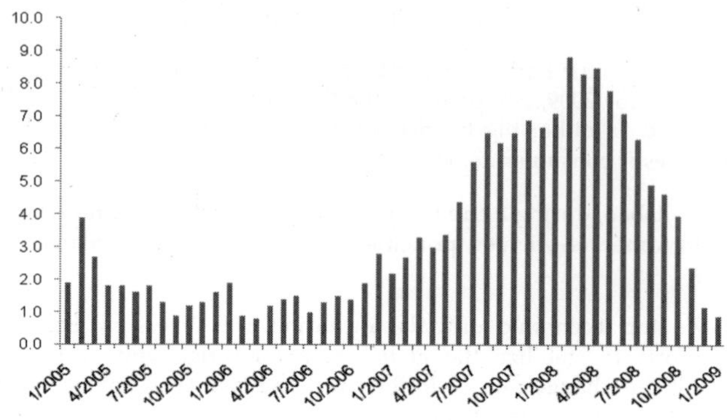

Source: Economic Intelligence Unit Database, accessed March 6, 2009.

Exhibit 2 China's Stock Markets

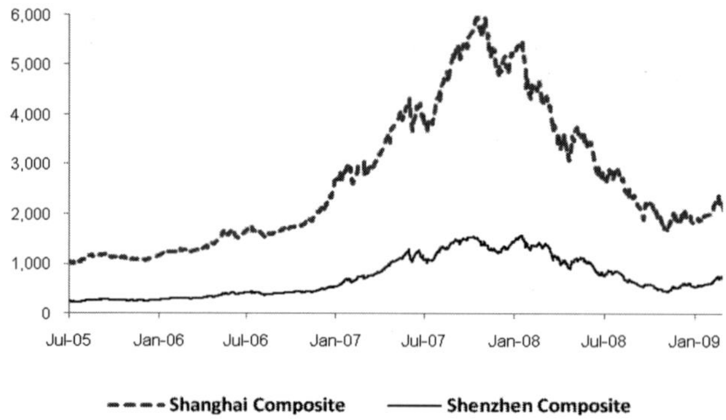

Source: Global Financial Database, accessed March 6, 2009.

Exhibit 3 People's Bank of China's Benchmark One-Year Lending Rate (%)

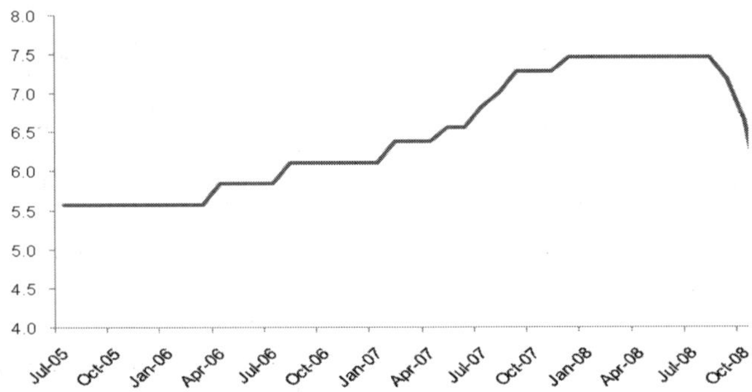

Source: Global Financial Database, accessed March 6, 2009.

Exhibit 4 Chinese Yuan Exchange Rate's Relative Performance, July 2005 – February 2009

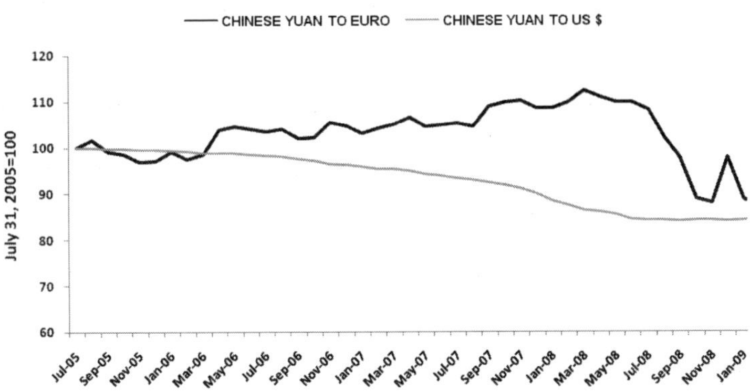

Source: Thomson Financials Database, accessed March 11, 2009.

Endnotes

1 These are listed in the "Notice of the People's Bank of China on Issues Regarding Expanding Designated Banks' Forward Sale and Purchase of Foreign Exchange Businesses to Customers and Launching RMB Swaps against Foreign Currencies," PBC Document No. 201, August 2, 2005, as "repayment of foreign exchange loans issued by the banks; repayment of external borrowings registered with SAFE; receipt and payment arising from overseas direct investment registered with SAFE; receipt of equity funds of foreign-funded enterprises registered with SAFE; receipt of foreign exchange arising from a domestic entity's overseas listing registered with SAFE; other receipt and payment of foreign exchange approved by SAFE."

2 Neil King, Jr., "Beijing Assures U.S. Over Efforts To Adjust Yuan," *The Wall Street Journal,* October 18, 2005.

3 "Senators Delay China Currency Vote," *AFX International Focus,* November 16, 2005.

4 "China, US to cooperate on Yuan: Bush," *Associated Press,* November 21, 2005, available at www.chinadaily.com.cn/english/doc/2005-11/21/content_496663.htm, accessed December 8, 2005.

5 "DJ BOJ Fukui: Chinese Forex System Not Flexible Enough," Dow Jones Commodities Service, December 7, 2005.

6 Public Announcement of the People's Bank of China No. 1 [2006], Public Announcement of the People's Bank of China on Further Improving the Inter-Bank Spot Foreign Exchange Market, January 3, 2006. See also "Finance: Under-appreciated currency," Economist Intelligence Unit—Business Asia, January 23, 2006, for further explanation of the measures.

7 Data from Andrew Browne, "China foreign-currency reserves soar," *The Wall Street Journal Asia,* January 16, 2006.

8 Farah Stockman, "China's leader vows trade changes," *The Boston Globe,* April 21, 2006.

9 "G7 Meeting: Snow says global stability needs help from China, others," *Xinhua Financial Network (XFN) News,* April 24, 2006.

10 John Authers and Tony Tassell, "Dollar Edges off lows after China avoids Currency Manipulator Tag," *Financial Times,* May 11, 2006, p. 30.

11 "China to Widen Yuan Trading Band Sooner or Later," *AFX Asia,* September 16, 2006.

12 Michael Phillips and Andrew Browne, "Paulson Prods Beijing on Currency," *Wall Street Journal,* September 22, 2006.

13 "China's Foreign Currency Reserves Surpass $1 Trillion," *Associated Press Newswires,* January 15, 2007.

14 "The China Tariffs," *The Wall Street Journal,* April 2, 2007.

15 "PBOC Zhou: No timetable for full yuan convertibility," *Dow Jones International News,* September 21, 2007.

16 "New policy gives yuan biggest weekly gain vs dlr," *Reuters News,* November 9, 2007.

17 Scott McDonald, "China says it will tighten monetary policy in 2008, exert greater control over lending," *Associated Press,* December 5, 2007.

18 "IMF's Strauss-Kahn: IMF wants faster yuan appreciation," *Market News International,* February 14, 2008.

19 Andrew Batson and Jason Leow, "Central banker dismisses prospects of yuan surge," *The Wall Street Journal,* March 7, 2008.

20 Takashi Nakamichi, "Update: Japan MOF Asks China to Make Yuan More Flexible," Dow Jones International News, March 23, 3008.

[21] Glenn Somerville, "Update 1: US's Paulson Praises China on Currency Progress," Reuters News, April 2, 2008.

[22] "IMF Chief: China must let Yuan Appreciate More Quickly," Dow Jones Chinese Financial Wire, May 7, 2008, accessed via Factiva on March 6, 2009.

[23] "Update: PBOC: Yuan Exchange Rate can Curb Inflation Concerns," Dow Jones International News, May 14, 2008.

[24] Tania Branigan, "China: Beijing to Pump 4tn Yuan into Economy to Offset Fall in Exports," *The Guardian*, November 10, 2008.

[25] "Geithner Backs Strong Dlr; Says China Manipulates Yuan," Dow Jones News Service, January 22, 2009.

[26] J.R. Wu, "World News: Beijing Snaps Back Over Yuan," *The Wall Street Journal*, January 26, 2009.

[27] "Crisis 'has hit China's Economy'", BBC News, January 28, 2009, http://www.bbc.co.uk/2/hi/business/davos/7856636.stm., accessed March 12, 2009.

[28] Michael M. Phillips and Stacy Meichtry, "G-7 Mutes Criticism of China—Officials Praise Beijing's Stabilizing Role in Crisis, No Longer Fault Yuan Policy," *The Wall Street Journal Asia*, February 16, 2009.

HARVARD | BUSINESS | SCHOOL

9-706-023
REV: NOVEMBER 20, 2006

LAURA ALFARO
RAFAEL DI TELLA

China: To Float or Not To Float? (C)

Esquel Group and the Chinese Renminbi

In July 2005, China revalued its currency by 2.1% and adjusted its exchange rate regime toward a more market-based system. Initially, China's central bank allowed only minor movement in the yuan's value. Observers were uncertain what would happen to the yuan in the short and medium term, especially with some experts estimating that it was undervalued by up to 35%. Would the central bank introduce further discreet steps revaluing the yuan? Would the yuan eventually be allowed to float more freely? Would China's currency appreciate as substantially against the U.S. dollar as predicted by economists? When would further change occur?[1]

The stakes were high; a freer yuan float would impact groups very differently. The Hong Kong-based Esquel Group was one keenly interested party.

Esquel Group

Esquel Group was a family-run, privately held textiles firm specializing in high-quality cotton shirts. Shanghai-born Y.L. Yang started the company in 1978 with his daughter Marjorie Yang, who was returning to Hong Kong from the United States after earning a degree in mathematics from MIT, completing an MBA at Harvard Business School, and working in mergers and acquisitions at an investment bank.[2]

In 1995, Ms. Yang became chairperson of the company and launched a major expansion. Esquel Group became a vertically integrated business with its own cotton production in northwest China combined with operations focused on spinning yarn; weaving, knitting, and dying fabric; and assembling, accessorizing, and packaging final garments for shipment. Production facilities—based in China, Malaysia, Vietnam, Mauritius, and Sri Lanka—were complemented by product development and merchandising capabilities carried out in worldwide branches near major customers. Facing an insecure electric power supply in China, Esquel even came to build its own power plants for its key factories in the country.[3]

---

1 Refer to "China: To Float or Not To Float (A)," HBS No. 706-021, November 2005, for a more detailed discussion on this topic.

2 Andrew Tanzer, "The Great Quota Hustle: Is the U.S. Really Taking Down Trade Barriers?" *Forbes*, March 6, 2000.

3 Andreas Haslauer, "Schneider Der Welt," *Focus-Money*, August 31, 2005.

Professors Laura Alfaro and Rafael Di Tella and Research Associate Ingrid Vogel prepared this case. HBS cases are developed solely as the basis for class discussion. Cases are not intended to serve as endorsements, sources of primary data, or illustrations of effective or ineffective management.

By 2000, Esquel had become one of the world's largest manufacturers of cotton shirts, with approximately US$500 million in revenues.[4] In 2005, customers included well-known brands and retailers such as Abercrombie & Fitch, Banana Republic, Hugo Boss, J. Crew, Lands' End, Marks & Spencer, Muji, Nike, Nordstrom, and Tommy Hilfiger.[5] The company produced in excess of 60 million garments annually. Approximately 60% were exported to the United States, 15% to Europe, and 15% to Japan, and the remainder were sold in the rest of Asia. Esquel had a total of 46,000 employees comprising approximately 25,000 factory workers and 3,000 other staff in mainland China and Hong Kong; 15,000 factory workers in Malaysia, Vietnam, the Philippines, Mauritius, and Sri Lanka; plus 3,000 other staff around the world.[6] Yang was regularly featured in *Fortune* magazine's list of the 50 most powerful businesswomen in the world.

China's Textile Industry

In 2005, the $350 billion textile manufacturing industry faced a number of challenges. The system of global quotas that had once specified exactly how much each country could export to other countries had been dismantled on January 1. The less cost effective of the more than 60 countries that had once exported textiles to Western countries under specified allotments risked losing their textile industries to those countries that proved most competitive.

Many analysts expected China to become one of the primary bases of textile production. China's garment industry, which accounted for 20% of global production in 2004,[7] had already grown from $10 billion in 1990 to $50 billion in 2005. Garment factories numbering around 40,000 employed 15 million workers and produced 20 billion finished items per year in addition to billions more items that were prepared in China but finished elsewhere. Many analysts believed China, with more than 200 million surplus workers, would create additional capacity quickly and cost effectively in support of the country's export-driven development strategy to drive rapid economic growth.[8]

However, the Chinese textile industry faced its own challenges. First, the United States and Europe imposed new quotas on imports of Chinese textiles after a surge in imports resulting from the lifting of quotas on January 1, 2005. (See **Appendix** for text of the June 12, 2005 official EU China Textiles Memorandum.) This created uncertainty for the industry, since how long these new quotas might last and whether they might be increased or reduced remained unclear.[9]

Second, China faced wages that were higher than in other textile-producing countries and was experiencing upward wage pressure as it rapidly developed, particularly in the coastal areas where much current production was based. Estimates from 2002 placed hourly compensation in sewing and weaving in China's coastal area at $0.69, compared with $0.41 for China's noncoastal areas, $0.25 for Bangladesh, $0.40 for Sri Lanka, $0.50 for Indonesia, and $0.57 for India. For apparel, 2002 estimates

[4] Tanzer, "The Great Quota Hustle."

[5] Company website, www.esquel.com.

[6] Toh Han Shih, "Esquel to Reshuffle 20,000 Jobs as Quotas End; Labor Location Hinges on the Outcome of the Textile Dispute," *South China Morning Post*, November 22, 2003.

[7] See EIU China Country Report June 2005; and George Wehrfritz and Alexandra A. Seno with Sudip Mazumdar, "Succeeding at Sewing; The Most Sweeping Reform in Industrial History Leaves China Poised to Rule the Garment Trade," *Newsweek International*, January 10, 2005.

[8] For more on this topic, refer to "China: To Float or Not To Float (A)," HBS No. 706-021.

[9] See "China: To Float or Not To Float (B): Timeline of Changes Relevant to the Chinese Renminbi," HBS No. 706-022, for latest updates on textile quotas.

of hourly compensation were $0.68 for China, $0.39 for Bangladesh, $0.48 for Sri Lanka, $0.27 for Indonesia, $0.38 for India, and $0.88 for better-quality apparel in China.[10] Total costs, however, remained lower in China. According to one study, the total cost of a shirt made in China was approximately US$11.15, compared with almost one dollar more in Bangladesh, even though labor on a Chinese shirt amounted to US$2.28, compared with US$1.52 in Bangladesh.[11] Among other advantages, the Chinese had invested in roads and ports, reducing transportation costs for Chinese manufacturers. Chinese textile factories also tended to be more advanced with more automated processes. In addition, Chinese textile and apparel workers were considered more skilled than workers in other countries, and middle management was thought to be stronger.[12]

A third major challenge faced by China's textile industry was the yuan revaluation. Not only did the 2.1% revaluation threaten to reduce profit margins, but, like the new quotas, the possibility for future changes to the yuan-dollar exchange rate introduced considerable uncertainty to the industry.

Esquel Group's Response to Renminbi Issues

Esquel Group, with its most significant manufacturing base located in China, was among those companies confronted with the challenge of addressing the revaluation of the yuan and the possibility of future appreciation. Esquel Executive Director K. L. Lee explained:

> The appreciation in the value of the yuan will have a big impact on our business. Most of our customers are invoiced in dollars, yet a very large percentage of our cost structure is in renminbi. In our industry, we are facing a situation of excess global capacity and, as a result, a very high level of competition. Therefore, we cannot simply pass on the increase in our costs caused by the revaluation to our customers. Instead, we will need to address this cost increase in other ways.

Financial hedging was not a viable method by which to address future uncertainty. Without a fully convertible local currency, Chinese companies were limited in their ability to hedge currency risk in financial markets. Although nondeliverable forward (NDF) markets[13] had developed in the last few years—which allowed investors with local currency exposure to hedge against future renminbi movements without needing to exchange renminbi—NDF contracts could be expensive to buy. Lee noted: "Oftentimes companies needed to pay a 5% premium, and when the appreciation was only around 2%, it didn't pay out. "

---

[10] U.S. International Trade Commission, "Textiles and Apparel: Assessment of the Competitiveness of Certain Foreign Suppliers to the U.S. Market Volume I," Investigation No. 332-448, declassified January 26, 2004, available at http://hotdocs.usitc.gov/pub3671/pub3671.pdf, accessed November 2005, compiled for the textile industries from Werner International Management Consultants, "Spinning and Weaving Labor Cost Comparisons 2002," (Reston, VA); and for the apparel industries from Jassin-O'Rourke Group, "Global Competitiveness Report: Selling to Full Package Providers" (New York, NY), November 2002.

[11] A.T. Kearney study cited in "Succeeding at Sewing," 2005.

[12] U.S. International Trade Commission, 2004.

[13] A Bank for International Settlements (BIS) paper defines NDFs as "foreign exchange derivative products traded over the counter. The parties of the NDF contract settle the transaction, not by delivering the underlying pair of currencies, but by making a net payment in a convertible currency (typically the U.S. dollar) proportional to the difference between the agreed forward exchange rate and the subsequently realized spot rate. NDFs are also distinct from deliverable forwards in that NDFs trade outside the direct jurisdiction of the authorities of the corresponding currencies and their pricing need not be constrained by domestic interest rates." Guonan Ma, Corrinne Ho, and Robert N. McCauley, "The Markets for Non-Deliverable Forwards in Asian Currencies," *BIS Quarterly Review*, June 2004 (accessed November 2005).

Esquel had some operational protection against renminbi movement. Production facilities outside of China offered limited opportunities to shift production. Furthermore, a small proportion of Esquel's costs were dollar denominated, such as oil supply for energy and other imported materials. But these protections were insufficient to protect the company adequately from the yuan's appreciation and possible future appreciation. Instead, as described by Lee:

> China faces lots of pressure from the international community to further adjust its currency regime. It remains, of course, unclear for companies like ours what will ultimately happen—whether China will make further adjustments, when, and by how much. So it is important for us to make changes as we can in preparation. It will have a significant impact on our business strategy.
>
> First, we are working on further improvements to our cost structure through becoming even more productive. Of course, such improvement won't happen overnight. But it is an important step, especially given the possibility for further renminbi appreciation.
>
> Second, we are working toward growing our sales in China. Having more renminbi revenue to match against our renminbi costs will create a natural hedge to protect against currency risks. We are already supplying to international brands selling inside China and some domestic brands as well. In 2000, we launched our own apparel brand in China, called PYE. We believe it is poised to become one of China's best-known labels. Currently, China accounts for around 5% of our sales. The opportunity is for us to grow this to 10% to 15% shortly. Obviously, the market has huge potential; there is no reason we should not be able to grow our renminbi revenue stream substantially.

Esquel also had the opportunity to continue to focus on creating more specialized products and offering more extensive service in order to present an advantage over its competitors. In terms of specialized products, Esquel already produced antiwrinkle, odor-free, UV-protective, antibacterial, performance care, as well as water and stain-resistant fabrics /garments. Some of these were using Esquel's proprietary technology under its own patents. In terms of service, customers were increasingly calling on Esquel to participate in design. In a *Financial Times* feature on the company, Yang described Esquel's response to a request from Hugo Boss to develop a "new style classic shirt": "We are in the middle of fundamental change in the way we run the business. We are turning from a hard-core manufacturer into a service company. Hugo Boss customers want to look good but they are quite conservative. Any changes had to be subtle."[14] Yang commented that Esquel was "introducing better supply chain management and better systems generally. I've no doubt we'll be able to take on our competitors and bust ass."[15]

---

[14] Angela Mackay, "Esquel Chairman Stays Private by Design—Marjorie Yang Values Her Freedom at the World's Largest Cotton Shirts Manufacturer," *The Financial Times*, October 28, 2003.

[15] Ibid. (2003, comment in response to anticipation of lifting of quotas).

Appendix

June 12, 2005 Memo of the European Union, The EU-China Textile Agreement, Brussels

The EU and China have agreed to a deal that will manage the growth of Chinese textile imports to the EU until 2008. The agreement on 10 product categories of concern limits the rate of imports while allowing fair and reasonable growth for Chinese exports. By finding a wide and balanced agreement, the EU and China ensure a period of adjustment for textile industries in the EU and developing countries, provide greater predictability for importers and retailers, and preserve the prize of market liberalization for China.

The agreement The European Commission and the Ministry of Commerce of the People's Republic of China, pursuant to the WTO principle of encouraging its Members to settle their differences by way of consultation, engaged in consultations on the export of certain Chinese textile and clothing products to the European Union until the end of the year 2008 in Shanghai, China on June 10, 2005. They reached the following understanding:

- Chinese textile exports to the EU in 10 categories of concern will be limited to agreed growth levels until the end of 2007.
- This agreement will cover 10 of the 35 categories of Chinese imports liberalized on 1 January 2005: pullovers, men's trousers, blouses, t-shirts, dresses, bras, flax yarn, cotton fabrics, bed linen, table and kitchen linen. It covers the categories of serious concern, including most of the categories identified by the European Textile Association Euratex and the two categories for which the EU had already launched formal WTO consultations with the Chinese: t-shirts and flax yarn (see table below).
- The EU agrees to end the ongoing investigations concerning these product categories.
- The agreement limits growth in imports in the 10 categories to between 8 and 12.5% per year for 2005, 2006 and 2007. These levels will be calculated on a base that includes either two or three months of post-quota trade levels (see table below). In those categories for which growth is initially set at 8%, agreed growth rates will rise over the three-year period.
- Quantitative levels will apply from 11 June 2005. Both sides will at once put in place the necessary administrative arrangements for the management of agreed import levels.
- In categories not covered by the agreement, and for 2008, the European Union will undertake to exercise restraint in the application of its rights under Article 242 of China's Protocol of Accession to the WTO.
- The two sides stand ready to discuss promptly any aspect regarding the implementation of this agreement.
- This agreement takes the form of a Memorandum of Understanding between the European Commission and the Chinese Ministry of Commerce. It will now be submitted to Member States and the competent authorities in China for endorsement or approval.

	Unit	Actual Imports January–March 2005	Percentage Increase Compared to January–March 2004	Agreed Growth Rate 2005	Agreed Growth Rate 2006	Agreed Growth Rate 2007
5 – pullovers	1000 units	65.02	534%	8%	10%	10%
6 – men's trousers	1000 units	104.195	413%	8%	10%	10%
7 – blouses	1000 units	21.927	186%	8%	10%	10%
4 – T-shirts	1000 units	150.665	164%	10%	10%	10%
26 – dresses	1000 units	5.834	139%	10%	10%	10%
31 – brassieres	1000 units	44.229	63%	10%	10%	10%
115 – flax yarn	tons	1.098	51%	10%	10%	10%
2 – cotton fabrics	tons	14.048	60%	12.50%	12.50%	12.50%
20 – bed linen	tons	4.058	164%	12.50%	12.50%	12.50%
39 – table+kitchen linen	tons	2.859	61%	12.50%	12.50%	12.50%

What the agreement achieves The agreement reached with China represents a common, broad and forward-looking strategy for dealing with textile imports from China.

- Whereas EU unilateral safeguards under the Textiles Specific Safeguard Clause in China's WTO Accession Protocol would have provided limited protection in some categories only until the end of the year, this agreement gives wider coverage over a longer period. It gives the EU textile industry three years in which to adapt to changed market conditions.
- The agreement's limits on growth for Chinese exports are higher than the 7.5% growth that would have been permitted under safeguard measures. This reflects the fact that they were reached by agreement. They allow China fair and reasonable growth, at levels which in some cases increase over the three-year period.
- The agreement allows importers and retailers to plan and purchase in China in conditions of maximum predictability and minimum market distortion.
- The agreement preserves the strong and constructive wider trading relationship that Europe prizes with China. It preserves the prospect of market opening in China for EU businesses. It is a strong signal that China takes its international trading responsibilities seriously—and that Europe respects China's right to benefit from trade liberalization.
- The agreement also provides a window for adaptation for producers in developing countries whose textiles exports to the EU were being displaced by a surge in imports from China. This is particularly important for textile industries in the EU's Mediterranean neighbors.

Context With the expiry of the WTO Agreement on Textiles and Clothing on 1 January 2005, all WTO members were required to lift their remaining quotas on textiles trade. The Uruguay Round provided for the gradual liberalization of this trade over a period of ten years from 1 January 1995 to 31 December 2004, allowing time for adjustment.

The European Commission believes that the removal of quotas in global textile trade is an important prize for progressive trade liberalization. Free trade in textiles will provide global competitive disciplines that will improve productivity and lower prices for consumers.

This competitive pressure is being driven chiefly by China, whose formidable production and export capacity will quickly reinforce its status as one of the world's largest producers and exporters of textile and clothing products.

Managing this transition presents a challenge both for China and its trading partners, many of whom have textile industries of their own. European textiles producers face tough competition from China. European industry has a huge capacity for innovation and adjustment, but a sudden, steep and sustained surge in Chinese textiles exports could be highly damaging.

The agreement between China and the EU reflects this by providing a three-year breathing space where growth in Chinese imports in sensitive categories will be capped at reasonable levels. These caps will nevertheless be high enough to allow China to benefit from liberalization, as it has a right to expect. Commissioner Mandelson has described such measures as an attempt to "manage change and adjustment, rather than manage trade."

Annex 1: EU-China Textiles Negotiations 2005

1 January 2005. With the end of the Multi-Fibre Arrangement all remaining quotas in international textile trade are lifted.

6 April 2005. The European Commission publishes guidelines for the use of the Textile Specific Safeguard Clause (TSSC) written into China's protocol of accession to the WTO. These guidelines set alert levels for categories of Chinese textiles imports beyond which the Commission will consider launching market disruption investigations that could ultimately lead to the use of temporary safeguards, as permitted by the TSSC.

24 April 2005. Presenting data showing substantial rises in exports in some liberalized categories for the first three months of 2005, the Commission launches investigations into 9 categories of textile imports from China: t-shirts, pullovers, blouses, stockings and socks, men's trousers, women's overcoats, brassieres, flax or ramie yarn and woven fabrics flax.

5 May 2005. Commissioner Mandelson meets Chinese Commerce Minister Bo Xilai in Paris.

17 May 2005. The Commission requests use of urgency procedure written into the Commission Guidelines on two categories of textile products: t-shirts and flax yarn. This allows the EU to request immediate formal consultations with China in these two categories.

23 May 2005. EU Member States approve urgency procedures in two categories of textile exports: t-shirts and flax yarn.

24 May 2005. Commissioner Mandelson and Vice Minister and Textile Negotiator Gao Hucheng meet in Brussels and agree to continue and intensify negotiations.

27 May 2005. European Commission requests formal consultations on two categories of Chinese textiles exports: t-shirts and flax yarn; under the terms of the TSSC China has 15 days to take action to restrain export growth in these two categories to the level of the first twelve of the previous fourteen months plus 7.5%. If China does not act, the EU is authorized to act to limit exports to the same effect. Negotiations with the Chinese continue and intensify.

10 June 2005. Peter Mandelson and Bo Xilai agree to a deal that will manage the growth of Chinese textile imports to the EU until the end of 2008.

Annex 2: The Wider EU-China Trading Relationship

- China is the EU's second largest trading partner. Their trading relationship was worth 174 billion euro in 2004.
- China is the second largest exporter to the EU after the US. The EU imported more than 126 billion euros worth of goods in 2004—12% of the EU import market. EU imports from China rose by 17% between 2002 and 2003 and 20% between 2003 and 2004.
- EU exports to China have also been growing. China is now the third export partner of the EU. In 2004 the EU exported 48 billion worth of goods to China—some 5% of all EU exports. This is an increase of 16% on 2003. It is estimated that in less than a decade the Chinese market for luxury European goods will have risen to about 250 million people.
- The EU is the world's second largest textiles exporter after China. In 2004 Europe exported 514 million euros worth of textiles to China. In the same year China exported 16 billion euros worth of textiles to Europe.
- The EU's main exports to China are non-electrical machinery, transport equipment and chemical products. China's main exports to the EU are office and telecommunications equipment and textiles and clothing.
- China is a large market for EU foreign investment: some 3.1 billion in 2003. With reform in the Chinese services sector and full implementation of WTO obligations this is a huge market for EU investors.[16]

[16] Memo of the European Union, The EU-China Textile Agreement, Brussels, June 12, 2005, available at http://europa.eu.int/comm/trade/issues/sectoral/industry/textile/memo100605_en.htm, accessed November 2005.

9-706-031
REV: NOVEMBER 20, 2006

LAURA ALFARO
RAFAEL DI TELLA

China: To Float or Not To Float? (D)

Bank of America's Strategic Investment in China Construction Bank

In July 2005, China revalued its currency by 2.1% and adjusted its exchange rate regime toward a more market-based system. Initially, China's central bank allowed only minor movement in the yuan's value. It remained uncertain what would happen to the yuan in the short and medium term, especially with some experts estimating that the currency was undervalued by up to 35%. Would the central bank introduce further discreet steps revaluing the yuan? Would the yuan eventually be allowed to float more freely? Would China's currency appreciate as substantially against the U.S. dollar as predicted by economists? When would further change occur?[a]

Observers noted the importance of sequencing further changes to China's exchange rate regime with banking sector reform and capital account liberalization. Alan Greenspan summarized the argument: "Many in China fear that removal of capital controls that restrict the ability of domestic investors to invest abroad and to sell or to purchase foreign currency—which is a necessary step to allow a currency to float freely—could cause an outflow of deposits from Chinese banks, destabilizing the system."[1]

With its $3 billion investment in Chinese state bank China Construction Bank, Bank of America—the second U.S. bank behind Citigroup in terms of assets and market capitalization[2]—was one of several foreign banks directly participating in China's banking sector reform.

China's Banking Sector

Overview Faced with underdeveloped equity and bond markets in China, firms tended to rely predominately on bank loans for financing. As such, banks played a major role in intermediating private savings. At year-end 2004, Chinese banks had approximately $3.7 trillion in assets, equivalent to 210% of gross domestic product (GDP).[3] The ratio of bank assets to stock market capitalization plus bonds outstanding in China exceeded 300%, a far higher ratio than in most industrial countries and in many developing countries. For example, India, Japan, Mexico, South Africa, and the United States all had ratios less than 100%.[4]

---

[a] See "China: To Float or Not To Float (A)," HBS No. 706-021, for an extensive discussion on this topic.

Professors Laura Alfaro and Rafael Di Tella and Research Associate Ingrid Vogel prepared this case. This case was developed from published sources. HBS cases are developed solely as the basis for class discussion. Cases are not intended to serve as endorsements, sources of primary data, or illustrations of effective or ineffective management.

The Chinese banking system comprised five categories of banks. Four state banks—Industrial and Commercial Bank of China (ICBC), China Construction Bank (CCB), Agricultural Bank of China (ABC), and Bank of China (BOC)—accounted for 53% of total bank assets. (See **Exhibit 1** for basic statistics.) Created in 1994 to take over the policy-lending role of China's state banks, three policy banks—China Development Bank, Export-Import Bank of China, and Agricultural Development Bank of China—had a 14% share of assets. The remainder of China's banking sector included 12 joint-stock commercial banks with mixed government and private ownership accounting for 15% of total bank assets, 112 urban commercial banks for 5%, 34,000 rural credit cooperatives for 10%, and 60 foreign banks for 2% (although their share in major commercial areas such as Shanghai and Beijing was closer to 12%).[5] The share of assets in foreign banks had actually decreased slightly over the prior three years.[6]

Challenges China's banking sector faced a number of challenges, including the relatively poor quality of its assets. At year-end 2001, official estimates of the share of nonperforming loans (NPLs) in total loans of the four state banks stood at more than 30%. By mid-2005, after the government facilitated bank transfers of $240 billion in NPLs to asset-management companies, official data showed that NPLs at the four state banks had fallen to $122 billion, representing 10% of their total loans. (See **Exhibit 2** for data on NPLs.) Independent estimates, however, put bad debts much higher, at between 20% and 25%.[7] Furthermore, there was concern that NPLs would rise in the future with the surge in credit between 2003 and 2005.[8] Analysts noted that the share of "special mention" loans on bank balance sheets was high—for example, they stood at 15.4% for CCB. "Special mention" loans, which were caused by insufficient documentation, risked becoming nonperforming in a credit cycle downturn. Not only did insufficient documentation imply that credit decisions were likely not well informed but also that collateral would be difficult to seize.

The origin of China's high level of NPLs was attributed predominately to the role of state banks prior to 1994 in supporting loss-making state-owned enterprises. The lack of necessary commercial credit skills within Chinese banks was another contributing factor. In an analyst report, Morgan Stanley noted: "Building a credit culture, correcting the salary structure, and correctly incentivizing staff are key tasks to negate fraud and avoid excessive build-up of NPLs."[9] Market participants within China agreed; soon after becoming chairman of CCB in March 2005, Guo Shuqing commented on his own institution: "More than 90% of the bank's risk managers are unqualified."[10]

Widespread fraud and corruption within the banking sector proved another major challenge. In March 2005, the former chairman of CCB resigned following accusations that he had accepted $1 million from Alltel Information Services (later renamed Fidelity Information Services) to steer business toward the company.[11] His predecessor was serving a 12-year sentence on charges that he had accepted bribes while serving as chairman of BOC. Other high-level employees of BOC, as well as of other Chinese banks, were also involved in corruption and embezzlement scandals.

Reform In response to banking sector weaknesses, as well as to an anticipated surge in foreign competition after the required removal under WTO rules of all barriers to foreign competition in its banking sector by 2007, China embarked on an ambitious bank reform program. In 1998, China began to improve bank balance sheets and reduce the stock of NPLs through transfers and bailouts, including capital injections and the transfer of NPLs on attractive terms to asset-management companies. The process was expensive; for example, the total economic cost of recapitalizing CCB between 1998 and 2005 reached $71 billion.[12] Furthermore, the China Banking Regulatory Commission (CBRC) was introduced in 2003 with the mandate to improve the supervision and regulation of the banking system. The CBRC and central bank imposed measures such as removing the ceiling on interest rates to allow banks to price risks better and introducing differentiated reserve requirements based on asset quality and capital adequacy to limit expansion of weaker banks.

Furthermore, state banks were required to reorganize their boards such that independent directors represented a third of total members. In January 2004, China decided to use BOC and CCB as pilot banks in shareholder reform. Several months later, CCB was restructured from a state-owned commercial bank into a shareholding bank with the state holding the controlling share in preparation for an eventual overseas listing. It was expected that overseas regulators and public shareholders would subject banks to greater transparency and tighter supervision.[13]

Involving foreign "strategic investors"—who were allowed up to a 20% stake in Chinese banks and were expected to transfer knowledge and skills to Chinese banks in return—was considered an important prerequisite to going public. Goldman Sachs Managing Director Fred Hu explained:

> Foreign strategic investment provides a powerful catalyst to China's banking reforms. With mutual commitment and a proper deal structure, foreign partners can add real long-term value to Chinese banks, especially in credit policies, product expertise, risk control and corporate governance. In return, they can leverage Chinese banks' extensive branch networks and customer bases to offer services in the world's fastest growing economy.[14]

In less than two years, China's banking sector had attracted more than $17 billion in investment (see **Exhibit 3**). By November 2005, three of China's four state banks had attracted foreign partners; only Agricultural Bank of China, the weakest of China's four state banks, had failed to attract a strategic investor.

By December 2005, two of China's five largest banks had conducted initial public offerings. Bank of Communications, China's fifth-largest bank, successfully listed in Hong Kong in June 2005 after a $1.7 billion strategic investment by HSBC for a 19.9% stake in August 2004. CCB experienced similar success with its October 2005 listing.

Bank of America Strategic Investment in China Construction Bank

Not long ago, the China Construction Bank was besieged by scandals that further shook confidence in China's troubled banking system. It is nothing short of stunning, therefore, that just six months later, the bank pulled off an $8 billion initial public offering at a hefty price.[15]

—Goldman Sachs Managing Director Fred Hu

Background China Construction Bank was China's third-largest bank, with 14,250 branches, 300,000 staff,[b] 146 million personal deposit accounts, 3.2 million corporate deposit accounts, and relationships with 97% of China's top corporations. Earnings growth was strong and was expected to improve with continued efforts to restructure, including commitments to decrease the number of staff and branches. CCB had an NPL ratio of just 3.9%—the lowest among China's state banks. Although its share of "special mention" loans was higher than that of its peers, analysts believed CCB had the ability to tolerate a high enough share of NPLs to mitigate the risk posed.[16] (See **Exhibit 4** for basic financial indicators.)

With its low NPL ratio and extensive distribution network, CCB was the first of China's state banks to secure foreign strategic investment. Bank of America, which came to account for just below the 10% limit on U.S. deposits imposed on merging banks after aggressive U.S. expansion through acquisition, including through its $47 billion takeover of FleetBoston in 2004, was interested in opportunities overseas. To this end, in June 2005 Bank of America invested $2.5 billion for a 9% stake in CCB and agreed to invest an additional $500 million to maintain its stake at 9% once CCB

[b] These values are from October 2005 and are therefore more recent than data presented in **Exhibit 1**.

conducted its initial public offering. In addition, Bank of America retained an option for 66 months to increase its investment to 19.9%. Bank of America's CEO noted: "We've been looking for some time for a way to invest in this economy. CCB is the first to be ready for foreign investment of any size." Singapore's investment agency Temasek invested a further $1.4 billion for a 5.1% share.

After bringing in its foreign strategic partners, CCB conducted a successful initial public offering in Hong Kong in October 2005. The bank raised $8 billion from foreign investors for 12% of its shares, making the deal the largest global flotation for four years, China's largest flotation ever, and the biggest ever for any bank. With a total market capitalization at $66 billion, CCB was larger than Deutsche Bank or Barclays.[17]

Perspectives Observers differed in their view of Bank of America's investment. On the one hand, Bank of America paid 1.15 times book value for its stake in CCB, which floated at almost two times book value.[18] More importantly, as noted by a banker involved in Chinese equity deals: "These are huge opportunities to capitalize on China's untapped consumer finance, asset management and credit card sectors, as well as its maturing corporate sector."[19] It was also noted that the more flexible exchange rate gradually being implemented by the central bank would increase the demand for forward and swap transactions and cash management, services in which foreign banks had advantages.[20] From the perspective of CCB, Chairman Gao noted the expertise Bank of America would bring in risk management and in helping establish a solid credit culture in which lending decisions would be based on borrower credit rather than relationships and government policy. Gao commented on Bank of America's investment: "The biggest goal is not to absorb more capital, but to absorb experience in management."[21]

On the other hand, critics were aware that Bank of America would be restricted to one board member of a total of 16 to 19,[22] which could limit its influence in strategic or operational decisions. Furthermore, Communist Party involvement in bank activities had only recently been scaled down. After being appointed chairman of CCB in March 2005, Gao noted the influence and meeting regularity of the Communist Party Committee headed by the former chairman: "The party is not a commercial organization. There has been a misunderstanding of the party's role in the past, and wrong practices inside the bank as a result. That is why we are making some changes."[23] It remained unclear how much time such change would take and how comprehensive it would be. Moreover, there was some threat of political backlash against foreign investors, with some critics portraying sales of stakes in China's bank to foreigners as "nothing more than selling cheap national crown jewels" and suggesting that foreign investment posed a threat to China's financial sector independence and national security.[24]

Exhibit 1 Market Position of China's Main Commercial Banks

				Total Assets			Gross Loans			Total Deposits		
(US$ billions)	Abbrev.	Branch	Staff	2001	2002	2003	2001	2002	2003	2001	2002	2003
Industrial & Commercial Bank of China	ICBC	24,129	389,045	520.2	570.4	636.0	320.4	356.4	403.5	431.3	488.8	550.2
China Construction Bank	CCB	16,613	342,967	331.6	371.4	428.2	181.4	213.0	255.7	273.0	313.3	358.0
Agricultural Bank of China	ABC	36,138	511,425	304.6	358.7	421.0	198.3	230.5	273.3	251.9	298.8	341.6
Bank of China	BOC	11,609	171,777	312.9	350.1	378.3	150.1	168.6	196.4	216.7	251.6	292.4
Bank of Communications	BoComm	2,592	55,510	77.7	85.3	108.2	43.5	48.6	62.9	83.0	105.3	124.1
China Merchant Bank	CMB	1,400	15,965	32.0	44.8	60.7	13.3	19.2	29.5	24.3	34.0	49.0
CITIC Industrial Bank	CITIC	379	9,457	36.1	40.4	50.7	14.6	19.9	29.9	27.2	31.9	44.7
China Everbright Bank	CEB	31	8,569	31.9	39.5	47.5	15.3	19.3	28.7	21.6	28.2	41.4
Shanghai Pudong Development Bank	Pudong	329	7,796	21.0	33.6	44.7	10.7	17.1	30.8	16.3	27.5	38.7
China Minsheng Banking Corp.	Minsheng	214	6,400	16.7	29.4	43.5	6.5	12.4	21.6	11.4	20.6	33.1
Guangdong Development Bank		526	12,449	23.0	26.4	37.0	11.2	13.6	22.9	15.5	18.1	31.3
Fujian Industrial Bank		256	7,259	15.1	21.4	30.8	6.1	11.2	19.6	9.4	15.4	24.9
China Huaxia Bank	Huaxia	220	6,681	16.4	21.4	29.8	7.5	10.1	17.7	11.7	16.0	25.3
Shenzhen Development Bank		241	6,471	14.5	20.0	23.3	5.9	7.6	16.0	8.9	10.0	17.0
Evergrowing				1.8	1.9	1.9	0.6	0.8	0.8	1.1	1.3	1.3
CCB's ranking		**3**	**3**	**2**	**2**	**2**	**3**	**3**	**3**	**2**	**2**	**3**

Source: Deutsche Bank 2005, p. 52.

Exhibit 2 Nonperforming Loans as % Total Loans

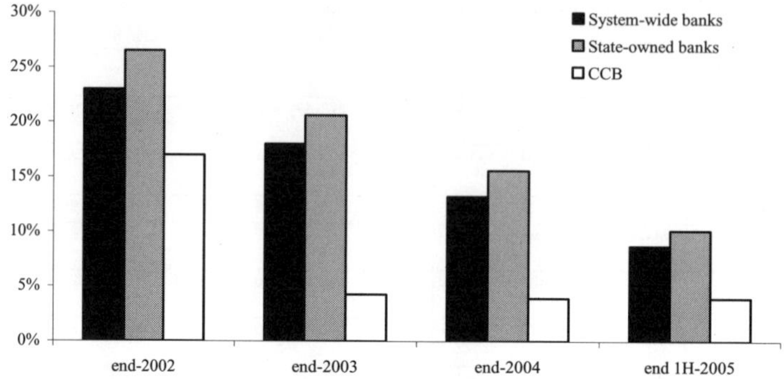

Source: Deutsche Bank 2005; Morgan Stanley 2005; and China Banking Regulatory Commission website, www.cbrc.gov.cn, accessed December 2005.

Exhibit 3 Foreign Investment in Chinese Banks

Target Bank	Type	Time	Foreign Investor	Stake (%)	Price (US$ mm)	PBV
Bohai Bank	JS	2006	Standard Chartered	20.00%	123	NA
Nanjing Bank	CC	Dec-01	IFC	15.00%	27	NA
		Oct-05	BNP Paribas	19.20%	87	NA
Hua Xia	JS	Oct-05	Deutsche Bank	9.90%	329	NA
		Oct-05	Sal. Oppenheim	4.10%		NA
Hang Zhou City Bank	CC	Sep-05	Commonwealth Bank of Australia	19.90%	76	NA
Jinana City Bank	CC	Sep-05	Commonwealth Bank of Australia	11.00%	17	NA
Bank of China	SB	Sep-05	UBS	1.60%	500	NA
		Aug-05	Temasek Holdings	10.00%	3,100	1.2x
		Aug-05	Royal Bank of Scotland	5.16%	1,600	1.2x
		Aug-05	Merrill Lynch and Li Ka Shing Found.	4.84%	1,500	1.2x
Industrial & Commercial Bank of China	SB	Aug-05	Goldman Sachs	6.00%	1,800	1.5x
		Aug-05	Allianz AZ	3.33%	1,000	1.5x
		Aug-05	American Express	0.67%	200	1.5x
Nanchong City Commerical Bank	CC	Jul-05	German Investment	10.00%	4	NA
		Jul-05	German Investment	3.30%	1	NA
China Construction Bank	SB	Jun-05	Bank of America	9.00%	2,500	1.1x
		Jul-05	Temasek	5.10%	1,400	1.1x
Bank of Beijing	CC	May-05	IFC	5.00%	54	1.2x
		Mar-05	ING	20.00%	215	1.2x
China Minsheng Bank	JS	Jan-05	Temasek	4.55%	107	1.5x
		Jul-04	IFC	1.60%	24	1.1x
Shenzhen Development Bank	JS	Oct-04	Newbridge Capital	18.00%	145	1.9x
Xi'an Bank	CC	Sep-04	Bank of Nova Scotia	11.50%	92	NA
		Sep-04	IFC	12.50%	100	NA
Bank of Communication	JVGP	Aug-04	HSBC	19.90%	1,750	1.6x
Dialien City Bank	CC	Nov-03	SHK Financial	10.00%	19	NA
Shanghai Pudong Development Bank	JS	Sep-03	Citigroup	5.00%	73	1.3x
Industrial Bank	JS	Dec-03	Hang Seng Bank	15.98%	208	1.8x
		Dec-03	GIC	5.00%	65	1.8x
		Dec-03	IFC	4.00%	52	1.8x
Bank of Shanghai	CC	Dec-01	HSBC	8.00%	63	1.1x
		Dec-01	Shanghai Commercial Bank (HK)	3.00%	23	1.1x
		Dec-01	IFC	7.00%	50	1.0x
China Everbright Bank	JS	1996	Asia Development Bank	3.30%	20	NA

Source: Deutsche Bank 2005, p. 55 (for transactions through September 2005); press clippings cited in endnotes for subsequent transactions.

Note: JS: Joint Stock; CC: City Commercial; SB: State-Owned; JVGP: Joint Venture Government Private.

Exhibit 4 Basic Financial Indicators

a. CCB Profit and Loss Statement ($ mms)	2002	2003	2004	1H05
Net Interest Income	9,502	10,957	12,227	6,719
Non-Interest Income	724	866	1,179	749
Fees and Commissions	*441*	*552*	*780*	
Trading Revenue	*45*	*83*	*98*	
Dividend Income	*126*	*115*	*94*	
Other Revenue	*112*	*116*	*208*	
Total Revenue	**10,226**	**11,822**	**13,407**	**7,469**
Staff costs	2,060	2,796	2,671	1,337
Property & equipment expense	1,263	1,287	1,457	586
Other general & administrative expense	1,179	1,366	1,530	597
Business tax expense	643	665	778	431
Total Operating Costs	**5,145**	**6,113**	**6,436**	**2,951**
Pre-provision Operating Profit	**5,082**	**5,709**	**6,971**	**4,518**
Bad Debt Expense	2,421	1,224	1,127	806
Operating Profit	**2,660**	**4,485**	**5,843**	**3,712**
Tax Expense	1,333	1,828	260	409
Pre-tax Associates	39	58	325	
Net profit	**1,366**	**2,715**	**5,908**	**3,303**

b. CCB Key Balance Sheet Items ($ mms)	2002	2003	2004	1H05
Interest-earning assets[a]	330,839	400,561	458,523	515,122
Risk-weighted assets[a]	223,676	234,557	273,189	306,886
Corporate deposits	183,886	204,108	220,905	235,289
Retail deposits	155,013	179,619	198,470	218,153
Overseas deposits	1,190	1,294	1,242	2,136
Subtotal deposits	340,090	385,021	420,617	455,578
Total deposits and borrowings	**353,416**	**399,383**	**439,644**	**476,230**
Total corporate loans	173,326	181,744	195,713	210,046
Total consumer loans	32,659	42,738	49,672	51,706
Total loan book	**205,985**	**224,483**	**245,385**	**261,752**
Stated Shareholder Equity[a]	**-16,049**	**22,555**	**23,560**	**34,997**

c. Cross-bank Comparison (2004)	CCB	BoComm	SPDB	CMB	Minsheng
Net Interest Income (as % bank assets)	2.72%	2.43%	2.55%	2.67%	2.26%
Non-Interest Income (as % bank assets)	0.33%	0.27%	0.23%	0.22%	0.08%
Total Revenue (as % bank assets)	3.05%	2.70%	2.78%	2.89%	2.34%
Total Operating Costs (as % bank assets)	1.43%	1.64%	1.27%	1.38%	1.30%
Pre-provision Operating Profit (as % assets)	1.62%	1.06%	1.51%	1.51%	1.04%
Bad Debt Expense (as % bank assets)	0.25%	0.31%	0.75%	0.57%	0.35%
Operating Profit (as % bank assets)	1.37%	0.75%	0.76%	0.94%	0.69%
Tax Expense (as % bank assets)	0.06%	0.59%	0.28%	0.35%	0.20%
ROA (return on assets; net profit as % assets)	1.31%	0.16%	0.48%	0.60%	0.50%
Equity Multiplier	19.5	29.5	32.2	26.8	35.8
ROE (return on equity)	25.63%	4.58%	15.40%	15.96%	17.76%

Source: Deutsche Bank 2005, pp. 2, 8, 9, 17, 21, 22.

[a]2005 values refer to expected year-end numbers.

Endnotes

1 Alan Greenspan wrote this in a letter to Senate Banking Committee Chairman Richard Shelby, as reported in Greg Ip, "Greenspan Warns About Yuan Float—Fed Chief Says Removing Currency's Peg to Dollar May Hurt China's Banks," *The Wall Street Journal,* March 2, 2004.

2 See Bank of America, "Investor Fact Book 1st Half 2005," available at www.bankofamerica.com/investor, accessed December 2005.

3 "A Great Big Banking Gamble—China's Banking Industry," *The Economist,* October 29, 2005, citing Nicholas Lardy at the Institute for International Economics in Washington.

4 Asian Development Bank, "Report and Recommendation of the President to the Board of Directors on a Proposed Equity Investment in Bank Of China Ltd. in the People's Republic of China," September 2005, available at http://adb.org/Documents/RRPs/PRC/38917-PRC-RRP.pdf, accessed December 2005.

5 Alan Chua, Tom Quarby, and Sandy Hu, "China Construction Bank: Built for a Positive Future; Initiate with a Buy," Deutsche Bank Company Focus Company Research, November 1, 2005.

6 Francesco Guerrera and Richard McGregor, "China's Banks Smarten Up as They Switch from State Control to Commercial Lending," *The Financial Times,* June 20, 2005.

7 "A Great Big Banking Gamble," *The Economist,* October 29, 2005.

8 See "China: To Float or Not To Float (A)," HBS No. 706-021, for more details.

9 Drew Brick, Ray Heung, and Jun Yuan, "Chinese Banks: Trip Report on Bank Reform," Morgan Stanley Fixed Income Research, July 21, 2005.

10 As quoted in "A Great Big Banking Gamble," *The Economist,* October 29, 2005.

11 Chris Buckley and Julie Creswell, "U.S. Bank Buys Stake in China," *The New York Times,* June 17, 2005.

12 Deutsche Bank 2005, p. 53.

13 For discussion, see, for example, Weijian Shan, "Will China's Banking Reform Succeed?" *The Wall Street Journal Asia,* October 17, 2005.

14 Fred Hu, "The Truth about Investing in China's Banks," *The Financial Times,* November 18, 2005; and as described in interview with casewriter on November 18, 2005.

15 Hu, "The Truth about Investing."

16 See, for example, Deutsche Bank 2005.

17 "A Great Big Banking Gamble," *The Economist,* October 29, 2005.

18 Ibid.

19 As quoted in "China's Banks Smarten Up," *The Financial Times,* June 20, 2005.

20 See discussion in "Foreign Banks to Have a 6% to 8% share in China's Banking Industry in 10 to 20 Years," *Xinhua's China Economic Information Service,* September 5, 2005.

21 As quoted in "Will China's Banking Reform Succeed?" *The Wall Street Journal Asia,* 2005.

22 As reported in "U.S. Bank Buys Stake in China," *The New York Times,* 2005.

23 As quoted in "China's Banks Smarten Up," *The Financial Times,* June 20, 2005.

24 Hu, "The Truth about Investing."

HARVARD | BUSINESS | SCHOOL

9-706-035

REV: NOVEMBER 21, 2006

LAURA ALFARO

RAFAEL DI TELLA

China: To Float or Not To Float? (E)

ABB Investment in China

In July 2005, China revalued its currency by 2.1% and adjusted its exchange rate regime toward a more market-based system. Initially, China's central bank allowed only minor movement in the yuan's value. It remained uncertain what would happen to the yuan in the short and medium term, especially with some experts estimating that the currency was undervalued by up to 35%. Would the central bank introduce further discreet steps revaluing the yuan? Would the yuan eventually be allowed to float more freely? Would China's currency appreciate as substantially against the U.S. dollar as predicted by economists? When would further change occur?[a]

The stakes were high; a freer yuan float would impact groups very differently. ABB, a global power and automation technologies company based out of Switzerland with operations in China, was one such keenly interested party.

ABB Overview

ABB—with shares listed on the SWX Swiss Exchange, the Stockholm Stock Exchange, and the New York Stock Exchange—had a history dating back to 1883. ABB was a global supplier of products and services including the transformers, breakers, substations, and technology needed to transmit and distribute power from where it is generated to the factory, building, or home where it is used; automation technologies to improve performance in factories and to operate robots that paint and assemble cars; and the drives that regulate air conditioning and move airport conveyor belts.[1] In 2004, ABB had revenues of $20.7 billion (see **Exhibit 1** for basic financial information) and approximately 103,000 employees.[2,b]

---

[a] See "China: To Float or Not To Float (A)," HBS No. 706-021, for an extensive discussion on this topic.

[b] In 2001, facing a slowdown in its key markets and threats of increased asbestos liability claims, ABB posted a net loss of $691 million. The company engaged in a major restructuring, including reducing its workforce from almost 161,000 at year-end 2000, focusing on its more successful core divisions, reducing debt, cutting costs, and negotiating the asbestos claims. (See, for example, ABB press release, "ABB posts US$691 million loss for 2001 after substantial charges, cuts net debt in Q4 by US$2.2 billion on record cash flow," February 13, 2002, available on company website.)

Professors Laura Alfaro and Rafael Di Tella and Research Associate Ingrid Vogel prepared this case. This case was developed from published sources. HBS cases are developed solely as the basis for class discussion. Cases are not intended to serve as endorsements, sources of primary data, or illustrations of effective or ineffective management.

ABB had a global presence both on the manufacturing side and on the revenue side with operations in around 100 countries. Revenues generated in Europe accounted for 52% of total 2004 revenues, compared with 21% generated in Asia, 17% in the Americas, and 10% in the Middle East and Africa. ABB achieved sales around $2.6 billion in China in 2004, making it ABB's largest market after the United States and Germany.[3]

ABB in China

I do not hesitate to say the China market is crucial to ABB's fate, as it has been for [the company's recent] turnaround. Driving through any city, you can see clearly the demand for power and automation technologies in China—our two core businesses.[4]

—ABB Chairman Jürgen Dormann, October 25, 2004

ABB's relationship with China dated back to the beginning of the twentieth century with the shipment of a steam boiler to the country in 1907. In 1974, ABB's China operation was formally established in Hong Kong, which was followed by its first permanent office in Beijing five years later. In 1994, ABB moved its China headquarters to Beijing and, one year later, established ABB (China) Limited. By 2005, ABB had more than 8,000 employees, an extensive sales and service network across 30 cities, and 25 joint ventures and wholly owned companies focused on production, engineering, and service in the fields of power transmission and distribution, automation products, and systems used in industrial, commercial, and utility applications.[5] A small selection of recent and major ABB projects in China included:[6]

- January 10, 2006—announcement of contracts totaling around $12.4 million from Shanghai Waigaoqiao Power Plant. ABB Chongqing Transformer Co. Ltd. will supply power transformers for the third phase of a coal-fired generating power plant in Shanghai.
- December 20, 2005—announcement of contract to form a 50:50 joint venture—ABB Datong Traction Transformers Co., Ltd.—for the production, sale, and service of traction transformers for rolling-stock manufacturers in China.
- December 7, 2005—announcement of a contract totaling around $4.9 million to deliver low-voltage switchgears for Guangzhou Metro project to ensure continuous, reliable, and high-efficient operation on Guangzhou Metro Line 4 and Line 5. The month before, ABB was awarded an $11 million contract to deliver gas-insulated switchgears for Metro Line 5.
- November 25, 2005—celebration of the production of its 100,000th circuit breaker at its Xiamen joint venture—ABB Xiamen Switchgear Co., Ltd.
- September 12, 2005—announcement of $10 million investment in a new facility in Beijing that makes a special energy-saving technology.
- September 9, 2005—announcement of move of headquarters of global robotics business to Shanghai. ABB migrated one of its robotics production lines from Europe to Shanghai in March 2005 and also set up a research and development (R&D) center there. In August 2005, ABB celebrated the 200th industrial robot rolling off the production line in Shanghai. The robots were widely used for material handling, picking, packing, palletizing, welding, painting, gluing, sealing, and assembling in various industries such as motor, IT, and manufacturing automation.
- June 14, 2004—announcement of order worth $390 million to build a key power link from the Three Gorges hydropower plant in central China to the coastal city of Shanghai. Working with

Chinese manufacturers, ABB was to build a 1,100-kilometer-long, 3,000-megawatt (MW) high-voltage direct current (HVDC) transmission link.

ABB remained committed to China for the long term. Chairman and President of ABB (China) Ltd. Peter Leupp reiterated ABB's commitment to China in ABB China's 2004 annual report: "ABB is committed to helping China meet its goal to be a well-off society in an all-around way by 2020. We understand the challenges ahead."[7] ABB CEO Fred Kindle explained ABB's aggressive targets for its China operations: "We remain on target for ABB in China to double orders to around $4 billion by 2008, overtaking the U.S. as ABB's largest market."[8] To meet its target, the company outlined a five-point plan:

1. **Organic growth.** ABB historically achieved double-digit growth rates in China, with individual product areas experiencing annual growth from at least 15% to more than 100%. ABB expected to grow 20% per year until at least 2008. To sustain its growth target, ABB explained that it planned to continue to invest in new facilities, develop new technologies, and launch new products.

2. **New investments.** ABB had invested more than $600 million in China through 2004 and planned to invest at least $100 million more by 2008. The company planned to start new companies and production facilities in areas in which it was strong globally. The new technologies and new products would be targeted specifically for the Chinese market. ABB also intended to improve manufacturing procedures and raise capacity to cut delivery times while meeting growth in demand.

3. **Cost migration.** ABB explained that it had a dedicated team buying materials from local suppliers and using those materials to build complete product lines, rather than importing certain components from Europe as it had done in the past. ABB wanted to couple the strategy of sourcing to achieve a cost advantage within China with using China as a base for global sourcing.

   Furthermore, ABB explained that it was opening new factories, transferring technologies and skills from Europe and North America, and relocating the engineering and production of high-end technologies such as industrial robots and relays for power-grid protection. The company explained that these measures were intended to bring ABB closer to its customers, reduce costs, shorten delivery times, develop skills and competence in China, and enable ABB to make a long-lasting and valuable contribution to China's development.

4. **Research and development.** In March 2005, ABB opened a global corporate research center in Beijing as part of its global network of laboratories. It was intended to drive innovation levels higher and enable ABB to better meet the needs of customers in China, as well as around the world.

5. **Developing local talent.** ABB China hired between 500 and 1,000 new employees each year between 1999 and 2004. Of these employees, 99% were Chinese. Between 2005 and 2008, the company intended to hire another 5,000, in order to reach 12,000.[9]

ABB China was also engaged in corporate social responsibility initiatives in China. For example, in May 2005, ABB donated $100,000 to help students from impoverished families finance their college education.[10] In November 2005, the company announced a cooperation agreement with Chongqing University to conduct research on the aging of transformers. Activities also extended into the political sphere. In 2004, China's vice premier Zeng Peiyan visited ABB Corporate Technology in Switzerland. In 1999, China's former president Jiang Zemin visited ABB's facilities for turbine leafs, coils, motors, rotors production, and welding in Switzerland. Furthermore, ABB Chairman Jürgen Dormann was an advisor to the mayor of Beijing, and Dinesh Paliwal, head of ABB's global automation technologies business and manager for the Americas, was an advisor to Guangdong Province.[11]

Foreign Direct Investment in China

In 1980, the Chinese government established four coastal special economic zones (SEZs) to experiment with new institutions to attract foreign investment bringing jobs, technical knowledge, and future tax revenues. The SEZs exempted foreign-invested firms from central government trade plans, released them from Chinese labor regulations, and introduced preferential tax treatment over domestically funded firms. Furthermore, unlike domestic companies, foreign-invested enterprises (FIEs) operating in the SEZs were allowed to retain foreign currency and to import and export freely. However, foreign firms initially faced restrictions including required partnerships with Chinese firms to ensure knowledge transfer as well as limitations on domestic sales.

Three SEZs—the cities of Shenzhen, Zhuhai, and Shantou—were located in the Guangdong Province near Hong Kong. The fourth SEZ was in the city of Xiamin, located in the Fujian Province across from Taiwan. (See **Exhibit 2** for a map of China.) Shenzhen was positioned to take advantage of the Hong Kong economy, which was beginning to transfer labor-intensive industry offshore. Shenzhen had almost no industrial base, but the local government moved quickly to upgrade the infrastructure and create a friendly legal environment. The results were immediate, with industrial output growth in excess of 75% per year between 1979 and 1984.[12]

As a result of this success, additional zones were created to attract FIEs. In April 1984, 14 economic development zones were opened along the coast in major industrial and commercial centers, including in Shanghai and Guangzhou.[13] In 1988, Hainan Province in its entirety was added as an SEZ. In 1990, the Pudong Development Zone in Shanghai was established as the focus of China's urban development strategy with the goal of transforming Pudong into Asia's new financial center. By June 2005, there were 56 export-oriented economic and technological development zones (ETDZs) also offering tax reductions and exemptions to encourage foreign investment in R&D and advanced technology. In addition, there were 15 free-trade zones, a number of export-processing zones, and national parks for high-tech industry.

In the 1990s, the government relaxed restrictions on FIEs. New rules allowed foreign investors to establish wholly foreign-owned enterprises with no knowledge-transfer requirements and to manufacture and sell a wide range of goods in China's increasingly attractive domestic market. By 2004, China was the world's largest recipient of foreign direct investment (FDI), with an annual inflow of $64 billion and a cumulative total balance of $564 billion. FDI was projected to exceed $66 billion in 2005.

Incentives offered in the various zones focused primarily on tax reductions. For example, all FIEs were exempt from import duties on equipment used to upgrade existing facilities if the equipment could not be produced domestically. FIEs operating in the original four SEZs were subject to a 15% income tax—lower than the normal income tax rate of 33%—and, in specific cases, a tax holiday. Furthermore, they were not subject to value-added tax on goods imported, produced, or sold within the SEZ. FIEs in the Hainan Province, China's fifth SEZ, were offered additional tax breaks, such as a 10% income tax rate for firms that exported at least 70% of their output. FIEs in ETDZs engaged in production, high-tech FIEs located in national high-tech industry parks, and FIEs producing for export in a free-trade zone were also subject to the 15% income tax rate. In comparison, in the 14 economic development zones and in the newer open cities of China's interior provinces, a 24% income tax applied to most FIEs engaged in production. Individual provinces and cities with provincial status (such as Beijing and Shanghai) offered their own additional tax incentives to foreign investors.[14]

China's system of incentives was often criticized. First, it was argued that it was too complex and encouraged manipulation and suboptimal investment decisions. As a result, the Chinese government intended to overhaul its policies on incentives, including implementing a more unified tax system applicable to all enterprises regardless of ownership. As part of this program, many local tax-relief policies were expected to be phased out by 2010. Second, it was argued that preferential policies fostered robust growth in investment zones while letting other regions lag, resulting in a growing wage gap (see **Exhibit 3**) between the SEZs and open cities on the coast on the one hand and poorer inland and rural regions, where the majority of China's 1.3 billion people lived, on the other hand.

In response, starting in 2000, the government made an effort to increase the attractiveness of the less developed areas of central and western China to help them catch up to the more prosperous coastal areas. Incentives included, for example, tax incentives broadly in line with those offered within SEZs for FIEs in encouraged industries, such as infrastructure and energy projects, operating in most of China's inland regions. In addition, Communist Party leaders of inland cities held investment fairs in Beijing, Shanghai, and Guangzhou to pitch their locations in person to foreign companies. Provincial officials from the interior also reduced the time required for investment approvals from more than six months to a few weeks.[15] Furthermore, in 2005, the Communist Party formulated its five-year plan for 2006–2010 with a strong emphasis on addressing growing inequities within the country.[16]

The Chinese government further encouraged foreign investment inland through billions of dollars worth of infrastructure development. Expressways and bridges linked once stranded inland cities to coastal ports and export markets. A national highway plan approved in 2005 aimed to double the 34,000-kilometer highway network. Investments in power plants further lifted inland economies, as well as almost $9 billion spent on new airports between 2001 and 2005 and $18 billion allocated for 2006–2010.[17]

The Wall Street Journal noted: "China's interior is starting to boom, raising consumer demand in out-of-the-way places where neither Chinese nor foreign companies once bothered to look."[18] Companies including General Motors, Honda, Intel, and Motorola were running operations in interior provinces where they reported abundant skilled labor and an increasingly vibrant consumer market, combined with much lower labor costs. The chairman of the American Chamber of Commerce in Beijing reported that 50% of U.S. member companies had already invested in second-tier cities and that manufacturers were looking as far inland as Inner Mongolia and Xinjiang (see **Exhibit 2**) for additional investment. He claimed: "Companies that don't look at inland China will find themselves disadvantaged."[19] (See **Exhibit 4** for data on FDI inflows by region within China.)

ABB Response to Yuan Revaluation

ABB, with a significant presence in China, was among those companies confronted with the challenge of addressing the revaluation of the yuan and the possibility of future appreciation. In 2004, approximately 6% of the company's total worldwide revenues were generated in renminbi.[20] In a May 2005 article, the *Financial Times* noted: "European companies that compete directly with Asian rivals are likely to enjoy a competitive advantage. . . . Companies generating a sizeable chunk of their turnover from Asia could also gain from the translation effect when these earnings are converted into euros. Winners here could include Lufthansa, Nestlé, ABB and Danone."[21] However, it remained unclear to outside observers how the possible future appreciation would affect ABB's strategy to intensify the use of China as a base for global sourcing.

Furthermore, the company was among those exploring opportunities to shift inland, where costs were much lower than in the more popular coastal and capital-city areas. At a media roundtable in Beijing in August 2005, ABB CEO Kindle noted:

> We are setting up more and more businesses in the West and we are creating new power and automation technologies to help China achieve its goal to be a resource-efficient society. . . . We now have two important ventures in Xian and two in Chongqing, including new sales offices dotting the West in places like Hohhot and Urumqi to support China's Go West initiative. In coming weeks, we plan to start the process for two more ventures, also in the West, so you can see we are clearly committed to China moving forward. . . . We built three of the high-voltage direct current links running power from the West to East of China. Each link provides power to about six million households and saves about 78 MW by avoiding losses—equivalent to a power supply for 156,000 households. That means we save enough power for around half a million households in China.[22]

Exhibit 1 ABB Financial Statements (millions of dollars)

Income Statement Items	1999	2000	2001	2002	2003[a]	2004	2005E
Sales	**24,356**	**22,967**	**23,726**	**18,295**	**18,795**	**20,721**	**21,877**
Operating profit	1,122	1,385	279	394	656	1,084	1,736
Net interest income / (expense)	(100)	(79)	(234)	(143)	(266)	(223)	(250)
Net income before taxes	**1,022**	**1,306**	**45**	**251**	**246**	**861**	**1,486**
Taxes	(343)	(377)	(105)	(83)	(78)	(311)	(505)
Minority interest	(36)	(48)	(70)	(72)	(82)	(102)	(133)
Net income from continuing operations	643	881	(130)	96	86	448	848
Results from discontinued operations	717	562	(561)	(880)	(853)	(483)	(93)
Net income	**1,360**	**1,443**	**(691)**	**(784)**	**(767)**	**(35)**	**755**

Balance Sheet Items	1999	2000	2001	2002	2003	2004	2005E
Total current assets	19,057	18,711	19,514	16,860	15,086	15,195	14,732
Assets held for sale	-	-	-	3,095	6,427	155	361
Financing receivables	3,427	3,875	4,263	1,802	1,330	1,233	675
Net fixed assets	3,813	3,243	3,003	2,792	2,840	2,981	2,705
Goodwill and other intangibles	2,904	3,155	3,299	2,878	2,880	3,095	2,903
Investments and other	1,377	1,978	2,265	2,106	1,850	2,018	1,950
Total assets	**30,578**	**30,962**	**32,344**	**29,533**	**30,413**	**24,677**	**23,326**
Current liabilities	5,880	5,738	6,701	5,135	4,375	5,709	5,251
Accrued liabilities (inc. asbestos provision)	6,635	6,127	7,587	8,319	5,140	6,436	6,298
Liabilities held for sale	-	-	-	2,384	5,100	290	467
Pension provision	1,954	1,790	1,688	1,659	1,794	1,551	1,500
Debt	6,953	7,363	9,790	7,952	7,887	5,534	4,190
Deferred taxes	1,656	1,528	1,360	1,166	969	953	719
Other liabilities	2,912	2,924	2,989	1,647	1,837	1,083	968
Minority interest	317	321	215	258	285	297	294
Total equity	4,271	5,171	2,014	1,013	3,026	2,824	3,639
Total liabilities and equity	**30,578**	**30,962**	**32,344**	**29,533**	**30,413**	**24,677**	**23,326**

Cash Flow Items	1999	2000	2001	2002	2003	2004	2005E
Operating cash flow	**1,164**	**1,323**	**700**	**(399)**	**(415)**	**706**	**1,581**
Operating free cash flow[b]	**736**	**469**	**1,432**	**(583)**	**(708)**	**183**	**625**
Dec/(inc) in financing receivable	(655)	(833)	(907)	264	390	176	133
Acquisitions (net of cash acquired)	(1,720)	(893)	(578)	(144)	(55)	(24)	(16)
Proceeds from divestiture & asset disposals	844	513	435	2,985	698	1,305	22
Dividends paid	(503)	(531)	(502)	-	-	-	-
Capital increase/treasury transactions	(165)	244	(1,393)	-	2,675	(36)	-
Other	(94)	(145)	(210)	-	(56)	(17)	(26)
Inc/(dec) in net financial position	**(834)**	**(1,190)**	**(2,320)**	**738**	**594**	**1,411**	**1,047**

Source: Compiled from Andreas Willi, Nick Paton, and Julia Varesko, "ABB: Downgrade to Neutral—in the sweet spot, but priced as such," JPMorgan European Equity Research, January 24, 2006; also includes author calculations.

[a]Unexplained data discrepancy in deriving net income from sales.

[b]Equivalent to operating cash flow less capex and increases in working capital.

Exhibit 2 Map of China

Source: Perry Castaneda Library Map Collection, www.lib.utexas.edu/maps/, accessed March 2006. Courtesy of the University of Texas Libraries, The University of Texas at Austin.

Exhibit 3 Monthly Salaries in Selected Chinese Cities (in U.S. dollars)

	Chengdu (interior city)	Shanghai (coastal city)	Beijing (capital city)
Worker	$126	$210	$211
Technician	213	493	298
Department Manager	376	1,264	1,370
Senior Manager	678	2,034	2,512

Source: Compiled from *BusinessWeek*, November 2005, based on data from the Sichuan provincial government.

Exhibit 4 FDI into China by Region (as % total FDI inflows, except where noted)

	Description of location	Average 1995–997	Average 2000–2003	2003
Guangdong	coastal	27.0	22.3	14.6
Jiangsu	coastal	12.8	17.4	19.7
Shanghai	coastal	8.8	8.8	10.2
Fujian	coastal	9.9	7.2	4.9
Shandong	coastal	6.2	8.8	11.2
Beijing	capital city area	3.4	3.8	4.1
Zhejiang	coastal	3.4	6.0	9.3
Tianjin	coastal	4.8	3.3	2.9
Liaoning	coastal (borders North Korea)	4.3	5.5	5.3
Hebei	one over from coast	2.0	1.6	1.8
Guangxi	one over from coast (borders Vietnam)	1.8	0.9	0.8
Hubei	inland central	1.7	2.6	2.9
Hainan	coastal	2.1	1.0	0.8
Hunan	one over from coast	1.7	1.8	1.9
Jiangxi	one over from coast	0.8	1.6	3.0
Henan	inland central	1.4	1.0	1.0
Anhui	one over from coast	1.2	0.7	0.7
Sichuan	inland central	1.0	1.0	0.8
Heilongjiang	inland north (borders Russia)	1.4	0.7	0.6
Jilin	inland north (borders North Korea)	1.0	0.6	0.4
Shaanxi	inland central	1.0	0.7	0.6
Chongqing	inland central	0.9	0.5	0.5
Shanxi	inland central	0.4	0.5	0.4
Inner Mongolia	inland north (borders Mongolia)	0.2	0.8	0.2
Yunnan	inland central (borders Burma)	0.3	0.2	0.2
Guizhou	inland central	0.1	0.1	0.1
Gansu	inland west	0.2	0.1	...
Qinghai	inland west	...	0.1	...
Ningxia	inland central	...	0.1	...
Xinjiang	inland west (borders Kazakhstan, Mongolia, Pakistan, and Kyrgyzstan)	0.1	0.1	...
Total annual FDI inflows (millions U.S. dollars)		*40,043*	*44,756*	*47,077*

Source: Compiled from International Monetary Fund, International Finance Statistics Online, December 2005; and Eswar Prasad and Shang-Jin Wei, "The Chinese Approach to Capital Inflows: Carrots and Sticks, or Deeper Forces at Work?" IMF Working Paper, April 2005, using data from CEIC database.

Note: The *2005 China Statistical Yearbook*, which would provide data for 2004, was not available at time of writing.

Endnotes

[1] Refer to ABB website at www.abb.com and ABB Annual Report 2004.

[2] ABB Ltd. SEC Form 20-F, filed May 27, 2005, available at company website.

[3] See company China-focused website, www.abb.com.cn, in particular page entitled, "ABB in China, ABB (China) Limited," edited December 20, 2005.

[4] As quoted in "ABB unveils major expansion plans in China," swissinfo, October 25, 2004. Note that Dormann was also CEO at time.

[5] See company China-focused website, www.abb.com.cn, in particular page entitled, "ABB in China, ABB (China) Limited," edited December 20, 2005.

[6] List compiled from company press releases (on dates specified) available on the company website, www.abb.com, accessed March 2006.

[7] As quoted in ABB China Annual Report 2005, available on company China-focused website, www.abb.com.cn, accessed March 2006.

[8] ABB press release, "CEO says ABB supporting China's goals; Pushing further West, helping create resource-efficient society," August 30, 2005.

[9] "CEO says ABB supporting China's goals," August 30, 2005.

[10] ABB press release, "ABB donates $100,000 to impoverished students; Fund will assist engineering students throughout China," May 28, 2005.

[11] See company China-focused website, www.abb.com.cn, in particular page entitled, "ABB in China, ABB (China) Limited," edited December 20, 2005.

[12] For more on the background of SEZs, see Robert E. Kennedy, "China: Facing the 21st Century," HBS No. 798-066, January 14, 2002. See also Federal Research Division of the Library of Congress Country Studies/Area Handbook Series sponsored by the U.S. Department of the Army, available at http://countrystudies.us/china/, accessed November 2005.

[13] Full list includes Dalian, Qinhuangdao, Tianjin, Yantai, Qingdao, Lianyungang, Nantong, Shanghai, Ningbo, Wenzhou, Fuzhou, Guangzhou, Zhanjiang, and Beihai.

[14] Economist Intelligence Unit—Country Commerce, China, "Incentives: Regional incentives," February 1, 2005.

[15] Andrew Browne and Kathy Chen, "Ripple Effects: A Booming Coast Breathes New Life Into China's Inland—Cities Benefit From Highways And Foreign Investment; Wal-Mart Sets Up Shop—Opening Day Brings 100,000," *The Wall Street Journal,* October 17, 2005.

[16] Kathy Chen, "China to Tackle Gap Between Rich, Poor—Next `Five-Year Blueprint' Will Boost Social Services, Address Growing Inequities," *The Asian Wall Street Journal,* September 30, 2005.

[17] Dexter Roberts, "Go West, Westerners; With growth slowing in the crowded and costly coastal centers, Beijing is urging business into the hinterlands," *BusinessWeek,* November 14, 2005.

[18] "Ripple Effects," *The Wall Street Journal,* October 17, 2005.

[19] *BusinessWeek,* 2005.

[20] ABB Ltd. SEC Form 20-F, filed May 27, 2005, available at company website, www.abb.com, accessed March 2006.

[21] Steve Johnson, "Renminbi revaluation means re-evaluation," *The Financial Times,* May 24, 2005.

[22] "CEO says ABB supporting China's goals," August 30, 2005.

HARVARD | BUSINESS | SCHOOL

9-706-036
REV: NOVEMBER 21, 2006

LAURA ALFARO
RAFAEL DI TELLA

China: To Float or Not To Float? (F)

Alcatel and Strong Chinese Competition

In July 2005, China revalued its currency by 2.1% and adjusted its exchange rate regime toward a more market-based system. Initially, China's central bank allowed only minor movement in the yuan's value. It remained uncertain what would happen to the yuan in the short and medium term, especially with some experts estimating that the currency was undervalued by up to 35%. Would the central bank introduce further discreet steps revaluing the yuan? Would the yuan eventually be allowed to float more freely? Would China's currency appreciate as substantially against the U.S. dollar as predicted by economists? When would further change occur?[a]

The stakes were high; a freer yuan float would impact groups very differently. Global communications solution provider Alcatel, based out of France with operations in China, was one such keenly interested party.

Alcatel Overview

Alcatel, founded in 1898 as General d'Electricite, was a leading global provider of telecommunications and services to telecom operators, Internet access providers, businesses, and the public sector. Products and services included broadband access, optical transmission, new-generation mobile networks, IP technologies, software application development, and integration of satellite telecommunications services and signaling networks for transport solutions. In 2005, the company—listed on the Paris Stock Exchange and the New York Stock Exchange—generated revenues of approximately $15 billion and operating profits of $1.4 billion with 56,000 employees (see **Exhibit 1**) and operations in 130 countries.[1]

Alcatel was a global or regional leader in many areas. For example, in 2004, Alcatel stood as the global leader in broadband access technology with 38% cumulative market share and over 58 million digital subscriber lines (DSLs) shipped.[2] In addition, Alcatel was the worldwide leader in optical networks with a 16% market share and second in wireless transmission networks with a 17% market share. Within Europe, Alcatel was number one in telecommunications satellites and enterprise IP communications systems, as well as a major player in railway management.[3]

---

[a] See "China: To Float or Not To Float (A)," HBS No. 706-021, for an extensive discussion on this topic.

Professors Laura Alfaro and Rafael Di Tella and Research Associate Ingrid Vogel prepared this case. This case was developed from public sources. HBS cases are developed solely as the basis for class discussion. Cases are not intended to serve as endorsements, sources of primary data, or illustrations of effective or ineffective management.

Alcatel had a global presence in its sales and operations. Alcatel had administrative, manufacturing, production, and research and development (R&D) facilities around the world. Its operations were spread across Germany, Italy, Spain, Belgium, Denmark, the United Kingdom, Canada, China, Mexico, Egypt, and the United States. In 1994, Western Europe accounted for 42% of Alcatel's sales, the rest of Europe for 7%, North America for 15%, Asia for 15%, and the rest of the world for 21%.[4] China was the second-largest market for Alcatel, after the United States, and two of Alcatel's top 10 global customers were Chinese.

Alcatel in China

Alcatel had been operating in China since 1983 when the company invested in Shanghai Bell, which became the first foreign-invested enterprise in China's telecommunications industry. By 2005, the company had invested more than $1 billion in China, was present in 31 Chinese provinces, was local supplier to all of China's four main telecommunications operators, and had approximately 5,800 employees in China—including more than 2,000 R&D staff.[5] Alcatel in China offered end-to-end communication solutions covering fixed and mobile networking, broadband access, next-generation networks, intelligent optical networking, network applications, network integration service, and multimedia solutions.[6]

In 2000, as China began to integrate itself more fully into the global economy and globalization became an important part of the country's agenda, Alcatel decided to move its regional headquarters from Sydney to Shanghai, a move the company claims it was the first to take.[7] In 2002, at a time when China was intent on globalizing its telecommunications industry and making it more export oriented, Alcatel and the Chinese government established Alcatel Shanghai Bell. Alcatel acquired a stake equal to 50% plus one share. As part of the arrangement, Alcatel agreed to make its worldwide technology base and R&D programs available to Alcatel Shanghai Bell. Analysts noted that this was a radical step, given the company was not wholly owned by Alcatel.[b] Alcatel consolidated its multiple Chinese operations and joint ventures under the Alcatel Shanghai Bell structure. By 2005, Alcatel Shanghai Bell came to represent approximately 10% of Alcatel's total sales.

After an Alcatel investor conference in Shanghai in November 2005, SG Equity research analysts noted:

> We estimate that Alcatel Shanghai Bell (ASB) is more than a low-cost manufacturing centre. Although it allows Alcatel to compete in China against the Chinese manufacturers, including primarily Huawei, ZTE and UTStarcom [see **Exhibit 2**], ASB also works as an export base for about 30 developing countries in Asia Pacific, Africa, Middle-East and CIS [Confederation of Independent States, i.e., former USSR]. . . . Being Chinese in China is the main positive for Alcatel. Especially, the Chinese government is both shareholder of ASB and highly influential with Chinese operators. As such, the Chinese government has a clear interest in supporting ASB operations in China.[8]

An important part of Alcatel's Chinese operations was its research and innovation center in Shanghai, which developed next-generation communications solutions. Vince Pizzica, Alcatel's Asia Pacific chief technology officer, noted: "It's part of our general policy to shift development activities to low-cost countries. There's lots of pressure on margins in the telecoms equipment industry. We need to find every opportunity we can to reduce the costs of bringing out equipment."[9] This was in line with the growing trend of multinational companies to shift from viewing China as a low-cost

---

[b] For example, Siemens Communications group also developed a strong R&D presence in China, but there was generally a relatively low level of technology transfer to China, with most first-tier technologies still developed in Germany.

manufacturing center to a low-cost R&D center—in addition to recognition of the importance of putting facilities closer to the customer. In part, this shift was driven by the fact that highly qualified Chinese engineers and information technology professionals commanded salaries just 25% of those in Europe and the United States.[10]

Chinese "National Champions" in High Technology

Alcatel faced strong local competition, particularly from state-owned Huawei Technologies and Hong Kong-listed ZTE. (See **Exhibit 3** for basic financials.) As of October 2005, Huawei—a telecommunications manufacturer serving many of the same markets as Alcatel—had over 35,000 employees and was active in 90 countries. Customers included 22 of the 50 largest global telecommunications companies. Huawei had 2004 revenues of $3.8 billion, including $2.3 billion in sales generated outside of China, and net income of $0.6 billion.[11] It had been successful bidding against European and U.S. rivals such as Siemens and Cisco in Latin America, Asia, and Africa and was starting to sell products in Europe and North America as well. In 2005, for example, Huawei was awarded a contract by BT Group PLC of the United Kingdom to be a part of BT's multibillion-dollar project to upgrade its infrastructure.[12] A French customer of Huawei's optical transmission equipment commented: "When we first saw Huawei we couldn't believe a Chinese company could match an occidental one—we were wrong. Their technology was better and they were 30% cheaper."[13] Huawei was targeting aggressive international expansion and, to that end, in late 2004 received a $10 billion credit facility from state-owned China Development Bank to support both Huawei and its customers abroad as well as a $360 million loan from a consortium of international banks.[14]

ZTE, with publicly listed shares on the Shenzhen Stock Exchange since 1997 and the Hong Kong Stock Exchange since December 2004, also focused on telecommunications equipment and related services. In 2004, ZTE had sales of $2.6 billion and employees numbering 25,500.[15] Like Huawei, it had become an important supplier in developing countries and was beginning to challenge European and U.S. rivals for a greater role in Europe and North America. For example, one month before Huawei's deal with BT, ZTE disclosed an agreement to become a global supplier of asymmetric DSL equipment to France Telecom.[16]

The success of Huawei and ZTE was attributed to many factors. First, analysts believed that both engaged in good business practices, such as continuous investment in R&D (of at least 10% of revenues) and strong marketing. For example, a Beijing-based consultant commented on Huawei's customer service focus, noting that the company offered better customer service than larger competitors by "asking the engineers to stay around the clients' central offices, get feedback on the products and provide customers with product design based on their demands."[17] Huawei was also engaged in a multimillion-dollar project to develop its brand.[18]

A second factor was that European and U.S. companies did not have deep-rooted business connections to block newcomers in emerging markets that were becoming major consumers of advanced technology. Instead, European and U.S. companies saw political, as well as economic, advantages in working with local manufacturers, such as China.[19]

A third factor often mentioned was related to state support. The U.S. Commercial Services of the American Embassy in Beijing noted:

> Chinese brands are strong and getting stronger in many sectors. In many Chinese markets there is a strong downward trend on prices. Chinese competitors, particularly those from the state-owned sector, often enjoy a very low cost of capital. Thus, they can enter markets quickly

and they can expect to receive strong encouragement from the government for their efforts. The Chinese government makes no secret of its support for state-owned enterprises (SOEs). Foreign companies should not expect a level playing field.[20]

China's central government targeted 30 to 50 of its strongest state firms to be built into "national champions" by 2010. These firms were provided with tax breaks, R&D subsidies, access to inexpensive real estate, government-organized contracts, and cheap or costless funding through the state-owned banking system.[21] JP Morgan Chase noted: "Local competition is strong and willing to 'buy' market share. . . . China wants to create national champions in areas such as telecom equipment."[22]

On the one hand, non-Chinese companies argued that government support gave these companies an unfair advantage. On the other hand, rivals conceded that although Huawei benefited from state support, China's telecommunications sector was less protected than those in other parts of the world.[23] Furthermore, some observers argued that local companies should have even more market protection, since liberalized markets made conditions difficult for local manufacturing brands to gain experience and develop scale to compete against global rivals with their own Chinese factories and R&D centers.[24] Gordon Orr, greater China chairman at management consultancy McKinsey, argued: "The pace at which China is opening up sectors gives local companies very limited time to develop."[25] Chairman and cofounder of ZTE Hou Weigui remained optimistic: "[We want] a reasonable degree of market protection and favor that would help enterprises get the exercise they need to get their blood moving. . . . However, I feel the current openness of the Chinese market and relative lack of protection for Chinese companies . . . offers very great training and challenges for us. . . . If we can grow in this kind of comparatively bad environment, then I think we will be even stronger when it comes to international competition."[26]

A fourth factor often mentioned in the success of Chinese firms was related to intellectual property. The U.S. Chamber of Commerce claimed in a September 2005 report that "China's IPR [intellectual-property rights] enforcement remains wholly inadequate and is the most visible area of WTO noncompliance."[27] *The Economist* appeared to concur, noting: "That Cisco, the industry leader, successfully sued Huawei for intellectual-property theft suggests weaknesses in its technological base. . . . Huawei tried to catch up with Cisco by bending the rules."[28]

Alcatel's Response to Yuan Revaluation

In an October 2005 *Financial Times* article, Alcatel Chief Executive Officer Serge Tchuruk described his approach in China:

> . . . we will have to continue to innovate and work hard because competition remains intense, not least from our home-grown Chinese rivals such as Huawei and ZTE. It is a challenge facing an increasing number of suppliers in the ICT [information communication technologies] environment, and indeed western economies in general—and one that must be confronted. We know and understand the strengths and weaknesses of our rivals, and we do not underestimate them. Chinese technology can be competitive—not in every area, but in a great many.
>
> There is a great well of talented, well-educated and well-trained people to draw from. You have to be very pragmatic in your areas of investment, as the Chinese can often devote four to five engineers to a project at the same cost of one elsewhere, while the competitive edge they enjoy in manufacturing is well documented. Equally we do not exaggerate the challenge of

Chinese rivals, but we do recognise that it presents us with some new tests, which I am not certain western governments and other companies are fully alive to.

At present, people in the west expect higher salaries and higher standards of living. To maintain these, western companies will need to push ever higher up the value chain, adding more innovation and more sophistication to their products and to their solution sets. If we cannot do so, life and business could become very tough indeed.[29]

Tchuruk's comments came amidst softness in the Chinese market for Alcatel. Although profit margins in China remained above the level of Alcatel's overall profit margin, revenues of Alcatel Shanghai Bell in 2005 fell over those in 2004, which Alcatel attributed to efforts of the Chinese government to try to cool down the economy, such as delaying the award of next-generation network contracts.[30] Furthermore, in May 2005, Alcatel was forced to unravel its mobile handset joint venture with TCL, China's largest consumer electronics manufacturer, after just nine months of operations. Alcatel sold its 45% stake back to TCL at a sharp discount to its asset value.[31]

The company responded to softness in Chinese market conditions in a number of ways. Facing strong competition from Chinese telecommunications equipment manufacturers in the global equipment market, Tchuruk announced a shift to focus more heavily on services. At an industry conference in January 2006, he described Alcatel's service range—including a range of professional, outsourcing, and network management services—to telecommunications operators.[32]

Even more significant, in March 2006, Alcatel was considering a major merger with competitor Lucent Technologies.[33] Analysts attributed the proposed merger in large part to the competitive threat from China (see **Exhibit 4** for data on growing Chinese exports of information communication technologies), most visible in the huge price differentials between Chinese and European or U.S. producers for telecommunications products.[34] It remained unclear what effect the expected yuan appreciation against the dollar would have on this price differential.

Exhibit 1 Alcatel Financials, 2002–2004

Income statement (millions euros)	2004	2003	2002
Net sales	12,265	12,513	16,547
Cost of sales	-7,690	-8,415	-12,186
Gross profit	**4,575**	**4,098**	**4,361**
Administrative and selling expense	-2,010	-2,173	-2,862
R&D costs	-1,587	-1,593	-2,226
Income (loss) from operations	**978**	**332**	**-727**
Financial and other income (expenses)	-117	-1,483	-3,323
Income (loss) before amortization of goodwill and tax	**861**	**-1,151**	**-4,050**
Income tax	-9	-82	19
Share in net income of equity affiliates and disposed of or discontinued operations	-97	-113	-107
Consolidated net income (loss) before amortization of goodwill	**755**	**-1346**	**-4138**
Amortization and exceptional amortization of goodwill	-408	-578	-589
Minority interests	-66	-20	-18
Net income (loss)	**281**	**-1944**	**-4745**

Balance sheet (millions euros)	2004	2003	2002
Goodwill, net	3,586	3,839	4,597
Other intangible assets, net	397	284	312
Property, plant and equipment	4,849	6,317	8,236
Depreciation	-3,688	-4,817	-5,737
Investments and other financial assets, net	960	1,213	1,281
Total fixed assets	**6,104**	**6,836**	**8,689**
Inventories and work in progress, net	1,527	1,432	2,329
Accounts receivable, net	6,295	6,595	8,753
Cash and cash equivalents	5,111	6,269	6,109
Total current assets	**12,933**	**14,296**	**17,191**
Total assets	**19,037**	**21,132**	**25,880**
Shareholders' equity	3,368	3,030	5,007
Minority interests	376	363	343
Other equity	645	645	645
Total reserves for liabilities and charges	3,422	4,059	4,317
Total financial debt	4,359	5,293	5,783
Total other liabilities	6,867	7,742	9,785
Total liabilities and shareholders' equity	**19,037**	**21,132**	**25,880**

Cash Flow Statement	2004	2003	2002
Net cash provided (used) by operating activities	-289	444	2,723
Net cash provided (used) by investing activities	314	443	-429
Net cash provided (used) by financing activities	-1,102	-564	-1,092
Net effect of exchange rate changes	-51	-136	-150
Net increase (decrease) in cash and cash equivalents	-1128	187	1052
Total workforce	**15,971**	**18,519**	**24,229**

Source: Compiled from Alcatel Annual Report 2004, available at www.alcatel.com, accessed April 2006.

Exhibit 2 Chinese Fixed and Mobile Infrastructure Market Share, Local and Foreign Companies

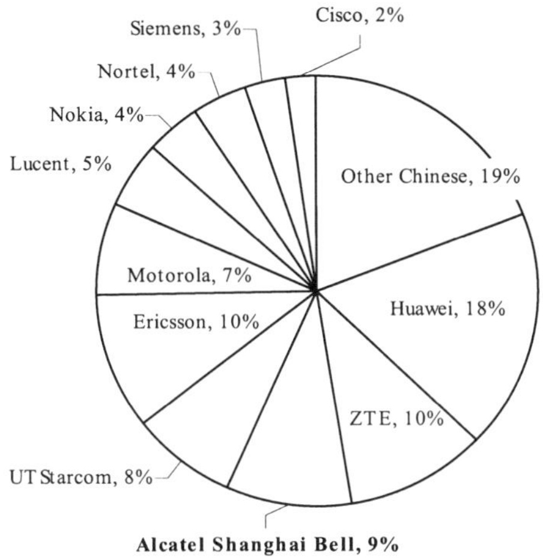

Source: Compiled from Surendran Panicker, Vincent Rech, Andy Perkins, and Bruce Gonyea, "Alcatel: Shanghai Investor Day Feedback," SG Equity Research, November 10, 2005.

Notes: "Other Chinese" includes a variety of relatively small software and hardware regional companies. Huawei, ZTE, and UTStarcom are Chinese.

Exhibit 3 Summary Financials for Huawei and ZTE

Huawei (nonaudited annual report)

Year Ended December 31	2004	2003	2002	2001[a]
Revenue	3,827	2,694	2,128	2,290
Net Income	624	384	108	258
Cash Flow from Operations	396	385	311	204
Operating Profit Margin	18%	19%	10%	17%
Return on Net Assets	31%	23%	7%	20%

Source: Compiled from Huawei Technologies Corporation Annual Report 2004.
[a]Excludes discontinued operations.

ZTE (Hong Kong accounting standards)

Year Ended December 31	2004	2003	2002	2001
Revenue	2,563	2,058	1,304	1,140
Net Income	154	124	85	50
Cash Flow from Operations	203	139	na	na
Operating Profit Margin	8%	9%	9%	7%
Return on Net Assets	14%	22%	19%	14%

Source: Compiled from ZTE Corporation Annual Report 2004.

Note: These financial numbers are not strictly comparable. Huawei's annual report is not audited and does not specify the accounting standard used, meaning the exact definitions of terms is unclear. The numbers from ZTE refer to Hong Kong accounting standards and are audited.

Exhibit 4 Imports and Exports of Information Communications Technology Goods (billions of U.S. dollars in current prices), 1996–2004

Imports (current US$ billions)	**1996**	**1997**	**1998**	**1999**	**2000**	**2001**	**2002**	**2003**	**2004**
United States	150	163	169	193	238	194	194	200	235
EU-15	106	112	127	137	167	148	140	164	226
China	17	20	26	35	51	57	76	111	149
Japan	48	46	41	49	67	58	55	61	73

Exports (current US$ billions)	**1996**	**1997**	**1998**	**1999**	**2000**	**2001**	**2002**	**2003**	**2004**
United States	124	141	135	148	182	152	133	137	149
China	19	23	27	33	47	55	79	123	180
EU-15	73	81	87	92	111	105	100	114	139
Japan	103	104	94	101	124	95	95	107	124

Source: Compiled from OECD, ITS database, available at ttp://www.oecd.org/document/8/0,2340,en_2649_33723_35833096_1_1_1_1,00.html, accessed May 2006.

Note: Data for the EU excludes intra-EU trade.

Endnotes

[1] Sara Silver, Dennis K. Berman, and Leila Abboud, "Enemy Lines: In Lucent Deal, Two Rivals Face Inroads From China—U.S. Firm, France's Alcatel See Bulking Up as a Key To Thriving in Telecom—Gearing for Beijing Olympics," *The Wall Street Journal*, March 25, 2006, and http://www.alcatel.com/finance/stock/paris.htm, accessed May 2006.

[2] http://www.alcatel-sbell.com.cn/alcatel_china/index_english.htm, accessed May 2006.

[3] Alcatel Annual Report 2004 (available on Alcatel website).

[4] Ibid.

[5] http://www.alcatel-sbell.com.cn/alcatel_china/index_english.htm, accessed May 2006.

[6] "Alcatel's 20 Year Presence in China," http://www.home.alcatel.com/vpr/vpr.nsf/va_TousByIDPere/IIACF95806552F4DF2C125700C003560B1II/$file/Alcatel_in_China.pdf, accessed May 2006.

[7] Serge Tchuruk, "China: A great well of talent to draw on—Serge Tchuruk: The Chinese have a hard-headed approach to business, but personal relationships have an important role to play as well," *The Financial Times*, October 19, 2005; and http://www.alcatel-sbell.com.cn/alcatel_china/index_english.htm, accessed May 2006.

[8] Surendran Panicker, Vincent Rech, Andy Perkins, and Bruce Gonyea, "Alcatel: Shanghai Investor Day Feedback," SG Cross Asset Research Equity Research, November 10, 2005.

[9] K.C. Swanson, "A threat rises in the East—China: KC Swanson analyses the implications for Western companies of R&D expansion," *The Financial Times*, June 2, 2005.

[10] Ibid.

[11] Huawei Technologies Corporation Annual Report 2004.

[12] Silver, Berman, and Abboud, "Enemy Lines."

[13] As quoted in "The Struggle of the Champions—China's Champions—China's Big Companies," *The Economist*, January 8, 2005, available at http://www.economist.com/displaystory.cfm?story_id=3535818, accessed December 30, 2005.

[14] Huawei Technologies Corporation Annual Report 2004.

[15] ZTE Corporation Annual Report 2004.

[16] Joanne Taaffe and Lorraine Turner, "Analysis: Telecoms equipment: China crisis," *Total Telecom Magazine*, January 6, 2006.

[17] Bruce Einhorn, "Cisco's Middle Kingdom Alliance, The networking giant teams up with China's ZTE to develop telecom gear for Asian markets—and ward off a common enemy," *BusinessWeek*, November 23, 2005.

[18] The Economist, 2005.

[19] Silver, Berman, and Abboud, "Enemy Lines."

[20] "Contact China 2005: A Resource Guide for Doing Business in the People's Republic of China," U.S. Commercial and Foreign Services of the American Embassy in Beijing, available at http://www.usembassy-china.org.cn/fcs/pdf/contact_china.pdf, accessed December 30, 2005.

[21] *The Economist*, 2005; and McGregor, *Financial Times*, 2005 (for information on research and development subsidies).

[22] Andreas Willi, Mark Davies-Jones, and Federica Cucé, "Siemens: Siemens China Analyst Meeting Feedback," Research Alert from J.P. Morgan Securities Limited European Equity Research, March 16, 2005.

[23] McGregor, *Financial Times*, 2005.

[24] Ibid.

[25] Ibid.

[26] Ibid.

[27] "China's WTO Implementation and Other Issues of Importance to American Business in the U.S.-China Commercial Relationship," U.S. Chamber of Commerce Report, September 2005.

[28] *The Economist*, 2005.

[29] Tchuruk, "China."

[30] See "Event Brief of Q3 2005 Alcatel Earnings Conference Call – Final," Voxant FD (FAIR DISCLOSURE) WIRE, October 27, 2005; and Inge Heydorn and Varun Khanna, "Alcatel: Shanghai Investor Update," Deutsche Bank Company Research Company Bulletin, November 8, 2005.

[31] Francesco Guerrera, Peggy Hollinger, and Justine Lau, "TCL link-up with Alcatel unravels in tough market," *The Financial Times*, May 17, 2005.

[32] Taaffe and Turner, "Analysis."

[33] See, for example, Alcatel press release, "Alcatel and Lucent Technologies respond to merger talk rumors," March 24, 2006, available at http://www.alcatel.com/vpr/, accessed May 2006.

[34] Silver, Berman, and Abboud, "Enemy Lines."

The U.S. Current Account Deficit and Global Imbalances

9-706-002
REV: JANUARY 20, 2009

LAURA ALFARO
RAFAEL DI TELLA

The U.S. Current Account Deficit

In the fall of 2008, investors and policymakers throughout the world were confronted with the challenge of deciding whether and how to respond to global economic imbalances exemplified by the large current account deficit in the United States. Already in 1998, many analysts believed the U.S. current account deficit—which, at $215 billion, was equivalent to 2.5% of GDP—was on an unsustainable trajectory.[1] Defying forecasts, the deficit continued to climb. By 2007, it was $731 billion, equivalent to 5.3% of GDP, from a peak of $788 billion in 2006, close to 6% of GDP. Since the mid-1970s, among the world's industrial countries, only smaller economies such as Australia, New Zealand, and Ireland had experienced current account deficits exceeding 5% of GDP.[2]

Yearly current account deficits were accompanied by substantial capital inflows from abroad as foreigners financed U.S. spending in excess of income. As these inflows accumulated, the gap between U.S. holdings of foreign assets and foreign holdings of U.S. assets (known as the net international investment position) was widening to unprecedented levels. By 2007, it stood at -17.7% of GDP, up from balance in 1985.[3]

Most U.S. policymakers downplayed the risks implied by the growing current account deficit and net international investment position (NIIP). They insisted that the deficit and NIIP simply reflected the attractiveness of the U.S. economy as a destination for global investment. For example, the 2006 Economic Report of the President focused on the current account's counterpart. A 24-page chapter of the report entitled "The U.S. Capital Account Surplus" noted: "What factors encourage large and persistent U.S. foreign capital inflows? Several factors, which reflect U.S. economic strengths, encourage these inflows. In particular, a high rate of U.S. growth encourages foreign capital to be 'pushed' toward the United States."[4]

Many analysts agreed that the current account could continue to be funded at much higher levels, focusing in particular on the "insatiable appetite" of Asian central banks—most notably China—to invest in U.S. assets as a means of keeping the dollar strong and supporting U.S. spending on Asian exports.[5] In 2006, China's current account surplus was $250 billion (up from $69 billion in 2004) while its increase in international reserves (the majority in U.S. dollar assets such as Treasuries) was over $245 billion.[6]

Other observers were less optimistic about the implications of the widening U.S. current account deficit. They believed the United States was mortgaging its future in favor of consumption in the present and argued that delaying adjustment to end U.S. external imbalances would only increase the severity of the eventual inevitable adjustment.[7] Berkeley economist Maurice Obstfeld and Harvard economist Kenneth Rogoff remarked: "In our view, any sober policymaker or financial market

---

Professors Laura Alfaro and Rafael Di Tella and Research Associates Ingrid Vogel and Renee Kim prepared this case. This case was developed from published sources. HBS cases are developed solely as the basis for class discussion. Cases are not intended to serve as endorsements, sources of primary data, or illustrations of effective or ineffective management.

analyst ought to regard the U.S. current account deficit as a sword of Damocles hanging over the global economy."[8] They forecasted further depreciation of the trade-weighted dollar, which fell by roughly 20% between early 2002 and June 2007.[9] The World Bank was also concerned about the strong dollar. Its 2005 Global Development Finance Report identified the "gravest risk" for emerging markets as a deep and disorderly dollar decline that would create financial market volatility and push up interest rates.

Furthermore, it was noted that high levels of external indebtedness made the U.S. financial system vulnerable to a loss of market confidence that could induce a "sudden stop" in capital inflows. Of course, unlike emerging economies more commonly associated with sudden stops, the U.S. could borrow in its own currency, meaning that it could pass the risk of future real depreciations on to its creditors.[10] Even so, former U.S. Treasury Secretary Robert Rubin warned that "the traditional immunity of advanced countries like America to third-world-style crises is not a birthright."[11]

Many global investors appeared to be in agreement with these concerns. Berkshire Hathaway, a holding company run by world famous investor Warren Buffett, increased the value of its foreign exchange contracts, consisting predominantly of short positions against the dollar, from $12 billion in 2003 to $21 billion in 2004. By the time of Berkshire's annual shareholder meeting in May 2006—given the climb of the dollar in 2005—such positions had cost the company around $500 million.[12] Even so, Buffett continued to emphasize the need to protect against further dollar declines. At the meeting, he postulated that current account imbalances would lead to "some chaotic markets in which currency adjustments play a part" and announced to shareholders a plan to shift from direct currency bets to increased investment in overseas companies to protect against this risk.[13] (See **Exhibits 1–4** for basic U.S. macroeconomic data.) There were also questions about how global imbalances would influence the short and long-term future of the dollar as a world currency and the United States' role in trade and finance.

A Historical Perspective on U.S. External Balances

Global Gold Standard (1870–1914)

Only in the late 19th century when the United States was rapidly industrializing were the U.S. current account deficit and NIIP close to their early 21st-century levels.[14] During this period, large current account imbalances were common throughout the world, with long-term "development finance" capital tending to flow from already industrialized countries of Western Europe with current account surpluses to emerging economies that needed to fund major infrastructure projects.[15] For example, in the 19th century most British investment in the United States flowed into bonds issued by canal, turnpike, and railroad companies or state governments that used the revenues to build public works.[16]

The global gold standard, which fixed major currencies against one another—and which the United States joined in 1879—encouraged these high levels of capital mobility. In 1879, global holdings of foreign assets were estimated at approximately 7% of world GDP. This rose quickly to close to 20% in 1900–1914 (see **Exhibit 5**).[17] Academics noted that the gold standard acted as a "seal of approval" for countries issuing sovereign debt.[18] Participating countries had much smaller spreads than nonparticipants over interest rates in London, where global capital markets were centered, with the British serving as "bankers to the world."[19]

U.S. adherence to the gold standard, however, generated opposition at home. A large faction of the Democratic Party, often called "populists," pressed for the United States to abandon gold in favor of a *de facto* silver standard. Although the movement was ultimately unsuccessful, speculators put pressure on the dollar in anticipation of an eventual departure from the gold standard. Between 1891 and 1897, the U.S. Treasury was forced to deter continued speculative dollar sales and maintain the fixed exchange rate by increasing interest rates dramatically. This resulted in a harsh recession.[20]

The Interwar Period (1914–1939)

After the commencement of World War I in 1914, worldwide holdings of foreign assets fell dramatically, only rising to their prewar levels around 1980. The gold standard fell apart, and monetary policy around the world became directed toward domestic goals, such as financing war efforts through issuing bonds and printing money.[21] Countries limited both international trade and investment through tariffs and capital controls.

After the war ended in 1918, there was interest in returning to the prewar gold standard that seemed to have offered stability and prosperity. Initial attempts failed in the face of inflation in Europe and high levels of European debt to the United States. Only in 1925 was a new gold standard finally initiated, under which countries held reserves in dollars, sterling, or gold, and the United States and United Kingdom agreed to exchange dollars or sterling, respectively, for gold on demand.[22]

Under the new gold standard, the United Kingdom made the political decision to set the value of the sterling against the dollar at the prewar exchange rate. Since there had been inflation during the war, this rate implied that the pound was overvalued, which encouraged investors to sell pounds in exchange for gold. With the United Kingdom politically unable to raise interest rates to prevent such outflows of gold, the Federal Reserve intervened, increasing U.S. money supply in order to decrease interest rates in the United States to levels comparable to levels in Great Britain.

Gold outflows from Great Britain halted, but excess credit in the United States was thought to have contributed to a major stockmarket boom. In 1928 and early 1929, the Federal Reserve raised interest rates to respond to the speculative bubble, but failed to prevent the stockmarket crash of October 1929. After lowering interest rates through 1930, the Federal Reserve was forced to raise interest rates in 1931 to defend its gold reserves after Great Britain's withdrawal of the pound from the gold standard following massive gold and capital outflows from Great Britain.[23] It was argued that tighter monetary conditions in the United States contributed to waves of bank failures in 1931 and 1932.[24] The United States withdrew from the gold standard in 1933. With the withdrawal in 1936 of Switzerland, France, and the Netherlands, this period of gold standard came to a definitive end.

The unified monetary system implied by the gold standard was blamed by some economists for spreading economic problems from the United States to Europe and precipitating the Great Depression of the 1930s. It was argued that governments were forced to protect their reserves of gold by keeping interest rates high and credit tight for too long, which had a devastating impact on credit, spending, and prices.

The Bretton Woods System of Fixed Exchange Rates (1950–1971)

In 1944, in the later stages of World War II, 44 countries met in Bretton Woods, New Hampshire to establish a new global monetary regime. Under the Bretton Woods system of fixed exchange rates, the dollar was pegged to gold while other currencies were pegged to the dollar.[25] The U.S. government agreed to make dollars convertible upon demand by foreign central banks into gold at the agreed price of $35 per ounce. All other countries were required to maintain their pegs to the dollar through active foreign exchange intervention, but were allowed to alter their par values to correct any "fundamental disequilibrium" in their balance of payments. They were formally encouraged to make use of capital controls to maintain external balance in the face of potentially destabilizing 'hot money' flows.[26] In 1945, the United States overtook Britain as the major international asset holder and became the new "banker to the world."[27]

In the initial years of the Bretton Woods arrangement, current account transactions had to be regulated. Strong European demand for U.S. products as European nations engaged in rebuilding efforts drove up U.S. current account surpluses (see **Exhibit 4b**) and caused a "dollar shortage." In order to control the usage of scarce dollars, European policymakers chose to prevent open purchases and sales of foreign exchange. The United States officially encouraged European countries to build dollar exchange reserves by expanding European exports to the U.S. market while maintaining restrictions on U.S. imports. By the end of the 1950s, European nations had accumulated sufficient dollar reserves to defend their chosen par values and to allow currency trading associated with international trade in goods and services. Current account convertibility was thus restored for the major European currencies.

Beginning in 1958, U.S. monetary authorities as well as other analysts and policymakers worldwide became concerned about what were considered "balance-of-payments imbalances" in the United States. These imbalances—which focused on liquidity within the balance of payments rather than on modern definitions of current and financial accounts—emerged as current account surpluses became insufficient to fund U.S. long-term investments abroad.[28] External balance was maintained through foreign central bank accumulation of short–term liquid claims on the United States. As the stock of official dollar liabilities held by foreign monetary authorities mounted, the risk of a run on U.S. monetary gold reserves increased. By 1964, official liabilities exceeded the U.S. monetary gold stock.[29] A shared interest among countries in maintaining the system as well as U.S. pressure on monetary authorities to refrain from converting dollar holdings into gold helped prevent such a run. As such, in 1968 the system switched to a *de facto* dollar standard—although the threat of gold conversion was still present.[30]

The problems associated with the official settlements deficit were exacerbated by U.S. economic expansion. After 1965, the U.S. economy began to overheat and inflation began rising in the face of major increases in social spending and escalating military expenditure in support of the Vietnam War (see **Exhibit 3b**). As the dollar became overvalued against other currencies, foreign central banks were forced to defend their pegged rates by buying dollars. Buying dollars increased foreign domestic money supply, which led to inflation abroad.[31]

In 1971, the U.S. trade balance turned negative for the first time since 1893.[32] Facing low returns on dollar assets and worried about a possible future devaluation of the dollar against gold to restore competitiveness, private investors began to flee from the dollar and many countries began to request the exchange of dollars into gold.[33] When Britain also revealed its intent to convert to gold, flight from the dollar intensified. Reluctant to raise interest rates to defend the currency (particularly in an election year) and aware that support for the Bretton Wood system was failing—both internationally and domestically with growing protectionist pressures—President Richard Nixon suspended convertibility of the dollar into gold, thereby "closing the gold window." Nixon remarked:

> In recent weeks, [international money] speculators have been waging an all-out war on the American dollar. . . . I have directed the Secretary of the Treasury to . . . suspend temporarily the convertibility of the dollar into gold or other reserve assets. . . . Now this action will not win us any friends among the international money trader. But our primary concern is with the American workers, and with fair competition around the world . . . . I am determined that the American dollar must never again be hostage in the hands of international speculators.[34]

Later in 1971 new par values were set for currencies, no longer backed by gold, but persistent speculation against the new values forced the system's collapse. In 1973, the world's currencies became independently floating. A worldwide recession followed as inflationary pressures took hold, exacerbated by the 1973 oil crisis.

Twin Deficits of the 1980s

After remaining close to balance through the rest of the 1970s—ranging from a surplus of 1.1% of GDP in 1975 to a deficit of 0.7% in 1977—the U.S. current account dramatically changed course in the 1980s. After Ronald Reagan became president in 1981, taxes were cut and defense spending increased in an effort to spur supply-driven growth of the sluggish U.S. economy. Expansionary fiscal policy was successful in encouraging domestic spending that supported GDP growth. In order to reduce inflation, the Federal Reserve kept interest rates high. High interest rates, in turn, attracted foreign investment, dramatically appreciating the value of the dollar. The appreciated dollar made U.S. exports more expensive for foreigners and imports cheaper for the United States, resulting in a widening trade deficit. In addition, economic growth rates of U.S. trading partners slowed relative to growth in the United States, implying that foreigners had less demand for U.S. exports while the United States had more demand for imports. These factors contributed to a widening of the current account balance, which passed from 0.1% of GDP in 1980 to a deficit of 3.3% in 1986. Over the same period, the government budget deficit increased from 2.8% to 4.8% of GDP. With changes in the same direction and of roughly the same magnitude, the current account and fiscal budget deficits became known as the "twin deficits."[35]

In order to address problems associated with the appreciated dollar, the United States, France, West Germany, Japan, and the United Kingdom (the G5 at the time) decided to intervene actively in currency markets to devalue the dollar against the yen and Deutsche Mark. They formalized this agreement in September 1985 with the Plaza Accord. The agreement proved successful, with the trade-weighted dollar falling 40% over two years.[36] (In fact, the program proved too successful: In February 1987, participants in the Plaza Accord plus Canada—the G6 at the time—signed the Louvre Accord outlining steps to halt continued decline of the dollar.)

The U.S. current account balance improved between 1987 and 1989, from a deficit of 3.4% to a deficit of 1.8% of GDP. GDP growth in the rest of the world increased relative to growth in the United States, which helped to shrink the current account deficit through trade channels as well as through increasing income on U.S. holdings of foreign assets relative to foreign holdings of U.S. assets. However, the effect was not large enough to shift the current account balance to a surplus. By 1986, as a result of the continual current account deficits, the U.S. NIIP (with assets and liabilities valued at market prices) turned negative on a current cost basis, implying that the country had become a net debtor to the rest of the world.[37]

New Economy of the Late 1990s

By the late 1990s, the "twin deficits" appeared to have become separated. As the government budget deficit moved into surplus, the current account widened. In the second half of the 1990s, with the backdrop of the "new economy" defined by accelerated gains in productivity growth through effective use of information and communication technology,[38] the U.S. stock market and other U.S. equity returns experienced a boom. Business investment rose dramatically, particularly on information technologies, from 5.5% of GDP in 1992 to 8.6% in 2000. Low unemployment rates, growing wealth, and optimistic assessments of future income led to increased consumer spending and lower household savings rates, which dropped from 6.5% of GDP in 1992 to less than 1% in 2000. Rising stock prices drove up taxable income and government savings—which helped to move the federal budget from a deficit of 5% of GDP in 1992 to a surplus of 2% in 2000. But this was insufficient to close the widening gap between private investment and domestic private savings.[39]

At the same time, as outlined by Federal Reserve Board Chairman Ben Bernanke, there was evidence of a "global savings glut" driven by demographic factors. With slowly growing or declining workforces, many advanced economies outside the U.S. faced a dearth of domestic investment opportunities. The aging populations of these countries required high current savings to provide for impending sharp increases in the number of retirees relative to the number of workers.[40] Foreign investors, attracted by rapidly rising equity returns and productivity gains, chose to invest a portion of their excess savings in the United States. Foreign capital inflows became increasingly focused on private-sector investments, thereby helping to finance the innovation and productivity growth of the "new economy." The share of U.S. assets in foreign portfolios in the rest of the world increased to 35% in 1999, heavily weighted toward U.S. equities, which increased to 51% of foreign equity portfolios (see **Exhibit 6**).[41] Overall, the U.S. NIIP fell from -$291 billion in 1994 to -$-1,331 billion in 2000, equivalent to a move from -4% to -14% of GDP (see **Exhibit 7**).[42]

With the creation of the euro currency in 1999, many analysts anticipated a decline in the ability of the United States to finance its large and growing current account deficit. Nobel Laureate Robert Mundell, on the eve of euro creation, warned:

> It would be a mistake to ignore [the fact that] in the last 15 years U.S. current account deficits have turned the U.S. from the world's biggest creditor to its biggest debtor. . . . The low-saving high-debt problems will one day come home to roost. . . . There will come a time when the pileup of international indebtedness makes reliance on the dollar as the world's only main currency untenable.[43]

However, contrary to predictions, the dollar strengthened (see **Exhibit 8**) and the current account deficit continued to widen.

Escalating Current Account Deficits (2000–2005)

In 2000, the dot-com bubble burst, leading to a mild recession in the United States between 2001 and 2002. Furthermore, oil prices increased the value of U.S. petroleum imports from $68 billion in 1999 to $104 billion in 2002 (see **Exhibit 4c** and **4d**). The government responded with a fiscal stimulus in the form of a tax cut, and the Federal Reserve responded with a monetary stimulus in the form of record-low interest rates. Rising government expenditures and falling tax receipts decreased the federal budget balance from a surplus of 2.4% in 2000 to a deficit of 3.4% in 2003.[44]

In spite of the worsening fiscal situation, funding of the U.S. current account deficit continued, led by official investment from foreign central banks. Between 2000 and 2004, all of the net new supply of U.S. Treasuries was purchased by foreigners, and between 80% and 90% by foreign central banks. In 2003, central banks around the world, particularly in Asia, accumulated $490 billion in dollar reserves, equivalent to more than 90% of the 2003 U.S. current account deficit of $523 billion. It was estimated that central banks increased their stock of dollar assets by $465 billion in 2004 (see **Exhibit 9**).[45] In fact, Asian accumulation of dollar reserves far exceeded the region's large current account surpluses (see **Exhibits 9a, 9b,** and **10**).[46] By intervening to prevent appreciation of their currencies against the dollar, Asian central banks maintained competitiveness of their countries' export sectors. The strategy was particularly important for China's economy; exports to the United States accounted for 15% of China's 2006 GDP, up from 8% in 2000.

The strategy also supported low U.S. interest rates, which served to increase the value of a wide range of assets, particularly in the nontraded goods sector. This was particularly clear in residential real estate,[47] where dramatic increases in value raised the wealth of many U.S. residents, many of whom chose to borrow against their assets as well as let asset price appreciation substitute for savings.[48] Low interest rates also drove high levels of household debt. In 2003, for example, household credit card debt averaged $9,205, which represented a 25% increase with respect to the previous five years.[49]

In contrast to Asian central banks, European central banks did not intervene to prevent appreciation of the euro and the pound against the dollar. In nominal terms, after appreciating by 53% against the euro and 12% against the pound between summer 1995 and early 2002, the dollar depreciated 54% against the euro and 36% against the pound through December 2004.[50]

Depreciation of the U.S. dollar against European currencies helped offset some of the impact of accumulated current account deficits on the NIIP. While current account deficits between 2001 and 2007 totaled $-4,242 billion, the NIIP deteriorated by only $-573 billion over the same period (see **Exhibit 11a**). The difference reflected changes in the valuation of the existing stock of U.S. assets and liabilities. Since a large portion of U.S.-owned assets abroad were located in Europe (see **Exhibit 12**), the fall in the value of the dollar against European currencies increased the dollar value of U.S. holdings of foreign assets.[51]

Regardless of valuation effects, U.S. liabilities to foreigners remained far in excess of U.S. claims on foreigners. Even so, the net investment income portion of the current account balance of the United States remained positive; the United States continued to receive more income from its investments abroad than foreigners received on their U.S. assets (see **Exhibit 4a**). In part, this was due to low U.S. interest rates. Harvard economists Ricardo Hausmann and Federico Sturzenegger had another more controversial explanation. They labeled the gap between official statistics indicating a negative U.S. NIIP and positive net income payments suggesting a positive NIIP "dark matter." They postulated that official data underestimated the true economic value of U.S. assets abroad by failing to capture important factors. These included "know-how" such as, for example, business ideas (rather than just plant, property, and equipment) that made U.S. foreign direct investment particularly productive; the provision of "liquidity services" in the form of foreign holdings of dollars in cash (on which the United States earned seignorage[52]); and the selling of "insurance" in that investors were willing to hold safer U.S. debt and equity at returns that were lower than those required to invest in the foreign countries where U.S. residents invested.[53] Hausmann and Sturzenegger concluded that "once dark matter is taken into account, the world is not far from balance. The stock of dark matter has been growing quite steadily. If this persists, the picture does not look that bad."[54]

Soft or Hard Landing for the U.S. Economy?

The implications of the U.S. current account deficit were debated with intensity. At one extreme, it was argued that large deficits would eventually resolve themselves smoothly, even if they persisted for many more years. For example, in an August 2006 report, the U.S. Congressional Budget Office estimated that current account deficits would grow more slowly than GDP through 2008 before stabilizing in 2016, implying shrinking deficits in terms of GDP over time.[55] Other groups believed the large deficits would soon lead to a necessary macroeconomic adjustment that could be painful for the United States as well as the rest of the world. Focusing in particular on the U.S. current account deficit, European Central Bank President Jean-Claude Trichet expressed concern over "global imbalances" exemplified by capital flowing, in aggregate, from the developing to the industrialized world.

A "Benign Resolution"

Some economists attributed "global imbalances" to potential growth differentials among various regions of the world and to differences in these regions' abilities to produce financial assets for global savers. They argued that imbalances could be maintained if these differences persisted.[56] Other studies focused on trade aspects, forecasting that faster economic growth outside of the United States would coincide with slower U.S. economic growth, leading to an improvement in the U.S. trade balance as foreign demand for U.S. products increased while U.S. demand for imports fell.[57] However, many economists argued that this analysis was too simplistic and failed to account for the fact that GDP growth in the United States increased U.S. imports more than foreign GDP growth increased U.S. exports.[58] The asymmetry was even more extreme for imports and exports of goods, but was reversed for imports and exports of services. The asymmetry implied that, assuming a constant exchange rate, the U.S. current account deficit could fail to improve even if the rest of the world grew at a faster rate.[59]

Meanwhile, in 2004 and 2005 Alan Greenspan, then chairman of the Federal Reserve, focused on financing the deficit. He noted that the ratio of global debt and equity claims to trade, as well as to GDP, had been rising for almost half a century, most rapidly since 1995. He argued that steady increases in financial intermediation (driven, for example, by global financial deregulation) facilitated the financing of continually widening current account deficits and surpluses around the world. At the same time, there appeared to be a trend toward reversal in the "home bias" phenomenon describing investors' tendency to put the majority of their wealth into assets from their own country rather than into foreign assets.[60] In 1993, 95% of domestic savings around the world flowed into domestic investments. By 2002, this value fell to 80%. In particular, global savings flowed into the United States with its favorable investment climate, strong investor protection framework, and expected real rates of return higher than in other countries.[61] Greenspan concluded: "Spreading globalization has fostered a degree of international flexibility that has raised the probability of a benign resolution to the U.S. current account imbalance."[62] Other members of the Federal Reserve Board of Governors were in agreement.[63]

Rather than playing down the risks of the current account deficit, U.S. Treasury Assistant Secretary for International Affairs Randal Quarles referred to it as "our gift to the world."[64] He was supported by economists who agreed that the widening deficit provided "the engine for growth for the rest of the world"[65] by encouraging export-led economic expansion, particularly in Asia. A major issue, therefore, was the degree to which Asian central bank dollar purchases would continue. Many observers believed that Asian countries would choose to maintain their heavily managed exchange rates against the dollar since the benefits to Asian export sectors outweighed the costs of holding U.S. assets yielding low—or even negative if further dollar depreciation was expected—returns. In part, this was due to the major structural changes taking place in industrializing Asia. For example, it was noted that China relied on rapid export-led growth to absorb 200 million surplus agricultural workers into the modern industrial traded sector.[66]

In 2004, former U.S. Treasury Secretary Larry Summers (Harvard University President at the time) used the term "balance of financial terror" to refer to the situation in which the United States was relying on the costs to the rest of the world of not financing the U.S. current account deficit as assurance that financing would continue.[67] In particular, it was argued that China would continue to buy billions of U.S. dollars each month in order to avoid a dollar collapse that would undermine U.S. consumption and the global stability upon which China's economic miracle was based. It followed that the United States would avoid tough sanctions to punish China's undervalued currency because such action would trigger inflation, higher interest rates, and recession.[68] Other economists referred to the situation more mildly as "vendor finance" or "Bretton Woods II."[69]

A Change in Trajectory

There was no guarantee, however, that Asian central banks would continue to support the dollar.[70] In mid-March 2005, Yoon Jeung Hyun, South Korea's top banking regulator, hinted at a gradual move away from this system: "There is widespread recognition that the ongoing trade imbalance between Asia and the United States—that is, Asian savings financing U.S. consumption—cannot be sustained and could potentially pose a systemic risk to the global financial system." Just days before, Japanese Prime Minister Junichiro Koizumi said his country should consider diversifying its currency holdings.[71]

Pressure on Asian countries to reduce purchases of U.S. dollar assets also came from the United States itself. Although foreign investment in U.S. Treasuries helped to keep U.S. interest rates low and U.S. consumption high, it also contributed to growing U.S. trade deficits, which intensified protectionist pressures. As such, the United States demanded that China allow its currency to become stronger against the dollar, even after the country loosened its exchange rate regime in mid-2005. U.S. imports from China were growing at a rapid pace, implying major shifts in U.S. employment (see **Exhibit 13a** and **13b**), especially as Chinese production moved up the value-added chain from textiles to furniture and auto parts[72] (See **Exhibit 14**). In 2004 and 2005, Congress introduced various bills that would levy extra tariffs on Chinese goods.[73] Six U.S. Senators wrote to Vice President Dick Cheney that China's exchange rate policy "has become a destabilizing force in the world economy, has led to major international exchange rate and trade imbalances throughout the world."[74] In mid-May 2006, the U.S. Treasury warned China that it could be cited by the U.S. as a currency manipulator, a process that could lead to economic sanctions, if it did not move toward a more flexible exchange rate. To similar threats in 2005, China's Deputy Chief of the State Administration of Foreign Exchange Wei Benhua responded: "There is no timeframe for such a change as conditions are not ready yet," and noted that the United States should "put its own house in order before blaming others" for its trade deficit.[75]

Furthermore, it was thought that continued U.S. current account deficits could lead to the U.S. NIIP becoming unsustainable. In 2005, it was estimated that maintaining current account deficits at 5% of GDP would imply that the NIIP would eventually stabilize at -83% of GDP (or, alternatively, that stabilizing the U.S. NIIP at -25% of GDP would require the U.S. current account deficit to fall to 1.5% of GDP).[76] Among large industrial countries, the 2005 U.S. NIIP of -15.5% of GDP was already among the highest, although some commentators noted that some smaller industrial countries had accumulated positions higher than -50% of GDP without obvious adverse effects. For example, Australia's NIIP stood at -59% of GDP and New Zealand's at -131% in 2003.[77] Most economists, however, doubted whether the United States, with a share of exports to GDP of only 10% versus 17% for Australia and 35% for New Zealand, could sustain an NIIP at equivalent levels.[78]

Analysts also noted that income payments associated with the growing stock of external financial obligations that had to be paid out of current production would become increasingly difficult for the United States to meet. They disregarded the "dark matter" argument that official statistics incorrectly valued U.S. assets abroad. For example, Goldman Sachs advisor Willem Buiter concluded that only possibly up to $0.5 trillion—representing seignorage on dollar cash holdings abroad—of the $3 trillion of "dark matter" identified by Hausmann and Sturzenegger was valid. He concluded that the paradox of the net investment income portion of the current account balance remaining positive even as the U.S. NIIP widened would be resolved simply by net income payments becoming negative: "In short, Hausmann and Sturzenegger believe they have found dark matter. Instead they have, thus far, found mainly cold fusion."[79]

In 2007, net income payments were $82 billion, rising from $57 billion in 2006. Economists estimated that net interest payments could reach above 2.5% of GDP in 2010 if high current account deficits persisted.[80] They also pointed out that the longer current account deficits continued, thereby expanding the NIIP, the more disruptive the eventual adjustment would be.[81]

The problem of possible future U.S. difficulties meeting growing interest payments was compounded by the fact that capital inflows from abroad were not moving into the tradeables sector where extra export capacity generated could be used to service debt.[82] Economists Obstfeld and Rogoff noted: "As long as nontraded goods account for the lion's share of U.S. output, a sharp contraction in net imports—a significant closing of the U.S. current account—will lead to a large exchange rate adjustment under most plausible scenarios. That adjustment will be sharper the longer is the initial rope that global capital markets offer to the United States."[83] In 2004, they estimated a possible depreciation of the trade-weighted dollar of up to 40% or more.

Some economists pointed to valuation effects to argue that the further expected depreciation of the dollar would shrink the NIIP and, therefore, reduce future income payments abroad. More specifically, economists made a rough calculation that a further 10% depreciation of the dollar would represent a transfer of 5% of U.S. GDP from the rest of the world to the United States.[84] It was noted that the effect of a sufficiently large negative valuation effect could lead to a sudden stop in capital flows that would force the trade balance to move into surplus.[85]

Global "Hard Landing"

Unilateral exchange rate adjustments will run into very substantial competitive pressures against those who allow a unilateral exchange rate appreciation. And so exchange rate appreciation is likely to be more politically acceptable and more economically acceptable if it does not take place unilaterally but takes place in a coordinated fashion. This, too, is a remedy that doesn't work very well on its own, as exchange rate adjustment in Asia and an associated substantial reduction in foreign purchases of U.S. Treasury bills would put American interest rates and the American recovery at significant risk with, again, risks to the global economy.[86]

—Summers, 2004

Another scenario involved a "hard landing" for the United States and global economies.[87] Economists Nouriel Roubini and Brad Setser explained the risk: "The current account deficit will continue to grow on the back of higher and higher payments on U.S. foreign debt even if the trade deficit stabilizes. That is why sustained trade deficits will set off the kind of explosive debt dynamics that lead to financial crises."[88]

It was also noted that the widely projected inevitable large future dollar depreciation could lead to severe inflation and a rapid increase in U.S. long-term interest rates. A resulting sharp fall in the price of a range of assets, including equities and housing, could lead to a severe slowdown in the United States. The fall in U.S. imports associated with the U.S. slowdown and the depreciated dollar could lead to a global severe economic slowdown or even recession.[89] Some economists predicted that the impact would be much more severe in Europe and Japan than in the United States.[90] With initial signs of such a slowdown as the U.S. housing market showed signs of softening in September 2006, Morgan Stanley Chief Economist Stephen Roach noted the importance of countries reducing dependence on expansion of U.S. domestic demand to support their own growth:

> As the U.S. housing bubble bursts, the American consumer is likely to stumble....With consumers elsewhere in the world unlikely to fill the void, growth in the world economy could well be at risk. This could come as quite a surprise to global investors, most of whom are banking on a continuation of the four-year boom in world economic growth. Financial markets have begun to discount such a possibility, but further adjustments could well lie ahead.... But

> in the end, there must be more to rebalancing the global economy than a drop in U.S. consumption. An export-dependent world economy has leaned too hard for too long on the American consumer as the sustenance of economic growth. As the housing bubble bursts, overextended U.S. consumers can't afford to carry that load any longer. Other countries must now learn to grow the old-fashioned way—drawing greater support from their home markets rather than free-riding on the United States.[91]

Furthermore, U.S. policymakers were urged to reduce dependence on external financing.[92] For example, the IMF in its 2005 World Economic Outlook underscored the importance of reducing U.S. fiscal deficits as part of a cooperative approach also involving gradually allowing exchange rate flexibility in Asia and adopting structural economic reforms in Europe and Japan.[93] The report proceeded by chiding the United States for being insufficiently ambitious with its deficit reduction target, as well as for failing to meet that target. While chairman of the Federal Reserve, even Greenspan agreed that the federal budget, with open spending on homeland security and "the war on terror," needed to be brought closer to balance.[94] The *Economist* was blunter still in its complaints about U.S. fiscal profligacy:

> America's commitment to budget discipline is a sham... Anyone who thinks more tax cuts and fewer spending cuts add up to budget discipline lives in fiscal fantasyland. ...The cowardice surrounding spending cuts makes the obsession with cutting taxes still further even harder to forgive. Despite healthy economic growth, federal revenues stand at 16% of GDP, the lowest in 50 years. Yet Mr. Bush and majorities in both houses of Congress want to make existing tax cuts permanent and push through new ones. ... Proposing such tax cuts just as the baby-boom generation retires is fiscal delusion not fiscal discipline.[95]

It remained to be seen how, when, and even whether policymakers around the world would respond, and what the impact would be on investors and currency speculators as well as the global economy.

Exhibit 1a U.S. General Economic Indicators

units as indicated	1960	1965	1970	1975	1980	1985	1990	1995	2000	2001	2002	2003	2004	2005	2006	2007
Per capita GDP (thousands 2000 dollars)	13.8	16.4	18.4	20.0	22.7	25.4	28.4	30.1	34.8	34.7	34.9	35.4	36.4	37.1	37.8	38.1
Nominal GDP (current trillions dollars)	0.5	0.7	1.0	1.6	2.8	4.2	5.8	7.4	9.8	10.1	10.5	11.0	11.7	12.4	13.2	13.8
Real GDP growth (% change on prior year)	2.5%	6.4%	0.2%	-0.2%	-0.2%	4.1%	1.9%	2.5%	3.7%	0.8%	1.6%	2.5%	3.6%	2.9%	2.8%	2.0%
Consumer prices (% change on prior year)	1.0%	1.6%	5.7%	9.1%	13.5%	3.6%	5.4%	2.8%	3.4%	2.8%	1.6%	2.3%	2.7%	3.4%	3.2%	2.8%
M2 (% change on prior year)	4.9%	8.1%	6.6%	12.6%	8.6%	8.0%	3.8%	4.1%	6.1%	10.4%	6.4%	5.1%	5.8%	4.2%	5.1%	5.9%
Real exchange rate (% change on prior year)	na	na	na	2.6%	-23.2%	3.5%	-4.3%	-3.3%	4.9%	5.7%	-0.2%	-6.4%	-4.6%	-1.4%	-0.4%	-3.9%
Federal deficit (% GDP)	0.1%	-0.2%	-0.3%	-3.4%	-2.7%	-5.1%	-3.9%	-2.2%	2.4%	1.3%	-1.5%	-3.5%	-3.6%	-2.6%	-1.9%	-1.2%
Stockmarket Index (annual % change)[a]	na	9.1%	0.1%	31.5%	25.8%	26.3%	-6.6%	34.1%	-10.1%	-13.0%	-23.4%	26.4%	9.0%	3.0%	13.6%	3.5%
Unemployment (% civilian population)	5.5%	4.5%	4.9%	8.5%	7.1%	7.2%	5.6%	5.6%	4.0%	4.7%	5.8%	6.0%	5.5%	5.1%	4.6%	4.6%
Productivity (output/hr; index; 1992=100)[b]	49	59	66	75	79	87	95	102	116	119	124	129	132	135	136	138
Compensation (per/hr, index; 1992=100[b]	14	17	24	35	54	73	91	106	135	140	145	151	157	163	170	177
Unit labor costs (index; 1992=100)[b]	28	29	36	47	68	83	96	104	116	118	117	118	119	121	124	128

Source: Adapted from Economic Report of the President, 2008; Department of Labor; World Development Indicators; and Economist Intelligence Unit Country Data database, Nov. 19, 2008.

[a]Standard and Poor 500 Index from Global Financial Database, accessed Dec. 1, 2008.

[b] 2007 figures based on data from the first three quarters of the year.

Exhibit 1b U.S. Interest Rates (annual average rate) and Consumer Price Inflation, 1962-2008[a] (%)

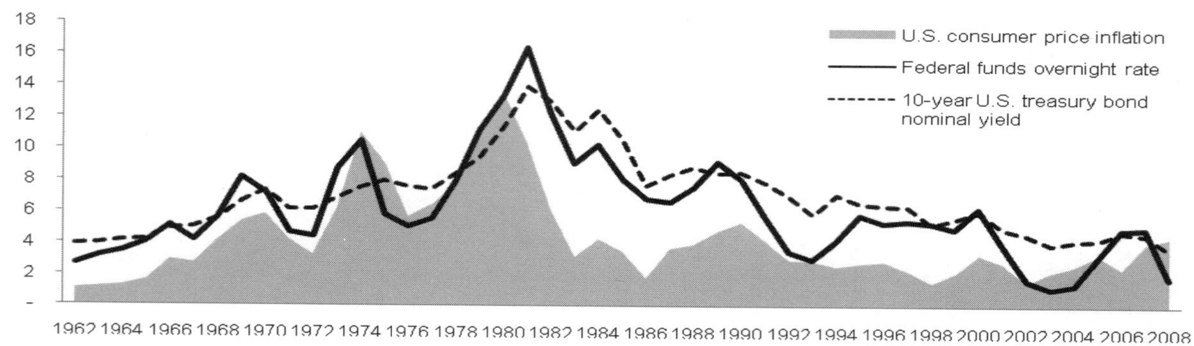

Source: Adapted from Federal Reserve Board, http://www.federalreserve.gov/releases/h15/data.htm and International Monetary Fund, International Financial Statistics, accessed Nov. 21, 2008.

[a]2008 figures as of September's end.

Exhibit 2a U.S. National Income Accounts (% GDP, except where noted)

	1980	1984	1988	1992	1996	2000	2002	2004	2005	2006	2007
GDP (current billion dollars)	**2,790**	**3,933**	**5,104**	**6,338**	**7,817**	**9,817**	**10,470**	**11,686**	**12,422**	**13,178**	**13,808**
Household Consumption:[a]	63%	64%	66%	67%	67%	69%	70%	70%	70%	70%	70%
Durable goods	8%	8%	9%	8%	8%	9%	9%	8%	8%	8%	8%
Nondurable goods	25%	22%	21%	21%	20%	20%	20%	20%	20%	20%	21%
Services	30%	33%	36%	38%	39%	40%	42%	42%	42%	42%	42%
Government Consumption:	20%	20%	20%	20%	18%	18%	19%	19%	19%	19%	19%
Federal Nondefense	3%	2%	2%	2%	2%	2%	2%	2%	2%	2%	2%
Federal defense	6%	7%	7%	6%	5%	4%	4%	5%	5%	5%	5%
State and local	12%	11%	11%	12%	11%	12%	12%	12%	12%	12%	12%
Gross Private Domestic Investment:	17%	19%	16%	14%	16%	18%	15%	16%	17%	17%	15%
Nonresidential	13%	12%	11%	10%	11%	13%	10%	10%	10%	11%	11%
Residential	4%	5%	5%	4%	4%	5%	5%	6%	6%	6%	5%
Change in private inventories	0%	2%	0%	0%	0%	1%	0%	1%	0%	0%	0%
Exports	**10%**	**8%**	**9%**	**10%**	**11%**	**11%**	**10%**	**10%**	**11%**	**11%**	**12%**
Imports	**11%**	**10%**	**11%**	**11%**	**12%**	**15%**	**14%**	**15%**	**16%**	**17%**	**17%**
Addendum: Real GDP (bns 2000 $)	5,162	5,814	6,743	7,337	8,329	9,817	10,049	10,676	10,990	11,295	11,524

Source: Adapted from Bureau of Economic Analysis (BEA), Table 1.1.5 Gross Domestic Product, and Table 1.1.6 Real Gross Domestic Product, Oct. 30, 2008.

[a] Figures may not add up precisely due to rounding.

Exhibit 2b U.S. Investment and Savings, 1970–2007[a] (% GDP)

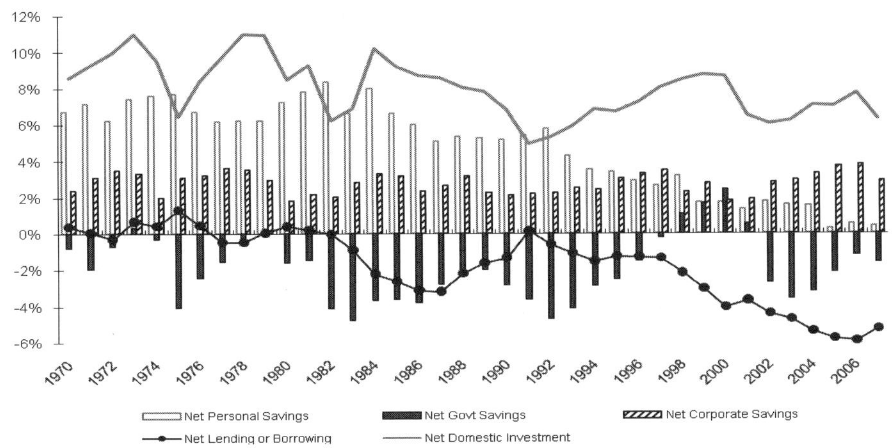

Source: Adapted from BEA, Table 5.1 Saving and Investment, Oct. 30, 2008.

[a] Net domestic investment referred to public and private investment and was net of depreciation. In 2007, net domestic investment amounted to 6% of GDP; gross private domestic investment was 15% of GDP; gross public domestic investment was 3%; and depreciation amounted to 12% of GDP.

Exhibit 3a U.S. Federal Government Fiscal Accounts

% GDP, except where noted	1980	1984	1988	1992	1996	2000	2002	2004	2005	2006	2007
Income (current billion dollars)	**517**	**667**	**909**	**1,091**	**1,453**	**2,026**	**1,853**	**1,880**	**2,154**	**2,407**	**2,568**
Income (% GDP)	19%	17%	18%	17%	19%	21%	18%	16%	17%	18%	19%
Individual Income Tax (% GDP)	8.8%	7.6%	7.9%	7.5%	8.4%	10.2%	8.2%	6.9%	7.5%	7.9%	7.6%
Corporation Income Tax	2.3%	1.4%	1.9%	1.6%	2.2%	2.1%	1.4%	1.6%	2.2%	2.7%	2.6%
Social Security and Retirement Receipts	5.7%	6.1%	6.6%	6.5%	6.5%	6.7%	6.7%	6.3%	6.4%	6.3%	6.1%
Other	1.8%	1.8%	1.6%	1.6%	1.5%	1.6%	1.4%	1.3%	1.2%	1.3%	2.4%
Expenditure (current billion dollars)	**591**	**852**	**1,065**	**1,382**	**1,561**	**1,789**	**2,011**	**2,293**	**2,472**	**2,654**	**2,730**
Expenditure (% GDP)	21%	22%	21%	22%	20%	18%	19%	20%	20%	20%	20%
National Defense (% GDP)	4.8%	5.8%	5.7%	4.7%	3.4%	3.0%	3.3%	3.9%	4.0%	4.0%	3.8%
International Affairs	0.5%	0.4%	0.2%	0.3%	0.2%	0.2%	0.2%	0.2%	0.3%	0.2%	0.2%
Health	0.8%	0.8%	0.9%	1.4%	1.5%	1.6%	1.9%	2.1%	2.0%	1.9%	1.8%
Medicare and Income & Social Security	8.5%	8.9%	8.4%	9.6%	9.6%	8.8%	8.8%	9.4%	9.4%	9.3%	9.6%
Net Interest	1.9%	2.8%	3.0%	3.1%	3.1%	2.3%	1.6%	1.4%	1.5%	1.7%	1.7%
Other	4.7%	3.0%	2.7%	2.7%	2.1%	2.4%	2.6%	2.7%	2.7%	2.9%	2.6%
Surplus (+)/Deficit (-) (current $ bn)	-74	-185	-155	-290	-107	236	-158	-413	-318	-248	-162
Surplus (+)/Deficit (-) (% GDP)	-3%	-5%	-3%	-5%	-1%	2%	-2%	-4%	-3%	-2%	-1%
Addendum: State and Local Government											
Surplus (+)/Decifit (-) (current $ bn)	8.8	23.9	17.9	0.7	25.8	50.0	-34.2	1.5	15.2	24.6	na

Source: Adapted from Economic Report of the President, 2008, Tables B-80 and B-82.

Exhibit 3b U.S. Federal Fiscal Balance as % GDP, 1934–2008[a]

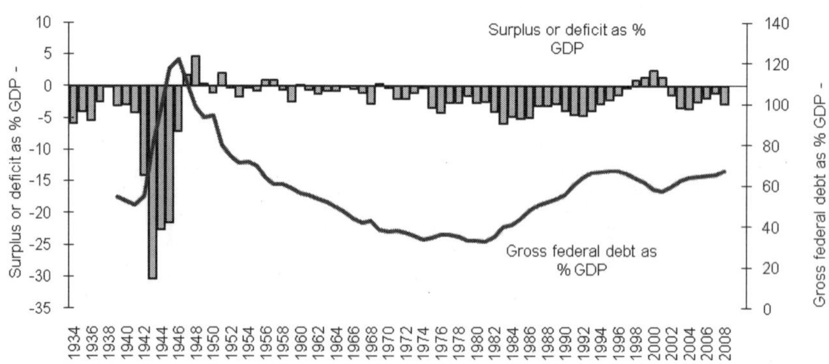

Source: Adapted from Economic Report of the President, 2008, Table B-79.

[a] Preliminary estimate for 2008 figures as of November 2008.

Exhibit 4a U.S. Balance of Payments

current billion dollars	1970[a]	1976	1980	1984	1988	1992	1996	2000	2001	2002	2003	2004	2005	2006	2007
Current Account	**2**	**4**	**2**	**-94**	**-121**	**-50**	**-125**	**-417**	**-385**	**-461**	**-523**	**-625**	**-729**	**-788**	**-731**
Net Goods	3	-9	-26	-112	-127	-97	-191	-455	-430	-485	-551	-670	-787	-838	-819
Exports of Goods	42	115	224	220	320	440	612	772	719	682	713	808	895	1,023	1,148
Imports of Goods	-40	-124	-250	-332	-447	-537	-803	-1,227	-1,148	-1,167	-1,264	-1,477	-1,682	-1,861	-1,968
Net Services	0	3	6	3	12	58	87	75	64	61	54	62	76	85	119
Exports of Services	14	28	48	71	111	177	239	299	286	292	304	353	389	434	497
Imports of Services	-15	-25	-41	-68	-99	-120	-153	-224	-222	-231	-250	-291	-314	-349	-378
Net Income	6	16	30	35	19	24	22	21	32	27	45	67	72	57	82
Income receipts on U.S.-owned assets abroad	12	29	73	109	137	134	226	351	291	281	320	414	535	685	818
Income payments on foreign-owned assets in U.S.	-6	-13	-43	-74	-118	-110	-204	-330	-259	-254	-275	-347	-463	-628	-736
Net Compensation of Employees	na	na	na	na	-1	-3	-4	-5	-5	-6	-6	-6	-6	-7	-7
Net Unilateral Transfers[b]	-6	-6	-8	-20	-25	-35	-43	-59	-51	-65	-72	-84	-90	-92	-113
Financial Account	**-2**	**-13**	**-25**	**76**	**138**	**94**	**134**	**478**	**400**	**501**	**533**	**532**	**701**	**809**	**768**
Increase (+) in U.S.-owned assets abroad, net (Financial outflow (-))	-8	-51	-86	-40	-107	-74	-413	-561	-383	-295	-325	-1,001	-547	-1,252	-1,290
U.S. Official Reserve Assets, net	3	-3	-7	-3	-4	4	7	0	-5	-4	2	3	14	2	0
U.S. Government (nonofficial) Assets, net	-2	-4	-5	-5	3	-2	-1	-1	0	0	1	2	6	5	-22
U.S. Private Direct Investment, net	-8	-12	-19	-16	-23	-48	-92	-159	-142	-154	-150	-316	-36	-241	-333
U.S. Private Foreign Securities, net	-1	-9	-4	-5	-8	-49	-149	-128	-91	-49	-147	-171	-251	-365	-289
U.S. Other Private Assets, net	-2	-24	-51	-11	-75	21	-178	-272	-144	-88	-31	-519	-279	-653	-645
Increase in Foreign-owned assets in the U.S., net (financial inflow (+))	6	38	61	116	245	168	548	1,038	783	795	858	1,533	1,247	2,061	2,058
Foreign Official Assets, net	7	18	15	3	40	40	127	43	28	116	278	398	259	488	411
Direct investment	1	4	17	24	58	20	87	321	167	84	64	146	113	242	238
U.S. Treasury securities	0	3	3	23	20	37	147	-70	-14	100	91	94	132	-58	157
U.S. Securities excl U.S. Treasury Secs	2	1	5	13	26	30	103	460	394	283	221	381	450	683	574
U.S. currency	na	1	3	2	4	11	14	-3	24	19	11	13	8	2	-11
Other	-4	10	18	50	97	30	70	288	184	192	194	501	284	704	689
Financial derivatives, net	**na**	**na**	**na**	**na**	**na**	**na**	**na**	**na**	**na**	**na**	**na**	**na**	**na**	**30**	**6**
Capital account transactions, net	**na**	**na**	**na**	**0**	**0**	**-1**	**-1**	**-1**	**-1**	**-1**	**-3**	**-2**	**-4**	**-4**	**-2**
Statistical discrepancy	**0**	**9**	**23**	**18**	**-18**	**-43**	**-9**	**-59**	**-14**	**-38**	**-6**	**95**	**32**	**-47**	**-41**

Source: Adapted from BEA, U.S. International Transactions Accounts Data, Sept. 17, 2008.

[a] Figures may not add up precisely due to rounding.

[b] Unilateral Transfers consisted of U.S. government grants, taxes paid by foreign residents to the U.S. government less taxes paid by U.S. residents to foreign governments, and other payments.

Exhibit 4b U.S. Current Account and Real Exchange Rate, 1948–2007

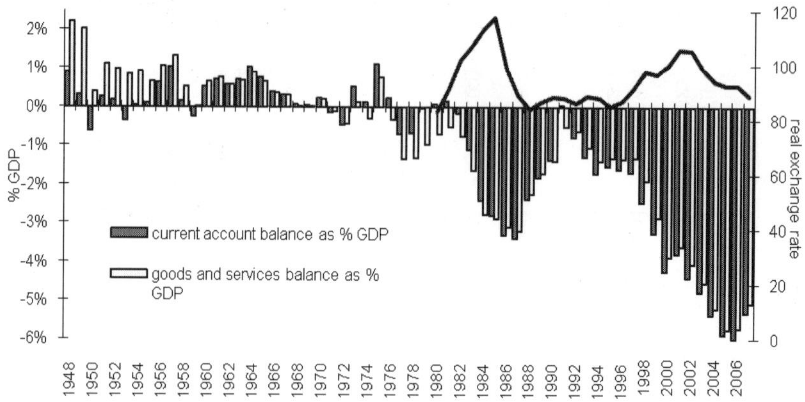

Source: Adapted from Economic Report of the President, 2008, Table B-103 and B-1; IMF International Financial Statistics; and BEA data.

Exhibit 4c U.S. Trade Balance by Sector, 1979–2007

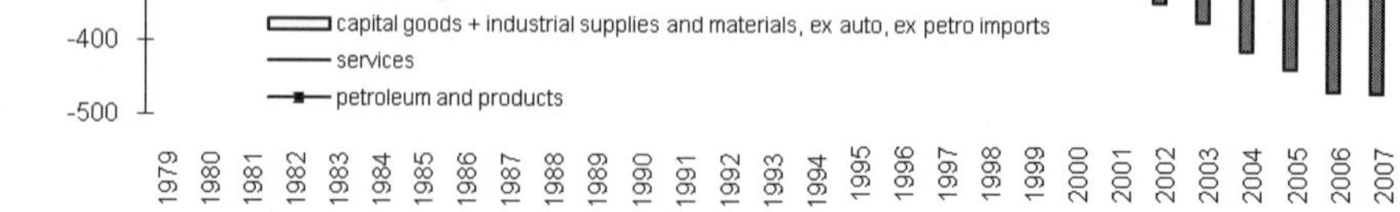

Source: Adapted from Economic Report of the President, 2006 and 2008 versions, Table B-106, and BEA, Table 2a, U.S. Trade in goods, Sept. 17, 2008.

Exhibit 4d Imported Crude Oil Prices, 1980-2008

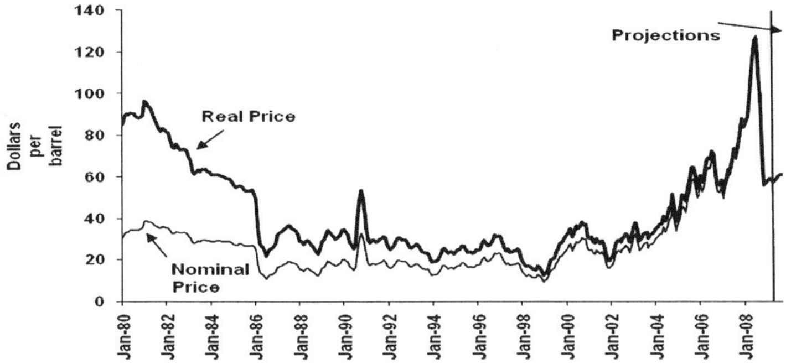

Source: Energy Information Administration (EIA), Refiner average imported crude oil acquisition cost historical series. Projections were based on EIA's Short-Term Energy Outlook Model, November 2008.

Exhibit 5 Worldwide Foreign Assets and Liabilities (current billion dollars)

	1825	1855	1870	1900	1914	1930	1938	1945	1960	1971	1980	1985	1990	1995
Assets														
United Kingdom	0.5	0.7	4.9	12.1	19.5	18.2	22.9	14.2	26.4	-	551	857	1,760	2,490
France	0.1	-	2.5	5.2	8.6	3.5	3.9	-	-	-	268	428	736	1,100
Germany	-	-	-	4.8	6.7	1.1	0.7	-	1.2	-	257	342	1,100	1,670
Netherlands	0.3	0.2	0.3	1.1	1.2	2.3	4.8	3.7	27.6	-	99	178	418	712
Other Europe	-	-	-	-	-	-	4.6	-	-	-	503	715	1,777	2,855
United States	-	-	-	0.5	2.5	14.7	11.5	15.3	63.6	-	775	1,300	2,180	3,350
Canada	-	-	-	0.1	0.2	1.3	1.9	-	-	-	92	129	227	302
Japan	-	-	-	-	-	-	1.2	-	-	-	160	437	1,860	2,720
Other	-	-	-	-	-	-	6.0	2.0	5.9	-	94	123	214	337
Total	0.9	0.9	7.7	23.8	38.7	41.1	57.5	35.2	124.7	-	2,799	4,509	10,272	15,536
World GDP	-	-	111	128	221	491	491	722	1,942	4,733	11,118	12,455	21,141	25,110
Sample GDP	-	-	16	43	76	149	182	273	671	-	7,806	9,705	17,250	21,956
Assets/Sample GDP	-	-	48%	55%	51%	28%	32%	13%	19%	-	36%	46%	60%	71%
Assets/World GDP	-	-	7%	19%	18%	8%	12%	5%	6%	-	25%	36%	49%	62%
Liabilities														
Europe	-	-	-	5.4	12.0	-	10.3	-	7.6	-	1,457	2,248	5,406	8,592
North America	-	-	-	2.6	11.1	-	13.7	-	12.5	-	684	1,412	2,830	4,681
Australia and NZ	-	-	-	1.6	2.0	-	4.5	-	2.2	-	71	118	216	318
Japan	-	-	-	0.1	1.0	-	0.6	-	0.3	-	147	307	1,530	1,970
Latin America	-	-	-	2.9	8.9	-	11.3	-	9.2	57	250	-	505	768
Asia (excl. Japan)	-	-	-	2.4	6.8	-	10.6	-	2.7	29	129	-	524	960
Africa	-	-	-	3.0	4.1	-	4.0	-	2.2	19	124	-	306	353
Developing Countries	-	-	-	6.0	13.0	-	25.9	-	14.1	107	506	-	1,338	2,086
All (includes others)	-	-	-	18.0	45.5	-	55.0	-	39.9	-	3,368	-	12,655	19,728

Source: Adapted from Maurice Obstfeld and Alan M. Taylor, "Globalization and Capital Markets," National Bureau of Economic Research Working Paper 8846, March 2002, p. 57; and Greenspan, 2004, footnote 7, p. 22, Table 2.

Exhibit 6 Share of U.S. Assets in Foreign Asset Portfolio of Rest of World, 1980–2003

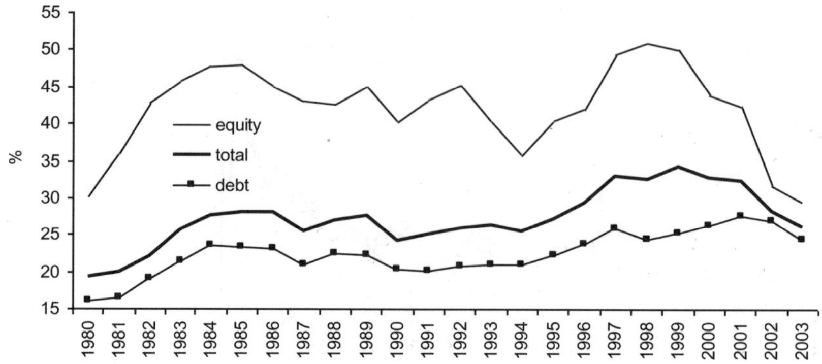

Source: Adapted from Philip R. Lane and Gian Maria Milesi-Ferretti, "A Global Perspective on External Positions," prepared for the NBER conference G7 Current Account Imbalances: Sustainability and Adjustment, May 3, 2005, p. 34, Figure 7.

Exhibit 7 U.S. International Investment Position

current billion dollars	1980	1984	1988	1990	1994	1998	2000	2001	2002	2003	2004	2005[a]	2006	2007[b]
Net International Investment Position	366	172	-161	-223	-291	-851	-1,331	-1,869	-2,038	-2,087	-2,245	-1,925	-2,226	-2,442
U.S.-Owned Assets Abroad	930	1,205	1,830	2,179	2,987	5,096	6,239	6,309	6,649	7,638	9,341	11,962	14,381	17,640
as % category:														
U.S. Official Reserve Assets	18%	9%	8%	8%	5%	3%	2%	2%	2%	2%	2%	2%	2%	2%
U.S. Government (nonofficial) Assets	7%	7%	5%	4%	3%	2%	1%	1%	1%	1%	1%	1%	1%	1%
U.S. Private Direct Investment[c]	42%	29%	28%	28%	26%	23%	25%	27%	28%	27%	27%	22%	20%	19%
U.S. Private Foreign Bonds	5%	5%	6%	7%	10%	12%	9%	9%	11%	11%	11%	8%	9%	8%
U.S. Private Foreign Corporate Stocks	2%	2%	7%	9%	21%	29%	30%	26%	21%	27%	27%	28%	30%	29%
U.S. Private Other	26%	48%	47%	44%	34%	31%	33%	35%	37%	31%	32%	39%	39%	41%
Foreign-Owned Assets in the U.S.	564	1,033	1,991	2,402	3,278	5,947	7,569	8,178	8,687	9,725	11,586	13,887	16,607	20,082
as % category:														
Foreign Official Assets	31%	19%	16%	16%	16%	15%	14%	14%	14%	16%	17%	17%	17%	17%
Direct Investment[c]	23%	22%	20%	21%	19%	15%	19%	19%	17%	16%	15%	14%	13%	12%
U.S. Treasury Securities	3%	6%	5%	6%	7%	9%	5%	5%	5%	5%	5%	5%	3%	4%
U.S. Corporate and other Bonds (excl Treasury)	2%	3%	10%	10%	11%	12%	14%	16%	18%	18%	18%	16%	17%	16%
U.S. Corporate Stocks	11%	9%	10%	9%	11%	20%	21%	18%	14%	18%	17%	15%	15%	14%
U.S. Currency	3%	3%	2%	3%	4%	3%	3%	3%	3%	3%	2%	2%	2%	1%
Other	27%	38%	37%	35%	31%	25%	25%	26%	28%	24%	26%	32%	33%	36%
Addendum: NIIP as % GDP	13.1%	4.4%	-3.2%	-3.8%	-4.1%	-9.7%	-13.6%	-18.5%	-19.5%	-19.0%	-19.2%	-15.5%	-16.9%	-17.7%

Source: Adapted from BEA, Table 2, International Investment Position at the year-end, 1976-2007, accessed Nov. 18, 2008.

[a] A break in series in 2005 reflected the introduction of U.S. Department of the Treasury data on financial derivatives, which was included in "U.S. Private Other" category starting in 2005.

[b] Preliminary figures as of November 2008.

[c] Direct investments were valued at current cost, under which NIIP turned negative in 1986. Under prior classifications of direct investments valued at market cost, NIIP turned negative in 1989.

Exhibit 8 U.S. Exchange Rates, January 1993–October 2008

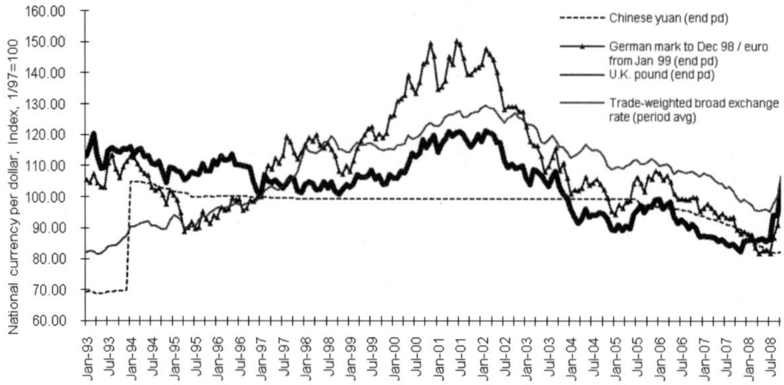

Sources: Adapted from Global Financial Data and Federal Reserve Board Historical Releases, H10, accessed Nov. 21, 2008.

Exhibit 9a Change in Reserves of Selected Asian Countries

current billion dollars	**2002**	**2003**	**2004**
Increase in reserves[a]	351	696	690
Asia	328	465	532
Japan	*64*	*202*	*178*
China	*74*	*162*	*202*
Other Asia	*190*	*101*	*152*
Increase in dollar reserves	185	486	465
Increase in euro/other reserves	74	62	165
Valuation gain (implicit)	92	103	60
U.S. current account deficit	-474	-531	-670
% financed by increase in dollar reserve	39%	92%	69%
U.S. financing need (net of FDI)	-536	-665	-760
% financed by increase in dollar reserve	35%	73%	61%
Reserves	2378	3029	3720
Dollar reserves	1607	2093	2558
Dollar reserves as % total	67.6%	69.1%	68.8%

Source: Adapted from Nouriel Roubini and Brad Setser, "Will the Bretton Woods 2 Regime Unravel Soon? The Risk of a Hard Landing in 2005–2006," written for the Symposium on the "Revived Bretton Woods System: A New Paradigm for Asian Development?," p. 34.

Exhibit 9b Countries with the Largest Foreign Reserve Holdings (in billion dollars)

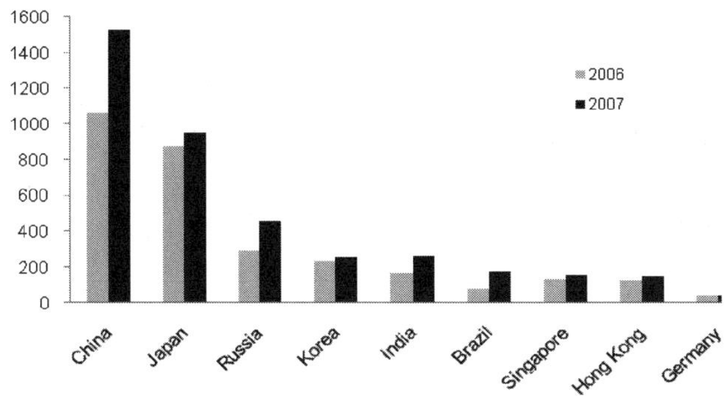

Source: Adapted from World Development Indicators, 2008.

Exhibit 10 Global Current Account Balances

current billion dollars	1997	2001	2005	2006	2007
United States[a]	-140.4	-384.7	-729.0	-788.1	-731.2
Australia	-11.9	-7.2	-41.3	-41.7	-56.2
Canada	-8.2	16.2	23.1	20.8	13.3
Japan	96.6	87.8	165.7	170.4	212.8
Euro Area	96.0	8.4	23.6	-6.4	-30.0
United Kingdom	-1.4	-31.5	-56.4	-92.6	-136.2
Switzerland	25.5	20.0	50.5	58.7	72.8
Oil exporters[b]	20.6	48.6	220.8	272.9	303.3
China	37.0	17.4	160.8	249.9	360.7
Developing Asia, excluding China	-27.4	19.3	0.6	27.6	22.8
Latin America	-65.4	-54.0	35.0	45.4	16.4
Russia	-0.1	33.9	84.4	94.3	76.6
Rest of Central and Eastern Europe	-21.5	-49.8	-145.7	-185.2	-198.1
Rest of the world	1.1	111.8	208.9	255.4	240.5

Source: Adapted from World Economic Outlook Database, April 2008.

[a] United States' figures from BEA, U.S. International Transaction Data, Sept. 17, 2008.

[b] Oil exporters defined as: Algeria, Bahrain, Iran, Kuwait, Libya, Oman, Qatar, Saudi Arabia, Sudan, Syrian Arab Republic, UAE, and Yemen.

Exhibit 11a U.S. NIIP Changes

current billion dollars	1998	1999	2000	2001	2002	2003	2004	2005	2006	2007[a]	Total (1998-2007)
NIIP	-851	-724	-1,331	-1,869	-2,038	-2,087	-2,245	-1,925	-2,226	-2,442	**-17,738**
Change in NIIP	-72	127	-606	-538	-169	-49	-159	320	-301	-216	**-1,662**
Current Account Deficit	-215	-302	-417	-385	-461	-523	-625	-729	-788	-731	**-5,176**
Valuation Change	143	429	-189	-153	292	474	466	1,049	487	515	**3,514**

Source: Adapted from BEA International Investment Position, Year-End, 1976-2007 accessed Nov. 18, 2008.

Exhibit 11b U.S. NIIP Source of Changes, 1983–2007[a] (in billion dollars)

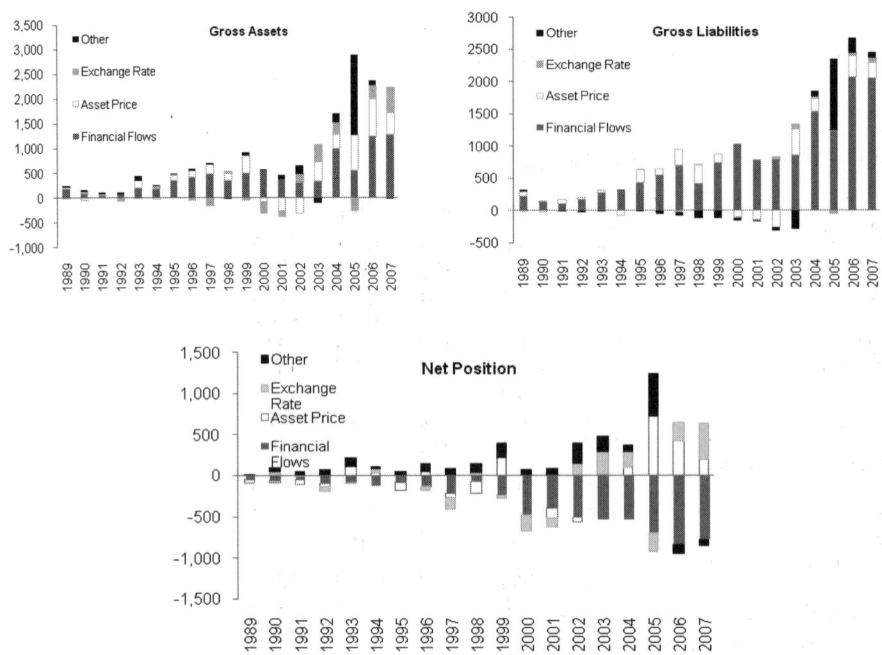

Source: BEA, Components of changes in foreign-owned assets in the United States, accessed Nov. 19, 2008.

[a] Exchange rate change represented gains or losses on foreign-currency-denominated assets and liabilities due to their revaluation at current exchange rates. Other included changes in coverage, capital gains and losses of direct investment affiliates, and other adjustments to the value of assets and liabilities. Data from 2005 included new derivatives positions.

Exhibit 12 Currency Composition of Selected U.S. External Assets

current billion dollars	1994	1997	2001	2004	2005	2006	2007
Long-term debt securities[a]	**304**	**547**	**502**	**993**	**1,028**	**1,294**	**1,607**
% U.S. dollar-denominated	48%	60%	66%	72%	76%	75%	73%
% German mark, French franc, Italian lira, Spanish peseta-denominated	19%	13%	na	na	na	na	na
% Euro-denominated	na	na	18%	15%	11%	10%	12%
% U.K. pound sterling-denominated	4%	5%	3%	3%	3%	3%	4%
% Yen-denominated	10%	6%	5%	4%	3%	3%	4%
% Canadian dollar-denominated	6%	8%	4%	3%	3%	3%	3%
% Other currency-denominated	13%	9%	3%	3%	4%	5%	5%
Short-term debt securities	na	na	**147**	**233**	**263**	**368**	**357**
% U.S. dollar-denominated	na	na	84%	84%	87%	92%	92%
FDI (at historical cost basis)[b]	**613**	**871**	**1,460**	**2,161**	**2,242**	**2,455**	**2,791**
% in Canada	12%	11%	10%	10%	10%	9%	9%
% in Europe	48%	49%	53%	55%	54%	55%	56%
% in Latin America/Caribbean	19%	21%	19%	16%	17%	17%	17%
% in Africa and Middle East	2%	2%	2%	2%	2%	2%	2%
% in Australia and New Zealand	4%	4%	2%	na[c]	4%	3%	3%
% in Japan	6%	4%	4%	3%	4%	4%	4%
% in rest of Asia	8%	9%	10%	14%	10%	10%	10%
Portfolio equity	**567**	**1,208**	**1,613**	**2,560**	**3318**	**4,329**	**5,248**
% in Europe	48%	61%	58%	53%	49%	51%	49%
% in Asia	26%	18%	19%	22%	26%	24%	23%
% in Canada/Latin America/Caribbean	21%	17%	20%	21%	22%	21%	24%
% in Australia/New Zealand	4%	3%	2%	3%	2%	3%	3%
% in Other	1%	1%	1%	1%	1%	1%	1%
(note: % of total foreign portfolio equity in ADRs)	na	21%	20%	15%	16%	17%	17%
Total of Selected Assets	**1,484**	**2,626**	**3,722**	**5,947**	**6,851**	**8,446**	**10,003**
Total U.S. External Assets (at cost basis)[d]	**2,754**	**4,032**	**6,239**	**9,341**	**11,962**	**14,381**	**17,640**

Source: Calculated based on data in U.S. Treasury, U.S. Portfolio Holdings of Foreign Securities at end-year 2003, March 31, 2005, and subsequent years.

[a] Based on Appendix Table 18; Canada was based on text Table 8.

[b] Historical cost basis data for FDI differs from BEA IIP data

[c] BEA reported that data for this year was suppressed to avoid disclosure of individual companies' data.

[d] Other remaining assets included, for example, claims reported by banks and non-banking concerns, mostly denominated in dollars. R-S and Gourinchas Rey both estimated that 55% of foreign U.S. assets were denominated in foreign currency.

Exhibit 13a Changes in Manufacturing Employment by Industry, 2000-2008

	Change in Employment (Thousands of jobs)			Change in Employment (Percent)
	2000–2004[a]	2004–2007[b]	2007–2008[c]	2000–2008[d]
Manufacturing Sector				
Production workers	-2,314	-82	-304	-21.9
Nonproduction Workers	-599	-416	-60	-22.1
Total, manufacturing sector	**-2,913**	**-498**	**-364**	**-22.0**
Industry Classification				
Durable Goods	-2,002	-114	-269	-21.9
Wood products	-55	-33	-42	-21.7
Nonmetallic mineral products	-55	1	-25	-14.2
Primary metals	-151	-12	-8	-27.9
Fabricated metal products	-284	87	-35	-13.2
Machinery	-323	56	2	-18.2
Computer and electronic products	-541	-62	-12	-33.0
Electrical equipment and appliances	-141	-21	-6	-28.6
Transportation equipment	-263	-73	-96	-21.3
Motor vehicles and parts	-176	-146	-97	-32.4
Furniture and related products	-109	-47	-38	-28.3
Miscellaneous manufacturing	-81	-10	-10	-13.8
Nondurable Goods	-911	-384	-95	-22.0
Food manufacturing	-51	-18	-7	-4.9
Beverages and tobacco products	-15	0	-2	-8.0
Textile mills	-130	-77	-15	-59.6
Textile product mills	-44	-27	-8	-34.9
Apparel	-178	-80	-11	-58.0
Leather and allied products	-23	-9	1	-47.2
Paper and paper products	-101	-40	-7	-24.6
Printing and related support activities	-136	-46	-24	-25.6
Petroleum and coal products	-9	-1	2	-6.1
Chemicals	-87	-29	-6	-12.5
Plastics and rubber products	-138	-58	-19	-22.9
Memorandum:				
Private Employment (Excluding Manufacturing)	355	7,249	-548	7.5

Source: Congressional Budget Office, "Economic and Budget Issue Brief," December 23, 2008, p.2.

[a]From the fourth quarter of 2000 to the first quarter of 2004.

[b]From the first quarter of 2004 to the fourth quarter of 2007.

[c]From the fourth quarter of 2007 to the third quarter of 2008.

[d]From the fourth quarter of 2000 through the third quarter of 2008.

Exhibit 13b Manufacturing Employment[a]

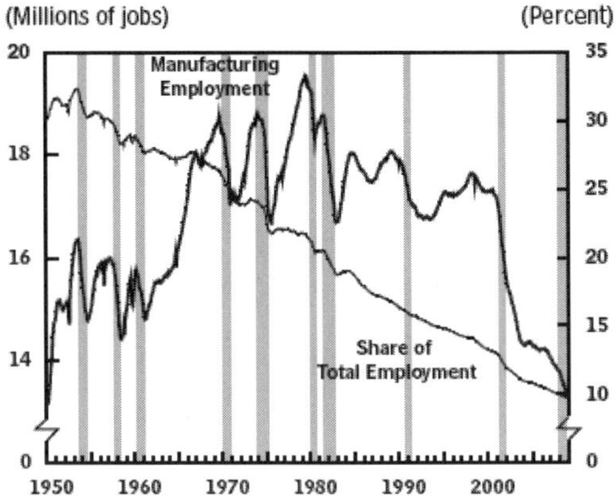

Source: Congressional Budget Office, "Economic and Budget Issue Brief," December 23, 2008, p. 3.

[a]Data represented through the third quarter of 2008. Shaded vertical bars indicated recessions, as defined by the National Bureau of Economic Research.

Exhibit 14 U.S. Bilateral Trade Patterns

current billion dollars	1978	1982	1986	1990	1994	1998	2002	2004	2005	2006	2007
Exports of Goods	**142**	**211**	**223**	**387**	**503**	**670**	**682**	**808**	**895**	**1,023**	**1,148**
as % exports											
European Union	22%	22%	23%	26%	21%	22%	21%	21%	21%	21%	24%
Canada	22%	19%	25%	22%	23%	23%	24%	24%	24%	23%	22%
Latin America + Rest of Western Hem.	16%	16%	14%	14%	18%	21%	22%	21%	22%	22%	21%
China	1%	1%	1%	1%	2%	2%	3%	4%	5%	5%	6%
Japan	9%	10%	12%	12%	10%	8%	7%	6%	6%	6%	5%
Other Asia[a]	14%	17%	15%	17%	19%	17%	17%	17%	16%	16%	16%
Remainder	16%	15%	10%	8%	7%	6%	7%	7%	8%	8%	6%
Imports of Goods	**176**	**248**	**368**	**498**	**669**	**917**	**1,167**	**1,477**	**1,682**	**1,861**	**1,968**
as % imports											
European Union	16%	17%	20%	20%	18%	19%	19%	19%	18%	18%	18%
Canada	19%	20%	19%	19%	20%	19%	18%	18%	17%	16%	16%
Latin America + Rest of Western Hem.	13%	16%	11%	13%	13%	16%	18%	17%	18%	18%	17%
China	0%	1%	1%	3%	6%	8%	11%	13%	14%	15%	15%
Japan	14%	15%	22%	18%	18%	13%	10%	9%	8%	8%	7%
Other Asia	21%	18%	18%	21%	20%	19%	16%	15%	14%	13%	13%
Remainder	16%	13%	8%	7%	5%	5%	8%	10%	11%	11%	14%

Source: Adapted from BEA International Transactions Accounts, Table 2, U.S. Trade in Goods, Sept. 17, 2008.

[a]'Other Asia' redefined as Asia Pacific, excluding Japan and China, following BEA's reclassification of Asia from 1999.

Endnotes

[1] For earlier discussions of concerns about the U.S. current account deficit, see, for example: mention of Federal Reserve staff concerns in Edwin M. Truman, "The U.S. Current Account Deficit and the Euro Area," speech prepared for "The ECB and Its Watchers VI" Conference, Frankfurt, Germany, July 2, 2004; and Robert Mundell, "The Case for the Euro – I and II," *Wall Street Journal,* March 24 and 25, 1998, as cited in Fred Bergsten, "The Euro Versus the Dollar: Will There be a Struggle for Dominance?" Presented to a Roundtable at the Annual Meeting of the American Economic Association Atlanta January 4, 2002, available at http://www.iie.com/publications/papers/bergsten0102-1.pdf, accessed June 9, 2005; and Maurice Obstfeld and Kenneth Rogoff, "Perspectives on OECD Capital Market Integration: Implications for U.S. Current Account Adjustment," in Federal Reserve Bank of Kansas City, *Global Economic Integration: Opportunities and Challenges,* March 2000, pp. 169–208.

[2] Full list: Australia, Austria, Denmark, Finland, Greece, Iceland, Ireland, Malta, New Zealand, Norway and Portugal, according to Sebastian Edwards, "Is the U.S. Current Account Deficit Sustainable? And if Not, How Costly is Adjustment Likely To Be?" prepared for presentation at the Spring 2005 meeting of the Brookings Panel on Economic Activity, March 16, 2005, p. 10.

[3] More precisely, BEA data from June 2008, showed U.S. NIIP in 1985 to be $67,121 million and $-21,766 million in 1986.

[4] 2006 Economic Report of the President, p. 140, available at http://www.gpoaccess.gov/eop/index.html, accessed September 6, 2006.

[5] This view was most famous in Michael P. Dooley, David Folkerts-Landau, and Peter Garber, "An Essay on the Revived Bretton Woods System," National Bureau of Economic Research Working Paper 9971, September 2003 and Michael P. Dooley, David Folkerts-Landau, and Peter Garber, "The Revived Bretton Woods System: The Effects of Periphery Intervention and Reserve Management on Interest Rates and Exchange Rates in Center Countries," Bureau of Economic Research Working Paper 10332, March 2004.

[6] International Monetary Fund, International Financial Statistics Database (online), accessed July 27, 2007. Economist Intelligence Unit, Country Report July 1, 2007

[7] Economists Nouriel Roubini and Brad Setser noted: "The core contradiction in the current international monetary order is simple. The United States is currently financing itself by selling low-yielding dollar debt, which offers foreign investors little protection against a future fall in the dollar. Yet the United States' large trade deficit and rapidly rising external debt to GDP ratio imply that a large future fall in the dollar will be needed to reduce the U.S. trade deficit to more sustainable levels. The longer foreign investors finance the United States on current terms—particularly investors from countries whose currencies have yet to fall at all against the dollar—the larger their likely capital losses on their dollar assets." Nouriel Roubini and Brad Setser, "Will the Bretton Woods 2 Regime Unravel Soon? The Risk of a Hard Landing in 2005–2006," written for the Symposium on the "Revived Bretton Woods System: A New Paradigm for Asian Development?" organized by the Federal Reserve Bank of San Francisco and U.C. Berkeley, San Francisco, February 4, 2005, p. 11.

[8] Maurice Obstfeld and Kenneth Rogoff, "Global Current Account Imbalances and Exchange Rate Adjustments," May 17, 2005, available at elsa.berkeley.edu/~obstfeld/global_current.pdf, accessed September 19, 2006.

[9] Based on data at Federal Reserve website, available at http://www.federalreserve.gov/releases/H10/Summary/indexb_m.txt, accessed July 27, 2007.

[10] Nouriel Roubini and Brad Setser, "The US as a Net Debtor: The Sustainability of the US External Imbalances," NYU, August 2004, revised: November 2004, available at http://www.stern.nyu.edu/globalmacro/Roubini-Setser-US-External-Imbalances.pdf, accessed September 14, 2006, p. 45.

[11] Roubini and Setser 2004, p. 44, citing Peter G. Peterson, "Presentation of the Book (Running on Empty: How the Democratic and Republican Parties are Bankrupting Our Future and What Americans Can Do about

It)." Institute for International Economics, August 9, 2004, available at http://www.iie.com/publications/papers/peterson0804.pdf, accessed June 9, 2005.

12 Alistair Barr, "Deficits may hit dollar, fuel inflation: Buffett says Iscar deal is part of strategy to protect against a drop in buck," May 6, 2006 available at http://www.marketwatch.com, accessed September 14, 2006.

13 Financial Times, "Buffett skeptical about soft landing for dollar" May 6, 2006.

14 In 1894, the U.S. NIIP was estimated to have reached a level close to the 2004 level of -22% of GDP. Around the same time, the current account deficit fluctuated around 4% of GDP. From Maurice Obstfeld and Kenneth Rogoff, "The Unsustainable U.S. Current Account Position Revisited," National Bureau of Economic Research Working Paper 10869, October 2004, pp. 5–6, referring to Maurice Obstfeld and Alan M. Taylor, *Global Capital Markets: Integration, Crisis, and Growth* (Cambridge: Cambridge University Press, 2004).

15 See Maurice Obstfeld and Alan M. Taylor, "Globalization and Capital Markets," National Bureau of Economic Research Working Paper 8846, March 2002, p. 57; and Greenspan 2004, footnote 7.

16 For an interesting discussion of the financing of railroad construction in the United States see Bradford DeLong, "Slouching Towards Utopia?: The Economic History of the Twentieth Century," available at http://www.j-bradford-delong.net/TCEH/Slouch_Gold8.html, accessed June 9, 2005.

17 Obstfeld and Taylor 2002.

18 Michael D. Bordo and Hugh Rockoff, "The Gold Standard as a "Good Housekeeping Seal of Approval," *Journal of Economic History* 56, June 1996, pp. 389–428.

19 Obstfeld and Taylor 2002, p. 21.

20 Obstfeld and Taylor 2002, p. 10.

21 See, for example, Obstfeld and Taylor 2002, p. 5.

22 For more on the gold standard, see Daniel Pope and Thomas K. McCraw, "The U.K. and the Gold Standard in 1925," HBS No. 383-081, revised April 24, 1998.

23 Michael D. Bordo, "The Classical Gold Standard—Some Lessons for Today," *Federal Reserve Bank of St. Louis Review* 63, no. 5, May 1981, pp: 2-17.

24 See for example Milton Friedman and Anna J. Schwartz, *A Monetary History of the United States, 1867-1960* (Princeton: Princeton University Press, 1971).

25 See also Louis T. Wells Jr., "The Bretton Woods System of Exchange Rates," HBS No. 797-093, March 25, 1997.

26 For more on Bretton Woods, see Michael D. Bordo, "The Bretton Woods International Monetary System: An Historical Overview," National Bureau of Economic Research Working Paper 4033, March 1992; Michael D. Bordo and Barry Eichengreen (eds.) *A Retrospective on the Bretton Woods System: Lessons for International Monetary Reform* (Chicago: University of Chicago Press, 1993); Barry Eichengreen, "From Benign Neglect to Malignant Preoccupation: U.S. Balance-Of-Payments Policy in the 1960s," National Bureau of Economic Research Working Paper 7630, March 2000; and Barry Eichengreen, *Globalizing Capital: A History of the International Monetary System* (Princeton, NJ: Princeton University Press, 1996).

27 Obstfeld and Taylor 2002, p. 25.

28 For more on this, see Bordo 1992, p. 37; and Michael Dooley and Peter Garber, "Is It 1958 or 1968? Three Notes on the Longevity of the Revived Bretton Woods System," Paper prepared for Brookings Panel on Economic Activity, March 31–April 1, 2005, which addresses the difference between the then-definition of Balance of Payment deficit and current account and financial account deficits focused on today.

29 Bordo 1992, p. 37.

[30] Michael D. Bordo, "Historical Perspective on Global Imbalances," NBER Working Paper 11383, May 2005, p. 13; and Bordo 1992, p. 48.

[31] As described in Eichengreen 2000, the United States did not follow a policy of "benign neglect" and did try to counteract associated problems with other measures. As he describes on p. 2: "The Kennedy, Johnson and Nixon Administrations resorted to a series of indirect policy initiatives—differential tax treatment of domestic and foreign investments, reductions in the value of the goods American tourists could bring into the country, tied foreign aid, and finally an across-the-board import surcharge—in an effort to remedy the balance of payments problem and free up monetary and fiscal policies for the pursuit of domestic objectives."

[32] See Bordo 1992, Eichengreen 2000, and Michael G. Rukstad, "Nixon's New Economic Policy: 1971," HBS No. 386-063, revised March 8, 2000. For more on U.S. balance of payments issues in the late 1960s, see also John W. Rosenblum, "Nixon's Economic Strategy—1969," HBS No. 378-258, revised March 8, 2000.

[33] Bordo 1992, p. 55 and Eichengreen 2000, p. 34 discuss countries wanting to convert.

[34] Richard Nixon, Presidential Message, August 15, 1971, as quoted in HBS No. 386-063.

[35] Catherine L. Mann, "Perspectives on the U.S. Current Account Deficit and Sustainability," *Journal of Economic Perspectives* Vol. 16, No. 3, summer 2002, p. 138.

[36] Obstfeld and Rogoff 2004, p. 5.

[37] Exactly when the NIIP turned negative depended on whether direct investments were valued at current cost or market values. Under direct investments at current costs, NIIP turned negative in 1986. Under market values, NIIP turned negative in 1989.

[38] See Mann 2002 for further citations of definition of new economy. See also, Huw Pill, "The U.S. in 2001: Macroeconomic Policy and the New Economy," HBS No. 701-113, revised February 25, 2002.

[39] Mann 2002 and Greenspan 2004.

[40] (At the time of publication of this article, Bernanke was a Federal Reserve Board Governor.) Ben S. Bernanke, "The Global Saving Glut and the U.S. Current Account Deficit," Remarks at the Sandridge Lecture, Virginia Association of Economics, Richmond, Virginia, March 10, 2005, available at http://www.federalreserve.gov/boarddocs/speeches/2005/200503102/default.htm, accessed June 9, 2005.

[41] Philip R. Lane and Gian Maria Milesi-Ferretti, "A Global Perspective on External Positions," prepared for the NBER conference *G7 Current Account Imbalances: Sustainability and Adjustment*, May 3, 2005, p.12.

[42] Calculated from Bureau of Economic Analysis, International Investment Position data.

[43] Mundell 1998.

[44] Roubini and Setser 2004, p. 21, and Roubini and Setser 2005.

[45] Roubini and Setser 2005, pp. 6 and 34.

[46] Roubini and Setser 2005, p. 17.

[47] Lawrence H. Summers, "The U.S. Current Account Deficit and the Global Economy," Per Jacobsson Lecture, October 3, 2004, p. 6.

[48] Roubini and Setser 2005.

[49] Roger Cohen, "China and the Politics of a U.S. Awash in Debt," *International Herald Tribune*, May 21, 2005.

[50] Calculations based on Federal Reserve data.

[51] See valuation discussion in Tille 2003, which noted: "while changes in foreign trade patterns are likely to emerge only over time, valuation changes have the advantage of taking effect immediately."

52 The Federal Reserve Bank defined seignorage as: "The profit which results from the difference between the cost of making coins and currency and the exchange value of coin and currency in the market." (See www.minneapolisfed.org/glossary.cfm.) In essence, the coins and notes outstanding were like an interest-free loan from currency holders to the issuing central bank.

53 Ricardo Hausmann and Federico Sturzenegger, "Dark Matter Makes the U.S. Deficit Disappear," Financial Times December 8, 2005, p. A15. See also overview in Barry Eichengreen "Global Imbalances: The New Economy, the Dark Matter, the Savvy Investor, and the Standard Analysis," University of California, Berkeley March 2006.

54 Ricardo Hausmann and Federico Sturzenegger, "Can Dark Matter Prevent a Big Bang?" presentation in Cambridge, March 1, 2006.

55 Congress of the United States, Congressional Budget Office, "The Budget and Economic Outlook: An Update; Total Outlays and Revenues as a percentage of gross domestic product," August 2006, available at http://www.cbo.gov/ftpdocs/74xx/doc7492/08-17-BudgetUpdate.pdf, accessed September 14, 2006.

56 Ricardo J. Caballero, Emmanuel Farhi, and Pierre-Olivier Gourinchas, "An Equilibrium Model of 'Global Imbalances' and Low Interest Rates," February 8, 2006.

57 Chairman of the Council of Economic Advisors, 2005 Economic Report of the President, p. 38, available at http://www.gpoaccess.gov/eop, accessed June 9, 2005.

58 The long-run elasticity of U.S. imports with respect to U.S. GDP was 1.8, while the long-run elasticity of U.S. exports with respect to foreign GDP was 0.8, as calculated by Peter Hooper, Karen Johnson, and Jaime Marquez, in "Trade Elasticities for G-7 Countries," Federal Reserve Board of Governors, International Finance Discussion Papers 609, 1998.

59 Mann 2002, p. 138. Phenomenon first noted, as cited in Greenspan 2004, footnote 2, in H. S. Houthakker, and S. P. Magee, "Income and Price Elasticities in World Trade," *Review of Economics and Statistics* 51, May 1969, pp. 111–25.

60 See Mann 2002 for description of "home bias" and Remarks by Chairman Alan Greenspan at the European Banking Congress 2004, Frankfurt, Germany November 19, 2004 for discussion of decrease.

61 Remarks by Vice Chairman Roger W. Ferguson, Jr. to the Economics Club of the University of North Carolina at Chapel Hill, Chapel Hill, North Carolina, April 20, 2005, "U.S. Current Account Deficit: Causes and Consequences," available at http://www.federalreserve.gov/boarddocs/Speeches/2005/20050420/default.htm, accessed October 3, 1996.

62 Remarks by Chairman Alan Greenspan at the 21st Annual Monetary Conference, Cosponsored by the Cato Institute and The Economist, Washington, D.C., November 20, 2003. See also Greenspan 2004, in which Greenspan remarked: "Should globalization be allowed to proceed and thereby create an ever more flexible international financial system, history suggests that current imbalances will be defused with little disruption."

63 See "Wise Men at Ease; the American Economy," *The Economist*, April 30, 2005.

64 Comment made at Foreign Correspondents' Club of Japan March 10, 2005, quoted in various sources, including James Simms, "U.S. Treasury Quarles: Need More Global FX Flexibility," *Dow Jones Newswires*, March 11, 2005.

65 Michael P. Dooley, David Folkerts-Landau, and Peter Garber, "An Essay on the Revived Bretton Woods System," National Bureau of Economic Research Working Paper 9971, September 2003, p. 5.

66 Dooley and Garber 2005, see China: To Float or Not to Float (A), HBSP No. 706-021 for more on this.

67 Lawrence H. Summers, "The U.S. Current Account Deficit and the Global Economy," Per Jacobsson Lecture, October 3, 2004, p. 8.

[68] See summary of Summers' argument in Frederick Kempe, "Thinking Global: U.S., China Stage an Economic Balancing Act; Growing Tensions Will Test Logic That Neither Wants To Declare a Trade War," *The Wall Street Journal,* March 28, 2006.

[69] Summers 2004 for discussion of "balance of financial terror" and for reference to "vendor finance" and Dooley et al., 2003 and 2004 for discussion of "revived Bretton Woods."

[70] See, for example, Lane and Milesi-Ferretti 2005, pp. 16–17.

[71] Jag Dhaliwall and Daniel Moss, "S. Korean Regulator Says Asia Can't Keep Funding U.S. Spending," Bloomberg, March 15, 2005.

[72] Roubini and Setser 2005, pp. 14–15.

[73] Summers 2004, p. 8. See also Elizabeth Becker, "Trade Deficit Narrows to a 6-Month Low," *The New York Times,* May 12, 2005.

[74] Mervyn King, "The International Monetary System," Speech by Mervyn King, Governor of the Bank of England, at the "Advancing Enterprise 2005" conference, London, February 4, 2005, available at http://www.bis.org/review/r050217b.pdf, accessed June 9, 2005. (The open letter was from U.S. senators Schumer, Bunning, Durbin, Graham, Dodd and Bayh to Vice President Richard Cheney, January 22, 2004.)

[75] "China Hits Back in War of Words: Officials Dismiss U.S. Criticism of Yuan Policy; Call Steps to Curb Textile Exports Unfair," May 18, 2005, http://money.cnn.com/2005/05/18/news/international/china.reut/, accessed June 9, 2005.

[76] Truman 2004 (referred to it as "back-of-envelope" calculation).

[77] Michael Mussa, "Exchange Rate Adjustments Needed to Reduce Global Payments Imbalance," in Bergsten, C.F. and J. Williamson (Editors): *Dollar Adjustment: How Far? Against What?* (Institute for International Economics: Washington D.C., November 2004.

[78] Roubini and Setser 2004, pp. 25–26, footnote 38.

[79] Willem Buiter, "Dark Matter or Cold Fusion?" Global Economics Paper No. 136, Goldman Sachs Global Economic Website, January 16, 2006, available at http://www.nber.org/~wbuiter/dark.pdf, September 26, 2006.

[80] Mann 2002, p. 132; and Roubini and Setser 2004, p. 43.

[81] Roubini and Setser 2005, p. 11.

[82] Summers 2004.

[83] Obstfeld and Rogoff 2004.

[84] See, for example, Pierre-Olivier Gourinchas and Hélène Rey "International Financial Adjustment," National Bureau of Economic Research Working Paper 11155, February 2005. They gave a "back-of-envelope" calculation that a 10% depreciation of the dollar represented a transfer of 5% of U.S. GDP from the rest of the world to the United States—compared with a trade deficit on goods and services of 4.4% of GDP in 2003 (p. 2). The paper modeled the problem in detail.

[85] Lane and Milesi-Ferretti 2004.

[86] Summers 2004, p. 12. At the time, Summers was President of Harvard University.

[87] Term "hard landing" used, for example, in "Wise Men at Ease; The American Economy," *The Economist,* April 30, 2005.

[88] Roubini and Setser 2005.

[89] Roubini and Setser 2005, p. 5.

[90] Olivier Blanchard, Francesco Giavazzi, and Filipa Sa, "The U.S. Current Account and the Dollar," National Bureaus for Economic Research Working Paper 11137, January 26, 2005.

[91] Stephen Roach, "In Search of Big Spenders; American consumers spend nearly $9 trillion a year, or 20% more than Europeans. But the binge is now coming to an end," *Newsweek International*, September 11, 2006.

[92] Roubini and Setser 2005, p. 2.

[93] This strategy was first outlined in Communiqué of the International Monetary and Financial Committee (IMFC) of the Board of Governors of the International Monetary Fund October 2, 2004, available at http://www.imf.org/external/np/cm/2004/100204.htm, accessed June 9, 2005. See also IMF World Economic Outlook 2005, pp. 114–115 and 26–27. The report proceeded by chiding the United States for being insufficiently ambitious with the fiscal goal, for failing to include expenses associated with Iraq and Afghanistan, and because of the substantial risk that the objective will not be met.

[94] See, for example, Testimony of Chairman Alan Greenspan before the Committee on the Budget, U.S. House of Representatives, "Economic Outlook and Current Fiscal Issues," March 2, 2005.

[95] "Fiscal Fantasyland; America's budget," *The Economist*, April 9, 2005.

The U.S. Current Account Deficit, Spreadsheet

Harvard Business School Case 706-002
Courseware 706-701

ASSUMPTIONS AND FACTS

Change assumptions (grey fields)
Modify baseline facts (white fields)
Hit Ctrl+r for results
Fill in results table (end of workbook)

theta	1	substitution elasticity between tradable and nontradable goods
mu	2	substition elasticity between imported and domestically produced tradable goods (if *mu*=100, all tradable goods perfect substitutes)
alpha	0.7	US and European weight on home products in tradable goods basket
beta	0.8	(*beta-alpha*)=US and European weight on each others' tradables; [1-*alpha*-(*beta-alpha*)]=US and European weight on Asian tradables
delta	0.7	Asian weight on home products in tradable goods basket
gamma	0.25	share of traded goods in total consumption

notes: 1>*beta*>*alpha*>0.5; *delta*>0.5; (increasing *theta* and *mu* simulates a more gradual unwinding: 2&4 for 5-7 years, 4&8 for 10-12 years).

	start	**new**
US production nontradables/GDP	0.75	
US production tradables/GDP	0.25	
EUR production nontradables/GDP	0.75	
EUR production tradables/GDP	0.25	
Asia production nontradables/GDP	0.75	
Asia production tradables/GDP	0.25	
US current account/tradable US GDP	-0.2	0
EUR current account/tradable US GDP	0.05	0
Asia current account/tradable US GDP	0.15	0
US gross foreign assets ($tns)	8.25	10.02
US gross foreign liab ($tns)	11.00	11.14
EUR gross foreign assets ($tns)	11.00	13.60
EUR gross foreign liab ($tns)	11.00	13.94
Asia gross foreign ass ($tns)	11.00	11.74
Asia gross foreign liab ($tns)	8.25	10.27
interest rate on US liabilities	3.75%	3.75%
interest rate on non-US liabilities	5.00%	

US share of external liab in dollars	96.4%
US shr ext liab in EUR currencies	3.0%
US shr ext liab in Asian currencies	0.6%
US share of ext assets in dollars	40.2%
US shr ext ass in EUR currencies	40.5%
US shr ext ass Asian currencies	19.3%
EUR share of external liab in dollars	20.0%
EUR shr ext liab in EUR currencies	80.0%
EUR shr ext liab in Asian currencies	0.0%
EUR share external assets in dollars	31.8%
EUR shr ext ass in EUR currencies	57.4%
EUR shr ext ass Asian currencies	10.9%
Asia share of external liab in dollars	34.0%
Asia shr ext liab in EUR currencies	33.0%
Asia shr ext liab in Asian currencies	33.0%
Asia share of external assets dollars	80.0%
Asia shr ext ass EUR currencies	20.0%
Asia shr ext ass Asian currencies	0.0%

US tradable GDP ($tns)	2.75
Asia shr ass inv in US (not $ specific)	0.6
EUR shr ass inv in US (not $ specific)	0.4
US shr short-term liab in total liab	0.3

Calculations needed for model:

US prod tradables/EUR prod tradables and US prod tradables/Asian prod tradables

sigma U/E	1.00
sigma U/A	1.00

net income payments as % US tradable GDP

	step 1	**step 2**	**step 3**
r*f U	0.00%	0.00%	3.03%
r*f E	-2.00%	-2.00%	-3.10%
r*f A	2.00%	2.00%	-0.54%

Source: Model developed based on equations presented in Maurice Obstfeld and Kenneth Rogoff, "Global Current Account Imbalances and Exchange Rate Adjustments," prepared for spring 2005 meeting of the Brookings Panel on Economic Activity, draft dated May 16, 2005.

STEP 1					Location in O&R paper
t U,E	0.83847844	terms of trade US versus Europe			
t U,A	0.95308793	terms of trade US versus Asia			
x U	1.23514091	US prices nontraddables/prices tradables			
x E	0.87980267	Europe prices nontradables/price tradedables			
x A	0.87540272	Asia prices nontradables/price tradables			
Equ 1	1.00		1.00	0.000	see page 59
Equ 2	1.00		1.00		see page 60
Equ 3	3.00	sigma N/U	3.00	US production nontradables/production tradables	see page 60
Equ 4	3.00	sigma N/E	3.00	Eur production nontradables/production tradables	see page 60
Equ 5	3.00	sigma N/A	3.00	Asia production nontradables/production tradables	see page 60
q U, E	0.6971	real exchange rate dollar versus European currencies			see page 55
q U, A	0.7476	real exchange rate dollar versus Asian currencies			see page 55

STEP 2				
t U,E	0.98787966	terms of trade US versus Europe		
t U,A	1.12754991	terms of trade US versus Asia		
x U	0.97890446	US prices nontraddables/prices tradables		
x E	0.95416842	Europe prices nontradables/price tradedables		
x A	1.05886981	Asia prices nontradables/price tradables		
Equ 1	1.00		1.00	0.000
Equ 2	1.00		1.00	
Equ 3	3.00	sigma N/U	3.00	US production nontradables/production tradables
Equ 4	3.00	sigma N/E	3.00	Eur production nontradables/production tradables
Equ 5	3.00	sigma N/A	3.00	Asia production nontradables/production tradables
q U, E	0.9737	real exchange rate dollar versus European currencies		
q U, A	1.1250	real exchange rate dollar versus Asian currencies		

STEP 3				
t U,E	0.96286997	terms of trade US versus Europe		
t U,A	1.1018245	terms of trade US versus Asia		
x U	1.0152186	US prices nontraddables/prices tradables		
x E	0.93997234	Europe prices nontradables/price tradedables		step 1
x A	1.0376306	Asia prices nontradables/price tradables		
Equ 1	1.00		1.00	(0.000)
Equ 2	1.00		1.00	
Equ 3	3.00	sigma N/U	3.00	US production nontradables/production tradables
Equ 4	3.00	sigma N/E	3.00	Eur production nontradables/production tradables
Equ 5	3.00	sigma N/A	3.00	Asia production nontradables/production tradables
q U, E	0.9222	real exchange rate dollar versus European currencies		
q U, A	1.0643	real exchange rate dollar versus Asian currencies		

OUTPUT

	step 1	step 2	**change**	step 3	**change (including reval)**	
q u,e	0.6971	0.9737	**33.4%**	0.9222	**28.0%**	real depreciation of $ against european currencies
q u,a	0.7476	1.1250	**40.9%**	1.0643	**35.3%**	real depreciation of the $ against asian currencies
q e,a	1.07245338	1.155406173	**7.5%**	1.154099013	**7.3%**	real depreciation of the european against asian currencies
t u, e	0.83847844	0.987879658	**16.4%**	0.962869967	**13.8%**	real depreciation of terms of trade in US versus Europe
t u, a	0.95308793	1.127549909	**16.8%**	1.101824499	**14.5%**	real depreciation of terms of trade in US versus Asia
t e, a	1.13668746	1.141383871	**0.4%**	1.144312873	**0.7%**	real depreciation of terms of trade in Europe versus Asia

Source: Model developed based on equations presented in Maurice Obstfeld and Kenneth Rogoff, "Global Current Account Imbalances and Exchange Rate Adjustments," prepared for spring 2005 meeting of the Brookings Panel on Economic Activity, draft dated May 16, 2005.

OUTPUT (based on assumptions and facts below)

	log change excluding revaluation effects	log change including revaluation effects	(changes are against two-year average reference rates)
q u,e	**33.4%**	**28.0%**	real depreciation of dollar against European currencies
q u,a	**40.9%**	**35.3%**	real depreciation of dollar against Asian currencies
q e,a	**7.5%**	**7.3%**	real depreciation of European against Asian currencies
t u,e	**16.4%**	**13.8%**	terms of trade US versus European countries
t u,a	**16.8%**	**14.5%**	terms of trade US versus Asian countries
t e,a	**0.4%**	**0.7%**	terms of trade European versus Asian countries

ASSUMPTIONS AND FACTS

theta	1	substitution elasticity between tradable and nontradable goods
mu	2	substition elasticity between imported and domestically produced tradable goods (if mu=100, all tradable goods perfect substitutes)
alpha	0.7	US and European weight on home products in tradable goods basket
beta	0.8	(beta-alpha)=US and European weight on each others' tradables; [1-alpha-(beta-alpha)]=US and European weight on Asian tradables
delta	0.7	Asian weight on home products in tradable goods basket
gamma	0.25	share of traded goods in total consumption

notes: 1>beta>alpha>0.5; delta>0.5; (increasing theta and mu simulates a more gradual unwinding: 2&4 for 5-7 years, longer for 4&8).

	start	new
US production nontradables/GDP	0.75	
US production tradables/GDP	0.25	
EUR production nontradables/GDP	0.75	
EUR production tradables/GDP	0.25	
Asia production nontradables/GDP	0.75	
Asia production tradables/GDP	0.25	
US current account/tradable US GDP	-0.2	0
EUR current account/tradable US GDP	0.05	0
Asia current account/tradable US GDP	0.15	0
US gross foreign assets ($tns)	8.25	10.02
US gross foreign liab ($tns)	11.00	11.14
EUR gross foreign assets ($tns)	11.00	13.60
EUR gross foreign liab ($tns)	11.00	13.94
Asia gross foreign ass ($tns)	11.00	11.74
Asia gross foreign liab ($tns)	8.25	10.27
interest rate on US liabilities	3.75%	3.75%
interest rate on non-US liabilities	5.00%	

US share of external liab in dollars	96.4%
US shr ext liab in EUR currencies	3.0%
US shr ext liab in Asian currencies	0.6%
US share of ext assets in dollars	40.2%
US shr ext ass in EUR currencies	40.5%
US shr ext ass Asian currencies	19.3%
EUR share of external liab in dollars	20.0%
EUR shr ext liab in EUR currencies	80.0%
EUR shr ext liab in Asian currencies	0.0%
EUR share external assets in dollars	31.8%
EUR shr ext ass in EUR currencies	57.4%
EUR shr ext ass Asian currencies	10.9%
Asia share of external liab in dollars	34.0%
Asia shr ext liab in EUR currencies	33.0%
Asia shr ext liab in Asian currencies	33.0%
Asia share of external assets dollars	80.0%
Asia shr ext ass EUR currencies	20.0%
Asia shr ext ass Asian currencies	0.0%

US tradable GDP ($tns)	2.75
Asia shr ass inv in US (not $ specific)	0.6
EUR shr ass inv in US (not $ specific)	0.4
US shr short-term liab in total liab	0.3

Calculations needed for model:

US prod tradables/EUR prod tradables and US prod tradables/Asian prod tradables

sigma U/E	1.00
sigma U/A	1.00

net income payments as % US tradable GDP

	step 1	step 2	step 3
r*f U	0.00%	0.00%	3.03%
r*f E	-2.00%	-2.00%	-3.10%
r*f A	2.00%	2.00%	-0.54%

Source: Model developed based on equations presented in Maurice Obstfeld and Kenneth Rogoff, "Global Current Account Imbalances and Exchange Rate Adjustments," prepared for spring 2005 meeting of the Brookings Panel on Economic Activity, draft dated May 16, 2005.

RESULTS TABLE

	real depreciation of dollar against European currencies	real depreciation of dollar against Asian currencies	real depreciation of European against Asian currencies	change in terms of trade US vs European countries	change in terms of trade US vs Asian countries	change in terms of trade European vs Asian countries
1. Initial baseline facts, all current account balances go to zero, no change in interest rates, no revaluation effects						
2. Initial baseline facts, all current account balances go to zero, no change in interest rates, including revaluation effects						
3. Initial baseline facts, all current account balances go to zero, U.S. interest rates increase to 5%, including revaluation effects						
4. "Slow adjustment" – *theta* set to 2, *mu* to 4, current accounts to 0, with revaluation effects						
5. "Conservative test" – same as 2., but *theta* set to 2 instead of 1						
6. "Testing elimination of terms of trade" – same as 2., but *mu* set to 100 instead of 2						
7. "Milder global rebalancing" – same as 2., but current account balances halve rather than fall to 0						
8. "Symmetric country preferences" – same as 2., but *beta* set to .85						

The U.S. Subprime Mortgage Crisis

HARVARD | BUSINESS | SCHOOL

9-708-036
REV: NOVEMBER 20, 2008

LAURA ALFARO
RENEE KIM

U.S. Subprime Mortgage Crisis: Policy Reactions

Creditworthiness is like oxygen; you don't notice it when it is around.

—Warren Buffet[1]

In March 2008, the U.S. Federal Reserve Board (the "Fed"), in an unprecedented move, played a critical role in orchestrating JPMorgan Chase's purchase of Bear Stearns, the fifth-largest U.S. investment bank. This was no ordinary deal between two investment banks on Wall Street. The Fed had consented to cover up to $29 billion in potential losses from Bear Stearns' risky assets, which were linked to the U.S. subprime mortgage crisis. In a separate move, to ease the economy's credit crunch, the central bank also opened a direct credit line for investment banks for the first time in history. The policy broke away from the traditional practice of directly lending to commercial banks only. These moves were all aimed at restoring investors' confidence amid concerns of the widespread impact of the mortgage crisis.

Even before the Bear Stearns deal, the Fed had made several efforts to prevent the crisis from turning from bad to worse. The Fed had slashed interest rates at the fastest pace in decades, to 2.25% as of March 2008 (see **Exhibit 1**). In a parallel effort, the Bush administration approved a fiscal stimulus package exceeding $150 billion. Yet such measures failed to restore confidence; the dollar tumbled to record lows against major currencies, and many financial markets suffered from declines not seen since the September 11, 2001 terrorist attacks (see **Exhibits 2** and **3**). The International Monetary Fund (IMF) pointed to the U.S. as the "epicenter of the global slowdown" amid lower world growth forecasts[2] (see **Exhibit 4**).

Policy makers, academics, and business leaders were caught in an intense debate over what the best policy response would be moving forward. Some argued for an aggressive monetary and fiscal expansion to prevent a recession in the United States. Additional proposals ranged from the Fed and the Treasury taking on more direct responsibility for financial regulation of investment banks to the provision of aid for the millions of homeowners who faced foreclosures, unable to meet their housing payments. Many critics, however, viewed the Fed's involvement in the Bear Stearns crisis and some of the other proposals advanced to date as a bailout for financial institutions' imprudent lending practices, which had been conducted especially in the subprime mortgage sector; and as a bailout for homeowners' irresponsible borrowings to purchase homes beyond their means.

Professor Laura Alfaro and Research Associate Renee Kim prepared this case. This case was developed from published sources. HBS cases are developed solely as the basis for class discussion. Cases are not intended to serve as endorsements, sources of primary data, or illustrations of effective or ineffective management.

The Housing Boom

Expanding the American dream of homeownership must continue to be our mission. . . . Let's look for every possible reason to approve applicants, not to reject them.

—Angelo Mozilo, CEO, Countrywide Financial[3]

A frenzy of multiple bids on a single house; quick sales and turnover of housing inventory; massive new home constructions. These were just some of the happenings that characterized the booming U.S. housing market in the early 2000s (see **Exhibit 5**). Low interest rates and attractive mortgage rates fueled housing starts to a 25-year high by the end of 2003.[4] House prices surged by 124% in 1997–2006, according to the S&P/Case-Shiller national home-price index.

Financial innovation[5] One sector that particularly benefited during this period was the subprime mortgage market. A subprime mortgage was a loan given to people with poor or no credit history at higher-than-normal rates. Housing for these borrowers, was quite affordable during the boom even at higher premium rates, because interest rates were so low (see **Exhibit 1**). According to the U.S. Department of Housing and Urban Development, the number of lenders, including leading financial institutions such as Merrill Lynch and Citibank, specializing in this type of loans more than tripled to 209 in 2005.

From financial institutions' point of view, the historically low interest rates, coupled with the institutions' own ample liquidity, left them in search of a new sector where they could generate higher returns. They found it in the subprime market. A popular type of subprime mortgage was a "2/28" or "3/27" loan, whereby the borrower would pay a fixed rate for the first two or three years, then pay a variable rate for the remaining years. The initial rate was usually 6% higher than the benchmark six-month London Interbank Offer Rate (LIBOR).[6] With high housing inflation, delinquencies on subprime products went down, permitting favorable rates to continue. Consequently, many subprime borrowers assumed that they could easily refinance at the existing market rates.

In addition, the advancement of sophisticated financial products played a critical role in the expansion of the subprime mortgage market. With traditional mortgage loans, banks' lending capacity had been dependent on the size of their customer deposits. Under the new model, banks sold the mortgages to the bond market, which not only made it easier to fund additional borrowing but also allowed them to make a commission on every mortgage they sold. Loans were often repackaged and sold as securities or instruments known as "collateralized debt obligations" (CDOs). Although estimates varied, one financial institution said there were about $500 to $600 billion in CDOs made of bonds backed by subprime mortgages, out of the $1.5 trillion in global collateralized CDOs.[7] What made CDOs unique was that they represented different types of debts and credit risks. Investment banks believed that they were minimizing risk by selling pooled assets rather than keeping a lump sum of a single high-risk loan on their balance sheets. This new practice allowed these products to receive "AAA" or higher credit ratings from agencies such as Moody's or Standard and Poor's.

Hedge funds, which faced less regulation or supervision compared with traditional banks, were active buyers of these new innovative mortgage-related financial products, willing to risk high leverage for the promise of high capital gains. European and Asian financial institutions also fueled the demand for such securities, which exposed them to subprime-related mortgage products. As one banker noted, "There was fierce competition for these loans. They were a major source of revenues and perceived profits for both the originators and investment banks."[8]

Burst of the bubble When concerns about inflation finally began to emerge in 2004, in June of that year the U.S. Federal Reserve started to hike rates and did not stop until the rate reached 5.25% in June 2006. Homeowners, especially those who took out subprime mortgages, started to feel the impact of higher rates. With homeowners facing the burden of monthly payments beyond their means, the number of defaults on such mortgages and consequent foreclosures of homes rose in early 2007 (see **Exhibit 6**). In his March testimony to the Joint Economic Committee, however, Federal Chairman Ben Bernanke assured Congress that the housing market weakness did not appear "to have spilled over to a significant extent."[9]

The following month, California-based New Century Financial, the second largest subprime lender in 2006, filed for bankruptcy after struggling with buyback demands for defaulting mortgages. Financial institutions started to tighten credit conditions. Additional subprime mortgage-related troubles hit the markets, triggering anxiety and concerns among investors about the level of their exposure to such mortgages (see **Appendix** for chronology of events). Many analysts noted the difficulty of accurately assessing potential losses because the products that made up CDOs had been sliced and re-packaged many times. In July 2007, two hedge funds run by Bear Stearns that were heavily involved in subprime mortgages, were shut down. On August 9, French bank BNP Paribas decided to suspend three funds worth two billion euros, citing difficulty in valuing the funds' assets.

As investors realized that the subprime mortgage problem had spiraled beyond borders, panic struck markets across the globe. On the same day, August 9, the European Central Bank, in what would mark the beginning of many operations, injected 95 billion euros into the market to soothe fears about the subprime credit crunch. The U.S. Federal Reserve took similar action; in fact, its $35 billion injection on August 10 was the largest since the 9/11 terrorist attacks in 2001. Despite these interventions, the crisis continued to unravel and became a global credit crunch, striking major Wall Street firms such as Citibank and Merrill Lynch, which not only wrote off billions of dollars in mortgage-related losses but also forced their CEOs to resign before the year's end (see **Exhibit 7**). On January 22, 2008, the Fed even slashed its federal funds rates by three quarters of a percentage point to 3.5% before its regular monthly meeting, the biggest cut since 1982. As a Fed governor described the situation, "In informal terms, we are uncertain about where the economy has been, where it is now, and where it is going."[10]

What Went Wrong?

The upheaval that began more than two months ago has been called not only a subprime crisis but also a banking crisis, a crisis of liquidity and a crisis of collateral. It has been each of those things, but most of all it has been a crisis of central banking.

—*The Economist*, October 2007[11]

Monetary policy Many experts blamed the crisis on the expansionary monetary policy during the early 2000s that kept interest rates low for so long despite rising asset prices. Among them was Anna Schwartz, an influential economist at the National Bureau of Economic Research, who claimed that "there never would have been a sub-prime mortgage crisis if the Fed had been alert. This is something Alan Greenspan must answer for."[12] John Taylor, an economics professor at Stanford University, argued that the housing bubble could have been avoided if the Fed had applied the "Taylor rule" to determine the interest levels.[13] In his view, the Fed Funds rate should have been higher than its actual rate by at least three percentage points during the early 2000s (see **Exhibit 8**). Even William Poole, president of the Federal Reserve Bank of St. Louis and a voting member of the Fed's policy panel that determined interest rates, admitted, "With the benefit of hindsight . . . it is not hard to argue that the [Fed] was too slow to raise the federal funds target after taking the target down to 1% in 2003."[14]

However, according to then-Fed Chairman Alan Greenspan, he and his colleagues at the Fed believed that "the potential threat of corrosive deflation in 2003 was real" (see **Exhibit 9**). The 1% rate set in mid-2003 was targeted to counter potential deflation after the economy tumbled into a recession after the burst of the dot-com bubble and the 9/11 terrorist attacks.[15] Greenspan also highlighted that long-term interest rates did not rise after the Fed started to raise rates in mid-2004. This puzzling situation, which Greenspan termed a "conundrum," was a deviation from past experiences when long-term interest rates had corresponded to changes in short-term interest rates.

One possible explanation for such trends was that consumers expected housing prices to continue to rise as they had until then. Another explanation was the surge in global savings led by many Asian countries following the 1997–1998 financial crisis and by oil-exporting countries after the increase in oil prices in the 2000s. Bernanke had labeled this phenomenon the "global savings glut," in which worldwide savings soared to 33% of nominal GDP in 2006 from 24% in 1999, outpacing investments, and thus holding down long-term interest rates.[16] Coupled with the worldwide trend of lower inflation, long-term rates seemed to have become less sensitive to movements in short-term rates[17] (see **Exhibit 10**).

In addition, some critics argued that the financial crisis stemmed from the central bank's failure to target asset prices. There were parallels drawn between the United States' current crisis and Japan's economic problems after the burst of its housing and stock market in the 1990s.[18] Stephen Cecchetti, professor at Brandeis University, asserted that a central bank should adjust its policy to *both* inflation and asset prices, since the inclusion of the latter could reduce the likelihood of an asset price bubble.[19] Others disagreed, including Fed Chairman Bernanke, who believed that changes in asset prices should affect monetary policy only to the extent that they affect the central bank's inflation forecast. Bernanke's theory was that as long as there was an aggressive response to inflation, there was no significant benefit to responding to asset prices.[20] Similarly, Greenspan noted that monetary policy had its limits—that "bubbles cannot be safely defused by monetary policy or other policy initiatives before the speculative fever breaks on its own."[21]

Financial supervision Poor regulation was also highlighted as one of the primary causes of the crisis, as financial institutions came under scrutiny about how they actually managed their risk and enforced loan standards. Standard & Poor's estimated that subprime writedowns could reach $285 billion, but other investment banks expected the figure to reach $400 billion.[22] Carmen Reinhart and Kenneth Rogoff, former research directors at the IMF, pointed out: "New unregulated, or lightly regulated, financial entities have come to play a much larger role in the financial system, undoubtedly enhancing stability against some kinds of shocks, but possibly increasing vulnerabilities against others."[23]

The central bank had federal supervision over traditional commercial banks, but not over investment banks, hedge funds, or other firms involved in derivatives or complex financial products such as CDOs. The Securities and Exchange Commission, Bear Stearns' primary regulator, insisted that it had fulfilled its responsibilities, and that the investment bank's failure was "a lack of confidence, not a lack of capital."[24] Half of all subprime loans were written by state-chartered mortgage companies with little supervision. Rating agencies were paid by the very companies whose securities were being rated. Lenders sold products such as "piggyback" loans that did not require the borrower to make a downpayment. One research firm reported that borrowers who did not provide full documents that proved their income or assets surged from 17% of subprime borrowers to 44% in 2006.[25]

But as long as Wall Street was raking in fat profits from innovative financial products during the housing boom, the idea of imposing stricter regulations or control seemed unnecessary. An observer commented that even though some attempts had been made to impose regulations, they were "obstructed by the prevailing belief that the economy did best when financial markets operated as freely as possible."[26] Barney Frank, chair of the House Financial Services Committee, recalled that former Fed Chairman Alan Greenspan "specifically refused to act," while others voiced their doubts that more regulation would have been able to prevent the current crisis.[27]

Closely related to the issue of regulation was the criticism of the financial compensation system of investment banks. Raghuram Rajan, professor at the University of Chicago and former IMF chief economist, blamed the practice of compensating employees regardless of the losses banks had accumulated as contributing to the outbreak of such financial crises. Martin Wolf of the *Financial Times* noted, "By paying huge bonuses on the basis of short-term performance in a system in which negative bonuses are impossible, banks create gigantic incentives to disguise risk-taking as value-creation."[28]

Possible Solutions

Some say the world will end in fire [financial collapse]
Some say in ice [inflation]. . . .

—Robert Frost, as quoted by Harvard economist Kenneth Rogoff[29]

Monetary policy In the short run, the Fed seemed more preoccupied with weak economic growth than price stability, suggesting the possibility of further rate cuts. In February 2008, Fed Chairman Bernanke stated that ". . . it is important to recognize that downside risks to growth remain. The FOMC . . . will act in a timely manner as needed to support growth and to provide adequate insurance against downside risks."[30] Yet the central bank faced a dilemma. Lower interest rates were aimed at reviving liquidity, largely because banks were hesitant to lend amid concerns of a further credit squeeze. Loose monetary policy could also encourage the dollar, which had reached an all-time low against the euro, to remain weak, which could increase net exports and improve the U.S. current account deficit.[31] However, opponents fretted that the Fed was walking down a dangerous path by focusing on economic stimulation while overlooking rising inflation. Inflation, as measured by the Consumer Price Index, had risen 4.3% over the last 12 months as of January, coming close to a 16-year high and even sparking fear of stagflation.[32] Core inflation, which excluded food and energy prices, showed a 2.5% year-on-year increase in January, higher than the Fed's unofficial inflation target range of 1%–2%. Rising oil and commodity prices, coupled with a weak U.S. dollar, reinforced the current upward trend (see **Exhibit 11**). Low interest rates would not help the extremely low U.S. savings rate either, another key factor behind the huge U.S. deficit.

Critics argued that the Fed should rein in inflation now and stop cutting interest rates, rather than risking the chance of inflation spiraling out of control. Allen Meltzer, professor at Carnegie Mellon, argued that the 1970s experience with stagflation was that a country unwilling to accept the possibility of a small recession would end up paying the larger cost of inflation, thus questioning the Fed's willingness to cut interest rates so drastically and quickly.[33] Others claimed that the Fed was risking its commitment to price stability and anti-inflation; this credibility, if lost, could be a lengthy and costly process in contrast to recessions, which tended to be short. However, Bernanke refuted that the economy was heading toward stagflation and suggested that inflation could come down ". . . if slower-than-expected global growth moderates the pressure on the prices of energy and other commodities or if rates of domestic resource utilization fall more than we currently expect."[34]

In addition, the large amount of liquidity injected into the financial system over recent months raised concerns that the Fed contributed to moral hazard, the mentality that banks might escape from taking full responsibility for their actions since the central bank would bail them out. For example, Countrywide, the largest U.S. mortgage lender, received $51 billion in public funds through the Federal Bank Home Loan. Nouriel Roubini, an economics professor at New York University, argued that this was a clear bailout of insolvent mortgage lenders who had engaged in reckless practices.[35]

Many observers questioned the extent to which government should provide assistance and be responsible for "cleaning up" the mess created by financial institutions, especially in light of the dramatic role the Fed played in helping to rescue Bear Stearns from collapsing. On March 14, the Fed and JPMorgan agreed to provide 28-day emergency loans to Bear Stearns, which was facing a severe liquidity squeeze. Two days later, JPMorgan announced that it would buy Bear Stearns for $2 per share, a 93% discount from its last closing price of $30 per share, with a promised $30 billion credit line from the Fed for JPMorgan to purchase the troubled investment bank.[a] The Fed's involvement raised questions about its appropriate role. Critics claimed that the Fed essentially bailed out Bear Stearns which created the danger of encouraging irresponsible financial practices to continue in the future. Alan Blinder, a former Fed vice chairman, insisted that "You're taking on substantial risks when you do something virtually unprecedented or you put money at risk. The Fed has now done both."[36] Former Fed Chairman Paul Volcker, although agreeing that the Fed's judgment was "understandable," argued that the unprecedented move was not "what you want for the longstanding regulatory support system."[37] Others, however, applauded the bold moves by the Fed in times of unprecedented uncertainty. Treasury Secretary Henry Paulson claimed that "We're very aware of moral hazard. But our primary concern right now . . . is the stability of our financial system, the orderliness of the markets."[38]

Fiscal policy Another proposal was to accompany monetary expansion with fiscal stimulus. Former Treasury Secretary Lawrence Summers, for example, argued that fiscal policies would be felt by families bearing the brunt of the recession, contrary to monetary policies that had a more direct impact on financial institutions. In his view, the use of fiscal policy would also "mitigate the various risks of bubble creation associated with excessively low interest rates."[39]

The Bush administration's $150 billion fiscal package included tax rebates for households and individuals and tax cuts for businesses. Most analysts agreed that a fiscal stimulus should be "timely, targeted, and temporary" to be effective.[40] Yet there were doubts as to whether the stimulus package met these requirements. First, the tax rebates were expected for early summer 2008, creating a time lag. However, a fiscal stimulus would need to be implemented more quickly in order to maximize its effectiveness. Second, as Stephen Roach, chairman of Morgan Stanley Asia, argued, "Government aid is being aimed, mistakenly, at maintaining unsustainably high rates of personal consumption"; Roach asserted that this was exactly what got the U.S. into the subprime mess in the first place in the form of low national savings and a huge trade deficit.[41] He asserted that aid should target low-income consumers or unemployed workers who would spend the money they'd received and thus boost demand. A greater concern was that as households faced excessive debt, the rebates could be used to repay existing debts rather than for consumer spending. In fact, one poll found that 45% of the people planned to pay off bills and only 19% planned to spend their rebates.[42] Third, some worried that if stimulus measures such as tax cuts dragged on rather than being short-term temporary measures, they might only worsen the nation's budget deficit.

---

[a] The deal was revised a week later with JPMorgan raising the purchase price to $10 per share amid intense opposition from Bear Stearns' shareholders and trading partners. The Fed's agreement to cover up to $30 billion in potential losses from Bear Stearns' risky assets was reduced to $29 billion, with JP Morgan agreeing to meet the other $1 billion.

Financial regulation Many critics advanced the need for more stringent regulation standards and supervision. This applied to financial institutions' failure to fully disclose the risks of their loans and the possibility of higher interest rates that subprime mortgages borrowers would have to pay at a later date. In other words, the riskiest products were sold to borrowers who lacked proper information and tools to properly assess the loans they were taking out. And buyers of the special asset-backed securities had little idea of the quality of the different underlying assets that were pooled. Some argued that the central bank should focus more on financial institutions' liquidity management to better assess risks associated with liquidity, or even take on the responsibility of supervising investment banks. James Dimon, JPMorgan's chief executive, admitted that "We have a terribly global world and, over all, financial regulation has not kept up with that."[43] However, greater financial regulation touched on the broader debate of *laissez-faire* economics—to what extent should governments and policy makers leave the financial sector to operate according to free market principles?

Other measures Given that the crisis had originated with the burst of the housing bubble, some analysts advocated that policies should focus on fixing problems in the housing sectors rather than trying to use low interest rates to solve the problem. In March 2008, the government had temporarily the increased mortgage loan limit of federal housing agencies such as Fannie Mae and Freddie Mac to $729,750 from $417,000, with the hope that it would stimulate home purchases and mortgage refinances and thus increase actual consumer spending or investment. The fear was that the higher Fannie Mae and Freddie Mac loan limits could lead to more homeowners overextending their finances again and creating bigger additional bad loans, a burden which would ultimately fall on taxpayers.

Additional proposals involved increasing the government's role in resolving the crisis, such as allowing bankruptcy judges to alter the terms of some mortgages facing foreclosure and making it easier for borrowers to switch into more affordable loans backed by the government. Yet Treasury Secretary Paulson opposed such measures, claiming that "Most of the proposals I've seen would do more harm than good—bailing out investors, lenders or speculators who, instead of getting a free-pass, should be accountable for the risks they took."[44]

As the global credit crunch and anxieties over the subprime meltdown showed few signs of easing as of March 2008, additional policy measures seemed necessary. Volcker commented, "We've got a lot of work to do [regarding] what we do with the regulatory system, the supervisory system, what the role of the Federal Reserve is, what the role of the Treasury and the government is, because this is a different financial market."[45]

Appendix

Timeline of Events

2007	
February 7	California-based New Century Financial Corp., the second-largest subprime lender in 2006, said it would have to restate earnings for the first three quarters of last year amid losses from higher-than-expected loan repurchases. HSBC Holdings, Europe's biggest bank, also warned that its bad debts would surge beyond $10 billion in 2006, about 20% higher than analysts' average forecast, blaming rising delinquencies in its subprime loans in the U.S. market.
March 12	Trading of New Century Financial shares were suspended amid rumors of a possible bankruptcy and after the lender said it could not meet creditors' demands to buy back defaulting mortgages. A few days earlier, the company stopped making loans because its own lenders, including Bank of America and Citigroup, cut off financing to New Century.
April 2	New Century Financial filed for bankruptcy protection. It announced that it would slash 3,200 jobs, more than half of its work force.
April 24	The National Association of Realtors said sales of existing homes tumbled 8.5% in March from February, the biggest month-to-month drop in 18 years.
June 12	RealtyTrac, which provided foreclosure listings in the United States, said foreclosure filings jumped 90% in May compared with the same period last year.
June 22	Bear Stearns announced that it would spend $3.2 billion to bail out one of its subprime hedge funds. At the same time, it tried to raise external funds from other banks to rescue another fund.
July 18	Bear Stearns said its two hedge funds with heavy exposure to the subprime market had lost over 90% of their value, equivalent to over $1.4 billion.
July 20	Fed Chairman Bernanke warned that there would be "significant losses" from subprime mortgages and that problems were likely to "get worse before they get better."[46]
July 27	Fears about the subprime mortgage crisis spread rapidly and hammered global stock markets; the Dow Jones dove 4.2% in five sessions.
July 31	Bear Stearns turned back clients trying to withdraw their money from a third hedge fund, citing that it had been overwhelmed with withdrawal requests. The bank also filed for bankruptcy protection for the two funds it unsuccessfully tried to bail out.
August 5	Warren Spector, Bear Stearns' co-president, resigned.
August 6	American Home Mortgage, another home loan provider, filed for bankruptcy, citing the slumping housing market and problems with subprime mortgages.
August 9	BNP Paribas, a French bank, suspended three investment funds worth two billion euros, citing that it could not value the assets in the fund due to problems with their subprime exposure. The European Central Bank (ECB) decided to inject 95 billion euros into the market to try and calm it down. The U.S. Federal Reserve and Bank of Japan took similar action.
August 10	The ECB provided an additional 61 billion euros in funds; London's benchmark FTSE 100 lost 3.7%, its worse trading day in more than four years.
August 13	The ECB conducted its third cash injection that month, 47.7 billion euros; the U.S. Fed and Bank of Japan took similar measures as well.
August 17	The Fed cut the Fed discount rate by half a point.
August 31	Fed Chairman Bernanke tried to reassure investors that the Fed would "act as needed" to contain the mortgage crisis from spreading even further.
September 14	Northern Rock, the biggest mortgage lender in the United Kingdom, received emergency funding from the Bank of England, as it suffered from a severe liquidity squeeze linked to the U.S. subprime mortgage problems. The news sparked a bank run for a few days, the first in the nation in over a century, which was contained only after the government said it would guarantee all deposits held at Northern Rock.
September 18	RealtyTrac revealed that home foreclosure filings in the U.S. surged 115% in August from the same period last year, the highest number of such filings since the company started to keep records of the foreclosures. The same day, the Fed cut the Fed Funds rate by half a percentage point to 4.75%, the biggest rate cut in almost five years. The Dow Jones rallied to close up 2.51% to 13,739.39.

October 1	Former Fed Chairman Alan Greenspan warned, "As in similar situations of inventory excess, I would expect home price declines to continue until the rate of inventory liquidation reaches its peak."[47]
October 29	Merrill Lynch's CEO Stanley E. O'Neal resigned after the company suffered its biggest quarterly loss in its history due to subprime-related losses.
November 4	Citigroup announced that it would suffer an additional $8–$11 billion subprime-related writedown, on top of the $6 billion writedown announced in the previous month. CEO Charles Prince tendered his resignation.
November 29	RealtyTrac said foreclosure filings now represented one closure for every 555 households in the nation, indicating that the situation was getting worse.
December 18	The U.S. Commerce Department reported that housing construction fell 3.7% to a seasonally adjusted rate of 1.2 million units in November, marking the lowest level of home constructions in more than 16 years.
December 20	Bear Stearns posted its first quarterly loss in eight decades, including a $1.9 billion writedown on its mortgage assets. The announcement brought Wall Street's combined losses from the subprime mortgage crisis to $40 billion.
2008	
January 11	Bank of America agreed to buy Countrywide Financial Corp for $4 billion, rescuing the nation's largest mortgage lender from declaring bankruptcy. The previous day, Countrywide said its late mortgage payments and foreclosures in December 2006 reached their highest level ever recorded, causing its shares to nosedive.
January 22	The Fed slashed interest rates by three-quarters of a percentage point before its regularly scheduled meeting.
February 17	Northern Rock was nationalized, and trading of its shares was suspended after two failed attempts to sell the troubled lender.
February 28	Bernanke, at his congressional testimony, denied concerns of stagflation, saying, "I don't think we were anywhere near the situation that prevailed in the 1970s."[48]
March 6	The latest quarterly housing market survey from Mortgage Bankers Association's revealed that over 900,000 households were in the foreclosure process, up 71% from a year ago; subprime adjustable-rate mortgages accounted for 42% of the foreclosures.
March 11	The Federal Reserve announced that it would lend up to $200 billion to major investment banks and accept a wider variety of securities as collateral, including hard-to-sell mortgage-backed securities, to ease the credit squeeze. Other foreign central banks, including the European Central Bank and Bank of England, agreed to participate as well. The Dow Jones index surged 416.66 points to 12,156.81, the biggest point gain in over five years. However, enthusiasm was short-lived, and the Dow retreated the next day amid skepticism that the Fed's move was only a short-term solution.
March 13	The U.S. dollar fell below 100 yen during trading for the first time since November 1995.
March 13	Carlyle Capital Corporation, a major hedge fund, collapsed from its exposure to mortgage-backed securities. Bear Stearns' shares tumbled amid concerns of the investment bank's exposure to Carlyle as its major creditor.
March 14	Bear Stearns' CEO Alan Schwartz said its liquidity position had "significantly deteriorated" and would receive an emergency credit line from JPMorgan and the Federal Reserve.
March 16	JPMorgan agreed to buy Bear Stearns for $236 million, or $2 per share. The Fed also agreed to shoulder up to $30 billion in potential losses from Bear Stearns' troubled assets.
March 18	The Federal Reserve cut rates again (by an 8-2 vote), reducing its Fed Funds target rate by 75 basis points to 2.25%. Short-term rates were now three full points lower than September 7, signalling the fastest pace of cutting rates in decades. The Dow Jones surged 420.41 points, or 3.5%, to close at 12,392.66.
March 24	JPMorgan revised the terms of its Bear Stearns deal after bitter protest from Bear's shareholders and employees over the initial deal. The new bid valued Bear Stearns at about $1.2 billion, or $10 per share, and gave JPMorgan a 39.5% stake in the company. The Fed's agreement to take up to $30 billion of potential losses from Bear Stearns' illiquid assets, such as mortgage securities, was reduced to $29 billion, with JPMorgan agreeing to take on $1 billion.

Source: Casewriters.

Exhibit 1a Effective Fed Funds Rate (%)

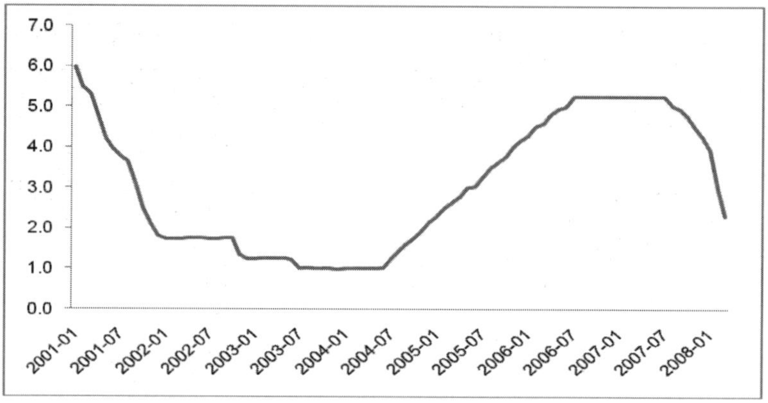

Exhibit 1b 10-Year Treasury Rate—Constant Maturity, Quoted on Investment Basis, and Inflation-Indexed (%)

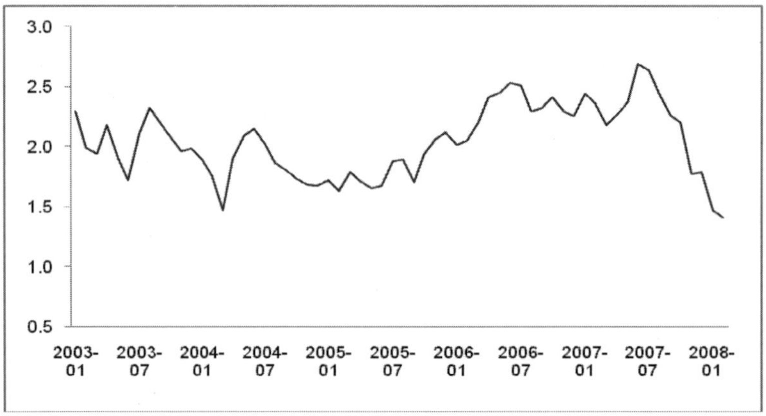

Source: Created by casewriter using data from the U.S. Federal Reserve Board.

Exhibit 2a Japanese Yen/US Dollar Exchange Rate

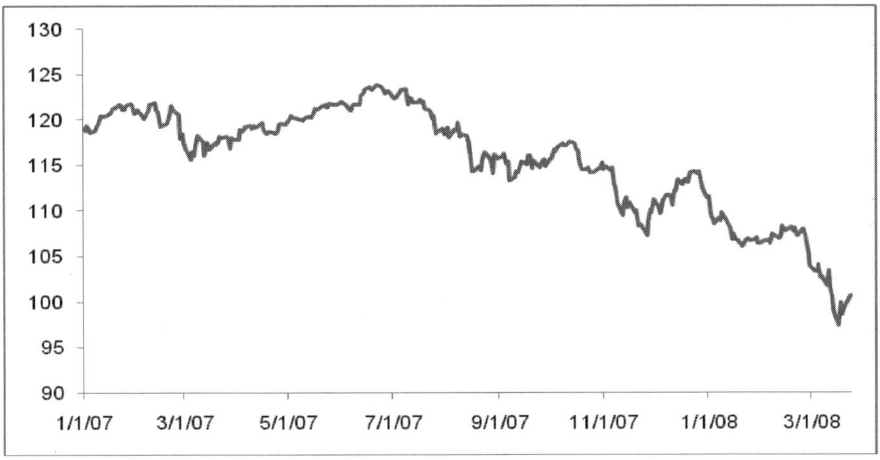

Exhibit 2b Euro/US Dollar and British Pound/US Dollar Exchange Rate

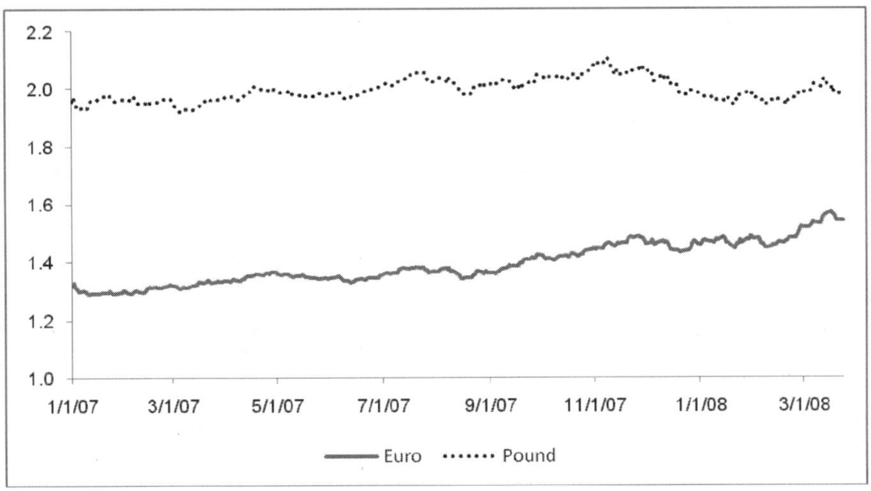

Source: Created by casewriter using data from Global Financial Data, Inc.

Exhibit 3 Global Financial Markets

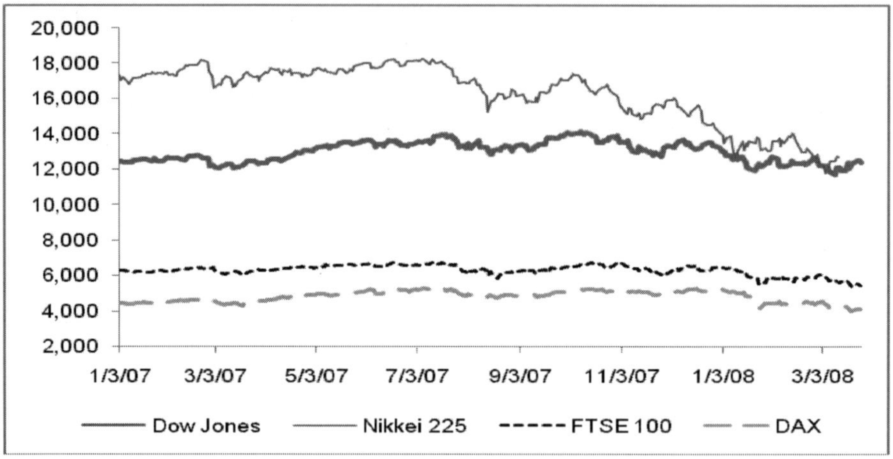

Source: Created by casewriter using data from Global Financial Data, Inc.

Exhibit 4 IMF World Economic Outlook Global Growth Forecast (%)

	2005	2006	Estimates 2007	Projections 2008	Difference from October 2007 Projections 2007	Difference from October 2007 Projections 2008
World Output	4.4	5.0	4.9	4.1	0.2	-0.3
Advanced Economics	2.5	3.0	2.6	1.8	0.1	-0.4
Of which:						
United States	3.1	2.9	2.2	1.5	0.3	-0.4
Euro Area (15)	1.5	2.8	2.6	1.6	0.1	-0.5
Japan	1.9	2.4	1.9	1.5	-0.1	-0.2
Other advanced economies	3.2	3.7	3.8	2.8	0.1	-0.2
Emerging market and developing economies	7.0	7.7	7.8	6.9	0.2	-0.2
Africa	5.9	5.8	6.0	7.0	-	-0.2
Central and eastern Europe	5.6	6.4	5.5	4.6	-0.3	-0.6
Commonwealth of Indep. States	6.6	8.1	8.2	7.0	0.5	-
Developing Asia	9.0	9.6	9.6	8.6	-	-0.1
Of which						
China	10.4	11.1	11.4	10.0	-0.1	-
Middle East	5.6	5.8	6.0	5.9	0.1	-0.1
Western Hemisphere	4.6	5.4	5.4	4.3	0.5	-

Source: International Monetary Fund, "World Economic Outlook Update," January 2008, http://www.imf.org/external/pubs/ft/weo/2008/update/01/index.htm, accessed March 3, 2008.

Exhibit 5 S&P/Case-Shiller Home Price Indices[a]

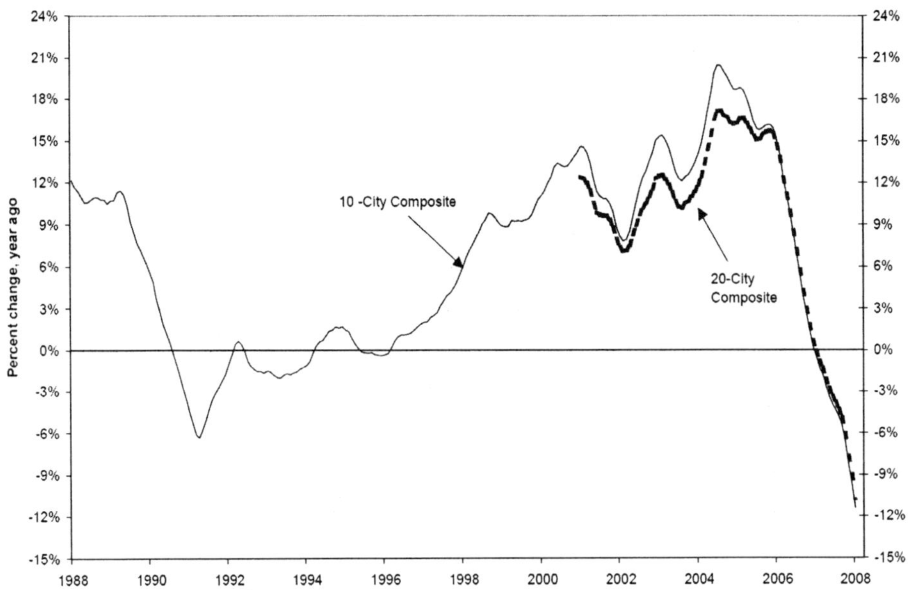

Source: Standard & Poor's, "Record declines in home prices continued in 2008, according to the S&P/Case-Shiller home price indices," press release, March 25, 2008, p. 1.

[a]The S&P/Case-Shiller U.S. National index tracks the value of single-family housing and covers all loans, including non-traditional loans, "jumbo" loans exceeding $417,000, and subprime loans. Geographically, it covers about 70% of the country. The 10-City Composite Index is a value-weighted average of 10 metro areas including Boston, Chicago, Denver, Las Vegas, Los Angeles, Miami, New York, San Diego, San Francisco, and Washington, D.C. The 20-City Composite index includes those in the 10-City Index plus Atlanta, Charlotte, Cleveland, Dallas, Detroit, Minneapolis, Phoenix, Portland, Seattle, and Tampa.

Exhibit 6 Mortgage Defaults and Foreclosures Rates[a]

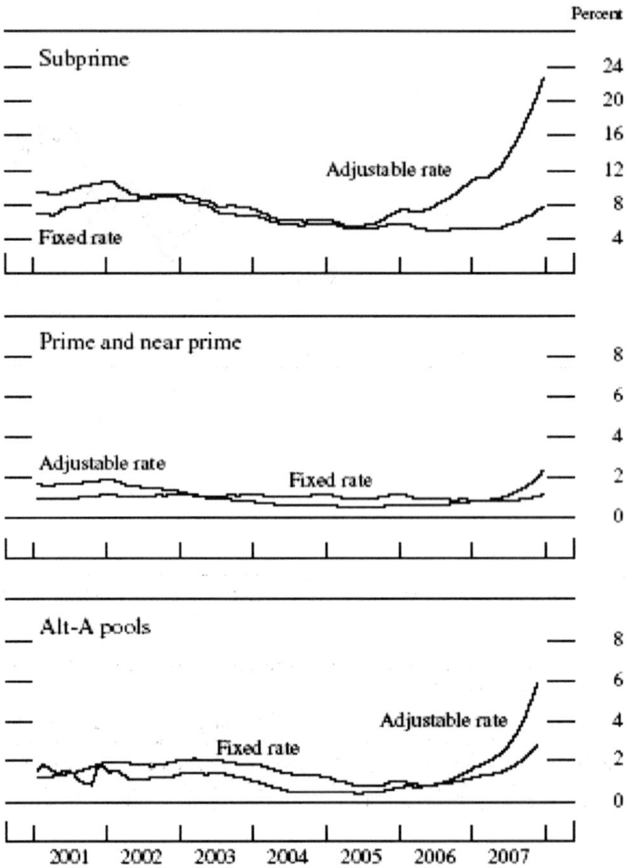

Source: "Monetary Policy Report to the Congress," Board of Governors of the Federal Reserve System, February 27, 2008, p. 5.

[a] Data is monthly and extends through December 2007, except the "Alt-A pools," which extends through November 2007. "Alt-A" pool mortgages refers to a mix of prime, near-prime, and subprime mortgages.

Exhibit 7 Global Financial Institutions' Writedowns Related to the Subprime Crisis

	Writedowns for 4Q 2007 (in $ billions)
Bear Stearns	1.9
Citigroup	18.0
Credit Suisse Group[a]	2.9
Goldman Sachs[b]	-
JPMorgan	1.3
Lehman Brothers[b]	3.5
Merrill Lynch[c]	16.7
Morgan Stanley	9.4
UBS AG	13.7
HSBC	3.4

Source: Created by casewriter using data from "Global investment banks and brokers remain challenged after dismal fiscal year end," Standard & Poor's, February 26, 2008.

[a]Chris Hughes, "Credit Suisse plunges on $2.85bn writedown," *Financial Times*, February 19, 2008.

[b]Stephen Bernard, "Goldman Sachs 4th-quarter earnings, risk management make it winner among U.S. investment banks," Associated Press, December 20, 2007.

[c] Includes ABS CDOs, subprime mortgages, and leveraged finance exposures.

Exhibit 8 Fed Funds Rate versus the Counterfactual Fed Funds Rate (%)

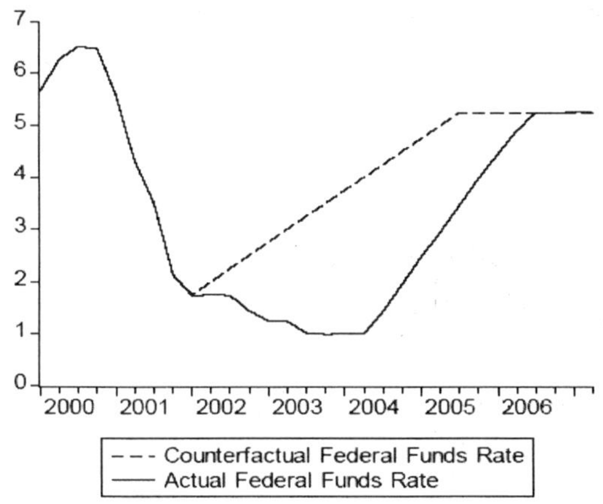

Source: John B. Taylor, "Housing and Monetary Policy," September 2007, p. 3, http://www.stanford.edu/~johntay/, accessed February 15, 2008.

Exhibit 9 Consumer Price Inflation (%)

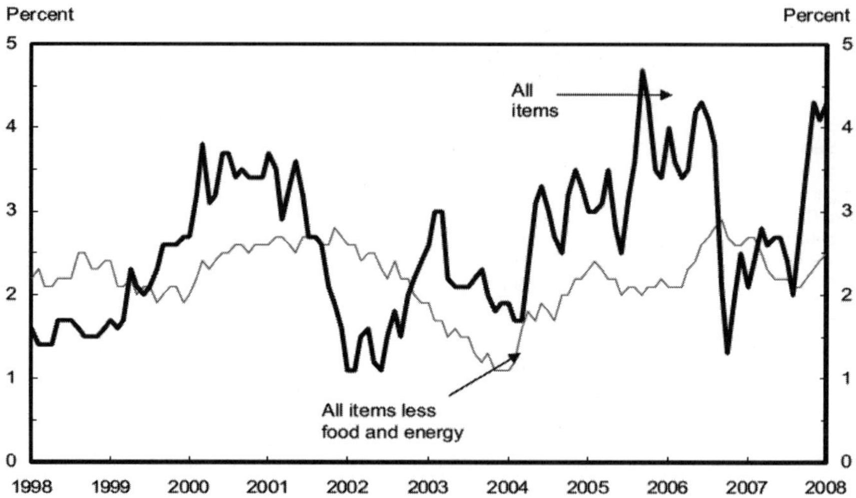

Source: Bureau of Labor Statistics, "Consumer Price Index Detailed Report," January 2008, p. 3.

Exhibit 10 Trend of Consumer Prices for Major Foreign Economics (%)

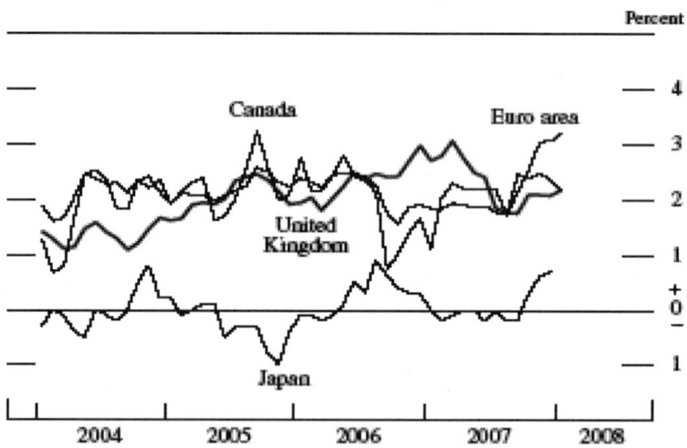

Source: Board of Governors of the Federal Reserve System, "Monetary Policy Report to the Congress," February 27, 2008, p. 34.

Exhibit 11 Oil Prices (US$ per barrel)[a]

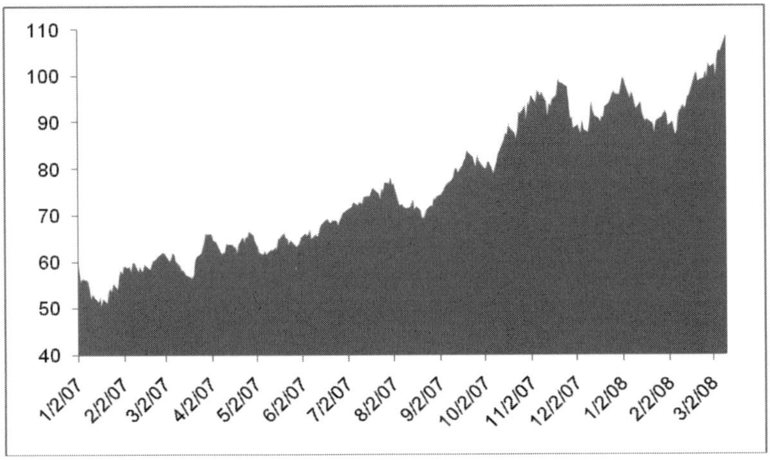

Source: Created by casewriter using data from Global Financial Data, Inc.

[a]Based on the spot price of West Texas intermediate crude oil.

Endnotes

[1] Francesco Guerrera, "Man in the news; the veteran of value," *Financial Times*, February 15, 2008.

[2] Suzy Jagger and Grainne Gilmore, "IMF pulls down forecast for global growth as problems mount in US," *The Times*, January 30, 2008.

[3] "Countrywide's Chairman Mozilo delivers John T. Dunlop Lecture," PR Newswire, February 4, 2003.

[4] John B. Taylor," Housing and monetary policy," National Bureau of Economic Research working paper 13682, http://www.nber.org/papers/w13682, accessed January 30, 2008.

[5] This section is largely based on Julio Rotemberg, "Subprime Meltdown: American Housing and Global Financial Turmoil," HBS No. 708-042 (Boston: Harvard Business School Publishing, 2008).

[6] Eric Rosengren, president and CEO of Federal Reserve Bank of Boston, in a speech titled "Subprime mortgage problems: Research, opportunities and policy considerations," Boston, Mass., December 3, 2007, http://www.bos.frb.org/news/speeches/rosengren/2007/120307.pdf, accessed February 5, 2008.

[7] Jenny Anderson and Heather Timmons, "Why a U.S. subprime mortgage crisis is felt around the world," *New York Times*, August 31, 2007.

[8] Jenny Anderson and Vikas Bajaj, "Wary of risk, bankers sold shaky mortgage debt," *New York Times*, December 6, 2007.

[9] Joint Economic Committee, "Subprime Mortgage Crisis Timeline," January 2008, http://jec.senate.gov/Documents/Reports/01%2023%2008%20subprime%20timeline.pdf, accessed February 22, 2008.

[10] "Only Human," *The Economist*, October 20, 2007.

[11] "CSI: Credit Crunch," *The Economist*, October 20, 2007.

[12] Ambrose Evans-Pritchard, "Anna Schwartz blames Fed for sub-prime crisis," *The Telegraph*, January 13, 2008.

[13] The "Taylor Rule" claimed that if output exceeded long-run capacity, or if inflation was higher than the Fed's target level, interest rates should be higher (i.e., adopt a "tight" monetary policy). See John Taylor, "Discretion versus policy rules in practice," Carnegie-Rochester Conference Series on Policy 39 (1993): 195–214.

[14] Greg Ip, "For the Fed, a recession—not inflation—poses a greater threat," *The Wall Street Journal*, March 3, 2008.

[15] Alan Greenspan, "The roots of the mortgage crisis," *The Wall Street Journal*, December 12, 2007.

[16] Ibid. For more information about Asian countries, such as China, building up their foreign reserves, see Laura Alfaro, Rafael Di Tella, and Ingrid Vogel, "China: To Float or Not to Float? (A)," HBS No. 706-021 (Boston: Harvard Business School Publishing, 2006). See also Ben Bernanke speech, "The global savings glut and the U.S. current account deficit," presented at Virginia Association of Economists, Richmond, Va., March 10, 2005, http://www.federalreserve.gov/ boarddocs/speeches/2005/20050414/default.htm, accessed February 14, 2008.

[17] For more information, see Tao Wu, "Globalization's Effects on Interest Rates and the Yield Curve," Federal Reserve Bank of Dallas, September 2006, http://www.dallasfed.org/research/eclett/2006/e10609.html, accessed February 14, 2008. For a counter explanation, see Josephine M. Smith and John Taylor, "The Long and the Short End of the Term Structure of Policy Rules," Stanford University, November 2007.

[18] For more on Japan's asset bubble and its monetary policy, see Laura Alfaro and Akiko Kanno, "*Kinyuseisaku*: Monetary Policy in Japan," HBS No. 708-017 (Boston: Harvard Business School Publishing, 2008).

[19] Stephen G. Cecchetti et al., "Asset Prices and Central Bank Policy," Geneva Reports on the World Economy 2 (London: Centre for Economic Policy Research, 2000), p. 2.

[20] Ben S. Bernanke and Mark Gertler, "Should Central Banks Respond to Movements in Asset Prices?" http://www.princeton.edu/~bernanke/asset.doc, p. 1, accessed August 13, 2007.

[21] Greenspan, "The roots of the mortgage crisis."

[22] Maurna Desmond, "S&P sights end of subprime nightmare," *Forbes*, March 13, 2008.

[23] Carmen Reinhart and Kenneth Rogoff, "Is the 2007 U.S. Subprime financial crisis so different? An international historical comparison," January 7, 2008, http://www.economics.harvard.edu/faculty/rogoff/files/Is_The_US_Subprime_Crisis_So_Different.pdf, accessed February 1, 2008.

[24] Nelson D. Schwartz and Julie Creswell, "What created this monster?" *New York Times*, March 23, 2008.

[25] Greg Ip, James Hagerty, and Jonathan Karp, "Housing bust fuels blame game," *The Wall Street Journal*, February 27, 2008.

[26] Ibid.

[27] Schwartz and Creswell, "What created this monster?"

[28] Martin Wolf, "Why regulators should intervene in bankers' pay," *Financial Times*, January 16, 2008.

[29] Martin Wolf, "The rescue of Bear Stearns makes liberalisation's limit," *Financial Times*, March 25, 2008.

[30] Ben S. Bernanke, "Semiannual Monetary Policy Report to the Congress," Testimony, February 27, 2008, http://www.federalreserve.gov/newsevents/testimony/bernanke20080227a.htm, accessed February 28, 2008. ("FOMC" stands for Federal Open Market Committee.)

[31] Bernanke indicated that U.S. real exports of goods and services increased about 11% in the second half of 2007, which probably narrowed the U.S. current account deficit for the first time since 2001. See Ben S. Bernanke, "Semiannual Monetary Policy Report to the Congress," February 27, 2008. For more about the U.S. current account deficit, see Laura Alfaro, Rafael Di Tella, and Ingrid Vogel, "The U.S. Current Account Deficit," HBS No. 706-002 (Boston: Harvard Business School Publishing, 2006).

[32] "Stagflation" refers to the U.S. economy during 1970–1981 when inflation was in the double digits while the economy suffered from a recession and high unemployment. Inflation was finally brought down, but only after then-Fed Chairman Paul Volcker raised interest rates, which caused a recession in 1981–1982.

[33] Allan H. Meltzer, "That '70s show," *The Wall Street Journal*, February 28, 2008.

[34] Bernanke, "Semiannual Monetary Policy Report to the Congress."

[35] Nouriel Roubini, "The stealth public bailout of reckless 'Countrywide'," RGE Monitor, November 27, 2007. One barometer of "best-practice" lending was Walter Bagehot's idea that the central bank should act as the lender of last resort by lending "quickly, freely and readily" during times of crises against good collateral, but at a penalty rate to minimize moral hazard. See "What would Bagehot do?" *The Economist*, August 17, 2007.

[36] Edmund L. Andrews, "Rescue tests the Fed's credibility," *New York Times*, March 18, 2008.

[37] "Volcker: Fed's 'extreme' intervention 'raises some real questions,'" March 18, 2008, http://blogs.wsj.com/economics/2008/03/18/volcker-feds-extreme-intervention-raises-some-real-questions.

[38] "Paulson defends bailout of Bear," Associated Press, March 16, 2008.

[39] Lawrence Summers, "Why America must have a fiscal stimulus," *Financial Times*, January 7, 2008.

[40] Ibid.

[41] Stephen Roach, "Double bubble trouble," *New York Times*, March 5, 2008.

[42] "Rebate checks in the mail by spring," Associated Press, February 14, 2008.

[43] Schwartz and Creswell, "What created this monster?"

[44] Secretary Henry M. Paulson, Jr., "US Housing and Mortgage Market Update Before the National Association of Business Economists," Department of the Treasury, Press Release No. HP-856, March 3, 2008.

[46] Bernanke, "Semiannual Monetary Policy Report to Congress," July 18, 2007.

[47] Joint Economic Committee, "Subprime Mortgage Crisis Timeline," January 2008.

[48] Neil Irwin, "Bernanke doesn't see stagflation; picture, however, isn't pretty," *Washington Post*, February 29, 2008.

9-709-045
REV: APRIL 16, 2009

LAURA ALFARO
RENEE KIM

U.S. Subprime Mortgage Crisis: Policy Reactions (B)

Now is the time to act boldly and wisely – to not only revive this economy, but to build a new foundation for lasting prosperity.

—President Barack Obama[1]

By March 2009, one year had passed since the U.S. Federal Reserve Board (the "Fed") had orchestrated JPMorgan Chase's purchase of investment bank Bear Stearns in an effort to stem the subprime mortgage crisis from spiraling out of control.[2] However, the situation had turned from bad to worse. Several big companies that represented the heart of America's financial system, including Lehman Brothers and insurance giant AIG, had faltered. In fact, the United States had plunged into the worst financial crisis and recession not seen since the Great Depression. More than five million jobs had been axed since the recession began, coupled with a massive loss of wealth and depressed consumer confidence.

The Bush administration attempted to breathe life back into the economy by pushing for a stimulus package and creating various lending programs for debt-ridden banks. The Fed dropped interest rates to near zero percent and expanded the type of assets it would buy from financial institutions in an effort to ease credit and restore confidence. Yet as the economy showed few signs of turning around anytime soon, now, the responsibility fell on newly elected President Barack Obama. One of his first agendas was to push for a massive $787 billion bailout package within a month of taking over the oval office.

The question was—would the various rescue plans work? What really had to be done to tackle the battered financial system that traced its origins back to the subprime mortgage crisis that first broke out in 2007? What were the short and long-term consequences of the new stimulus measures that provoked fierce debates about rising nationalism and protectionism?

Monetary Policy

The economic repercussions of a stock market crash depend less on the severity of the crash itself than on the response of economic policymakers, particularly central bankers.

—Ben Bernanke, 2000[3]

Professor Laura Alfaro and Research Associate Renee Kim prepared this case. This case was developed from published sources. HBS cases are developed solely as the basis for class discussion. Cases are not intended to serve as endorsements, sources of primary data, or illustrations of effective or ineffective management.

Following the Bear Stearns deal, U.S. policymakers had hoped that the stressful U.S. financial situation would come under control. Yet neither the housing market nor credit market showed signs of improvement. Then in September 2008, the Treasury nationalized Fannie Mae and Freddie Mac, two of the nation's biggest mortgage lenders, which collectively held more than $5 trillion in assets. Their problems were rooted in using government subsidized financing to buy mortgage-backed securities, including subprime mortgages, which ended up ballooning into billions of dollars of losses they could no longer cover with their capital anymore.

One week later, Lehman Brothers, the fourth largest U.S. investment bank, filed for bankruptcy, rattling markets into a panic attack. It was the biggest corporate bankruptcy since telecom company WorldCom in 2002. Rumors of financial troubles sent shares to nosedive 95% within a few days while Lehman feverishly sought to find a buyer. Yet potential candidates walked away. Some observers claimed that Lehman's CEO Dick Fuel acted too late by failing to come to terms with the extent of the company's problems to seek a buyer sooner. Others pointed out that the Fed did not help to bailout Lehman, such as offering prospective buyers the kind of financial backing it did for JPMorgan's takeover of Bear Stearns.

In making a stance that the government would not always bailout banks for their reckless behaviors, the *Economist* noted that "...the government had provided a painful lesson in the dangers of doing the right thing at the wrong time."[4] Markets interpreted the event as a signal that if Lehman could fall, no major financial institution was safe. Adding to the escalating anxiety was Merrill Lynch's announcement that the venerable investment bank decided to sell itself to Bank of America for $50 billion amid fears of its own survival. Credit markets froze, banks bolted their lending doors to one another, and even the Fed's decision to save AIG with an emergency $85 billion loan in exchange for a 80% stake in the insurance company a few days later did little to halt the shock waves that were spreading throughout the global financial markets like a tsunami (see **Appendix** and **Exhibit 1**).

The Fed reacted by continuing its path of aggressively cutting interest rates. During October, the Fed funds rate (the rate banks charge to each other for lending their reserves) was lowered a full percentage point to 1%, which included a coordinated rate cut with other central banks around the world (see **Exhibit 2**). At the same time, collapsing consumer demand meant that rising inflation no longer represented a threat as prices, especially oil, reversed their trend and started to tumble rapidly within a short period; in November, the seasonally adjusted consumer price index (CPI) fell 1.7%, following October's 1% drop (see **Exhibit 3**). This triggered a different concern, the dreaded "D" word—deflation—a persistent decline of goods and services.

As seen in the 1930's, many feared that prolonged deflation could lead to a deeper and longer recession as deflation encouraged people to defer purchases under the expectation that goods would probably be cheaper in a few months. Weak demand would also cause businesses to refrain from making new investments or increasing production. Perhaps more troubling was that deflation raised the real value of debt at a time when the average U.S. household debt already reached more than 140% of their disposable income.

"Helicopter" Ben?

As the situation failed to improve, the Fed took a drastic measure in December 2008. For the first time in its 95-year history, the central bank set a target Fed funds rate range of 0%-0.25%. Prepared to "employ all available tools to promote the resumption of sustainable growth and to preserve price stability," the Fed deployed a new policy measure aimed at creating liquidity which would thereby increase the central bank's balance sheet.[5] This was similar to 'quantitative easing,' an approach used by Japan between 2001 and 2006 when it was trying to combat deflation.[6] The main difference with Japan's quantitative easing and the Fed's action was that the Bank of Japan targeted to increase the amount of reserves while the Fed focused to increase its assets. Often referred to as a central bank's last resort, the idea was to directly buy government and other bank assets, including mortgage-based securities, to hopefully resume private credit market functions back to more normal levels.[7] Indeed, between September 2008 and January 2009, the monetary base had nearly doubled (see **Exhibit 4**).

The new attempt came with its share of high risks. The Fed had to keep a vigilant watch over inflation to make sure it did not get out of hand once growth resumed. It would also require the willingness to take rapid action to quickly withdraw the trillions of dollars the Fed had pumped into the economy once the situation improved. Another problem was that if nominal interest rates reached zero, the Fed would be unable to use its *traditional* tool to influence monetary policy. Fed Chairman Ben Bernanke noted in a 2002 speech about deflation that, "...people know that inflation erodes the real value of the government's debt and, therefore, that it is in the interest of the government to create some inflation."[8] The Fed's new direction echoed Bernanke's famous "helicopter speech" when he indicated that the easiest way to tackle deflation was by printing more money, in reference to Noble laureate economist Milton Friedman's helicopter analogy of dropping money from the sky to get people to spend and escape deflation.[9]

Skeptics pointed to Japan's experience, and questioned the effectiveness of quantitative easing in achieving its goal; the tool was employed for more than five years with little results, although Japan's circumstances were different from what the United States faced. The *Wall Street Journal* noted that "The larger economic problem today isn't an overall lack of liquidity. It is fear and uncertainty...what the economy really needs is a revival of confidence."[10] Harvard professor Kenneth Rogoff, who used to be fearful of inflation, argued, "It will take every tool in the box to fix today's once-in-a-century financial crisis. Fear of inflation, when viewed in the context of a possible global depression, is like worrying about getting the measles when one is in danger of getting the plague."[11]

The Fed's Other Measures

In a parallel effort, the Fed tried encouraging banks to start lending again by expanding the *types* of assets that the Fed would buy from financial institutions. New, unconventional asset purchases on the Fed's balance sheet not only included debt and mortgage-backed securities, but also selected long-term bonds and consumer loans (see **Exhibit 5**). One program was named Term Auction Facility (TAF), aimed at injecting funds to a wider range of depository institutions against a broader range of collateral. The Fed would auction short-term, collateral-backed loans to depository institutions, allowing financial institutions to borrow money from the Fed at rates even lower that the discount rate. Another program was Term Asset-Backed Securities Loan Facility (TALF), which would lend up to $200 billion to support the issue of new securities backed by auto, student, or credit card loans. Other aggressive moves continued, such as the Fed's plan, announced in March 2009, to buy long-term Treasuries, aimed at trying to bring down yields on long-term securities. It was estimated that the purchase would further increase the Fed's balance sheet by more than $1 trillion to reach nearly $4 trillion, about a third of the size of the U.S. economy.[12]

Fixing the Financial Sector

I feel like Butch Cassidy and the Sundance Kid. Who are these guys that just keep coming?

—Former U.S. Treasury Secretary, Henry Paulson, Jr.[13]

I believe that banking institutions are more dangerous to our liberties than standing armies.

—Thomas Jefferson[14]

Meanwhile, the Treasury Department had focused on addressing the troubled financial sector. A major initiative came in October 2008, a $700 billion financial bailout program called the Trouble Asset Relief Program (TARP). Initially, the program targeted to purchase toxic financial assets at a premium over their current value, thereby providing banks with liquidity. However, as financial markets continued their roller coaster ride, markets indicated that illiquidity was not the main problem; it was insolvency amid the lack of confidence in the value of banks' liabilities. In other words, there was growing distrust that a $100 million loan was really worth less than the face value, prompting financial institutions to refrain from lending to each other, especially in terms of short-term loans. Rumor of financial troubles also quickly led to runs on deposits, as seen with the case of Lehman Brothers.

Henry Paulson Jr., the Treasury Secretary at that time, scrapped the initial plan and decided the Treasury would directly invest $250 billion in banks instead by buying preferred shares. Other key provisions included a guarantee of new debt issued by banks up to three years, and the Federal Deposit Insurance Corp.'s (FDIC) unlimited insurance on non-interest bearing accounts, usually used by businesses. Major financial institutions, from Bank of America to Citibank quickly lined up to receive a portion of TARP (see **Exhibit 6**). By mid-December, only $15 billion of the $350 billion first tranche of the TARP program was left.[15] Then, the remainder ended up in the hands of U.S. auto giants General Motors and Chrysler, who marched up to Congress in November 2008 asking for financial assistance as well, claiming that they needed emergency aid to stay in business.

Overall, TARP provoked more backlash and criticism than praises. Why did the Treasury 'reward' financial institutions by recapitalizing them when it was their reckless financing behavior that led them to their current positions in the first place? Why did the program end up covering automakers? Why wasn't more being done to address the massive home foreclosures and the average taxpayer? As defaults on mortgages had shown few signs of improving, Martin Feldstein, a Harvard professor, argued that, "...the fundamental problem is in the housing market...and that hangs as a cloud over financial institutions, because we don't know how much more we're going to see defaults and foreclosures driving down house prices and driving down the value of those mortgage-backed securities that are a large part of the bank's balance sheet" (see **Exhibit 7**).[16] Others questioned why the Treasury did not use the money to directly tackle the bad loans on the banks' balance sheets. Above all, TARP had been poorly executed—there had been few, if any, condition attached to the funds. The money could have been used for lending or just kept in the vaults at the banks' own discretion. As the Congressional oversight panel created to oversee TARP noted in its report, "While both tightened credit standards and the economic slowdown undoubtedly have depressed lending, these events do not justify the failure to measure whether the TARP capital investments are having a positive effect on lending."[17]

The Debate over Nationalization

The pressure to create a better, more accountable plan to tackle the financial system fell onto Timothy Geithner, the newly appointed Treasury Secretary. In February 2009, Geithner announced a new TARP 2 plan, labeled the 'Financial Stability Plan.' It called for up to $2 trillion in public and private funds to rescue the financial system (including the remaining $350 billion from the original TARP plan):

1. Recruit the private sector to buy toxic bank assets in a Private-Public Partnership. The government would raise somewhere between $500 billion and $1 trillion to offer low-cost financing for this purpose.
2. Expand TALF by up to $1 trillion to buy new car, home, and student loans.
3. Offer direct help for the banks, which would involve a 'stress test' to see which banks with assets over $100 billion would be worth saving, aimed at creating better accountability and oversight over the funds.

Markets reacted negatively with the Dow Jones industrial average falling 4.6% as Geithner's initial plan generated more questions than answers. One of the most troubling aspects was the lack of detail on how the plan would encourage the private sector to buy bad loans. There was a huge gap between what private investors were willing to pay for banks' assets from what financial institutions deemed was a reasonable price for their toxic holdings. This difficulty in valuing the distressed assets was a situation that had prevailed for months, creating the deadlock in credit markets. Many economists believed that there were a good number of banks that were already insolvent but have not been revealed yet based on the toxic assets that they possessed that were simply too hard to value under current market conditions or were simply unwilling to admit to.

In a more detailed plan announced a month later, Geithner said the government would lend private investors up to 85% of the purchase price for banks' mortgage sales. The FDIC would be in charge of running a program for banks to bundle up their troubled mortgages and put them on the sale block.[18] The chairman of Pimo, the world's largest bond fund, welcomed the new plan, calling it "perhaps the first win-win policy to be put on the table" while skeptic Nobel laureate economist Paul Krugman bashed the plan, calling it "cash for trash."[19]

The Financial Stability Plan also subjected 19 of the nation's largest banks with assets over $100 billion to a stress test. Banks' financial strength would be tested under a potential scenario that involved a two-year recession, an unemployment rate that could rise above 10%, and further declines in housing prices. If the test indicated that a bank needed more capital, the government would first give the financial institution six months to try and raise capital on its own. If unsuccessful, the government would then step in by taking preferred shares with voting rights that could convert into common equity. In banks that had received government aid through the initial TARP plan, those preferred non-voting shares would be replaced with the new preferred shares. Additional ceilings on executive compensation would be imposed as well.

In essence, the financial sector's dire situation triggered a contentious debate over whether the banking sector should be nationalized. For some critics, one lesson drawn from Japan's painful experience was that no amount of monetary easing and fiscal stimulus could save an economy without fixing the financial system. Failure to act quickly and boldly dragged the Japanese economy into stagnation for years, in what became known as Japan's "lost decade." Estimates for the total losses by U.S. financial institutions ranged from $2 trillion to as high as $3.2 trillion. Such figures sparked widespread concerns that the Fed's plan would fall short of addressing the losses and helping to resume lending.

Nationalization was not without precedence. Sweden had completely overhauled its banking system in the 1990s when the government took over insolvent banks to clean up their balance sheets. Shareholders were basically wiped out and management was replaced. Banks were forced to write down their bad assets before recapitalization took place, something the U.S. had been unwilling to do so far. In addition, Sweden created a 'bad bank', a government agency that was specifically in charge of taking the bad assets off banks' balance sheets and selling them later when market conditions improved. Albeit painful, Sweden managed to pull itself out of its banking crisis remarkably quickly.

Korea had taken similar action with its 1997 financial crisis, empowering an agency specifically to buy bank's non-performing loans and dispose of them. During the Savings and Loans crisis in the 1980s, the U.S. also ended up briefly taking over such institutions.

Paul Krugman suggested that Geithner's proposal for "...stress testing may end up sort of being the Trojan horse to smuggle the good guys into the fortress, that the public isn't ready. Congress isn't ready for major nationalization..."[20] Although the stress test may result in the government taking larger stakes in several banks, Geithner insisted that the government was not seeking nationalization, which would be, "the wrong strategy for the country and I don't think it's the necessary strategy."[21] For a country that had long embraced free market capitalism, nationalization was not a concept that neither boded well among financial institutions nor the government. Many policymakers associated nationalization as an antithesis to *lassaire-faire* economics, something one would see in an emerging market economy or under an oligarchy government. Simon Johnson, former IMF research director and MIT professor, also indicated that the U.S. banking culture of banks exerting tremendous power through their vested interests and wealth created their "feeling of invisibility", adding more complications and challenges to tackle necessary banking reforms.[22]

In addition, the U.S. financial sector was much bigger and complex than Sweden's, posing greater challenges. Another fear was that the government lacked the experience and guidance to run banks. The interplay of politics could not be ignored either; for instance, powerful key election states could put pressure on the government to lend them money for projects and influence their decisions. Valuation problems emerged again—what kind of standards would be applicable to determine which banks were worth saving or not? How could the government ensure that it would not over or under pay for the banks? There was also the concern that the government may struggle to find suitable buyers quickly, running into the risk of controlling the banks longer than expected or necessary.

Yet those in favor of some form of nationalization argued that only the government was in position to swiftly recapitalize the banking sector, given the massive price tag of cleaning up the banks. Nouriel Roubini, a New York University professor who became well known for his prediction of a crisis, claimed that the Treasury's plan, though well intended, was too late: "Basically, we're all Swedes now. We have used all our bullets, and the boogeyman is still coming. Let's pull out the bazooka and be done with it."[23] Simon Johnson argued that if the IMF was presented with the current financial meltdown of the United States based on just the numbers, "There is no doubt what old International Monetary Fund hand would say... Nationalize the banking system."[24] Even former Fed chairman Alan Greenspan, well known for his firm conviction in free market capitalism, indicated that he was in favor of temporarily nationalizing some banks, citing that, "I understand that once in a hundred years this is what you do."[25]

Fiscal Stimulus – Turning Keynesians Again

We are all Keynesians now... The ghost of John Maynard Keynes, the father of macroeconomics, has returned to haunt us.

—Martin Wolf, *Financial Times'* Chief Economic Commentator[26]

"The ideas of economists and political philosophers, both when they are right and when they are wrong, are more powerful than is commonly understood. Indeed the world is ruled by little else. Practical men, who believe themselves to be quite exempt from any intellectual influences, are usually the slaves of some defunct economist."

—John Maynard Keynes[27]

The scale and scope of the financial crisis steered policymakers towards the general consensus of accompanying monetary tools with a massive fiscal stimulus package to pull the U.S. economy out of its recession. A systematic financial crisis was forecasted to have a lasting effect; one study published by former IMF economist Carmen Reinhart and Kenneth Rogoff and revealed that in the aftermath of a financial crises, rising unemployment and declining housing prices lasted for five and six years respectively.[28] Thus, the new theme was to become Keynesians again, following the economic theory of the famous British economist John Maynard Keynes that advocated massive government spending to combat a recession. The International Monetary Fund concurred, citing that "...the timely implementation of fiscal stimulus across a broad range of advanced and emerging economies must provide a key support to world growth" in its latest world economic outlook.[29] It seemed as if the world had fallen into a "Minsky moment", when a financial mania turned into panic (a situation named after Keynes' follower Hyman Minsky).

President Obama tried to act quickly by pushing for a massive stimulus package, which was finally approved in February 2009 after weeks of political wrangling. The $787 billion stimulus package dedicated a third to tax cuts with the rest focused on expanding unemployment benefits, constructing new infrastructure, increasing aid for health insurance, and booting education spending (see **Exhibit 8**). Some $116 billion would go to payroll tax relief for low-income families while companies that received TARP funds would see a cap on executive compensation and bonuses. The Obama administration hoped the stimulus would create 3.5 million jobs with more than two thirds of the money aimed to be spent by Sept. 30, 2010.

Several compromises had been made to get approval, including the size of the overall package and greater tax cuts for the middle class. With the last fiscal stimulus package carried out by the Bush administration, less than 40% was spent as consumers opted to use the rebates to pay off existing debt or simply save the money.[30] Thus, it was questionable whether consumers would spend the tax cuts this time around when their personal wealth and the value of their own assets had eroded even more in just a year's time. While observers agreed that a fiscal boost was necessary given the dire status of the economy, the plan fell short of expectations, especially over the polarized opinions among the political parties. Bickering between the Democrats and Republicans had translated into each party trying to promote their own agenda and interests; as the *Economist* noted, "The compromised bill is larded with spending determined more by Democrat lawmakers' pet projects than by the efficiency with which the economy will be boosted."[31] Many observers feared that political wrangling could get into the way of collective action and support to find a remedy for the dire status of the economy. Economist Jeffrey Sachs even claimed that the stimulus package had turned into a "fiscal piñata—with a mad scramble for candy on the floor."[32]

Also troubling was the sign of economic protectionism. The package included a "Buy American" provision, requiring the use of America-made steel and iron in certain stimulus-funded public projects.[33] Although President Obama had watered down the original provision, adding that it must comply with World Trade Organization rules, the clause evoked memories of the Smoot-Hawley Tariff Act. Adopted in 1930, Smoot-Hawley raised U.S. tariffs on some 20,000 imports to record levels. Not only did it spark a trade war with many trade partner countries retaliating, but it also became one of the main contributors to the outbreak of the Great Depression.

Lawmakers and U.S. steel companies (who lobbied hard for the provision), claimed that "Buy American" was not an act of protectionism; House Speaker Nancy Pelosi insisted that, "We want them [workers] to be assured that we're looking out for their interest as we look to grow the U.S. economy. I don't think that's protectionism."[34] However, the inclusion of the provision itself had instigated fears of backlash and possible trade wars. A study conducted by the Peterson Institute for International Economics, a leading think tank in Washington DC, indicated that the "Buy American" provision would create about 1,000 jobs in the steel industry, a paltry figure considering the 140 million labor force in the United States.[35] Several countries, including China and Canada, two of the United States' biggest trade partners, vowed to keep a close eye on the provision.

Other Policies

It is not from the benevolence of the butcher, the brewer, or the baker that we expect our dinner, but from their regard to their own interest.

—Adam Smith[36]

Capitalism is the astounding belief that the most wickedest of men will do the most wickedest of things for the greatest good of everyone.

—John Maynard Keynes[37]

The Obama administration continued to roll out other policies and measures to combat the crisis that continued to infect all corners of the economy. One plan was to set aside as much as $275 billion to help homeowners refinance their loans through Fannie Mae and Freddie Mac. Part of the fund would also be used to encourage lenders to restructure loan conditions for those either already in foreclosure or in risk of facing one. In his first budget proposal, President Obama laid out an ambitious plan to cut the budget deficit from a projected $1.75 trillion, or 12% of GDP, to $533 billion, or 3% of GDP, by 2013. The projection was contingent on the assumptions that the stimulus and bailouts would actually work and the economy would recover to generate higher tax income and lower spending for programs such as unemployment benefits. History also indicated that financial bailouts were costly with the risk that actual spending could be even greater than projections (see **Exhibit 9**). Even within weeks of taking office, the Obama administration found itself taking up to a 36% stake in Citigroup to become the largest shareholder in the battered financial institution, and extending an additional $30 billion credit line to AIG.

Above all, there was a growing sense of anger and frustration that directly attacked the lax financial regulations that allowed institutions to take unsupervised risks and slip through the system without notice until it was too late. In response to the overwhelming criticisms, both at home and abroad, Secretary Geithner proposed to overhaul regulation, which would include greater supervision over hedge funds, private equity, and even derivatives. Capital requirements held against liabilities could increase as well. Separately, Geithner and Bernanke also sought unprecedented federal government power to take over non-banking financial firms, if deemed necessary to save the financial system.[38]

Financial markets across the world showed few signs of finding comfort in the various plans that had been unveiled and as economic indicators showed more disturbing signs of the deep recession the world's biggest economy had fallen into. Revised fourth quarter 2008 GDP growth indicated that the U.S. economy had contracted by 6.2%, the sharpest contraction since 1982. The unemployment rate was above 8% with economists predicting it to reach 10% by the year's end (see **Exhibit 10**). Anxiety and tension rose in the Obama administration as it continued to ponder—would the combined efforts of monetary easing, fiscal stimulus, and the various bank recapitalization programs work effectively? How soon would the U.S. economy be able to pull itself out of the worst recession since the Great Depression, with the consequences of U.S. actions having a far reaching impact across the global economy?

Appendix - Timeline of the Crisis

Date	Event
Sept. 7 '08	The government decided to nationalize Fannie Mae and Freddie Mac, the nation's two biggest mortgage finance companies, and commit up to $100 billion in government funds to each company to meet possible capital shortages.
Sept. 9, '08	Shares of Lehman Brothers lost nearly half of its value amid rumors that it was on the brink of bankruptcy.
Sept. 14, '08	Lehman Brothers filed for bankruptcy, unable to find a buyer or receive government aid. Bank of America said it would buy the venerable investment bank, Merrill Lynch, for $50 billion. Meanwhile, insurance giant AIG sought a $40 billion lifeline from the Fed.
Sept. 15, '08	AIG shares nosedived about 60% after the government rejected its rescue fund request.
Sept. 16, '08	The Fed reversed its stance and agreed to extend an $85 billion credit line to the ailing AIG, effectively nationalizing the insurer.
Sept. 20, '08	The government revealed a new plan to buy $700 billion worth of distressed mortgages, which immediately sparked criticisms and doubts whether the package could work.
Sept. 21, '08	Goldman Sachs and Morgan Stanley—the last two major investment banks on Wall Street—voluntarily decided to convert themselves into bank holding companies and subject themselves to greater regulation.
Sept. 25, 08	Washington Mutual was saved by the government as it intervened to sell the biggest savings and loan company in the United States to JP Morgan Chase for $1.9 billion.
Sept. 29, '08	The House rejected the proposed $700 billion bailout plan, also known as Troubled Asset Relief Program (TARP). The Dow Jones industrial average tumbled 778 points, or 7%, wiping out more than $1 trillion in the Dow's worst single day decline in a decade.
Oct. 3, '08	The House finally accepted a revised version of TARP, a few days after the Senate approved the rescue package. Separately, Wachovia agreed to be bought by San Francisco-based Wells Fargo for $15 billion, reversing an earlier agreement to be sold to Citigroup.
Oct 8, '08	Following days of jittery stock markets and credit squeezes across the globe, the Fed and other central banks coordinate their efforts and simultaneously cut interest rates.
Oct. 10 '08	The Dow Jones ended its worst trading week, plunged 18% to below the 8,500 level as rate cuts failed to reassure investors, who grew increasingly concerned that a global recession was in sight. G7 leaders met to try and address the turmoil which had turned into a massive global crisis.
Oct. 13, '08	The government revealed a new plan, which included spending up to $250 billion to buy banks' preferred shares, and guarantee new debt issued by banks up to three years. The Dow Jones reacted positively with a 936 point, or 11% gain.
Oct. 20, '08	Money markets showed signs of easing for the first time in weeks as the Dow Jones gained more than 400 points.
Oct. 22 '08	Hedge funds announced that they lost $180 billion in the last three months. Separately, Wachovia reported a third quarter loss of about $24 billion.
Oct. 29, '08	The Fed cut the Fed funds rate by half a percentage point to 1%, its lowest level since 2004.

Oct. 30, '08	Economic data indicated that the U.S. economy shrank 0.3% in the third quarter compared to the same period a year ago while consumer spending declined for the first time in 17 years.
Nov. 7 '08	The jobless rate hit a 14-year high with about 1.2 million people losing their jobs since the beginning of the year.
Nov. 14, '08	Treasury Secretary Paulson changed plans for the $700 billion rescue package to directly help consumers instead, shifting the focus away from helping financial institutions.
Nov. 18, '08	The big three automakers—Ford, GM, and Chrysler—made an appeal to Congress for billions of dollars in government aid, claiming that they may exhaust their cash reserves by the year's end without any aid.
Nov. 19, '08	Data indicated that inflation fell 1% in October, the biggest one-month decline in the Consumer Price Index.
Nov. 25, '08	The Fed decided to purchase up to $100 billion worth of Fannie Mae and Freddie Mac's mortgages, which allowed fixed 30-year home loan rates to drop from 6.3% to 5.5%. Another new credit facility—Term Asset-Backed Securities Loan Facility (TALF)—was announced that would lend up to $200 billion against consumer-debt-backed securities, aimed at trying to revive liquidity in the nearly paralyzed consumer credit markets.
Dec. 1 '08	The National Bureau of Economic Research (NBER) announced that the United States was in a recession and had been since December 2007. NBER defined a recession as, "a period of significant decline in total output, income, employment, and trade, usually lasting from six months to a year, and marked by widespread contractions in many sectors of the economy."
Jan. 10, '09	The unemployment rate for December reached 7.2%, a 16-year high, bringing the total loss of jobs to 2.6 million for 2008.
Jan. 12, '09	President Bush sought for the release of the remaining $350 billion of the TARP funds.
Jan. 15, '09	Foreclosures surged 81% in 2008 from the previous year, according to RealtyTrac, a foreclosure filing firm.
Jan. 20, '09	Barack Obama was sworn in as the 44th President of the United States.
Feb 10, '09	New Treasury Secretary Timothy Geithner announced a new financial stability plan, which fell short of expectations. The Dow declined 4.6%.
Feb 14, '09	President Obama's new $787 billion fiscal stimulus plan received congressional approval after weeks of wrangling between the two political parties.
Feb. 19, '09	President Obama outlined a $275 billion plan to help struggling homeowners refinance their loans through Fannie Mae and Freddie Mac.
Feb. 27, '09	Citigroup announced that the government would take as much as a 36% stake to become the largest shareholder. The deal could dilute existing common shareholders' shares to dilute by almost 75%. In return, the government demanded Citi to revamp its board of directors while CEO Vikram Pandit was expected to stay in place.
Mar. 2, '09	AIG posted a $61.7 billion fourth quarter loss, the biggest quarterly loss for a corporation. The Fed decided to provide a new $30 billion credit line, in addition to the $150 billion already committed to the insurance agency. Concerns about the health of financial institutions sent the Dow to close below 7,000, its lowest level in 12 years.
Mar. 14 '09	Reports leaked that AIG was scheduled to pay $165 million in bonus, causing an uproar on Capitol Hill and among the public. The bonus agreements were made prior to the insurance company's financial woes that led to a government bailout.

Mar. 16, '09	President Obama said he would "pursue every single legal avenue to block" the $165 million bonus payments to AIG executives. Several managers ended up returning their bonuses.
Mar. 24, '09	Secretary Geithner unveiled details for his Public-Private Investment Plan to remove up to $1 trillion in toxic mortgage assets off banks' balance sheets. The Dow Jones reacted positively, gaining 6.8% to close at 7775.86.
Mar. 25, '09	Geithner and Fed Chairman Bernanke testified in front of Congress and called for new powers to take control of financial firms beyond banks in cases of a crisis, the way the FDIC was authorized to take over banks in an emergency.
Mar. 29, '09	The government directly intervened in the auto sector by forcing General Motors' CEO Rick Wagoner to leave. The media reported that the government threatened to withhold bailout funds if Wagoner did not resign, amid greater doubts of the company's potential to survive.

Source: Created by casewriter based on various public sources.

Exhibit 1 Global Financial Markets, February 2008 - March 2009

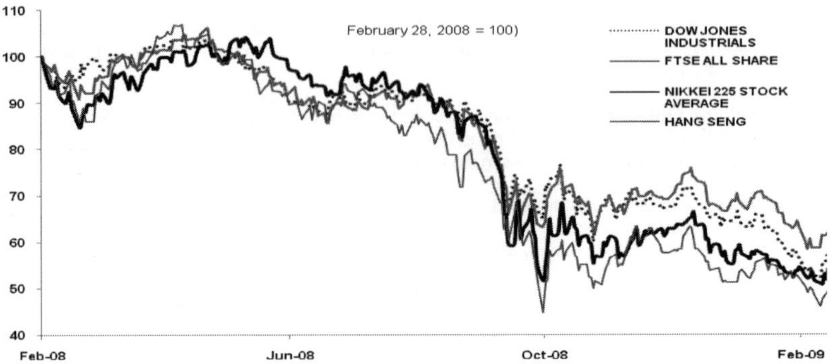

Source: Thomson ONE Banker, accessed April 3, 2009.

Exhibit 2 Fed Funds Rate and Discount Rate (%) - January to December, 2008

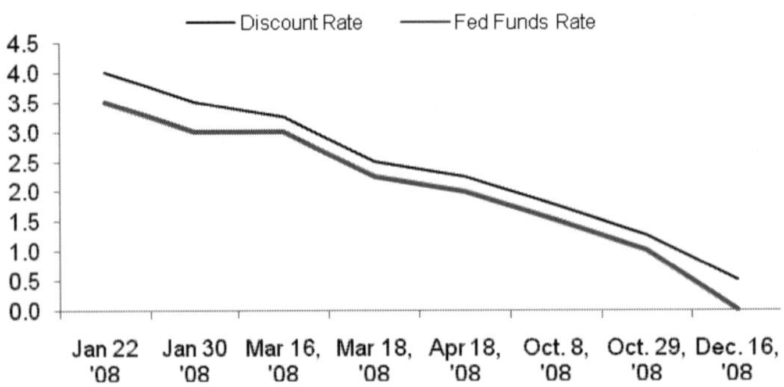

Source: Federal Reserve Board.

Exhibit 3 Consumer Price Index (% Change)

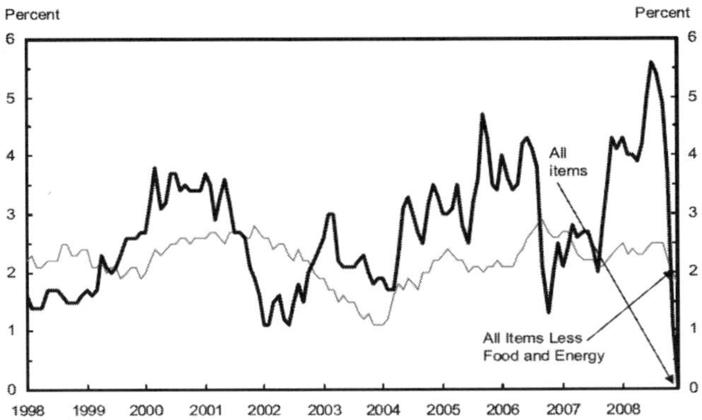

Source: Bureau of Labor Statistics, "CPI Detailed Report," December 2008.

Exhibit 4 Monetary Base

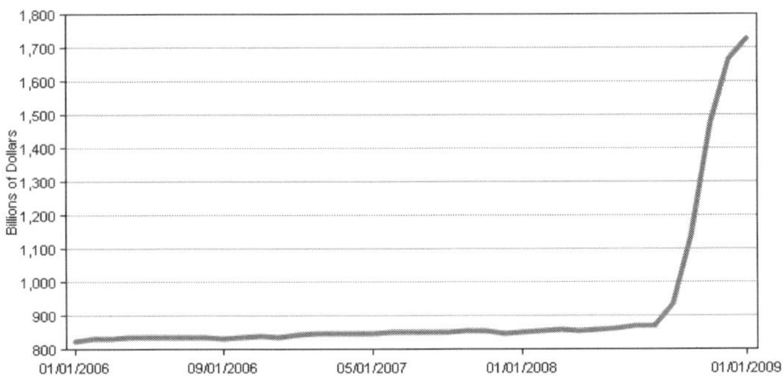

Source: Federal Reserve Bank of St. Louis, Adjusted Monetary Base Data.

Exhibit 5 Federal Reserve's Main Lending Programs

Measure	Announcement	Description	Amount	Maturity Date
Term Auction Facility (TAF)	Dec. 12, '07	Auction term funds to a wider range of financial institutions against a wider range of acceptable collateral for 28 or 84-day loans.	Up to $450 billion	Undecided
Temporary Reciprocal Currency Arrangements	Dec. 12 '07 and onward	Swap dollar funding for other currencies with other central banks.	Unlimited	NA
Primary Dealer Credit Facility (PDCF)	Mar. 16, '08	Provide overnight funds at the prime rate to primary dealers, which was previously available to depository institutions only.	Not specified, but used up to $38 billion as of Jan. '09	Extended to Oct. 30, '09 from Apr. 30, '09.
Discount Facility Adjustments	Mar. 16, '08	Maximum maturity of primary credit loans extended from 30 to 90 days and the discount rate premium cut 25 basis points over policy rate.	Not specified, but $87 billion of window credit as of Dec. '08	NA
Term Securities Lending Facility Options Program (TOP)	Jul. 30, '08	Auction options to borrow Treasury securities against collateral regarding important financing dates.	Up to $50 billion	Apr. 30, '09
Asset-Backed Commercial Paper Money Market Mutual Fund Liquidity Facility (AMLF)	Sept. 19, '08	Provide loans to depository institutions to buy asset-backed CP from money market mutual funds.	Not specified, but $24 billion used as of Jan. '09.	Extended to Oct. 30, '09 from Apr. 30, '09.
Commercial Paper Funding Facility (CPFF)	Oct. 7, '08	New York Fed to provide finance to a special purpose vehicle (SPV) to purchase three-month CP and asset-based CP from issuers and hold them until maturity.	Not specified, but $332 billion used as of Jan. '09.	Extended to Oct. 30, '09 from Apr. 30, '09.
Pay Interest on Reserves	Oct. 9, '08	Fed to pay interest on depository institutions' required and excess reserve balances, which will allow the Fed to increase its own balance sheet to fund the various liquidity programs.	NA	NA
Money Market Investor Funding Facility (MMIFF)	Oct. 21, '08	Provide senior secured funding to private SPV's to buy short-term CDs and commercial paper (CP) from money market mutual funds and other money market investors	Up to $540 billion	Extended to Oct. 30, '09 from Apr. 30, '09.
Term Asset Backed Securities Loan Facility (TALF)	Nov. 25, '08	NY Fed support for issuance of asset-backed securities collateralized by auto, credit, and student loans guaranteed by the Small Business Administration.	Up to $200 billion	Dec. 31, '09
Agency Market Intervention	Nov. 25, '08	Purchase direct obligations of Freddie Mac, Fannie Mae, and Federal Home Loan Banks. Purchase mortgage-backed securities of Freddie Mac, Fannie Mae, and Ginnie Mae.	Up to $100 billion Up to $500 billion	Undecided

Source: Created by casewriter based on data from the Federal Reserve Board.

Exhibit 6 TARP Funding Disbursement (as of February 18, 2009)

Name	Bailout (in $ millions)
Funds Committed Under Bush Administration	**379,800**
Funds Disbursed to Financial Firms	281,000
of which:	
Citigroup	50,000
Bank of America	45,000
AIG	40,000
JP Morgan Chase	25,000
Wells Fargo	24,800
Goldman Sachs Group	10,000
Morgan Stanley	10,000
PNC Financial Services	7,579
U.S. Bancorp	6,599
SunTrust	4,850
Capital One Financial Corp.	3,555
Regions Financial Corp.	3,500
Fifth Third Bancorp	3,408
American Express	3,389
Others	43,320
Pending	54,000
Automakers[a]	23,400
Other (including some funding for TALF)	21,400
Funds Allowed under the Obama Administration	**320,000**
TOTAL	**699,800**

Source: Adapted by casewriter based on data from the U.S. Treasury Department.

[a]Automakers include General Motors, Chrysler, and GMAC, General Motors' financing arm. The automakers requested for additional funding in February 2009.

Exhibit 7a Standard & Poor's Residential Real Estate Indicators

	Q307	Q407	Q108	Q208	Q308
U.S. National Home Price Index (% change)	-1.8%	-5.3%	-6.6%	-2.2%	-3.5%
Mortgage Delinquency Rate (%):					
On All loans	5.59%	5.82%	6.35%	6.41%	6.99%
On Prime Loans	3.12%	3.24%	3.71%	3.93%	4.34%
On Subprime Loans	16.31%	17.31%	18.79%	18.67%	20.03%
Foreclosures Started in Quarter:					
On All loans	0.78%	0.83%	0.99%	1.19%	1.07%
On Prime Loans	0.37%	0.41%	0.54%	0.67%	0.61%
On Subprime Loans	3.12%	3.44%	4.06%	4.70%	4.13%

Source: Adapted by casewriter based on Standard & Poor's "Residential Real Estate Indicators," January 2009.

Exhibit 7b S&P/Case-Shiller Home Price Indices[a]

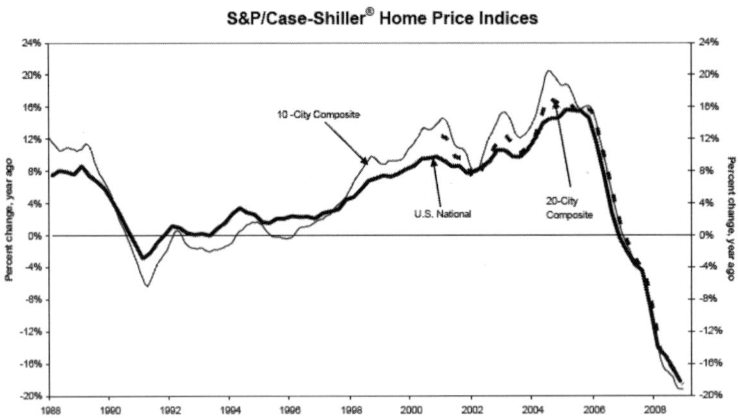

Source: Standard and Poor's, "Home Price Declines Continue as the S&P/Case-Shiller Home Price Indices Set New Record Annual Declines," Press Release, January 27, 2009, pg. 1.

[a] The S&P/Case-Shiller U.S. National index tracks the value of single-family housing and covers all loans, including non-traditional, "jumbo" loans exceeding $417,000, and subprime loans. Geographically, it covers about 70% of the country. The 10-City Composite Index is a value-weighted average of ten metro areas: Boston, Chicago, Denver, Las Vegas, Los Angeles, Miami, New York, San Diego, San Francisco, and Washington D.C. The 20-City Composite index includes those in the 10-City Index and: Atlanta, Charlotte, Cleveland, Dallas, Detroit, Minneapolis, Phoenix, Portland, Seattle, and Tampa.

Exhibit 8 Fiscal Stimulus Package Breakdown

Category	Amount (in US$ bln)	% of Total
Spending, of which:	**308,481**	**39.2%**
Labor, Health, Education, Volunteering, and Social Services	71,271	
Transportation and Housing	61,051	
Environment and Energy	50,775	
Farming and Food	26,431	
Commerce, Science and Justice	15,810	
Government	6,707	
Defense, Military, and Veterans	18,590	
Other	14,059	
Tax Cuts, of which:	**288,339**	**36.6%**
Individual	232,426	
Business	6,150	
Manufacturing	1,850	
Economy	6,501	
Infrastructure	19,638	
Energy and Other	20,127	
Individual Aid	14,443	
Aid (including individual and health care)	**190,421**	**24.2%**
TOTAL	**787,241**	**100.0%**

Source: Adapted by case writer based on various government documents.

Exhibit 9 Fiscal Balance as a % of GDP (Projections from 2009 and Onward)

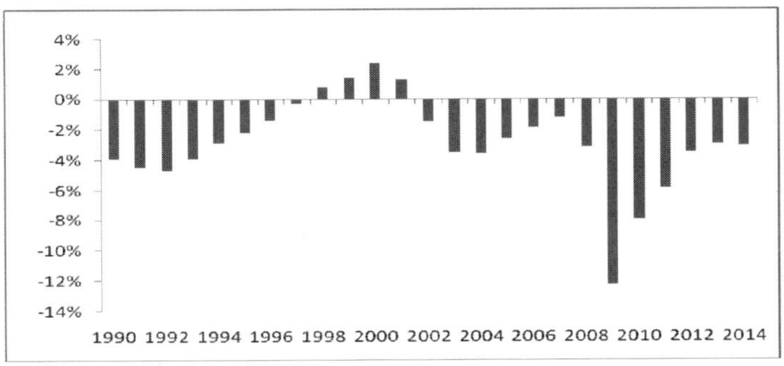

Source: Created by casewriter based on White House Budget Projections, February 26, 2009.

Exhibit 10 U.S. Unemployment Rate (% Change)

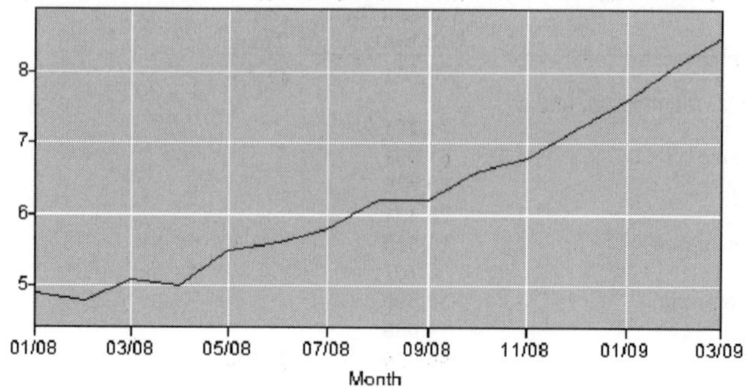

Source: U.S. Bureau of Labor of Statistics.

Endnotes

[1] "Remarks of President Barack Obama – Address to Joint Session of Congress," The White House Briefing Room, February 24, 2009.

[2] For more, see Laura Alfaro and Renee Kim, "U.S. Subprime Mortgage Crisis: Policy Reactions," HBS No. 708-036, March 2008.

[3] Ben Bernanke, "A Crash Course for Central Bankers," *Foreign Affairs*, September/October 2000.

[4] "Rethinking Lehman Brothers: The Price of Failure," *The Economist*, October 4, 2008.

[5] Federal Open Market Committee Monetary Policy Press Release, Washington DC., December 16, 2008,

[6] For more about Japan's monetary policy and use of quantitative easing, see Laura Alfaro and Akiko Kanno, "*Kinyuseisaku*: Monetary Policy in Japan (A)," HBS No. 708-017, January 2008.

[7] For more, see Ben S. Bernanke, "The Crisis and the Policy Response," Speech at the Stamp Lecture, London School of Economics, London, England, January 13, 2009, http://www.federalreserve.gov/newsevents/speech/bernanke200901132,htm, accessed February 4, 2009.

[8] See Ben S. Bernanke, "Deflation: Making Sure "It" Doesn't Happen Here," Remarks before the National Economists Club, Washington DC, November 21, 2002, http://www.federalreserve.gov/boardDocs/speeches/2002/20021121/default.htm, accessed February 3, 2009.

[9] For the full text of Bernanke's speech, see "Deflation: Making sure 'It' Doesn't Happen Here," 2002. For more about Friedman's "helicopter drop" theory, see Milton Friedman, "The Optimum Quantity of Money," in Milton Friedman, *The Optimum Quantity of Money and Other Essays* (Chicago: Adline Publishing Company, 1967), pp. 1-50.

[10] "Bernanke Goes All In," *The Wall Street Journal Editorial*, December 17, 2008.

[11] Kenneth Rogoff, "Inflation is Now the Lesser Evil," Project Syndicate, 2008, http://www.project-syndicate.org/commentary/rogoff51, accessed February 12, 2009.

[12] Krishna Guha, "Federal Reserve Plan Stuns Investors," *Financial Times*, March 18, 2009.

[13][13] Joe Nocera and Edmund L. Andrews, "Struggling to Keep up as the Crisis Raced on," *The New York Times*, October 23, 2008.

[14] "Historical Documents in United States History," http://www.historicaldocuments.com/HistoricQuotes.htm, accessed March 20, 2009.

[15] Although Congress had approved $700 billion for TARP, only half was released initially. The second half of the bailout fund was released by the Bush administration, a few days prior to Obama's inauguration.

[16] PBS Online NewsHour Transcript, "Following the Bailout Money Trail Yields Few Answers," December 24, 2008, http://www.pbs/org/newshour/bb/business/july-dec08/tarp_12-24.html, accessed February 3, 2009.

[17] Michael R. Crittenden, "Crisis on Wall Street: Treasury Plans to Better Track TARP Funds," *The Wall Street Journal*, January 9, 2009.

[18] Another key component of the plan was to provide the taxpayer a matching dollar of equity and up to $12 in other financing for every private dollar invested.

[19] Tom Baldwin, "Obama's Rescue Plan Hailed as 'Light at the End of the Tunnel'" *The Times*, March 24, 2009.

[20] Ibid.

[21] Deborah Solomon and Jon Hilsenrath, "US News: Bank Capital gets Stress Test – Dark Scenario Includes Jobless rate above 10% and Further 25% Drop in Home Prices," *The Wall Street Journal*, February 26, 2009, p. A3.

[22] For more, see PBS, "Bill Moyers Journal," interview transcript with Simon Johnson, February 13, 2009, http://www.pbs.org/moyers/journal/02132009/transcript1.html, accessed February 27, 2009.

[23] Matthew Richardson and Nouriel Roubini, "Nationalize the Banks! We're all Swedes now," *The Washington Post*, February 13, 2009.

[24] Peter Boone and Simon Johnson, "To Save the Banks We Must Stand Up to the Bankers," *Financial Times*, January 27, 2009.

[25] Krishna Guha and Edward Luce, "Greenspan Suggests Nationalising Banks," *Financial Times*, February 18, 2009.

[26] Martin Wolf, "Keynes Offers us the Best Way to Think about the Crisis," *Financial Times*, December 24, 2008.

[27] John Maynard Keynes, *The General Theory of Employment, Interest, and Money*, 1936.

[28] For more, see Carmen Reinhart and Kenneth Rogoff, "The Aftermath of Financial Crises," Harvard University manuscript, December 2008, http://www.economics.harvard.edu/faculty/rogoff/files/Aftermath.pdf, accessed January 31, 2009.

[29] "World Economic Outlook Update, Global Economic Slump Challenges Policies," International Monetary Fund, January 28, 2009, http://www.imf.org/external/pubs/ft/weo/2009/update/01/index.htm, accessed February 10, 2009.

[30] RGE Monitor, "U.S. Congress Passes the Fiscal Stimulus Package: Will it Alleviate the Recession in 2009?", http://www.rgemonitor.com/index.php, accessed February 17, 2009.

[31] "The Obama Rescue," *The Economist*, February 14, 2009.

[32] Jeffrey Sachs, "The Tarp is a Fiscal Straitjacket," *Financial Times*, January 28, 2009.

[33] The provision included a waiver if the project's total funding cost would increase by more than 25% by purchasing American goods.

[34] "United States is Not Protectionist, Pelosi Says," *Reuters*, February 16, 2009, accessed via Factiva, February 17, 2009.

[35] For more, see Gary Clyde Hufbauer and Jeffrey J. Schott, "Buy American: Bad for Jobs, Worse for Reputation," Peterson Institute for International Economics, No. PB09-2, February 2009.

[36] The Concise Encyclopedia of Economics, "Adam Smith (1723-1790)," http://www.econlib.org/library/Enc/bios/Smith.html, accessed March 20, 2009.

[37] Nancy Gibbs, "In Defense of the Recession Blame Game," *Time*, February 12, 2009, http://www.time.com/time/business/article/0,8599,1878939,00.html, accessed February 28, 2009.

[38] The call for greater powers came following the uproar over AIG's bonus payments to executive worth $165 million. The government held an 80% stake in AIG yet it did not have the legal authority over management decisions such as the bonus payments. More than $170 billion in taxpayers' money had been committed to save AIG.

HARVARD | BUSINESS | SCHOOL

9-708-053
MAY 9, 2008

LAURA ALFARO
RENEE KIM

Sovereign Wealth Funds: For Profits or Politics?

Money is naturally going to gravitate toward dollar-based assets because of the strength of our economy. I'd like nothing more than to get more of that money. But I understand that there's a natural fear that they're going to buy up America.

Henry M. Paulson Jr., U.S. Treasury Secretary[1]

It's our policy not to control anything

Gao Xiqing, Head of China Investment Corporation[2]

U.S. Treasury Secretary Henry M. Paulson Jr. appeared pleased. On March 21, 2008, the U.S. government had secured an agreement from two leading sovereign wealth funds (SWFs) to adopt a new set of investment principles. Singapore and the United Arab Emirates, which ran two of the biggest sovereign funds in the world, agreed to a new code of conduct for both the investing and recipient countries. For SWFs, the agreement involved refraining from making investments linked to "geopolitical goals" and increasing disclosure regarding the Funds' activities (see **Appendix**). Secretary Paulson hoped that the code of conduct would set a new framework that could be embraced by other SWFs.

The U.S. government defined a SWF as a government investment vehicle, funded by foreign exchange assets, which managed those assets separately from the official reserves of the monetary authorities. A broader definition was an investment fund owned by a national or state government. Investments made by global SWFs reached a record $48.5 billion in 2007 and $24.4 billion in just the first two months of 2008 alone.[3] Their investments had a multi-dimensional effect across the globe, affecting cross border capital flows to financial regulations to exchange rates. Recently, several SWFs had made large investments into troubled U.S. investment banks that needed new equity after suffering from huge losses linked to the subprime mortgage crisis. Yet given that the majority of funds provided little information about their activities or investment goals, anxiety was escalating to reach some kind of governing principles that could be applicable to this new financial vehicle. Many policymakers feared that SWFs, by nature, did not represent just a pure investment, such as a hedge fund, a concern that the majority of SWFs decried as unfair given their investment track record up to now. Were the concerns surrounding SWFs justified? Would it be possible for the United States to orchestrate a coordinated effort to impose an international regulation?

Professor Laura Alfaro and Research Associate Renee Kim prepared this case. HBS cases are developed solely as the basis for class discussion. Cases are not intended to serve as endorsements, sources of primary data, or illustrations of effective or ineffective management.

The Rise of Sovereign Funds

This is our doing, not some nefarious plot by foreign governments... Our trade equation guarantees massive foreign investment in the U.S.... why should we complain when they choose stocks over bonds?

Warren Buffett, Investor[4]

The first government investment fund was created back in 1953, the Kuwait Investment Authority, out of oil revenues even before Kuwait became independent from Great Britain. Others emerged later; Singapore's Temasek Holdings, established in 1974, claimed itself to be an "Asian investment house" with a total annual compounded return of 18% since its inception.[5] UAE's Abu Dhabi Investment Authority, currently considered the biggest SWF, started out in 1976 with foreign currency reserves from oil exports. However, it was the growth in size of such funds that ballooned over the last few years that grabbed the world's attention. The number of SWFs had risen to about 40 from just a handful a decade ago. Stephen Jen, managing director and chief currency economist at Morgan Stanley, projected them to hold nearly $12 trillion by 2015 from about $3 trillion as of late 2007 (see **Exhibit 1**).

Analysts traced the rise of these government investment vehicles to two major sources and trends: rising surplus of oil-producing countries and excess foreign currency reserves held by Asian countries that also helped to fund the U.S. current account deficit (see **Exhibit 2**). Countries such as Norway and Russia accumulated current account surpluses thanks to export of commodities, especially with the surge in oil prices. Over the last four years alone, Russia accumulated $157 billion in its oil proceeds fund.[6] The Gulf Cooperative Council (GCC) members' annual oil reports stood at $610 billion with close to 500 billion barrels of proven oil reserves, marking GCC countries' SWFs among the biggest in the world with greater potential for growth.[7] In addition, most analysts cited that the 1997 Asian financial crisis prompted many Asian countries, including China and Korea, to reassess their policy and stock up on their reserves to defend themselves against future potential shocks. Some observers also indicated that the accumulation of reserves was an exchange rate management mechanism to prevent the appreciation of their currency.[8]

Like petrodollar surplus countries, the IMF projected that Asian countries would continue to amass foreign assets with persistent current account surpluses.[9] Initially, the reserves were invested in safe government bonds such as U.S. Treasuries. Yet as the stockpile of their reserves surpassed what governments deemed a comfortable and necessary level, they started to look for alternative investments to generate higher returns. Thus, countries started to create funds to specifically manage their assets, such as China's $200 billion sovereign fund in 2007. Latin American countries were about to join the trend as well; late last year, Brazil's finance minister discussed plans for a SWF to handle volatility in the foreign exchange markets while Chile said in April 2008 that it would invest up to $5.9 billion in equities and corporate bonds.[10]

The IMF classified the various motivations behind the establishment of SWFs into roughly five different categories based on their purpose:

- Stabilization funds: Protect the budget and economy against volatility in commodities prices (such as oil)
- Savings funds: Convert nonrenewable assets into a more diversified portfolio of assets for future generations
- Reserve Investment Corporations: Increase the rate of return on reserves, which are used as investment assets

- Development Funds: Fund socio-economic projects or promote industrial policies that may promote future economic growth
- Contingent Pension Reserve Funds: Provide contingent unspecified pension liabilities on the government's balance sheets[11]

The purpose of SWFs could be limited to one purpose or inclusive of a combination of different motivations, including others that did not fall into these five categories, based on countries' economic situation and government balances (see **Exhibit 3**). For instance, stabilization funds would typically focus on fiscal stabilization and to keep foreign exchange inflows from stroking inflation; a large surge in oil prices for a country dependent on imported oil could raise commodity prices and translate into higher inflation. In the case of Russia, part of its fund has evolved to boost the national pension system with plans to invest in foreign stocks and bonds in the future. Jeffrey Frankel, a Harvard economist, noted that a producer of a natural commodity may also use SWFs to avoid the 'Dutch Disease' – real appreciation of the exchange rate, loss of manufacturing exports, and reduced international investment position.[12]

Although there was a lack of comprehensive data to conduct a detailed analysis of SWFs' investment trends, several commonalities characterized their investment strategies. Most SWFs were long-term investors with no explicit liabilities, given that they were primarily funded by foreign currency reserves, and held a diversified portfolio, investing in anything from long-term government bonds to equities to real estate. For example, Norway's Fund aimed to allocate 60% of its funds into equities from the current level of 40% by 2010, with the remaining balance in fixed income.[13] Emerging markets, usually considered a high risk yet high return investment, were an attractive destination; McKinsey Global Institute estimated that nearly a quarter of investment from the Gulf were in Asia, the Middle East, and Africa.

U.S. Subprime Crisis: An Investment Opportunity?

The big emergence of SWFs investments in a particular sector came in 2007 with the U.S. subprime mortgage crisis. Many investment banks on Wall Street had suffered billions of dollars of mortgage-related losses and found themselves in need of new capital. They found a willing investor in SWFs. On the surface, it seemed like an ideal match. Investment banks needed fresh equity. From SWFs' point of view, as one managing director stated, "There are certain opportunities which do not come every day. We consider the recent crisis as creating some opportunities in certain sectors."[14]

Singapore's Government of Singapore Investment Corp (GIC), with Saudi Arabian Monetary Agency, purchased a 9% minority stake in UBS, which wrote down nearly $14 billion in its fourth quarter due to subprime related losses. Temasek invested in Merrill Lynch and British financial institutions such as Barclays and Standard Chartered. Lim Hwee Hua, Singapore's Minister of State for Finance and Transportation, said "These investments were made after thorough assessments of the market developments, risk and potential returns, including factoring the opportunities and risks that they can afford to take in a down market. GIC and Temasek are long-term players, out to seek long-term returns."[15] On January 14, 2008, Citigroup and Merrill Lynch, two of the hardest hit investment firms from the subprime meltdown, announced that they received about $14 billion and $6 billion respectively from SWFs based mostly Asia and the Middle East. In fact, financials represented more than two thirds of the $73 billion invested by SWFs since January 2007[16] (see **Exhibit 4**).

The investments did not go through a formal review under U.S. banking law. Regulations under the Bank Holding Company (BHC) Act stipulated that an investment would require a review if a company 1) purchased or controlled 25% or more of voting securities of the bank or bank holding company, 2) controlled the election of a majority of the board of directors, or 3) had the ability to exercise a controlling influence over management or policies.[17] In addition, the BHC Act only applied to investments in banks and bank holding companies made by "companies," not direct investments made by foreign governments, even though the Federal Reserve leaned towards the idea of treating a SWF as a company if the a SWF made an investment that met any of the three conditions.[18]

Not all SWF investments had been profitable. The Chinese investment fund purchased a $3 billion stake in the private equity and real estate company, Blackstone Group, only to see the value of its investment tumble in the months to follow. Abu Dhabi's SWF paid $7.6 billion for a stake in Citigroup, whose share price had declined by nearly a third. In fact, research indicated that historically, foreign investment in the U.S. yielded lower returns compared to U.S. investments abroad (see **Exhibit 5**). Nevertheless, the sudden increase in SWF investments in U.S. financial institutions rose to the spotlight of attention and speculations. While investor Warren Buffet pointed to the U.S. trade deficit, national debt, and weak dollar as factors that lured foreign investors to the U.S., the primary fear was that the investments may not be purely driven by profit but tangled with some kind of political motivation. Bader al-Saad, managing director of Kuwait Investment Authority, bitterly complained about such talks, claiming "Why is everybody after sovereign wealth funds? What have they done?... All they are talking about is a fear of something that did not happen and will not happen."[19] Simon Israel, Temasek's executive director, echoed al-Saad's sentiments, commenting that "If the shoes was on the other foot, if these were sovereign wealth investors in France, Germany, the UK or the US earning fabulous returns, reducing countries' national deficits, funding social security costs and investing into the rest of the world, would they think it was an issue? I suspect they wouldn't."[20]

The Debate

Governments are very different from other economic actors. Their investments should be governed by rules designed with that reality very clearly in mind.

Lawrence Summers, Harvard Economist and former Treasury Secretary[21]

Lack of information One of the biggest concerns regarding SWFs was their level of transparency and disclosure (see **Exhibit 6**). Given that there was no universal standard or governing regulation institution that was applicable to SWFs, the amount of information available ran the gamut. On one hand, there were funds such as Norway's Government Pension Fund, which was hailed as an outstanding example of disclosure and transparency among SWFs. In 2004, it had even established a Council on Ethics to ensure that its investments were consistent with its established ethical guidelines. The Fund had withdrawn several investments, such as that in Wal-Mart Stores Inc., following the adoption of this practice.[22] Norway's finance ministry official claimed that "In every country that has a fund, they are the cornerstone of macroeconomic policy so... there is nothing illegitimate or sinister about these funds."[23] Yet on the opposite end were funds that neither publicized the size of their total assets nor portfolio structure.

In Europe, countries such as Germany and France had made no secret about their distrust regarding SWFs for their lack of transparency. German Chancellor Angela Merkel pledged to keep a close watch on foreign investments in the country amid Russia's state-owned natural gas company buying pipelines and energy infrastructure in Europe. In April 2008, the German government announced a new legislature that would allow the ministry of labor to stop any major investment in local firms if they threaten local job security or take place in a strategic sector such as electricity. The government had also considered creating a similar agency such as the U.S. Committee on Foreign Investment, which reviewed foreign takeover bids. French President Nicolas Sarkozy vowed that

France would defend "the primordial economic interests of the nation" against such government funds that "don't respect economic logic."[24] Meanwhile, Britain's Trade Minister Digby Jones said his country welcomed sovereign investments and was against any movement by the European Union to impose greater restrictions on SWFs, claiming that "We do not discriminate, we do not start to make judgment calls on whose capital it is."[25]

Political concerns Up to now, most SWFs' investments were in the form of 'passive investments' whereby they did not take direct management control. In fact, "Sovereign Wealth Funds have a track record that is almost impeccable. To my knowledge, there has been no investment made directly tied to politics" according to Morgan Stanley's Stephen Jen. Yet it was the very fear of such an activity that put government authorities on edge. The Bush administration emphasized the potential threat of national security, whereby SWFs would use their investments as a vehicle to assert their own political or national interests.

Although they were not in the form of SWF investments, China National Offshore Oil Company (CNOOC)'s attempt to purchase an American oil company or Dubai Port World's attempt to takeover operations of U.S. ports in previous years were all blocked amid fierce opposition citing conflict with national security interests. In 1992, the U.S. passed a specific act to review any state-controlled investment that would raise a national security concern. Then in 2007, Congress passed the Foreign Investment National Security Act which formalized the government's review of foreign investments to a wider range of areas, such as those that affect "critical US infrastructure" and subjected all acquisitions by state-owned entities to be investigated, unless a senior government official certified that the transaction did not conflict with national security interests. Under the same theme, the U.S. Treasury also made a new proposal in April 2008 to subject foreign investments under 10% to an investigation by the Committee on Foreign Investment, a departure from the previous notion that exempted, in most cases, investments under 10% that did not constitute a "change in control."[26] The new regulation, if approved, however, would exempt investments, including those made by SWFs, made solely for investment purposes and those that do not involve any other rights that would represent a form of control over a company, such as representation on the board or the right to question management's business policies or financial transactions.

Analysts also pointed out the risk that SWFs may target specific industries in the future, such as high tech, energy, and the financial sectors and use them to gain access to valuable technology, research, or know-how. For example, China grabbed the world's attention for its voracious appetite for commodities to help its booming economy sustain its growth path, accounting for 26% of total global demand for key industrial commodities in 2006 from 21% in 2004.[27] In early 2008 alone, the Chinese investment fund had acquired stakes in BP, the world's third largest integrated oil company, and in Total, the giant French oil corporation.

Singapore's Temasek had already had its share of political friction with other Asian governments regarding its investments. In 2006, Temasek bought a controlling stake in Thailand's telecom giant, Shin Corp., from the former Prime Minister Thaksin Shinawatrathe, and his family. The tax-free purchase triggered a massive public outcry and eventually led to a coup that pushed him out of office. The core objection, as *Euromoney* commented, was the concept of a big national asset being owned by Singapore.[28] The Singapore fund was also caught in an anti-trust lawsuit over accusations that Temasek's purchase of stakes in two major mobile phone companies in Indonesia violated anti-trust laws.

Source of market volatility? The U.S. Council on Foreign Relations claimed that the total value of all trade securities in Africa, the Middle East, and emerging Europe came to about $4 trillion.[29] Given SWFs' interest in these markets and the projected future growth trend of these funds, many observers cited concerns that they could become a source of major market volatility. For instance, if SWFs started to further diversify away from long-term stable governments bonds into riskier assets or equity stakes, this could drive interest rates higher. If governments chose to reduce their dollar holdings, especially in terms of foreign reserves, that could weaken the dollar. Morgan Stanley estimated that a 1% per year decline in the U.S. dollar's share of total reserves would translate into $60 billion worth of currency outflows of the greenback.[30] The IMF even cited concerns that SWFs' growing involvement in the financial sector could hinder the central bank's ability to coordinate and resolve domestic financial crises.

Other issues Lawrence Summers, Harvard economist and former Treasury Secretary, highlighted the risks associated with ownership of government-controlled entities, questioning whether SWFs would act like ordinary shareholders whose goal is to maximize the value of their investment. Summers stated that "they [SWFs] may want to see their national companies compete effectively, or to extract technology or to achieve influence."[31] In other words, a conflict of interest may arise between SWFs and the managers of those assets. Given all the uncertainty and uneasiness about these government funds, many policymakers felt the need to not only clarify the rules of investments for SWFs, but also to reassess the guidelines for recipient countries as well.

The Need for Regulation?

National Security is a legitimate concern but should not be a cover for protectionist policies

—OECD[32]

Several proposals were being made to address investment recipient countries' concerns. In March, European Union leaders called for an international code of conduct governing sovereign wealth funds, leaving national governments the power to shield strategic industries such as defense. Under a voluntary code being drafted by the IMF, the organization called for sovereign investors to disclose details on their assets, investment strategy, and how they are shielded from political influence. Talks were being held with various SWFs and the Organization for Economic Co-operation and Development (OECD) agreed to coordinate the effort to develop a best set of practices and principles. Edwin Truman, an economist and former assistant secretary for International Affairs at the Treasury during the Clinton administration, argued that an adoption of a set of best practice guidelines would be in the interest of all parties involved, especially given that most advanced Western economies built their economic architecture under the basic assumption that the government's role should be limited.[33] As Morgan Stanley's Jen pointed out, "Overhaul of cross-border regulations is necessary because the existing rules were written for private players, not government entities."[34] For instance, government support and funding for SWFs could provide them with an advantage in terms of financing or access to classified information that may not be accessible to private companies.

Yet representatives from funds in the Persian Gulf voiced out their complaints that a 'best practice' code was not desirable, especially given that they had not done anything to arouse suspicions and receive the 'guilty until proven innocent' treatment. Bader al-Saad of the Kuwait Investment Authority argued that, "The consequences of imposing regulations on sovereign wealth funds will result in an adverse impact on global capital flows. These regulations will not solve or prevent any future financial crises."[35] Gao Xiqing, who ran China's China Investment Corporation, claimed that although it would eventually publish annual reports and adopt voluntary practices that would increase transparency, he viewed the push for such regulations as economically "stupid and unfair," especially when they were not required for U.S. hedge funds or private equity and he did not consider his fund a "vulture" as some critics called SWFs, just a typical investor.[36] Angela Gurria, Secretary General of the OECD, agreed that "...there should not be any legislation or any regulation or any code applied that unduly restricts the freedom of investment, because we would be doing ourselves a disservice," as long as the funds are transparent and motivated by profit.[37] In addition, several observers raised the concern that regulations could impose barriers that would hinder the free flow of capital, a potential phenomena that Truman warned would have a detrimental effect on the prosperity of the domestic and global economy; "We may not in all cases be comfortable with the consequences of the free flow of finance and investment either internally or across borders, but on balance it promotes competition and efficiency."[38]

Others, including Lawrence Summer and Kenneth Rogoff, former IMF chief economist and Harvard professor, favored the idea of requiring SWFs to invest through an intermediary asset manager, such as the way pension funds operate. Summers argued that this approach was likely to produce the best risk-adjusted returns. Yet how could organizations such as the IMF and OECD convince SWFs to voluntary agree to a set of common rules? Such talks touched upon the sensitive issue of how, if any, rules that governed international capital flows would affect national regulations on a country level. Each nation with a SWF had their own objectives and goals, not to mention different economic statuses and foreign investment policies. As OECD Secretary General Gurria noted, "On the one hand, formal rules and their application must be tailored to specific domestic needs and realities. On the other hand, this approach entails the risk that regulatory authorities with different mandates and constituencies will take inconsistent measures to solve similar problems."[39] Some critics also pointed to the IMF's past attempt to create a common international practice for sovereign debt restructuring. The Sovereign Debt Restructuring Mechanism (SDRM) proposal failed to gain enough support to materialize amid various concerns such as requiring individual countries to change their own legal regulations. Thus, observers wondered, what could be done to make SWFs an investment vehicle that both investing and recipient countries would be comfortable with?

Appendix U.S. Treasury Department Press Release

March 20, 2008
hp-881

Treasury Reaches Agreement on Principles for Sovereign Wealth Fund Investment with Singapore and Abu Dhabi

Washington, DC--Officials from the U.S. Treasury, the governments of Singapore and Abu Dhabi, and sovereign wealth funds ADIA and GIC met today in Washington, DC to discuss issues surrounding sovereign wealth funds, recipient country inward investment regimes, and efforts to develop best practices. Joining Treasury Secretary Henry M. Paulson, Jr. and Deputy Secretary Robert M. Kimmitt were Government of Abu Dhabi Executive Council Member Hamad Al Hurr Al Suwaidi, ADIA Executive Director Hareb Masood Al-Darmaki, Singapore Finance Minister Tharman Shanmugaratnam and GIC Deputy Chairman Tony Tan.

"We had a good discussion today on the issues surrounding sovereign wealth funds. Singapore and UAE have long-established, well-respected funds and are showing real leadership by joining with us today. The U.S. welcomes sovereign wealth fund investment and looks forward to continuing to work with these two countries and others to support the initiatives underway at the IMF and OECD to develop best practices for sovereign wealth funds and recipient countries," said Paulson. "The principles we agreed to here today will further those efforts."

Following today's meeting the three nations released the following joint statement and accompanying policy principles:

Sovereign wealth funds (SWFs) represent government-owned investment vehicles, funded by foreign exchange assets and commodity export receipts, etc., which invest internationally for financial objectives such as stabilization and intergenerational savings.

The United States, Abu Dhabi, and Singapore, being a group of nations with SWFs and a country receiving investments from SWFs, have a common interest in an open and stable international financial system. We support the processes underway in the International Monetary Fund (IMF) and the Organization for Economic Cooperation and Development (OECD) to develop voluntary best practices for SWFs and inward investment regimes for government-controlled investment in recipient countries, respectively. International agreement on a set of voluntary best practices will create a strong incentive among SWFs and investment-recipient countries to hold themselves to high standards. We hope that the IMF and OECD's work can build upon these basic principles:

Policy Principles for Sovereign Wealth Funds (SWFs)

1. SWF investment decisions should be based solely on commercial grounds, rather than to advance, directly or indirectly, the geopolitical goals of the controlling government. SWFs should make this statement formally as part of their basic investment management policies.

2. Greater information disclosure by SWFs, in areas such as purpose, investment objectives, institutional arrangements, and financial information particularly asset allocation, benchmarks, and rates of return over appropriate historical periods can help reduce uncertainty in financial markets and build trust in recipient countries.

3. SWFs should have in place strong governance structures, internal controls, and operational and risk management systems.

4. SWFs and the private sector should compete fairly.

5. SWFs should respect host-country rules by complying with all applicable regulatory and disclosure requirements of the countries in which they invest.

Policy Principles for Countries Receiving SWF Investment

1. Countries receiving SWF investment should not erect protectionist barriers to portfolio or foreign direct investment.

2. Recipient countries should ensure predictable investment frameworks. Inward investment rules should be publicly available, clearly articulated, predictable, and supported by strong and consistent rule of law.

3. Recipient countries should not discriminate among investors. Inward investment policies should treat like-situated investors equally.

4. Recipient countries should respect investor decisions by being as unintrusive as possible, rather than seeking to direct SWF investment. Any restrictions imposed on investments for national security reasons should be proportional to genuine national security risks raised by the transaction.

Source: U.S. Treasury Department.

Exhibit 1a Major Sovereign Wealth Funds as of October 2007

Country	Fund Name	Assets (US$ billions)	Inception Year	Source of Funds
UAE	Abu Dhabi Investment Authority	875.0	1976	Oil
Norway	Govt Pension Fund – Global	341.2	1996	Oil
Singapore	GIC	330.0	1981	Other
Saudi Arabia	Various	300.0	n/a	Oil
Kuwait	Reserve Fund for Future Generation	250.0	1953	Oil
China	State FX Investment Corp and Huejing Co.[a]	200.0	2007	Other
Singapore	Temasek Holdings	159.2	1974	Other
Libya	Oil Reserve Fund	50.0	2005	Oil
Algeria	Fond de regulation des recettes	42.6	2000	Oil
Qatar	Qatar Investment Authority	40.0	n/a	Oil, gas
US (Alaska)	Permanent Reserve Fund	38.0	1976	Oil
Brunei	Brunei Investment Authority	30.0	1983	Oil
Malaysia	Khazanah Nasional BHD	25.7	1993	Other
Russia	Stabilisation Fund	24.0	2003	Oil
Korea	Korea Investment Corp.	20.0	2006	Other
Other		194.4		
TOTAL		**2,827.5**		

Source: Stephen Jen, "Sovereign Wealth Funds," Morgan Stanley, October 2007, p. 2.
[a]Operation of Huejing Co. not yet finalized

Exhibit 1b SWF Investments by Value (in US$ billions)

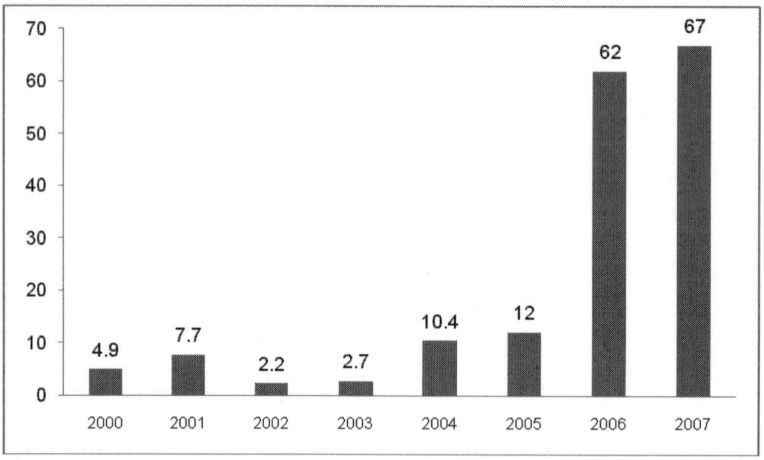

Source: Karen Yourish and Laura Stanton, "Top sovereign wealth funds," *Washington Post*, March 27, 2008.

Exhibit 2a Foreign Currency Reserves

	Foreign Exchange Reserves				
	2006 (in billions of US$)	Change 2001-2006 (%)	Share of GDP 2006 (%)	Reserves/GDP[a] 2002-2006 (%)	Current Account/GDP[b] 2002-2006 (%)
China[c]	1,066	403	41	8.6	5.5
Japan	875	126	20	2.2	3.5
Russia[cd]	295	807	30	8.4	9.7
Taiwan	266	118	75	8.9	7.1
Korea[cd]	238	133	27	3.9	1.9
India	170	276	19	3.7	-0.3
Singapore[cd]	136	81	103	11.3	22.5
Hong Kong	133	20	70	2.6	9.9
Brazil	86	139	8	1.4	1.0
Malaysia[c]	82	185	54	8.9	13.3
Algeria[c]	78	333	68	14.0	17.2
Norway[c]	56	153	17	2.6	14.3
United Arab Emirates[c]	28	98	16	2.4	12.3
Kuwait[c]	12	32	13	0.9	32.9
Qatar[c]	5	346	10	2.4	20.0

Source: Edwin M. Truman, "A Scoreboard for Sovereign Wealth Funds," Paper presented at the Conference on China's Exchange Rate Policy, October 17, 2007, Peterson Institute, Washington, DC, p. 11.

[a] Sum of changes in reserves as a ratio to sum of total output

[b] Sum of current account balances as a ratio to sum of total output

[c] Has one or more SWFs

[d] Reserves include SWF in whole of in part

Exhibit 2b U.S. Balance of Payments (in current million dollars)

	2005	2006	2007[a]
Current Account			
Exports of goods and services and income receipts	**1,788,557**	**2,096,165**	**2,410,587**
Exports of goods and services	1,283,070	1,445,703	1,628,358
Goods (balance of payments basis)	894,631	1,023,109	1,149,208
Services	388,439	422,594	479,150
Income receipts	505,488	650,462	782,229
Imports of goods and services and income payments	**-2,454,871**	**-2,818,047**	**-3,044,786**
Imports of goods and services	-1,997,441	-2,204,225	-2,336,873
Goods (balance of payments basis)	-1,681,780	-1,861,380	-1,964,577
Services	-315,661	-342,845	-372,296
Income payments	-457,430	-613,823	-707,913
Unilateral current transfers, net	**-88,535**	**-89,595**	**-104,438**
Capital Account	**-4,054**	**-3,913**	**-2,317**
Financial Account			
U.S.-owned assets abroad[b]	**-426,875**	**-1,055,176**	**-1,206,332**
U.S. official reserve assets	14,096	2,374	-122
U.S. Government assets, other than official reserve assets	5,539	5,346	-22,931
U.S. private assets	-446,510	-1,062,896	-1,183,278
Direct Investment	7,662	-235,358	-335,415
Foreign Securities	-197098	-289422	-273851
Other	797,813	864,352	1,461,766
Foreign-owned assets in the U.S.[b]	**1,204,231**	**1,859,597**	**1,863,697**
Foreign official assets in the U.S.	259,268	440,264	412,698
Other foreign assets in the U.S.	944,963	1,419,333	1,450,999
Direct investment	108,996	180,580	204,414
U.S. Treasury securities	132,300	-35,931	166,301
U.S. securities other than U.S. Treasury securities	450,386	591,951	391,884
U.S. currency	18,969	12,571	10,937
Other	234,312	670,162	677,463
Financial derivatives, net	**n.a.**	**28,762**	**n.a.**
Statistical discrepancy	**-18,454**	**-17,794**	**83,590**
GDP in current million dollars	**12,433,900**	**13,194,700**	**13,841,300**

Source: Bureau of Economic Analysis, International Transactions Data

[a]Preliminary figures

[b]Excluding financial derivatives

Exhibit 3 Selected Data on Countries with SWFs

Country	Year	GDP (current US$ bln)	GDP growth (annual %)	GDP per capita, PPP (current int'l $)	FDI, net inflows (% of GDP)	Current Account (BoP, current US$ bln)	Budget balance (% of GDP)	Inflation, consumer prices (%)	Gross domestic savings (% of GDP)	Lending Interest Rate (%)
UAE	2000	70.6	5.0	25,442.6	0.7[b]	12.2[b]	-3.8	2.0[b]	41.2	9.7
	2005	129.7	8.5	33,484.0	8.3[b]	35.9[b]	8.1	13.8[b]	42.4	7.2
Norway	2000	168.3	3.3	38,916.6	4.1	25.1	15.4	3.1	37.5	8.2
	2006	334.9	2.9	50,078.0	1.4	55.2	17.9	2.3	40.0	4.3
Singapore	2000	92.7	10.1	32,610.1	17.8	10.7	2.0	1.4	46.9	5.8
	2006	132.2	7.9	44,708.2	18.3	36.3	0.6	1.0	50.5	5.3
Saudi Arabia	2000	188.4	4.9	17,402.5	-1.0	14.3	3.2	-1.1	37.5	11.2
	2006	349.1	4.3	22,296.3	0.2	99.1	21.4	2.2	49.3	-2.5
Kuwait	2000	37.7	4.7	32,328.2	0.0	14.7	25.3	2.5	37.0	8.9
	2005	80.8	8.5	43,551.0	0.3	51.0	37.9	4.1	57.0	7.5
China	2000	1,198.5	8.4	2,371.3	3.2	20.5	-2.5	0.3	37.5	5.9
	2006	2,644.7	10.7	4,644.0	3.0	249.9	-0.8	1.5	52.5	6.1
Libya	2000	34.5	1.1	9,122.0	0.4[b]	6.3	14.4	-2.9	32.9	7.0
	2006	50.3	5.6	11,622.0	4.0[b]	22.2	32.8[a]	3.4	na	6.3
Algeria	2000	54.8	2.2	4,552.0	0.8	8.9	9.7	0.3	44.8	10.0
	2006	114.7	3.0	6,347.1	1.6	21.7[a]	13.7[a]	2.5	54.4[a]	8.0
Qatar	2000	17.8	9.1	na	5.1b	4.6[b]	7.9	1.7	65.1	11.4
	2005	42.5	6.1	70,715.8	5.5b	7.5[b]	9.2	8.8	70.3	6.4
U.S.	2000	9,764.8	3.7	34,600.3	3.3	-417.3	2.4	3.4	16.6	9.2
	2006	13,163.9	2.9	43,967.8	1.4	-811.5	-1.9	3.2	13.5[a]	8.0
Brunei	2000	6.0	2.8	42,166.3	na	na	na	1.6	44.6	na
	2006	11.6	5.1	49,897.7	na	na	na	0.1	56.5	na
Malaysia	2000	90.3	8.9	9,219.8	4.2	8.5	-5.5	1.5	47.3	7.5
	2006	150.7	5.9	12,536.1	4.0	25.5	-3.3	3.6	37.7	6.6
Russia	2000	259.7	10.0	7,639.2	1.0	46.8	2.4	20.8	38.7	24.4
	2006	986.9	6.7	13,115.7	3.1	94.3	7.4	9.7	32.9	10.5
Korea	2000	511.7	8.5	15,511.3	1.8	12.3	1.1	2.3	34.2	8.5
	2006	888.0	5.0	22,988.1	0.4	6.1	0.4	2.2	30.9	6.0

Source: Created by casewriter using World Development Indicators, World Bank; data on budget balance and lending interest rates from Economic Intelligence Unit database.

[a] 2005 figure.

[b] Data from Economic Intelligence Unit database.

Exhibit 4a Recent Sovereign Wealth Fund Activities

Investment Announcement	Acquirer	Target (Stake)	Target Country	Value (in $ billions)	Status[a]
January 14, '08	Govt of Singapore Investment Corp., Kuwait Investment Authority & others[b]	Citigroup	United States	12.5	Preliminary Discussions
January 14, '08	Kuwait Investment Authority; Mizuho Financial; Korea Investment Fund	Merrill Lynch	United States	6.2	Preliminary Discussions
December 24, '07	Temasek Holdings Ltd; Davis Selected Advisors	Merrill Lynch	United States	6.2	Pending
December 19, '07	China Investment Corp.	Morgan Stanley (9.9%)	United States	5.0	Preliminary Discussions
December 10, '07	Govt of Singapore Investment Corp; Saudi Arabian Monetary Agency	UBS AG (9%)	Switzerland	11.5	Preliminary Discussions
November 27, '07	Abu Dhabi Investment Authority	Citigroup (4.9%)	United States	7.5	Preliminary Discussions
November 7, '07	China Investment Corp.	China Everbright Bank Co. Ltd (70.92%)	China	2.7	Completed
October 30, '07	Dubai Int'l Capital LLC	Och-Ziff Capital Management Group (9.9%)	United States	1.3	Pending
September 20,'07	Mubadala Development Co.	Carlyle Group (7.5%)	United States	1.4	Pending
September 20, 07	Qatar Investment Authority	London Stock Exchange Plc – LSE Group (20%)	United Kingdom	1.3	Completed
July 23, '07	Temasek Holdings (Pte) Ltd.	Barclays Plc (1.77%)	United Kingdom	2.0	Completed
May 21 '07	China Investment Corp	Blackstone Group (10%)	United States	3.0	Completed
March 7, '07	Temasek Holdings (Pte) Ltd.	Standard Chartered Plc (3.74%)	United Kingdom	1.4	Completed
March 27, '06	Temasek Holdings (Pte) Ltd.	Standard Chartered plc (11.55%)	United Kingdom	4.0	Completed
September 1 '05	Temasek Holdings (Pte) Ltd.	Bank of China Ltd (5%)	China	1.6	Completed
June 27, '05	Temasek Holdings (Pte) Ltd.	China Construction Bank Corp (5.1%)	China	2.5	Completed

Source: Adapted by casewriter using Stephen Grocer, "Sovereign Power," *Wall Street Journal*, http://online.wsj.com/public/resources/documents/info-launch.html?project=foreignSWF08&w=980&h=530, accessed March 20, 2008.

[a] As of March 2008

b Private investors; Capital Research Global investors

Exhibit 4b Global Financial Institutions' Writedowns Related to the Subprime Crisis

	Writedowns for 4Q07 (in $ billions)
Bear Stearns	1.9
Citigroup	18.0
Credit Suisse Group[a]	2.9
Goldman Sachs[b]	-
JP Morgan	1.3
Lehman Brothers[b]	3.5
Merrill Lynch[c]	16.7
Morgan Stanley	9.4
UBS AG	13.7
HSBC	3.4

Source: Created by case writer using "Global investment banks and brokers remain challenged after dismal fiscal year end," *Standard & Poor's*, February 26, 2008, as published in Laura Alfaro and Renee Kim, "U.S. Subprime Mortgage Crisis: Policy Reactions," HBS Case No. N9-708-036 (Boston: Harvard Business School Publishing, 2008), p. 16.

Exhibit 5 U.S. Return on Foreign Investments vs. Foreign Investment in the U.S., 1990–2005

	Claims (U.S. foreign investment)	Liabilities (Foreigners' investment in the U.S.)	Diff
Aggregate			
Total Return	7.4	6.4	1.0
Yield	5.0	4.1	0.9
Capital Gains	2.4	2.4	0.0
Direct Investment			
Total Return	10.4	7.9	2.5
Yield	6.9	2.4	4.5
Capital Gains	3.6	5.5	-1.9
Bonds			
Total Return	8.3	6.7	1.6
Yield	7.6	6.2	1.4
Capital Gains	0.7	0.5	0.2
Equities			
Total Return	10.2	12.1	-1.9
Yield	2.5	2.2	0.3
Capital Gains	7.7	9.9	-2.2
Other			
Total Return	4.3	4.0	0.3
Yield	4.0	4.2	-0.2
Capital Gains	0.2	-0.2	0.4

Source: Adapted by casewriter based on Stephanie E. Curcuru, Tomas Dvorak, and Francis E. Warnock, "Cross-Border Returns Differentials," Federal Reserve Bank of Dallas Globalization and Monetary Policy Institute Working Paper No. 4, p. 27, http://www.dallasfed.org/gmpi/wpapers/2007/0004.pdf, accessed April 11, 2008.

Exhibit 6 SWF's Investment Approach and Transparency

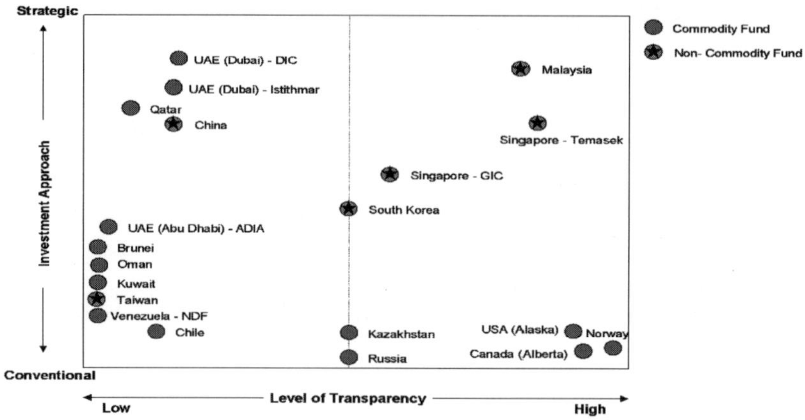

Source: Gerard Lyons, "State Capitalism: the rise of sovereign wealth funds," Standard Chartered, October 15, 2007.

Endnotes

[1] Steven Weisman, "A fear of foreign investments," *New York Times*, August 21, 2007.

[2] "China investment an open book? Sovereign Wealth Fund's president promises transparency," *CBS News*, April 6, 2008.

[3] John Burton, "Wealth funds exploit credit squeeze," *Financial Times*, March 23, 2008.

[4] Francesco Guerrera and Justin Baer, "Buffett defends sovereign wealth funds," *Financial Times*, February 29, 2008.

[5] Temasek Holdings Corporate Profile, http://www.temasekholdings.com.sg/about_us.htm, accessed April 14, 2008.

[6] Andrew Kramer, "Russia creates a $32 billion sovereign wealth fund," *New York Times*, February 1, 2008.

[7] Stephen Jen, "CGG: Transforming oil into financial wealth," Morgan Stanley Research, November 15, 2007. The six member countries of GCC are: Bahrain, Kuwait, Oman, Qatar, Saudi Arabia and UAE.

[8] For more, see Ronald McKinnon and G. Schnabl, "China: a stabilizing or deflationary influence in East Asia? The problem of conflicted virtue," Stanford Center for Int'l Development Working Paper No. 196, Stanford University, 2003, and Akiko Terada-Hagiwara, "Foreign Exchange Reserves, Exchange Rate Regimes, and Monetary Policy: Issues in Asia," Asian Development Bank Economics and Research Department Working Paper Series No. 61, January 2005.

[9] Mark Allen and Jaime Caruana, "Sovereign Wealth Funds – A Work Agenda," IMF, February 29, 2008, http://www.imf.org/external/np/pp/eng/2008/02282008/pdf, accessed April 3, 2008.

[10] Laura Dixon and Richard Lapper, "Chile to invest dollar 5.9bn surplus in new sovereign fund," *Financial Times*, April 9, 2008.

[11] Mark Allen and Jaime Caruana, "Sovereign Wealth Funds – A Work Agenda," International Monetary Fund, February 29, 2008, http://www.imf.org/external/np/pp/eng/2008/02282008/pdf, accessed April 3, 2008

[12]"Sovereign funds shake the logic of capitalism," Financial Times blog, blogs.ft.com/wolfforum/2007/07/sovereign-funds.html/, accessed March 20, 2008.

[13] Ibid.

[14] Ariana Eunjung Cha, "Foreign wealth funds defend U.S. investments," *Washington Post*, March 27, 2008.

[15] "Singapore Min: Open to sovereign wealth fun transparency," *Dow Jones International News*, March 3, 2008.

[16] John Burton, "Wealth funds exploit credit squeeze," *Financial Times*, March 23, 2008.

[17] General Counsel Scott G. Alvarez, "Sovereign Wealth Funds" testimony before the Subcommittee on Domestic and International Monetary Policy, Trade, and Technology, Board of Governors of the Federal Reserve System, March 5, 2008.

[18] Ibid.

[19] Ariana Eunjung Cha, "Foreign wealth funds defend U.S. investments," *Washington Post*, March 27, 2008.

[20] Chris Wright, "Temasek: a fund apart?" *Euromoney*, December 1, 2007.

[21] Lawrence Summers, "Sovereign funds shake the logic of capitalism," *Financial Times*, July 30, 2007.

[22] For more, see Robert Posen and Also Sesia Jr., "Norway Sells Wal-Mart," HBS No. 308-019 (Boston: Harvard Business School Publishing, 2008).

[23] "Transparency concerns for sov wealth funds – Norway official," *Reuters News*, March 31, 2008.

[24] Christopher S. Rugaber, "Proliferation of multibillion-dollar foreign investments in US banks raises concerns," *Associated Press*, January 15, 2008.

[25] Andrew Peaple, "Interview: UK open to China Sovereign Wealth Fund Investment," *Dow Jones*, November 20, 2007.

[26] Stephanie Kirchgassner, "US invites foreign investors to forgo 'control'", *Financial Times*, April 21, 2008.

[27] Gerard Lyons, "State capitalism: the rise of sovereign wealth funds," Standard Chartered, October 15, 2007.

[28] Chris Wright, "Temasek: a fund apart?" *Euromoney*, December 1, 2007.

[29] "Sovereign Wealth Funds," Council on Foreign Relations, http://www.cfr.org/publication/15251/, accessed March 15, 2008.

[30] Stephen Jen, "Full Deployment of SWFs to hurt both USD & EUR," Morgan Stanley Research, October 18, 2007. According to Jen, USD, EUR and GBP assets account for about 95% of the world's reserve holdings

[31] Lawrence Summers, "Sovereign funds shake the logic of capitalism," *Financial Times*, July 30, 2007.

[32] "Sovereign Wealth Funds and the recipient country policies," OECD Investment Committee Report, April 4, 2008, p. 4.

[33] For more, see Edwin Truman, "Sovereign Wealth Fund Acquisitions and Other Foreign Government Investments in the United States: Assessing the Economic and national Security Implications," Testimony before the Committee on Banking, Housing, and Urban Affairs, U.S. Senate, November 14, 2007.

[34] Stephen Jen, case writer interview, April 7, 2008.

[35] Will McSheehy and John Rega, "Kuwait Sovereign Fund Attacks Plans for More Scrutiny," *Bloomberg News*, April 9, 2008.

[36] "China investment an open book? Sovereign Wealth Fund's President promises transparency," *CBS News*, April 6, 2008.

[37] "OECD sees no need for sovereign wealth fund rules," *Reuters News*, March 25, 2008.

[38] Edwin Truman testimony, p. 6.

[39] Angel Gurria, "'The 17th European Banking Congress: Global Capital – Threat or Salvation?"Opening Remarks, Frankfurt, November 23, 2007, http://www.oecd.org/document/31/0,3343,de_2649_34487_39677151_1_1_1_1,00.html, accessed April 1, 2008.

Global Financial Crisis

HARVARD | BUSINESS | SCHOOL

9-709-057
APRIL 7, 2009

LAURA ALFARO
RENEE KIM

The First Global Financial Crisis of the 21st Century

But there is one enduring lesson of the history of financial crises: ***they all end.***

—Lawrence Summers, Director of U.S. National Economic Council[1]

In March 2009, the World Bank presented its most dismal outlook for the global economy to date, forecasting negative growth for the full year, a phenomenon not seen since World War II. The World Bank's sister organization, the International Monetary Fund (IMF) released a similar outlook (see **Exhibit 1**). It also warned that the global recession was getting worse with world growth falling 5% in the fourth quarter of 2008. More than $50 trillion in wealth had been wiped out across borders over the last 18 months.[2] Policymakers across the world found themselves trying to tackle a dizzying array of problems from rising unemployment to frightened investors to plunging exports. Consumer confidence levels for the Organization for Economic Cooperation and Development (OECD) members stood at their lowest level since 1978 (see **Exhibit 2**).

The instigator behind the unprecedented global situation was none other than the U.S. subprime mortgage crisis, which had caused havoc across the global economy. Many academics and policymakers also argued that the financial debacle's origins were rooted in the "global imbalances"—the phenomenon of the United States' large current account deficit funded by large current account surpluses in China and other countries.[3] The situation was also a true testimony of how intertwined individual economies had become over the years. With the explosion of international capital flows, financial institutions in various corners of the world had inadvertently participated in the United States' debt-financing boom.

Individual nations tried to stabilize and steer their economies towards recovery through monetary, fiscal, and financial policies. At the same time, they recognized that the scope and scale of the financial crisis required a greater coordinated effort. Harvard Professor Dani Rodrik claimed that policymakers, "Need to come to grips with the reality that national regulations and international markets are inextricably linked with—and in need of—each other."[4] Yet at the Group of 20's (G20) summit of top level financial ministers held in the first week of April, 2009, there was discord among the nations that accounted for 80% of the world economy on what kind of action had to be taken to meet their goals. The United States wanted more countries to spend in fiscal stimulus measures while several European nations, led by France and Germany, stressed the need for sweeping financial regulations at the global level instead.

Professor Laura Alfaro and Research Associate Renee Kim prepared this case. This case was developed from published sources. HBS cases are developed solely as the basis for class discussion. Cases are not intended to serve as endorsements, sources of primary data, or illustrations of effective or ineffective management.

Although there were underlying differences in domestic economic constraints that caused the discord among nations on what had to be done, there were also contrasting views on what kind of short and long-term policies would really work. As Lawrence Summers, the chief economic advisor to President Barack Obama noted, all crises did come to an end. The issue was—how fast and efficiently could nations recover from the first global financial crisis of the 21st century?

Monetary Policy

The history of the City is in large part the history of banking crises…[But] a collapse of confidence in the coffee houses of Lombard Street was one thing; a collapse of confidence in the world economy is quite another.

—Mervyn King, Governor of the Bank of England[5]

One of the first actions central banks took in response to the crisis was to lower interest rates. The European Central Bank (ECB) had moved a little less aggressively compared to the United States or the United Kingdom (see **Exhibit 3**). However, by early 2009, several central banks around the world had dropped their rates to near zero percent and increasingly shifted towards non-conventional tools. The Bank of England started to buy selected debt from the private sector in 2009. The Bank of Japan, which had been forced to hold interest rates below the one percent level for more than a decade, opted to purchase commercial paper and corporate bonds.[6] In countries such as Australia and South Korea where concerns over rising inflation had hindered any move to reduce interest rates prior to the crisis, central banks found themselves with greater room for rate cuts as growth slowed and upward pressure on prices subsided.

Much attention was focused on whether the ECB would have to implement additional rate cuts given the dire state of EU member countries. Although ECB President Jean-Claude Trichet did not rule out zero interest rates, he said, "We felt there were a certain number of disadvantages associated with zero rates," while Juergen Stark on the Executive Board stated that "overly aggressive reductions in our policy rate when we cannot see any risk of deflation would exacerbate and not resolve uncertainty."[7]

In addition, despite the various monetary easing measures central banks had adopted, many analysts argued that monetary policy was simply not enough to ease the credit crunch or encourage domestic demand. In March 2009, the United Kingdom saw its bond auction to sell gilts fail for the first time since 2002, unable to attract enough debt investors for the 40-year offering which was part of its quantitative easing plan. Thus, the world's attention increasingly shifted towards fiscal policy.

Fiscal Stimulus – Keynes to the Rescue?

And in the long run, it turns out, Keynes is anything but dead.

—Paul Krugman, Economics Nobel Prize Winner[8]

The IMF stood at the front lines advocating for a greater fiscal stimulus beyond what had already been announced to promote growth and cushion the effects of the global recession. The message was that time was of essence and countries should increase fiscal stimulus by 2% of GDP, equivalent to about $1,200 billion. Washington pushed forward with an aggressive $787 billion fiscal package, which represented more than 5% of GDP. In November 2008, China revealed a four trillion yuan stimulus package, about 6% of the country's GDP to combat slowing growth as well. The various packages came in the form of tax cuts, increases in infrastructure spending, and greater social safety net benefits (see **Exhibit 4**). However, the United States urged more countries to do the same, insisting that the global recession had to be combated on a global level.

The argument behind a global fiscal stimulus package was that it had to be done on a bigger scale to have a collective real impact on the global economy. Another belief was that only widespread group action would prevent one country from being singled out and punished for temporarily expanding its fiscal deficit. Others expressed concerns that a country could try to reap the benefit from another's stimulus package rather than pursuing one on its own. As President Obama noted, "We don't want a situation in which some countries are making extraordinary efforts, and other countries aren't, with the hope that somehow the countries that are making those important steps lift everybody up."[9] Australia's Prime Minister Kevin Rudd was also a strong advocator for global coordination, urging that such a failure would slow recovery and reduce the aggregate impact of the stimulus packages.

Many nations, however, were not in a position to expand their fiscal balance In fact, the IMF recognized that only five nations—The United States, China, Australia, Spain, and Saudi Arabia—would reach the goal of creating a stimulus package worth 2% of GDP in 2009.[10]. For instance, Latin America and the Middle East had withstood the global recession relatively well into the mid-2008s, thanks to the high price of commodities. However, the recent slump in commodity prices no longer made their economies immune to the rest of the world (see **Exhibit 5**). As a result, oil rich countries had less money to invest abroad and tended to keep their capital for domestic purposes, such as supporting infrastructure projects.

Ban Ki-Moon, United Nations' Secretary-General, called on the G-20 leaders to support a $1,000 billion stimulus package for developing countries threatened by the global financial crisis: "If we don't handle the current economic crisis properly with a sense of strong determination and very strong and solid political leadership I'm concerned that this may not only be an economic crisis, but may develop into global political instability,"[11] IMF's Strauss-Kahn identified the impact of the crisis on low-income countries the third wave of the global financial crisis. For these countries, he noted, their sufferings stemmed from their increased integration with the world economy through trade and financing rather than having a direct exposure to the toxic bad assets.[12]

The impact of the crisis on emerging and low-income countries was evident in the sudden reversal of international capital flows. Net private capital flows in 2008 tumbled to half of their previous year's level at $466 billion and were projected to fall in 2009 to $165 billion (see **Exhibit 6**). Foreign direct investment showed signs of sudden stoppages as investors found themselves in a more difficult financing position amid uncertainty of the prospects of investment returns with the dismal global economic outlook (see **Exhibit 7**). In addition, external financing requirements were expected to exceed private sources of financing in more than two thirds of 104 developing countries, indicating a cumulative financing gap of $268 billion, according to the World Bank. At the same time, foreign investors were drawn to U.S. Treasury bills; "It's a huge safe haven effect. The basic assumption that people are making is that the U.S. government will never default on its debt," claimed an economist at a Washington D.C.-based think tank.[13]

Europe, on the other hand, was not in favor of boosting additional spending, following the European Union's (EU) approval for a 200 billion euros stimulus package in November 2008. Rather, some EU member countries wanted to focus on tightening regulations, especially over hedge funds and private equity that would address the international financial system. Trichet of the ECB insisted that, "Nothing will really work until the financial sector is back on track and ready to lend on a sustainable basis. I would say the exact same with the budget... Quick implementation, quick disbursement is what is needed."[14] Trichet expressed concerns that too much government debt would push up long-term interest rates and ultimately hurt consumers and investors' already tattered confidence. Jean-Claude Juncker, head of the Euro Group of finance ministers, echoed this view, insisting that, "Europe has done what it needs to do."[15]

In Germany, one of the most vocal opponents to an increase in fiscal stimulus, Chancellor Angela Merkel noted that its social welfare benefits were already more generous than other countries. A 50 billion euro package had already been approved and Meeker argued, "It is not time to look at more growth measures. I disagree with this idea completely."[16] In addition, Germany had traditionally been conservative when it came to increasing budget deficit, especially as it grew increasingly concerns about Eastern European EU members' alarming debt levels. Czech Republic Prime Minister Mirek Topolanek went as far as claiming that the U.S. fiscal stimulus measures were "the road to hell."[17] Such positions stood in direct conflict with the IMF's chief Dominique Strauss-Kahn who insisted that, "[...] the fact that some advanced and emerging economies cannot or should not engage in fiscal stimulus, makes it all the more important that other countries do their part."[18] The United States and Britain also showed uneasiness of how tighter financial regulations could affect their positions as two of the most important financial centers in the world.

The Politics of Protectionism

Protectionism is the road to ruin.

—Gordon Brown, U.K. Prime Minister[19]

The global financial crisis was also having a detrimental effect on the flow of international trade. Demand had declined dramatically while the World Trade Organization (WTO) highlighted the problem in accessing trade financing to support exports and imports as another major cause behind the steep contraction in trade (see **Exhibit 8**). In 2009, the WTO forecasted a 9% decline in exports led by weaker demand from advanced nations. The decline in trade was particularly disturbing for leading to another trend—a growing number of countries that were implementing some kind of form of economic protectionism. The World Bank reported that 17 of the G20 countries had implemented trade restrictions since the outbreak of the financial crisis. Anti-dumping claims also rose 20% in 2008 from the previous year (see **Exhibit 9**). Governments were adopting measures that would support specific industries as part of their fiscal stimulus packages, as seen in the United States' "Buy American" provision of requiring use of domestic steel for certain projects.[20] In other corners of the world, India banned Chinese toys while Argentina imposed tougher licensing requirements on textiles and leather goods.

Pascal Lamy, WTO Director-General, urged that, "Government must avoid making this bad situation worse by reverting to protectionist measure which in reality protect no nation and threaten the loss of more jobs."[21] In particular, several nations had provided support for their ailing auto sector, long hailed as a symbolic industry for each country but strained by problems ranging from overcapacity to legacy loans even before the outbreak of the credit crisis (see **Exhibit 10**). France, whose auto sector was estimated to account for nearly 10% of the French working age population, provided about $8 billion in loans to Renault and Peugeot-Citroen under the condition that they would not close factories in France. French President Nicolas Sarkozy even went as far stating that, "We want to stop factories from relocating abroad, and if possible to bring them back,"[22] provoking anger among its eastern European neighbors where many production factories were located.

Other Proposals

Every day brings new evidence that psychologies have changed.

—Dominique Strauss-Kahn, IMF Managing Director[23]

Other proposals to address the mounting crisis shifted attention to the IMF, which strived to play a greater role in the global financial turmoil. G20 leaders pledged to double the IMF's coffers to $750 billion.[24] The agency was also promised $250 billion in Special Drawing Rights, which would allow countries to secure loans from the IMF without stringent loan conditions. The availability of the loans were previously limited and allocated based on member countries' quotas with the IMF, which meant that emerging economies and low-income countries' had access to fewer funds than the G7 countries.

IMF Managing Director Strauss-Kahn embraced the latest arrangement, calling it "the beginning of increasing the role of the IMF not only as a lender of last resort... but also in providing liquidity to the rest of the world which is the role of a monetary institution like ours."[25] On the other hand, Kenneth Rogoff, Harvard professor and former IMF research director, disagreed with the idea of increasing the IMF"s lending capabilities, insisted that "the IMF's role, even in the current crisis, should be sharpened as an interlocutor between lenders and developing country borrowers, rather than simply as a replacement for all other loan sources."[26]

Even if the IMF had more money to lend, it was questionable whether countries would be willing to seek help from the institution. For instance, the Fund ended up altering the terms of a $100 billion lending program, announced in October 2008, attaching fewer conditions on longer-term loans and significantly raising the ceiling on how much qualified countries could borrow after attracting no borrowers. Yet many nations still held back, out of fear of the negative message that could be projected by taking out an IMF loan. Countries such as South Korea, an export-oriented nation struggling from sluggish demand, said it would rely on other financing means, such as its foreign currency reserves instead. The reluctance was closely associated with the negative stigma the IMF had generated in Asia for its role during the 1997-1998 Asian financial crisis. Many critics blamed the IMF for aggravating the recipient countries' dire situation in the wrong direction by imposing harsh and wide-ranging loan conditions.[27] Thus, it remained to be seen whether the expanded funding would empower the institution to play a better and more important role in solving the current global financial crisis.

Another controversial proposal came from China's central bank governor Zhou Xiaochuan, who called for a new global currency that would essentially replace the U.S. dollar as the world's representative reserve currency. As the global financial turmoil exhibited the vulnerability and weaknesses of the international financial community's dependency on the greenback, Zhou said a new currency, consisting of a basket of global currencies and monitored by the IMF, could "achieve the objective of safeguarding global economic and financial stability"[28] (see **Exhibit 11**). Russia had voiced out such a proposal earlier as well. Yet such a move was unlikely to gain wider support, given the political and economic obstacles such a move would require. President Obama and Treasury Secretary Geithner were quick to dismiss the proposal.

With the major advanced economies all in a recession, the crisis had diminished the once prominent theory of decoupling. Leaders of the G20 left the London summit with promises to help revive world trade and work towards financial regulations. Developing nations were promised a greater role in the global financial system with the agreement to create a new Financial Stability Board that would include all G20 members for the first time. Did the current status leave the global economy towards a recovery path? Was the world economy truly at risk of falling into a deeper recession without more fiscal stimulus? What should be done at the international level to prevent future global chaos?

Exhibit 1 IMF's World Economic Outlook (as of January 2009)

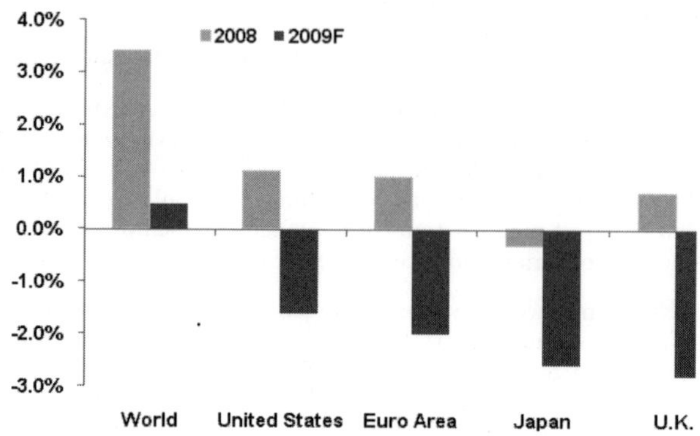

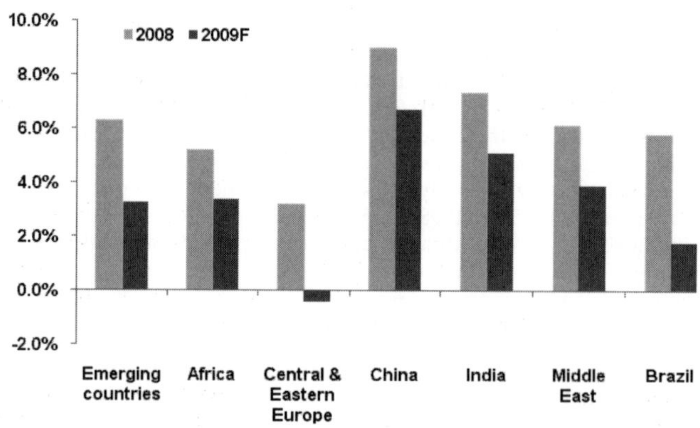

Source: Adapted by casewriter from IMF, "World Economic Outlook Update," January 28, 2009.

Exhibit 2 Consumer Confidence in OECD Area

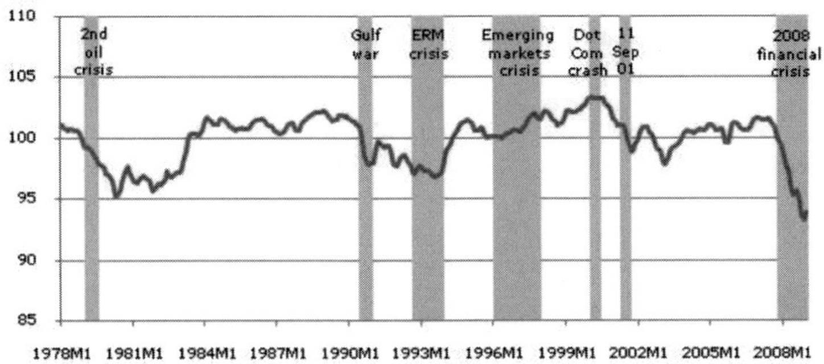

Source: OECD, "Financial Crisis Sees Collapse in OECD Consumer Confidence," http://www.oecd.org, accessed March 13, 2009.

Exhibit 3 Central Banks' Key Interest Rates (%)

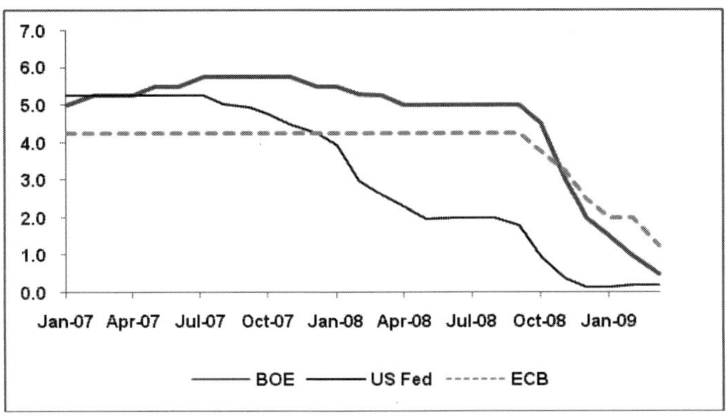

Source: Bank of England, European Central Bank, and the U.S. Federal Reserve Board.

Exhibit 4a Composition of Fiscal Stimulus Measures in G-7 Nation and China

Measure	Canada	China	France	Germany	India	Italy	Japan	UK	US
Expenditure:									
Infrastructure investment	X	X	X	X	X		X	X	X
Support to SMEs and/or farmers				X			X		
Safety nets	X	X	X	X		X	X	X	X
Housing/construction support	X	X	X	X			X	X	
Strategic industries support	X	X		X	X				
Other	X	X	X	X	X		X	X	X
Revenue:									
Corporate Tax/depreciation/incentives	X		X				X		X
Personal Tax/exemptions/deductions	X			X			X	X	X
Indirect tax reductions/exemptions		X	X	X	X			X	
Other							X	X	

Source: Adapted by casewriter from IMF, "The Size of the Fiscal Expansion: An Analysis for the Largest Countries," February 2009.

Exhibit 4b Fiscal Balance Projections for 2009 (% of GDP)

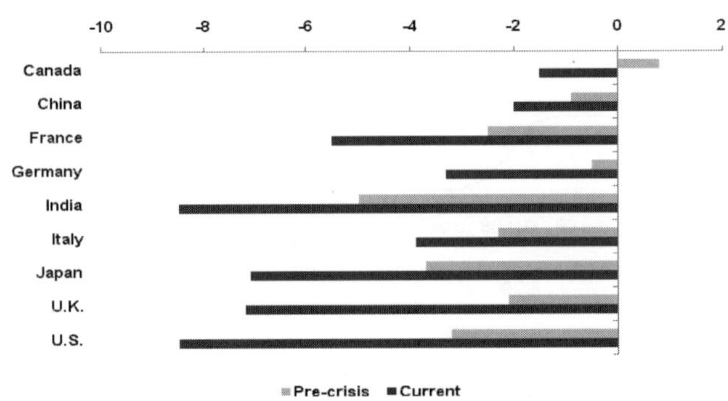

Source: Adapted by casewriter from IMF, "The Size of the Fiscal Expansion: An Analysis for the Largest Countries," February 2009.

Exhibit 5a Commodity Prices (1995=100)

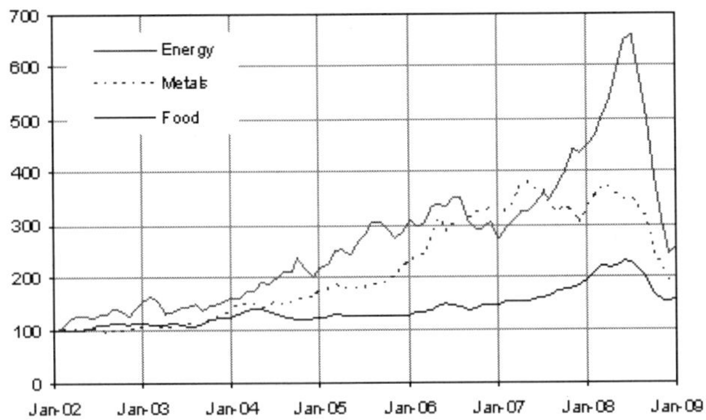

Source: World Trade Organization, "WTO Sees 9% Global Trade Decline in 2009 as Recession Strikes," Press Release No. 554, March 23, 2009.

Exhibit 5b Loss of Fiscal Revenue from Movement in Commodity Prices (% of GDP)

	2008	2009
Argentina	0.0	-0.3
Australia	0.0	-0.4
Brazil	1.0	-2.8
Canada	-0.1	-0.3
Indonesia	0.2	0.0
Mexico	0.3	-0.1
Russia	1.3	-6.4
Saudi Arabia	15.0	-26.8
South Africa	0.2	-0.1

Source: IMF, "The State of Public Finances: Outlook and Medium-Term Policies after the 2008 Crisis," March 6, 2009, p. 13.

Exhibit 6a Emerging Market Economies' External Financing (in billion US$)

	2006	2007	2008e	2009f
Current account balance	383.9	434.0	387.4	322.8
External financing, net:				
Private flows, net	564.9	928.6	465.8	165.3
Equity investment, net	222.3	296.1	174.1	194.8
Direct investment, net	170.9	304.1	263.4	197.5
Portfolio investment, net	51.5	-8.0	-89.3	-2.7
Private creditors, net	342.6	632.4	291.7	-29.5
Commercial banks, net	211.9	410.3	166.6	-60.6
Nonbanks, net	130.7	222.2	125.1	31.1
Official flows, net	-57.5	11.4	41.0	29.4
IFIs	-30.4	2.7	16.6	31.0
Bilateral creditors	-27.1	8.7	24.3	-1.6
Resident lending/other, net[1]	-336.5	-425.3	-449.8	-271.6
Reserves (- = increase)	-554.8	-948.7	-444.3	-245.9

e = estimate, f = IIF forecast
[1]Including net lending, monetary gold, and errors and omissions.

Source: Institute of International Finance, "Capital Flows to Emerging Market Economies," January 27, 2009, p. 1.

Exhibit 6b Net Private Capital Flows, by Region (% of Emerging Market's GDP)

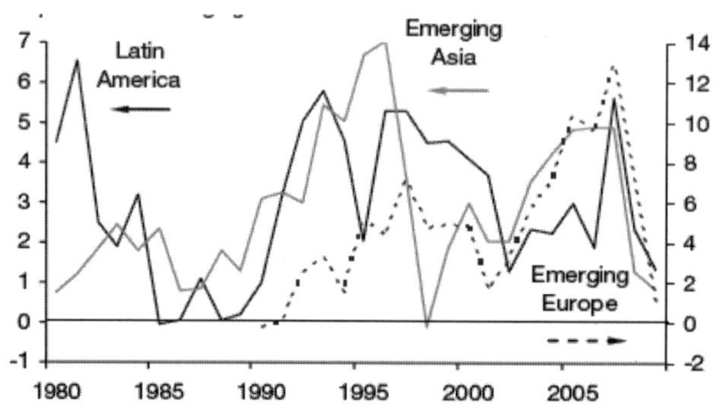

Source: Institute of International Finance, "Capital Flows to Emerging Market Economies," January 27, 2009, p. 1.

Exhibit 7a Emerging Market Bond Spreads[a] (in basis points)

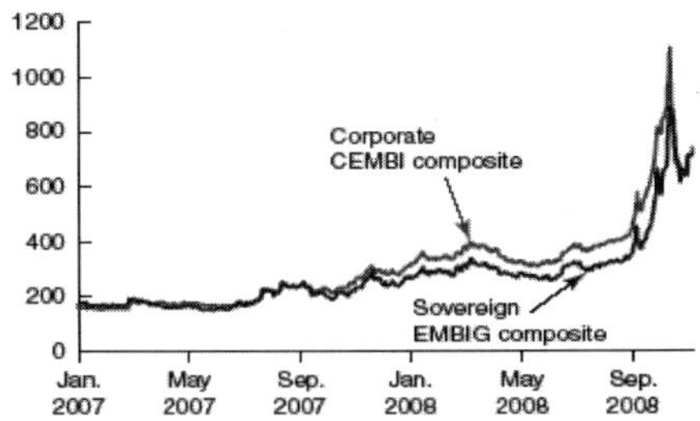

Source: World Bank, "Global Economic Prospects 2009," December 9, 2008, p. 22, http://siteresources.worldbank.org/INTGEP2009/Resources/10363_WebPDF-w47.pdf, accessed March 4, 2009.

[a] CEMBI = Corporate Emerging Markets Bond Index and EMBIG = Emerging Markets Bond Index Global.

Exhibit 7b Emerging Market Equities (January 2005 = 100)

Source: World Bank, "Global Economic Prospects 2009," December 9, 2008, p. 22, http://siteresources.worldbank.org/INTGEP2009/Resources/10363_WebPDF-w47.pdf, accessed March 4, 2009.

Exhibit 8 Real GDP and Trade Growth in OECD Countries

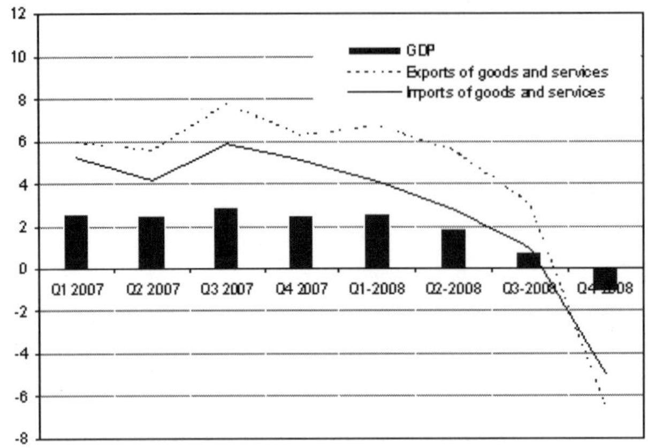

Source: World Trade Organization, "WTO Sees 9% Global Trade Decline in 2009 as Recession Strikes," Press Release No. 554, March 23, 2009.

Exhibit 9 Anti-Dumping Measures

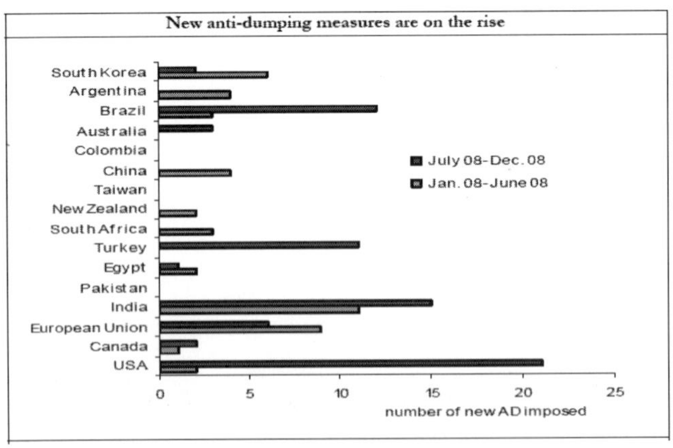

Source: World Bank, "Swimming Against the Tide: How Developing Countries are Coping with the Global Crisis," Background Paper prepared for the G20 Finance Ministers and Central Bank Governors Meeting, Horsham, United Kingdom on March 13-14, 2009.

Exhibit 10 Auto Industry Bailouts (in billion US$)

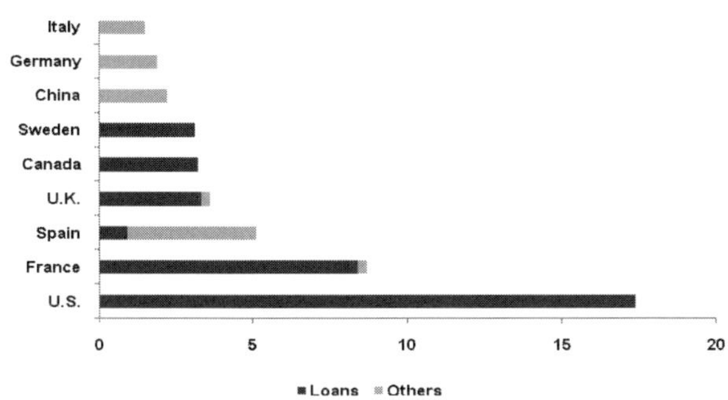

Source: Adapted by casewriter from "Automotive industry bail-outs around the world," *Financial Times*, February 18, 2009, http://www.ft.com, accessed March 24, 2009.

Exhibit 11 Exchange Rates

Country	Unit Per US$ (on March 25, 2009)	Unit per US$ (one year ago)
Australia	1.43	1.09
Brazil	2.24	1.74
Britain	0.69	0.50
Canada	1.22	1.02
China	6.82	7.04
Euro Area	0.74	0.63
Hong Kong	7.75	7.78
Hungary	221	163
India	50.8	40.2
Japan	97.7	99.1
Mexico	14.2	10.7
Poland	3.35	2.24
South Africa	9.51	8.08
South Korea	1,362	987
Russia	33.6	23.5

Source: Adapted by casewriter from "Trade, Exchange Rates, Budget Balances and Interest Rates," *The Economist*, March 25, 2009.

Endnotes

[1] Larry H. Summers, "Responding to a Historical Economic Crisis: The Obama Program," remarks at the Brookings Institute, Washington DC, March 13, 2009, Office of the Press Secretary, the White House.

[2] Ibid.

[3] For more about the U.S. current account deficit, see Laura Alfaro et al., "The U.S. Current Account Deficit," HBS No. 706-002 (Boston: Harvard Business School Publishing, 2005). For more on the causes of the subprime mortgage crisis, see Julio Rotenberg, "Subprime Meltdown: American Housing and Global Financial Turmoil," HBS No. 708-042 (Boston: Harvard Business School Publishing, 2008). For policy analysis, see Laura Alfaro and Renee Kim, "U.S. Subprime Mortgage Crisis: Policy Reactions," HBS No. 708-036 (Boston: Harvard Business School Publishing, 2008) and "U.S. Subprime Mortgage Crisis: Policy Reactions (B)," HBS No. N9-709-045 (Boston: Harvard Business School Publishing, 2009).

[4] Dani Rodrik, "A Time to Experiment," Project Syndicate, http://www.project-syndicate.org/commentary/rodrik27, accessed March 25, 2009.

[5] Mervyn King, "Finance: A Return from Risk," speech to the Worshipful Company of International Bankers, Mansion House, London, United Kingdom, March 17, 2009.

[6] For more about Japan's monetary policy history, see Laura Alfaro and Akiko Kano, "*Kinyuseisaku*: Monetary Policy in Japan," HBS No. 708-017 (Boston: Harvard Business School Publishing, 2008).

[7] "Factbox – ECB Policymakers' Recent Rate Comments," Reuters News, March 4, 2009.

[8] Paul Krugman, "The Keynesian Moment," *The New York Times*, November 29, 2008.

[9] Office of the Press Secretary, "News Conference by the President," White House, March 24, 2009.

[10] Bob Davis, "U.S. to Push for Global Stimulus—Stance Risks Angering Europeans Who Want to Focus on Regulation at G-20 Summit," *The Wall Street Journal*, March 9, 2009.

[11] "UN urges $1,000bn for developing world," *Financial Times*, March 25 2009 23:14

[12] For more, see Dominique Strauss-Kahn, "The Impact of the Financial Crisis on Low-Income Countries," remarks at the Brookings Institution, Washington DC, March 3, 2009..

[13] Ibid.

[14] Joellen Perry and Stephen Fidler, "ECB Chief Says Boost in Stimulus Not Needed," *The Wall Street Journal*, March 23, 2009.

[15] Laurence Norman and Paul Hannon, "Focus: G20 Fin Mins Gather to Chart Path Through Econ Crisis," Dow Jones International News, March 12, 2009, via Factiva, accessed March 13, 2009.

[16] Ian Traynor and David Gow, "Brown's Plan for Recovery Rejected by Germany," *The Guardian*, March 20, 2009.

[17] "EU leader condemns US 'road to hell'", *Financial Times*, March 25, 2009.

[18] "IMF Outlines Dire Consequences if World Fails to Act on Banks," News Press, February 10, 2009, via Factiva, accessed March 13, 2009.

[19] Catherine Mayer and Simon Robinson, "Gordon Brown: 'Sometimes a Crisis Forces Change,'" *Time*, March 25, 2009.

[20] The United States claimed that the "Buy American" provision were consistent with WTO rules and would be implemented within the WTO boundaries.

[21] World Trade Organization, "WTO Sees 9% Global Trade Decline in 2009 as Recession Strikes," Press Release 554, March 23, 2009.

[22] "Sarkozy under Fire in Europe for 'Protectionism,'" Agence France Presse, February 6, 2009.

[23] "Update: IMF Strauss-Kahn Urges More Active Response to Crisis," Dow Jones International News, December 15, 2008, via Factiva, accessed March 26, 2009.

[24] Out of the $500 billion pledge to increase the IMF's loan window, Japan, the European Union, and China pledged to provide $250 billion, while the rest remained to be raised.

[25] Gonzalo Vina, "IMF Makes Comeback Wielding $1 Trillion for Rescue (Update1)," Bloomberg, April 3, 2009.

[26] Kenneth Rogoff, "Super-Sizing the IMF is Wrong," RGE Monitor, November 10, 2008, http://www.rgemonitor/com/financemarkets-monitor, accessed March 13, 2009.

[27] For more about Korea and the IMF's role in its 1997-1998 financial crisis, see Laura Alfaro and Renee Kim, "Transforming Korea Inc: Financial Crisis and Institutional Reform," HBS No. 708-007 (Boston: Harvard Business School Publishing, 2008). For Malaysia's experience, see Rawi Abdelal and Laura Alfaro, "Malaysia: Capital and Control," HBS No. 702-040 (Boston: Harvard Business School Publishing, 2002).

[28] "China Calls for New Global Currency," The Associated Press, March 24, 2009.